Lecture Notes in Computer Science 11273

Commenced Publication in 1973
Founding and Former Series Editors:
Gerhard Goos, Juris Hartmanis, and Jan van Leeuwen

More information about this series at http://www.springer.com/series/7410

Thomas Peyrin · Steven Galbraith (Eds.)

Advances in Cryptology – ASIACRYPT 2018

24th International Conference on the Theory and Application of Cryptology and Information Security
Brisbane, QLD, Australia, December 2–6, 2018
Proceedings, Part II

Springer

Editors
Thomas Peyrin
Nanyang Technological University
Singapore, Singapore

Steven Galbraith
University of Auckland
Auckland, New Zealand

ISSN 0302-9743 ISSN 1611-3349 (electronic)
Lecture Notes in Computer Science
ISBN 978-3-030-03328-6 ISBN 978-3-030-03329-3 (eBook)
https://doi.org/10.1007/978-3-030-03329-3

Library of Congress Control Number: 2018959424

LNCS Sublibrary: SL4 – Security and Cryptology

This Springer imprint is published by the registered company Springer Nature Switzerland AG
The registered company address is: Gewerbestrasse 11, 6330 Cham, Switzerland

Preface

ASIACRYPT 2018, the 24th Annual International Conference on Theory and Application of Cryptology and Information Security, was held in Brisbane, Australia, during December 2–6, 2018.

The conference focused on all technical aspects of cryptology, and was sponsored by the International Association for Cryptologic Research (IACR).

Asiacrypt 2018 received a total of 234 submissions from all over the world. The Program Committee selected 65 papers for publication in the proceedings of this conference. The review process was made by the usual double-blind peer review by the Program Committee, which consisted of 47 leading experts of the field. Each submission was reviewed by at least three reviewers and five reviewers were assigned to submissions co-authored by Program Committee members. This year, the conference operated a two-round review system with rebuttal phase. In the first-round review the Program Committee selected the 145 submissions that were considered of value for proceeding to the second round. In the second-round phase the Program Committee further reviewed the submissions by taking into account their rebuttal letter from the authors. The selection process was assisted by a total of 347 external reviewers. These three-volume proceedings contain the revised versions of the papers that were selected. The revised versions were not reviewed again and the authors are responsible for their contents.

The program of Asiacrypt 2018 featured three excellent invited talks by Mitsuru Matsui, Melissa Chase, and Vanessa Teague. The conference also featured a traditional rump session that contained short presentations on the latest research results of the field. The Program Committee selected the work "Block Cipher Invariants as Eigenvectors of Correlation Matrices" by Tim Beyne for the Best Paper Award of Asiacrypt 2018. Two more papers, "Learning Strikes Again: the Case of the DRS Signature Scheme" by Yang Yu and Léo Ducas, and "Tighter Security Proofs for GPV-IBE in the Quantum Random Oracle Model" by Shuichi Katsumata, Shota Yamada, and Takashi Yamakawa, were solicited to submit the full versions to the *Journal of Cryptology*. The program chairs selected Chris Brzuska and Bart Mennink for the Best PC Member Award.

Many people contributed to the success of Asiacrypt 2018. We would like to thank the authors for submitting their research results to the conference. We are very grateful to all of the PC members as well as the external reviewers for their fruitful comments and discussions on their areas of expertise. We are greatly indebted to Josef Pieprzyk, the general chair, for his efforts and overall organization. We would also like to thank Waleed Alkalabi, Niluka Arasinghe, Mir Ali Rezazadeh Baee, Lynn Batten, Xavier Boyen, Ed Dawson, Ernest Foo, Mukhtar Hassan, Udyani Herath, Qingyi Li, Georg Lippold, Matthew McKague, Basker Palaniswamy, Anisur Rahman, Leonie Simpson, Shriparen Sriskandarajah, Gabrielle Stephens, and Chathurika Don Wickramage, the local Organizing Committee for their continuous support. We thank Craig Costello, Léo Ducas, and Pierre Karpman for expertly organizing and chairing the rump session.

Finally we thank Shai Halevi for letting us use his nice software for the paper submission and review process. We also thank Alfred Hofmann, Anna Kramer, and their colleagues for handling the editorial process of the proceedings published in Springer's LNCS series.

December 2018

Thomas Peyrin
Steven Galbraith

ASIACRYPT 2018

The 24th Annual International Conference on Theory and Application of Cryptology and Information Security

Sponsored by the International Association for Cryptologic Research (IACR)

December 2–6, 2018, Brisbane, Australia

General Chair

Josef Pieprzyk	CSIRO, Data61, Australia

Program Co-chairs

Thomas Peyrin	Nanyang Technological University, Singapore
Steven Galbraith	University of Auckland, New Zealand

Program Committee

Martin Albrecht	Royal Holloway University of London, UK
Prabhanjan Ananth	MIT, USA
Lejla Batina	Radboud University, The Netherlands
Sonia Belaïd	CryptoExperts, France
Daniel J. Bernstein	University of Illinois at Chicago, USA
Chris Brzuska	Aalto University, Finland
Bernardo David	Tokyo Institute of Technology, Japan
Nico Döttling	Friedrich-Alexander University Erlangen-Nürnberg, Germany
Léo Ducas	CWI, The Netherlands
Jens Groth	University College London, UK
Dawu Gu	Shanghai Jiao Tong University, China
Goichiro Hanaoka	AIST, Japan
Viet Tung Hoang	Florida State University, USA
Takanori Isobe	University of Hyogo, Japan
Jérémy Jean	ANSSI, France
Stefan Kölbl	Technical University of Denmark, Denmark
Ilan Komargodski	Cornell Tech, USA
Kaoru Kurosawa	Ibaraki University, Japan
Virginie Lallemand	Ruhr-Universität Bochum, Germany
Gaëtan Leurent	Inria, France
Benoît Libert	CNRS and ENS de Lyon, France
Helger Lipmaa	University of Tartu, Estonia

Atul Luykx	Visa Research, USA
Stefan Mangard	TU Graz, Austria
Bart Mennink	Radboud University, The Netherlands
Brice Minaud	Royal Holloway University of London, UK
Mridul Nandi	Indian Statistical Institute, India
Khoa Nguyen	Nanyang Technological University, Singapore
Svetla Nikova	KU Leuven, Belgium
Elisabeth Oswald	University of Bristol, UK
Arpita Patra	Indian Institute of Science, India
Giuseppe Persiano	Università di Salerno, Italy and Google, USA
Carla Ràfols	Universitat Pompeu Fabra, Spain
Amin Sakzad	Monash University, Australia
Jae Hong Seo	Hanyang University, Korea
Ling Song	Institute of Information Engineering, Chinese Academy of Sciences, China Nanyang Technological University, Singapore
Douglas Stebila	University of Waterloo, Canada
Marc Stevens	CWI, The Netherlands
Qiang Tang	New Jersey Institute of Technology, USA
Mehdi Tibouchi	NTT laboratories, Japan
Yosuke Todo	NTT Secure Platform Laboratories, Japan
Dominique Unruh	University of Tartu, Estonia
Gilles Van Assche	STMicroelectronics, Belgium
Frederik Vercauteren	KU Leuven, Belgium
Bo-Yin Yang	Academia Sinica, Taiwan
Yu Yu	Shanghai Jiao Tong University, China
Aaram Yun	UNIST, Korea

External Reviewers

Behzad Abdolmaleki
Aysajan Abidin
Shweta Agrawal
Estuardo Alpirez Bock
Joël Alwen
Abdelrahaman Aly
Andris Ambainis
Elena Andreeva
Jan-Pieter d'Anvers
Kazumaro Aoki
Nuttapong Attrapadung
Karim Baghery
Shi Bai
Gustavo Banegas
Subhadeep Banik
Paulo Barreto
Gilles Barthe
Hridam Basu
Aurélie Bauer
Carsten Baum
Christof Beierle
Adi Ben-Zvi
Ela Berners-Lee
David Bernhard
Pauline Bert
Ward Beullens
Rishiraj Bhattacharyya
Jean-Francois Biasse
Nina Bindel
Bruno Blanchet

Olivier Blazy
Xavier Bonnetain
Charlotte Bonte
Carl Bootland
Jonathan Bootle
Cecilia Boschini
Raphael Bost
Christina Boura
Florian Bourse
Dusan Bozilov
Andreas Brasen Kidmose
Jacqueline Brendel
Ignacio Cascudo
Dario Catalano
Andrea Cerulli
Avik Chakraborty
Debrup Chakraborty
Long Chen
Yu Chen
Yu Long Chen
Wonhee Cho
Ashish Choudhury
Chitchanok Chuengsatiansup
Michele Ciampi
Sandro Coretti
Alain Couvreur
Ben Curtis
Dana Dachman-Soled
Joan Daemen
Nilanjan Datta
Pratish Datta
Alex Davidson
Thomas De Cnudde
Luca De Feo
Lauren De Meyer
Gabrielle de Micheli
Fabrizio De Santis
Rafael Del Pino
Cyprien Delpech de Saint Guilhem
Yi Deng
Amit Deo
David Derler
Apoorvaa Deshpande
Lin Ding
Ning Ding
Christoph Dobraunig
Rafael Dowsley
Alexandre Duc
Avijit Dutta
Ratna Dutta
Sébastien Duval
Edward Eaton
Maria Eichlseder
Ali El Kaafarani
Keita Emura
Naomi Ephraim
Muhammed Esgin
Thomas Espitau
Martianus Frederic Ezerman
Leo (Xiong) Fan
Antonio Faonio
Oriol Farràs
Prastudy Fauzi
Serge Fehr
Dario Fiore
Tore Frederiksen
Thomas Fuhr
Eiichiro Fujisaki
Benjamin Fuller
Philippe Gaborit
Clemente Galdi
Nicolas Gama
Chaya Ganesh
Si Gao
Luke Garratt
Romain Gay
Nicholas Genise
Rosario Gennaro
Essam Ghadafi
Anirban Ghatak
Satrajit Ghosh
Junqing Gong
Alonso González
Hannes Gross
Paul Grubbs
Charles Guillemet
Siyao Guo
Qian Guo
Kyoohyung Han
Javier Herranz
Julia Hesse
Harunaga Hiwatari

Thang Hoang
Dennis Hofheinz
Seungwan Hong
Akinori Hosoyamada
Kathrin Hövelmanns
James Howe
Andreas Huelsing
Ilia Iliashenko
Ai Ishida
Masahito Ishizaka
Mitsugu Iwamoto
Tetsu Iwata
Håkon Jacobsen
Christian Janson
Dirmanto Jap
Jinhyuck Jeong
Ashwin Jha
Luke Johnson
Antoine Joux
Pierre Karpman
Shuichi Katsumata
Andrey Kim
Dongwoo Kim
Duhyeong Kim
Jeongsu Kim
Jihye Kim
Jiseung Kim
Myungsun Kim
Elena Kirshanova
Fuyuki Kitagawa
Susumu Kiyoshima
Yashvanth Kondi
Ben Kreuter
Toomas Krips
Veronika Kuchta
Marie-Sarah Lacharite
Junzuo Lai
Esteban Landerreche
Tanja Lange
Joohee Lee
Iraklis Leontiadis
Tancrède Lepoint
Jie Li
Qinyi Li
Shun Li
Wei Li
Xiangyu Li
Fuchun Lin
Donxi Liu
Fukang Liu
Hanlin Liu
Junrong Liu
Shengli Liu
Ya Liu
Zhen Liu
Zhiqiang Liu
Victor Lomne
Yu Long
Xianhui Lu
Yuan Lu
Chen Lv
Shunli Ma
Xuecheng Ma
Rusydi Makarim
Giulio Malavolta
Mary Maller
Alex Malozemoff
Yoshifumi Manabe
Avradip Mandal
Mark Manulis
Marco Martinoli
Daniel Masny
Pedro Maat Costa Massolino
Takahiro Matsuda
Alexander May
Sogol Mazaheri
Patrick McCorry
Florian Mendel
Peihan Miao
Vincent Migliore
Kazuhiko Minematsu
Matthias Minihold
Takaaki Mizuki
Andrew Morgan
Paz Morillo
Fabrice Mouhartem
Pratyay Mukherjee
Alireza Naghipour
Yusuke Naito
Maria Naya-Plasencia
Ryo Nishimaki
Ariel Nof

Wakaha Ogata
Emmanuela Orsini
Rafail Ostrovsky
Carles Padró
Tapas Pandit
Louiza Papachristodoulou
Alain Passelègue
Kenny Paterson
Goutam Paul
Michaël Peeters
Chris Peikert
Massimo Perillo
Léo Perrin
Edoardo Persichetti
Peter Pessl
Thomas Peters
Christophe Petit
Stjepan Picek
Zaira Pindado
Bertram Poettering
Eamonn Postlethwaite
Thomas Prest
Emmanuel Prouff
Elizabeth Quaglia
Adrián Ranea
Shahram Rasoolzadeh
Divya Ravi
Ling Ren
Guénaël Renault
Joost Renes
Joost Rijneveld
Thomas Roche
Paul Rösler
Mélissa Rossi
Dragos Rotaru
Yann Rotella
Arnab Roy
Sujoy Sinha Roy
Sylvain Ruhault
Mohammad Sabt
Mohammad Reza Sadeghi
Yusuke Sakai
Simona Samardzijska
Olivier Sanders
John Schanck
Peter Scholl
André Schrottenloher
Jacob Schuldt
Peter Schwabe
Danping Shi
Kyoji Shibutani
SeongHan Shin
Ferdinand Sibleyras
Janno Siim
Javier Silva
Thierry Simon
Luisa Siniscalchi
Kit Smeets
Yongha Son
Gabriele Spini
Christoph Sprenger
Martijn Stam
Damien Stehle
Ron Steinfeld
Joshua Stock
Ko Stoffelen
Shifeng Sun
Siwei Sun
Moon Sung Lee
Koutarou Suzuki
Alan Szepieniec
Akira Takahashi
Katsuyuki Takashima
Benjamin Tan
Adrian Thillard
Jean-Pierre Tillich
Elmar Tischhauser
Radu Titiu
Junichi Tomida
Ni Trieu
Boaz Tsaban
Thomas Unterluggauer
Christine Van Vredendaal
Prashant Vasudevan
Serge Vaudenay
Philip Vejre
Muthuramakrishnan Venkitasubramaniam
Daniele Venturi
Benoît Viguier
Jorge L. Villar
Srinivas Vivek

Antonia Wachter-Zeh
Alexandre Wallet
Michael Walter
Peng Wang
Ping Wang
Yuyu Wang
Man Wei
Zihao Wei
Friedrich Wiemer
Tim Wood
Joanne Woodage
Thomas Wunderer
Keita Xagawa
Haiyang Xue
Shota Yamada
Takashi Yamakawa
Avishay Yanai
Kang Yang
Qianqian Yang
Kan Yasuda
Kevin Yeo
Scott Yilek
Kazuki Yoneyama
Jingyue Yu
Yang Yu
Xingliang Yuan
Thomas Zacharias
Michal Zajac
Rina Zeitoun
Mark Zhandry
Bin Zhang
Cong Zhang
Fan Zhang
Jiang Zhang
Juanyang Zhang
Ren Zhang
Yingjie Zhang
Raymond K. Zhao
Shuoyao Zhao
Linfeng Zhou
Vincent Zucca

Local Organizing Committee

General Chair

Josef Pieprzyk	CSIRO, Data61, Australia

Advisors

Lynn Batten	Deakin University, Australia
Ed Dawson	QUT, Australia

Members

Waleed Alkalabi	QUT, Australia
Niluka Arasinghe	QUT, Australia
Mir Ali Rezazadeh Baee	QUT, Australia
Xavier Boyen	QUT, Australia
Ernest Foo	QUT, Australia
Mukhtar Hassan	QUT, Australia
Udyani Herath	QUT, Australia
Qingyi Li	QUT, Australia
Georg Lippold	Mastercard, Australia
Matthew McKague	QUT, Australia
Basker Palaniswamy	QUT, Australia
Anisur Rahman	QUT, Australia

Contents – Part II

Symmetric-Key Cryptanalysis

Public Key and Identity-Based Encryption

Asiacrypt 2018 Award Paper I

Side-Channels

Signatures

Asiacrypt 2018 Award Paper II

Leakage-Resilient Cryptography

Functional/Inner Product/Predicate Encryption

Symmetric-Key Cryptanalysis

Programming the Demirci-Selçuk Meet-in-the-Middle Attack with Constraints

Danping Shi[1,2], Siwei Sun[1,2,3](✉), Patrick Derbez[4], Yosuke Todo[5], Bing Sun[6], and Lei Hu[1,2,3]

[1] State Key Laboratory of Information Security, Institute of Information Engineering, Chinese Academy of Sciences, Beijing, China
{shidanping,sunsiwei,hulei}@iie.ac.cn
[2] Data Assurance and Communication Security Research Center, Chinese Academy of Sciences, Beijing, China
[3] School of Cyber Security, University of Chinese Academy of Sciences, Beijing, China
[4] Univ Rennes, CNRS, IRISA, Rennes, France
patrick.derbez@irisa.fr
[5] NTT Secure Platform Laboratories, Tokyo, Japan
todo.yosuke@lab.ntt.co.jp
[6] College of Liberal Arts and Sciences, National University of Defense Technology, Changsha, China
happy_come@163.com

Abstract. Cryptanalysis with SAT/SMT, MILP and CP has increased in popularity among symmetric-key cryptanalysts and designers due to its high degree of automation. So far, this approach covers differential, linear, impossible differential, zero-correlation, and integral cryptanalysis. However, the Demirci-Selçuk meet-in-the-middle ($\mathcal{DS}$-MITM) attack is one of the most sophisticated techniques that has not been automated with this approach. By an in-depth study of Derbez and Fouque's work on $\mathcal{DS}$-MITM analysis with dedicated search algorithms, we identify the crux of the problem and present a method for automatic $\mathcal{DS}$-MITM attack based on general constraint programming, which allows the cryptanalysts to state the problem at a high level without having to say how it should be solved. Our method is not only able to enumerate distinguishers but can also partly automate the key-recovery process. This approach makes the $\mathcal{DS}$-MITM cryptanalysis more straightforward and easier to follow, since the resolution of the problem is delegated to off-the-shelf constraint solvers and therefore decoupled from its formulation. We apply the method to SKINNY, TWINE, and LBlock, and we get the currently known best $\mathcal{DS}$-MITM attacks on these ciphers. Moreover, to demonstrate the usefulness of our tool for the block cipher designers, we exhaustively evaluate the security of $8! = 40320$ versions of LBlock instantiated with different words permutations in the F functions. It turns out that the permutation used in the original LBlock is one of the 64 permutations showing the strongest resistance against the $\mathcal{DS}$-MITM

T. Peyrin and S. Galbraith (Eds.): ASIACRYPT 2018, LNCS 11273, pp. 3–34, 2018.
https://doi.org/10.1007/978-3-030-03329-3_1

attack. The whole process is accomplished on a PC in less than 2 h. The same process is applied to TWINE, and similar results are obtained.

Keywords: Demirci-Selçuk meet-in-the-middle attack
Automated cryptanalysis · Constraint programming · MILP

1 Introduction

Cryptanalysis of block ciphers is a highly technical, time consuming and error-prone process. On the one hand, the attackers have to perform a variety of cryptanalytic techniques, including differential attack [1], linear attack [2], integral attack [3–5], etc., to see which technique leads to the best attack. On the other hand, the designers need to repeat all these different attacks again and again to identify the optimal choices of parameters and building blocks which meet the security and implementation requirements. Therefore, automatic tools are indispensable to the community, which significantly reduce the manual work and make a thorough exploration of the design/analysis space possible.

One paradigm for automatic symmetric-key cryptanalysis getting increasing popularity in recent years is to model the problem by means of constraints, which includes the methods based on SAT/SMT (satisfiability modulo theory) [6–8], MILP (mixed-integer linear programming) [9–13], and classical constraint programming [14,15]. In this paper, these methods are collectively referred to as the general constraint programming (CP) based approach, or just CP based approach for short. So far, the CP based approach covers a wide range of symmetric-key cryptanalysis techniques. For instance, we can determine the minimum number of differentially or linearly active S-boxes of a block cipher with MILP [9]; we can search for actual differential characteristics, linear characteristics, and integral distinguishers with SAT/SMT, MILP or classical constraint programming [8,10,11,14]; and we can search for impossible differentials and zero-correlation linear approximations [12,16] in a similar way.

Compared with search algorithms implemented from scratch in general purpose programming languages [17–24], the CP based approach allows the cryptanalysts to state the problem very naturally, and at a high level without having to say how it should be solved. The resolution of the problem is delegated to generic solvers, and therefore decoupled from the formulation of the problem. As Eugene C. Freuder stated [25]: *Constraint programming represents one of the closest approaches computer science has yet made to the Holy Grail of programming : the user states the problem, the computer solves it.*

However, the Demirci-Selçuk meet-in-the-middle attack ($\mathcal{DS}$-MITM) attack [26], introduced by Demirci and Selçuk at FSE 2008 to attack the famous Advanced Encryption Standard (AES) [27], is one of the cryptanalytic techniques which has not been automated with general constraint programming due to its extraordinary sophistication. After a series of improvements of the attack with various creative techniques [28–32], the $\mathcal{DS}$-MITM attack reaches the best known attack on 7-round AES-128, 9-round AES-256 and 10-round AES-256 in the single-key model. The attack has been applied to several specific block ciphers [33–36] as well as on generic balanced Feistel constructions [37]. Most recently, Guo et al. show generic attacks on unbalanced Feistel ciphers based on the $\mathcal{DS}$-MITM technique which penetrate a large number of rounds of some specific class of unbalanced Feistels [38]. Note that despite sharing the same name with the traditional MITM attacks in some literature (the attacks on some block ciphers [39,40] and on a number of hash functions, e.g. [41,42]), the $\mathcal{DS}$-MITM attack concerned in this paper follows a different and a more complex strategy.

Related Work and Our Contribution. In [30,31], Derbez and Fouque presented a tool implemented in C/C++ for finding the $\mathcal{DS}$-MITM attack with dedicated search algorithm. In this paper, we present the first CP-based tool for finding the $\mathcal{DS}$-MITM attack automatically. Our approach is based on a novel modelling technique in which we introduce several different types of variables for every input/output word of all operations, and impose constraints on these variables such that from a solution of these variables satisfying all the constraints we can deduce a $\mathcal{DS}$-MITM distinguisher or $\mathcal{DS}$-MITM attack.

Compared with Derbez and Fouque's tool [30,31] which was implemented in the general purpose programming language C/C++, the CP based method allows the cryptanalysts to state the problem at a high level very naturally, without considering how to maintain the relationships between the variables explicitly with dedicated algorithms. Therefore, our tool should be very useful in fast prototyping in the process of block cipher design.

In [43], Lin et al. modeled the problem of searching for $\mathcal{DS}$-MITM distinguishers as an integer programming model. However, their integer programming model is incomplete and is solved by a dedicated search algorithm. Secondly, Lin et al. 's work only focuses on the distinguisher part. Our CP based approach can not only enumerate distinguishers but also partly automate the key-recovery process of the attack. Moreover, by applying our CP based approach to LBlock, the same cipher targeted in [43], we show it finds better distinguishers as well as better attacks. To demonstrate the effectiveness of our approach, we apply it to SKINNY [44], TWINE [45], and LBlock [46]. We produce so far the best $\mathcal{DS}$-MITM attacks on these well-known ciphers automatically.

For LBlock, we can not only find an 11-round $\mathcal{DS}$-MITM distinguisher which is 2 rounds longer than the one(s) presented in [43], but also construct the first $\mathcal{DS}$-MITM attack on 21-round LBlock. We also rediscover the same attack on TWINE-128 given in [34], and identify the first $\mathcal{DS}$-MITM attack on 20-round TWINE-80. In addition, we report the first concrete $\mathcal{DS}$-MITM analysis of SKINNY. A remarkable fact is that our tool identify an 10.5-round $\mathcal{DS}$-MITM distinguisher in a few seconds, while its designers expect an upper-bound of 10 rounds against such distinguishers in [44]. A summary of these results are given in Table 1.

We also show how helpful our tool can be in the block cipher design process by searching for the best choices of block shuffles in LBlock and TWINE. We scan over 40320 variants of LBlock, and 887040 variants of TWINE. We identify permutations which are potentially stronger than the permutations in the original designs. We make the source code of this work publicly available at https://github.com/siweisun/MITM.

In addition, all supplementary materials referred later on are provided in an extended version of this paper at https://github.com/siweisun/MITM.

Organization. In Sect. 2, we give the notations used in this paper. An introduction of the $\mathcal{DS}$-MITM attack is presented in Sect. 3. We show the general principle of how to model the $\mathcal{DS}$-MITM attack in Sect. 4, and subsequently in Sect. 5 the technical detail of the modelling method is given. Section 6 discusses how to use our method in practice. In Sect. 7, we apply our approach to SKINNY, TWINE, LBlock, AES, ARIA, and SIMON. In Sect. 8, we discuss how to use our tool to find high-quality building blocks (with respect to the $\mathcal{DS}$-MITM attack) in the process of block cipher design. Section 9 is the conclusion.

Table 1. A summary of the results. Though the focus of this paper is the $\mathcal{DS}$-MITM attack, we also list other types of attacks which achieve currently known best results against the ciphers targeted. For the $\mathcal{DS}$-MITM attack, the number of rounds attacked is presented in the form of $a + b$, where a shows how many rounds are covered by the underlying $\mathcal{DS}$-MITM distinguisher, while b is the number orouter rounds added when performing a key-recovery attack. Therefore, $b = 0$ indicates a distinguishing attack.

Target	Rounds	Time	Data	Memory	Method	Ref
LBlock	$11+10$	$2^{70.20}$	2^{48} CP	$2^{61.91}$	$\mathcal{DS}$-MITM	Sect. 7.2
	$9+0$	$2^{74.5}$	–	–	$\mathcal{DS}$-MITM Dist.	[43]
	23	$2^{74.5}$	$2^{59.5}$CP	$2^{74.3}$	ID	[47]
	23	$2^{75.36}$	2^{59}CP	2^{74}	ID	[48]
	23	2^{72}	$2^{62.1}$ Kp	2^{60}	MultiD ZC	[47]
	23	2^{76}	$2^{62.1}$ Kp	2^{60}	MultiD ZC	[49]
TWINE80	$11+9$	$2^{77.44}$	2^{32} CP	$2^{82.91}$	$\mathcal{DS}$-MITM	Sect. 7.3
	23	$2^{79.09}$	$2^{57.85}$ CP	$2^{84.06}$	ID	[50]
	23	2^{73}	$2^{62.1}$ KP	2^{60}	MultiD ZC	[47]
TWINE128	$11+14$	$2^{124.7}$	2^{48} CP	2^{109}	$\mathcal{DS}$-MITM[a]	[34]
	25	$2^{124.5}$	$2^{59.1}$ CP	$2^{78.1}$	ID	[34]
	25	2^{119}	$2^{62.1}$ KP	2^{60}	MultiD ZC	[47]
	25	$2^{122.12}$	$2^{62.1}$ KP	2^{60}	MultiD ZC	[49]
SKINNY-128-384	10.5+11.5	$2^{382.46}$	2^{96} CP	$2^{330.99}$	$\mathcal{DS}$-MITM	Sect. 7.1
	$11+11$	$2^{373.48}$	$2^{92.22}$ CP	$2^{147.22}$	ID	[51]

[a] We find the attacks with the same complexity.

2 Notations

An n-bit state state with $n = cn_c$ is alternatively regarded as a sequence $(\mathsf{state}[0], \mathsf{state}[1], \cdots, \mathsf{state}[n_c - 1])$ of n_c c-bit words. Let $\mathcal{A} = [j_0, j_1, \cdots, j_{s-1}]$ be an ordered set of integers such that $0 \le j_0 < \cdots < j_{s-1} < n_c$. Then $\mathsf{state}[\mathcal{A}]$ is used to represent $\mathsf{state}[j_0]\|\cdots\|\mathsf{state}[j_{s-1}]$, where $\mathsf{state}[j]$ is the j-th c-bit word of state and $\|$ is the operation of bit string concatenation.

Definition 1. *A set* $\{P^0, \cdots, P^{N-1}\} \subseteq \mathbb{F}_2^{cn_c} = \mathbb{F}_2^n$ *of* $N = 2^{sc}$ *n-bit values for* state *is a* $\delta(\mathcal{A})$*-set for* state *with* $\mathcal{A} = [k_0, k_1, \cdots, k_{s-1}]$ *if* $P^0[\mathcal{A}] \oplus P^j[\mathcal{A}] = j$ $(1 \leq j < N)$*, and* $P^i[k] = P^j[k]$ *for all* $i, j \in \{0, \cdots, N-1\}$ *and* $k \notin \mathcal{A}$*. That is,* $\{P^0, \cdots, P^{N-1}\}$ *traverse the s c-bit words specified by* $\mathcal{A}$ *while share the same value in other word positions.*

An r-round iterative block cipher E with $r = r_0 + r_1 + r_2$, depicted in Fig. 1, is a keyed permutation which transforms an n-bit state state_0 into state_{2r} step by step with nonlinear and linear operations. In our indexing scheme, as illustrated in Fig. 1, state_{2k} is the input state of round k, state_{2k+1} is the output state of the nonlinear operation of round k, and $\mathsf{state}_{2(k+1)}$ is the output of round k or the input of round $k+1$ for $k \in \{0, \cdots, r_0 + r_1 + r_2 - 1\}$. For the sake of simplicity and concreteness, we will conduct the discussion based on Fig. 1, which visualizes the structure of a common SP cipher. Without loss of generality, we assume that the key addition is performed after the linear layer L as illustrated in Fig. 1. The basic rule is that we should always introduce a new state for the direct input to the nonlinear layer. For example, if the key addition is performed in between state_{2i} and the NL operation, then a new state (representing the direct input to NL) should be introduced in between the key addition and the NL operation, and the original state may be omitted (regarding the new state as an output obtained by masking the output of the previous round with the subkey).

Note that though our discussion are based on a SP cipher illustrated in Fig. 1, the ideas and techniques presented in this paper are general enough to be applied to other structures, such as Feistel and Generalized Feistel structures.

For convenience, a $\delta(\mathcal{A})$-set $\{P^0, \cdots, P^{N-1}\}$ is denoted by $\mathbb{P}_{\delta(\mathcal{A})}$, and let $\Delta_E(\mathbb{P}_{\delta(\mathcal{A})}, \mathcal{B})$ be the sequence $[C^0[\mathcal{B}] \oplus C^1[\mathcal{B}], \cdots, C^0[\mathcal{B}] \oplus C^{N-1}[\mathcal{B}]]$, where $C^i = E(P^i)$ and $\mathcal{B} = [j_0, \cdots, j_{t-1}]$ such that $0 \leq j_0 < \cdots < j_{t-1} < n_c$.

Let P, $P' \in \mathbb{F}_2^n$ be two values of state_0 shown in Fig. 1, which are often regarded as plaintexts since state_0 is the input of the encryption algorithm. The value P creates a series of intermediate values during the encryption process. We define $P(\mathsf{state}_i)$ as the intermediate value at state_i created by the partial encryption of P. Sometimes we only care about the value of $P(\mathsf{state}_i)$ at some specified word positions indexed by an ordered set $\mathcal{I}$, which is denoted by $P(\mathsf{state}_i[\mathcal{I}])$. We define $P \oplus P'(\mathsf{state}_i)$ and $P \oplus P'(\mathsf{state}_i[\mathcal{I}])$ to be the intermediate differences $P(\mathsf{state}_i) \oplus P'(\mathsf{state}_i)$ and $P(\mathsf{state}_i[\mathcal{I}]) \oplus P'(\mathsf{state}_i[\mathcal{I}])$ respectively. Let C and C' be the ciphertexts of P and P'. An intermediate value can also be regarded as the result of a partial decryption of the ciphertext C. Therefore, we define $C(\mathsf{state}_i)$, $C(\mathsf{state}_i[\mathcal{I}])$, $C \oplus C'(\mathsf{state}_i)$, and $C \oplus C'(\mathsf{state}_i[\mathcal{I}])$ similarly. Note that in the above notations, the intermediate values or differences of intermediate values are specified with respect to some plaintexts or ciphertexts. We may as well specify them with respect to some intermediate values, say $Q = P(\mathsf{state}_j)$ and $Q' = P'(\mathsf{state}_j)$. Hence, we may have notations such as $Q(\mathsf{state}_i)$, $Q(\mathsf{state}_i[\mathcal{I}])$, $Q \oplus Q'(\mathsf{state}_i)$, and $Q \oplus Q'(\mathsf{state}_i[\mathcal{I}])$, whose meanings should be clear from the context.

To make the notation succinct, if not stated explicitly, we always assume that $\mathcal{A} = [k_0, \cdots, k_{s-1}]$, $\mathcal{B} = [j_0, \cdots, j_{t-1}]$, and a state state is viewed as a

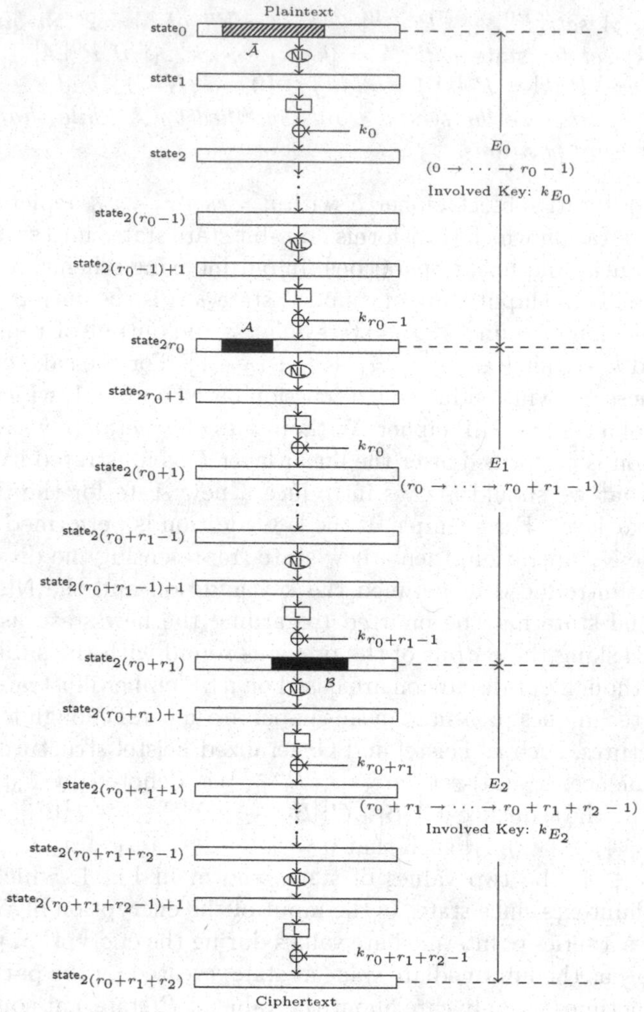

Fig. 1. An r-round SP block cipher $E = E_2 \circ E_1 \circ E_0$ with $r = r_0 + r_1 + r_2$, whose round function consists of a layer of nonlinear operation and a layer of linear operation. A $\mathcal{DS}$-MITM key-recovery attack is performed based on a $\mathcal{DS}$-MITM distinguisher placed at E_1. A more detailed explanation of this figure will be given in Sect. 3.2.

a sequence of n bits or a sequence of n_c c-bit words. Moreover, we make the following assumption which is very natural for a block cipher.

Assumption 1. *Let the nonlinear layer in Fig. 1 be a parallel application of* n_c $c \times c$ *invertible S-boxes, and* $\mathcal{I} = [j : Q \oplus Q'(\text{state}_{2k}[j]) \neq 0,\ 0 \leq j < n_c]$ *be an ordered set, where* Q *and* Q' *are two values for* state_{2k}*. If we know the value of* $Q(\text{state}_{2k}[\mathcal{I}])$*, then we can derive the value of* $Q \oplus Q'(\text{state}_{2k+1})$ *with the knowledge of* $Q \oplus Q'(\text{state}_{2k}[\mathcal{I}])$*. Similarly, we can derive the value of*

$Q \oplus Q'(\mathsf{state}_{2k})$ *with the knowledge of* $Q(\mathsf{state}_{2k+1}[\mathcal{I}])$ *and* $Q \oplus Q'(\mathsf{state}_{2k+1}[\mathcal{I}])$. *In other words, we can derive the value of the output/input differences if we know the value of input/output values and differences at the active positions.*

3 The Demirci-Selçuk Meet-in-the-Middle Attack

3.1 The $\mathcal{DS}$-MITM Distinguisher

The $\mathcal{DS}$-MITM attack relies on a special differential-type distinguisher. Compared with ordinary differential distinguishers, the $\mathcal{DS}$-MITM distinguishers generally lead to much stronger filters.

Let F be a keyed permutation, and $\mathbb{Q}_{\delta(\mathcal{A})} = \{Q^0, \cdots, Q^{N-1}\}$ be a $\delta(\mathcal{A})$-set for the input state of F. If F is a random permutation, then it can be shown that there are $(2^{ct})^{2^{cs}-1}$ possibilities for $\Delta_F(\mathbb{Q}_{\delta(\mathcal{A})}, \mathcal{B})$. But for a block cipher F, it is possible that the sequence $\Delta_F(\mathbb{Q}_{\delta(\mathcal{A})}, \mathcal{B})$ can be fully determined with the knowledge of d c-bit words. For instance, from the values of one internal state and the master key one can derive the values for all the internal states. Therefore, given $\mathbb{Q}_{\delta(\mathcal{A})}$, we can get at most 2^{cd} possible cases of $\Delta_F(\mathbb{Q}_{\delta(\mathcal{A})}, \mathcal{B})$ by traversing the d c-bit words. We call d the $(\mathcal{A}, \mathcal{B})$-degree of F, which is denoted by $\mathsf{Deg}_F(\mathcal{A}, \mathcal{B})$, or simply $\mathsf{Deg}(\mathcal{A}, \mathcal{B})$ if F can be inferred from the context. If $\mathsf{Deg}_F(\mathcal{A}, \mathcal{B}) = d$ is small enough such that $\lambda = 2^{cd}/(2^{ct})^{2^{cs}-1} = 2^{c(d-t\cdot(2^{cs}-1))} < 1$, or $d < t \cdot (2^{cs} - 1)$, then we can use this property as a distinguisher and construct a key-recovery attack on F. Therefore, a $\mathcal{DS}$-MITM distinguisher of a keyed permutation F can be regarded as a tuple $(\mathcal{A}, \mathcal{B}, \mathsf{Deg}_F(\mathcal{A}, \mathcal{B}))$.

3.2 Key Recovery Attack Based on $\mathcal{DS}$-MITM Distinguisher

We now describe how a key-recovery attack can be performed with a $\mathcal{DS}$-MITM distinguisher. This part should be read while referring to Fig. 1.

As shown in Fig. 1, we divide the target cipher E into 3 parts: E_0, E_1, and E_2, where E_i is a keyed permutation with r_i rounds. As depicted in Fig. 1, E_0 covers rounds $(0 \to \cdots \to r_0 - 1)$, E_1 covers rounds $(r_0 \to \cdots \to r_0 + r_1 - 1)$, and E_2 covers rounds $(r_0 + r_1 \to \cdots \to r_0 + r_1 + r_2 - 1)$. According to our indexing scheme, as illustrated in Fig. 1, state_0 is the input state of E_0; state_{2r_0} is the output state of E_0 which is also the input state of E_1; $\mathsf{state}_{2(r_0+r_1)}$ is the output of E_1 or the input of E_2; finally, $\mathsf{state}_{2(r_0+r_1+r_2)}$ is the output of E_2.

In the attack, we place a $\mathcal{DS}$-MITM distinguisher $(\mathcal{A}, \mathcal{B}, \mathsf{Deg}_{E_1}(\mathcal{A}, \mathcal{B}))$ at E_1, and prepare a $\delta(\bar{\mathcal{A}})$-set $\mathbb{P}_{\delta(\bar{\mathcal{A}})}$ of chosen plaintexts for state_0, where $\bar{\mathcal{A}}$ is the ordered set of integers k $(0 \le k < n_c)$ such that $V^0 \oplus V^j(\mathsf{state}_0[k]) \neq 0$ for some $\delta(\mathcal{A})$-set $\mathbb{V}_{\delta(\mathcal{A})} = \{V^0, \cdots, V^{N-1}\}$ for state_{2r_0} (the input state of E_1) and some $j \in \{0, \cdots, N-1\}$. Note that $\bar{\mathcal{A}}$ can be obtained by propagating the differences created by $\mathbb{V}_{\delta(\mathcal{A})}$ for state_{2r_0} (the input of E_1) reversely against E_0.

Then we select an arbitrary plaintext P^0 from $\mathbb{P}_{\delta(\bar{\mathcal{A}})}$, and guess the secret key information $k_{E_0} \in \mathbb{F}_2^{e_0}$ with which we can find $P^1, \cdots, P^{N-1}$ in $\mathbb{P}_{\delta(\bar{\mathcal{A}})}$ such that $\mathbb{Q}_{\delta(\mathcal{A})} = \{Q^0, \cdots, Q^{N-1}\}$ where $Q^j = E_0(P^j)$ forms a $\delta(\mathcal{A})$-set for state_{2r_0}.

Finally, we guess the secret key information $k_{E_2} \in \mathbb{F}_2^{e_2}$ involved in E_2 with which we can determine the sequence

$$\Delta_{E_1}(\mathbb{Q}_{\delta(\mathcal{A})}, \mathcal{B}) = [C^0 \oplus C^1(\mathsf{state}_{2(r_0+r_1)}[\mathcal{B}]), \cdots, C^0 \oplus C^{N-1}(\mathsf{state}_{2(r_0+r_1)}[\mathcal{B}])]$$

by partial decryption with E_2, where $C^j = E(P^j)$.

If the resulting sequence is not one of the possible $\Delta_{E_1}(\mathbb{Q}_{\delta(\mathcal{A})}, \mathcal{B})$ sequences which can be determined with the $\mathsf{Deg}_{E_1}(\mathcal{A}, \mathcal{B}) = d$ c-bit parameters, the guesses of k_{E_0} and k_{E_2} are certainly incorrect and therefore rejected. Similar to [52], we adopt the notion of $|k_{E_0} \cup k_{E_2}|$ to represent the log of the entropy of the involved secret key bits in the outer rounds from an information theoretical point of view.

3.3 Complexity Analysis

Offline Phase. Store all the 2^{cd} possibilities of the sequence $\Delta_{E_1}(\mathbb{Q}_{\delta(\mathcal{A})}, \mathcal{B})$ in a hash table. The time complexity is $2^{cd} \cdot 2^{cs} \cdot \rho_{E_1} C_E$, and the memory complexity is $(2^{cs} - 1) \cdot ct \cdot 2^{cd}$ bits, where C_E is the time complexity of one encryption with E, and ρ_{E_1} is typically computed in literature as $\mathsf{Deg}(\mathcal{A}, \mathcal{B})$ divided by the total number of S-boxes in E.

Online Phase. For each of the $2^{|k_{E_0} \cup k_{E_2}|}$ possible guesses, if the resulting sequence $\Delta_{E_1}(\mathbb{Q}_{\delta(\mathcal{A})}, \mathcal{B})$ is not in the hash table precomputed, then the guess under consideration is certainly not correct and is discarded. The time complexity of this step is $2^{|k_{E_0} \cup k_{E_2}|} \cdot 2^{sc} \cdot \rho_{E_0 \cup E_2} C_E$, where $\rho_{E_0 \cup E_2}$ is typically computed as the number of S-boxes involved in the outer rounds divided by the total number of S-boxes in E. After this step, the $2^{|k_{E_0} \cup k_{E_2}|}$ key space is reduced approximately to $\lambda \cdot 2^{|k_{E_0} \cup k_{E_2}|}$, where $\lambda = 2^{c(d - t \cdot (2^{cs} - 1))}$.

4 Modelling the $\mathcal{DS}$-MITM Attack with Constraints: A High Level Overview

In this section, we give a high level overview of our modelling method with the aid of Figs. 1 and 2, which serves as a road map for the next section (Sect. 5), where the technical details are presented. To model the attack with constraint programming (CP) for the cipher $E = E_2 \circ E_1 \circ E_0$ shown in Fig. 1, we proceed as the following steps.

Step 1. Modelling the distinguisher part

- Introduce three types (X, Y, and Z) of 0-1 variables for each word of the states $\mathsf{state}_{2r_0}, \cdots, \mathsf{state}_{2(r_0+r_1)}$ involved in E_1. We denote the sets of all type-X, type-Y and type-Z variables by $\mathsf{Vars}(X)$, $\mathsf{Vars}(Y)$ and $\mathsf{Vars}(Z)$, respectively.
- Introduce a set of constraints over $\mathsf{Vars}(X)$ to model the propagation of the *forward differential*, and introduce a set of constraints over $\mathsf{Vars}(Y)$ to model the *backward determination relationship.*
- Impose a set of constraints on $\mathsf{Vars}(Z)$ such that a type-Z variable for $\mathsf{state}_i[j]$ is 1 if and only if the type-X and type-Y variables for $\mathsf{state}_i[j]$ are 1 simultaneously.

Remark 1. Under the above configuration, every instantiation of the variables in $\mathsf{Vars}(X)$, $\mathsf{Vars}(Y)$, and $\mathsf{Vars}(Z)$ corresponds to a potential $\mathcal{DS}$-MITM distinguisher. Therefore, all distinguishers can be enumerated with the above model. Also note that the key addition can be omitted while searching for distinguishers if it does not affect the propagation of the forward differential and backward determination relationship. This is the case for all the examples presented in this paper, where key additions are only involved in computing the actual complexities.

Step 2. Modelling the outer rounds

- Introduce a type-M variable for each word of the states $\mathsf{state}_0, \cdots, \mathsf{state}_{2r_0}$ involved in E_0, and impose a set of constraints over $\mathsf{Vars}(M)$ to model the *backward differential.* Note that there are both type-X and type-M variables for state_{2r_0}. We require that the corresponding type-X and type-M variables for each of the n_c words of state_{2r_0} are equal.
- Introduce a type-W variable for each word of the states $\mathsf{state}_{2(r_0+r_1)}, \cdots,$ $\mathsf{state}_{2(r_0+r_1+r_2)}$ involved in E_2, and impose a set of constraints over $\mathsf{Vars}(W)$ to model the *forward determination relationship.* Note that there are both type-Y and type-W variables for $\mathsf{state}_{2(r_0+r_1)}$. We require that the corresponding type-Y and type-W variables for each of the n_c words of $\mathsf{state}_{2(r_0+r_1)}$ are equal.

Remark 2. Every solution of $\mathsf{Vars}(M)$ and $\mathsf{Vars}(W)$ helps us to identify the information that needs to be guessed in the outer rounds, which will be clearer in the following.

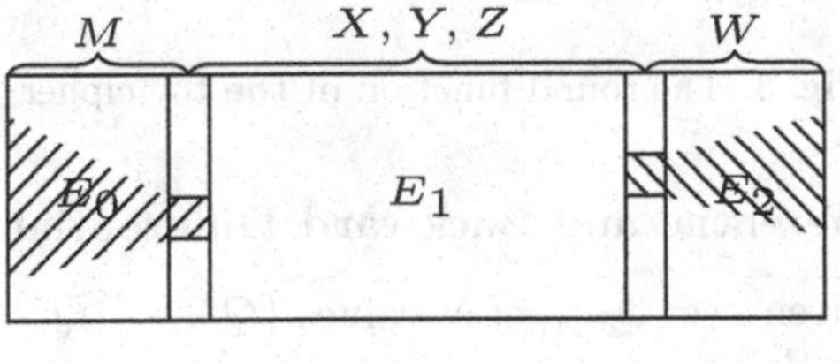

Fig. 2. A high level overview of the modelling method for $\mathcal{DS}$-MITM attack

The overall modelling strategy is depicted in Fig. 2. In summary, given a full solution of the variables such that all constraints are fulfilled, we can extract the following information

- $\mathcal{A}$: The variables in $\mathsf{Vars}(X)$ for state_{2r_0} whose values are 1 indicate $\mathcal{A}$;
- $\mathcal{B}$: The variables in $\mathsf{Vars}(Y)$ for $\mathsf{state}_{2(r_0+r_1)}$ whose values are 1 indicate $\mathcal{B}$;
- $\mathsf{Deg}_{E_1}(\mathcal{A}, \mathcal{B})$: The variables in $\mathsf{Vars}(Z)$ for state_{2j}, $r_0 \le j < r_0 + r_1$ whose values are 1 indicate $\mathsf{Deg}_{E_1}(\mathcal{A}, \mathcal{B})$;

- $\bar{\mathcal{A}}$ and guessed materials in E_0 : The variables in $\mathsf{Vars}(M)$ whose values are 1 indicate $\bar{\mathcal{A}}$ and guessed materials in E_0 which tells us how to prepare the plaintexts leading a $\delta(\mathcal{A})$ set at state_{2r_0};
- Guessed materials in E_2 : The variables in $\mathsf{Vars}(W)$ whose values are 1 indicate the Guessed materials in E_2 with which we can derive the sequence of differences at $\mathsf{state}_{2(r_0+r_1)}$ from the ciphertexts.

Together this information forms a $\mathcal{DS}$-MITM attack on E. Note that the guessed materials in E_0 and E_2 still need to be converted to guessed key materials, which can be done manually or automatically fairly straightforwardly.

According to the semantics of $\mathsf{Vars}(Z)$, if we draw the propagation patterns of $\mathsf{Vars}(X)$ and $\mathsf{Vars}(Y)$ in two figures, then the propagation pattern of $\mathsf{Vars}(Z)$ can be obtained by superposition of the two figures. Therefore, the key to understand the details of the modelling of $\mathcal{DS}$-MITM attack is the so-called *forward/backward differential* and *forward/backward determination relationship.* To make the description succinct and without loss of generality, we introduce the concepts based on a 5-round keyed permutation shown in Figs. 4 and 6. We will also give two concrete examples of the forward differential and backward determination of a 3-round toy SPN block cipher with 32-bit (4-byte) block size. The round function shown in Fig. 3 of the toy cipher consists of an S-box layer (a parallel application of four 8 × 8 Sboxes), and a linear layer L with $y_i = \bigoplus_{j\in\{0,1,2,3\}-\{i\}} x_j$ for $i \in \{0, 1, 2, 3\}$.

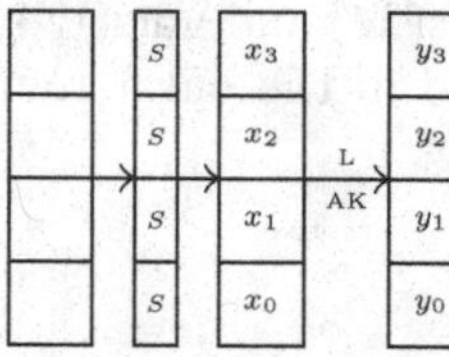

Fig. 3. The round function of the toy cipher

4.1 Forward Differential and Backward Differential

As shown in Fig. 4, given a set $\mathbb{Q}_{\delta(\mathcal{A})}$ of N values $\{Q^0, \cdots, Q^{N-1}\}$ for state_4 which forms a $\delta(\mathcal{A})$ set for the input state of round 2. For every word $\mathsf{state}_i[j]$ ($4 \le i \le 10, 0 \le j < n_c$), we introduce a 0-1 variable $X_i[j]$. We say that the set of 0-1 variables $\{X_i[j] : 4 \le i \le 10, 0 \le j < n_c\}$ models the *forward differential* of $\mathbb{Q}_{\delta(\mathcal{A})}$ in rounds ($2 \to 3 \to 4$) if the following conditions are satisfied.

- Conditions for state_4 (the starting point of the forward differential, which is also the input of round 2) : $\forall j \in \mathcal{A}$, $X_4[j] = 1$ and $\forall j \notin \mathcal{A}$, $X_4[j] = 0$
- Conditions for rounds ($2 \to 3 \to 4$): $X_i[j] = 0$ ($5 \le i \le 10, 0 \le j < n_c$) if and only if $\forall Q^k \in \mathbb{Q}_{\delta(\mathcal{A})}$, $Q^0 \oplus Q^k(\mathsf{state}_i[j]) = 0$

Similarly, as depicted in Fig. 4, we say that the set of variables $\{X_i[j] : 0 \le i \le 4, 0 \le j < n_c\}$ models the *backward differential* of $\mathbb{Q}_{\delta(\mathcal{A})}$ in rounds ($1 \to 0$) if the following conditions are satisfied.

- Conditions for state_4 (the starting point of the backward differential, which is also the output of round 1): $\forall j \in \mathcal{A}$, $X_4[j] = 1$ and $\forall j \notin \mathcal{A}$, $X_4[j] = 0$
- Conditions for rounds $(1 \to 0)$: $X_i[j] = 0$ $(0 \le i < 4, 0 \le j < n_c)$ if and only if $\forall Q^k \in \mathbb{Q}_{\delta(\mathcal{A})}$, $Q^0 \oplus Q^k(\mathsf{state}_i[j]) = 0$

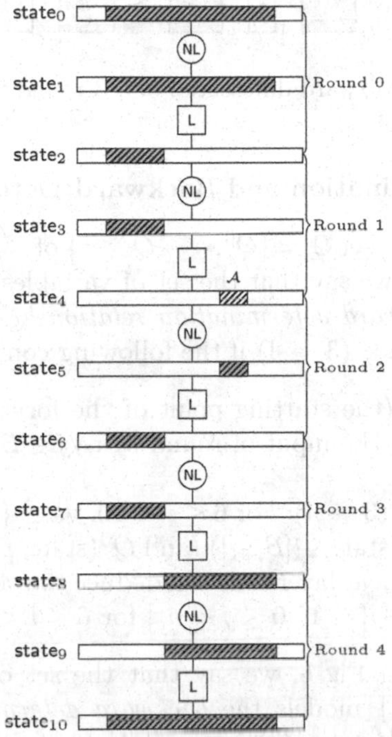

Fig. 4. Forward/backward differential illustrated on a 5-round keyed permutation

Let us give a concrete example. Let $\mathcal{A} = [3]$ and $\mathbb{Q}_{\delta(\mathcal{A})} = \{(0, 0, 0, x) \in (\mathbb{F}_2^8)^4 : x \in \mathbb{F}_2^8\}$. Then the set of variables $X_i[j]$ with $0 \le i \le 6$ and $0 \le j < 4$ shown in Fig. 5 models forward differential of $\mathbb{Q}_{\delta(\mathcal{A})}$ in rounds $(0 \to 1 \to 2)$ if we impose the following constraints on $X_i[j]$. Since the values in $\mathbb{Q}_{\delta(\mathcal{A})}$ are active at the third byte, we have $X_0[0] = X_0[1] = X_0[2] = 0, X_0[3] = 1$. For the S-layers in the toy cipher, we have $X_{2i}[j] = X_{2i+1}[j], 0 \le i \le 2, 0 \le j < 4$. For the linear layers, we enforce $3X_{2(i+1)}[j] - X_{2i+1}[j+1] - X_{2i+1}[j+2] - X_{2i+1}[j+3] \ge 0$ to ensure that $X_{2(i+1)}[j]$ will be equal to 1 when any one of $X_{2i+1}[j+1]$, $X_{2i+1}[j+2]$, $X_{2i+1}[j+3]$ is 1. We also add the constraint

$$X_{2i+1}[j+1] + X_{2i+1}[j+2] + X_{2i+1}[j+3] - X_{2(i+1)}[j] \ge 0$$

to dictate that $X_{2(i+1)}[j]$ must be 0 when all of $X_{2i+1}[j+1]$, $X_{2i+1}[j+2]$, $X_{2i+1}[j+3]$ are 0, where $0 \le i \le 2$, $0 \le j < 4$ and the indexes are computed modulo 4. With these constraints, the $X_i[j]$ variables propagate in a pattern depicted in Fig. 5.

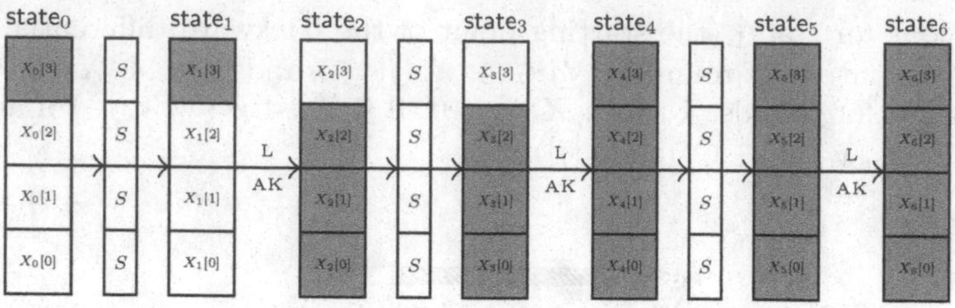

Fig. 5. The forward differential of a 3-round toy cipher

4.2 Forward Determination and Backward Determination

As shown in Fig. 6, given a set $\mathbb{Q} = \{Q^0, \cdots, Q^{N-1}\}$ of N values for state_6 and an ordered set $\mathcal{B}$ of indices, we say that the set of variables $\{Y_i[j] : 6 \leq i \leq 10, 0 \leq j < n_c\}$ models the *forward determination relationship* of $\{Q^0(\mathsf{state}_6[\mathcal{B}]), \cdots, Q^{N-1}(\mathsf{state}_6[\mathcal{B}])\}$ in rounds $(3 \to 4)$ if the following conditions hold.

- Conditions for state_6 (the starting point of the forward determination relationship, which is also the input of round 3) : $\forall j \in \mathcal{B}$, $Y_6[j] = 1$ and $\forall j \notin \mathcal{B}$, $Y_6[j] = 0$
- Conditions for rounds $(3 \to 4)$: For $6 \leq i < 10$, $\forall k \in \{0, \cdots, N-1\}$, with the knowledge of $Q^0 \oplus Q^k(\mathsf{state}_{i+1}[\mathcal{B}_{i+1}])$ (and $Q^0(\mathsf{state}_{i+1}[\mathcal{B}_{i+1}])$ if state_{i+1} is an output state of a nonlinear layer) one can deduce the value $Q^0 \oplus Q^k(\mathsf{state}_i[\mathcal{B}_i])$, where $\mathcal{B}_{i+1} = [j : Y_{i+1}[j] = 1,\ 0 \leq j < n_c]$ for $6 \leq i < 10$ and $\mathcal{B}_6 = \mathcal{B}$.

Similarly, as shown in Fig. 6, we say that the set of 0-1 variables $\{Y_i[j] : 0 \leq i \leq 6, 0 \leq j < n_c\}$ models the *backward determination relationship* of $\{Q^0(\mathsf{state}_6[\mathcal{B}]), \cdots, Q^{N-1}(\mathsf{state}_6[\mathcal{B}])\}$ in rounds $(2 \to 1 \to 0)$ if the following conditions hold.

- Conditions for the state_6 (the starting point of the backward determination relationship, which is also the output of round 2): $\forall j \in \mathcal{B}$, $Y_6[j] = 1$ and $\forall j \notin \mathcal{B}$, $Y_6[j] = 0$
- Conditions for rounds $(2 \to 1 \to 0)$: For $0 < i \leq 6$, $\forall k \in \{0, \cdots, N-1\}$ from the knowledge of the values $Q^0 \oplus Q^k(\mathsf{state}_{i-1}[\mathcal{B}_{i-1}])$, (and $Q^0(\mathsf{state}_{i-1}[\mathcal{B}_{i-1}])$ if state_{i-1} is an input state of a nonlinear layer), one can determine the value $Q^0 \oplus Q^k(\mathsf{state}_i[\mathcal{B}_i])$, where $\mathcal{B}_{i-1} = [j : Y_{i-1}[j] = 1, 0 \leq j < n_c]$ for $0 < i \leq 6$, and $\mathcal{B}_6 = \mathcal{B}$.

Now we show a concrete example. Assume that we have a set $\{Q^0, \cdots, Q^{255}\} = \{(0, 0, 0, x) \in (\mathbb{F}_2^8)^4 : x \in \mathbb{F}_2^8\}$ of 2^8 values for state_0, as depicted in Fig. 7. After the 3-round encryption of the toy cipher, we get a set $\{C^0, \cdots C^{255}\}$ of 2^8 values for state_6. Let $\mathcal{B} = [3]$. The set of variables $Y_i[j]$ with $0 \leq i \leq 6$ and $0 \leq j < 4$ shown in Fig. 7 models backward determination of $\{C^0, \cdots C^{255}\}$ in rounds $(2 \to 1 \to 0)$ if we impose the following constraints on $Y_i[j]$.

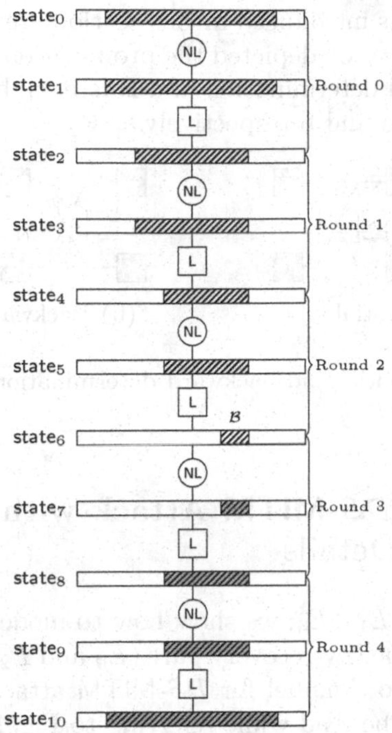

Fig. 6. The forward/backward determination relationship illustrated on a 5-round keyed permutation

Since $\mathcal{B} = [3]$, we have $Y_6[0] = Y_6[1] = Y_6[2] = 0, Y_6[3] = 1$. For the S layers in the toy cipher, we have $Y_{2i}[j] = Y_{2i+1}[j], 0 \leq i \leq 2, 0 \leq j < 4$. For the linear layers, we add $3Y_{2i+1}[j] - Y_{2(i+1)}[j+1] - Y_{2(i+1)}[j+2] - Y_{2(i+1)}[j+3] \geq 0$ to ensure that $Y_{2i+1}[j]$ must be 1 when any one of $Y_{2(i+1)}[j+1], Y_{2(i+1)}[j+2], Y_{2(i+1)}[j+3]$ is 1, and $Y_{2(i+1)}[j+1] + Y_{2(i+1)}[j+2] + Y_{2(i+1)}[j+3] - Y_{2i+1}[j] \geq 0$ to dictate that $Y_{2i+1}[j]$ must be 0 when all of $Y_{2(i+1)}[j+1], Y_{2(i+1)}[j+2], Y_{2(i+1)}[j+3]$ are 0, where the indexes are computed modulo 4. With these constraints, the $Y_i[j]$ variables propagate in a pattern depicted in Fig. 7.

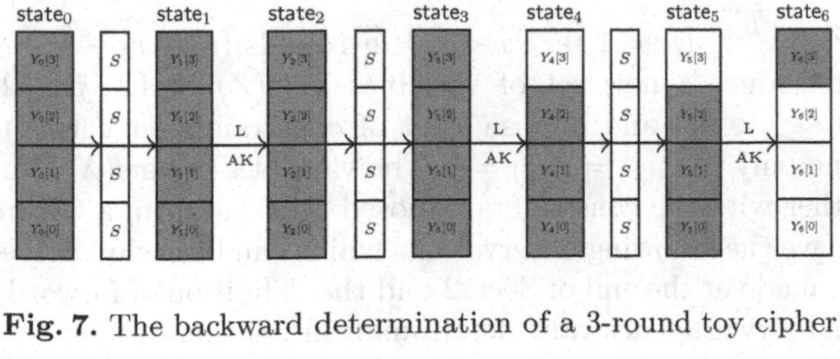

Fig. 7. The backward determination of a 3-round toy cipher

Note that the concepts introduced in this section are generic and not limited to SP ciphers. For instance, we depicted the propagation patterns of the forward differential and backward determination of a Feistel cipher with 8-bit block size and 4×4 S-box in Fig. 8a and b respectively.

(a) Forward differential (b) Backward determination

Fig. 8. The forward differential and backward determination of a 3-round toy cipher with Feistel structure

5 Modelling the $\mathcal{DS}$-MITM Attack with Constraints: The Technical Details

Given a cipher $E = E_2 \circ E_1 \circ E_0$, we show how to model the distinguisher part (E_1), and subsequently the key-recovery part (E_0 and E_2). These models for E_1, E_0 and E_2 jointly lead to a model for $\mathcal{DS}$-MITM attack on E. Note that this part of the paper should be read while referring to Fig. 1.

5.1 CP Model for E_1: The Distinguisher Part

We introduce 2 sets of variables $\mathsf{Vars}(X) = \{X_i[j] : 2r_0 \le i \le 2(r_0 + r_1),\ 0 \le j < n_c\}$ and $\mathsf{Vars}(Y) = \{Y_i[j] : 2r_0 \le i \le 2(r_0 + r_1),\ 0 \le j < n_c\}$ for all the words of the states $\{\mathsf{state}_i[j] : 2r_0 \le i \le 2(r_0 + r_1),\ 0 \le j < n_c\}$ involved in the r_1 rounds of E_1 as shown in Fig. 1.

We then impose a set of constraints on $\mathsf{Vars}(X)$ such that $\mathsf{Vars}(X)$ models the forward differential of a $\delta(\mathcal{A})$-set $\mathbb{Q}_{\delta(\mathcal{A})} = \{Q^0, \cdots, Q^{N-1}\}$ for state_{2r_0} with $\mathcal{A} = [j : X_{2r_0}[j] = 1,\ 0 \le j < n_c]$ in rounds $(r_0 \to r_0 + 1 \to \cdots \to r_0 + r_1 - 1)$. Also, another set of constraints is imposed on $\mathsf{Vars}(Y)$ such that $\mathsf{Vars}(Y)$ models the backward determination relationship of

$$\{Q^0(\mathsf{state}_{2(r_0+r_1)}[\mathcal{B}]), \cdots, Q^{N-1}(\mathsf{state}_{2(r_0+r_1)}[\mathcal{B}])\}$$

with $\mathcal{B} = [j : Y_{2(r_0+r_1)}[j] = 1, 0 \le j < n_c]$ in rounds $(r_0 + r_1 - 1 \to \cdots \to r_0)$. Finally, we introduce a new set of variables $\mathsf{Vars}(Z) = \{Z_i[j] : 2r_0 \le i \le 2(r_0 + r_1),\ 0 \le j < n_c\}$ and impose a set of constraints on $\mathsf{Vars}(Z)$ such that $Z_i[j] = 1$ if and only if $X_i[j] = Y_i[j] = 1$. The variables in $\mathsf{Vars}(X)$, $\mathsf{Vars}(Y)$, and $\mathsf{Vars}(Z)$ together with the constraints imposed on them form a CP model.

Then we have the following observations which can be easily derived from the Assumption 1 made at the end of Sect. 2 and the definition of forward/backward differential and forward/backward determination relationship.

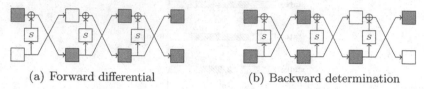

Observation 1. *If* $\mathsf{Vars}(X)$ *models the forward differential of a* $\delta(\mathcal{A})$*-set*

$$\mathbb{Q}_{\delta(\mathcal{A})} = \{Q^0, \cdots, Q^{N-1}\}$$

for state_{2r_0} *(Fig. 1) with* $\mathcal{A} = [j : X_{2r_0}[j] = 1,\ 0 \le j < n_c]$ *in rounds* $(r_0 \to r_0 + 1 \to \cdots \to r_0 + r_1 - 1)$*, then for an arbitrary ordered set* $\mathcal{B}$ *of indices, we can determine the sequence of differences*

$$\Delta_{E_1}(\mathbb{Q}_{\delta(\mathcal{A})}, \mathcal{B}) = [Q^0 \oplus Q^1(\mathsf{state}_{2(r_0+r_1)}[\mathcal{B}]), \cdots, Q^0 \oplus Q^{N-1}(\mathsf{state}_{2(r_0+r_1)}[\mathcal{B}])]$$

from the knowledge of the following set of intermediate values of Q^0*.*

$$\{Q^0(\mathsf{state}_{2i}[j]) : X_{2i}[j] = 1, r_0 \le i < r_0 + r_1, 0 \le j < n_c\}.$$

Observation 2. *Let* $\mathbb{Q}_{\delta(\mathcal{A})} = \{Q^0, \cdots, Q^{N-1}\}$ *be a* $\delta(\mathcal{A})$ *set for* state_{2r_0} *for an arbitrary* $\mathcal{A}$*. If* $\mathsf{Vars}(Y)$ *models the backward determination relationship of*

$$\{Q^0(\mathsf{state}_{2(r_0+r_1)}[\mathcal{B}]), \cdots, Q^{N-1}(\mathsf{state}_{2(r_0+r_1)}[\mathcal{B}])\}$$

with $\mathcal{B} = [j : Y_{2(r_0+r_1)}[j] = 1, 0 \le j < n_c]$ *in rounds* $(r_0 + r_1 - 1 \to \cdots \to r_0)$*, then we can determine the sequence of differences*

$$\Delta_{E_1}(\mathbb{Q}_{\delta(\mathcal{A})}, \mathcal{B}) = [Q^0 \oplus Q^1(\mathsf{state}_{2(r_0+r_1)}[\mathcal{B}]), \cdots, Q^0 \oplus Q^{N-1}(\mathsf{state}_{2(r_0+r_1)}[\mathcal{B}])]$$

from the knowledge of the following set of intermediate values of Q^0

$$\{Q^0(\mathsf{state}_{2i}[j]) : Y_{2i}[j] = 1, r_0 \le i < r_0 + r_1, 0 \le j < n_c\}.$$

Note that Observations 1 and 2 are stated with an arbitrary ordered set $\mathcal{A}$ and $\mathcal{B}$ respectively. Therefore, if we know the intermediate values of $Q^0(\mathsf{state}[j])$ such that $X_{2i}[j]$ and $Y_{2i}[j]$ are equal to 1 simultaneously, we can determine the sequence $\Delta_{E_1}(\mathbb{Q}_{\delta(\mathcal{A})}, \mathcal{B})$ with the specific $\mathcal{A}$ and $\mathcal{B}$ corresponding to the underlying values of $\mathsf{Vars}(X)$ and $\mathsf{Vars}(Y)$.

Observation 3. *Let* $\mathcal{A} = [j : X_{2r_0}[j] = 1,\ 0 \le j < n_c]$*,* $\mathcal{B} = [j : Y_{2(r_0+r_1)}[j] = 1,\ 0 \le j < n_c]$*, and* $\mathbb{Q}_{\delta(\mathcal{A})} = \{Q^0, \cdots, Q^{N-1}\}$ *be a* $\delta(\mathcal{A})$ *set for* state_{2r_0}*. Then from the knowledge of the following* $\sum_{i=r_0}^{r_0+r_1-1} \sum_{j=0}^{n_c-1} Z_{2i}[j]$ *c-bit words*

$$\{Q^0(\mathsf{state}_{2i}[j]) : Z_{2i}[j] = 1, r_0 \le i < r_0 + r_1, 0 \le j < n_c\},$$

we can determine the value of the sequence of differences

$$\Delta_{E_1}(\mathbb{Q}_{\delta(\mathcal{A})}, \mathcal{B}) = [Q^0 \oplus Q^1(\mathsf{state}_{2(r_0+r_1)}[\mathcal{B}]), \cdots, Q^0 \oplus Q^{N-1}(\mathsf{state}_{2(r_0+r_1)}[\mathcal{B}])].$$

From the above observations, it is easy to see that any solution of $\mathsf{Vars}(X)$, $\mathsf{Vars}(Y)$, and $\mathsf{Vars}(Z)$ corresponds to a $\mathcal{DS}$-MITM distinguisher $(\mathcal{A}, \mathcal{B}, \mathsf{Deg}_{E_1}(\mathcal{A}, \mathcal{B}))$ with $\mathcal{A} = [j : X_{2r_0}[j] = 1,\ 0 \le j < n_c]$, $\mathcal{B} = [j : Y_{2(r_0+r_1)}[j] = 1,\ 0 \le j < n_c]$, and $\mathsf{Deg}_{E_1}(\mathcal{A}, \mathcal{B}) = \sum_{i=r_0}^{r_0+r_1-1} \sum_{j=0}^{n_c-1} Z_{2i}[j]$.

5.2 CP Model for the Outer Rounds E_0 and E_2

The CP Model for E_0. As discussed in Sect. 3, the attacker needs to prepare a set $\mathbb{P}_{\delta(\bar{\mathcal{A}})}$ of chosen plaintexts based on the distingusher $(\mathcal{A}, \mathcal{B}, \mathsf{Deg}_{E_1}(\mathcal{A}, \mathcal{B}))$ placed at E_1. According to the definition of $\bar{\mathcal{A}}$, there must be $P^1, \cdots, P^{N-1}$ in $\mathbb{P}_{\delta(\bar{\mathcal{A}})}$ such that $\mathbb{Q}_{\delta(\mathcal{A})} = \{Q^0, \cdots, Q^{n-1}\}$ forms a $\delta(\mathcal{A})$-set for state_{2r_0}, where $Q^j = E_0(P^j)$.

For E_0 we introduce a set of 0-1 variables $\mathsf{Vars}(M) = \{M_i[j] : 0 \leq i \leq 2r_0, 0 \leq j < n_c\}$ and impose a set of constraints on $\mathsf{Vars}(M)$ such that $\mathsf{Vars}(M)$ models the backward differential of the $\delta(\mathcal{A})$-set $\mathbb{Q}_{\delta(\mathcal{A})}$ with $\mathcal{A} = \{j : X_{2r_0}[j] = 1, 0 \leq j < n_c\}$ in rounds $(r_0 - 1 \to \cdots \to 0)$. Then according to the definition of backward differential and assumption 1, we have the following observation.

Observation 4. *Given $P^0 \in \mathbb{P}_{\delta(\bar{\mathcal{A}})}$, the set*

$$\mathsf{Guess}(E_0) = \{P^0(\mathsf{state}_{2i}[j]) : M_{2i}[j] = 1, 0 < i < r_0, 0 \leq j < n_c\}$$

of $\sum_{i=1}^{r_0-1} \sum_{j=0}^{n_c-1} M_{2i}[j]$ c-bit words needs to be guessed to find $P^1, \cdots, P^{N-1}$ in $\mathbb{P}_{\delta(\bar{\mathcal{A}})}$.

The CP Model for E_2. After the guess of $\mathsf{Guess}(E_0)$, we obtain a set $\{P^0, \cdots, P^{N-1}\} \subseteq \mathbb{P}_{\delta(\bar{\mathcal{A}})}$ such that $\mathbb{Q}_{\delta(\mathcal{A})} = \{Q^0, \cdots, Q^{N-1}\}$ with $Q^j = E_0(P^j)$ forms a $\delta(\mathcal{A})$ set for state_{2r_0} (under the guess). Let $C^j = E(P^j)$, $0 \leq j < N$. Then we want to get the sequence

$$\Delta_{E_1}(\mathbb{Q}_{\delta(\mathcal{A})}, \mathcal{B}) = \{Q^0(\mathsf{state}_{2(r_0+r_1)}[\mathcal{B}]), \cdots, Q^{N-1}(\mathsf{state}_{2(r_0+r_1)}[\mathcal{B}])\}$$

by decrypting $\{C^0, \cdots, C^{N-1}\}$ with E_2.

For E_2 we introduce a set of 0-1 variables $\mathsf{Vars}(W) = \{W_i[j] : 2(r_0 + r_1) \leq i \leq 2(r_0 + r_1 + r_2), 0 \leq j < n_c\}$ and impose a set of constraints on $\mathsf{Vars}(W)$ such that $\mathsf{Vars}(W)$ models the forward determination of the set $\{Q^0(\mathsf{state}_{2(r_0+r_1)}[\mathcal{B}]), \cdots, Q^{N-1}(\mathsf{state}_{2(r_0+r_1)}[\mathcal{B}])\}$ with $\mathcal{B} = \{j : Y_{2(r_0+r_1)}[j] = 1, 0 \leq j < n_c\}$ in rounds $(r_0 + r_1 \to \cdots \to r_0 + r_1 + r_2 - 1)$.

Observation 5. *Given $\{C^0, \cdots, C^{N-1}\}$, the set*

$$\mathsf{Guess}(E_2) = \{Q^0(\mathsf{state}_{2i}[j]) : W_{2i}[j] = 1, r_0 + r_1 \leq i < r_0 + r_1 + r_2, 0 \leq j < n_c\}$$

of $\sum_{i=r_0+r_1}^{r_0+r_1+r_2-1} \sum_{j=0}^{n_c-1} W_{2i}[j]$ c-bit words needs to be guessed to determine the sequence

$$\Delta_{E_1}(\mathbb{Q}_{\delta(\mathcal{A})}, \mathcal{B}) = [C^0 \oplus C^1(\mathsf{state}_{2(r_0+r_1)}[\mathcal{B}]), \cdots, C^0 \oplus C^{N-1}(\mathsf{state}_{2(r_0+r_1)}[\mathcal{B}])].$$

Remark. There is still a gap between $\mathsf{Guess}(E_i)$ and k_{E_i} for $i \in \{0, 2\}$. To perform the attack (see Sect. 3), we need to identify k_{E_i} rather than $\mathsf{Guess}(E_i)$. As we will show in Sects. 7.1, 7.2 and 7.3, it is fairly straightforward to convert $\mathsf{Guess}(E_i)$ to k_{E_i}.

6 How to Use the Modelling Technique in Practice?

The modelling technique for $\mathcal{DS}$-MITM attack can be applied in several scenarios. In the following, we identify two of them and give a discussion of possible extensions.

6.1 Enumeration of $\mathcal{DS}$-MITM Distinguishers

In Sect. 5, the descriptions of the modelling of E_1 (the distinguisher part) and the outer rounds (E_0 and E_2) are intentionally separated to have a method whose only purpose is to search for $\mathcal{DS}$-MITM distinguishers.

When we target a cipher with $\mathcal{DS}$-MITM attack, probably the first that come into mind is to identify a $\mathcal{DS}$-MITM distinguisher covering as many rounds as possible. To this end, we can build a model with the method presented in Sect. 5 for k rounds of the target cipher, and add one more constraint dictating that

$$\mathsf{Deg}(\mathcal{A},\mathcal{B}) = \sum_{i=r_0}^{r_0+r_1-1}\sum_{j=0}^{n_c-1} Z_{2i}[j] < |K|_c$$

to prevent the complexity of the offline phase from being too high, where $|K|_c$ is the number of c-bit words in the master key of the target cipher. Then we can enumerate all solutions using a constraint solver. If the solutions of the model lead to valid distinguishers, we can increase k and try to find distinguishers covering more rounds.

6.2 Fast Prototyping for $\mathcal{DS}$-MITM Attacks

Given a keyed permutation $E = E_2 \circ E_1 \circ E_0$, it is difficult to determine which $\mathcal{DS}$-MITM distinguisher covering E_1 will lead to the best attack, though intuitively a distinguisher $(\mathcal{A},\mathcal{B},\mathsf{Deg}(\mathcal{A},\mathcal{B}))$ with smaller $\mathsf{Deg}(\mathcal{A},\mathcal{B})$ is preferred. In this situation, we can set up a model for the whole $E_2 \circ E_1 \circ E_0$ with the constraints

$$\begin{cases} \mathsf{Deg}(\mathcal{A},\mathcal{B}) = \sum_{i=r_0}^{r_0+r_1-1}\sum_{j=0}^{n_c-1} Z_{2i}[j] < |K|_c \\ \sum\limits_{i=1}^{r_0-1}\sum\limits_{j=0}^{n_c-1} M_{2i}[j] + \sum\limits_{i=r_0+r_1}^{r_0+r_1+r_2-1}\sum\limits_{j=0}^{n_c-1} W_{2i}[j] < |K|_c \end{cases}$$

The resolution of the model leads to both a distinguisher covering E_1 and an attack based on the distinguisher simultaneously, which should be very useful in fast prototyping of $\mathcal{DS}$-MITM attack in the analysis and design of block ciphers. Note that the output of the tool is a distinguisher $(\mathcal{A},\mathcal{B},\mathsf{Deg}(\mathcal{A},\mathcal{B}))$ and the secret information $\mathsf{Guess}(E_0)$ and $\mathsf{Guess}(E_2)$, which needs to be converted to k_{E_0} and k_{E_2} automatically or manually. Then the so-called key-bridging technique [29,47] can be applied to give an estimation of $|k_{E_0} \cup k_{E_2}|$.

Another strategy is to find all k-round distinguishers $(\mathcal{A},\mathcal{B},\mathsf{Deg}(\mathcal{A},\mathcal{B}))$ with $\mathsf{Deg}(\mathcal{A},\mathcal{B}) < d$ for some integer d. Then various generic or dedicated optimization techniques [29] (some of which may be unknown at present) can be applied based on these distinguishers to see which one leads to the best attack.

7 Applications

7.1 Application to SKINNY

In this section, we apply our method to SKINNY-128-384 (the TK3 version with 128-bit block size, 384-bit key, and 0-bit tweak) to have a concrete example demonstrating the method presented in Sect. 4. The specification of SKINNY can be found in [44], and we omit it from this paper due to space restrictions.

The indexing scheme we used for analyzing SKINNY is illustrated in Fig. 9, which is essentially the same as Fig. 1, except that the states are drawn as 4×4 squares and the NL layer is composed of a parallel application of 16 Sboxes and a shift row operation.

To model an r-round $\mathcal{DS}$-MITM distinguisher, we introduce 3 sets $\mathsf{Vars}(X)$, $\mathsf{Vars}(Y)$, and $\mathsf{Vars}(Z)$ of variables for all the states involved in rounds $(k, k+1, \cdots, k+r-1)$, where $\mathsf{Vars}(X) = \{X_i[j] : 2k \leq i \leq 2(k+r), 0 \leq j < n_c\}$ models the forward differential, $\mathsf{Vars}(Y) = \{Y_i[j] : 2k \leq i \leq 2(k+r), 0 \leq j < n_c\}$ models the backward determination relationship, and $\mathsf{Vars}(Z) = \{Z_i[j] : 2k \leq i \leq 2(k+r), 0 \leq j < n_c\}$ such that $Z_i[j] = 1$ if and only if $X_i[j] = Y_i[j] = 1$. Note that the logical statement of $Z_i[j]$ can be converted into allowed tuples of $(Z_i[j], X_i[j], Y_i[j])$, that is $(Z_i[j], X_i[j], Y_i[j]) \in \{(0,0,0), (0,0,1), (0,1,0), (1,1,1)\}$, which can be modeled in CP or MILP trivially [10,14]. So the only question left is what kind of constraints should be imposed on $\mathsf{Vars}(X)$ and $\mathsf{Vars}(Y)$ such that they model the intended properties.

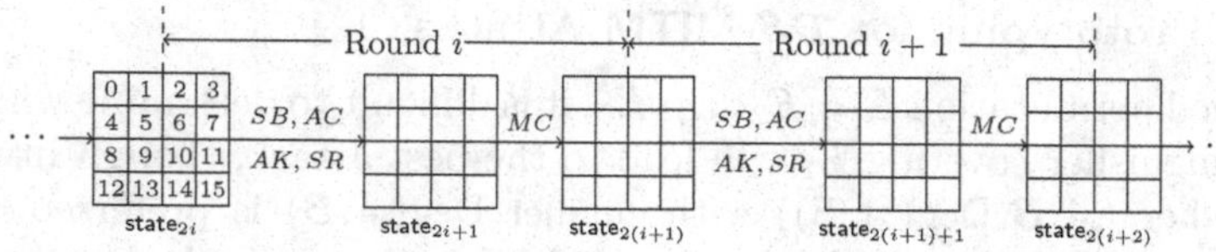

Fig. 9. The indexing scheme used for the rounds, states, and words of SKINNY

The Constraints Imposed on $\mathsf{Vars}(X)$. Firstly, according to the definition of forward differential and the SB, AC, AK, SR operations of SKINNY, we have $X_{2i+1}[4a+b] = X_{2i}[4a+(b-a) \mod 4]$ for $k \leq i < k+r$, where $a, b \in \{0,1,2,3\}$ are used to index the rows and columns of a state respectively. Secondly, for every column $b \in \{0,1,2,3\}$ and $k \leq i < k+r$, we impose the following constraints due to the MC operation

- $X_{2(i+1)}[b] = 0$ if and only if $X_{2i+1}[b] = X_{2i+1}[b+8] = X_{2i+1}[b+12] = 0$;
- $X_{2(i+1)}[b+4] = X_{2i+1}[b]$;
- $X_{2(i+1)}[b+8] = 0$ if and only if $X_{2i+1}[b+4] = X_{2i+1}[b+8] = 0$;
- $X_{2(i+1)}[b+12] = 0$ if and only if $X_{2i+1}[b] = X_{2i+1}[b+8] = 0$.

Note that all constraints given in the above can be converted to allowed tuples of some variables and therefore can be easily modeled by the CP approach.

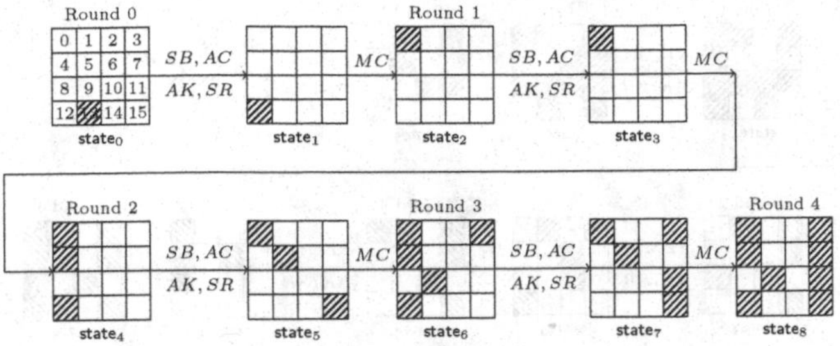

Fig. 10. Forward differential of a $\delta(\mathcal{A})$ set for state_0 in rounds $(0 \to 1 \to 2 \to 3)$ with $\mathcal{A} = [13]$

An example solution of a set of variables modelling the forward differential of 4-round SKINNY is visualized in Fig. 10.

The Constraints Imposed on $\mathsf{Vars}(Y)$**.** Similarly, according to the definition of backward determination relationship and the SB, AC, AK, SR operations of SKINNY, we have $Y_{2i+1}[4a+b] = Y_{2i}[4a+(b-a) \mod 4]$ for $k \le i < k+r$ and $a, b \in \{0,1,2,3\}$. In addition, for every column $b \in \{0,1,2,3\}$ and $k \le i < k+r$, we impose the following constraints

- $Y_{2i+1}[b] = 0$ if and only if $Y_{2(i+1)}[b] = Y_{2(i+1)}[b+4] = Y_{2(i+1)}[b+12] = 0$;
- $Y_{2i+1}[b+4] = Y_{2(i+1)}[b+8]$;
- $Y_{2i+1}[b+8] = 0$ if and only if $Y_{2(i+1)}[b] = Y_{2(i+1)}[b+8] = Y_{2(i+1)}[b+12] = 0$;
- $Y_{2i+1}[b+12] = Y_{2(i+1)}[b]$.

An example solution of a set of variables modelling the backward determination relationship of 4-round SKINNY is visualized in Fig. 11. According to the constraints imposed on $\mathsf{Vars}(Z)$, if $\mathsf{Vars}(X)$ and $\mathsf{Vars}(Y)$ are assigned to values as illustrated in Figs. 10 and 11 respectively, then we can derive the values of $\mathsf{Vars}(Z)$ by superposition of Figs. 10 and 11, as depicted in Fig. 12.

Additional Constraints. We require $\sum X_i[j] \neq 0$, $\sum Y_i[j] \neq 0$, and $\sum Z_i[j] \neq 0$ to exclude the trivial solution where all variables are assigned to 0. Also, to

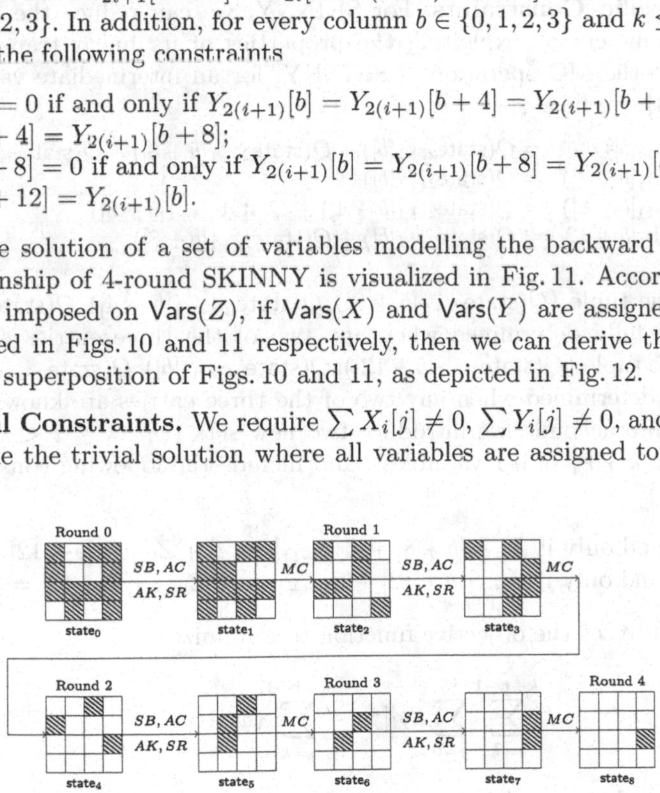

Fig. 11. The backward determination relationship of $\{Q^0(\mathsf{state}_8[\mathcal{B}]), \cdots, Q^{N-1}(\mathsf{state}_8[\mathcal{B}])\}$ for state_8 in rounds $(3 \to 2 \to 1 \to 0)$ with $\mathcal{B} = [11]$

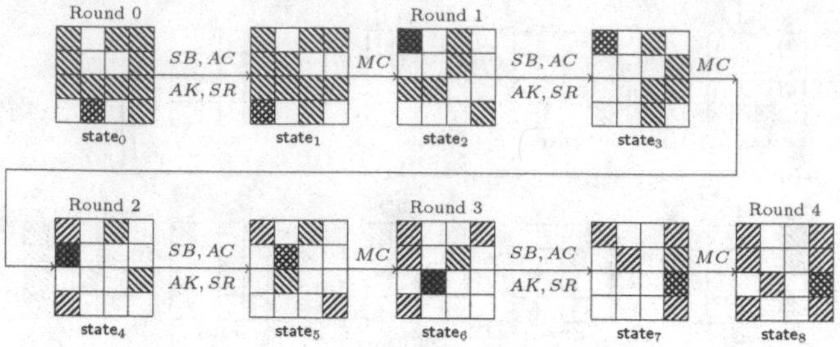

Fig. 12. A visualization of an instantiation of $\mathsf{Vars}(Z)$ according to the values assigned to $\mathsf{Vars}(X)$ and $\mathsf{Vars}(Y)$, which can be regarded as a superposition of Figs. 10 and 11

make the time complexity of the offline phase not exceeding the complexity of the exhaustive search attack, we require $\sum Z_{2i}[j] \leq |K|_c = 384/8 = 48$.

Objective Functions. The objective function is to minimize $\sum_{i=k}^{k+r-1} \sum_{j=0}^{15} Z_{2i}[j]$ to make $\mathsf{Deg}(\mathcal{A}, \mathcal{B})$ as small as possible.

Cipher-Specific Constraints. For SKINNY, we can reduce the number of guessed parameters by exploiting the properties of its linear transformation. According to the MC operation of SKINNY, for an intermediate value Q and $b \in \{0, 1, 2, 3\}$, we have

$$\begin{cases} Q(\mathsf{state}_{2(i+1)}[b]) &= Q(\mathsf{state}_{2i+1}[b]) + Q(\mathsf{state}_{2i+1}[b+8]) + Q(\mathsf{state}_{2i+1}[b+12]) \\ Q(\mathsf{state}_{2(i+1)}[b+4]) &= Q(\mathsf{state}_{2i+1}[b]) \\ Q(\mathsf{state}_{2(i+1)}[b+8]) &= Q(\mathsf{state}_{2i+1}[b+4]) + Q(\mathsf{state}_{2i+1}[b+8]) \\ Q(\mathsf{state}_{2(i+1)}[b+12]) &= Q(\mathsf{state}_{2i+1}[b]) + Q(\mathsf{state}_{2i+1}[b+8]) \end{cases}$$

Hence, the tuple $(Q(\mathsf{state}_{2i+1}[b+8]), Q(\mathsf{state}_{2(i+1)}[b+4]), Q(\mathsf{state}_{2(i+1)}[b+12]))$ can be fully determined when any two of the three entries are known. Similarly, the tuple $(Q(\mathsf{state}_{2i+1}[b+12]), Q(\mathsf{state}_{2(i+1)}[b]), Q(\mathsf{state}_{2(i+1)}[b+12]))$ can be fully determined when any two of the three entries are known. To take these facts into account, we introduce two new sets $\{\phi_i : k \leq i < k+r\}$ and $\{\varphi_i : k \leq i < k+r\}$ of 0-1 variables , and include the following constraints for $b \in \{0, 1, 2, 3\}$

- $\phi_i = 1$ if and only if $Z_{2i+1}[b+8] + Z_{2(i+1)}[b+4] + Z_{2(i+1)}[b+12] = 3$;
- $\psi_i = 1$ if and only if $Z_{2i+1}[b+12] + Z_{2(i+1)}[b] + Z_{2(i+1)}[b+12] = 3$;

We also need to set the objective function to minimize

$$\sum_{i=k}^{k+r-1} \sum_{j=0}^{15} Z_{2i}[j] - \sum_{i=k}^{k+r-1} (\phi_i + \psi_i).$$

Using the above model, we can find a $\mathcal{DS}$-MITM distinguisher for 10.5-round SKINNY-128-384 in 2 s. In [44], the designers of SKINNY expected that there should be no $\mathcal{DS}$-MITM distinguisher covering more than 10 rounds of

SKINNY since partial-matching can work at most $(6-1)+(6-1)=10$ rounds. Hence, our result concretize the 10-round distinguisher, and actually our tool found $\mathcal{DS}$-MITM distinguishers of SKINNY covering more than 10 rounds. An enumeration of all $\mathcal{DS}$-MITM distinguishers covering 10.5-round SKINNY with $40 \le \mathsf{Deg}(\mathcal{A},\mathcal{B}) \le 48$ is performed and the results are listed in Table 2. Note that distinguishers with $\mathsf{Deg}(\mathcal{A},\mathcal{B}) > 48$ are ineffective for an attack. We then try to get an attack on SKINNY by modelling E_1 (the distinguisher part), E_0 and E_2 (the outer rounds) as a whole with the method presented in Sect. 4. We omit the detailed description of the constraints for $\mathsf{Vars}(M)$ and $\mathsf{Vars}(W)$ introduced for E_0 and E_2 since they are similar to the constraints imposed on $\mathsf{Vars}(X)$ and $\mathsf{Vars}(Y)$ given previously. As a result, we identify a $\mathcal{DS}$-MITM attack on 22-round SKINNY-128-384 based on a distinguisher $(\mathcal{A},\mathcal{B},\mathsf{Deg}(\mathcal{A},\mathcal{B}))$ with $\mathcal{A}=[14]$, $\mathcal{B}=[7]$, and $\deg(\mathcal{A},\mathcal{B})=40$, which is shown in Fig. 17 in [supplementary material]. The secret intermediate values $\mathsf{Guess}(E_0)$ and $\mathsf{Guess}(E_2)$ created by P^0 in the outer rounds are presented in Fig. 18 in [supplementary material A]. To perform the attack, we still need to convert $\mathsf{Guess}(E_0)$ and $\mathsf{Guess}(E_2)$ into the secret information of subkeys manually, which is visualized in Fig. 19 in [supplementary material A]. Then we perform the key-bridging technique [29,47] on k_{in} and k_{out}, and find that $|k_{in} \cup k_{out}| \le 376$.

Complexity Analysis. According to the discussion of Sect. 3.3, in the offline phase, the time complexity is $2^{8\times 40} \times 2^{8\times 1} \times \frac{40}{16\times 22} C_E \approx 2^{324.86} C_E$, and the memory complexity is $(2^8-1) \times 8 \times 1 \times 2^{8\times 40} \approx 2^{330.99}$ bits. In the online phase, the time complexity is $2^{47\times 8} \times 2^{8\times 1} \times \frac{57+64}{22\times 16} C_E \approx 2^{382.46} C_E$. The data complexity of the attack is $2^{8\times 12} = 2^{96}$, which can be obtained from the input state of Fig. 18 in [supplementary material A].

7.2 Application to LBlock

The indexing scheme we used for analyzing LBlock is shown in Fig. 13, where the AK is the subkey xor operation, SB is a parallel application of 8 4×4 S-boxes, and LN is a permutation permuting j to $\mathrm{LN}[j]$.

To model an r-round $\mathcal{DS}$-MITM distinguisher of LBlock, we introduce 3 sets $\mathsf{Vars}(X)$, $\mathsf{Vars}(Y)$, and $\mathsf{Vars}(Z)$ of variables for all the states involved in rounds $(k, k+1, \cdots, k+r-1)$, where $\mathsf{Vars}(X) = \{X_i^L[j], X_i^R[j] : k \le i \le k+r, 0 \le j < n_c\} \cup \{X_i^S[j], X_i^M[j] : k \le i < k+r, 0 \le j < n_c\}$ models the forward differential, $\mathsf{Vars}(Y) = \{Y_i^L[j], Y_i^R[j] : k \le i \le k+r, 0 \le j < n_c\} \cup \{Y_i^S[j], Y_i^M[j] : k \le i < k+r, 0 \le j < n_c\}$ models the backward determination relationship, and $\mathsf{Vars}(Z) = \{Z_i^L[j], Z_i^R[j] : k \le i \le k+r, 0 \le j < n_c\} \cup \{Z_i^S[j], Z_i^M[j] : k \le i < k+r, 0 \le j < n_c\}$ such that

- $Z_i^L[j]=1$ if and only if $X_i^L[j]=Y_i^L[j]=1$
- $Z_i^R[j]=1$ if and only if $X_i^R[j]=Y_i^R[j]=1$
- $Z_i^S[j]=1$ if and only if $X_i^S[j]=Y_i^S[j]=1$
- $Z_i^M[j]=1$ if and only if $X_i^M[j]=Y_i^M[j]=1$

Table 2. An enumeration of all $\mathcal{DS}$-MITM distinguishers for 10.5-round SKINNY-128-384 with $40 \leq \mathsf{Deg}(\mathcal{A}, \mathcal{B}) \leq 48$.

No.	$\mathcal{A}$	$\mathcal{B}$	$\mathsf{Deg}(\mathcal{A}, \mathcal{B})$	No.	$\mathcal{A}$	$\mathcal{B}$	$\mathsf{Deg}(\mathcal{A}, \mathcal{B})$	No.	$\mathcal{A}$	$\mathcal{B}$	$\mathsf{Deg}(\mathcal{A}, \mathcal{B})$
1	[15]	[4]	40	21	[13]	[6, 4]	45	41	[13]	[5]	46
2	[12]	[5]	40	22	[14]	[7, 5]	45	42	[12]	[4]	46
3	[13]	[6]	40	23	[13]	[6, 4]	45	43	[14]	[6]	46
4	[14]	[7]	40	24	[15]	[4, 6]	45	44	[15]	[7]	46
5	[15]	[5]	42	25	[13]	[5]	45	51	[13]	[4, 6]	47
6	[12]	[6]	42	26	[15]	[6]	45	52	[12]	[7, 5]	47
7	[13]	[7]	42	27	[14]	[4]	45	53	[14]	[5, 7]	47
8	[14]	[4]	42	28	[13]	[4]	45	54	[15]	[6, 4]	47
9	[13]	[5]	43	29	[14]	[5]	45	49	[13]	[6]	47
10	[14]	[6]	43	30	[14]	[6]	45	50	[13]	[6]	47
11	[12]	[4]	43	31	[12]	[4]	45	51	[14]	[7]	47
12	[15]	[7]	43	32	[15]	[5]	45	52	[12]	[5]	47
13	[12]	[7]	44	33	[13]	[7]	45	53	[12]	[5]	47
14	[13]	[4]	44	34	[12]	[6]	45	54	[14]	[7]	47
15	[12]	[7]	44	35	[15]	[7]	45	55	[15]	[4]	47
16	[13]	[4]	44	36	[12]	[7]	45	56	[15]	[4]	47
17	[13]	[4]	44	37	[14]	[4, 6]	46	57	[15]	[7, 5]	48
18	[14]	[5]	44	38	[13]	[7, 5]	46	58	[14]	[6, 4]	48
19	[14]	[5]	44	39	[15]	[5, 7]	46	59	[12]	[4, 6]	48
20	[13]	[4]	44	40	[12]	[6, 4]	46	60	[13]	[5, 7]	48

Note that the logical statement of $\mathsf{Vars}(Z)$ can be converted into allowed tuples, e.g. $(Z_i^L[j], X_i^L[j], Y_i^L[j]) \in \{(0,0,0), (0,0,1), (0,1,0), (1,1,1)\}$, which can be modeled in CP or MILP trivially [10,14]. So the only question left is what kind of constraints should be imposed on $\mathsf{Vars}(X)$ and $\mathsf{Vars}(Y)$ such that they model the intended properties.

The Constraints Imposed on $\mathsf{Vars}(X)$. According to the definition of forward differential and the AK, SB, LN, $\lll 8$, XOR operations of LBlock, we have the following constraints

- $X_i^L[j] = X_i^S[j] = X_{i+1}^R[j]$, for $k \leq i < k+r$ and $0 \leq j \leq 7$;
- $X_i^M[LN[j]] = X_i^S[j]$, for $k \leq i < k+r$ and $0 \leq j \leq 7$;
- $X_{i+1}^L[j] = 0$ if and only if $X_i^R[(j+2) \mod 8] = X_i^M[j] = 0$, for $k \leq i < k+r$ and $0 \leq j \leq 7$.

The Constraints Imposed on $\mathsf{Vars}(Y)$. Similarly, according to the definition of the backward determination relationship and the AK, SB, LN, $\lll 8$, XOR operations of LBlock, we have the following constraints

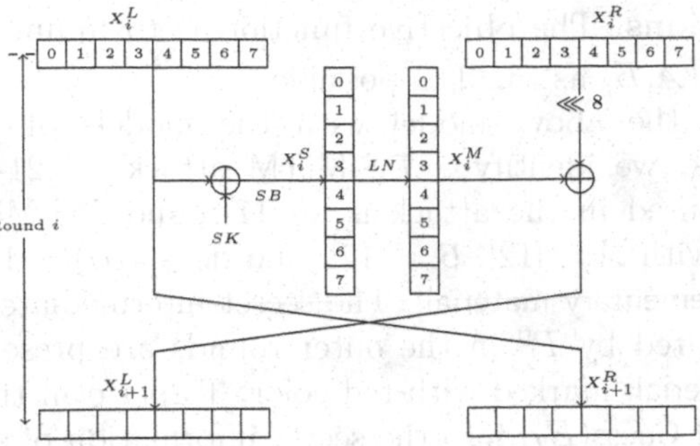

Fig. 13. The indexing scheme used for LBlock

- For $k \leq i < k+r$ and $0 \leq j \leq 7$, $Y_i^L[j] = 0$ if and only if $Y_{i+1}^R[j] = Y_i^S[j] = 0$;
- $Y_i^M[LN[j]] = Y_i^S[j]$, for $k \leq i < k+r$ and $0 \leq j \leq 7$;
- For XOR and SR operations: $Y_i^M[j] = Y_i^R[(j+2) \mod 8] = Y_{i+1}^L[j]$

According to the constraints imposed on $\mathsf{Vars}(Z)$, if $\mathsf{Vars}(X)$ and $\mathsf{Vars}(Y)$ are assigned to values as illustrated in Fig. 14a and b, then we can derive the values of $\mathsf{Vars}(Z)$ by superposition of Fig. 14a and b, which is depicted in Fig. 14c.

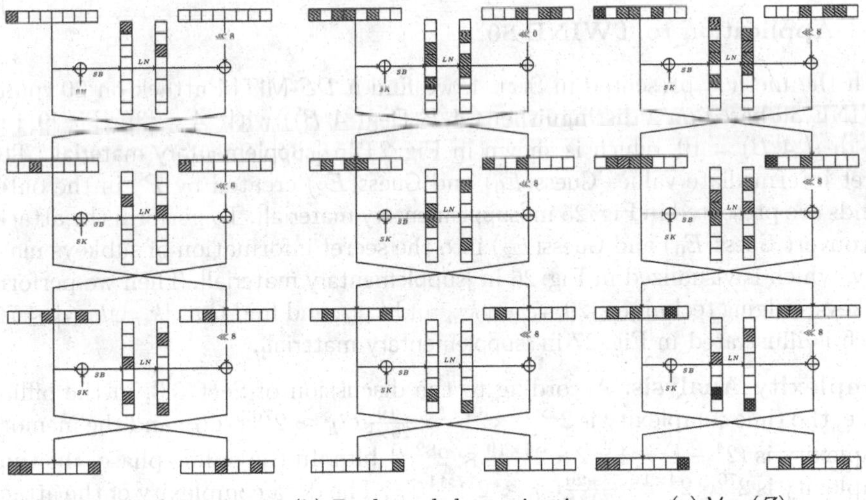

(a) Forward differential (b) Backward determination (c) $\mathsf{Vars}(Z)$

Fig. 14. An instantiation of the $\mathsf{Vars}(X)$, $\mathsf{Vars}(Y)$ and $\mathsf{Vars}(Z)$

Additional Constraints. We require $\sum X_k^L[j] + \sum X_k^R[j] \neq 0$, $\sum Y_{k+r}^L[j] + \sum Y_{k+r}^R[j] \neq 0$, to exclude the trivial solution where all variables are assigned to 0. Also, to make the time complexity of the offline phase not exceeding the complexity of the exhaustive search, we require $\sum Z_i^S[j] < |K|_c = 80/4 = 20$.

Objective Functions. The objective function is to minimize $\sum_{i=k}^{k+r-1}\sum_{j=0}^{7} Z_i^S[j]$ to make $\mathsf{Deg}(\mathcal{A},\mathcal{B})$ as small as possible.

By integrating the above model with the models of E_0 and E_2 with some simple tweak, we identify a $\mathcal{DS}$-MITM attack on 21-round LBLOCK. The distinguisher used in the attack is an 11-round $\mathcal{DS}$-MITM distinguisher $(\mathcal{A},\mathcal{B},\mathsf{Deg}(\mathcal{A},\mathcal{B}))$ with $\mathcal{A}=[12]$, $\mathcal{B}=[12]$, and $\deg(\mathcal{A},\mathcal{B})=14$, which is shown in Fig. 20 in [supplementary material]. The secret intermediate values $\mathsf{Guess}(E_0)$ and $\mathsf{Guess}(E_2)$ created by P^0 in the outer rounds are presented in Fig. 21 in [supplementary material] marked with red color. To perform the attack, we convert $\mathsf{Guess}(E_0)$ and $\mathsf{Guess}(E_2)$ into the secret information of subkeys manually, which is visualized in Fig. 22 in [supplementary material], where there are 22 nibbles in k_{in} and 12 nibbles in k_{out}. Then we perform the key-bridging technique [29,47] on k_{in} and k_{out}, and find that $|k_{in}\cup k_{out}|\leq 69$, which is illustrated in Fig. 23 in [supplementary material].

Complexity Analysis. According to the discussion of Sect. 3.3, in the offline phase, the time complexity is $2^{4\times14}\times2^{4\times1}\times\frac{14}{21\times8}C_E\approx2^{56.42}C_E$, and the memory complexity is $(2^4-1)\times4\times1\times2^{4\times14}\approx2^{61.91}$ bits. In the online phase, the time complexity is $2^{69}\times2^{4\times1}\times\frac{12+12}{21\times8}C_E\approx2^{70.20}C_E$. The data complexity of the attack is $2^{4\times12}=2^{48}$, which can be obtained from input state (Round 0) of Fig. 21 in [supplementary material].

7.3 Application to TWINE-80

With the method presented in Sect. 4, we find a $\mathcal{DS}$-MITM attack on 20-round TWINE-80 based on a distinguisher $(\mathcal{A},\mathcal{B},\mathsf{Deg}(\mathcal{A},\mathcal{B}))$ with $\mathcal{A}=[3]$, $\mathcal{B}=[9,13]$, and $\deg(\mathcal{A},\mathcal{B})=19$, which is shown in Fig. 24 in [supplementary material]. The secret intermediate values $\mathsf{Guess}(E_0)$ and $\mathsf{Guess}(E_2)$ created by P^0 in the outer rounds are presented in Fig. 25 in [supplementary material]. To perform the attack, we convert $\mathsf{Guess}(E_0)$ and $\mathsf{Guess}(E_2)$ into the secret information of subkeys manually, which is visualized in Fig. 26 in [supplementary material]. Then we perform the key-bridging technique [29,47] on k_{in} and k_{out}, and find that $|k_{in}\cup k_{out}|\leq 76$, which is illustrated in Fig. 27 in [supplementary material].

Complexity Analysis. According to the discussion of Sect. 3.3, in the offline phase, the time complexity is $2^{4\times19}\times2^{4\times1}\times\frac{19}{20\times8}C_E\approx2^{76.93}C_E$, and the memory complexity is $(2^4-1)\times4\times2\times2^{4\times19}\approx2^{82.91}$ bits. In the online phase, the time complexity is $2^{76}\times2^{4\times1}\times\frac{7+20}{20\times8}C_E\approx2^{77.44}C_E$. The data complexity of the attack is $2^{4\times8}=2^{32}$, which can be obtained from input state (Round 0) of Fig. 25 in [supplementary material].

7.4 Applications to AES, ARIA, and SIMON

We also apply our method to AES, ARIA, and SIMON. However, no better result is obtained. Still, We would like to provide some information about our analysis for the sake of completeness.

For AES, our tool can recover the base $\mathcal{DS}$-MITM attacks behind all attacks (including the best ones) presented in [28–30,32,53]. However, currently known best attacks on AES exploit the *differential enumeration technique* [28] which our tool cannot take into account automatically. To deal with this, we use a 2-step approach. First, we list all the distinguishers that may lead to a valid attack using the fact that, at best, the differential enumeration technique can decrease the memory complexity by a factor strictly less than 2^n, where n is the state size. For AES-128 we would only add the constraint dictating that two consecutive states cannot be fully active in the distinguisher. Then in a second step, we can obtain the concrete complexities of the attacks derived from the distinguishers by applying known techniques. Usually, the distinguisher leading to the best attack has the lowest number of active bytes. But some manual work is inevitable to really optimize the attacks. Actually, during our analysis, our code generates figures based on the distinguishers automatically, which greatly facilitates subsequent manual analysis and the checking of correctness. Note that the first step alone can be used to get an upper bound on the number of rounds one may attack (independent of any tricks involving manual work): if there is no distinghuisher then there is no attack.

For ARIA, we obtain the same result presented in [54]. Unlike the other targets presented in the paper which are modeled using MILP, we also provide a Choco [55] implementation for finding the $\mathcal{DS}$-MITM distinguishers of the ARIA cipher to show that we can choose from MILP/SAT/SMT/CP as the modeling language freely. This fact is important since the solvers are being improved constantly, and thus we can expect the resolution of more difficult instances in the future. We also try our tool on bit-oriented ciphers like SIMON. For SIMON32/64, only an 8-round $\mathcal{DS}$-MITM distinguisher is identified, which is far less than the rounds can be penetrated by differential attacks.

8 Applications in the Process of Block Cipher Design

In the design process, the designer typically first fixes the general structure of the block cipher. Then she or he tries to identify the optimal local components in terms of security, efficiency, power consumption etc. by a tweaking-and-analysis style iterative approach. Therefore, it is important to have efficient tools at hands such that a thorough exploration of the design space can be performed. In this section, we show that our tool can be applied in this situation by tweaking the block ciphers LBlock and TWINE. Note that unlike Ivica's tool [56], where nature-inspired meta-heuristics are employed, our method essentially performs an $\mathcal{DS}$-MITM distinguishing attack for each possible instantiation of the target cipher, and pick the optimal ones according to the results.

For LBlock-80, we tweak the 8-nibble to 8-nibble permutation. We exhaustively search for the 11-round $\mathcal{DS}$-MITM distinguishers with the lowest $\mathsf{Deg}(\mathcal{A}, \mathcal{B})$ for the $8! = 40320$ cases. The distribution of the 40320 cases in terms of $\mathsf{Deg}(\mathcal{A}, \mathcal{B})$ is shown in Fig. 15. According to Fig. 15, we can make several interesting observations. Firstly, there are many very weak permutations with very

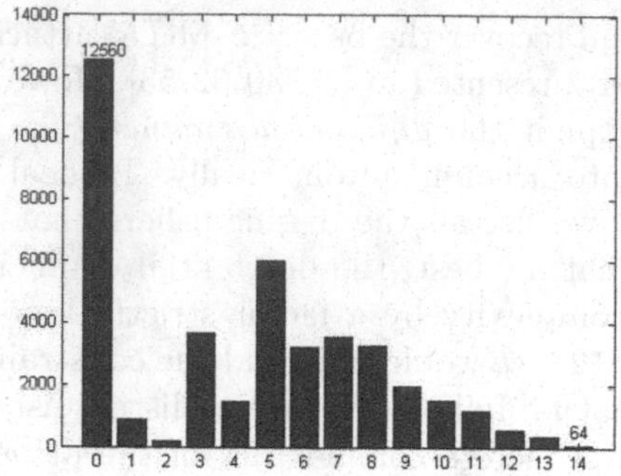

Fig. 15. The horizontal axis shows $\mathsf{Deg}(\mathcal{A},\mathcal{B})$ of the 11-round distinguisher (N/A means there is no valid distinguisher found), while the vertical axis indicates the corresponding numbers of permutations

low $\deg(\mathcal{A},\mathcal{B})$ which obviously should be avoided. In extreme cases, there are 12560 permutations with $\mathsf{Deg}(\mathcal{A},\mathcal{B}) = 0$. Secondly, the number of permutations with high resistance against $\mathcal{DS}$-MITM attack is small. There are 64 permutations (listed in Table 3 in [supplementary material]) among the 40320 ones with $\mathsf{Deg}(\mathcal{A},\mathcal{B}) = 14$, and actually the original permutation of LBlock is chosen from these good permutations.

For TWINE-80, we tweak the word shuffle of 16 nibbles. There are totally $16! \approx 2^{44.25}$ possibilities, which is out of reach of our computational power. However, according to [57], we only need to consider the $8! \times 8!$ *even-odd* shuffles. Let $P = (P_0, P_1)$, be the word shuffle where P_0 is the shuffle of all even positions while P_1 is the shuffle of all odd positions. Then it can be shown that (P_0, P_1) is equivalent to $(Q \circ P_1 \circ Q^{-1}, Q \circ P_2 \circ Q^{-1})$, where Q is an arbitrary word shuffle. Therefore, the number of cases can be further reduced since the $8! \times 8!$ shuffles can be divided into $22 \times 8! = 887040$ equivalent classes with respect to the $\mathcal{DS}$-MITM attack. We exhaustively search for the 11-round $\mathcal{DS}$-MITM distinguishers with the lowest $\mathsf{Deg}(\mathcal{A},\mathcal{B})$ for the 887040 cases. The distribution of the 887040 cases in terms of $\mathsf{Deg}(\mathcal{A},\mathcal{B})$ is shown in Fig. 16. According to Fig. 16, we can make several interesting observations. Firstly, there are many very weak permutations with very low $\deg(\mathcal{A},\mathcal{B})$ which obviously should be avoided. In extreme cases, there are 528631 permutations with $\mathsf{Deg}(\mathcal{A},\mathcal{B}) = 0$. Secondly, the number of permutations with high resistance against $\mathcal{DS}$-MITM attack is small. There are only 344 permutations among the 887040 ones with $\mathsf{Deg}(\mathcal{A},\mathcal{B}) = 14$, and actually the original permutation of TWINE is chosen from these good permutations. Finally, we identify a set of 12 permutations for which we can not find any 11-round distinguisher, indicating that they are stronger than the original permutation in TWINE-80 with respect to the $\mathcal{DS}$-MITM attack.

Since both the $\mathcal{DS}$-MITM attack in this paper and the word-oriented truncated impossible differential attack are structure attacks whose effectiveness is not affected by the details of the underlying S-boxes, we are wondering whether there is a set of strongest word shuffles with respect to the $\mathcal{DS}$-MITM attack

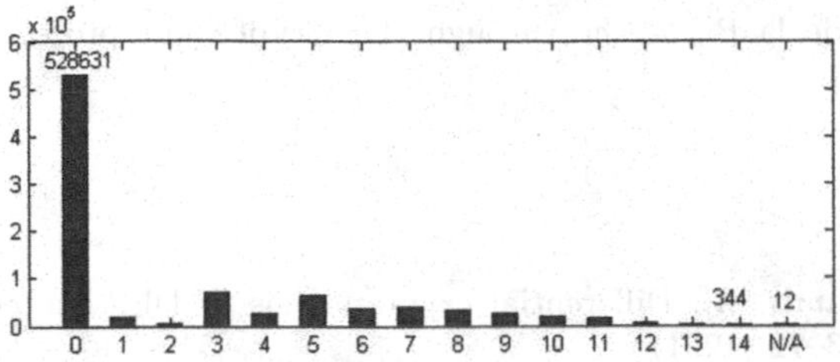

Fig. 16. The horizontal axis shows $\mathsf{Deg}(\mathcal{A},\mathcal{B})$ of the 11-round distinguisher (N/A means there is no valid distinguisher found), while the vertical axis indicates the corresponding numbers of permutations

and impossible differential attack simultaneously. We exhaustively analysis the 887040 TWINE variants. It turns out that for any variant there is a 14-round impossible differential, and there are 144 variants with no 15-round impossible differential. Finally, we identify a set of 12 word shuffles with no 15-round impossible differential and no 11-round $\mathcal{DS}$-MITM distinguisher (listed in Table. 4 in [supplementary material]). Note that the word shuffle used in TWINE is not in this set. Therefore, it is potentially better to use one from these 12 word shuffles.

9 Conclusion and Discussion

In this paper, we present the first tool for automatic Demirci-Selçuk meet-in-the-middle analysis based on constraint programming. In our approach, the formulation and resolution of the model are decoupled. Hence, the only thing needs to do by the cryptanalysts is to specify the problem in some modeling language, and the remaining work can be done with any open-source or commercially available constraint solvers. This approach should be very useful in fast prototyping block cipher designs. Finally, we would like to identify a set of limitations of our approach, overcoming which is left for future work.

Limitations. First of all, some important techniques for improving the $\mathcal{DS}$-MITM attack have not been integrated into our framework yet, including (but not limited to) the differential enumeration technique, and using several distinguishers in parallel. Secondly, we cannot guarantee the optimality of the attacks produced by our tool, due to the heuristic natures of the key-recovery process, and the lack of automatically considering cipher specific properties. Finally, we do not know how to apply our method to ARX based constructions.

Acknowledgments. The authors thank the anonymous reviewers for many helpful comments, and Gaëtan Leurent for careful reading and shepherding our paper. The work is supported by the Chinese Major Program of National Cryptography Development Foundation (Grant No. MMJJ20180102), the National Natural Science Foundation of China (61732021, 61802400, 61772519, 61802399), the Youth Innovation Promotion Association of Chinese Academy of Sciences, and the Institute of Information Engineering, CAS (Grant No. Y7Z0251103). Patrick Derbez is supported by the French

Agence Nationale de la Recherche through the CryptAudit project under Contract ANR-17-CE39-0003.

References

1. Biham, E., Shamir, A.: Differential cryptanalysis of DES-like cryptosystems. J. Cryptol. **4**(1), 3–72 (1991)
2. Matsui, M.: Linear cryptanalysis method for DES cipher. In: Helleseth, T. (ed.) EUROCRYPT 1993. LNCS, vol. 765, pp. 386–397. Springer, Heidelberg (1994). https://doi.org/10.1007/3-540-48285-7_33
3. Daemen, J., Knudsen, L., Rijmen, V.: The block cipher square. In: Biham, E. (ed.) FSE 1997. LNCS, vol. 1267, pp. 149–165. Springer, Heidelberg (1997). https://doi.org/10.1007/BFb0052343
4. Knudsen, L., Wagner, D.: Integral cryptanalysis. In: Daemen, J., Rijmen, V. (eds.) FSE 2002. LNCS, vol. 2365, pp. 112–127. Springer, Heidelberg (2002). https://doi.org/10.1007/3-540-45661-9_9
5. Todo, Y.: Structural evaluation by generalized integral property. In: Oswald, E., Fischlin, M. (eds.) EUROCRYPT 2015, Part I. LNCS, vol. 9056, pp. 287–314. Springer, Heidelberg (2015). https://doi.org/10.1007/978-3-662-46800-5_12
6. Liu, Y., Wang, Q., Rijmen, V.: Automatic search of linear trails in ARX with applications to SPECK and chaskey. In: Manulis, M., Sadeghi, A.-R., Schneider, S. (eds.) ACNS 2016. LNCS, vol. 9696, pp. 485–499. Springer, Cham (2016). https://doi.org/10.1007/978-3-319-39555-5_26
7. Mouha, N., Preneel, B.: Towards finding optimal differential characteristics for ARX: application to Salsa20. IACR Cryptology ePrint Archive, Report 2013/328 (2013). http://eprint.iacr.org/2013/328
8. Kölbl, S., Leander, G., Tiessen, T.: Observations on the SIMON block cipher Family. In: Gennaro, R., Robshaw, M. (eds.) CRYPTO 2015. LNCS, vol. 9215, pp. 161–185. Springer, Heidelberg (2015). https://doi.org/10.1007/978-3-662-47989-6_8
9. Mouha, N., Wang, Q., Gu, D., Preneel, B.: Differential and linear cryptanalysis using mixed-integer linear programming. In: Wu, C.-K., Yung, M., Lin, D. (eds.) Inscrypt 2011. LNCS, vol. 7537, pp. 57–76. Springer, Heidelberg (2012). https://doi.org/10.1007/978-3-642-34704-7_5
10. Sun, S., Hu, L., Wang, P., Qiao, K., Ma, X., Song, L.: Automatic security evaluation and (related-key) differential characteristic search: application to SIMON, PRESENT, LBlock, DES(L) and other bit-oriented block ciphers. In: Sarkar, P., Iwata, T. (eds.) ASIACRYPT 2014, Part I. LNCS, vol. 8873, pp. 158–178. Springer, Heidelberg (2014). https://doi.org/10.1007/978-3-662-45611-8_9
11. Xiang, Z., Zhang, W., Bao, Z., Lin, D.: Applying MILP method to searching integral distinguishers based on division property for 6 lightweight block ciphers. In: Cheon, J.H., Takagi, T. (eds.) ASIACRYPT 2016, Part I. LNCS, vol. 10031, pp. 648–678. Springer, Heidelberg (2016). https://doi.org/10.1007/978-3-662-53887-6_24
12. Sasaki, Y., Todo, Y.: New impossible differential search tool from design and cryptanalysis aspects. In: Coron, J.-S., Nielsen, J.B. (eds.) EUROCRYPT 2017, Part III. LNCS, vol. 10212, pp. 185–215. Springer, Cham (2017). https://doi.org/10.1007/978-3-319-56617-7_7

13. Fu, K., Wang, M., Guo, Y., Sun, S., Hu, L.: MILP-based automatic search algorithms for differential and linear trails for speck. In: Peyrin, T. (ed.) FSE 2016. LNCS, vol. 9783, pp. 268–288. Springer, Heidelberg (2016). https://doi.org/10.1007/978-3-662-52993-5_14
14. Gerault, D., Minier, M., Solnon, C.: Constraint programming models for chosen key differential cryptanalysis. In: Rueher, M. (ed.) CP 2016. LNCS, vol. 9892, pp. 584–601. Springer, Cham (2016). https://doi.org/10.1007/978-3-319-44953-1_37
15. Sun, S., Gerault, D., Lafourcade, P., Yang, Q., Todo, Y., Qiao, K., Hu, L.: Analysis of AES, SKINNY, and others with constraint programming. IACR Trans. Symmetric Cryptol. **2017**(1), 281–306 (2017)
16. Cui, T., Jia, K., Fu, K., Chen, S., Wang, M.: New automatic search tool for impossible differentials and zero-correlation linear approximations. IACR Cryptology ePrint Archive 2016, 689 (2016)
17. Matsui, M.: On correlation between the order of S-boxes and the strength of DES. In: De Santis, A. (ed.) EUROCRYPT 1994. LNCS, vol. 950, pp. 366–375. Springer, Heidelberg (1995). https://doi.org/10.1007/BFb0053451
18. Dobraunig, C., Eichlseder, M., Mendel, F.: Heuristic tool for linear cryptanalysis with applications to CAESAR candidates. In: Iwata, T., Cheon, J.H. (eds.) ASIACRYPT 2015, Part II. LNCS, vol. 9453, pp. 490–509. Springer, Heidelberg (2015). https://doi.org/10.1007/978-3-662-48800-3_20
19. Biryukov, A., Velichkov, V.: Automatic search for differential trails in ARX ciphers. In: Benaloh, J. (ed.) CT-RSA 2014. LNCS, vol. 8366, pp. 227–250. Springer, Cham (2014). https://doi.org/10.1007/978-3-319-04852-9_12
20. Biryukov, A., Nikolić, I.: Search for related-key differential characteristics in DES-like ciphers. In: Joux, A. (ed.) FSE 2011. LNCS, vol. 6733, pp. 18–34. Springer, Heidelberg (2011). https://doi.org/10.1007/978-3-642-21702-9_2
21. Fouque, P.-A., Jean, J., Peyrin, T.: Structural evaluation of AES and chosen-key distinguisher of 9-round AES-128. In: Canetti, R., Garay, J.A. (eds.) CRYPTO 2013. LNCS, vol. 8042, pp. 183–203. Springer, Heidelberg (2013). https://doi.org/10.1007/978-3-642-40041-4_11
22. Bouillaguet, C., Derbez, P., Fouque, P.-A.: Automatic search of attacks on round-reduced AES and applications. In: Rogaway, P. (ed.) CRYPTO 2011. LNCS, vol. 6841, pp. 169–187. Springer, Heidelberg (2011). https://doi.org/10.1007/978-3-642-22792-9_10
23. Dobraunig, C., Eichlseder, M., Mendel, F.: Analysis of SHA-512/224 and SHA-512/256. In: Iwata, T., Cheon, J.H. (eds.) ASIACRYPT 2015, Part II. LNCS, vol. 9453, pp. 612–630. Springer, Heidelberg (2015). https://doi.org/10.1007/978-3-662-48800-3_25
24. Mella, S., Daemen, J., Assche, G.V.: New techniques for trail bounds and application to differential trails in Keccak. IACR Trans. Symmetric Cryptol. **2017**(1), 329–357 (2017)
25. Freuder, E.C.: In pursuit of the holy grail. Constraints **2**(1), 57–61 (1997)
26. Demirci, H., Selçuk, A.A.: A meet-in-the-middle attack on 8-round AES. In: Nyberg, K. (ed.) FSE 2008. LNCS, vol. 5086, pp. 116–126. Springer, Heidelberg (2008). https://doi.org/10.1007/978-3-540-71039-4_7
27. Daemen, J., Rijmen, V.: The Design of Rijndael: AES - The Advanced Encryption Standard. Information Security and Cryptography. Springer, Heidelberg (2002). https://doi.org/10.1007/978-3-662-04722-4

28. Dunkelman, O., Keller, N., Shamir, A.: Improved single-key attacks on 8-round AES-192 and AES-256. In: Abe, M. (ed.) ASIACRYPT 2010. LNCS, vol. 6477, pp. 158–176. Springer, Heidelberg (2010). https://doi.org/10.1007/978-3-642-17373-8_10
29. Derbez, P., Fouque, P.-A., Jean, J.: Improved key recovery attacks on reduced-round AES in the single-key setting. In: Johansson, T., Nguyen, P.Q. (eds.) EUROCRYPT 2013. LNCS, vol. 7881, pp. 371–387. Springer, Heidelberg (2013). https://doi.org/10.1007/978-3-642-38348-9_23
30. Derbez, P., Fouque, P.-A.: Exhausting Demirci-Selçuk meet-in-the-middle attacks against reduced-round AES. In: Moriai, S. (ed.) FSE 2013. LNCS, vol. 8424, pp. 541–560. Springer, Heidelberg (2014). https://doi.org/10.1007/978-3-662-43933-3_28
31. Derbez, P., Fouque, P.-A.: Automatic search of meet-in-the-middle and impossible differential attacks. In: Robshaw, M., Katz, J. (eds.) CRYPTO 2016, Part II. LNCS, vol. 9815, pp. 157–184. Springer, Heidelberg (2016). https://doi.org/10.1007/978-3-662-53008-5_6
32. Li, R., Jin, C.: Meet-in-the-middle attacks on 10-round AES-256. Des. Codes Cryptogr. **80**(3), 459–471 (2016)
33. Derbez, P., Perrin, L.: Meet-in-the-middle attacks and structural analysis of round-reduced PRINCE. In: Leander, G. (ed.) FSE 2015. LNCS, vol. 9054, pp. 190–216. Springer, Heidelberg (2015). https://doi.org/10.1007/978-3-662-48116-5_10
34. Biryukov, A., Derbez, P., Perrin, L.: Differential analysis and meet-in-the-middle attack against round-reduced TWINE. In: Leander, G. (ed.) FSE 2015. LNCS, vol. 9054, pp. 3–27. Springer, Heidelberg (2015). https://doi.org/10.1007/978-3-662-48116-5_1
35. Li, L., Jia, K., Wang, X., Dong, X.: Meet-in-the-middle technique for truncated differential and its applications to CLEFIA and camellia. In: Leander, G. (ed.) FSE 2015. LNCS, vol. 9054, pp. 48–70. Springer, Heidelberg (2015). https://doi.org/10.1007/978-3-662-48116-5_3
36. Dong, X., Li, L., Jia, K., Wang, X.: Improved attacks on reduced-round camellia-128/192/256. In: Nyberg, K. (ed.) CT-RSA 2015. LNCS, vol. 9048, pp. 59–83. Springer, Cham (2015). https://doi.org/10.1007/978-3-319-16715-2_4
37. Guo, J., Jean, J., Nikolić, I., Sasaki, Y.: Meet-in-the-middle attacks on generic feistel constructions. In: Sarkar, P., Iwata, T. (eds.) ASIACRYPT 2014, Part I. LNCS, vol. 8873, pp. 458–477. Springer, Heidelberg (2014). https://doi.org/10.1007/978-3-662-45611-8_24
38. Guo, J., Jean, J., Nikolic, I., Sasaki, Y.: Meet-in-the-middle attacks on classes of contracting and expanding feistel constructions. IACR Trans. Symmetric Cryptol. **2016**(2), 307–337 (2016)
39. Diffie, W., Hellman, M.E.: Special feature exhaustive cryptanalysis of the NBS data encryption standard. IEEE Comput. **10**(6), 74–84 (1977)
40. Bogdanov, A., Rechberger, C.: A 3-subset meet-in-the-middle attack: cryptanalysis of the lightweight block cipher KTANTAN. In: Biryukov, A., Gong, G., Stinson, D.R. (eds.) SAC 2010. LNCS, vol. 6544, pp. 229–240. Springer, Heidelberg (2011). https://doi.org/10.1007/978-3-642-19574-7_16
41. Aoki, K., Sasaki, Y.: Meet-in-the-middle preimage attacks against reduced SHA-0 and SHA-1. In: Halevi, S. (ed.) CRYPTO 2009. LNCS, vol. 5677, pp. 70–89. Springer, Heidelberg (2009). https://doi.org/10.1007/978-3-642-03356-8_5

42. Guo, J., Ling, S., Rechberger, C., Wang, H.: Advanced meet-in-the-middle preimage attacks: first results on full tiger, and improved results on MD4 and SHA-2. In: Abe, M. (ed.) ASIACRYPT 2010. LNCS, vol. 6477, pp. 56–75. Springer, Heidelberg (2010). https://doi.org/10.1007/978-3-642-17373-8_4
43. Lin, L., Wu, W., Wang, Y., Zhang, L.: General model of the single-key meet-in-the-middle distinguisher on the word-oriented block cipher. In: Lee, H.-S., Han, D.-G. (eds.) ICISC 2013. LNCS, vol. 8565, pp. 203–223. Springer, Cham (2014). https://doi.org/10.1007/978-3-319-12160-4_13
44. Beierle, C., et al.: The SKINNY Family of block ciphers and its low-latency variant MANTIS. In: Robshaw, M., Katz, J. (eds.) CRYPTO 2016, Part II. LNCS, vol. 9815, pp. 123–153. Springer, Heidelberg (2016). https://doi.org/10.1007/978-3-662-53008-5_5
45. Suzaki, T., Minematsu, K., Morioka, S., Kobayashi, E.: *TWINE*: a lightweight block cipher for multiple platforms. In: Knudsen, L.R., Wu, H. (eds.) SAC 2012. LNCS, vol. 7707, pp. 339–354. Springer, Heidelberg (2013). https://doi.org/10.1007/978-3-642-35999-6_22
46. Wu, W., Zhang, L.: LBlock: a lightweight block cipher. In: Lopez, J., Tsudik, G. (eds.) ACNS 2011. LNCS, vol. 6715, pp. 327–344. Springer, Heidelberg (2011). https://doi.org/10.1007/978-3-642-21554-4_19
47. Lin, L., Wu, W., Zheng, Y.: Automatic search for key-bridging technique: applications to LBlock and TWINE. In: Peyrin, T. (ed.) FSE 2016. LNCS, vol. 9783, pp. 247–267. Springer, Heidelberg (2016). https://doi.org/10.1007/978-3-662-52993-5_13
48. Boura, C., Minier, M., Naya-Plasencia, M., Suder, V.: Improved impossible differential attacks against round-reduced lblock. IACR Cryptology ePrint Archive 2014, 279 (2014)
49. Wang, Y., Wu, W.: Improved multidimensional zero-correlation linear cryptanalysis and applications to LBlock and TWINE. In: Susilo, W., Mu, Y. (eds.) ACISP 2014. LNCS, vol. 8544, pp. 1–16. Springer, Cham (2014). https://doi.org/10.1007/978-3-319-08344-5_1
50. Zheng, X., Jia, K.: Impossible differential attack on reduced-round TWINE. In: Lee, H.-S., Han, D.-G. (eds.) ICISC 2013. LNCS, vol. 8565, pp. 123–143. Springer, Cham (2014). https://doi.org/10.1007/978-3-319-12160-4_8
51. Tolba, M., Abdelkhalek, A., Youssef, A.M.: Impossible differential cryptanalysis of reduced-round SKINNY. In: Joye, M., Nitaj, A. (eds.) AFRICACRYPT 2017. LNCS, vol. 10239, pp. 117–134. Springer, Cham (2017). https://doi.org/10.1007/978-3-319-57339-7_7
52. Boura, C., Naya-Plasencia, M., Suder, V.: Scrutinizing and improving impossible differential attacks: applications to CLEFIA, camellia, LBlock and SIMON. In: Sarkar, P., Iwata, T. (eds.) ASIACRYPT 2014, Part I. LNCS, vol. 8873, pp. 179–199. Springer, Heidelberg (2014). https://doi.org/10.1007/978-3-662-45611-8_10
53. Li, L., Jia, K., Wang, X.: Improved single-key attacks on 9-round AES-192/256. In: Cid, C., Rechberger, C. (eds.) FSE 2014. LNCS, vol. 8540, pp. 127–146. Springer, Heidelberg (2015). https://doi.org/10.1007/978-3-662-46706-0_7
54. Akshima, Chang, D., Ghosh, M., Goel, A., Sanadhya, S.K.: Improved meet-in-the-middle attacks on 7 and 8-round ARIA-192 and ARIA-256. In: Biryukov, A., Goyal, V. (eds.) INDOCRYPT 2015. LNCS, vol. 9462, pp. 198–217. Springer, Cham (2015). https://doi.org/10.1007/978-3-319-26617-6_11
55. Prud'homme, C., Fages, J.G., Lorca, X.: Choco Documentation. TASC - LS2N CNRS UMR 6241, COSLING S.A.S. (2017)

56. Nikolić, I.: How to use metaheuristics for design of symmetric-key primitives. In: Takagi, T., Peyrin, T. (eds.) ASIACRYPT 2017, Part III. LNCS, vol. 10626, pp. 369–391. Springer, Cham (2017). https://doi.org/10.1007/978-3-319-70700-6_13
57. Suzaki, T., Minematsu, K.: Improving the Generalized Feistel. In: Hong, S., Iwata, T. (eds.) FSE 2010. LNCS, vol. 6147, pp. 19–39. Springer, Heidelberg (2010). https://doi.org/10.1007/978-3-642-13858-4_2

Cryptanalysis of MORUS

Tomer Ashur[1](✉), Maria Eichlseder[2](✉), Martin M. Lauridsen[7](✉), Gaëtan Leurent[3](✉), Brice Minaud[4](✉), Yann Rotella[3](✉), Yu Sasaki[5](✉), and Benoît Viguier[6](✉)

[1] imec-COSIC, KU Leuven, Leuven, Belgium
tomer.ashur@esat.kuleuven.be
[2] Graz University of Technology, Graz, Austria
maria.eichlseder@iaik.tugraz.at
[3] Inria, Paris, France
{gaetan.leurent,yann.rotella}@inria.fr
[4] Royal Holloway University of London, Egham, UK
brice.minaud@gmail.com
[5] NTT, Tokyo, Japan
sasaki.yu@lab.ntt.co.jp
[6] Radboud University, Nijmegen, Netherlands
b.viguier@science.ru.nl
[7] Paris, France
mail@martinlauridsen.info@inria.fr

Abstract. MORUS is a high-performance authenticated encryption algorithm submitted to the CAESAR competition, and recently selected as a finalist. There are three versions of MORUS: MORUS-640 with a 128-bit key, and MORUS-1280 with 128-bit or 256-bit keys. For all versions the security claim for confidentiality matches the key size. In this paper, we analyze the components of this algorithm (initialization, state update and tag generation), and report several results.

As our main result, we present a linear correlation in the keystream of full MORUS, which can be used to distinguish its output from random and to recover some plaintext bits in the broadcast setting. For MORUS-1280, the correlation is 2^{-76}, which can be exploited after around 2^{152} encryptions, less than what would be expected for a 256-bit secure cipher. For MORUS-640, the same attack results in a correlation of 2^{-73}, which does not violate the security claims of the cipher.

To identify this correlation, we make use of rotational invariants in MORUS using linear masks that are invariant by word-rotations of the state. This motivates us to introduce single-word versions of MORUS called MiniMORUS, which simplifies the analysis. The attack has been implemented and verified on MiniMORUS, where it yields a correlation of 2^{-16}.

We also study reduced versions of the initialization and finalization of MORUS, aiming to evaluate the security margin of these components. We show a forgery attack when finalization is reduced from 10 steps to 3, and a key-recovery attack in the nonce-misuse setting when initialization is reduced from 16 steps to 10. These additional results do not

T. Peyrin and S. Galbraith (Eds.): ASIACRYPT 2018, LNCS 11273, pp. 35–64, 2018.
https://doi.org/10.1007/978-3-030-03329-3_2

threaten the full MORUS, but studying all aspects of the design is useful to understand its strengths and weaknesses.

Keywords: MORUS · CAESAR · Authenticated encryption
Nonce respecting · Linear cryptanalysis · Confidentiality

1 Introduction

Authenticated Encryption (AE) schemes combine the functionality of symmetric encryption schemes and message authentication codes. Based on a shared secret key K, they encrypt a plaintext message M to a ciphertext C and authentication tag T in order to protect both the confidentiality and the authenticity of M. Most modern authenticated encryption algorithms are nonce-based schemes with associated data (AEAD), where (C, T) additionally depends on a unique nonce N (or initialization value IV) and optional associated metadata A. One of the most prominent standardized AEAD designs is AES-GCM [8,13], which is widely deployed in protocols such as TLS (since v1.2).

To address the growing need for modern authenticated encryption designs for different application scenarios, the CAESAR competition was launched in 2013 [4]. The goal of this competition is to select a final portfolio of AEAD designs for three different use-cases: (1) lightweight hardware characteristics, (2) high-speed software performance, and (3) robustness. The competition attracted 57 first-round submissions, 7 of which were recently selected as finalists in the fourth selection round.

MORUS is one of the three finalists for use-case (2), together with OCB and AEGIS. This family of authenticated ciphers by Wu and Huang [19] provides three main variants: MORUS-640 with a 128-bit key and MORUS-1280 with either a 128-bit or a 256-bit key. The design approach is reminiscent of classical stream cipher designs and continuously updates a relatively large state with a few fast operations. MORUS can be efficiently implemented in both software and hardware; in particular, the designers claim that the software performance even surpasses AES-GCM implementations using Intel's AES-NI instructions, and that MORUS is the fastest authenticated cipher not using AES-NI [19].

Related Work. In the MORUS submission document, the designers discuss the security of MORUS against several attacks, including algebraic, differential, and guess-and-determine attacks. The main focus is on differential properties, and not many details are given for other attack vectors. In third-party analysis, Mileva et al. [14] propose a distinguisher in the nonce-reuse setting and practically evaluate the differential behaviour of toy variants of MORUS. Shi et al. [17] analyze the differential properties of the finalization reduced to 2 out of 10 steps, but find no attacks. Dwivedi et al. [6] discuss the applicability of SAT solvers for state recovery, but the resulting complexity of 2^{370} for MORUS-640 is well beyond the security claim. Dwivedi et al. [7] also propose key-recovery attacks for MORUS-1280 if initialization is reduced to 3.6 out of 16 steps, and discuss the security of MORUS against internal differentials and rotational cryptanalysis. Salam et al. [16] apply cube attacks to obtain distinguishers for up to 5 out of 16 steps of the initialization of MORUS-1280 with negligible complexity. Additionally, Kales et al. [9] and Vaudenay and Vizár [18] independently propose state-recovery and forgery attacks on MORUS in a nonce-misuse setting with negligible data and time complexities.

Finally, a keystream correlation similar in nature to our main attack was uncovered by Minaud [15] on the authenticated cipher AEGIS [20,21], another CAESAR finalist. AEGIS shares the same overall structure as MORUS, but uses a very different state update function, based on the parallel application of AES rounds, rather than the shift/AND/XOR operations used in MORUS. Similar to our attack, the approach in [15] is to build a linear trail linking ciphertext bits, while canceling the contribution of inner state bits. How the trail is built depends primarily on the state update function, and how it lends itself to linear cryptanalysis. Because the state update function differs significantly between AEGIS and MORUS, the process used to build the trail is also quite different.

Our Contributions. Our main contribution is a keystream distinguisher on full MORUS-1280, built from linear approximations of its core `StateUpdate` function. In addition, we provide results for round-reduced MORUS, targeting both the initialization or finalization phases of the cipher.

In more detail, our main result is a linear approximation [11,12] linking plaintext and ciphertext bits spanning five consecutive encryption blocks. Moreover, the correlation does not depend on the secret key of the cipher. In principle, this property could be used as a known-plaintext distinguisher, or to recover unknown bits of a plaintext encrypted a large number of times. For MORUS-1280 with 256-bit keys, the linear correlation is 2^{-76} and can be exploited using about 2^{152} encrypted blocks.

To the best of our knowledge, this is the first attack on full MORUS in the nonce-respecting setting. We note that rekeying does not prevent the attack: the biases are independent of the secret encryption key and nonce, and can be exploited for plaintext recovery as long as a given plaintext segment is encrypted sufficiently often, regardless of whether each encryption uses a different key. A notable feature of the linear trail underpinning our attack is also that it does not depend on the values of rotation constants: a very similar trail would exist for most choices of round constants.

To obtain this result, we propose a simplified abstraction of MORUS, called MiniMORUS. MiniMORUS takes advantage of certain rotational invariants in MORUS and simplifies the description and analysis of the attack. We then show how the attack can be extended from MiniMORUS to the real MORUS. To confirm the validity of our analysis, we practically verified the correlation of the full linear trail for MiniMORUS, as well as the correlation of trail fragments for the full MORUS. Our analysis is also backed by a symbolic evaluation of the full trail equation and its correlation on all variants of MORUS.

In addition to the previous attack on full MORUS, we provide two secondary results: (1) we analyze the security of MORUS against forgery attacks with round-reduced finalization; and (2) we analyze its security against key recovery in a nonce-misuse setting, with round-reduced initialization. While this extra analysis does not threaten full MORUS, it complements the main result to provide a better overall understanding of the security of MORUS. More precisely, we present a forgery attack for round-reduced MORUS-1280 with success probability 2^{-88} for a 128-bit tag if the finalization is reduced to 3 out of 10 steps. This nonce-respecting attack is based on a differential analysis of the padding rule. The second result targets round-reduced initialization with 10 out of 16 steps, and extends a state-recovery attack (which can be mounted e.g. in a nonce-misuse setting) into a key-recovery attack.

Outline. This paper is organized as follows. We first provide a brief description of MORUS in Sect. 2. In Sect. 3, we introduce MiniMORUS, an abstraction of MORUS based on a certain class of rotational invariants. We analyze this simplified scheme in Sect. 4 and provide a ciphertext-only linear approximation with a weight of 16. We then extend our result to the full scheme in Sect. 5, showing a correlation in the keystream over 5 steps, and discuss the implications of our observation for the security of MORUS in Sect. 6. In Sect. 7, we present our results on the security of MORUS with round-reduced initialization (in a nonce-misuse setting) or finalization. We conclude in Sect. 8.

2 Preliminaries

MORUS is a family of authenticated ciphers designed by Wu and Huang [19]. An instance of MORUS is parametrized by a secret key K. During encryption, it takes as input a plaintext message M, a nonce N, and possibly some associated data A, and outputs a ciphertext C together with an authentication tag T. In this section, we provide a brief description of MORUS and introduce the notation for linear approximations.

2.1 Specification of MORUS

The MORUS family supports two internal state sizes: 640 and 1280 bits, referred to as MORUS-640 and MORUS-1280, respectively. Three parameter sets are recommended: MORUS-640 supports 128-bit keys and MORUS-1280 supports either 128-bit or 256-bit keys. The tag size is 128 bits or shorter. The designers strongly recommend using a 128-bit tag. With a 128-bit tag, integrity is claimed up to 128 bits and confidentiality is claimed up to the number of key bits (Table 1).

State. The internal state of MORUS is composed of five q-bit *registers* S_i, $i \in \{0, 1, 2, 3, 4\}$, where $q = 128$ for MORUS-640 and $q = 256$ for MORUS-1280. The internal state of MORUS may be represented as $S_0 \| S_1 \| S_2 \| S_3 \| S_4$. Registers are themselves divided into four $q/4$-bit *words*. Throughout the paper, we denote the word size by $w = q/4$, i.e., $w = 32$ for MORUS-640 and $w = 64$ for MORUS-1280.

Table 1. Security goals of MORUS.

	Confidentiality (bits)	Integrity (bits)
MORUS-640-128	128	128
MORUS-1280-128	128	128
MORUS-1280-256	256	128

Table 2. Rotation constants b_i for $\lll_w$ and b'_i for $\lll$ in round i of MORUS.

	Bit-wise rotation $\lll_w$					Word-wise rotation $\lll$				
	b_0	b_1	b_2	b_3	b_4	b'_0	b'_1	b'_2	b'_3	b'_4
MORUS-640	5	31	7	22	13	32	64	96	64	32
MORUS-1280	13	46	38	7	4	64	128	192	128	64

The encryption process of MORUS consists of four parts: initialization, associated data processing, encryption, and finalization. During the initialization phase, the value of the state is initialized using a key and nonce. The associated data and the plaintext are then processed block by block. Then the internal state undergoes the finalization phase, which outputs the authentication tag.

Every part of this process relies on iterating the `StateUpdate` function at the core of MORUS. Each call to the `StateUpdate` function is called a step. The internal state at step t is denoted by $S_0^t \| S_1^t \| S_2^t \| S_3^t \| S_4^t$, where $t = -16$ before the initialization and $t = 0$ after the initialization.

The `StateUpdate` Function. `StateUpdate` takes as input the internal state $S^t = S_0^t \| S_1^t \| S_2^t \| S_3^t \| S_4^t$ and an additional q-bit value m^t (recall that q is the size of a register), and outputs an updated internal state.

`StateUpdate` is composed of 5 rounds with similar operations. The additional input m^t is used in rounds 2 to 5, but not in round 1. Each round uses the bit-wise rotation (left circular shift) operation inside word, denoted $\lll_w$ in the following and `Rotl_xxx_yy` in the design document. It divides a q-bit register value into 4 words of $w = q/4$ bits, and performs a rotation on each w-bit word. The bit-wise rotation constants b_i for round i are defined in Table 2. Additionally, each round uses rotations on a whole q-bit register by a multiple of the word size, denoted $\lll$ in the following and `<<<` in the design document. The word-wise rotation constants b'_i are also listed in Table 2.

$S^{t+1} \leftarrow$ `StateUpdate`(S^t, m^t) is defined as follows, where $\cdot$ denotes bit-wise AND, $\oplus$ is bit-wise XOR, and m_i is defined depending on the context:

$$\text{Round 1:} \quad S_0^{t+1} \leftarrow (S_0^t \oplus (S_1^t \cdot S_2^t) \oplus S_3^t) \lll_w b_0, \qquad S_3^t \leftarrow S_3^t \lll b'_0.$$
$$\text{Round 2:} \quad S_1^{t+1} \leftarrow (S_1^t \oplus (S_2^t \cdot S_3^t) \oplus S_4^t \oplus m_i) \lll_w b_1, \qquad S_4^t \leftarrow S_4^t \lll b'_1.$$
$$\text{Round 3:} \quad S_2^{t+1} \leftarrow (S_2^t \oplus (S_3^t \cdot S_4^t) \oplus S_0^t \oplus m_i) \lll_w b_2, \qquad S_0^t \leftarrow S_0^t \lll b'_2.$$

Round 4: $S_3^{t+1} \leftarrow (S_3^t \oplus (S_4^t \cdot S_0^t) \oplus S_1^t \oplus m_i) \lll_w b_3, \quad S_1^t \leftarrow S_1^t \lll b_3'.$

Round 5: $S_4^{t+1} \leftarrow (S_4^t \oplus (S_0^t \cdot S_1^t) \oplus S_2^t \oplus m_i) \lll_w b_4, \quad S_2^t \leftarrow S_2^t \lll b_4'.$

Initialization. The initialization of MORUS-640 starts by loading the 128-bit key K_{128} and the 128-bit nonce N_{128} into the state together with constants c_0, c_1:

$$S_0^{-16} = N_{128}, \quad S_1^{-16} = K_{128}, \quad S_2^{-16} = 1^{128}, \quad S_3^{-16} = c_0, \quad S_4^{-16} = c_1.$$

Then, $\texttt{StateUpdate}(S^t, 0)$ is iterated 16 times for $t = -16, -15, \ldots, -1$. Finally, the key is XORed into the state again with $S_1^0 \leftarrow S_1^0 \oplus K_{128}$.

The initialization of MORUS-1280 differs slightly due to the difference in register size and the two possible key sizes, and uses either $K = K_{128} \| K_{128}$ (for MORUS-1280-128) or $K = K_{256}$ (for MORUS-1280-256) to initialize the state:

$$S_0^{-16} = N_{128} \parallel 0^{128}, \quad S_1^{-16} = K, \quad S_2^{-16} = 1^{256}, \quad S_3^{-16} = 0^{256}, \quad S_4^{-16} = c_0 \parallel c_1.$$

After iterating StateUpdate 16 times, the state is updated with $S_1^0 \leftarrow S_1^0 \oplus K$.

Associated Data Processing. After initialization, the associated data A is processed in blocks of $q \in \{128, 256\}$ bits. For the padding, if the last associated data block is not a full block, it is padded to q bits with zeroes. If the length of A, denoted by $|A|$, is 0, then the associated data processing phase is skipped; else, the state is updated as

$$S^{t+1} \leftarrow \texttt{StateUpdate}(S^t, A^t) \qquad \text{for } t = 0, 1, \ldots, \lceil |A|/q \rceil - 1.$$

Encryption. Next, the message is processed in blocks M_t of $q \in \{128, 256\}$ bits to update the state and produce the ciphertext blocks C_t. If the last message block is not a full block, a string of 0's is used to pad it to 128 or 256 bits for MORUS-640 and MORUS-1280, respectively, and the padded full block is used to update the state. However, only the partial block is encrypted. Note that if the message length denoted by $|M|$ is 0, encryption is skipped. Let $u = \lceil |A|/q \rceil$ and $v = \lceil |M|/q \rceil$. The following is performed for $t = 0, 1, \ldots, v-1$:

$$C^t \leftarrow M^t \oplus S_0^{u+t} \oplus (S_1^{u+t} \lll b_2') \oplus (S_2^{u+t} \cdot S_3^{u+t}),$$
$$S^{u+t+1} \leftarrow \texttt{StateUpdate}(S^{u+t}, M^t).$$

Finalization. The finalization phase generates the authentication tag T using 10 more StateUpdate steps. We only discuss the case where T is not truncated. The associated data length and the message length are used to update the state:

1. $L \leftarrow |A| \parallel |M|$ for MORUS-640 or $L \leftarrow |A| \parallel |M| \parallel 0^{128}$ for MORUS-1280, where $|A|, |M|$ are represented as 64-bit integers.
2. $S_4^{u+v} \leftarrow S_4^{u+v} \oplus S_0^{u+v}$.
3. For $t = u+v, u+v+1, \ldots, u+v+9$, compute $S^{t+1} \leftarrow \texttt{StateUpdate}(S^t, L)$.
4. $T = S_0^{u+v+10} \oplus (S_1^{u+v+10} \lll b_2') \oplus (S_2^{u+v+10} \cdot S_3^{u+v+10})$, or the least significant 128 bits of this value in case of MORUS-1280.

2.2 Notation

In the following, we use linear approximations [11] that hold with probability $\Pr(E) = \frac{1}{2} + \varepsilon$, i.e., they are biased with bias ε. The *correlation* $\mathrm{cor}(E)$ of the approximation and its *weight* $\mathrm{weight}(E)$ are defined as

$$\mathrm{cor}(E) := 2\Pr(E) - 1 = 2\varepsilon,$$
$$\mathrm{weight}(E) := -\log_2 |\mathrm{cor}(E)|,$$

where $\log_2()$ denotes logarithm in base 2. By the Piling-Up Lemma, the correlation (resp. weight) of an XOR of independent variables is equal to the product (resp. sum) of their individual correlations (resp. weights) [11].

We also recall the following notation from the previous section, where an *encryption step* refers to one call to the `StateUpdate` function:

C^t : the ciphertext block output during the t-th encryption step.
C^t_j : the j-th bit of C^t, with C^t_0 being the rightmost bit.
S^t_i : the i-th register at the beginning of t-th encryption step.
$S^t_{i,j}$: the j-th bit of S^t_i, with $S^t_{i,0}$ being the rightmost bit.

In the above notation, bit positions are always taken modulo the register size q, i.e., $q = 128$ for MORUS-640 and $q = 256$ for MORUS-1280.

For simplicity, in the remainder, the 0-th encryption step will often denote the encryption step where our linear trail starts. Any encryption step could be chosen for that purpose, as long as at least four more encryption steps follow. In particular the 0-th encryption step from the perspective of the trail does not have to be the first encryption step after initialization.

3 Rotational Invariance and MiniMORUS

To simplify the description of the attack, we assume all plaintext blocks are zero. This assumption will be removed in Sect. 5.3, where we will show that plaintext bits only contribute linearly to the trail. Recall that the inner state of the cipher consists of five $4w$-bit registers $S_0, \ldots, S_4$, each containing four w-bit words.

3.1 Rotationally Invariant Linear Combinations

We begin with a few observations about the `StateUpdate` function. Besides XOR and AND operations, the `StateUpdate` function uses two types of bit rotations:

1. *bit-wise* rotations perform a circular shift on each word within a register;
2. *word-wise* rotations perform a circular shift on a whole register.

The second type of rotation always shifts registers by a multiple of the word size w. This amounts to a (circular) permutation of the words within the register: for example, if a register contains the words (A, B, C, D), and a word-wise rotation by w bits to the left is performed, then the register now contains the words (B, C, D, A).

To build our linear trail, we start with a linear combinations of bits within a single register.

Definition 1 (Rotational Invariance). *Recall that w denotes the word size in bits, and $4w$ is the size of a register. A linear combination of the form:*

$$S^t_{i,j(0)} \oplus S^t_{i,j(1)} \oplus \cdots \oplus S^t_{i,j(k)}$$

is said to be rotationally invariant *iff the set of bits $S^t_{i,j(0)}, \ldots, S^t_{i,j(k)}$ is left invariant by a circular shift by w bits; that is, iff:*

$$\{j(i) : i \leq k\} = \{j(i) + w \bmod 4w : i \leq k\}.$$

Example. The following linear combination is rotationally invariant for MORUS-640, i.e. $w = 32$:

$$S^t_{0,0} \oplus S^t_{0,32} \oplus S^t_{0,64} \oplus S^t_{0,96}. \tag{1}$$

This definition naturally extends to a linear combination across multiple registers, and also across ciphertext blocks. The value of such a linear combination is unaffected by word-wise rotations, since those rotations always shift registers by a multiple of the word size. On the other hand, since bit-wise rotations always shift all four words within a register by the same amount, bit-wise rotations preserve the rotational invariance property. Moreover, the XOR of two rotationally invariant linear combinations is also rotationally invariant.

This naturally leads to the idea of building a linear trail using only rotationally invariant linear combinations, which is what we are going to do. As a result, the effect of word-wise rotations can be ignored. Moreover, since all linear combinations we consider are going to be rotationally invariant, they can be described by truncating the linear combination to the first word of a register. Indeed, an equivalent way of saying a linear combination is rotationally invariant, is that it involves the same bits in each word within a register. For example, in the case of (1) above, the four bits involved are the first bit of each of the four words.

3.2 MiniMORUS

In fact, we can go further and consider a reduced version of MORUS where each register contains a single word instead of four. The `StateUpdate` function is unchanged, except for the fact that word-wise rotations are removed: see Fig. 1. We call these reduced versions MiniMORUS-640 and MiniMORUS-1280, for MORUS-640 and MORUS-1280 respectively. Since registers in MiniMORUS contain a single word, bit-wise and word-wise rotations are the same operation; for simplicity we write $\lll$ for bit-wise rotations.

Since the trail we are building is relatively complex, we will first describe it on MiniMORUS. We will then extend it to the full MORUS via the previous rotational invariance property.

4 Linear Trail for MiniMORUS

In this section, we describe how we build a trail for MiniMORUS, then compute its correlation and validate the correlation experimentally.

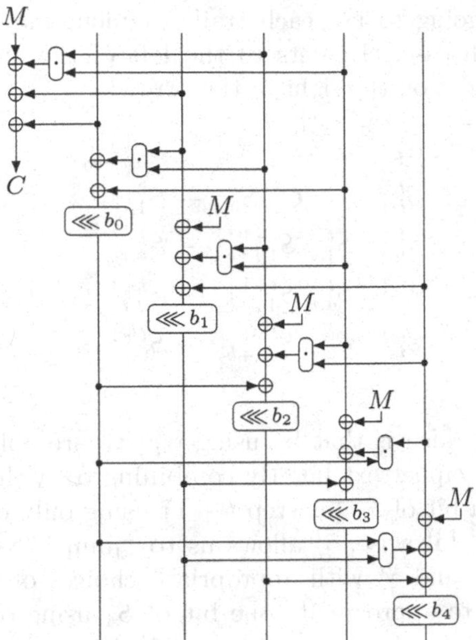

Fig. 1. MiniMORUS state update function.

4.1 Overview of the Trail

To build a linear trail for MiniMORUS, we combine the following five trail fragments α_i^t, β_i^t, γ_i^t, δ_i^t, ε_i^t, where the subscript i denotes a bit position, and the superscript t denotes a step number:

- α_i^t approximates (one bit of) state word S_0 using the ciphertext;
- β_i^t approximates S_1 using S_0 and the ciphertext;
- γ_i^t approximates S_4 using two approximations of S_1 in consecutive steps;
- δ_i^t approximates S_2 using two approximations of S_4 in consecutive steps;
- ε_i^t approximates S_0 using two approximations of S_2 in consecutive steps.

The trail fragments are depicted on Fig. 2. In all cases except α_i^t, the trail fragment approximates a single AND gate by zero, which holds with probability 3/4, and hence the trail fragment has weight 1. In the case of α_i^t, two AND gates are involved; however the two gates share an entry in common, and in both cases the other entry also has a linear contribution to the trail, which results in an overall contribution of the form (see [3, Sect. 3.3])

$$x \cdot y \oplus x \cdot z \oplus y \oplus z = (x \oplus 1) \cdot (y \oplus z).$$

As a result, the trail fragment α_i^t also has a weight of 1. Another way of looking at this phenomenon is that the trail holds for two different approximations of the AND gates: the alternative approximation is depicted by a dashed line on Fig. 2.

The way we are going to use each trail fragment may be summarized as follows, where in each case, elements to the left of the arrow → are used to approximate the element on the right of the arrow:

$$\begin{aligned}
\alpha_i^t : &\quad C_i^t \rightarrow S_{0,i+b_0}^{t+1} \\
\beta_i^t : &\quad C_i^t, S_{0,i}^t \rightarrow S_{1,i}^t \\
\gamma_i^t : &\quad S_{1,i}^t, S_{1,i+b_1}^{t+1} \rightarrow S_{4,i}^t \\
\delta_i^t : &\quad S_{4,i}^t, S_{4,i+b_4}^{t+1} \rightarrow S_{2,i}^{t+1} \\
\varepsilon_i^t : &\quad S_{2,i}^t, S_{2,i+b_2}^{t+1} \rightarrow S_{0,i}^{t+1}.
\end{aligned}$$

In more detail, the idea is that by using α_i^t, we are able to approximate a bit of S_0 using only a ciphertext bit. By combining α_i^t with $\beta_{i+b_0}^{t+1}$, we are then able to approximate a bit of S_1 (at step $t+1$) using only ciphertext bits from two consecutive steps. Likewise, γ_i^t allows us to "jump" from S_1 to S_4, i.e. by combining α_i^t with β_i^t and γ_i^t with appropriate choices of parameters t and i for each, we are able to approximate one bit of S_4 using only ciphertext bits. Notice however that γ_i^t requires approximating S_1 in two consecutive steps; and so the previous combination requires using α_i^t and β_i^t *twice* at different steps. In the same way, δ_i^t allows us to jump from S_4 to S_2; and ε_i^t allows jumping from S_2 back to S_0. Eventually, we are able to approximate a bit of S_0 using only ciphertext bits via the combination of all trail fragments α_i^t, β_i^t, γ_i^t, δ_i^t, and ε_i^t.

However, the same bit of S_0 can also be approximated directly by using α_i^t at the corresponding step. Thus that bit can be linearly approximated from two different sides: the first approximation uses a combination of all trail fragments, and involves successive approximations of all state registers (except S_3) spanning several encryption steps, as explained in the previous paragraph. The second approximation only involves using α_i^t at the final step reached by the previous trail. By XORing up these two approximations, we are left with only ciphertext bits, spanning five consecutive encryption steps.

Of course, the overall trail resulting from all of the previous combinations is quite complex, especially since γ_i^t, δ_i^t, and ε_i^t each require two copies of the preceding trail fragment in consecutive steps: that is, ε_i^t requires two approximations of S_2, which requires using δ_i^t twice; and δ_i^t in turn requires using γ_i^t twice, which itself requires using α_i^t and β_i^t twice. Then α_i^t is used one final time to close the trail. The full construction with the exact bit indices for MiniMORUS-640 and MiniMORUS-1280 is illustrated in Fig. 3, where the left and right half each show half of the full trail. One may naturally wonder if some components of this trail are in conflict. In particular, products of bits from registers S_2 and S_3 are approximated multiple times, by α_i^t, β_i^t and γ_i^t. To address this concern, and ensure that all approximations along the trail are in fact compatible, we now compute the full trail equation explicitly.

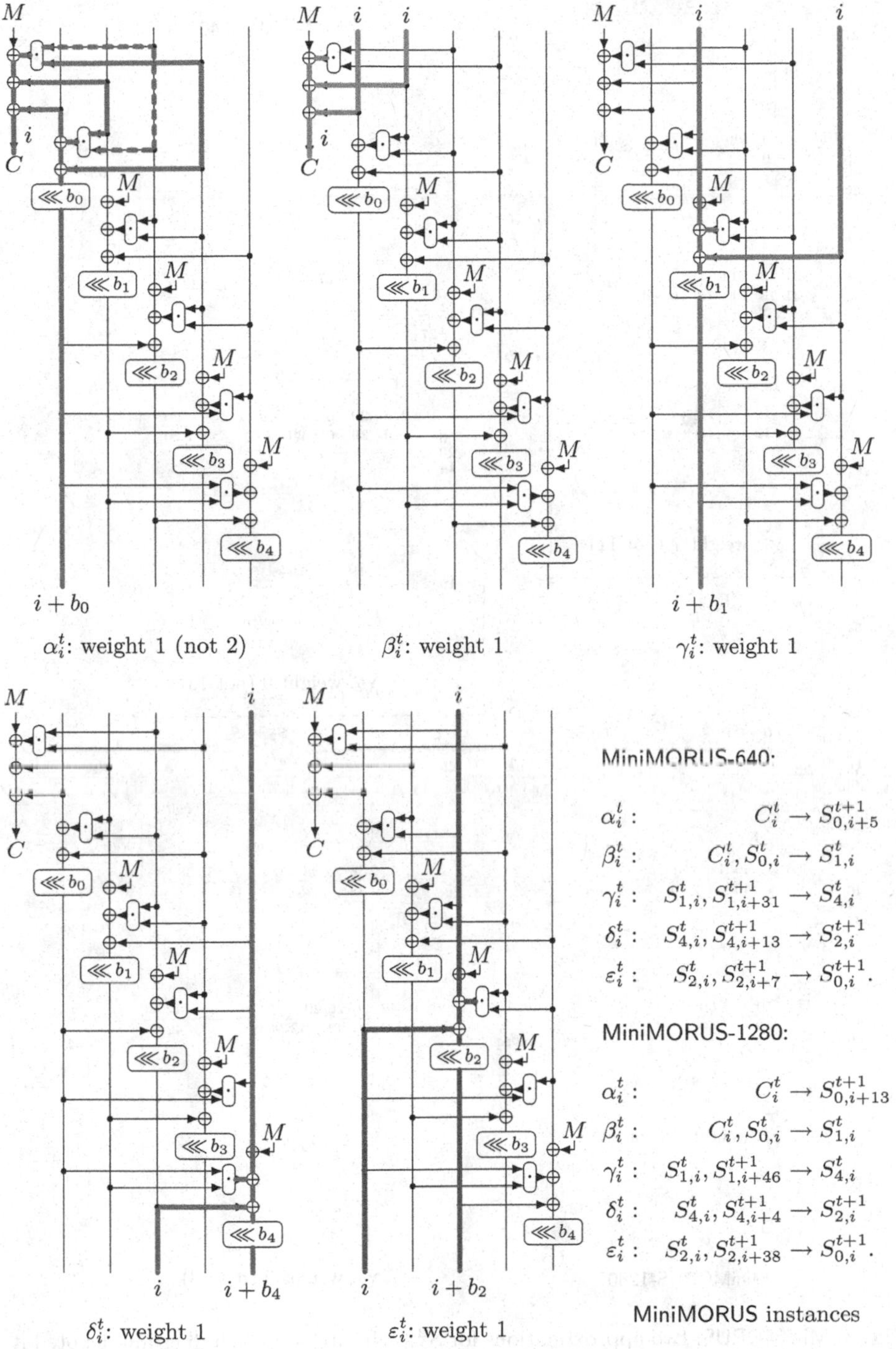

Fig. 2. MiniMORUS linear trail fragments.

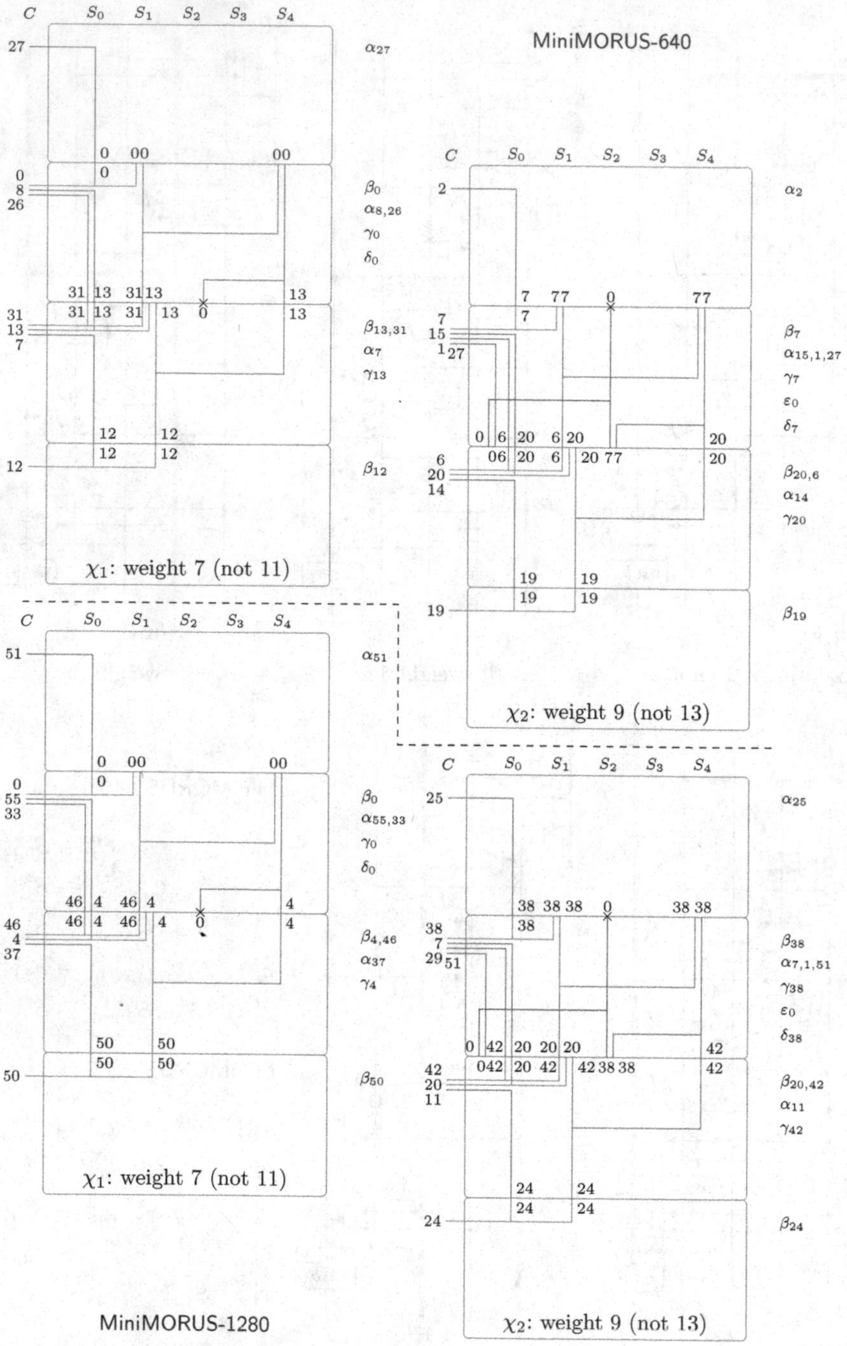

Fig. 3. MiniMORUS: two approximations for $S^2_{2,0}$. Numbers in each diagram denote bit positions used in the linear approximation, i.e. subscripts of $\alpha, \beta, \gamma, \delta$ and ε. χ_1 and χ_2 are two halves of the full trail which we experimentally verify.

4.2 Trail Equation

The equation corresponding to each of the five trail fragments α_i^t, β_i^t, γ_i^t, δ_i^t, ε_i^t may be written explicitly as $\mathbf{A}_i^t$, $\mathbf{B}_i^t$, $\mathbf{C}_i^t$, $\mathbf{D}_i^t$, $\mathbf{E}_i^t$ as follows. For each equation, we write on the left-hand side of the equality the biased linear combination used in the trail; and on the right-hand side, the remainder of the equation, which must have non-zero correlation (in all cases the correlation is 2^{-1}).

$$\begin{aligned}
\mathbf{A}_i^t: &\quad C_i^t \oplus S_{0,i+b_0}^{t+1} = S_{1,i}^t \oplus S_{3,i}^t \oplus S_{1,i}^t \cdot S_{2,i}^t \oplus S_{2,i}^t \cdot S_{3,i}^t \\
\mathbf{B}_i^t: &\quad C_i^t \oplus S_{0,i}^t \oplus S_{1,i}^t = S_{2,i}^t \cdot S_{3,i}^t \\
\mathbf{C}_i^t: &\quad S_{1,i}^t \oplus S_{1,i+b_1}^{t+1} \oplus S_{4,i}^t = S_{2,i}^t \cdot S_{3,i}^t \\
\mathbf{D}_i^t: &\quad S_{4,i}^t \oplus S_{4,i+b_4}^{t+1} \oplus S_{2,i}^{t+1} = S_{0,i}^{t+1} \cdot S_{1,i}^{t+1} \\
\mathbf{E}_i^t: &\quad S_{2,i}^t \oplus S_{2,i+b_2}^{t+1} \oplus S_{0,i}^{t+1} = S_{3,i}^t \cdot S_{4,i}^t
\end{aligned}$$

From an algebraic point of view, building the full trail amounts to adding up copies of the previous equations for various choices of t and i, so that eventually all $S_{y,z}^x$ terms on the left-hand side cancel out. Then we are left with only ciphertext terms on the left-hand side, while the right-hand side consists of a sum of biased expressions. By measuring the correlation of the right-hand side expression, we are then able to determine the correlation of the linear combination of ciphertext bits on the left-hand side. We now set out to do so.

In order to build the equation for the full trail, we start with $\mathbf{E}_0^2$:

$$S_{2,0}^2 \oplus S_{2,b_2}^3 \oplus S_{0,0}^3 = S_{3,0}^2 \cdot S_{4,0}^2.$$

In order to cancel the $S_{0,0}^3$ term on the left-hand side, we add to the equation $\mathbf{A}_{-b_0}^2$ (where the sum of two equations of the form $a = b$ and $c = d$ is defined to be $a + c = b + d$). This yields:

$$\begin{aligned}
&S_{2,0}^2 \oplus S_{2,b_2}^3 \oplus C_{-b_0}^2 \\
&= S_{3,0}^2 \cdot S_{4,0}^2 \oplus S_{1,-b_0}^2 \oplus S_{3,-b_0}^2 \oplus S_{1,-b_0}^2 \cdot S_{2,-b_0}^2 \oplus S_{2,-b_0}^2 \cdot S_{3,-b_0}^2.
\end{aligned}$$

We then need to cancel two terms of the form $S_{2,i}^t$. To do this, we add to the equations $\mathbf{D}_i^t$ for appropriate choices of t and i. This replaces the two $S_{2,i}^t$ terms by four $S_{4,i}^t$ terms. By using equation $\mathbf{B}_i^t$ four times, we can then replace these four $S_{4,i}^t$ terms by eight $S_{1,i}^t$ terms. By applying equation $\mathbf{B}_i^t$ eight times, these eight $S_{1,i}^t$ terms can in turn be replaced by eight $S_{0,i}^t$ terms (and some ciphertext terms). Finally, applying $\mathbf{A}_i^t$ eight times allows to replace these eight $S_{0,i}^t$ terms by only ciphertext bits. Ultimately, for MiniMORUS-1280, this yields the equation:

$$\begin{aligned}
&C_{51}^0 \oplus C_0^1 \oplus C_{25}^1 \oplus C_{33}^1 \oplus C_{55}^1 \oplus C_4^2 \oplus C_7^2 \oplus C_{29}^2 \oplus C_{37}^2 \\
&\oplus C_{38}^2 \oplus C_{46}^2 \oplus C_{51}^2 \oplus C_{11}^3 \oplus C_{20}^3 \oplus C_{42}^3 \oplus C_{50}^3 \oplus C_{24}^4 \\
&= S_{1,51}^0 \cdot S_{2,51}^0 \oplus S_{2,51}^0 \cdot S_{3,51}^0 \oplus S_{1,51}^0 \oplus S_{3,51}^0 && \text{weight 1} \\
&\oplus S_{1,25}^1 \cdot S_{2,25}^1 \oplus S_{2,25}^1 \cdot S_{3,25}^1 \oplus S_{1,25}^1 \oplus S_{3,25}^1 && \text{weight 1}
\end{aligned}$$

$$\oplus S^1_{1,33} \cdot S^1_{2,33} \oplus S^1_{2,33} \cdot S^1_{3,33} \oplus S^1_{1,33} \oplus S^1_{3,33} \qquad \text{weight 1}$$
$$\oplus S^1_{1,55} \cdot S^1_{2,55} \oplus S^1_{2,55} \cdot S^1_{3,55} \oplus S^1_{1,55} \oplus S^1_{3,55} \qquad \text{weight 1}$$
$$\oplus S^2_{1,7} \cdot S^2_{2,7} \oplus S^2_{2,7} \cdot S^2_{3,7} \oplus S^2_{1,7} \oplus S^2_{3,7} \qquad \text{weight 1}$$
$$\oplus S^2_{1,29} \cdot S^2_{2,29} \oplus S^2_{2,29} \cdot S^2_{3,29} \oplus S^2_{1,29} \oplus S^2_{3,29} \qquad \text{weight 1}$$
$$\oplus S^2_{1,37} \cdot S^2_{2,37} \oplus S^2_{2,37} \cdot S^2_{3,37} \oplus S^2_{1,37} \oplus S^2_{3,37} \qquad \text{weight 1}$$
$$\oplus S^2_{1,51} \cdot S^2_{2,51} \oplus S^2_{2,51} \cdot S^2_{3,51} \oplus S^2_{1,51} \oplus S^2_{3,51} \qquad \text{weight 1}$$
$$\oplus S^3_{1,11} \cdot S^3_{2,11} \oplus S^3_{2,11} \cdot S^3_{3,11} \oplus S^3_{1,11} \oplus S^3_{3,11} \qquad \text{weight 1}$$
$$\oplus S^2_{0,0} \cdot S^2_{1,0} \qquad \text{weight 1}$$
$$\oplus S^2_{2,46} \cdot S^2_{3,46} \qquad \text{weight 1}$$
$$\oplus S^2_{3,0} \cdot S^2_{4,0} \qquad \text{weight 1}$$
$$\oplus S^3_{0,38} \cdot S^3_{1,38} \qquad \text{weight 1}$$
$$\oplus S^3_{2,20} \cdot S^3_{3,20} \qquad \text{weight 1}$$
$$\oplus S^3_{2,50} \cdot S^3_{3,50} \qquad \text{weight 1}$$
$$\oplus S^4_{2,24} \cdot S^4_{3,24} \qquad \text{weight 1}$$

The equation for MiniMORUS-640 is very similar, and is given in the full version of this paper [2].

4.3 Correlation of the Trail

In the equation for MiniMORUS-1280 from the previous section, each line on the right-hand side of the equality involves distinct $S^t_{i,j}$ terms (in the sense that no two lines share a common term), and each line has a weight of 1. By the Piling-Up Lemma, it follows that if we assume distinct $S^t_{i,j}$ terms to be uniform and independent, then the expression on the right-hand side has a weight of 16. Hence the linear combination of ciphertext bits on the left-hand side has a correlation of 2^{-16}. The same holds for MiniMORUS-640.

The correlation is surprising high. The full trail uses trail fragments ε^t_i, δ^t_i, γ^t_i, β^t_i, and α^t_i, once, twice, 4 times, 8 times, and 9 times, respectively. Since each trail fragment has a weight of 1, this would suggest that the total weight should be $1 + 2 + 4 + 8 + 9 = 24$ rather than 16. However, when combining trail fragments β_i and γ_i, notice that the same AND is computed at the same step between registers S_2 and S_3 (equivalently, notice that the right-hand side of equations $\mathbf{B}^t_i$ and $\mathbf{C}^t_i$ is equal). In both cases it is approximated by zero. When XORing the corresponding equations, these two ANDs cancel each other, which saves two AND gates. Since γ^t_i is used four times in the course of the full trail, this results in saving 8 AND gates overall, which explains why the final correlation is 2^{-16} rather than 2^{-24}.

4.4 Experimental Verification

To confirm that our analysis is correct, we ran experiments on an implementation of MiniMORUS-1280 and MiniMORUS-640. We consider two halves χ_1 and χ_2 of the full trail (depicted on Fig. 3), as well as the full trail itself, denoted by χ. In each case, we give the weight predicted by the analysis from the previous section, and the weight measured by our experiments. Results are displayed on Table 3. While our analysis predicts a correlation of 2^{-16}, experiments indicate a slightly better empirical correlation of $2^{-15.5}$ for MORUS-640. The discrepancy of $2^{-0.5}$ probably arises from the fact that register bits across different steps are not completely independent.

The programs we used to verify the bias experimentally are available at: https://github.com/ildyria/MorusBias

Table 3. Experimental verification of trail correlations.

Approximations for MiniMORUS-640	Weight	
	Predicted	Measured
χ_1 $S_0^{2,2} = C_{27}^0 \oplus C_{0,8,26}^1 \oplus C_{7,13,31}^2 \oplus C_{12}^3$	7	7
χ_2 $S_0^{2,2} = C_2^1 \oplus C_{1,7,15,27}^2 \oplus C_{6,14,20}^3 \oplus C_{19}^4$	9	9
χ $0 = C_{27}^0 \oplus C_{0,2,26,8}^1 \oplus C_{1,13,15,27,31}^2 \oplus C_{6,12,14,20}^3 \oplus C_{19}^4$	16	15.5
Approximations for MiniMORUS-1280		
χ_1 $S_0^{2,2} = C_{51}^0 \oplus C_{0,33,55}^1 \oplus C_{4,37,46}^2 \oplus C_{50}^3$	7	7
χ_2 $S_0^{2,2} = C_{25}^1 \oplus C_{7,29,38,51}^2 \oplus C_{11,20,42}^3 \oplus C_{24}^4$	9	9
χ $0 = C_{51}^0 \oplus C_{0,25,33,55}^1 \oplus C_{4,7,29,37,38,46,51}^2 \oplus C_{11,20,42,50}^3 \oplus C_{24}^4$	16	15.9

5 Trail for Full MORUS

In the previous section, we presented a linear trail for the reduced ciphers MiniMORUS-1280 and MiniMORUS-640. We now turn to the full ciphers MORUS-1280 and MORUS-640.

5.1 Making the Trail Rotationally Invariant

In order to build a trail for the full MORUS, we proceed exactly as we did for MiniMORUS, following the same path down to step and word rotation values, with one difference: in order to move from the one-word registers of MiniMORUS to the four-word registers of full MORUS, we make every term $S_{i,j}^t$ and C_j^t rotationally invariant, in the sense of Sect. 3. That is, for every $S_{i,j}^t$ (resp. C_j^t) component in every trail fragment and every equation, we expand the term by adding in the terms $S_{i,j+w}^t$, $S_{i,j+2w}^t$, $S_{i,j+3w}^t$ (resp. C_{j+w}^t, C_{j+2w}^t, C_{j+3w}^t), where as usual w denotes the word size. For example, if $w = 64$ (for MORUS-1280), the term $S^3_{2,0}$ is expanded into:

$$S^3_{2,0} \oplus S^3_{2,64} \oplus S^3_{2,128} \oplus S^3_{2,192}.$$

Thus, translating the trail from one of the MiniMORUS ciphers to the corresponding full MORUS cipher amounts to making every linear combination rotationally invariant—indeed, that was the point of introducing MiniMORUS in the first place. Concretely, in order to build the full trail equation for MORUS, we write rotationally invariant versions of equations $\mathbf{A}^t_i$, $\mathbf{B}^t_i$, $\mathbf{C}^t_i$, $\mathbf{D}^t_i$, $\mathbf{E}^t_i$ from Sect. 4.2, and then combine them in exactly the same manner as before. This way, the biased linear combination on MiniMORUS-1280 given in Sect. 4.2, namely:

$$C^0_{51} \oplus C^1_0 \oplus C^1_{25} \oplus C^1_{33} \oplus C^1_{55} \oplus C^2_4 \oplus C^2_7 \oplus C^2_{29} \oplus C^2_{37}$$
$$\oplus C^2_{38} \oplus C^2_{46} \oplus C^2_{51} \oplus C^3_{11} \oplus C^3_{20} \oplus C^3_{42} \oplus C^3_{50} \oplus C^4_{24}$$

ultimately yields the following biased rotationally invariant linear combination on the full MORUS-1280:

$$C^0_{51} \oplus C^0_{115} \oplus C^0_{179} \oplus C^0_{243} \oplus C^1_0 \oplus C^1_{25} \oplus C^1_{33} \oplus C^1_{55} \oplus C^1_{64} \oplus C^1_{89}$$
$$\oplus C^1_{97} \oplus C^1_{119} \oplus C^1_{128} \oplus C^1_{153} \oplus C^1_{161} \oplus C^1_{183} \oplus C^1_{192} \oplus C^1_{217} \oplus C^1_{225} \oplus C^1_{247}$$
$$\oplus C^2_4 \oplus C^2_7 \oplus C^2_{29} \oplus C^2_{37} \oplus C^2_{38} \oplus C^2_{46} \oplus C^2_{51} \oplus C^2_{68} \oplus C^2_{71} \oplus C^2_{93}$$
$$\oplus C^2_{101} \oplus C^2_{102} \oplus C^2_{110} \oplus C^2_{115} \oplus C^2_{132} \oplus C^2_{135} \oplus C^2_{157} \oplus C^2_{165} \oplus C^2_{166} \oplus C^2_{174}$$
$$\oplus C^2_{179} \oplus C^2_{196} \oplus C^2_{199} \oplus C^2_{221} \oplus C^2_{229} \oplus C^2_{230} \oplus C^2_{238} \oplus C^2_{243} \oplus C^3_{11} \oplus C^3_{20}$$
$$\oplus C^3_{42} \oplus C^3_{50} \oplus C^3_{75} \oplus C^3_{84} \oplus C^3_{106} \oplus C^3_{114} \oplus C^3_{139} \oplus C^3_{148} \oplus C^3_{170} \oplus C^3_{178}$$
$$\oplus C^3_{203} \oplus C^3_{212} \oplus C^3_{234} \oplus C^3_{242} \oplus C^4_{24} \oplus C^4_{88} \oplus C^4_{152} \oplus C^4_{216}$$

We refer the reader to the full version of this paper [2] for the corresponding linear combination on MORUS-640.

5.2 Correlation of the Full Trail

The rotationally invariant trail on full MORUS may be intuitively understood as consisting of four copies of the original trail on MiniMORUS. Indeed, the only difference between full MORUS (for either version of MORUS) and four independent copies of MiniMORUS comes from word-wise rotations, which permute words within a register. But as observed in Sect. 3, word-wise rotations preserves the rotational invariance property; and so, insofar as we only ever use rotationally invariant linear combinations on all registers along the trail, word-wise rotations have no effect.

Following the previous intuition, one may expect that the weight of the full trail should simply be four times the weight of the corresponding MiniMORUS trail, namely 64 for both MORUS-1280 and MORUS-640. However, reality is a little more complex, as the full trail does not exactly behave as four copies of the original trail when one considers nonlinear terms.

To understand why that might be the case, assume a nonlinear term $S_{2,0}^0 \cdot S_{3,0}^0$ arising from some part of the trail, and another term $S_{2,0}^0 \cdot S_{3,w}^0$ arising from a different part of the trail (where w denotes the word size). Then when we XOR the various trail fragments together, in MiniMORUS these two terms are actually equal and will cancel out, since word-wise rotations by multiples of w bits are ignored. However in the real MORUS these terms are of course distinct and do not cancel each other.

In the actual trail for (either version of) full MORUS, this exact situation occurs when combining trail fragments β_i^t and γ_i^t. Indeed, β_i^t requires approximating the term $S_{2,i}^t \cdot S_{3,i}^t$, while γ_i^t requires approximating the term $S_{2,i}^t \cdot S_{3,i-w}^t$ (cf. Fig. 4). While in MiniMORUS, these terms cancel out, in the full MORUS, when adding up four copies of the trail to achieve rotational invariance, we end up with the sum:

$$\begin{aligned} &S_{2,i}^t \cdot S_{3,i}^t \oplus S_{3,i}^t \cdot S_{2,i+w}^t \oplus S_{2,i+w}^t \cdot S_{3,i+w}^t \oplus S_{3,i+w}^t \cdot S_{2,i+2w}^t \\ \oplus\, &S_{2,i+2w}^t \cdot S_{3,i+2w}^t \oplus S_{3,i+2w}^t \cdot S_{2,i+3w}^t \oplus S_{2,i+3w}^t \cdot S_{3,i+3w}^t \oplus S_{3,i+3w}^t \cdot S_{2,i}^t. \end{aligned} \quad (2)$$

It may be observed that the products occurring in the equation above involve eight terms forming a ring. The weight of this expression can be computed by brute force, and is equal to 3.

For MORUS-1280, since the trail fragment γ_i^t is used four times, this phenomenon adds a contribution of $4 \cdot 3 = 12$ to the overall weight of the full trail. This results in a total weight of $4 \cdot 16 + 12 = 76$ (recall that the weight of the trail on MiniMORUS-1280 is 16). We have confirmed this by explicitly computing the full trail equation in Appendix A, and evaluating its exact weight like we did for MiniMORUS in Sect. 4.3. That is, since the equation is quadratic, we may view it as a graph, which we split into connected components; we then compute the weight of each connected component separately by brute force, and then add up the weights of all components per the Piling-Up Lemma. Overall, the full trail equation given in Appendix A yields a weight of 76 for the full trail on MORUS-1280.

In the case of MORUS-640, collisions between rotation constants further complicate the analysis. Specifically, when using trail fragment β_i^t, the term $S_{2,i}^t \cdot S_{3,i}^t$ occurs. As explained previously, a partial collision with the term $S_{2,i}^t \cdot S_{3,i-w}^t$ from trail fragment γ_i^t results in Eq. (2). However trail fragment α_{i+d}^t is once used in the course of the full trail with an offset of $d = b_1 + b_4 - b_0 - b_2$ (relative to γ_i^t), which in the case of MORUS-640 is equal to $31 + 13 - 5 - 7 = 0 \bmod 32$. This creates another term $S_{2,i}^t \cdot S_{3,i}^t$, which ultimately destroys one of the four occurrences of Eq. (2). Therefore, when computing the full trail equation on MORUS-640, we get that the weight of the trail is 73 (cf. the full version of this paper for the full trail equation for MORUS-640).

5.3 Taking Variable Plaintext into Account

In our analysis so far, for the sake of simplicity, we have assumed that all plaintext blocks are zero. We now examine what happens if we remove that assumption, and integrate plaintext variables into our analysis. What we show is that

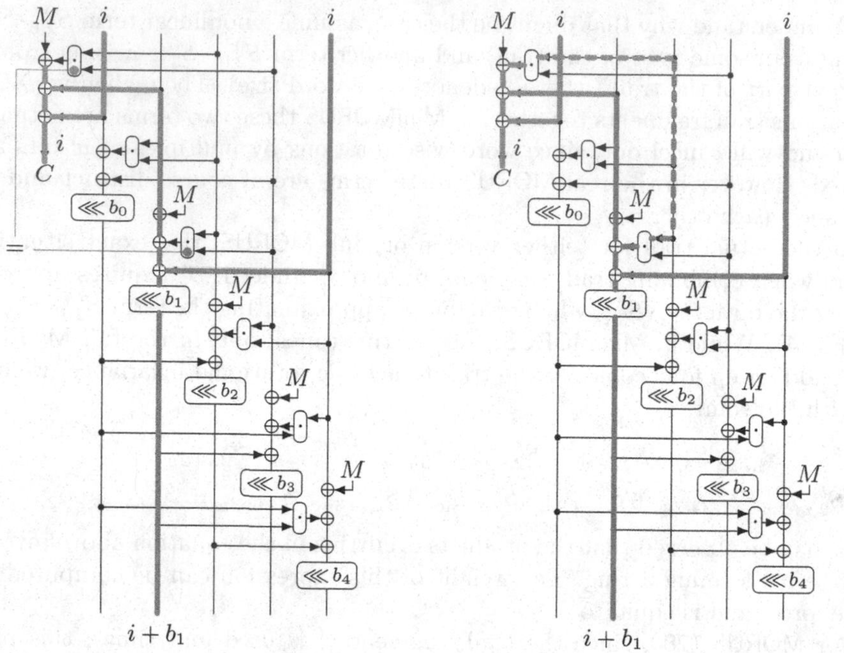

MiniMORUS: weight 0 (not 2) MORUS: weight 4×1 (not 4×2)

Fig. 4. Weight of $\beta_i^t \oplus \gamma_i^t$ for MiniMORUS and MORUS.

plaintext variables only contribute linearly to the trail. In other words, the full trail equation with plaintext variables is equal to the full trail equation with all-zero plaintext XORed with a linear combination of plaintext variables.

To see this, recall that plaintext bits contribute to the encryption process in two ways (cf. Sect. 2.1):

1. They are added to some bits derived from the state to form the ciphertext.
2. During each encryption step, the `StateUpdate` function adds a plaintext block to every register except S_0.

The effect of Item 1 is that whenever we use a ciphertext bit in our full trail equation, the corresponding plaintext bit also needs to be XORed in. Because ciphertext bits only contribute linearly to the trail equation, this only adds a linear combination of plaintext bits to the equation.

Regarding Item 2, recall that the full trail equation is a linear combination of (the rotationally invariant version of) equations $\mathbf{A}_i^t$, $\mathbf{B}_i^t$, $\mathbf{C}_i^t$, $\mathbf{D}_i^t$, $\mathbf{E}_i^t$ in Sect. 4.2. Also observe that in each equation, state bits that are shifted by a bit-wise rotation only contribute linearly. Because plaintext bits are XORed into each register at the same time bit-wise rotation is performed, this implies that plaintext bits resulting from Item 2 also only contribute linearly. In fact in all cases, it so happens that updating the equation to take plaintext variables into account simply involves XORing in the plaintext bit M_i^t.

It may be observed that message blocks in the `StateUpdate` function only contribute linearly to the state, and in that regard play a role similar to key bits in an SPN cipher; and indeed in SPN ciphers, it is the case that key bits contribute linearly to linear trails [11]. In this light the previous result may not be surprising.

In the end, with variable plaintext, our trail yields a biased linear combination of ciphertext bits and plaintext bits. In regards to attacks, this means the situation is effectively the same as with a biased stream cipher: in particular if the plaintext is known we obtain a distinguisher; and if a fixed unknown plaintext is encrypted multiple times (possibly also with some known variable part) then our trail yields a plaintext recovery attack.

6 Discussion

We now discuss the impact of these attacks on the security of MORUS.

Keystream Correlation. We emphasize that the correlation we uncover between plaintext and ciphertext bits is *absolute*, in the sense that it does not depend on the encryption key, or on the nonce. This is the same situation as the keystream correlations in AEGIS [15]. As such, they can be leveraged to mount an attack in the broadcast setting, where the same message is encrypted multiple times with different IVs and potentially different keys [10]. In particular, the broadcast setting appears in practice in man-in-the-browser attacks against HTTPS connections following the BEAST model [5]. In this scenario, an attacker uses Javascript code running in the victim's browser (by tricking the victim to visit a malicious website) to generate a large number of request to a secure website. Because of details of the HTTP protocol, each request includes an authentication token to identify the user, and the attacker can target this token as a repeated plaintext. Concretely, correlations in the RC4 keystream have been exploited in this setting, leading to the recovery of authentication cookies in practice [1].

Data Complexity. The design document of MORUS imposes a limit of 2^{64} encrypted blocks for a given key. However, since our attack is independent of the encryption key, and hence immune to rekeying, this limitation does not apply: all that matters for our attack is that the same plaintext be encrypted enough times.

With the trail presented in this work, the data complexity is clearly out of reach in practice, since exploiting the correlation would require 2^{152} encrypted blocks for MORUS1280, and 2^{146} encrypted blocks for MORUS640. The data complexity could be slightly lowered by leveraging multilinear cryptanalysis; indeed, the trail holds for any bit shift, and if we assume independence, we could run w copies of the trail in parallel on the same encrypted blocks (recall that w is the word size, and the trail is invariant by rotation by w bits). This would save a factor 2^5 on the data complexity for MORUS640, and 2^6 for MORUS1280; but the resulting complexity is still out of reach.

However, MORUS1280 with a 256-bit key claims a security level of 256 bits for confidentiality, and an attack with complexity 2^{152} violates this claim, even if it is not practical.

Design Considerations. The existence of this trail does hint at some weakness in the design of MORUS. Indeed, a notable feature of the trail is that the values of rotation constants are mostly irrelevant: a similar trail would exist for most choices of the constants. That it is possible to build a trail that ignores rotation constants may be surprising. This would have been prevented by adding a bit-wise rotation to one of the state registers at the input of the ciphertext equation.

7 Analysis on Initialization and Finalization of Reduced MORUS

The bias in the previous sections analysed the encryption part of the MORUS. In this section, for comprehensive security analysis of MORUS, we provide new attacks on reduced version of the initialization and the finalization. We emphasize that the results in this section do not threaten any security claim by the designers. However, we believe that investigating all parts of the design with different approaches from the existing work on MORUS provides a better understanding and will be useful especially when the design will be tweaked in future.

7.1 Forgery with Reduced Finalization

We present forgery attacks on 3 out of 10 steps of MORUS-1280 that claims 128-bit security for integrity. The attack only works for a limited number of steps, while it works in the nonce-respecting setting. As far as we know, this is the first attempt to evaluate integrity of MORUS in the nonce-respecting setting.

Overview. A general strategy for forgery attacks in the nonce-respecting setting is to inject some difference in a message block and propagate it so that it can be canceled by a difference in another message block. However this approach does not work well against MORUS due to its large state size which prevents an attacker from easily controlling the differences in different registers.

Here we focus on the property that the padding for an associated data A and a message M is the zero-padding, hence A and $A' = A\|0^*$ and M and $M' = M\|0$ result in identical states after the associated data processing and the encryption parts, as long as A, A' and M, M' fit in the same number of blocks. During the finalization, since A, A' (resp. M, M') have different lengths, the corresponding 64-bit values $|A|$ (resp. $|M|$) are different, which appears as $\Delta|A|$ (resp. $\Delta|M|$)

during the finalization, and is injected through the message input interface. Our strategy is to propagate this difference to the 128-bit tags T and T' such that their difference ΔT appears with higher probability than 2^{-128}. All in all, the forgery succeeds as long as the desired ΔT is obtained or in other words, the attacker does not have to cancel the state difference, which is the main advantage of attacking the finalization part of the scheme.

Note that if the attacker uses different messages M, M', not only the new tag T' but also new ciphertext C' must be guessed correctly. Because the encryption of MORUS is a simple XOR of the key stream, C' can be easily guessed. For this purpose, the attacker should first query a longer message $M' = M\|0^*$ to obtain C'. Then, C can be obtained by truncating C'.

Differential Trails. Recall that the message input during the finalization of MORUS-1280 is $|A| \,\|\, |M| \,\|\, 0^{128}$ where $|A|$ and $|M|$ are 64-bit strings. We set $\Delta|A|$ to be of low Hamming weight, e.g., 0x0000000000000001. This difference propagates through 3 steps as specified in Table 4.

Recall that each step consists of 5 rounds and the input message is absorbed to the state in rounds 2 to 5. The trail in Table 4 initially does not have any difference and the same continues even after round 1. Differences start to appear from round 2 and they will go through the bitwise-AND operation from round 4. We need to pay 1 bit to control each active AND gate. The probability evaluation for round 15 can be ignored since in this round only S_4 is non-linearly updated, while S_4 is never used for computing the tag. Finally, bitwise-AND in the tag computation is taken into account. Note that the tag is only 128 LSBs, thus the number of active AND gates should be counted only for those bits. As shown in Table 4, we can have a particular tag difference ΔT with probability 2^{-88}. Thus after observing A and corresponding T, $A\|0$ and $(T \oplus \Delta T)$ is a valid pair with probability 2^{-88}.

Remarks. The fact that the S_4 is updated in the last round but is not used in the tag generation implies that the MORUS finalization generally includes unnecessary computations with respect to security. It may be interesting to tweak the design such that the tag can also depend on S_4. Indeed in Table 4, we can observe some jump-up of the probability in the tag computation. This is because the non-linearly involved terms are $S_2 \cdot S_3$, and S_3 that was updated 2 rounds before has a high Hamming weight. In this sense, involving S_4 in non-linear terms of the tag computation imposes more difficulties for the attacker.

7.2 Extending State Recovery to Key Recovery

Kales et al. [9] showed that the internal state of MORUS-640 can be recovered under the nonce-misuse scenario using 2^5 plaintext-ciphertext pairs. As claimed by [9] the attack is naturally extended to MORUS-1280 though Kales et al. [9] did not demonstrate specific attacks. The recovered state allows the attacker to mount a universal forgery attack under the same nonce. However, the key still cannot be recovered because the key is used both at the beginning and end of the initialization, which prevents the attacker from backtracking the state value to the initial state. In this section, we show that meet-in-the-middle attacks allow the attacker to recover the key faster than exhaustive search for a relatively large number of steps, i.e., 10 out of 16 steps in MORUS-1280.

Overview. We divide the 10 steps of the initialization computation into two subsequent parts F_0 and F_1. (We later set that F_0 is the first 4 steps and F_1 is the last 6 steps.) Let S^{-10} be the initial state value before setting the key, i.e., $S^{-10} = (N \parallel 0^{128}, 0^{256}, 1^{256}, 0^{256}, c_0 \parallel c_1)$. Also let S^0 be 1280-bit state value after the initialization, which is now assumed to be recovered with the nonce-misuse analysis [9]. We then have the following relation.

$$F_1 \circ F_0(S^{-10} \oplus (0, K, 0, 0, 0)) \oplus (0, K, 0, 0, 0) = S^0.$$

We target the variant MORUS-1280-128, where $K = K_{128} \parallel K_{128}$.

Here, our strategy is to recover K_{128} by independently processing F_0 and F_1^{-1} to find the following match.

$$F_0(S^{-10} \oplus (0, K_{128} \| K_{128}, 0, 0, 0)) \stackrel{?}{=} F_1^{-1}(S^0 \oplus (0, K_{128} \| K_{128}, 0, 0, 0)).$$

To evaluate the attack complexity, we consider the following parameters.

- G_0: a set of bits of K_{128} that are guessed for computing F_0.
- G_1: a set of bits of K_{128} that are guessed for computing F_1^{-1}.
- G_2: a set of bits in the intersection of G_0 and G_1.
- x bits can match after processing F_0 and F_1^{-1}.

Suppose that the union of G_0 and G_1 covers all the bits of K_{128}. The attack exhaustively guesses G_2 and performs the following procedure for each guess.

1. F_0 is computed $2^{|G_0|-|G_2|}$ times and the results are stored in a table T. (Because $|G_1| - |G_2|$ bits are unknown, only a part of the state is computed.)
2. F_1^{-1} is computed $2^{|G_1|-|G_2|}$ times and for each result we check the match with any entry in T.
3. There are $2^{|G_0|-|G_2|+|G_1|-|G_2|}$ combinations, and the number of valid matches reduces to $2^{|G_0|-|G_2|+|G_1|-|G_2|-x}$ after matching the x bits.
4. Check the correctness of the guess by using one plaintext-ciphertext pair.

In the end, F_0 is computed $2^{|G_2|} \cdot 2^{|G_0|-|G_2|} = 2^{|G_0|}$ times. Similarly, F_1^{-1} is computed $2^{|G_1|}$ times. The number of the total candidates after the x-bit match is $2^{|G_2|} \cdot 2^{|G_0|-|G_2|+|G_1|-|G_2|-x} = 2^{|G_0|+|G_1|-|G_2|-x}$. Hence, the key K_{128} is recovered with complexity

$$\max(2^{|G_0|}, 2^{|G_1|}, 2^{|G_0|+|G_1|-|G_2|-x}).$$

Suppose that we choose $|G_0|$ and $|G_1|$ to be balanced i.e., $|G_0| = |G_1|$. Then, the complexity is

$$\max(2^{|G_0|}, 2^{2|G_0|-|G_2|-x}).$$

Two terms are balanced when $x = |G_0| - |G_2|$. Hence, the number of matched bits in the middle of two functions must be greater than or equal to the number of independently guessed bits to compute F_0 and F_1^{-1}.

In the attack below, we choose $|G_0| = |G_1| = 127$ and $|G_2| = 126$ (equivalently $|G_2| - |G_0| = |G_2| - |G_1| = 1$) in order to aim $x = 1$-bit match in the middle, which maximizes the number of attacked rounds.

Full Diffusion Rounds. We found that `StepUpdate` was designed to have good diffusion in the forward direction. Thus, once the state is recovered, the attacker can perform the partial computation in the backward direction longer than the forward direction. We set G_0 and G_1 as follows.

$$G_0 = \{1, 2, \cdots, 127\} \qquad \text{Bit position 0 is unknown.}$$
$$G_1 = \{0, 1, \cdots, 7, 9, 10, \cdots, 127\} \qquad \text{Bit position 8 is unknown.}$$

Those will lead to 4 matching bits after the 4-step forward computation and the 6-step backward computation. The analysis of the diffusion is given in Table 5. In the end, K_{128} can be recovered faster than the exhaustive search by 1 bit, i.e., with complexity 2^{127}.

Remarks. The matching state does not have to be a border of a step. It can be defined on a border of a round, or even in some more complicated way. We did not find the extension of the number of attacked steps even with this way.

As can be seen in Table 5, the updated register in step i is independent of the update function in step $i+1$ in the forward direction, and starts to impact from step $i+2$. By modifying this point, the diffusion speed can increase faster, which makes this attack harder.

8 Conclusion

This work provides a comprehensive analysis of the components of MORUS. In particular, we show that MORUS-1280's keystream exhibits a correlation of 2^{-76} between certain ciphertext bits. This enables a plaintext recovery attack in the broadcast setting, using about 2^{152} blocks of data. While the amount of data required is impractical, this seems to violate the security claims of MORUS-1280 because the attack works even if the key is refreshed regularly. Moreover, the broadcast setting is practically relevant, as was shown with attacks against RC4 as used in TLS [1].

We have shared an earlier version of this paper with the authors of MORUS and they agree with the technical details of the keystream bias. However they consider that it is not a significant weakness in practice because it requires more than 2^{64} ciphertexts bits. In the context of the CAESAR competition, we believe that certificational attacks such as this one should be taken into account, in order to select a portfolio of candidates that reflects the state of the art in terms of cryptographic design.

Acknowledgments. The results presented here were originally found during the Flexible Symmetric Cryptography workshop held at the Lorentz Center in Leiden, Netherlands. The authors would like to thank Meltem Sonmez Turan, who participated in the initial discussion. The second author was supported by the European Union's H2020 grant 644052 (HECTOR). The fourth and sixth authors are partially supported by the French Agence Nationale de la Recherche through the BRUTUS project under Contract ANR-14-CE28-0015. The fifth author was supported by EPSRC Grant EP/M013472/1.

A Trail Equations

In this section, we provide the full trail equation for MORUS-1280. Trail equations for MORUS-640 are available in the full version of this paper [2]. In each case, we decompose the right-hand side of the equality (involving state bits) into connected components, and compute the weight of each of these connected components. If we assume that distinct state bits are uniformly random and independent, then each connected component is independent. By the Piling-Up Lemma, it follows that the weight of the full equation is equal to the sum of the weights of the connected components.

A.1 Trail Equation for Full MORUS-1280

$$
\begin{aligned}
& C^0_{51} \oplus C^0_{115} \oplus C^0_{179} \oplus C^0_{243} \oplus C^1_0 \oplus C^1_{25} \oplus C^1_{33} \oplus C^1_{55} \oplus C^1_{64} \oplus C^1_{89} \\
& \oplus C^1_{97} \oplus C^1_{119} \oplus C^1_{128} \oplus C^1_{153} \oplus C^1_{161} \oplus C^1_{183} \oplus C^1_{192} \oplus C^1_{217} \oplus C^1_{225} \oplus C^1_{247} \\
& \oplus C^2_4 \oplus C^2_7 \oplus C^2_{29} \oplus C^2_{37} \oplus C^2_{38} \oplus C^2_{46} \oplus C^2_{51} \oplus C^2_{68} \oplus C^2_{71} \oplus C^2_{93} \\
& \oplus C^2_{101} \oplus C^2_{102} \oplus C^2_{110} \oplus C^2_{115} \oplus C^2_{132} \oplus C^2_{135} \oplus C^2_{157} \oplus C^2_{165} \oplus C^2_{166} \oplus C^2_{174} \\
& \oplus C^2_{179} \oplus C^2_{196} \oplus C^2_{199} \oplus C^2_{221} \oplus C^2_{229} \oplus C^2_{230} \oplus C^2_{238} \oplus C^2_{243} \oplus C^3_{11} \oplus C^3_{20} \\
& \oplus C^3_{42} \oplus C^3_{50} \oplus C^3_{75} \oplus C^3_{84} \oplus C^3_{106} \oplus C^3_{114} \oplus C^3_{139} \oplus C^3_{148} \oplus C^3_{170} \oplus C^3_{178} \\
& \oplus C^3_{203} \oplus C^3_{212} \oplus C^3_{234} \oplus C^3_{242} \oplus C^4_{24} \oplus C^4_{88} \oplus C^4_{152} \oplus C^4_{216} \\
& = S^1_{2,0} \cdot S^1_{3,192} \oplus S^1_{2,0} \cdot S^1_{3,0} \oplus S^1_{2,64} \cdot S^1_{3,0} \oplus S^1_{2,64} \cdot S^1_{3,64} \\
& \qquad \oplus S^1_{2,128} \cdot S^1_{3,64} \oplus S^1_{2,128} \cdot S^1_{3,128} \oplus S^1_{2,192} \cdot S^1_{3,128} \oplus S^1_{2,192} \cdot S^1_{3,192} && \text{weight 3} \\
& \oplus S^2_{2,4} \cdot S^2_{3,4} \oplus S^2_{2,68} \cdot S^2_{3,4} \oplus S^2_{2,68} \cdot S^2_{3,68} \oplus S^2_{2,132} \cdot S^2_{3,68} \\
& \qquad \oplus S^2_{2,132} \cdot S^2_{3,132} \oplus S^2_{2,196} \cdot S^2_{3,132} \oplus S^2_{2,196} \cdot S^2_{3,196} \oplus S^2_{2,4} \cdot S^2_{3,196} && \text{weight 3} \\
& \oplus S^2_{2,102} \cdot S^2_{3,38} \oplus S^2_{2,102} \cdot S^2_{3,102} \oplus S^2_{2,166} \cdot S^2_{3,102} \oplus S^2_{2,166} \cdot S^2_{3,166} \\
& \qquad \oplus S^2_{2,230} \cdot S^2_{3,166} \oplus S^2_{2,230} \cdot S^2_{3,230} \oplus S^2_{2,38} \cdot S^2_{3,230} \oplus S^2_{2,38} \cdot S^2_{3,38} && \text{weight 3} \\
& \oplus S^3_{2,42} \cdot S^3_{3,42} \oplus S^3_{2,106} \cdot S^3_{3,42} \oplus S^3_{2,106} \cdot S^3_{3,106} \oplus S^3_{2,170} \cdot S^3_{3,106} \\
& \qquad \oplus S^3_{2,170} \cdot S^3_{3,170} \oplus S^3_{2,234} \cdot S^3_{3,170} \oplus S^3_{2,234} \cdot S^3_{3,234} \oplus S^3_{2,42} \cdot S^3_{3,234} && \text{weight 3} \\
& \oplus S^0_{1,51} \cdot S^0_{2,51} \oplus S^0_{1,51} \oplus S^0_{2,51} \cdot S^0_{3,51} \oplus S^0_{3,51} && \text{weight 1} \\
& \oplus S^0_{1,115} \cdot S^0_{2,115} \oplus S^0_{1,115} \oplus S^0_{2,115} \cdot S^0_{3,115} \oplus S^0_{3,115} && \text{weight 1} \\
& \oplus S^0_{1,179} \cdot S^0_{2,179} \oplus S^0_{1,179} \oplus S^0_{2,179} \cdot S^0_{3,179} \oplus S^0_{3,179} && \text{weight 1} \\
& \oplus S^0_{1,243} \cdot S^0_{2,243} \oplus S^0_{1,243} \oplus S^0_{2,243} \cdot S^0_{3,243} \oplus S^0_{3,243} && \text{weight 1}
\end{aligned}
$$

$\oplus S^1_{1,25} \cdot S^1_{2,25} \oplus S^1_{1,25} \oplus S^1_{2,25} \cdot S^1_{3,25} \oplus S^1_{3,25}$ weight 1

$\oplus S^1_{1,33} \cdot S^1_{2,33} \oplus S^1_{1,33} \oplus S^1_{2,33} \cdot S^1_{3,33} \oplus S^1_{3,33}$ weight 1

$\oplus S^1_{1,55} \cdot S^1_{2,55} \oplus S^1_{1,55} \oplus S^1_{2,55} \cdot S^1_{3,55} \oplus S^1_{3,55}$ weight 1

$\oplus S^1_{1,89} \cdot S^1_{2,89} \oplus S^1_{1,89} \oplus S^1_{2,89} \cdot S^1_{3,89} \oplus S^1_{3,89}$ weight 1

$\oplus S^1_{1,97} \cdot S^1_{2,97} \oplus S^1_{1,97} \oplus S^1_{2,97} \cdot S^1_{3,97} \oplus S^1_{3,97}$ weight 1

$\oplus S^1_{1,119} \cdot S^1_{2,119} \oplus S^1_{1,119} \oplus S^1_{2,119} \cdot S^1_{3,119} \oplus S^1_{3,119}$ weight 1

$\oplus S^1_{1,153} \cdot S^1_{2,153} \oplus S^1_{1,153} \oplus S^1_{2,153} \cdot S^1_{3,153} \oplus S^1_{3,153}$ weight 1

$\oplus S^1_{1,161} \cdot S^1_{2,161} \oplus S^1_{1,161} \oplus S^1_{2,161} \cdot S^1_{3,161} \oplus S^1_{3,161}$ weight 1

$\oplus S^1_{1,183} \cdot S^1_{2,183} \oplus S^1_{1,183} \oplus S^1_{2,183} \cdot S^1_{3,183} \oplus S^1_{3,183}$ weight 1

$\oplus S^1_{1,217} \cdot S^1_{2,217} \oplus S^1_{1,217} \oplus S^1_{2,217} \cdot S^1_{3,217} \oplus S^1_{3,217}$ weight 1

$\oplus S^1_{1,225} \cdot S^1_{2,225} \oplus S^1_{1,225} \oplus S^1_{2,225} \cdot S^1_{3,225} \oplus S^1_{3,225}$ weight 1

$\oplus S^1_{1,247} \cdot S^1_{2,247} \oplus S^1_{1,247} \oplus S^1_{2,247} \cdot S^1_{3,247} \oplus S^1_{3,247}$ weight 1

$\oplus S^2_{1,7} \cdot S^2_{2,7} \oplus S^2_{1,7} \oplus S^2_{2,7} \cdot S^2_{3,7} \oplus S^2_{3,7}$ weight 1

$\oplus S^2_{1,29} \cdot S^2_{2,29} \oplus S^2_{1,29} \oplus S^2_{2,29} \cdot S^2_{3,29} \oplus S^2_{3,29}$ weight 1

$\oplus S^2_{1,37} \cdot S^2_{2,37} \oplus S^2_{1,37} \oplus S^2_{2,37} \cdot S^2_{3,37} \oplus S^2_{3,37}$ weight 1

$\oplus S^2_{1,51} \cdot S^2_{2,51} \oplus S^2_{1,51} \oplus S^2_{2,51} \cdot S^2_{3,51} \oplus S^2_{3,51}$ weight 1

$\oplus S^2_{1,71} \cdot S^2_{2,71} \oplus S^2_{1,71} \oplus S^2_{2,71} \cdot S^2_{3,71} \oplus S^2_{3,71}$ weight 1

$\oplus S^2_{1,93} \cdot S^2_{2,93} \oplus S^2_{1,93} \oplus S^2_{2,93} \cdot S^2_{3,93} \oplus S^2_{3,93}$ weight 1

$\oplus S^2_{1,101} \cdot S^2_{2,101} \oplus S^2_{1,101} \oplus S^2_{2,101} \cdot S^2_{3,101} \oplus S^2_{3,101}$ weight 1

$\oplus S^2_{1,115} \cdot S^2_{2,115} \oplus S^2_{1,115} \oplus S^2_{2,115} \cdot S^2_{3,115} \oplus S^2_{3,115}$ weight 1

$\oplus S^2_{1,135} \cdot S^2_{2,135} \oplus S^2_{1,135} \oplus S^2_{2,135} \cdot S^2_{3,135} \oplus S^2_{3,135}$ weight 1

$\oplus S^2_{1,157} \cdot S^2_{2,157} \oplus S^2_{1,157} \oplus S^2_{2,157} \cdot S^2_{3,157} \oplus S^2_{3,157}$ weight 1

$\oplus S^2_{1,165} \cdot S^2_{2,165} \oplus S^2_{1,165} \oplus S^2_{2,165} \cdot S^2_{3,165} \oplus S^2_{3,165}$ weight 1

$\oplus S^2_{1,179} \cdot S^2_{2,179} \oplus S^2_{1,179} \oplus S^2_{2,179} \cdot S^2_{3,179} \oplus S^2_{3,179}$ weight 1

$\oplus S^2_{1,199} \cdot S^2_{2,199} \oplus S^2_{1,199} \oplus S^2_{2,199} \cdot S^2_{3,199} \oplus S^2_{3,199}$ weight 1

$\oplus S^2_{1,221} \cdot S^2_{2,221} \oplus S^2_{1,221} \oplus S^2_{2,221} \cdot S^2_{3,221} \oplus S^2_{3,221}$ weight 1

$\oplus S^2_{1,229} \cdot S^2_{2,229} \oplus S^2_{1,229} \oplus S^2_{2,229} \cdot S^2_{3,229} \oplus S^2_{3,229}$ weight 1

$\oplus S^2_{1,243} \cdot S^2_{2,243} \oplus S^2_{1,243} \oplus S^2_{2,243} \cdot S^2_{3,243} \oplus S^2_{3,243}$ weight 1

$\oplus S^3_{1,11} \cdot S^3_{2,11} \oplus S^3_{1,11} \oplus S^3_{2,11} \cdot S^3_{3,11} \oplus S^3_{3,11}$ weight 1

$\oplus S^3_{1,75} \cdot S^3_{2,75} \oplus S^3_{1,75} \oplus S^3_{2,75} \cdot S^3_{3,75} \oplus S^3_{3,75}$ weight 1

$\oplus S^3_{1,139} \cdot S^3_{2,139} \oplus S^3_{1,139} \oplus S^3_{2,139} \cdot S^3_{3,139} \oplus S^3_{3,139}$ weight 1

$\oplus S^3_{1,203} \cdot S^3_{2,203} \oplus S^3_{1,203} \oplus S^3_{2,203} \cdot S^3_{3,203} \oplus S^3_{3,203}$ weight 1

$\oplus S^2_{0,0} \cdot S^2_{1,0}$ weight 1

$\oplus S^2_{0,64} \cdot S^2_{1,64}$ weight 1

$\oplus S^2_{0,128} \cdot S^2_{1,128}$	weight 1
$\oplus S^2_{0,192} \cdot S^2_{1,192}$	weight 1
$\oplus S^3_{0,230} \cdot S^3_{1,230}$	weight 1
$\oplus S^2_{2,46} \cdot S^2_{3,46}$	weight 1
$\oplus S^2_{2,110} \cdot S^2_{3,110}$	weight 1
$\oplus S^2_{2,174} \cdot S^2_{3,174}$	weight 1
$\oplus S^2_{2,238} \cdot S^2_{3,238}$	weight 1
$\oplus S^2_{3,64} \cdot S^2_{4,0}$	weight 1
$\oplus S^2_{3,128} \cdot S^2_{4,64}$	weight 1
$\oplus S^2_{3,192} \cdot S^2_{4,128}$	weight 1
$\oplus S^2_{3,0} \cdot S^2_{4,192}$	weight 1
$\oplus S^3_{0,38} \cdot S^3_{1,38}$	weight 1
$\oplus S^3_{0,102} \cdot S^3_{1,102}$	weight 1
$\oplus S^3_{0,166} \cdot S^3_{1,166}$	weight 1
$\oplus S^3_{2,20} \cdot S^3_{3,20}$	weight 1
$\oplus S^3_{2,50} \cdot S^3_{3,50}$	weight 1
$\oplus S^3_{2,84} \cdot S^3_{3,84}$	weight 1
$\oplus S^3_{2,114} \cdot S^3_{3,114}$	weight 1
$\oplus S^3_{2,148} \cdot S^3_{3,148}$	weight 1
$\oplus S^3_{2,178} \cdot S^3_{3,178}$	weight 1
$\oplus S^3_{2,212} \cdot S^3_{3,212}$	weight 1
$\oplus S^3_{2,242} \cdot S^3_{3,242}$	weight 1
$\oplus S^4_{2,24} \cdot S^4_{3,24}$	weight 1
$\oplus S^4_{2,88} \cdot S^4_{3,88}$	weight 1
$\oplus S^4_{2,152} \cdot S^4_{3,152}$	weight 1
$\oplus S^4_{2,216} \cdot S^4_{3,216}$	weight 1

The total weight of the trail is 76.

Table 4. Differential propagation through 3 Steps. Five lines for round i denote the difference of $S_0, \cdots, S_4$ after the round i transformation.

Round	State difference				Weight	Accumulated probability
	0000000000000000	0000000000000000	0000000000000000	0000000000000000	0	
	0000000000000000	0000000000000000	0000000000000000	0000000000000000	0	
Ini	0000000000000000	0000000000000000	0000000000000000	0000000000000000	0	–
	0000000000000000	0000000000000000	0000000000000000	0000000000000000	0	
	0000000000000000	0000000000000000	0000000000000000	0000000000000000	0	
	0000000000000000	0000000000000000	0000000000000000	0000000000000000	0	
	0000000000000000	0000000000000000	0000000000000000	0000000000000000	0	
1	0000000000000000	0000000000000000	0000000000000000	0000000000000000	0	1
	0000000000000000	0000000000000000	0000000000000000	0000000000000000	0	
	0000000000000000	0000000000000000	0000000000000000	0000000000000000	0	
	0000000000000000	0000000000000000	0000000000000000	0000000000000000	0	
	0000400000000000	0000000000000000	0000000000000000	0000000000000000	1	
2	0000000000000000	0000000000000000	0000000000000000	0000000000000000	0	1
	0000000000000000	0000000000000000	0000000000000000	0000000000000000	0	
	0000000000000000	0000000000000000	0000000000000000	0000000000000000	0	
	0000000000000000	0000000000000000	0000000000000000	0000000000000000	0	
	0000400000000000	0000000000000000	0000000000000000	0000000000000000	1	
3	0000004000000000	0000000000000000	0000000000000000	0000000000000000	1	1
	0000000000000000	0000000000000000	0000000000000000	0000000000000000	0	
	0000000000000000	0000000000000000	0000000000000000	0000000000000000	0	
	0000000000000000	0000000000000000	0000000000000000	0000000000000000	0	
	0000000000000000	0000000000000000	0000400000000000	0000000000000000	1	
4	0000004000000000	0000000000000000	0000000000000000	0000000000000000	1	1
	0020000000000080	0000000000000000	0000000000000000	0000000000000000	2	
	0000000000000000	0000000000000000	0000000000000000	0000000000000000	0	
	0000000000000000	0000000000000000	0000000000000000	0000000000000000	0	
	0000000000000000	0000000000000000	0000400000000000	0000000000000000	1	
5	0000000000000000	0000000000000000	0000000000000000	0000004000000000	1	2^{-1}
	0020000000000080	0000000000000000	0000000000000000	0000000000000000	2	
	0000040000000010	0000000000000000	0000000000000000	0000000000000000	2	
	0000000000100004	0000000000000000	0000000000000000	0000000000000000	2	
	0000000000000000	0000000000000000	0000400000000000	0000000000000000	1	
6	0000000000000000	0000000000000000	0000000000000000	0000004000000000	1	2^{-3}
	0000000000000000	0000000000000000	0000000000000000	0020000000000080	2	
	0000040000000010	0000000000000000	0000000000000000	0000000000000000	2	
	0000000000100004	0000000000000000	0000000000000000	0000000000000000	2	
	0004400001000000	0000000000000000	0000000010000000	0000000000000000	4	
7	0000000000000000	0000000000000000	0000000000000000	0000004000000000	1	2^{-6}
	0000000000000000	0000000000000000	0000000000000000	0020000000000080	2	
	0000000000000000	0000000000000000	0000040000000010	0000000000000000	2	
	0000000000000000	0000000000100004	0000000000000000	0000000000000000	2	
	0004400001000000	0000000000000000	0000000010000000	0000000000000000	4	
8	0400014000000000	0000000000000000	0000000000000000	0000000000001000	4	2^{-10}
	0000000000000000	0000000000000000	0000000000000000	0010000000000000	1	
	0000000000000000	0000000000000000	0000040000000010	0000000000000000	2	
	0000000000000000	0000000000100004	0000000000000000	0000000000000000	2	
	0000000010000000	0000000000000000	0004400001000000	0000000000000000	4	
9	0400014000000000	0000000000000000	0000000000000000	0000000000001000	4	2^{-14}
	0220000080000080	0000000000000000	0000000800000000	1000000000004000	7	
	0000000000000000	0000000000000000	0000040000000010	0000000000000000	2	
	0000000000000000	0000000000100004	0000000000000000	0000000000000000	2	
	0000000010000000	0000000000000000	0004400001000000	0000000000000000	4	
10	0000000000000000	0000000000000000	0000000000001000	0400014000000000	4	2^{-20}
	0220000080000080	0000000000000000	0000000800000000	1000000000004000	7	
	4000140000000010	0000000000000000	0000400000000100	0000000000010000	7	
	0000100000100044	0000000200008000	0001000000000000	0000000008000200	9	
	0000000010000000	0000000000000000	0004400001000000	0000000000000000	4	
11	0000000000000000	0000000000000000	0000000000001000	0400014000000000	4	2^{-28}
	0000000000000000	0000000800000000	1000000000004000	0220000080000080	7	
	4000140000000010	0000000000000000	0000400000000100	0000000000010000	7	
	0000100000100044	0000000200008000	0001000000000000	0000000008000200	9	
	0004500005000400	0000000000000000	0040000100000040	4000000000000000	10	
12	0000000000000000	0000000000000000	0000000000001000	0400014000000000	4	2^{-39}
	0000000000000000	0000000800000000	1000000000004000	0220000080000080	7	
	0000400000000100	0000000000010000	4000140000000010	0000000000000000	7	
	0000000008000200	0000100000100044	0000000200008000	0001000000000000	9	
	0004500005000400	0000000000000000	0040000100000040	4000000000000000	10	
13	0400114000040000	0020000000000080	0004000000400000	0000800100005002	14	2^{-53}
	0000000000000000	0000000800000000	1000000000004000	0220000080000080	7	
	0000400000000100	0000000000010000	4000140000000010	0000000000000000	7	
	0000000008000200	0000100000100044	0000000200008000	0001000000000000	9	
	0040000100000040	4000000000000000	0004500005000400	0000000000000000	10	
14	0400114000040000	0020000000000080	0004000000400000	0000800100005002	14	2^{-69}
	0228000280020080	0000040000000000	2000008000202008	1000004000004021	18	
	0000400000000100	0000000000010000	4000140000000010	0000000000000000	7	
	0000000008000200	0000100000100044	0000000200008000	0001000000000000	9	
	0040000100000040	4000000000000000	0004500005000400	0000000000000000	10	
15	0020000000000080	0004000000400000	0000800100005002	0400114000040000	14	–
	0228000280020080	0000040000000000	2000008000202008	1000004000004021	18	
	0000400000000100	0000000000010000	4000140000000010	0000000000000000	7	
ΔT			600080830020f00a	1405414005044421		2^{-88}

Table 5. Analysis of the diffusion and matching bits over 10 steps. '0' and '1' denote that the state bit can and cannot be computed from a partial knowledge of K_{128}, respectively. After the partial computations from each direction, 4 bits of S^{-6} can match.

Round	State Difference			
	0000000000000000	0000000000000000	0000000000000000	0000000000000000
	0000000000000000	0000000000000001	0000000000000000	0000000000000001
$S^{-10} \oplus K_{128}$	0000000000000000	0000000000000000	0000000000000000	0000000000000000
	0000000000000000	0000000000000000	0000000000000000	0000000000000000
	0000000000000000	0000000000000000	0000000000000000	0000000000000000
	0000000000002000	0000000000000000	0000000000002000	0000000000000000
	0000000000000000	0000400000000000	0000000000000000	0000400000000000
1	0008000000000000	0000000000000000	0008000000000000	0000000000000000
	0000000000100000	0020000000000000	0000000000100000	0020000000000000
	0000000000020000	0084000000000000	0000000000020000	0084000000000000
	0800000000000004	0000000204000001	0800000000000004	0000000204000001
	8000000a00000000	0000002110000004	8000000a00000000	0000002110000004
2	0400010221000000	008000400a000081	0400010221000000	008000400a000081
	1000050001000244	4200118a08000280	1000050001000244	4200118a08000280
	880004a0a0200858	4840123350000050	880004a0a0200858	4840123350000050
	023d63c00050a850	00a1442000489380	023d63c00050a850	00a1442000489380
	02b63380056aaa48	00b5563005dcd6c0	02b63380056aaa48	00b5563005dcd6c0
3	d42ab556bf5dfcd6	5a26f633a8556aaa	d42ab556bf5dfcd6	5a26f633a8556aaa
	5fbbf556bd556c65	7aab99aaee6bea2c	5fbbf556bd556c65	7aab99aaee6bea2c
	abff7f3ad7feafad	cfff777ffddffd6d	abff7f3ad7feafad	cfff777ffddffd6d
	fff77dfffffdcf57	fefad7efffdffbf7	fff77dfffffdcf57	fefad7efffdffbf7
	fffffffffffbfff	fffbf7fffddfff77	fffffffffffbfff	fffbf7fffddfff77
4	ffffffffffffffff	ffffffffffffffff	ffffffffffffffff	ffffffffffffffff
	ffffffffffffffff	fffbfffeffffffff	ffffffffffffffff	fffbfffeffffffff
	ffffffffffffffff	ffffffffffffffff	ffffffffffffffff	ffffffffffffffff
		2-bits match		2-bits match
	ffffffffffffffff	ffffffffffffffff	ffffffffffffffff	ffffffffffffffff
	ffffffffffffffff	ffffffffffffffff	ffffffffffffffff	ffffffffffffffff
5	ffffffffffffffff	ffffffffffffffff	ffffffffffffffff	ffffffffffffffff
	fffff7ffedfffff7	ffffffffedffffff	fffff7ffedfffff7	ffffffffedffffff
	ffffffffedffffff	fffff7ffedfffff7	ffffffffedffffff	fffff7ffedfffff7
	ffffffffedffffff	fffff7ffedfffff7	ffffffffedffffff	fffff7ffedfffff7
	fffbf5e7cdfffbf7	fffff7bfcdfff757	fffbf5e7cdfffbf7	fffff7bfcdfff757
6	fffbf5e7cdfffbf7	fffff7bfcdfff757	fffbf5e7cdfffbf7	fffff7bfcdfff757
	7ffd75b6cdfff357	fffbf5a6ccfcfb73	7ffd75b6cdfff357	fffbf5a6ccfcfb73
	7ffbf5a6ccfcf373	7ff975b6ccfff353	7ffbf5a6ccfcf373	7ff975b6ccfff353
	7efbf5a6cc7cf353	7fd975a6cceff353	7efbf5a6cc7cf353	7fd975a6cceff353
	7eb950a4cc78e353	7dd07184cced7153	7eb950a4cc78e353	7dd07184cced7153
7	7eb950a4cc78e353	7dd07184ccec7153	7eb950a4cc78e353	7dd07184ccec7153
	7cd051044c6c3153	3e985024cc48a313	7cd051044c6c3153	3e985024cc48a313
	3c905004cc482313	7c9051044c6c2113	3c905004cc482313	7c9051044c6c2113
	2c905004c4482113	7c9050040c682113	2c905004c4482113	7c9050040c682113
	2810100444082112	5c1010040c402113	2810100444082112	5c1010040c402113
8	2810100444082112	1c1010040c402113	2810100444082112	1c1010040c402113
	0c00100404400113	2800000404082112	0c00100404400113	2800000404082112
	0800000404002112	0800100404400113	0800000404002112	0800100404400113
	0800000404002112	0800100004000112	0800000404002112	0800100004000112
	0000000404000102	0000100004000110	0000000404000102	0000100004000110
9	0000000404000102	0000000004000110	0000000404000102	0000000004000110
	0000000004000110	0000000000000102	0000000004000110	0000000000000102
	0000000000000100	0000000004000110	0000000000000100	0000000004000110
	0000000000000100	0000000004000100	0000000000000100	0000000004000100
	0000000000000000	0000000004000100	0000000000000000	0000000004000100
10	0000000000000000	0000000000000100	0000000000000000	0000000000000100
	0000000000000100	0000000000000000	0000000000000100	0000000000000000
	0000000000000000	0000000000000100	0000000000000000	0000000000000100
	0000000000000000	0000000000000000	0000000000000000	0000000000000000
	0000000000000000	0000000000000100	0000000000000000	0000000000000100
$S^{0} \oplus K_{128}$	0000000000000000	0000000000000000	0000000000000000	0000000000000000
	0000000000000000	0000000000000000	0000000000000000	0000000000000000
	0000000000000000	0000000000000000	0000000000000000	0000000000000000

References

1. AlFardan, N.J., Bernstein, D.J., Paterson, K.G., Poettering, B., Schuldt, J.C.N.: On the security of RC4 in TLS. In: USENIX Security Symposium 2013, pp. 305–320. USENIX Association (2013)
2. Ashur, T., et al.: Cryptanalysis of MORUS. Cryptology ePrint Archive, Report 2018/464 (2018). https://eprint.iacr.org/2018/464

3. Ashur, T., Rijmen, V.: On linear hulls and trails. In: Dunkelman, O., Sanadhya, S.K. (eds.) INDOCRYPT 2016. LNCS, vol. 10095, pp. 269–286. Springer, Cham (2016). https://doi.org/10.1007/978-3-319-49890-4_15
4. CAESAR Committee: CAESAR: Competition for authenticated encryption: security, applicability, and robustness. Call for submissions (2013). http://competitions.cr.yp.to/caesar-call.html
5. Duong, T., Rizzo, J.: Here come the ⊕ ninjas. Ekoparty (2011)
6. Dwivedi, A.D., Klouček, M., Morawiecki, P., Nikolić, I., Pieprzyk, J., Wójtowicz, S.: SAT-based cryptanalysis of authenticated ciphers from the CAESAR competition. Cryptology ePrint Archive, Report 2016/1053 (2016). https://eprint.iacr.org/2016/1053
7. Dwivedi, A.D., Morawiecki, P., Wójtowicz, S.: Differential and rotational cryptanalysis of round-reduced MORUS. In: Samarati, P., Obaidat, M.S., Cabello, E. (eds.) E-Business and Telecommunications - ICETE/SECRYPT 2017, pp. 275–284. SciTePress (2017)
8. Dworkin, M.J.: NIST SP 800–38D: Recommendation for block cipher modes of operation: Galois/Counter Mode (GCM) and GMAC. National Institute of Standards and Technology (NIST) Special Publication (SP) (2007). https://www.nist.gov/node/562956
9. Kales, D., Eichlseder, M., Mendel, F.: Note on the robustness of CAESAR candidates. IACR Cryptology ePrint Archive, Report 2017/1137 (2017). https://eprint.iacr.org/2017/1137
10. Mantin, I., Shamir, A.: A practical attack on broadcast RC4. In: Matsui, M. (ed.) FSE 2001. LNCS, vol. 2355, pp. 152–164. Springer, Heidelberg (2002). https://doi.org/10.1007/3-540-45473-X_13
11. Matsui, M.: Linear cryptanalysis method for DES cipher. In: Helleseth, T. (ed.) EUROCRYPT 1993. LNCS, vol. 765, pp. 386–397. Springer, Heidelberg (1994). https://doi.org/10.1007/3-540-48285-7_33
12. Matsui, M., Yamagishi, A.: A new method for known plaintext attack of FEAL cipher. In: Rueppel, R.A. (ed.) EUROCRYPT 1992. LNCS, vol. 658, pp. 81–91. Springer, Heidelberg (1993). https://doi.org/10.1007/3-540-47555-9_7
13. McGrew, D.A., Viega, J.: The security and performance of the Galois/Counter Mode (GCM) of operation. In: Canteaut, A., Viswanathan, K. (eds.) INDOCRYPT 2004. LNCS, vol. 3348, pp. 343–355. Springer, Heidelberg (2004). https://doi.org/10.1007/978-3-540-30556-9_27
14. Mileva, A., Dimitrova, V., Velichkov, V.: Analysis of the authenticated cipher MORUS (v1). In: Pasalic, E., Knudsen, L.R. (eds.) BalkanCryptSec 2015. LNCS, vol. 9540, pp. 45–59. Springer, Cham (2016). https://doi.org/10.1007/978-3-319-29172-7_4
15. Minaud, B.: Linear biases in AEGIS keystream. In: Joux, A., Youssef, A. (eds.) SAC 2014. LNCS, vol. 8781, pp. 290–305. Springer, Cham (2014). https://doi.org/10.1007/978-3-319-13051-4_18
16. Salam, M.I., Simpson, L., Bartlett, H., Dawson, E., Pieprzyk, J., Wong, K.K.: Investigating cube attacks on the authenticated encryption stream cipher MORUS. In: IEEE Trustcom/BigDataSE/ICESS 2017, pp. 961–966. IEEE (2017)
17. Shi, T., Guan, J., Li, J., Zhang, P.: Improved collision cryptanalysis of authenticated cipher MORUS. In: Artificial Intelligence and Industrial Engineering - AIIE 2016. Advances in Intelligent Systems Research, vol. 133, pp. 429–432. Atlantis Press (2016)

18. Vaudenay, S., Vizár, D.: Under pressure: security of CAESAR candidates beyond their guarantees. Cryptology ePrint Archive, Report 2017/1147 (2017). https://eprint.iacr.org/2017/1147
19. Wu, H., Huang, T.: The authenticated cipher MORUS (v2). Submission to CAESAR: competition for authenticated encryption. Security, applicability, and robustness (Round 3 and Finalist), September 2016. http://competitions.cr.yp.to/round3/morusv2.pdf
20. Wu, H., Preneel, B.: AEGIS: a fast authenticated encryption algorithm. In: Lange, T., Lauter, K., Lisoněk, P. (eds.) SAC 2013. LNCS, vol. 8282, pp. 185–201. Springer, Heidelberg (2014). https://doi.org/10.1007/978-3-662-43414-7_10
21. Wu, H., Preneel, B.: AEGIS: A fast authenticated encryption algorithm (v1.1). Submission to CAESAR: Competition for Authenticated Encryption. Security, Applicability, and Robustness (Round 3 and Finalist), September 2016. http://competitions.cr.yp.to/round3/aegisv11.pdf

New MILP Modeling: Improved Conditional Cube Attacks on Keccak-Based Constructions

Ling Song[1,2(✉)], Jian Guo[1(✉)], Danping Shi[2(✉)], and San Ling[1(✉)]

[1] Division of Mathematical Sciences, School of Physical and Mathematical Sciences, Nanyang Technological University, Singapore, Singapore
{guojian,lingsan}@ntu.edu.sg

[2] State Key Laboratory of Information Security, Institute of Information Engineering, Chinese Academy of Sciences, Beijing, China
{songling,shidanping}@iie.ac.cn

Abstract. In this paper, we propose a new MILP modeling to find better or even optimal choices of conditional cubes, under the general framework of conditional cube attacks. These choices generally find new or improved attacks against the keyed constructions based on KECCAK permutation and its variants, including KECCAK-MAC, KMAC, KEYAK, and KETJE, in terms of attack complexities or the number of attacked rounds. Interestingly, conditional cube attacks were applied to round-reduced KECCAK-MAC, but not to KMAC despite the great similarity between KECCAK-MAC and KMAC, and the fact that KMAC is the NIST standard way of constructing MAC from SHA-3. As examples to demonstrate the effectiveness of our new modeling, we report key recovery attacks against KMAC128 and KMAC256 reduced to 7 and 9 rounds, respectively; the best attack against Lake KEYAK with 128-bit key is improved from 6 to 8 rounds in the nonce-respected setting and 9 rounds of Lake KEYAK can be attacked if the key size is of 256 bits; attack complexity improvements are found generally on other constructions. Our new model is also applied to KECCAK-based full-state keyed sponge and gives a positive answer to the open question proposed by Bertoni *et al.* whether cube attacks can be extended to more rounds by exploiting full-state absorbing. To verify the correctness of our attacks, reduced-variants of the attacks are implemented and verified on a PC practically. It is remarked that this work does not threaten the security of any full version of the instances analyzed in this paper.

Keywords: KECCAK · SHA-3 · KMAC · KEYAK · KETJE · Full-state Conditional cube attack · MILP

1 Introduction

The KECCAK hash function family [5] is a proposal designed by Bertoni *et al.* and submitted to the SHA-3 competition [22] in 2008. It was selected as the final winner of the competition in 2012, and subsequently standardized as SHA-3 [29] in

T. Peyrin and S. Galbraith (Eds.): ASIACRYPT 2018, LNCS 11273, pp. 65–95, 2018.
https://doi.org/10.1007/978-3-030-03329-3_3

2015 by the National Institute of Standards and Technology of the U.S. (NIST). It supports four digest sizes from $\{224, 256, 384, 512\}$ to achieve different security levels. The standard SHA-3 and the original KECCAK design differ only in the way how messages are padded, and hence share almost all security analysis.

Since the KECCAK hash function was made public in 2008, it has attracted intensive cryptanalysis from the research community in many different settings. Against the three major properties of hash functions: collision, preimage and second-preimage resistance, the best practical collision/preimage attacks are up to 6 and 4 out of the total 24 rounds, respectively. By observing the low algebraic degree of the Sbox in KECCAK, Guo *et al.* [17] proposed the linear structures for up to 3 rounds of KECCAK, where the Sbox can be re-expressed as linear transformations when the input is restricted to specific affine subspaces. In [27], Song *et al.* found the first practical collision against 5-round KECCAK-224, where they used 3-round "connectors" based on the pioneer work by Qiao *et al.* [23] and Dinur *et al.* [12].

There is also a line of research on analyzing the security of keyed constructions based on KECCAK-*p*—the KECCAK permutations with variable width and rounds. Message authentication codes are naturally among the first keyed constructions based on KECCAK-*p*, *e.g.*, KECCAK-MAC [4] and KMAC [30]. In [13], Dinur *et al.* proposed the first cube attack against KECCAK-MAC for up to 7-round key recovery and 8-round forgery attacks. The attack complexities were subsequently improved by Huang *et al.* using conditional cube attacks [19]. The authenticated encryption schemes KEYAK [7] and KETJE [6] are also based on KECCAK-*p* and its variants. Similar to the attacks against KECCAK-MAC, the conditional cube attack was applied to KEYAK for up to 8 out of 12 rounds [19], and to KETJE [15,20] for up to 7 out of 13 rounds. Differently from the traditional way of reducing the strength of the design by round number, there is a recent attack against full KETJE with tweaked rate size by Fuhr *et al.* [16]. KRAVATTE [2] is a pseudorandom function by instantiating the Farfalle construction with KECCAK-*p*. Algebraic attacks on KRAVATTE, including cube attacks, which take advantage of structural properties of Farfalle, were proposed in [9].

Following a similar design strategy used for KECCAK-MAC, KMAC [30] is the standard way of constructing MAC from SHA-3 by NIST. The major design difference is that, the master key is processed as an independent data block before processing the message in KMAC, while it was processed together with some message bits as the first data block in KECCAK-MAC. Hence, at the point of injecting the first message block, the internal state for KMAC is totally unknown, while most bits of that for KECCAK-MAC are known. Similar observations were discovered and made use of in the so-called "Full-State Keyed Duplex (FKD)" [10,21] to improve the efficiency of keyed sponge constructions. It is interesting to note, despite the great similarity between KECCAK-MAC and KMAC, there is no existing cryptanalysis result against KMAC to the best of our knowledge. Also, for FKD no cube attack is proposed by exploiting the full-state absorption, as stated by the KEYAK designers in [7]:

Whether these attacks can still be extended to more rounds by exploiting full-state absorbing remains an open question.

Our Contributions. Based on the previous works [15,19,20] on conditional cube attacks against KECCAK-based keyed constructions, we propose a new Mixed Integer Linear Programming (MILP) modeling. While the length of cube tester (the zero-sum property) is determined entirely by the algebraic degrees of the underlying permutations, the conditional cube attack could only be improved by finding cube variables with lesser conditions and keeping the cube size large enough meanwhile. Our new MILP modeling is able to capture the characteristics of 2 KECCAK rounds, as well as the linear structures used in the first round. This new modeling is generic and imposes no unnecessary conditions, hence could be able to find optimal conditional cubes, in terms of cube size and number of conditions, whenever possible. This comes with a few key techniques:

1. We are able to model 2 KECCAK rounds together, *i.e.*, Sbox layer of the first round, the linear layer followed by the Sbox layer again of the second round. To do this, we exhaustively list the propagations of variables through the first Sbox layer so to keep the output of the Sbox linear. The second round is dealt in different ways.
   - For normal KECCAK-based constructions, we classify the situation of the linear layer in the second round into two cases depending on whether there is spreading of variables and model them each individually.
   - For FKD, we describe column sums of the state after the Sbox layer of the first round with inequalities. With this, the diffusion of the second round can be described precisely with MILP.

   With all these together, we are able to convert all the necessary constraints in the search of conditional cubes into the MILP language.
2. For FKD, instead of the initial state, the internal state value just before the first Sbox layer are used as (conditional) variables by setting the variables in the column parity kernel. This simple change removes all the unnecessary constraints brought up by the linear layer of the first KECCAK round, and enlarges the space covered by our search program.

We apply this new MILP modeling to KECCAK-based keyed constructions including KECCAK-MAC, KMAC, KEYAK, KETJE, and FKD and find new or better results for each of the constructions. Specifically

- For KMAC, due to the fact that it processes the key as an independent block compared with KECCAK-MAC, it should provide better security and hence becomes harder for the attacker. With the same security level of 128 bits, we find attacks against KMAC128 reduced to 7 rounds, the same number of rounds found for KECCAK-MAC in previous works. For KMAC256 aiming for 256 bits security, we find attacks up to 9 rounds combining a technique to invert the last round. Details are summarized in Table 1.

- General complexity improvements are also found on the attacks against Keyak and Ketje. Notably, we improve the attack against Lake Keyak with 128-bit keys from 6 to 8 rounds in the nonce-respected setting and 9 rounds of Lake Keyak can be attacked if the key size is 256 bits. Details are summarized in Table 2.
- Conditional cubes that fully linearize the first two rounds are targeted by our modeling and the open question of FKD is answered by extending cube attacks by one additional round.

Table 1. Summary of our attacks on KMAC, and Keccak-MAC with related works.

Target	Key size	Capacity	Rounds	Time (Data)	Reference
KMAC128	128	256	7/24	2^{76}	Section 6.1
KMAC256	256	512	9/24	2^{147}	
Keccak-MAC	128	256/512	7/24	2^{72}	[19]
		768	7/24	2^{75}	[20]
		1024	6/24	$2^{58.3}$	
		1024	6/24	2^{40}	Section 5.3
		1024	7/24	2^{111}	[25]

Very recently, another two MILP models [8,25] were proposed for cube-attack-like cryptanalysis [13], together with some new results for keyed Keccak modes. In particular, 7 rounds of Keccak-MAC-512 can be attacked. In cube-attack-like cryptanalysis, only the first round is linearized and the idea is to choose cube variables such that they multiply with a small number of key bits in the first round. Therefore, one only needs to pay attention to the diffusion of the linear layer in the first round. Due to this, cube-attack-like cryptanalysis performs well especially when the degrees of freedom is limited, *e.g.*, smaller versions of Ketje. The drawback is that cube-attack-like cryptanalysis is not suitable for constructions with fully unknown internal state, *e.g.*, KMAC and Keccak-based FKD which are our main targets of conditional cube attacks. Whereas, in conditional cube attacks, one has to deal with two rounds in which more degrees of freedom are needed to control the diffusion of cube variables. Also, finding good conditional cubes is more challenging. However, if sufficient degrees of freedom are available, conditional cube attacks can exploit this and provide better attacks. Examples include attacks on all instances of Keyak, Ketje Major and Ketje Minor.

Organization. The remaining part of the paper is organized as follows. Section 2 gives a detailed description of Keccak-p based constructions, including Keccak, KMAC, Keyak and Ketje, followed by an introduction in Sect. 3 to related works. Our new MILP model is presented in Sects. 4 and 5, and applied

Table 2. Summary of our attacks on KEYAK, KETJE and comparison with related works

Target	Key size	Rounds	Time (Data)	Memory	nonce-respected	Reference
Lake KEYAK	128	6/12	2^{37}	-	Yes	[13]
	128	8/12	2^{74}	-	No	[19]
	128	8/12	$2^{71.01}$	-	Yes	Section 6.2
	256	9/14	$2^{137.05}$	-	Yes	
River KEYAK	128	8/12	2^{77}	-	Yes	Section 6.2
KETJE Major	128	7/13	2^{83}	-	Yes	[20]
	128	7/13	$2^{71.24}$	-	Yes	Section 6.2
KETJE Minor	128	7/13	2^{81}	-	Yes	[20]
	128	7/13	$2^{73.03}$	-	Yes	Section 6.2
KETJE SR v1	128	7/13	2^{115}	2^{50}	Yes	[15]
	128	7/13	2^{91}	-	Yes	Section 6.2
FKD[1600]	128	9/-	2^{90}	-	No	Section 6.3
KETJE Jr v1	96	5/13	$2^{36.86}$	2^{18}	Yes	[25]
KETJE Jr v2	96	5/13	$2^{34.91}$	2^{15}	Yes	
KETJE Sr v2	128	7/13	2^{99}	2^{33}	Yes	

to the key recovery attacks of KMAC, KEYAK, KETJE and full-state keyed duplex (FKD) in Sect. 6. Finally, Sect. 7 concludes the paper. Details of cubes are provided in the full version of this paper [26].

2 Description of KMAC, KEYAK and KETJE

2.1 KECCAK-p

The KECCAK-p permutations are specified with two parameters: the width of the permutation in bits $\boldsymbol{b}$ and the number of rounds $\boldsymbol{n_r}$. The KECCAK-p permutation with $\boldsymbol{n_r}$ rounds and width $\boldsymbol{b}$ is denoted by KECCAK-$p[\boldsymbol{b}, \boldsymbol{n_r}]$, where $\boldsymbol{n_r}$ is any positive integer and $\boldsymbol{b}$ can be any value of the form $25 \cdot 2^l$ for $l = 0, \cdots, 6$. The $\boldsymbol{b}$-bit state a for the KECCAK-$p[\boldsymbol{b}, \boldsymbol{n_r}]$ permutation is seen as a three-dimensional array of bits, namely $a[5][5][w]$ with $w = 2^l$. The expression $a[x][y][z]$ with $0 \leq x, y < 5$, $0 \leq z < w$, denotes the bit with (x, y, z) coordinate. The coordinates are always considered within modulo 5 for x and y and modulo w for z. The one-dimensional portion $a[*][y][z]$ is called a *row*, $a[x][*][z]$ a *column* and $a[x][y][*]$ a *lane*. A lane of the state is also denoted by $a[x][y]$ by omitting the z index. At lane level, the state $a[x][y]$ becomes a 5×5 array as shown in Fig. 1 with x for the column index and y for the row index.

The KECCAK-$p[\boldsymbol{b}, \boldsymbol{n_r}]$ permutation iterates an identical round function (up to a difference of round-dependent constant addition) $\boldsymbol{n_r}$ times, each of which consists of five steps $\mathtt{R} = \iota \circ \chi \circ \pi \circ \rho \circ \theta$, with details as follows.

θ: $a[x][y][z] = a[x][y][z] \oplus \bigoplus_{y=0}^{4} a[x-1][y][z] \oplus \bigoplus_{y=0}^{4} a[x+1][y][z-1]$.

0,0	1,0	2,0	3,0	4,0
0,1	1,1	2,1	3,1	4,1
0,2	1,2	2,2	3,2	4,2
0,3	1,3	2,3	3,3	4,3
0,4	1,4	2,4	3,4	4,4

Fig. 1. Lane coordinates. Each square stands for a lane in the state.

ρ: $a[x][y][z] = a[x][y][(z - T(x, y))]$, where $T(x, y)s$ are rotation constants.
π: $a[y][2x + 3y][z] = a[x][y][z]$.
χ: $a[x][y][z] = a[x][y][z] \oplus (a[x + 1][y][z] \oplus 1) \cdot a[x + 2][y][z]$.
ι: $a[0][0] = a[0][0] \oplus RC_{i_r}$, where RC_{i_r} is the i_r-th round constant.

Here, '$\oplus$' denotes XOR and '$\cdot$' denotes logic AND. Expressions in the x and y coordinates should, as mentioned, be taken in modulo 5 and expressions in the z coordinate modulo w.

The KECCAK-f family of permutations is a specification of the KECCAK-p family to the case of $\boldsymbol{n_r} = 12 + 2l$, that is KECCAK-$f[\boldsymbol{b}]$ = KECCAK-$p[\boldsymbol{b}, 12 + 2l]$. The permutation underlying SHA-3 and KMAC is of width 1600 bits and 24 rounds, *i.e.*, KECCAK-$f[1600]$ = KECCAK-$p[1600, 24]$.

2.2 The Sponge Construction and KMAC

The sponge construction is a framework for constructing hash functions from permutations, as depicted in Fig. 2. The construction consists of three components: an underlying $\boldsymbol{b}$-bit permutation f, a parameter $\boldsymbol{r}$ called *rate* and a padding rule. The *capacity* is defined as $\boldsymbol{c} := \boldsymbol{b} - \boldsymbol{r}$. A hash function following this construction takes in a message M as input and outputs a digest of $\boldsymbol{d}$ bits. Given the message M, it is first padded and split into $\boldsymbol{r}$-bit blocks. The $\boldsymbol{b}$-bit state is initialized to be all zeros. The sponge construction then proceeds in two phases. In the absorbing phase, each message block is XORed into the first $\boldsymbol{r}$ bits of the state, followed by application of the permutation f. This process is repeated until all message blocks are processed. Then, the sponge construction switches to the squeezing phase, where each iteration returns the first $\boldsymbol{r}$ bits of the state as output and then applies the permutation f to the current state. This repeats until $\boldsymbol{d}$ bits digest are obtained.

The KECCAK hash function follows the sponge construction and takes KECCAK-$f[1600]$ as the underlying permutation. In 2015, KECCAK was formally standardized by NIST as SHA-3 [29], based on which more functions, including cSHAKE128, cSHAKE256 and KMAC, are derived in the NIST Special Publication 800-185 [30].

KMAC (KECCAK Message Authentication Code) is a keyed hash function with a variable-length output, and can be used as a pseudorandom function. It has

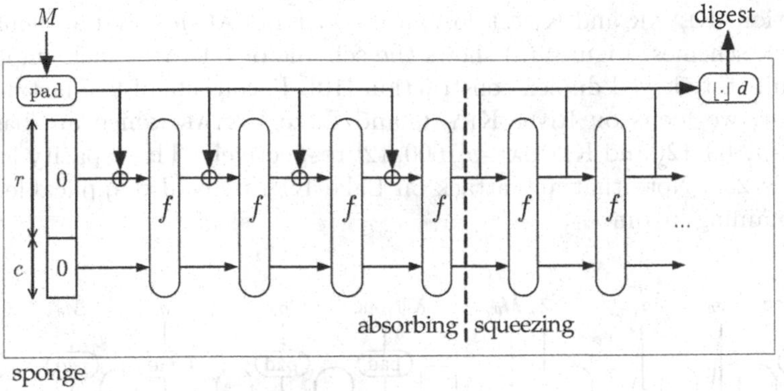

Fig. 2. Sponge construction [3].

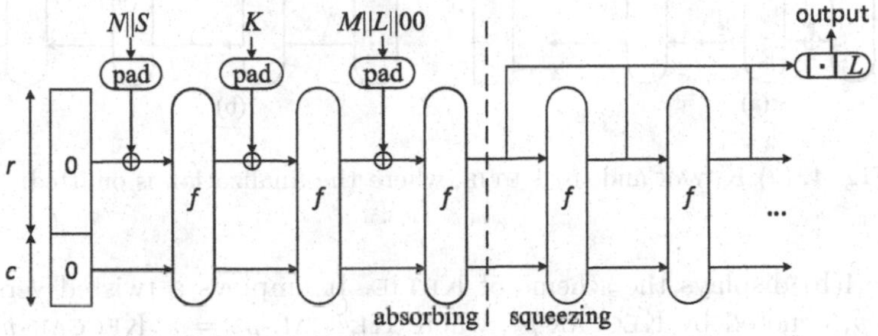

Fig. 3. KMAC processing one message block

two variants: KMAC128 and KMAC256, based on KECCAK$[c = 256](M, L)$ and KECCAK$[c = 512](M, L)$, whose capacities are set to be 256 and 512 bits, respectively. The input of KMAC consists of the key K, the main message M, the output length L, the name string $N =$ "KMAC" and the optional customization bit string S of any length (including 0). Given these inputs, KMAC first processes a block encoded from the public values N and S. Then it accepts a block of the padded key, and absorbs message blocks from the third call of permutation f onwards. Figure 3 demonstrates the procedure of KMAC processing one message block. Different from KECCAK, KMAC supports variable-length output, e.g., KMAC128 supports any output of length no less than 256 bits and at least 512 bits for KMAC256.

KECCAK-MAC [4] is a KECCAK-based MAC where KECCAK directly takes the combination of a key and a message, *i.e.*, $K||M$ as input. The key size is assumed to be 128 bits.

2.3 The Duplex Construction and KEYAK, KETJE

The duplex construction [4] is closely related to the sponge construction, and is mostly used for authenticated encryption. Following variants of the duplex construction, KEYAK and KETJE [6,7] are two KECCAK-p based authenticated encryption schemes. Figure 4(a) shows the scheme of KEYAK which employs an almost full-state keyed duplex construction [10]. It consists of five instances. In this paper, we focus on River KEYAK and Lake KEYAK which are based on KECCAK-$p[800, 12]$ and KECCAK-$p[1600, 12]$ respectively. The capacity for both versions is 256. Note that any attack on Lake KEYAK is also applicable to the three remaining instances.

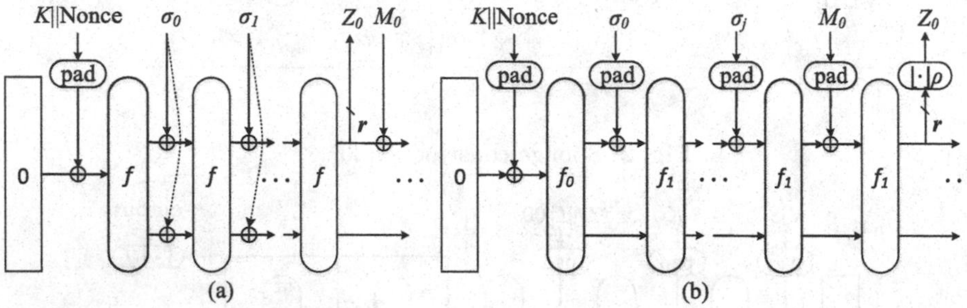

Fig. 4. (a) KEYAK and (b) KETJE, where the finalization is omitted.

Figure 4(b) displays the scheme of KETJE. It employs a twisted version of KECCAK-p, denoted by KECCAK-$p^\star$, where KECCAK-$p^\star = \pi \circ$KECCAK-$p \circ \pi^{-1}$. Specifically, the underlying permutations f_0 = KECCAK-$p[\boldsymbol{b}, 12]$ and f_1 = KECCAK-$p[\boldsymbol{b}, 1]$. KETJE has four instances which are:

Name	$\boldsymbol{b}$	ρ
KETJE JR	200	16
KETJE SR	400	32
KETJE Minor	800	128
KETJE Major	1600	256

In the old version of KETJE, KECCAK-p, instead of KECCAK-$p^\star$, is used.

Full-state Keyed Duplex (resp. Full-state Keyed Sponge) [10,21] is generalized from duplex (resp. sponge) for better efficiency by allowing full-state absorption. This idea has been applied to KEYAK which absorbs data blocks of length greater than $\boldsymbol{r}$ bits.

2.4 Notations

In this paper, $\boldsymbol{r}$ and $\boldsymbol{c}$ in bold denote the rate and capacity for the sponge construction. $\boldsymbol{b}$ in bold stands for the width in bits of the permutation. The first three mappings θ, π, ρ of the round function of KECCAK-p are linear, and we denote their composition by $\lambda \triangleq \pi \circ \rho \circ \theta$. The nonlinear layer χ applying to each row is called an Sbox. Only one-block padded messages are considered in our attacks for KMAC while there is no restriction on message length for attacks on other instances.

For describing the model, we use variables a, b, c, d in lowercase to denote states and the capital ones, namely A, B, C, D to denote their activeness, *i.e.*, a bit is active if it contains cube variables. The demension of the cube is denoted by d, and the number of conditions is denoted by t.

3 Related Works and Motivations

3.1 Cube Attacks

The cube attack, a variant of higher order differential attacks, was introduced by Dinur and Shamir [14] in 2009. It considers the output bit of a cipher as an unknown Boolean polynomial $f(k_0, \cdots, k_{n-1}, v_0, \cdots, v_{m-1})$ where $k_0, \cdots, k_{n-1}$ are secret input variables and $v_0, \cdots, v_{m-1}$ are public input variables. Given a monomial $t_I = v_{i_1} \cdots v_{i_d}$, $I = \{i_1, \cdots, i_d\}$ $(d \leq m)$, any Boolean polynomial f can be written as the sum of terms which are supersets of t_I and terms that are not divisible by t_I:

$$f(k_0, \cdots, k_{n-1}, v_0, \cdots, v_{m-1}) = t_I \cdot p_{S_I} + q(k_0, \cdots, k_{n-1}, v_0, \cdots, v_{m-1}),$$

where p_{S_I} is called the superpoly of I in f. The basic idea of cube attacks and cube testers [1] is that the sum of the outputs over the cube which contains all possible values for $v_{i_1}, \cdots, v_{i_d}$ (called *cube variables*) is exactly p_{S_I}, while this is a random function for a random polynomial. By carefully selecting I, cube attacks aim to find a low-degree polynomial p_{S_I} in secret variables, and cube testers aim to distinguish p_{S_I} from a random function, *e.g.*, $p_{S_I} = 0$.

In [13], Dinur *et al.* applied cube attacks and cube testers to the keyed variants of KECCAK, including KECCAK-MAC, KEYAK and a KECCAK stream cipher.

3.2 Conditional Cube Attacks

In [19], Huang *et al.* developed conditional cube testers for the keyed KECCAK sponge function, where the propagation of certain cube variables are controlled in the first few rounds if some conditions are satisfied. There are two major advantages of conditional cube testers over ordinary cube testers. One is to potentially reduce the algebraic degree of the permutation under the conditions, and hence the required cube dimension to carry out the attack can be reduced accordingly. The other advantage of conditional cubes is that the conditions, which control how the conditional cube variables propagate in the first few rounds, are related to the initial state values, which may contain the key information. By observing the cube sum of the final output, one may recover the key.

To proceed further, we recall the definition of conditional cube variables and a theorem from [19] below.

Definition 1 ([19]). *Cube variables that have propagation controlled in the first round and are not multiplied with each other in the second round of* KECCAK *are called* **conditional cube variables**. *Cube variables that are not multiplied with each other in the first round and are not multiplied with any conditional cube variable in the second round are called* **ordinary cube variables**.

Theorem 1 ([19]). *For $(n+2)$-round* KECCAK *sponge function $(n > 0)$, if there are p $(0 \le p < 2^n + 1)$ conditional cube variables $v_0, \cdots, v_{p-1}$, and $q = 2^{n+1} - 2p + 1$ ordinary cube variables, $u_0, \cdots, u_{q-1}$ (If $q = 0$, we set $p = 2^n + 1$), then the term $v_0 v_1 \cdots v_{p-1} u_0 \cdots u_{q-1}$ will not appear in the output polynomials of $(n+2)$-round* KECCAK *sponge function.*

Using conditional cube testers, better key recovery attacks were obtained for KECCAK-MAC and KEYAK in [19]. Later, the attacks on KECCAK-MAC were further improved with better conditional cubes found by an MILP model in [20].

Attack Procedure. In previous works [19,20], the number of conditional cube variables is chosen to be 1, *i.e.*, $p = 1$. Then, over a conditional cube with dimension $d = 2^n$, the cube sum is zero for $(n+1)$-round KECCAK sponge function if the conditions are satisfied. For such a conditional cube whose conditions involve t-bit secret information, the $(n+1)$-round attack proceeds in two steps as follows.

1. Guess the t-bit secret information and set the conditions accordingly.
2. Query the $2^d = 2^{2^n}$ outputs and calculate the cube sum. If the cube sum is zero, mark the guess as a candidate for the t-bit secret information.

The attack has a time and data complexity of $2^{d+t} = 2^{2^n+t}$. If t is far less than the output length, the t-bit secret information can be recovered uniquely. There may exist conditions that do not involve any secret information, but only conditions involving secret information affect the complexities. In the following, t is referred to the number of bits of secret information in conditions.

3.3 Linear Structures

In [17], Guo *et al.* developed a technique named *linear structure* which allows linearization of KECCAK-f for up to 3 rounds. Based on the linear structures, a series of new zero-sum distinguishers of KECCAK-f were proposed, as well as several new preimage attacks against KECCAK.

Let $a[x][y]$, $x = 0, 2, y = 0, 1, 2, 3$ be variables and $a[x][4] = \bigoplus_{y=0}^{3} a[x][y] \oplus \alpha_x$ with any constant α_x so that variables in each column sum to a constant. The core idea is to reduce the diffusion effect of θ. With all columns sum to constants, the variables do not propagate through θ. Note θ is the only mapping in λ with diffusion property, so λ does not diffuse the variables under this setting. Figure 5 shows how the variables influence the internal state under the transformation of KECCAK-f round function $\mathtt{R} = \iota \circ \chi \circ \pi \circ \rho \circ \theta$. All bits of the lanes with orange slashes have algebraic degree 1, those lanes with orange dots have algebraic degree at most 1 (meaning it is either a variable of degree 1 or a constant), and the other lanes are all constants where gray, light gray and white bits stand for values 1, 0, and arbitrary constants, respectively. Note the algebraic degrees remain through the linear operations θ, ρ, π, and ι. The only non-linear operation is the χ which increases the algebraic degree through the AND operation of two adjacent bits. As shown in the figure, all variables before χ are not adjacent to each other, which makes sure that the algebraic degree of the state bits remains at most 1 after one round function R.

Moreover, bit 1 (0) on the left (right) of the variable helps to restrict the diffusion of variables through χ, while an unknown neighboring constant diffuses the variable in an uncertain way, as denoted by lanes with orange dots where the variable has an uncertain coefficient. This structure has degrees of freedom 512. Also, it can be regarded as a cube of dimension 512 that linearizes the first round.

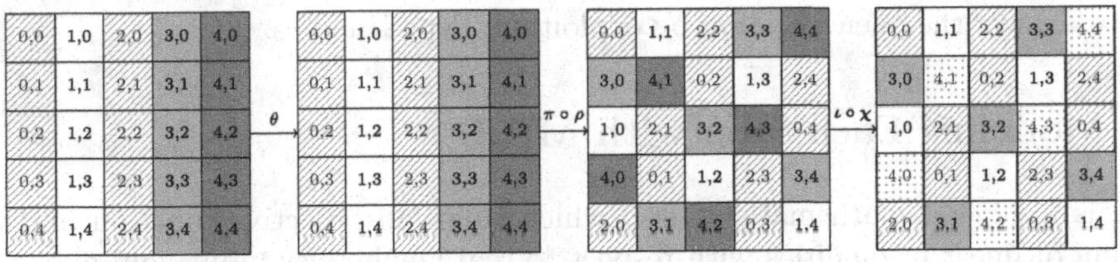

Fig. 5. 1-round linear structure of KECCAK-p with the degrees of freedom up to 512, with bits in orange slashes (resp. dots) of degree 1 (resp. at most 1), and gray, light gray and white bits being values 1, 0, and arbitrary unknown constants, respectively.

3.4 Motivations

Through the linear structure, the diffusion effect of variables through χ is illustrated, which enables us to give a full description of χ using MILP. Then we consider the possibility of building a new MILP model for searching conditional cube attacks for KECCAK-p based constructions, especially for finding optimal conditional cubes for constructions with fully unknown internal state.

Impact of p. If the number of conditional cube variables p increases by 1, the dimension d of the required cube reduces by 1 but t increases by at least 1. So there is no need to have more than one conditional cube variable for most cases. Therefore, we set $p = 1$ in our attacks on KMAC, KEYAK and KETJE.

However, multiple conditional cube variables may be useful for analyzing Full-state Keyed Sponge (FKS) or Full-state Keyed Duplex (FKD) [10,21] where full-state message absorption is used. Due to full-state degrees of freedom, a large number of conditional cube variables may exist and even without any condition. The following table shows the comparison between two extreme cases where $p = 1$ and $p = 2^n + 1$, latter of which means all cube variables are conditional cube variables and thus the first two rounds are fully linearized. If p is large

p	Dimension	n_r rounds with zero sum
1	2^n	$n+1$
2^n+1	2^n+1	$n+2$

enough and $2^{d+t} = 2^{2^{n+1}-p+1+t} < 2^{|K|}$, the cube attack can be extended by one round.

For clarity, we define two types of conditional cubes as follows.

Type I. Among all cube variables, there is only one conditional cube variable.
Type II. All cube variables are conditional cube variables, *i.e.*, all the cube variables do not multiply with each other in the first two rounds.

In [7], it is stated that whether cube attacks can be extended to more rounds by exploiting full-state absorbing remains an open question. In this paper, we try to answer the open question by exploiting Type II cubes.

4 Modeling Each Step with MILP

MIL is a general mathematical tool, which takes an objective function and a system of linear inequalities with respect to real numbers as input, and aims to search for an optimal solution which not only satisfies all the inequalities but also minimizes/maximizes the objective function.

Cryptanalysis using MILP takes five main steps as shown in Fig. 6. Firstly, one defines variables which are mostly binary for the cryptanalytical problem. Secondly, she identifies links between the variables, which deeply depend on the cryptanalytical problem. Based on the links, she then generates all valid patterns for the variables which can be described with inequalities, using existing methods. In this paper, we use the convex hull method [28] together with a selection algorithm from [24]. Once the cryptanalytical problem is converted to an MILP problem, it can be solved with an MILP solver. Cryptanalysis using other tools such as SAT solvers works in a similar way. Since the last two steps are straightforward, the first three steps are the core part for MILP-based cryptanalysis which will be our focus in Sects. 4 and 5.

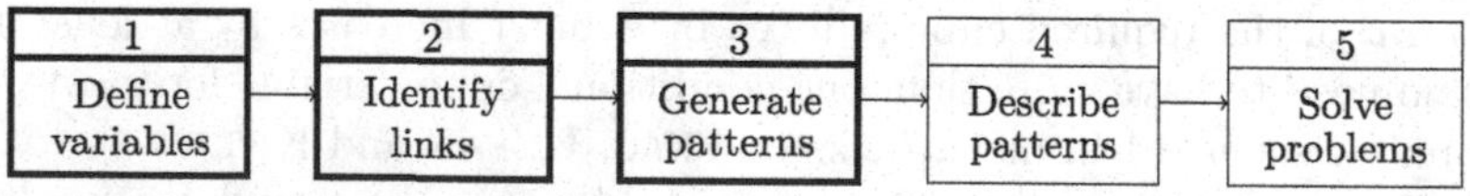

Fig. 6. Workflow of cryptanalysis using MILP

In this section, through a 1-round linear structure of KMAC we first show where the conditions come from, and formulate the time complexity of conditional cube attacks. Then we describe each step of the KECCAK-p round function using inequalities. The full model for searching conditional cubes will be introduced in the next section. Note that our modeling is described under the assumption that the internal state of the target constructions is fully unknown. The difference of the model for constructions with partially known internal state will be discussed in Sect. 5.3.

4.1 A 1-Round Linear Structure of KMAC

Suppose the internal state before injecting messages is denoted by $k[x][y]$, $0 \leq x, y < 5$. For convenience, the r-bit message block is denoted as $a[x][y]$, $0 \leq x, y < 5$, where the last c bits are set to 0. Figure 7 provides a 1-round linear structure of KMAC128 and shows the transformation of the internal state under the first round function R after absorbing the message block. Following the same notations in Sect. 3.3, lanes with orange slashes denote variables, lanes with orange dots have algebraic degree at most 1, and bits in white lanes are constants. Here, the first four lanes of the first and the third columns of $a[x][y]$ are set to be variables such that the sum $\bigoplus_{y=0}^{3} a[x, y]$ equals to certain constants for $x = 0, 2$. The capacity of KMAC128 consists of four lanes, so these lanes can not be chosen as variables. As can be seen from Fig. 7, the output of the first round function is linear since there are no adjacent variables at the input of χ. This 1-round linear structure of KMAC128 has a degree of freedom up to 384. A similar 1-round linear structure can also be constructed for KMAC256.

As can be seen, the first round can be linearized without any condition on constants by just excluding neighbouring variables before χ. Let us consider constructing a conditional cube, where at least one variable should be selected such that it is not multiplied with any other variables in the second round, while there is no such restriction for the rest of the variables. Specifically, if an input bit of the χ in the second round contains the conditional variable, its two neighbouring bits should be constants. According to the property of Keccak-p (specifically the θ), each neighbouring bit is calculated from 11 output bits of the first round. These 11 bits may be variables or constants, depending on the actual constant values involved in the χ of the first round.

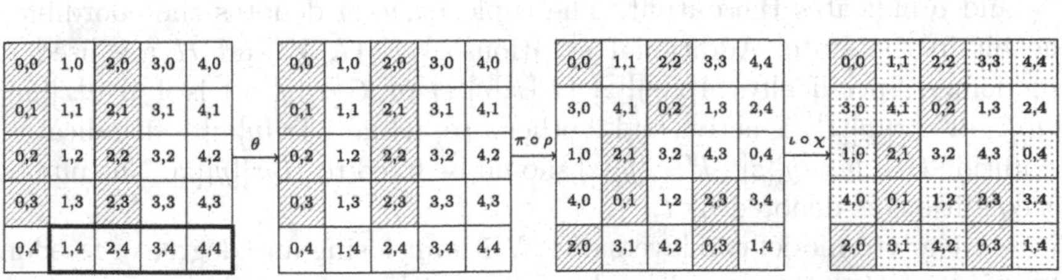

Fig. 7. 1-round linear structure of KMAC128 with the degrees of freedom up to 384, with bits in orange slashes (resp. dots) of degree 1 (resp. at most 1), and white bits being arbitrary unknown constants, respectively.

Unlike the linear structure proposed in [17], all the constants before χ of the first round are not controllable because of the unknown initial state. Hence, it is impossible to determine how the variables are propagated due to the logic AND, where ANDing with 1 allows propagation, and no propagation otherwise. This makes it hard to track the positions of all variables in the second round deterministically, hence increases the difficulty to find conditional cubes fulfilling the requirement that there is no multiplication (a.k.a. AND operation) with any conditional cube variables in the second round. However, if part of constants meets certain conditions, then it can be guaranteed that the conditional cube variable do not multiply with any variable in the second round and thus conditional cubes can be constructed. This is where bit conditions come from for conditional cubes.

Given a 2^n-dimensional conditional cube with one conditional cube variable and t bit conditions, it requires a time complexity of 2^{2^n+t} to recover t bits of the internal state for an $(n+1)$-round KECCAK-p based construction. Hence the overall complexity to recover the internal state is around $\lceil \frac{|b|}{t} \rceil \cdot 2^{2^n+t}$. Once the internal state is recovered, the key can be computed directly. It is inferred that the smaller t is, the lower the time complexity would be. So the aim of our new MILP model is to find conditional cubes with minimal bit conditions, meanwhile keeping the cube dimension large enough.

4.2 Modeling the Non-linear Layer

The first observation before giving the MILP model is that, although one input bit to the first χ is calculated from 11 bits of the initial state, it is unnecessary for us to start from the initial state, as there is a bijective relation (the λ) between it and the state just before the χ. In the meanwhile, the 1-round linear structure could be started from the middle as well. Hence, instead of trying to derive everything from the very beginning, we start from the state just before χ. This simple yet crucial observation will reduce the complexity of the problem significantly, as will be seen later.

Recall that the message block is denoted by a, and $b = \lambda(a)$, and k stands for the secret internal state. Let $k' = \lambda(k)$. Thus, $b \oplus k'$ is the input of the first χ and c indicates the output. The tuple (x, y, z) denotes the coordinates of one bit in the state. Additional notations A, B, C, V and H are used for the modeling. Specifically, $A[x][y][z]$ ($B[x][y][z]$ or $C[x][y][z]$) is 1 if $a[x][y][z]$ ($b[x][y][z]$ or $c[x][y][z]$) is active and 0 otherwise, while $V[x][y][z] = 1$ indicates a bit condition that $b[x][y][z]+k'[x][y][z]$ should be fixed to $H[x][y][z]$. The number of bit conditions is denoted by t.

Note, we are to model two layers of χ. Without losing any degree of freedom, we do it in two steps by modeling the first χ without imposing any additional condition, and the second χ using the output from our modeling of the first χ, *i.e.*, nested modeling. This may cost higher search complexity compared with previous works at first glance, we will see the effectiveness and power later. Due to the generality of our modeling, we could find optimal solutions whenever it is practical to solve.

Although χ is the only non-linear operation of KECCAK-p, modeling it into inequalities is non-trivial. Let us look at the computation of one bit through χ. According to the algebraic expression of χ, $c[x][y][z] = b[x][y][z] \oplus (1 \oplus b[x+1][y][z]) \cdot b[x+2][y][z]$. For a conditional cube, the output bits of the first round should be linear, which can be guaranteed by the constraint that variables do not appear in adjacent input bits, namely $B[x][y][z] + B[x+1][y][z] \leq 1$. However, the value of input constants influences the diffusion of variables through χ and further influences the second round, as shown in Fig. 5. However, as we find out, the diffusion patterns of variables through χ fall in a smaller than expected set as listed in Table 3, which makes the modeling of all cases possible without imposing any additional conditions. To make it clear, we explain some rows of Table 3. The first two rows mean that if both $b[x+1][y][z]$ and $b[x+2][y][z]$ are constants, then the constants can be any value and $c[x][y][z]$ will inherit the same activeness from $b[x][y][z]$. The third row means that if $b[x+2][y][z]$ is active and $b[x][y][z], b[x+1][y][z]$ are constants but the value of $b[x+1][y][z]$ is uncertain, then $c[x][y][y]$ contains uncertain propagation from $b[x+2][y][z]$ and its algebraic degree is at most 1. On the contrary, if the value of $b[x+1][y][z]$ is restricted to 1 (resp. 0) as in the fourth (resp. fifth) row, $c[x][y][z]$ turns to be inactive (active) definitely. The fifth row can be ignored since it costs a bit condition but still diffuses the variable from $b[x+2][x][y]$ to $c[x][y][z]$, making the second round denser. The remaining rows can be explained similarly. Next, we generate a set of inequalities (see Table 7 in Appendix B) to describe these 0–1 patterns.

Table 3. Diffusion of variables through χ, where coordinates $[y][z]$s are omitted and symbol '*' denotes arbitrary value.

$B[x]$	$B[x+1]$	$B[x+2]$	$V[x+1]$	$V[x+2]$	$H[x+1]$	$H[x+2]$	$C[x]$
0	0	0	*	*	*	*	0
1	0	0	*	*	*	*	1
0	0	1	0	0	*	*	1
0	0	1	1	0	1	*	0
0	0	1	1	0	0	*	1[a]
0	1	0	0	0	*	*	1
0	1	0	0	1	*	0	0
0	1	0	0	1	*	1	1
1	0	1	0	0	*	*	1
1	0	1	1	0	*	*	1

[a] This row can be excluded

4.3 Modeling the Linear Layer

The linear layer λ consists of three steps: θ, ρ and π, the latter two of which just change the positions of the state bits. Hence, we focus on modeling θ. θ adds two columns to a bit. If both columns have even parity, then the bit does not change at all after θ. If all columns have even parity, then it is said that the state is in the column parity kernel (CP-kernel). While the original column parity is defined on values, in the context of cube attacks, it refers to activeness.

Following [25], we introduce $F[x][z]$ and $G[x][z]$ to describe the parity of a column in the state.

- The column is not active, *i.e.*, there is no variable: $G[x][z] = 0, F[x][z] = 0$;
- The column is active and the column sum is active: $G[x][z] = 1, F[x][z] = 0$;
- The column is active and the column sum is inactive: $G[x][z] = 0, F[x][z] = 1$;

As can be seen, $G[x][z] = 1$ indicates that the column sum contains variables, and only constants otherwise. If $G[x][z] = 0$ for all columns, then the cube lies in the CP-kernel. $F[x][z] = 1$ means that the column contains variables but the variables sum to certain constant, by consuming one bit degree of freedom. Suppose $A[x][y][z], y = 0, \cdots, 4$ stands for the activeness of column (x, z), then the patterns of $A[x][y][z], y = 0, \cdots, 4$ and $F[x][z]$, $G[x][z]$ fall into a set of $1 + 5 + (32 - 6) \times 2 = 58$ discrete points in $\mathbb{R}^7$. The inequalities model this set are derived and listed in Table 8.

The activeness of the output of θ now can be calculated from $A[x][y][z]$ and $G[x][z]$. Assume $B[x][y][z]$ denotes the activeness of θ's output (elsewhere $B[x][y][z]$ denotes the activeness of the output of the linear layer). Then $B[x][y][z] = 1$ if any of $A[x][y][z]$, $G[x-1][z]$ and $G[x+1][z-1]$ is 1; otherwise $B[x][y][z] = 0$. This can be modeled by the following inequalities.

$$
\begin{aligned}
B[x][y][z] - A[x][y][z] \geq 0,\\
B[x][y][z] - G[x-1][z] \geq 0, B[x][y][z] - G[x+1][z-1] \geq 0,\\
A[x][y][z] + G[x-1][z] + G[x+1][z-1] - B[x][y][z] \geq 0.
\end{aligned}
\tag{1}
$$

If only cubes in the CP-kernel are of interest, set $G[x][z] = 0$ and inequalities in (1) can be replaced with $B[x][y][z] = A[x][y][z]$. In this way, the model of the linear layer is simplified.

5 Modeling the Search for Conditional Cubes

This section presents a full model for searching conditional cubes of both types. The conditional cube requires conditional cube variables not to multiply with any variable even in the second round, which means their neighboring bits before the second χ should be constants. For the Type I, we could fix the positions of the conditional cube variable (we place the same variable at two bit positions in the same column of the initial state) and focus only on it and its neighboring bits. Whereas for Type II, attention should be paid to the diffusion of all variables in the second round. Due to this difference for the second round, our model for searching conditional cubes of both types will be constructed separately.

5.1 Model for Searching Conditional Cubes of Type I

Modeling the Second Round. The neighboring bits of the conditional cube variable before the second χ should be constants. Suppose these neighboring bits are denoted by s_i. According to the round function R, each neighboring bit s_i is calculated from 11 bits of $c[x][y][z]$. There are two cases depending on whether there is any variable among the 11 bits:

Case 1. For these 11 bits, none of them are variables, *i.e.*, $C[x][y][z] = 0$;
Case 2. There are variables among the 11 bits and the XOR of these 11 bits form a linear equation which consumes one bit degree of freedom.

We introduce one more dummy variable S_i for s_i to indicate which case happens, where $S_i = 0$ for Case 1 and $S_i = 1$ for Case 2. Case 1 is simple, while for Case 2 one needs to pay attention to "uncertain propagations" or lanes with orange dots in Fig. 7 since no exact information can be derived from a linear equation containing variables with uncertain coefficients. So once Case 2 happens, additional conditions should be imposed to avoid uncertain propagations.

Similarly, all possible patterns of S_i and its related bits can be enumerated as shown in Table 4 and the set of inequalities are provided in Table 9. Specifically, if $c[x][y][z]$ is required in calculating s_i, the inequalities in Table 9 are added to the MILP model.

Table 4. Influence of conditional cube variables in the second round. Symbol '*' denotes arbitrary value.

S_i	$B[x][y][z]$	$B[x+1][y][z]$	$B[x+2][y][z]$	$V[x+1][y][z]$	$V[x+2][y][z]$
0	*	*	*	*	*
1	0	0	0	*	*
1	1	0	0	*	*
1	1	0	1	1	0
1	0	0	1	1	0
1	0	1	0	0	1

Modeling the Search for Conditional Cubes. The following constraints are generated for searching conditional cubes of Type I.

1. Constraints for the linear layer of the first round, according to Sect. 4.3;
2. Constraints for the nonlinear layer of the first round, according to Table 7;
3. Constraints for the conditional cube variable in the first round. If a input bit $b[x][y][z]$ of χ involves the *conditional* cube variable, then we fix its neighboring bits to constants such that it does not diffuse to other positions. It requires

$$\begin{aligned} B[x-1][y][z] = 0, B[x+1][y][z] = 0,\\ V[x-1][y][z] = 1, V[x+1][y][z] = 1.\\ H[x-1][y][z] = 1, H[x+1][y][z] = 0. \end{aligned} \tag{2}$$

4. Constraints for the conditional cube variable in the second round, according to Table 9;
5. Constraint for the dimension. If a 2^n-dimensional conditional cube is required, then set

$$\sum A[x][y][z] - \sum F[x][z] - \sum S_i = 2^n, \tag{3}$$

where $\sum F[x][z] + \sum S_i$ is the number of consumed degrees of freedom.
6. Objective. The objective is to minimize bit conditions. That is

$$\text{Minimize}: \quad \sum V[x][y][z]. \tag{4}$$

Besides, there may exist additional constraints. For example, the last **c** bits and some padded bits cannot be variables. When all constraints are generated, an MILP solver is invoked to find a solution that minimizes the objective.

5.2 Model for Searching Conditional Cubes of Type II

Modeling the Second Round. For Type II conditional cubes, all the cube variables should not multiply with each other in the second round. Therefore the diffusion of each cube variable in the second round becomes indispensable and must be modeled. Beside the activeness of the input of the second round, the diffusion of cube variables also depends on the activeness of column sums which is the core part to be modeled.

Recall that we start from b, the input of χ in the first round and $c = \chi(b)$. Let $d = \lambda(c)$ by omitting the ι step of the first round, and $D[x][y][z]$ denotes the activeness of d. From the algebraic expression of χ, namely, $c[x][y][z] = b[x][y][z] \oplus (1 \oplus b[x+1][y][z]) \cdot b[x+2][y][z]$, it is known that if $B[x][y][z] = 1$, then $C[x][y][z] = 1$. If the sum of column (x, z) of b is inactive, then in what circumstance the sum of column (x, z) of c is also active? This is what we need to explore. Note that, columns with an inactive sum do not diffuse to other columns, which is beneficial to the linearization of the second round.

Suppose $G_1[x][z] = 1$ means the sum of column (x, z) in b is active and $G_1[x][z = 0]$ otherwise. Let $G_2[x][z]$ play the same role for c. With $G_2[x][z]$ and $C[x][y][z]$, the linear layer in the second round can be modeled just as the linear layer in the first round. To make the second round linear, we only need to add the constraint $D[x][y][z] + D[x+1][y][z] \leq 1$. So the only problem unsolved is to model the activeness of columns of c.

The value of $G_2[x][z]$ is influenced by three columns of b at $(x, z), (x+1, z)$ and $(x+1, z)$. This is the most complex relation to be modeled in this paper. Specifically, variables at position (x, y, z) of b propagate to position (x, y, z) of c for sure; variables at positions $(x+1, y, z)$ and $(x+2, y, z)$ of b may diffuse to position (x, y, z) of c. The sum of column (x, z) of c is inactive, *i.e.*, $G_2[x][z] = 0$ only if all the following three conditions hold.

- $G_1[x][z] = 0$.
- No variable in column $(x+1)$ of b propagates to column (x, z) of c.
- (a) No variable in column $(x+2)$ of b propagates to column (x, z) of c, or (b) all the variables in column $(x+2)$ of b propagate to column (x, z) of c and $G_1[x+2][z] = 0$[1].

In the following, the three conditions will be analyzed in detail individually.

1. The effect of variables in column (x, z). $C[x][z] = 1$ if $B[x][z] = 1$, so $G_2[x][z] = 1$ if $G_1[x][z] = 1$.
2. The effect of variables in column $(x+1, z)$ of b depends on conditions in column $(x+2, z)$. If there is any uncertain propagation of variables from column $(x+1, z)$, $G[x][z] = 1$. Additionally, $P[x][y][z]$ is introduced where $P[x][y][z] = 1$ if the variable at $(x+1, y, z)$ is propagated to (x, y, z) with an uncertain coefficient and $P[x][y][z] = 0$ otherwise. The relation of $P[x][y][z]$ and $B[x+1][y][z], V[x+2][y][z]$ is described in the following table.

$P[x]$	$B[x+1]$	$V[x+2]$	inequalities
0	0	*	$-P[x] + B[x+1] \geq 0$
1	1	0	$-P[x] - V[x+2] \geq -1$
0	1	1	$P[x] - B[x+1] + V[x+2] \geq 0$

   The effect of column $(x+1, z)$ to column (x, z) is denoted by $M[x][z]$ where $M[x][z] = 1$, *i.e.*, there exist uncertain propagations of variables from column $(x+1, z)$ if any $P[x][y][z], y = 0, \cdots, 4$ is 1. This can be described with inequalities in (5).

$$\begin{aligned} &M[x][z] - P[x][y][z] \geq 0, y = 0, \cdots, 4. \\ &\sum_y P[x][y][z] - M[x][z] \geq 0. \end{aligned} \tag{5}$$

3. The effect of variables in column $(x+2, z)$ of b is relatively complicated. As shown previously, there are two cases that column $(x+2, z)$ of b does not affect $G_2[x][z]$. To identify these two cases, we introduce $Q_1[x][y][z], Q_2[x][y][z]$, $N_1[x][z], N_2[x][z]$ and $N_3[x][z]$. $Q_1[x][y][z]$ and $N_1[x][z]$ play similar roles as $P[x][y][z]$ and $M[x][z]$, *i.e.*, $N_1[x][z] = 1$ if there is uncertain propagation from column $(x+2, z)$.
   $Q_2[x][y][z] = 1$ if the variable at $(x+2, y, z)$ of b is propagated to (x, y, z) of

[1] The reason why the modeling for the effects of column $(x+2, z)$ and column $(x+1, z)$ are different lies in the following fact. If the constant on the right side of a cube variable consumes a condition, we can constrained the constant to 0 directly, since 1 is worse under all circumstance as shown in Table 3. On the contrary, if the condition is imposed to the constant on the left side of a cube variable, the constant can be restricted to either 0 or 1 and no one has an absolute advantage over the other.

c for sure. Let $N_2[x][z] = 0$ if and only if $\sum_y Q_2[x][y][z] = 0$. Let $N_3[x][z] = 0$ if $\sum_y Q_2[x][y][z] = \sum_y B[x+2][y][z]$, *i.e.*, all variables in column $(x+2, z)$ of b are diffused to column (x, z) of c.

$Q_1[x][y][z]$ and $Q_2[x][y][z]$ can be modeled as shown in the following table.

$Q_1[x]$	$Q_2[x]$	$B[x+2]$	$V[x+1]$	$H[x+1]$	Inequalities
0	0	0	0	*	$-Q_1[x] - Q_2[x] + B[x+2] \geq 0$
0	0	0	1	*	$Q_1[x] - B[x+2] + V[x+1] \geq 0$
1	0	1	0	*	$-Q_1[x] - V[x+1] \geq -1$
0	1	1	1	0	$Q_1[x] + Q_2[x] - B[x+2] + H[x+1] \geq 0$
0	0	1	1	1	$-Q_2[x] - H[x+1] \geq -1$

The relation between $N_1[x][z], N_2[x][z]$ and $Q_1[x][y][z], Q_2[x][y][z]$ can also be described in the same way as in (5). To model $N_3[x][z]$, a large integer I is used to express the IF-ELSE logic that $N_3[x][z] = 0$ if $\sum_y Q_2[x][y][z] = \sum_y B[x+2][y][z]$ as long as I is larger than 5, say 100. The exact inequalities are shown in (6).

$$\sum_y Q_2[x][y][z] - \sum_y B[x+2][y][z] + I \cdot N_3[x][z] \leq I - 1,$$
$$\sum_y Q_2[x][y][z] - \sum_y B[x+2][y][z] + I \cdot N_3[x][z] \geq 0. \tag{6}$$

According to our model, $(N_1[x][z], N_2[x][z], N_3[x][z]) = (0, 0, *)$ indicates the first case, and $(N_1[x][z], N_2[x][z], N_3[x][z]) = (0, 1, 0)$ stands for the second case.

As can be derived from the above analysis, when (a) $(M[x][z], N_1[x][z], N_2[x][z], N_3[x][z]) = (0, 0, 0, *)$, or (b) $(M[x][z], N_1[x][z], N_2[x][z], N_3[x][z]) = (0, 0, 1, 0)$, and $G_1[x+2][z] = 0$, $G_2[x][z] = G_1[x][z]$; otherwise $G_2[x][z]$ is 1. The inequalities in Table 10 can be used to model this property.

Modeling the Search for Conditional Cubes. After introducing special techniques for modeling the column parity of the state in the second round, we can build the whole model for searching conditional cubes that linearize the first two rounds. Note that we start from the input of χ in the first round.

1. Describe the column parity of b using $G_1[x][z], F_1[x][z]$, according to Table 8.
2. Constraints for χ in the first round, according to Sect. 4.2;
3. Constraints for modeling the column parity of c, according to this subsection.
4. Constraints for the linear layer in the second round, according to Sect. 4.3;
5. Constraints for χ in the second round, *i.e.*, $D[x][y][z] + D[x+1][y][z] \leq 1$.

6. Constraint for the dimension. If a (2^n+1)-dimensional conditional cube is required, then set

$$\sum C[x][y][z] - \sum F_1[x][z] = 2^n + 1, \tag{7}$$

where $\sum F_1[x][z]$ is the number of consumed degrees of freedom.
7. Objective. The objective is to minimize bit conditions. That is

$$\text{Minimize}: \sum V[x][y][z]. \tag{8}$$

5.3 Discussion and Comparison

Model for Constructions with Partially Known Internal State. While minimal conditions means optimal conditional cubes for KECCAK-p-based construction with fully unknown internal state, such as KMAC, it is not the case if the internal state is partially known even though the number of conditions involving the key is still minimized. Note that the conditions are imposed on certain input bits of the first χ and each bit involves some key information. For KECCAK-p-based construction with partially unknown internal state, t bit conditions do not necessarily contain t-bit key information. For example, in the 64-dimensional cube of KETJE SR v1, there are 27 bit conditions all of which involve the key but contain only 26-bit information of the key due to dependency.

Comparison with the Existing MILP Model. Recently, Li *et al.* proposed an MILP model for searching cubes of Type I [20]. Their model sets every $b[x][y][z]$ to a constant if it relates to the neighboring bits of the conditional variable in the first two rounds. In our model, we incorporate the full diffusion effect of χ and hence consider a broader class of conditional cubes. In particular, $b[x][y][z]$ can be a variable even if it relates to the neighboring bits of the conditional variable in the second round. As a result, more conditional cubes can be found with a greater range of dimension. As demonstrated in Table 5, better conditional cubes are found using our model under the same setting. In particular, given the dimension, our model returns conditional cubes with much fewer bit conditions. For example, the 32-dimensional conditional cube of KECCAK-MAC-512 in [20] requires 24 bit conditions involving the key, while using our model, the number of bit conditions can be only 3 ($n = 5$ and $t = 3$), which reduces the time complexity of attacking 6-round KECCAK-MAC-512 from $2^{58.3}$ [20] to $\lceil\frac{|k|}{t}\rceil \cdot 2^{2^n+t} = \lceil\frac{128}{3}\rceil \cdot 2^{2^5+3} \approx 2^{40}$. Our cube of KECCAK-MAC-512 is provided in Table 5. Moreover, our models cover both types of conditional cubes while Li *et al.*'s model aims for only Type I conditional cubes.

6 Applications

In this section, we apply our models to conditional cubes attacks on KMAC, KEYAK and KETJE where Type I cubes are used. In order to extend the cube attacks on KECCAK-p based constructions with full-state absorption, we exploit Type II cubes.

Table 5. Comparison with the previous MILP model on KECCAK-MAC with the conditional cube placed at (2, 0, 0) and (2, 1, 0). The number of bit conditions only takes those involving key bits into account.

Variant	Dimension	#Conditions	Reference
KECCAK-MAC-384	65	8	[20]
	97	8	This
	65	**2**	
KECCAK-MAC-512	32	24	[20]
	32	**3**	This
	50	24	

6.1 Conditional Cube Attacks on KMAC

In this subsection, techniques described in Sects. 4 and 5.1 are used to find conditional cubes for KMAC, based on which key recovery attacks can be mounted on 7-round KMAC128 and 9-round KMAC256 respectively.

Cube Attack on KMAC128. For KMAC128, the capacity is 256, which covers only four lanes. By placing the conditional cube variable at two bits in a column of a^2, our MILP model could find large conditional cubes with 4 bit conditions which are least possible conditions. To make the attack clear, a toy cube of KMAC is introduced first, as shown in Table 6. This cube is selected from the CP-kernel and has dimension 16, and the conditional cube variable is placed at $a[0][0][0], a[0][1][0]$. The 4-bit conditions can be derived directly from the positions of the conditional cube variable since only the conditional cube variable contributes to bit conditions in this case. Note that, $b = \lambda(a)$ and the relation between $a[x][y][z]$ and $b[x][y][z]$ is not expressed explicitly in the bit conditions. The remaining 15 ordinary cube variables can be extracted from $A[x][y][z]$, $0 \leq x, y < 5, 0 \leq z < 64$ which are represented as a 5×5 array of lanes and labeled as 'Positions of cube variables' in the table. In the remainder of the paper, the bit conditions are omitted if they come only from the conditional cube variable.

For KMAC128, 64-dimensional conditional cubes are enough for attacking 7 rounds of KMAC128. In the following, multiple 64-dimensional conditional cubes are used for the recovery of the internal state. Once the internal state is recovered, the key can be derived directly.

1. **Recover t bits of the internal state.** Given a 64-dimensional conditional cube with t bit conditions where $t = 4$ for KMAC128, the t bits of the secret internal state $k'[x][y][z]$ involving in the conditions are guessed and then the constant part of the messages is chosen such that the t bit conditions are satisfied. The right guess is detected by assigning all possible values to each

[2] There is an exception that no conditional cube can be found when the conditional variable is placed in lanes $(1, 0), (1, 1)$.

Table 6. A conditional cube of KMAC in the CP-kernel. Positions of cube variables are derived from a 5×5 array of lanes in hexadecimal using the little-endian format where '0' is replaced with '–'.

Positions of cube variables

```
4----------2---1|----------------|---------------1|----------------|----------------
66------41-28-11|----------------|---------1-----1|----------------|----------------
26------414-8-1-|----------------|---------1------|----------------|----------------
24--------4---1-|----------------|----------------|----------------|----------------
----------------|----------------|----------------|----------------|----------------
```

The conditional cube variable: $a[0][0][0] = a[0][1][0] = v_0$

Ordinary cube variables

$a[0][1][4] = v_1$,	$a[0][1][24] = a[0][2][24] = v_6$,	$a[0][1][61] = v_{11}$,
$a[0][2][4] = v_2$,	$a[0][1][30] = a[0][2][30] = v_7$,	$a[0][2][61] = v_{12}$,
$a[0][3][4] = v_1 + v_2$,	$a[0][1][57] = a[0][2][57] = v_8$,	$a[0][3][61] = v_{11} + v_{12}$,
$a[0][1][15] = a[0][2][15] = v_3$,	$a[0][1][58] = v_9$,	$a[0][0][62] = a[0][1][62] = v_{13}$,
$a[0][0][17] = a[0][1][17] = v_4$,	$a[0][2][58] = v_{10}$,	$a[2][0][0] = a[2][1][0] = v_{14}$,
$a[0][2][22] = a[0][3][22] = v_5$,	$a[0][3][58] = v_9 + v_{10}$,	$a[2][1][24] = a[2][2][24] = v_{15}$.

Conditions

$b[0][3][36] = k'[0][3][36] + 1$, $b[2][3][36] = k'[2][3][36]$,

$b[4][0][0] = k'[4][0][0] + 1$, $b[1][0][0] = k'[1][0][0]$.

cube variable and checking the sum of all outputs under the guess. If the cube sum is zero, then the corresponding guess is the right one with overwhelming probability and then the t bits of the secret internal state are recovered. The time complexity for recovering the t bits of the internal state is $2^{64+t} = 2^{68}$.

2. **Recover t lanes of the internal state.** Due to the z-axis translation invariance of KECCAK-p, a conditional cube is still a conditional cube after being rotated along the z-axis. A cube and all its rotations are z-axis equivalent. However, for KMAC the padding rule may break the z-axis equivalence. To avoid it from happening, the last lane of the r-bit message block is set to be inactive. Therefore, by rotating the cube bit by bit, t lanes of the internal state would be recovered in $2^6 \cdot 2^{68} = 2^{74}$ calls of 7-round KMAC128.
3. **Recover the whole internal state.** Ten z-axis equivalent conditional cubes are used to recover the full internal state. The details of these cubes are given in [26], and the order of the lanes recovered are displayed in Fig. 8. The total time complexity of recovering the whole internal state is $2^6 \cdot 2^{64}(1 \cdot 2^4 + 3 \cdot 2^3 + 6 \cdot 2^2) = 2^{76}$.

Cube Attack on KMAC256. KMAC256 has a capacity of 512 bits which is equivalent to 8 lanes. Including the last lane of the message block where certain bits are padded, there are 9 lanes which can not contain variables. Apart from this, the cube search for KMAC256 remains as that for KMAC128. Our MILP model could find many 128-dimensional conditional cubes which can be used to attack

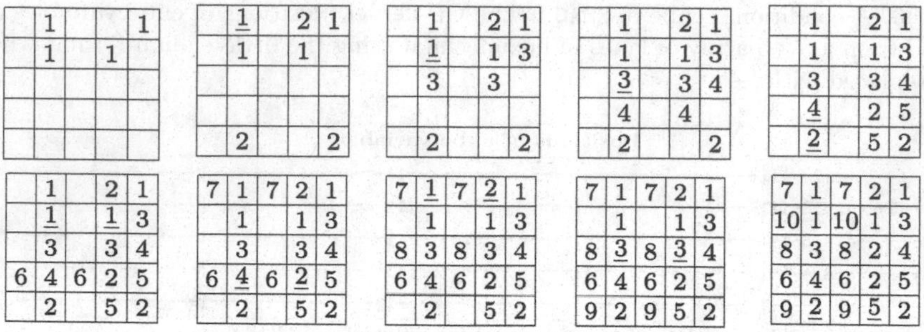

Fig. 8. The lanes recovered using ten z-axis equivalent conditional cubes. The underline means bits of these lanes are involved in conditions but they are already known.

8 rounds of KMAC256. Since the output length of KMAC256 can be more than 320 bits, the first 5 lanes of the output can be reversed through the χ of the last round. This immediately increases the attacked rounds by one, as this inversion covers the χ of the last round, while λ does not increase the algebraic degree. As a result, 9 rounds of KMAC256 can be attacked.

Choice of the Conditional Cube Variable. When we place the conditional cube variable at two bit positions of the same column in a, the obtained cubes generally have more than 30 bit conditions. The increase of bit conditions is caused by the increase of capacity. In order to reduce the number of bit conditions, we place the conditional cube variable in a 2-round CP-kernel so that it does not diffuse even in the second round, leading to a small set of constraints for the conditional cube variable. As studied in [11], the minimal Hamming weight of a 2-round CP-kernel differential trail of KECCAK-f[1600] is 6. Among all the 2-round CP-kernel differential trails, only those which have no difference in the last 9 lanes can be applied to the conditional cube search of KMAC256. Fortunately, there is one (only one) 2-round CP-kernel differential trail satisfying this requirement. The active bit positions of the 2-round CP-kernel differential trail are

$$[(0,0,0),(0,1,0),(1,0,63),(1,2,63),(2,1,30),(2,2,30)].$$

By setting the conditional cube variable to these six bit positions, our MILP model returns 128-dimensional cubes with 12 bit conditions, with which 11 lanes (one lane overlapped) of the internal state can be recovered. With these 11 lanes known, cubes with the conditional cube variable placed at two bit positions of a column of $a[x][y][z]$, $0 \leq y < 3$ can then be exploited to recover the remaining lanes.

To recover the whole internal state, three z-axis equivalent conditional cubes as shown in [26] are used and lanes recovered in each cube are displayed in Fig. 9. As can be learned from the figure, the time complexity of the internal state recovery is $2^6 \cdot 2^{128}(2^{12} + 2^{11} + 2^3) = 2^{146.58}$ calls of 9-round KMAC256.

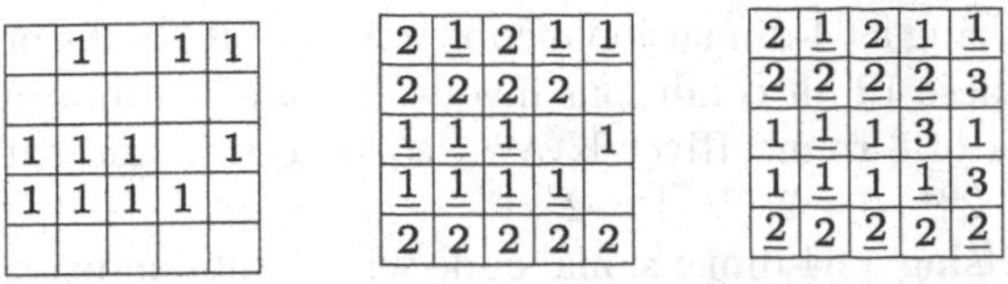

Fig. 9. The lanes recovered using three z-axis equivalent conditional cubes. The underline means bits of these lanes are involved in conditions but they are already known.

6.2 Conditional Cube Attacks on Keyak and Ketje

This subsection considers conditional cube attacks of Keyak and Ketje under the nonce respect setting, *i.e.*, the cube variables are placed among the positions where the nonce is loaded, and suppose there is no associated data to be processed.

Figure 10 shows the key pack of Keyak and Ketje respectively (for Ketje, it shows the key pack after π^{-1}), where blue positions stand for the key, light blue positions denote padded or encoded bits and white positions are the nonce. This means that the cube variable should be placed in white lanes. Unlike KMAC, the internal state of both Keyak and Ketje is known except the key part. Due to the dependence of key bits in conditions, our model may not guarantee optimal solutions.

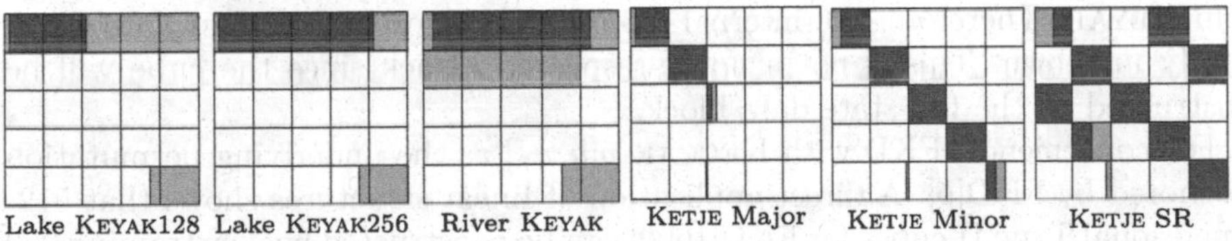

Fig. 10. Key pack of Keyak and Ketje where the blue part means the key, the light blue part denotes padded or encoded bits and the white part is the nonce.

All instances of Keyak and Ketje considered in this paper use 128-bit keys, except Lake Keyak, where 256-bit keys are supported by replacing Keccak-p[1600, 12] with Keccak-p[1600, 14]. Our main results are as follows and summarized in Table 2.

Lake Keyak128. Using a 64-dimensional cube with 2 bit conditions involving the key (see [26]), the key recovery attack of 8-round Lake Keyak128 costs a data and time complexities $2^2 \cdot 2^{64} \cdot 32 + 2^{64} = 2^{71.01}$ where the last χ can be partially reversed due to large output length.

Lake Keyak256. Using a 128-dimensional cube with 4 bit conditions involving the key (see [26]), the key recovery attack of 9-round Lake Keyak256 costs a data and time complexities less than $2^4 \cdot 2^{128} + 2^3 \cdot 2^{128} \cdot 63 + 2^{128} = 2^{137.05}$.

River KEYAK. Using a 64-dimensional cube with 12 bit conditions involving the key (see [26], these 12 bit conditions involve 11 bits key information), the key recovery attack of 8-round River KEYAK costs a data and time complexities $2^{11} \cdot 2^{64} + 2^{10} \cdot 2^{64} \cdot 6 + 2^{128-71} = 2^{77.00}$.

KETJE **Major.** Using a 64-dimensional cube with 3 bit conditions involving the key (see [26]), the key recovery attack of 7-round KETJE Major costs a data and time complexities $2^3 \cdot 2^{64} \cdot 3 + 2^2 \cdot 2^{64} \cdot 2 + 2^1 \cdot 2^{64} \cdot (64-5) + 2^{64} = 2^{71.24}$.

KETJE **Minor.** Using a 64-dimensional cube with 4 bit conditions involving the key (see [26]), the key recovery attack of 7-round KETJE Minor costs a data and time complexities less than $2^4 \cdot 2^{64} + 2^3 \cdot 2^{64} \cdot 63 + 2^{64} = 2^{73.03}$.

For KETJE SR and KETJE JR, our model could not find better attacks than the existing ones in [15]. However, for KETJE SR with KECCAK-p as the underlying permutation, namely, KETJE SR v1, better attacks on 7-round KETJE SR are found using a 64-dimensional cube with 27 bit conditions (see [26], involve 26 bits key information) and the time and data complexities are $2^{26} \cdot 2^{64} \cdot 2 + 2^{128-54} = 2^{91.00}$. Therefore, KETJE instances using KECCAK-$p^\star$ are stronger than those instances using KECCAK-p under our attacks.

6.3 Conditional Cube Attacks on Full-State Keyed Duplex

In this subsection, we consider conditional cube attacks on KECCAK-p based FKD (or FKS) which provides full-state degrees of freedom. We assume that the first data block is absorbed after the application of the underlying permutation, as in KEYAK. Therefore, the internal state before injecting the first data block is fully unknown. This is not a nonce-respected attack since the cube will be constructed on the full-state data block.

For convenience, FKD with KECCAK-$p[\boldsymbol{b}, n_r]$ as the underlying permutation is denoted by FKD[$\boldsymbol{b}$]. A direct application of linear structures shows that 512-dimensional Type II cubes for FKD[1600] can be constructed by constraining 960 bits to certain constants. However, in key/state recovery attacks the number of bit conditions allowed is limited. In this subsection, we apply our model for searching Type II cubes of FKD[$\boldsymbol{b}$], and try to find some useful cubes with a small number of bit conditions.

When the number of bit conditions is set to 0, Type II cubes of FKD[1600] can be found with dimension at least 48. If the dimension is set to 65, a Type II cube with 25 bit conditions is found, as shown in [26]. Since the first two rounds are linearized, the cube sum of 8-round KECCAK is zero. Thus, this cube can be used to attack 8-round FKD[1600] by recovering the internal state in a similar way to the attack on KMAC. As long as the rate $\boldsymbol{r}$ is greater than 320 bits, a 9-round attack of FKD[1600] can be achieved by partially reversing the last round. The time complexity is about $2^{65+25} = 2^{90}$. For more experimental results, please refer to Appendix A.

Compared with cube attacks on KECCAK-p based constructions where $\boldsymbol{r}$-bit messages are absorbed, cube attacks on FKD[1600] can be extended to one more round by exploiting the full-state absorption. With this, the open question proposed by the KEYAK designers in [7] now is answered.

The idea of full-state absorption has already been applied to KEYAK which absorbs data blocks of more than r bits each but less than b bits. For example, Lake KEYAK processes data blocks of 1536 bits, less than 1600 bits. A simple way to adapt our attack on 9-round FKD[1600] to Lake KEYAK is to find a Type II cube with dimension 129 (65+64). However, such a cube with increased dimension could not be found in a practical amount of time. Therefore, the extended attack does not apply to Lake KEYAK.

6.4 Experimental Verification and Codes

Since the attacks in this paper are impractical with current computation power, the correctness of the attacks is verified on cubes with small dimensions. We do no change to the attacks except reducing the number of rounds for the cube tester in the middle, so the attack complexity reduces to a practical level. We implement two Type I conditional cube attacks: one based on the 16-dimensional toy cube in Table 6 for fast verification, and the other based on a 32-dimensional cube for attacking 7-round `KMAC256` (or 6-round `KMAC128`). A conditional cube attack on 7-round FKD[1600] is also implemented with a 32-dimensional cube of Type II. Note that this cube has three bit conditions which are set intentionally; otherwise, there can be no condition. The correctness of our attacks are confirmed by these three experiments. The source codes for experimental verification are available via http://team.crypto.sg/VerificationCodesConCube.zip. The codes for building our models are available through http://team.crypto.sg/modelConCube.zip.

7 Conclusions

In the paper, we proposed new MILP models for searching two types of conditional cubes for KECCAK-p based keyed constructions. Particularly, we incorporated the diffusion effect of variables through the non-linear layer and took a broader class of Type I conditional cubes into account and we proposed a model for searching Type II conditional cube for the first time. With the new models, conditional cubes with desired dimensions and least bit conditions were found for `KMAC`. As a result, key recovery attacks of 7-round `KMAC128`, 9-round `KMAC256` can be mounted respectively. To the best of our knowledge, these are the first cryptanalysis results against `KMAC`. Using our model, we solve the open question of FKD by extending the conditional cube attack by one additional round. The application of our model to KEYAK and KETJE gives rise to new attacks or better attacks with reduced complexities. Specifically, the number of rounds attacked against Lake KEYAK with 128-bit keys is improved from 6 to 8 in the nonce-respected setting and 9 rounds of Lake KEYAK can be attacked when using 256-bit keys; attack complexities are reduced generally on other constructions.

Acknowledgement. Ling Song and Danping Shi are partially supported by the Fundamental Theory and Cutting Edge Technology Research Program of Institute of Information Engineering, CAS (Grant No. Y7Z0251103), Youth Innovation Promotion Association CAS, the National Natural Science Foundation of China (Grants No. 61802399, 61802400, 61732021, 61772519 and 61472415) and Chinese Major Program of National Cryptography Development Foundation (Grant No. MMJJ20180102).

A Experimental Details

The model for searching Type II cubes for FKD[1600] has 37440 inequalities on 15040 variables, which is about 1.8 times of the model for searching Type I conditional cubes. Even though the search for Type I conditional cubes takes seconds or minutes, the solving time of the model for Type II cubes increases exponentially. We solve the model for finding Type II conditional cubes with Gurobi optimizer [18] on a server with 64 cores at 2.3 GHz, and Gurobi could not finish the optimization in a practical amount of time.

Type II cubes for FKD[1600] can be found with dimension $d \geq 65$. However, for FKD[800], when we set the number of conditions $t \leq 62$ and the objective to maximize the dimension, Gurobi shows after running 8 days that the dimension falls in $[62, 94]$, but to extend the attack by one more round, a 65-dimensional Type II conditional cube is required.

B Inequalities

Table 7. Inequalities modeling the non-linear operation χ in the first round, where coordinates $[y][z]$s are omitted.

$$
\begin{aligned}
-B[x] - B[x+1] &\geq -1\\
-B[x] + C[x] &\geq 0\\
-B[x+2] - V[x+2] &\geq -1\\
-B[x+1] - V[x+1] &\geq -1\\
-B[x] - B[x+1] - H[x+2] + C[x] &\geq -1\\
B[x] - V[x+1] - H[x+1] - C[x] &\geq -2\\
B[x] - V[x+2] + H[x+2] - C[x] &\geq -1\\
B[x] + B[x+1] + B[x+2] - C[x] &\geq 0\\
-B[x+1] - B[x+2] + V[x+1] + V[x+2] + C[x] &\geq 0\\
-B[x+1] - B[x+2] + V[x+2] + H[x+1] + C[x] &\geq 0
\end{aligned}
$$

Table 8. Inequalities modeling the parity of a column

$$
\begin{aligned}
-F[x][z] - G[x][z] &\geq -1 \\
-A[x][0][z] + F[x][z] + G[x][z] &\geq 0 \\
-A[x][1][z] + F[x][z] + G[x][z] &\geq 0 \\
-A[x][2][z] + F[x][z] + G[x][z] &\geq 0 \\
-A[x][3][z] + F[x][z] + G[x][z] &\geq 0 \\
-A[x][4][z] + F[x][z] + G[x][z] &\geq 0 \\
A[x][0][z] + A[x][1][z] + A[x][2][z] + A[x][3][z] + A[x][4][z] - 2F[x][z] - G[x][z] &\geq 0
\end{aligned}
$$

Table 9. Inequalities modeling the non-linear operation χ in the second round

$$
\begin{aligned}
-S_i - B[x+1][y][z] - B[x+2][y][z] &\geq -2 \\
-S_i - B[x+1][y][z] + V[x+2][y][z] &\geq -1 \\
-S_i - B[x+2][y][z] + V[x+1][y][z] &\geq -1 \\
-S_i - B[x+1][y][z] - V[x+1][y][z] &\geq -2 \\
-S_i - B[x+2][y][z] - V[x+2][y][z] &> -2 \\
-S_i - B[x][y][z] - B[x+1][y][z] &\geq -2
\end{aligned}
$$

Table 10. Inequalities modeling the column parity of the input of the second round.

$$
\begin{aligned}
G_2[x][z] - G_1[x][z] &\geq 0 \\
G_2[x][z] - N_1[x][z] &\geq 0 \\
G_2[x][z] - M[x][z] &\geq 0 \\
-G_2[x][z] + G_1[x][z] + M[x][z] + N_1[x][z] + N_2[x][z] &\geq 0 \\
G_2[x][z] - G_1[x+2][z] - N_2[x][z] &\geq -1 \\
G_2[x][z] - N_2[x][z] - N_3[x][z] &\geq -1 \\
-G_2[x][z] + G_1[x][z] + G_1[x+2][z] + M[x][z] + N_1[x][z] + N_3[x][z] &\geq 0
\end{aligned}
$$

References

1. Aumasson, J., Dinur, I., Meier, W., Shamir, A.: Cube testers and key recovery attacks on reduced-round MD6 and Trivium. In: Handschuh, H., Lucks, S., Preneel, B., Rogaway, P. (eds.) Symmetric Cryptography, 11.01. - 16.01.2009. Dagstuhl Seminar Proceedings, vol. 09031. Schloss Dagstuhl - Leibniz-Zentrum für Informatik, Germany (2009). http://drops.dagstuhl.de/opus/volltexte/2009/1944/

2. Bertoni, G., Daemen, J., Hoffert, S., Peeters, M., Van Assche, G., Van Keer, R.: Farfalle: parallel permutation-based cryptography. IACR Trans. Symmetric Cryptol. **2017**(4), 1–38 (2017). https://tosc.iacr.org/index.php/ToSC/article/view/801
3. Bertoni, G., Daemen, J., Peeters, M., Van Assche, G.: Cryptographic Sponge functions. Submission to NIST (Round 3) (2011). http://sponge.noekeon.org/CSF-0.1.pdf
4. Bertoni, G., Daemen, J., Peeters, M., Van Assche, G.: Duplexing the sponge: single-pass authenticated encryption and other applications. In: Miri, A., Vaudenay, S. (eds.) SAC 2011. LNCS, vol. 7118, pp. 320–337. Springer, Heidelberg (2012). https://doi.org/10.1007/978-3-642-28496-0_19
5. Bertoni, G., Daemen, J., Peeters, M., Van Assche, G.: The Keccak Reference, January 2011. http://keccak.noekeon.org, version 3.0
6. Bertoni, G., Daemen, J., Peeters, M., Van Assche, G., Van Keer, R.: CAESAR Submission: Ketje v2. Candidate of CAESAR Competition, September 2016
7. Bertoni, G., Daemen, J., Peeters, M., Van Assche, G., Van Keer, R.: CAESAR Submission: Keyak v2. Candidate of CAESAR Competition, September 2016
8. Bi, W., Dong, X., Li, Z., Zong, R., Wang, X.: Milp-aided cube-attack-like cryptanalysis on Keccak keyed modes. Designs, Codes and Cryptography, August 2018. https://doi.org/10.1007/s10623-018-0526-x
9. Chaigneau, C., Fuhr, T., Gilbert, H., Guo, J., Jean, J., Reinhard, J., Song, L.: Key-recovery attacks on full kravatte. IACR Trans. Symmetric Cryptol. **2018**(1), 5–28 (2018). https://doi.org/10.13154/tosc.v2018.i1.5-28
10. Daemen, J., Mennink, B., Van Assche, G.: Full-state keyed duplex with built-in multi-user support. In: Takagi, T., Peyrin, T. (eds.) ASIACRYPT 2017. LNCS, vol. 10625, pp. 606–637. Springer, Cham (2017). https://doi.org/10.1007/978-3-319-70697-9_21
11. Daemen, J., Van Assche, G.: Differential propagation analysis of Keccak. In: Canteaut, A. (ed.) FSE 2012. LNCS, vol. 7549, pp. 422–441. Springer, Heidelberg (2012). https://doi.org/10.1007/978-3-642-34047-5_24
12. Dinur, I., Dunkelman, O., Shamir, A.: Improved practical attacks on round-reduced Keccak. J. Cryptol. **27**(2), 183–209 (2014). https://doi.org/10.1007/s00145-012-9142-5
13. Dinur, I., Morawiecki, P., Pieprzyk, J., Srebrny, M., Straus, M.: Cube attacks and cube-attack-like cryptanalysis on the round-reduced Keccak sponge function. In: Oswald, E., Fischlin, M. (eds.) EUROCRYPT 2015, Part I. LNCS, vol. 9056, pp. 733–761. Springer, Heidelberg (2015). https://doi.org/10.1007/978-3-662-46800-5_28
14. Dinur, I., Shamir, A.: Cube attacks on tweakable black box polynomials. In: Joux, A. (ed.) EUROCRYPT 2009. LNCS, vol. 5479, pp. 278–299. Springer, Heidelberg (2009). https://doi.org/10.1007/978-3-642-01001-9_16
15. Dong, X., Li, Z., Wang, X., Qin, L.: Cube-like attack on round-reduced initialization of Ketje Sr. IACR Trans. Symmetric Cryptol. **2017**(1), 259–280 (2017). https://doi.org/10.13154/tosc.v2017.i1.259-280
16. Fuhr, T., Naya-Plasencia, M., Rotella, Y.: State-recovery attacks on modified Ketje Jr. IACR Trans. Symmetric Cryptol. **2018**(1), 29–56 (2018). https://tosc.iacr.org/index.php/ToSC/article/view/843
17. Guo, J., Liu, M., Song, L.: Linear structures: applications to cryptanalysis of round-reduced KECCAK. In: Cheon, J.H., Takagi, T. (eds.) ASIACRYPT 2016, Part I. LNCS, vol. 10031, pp. 249–274. Springer, Heidelberg (2016). https://doi.org/10.1007/978-3-662-53887-6_9
18. Gurobi: Gurobi Optimizer. http://www.gurobi.com/

19. Huang, S., Wang, X., Xu, G., Wang, M., Zhao, J.: Conditional cube attack on reduced-round Keccak sponge function. In: Coron, J.-S., Nielsen, J.B. (eds.) EUROCRYPT 2017, Part II. LNCS, vol. 10211, pp. 259–288. Springer, Cham (2017). https://doi.org/10.1007/978-3-319-56614-6_9
20. Li, Z., Bi, W., Dong, X., Wang, X.: Improved conditional cube attacks on Keccak keyed modes with MILP method. In: Takagi, T., Peyrin, T. (eds.) ASIACRYPT 2017, Part I. LNCS, vol. 10624, pp. 99–127. Springer, Cham (2017). https://doi.org/10.1007/978-3-319-70694-8_4
21. Mennink, B., Reyhanitabar, R., Vizár, D.: Security of full-state keyed sponge and duplex: applications to authenticated encryption. In: Iwata, T., Cheon, J.H. (eds.) ASIACRYPT 2015, Part II. LNCS, vol. 9453, pp. 465–489. Springer, Heidelberg (2015). https://doi.org/10.1007/978-3-662-48800-3_19
22. NIST: SHA-3 COMPETITION. http://csrc.nist.gov/groups/ST/hash/sha-3/index.html (2007–2012)
23. Qiao, K., Song, L., Liu, M., Guo, J.: New collision attacks on round-reduced Keccak. In: Coron, J.-S., Nielsen, J.B. (eds.) EUROCRYPT 2017, Part III. LNCS, vol. 10212, pp. 216–243. Springer, Cham (2017). https://doi.org/10.1007/978-3-319-56617-7_8
24. Sasaki, Y., Todo, Y.: New algorithm for modeling S-box in MILP based differential and division trail search. In: Farshim, P., Simion, E. (eds.) SecITC 2017. LNCS, vol. 10543, pp. 150–165. Springer, Cham (2017). https://doi.org/10.1007/978-3-319-69284-5_11
25. Song, L., Guo, J.: Cube-Attack-like cryptanalysis of round-reduced Keccak using MILP. To appear in IACR Trans. Symmetric Cryptol. **2018**(3) (2018). https://eprint.iacr.org/2018/810
26. Song, L., Guo, J., Shi, D., Ling, S.: New MILP Modeling: Improved Conditional Cube Attacks on Keccak-based Constructions. Cryptology ePrint Archive, Report 2017/1030 (2017). https://eprint.iacr.org/2017/1030
27. Song, L., Liao, G., Guo, J.: Non-full Sbox linearization: applications to collision attacks on round-reduced Keccak. In: Katz, J., Shacham, H. (eds.) CRYPTO 2017, Part II. LNCS, vol. 10402, pp. 428–451. Springer, Cham (2017). https://doi.org/10.1007/978-3-319-63715-0_15
28. Sun, S., Hu, L., Wang, P., Qiao, K., Ma, X., Song, L.: Automatic security evaluation and (related-key) differential characteristic search: application to SIMON, PRESENT, LBlock, DES(L) and other bit-oriented block ciphers. In: Sarkar, P., Iwata, T. (eds.) ASIACRYPT 2014, Part I. LNCS, vol. 8873, pp. 158–178. Springer, Heidelberg (2014). https://doi.org/10.1007/978-3-662-45611-8_9
29. The U.S. National Institute of Standards and Technology: SHA-3 Standard: Permutation-Based Hash and Extendable-Output Functions. Federal Information Processing Standard, FIPS 202, 5th August 2015. http://nvlpubs.nist.gov/nistpubs/FIPS/NIST.FIPS.202.pdf
30. The U.S. National Institute of Standards and Technology: SHA-3 Derived Functions: cSHAKE, KMAC, TupleHash and ParallelHash. NIST Special Publication 800–185, 21 December 2016. http://nvlpubs.nist.gov/nistpubs/SpecialPublications/NIST.SP.800-185.pdf

On the Concrete Security of Goldreich's Pseudorandom Generator

Geoffroy Couteau[1](✉), Aurélien Dupin[2,3,4], Pierrick Méaux[5], Mélissa Rossi[2,6,7], and Yann Rotella[7]

[1] Karlsruhe Institute of Technology, Karlsruhe, Germany
geoffroy.couteau@kit.edu
[2] Thales Communications and Security, Gennevilliers, France
[3] CentraleSupélec, Rennes, France
[4] Irisa, Rennes, France
dupin.aurelien@gmail.com
[5] ICTEAM/ELEN/Crypto Group, Université catholique de Louvain, Louvain-la-Neuve, Belgium
pierrick.meaux@uclouvain.be
[6] École Normale Supérieure de Paris, Département d'informatique, CNRS, PSL Research University, Paris, France
melissa.rossi@ens.fr
[7] Inria, Paris, France
yann.rotella@inria.fr

Abstract. Local pseudorandom generators allow to expand a short random string into a long pseudo-random string, such that each output bit depends on a constant number d of input bits. Due to its extreme efficiency features, this intriguing primitive enjoys a wide variety of applications in cryptography and complexity. In the polynomial regime, where the seed is of size n and the output of size n^{s} for $\mathsf{s} > 1$, the only known solution, commonly known as *Goldreich's PRG*, proceeds by applying a simple d-ary predicate to public random size-d subsets of the bits of the seed.

While the security of Goldreich's PRG has been thoroughly investigated, with a variety of results deriving provable security guarantees against class of attacks in some parameter regimes and necessary criteria to be satisfied by the underlying predicate, little is known about its concrete security and efficiency. Motivated by its numerous theoretical applications and the hope of getting practical instantiations for some of them, we initiate a study of the concrete security of Goldreich's PRG, and evaluate its resistance to cryptanalytic attacks. Along the way, we develop a new guess-and-determine-style attack, and identify new criteria which refine existing criteria and capture the security guarantees of candidate local PRGs in a more fine-grained way.

Keywords: Pseudorandom generators · Algebraic attacks
Guess-and-determine · Gröbner basis

T. Peyrin and S. Galbraith (Eds.): ASIACRYPT 2018, LNCS 11273, pp. 96–124, 2018.
https://doi.org/10.1007/978-3-030-03329-3_4

1 Introduction

One of the most fundamental problems in cryptography is the question of what makes an efficiently computable function hard to invert. The quest for the simplest design which leads to a primitive resisting all known attacks is at the heart of both symmetric and asymmetric cryptography: while we might be able to build seemingly secure primitives by relying on more and more complex designs to thwart cryptanalysis attempts, such a "security by obscurity" approach is unsatisfying. Instead, as advocated almost two decades ago by Goldreich [Gol00], we should seek to construct the simplest possible function that we do not know how to invert efficiently. Only this way, Goldreich argued, can we better understand what really underlies the security of cryptographic constructions.

Random Local Functions. In an attempt to tackle this fundamental problem, Goldreich suggested a very simple candidate one-way function as a promising target for cryptanalysis: let (n, m) be integers, and let $(\sigma^1, \ldots, \sigma^m)$ be a list of m subsets of $[n]$, such that each subset is of small size: for any $i \leq m$, $|\sigma^i| = c(n)$, where $c(n) \ll n$ (in actual instantiations, $c(n)$ can for example be logarithmic in n, or even constant). Fix a simple predicate $P : \{0,1\}^{c(n)} \mapsto \{0,1\}$, and define the function $f : \{0,1\}^n \mapsto \{0,1\}^m$ as follows: on input $x \in \{0,1\}^n$, for any subset S of $[n]$, let $x[\sigma]$ denote the subset of the bits of x indexed by σ. Compute $f(x)$ as $P(x[\sigma^1])|| \cdots ||P(x[\sigma^m])$ (that is, $f(x)$ is computed by applying the predicate P to all subsets of the bits of x indexed by the sets $\sigma^1, \ldots, \sigma^m$). We call *random local functions* the functions obtained by instantiating this template.

In his initial proposal, Goldreich advocated instantiating the above methodology with $m \approx n$ and $c(n) = O(\log n)$, and conjectured that if the subsets $(\sigma^1, \ldots, \sigma^m)$ form an expander graph[1], and for an appropriate choice of the predicate P, it should be infeasible to invert the above function f in polynomial time. While setting $c(n)$ to $O(\log n)$ offers stronger security guarantees, the more extreme design choice $c(n) = O(1)$ (also discussed in Goldreich's paper) enhances the above candidate with an appealing feature: it enjoys constant input locality (which puts it into the complexity class NC^0), hence it is highly parallelizable (it can be computed in constant parallel time). It appeared in subsequent works that a stronger variant of Goldreich's conjecture, which considers $m \gg n$ and claims that f is in fact a *pseudorandom generator*, was of particular interest; we will elaborate on this later on.

Local Pseudorandom Generators. The question of whether cryptographic primitives can exist in weak complexity classes such as NC^0 has attracted a lot of attention in the cryptographic community. A primitive of particular interest, which has been the focus of most works on the subject, is the notion of pseudorandom generators (PRGs), which are functions $G : \{0,1\}^n \mapsto \{0,1\}^m$ extending a

[1] The subsets form an expander graph if for some k, every k subsets cover $k + \Omega(n)$ elements of $[n]$. In practice, it suffices to pick once for all the subsets $(\sigma^1, \ldots, \sigma^m)$ at random to guarantee that they will be expanding except with $o(1)$ probability.

short random seed into a longer, pseudorandom string. The existence of PRGs in NC^0 was first considered by Cryan and Miltersen in [CM01]. Remarkably, it was shown by Applebaum, Ishai, and Kushilevitz [AIK04, AIK08] that cryptographically secure pseudorandom generators (with linear stretch $m = O(n)$) exist in a complexity class as low as NC^0_4 (the class of constant depth, polysize circuits where each output bit depends on at most 4 input bits), under widely believed standard assumption for the case of PRG with sublinear stretch (such as factorization, or discrete logarithm), and under a specific intractability assumption related to the hardness of decoding "sparsely generated" linear codes, for the case of PRG with linear stretch. While this essentially settled the question of the existence of linear stretch PRGs in NC^0, an intriguing open question remained: could PRGs in NC^0 have *polynomial* stretch, $m = \mathsf{poly}(n)$?

Some early negative results were given by Cryan and Miltersen [CM01] (who ruled out the existence of PRGs in NC^0_3 with stretch $m > 4n$) and Mossel, Shpilka, and Trevisan [MST03] (who ruled out the existence of PRGs in NC^0_4 with stretch $m > 24n$). The authors of [CM01] also conjectured that any candidate PRG with superlinear stretch in NC^0 would be broken by simple, linear distinguishing tests[2]; this conjecture was refuted in [MST03], who gave a concrete candidate PRG in NC^0, by instantiating a random local function with $c = 5$, and the predicate

$$P_5 : (x_1, x_2, x_3, x_4, x_5) \mapsto x_1 + x_2 + x_3 + x_4 x_5.$$

where the + denotes the addition in $\mathbb{F}_2$ *i.e.* the xor.

They proved that this PRG fools linear tests, even when m is a (sufficiently small) polynomial in n. By the previously mentioned negative result on PRGs in NC^0_4, this candidate PRG, which has locality 5, achieves the best possible locality. Recently, there has been a renewed interest in the study of this local PRG, now commonly known as Goldreich's PRG, and its generalizations [BQ09, App12, OW14, CEMT14, App15, ABR16, AL16, IPS08, LV17, BCG+17].

1.1 Implications of Polynomial-Stretch Local Pseudorandom Generators

The original motivation for the study of local pseudorandom generators was the intriguing possibility of designing cryptographic primitives that can be evaluated in *constant time*, using polynomially many cores. While this is already a strong motivation in itself, it was observed in several works that the existence of (poly-stretch) local PRGs had a number of non-trivial implications, and is at the heart of feasibility results for several high-end cryptographic primitives. We provide below a brief overview.

- *Secure computation with constant computational overhead.* In the recent work [IKOS08], the authors explored the possibility of computing cryptographic primitives with essentially optimal efficiency, namely, constant overhead over a naive insecure implementation of the same task. One of their main

[2] A linear test attempts to distinguish a string from random by checking whether the xor of a subset of the bits of the string is biased toward either 0 or 1.

results establishes the existence of constant-overhead two-party computation protocols for any boolean circuit, assuming the existence of poly-stretch local PRGs (and oblivious transfers). In a recent work [ADI+17a], this result was extended to arithmetic circuits, using an arithmetic generalization of local PRGs.

- *Indistinguishability obfuscation (iO).* Introduced in the seminal paper of Barak et al. [BGI+01], iO is a primitive that has received a considerable attention from the crypto community in the past years, as a long sequence of works starting with [SW14] has demonstrated that iO had tremendous theoretical implications, to the point that it is often referred to as being a "crypto-complete" primitive. All known candidate constructions of iO rely, directly or indirectly, on a primitive called k-linear map, for some degree k. Recently, a sequence of papers (culminating with [LT17]) has attempted to find out the minimal k for which a k-linear map would imply the existence of iO (with the ultimate goal of reaching $k = 2$, as bilinear maps are well understood objects). These works have established a close relation between this value k and the existence of pseudorandom generators with poly-stretch, and locality k.[3]
- *MPC-friendly primitives.* Historically, the design of symmetric cryptographic primitives (such as block ciphers, pseudorandom generators, and pseudorandom functions) has been motivated by efficiency considerations (memory consumption, hardware compatibility, ease of implementation, ...). The field of multiparty computation (MPC), where parties want to jointly evaluate a function on secret inputs, has led to the emergence of new efficiency considerations: the efficiency of secure evaluation of symmetric primitives is strongly related to parameters such as the circuit depth of the primitive, and the number of its AND gates. This observation has motivated the design of MPC-friendly symmetric primitives in several recent works (*e.g.* [ARS+15, CCF+16, MJSC16, GRR+16]). Local pseudorandom generators make very promising candidate MPC-friendly PRGs (and lead, through the GGM transform [GGM84], to promising candidates for MPC-friendly pseudorandom functions). Secure evaluation of such symmetric primitives enjoys a wide variety of applications.
- *Cryptographic capsules.* In [BCG+17], Boyle et al. studied the recently introduced primitive of homomorphic secret sharing (HSS). An important implication of HSS is that, assuming the existence of a local PRG with poly-stretch, one can obtain multiparty computation protocols in the preprocessing model[4] where the amount of communication between the parties is considerably smaller than the circuit size of the function, by constructing a primitive

[3] The locality requirement can in fact be weakened to a related notion of *block locality*.

[4] In this model, n parties securely compute a function f on private inputs $(x_1, \ldots, x_n)$; in the preprocessing phase, the parties have access to f (but not to the input), and generate some preprocessing material. Then, in the online phase, the parties execute an *information-theoretically secure* protocol to compute $f(x)$, using the preprocessed material. MPC protocols in the preprocessing model are among the most promising candidates for getting practical solutions to the multiparty computation problem.

called cryptographic capsule which, informally, allows to compress correlated (pseudo-)random coins. MPC protocols with low-communication preprocessing have numerous appealing applications; however, the efficiency of the constructions of cryptographic capsule strongly depends on the locality and seed size of the underlying local PRG (both should be as small as possible to get a reasonably efficient instantiation).

In addition to the above (non-exhaustive) overview, we note that the existence of poly-stretch local pseudorandom generators also enjoys interesting complexity-theoretic implications. For example, they have been shown in [AIK08] to imply strong (tight) bounds on the average-case inapproximability of constraints satisfactions problems such as Max3SAT.

1.2 On the Security of Goldreich's PRG

In this section, we provide a brief overview of the state-of-the-art regarding the security of local pseudorandom generators. For a more detailed and well-written overview dating from 2015, we refer the reader to [App15].

Positive Results: Security Against Class of Attacks. The seminal paper of Goldreich [Gol00] made some preliminary observations on necessary properties for a local one-way function. Namely, the predicate P must satisfy some non-degeneracy properties, such as being non-linear (otherwise, one could inverse the function using Gaussian elimination). It also noted that to avoid a large class of natural "backtracking" attacks, which make a guess on the values of bit inputs based on local observations and attempt to combine many local solutions into a global solution, the subsets $(S_1, \ldots, S_m)$ should be sufficiently *expanding*: for some k, every k subsets should cover $k + \Omega(n)$ elements of $[n]$. The security of Goldreich's candidate one-way function against a large class of backtracking algorithm was formally analyzed in [AHI05, CEMT14], where it was proven that two restricted types of backtracking algorithms (called "drunk" and "myopic" backtracking algorithms) take exponential time to invert the function (with high probability). They also ran experiments to heuristically evaluate its security against SAT solvers (and observed experimentally an exponential increase in running time as a function of the input length).

The pseudorandomness of random local functions was originally analyzed in [MST03]. They proved (among other results) that the random local function instantiated with the predicate $P_5 : (x_1, x_2, x_3, x_4, x_5) \mapsto x_1 + x_2 + x_3 + x_4 x_5$ fools all $\mathbb{F}_2$-linear distinguishers for a stretch up to $m(n) = n^{1.25-\varepsilon}$ (for an arbitrary small constant ε). This result was later extended to a larger stretch $n^{1.5-\varepsilon}$ in [OW14]. In the same paper, the authors proved that this candidate PRG is also secure against a powerful class of attacks, the Lasserre/Parrilo semidefinite programming (SDP) hierarchy, up to the same stretch. Regarding security against $\mathbb{F}_2$-linear attacks, a general dichotomy theorem was proven in [ABR12], which identified a class of *non-degenerate* predicates and showed that for most graphs, a local PRG instantiated with a non-degenerate predicate is secure against linear attacks, and for most graphs, a local PRG instantiated with a degenerate predicate is insecure against linear distinguishers. In general, to fool $\mathbb{F}_2$-linear distinguishers, the predicate should have high *algebraic degree* (in particular, a random local function instantiated with a degree-ℓ predicate cannot be pseudorandom for a stretch ℓ ($m \equiv n^\ell$), as it is broken by a straightforward Gaussian elimination attack).

Being pseudorandom seems to be a much stronger security property than being one-way. Nevertheless, in the case of random local functions, it was shown in [App12] that the existence of local pseudorandom generators follows from the existence of *one-way* random local functions (with sufficiently large output size).

Negative Results. The result of O'Donnell and Witmer [OW14] regarding security against SDP attacks is almost optimal, as attacks from this class are known to break the candidate for a stretch $\Theta(n^{1.5} \log n)$. More generally, optimizing SDP attacks leads to a polytime inversion algorithm for any predicate P which is (even slightly) correlated with some number c of its inputs, as soon as the output size exceeds $m \in \Omega(n^{c/2} + n \log n)$ [OW14, App15]. Therefore, a good predicate should have high *resiliency* (*i.e.* it should be k-wise independent, for a k as large as possible). This result shows, in particular, that a random local function with a constant locality d and with an output size $m > \mathsf{poly}(d) \cdot n$ is insecure when instantiated with a uniformly random predicate P. Combining this observation with the result of Siegenthaler [Sie84], which studied the correlation of d-ary predicates, gives a polytime inversion algorithm for any random local function implemented with a d-ary predicate, and with an output size $m \in \Omega(n^{1/2\lfloor 2d/3 \rfloor} \log n)$.

Bogdanov and Qiao [BQ09] studied the security of random local functions when the output is sufficiently larger than the input (*i.e.*, $m \geq Dn$, for a large constant D). They proved that for sufficiently large D, inverting a random local function could be reduced to finding an *approximate inverse* (*i.e.* finding any x' which is close to the inverse x in Hamming distance), by showing how to invert the function with high probability given an advice x' close to x. For random local function with an output size polynomial in n, $m = n^{\mathsf{s}}$ for some s, this leads to a subexponential-time attack [App15]: fix a parameter ε, assign random values to the $(1 - 2\varepsilon)n$ first inputs, and create a list that enumerates over all possible $2\varepsilon n$ assignments for the remaining variables. Then the list is guaranteed to contain a value x' that agree with the preimage x on a $(1/2+\varepsilon)n$ fraction of the coordinates with good probability. By applying the reduction of [BQ09], using each element of the list as an advice string, one recovers the preimage in time $\mathsf{poly}(n) \cdot 2^{2\varepsilon n}$ provided that $m = \Omega(n/\varepsilon^{2d})$ (d is the arity of the predicate P). In the case of the 5-ary predicate P_5, this leads to an attack in subexponential-time $2^{O(n^{1-(\mathsf{s}-1)/2d})}$ (*e.g.* using $\mathsf{s} = 1.45$ gives an attack in time $2^{O(n^{0.955})}$).

By the previous observations, we know that the predicate of a random local function must have high resiliency and high algebraic degree to lead to a pseudorandom function. A natural question is whether this characterization is also sufficient; this question was answered negatively in [AL16], who proved that a predicate must also have high *bit-fixing degree* to fool linear attacks.[5] In particular, this observation disproved a previous conjecture of Applebaum that XOR-AND predicates (which are natural generalizations of the predicate P_5) could lead to local PRGs with stretch greater than 2 that fools all linear tests (see [AL16, Corollary 1.3]).

In the same work, Applebaum and Lovett considered the class of algebraic attacks on local pseudorandom function, which are incomparable to linear attacks. An algebraic attack against a function $f : \{0,1\}^n \mapsto \{0,1\}^m$ starts with an output y and uses it to initialize a system of polynomial equations over the input variables $x = (x_1, \ldots, x_n)$. The system is further manipulated and extended until a solution is found or until the system is refuted. Applebaum and Lovett proved that a predicate must also have high *rational degree* to fool algebraic attacks (a predicate P has rational degree e if it is the smallest integer for which there exist degree e polynomials Q and R, not both zero, such that $PQ = R$). Indeed, if $e < \mathsf{s}$ then P is not s-pseudorandom against algebraic attacks (see [AL16], Theorem 1.4). In the symmetric cryptography community, the rational degree denotes the well-known *algebraic immunity* criterion on Boolean function that underlies the so-called *algebraic attacks* on stream ciphers [CM03, Cou03]. An algebraic immunity of e implies an r-bit fixing degree greater than or equal to $e - r$ ([DGM05], Proposition 1), giving that an high algebraic immunity guarantees both high rational degree and high bit fixing degree. The algebraic degree is equivalent to the 0-bit fixing degree, then it leads to the following characterization: a predicate of a random local function must have high resiliency and high algebraic immunity. In light of this characterization, the authors of [AL16] suggested the XOR-MAJ predicate as a promising candidate for building high-stretch local PRGs, the majority function having optimal algebraic immunity [DMS05].

Security Against Subexponential Attacks. While there is a large body of work that studied the security of random local functions, leading to a detailed characterization of the parameters and predicates that lead to insecure instantiations, relatively little is known on the *exact* security of local PRGs instantiated with non-degenerated parameters. In particular, most papers only prove that some classes of polytime attacks provably fail to break candidates local PRGs; however, these results do not preclude the possible existence of non-trivial subexponential attacks (specifically, these polytime attacks do not "degrade gracefully" into subexponential attacks when appropriate parameters are chosen for the PRG; instead, they do always and provably not succeed). To our knowledge, the only results in this regard are the proof from [AHI05, CEMT14] that many backtracking-type attacks require exponential time to invert a random local function, and the subexponential-time attack arising from the work of Bogdanov and Qiao [BQ09]. However, as we saw above, the latter attack only gives

[5] A predicate P has r-bit fixing degree e if the minimal degree of the restriction of P obtained by fixing r inputs is e.

a slightly-subexponential algorithm, in time $2^{O(n^{1-(s-1)/2d})}$ for a d-ary predicate, and an n^s-stretch local PRG.

1.3 Our Goals and Results

In this work, we continue the study of the most common candidate local pseudorandom generators. However, we significantly depart from the approach of previous works, in that we wish to analyze the *concrete* security of local PRGs. To our knowledge, all previous works were only concerned about establishing asymptotic security guarantees for candidate local PRGs, without providing any insight on, *e.g.*, which parameters can be conjectured to lead to a primitive with a given bit-security. Our motivations for conducting this study are twofold.

- Several recent results, which we briefly overviewed in Sect. 1.1, indicate that (poly-stretch) local PRGs enjoy important theoretical applications. However, the possibility of instantiating these applications with concrete PRG candidates remains unclear, as their efficiency quickly deteriorates with the parameters of the underlying PRG. For example, the iO scheme of [LT17], which requires low-degree multilinear maps and therefore might be a viable approach to obtain efficiency improvements in iO constructions (as candidate high-degree multilinear maps are prohibitively expensive); however, it has a cost cubic in the seed size of a poly-stretch local PRG, which renders it practical only if we can safely use local PRGs with reasonably small seeds. Overall, we believe that there is a growing need for a better understanding of the exact efficiency of candidate local PRGs, and providing concrete estimations can prove helpful for researchers willing to understand which efficiency could potentially be obtained for local-PRG-based primitives.
- At a more theoretical level, previous works on (variants of) Goldreich's PRG have identified criteria which characterize the predicates susceptible to lead to secure local PRGs. Identifying such criteria is particularly relevant to the initial goal set up by Goldreich in [Gol00], which is to understand what characteristics of a function is the source of its cryptographic hardness, by designing the simplest possible candidate that resists all attacks we know of. However, existing criteria only distinguish predicates leading to insecure instances from those leading to instances for which no polynomial-time attack is known. We believe that it is also of particular relevance to this fundamental question to find criteria which capture in a more fine-grained way the cryptographic hardness of random local functions.

Our Results. We provide new cryptanalytic insights on the security of Goldreich's pseudorandom generator.

- *A new subexponential attack on Goldreich's PRG.* We start by devising a new attack on Goldreich's PRG. Our attack relies on a *guess-and-determine* technique, in the spirit of the recent attack [DLR16] on the FLIP family of stream ciphers [MJSC16]. The complexity of our attack is $2^{O(n^{2-s})}$ where s is

the stretch and n is the seed size. This complements O'Donnel and Witmer's result [OW14] showing that Goldreich's PRG is likely to be secure for stretch up to 1.5, with a more fine-grained complexity estimation. We implemented our attack and provide experimental results regarding its concrete efficiency, for various seed size and stretch parameters.
- *Generalization.* We generalize the previous attack to a large class of predicates, which are divided into two parts, a linear part and a non-linear part, XORed together. This captures all known candidate generalizations of Goldreich's PRG. Our attack takes subexponential time as soon as the stretch of the PRG is strictly above one. Importantly, our attack does not depend on the locality of the predicate, but only on the number of variables involved in the non-linear part. In a recent work [AL16], Applebaum and Lovett put forth an explicit candidate local PRG (of the form XOR-MAJ), as a concrete target for cryptanalytic effort. Our attack gives a new subexponential algorithm for attacking this candidate.
- *Extending the Applebaum-Lovett polynomial-time algebraic attack.* Applebaum and Lovett recently established that local pseudorandom generators can be broken in polynomial time, as long as the stretch s of the PRG is greater than the *rational degree* e of its predicate. We extend this result as follows: we show that the seed of a large class of local PRGs (which include all existing candidates) can be recovered in polynomial time whenever $\mathsf{s} \geq e - \log N_e / \log n$, where e is the rational degree, n is the seed size, and N_e is the number of independent annihilators of the predicate[6] of degree at most e.
- *Linearization and Gröbner attack.* We complement our study with an analysis of the efficiency of algebraic attacks *à la* Gröbner on Goldreich's PRG. While it is known that Goldreich's PRG (and its variants) provably resists such attacks for appropriate choices of (asymptotic) parameters [AL16], little is known about its exact security against such attacks for concrete choices of parameters. We evaluated the concrete security of Goldreich's PRG against an order-two linearization attack. The existence of such an attack allows to derive bounds on Gröbner basis performance. Using an implemented proof of concept, we introduce heuristic bounds for vulnerable parameters.

As illustrated by our attacks, both the number of annihilators of the predicate and the r bit fixing algebraic immunity play an important role in the security of Golreich's PRG. These criteria were overlooked in all previous works on local PRGs. Last but not least, our concrete analysis indicates that Gröbner basis attacks, although provably "ruled out" asymptotically, matters when studying the vulnerabilities of Goldreich's PRG, and the security of concrete instances.

1.4 Organization of the Paper

Section 2 introduces necessary preliminaries on predicates and local pseudorandom generators. Section 3 describes a guess-and-determine attack on Goldreich's

[6] An annihilator of a predicate P is a non-zero polynomials Q such that $Q \cdot P = 0$.

PRG instantiated with the predicate P_5 and analyzes it, where the proofs are given in the full version of our paper [CDM+18]. Section 4 extends this attack to all predicates of the form XOR-MAJ, where the proofs are given in the full version of our paper. Eventually, still in the full version of our paper, an order 2 linearization attack on Goldreich's PRG is described. The same full version of our paper considers the case of using Goldreich's PRG with ordered subset (as was initially advocated in [Gol00]) and provides indications that this weakens its concrete security. Finally, the full version of our paper improves the theorem of Applebaum and Lovett, by taking into account the number of annihilators of the predicate. The full version of our paper contains missing proofs on collisions.

2 Preliminaries

Throughout this paper, n denotes the size of the seed of the PRGs considered. A probabilistic polynomial time algorithm (PPT, also denoted *efficient* algorithm) runs in time polynomial in the parameter n. A positive function f is *negligible* if for any polynomial p there exists a bound $B > 0$ such that, for any integer $k \geq B$, $f(k) \leq 1/|p(k)|$. An event depending on n occurs with *overwhelming probability* when its probability is at least $1 - \mathsf{negl}(n)$ for a negligible function negl. Given an integer k, we write $[k]$ to denote the set $\{1, \ldots, k\}$. Given a finite set S, the notation $X \xleftarrow{\$} S$ means a uniformly random assignment of an element of S to the variable X. Given a string $x \in \{0,1\}^k$ for some k and a subset σ of $[k]$, we let $x[\sigma]$ denote the subsequence of the bits of x whose index belong to σ. Moreover, the i-th bit of $x[\sigma]$ will be denoted by x_{σ_i}.

2.1 Hypergraphs

Hypergraphs generalize the standard notion of graphs (which are defined by a set of nodes and a set of edges, an edge being a pair of nodes) to a more general object defined by a set of nodes and a set of *hyperedges*, each hyperedge being an arbitrary subset of the nodes. We define an (n, m, d)-hypergraph G to be a hypergraph with n vertices and m hyperedges, each hyperedge having cardinality d. The hyperedges are assumed to be ordered from 1 to m, and each hyperedge $\{i_1, i_2, \ldots, i_d\}$ is ordered and satisfies $i_j \neq i_k$ for all $j \leq d$, $k \leq d$, $j \neq k$. We will consider hypergraphs satisfying some expansion property, defined below.

Definition 1 (Expander Graph). *An (n, m, d)-hypergraph G, denoted $(\sigma^1, \ldots, \sigma^m)$, is* (α, β)-expanding *if for any $S \subset [m]$ such that $|S| \leq \alpha \cdot m$, it holds that $|\bigcup_{i \in S} \sigma^i| \geq \beta \cdot |S| \cdot d$.*

2.2 Predicates

The constructions of local pseudorandom generators that we will consider in this work rely on predicates satisfying some specific properties. Formally, a predicate P of arity d is a function $P : \{0,1\}^d \mapsto \{0,1\}$. We define below the two properties that were shown to be necessary for instantiating local PRGs:

- *Resiliency.* A predicate P is k-resilient if it has no nontrivial correlation with any linear combination of up to k of its inputs. An example of predicate with maximal resiliency is the parity predicate (*i.e.*, the predicate which xors all its inputs).
- *Algebraic Immunity.* A predicate P has algebraic immunity e, referred to as $\mathsf{AI}(P) = e$, if the minimal degree of a non null function g such that $Pg = 0$ (or $(P+1)g = 0$) on all its entries is e. A local PRG built from a AI-e predicate cannot be pseudorandom with a stretch n^e due to algebraic attacks.

Note that the algebraic immunity (also referred as rational degree in [AL16]) implies a lower bound on the degree and on the bit-fixing degree. Moreover, a high algebraic immunity implies at least the same degree. Hence, for now on, those two criterion are considered as the relevant criteria for evaluating the security of Goldreich's PRG.

We define a particular family of predicates which have been considered as a potential instantiation:

Definition 2 ($\mathsf{XOR}_\ell\mathsf{M}_k$ predicates). *We call $\mathsf{XOR}_\ell\mathsf{M}_k$ predicate a predicate P of arity $\ell + k$ such that M is a predicate of arity k and:*

$$P(x_1, \ldots, x_\ell, z_1, \ldots, z_k) = \sum_{i=1}^{\ell} x_i + M(z_1, \ldots, z_k).$$

We define also a subfamily of $\mathsf{XOR}_\ell\mathsf{M}_k$ predicates, which have been considered in [AL16]:

Definition 3 ($\mathsf{XOR}_\ell\mathsf{MAJ}_k$ predicates). *We call $\mathsf{XOR}_\ell\mathsf{MAJ}_k$ predicate a predicate P of arity $\ell + k$ such that P is a $\mathsf{XOR}_\ell\mathsf{M}_k$ predicate such that M is the majority function in k variables:*

$$M(z_1, \ldots, z_k) = 1 \Leftrightarrow \mathsf{w}_H(z_1, \ldots, z_k) \geq \left\lceil \frac{k}{2} \right\rceil,$$

where w_H denotes the Hamming weight.

2.3 Pseudorandom Generators

Definition. A pseudorandom generator is a deterministic process that expands a short random seed into a longer sequence, so that no efficient adversary can distinguish this sequence from a uniformly random string of the same length. Formally,

Definition 4 (Pseudorandom Generator). *A $m(n)$-stretch pseudorandom generator, for a polynomial m, is an efficient uniform deterministic algorithm PRG which, on input a seed $x \in \{0,1\}^n$, outputs a string $y \in \{0,1\}^{m(n)}$. It satisfies the following security notion: for any probabilistic polynomial-time adversary Adv,*

$$\begin{aligned}&\Pr[y \stackrel{\$}{\leftarrow} \{0,1\}^{m(n)} : \mathsf{Adv}(\mathsf{pp}, y) = 1]\\ \approx &\Pr[x \stackrel{\$}{\leftarrow} \{0,1\}^n, y \leftarrow \mathsf{PRG}(x) : \mathsf{Adv}(\mathsf{pp}, y) = 1]\end{aligned}$$

Here $\approx$ denotes that the absolute value of the difference of the two probabilities is negligible in the security parameters, and pp *stands for the public parameters of the* PRG. *For any $n \in \mathbb{N}$, we denote* PRG_n *the function* PRG *restricted to n-bit inputs. A pseudorandom generator* PRG *is d-*local *(for a constant d) if for any $n \in \mathbb{N}$, every output bit of* PRG_n *depends on at most d input bits.*

Goldreich's Pseudorandom Generator. Goldreich's candidate local PRGs form a family $\mathsf{F}_{G,P}$ of local PRGs: $\mathsf{PRG}_{G,P} : \{0,1\}^n \mapsto \{0,1\}^m$, parametrized by an (n, m, d)-hypergraph $G = (\sigma^1, \ldots, \sigma^m)$ (where $m = m(n)$ is polynomial in n), and a predicate $P : \{0,1\}^d \mapsto \{0,1\}$, defined as follows: on input $x \in \{0,1\}^n$, $\mathsf{PRG}_{G,P}$ returns the m-bit string $(P(x_{\sigma_1^1}, \ldots, x_{\sigma_d^1}), \ldots, P(x_{\sigma_1^m}, \ldots, x_{\sigma_d^m}))$.

Conjecture 1 (Informal). If G is a sufficiently expanding (n, m, d) hypergraph and P is a predicate with sufficiently high resiliency and high algebraic immunity, then the function $\mathsf{PRG}_{G,P}$ is a secure pseudorandom generator.

Note that picking an hypergraph G uniformly at random suffices to ensure that it will be expanding with probability $1 - o(1)$. However, picking a random graph will always give a non-negligible probability of having an insecure PRG. To see that, observe that when the locality d is constant, a random hypergraph G will have two hyperedges containing the same vertices with probability $1/\mathsf{poly}(n)$; for any such graph G, the output of $\mathsf{PRG}_{G,P}$ on a random input can be trivially distinguished from random. Therefore, the security of random local functions is usually formulated non-uniformly, by stating that for a $1 - o(1)$ fraction of all hypergraphs G (and appropriate choice of P), no polytime adversary should be able to distinguish the output of $\mathsf{PRG}_{G,P}$ from random with non-negligible probability.

Fixed Hypergraph Versus Random Hypergraphs. Goldreich's candidates local pseudorandom generators require to use a sufficiently expanding hypergraph. Unfortunately, building concrete graphs satisfying the appropriate expansion properties is a non-trivial task. Indeed, all known concrete constructions of expanding bipartite hypergraphs fail to achieve parameters which would allow to construct a PRG with constant locality. Therefore, to our knowledge, in all works using local PRG (see e.g. [IKOS08, App13, Lin17, ADI+17b, BCG+17]), it is always assumed (implicitly or explicitly) that the hypergraph G of the PRG is picked uniformly at random (which makes it sufficiently expanding with probability $1 - o(1)$, even in the constant-locality setting) in a one-time setup phase. Therefore, this is the setting we assume for our cryptanalysis.

Notations. In the first part of this work, we focus on the predicate P_5, assuming that the subsets σ^1, ..., σ^m are random subsets. The predicate P_5 can be regarded as a Boolean function of five variables:

$$P_5(x_1, x_2, x_3, x_4, x_5) = x_1 + x_2 + x_3 + x_4 x_5.$$

The predicate P_5 has algebraic degree 2 and an algebraic immunity of 2, and is 2-resilient. Let n be the size of the input, *i.e.* the number of initial random bits. We define the stretch s and denote the size m of the output as $m = n^{\mathsf{s}}$. Let $x_1, \ldots, x_n \in \mathbb{F}_2$ be the input random bits and $y_1, \ldots, y_m \in \mathbb{F}_2$ be the output bits. The m public equations E_i for $1 \leq i \leq m$ are drawn as follows:

– a subsequence of $[n]$ of size 5 is chosen uniformly at random. Let us call it

$$\sigma^i = [\sigma_1^i, \sigma_2^i, \sigma_3^i, \sigma_4^i, \sigma_5^i].$$

– E_i is the quadratic equation of the form

$$x_{\sigma_1^i} + x_{\sigma_2^i} + x_{\sigma_3^i} + x_{\sigma_4^i} x_{\sigma_5^i} = y_i.$$

The public system Σ that we consider is then defined with the m equations, that is $(E_i)_{1 \leq i \leq m}$.

Ordered and Unordered. There are two different cases to consider:

1. (Ordered case) σ^i is ordered, *i.e.* $\sigma_1^i < \sigma_2^i < \sigma_3^i < \sigma_4^i < \sigma_5^i$.
2. (Unordered case) The order σ^i's elements is arbitrary.

However, in the core of the paper, we will consider the **unordered case**, as we'll provide evidence that the vulnerabilities are even more important for the ordered case in the full version of our paper [CDM+18].

Matrix Inversion Complexity. Our attacks require a sparse matrix inversion algorithm. We consider the Wiedemann's algorithm [Wie86], the complexity of which is $O(n^2)$ in our context, since there are less than $d \cdot n$ non-zero elements of our matrices. Other algorithms could be used, but the complexity of our attacks would have to be modified accordingly.

3 Guess and Determine Cryptanalysis of Goldreich's PRG with P_5

In this section, we describe a new subexponential seed recovery attack on Goldreich's PRG when instantiated within the predicate P_5. Our attack is a *Guess and Determine* like attack, which is a widely used technique in symmetric cryptanalysis [HR00, EJ00]. As an example, a similar attack [DLR16] has been done on the preliminary version of the stream cipher FLIP [MJSC16] (which can be interpreted as an instance of Goldreich's PRG with linear locality and fixed security parameters). The idea of guessing elements before making algebraic analysis has been also introduced in [Bet11] under the name of *hybrid attacks*. In the following, we sketch a similar idea applied to the highly structured Goldreich's PRG.

3.1 Overview of the Attack

Using the above notations, we further make the following observations on Goldreich's PRG instantiated with P_5.

Observations

Quasi-linearity. If either $x_{\sigma_4^i}$ or $x_{\sigma_5^i}$ is known, then the corresponding equation becomes a linear equation. This is the main vulnerability that we use to mount our attack.
Collisions. If two equations have the same monomial of degree 2, then the sum of these equations becomes linear (details are given in Sect. 3.2). Using this phenomenon, we can also get linear equations. We first analyze the number c of pairs of equations that shares a monomial of degree 2. Let the notion of collision refer to this phenomenon.

Definition 5 (Collision). *A collision is a couple $(i, j) \in [m]^2$ such that $i \neq j$ and $\{\sigma_4^i, \sigma_5^i\} = \{\sigma_4^j, \sigma_5^j\}$.*

Combining both observations, a subexponential attack can be derived. The main idea is to find linear equations using collisions and quasi-linearity.

The Attack

step 1. Find all collisions and derive the corresponding linear equations. Let c be the number of linear equations obtained with this step.
step 2. Take a small subset of ℓ variables in $\{x_1, \ldots, x_n\}$, called $x_{i_1}, \ldots, x_{i_\ell}$, such that by guessing them, $n - c$ new equations are generated (ℓ is formally defined in Definition 6).
step 3. For all 2^ℓ possible values of $(x_{i_1}, \ldots, x_{i_\ell})$, build the system of at least n linear equations, solve it[7], find a candidate seed and check if that candidate matches the public evaluation of the PRG. If so, then it is the secret seed and the guess is correct.

Definition 6 (Number of guesses ℓ). *Let an instance of Goldreich's PRG be generated with n variables and m equations. Let c be the number of collisions. Let us define ℓ as a sufficient number of guesses required to build $n - c$ linear equations.*

The above attack works as long as the systems of linear equations obtained in step 2 and 3 above contain an invertible subsystem of size sufficiently large to recover the seed. Our experiments confirm that this is always the case. We formalize this observation with a combinatorial hypothesis: define $\mathcal{D}_n$ to be the distribution over $\mathbb{F}_2^{n \times n}$ obtained by sampling the hypergraph of Goldreich's PRG

[7] If more than n linear equations are recovered from Step 1 and 2, the system is unlikely to be solvable for an incorrect guess. In that case, it is not necessary to check if the public output matches with the candidate seed.

at random (with $d = 5$), finding c linear equations from the collisions, taking the smallest subset of variables which suffices to recover $n' \geq n - c$ additional linear equations, guessing at random the value of these variables, and outputting the $n \times n$ matrix A_n of the linear system (if $n' > n$, we truncate to n equations for simplicity).

Hypothesis 1. *There exists a constant γ such that for every sufficiently large $n \in \mathbb{N}$, the matrix A_n contains with overwhelming probability an invertible subsystem of $\gamma \cdot n$ equations, where the probability is taken over the coins of $A_n \xleftarrow{\$} \mathcal{D}_n$.*

In the full version of this work [CDM+18], we provide a detailed analysis of Hypothesis 1. Specifically:

- By applying the result of [BQ09], which describes a polytime seed recovery attack given an approximate preimage of the PRG, we formally show that Hypothesis 1 implies that our attack succeeds with overwhelming probability.
- We conduct detailed experimentations. In our experiments, the matrix A_n always contains an invertible subsystem of $\gamma \cdot n$ equations, with $\gamma > 0.9$.
- We show that Hypothesis 1 is related to well-established conjectures in mathematics, related to the distribution of the rank of random sparse matrices. Unfortunately, formally proving Hypothesis 1, even under some heuristics (e.g. replacing $\mathcal{D}_n$ by the uniform distribution over sparse matrices), appears to be a highly non-trivial mathematical problem, which requires techniques far out of the scope of the current paper.
- Eventually, we show that our attack can be modified to (provably) break the *pseudorandomness* of Goldreich's PRG, without having to rely on any unproved hypothesis. Hence, Hypothesis 1 seems to be only necessary for showing that our attack breaks the *one-wayness* of Goldreich's PRG.

In the next part, we give more details of our attack and we prove that the complexity of this attack will always be smaller than

$$O(n^2 2^{n^{2-s}}).$$

We later introduce experimental results in Sect. 3.3.

3.2 Complexity Analysis and Details

Assessing the Number of Collisions. As previously noticed, collisions can be used to build linear equations. For example, let us assume we have the following two equations in Σ:

$$x_{\sigma_1^i} + x_{\sigma_2^i} + x_{\sigma_3^i} + x_{\sigma_4^i} x_{\sigma_5^i} = y_i \tag{1}$$

$$x_{\sigma_1^j} + x_{\sigma_2^j} + x_{\sigma_3^j} + x_{\sigma_4^i} x_{\sigma_5^i} = y_j \tag{2}$$

then adding Eqs. (1) and (2) gives us the following linear equation:

$$x_{\sigma_1^i} + x_{\sigma_2^i} + x_{\sigma_3^i} + x_{\sigma_1^j} + x_{\sigma_2^j} + x_{\sigma_3^j} = y_i + y_j$$

However, we stress that if we had a third colliding equation:

$$x_{\sigma_1^k} + x_{\sigma_2^k} + x_{\sigma_3^k} + x_{\sigma_4^i} x_{\sigma_5^i} = y_k \tag{3}$$

then we could only produce a single other linear equation (w.l.o.g. (1) + (3)), since the other combination ((2) + (3)) would be linearly equivalent to the two previous linear equations.

Hence, this problem can be seen as a balls-into-bins problem: m balls are randomly thrown into $\binom{n}{2}$ bins and we want to know how many balls in average hit a bin that already contains at least one ball. Indeed, this number will approximate the value c of the algorithm.

Proposition 1 (Average number of collisions). *Let n be the number of variables, and m be the number of equations, let C be the random variable counting the number of collisions on the degree two monomials in the whole system. Then, the average number of collisions is:*

$$\mathbb{E}(C) = m - \binom{n}{2} + \binom{n}{2}\left(\frac{\binom{n}{2}-1}{\binom{n}{2}}\right)^m \in O(n^{2(s-1)}).$$

The proof of this proposition is given in the full version [CDM+18]. Table 1 gives the evaluation of this formula for some set of parameters. Our experimental results (see Sect. 3.3) corroborate these expectations and show that the number of collisions is always very close to this expected average.

Table 1. Average number of collisions

n	256	512	1024	2048	4096
s = 1.45	142	269	506	946	1771
s = 1.4	83	145	254	442	773
s = 1.3	28	42	64	97	147

We now assess the complexity of the first step.

Lemma 1. *In the worst case, Step 1 has complexity $O(m \cdot \log(m))$.*

The proof is given in the full version of our paper [CDM+18].

Finding the Smallest Subset of Guesses. The dominant term of the complexity of our attack is given by the number of guesses ℓ we have to make in the second step. Thus, minimizing ℓ is important. Consequently, the variables of the seed that we guess correspond to those appearing the most in the monomials of degree two. Then, the worst case happens when the instance of the PRG is such that there is no best set of guesses. In this specific unlikely setting, each guess generates the exact same amount of linear equations. Here, we bound the number of guesses with the minimum number of guesses for a worst case system.

Proposition 2 (Number of guesses). *For any instance with n variables, m equations and c collisions, an upper bound on the sufficient number of guesses required to build n − c linear equations is:*

$$\ell \leq \left\lfloor \frac{n(n-c)}{2(m-c)+n} + 1 \right\rfloor . \tag{4}$$

The proof is given in the full version of our paper [CDM+18]. Eventually, Eq. 4 can be approximated with

$$\left\lfloor \frac{n(n-c)}{2(m-c)+n} + 1 \right\rfloor \simeq O\left(\frac{n^{2-s}}{2}\right). \tag{5}$$

We show further in Sect. 3.3 that experimental results are much better. We stress that this theoretical worst case expectation is far from experience. Some explanations of this gap are given in the full version of our paper.

The complexity of Step 2 is given by the following lemma.

Lemma 2. *Step 2 has complexity $O(\ell \cdot m)$ which is $O(n^2)$ with Eq. 5 estimation.*

The proof is given in the full version of our paper.

Solving the Linear System. Now, ℓ variables $\{x_{i_1}, \ldots, x_{i_\ell}\}$ are chosen to be guessed and an exhaustion over all the 2^ℓ values of these variables is necessary. For every possible guess, one can try to solve the linear equations collected in the previous steps. In the case that more than n equations are collected, the system is overdetermined and thus may not be solvable. If so, then the guess is incorrect, else we obtain a candidate seed. This candidate can be either confirmed or rejected using the public quadratic system and the public output of the PRG. If the candidate is rejected, then the guess is also incorrect. However, if the candidate matches the public evaluation of the PRG, then the candidate seed is the secret seed with overwhelming probability[8] and the search can be stopped.

The complexity of this attack is given by the following lemma.

Lemma 3. *The complexity of Step 3 is*

$$O\left(n^\omega 2^{\frac{n^{2-s}}{2}}\right),$$

which is also the asymptotic complexity of the full attack.

The proof is given in the full version of our paper [CDM+18].

3.3 Experiment

Distribution of the Number of Collisions. The theoretical results of Table 1 are verified in practice, as shown in Fig. 1 for the particular case of $n = 1024$ and $s = 1.4$. As expected with the analytical formula, the number of collisions is very close to 254 in average. Moreover, our experimental results are very dense around the average, suggesting that the distribution has a low variance.

---

[8] It is very unlikely that two seeds give the same output by evaluating the same quadratic system. Even though, if it is the case, this procedure still finds an equivalent seed which makes the system insecure.

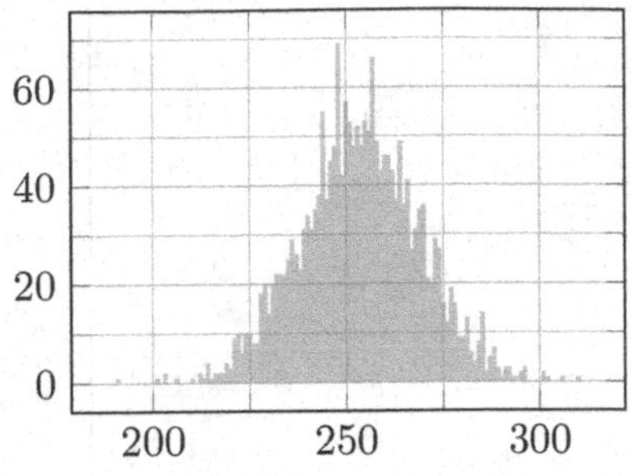

Fig. 1. Number of collisions for $n = 1024$ and $s = 1.4$ with 2000 tests

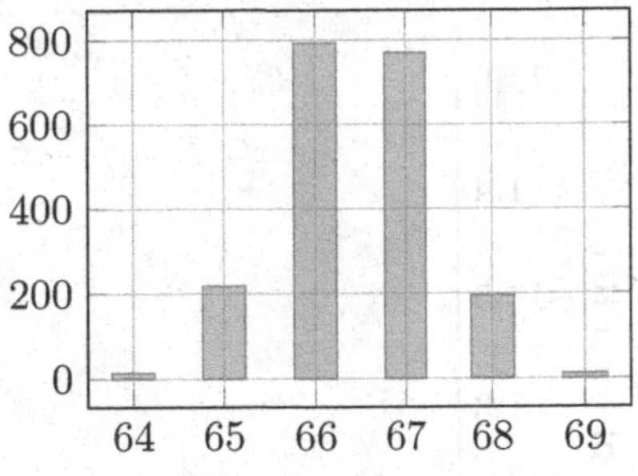

Fig. 2. Number of guesses for $n = 2048$ and $s = 1.3$ with 2000 tests

Table 2. Theoretical number of guesses in the worst case

n	256	512	1024	2048	4096
$\mathsf{s} = 1.45$	4	6	9	14	21
$\mathsf{s} = 1.4$	6	11	17	27	44
$\mathsf{s} = 1.3$	13	23	39	65	110

Table 3. Experimental number of guesses in average

n	256	512	1024	2048	4096
$\mathsf{s} = 1.45$	4	6	9	14	21
$\mathsf{s} = 1.4$	6	11	17	27	44
$\mathsf{s} = 1.3$	13	23	39	65	110

Implementation of the Attack. Since the study of this paper is the concrete security of Goldreich's PRG, it is important to practically check if the attack presented in Sect. 3.1 can be efficient when implemented. For this purpose, we provide a proof of concept in Python.

One can note that the practical attack should be on average more efficient than assessed theoretically. Indeed, the asymptotic complexity of Proposition 3 is estimated in the worst case and pessimistic approximations were made on $n - c$ and on the value of ℓ. Hence, we experimented this attack for different stretches and different values of n and we effectively noticed that the complexity in average is much smaller than the expected complexity. Table 2 represents the theoretical number of guesses necessary to recover the seed and Table 3 represents the average number of guesses actually needed in the experiment. Moreover, we also noticed that the number of guesses needed to invert the system has a very low variance, as shown in Fig. 2.

With this experiment, we were able to estimate the practical security of Goldreich's PRG against the guess and determine approach with 80 bits of security. Indeed, for one instance of the PRG, the complexity of the seed recovery can be easily derived from the number ℓ of guesses as $2^{\ell} n^{\omega}$. So to assess the 80 bits security, one can evaluate the average number of guesses necessary for one choice of (n, s) and check if the complexity is lower than 2^{80}. For that, for 30 values of $n \in [2^7, 2^{14}]$, we delimited the smallest stretch for which the average number of guesses allows a 80 bits attack. Each average has been done on 1000

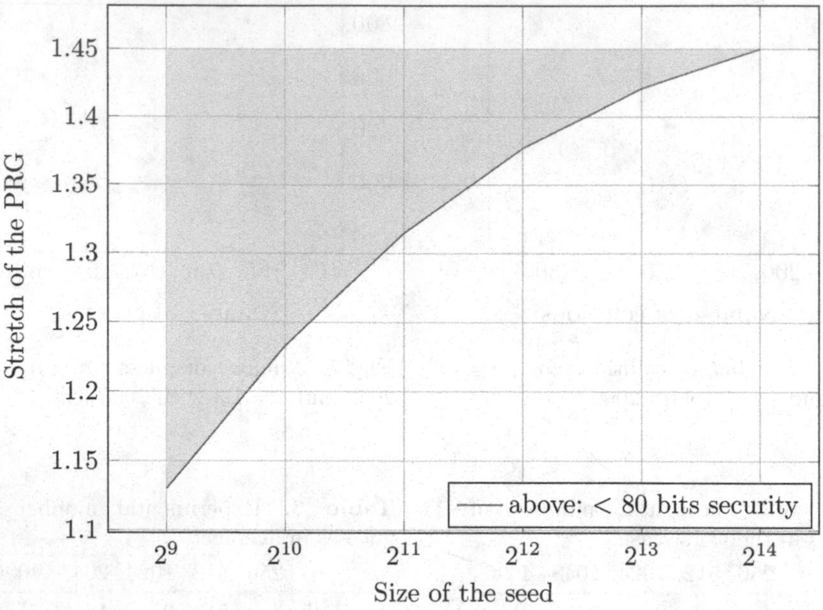

Fig. 3. Limit stretch for vulnerable instances. The gray zone above the curve denotes the insecure choices of parameters.

measurements because the variance was very small. Figure 3 represents the limit on vulnerable (n, s) parameters. Above the line, the parameters are on average insecure against the guess and determine attack.

Candidate Non-vulnerable Parameters. We were able to estimate the practical range of parameters that appear to resist to this attack. To assess them, we estimated the number of guesses necessary and deduced the bit security. With many measurements (1024 for each set of parameters), we could find the limit stretch for parameters that are, not vulnerable to our attack. The couples (n, s) that possess the maximal s with an expected security of 80 or 128 bits[9] are conjectured to be the limit for non vulnerable parameters. These couples[10] are represented by the two lines in Fig. 4.

We also introduce certain parameters in Table 4 as challenges for improving the cryptanalysis of Goldreich's PRG. These parameters correspond to choices of the seed size and the stretch which cannot be broken in less than 2^{80} (resp. 2^{128}) operations with the attacks of this paper. Further study is required to assess confidence in the security level given by these parameters.

[9] We actually took a margin of 10% to take into account the possible improvements of our implementation.

[10] This curve should not be extrapolated because outside of its range, Gröbner attacks seem more powerful, see Fig. 5.

Table 4. Challenge parameters for seed recovery attacks. The first line contains the parameter n and below are represented the associated stretches s.

Elementary operations	512	1024	2048	4096
$<2^{80}$	1.120	1.215	1.296	1.361
$<2^{128}$	1.048	1.135	1.222	1.295

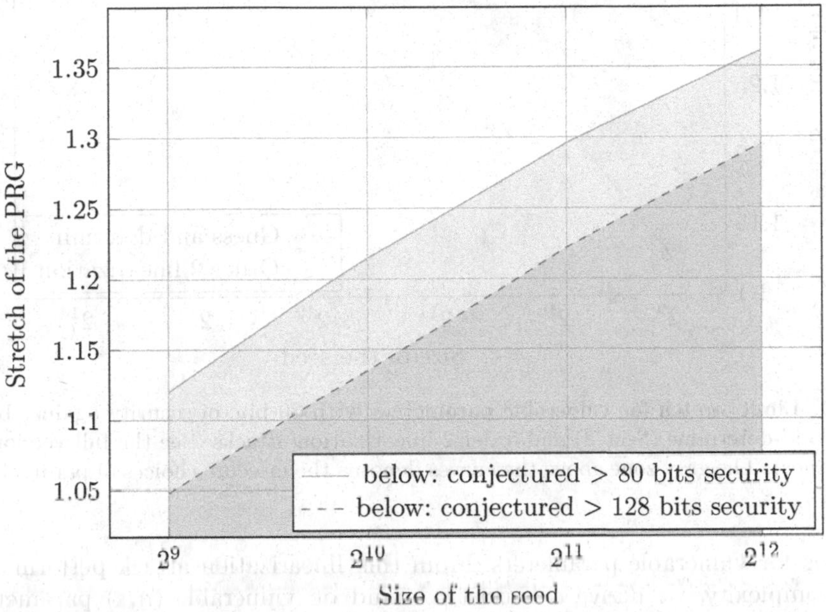

Fig. 4. Limit stretch for conjectured non vulnerable instances.

3.4 Other Algebraic Cryptanalysis

To complement this attack, we also made an analysis of the efficiency of algebraic attacks with Gröbner basis on Goldreich's PRG. While it is known that Goldreich's PRG (and its variants) provably resists such attacks for appropriate choices of (asymptotic) parameters ([AL16], Theorem 5.5), little is known about its exact security against such attacks for concrete choices of parameters.

Since Goldreich's PRG is far from a Boolean random quadratic system, the performance of a Gröbner basis strategy is hard to assess with the existing theory. In order to give an intuition on how Gröbner basis algorithms would behave on Goldreich's PRG with predicate P_5, we provide in the full version of our paper [CDM+18] an easy-to-understand order two linearization attack. This polynomial attack leads to a practical seed recovery for certain parameters (n, s) and we derive a heuristic bound for vulnerable (n, s) for 80 bits of security. The existence of such an attack allows to estimate bounds on Gröbner basis performance. Using an implemented proof of concept, we introduce heuristic

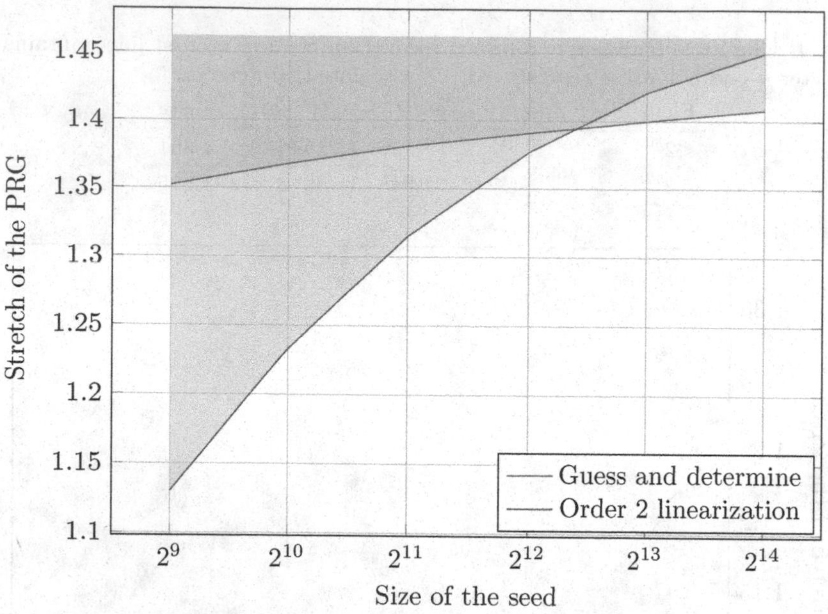

Fig. 5. Limit stretch for vulnerable parameters with 80 bits of security against both guess and determine (Sect. 3) and order 2 linearization attacks (See the full version of our paper). The gray zone above the curves denotes the insecure choices of parameters.

bounds for vulnerable parameters. From this linearization attack performance and complexity, we derive a heuristic bound on vulnerable (n, s) parameters against a Gröbner basis technique. We refer the reader to the full version of our paper for the complete analysis.

3.5 Conclusion

We described in this section a guess and determine attack against Goldreich's PRG. In the full version of our paper, we complement this result with an analysis of the security of Goldreich's PRG against an order 2 linearization attack (*à la* Gröbner). We represent on Fig. 5 the range of parameters for which Goldreich's PRG is conjectured to have 80 bits of security against those two attacks. As illustrated on the graph, the guess and determine approach targets more parameters for low n while the linearization attack performs better for $n > 4000$. Although Goldreich's PRG is conjectured to be theoretically secure for a stretch approaching 1.5 by an arbitrary constant, our analysis shows that a very large seed must be used to achieve at least 80 bits of security with such stretch. In particular, if a stretch of 1.4 is needed, no seed smaller than 5120 bits should be used. Similarly, for a stretch as small as 1.1, the seed must be at least 512 bits long.

4 Generic Attacks Against Goldreich's PRG

Beyond the predicate P_5 we investigate the security of other predicates for higher stretches, and show that the considered criteria are not sufficient to determine the security. In the full version of our paper, we prove that the number of independent annihilators of the predicate has to be taken into account. Hence, the algebraic immunity is not enough, as we provide a new bound on the stretch that refines the theorem of Applebaum and Lovett. On the other side, we provide in this section an improvement of the *guess and determine* technique, combined with an algebraic attack. This generalization can be seen as an hybrid attack as defined in [Bet11].

4.1 A Subexponential-Time Algorithm

The theorem of Applebaum and Lovett for polynomial-time algorithms regarding algebraic attacks can be improved, as shown in the full version of our paper. In this section, we focus on subexponential-time algorithms. The idea here is to generalize our initial attack of Sect. 3 against the PRG instantiated with the predicate P_5, to all other considered predicates. Therefore we generalize the attack to all $\mathsf{XOR}_\ell\mathsf{M}_k$ predicates and then more particularly to the $\mathsf{XOR}_\ell\mathsf{MAJ}_k$ predicates.

The Principle. Let n be the size of the seed of the PRG with stretch s, and let P be a predicate with locality d. The general idea is to guess r variables of the seed, and solve the corresponding system of equations for each possible value of those r bits. For each equation obtained, an equation of smaller or equal degree can be derived using the principle of the algebraic immunity. Then, the complexity of the attack mainly depends on the values of r and the algebraic immunity of the functions we obtain. It corresponds to the general principle of algebraic attacks with guess and determine [MJSC16], for which we can affine the complexity in the particular case of $\mathsf{XOR}_\ell\mathsf{M}_k$ predicates. We begin by considering the complexity of an attack targeting the degree of the M predicate after guessing some bits, based on the following remark:

Remark 1. As soon as $k-1$ variables among the k variables of M are fixed, a linear equation can be found, as the output of M depends on only one variable and as XOR_ℓ is linear.

The Attack. Our sub-exponential time algorithm works as follows:

step 1. Fix r variables of the seed $(x_{i_1}, \dots, x_{i_r})$, with $r \in O\left(n^{\frac{k-s}{k-1}}\right)$.
step 2. For all 2^r possible values of $x_{i_1}, \dots, x_{i_r}$, recover the corresponding linear system of equations.
step 3. Solve the system in $(n-r)^\omega$ operations; if there is a contradiction go back to step 2, otherwise add the solution to the list.
step 4. Return the list of solutions.

This attack works as long as the system of linear equations obtained in step 3 above contains an invertible subsystem of size sufficiently large to recover the seed. We then apply Hypothesis 1 with A_n being the linear system obtained by guessing at random the 2^r possible values of $x_{i_1}, \ldots, x_{i_r}$.

Complexity Analysis. The complexity is dominated by Step 3, as we repeat this step 2^r times (we have to solve a system of linear equations of size $n - r$ for each possible values of the r bits), the complexity of this algorithm is sub-exponential: $O(n^\omega 2^r)$. Eventually, the final complexity is determined by the following proposition:

Proposition 3. *For an overwhelming proportion of Goldreich's* PRG *instantiated with a* $\mathsf{XOR}_\ell\mathsf{M}_k$ *predicate, under Hypothesis 1 on step 2 system, the complexity order of the previous algorithm can be approximated by:*

$$2^{n^{\frac{k-s}{k-1}}} \cdot n^\omega.$$

The proof is given in the full version of our paper.

Remark 2. It is important to notice that the parameter of this attack does not rely directly on the locality, but only on the number k of variables that appear in the nonlinear part M, hence, it improves the complexity of [BQ09]. Indeed, the generic complexity of Bogdanov and Qiao is roughly $O(2^{n^{1-(s-1)/2d}})$ where d denotes the locality, as our algorithm has a complexity that is in $O\left(n^\omega \cdot 2^{n^{1-(s-1)/(k-1)}}\right)$, with $k - 1 < d$, by definition of k.

Moreover, the predicate requires a high resiliency to avoid linear attacks, and one of the most natural constructions to build a resilient function is to add an independent linear part to a function. It corresponds to the $\mathsf{XOR}_\ell\mathsf{M}_k$ predicates, which have a resiliency of at least $\ell - 1$ given by the xor part. It is also possible to build resilient functions differently, which seems to be a better choice regarding this attack. For the case of P_5, we have $k = 2$, that gives us an attack in $O(n^\omega 2^{n^{2-s}})$.

Possible Improvement. This algorithm only relies on the number of variables of the non-linear part, but not on its algebraic immunity. Instead of fixing variables in order to obtain linear equations in the non-linear part of a $\mathsf{XOR}_\ell\mathsf{M}_k$ predicate, an attacker can fix variables in order to recover equations of degree greater than 1. Indeed, using the algebraic immunity of the M predicate, the attacker can recover such equations by fixing less than k bits in the M part. By doing so, it appears that the relevant criterion regarding this attack is no longer the algebraic immunity, neither the r-bit fixing degree defined in [AL16], but a generalization of the two. The efficiency of the attack will depend on the algebraic immunity of the predicates obtained after doing some guesses, and on the probability of getting predicates (in fewer variables) with this algebraic immunity (or smaller). A lower bound on the algebraic immunity that can be obtained with r guesses is given by the r-bit fixing algebraic immunity (introduced first in term of recurrent algebraic immunity in [MJSC16] to bound the complexity of algebraic attacks combined with guess and determine) defined in the following sense:

Definition 7 *(r-bit fixing algebraic immunity). Let f be a Boolean function with d variables. For any $0 \leq r \leq d$, and $b = (b_1, \dots, b_r) \in \{0,1\}^r$, $i = (i_1, \dots, i_r) \in [d]^r$ such that $i_1 < i_2 < \cdots < i_r$, we note $f_{(b,i)}$ the restriction of f where the r variables indexed by $i_1, \dots, i_r$ are fixed to the value $b_1, \dots, b_r$. Then f has r-bit fixing algebraic immunity a if*

$$\min\left(\mathsf{AI}(f_{(b,i)}) : i = (i_1, \dots, i_r) \in [d]^r,\, i_1 < i_2 < \cdots < i_r,\, b \in \{0,1\}^r\right) = a$$

where AI denotes the algebraic immunity.

For the case of $\mathsf{XOR}_\ell\mathsf{M}_k$ predicates we prove in the full version of our paper [CDM+18] an upper bound on the r-bit fixing algebraic immunity. Thereafter, determining the number of predicates with this algebraic immunity that could be reached guessing r variables will lead to other sub-exponential time algorithms. The description and analysis of this algorithm applied on $\mathsf{XOR}_\ell\mathsf{M}_k$ predicates is given in the full version of our paper. However, this algorithm only generalizes the result given by the first algorithm as it considers systems of equations of degree greater than one. But it does not assume any property on the M predicate, and leads to consider the maximum algebraic immunity that can be provided by this part when some variables are fixed. Considering the principle of the r-bit fixing algebraic immunity, we can try to find guesses which lower this algebraic immunity, leading to an attack with even better complexity.

In the following, we show on the XOR-MAJ predicates how only taking into account specific values of guessed bits (but changing the positions that we guess) enables to target a low algebraic immunity with enough equations.

Application to XOR-MAJ Predicates. In the previous algorithms, we fix r bits that never change, but we test all possible values for those bits. However, it might be of interest to change the bits that we guess, by taking into account a specific value for those bits, such that we decrease more drastically the degree of the equations that we get. Using the notations of Definition 7, it boils down to finding values of $b \in \{0,1\}^r$ such that $\mathsf{AI}(f_{(i,b)})$ is low for enough i.

Let us consider the $\mathsf{XOR}_\ell\mathsf{MAJ}_k$ predicate (Definition 3), then our initial algorithm breaks the construction with complexity $O(n^\omega 2^{n^{(k-s)/(k-1)}})$, and its generalization with complexity $O\left(2^{n^{\frac{1+j-s+\lceil (k-j)/2\rceil}{j}}} n^{\omega(\lceil \frac{k-j}{2}\rceil+1)}\right)$ for all integer j such that $1 \leq j \leq k$. Moreover, this algorithm is an improvement only for bigger stretches. In the following, we change the way we make our guesses, in order to capture how the r-bit fixing algebraic immunity is a relevant criterion.

In these algorithms, one can notice that fixing j bits among the k variables that appear in the majority function can derive different degrees of equations, depending on the value of the bits that are guessed: fixing $\lceil \frac{k}{2} \rceil$ bits all to 0 (or all to 1) will derive directly linear equations. Indeed, for the majority function, if strictly more than half of the bits are supposed to be all zero, then the corresponding output has to be 0 by definition of the majority, and respectively 1 if all these bits are ones. On the other side, fixing a quarter of bits to be ones and a quarter of bits to be zero will derive an other majority function taken other half of the bits, which is clearly non-linear for k big enough.

Hence, instead of fixing r bits and guess all possible values of those bits, we choose r bits, guessing that all those bits are all one or all zero, and repeat this until the guess is right (the position of the r guessed variables changes, not the value). This particular guess-and-determine is exactly what Duval, Lallemand and Rotella investigated in [DLR16] on the FLIP family of stream ciphers (and which complexity can be bounded through the r-bit fixing algebraic immunity, [MJSC16] Sect. 3.4).

Description of the Algorithm

step 1. Fix randomly r variables of the seed $(x_{i_1}, \ldots, x_{i_r})$.
step 2. Assume that all of them are equal to zero, solve the corresponding linear system, add the solution to the list.
step 3. Assume that all the r variables are equal to one, solve the corresponding linear system, add the solution to the list.
step 4. If in the solution list there is one with no contradiction with the PRG output, output the solution as the seed. Otherwise, empty the list and go back to Step 1.

As for the first algorithm, we assume that Hypothesis 1 is verified with A_n representing the linear systems of Step 2 and 3.

Complexity Analysis. The complexity is dominated by the number of repetition of Step 2 and Step 3, we determine it through the following proposition:

Proposition 4. *For an overwhelming proportion of Goldreich's* PRG *instantiated with a* $\mathsf{XOR}_\ell\mathsf{MAJ}_k$ *predicate, under Hypothesis 1 for Step 2 and 3 systems, the seed can be recovered in time complexity of order:*

$$n^\omega 2^{n^{1-\frac{s-1}{\lceil \frac{k}{2} \rceil + 1}}}.$$

The proof is given in the full version of our paper.

This algorithm captures something else than the previous ones, as it shows that one has to consider all possible choices of guesses in order to evaluate exactly the security of such constructions. In other words, it shows that the r-bit fixing algebraic immunity is exactly the relevant criterion to resist our attack, as it defines the smallest algebraic immunity that can be considered for an attack. However, one must also take the probability that a corresponding guess happens on the equations into account. Hence there exists a trade-off between the choice of the good guesses, and the probability that the corresponding equation of small degree can be derived.

4.2 Open Questions

The attacks and their variants described here asked lot of open questions. For the polynomial time algorithm using the number of linearly independent annihilators, we do not take into account some dependencies into different equations as explained in the full version of our paper [CDM+18]. Hence, the condition on the stretch that we gave could be improved by considering dependencies on the subsets.

For the subexponential-time attack that uses the r bit fixing algebraic immunity, we do not know if the bound given in the full version of our paper is tight, that is if there exist predicates, such that fixing any bits will still derive Boolean functions with fewer variables that reach the maximal algebraic immunity. In other words, is it possible to have a perfect predicate regarding the r bit fixing algebraic immunity? Recalling that it is the relevant criterion in this context.

Moreover, this bound does not depend on the value of the bits that are guessed, whereas this might have an influence, as shown on the XOR-MAJ predicate. For example, the Boolean function $x_0 + x_1x_2x_3x_4$ is of algebraic immunity 2, but fixing x_1 to be 1 will derive a Boolean function that is still of algebraic immunity 2, but fixing $x_1 = 0$ will bring directly an equation of degree 1. Hence, all choices of guess are not equivalent, implying that different choices of guesses could improve the complexity of our subexponential-time algorithm, depending strongly on the predicate.

Last but not least, how the first idea of using different annihilators can improve the subexponential-time algorithms using guess and determine?

Acknowledgments. We thank Jean-Pierre Tillich and Benny Applebaum for useful discussions and observations. We also are indebted to Guénaël Renault for fruitful discussions about Gröbner basis approaches, and to the reviewers of ASIACRYPT for their useful comments. This research has been partially funded by ANRT under the programs CIFRE N 2015/1158 and 2016/1583. We acknowledge the support of the French Programme d'Investissement d'Avenir under national project RISQ P141580. The first author was supported by ERC grant 724307 (project PREP-CRYPTO). The fifth author was partially supported by the French Agence Nationale de la Recherche through the BRUTUS project under Contract ANR-14-CE28-0015.

References

[ABR12] Applebaum, B., Bogdanov, A., Rosen, A.: A dichotomy for local small-bias generators. In: Cramer, R. (ed.) TCC 2012. LNCS, vol. 7194, pp. 600–617. Springer, Heidelberg (2012). https://doi.org/10.1007/978-3-642-28914-9_34

[ABR16] Applebaum, B., Bogdanov, A., Rosen, A.: A dichotomy for local small-bias generators. J. Cryptol. **29**(3), 577–596 (2016)

[ADI+17a] Applebaum, B., Damgård, I., Ishai, Y., Nielsen, M., Zichron, L.: Secure arithmetic computation with constant computational overhead. Cryptology ePrint Archive, Report 2017/617 (2017). http://eprint.iacr.org/2017/617

[ADI+17b] Applebaum, B., Damgård, I., Ishai, Y., Nielsen, M., Zichron, L.: Secure arithmetic computation with constant computational overhead. In: Katz, J., Shacham, H. (eds.) CRYPTO 2017. LNCS, vol. 10401, pp. 223–254. Springer, Cham (2017). https://doi.org/10.1007/978-3-319-63688-7_8

[AHI05] Alekhnovich, M., Hirsch, E.A., Itsykson, D.: Exponential lower bounds for the running time of DPLL algorithms on satisfiable formulas. J. Autom. Reason. **35**(1–3), 51–72 (2005)

[AIK04] Applebaum, B., Ishai, Y., Kushilevitz, E.: Cryptography in NC^0. In: 45th FOCS, pp. 166–175. IEEE Computer Society Press, October 2004

[AIK08] Applebaum, B., Ishai, Y., Kushilevitz, E.: On pseudorandom generators with linear stretch in NC^0. Comput. Complex. **17**(1), 38–69 (2008)

[AL16] Applebaum, B., Lovett, S.: Algebraic attacks against random local functions and their countermeasures. In: 48th ACM STOC, pp. 1087–1100. ACM Press, June 2016

[App12] Applebaum, B.: Pseudorandom generators with long stretch and low locality from random local one-way functions. In: 44th ACM STOC, pp. 805–816. ACM Press, May 2012

[App13] Applebaum, B.: Pseudorandom generators with long stretch and low locality from random local one-way functions. SIAM J. Comput. **42**(5), 2008–2037 (2013)

[App15] Applebaum, B.: The cryptographic hardness of random local functions - survey. Cryptology ePrint Archive, Report 2015/165 (2015). http://eprint.iacr.org/2015/165

[ARS+15] Albrecht, M.R., Rechberger, C., Schneider, T., Tiessen, T., Zohner, M.: Ciphers for MPC and FHE. In: Oswald, E., Fischlin, M. (eds.) EUROCRYPT 2015, Part I. LNCS, vol. 9056, pp. 430–454. Springer, Heidelberg (2015). https://doi.org/10.1007/978-3-662-46800-5_17

[BCG+17] Boyle, E., Couteau, G., Gilboa, N., Ishai, Y., Orrù, M.: Homomorphic secret sharing: optimizations and applications. In: ACM CCS 2017, pp. 2105–2122. ACM Press (2017)

[Bet11] Bettale, L.: Cryptanalyse algebrique: outils et applications, Ph.D. thesis (2011)

[BGI+01] Barak, B., et al.: On the (Im)possibility of obfuscating programs. In: Kilian, J. (ed.) CRYPTO 2001. LNCS, vol. 2139, pp. 1–18. Springer, Heidelberg (2001). https://doi.org/10.1007/3-540-44647-8_1

[BQ09] Bogdanov, A., Qiao, Y.: On the security of Goldreich's one-way function. In: Dinur, I., Jansen, K., Naor, J., Rolim, J. (eds.) APPROX/RANDOM -2009. LNCS, vol. 5687, pp. 392–405. Springer, Heidelberg (2009). https://doi.org/10.1007/978-3-642-03685-9_30

[CCF+16] Canteaut, A., et al.: Stream ciphers: a practical solution for efficient homomorphic-ciphertext compression. In: Peyrin, T. (ed.) FSE 2016. LNCS, vol. 9783, pp. 313–333. Springer, Heidelberg (2016). https://doi.org/10.1007/978-3-662-52993-5_16

[CDM+18] Couteau, G., Dupin, A., Méaux, P., Rossi, M., Rotella, Y.: On the concrete security of Goldreich's pseudorandom generator (2018)

[CEMT14] Cook, J., Etesami, O., Miller, R., Trevisan, L.: On the one-way function candidate proposed by Goldreich. ACM Trans. Comput. Theor. (TOCT) **6**(3), 14 (2014)

[CM01] Cryan, M., Miltersen, P.B.: On pseudorandom generators in NC^0. In: Sgall, J., Pultr, A., Kolman, P. (eds.) MFCS 2001. LNCS, vol. 2136, pp. 272–284. Springer, Heidelberg (2001). https://doi.org/10.1007/3-540-44683-4_24

[CM03] Courtois, N.T., Meier, W.: Algebraic attacks on stream ciphers with linear feedback. In: Biham, E. (ed.) EUROCRYPT 2003. LNCS, vol. 2656, pp. 345–359. Springer, Heidelberg (2003). https://doi.org/10.1007/3-540-39200-9_21

[Cou03] Courtois, N.T.: Fast algebraic attacks on stream ciphers with linear feedback. In: Boneh, D. (ed.) CRYPTO 2003. LNCS, vol. 2729, pp. 176–194. Springer, Heidelberg (2003). https://doi.org/10.1007/978-3-540-45146-4_11

[DGM05] Dalai, D.K., Gupta, K.C., Maitra, S.: Cryptographically significant boolean functions: construction and analysis in terms of algebraic immunity. In: Gilbert, H., Handschuh, H. (eds.) FSE 2005. LNCS, vol. 3557, pp. 98–111. Springer, Heidelberg (2005). https://doi.org/10.1007/11502760_7

[DLR16] Duval, S., Lallemand, V., Rotella, Y.: Cryptanalysis of the FLIP family of stream ciphers. In: Robshaw, M., Katz, J. (eds.) CRYPTO 2016. LNCS, vol. 9814, pp. 457–475. Springer, Heidelberg (2016). https://doi.org/10.1007/978-3-662-53018-4_17

[DMS05] Dalai, D.K., Maitra, S., Sarkar, S.: Basic theory in construction of Boolean functions with maximum possible annihilator immunity. Cryptology ePrint Archive, Report 2005/229 (2005). http://eprint.iacr.org/2005/229

[EJ00] Ekdahl, P., Johansson, T.: SNOW - a new stream cipher. In: Proceedings of First NESSIE Workshop, Heverlee (2000)

[GGM84] Goldreich, O., Goldwasser, S., Micali, S.: How to construct random functions (extended abstract). In: 25th FOCS, pp. 464–479. IEEE Computer Society Press, October 1984

[Gol00] Goldreich, O.: Candidate one-way functions based on expander graphs. Cryptology ePrint Archive, Report 2000/063 (2000). http://eprint.iacr.org/2000/063

[GRR+16] Grassi, L., Rechberger, C., Rotaru, D., Scholl, P., Smart, N.P.: MPC-friendly symmetric key primitives. In: ACM CCS 2016, pp. 430–443. ACM Press, October 2016

[HR00] Hawkes, P., Rose, G.G.: Exploiting multiples of the connection polynomial in word-oriented stream ciphers. In: Okamoto, T. (ed.) ASIACRYPT 2000. LNCS, vol. 1976, pp. 303–316. Springer, Heidelberg (2000). https://doi.org/10.1007/3-540-44448-3_23

[IKOS08] Ishai, Y., Kushilevitz, E., Ostrovsky, R., Sahai, A.: Cryptography with constant computational overhead. In: 40th ACM STOC, pp. 433–442. ACM Press, May 2008

[IPS08] Ishai, Y., Prabhakaran, M., Sahai, A.: Secure arithmetic computation with no honest majority. Cryptology ePrint Archive, Report 2008/465 (2008)

[Lin17] Lin, H.: Indistinguishability obfuscation from SXDH on 5-linear maps and locality-5 PRGs. In: Katz, J., Shacham, H. (eds.) CRYPTO 2017, Part I. LNCS, vol. 10401, pp. 599–629. Springer, Cham (2017). https://doi.org/10.1007/978-3-319-63688-7_20

[LT17] Lin, H., Tessaro, S.: Indistinguishability obfuscation from trilinear maps and block-wise local PRGs. In: Katz, J., Shacham, H. (eds.) CRYPTO 2017, Part I. LNCS, vol. 10401, pp. 630–660. Springer, Cham (2017). https://doi.org/10.1007/978-3-319-63688-7_21

[LV17] Lombardi, A., Vaikuntanathan, V.: Limits on the locality of pseudorandom generators and applications to indistinguishability obfuscation. In: Kalai, Y., Reyzin, L. (eds.) TCC 2017, Part I. LNCS, vol. 10677, pp. 119–137. Springer, Cham (2017). https://doi.org/10.1007/978-3-319-70500-2_5

[MJSC16] Méaux, P., Journault, A., Standaert, F.-X., Carlet, C.: Towards stream ciphers for efficient FHE with low-noise ciphertexts. In: Fischlin, M., Coron, J.-S. (eds.) EUROCRYPT 2016, Part I. LNCS, vol. 9665, pp. 311–343. Springer, Heidelberg (2016). https://doi.org/10.1007/978-3-662-49890-3_13

[MST03] Mossel, E., Shpilka, A., Trevisan, L.: On e-Biased generators in NC0. In: 44th FOCS, pp. 136–145. IEEE Computer Society Press, October 2003

[OW14] ODonnell, R., Witmer, D.: Goldreich's PRG: evidence for near-optimal polynomial stretch. In: IEEE 29th Conference on Computational Complexity (CCC), pp. 1–12. IEEE (2014)

[Sie84] Siegenthaler, T.: Correlation-immunity of nonlinear combining functions for cryptographic applications (corresp.). IEEE Trans. Inf. Theor. **30**(5), 776–780 (1984)

[SW14] Sahai, A., Waters, B.: How to use indistinguishability obfuscation: deniable encryption, and more. In: 46th ACM STOC, pp. 475–484. ACM Press, May/June 2014

[Wie86] Wiedemann, D.: Solving sparse linear equations over finite fields. IEEE Trans. Inf. Theor. **32**(1), 54–62 (1986)

Public Key and Identity-Based Encryption

A Framework for Achieving KDM-CCA Secure Public-Key Encryption

Fuyuki Kitagawa(✉) and Keisuke Tanaka(✉)

Tokyo Institute of Technology, Tokyo, Japan
{kitagaw1,keisuke}@is.titech.ac.jp

Abstract. We propose a framework for achieving a public-key encryption (PKE) scheme that satisfies key dependent message security against chosen ciphertext attacks (KDM-CCA security) based on projective hash function. Our framework can be instantiated under the decisional diffie-hellman (DDH), quadratic residuosity (QR), and decisional composite residuosity (DCR) assumptions. The constructed schemes are KDM-CCA secure with respect to affine functions and compatible with the amplification method shown by Applebaum (EUROCRYPT 2011). Thus, they lead to PKE schemes satisfying KDM-CCA security for all functions computable by a-priori bounded size circuits. They are the first PKE schemes satisfying such a security notion in the standard model using neither non-interactive zero knowledge proof nor bilinear pairing. The above framework based on projective hash function captures only KDM-CCA security in the single user setting. However, we can prove the KDM-CCA security in the multi user setting of our concrete instantiations by using their algebraic structures explicitly. Especially, we prove that our DDH based scheme satisfies KDM-CCA security in the multi user setting with the same parameter setting as in the single user setting.

Keywords: Key dependent message security
Chosen ciphertext security · Projective hash function

1 Introduction

1.1 Backgrounds

Key dependent message (KDM) security, introduced by Black, Rogaway and Shrimpton [3], guarantees confidentiality of communication even if an adversary can get a ciphertext of secret keys. KDM security is useful for many practical applications including anonymous credential systems [7] and hard disk encryption systems (e.g., BitLocker [4]). KDM security is defined with respect to a function family $\mathcal{F}$. Let n denote the number of keys and $\mathbf{sk} = (\mathsf{sk}_1, \cdots, \mathsf{sk}_n)$ be secret keys. Informally, a PKE scheme is said to be $\mathcal{F}$-KDM secure if confidentiality of messages is protected even when an adversary can see a ciphertext of $f(\mathbf{sk})$ under the k-th public key for any $f \in \mathcal{F}$ and $k \in \{1, \cdots, n\}$. In this

T. Peyrin and S. Galbraith (Eds.): ASIACRYPT 2018, LNCS 11273, pp. 127–157, 2018.
https://doi.org/10.1007/978-3-030-03329-3_5

paper, we focus on constructing PKE schemes that satisfy KDM security against chosen ciphertext attacks, namely *KDM-CCA* security in the standard model.

Camenisch, Chandran and Shoup [6] proposed the first KDM-CCA secure PKE based on the Naor-Yung paradigm [16]. They showed that for any function class $\mathcal{F}$, $\mathcal{F}$-KDM-CPA secure PKE can be transformed into $\mathcal{F}$-KDM-CCA secure one assuming non-interactive zero knowledge (NIZK) proof. They also showed a concrete instantiation based on the decisional diffie-hellman (DDH) assumption on a bilinear pairing. Subsequently, Hofheinz [10] showed more efficient KDM-CCA secure PKE. His scheme is circular secure (KDM-CCA secure with respect to selection functions) relying on both the DDH and decisional composite residuosity (DCR) assumptions on a bilinear pairing.

The first KDM-CCA secure PKE using neither NIZK proof nor bilinear pairing was proposed by Lu, Li and Jia [14]. They claimed their scheme is KDM-CCA secure with respect to affine functions ($\mathcal{F}_{\mathsf{aff}}$-KDM-CCA secure) relying on both the DDH and DCR assumptions. However, a flow on their security proof was later discovered by Han, Liu and Lyu [9]. Han et al. also showed a new $\mathcal{F}_{\mathsf{aff}}$-KDM-CCA secure PKE scheme based on the construction methodology of Lu et al. In addition, they constructed KDM-CCA secure PKE with respect to bounded degree polynomial functions. Their schemes are efficient and secure relying on both the DDH and DCR assumptions.

Despite the above previous efforts, it is still open whether we can construct KDM-CCA secure PKE based on a single computational assumption using neither NIZK proof nor bilinear pairing. All existing KDM-CCA secure PKE schemes without NIZK proof were proved to be secure relying on both the DDH and DCR assumptions. These schemes are proposed based on a specific algebraic structure and it is crucial to assume the hardness of both the DDH and DCR problems on the specific algebraic structure. Thus, it seems difficult to construct KDM-CCA secure PKE based on a single computational assumption using their techniques.

Moreover, it is also an open question whether we can construct KDM-CCA secure PKE with respect to all functions computable by bounded size circuits ($\mathcal{F}_{\mathsf{all}}$-KDM-CCA secure) using neither NIZK proof nor bilinear pairing. The only existing way to construct $\mathcal{F}_{\mathsf{all}}$-KDM-CCA secure PKE is to utilize the amplification method shown by Applebaum [2]. Applebaum showed if a PKE scheme is KDM-CCA secure with respect to projection functions, we can transform it into a $\mathcal{F}_{\mathsf{all}}$-KDM-CCA secure one, where projection function is a function whose each output bit depends on only a single bit of an input. Kitagawa, Matsuda, Hanaoka and Tanaka [12] later showed we can perform such a transformation even if the underlying PKE is only KDM-CCA secure with respect to projection functions whose output is one bit.

Among existing KDM-CCA secure schemes, only Camenisch et al.'s scheme is compatible with those transformations. Thus, a construction of $\mathcal{F}_{\mathsf{all}}$-KDM-CCA secure PKE using neither NIZK proof nor bilinear pairing is not known so far.

1.2 Our Results

Based on the above back ground, we show the following results.

A framework achieving KDM-CCA *security in the single user setting.* First, we propose a framework to construct PKE that is $\mathcal{F}_{\mathsf{aff}}$-KDM-CCA secure in the single user setting based on *projective hash function.* Our framework can be instantiated based on the DDH, quadratic residuosity (QR), and DCR assumptions. More specifically, we obtain the following theorem.

Theorem 1 (Informal). *Under each of the DDH, QR, and DCR assumptions, there exists PKE that is* $\mathcal{F}_{\mathsf{aff}}$*-KDM-CCA secure in the single user setting.*

These schemes are also KDM-CCA secure with respect to projection functions of single-bit output thus compatible with the amplification method of Applebaum [2] and Kitagawa et al. [12]. Thus, we obtain the following corollary.

Corollary 1 (Informal). *Under each of the DDH, QR, and DCR assumptions, there exists PKE that is* $\mathcal{F}_{\mathsf{all}}$*-KDM-CCA secure in the single user setting.*

KDM-CCA secure PKE in the multi user setting. Then, we focus on KDM-CCA security in the multi user setting. Although the above framework based on projective hash function captures only KDM-CCA security in the single user setting, we can prove the KDM-CCA security in the multi user setting of our concrete instantiations by using their algebraic structures explicitly.

Our DDH based construction is an extension of the KDM-CPA secure scheme proposed by Boneh, Halevi, Hamburg and Ostrovsky [4]. Similarly to Boneh et al., using the self-reducibility of the DDH problem, we can prove the KDM-CCA security in the multi user setting of our DDH based construction with the same parameter setting as in the single user setting. Especially, we formally prove the following theorem.

Theorem 2 (Informal). *Under the DDH assumption, there exists PKE that is* $\mathcal{F}_{\mathsf{aff}}$*-KDM-CCA secure in the multi user setting.*

Since the DDH based construction is compatible with the results by Applebaum [2] and Kitagawa et al. [12], we obtain the following corollary.

Corollary 2 (Informal). *Under the DDH assumption, there exists PKE that is* $\mathcal{F}_{\mathsf{all}}$*-KDM-CCA secure in the multi user setting.*

Our QR and DCR based constructions are extensions of the KDM-CPA secure scheme proposed by Brakerski and Goldwasser [5]. If we allow the length of a secret key to depend on the number of users, we can also prove the KDM-CCA security in the multi user setting of our DCR and QR based schemes using a technique similar to Brakerski and Goldwasser. We briefly explain how to prove it after the proof of multi user security of the DDH based scheme.

We summarize our results and previous results in Fig. 1.

Scheme	Functions	Assumption	Free of pairing	Amplification	Flexible parameter
[6]	Affine	DDH		✓	✓
[10]	Circular	DDH+DCR			✓
[9]-1	Affine	DDH+DCR	✓		✓
[9]-2	polynomial	DDH+DCR	✓		✓
Ours 1	Affine	DDH	✓	✓	✓
Ours 2	Affine	QR	✓	✓	
Ours 3	Affine	DCR	✓	✓	

Fig. 1. Comparison of KDM-CCA secure PKE schemes. "Amplification" indicates whether we can transform the scheme into $\mathcal{F}_{\mathsf{all}}$-KDM-CCA secure one using the results of Applebaum [2] and Kitagawa et al. [12]. "Flexible parameter" indicates whether we can prove KDM-CCA security in the multi user setting of the scheme without making the length of a secret key depend on the number of users.

1.3 Technical Overview

Our starting point is the constructions of PKE proposed by Wee [19] that is KDM secure in the single user setting (hereafter, $\mathrm{KDM}^{(1)}$ security). He showed how to construct $\mathrm{KDM}^{(1)}$-CPA secure PKE based on *homomorphic* projective hash function. His framework captures the previous constructions proposed by Boneh et al. [4] and Brakerski and Goldwasser [5].

Projective hash function was originally introduced by Cramer and Shoup [8] to construct PKE satisfying indistinguishability against chosen ciphertext attacks (IND-CCA security). Thus, we have a natural question whether we can construct $\mathrm{KDM}^{(1)}$-CCA secure PKE based on projective hash function.

We answer the above question affirmatively with a simple construction. Below, we first review the construction proposed by Wee [19].

$\mathrm{KDM}^{(1)}$-CPA Secure PKE Based on Homomorphic Projective Hash Function. We consider a group $\mathcal{C}$ and its subgroup $\mathcal{V}$ satisfying *the subgroup indistinguishability*, that is, uniform distributions over $\mathcal{C}$ and $\mathcal{V}$ are computationally indistinguishable. Based on $\mathcal{C}$ and $\mathcal{V}$, we define projective hash function as follows. A projective hash function is a family $\mathcal{H}$ of hash functions $\Lambda_{\mathsf{sk}} : \mathcal{C} \to \mathcal{K}$ indexed by a key $\mathsf{sk} \in \mathcal{SK}$, where $\mathcal{K}$ is a group. Let μ be a projection map defined over $\mathcal{SK}$. We require Λ_{sk} be *projective*, that is, for every $c \in \mathcal{V}$, the value of $\Lambda_{\mathsf{sk}}(c)$ is determined by only c and $\mathsf{pk} = \mu(\mathsf{sk})$. In addition, we require that there exist a public evaluation algorithm Pub that given pk, $c \in \mathcal{V}$, and a witness w of $c \in \mathcal{V}$, outputs $\Lambda_{\mathsf{sk}}(c)$. Below, we denote group operations of $\mathcal{C}$ and $\mathcal{K}$ by "·" and "+", respectively.

Using a projective hash function $\mathcal{H}$, we can naturally construct a PKE scheme Π as follows. When generating a key pair $(\mathsf{pk}, \mathsf{sk})$, we sample random sk and compute $\mathsf{pk} = \mu(\mathsf{sk})$. When encrypting a message $m \in \mathcal{K}$, we first sample $c \xleftarrow{r} \mathcal{V}$ with a witness w of $c \in \mathcal{V}$. Then, we compute $d \leftarrow \mathsf{Pub}(\mathsf{pk}, c, w) + m$ and set (c, d) as a ciphertext. When decrypting (c, d), we compute $m \leftarrow d - \Lambda_{\mathsf{sk}}(c)$.

Π is IND-CPA secure if $\mathcal{H}$ is *smooth*, that is, the value of $\Lambda_{\mathsf{sk}}(c)$ is statistically chose to uniform given $\mathsf{pk} = \mu(\mathsf{sk})$ and c, where $\mathsf{sk} \xleftarrow{r} \mathcal{SK}$ and $c \xleftarrow{r} \mathcal{C}$.[1] We prove the IND-CPA security of Π as follows. We first switch c^* used to encrypt the challenge message to $c^* \xleftarrow{r} \mathcal{C}$ by using the subgroup indistinguishability. Then, the distribution of the resulting ciphertext is close to uniform due to the smoothness and thus IND-CPA security follows.

KDM security from homomorphism. Wee [19] showed Π is also KDM$^{(1)}$-CPA secure if $\mathcal{H}$ is *homomorphic*, that is, for every $c_0, c_1 \in \mathcal{C}$, it holds that $\Lambda_{\mathsf{sk}}(c_0 \cdot c_1) = \Lambda_{\mathsf{sk}}(c_0) + \Lambda_{\mathsf{sk}}(c_1)$. More precisely, Π is KDM$^{(1)}$-CPA secure with respect to functions defined as $f_e(\mathsf{sk}) = \Lambda_{\mathsf{sk}}(e)$, where $e \in \mathcal{C}$. Note that this function class corresponds to the set of affine functions in his instantiations.

If $\mathcal{H}$ is homomorphic, we can change the distribution of an encryption of $f_e(\mathsf{sk})$, that is $(c, \mathsf{Pub}(\mathsf{pk}, c, w) + \Lambda_{\mathsf{sk}}(e))$ as

$$\begin{aligned}
&(c, \mathsf{Pub}(\mathsf{pk}, c, w) + \Lambda_{\mathsf{sk}}(e)), \text{where } c \xleftarrow{r} \mathcal{V}\\
&= (c, \Lambda_{\mathsf{sk}}(c) + \Lambda_{\mathsf{sk}}(e)), \text{where } c \xleftarrow{r} \mathcal{V} \text{ (by projective property)}\\
&= (c, \Lambda_{\mathsf{sk}}(c \cdot e)), \text{where } c \xleftarrow{r} \mathcal{V} \text{ (by homomorphism)}\\
&\approx_{\mathsf{c}} (c, \Lambda_{\mathsf{sk}}(c \cdot e)), \text{where } c \xleftarrow{r} \mathcal{C} \text{ (by subgroup indistinguishability)}\\
&\approx_{\mathsf{s}} \left(c \cdot e^{-1}, \Lambda_{\mathsf{sk}}(c)\right), \text{where } c \xleftarrow{r} \mathcal{C} \text{ (since} e \in \mathcal{C})\\
&\approx_{\mathsf{c}} \left(c \cdot e^{-1}, \Lambda_{\mathsf{sk}}(c)\right), \text{where } c \xleftarrow{r} \mathcal{V} \text{ (by subgroup indistinguishability)}\\
&= \left(c \cdot e^{-1}, \mathsf{Pub}(\mathsf{pk}, c, w)\right), \text{where } c \xleftarrow{r} \mathcal{V} \text{ (by projective property),}
\end{aligned}$$

where w denotes a witness of $c \in \mathcal{V}$, and $\approx_{\mathsf{c}}$ and $\approx_{\mathsf{s}}$ denote computational indistinguishability and statistical indistinguishability, respectively. This means that we can simulate an encryption of $f_e(\mathsf{sk})$ without sk. Then, based on the standard hybrid argument, we can prove the KDM$^{(1)}$-CPA security of Π using the smoothness of $\mathcal{H}$ similarly to the proof for the IND-CPA security of Π.

Extension to KDM$^{(1)}$-CCA Secure PKE. We can construct IND-CCA secure PKE by adding 2-*universal* projective hash function to the construction of Π. More precisely, we use a projective hash function $\hat{\mathcal{H}}$ consisting of hash functions $\hat{\Lambda}_{\hat{\mathsf{sk}}}$ indexed by $\hat{\mathsf{sk}} \in \hat{\mathcal{SK}}$ defined on $\mathcal{C}$ and $\mathcal{V}$.[2] Let $\hat{\mu}$ and $\hat{\mathsf{Pub}}$ be the projection map and public evaluation algorithm of $\hat{\mathcal{H}}$. We require that $\hat{\mathcal{H}}$ be 2-*universal*, that is, for every $\hat{\mathsf{pk}}$, $c, c^* \in \mathcal{C} \setminus \mathcal{V}$, and $\mathsf{K}, \mathsf{K}^* \in \mathcal{K}$, $\hat{\Lambda}_{\hat{\mathsf{sk}}}(c) = \mathsf{K}$ holds with only negligible probability under the condition that $\hat{\mathsf{pk}} = \hat{\mu}\left(\hat{\mathsf{sk}}\right)$ and $\hat{\Lambda}_{\hat{\mathsf{sk}}}(c^*) = \mathsf{K}^*$, where $\hat{\mathsf{sk}} \xleftarrow{r} \hat{\mathcal{SK}}$.

We modify Π into IND-CCA secure Π' as follows. When generating a key pair, in addition to $(\mathsf{pk}, \mathsf{sk})$, we sample $\hat{\mathsf{sk}} \xleftarrow{r} \hat{\mathcal{SK}}$ and compute $\hat{\mathsf{pk}} = \hat{\mu}\left(\hat{\mathsf{sk}}\right)$. A public

[1] More specifically, this property is called average-case smoothness in general.

[2] In the actual construction of IND-CCA secure PKE, we need to use 2-universal projective hash function defined on $\mathcal{C} \times \mathcal{K}$ and $\mathcal{V} \times \mathcal{K}$. Such a primitive is called *extended* projective hash function [8]. For simplicity, we ignore this issue here.

key and secret key of Π' are $\left(\mathsf{pk}, \hat{\mathsf{pk}}\right)$ and $\left(\mathsf{sk}, \hat{\mathsf{sk}}\right)$, respectively. When encrypting a message, we first compute c and d in the same way as Π using pk. Then, we compute $\pi \leftarrow \hat{\mathsf{Pub}}\left(\hat{\mathsf{pk}}, c, w\right)$ and set (c, d, π) as the resulting ciphertext. When decrypting (c, d, π), we first check whether $\pi = \hat{\Lambda}_{\hat{\mathsf{sk}}}(c)$ holds and if so decrypt a message in the same way as Π using sk. Otherwise, we output $\perp$.

Since $\hat{\mathcal{H}}$ is 2-universal, an adversary cannot compute $\hat{\Lambda}_{\hat{\mathsf{sk}}}(c)$ correctly for $c \in \mathcal{C} \backslash \mathcal{V}$ even if he obtain a single hash value $\hat{\Lambda}_{\hat{\mathsf{sk}}}(c^*)$ for $c^* \in \mathcal{C} \backslash \mathcal{V}$ in the challenge ciphertext. In other words, the adversary cannot make a valid decryption query (c, d, π) for $c \in \mathcal{C} \setminus \mathcal{V}$. Then, from the projective property of $\mathcal{H}$, the adversary cannot obtain information of sk other than pk through decryption queries. Thus, we can reduce the IND-CCA security of Π' to the smoothness of $\mathcal{H}$.

Problems for proving KDM$^{(1)}$*-CCA security.* Even if $\mathcal{H}$ is homomorphic, we cannot prove the KDM$^{(1)}$-CCA security of Π' straightforwardly. In the security game of KDM$^{(1)}$-CCA security, an adversary can obtain an encryption of $\hat{\mathsf{sk}}$ in addition to that of sk. Thus, we need to eliminate $\hat{\mathsf{sk}}$ from the view of the adversary to use the 2-universal property of $\hat{\mathcal{H}}$.

Moreover, if we can do that, there is another problem. Consider functions of the form $f_e\left(\mathsf{sk}, \hat{\mathsf{sk}}\right) = \Lambda_{\mathsf{sk}}(e) + f\left(\hat{\mathsf{sk}}\right)$, where $e \in \mathcal{C}$ and $f : \hat{\mathcal{SK}} \rightarrow \mathcal{K}$ is a function. If $\mathcal{H}$ is homomorphic, using a similar argument as Wee [19], we can simulate an encryption of $f_e\left(\mathsf{sk}, \hat{\mathsf{sk}}\right)$ by

$$\left(c \cdot e^{-1}, \mathsf{Pub}(\mathsf{pk}, c, w) + f\left(\hat{\mathsf{sk}}\right), \hat{\Lambda}_{\hat{\mathsf{sk}}}\left(c \cdot e^{-1}\right)\right),$$

where $c \in \mathcal{V}$ and w is an witness of $c \in \mathcal{V}$. Even if we can eliminate $f\left(\hat{\mathsf{sk}}\right)$ from the second component, the third component $\hat{\Lambda}_{\hat{\mathsf{sk}}}\left(c \cdot e^{-1}\right)$ incurs another problem. e is an element chosen by an adversary in the security game, and thus $c \cdot e^{-1}$ might not be included in $\mathcal{V}$. Thus, the adversary can obtain a hash value $\hat{\Lambda}_{\hat{\mathsf{sk}}}\left(c \cdot e^{-1}\right)$ for $c \cdot e^{-1} \notin \mathcal{V}$ through each KDM query f_e. In this case, we cannot rely on the 2-universal property of $\hat{\mathcal{H}}$ to argue about decryption queries made by the adversary if he makes multiple KDM queries. Therefore, we also need to eliminate $\hat{\Lambda}_{\hat{\mathsf{sk}}}\left(c \cdot e^{-1}\right)$ from the view of the adversary.

Our solution: Double layered encryption. We solve the above two problems at once by extending double layered encryption techniques originally used to expand the plaintext space of an IND-CCA secure PKE scheme [11,15]. More precisely, by adding an outer encryption layer, we put the estimation of the probability that an adversary makes an "illegal" decryption query off till the end of the sequence of games where all information about the inner layer is eliminated from the challenge ciphertexts. We use an IND-CCA secure PKE scheme Π_{cca} as the outer layer encryption scheme. When encrypting a message, we first generate (c, d, π) in the same way as Π' and then encrypt them by Π_{cca}. We call the resulting PKE scheme Π_{kdm}.

Of course, if we just maintain a secret key csk of Π_{cca} as a part of a secret-key of Π_{kdm}, we cannot use the IND-CCA security of Π_{cca}. Thus, we add a modification. We maintain csk after encrypting by $\mathcal{H}$. More precisely, we modify the key generation procedure of Π_{kdm} as follows. We first generate $(\mathsf{pk}, \mathsf{sk})$ and $\left(\hat{\mathsf{pk}}, \hat{\mathsf{sk}}\right)$ in the same way as Π' and generate a key pair $(\mathsf{cpk}, \mathsf{csk})$ of Π_{cca}. Moreover, we sample $c^* \xleftarrow{\mathsf{r}} \mathcal{C}$ and compute $d^* \xleftarrow{\mathsf{r}} \Lambda_{\mathsf{sk}}(c^*) + \mathsf{csk}$.[3] The resulting public key and secret key of Π_{kdm} are $\left(\mathsf{pk}, \hat{\mathsf{pk}}, \mathsf{cpk}\right)$ and $\left(\mathsf{sk}, \hat{\mathsf{sk}}, c^*, d^*\right)$, respectively.

The overview of the security proof is as follows. Let $\mathcal{A}$ be an adversary for the KDM$^{(1)}$-CCA security of Π_{kdm}. We consider functions of the form

$$f_e\left(\mathsf{sk}, \hat{\mathsf{sk}}, c^*, d^*\right) = \Lambda_{\mathsf{sk}}(e) + f\left(\hat{\mathsf{sk}}, c^*, d^*\right),$$

where $e \in \mathcal{C}$ and $f : \hat{\mathcal{SK}} \times \mathcal{C} \times \mathcal{K} \to \mathcal{K}$ is a function. This set of functions includes affine functions in the actual instantiations.

1. We first change the security game so that we do not need sk to simulate KDM queries using the projective property and homomorphism of $\mathcal{H}$ and subgroup indistinguishability. Note that we do not need the smoothness of $\mathcal{H}$ to make this change as explained before.
   After this change, the answer to a KDM query f_e is of the form
   $$\mathsf{Enc}_{\mathsf{cpk}}\left(c \cdot e^{-1}, \mathsf{Pub}(\mathsf{pk}, c, w) + f\left(\hat{\mathsf{sk}}, c^*, d^*\right), \hat{\Lambda}_{\hat{\mathsf{sk}}}\left(c \cdot e^{-1}\right)\right) .$$
2. Then, we change the security game so that a decryption query CT made by $\mathcal{A}$ is replied with $\perp$ if $c \notin \mathcal{V}$, where $(c, d, \pi) \leftarrow \mathsf{Dec}_{\mathsf{csk}}(\mathsf{CT})$. The probability that this change affects the behavior of $\mathcal{A}$ is bounded by the probability that $\mathcal{A}$ makes a decryption query CT such that $c \notin \mathcal{V}$ and $\pi = \hat{\Lambda}_{\hat{\mathsf{sk}}}(c)$, where $(c, d, \pi) \leftarrow \mathsf{Dec}_{\mathsf{csk}}(\mathsf{CT})$. We call such a decryption query a *bad decryption query*. Since $\hat{\mathsf{sk}}$ is contained in answers to KDM queries, we cannot estimate the probability at this point. However, as noted above, we can put the estimation off till the end of the sequence of games, and thus we continue the sequence.
3. By the previous change on how decryption queries are replied, we can use the smoothness of $\mathcal{H}$. We eliminate csk encrypted in (c^*, d^*) using the smoothness of $\mathcal{H}$.
4. Then, we can use IND-CCA security of Π_{cca}. We change the security game so that a KDM query made by $\mathcal{A}$ is replied with $\mathsf{CT} \leftarrow \mathsf{Enc}_{\mathsf{cpk}}(0)$. In this game, the advantage of $\mathcal{A}$ is 0.

To complete the security proof, we need to estimate the probability that $\mathcal{A}$ makes a bad decryption query. In the final game, $\hat{\mathsf{sk}}$ is hidden from the view of $\mathcal{A}$ and he cannot obtain any hash value $\hat{\Lambda}_{\hat{\mathsf{sk}}}(c)$ for $c \notin \mathcal{V}$. Thus, the probability is negligible in the final game if $\hat{\mathcal{H}}$ is 2-universal. In fact, since the universal property of $\hat{\mathcal{H}}$ is sufficient for this argument, we use a universal projective

[3] Without loss of generality, we assume that the secret-key space of Π_{cca} is $\mathcal{K}$.

hash function instead of a 2-universal one in the actual construction. Then, the remaining problem is whether the probability that $\mathcal{A}$ makes a bad decryption query changes during the sequence of games.

The probability does not change by the third step since the view of $\mathcal{A}$ before the third step is statistically close to that after the third step from the smoothness of $\mathcal{H}$. In addition, if we can efficiently detect a bad decryption query made by $\mathcal{A}$, we can prove that the probability does not change by the fourth step based on the IND-CCA security of Π_{cca}. For the purpose, in this work, we require there exist a trapdoor that enables us to efficiently check the membership of $\mathcal{V}$ for projective hash function. We can complete the security proof under the existence of such a trapdoor.

Instantiations. We instantiate the above framework based on the DDH, QR, and DCR assumptions by extending the instantiations of $\mathrm{KDM}^{(1)}$-CPA secure PKE by Wee [19]. Therefore, the DDH based construction is also an extension of that proposed by Boneh et al. [4], and the QR and DCR based constructions are also extensions of those proposed by Brakerski and Goldwasser [5]. In all constructions, we can make a trapdoor for checking the membership of $\mathcal{V}$. We briefly review the DDH based instantiation.

The DDH based instantiation. In the DDH based instantiation, we set

$$\mathcal{C} = \mathbb{G}^{\ell} \text{ and } \mathcal{V} = \{(g_1^r, \ldots, g_\ell^r) \,|\, r \in \mathbb{Z}_p\},$$

where $\mathbb{G}$ is a cyclic group of order p, $g_1, \ldots, g_\ell$ are random generators of $\mathbb{G}$, and ℓ is a parameter determined in the analysis. The uniform distribution over $\mathcal{C}$ and $\mathcal{V}$ are computationally indistinguishable based on the DDH assumption on $\mathbb{G}$. Moreover, the discrete logarithms α_i such that $g_i = g^{\alpha_i}$ for every $i \in [\ell]$ can be used as a trapdoor to efficiently decide the membership of $\mathcal{V}$, where g is another generator and $[\ell]$ denotes $\{1, \ldots, \ell\}$.

We construct homomorphic projective hash function $\mathcal{H}$ exactly in the same way as Wee [19]. A secret key sk is randomly chosen $s = s_1 \cdots s_\ell \in \{0,1\}^\ell$. The corresponding public key is $g_0 = \prod_{i \in [\ell]} g_i^{s_i}$. When hashing $c = (c_1, \ldots, c_\ell) \in \mathcal{C}$, we compute $\prod_{i \in [\ell]} c_i^{s_i}$. We see that this construction satisfies the projective property and homomorphism. Moreover, we can prove the (average-case) smoothness of it based on the leftover hash lemma by taking ℓ appropriately.

We construct a universal projective hash function $\hat{\mathcal{H}}$ as follows. A secret key $\hat{\mathsf{sk}}$ is randomly chosen $(x_1, \ldots, x_\ell) \in \mathbb{Z}_p^\ell$. The corresponding public key is $\hat{g}_0 = \prod_{i \in [\ell]} g_i^{x_i}$. When hashing $c = (c_1, \ldots, c_\ell) \in \mathcal{C}$, we compute $\prod_{i \in [\ell]} c_i^{x_i}$. This construction can be seen as an extension of that proposed by Cramer and Shoup [8], and we can prove its projective property and universal property.

The QR and DCR based instantiations. In the QR based construction, we use the same $\mathcal{C}$, $\mathcal{V}$, and $\mathcal{H}$ as Wee [19]. However, in the QR based construction, we slightly modify how to mask csk in the key generation. Roughly speaking, this is because a hash value of $\mathcal{H}$ uniformly distributes over a group of order 2, and thus we need parallelization in order to mask csk using the smoothness of $\mathcal{H}$. In the modified version of construction, we avoid such parallelization. However, in the construction of a universal projective hash function $\hat{\mathcal{H}}$, we still need a parallelized construction similarly to IND-CCA secure PKE based on the QR assumption proposed by Cramer and Shoup [8]. When we consider CCA security, if the underlying group has a small prime factor, we need a parallelized construction.

In the DCR based construction, we also apply some modifications to the construction of $\mathcal{C}$, $\mathcal{V}$, and $\mathcal{H}$ used by Wee. In the construction of Wee, the underlying group has a small prime factor 2. Therefore, in a naive construction, we need parallelization. However, by defining hash functions so that every time we compute a hash value, we first perform a squaring, we can make the small factor useless to attack the scheme without parallelization. By this modification, the range of hash functions become a group whose order does not have a small prime factor and we can avoid parallelization.

Overhead of our constructions. The overhead of communicational complexity (that is, the size of public-keys and ciphertexts) of our KDM$^{(1)}$-CCA secure PKE schemes from its KDM$^{(1)}$-CPA secure counterparts [19] is very small in the DDH and DCR based constructions. A public-key and hash value of $\hat{\mathcal{H}}$ are just a single group element in the DDH and DCR based constructions. Moreover, we can use highly efficient IND-CCA secure PKE schemes [13,17] as the outer layer scheme. In this case, the overhead of communicational complexity is only few group elements.

Extension to Multi User Setting. Although the above framework based on projective hash function captures only KDM$^{(1)}$-CCA security, we can prove the KDM-CCA security in the multi user setting of concrete instantiations.

As noted before, our DDH based construction is an extension of that proposed by Boneh et al. [4], and our QR and DCR based constructions are extensions of those proposed by Brakerski and Goldwasser [5]. In both works, they first show the KDM$^{(1)}$-CPA security of their schemes, and then prove its KDM-CPA security in the multi user setting by extending the proof for KDM$^{(1)}$-CPA security.

By using similar techniques, we can prove KDM-CCA security in the multi user setting of our schemes. Especially, we prove the KDM-CCA security in the multi user setting of our DDH based construction with the same parameter setting as in the single user setting. We also briefly explain how to prove the KDM-CCA security in the multi user setting of our QR and DCR based constructions after proving the multi user security of the DDH based construction.

2 Preliminaries

We define some cryptographic primitives after introducing some notations and left-over hash lemma.

Notations. In this paper, $x \xleftarrow{r} X$ denotes choosing an element from a finite set X uniformly at random, and $y \leftarrow \mathsf{A}(x)$ denotes assigning to y the output of an algorithm A on an input x. For bit strings x and y, $x\|y$ denotes the concatenation of x and y. For an integer ℓ, $[\ell]$ denotes the set of integers $\{1,\ldots,\ell\}$.

λ denotes a security parameter. PPT stands for probabilistic polynomial time. A function $f(\lambda)$ is a negligible function if $f(\lambda)$ tends to 0 faster than $\frac{1}{\lambda^c}$ for every constant $c > 0$. We write $f(\lambda) = \mathsf{negl}(\lambda)$ to denote $f(\lambda)$ being a negligible function.

We introduce the left-over hash lemma.

Lemma 1 (Left-over hash lemma). *Let X, Y, and Z are sets. Let $\mathcal{H} := \{h : X \to Y\}$ be a family of 2-universal hash functions. Let $\mathsf{aux} : X \to Z$ be a function. Then, the distributions $(h, h(x), \mathsf{aux}(x))$ and $(h, y, \mathsf{aux}(x))$ are $\sqrt{\frac{|Y||Z|}{4\cdot|X|}}$-close, where $h \xleftarrow{r} \mathcal{H}$, $x \xleftarrow{r} X$, and $y \xleftarrow{r} Y$.*

2.1 Public Key Encryption

A public-key encryption (PKE) scheme PKE is a three tuple (KG, Enc, Dec) of PPT algorithms. Let $\mathcal{M}$ be the message space of PKE. The key generation algorithm KG, given a security parameter 1^λ, outputs a public key pk and a secret key sk. The encryption algorithm Enc, given a public key pk and message $m \in \mathcal{M}$, outputs a ciphertext CT. The decryption algorithm Dec, given a secret key sk and ciphertext CT, outputs a message $\tilde{m} \in \{\bot\} \cup \mathcal{M}$. As correctness, we require $\mathsf{Dec}(\mathsf{sk}, \mathsf{Enc}(\mathsf{pk}, m)) = m$ for every $m \in \mathcal{M}$ and $(\mathsf{pk}, \mathsf{sk}) \leftarrow \mathsf{KG}(1^\lambda)$.

Next, we define key dependent message security against chosen ciphertext attacks (KDM-CCA security) for PKE.

Definition 1 (KDM-CCA security). *Let PKE be a PKE scheme, $\mathcal{F}$ function family, and n the number of keys. We define the $\mathcal{F}$-KDM$^{(n)}$-CCA game between a challenger and an adversary $\mathcal{A}$ as follows. Let $\mathcal{SK}$ and $\mathcal{M}$ be the secret key space and message space of PKE, respectively.*

1. *First, the challenger chooses a challenge bit $b \xleftarrow{r} \{0,1\}$. Next, the challenger generates n key pairs $(\mathsf{pk}_k, \mathsf{sk}_k) \leftarrow \mathsf{KG}(1^\lambda)$ $(k \in [n])$. The challenger sets $\mathbf{sk} := (\mathsf{sk}_1, \ldots, \mathsf{sk}_n)$ and sends $(\mathsf{pk}_1, \ldots, \mathsf{pk}_n)$ to $\mathcal{A}$. Finally, the challenger prepares a list L_{kdm} which is initially empty.*
2. *$\mathcal{A}$ may adaptively make the following queries polynomially many times.*
   KDM queries *$\mathcal{A}$ sends $(j, f^0, f^1) \in [n]\times\mathcal{F}\times\mathcal{F}$ to the challenger. We require that f^0 and f^1 be functions such that $f : \mathcal{SK}^n \to \mathcal{M}$. The challenger returns $\mathsf{CT} \leftarrow \mathsf{Enc}\left(\mathsf{pk}_j, f^b(\mathbf{sk})\right)$ to $\mathcal{A}$. Finally, the challenger adds (j, CT) to L_{kdm}.*
   Decryption queries *$\mathcal{A}$ sends (j, CT) to the challenger. If $(j, \mathsf{CT}) \in L_{\mathsf{kdm}}$, the challenger returns $\bot$ to $\mathcal{A}$. Otherwise, the challenger returns $m \leftarrow \mathsf{Dec}\left(\mathsf{sk}_j, \mathsf{CT}\right)$ to $\mathcal{A}$.*
3. *$\mathcal{A}$ outputs $b' \in \{0,1\}$.*

We say that PKE is $\mathcal{F}$-KDM$^{(n)}$-CCA secure if for any PPT adversary $\mathcal{A}$, we have $\mathsf{Adv}^{\mathsf{kdmcca}}_{\mathsf{PKE},\mathcal{F},\mathcal{A},n}(\lambda) = \left|\Pr[b = b'] - \frac{1}{2}\right| = \mathsf{negl}(\lambda)$.

In addition, we say that PKE *is $\mathcal{F}$-KDM-CCA secure if it is $\mathcal{F}$-KDM$^{(n)}$-CCA secure for any polynomial $n = n(\lambda)$.*

Remark 1 (Difference with the previous definitions). In the original definition of KDM security defined by Black et al. [3], an adversary is required to distinguish an encryption of $f(\mathsf{sk})$ from that of some constant message such as 0, where f is a function chosen by the adversary.

In our definition of KDM-CCA security, an adversary chooses two functions (f^0, f^1) and is required to distinguish an encryption of $f^0(\mathsf{sk})$ from that of $f^1(\mathsf{sk})$. Such a definition was previously used by Alperin-sheriff and Peikert [1] when they defined KDM security for identity-based encryption to simplify their security proof. We also adopt this definition to simplify our security proofs.

These two types of definitions are equivalent if the function class $\mathcal{F}$ contains a constant function. This is the case for affine functions and projection functions that we focus on.

IND-CCA security is a special case of KDM-CCA security. More specifically, we can define IND-CCA security by restricting functions an adversary can query as KDM queries in the KDM-CCA game to constant functions. Thus, we omit the definition of IND-CCA security.

2.2 Projective Hash Function

We review the notion of projective hash function introduced by Cramer and Shoup [8] after introducing the notion of subset membership problem.

Definition 2 (Subset membership problem). *Let $\mathcal{C}$ be a group and $\mathcal{V}$ be a subgroup of $\mathcal{C}$. We say that the subset membership problem is hard for $(\mathcal{C}, \mathcal{V})$ if uniform distributions over $\mathcal{C}$ and $\mathcal{V}$ are computationally indistinguishable.*

In this work, for a subset membership problem $(\mathcal{C}, \mathcal{V})$, we require that there exist a trapdoor that enables us to efficiently check the membership of $\mathcal{V}$. Moreover, we require that we can efficiently sample c from $\mathcal{V}$ with a witness of $c \in \mathcal{V}$.

Definition 3 (Projective hash function). *A projective hash function $\mathcal{H}$ is a tuple $(\mathcal{C}, \mathcal{V}, \mathcal{K}, \mathcal{SK}, \mathcal{PK}, \Lambda, \mu)$. $\mathcal{C}$ and $\mathcal{K}$ are groups and $\mathcal{V}$ is a subgroup of $\mathcal{C}$. $\mathcal{SK}$ and $\mathcal{PK}$ are sets. The hash function Λ_{sk} indexed by $\mathsf{sk} \in \mathcal{SK}$, given $c \in \mathcal{C}$, outputs a hash value $\mathsf{K} \in \mathcal{K}$. The projection map μ, given $\mathsf{sk} \in \mathcal{SK}$, outputs $\mathsf{pk} \in \mathcal{PK}$. We require that $\mathcal{H}$ be projective, that is, for any $\mathsf{sk} \in \mathcal{SK}$ and $c \in \mathcal{V}$, the value of $\Lambda_{\mathsf{sk}}(c)$ is determined only by c and $\mathsf{pk} = \mu(\mathsf{sk})$. In addition, we require that there exist a public evaluation algorithm* Pub, *given $\mathsf{pk} = \mu(\mathsf{sk})$, $c \in \mathcal{V}$, and an witness w that $c \in \mathcal{V}$, outputs $\Lambda_{\mathsf{sk}}(c)$, where $\mathsf{sk} \in \mathcal{SK}$.*

In addition, we say that $\mathcal{H}$ is homomorphic if for any $\mathsf{sk} \in \mathcal{SK}$ and $c_0, c_1 \in \mathcal{C}$, it holds that $\Lambda_{\mathsf{sk}}(c_0 \cdot c_1) = \Lambda_{\mathsf{sk}}(c_0) + \Lambda_{\mathsf{sk}}(c_1)$, where "$\cdot$" and "$+$" denote operations in $\mathcal{C}$ and $\mathcal{K}$, respectively.

We define two security notions for projective hash function.

Definition 4 (Average-case smoothness). *Let $\mathcal{H} = (\mathcal{C}, \mathcal{V}, \mathcal{K}, \mathcal{SK}, \mathcal{PK}, \Lambda, \mu)$ be a projective hash function. We say that $\mathcal{H}$ is average-case smooth if the distributions $(\mathsf{pk}, c, \Lambda_{\mathsf{sk}}(c))$ and $(\mathsf{pk}, c, \mathsf{K})$ are statistically close, where $\mathsf{sk} \xleftarrow{r} \mathcal{SK}$, $\mathsf{pk} = \mu(\mathsf{sk})$, $c \xleftarrow{r} \mathcal{C}$, and $\mathsf{K} \xleftarrow{r} \mathcal{K}$.*

Definition 5 (Universal property). *Let $\mathcal{H} = (\mathcal{C}, \mathcal{V}, \mathcal{K}, \mathcal{SK}, \mathcal{PK}, \Lambda, \mu)$ be a projective hash function. We say that $\mathcal{H}$ is universal if for any $\mathsf{pk} \in \mathcal{PK}$, $c \in \mathcal{C} \setminus \mathcal{V}$, $\mathsf{K} \in \mathcal{K}$, we have $\Pr_{\mathsf{sk} \xleftarrow{r} \mathcal{SK}}[\Lambda_{\mathsf{sk}}(c) = \mathsf{K} | \mu(\mathsf{sk}) = \mathsf{pk}] = \mathsf{negl}(\lambda)$.*

3 KDM$^{(1)}$-CCA Secure PKE Based on Homomorphic Projective Hash Function

In this section, we show a framework for achieving KDM$^{(1)}$-CCA secure PKE based on homomorphic projective hash function.

Let $\mathcal{H} = (\mathcal{C}, \mathcal{V}, \mathcal{K}, \mathcal{SK}, \mathcal{PK}, \Lambda, \mu)$ be a homomorphic projective hash function with a public evaluation algorithm Pub. We denote the group operations of $\mathcal{C}$ and $\mathcal{K}$ by "$\cdot$" and "$+$", respectively. Let $\hat{\mathcal{H}} = \left(\mathcal{C}, \mathcal{V}, \hat{\mathcal{K}}, \hat{\mathcal{SK}}, \hat{\mathcal{PK}}, \hat{\Lambda}, \hat{\mu}\right)$ be a projective hash function with a public evaluation algorithm $\hat{\mathsf{Pub}}$. Let $\Pi_{\mathsf{cca}} = (\mathsf{KG}_{\mathsf{cca}}, \mathsf{Enc}_{\mathsf{cca}}, \mathsf{Dec}_{\mathsf{cca}})$ be a PKE scheme. We assume that the secret-key space of Π_{cca} is $\mathcal{K}$ for simplicity. Using these building blocks, we construct the following PKE scheme $\Pi_{\mathsf{kdm}} = (\mathsf{KG}_{\mathsf{kdm}}, \mathsf{Enc}_{\mathsf{kdm}}, \mathsf{Dec}_{\mathsf{kdm}})$. The message space of Π_{kdm} is $\mathcal{M}$. We use an invertible map $\phi : \mathcal{M} \to \mathcal{K}$ in the construction.

$\mathsf{KG}_{\mathsf{kdm}}(1^\lambda)$:
- Generate $\mathsf{sk} \xleftarrow{r} \mathcal{SK}$ and compute $\mathsf{pk} \leftarrow \mu(\mathsf{sk})$.
- Generate $\hat{\mathsf{sk}} \xleftarrow{r} \hat{\mathcal{SK}}$ and compute $\hat{\mathsf{pk}} \leftarrow \hat{\mu}\left(\hat{\mathsf{sk}}\right)$.
- Generate $(\mathsf{cpk}, \mathsf{csk}) \leftarrow \mathsf{KG}_{\mathsf{cca}}(1^\lambda)$.
- Generate $c^* \xleftarrow{r} \mathcal{C}$ and compute $d^* \leftarrow \Lambda_{\mathsf{sk}}(c^*) + \mathsf{csk}$.
- Return $\mathsf{PK} := \left(\mathsf{pk}, \hat{\mathsf{pk}}, \mathsf{cpk}\right)$ and $\mathsf{SK} := \left(\mathsf{sk}, \hat{\mathsf{sk}}, c^*, d^*\right)$.

$\mathsf{Enc}_{\mathsf{kdm}}(\mathsf{PK}, m)$:
- Parse $\left(\mathsf{pk}, \hat{\mathsf{pk}}, \mathsf{cpk}\right) \leftarrow \mathsf{PK}$.
- Generate $c \xleftarrow{r} \mathcal{V}$ with an witness w of $c \in \mathcal{V}$.
- Compute $\mathsf{K} \leftarrow \mathsf{Pub}(\mathsf{pk}, c, w)$ and $d \leftarrow \mathsf{K} + \phi(m)$.
- Compute $\pi \leftarrow \hat{\mathsf{Pub}}\left(\hat{\mathsf{pk}}, c, w\right)$.
- Return $\mathsf{CT} \leftarrow \mathsf{Enc}_{\mathsf{cca}}(\mathsf{cpk}, (c, d, \pi))$.

$\mathsf{Dec}_{\mathsf{kdm}}(\mathsf{SK}, \mathsf{CT})$:
- Parse $\left(\mathsf{sk}, \hat{\mathsf{sk}}, c^*, d^*\right) \leftarrow \mathsf{SK}$.
- Compute $\mathsf{csk} \leftarrow d^* - \Lambda_{\mathsf{sk}}(c^*)$.
- Compute $(c, d, \pi) \leftarrow \mathsf{Dec}_{\mathsf{cca}}(\mathsf{csk}, \mathsf{CT})$. If the decryption result is not in $\mathcal{C} \times \mathcal{K} \times \hat{\mathcal{K}}$, return $\bot$. Otherwise, compute as follows.
- If $\pi \neq \hat{\Lambda}_{\hat{\mathsf{sk}}}(c)$, return $\bot$. Otherwise, return $m \leftarrow \phi^{-1}(d - \Lambda_{\mathsf{sk}}(c))$.

Correctness. We have $\mathsf{Pub}(\mathsf{pk}, c, w) = \Lambda_{\mathsf{sk}}(c)$ and $\hat{\mathsf{Pub}}\left(\hat{\mathsf{pk}}, c, w\right) = \hat{\Lambda}_{\hat{\mathsf{sk}}}(c)$ for $c \in \mathcal{V}$, where w is a witness of $c \in \mathcal{V}$. Then, the correctness of Π_{kdm} follows from that of Π_{cca}.

Π_{kdm} is KDM-CCA secure with respect to the function family $\mathcal{F}_{\mathsf{phf}}$ consisting of functions described as

$$f_e\left(\mathsf{sk}, \hat{\mathsf{sk}}, c^*, d^*\right) = \phi^{-1}\left(\Lambda_{\mathsf{sk}}(e) + \phi\left(f\left(\hat{\mathsf{sk}}, c^*, d^*\right)\right)\right),$$

where $e \in \mathcal{C}$ and $f : \hat{\mathcal{SK}} \times \mathcal{C} \times \mathcal{K} \to \mathcal{M}$ is a function. This class corresponds to affine and projection functions in the instantiations. Formally, we prove the following theorem.

Theorem 3. *Let the subset membership problem $(\mathcal{C}, \mathcal{V})$ be hard. Let $\mathcal{H}$ be average-case smooth and $\hat{\mathcal{H}}$ universal. Let Π_{cca} be IND-CCA secure. Then, Π_{kdm} is $\mathcal{F}_{\mathsf{phf}}$-KDM$^{(1)}$-CCA secure.*

Proof of Theorem 3. Let $\mathcal{A}$ be an adversary that attacks the $\mathcal{F}_{\mathsf{phf}}$-KDM$^{(1)}$-CCA security of Π_{kdm}. We proceed the proof via a sequence of games. For every $t \in \{0, \ldots, 8\}$, let $\mathtt{SUC}_t$ be the event that $\mathcal{A}$ succeeds in guessing the challenge bit b in Game t.

Game 0: This is the original $\mathcal{F}_{\mathsf{phf}}$-KDM$^{(1)}$-CCA game regarding Π_{kdm}. We have $\mathsf{Adv}^{\mathsf{kdmcca}}_{\Pi_{\mathsf{kdm}}, \mathcal{F}_{\mathsf{phf}}, \mathcal{A}, 1}(\lambda) = \left|\Pr[\mathtt{SUC}_0] - \frac{1}{2}\right|$.

1. The challenger chooses a challenge bit $b \xleftarrow{r} \{0,1\}$, and runs as follows.
   (a) Generate $\mathsf{sk} \xleftarrow{r} \mathcal{SK}$ and compute $\mathsf{pk} \leftarrow \mu(\mathsf{sk})$.
   (b) Generate $\hat{\mathsf{sk}} \xleftarrow{r} \hat{\mathcal{SK}}$ and compute $\hat{\mathsf{pk}} \leftarrow \hat{\mu}\left(\hat{\mathsf{sk}}\right)$.
   (c) Generate $(\mathsf{cpk}, \mathsf{csk}) \leftarrow \mathsf{KG}_{\mathsf{cca}}\left(1^\lambda\right)$.
   (d) Generate $c^* \xleftarrow{r} \mathcal{C}$ and compute $d^* \leftarrow \Lambda_{\mathsf{sk}}(c^*) + \mathsf{csk}$.
   (e) Send $\mathsf{PK} := \left(\mathsf{pk}, \hat{\mathsf{pk}}, \mathsf{cpk}\right)$ to $\mathcal{A}$ and prepare a list L_{kdm}.
2. The challenger responds to queries made by $\mathcal{A}$.
   For a KDM query $((e^0, f^0), (e^1, f^1))$ made by $\mathcal{A}$, the challenger responds as follows.
   (a) Generate $c \xleftarrow{r} \mathcal{V}$ with a witness w of $c \in \mathcal{V}$.
   (b) Compute $\mathsf{K} \leftarrow \mathsf{Pub}(\mathsf{pk}, c, w)$ and $d \leftarrow \mathsf{K} + \Lambda_{\mathsf{sk}}(e^b) + \phi\left(f^b\left(\hat{\mathsf{sk}}, c^*, d^*\right)\right)$.
   (c) Compute $\pi \leftarrow \hat{\mathsf{Pub}}\left(\hat{\mathsf{pk}}, c, w\right)$.
   (d) Return $\mathsf{CT} \leftarrow \mathsf{Enc}_{\mathsf{cca}}(\mathsf{cpk}, (c, d, \pi))$ to $\mathcal{A}$ and add CT to L_{kdm}.
   For a decryption query CT made by $\mathcal{A}$, the challenger returns $\perp$ to $\mathcal{A}$ if $\mathsf{CT} \in L_{\mathsf{kdm}}$, and otherwise responds as follows.
   (a) Compute $(c, d, \pi) \leftarrow \mathsf{Dec}_{\mathsf{cca}}(\mathsf{csk}, \mathsf{CT})$. If the decryption result is not in $\mathcal{C} \times \mathcal{K} \times \hat{\mathcal{K}}$, return $\perp$ to $\mathcal{A}$. Otherwise, responds as follows.
   (b) Return $\perp$ if $\pi \neq \hat{\Lambda}_{\hat{\mathsf{sk}}}(c)$ and $m \leftarrow \phi^{-1}(d - \Lambda_{\mathsf{sk}}(c))$ otherwise.
3. $\mathcal{A}$ outputs $b' \in \{0,1\}$.

Game 1: Same as Game 0 except that when $\mathcal{A}$ makes a KDM query, the challenger computes $\mathsf{K} \leftarrow \Lambda_{\mathsf{sk}}(c)$ and $\pi \leftarrow \hat{\Lambda}_{\hat{\mathsf{sk}}}(c)$ instead of $\mathsf{K} \leftarrow \mathsf{Pub}(\mathsf{pk}, c, w)$ and $\pi \leftarrow \hat{\mathsf{Pub}}\left(\hat{\mathsf{pk}}, c, w\right)$, respectively.

Due to the projective property of $\mathcal{H}$ and $\hat{\mathcal{H}}$, this change is only conceptual and thus we have $|\Pr[\mathtt{SUC}_0] - \Pr[\mathtt{SUC}_1]| = 0$.

Game 2: Same as Game 1 except that when $\mathcal{A}$ makes a KDM query, the challenger generates $c \xleftarrow{r} \mathcal{C}$.

We have $|\Pr[\mathtt{SUC}_1] - \Pr[\mathtt{SUC}_2]| = \mathsf{negl}(\lambda)$ by the hardness of the subset membership problem $(\mathcal{C}, \mathcal{V})$.

Game 3: Same as Game 2 except that the challenger generates $c \xleftarrow{r} \mathcal{C}$ and uses $c' = c \cdot (e^b)^{-1}$ instead of c when $\mathcal{A}$ makes a KDM query $((e^0, f^0), (e^1, f^1))$.

We have $|\Pr[\mathtt{SUC}_2] - \Pr[\mathtt{SUC}_3]| = 0$ since if c uniformly distributes over $\mathcal{C}$, then so does $c \cdot (e^b)^{-1}$.

By this change, the answer to a KDM query $((e^0, f^0), (e^1, f^1))$ in Game 3 is $\mathsf{Enc}_{\mathsf{cca}}(\mathsf{cpk}, (c', d, \pi))$, where

$$c' = c \cdot (e^b)^{-1}, d = \Lambda_{\mathsf{sk}}(c \cdot (e^b)^{-1}) + \Lambda_{\mathsf{sk}}(e^b) + \phi\left(f^b\left(\hat{\mathsf{sk}}, c^*, d^*\right)\right), \pi = \hat{\Lambda}_{\hat{\mathsf{sk}}}(c'),$$

and $c \xleftarrow{r} \mathcal{C}$. Moreover, by the homomorphism of $\mathcal{H}$, $d = \Lambda_{\mathsf{sk}}(c) + \phi\left(f^b\left(\hat{\mathsf{sk}}, c^*, d^*\right)\right)$ holds.

Game 4: Same as Game 3 except that when $\mathcal{A}$ makes a KDM query, the challenger generates $c \xleftarrow{r} \mathcal{V}$ with a witness w of $c \in \mathcal{V}$.

We have $|\Pr[\mathtt{SUC}_3] - \Pr[\mathtt{SUC}_4]| = \mathsf{negl}(\lambda)$ by the hardness of the subset membership problem $(\mathcal{C}, \mathcal{V})$.

Game 5: Same as Game 4 except that when $\mathcal{A}$ makes a KDM query, the challenger computes $d \leftarrow \mathsf{Pub}(\mathsf{pk}, c, w) + \phi\left(f^b\left(\hat{\mathsf{sk}}, c^*, d^*\right)\right)$. Note that the challenger still computes π with $\pi \leftarrow \hat{\Lambda}_{\hat{\mathsf{sk}}}(c')$.

Due to the projective property of $\mathcal{H}$, this change is only conceptual and thus we have $|\Pr[\mathtt{SUC}_4] - \Pr[\mathtt{SUC}_5]| = 0$.

At this point, sk is not needed to compute answers to KDM queries. More precisely, the answer to a KDM query $((e^0, f^0), (e^1, f^1))$ is $\mathsf{Enc}_{\mathsf{cca}}(\mathsf{cpk}, (c', d, \pi))$, where

$$c' = c \cdot (e^b)^{-1}, d = \mathsf{Pub}(\mathsf{pk}, c, w) + \phi\left(f^b\left(\hat{\mathsf{sk}}, c^*, d^*\right)\right), \pi = \hat{\Lambda}_{\hat{\mathsf{sk}}}(c'),$$

$c \xleftarrow{r} \mathcal{V}$, and w is a witness of $c \in \mathcal{V}$.

Game 6: Same as Game 5 except how the challenger responds decryption queries made by $\mathcal{A}$. In this game, the challenger returns $\perp$ for a decryption query related to $c \notin \mathcal{V}$. More precisely, the challenger responds as follows.

For a decryption query CT made by $\mathcal{A}$, the challenger returns $\perp$ to $\mathcal{A}$ if $\mathsf{CT} \in L_{\mathsf{kdm}}$, and otherwise responds as follows.

1. Compute $(c, d, \pi) \leftarrow \mathsf{Dec_{cca}}(\mathsf{csk}, \mathsf{CT})$. If the decryption result is not in $\mathcal{V} \times \mathcal{K} \times \hat{\mathcal{K}}$, return $\perp$ to $\mathcal{A}$. Otherwise, respond as follows.
2. Return $\perp$ if $\pi \neq \hat{\Lambda}_{\hat{\mathsf{sk}}}(c)$ and $m \leftarrow \phi^{-1}(d - \Lambda_{\mathsf{sk}}(c))$ otherwise.

We define the following event in Game t $(t = 5, \cdots, 8)$.

BDQ_t**:** $\mathcal{A}$ makes a decryption query $\mathsf{CT} \notin L_{\mathsf{kdm}}$ which satisfies $c \in \mathcal{C} \setminus \mathcal{V}$ and $\pi = \hat{\Lambda}_{\hat{\mathsf{sk}}}(c)$, where $(c, d, \pi) \leftarrow \mathsf{Dec_{cca}}(\mathsf{csk}, \mathsf{CT})$. We call such a decryption query a "**bad decryption query**".

Games 5 and 6 are identical games unless $\mathcal{A}$ makes a bad decryption query in each game. Therefore, we have $|\Pr[\mathsf{SUC}_5] - \Pr[\mathsf{SUC}_6]| \leq \Pr[\mathsf{BDQ}_6]$.

Below, we let td be a trapdoor for efficiently deciding the membership of $\mathcal{V}$.

Game 7: Same as Game 6 except that the challenger generates $d^* \xleftarrow{r} \mathcal{K}$.

By the previous change, $\mathcal{A}$ cannot obtain information of sk other than pk through decryption queries in Games 6 and 7. Moreover, as noted above, KDM queries are replied without using sk in Games 6 and 7. Thus, the view of $\mathcal{A}$ in Games 6 and 7 can be perfectly simulated by $(\mathsf{pk}, c^*, \Lambda_{\mathsf{sk}}(c^*))$ and (pk, c^*, d^*), respectively, where $\mathsf{sk} \xleftarrow{r} \mathcal{SK}$, $\mathsf{pk} \leftarrow \mu(\mathsf{sk})$, $c^* \xleftarrow{r} \mathcal{C}$, and $d^* \xleftarrow{r} \mathcal{K}$. Therefore, we have $|\Pr[\mathsf{SUC}_6] - \Pr[\mathsf{SUC}_7]| = \mathsf{negl}(\lambda)$ and $|\Pr[\mathsf{BDQ}_6] - \Pr[\mathsf{BDQ}_7]| = \mathsf{negl}(\lambda)$ from the average-case smoothness of $\mathcal{H}$.[4]

csk is now eliminated from the view of $\mathcal{A}$. Thus, we can use IND-CCA security of Π_{cca}.

Game 8: Same as Game 7 except that when $\mathcal{A}$ makes a KDM query, the challenger computes $\mathsf{CT} \leftarrow \mathsf{Enc_{cca}}\left(\mathsf{cpk}, \left(1_{\mathcal{C}}, 1_{\mathcal{K}}, 1_{\hat{\mathcal{K}}}\right)\right)$, where $1_{\mathcal{C}}$, $1_{\mathcal{K}}$, and $1_{\hat{\mathcal{K}}}$ are identity elements of $\mathcal{C}$, $\mathcal{K}$, and $\hat{\mathcal{K}}$, respectively.

From the IND-CCA security of Π_{cca}, we have $|\Pr[\mathsf{SUC}_7] - \Pr[\mathsf{SUC}_8]| = \mathsf{negl}(\lambda)$.

Moreover, since reduction algorithms for IND-CCA security of Π_{cca} can detect a bad decryption query made by $\mathcal{A}$ by utilizing decryption queries, td, and $\hat{\mathsf{sk}}$, we obtain $|\Pr[\mathsf{BDQ}_7] - \Pr[\mathsf{BDQ}_8]| = \mathsf{negl}(\lambda)$ from the IND-CCA security of Π_{cca}.

[4] In terms of reduction, we can construct a computationally unbounded adversary $\mathcal{B}$ that given (pk, c^*, d^*), distinguishes whether $d^* \leftarrow \Lambda_{\mathsf{sk}}(c^*)$ or $d^* \xleftarrow{r} \mathcal{K}$ using $\mathcal{A}$. The only non-trivial part of the construction of $\mathcal{B}$ is how $\mathcal{B}$ responds to decryption queries made by $\mathcal{A}$. After Game 6, bad decryption queries made by $\mathcal{A}$ are replied with $\perp$. In addition, if a decryption query is not a bad decryption query, computationally unbounded $\mathcal{B}$ can reply to the decryption query correctly without using sk. This is done by extracting a witness related to the decryption query and computing the hash value with Pub.

We see that the value of b is information theoretically hidden from the view of $\mathcal{A}$ in Game 8. Thus, we have $|\Pr[\mathsf{SUC}_8] - \frac{1}{2}| = 0$.

We estimate $\Pr[\mathsf{BDQ}_8]$. In Game 8, $\hat{\mathsf{sk}}$ is hidden from the view of $\mathcal{A}$ except $\hat{\mathsf{pk}}$. Moreover, $\mathcal{A}$ cannot obtain any hash value $\hat{\Lambda}_{\hat{\mathsf{sk}}}(c)$ for $c \in \mathcal{C} \setminus \mathcal{V}$ since an answer to a KDM query is computed as $\mathsf{CT} \leftarrow \mathsf{Enc}_{\mathsf{cca}}(\mathsf{cpk}, (1_{\mathcal{C}}, 1_{\mathcal{K}}, 1_{\hat{\mathcal{K}}}))$ in Game 8. Therefore, from the universal property of $\hat{\mathcal{H}}$, we obtain $\Pr[\mathsf{BDQ}_8] = \mathsf{negl}(\lambda)$.[5]

From the above arguments, we see that $\mathsf{Adv}^{\mathsf{kdmcca}}_{\Pi_{\mathsf{kdm}}, \mathcal{F}_{\mathsf{phf}}, \mathcal{A}, 1}(\lambda) = \mathsf{negl}(\lambda)$. Since the choice of $\mathcal{A}$ is arbitrary, Π_{kdm} is $\mathcal{F}_{\mathsf{phf}}$-KDM$^{(1)}$-CCA secure. □ (**Theorem** 3)

Remark 2. (Shrink secret keys). We do not need to require any structure and homomorphism for $\hat{\mathsf{sk}}$ and csk. Then, we can shrink them into a single pseudorandom function key K_{prf} and modify the construction so that $\Lambda_{\mathsf{sk}}(c^*)$ masks K_{prf}. Moreover, we can maintain c^* and $d^* = \Lambda_{\mathsf{sk}}(c^*) + K_{\mathsf{prf}}$ as a part of the corresponding public key. If we do so, the resulting secret key is just sk.

4 Instantiation Based on the DCR Assumption

We can instantiate our framework shown in Sect. 3 under the DDH, QR, and DCR assumptions. Due to the space constraints, we show the instantiation under the DCR assumption only. For Instantiations under the DDH and QR assumptions, See full version of this paper.

Definition 6 (DCR assumption). *Let $N = PQ$ be a Blum integer for λ-bit safe primes $P, Q \equiv 3 \bmod 4$ such that $P = 2p + 1$ and $Q = 2q + 1$ for primes p and q. Let $n = pq$. We can decompose $\mathbb{Z}^*_{N^2}$ as an internal direct product $G_N \otimes \langle -1 \rangle \otimes G_n \otimes G_2$, where $\langle -1 \rangle$ is the subgroup of $\mathbb{Z}^*_{N^2}$ generated by $-1 \bmod N^2$, and G_N, G_n, and G_2 are cyclic groups of order N, n, and 2, respectively. Let $T = 1 + N \in \mathbb{Z}^*_{N^2}$. T has order N, and thus it generates G_N.*

We say that the DCR assumption holds if for any PPT algorithm $\mathcal{A}$, we have $|\Pr[\mathcal{A}(N, y) = 1] - \Pr[\mathcal{A}(N, y') = 1]| = \mathsf{negl}(\lambda)$, where $y \xleftarrow{r} G_N \otimes \langle -1 \rangle \otimes G_n$ and $y' \xleftarrow{r} \langle -1 \rangle \otimes G_n$.

We define N, G_N, G_n, $\langle -1 \rangle$, and T as in Definition 6. Let $g_1, \ldots, g_\ell$ be random generators of G_n, where ℓ is determined later. We can generate a random generator g of G_n by generating $\mu \xleftarrow{r} \mathbb{Z}^*_{N^2}$ and setting $g = \mu^{2N} \bmod N^2$. Then, g is a generator of G_n with high probability.

We define $\mathcal{C}$ and $\mathcal{V}$ as

$$\mathcal{C} = \left\{ (T^{d_1} \cdot (-1)^{\gamma_1} \cdot g_1^r, \ldots, T^{d_\ell} \cdot (-1)^{\gamma_\ell} \cdot g_\ell^r) \;\middle|\; d_1, \ldots, d_\ell \in \mathbb{Z}_N, \gamma_1, \ldots, \gamma_\ell \in \mathbb{Z}_2, r \in \mathbb{Z}_n \right\}, \text{and}$$

$$\mathcal{V} = \{((-1)^{\gamma_1} \cdot g_1^r, \ldots, (-1)^{\gamma_\ell} \cdot g_\ell^r) \,|\, \gamma_1, \ldots, \gamma_\ell \in \mathbb{Z}_2, r \in \mathbb{Z}_n\}.$$

[5] Similarly to the estimation of $|\Pr[\mathsf{SUC}_6] - \Pr[\mathsf{SUC}_7]|$, in terms of reduction, we can construct a computationally unbounded reduction that responds a decryption query from $\mathcal{A}$ correctly without knowing $\hat{\mathsf{sk}}$ by extracting a witness and using $\hat{\mathsf{Pub}}$.

$\mathcal{V}$ is a subgroup of $\mathcal{C}$ and subset membership problem of $(\mathcal{C}, \mathcal{V})$ is hard under the DCR assumption. As shown by previous works [5,19], two distributions $\{T^{d_i} \cdot (-g_i)^r\}_{i \in [\ell]}$ and $\{(-g_i)^r\}_{i \in [\ell]}$ are computationally indistinguishable under the DCR assumption, where $d_i \xleftarrow{r} \mathbb{Z}_N$ for every $i \in [\ell]$ and $r \xleftarrow{r} \mathbb{Z}_{2n}$. We see that uniform distributions over $\mathcal{C}$ and $\mathcal{V}$ are also computationally indistinguishable under the DCR assumption.

Let g be another generator of G_n. Then, there exists $\alpha_i \in \mathbb{Z}_n^*$ such that $g^{\alpha_i} = g_i$ for every $i \in [\ell]$. The trapdoor for checking the membership of $\mathcal{V}$ is P, Q, and $\{\alpha_i\}_{i \in [\ell]}$.

When sampling a random element $c = (c_1, \ldots, c_\ell)$ from $\mathcal{V}$, we randomly choose $r \xleftarrow{r} \mathbb{Z}_{\frac{N-1}{4}}$ and $\gamma_i \xleftarrow{r} \mathbb{Z}_2$ for every $i \in [\ell]$, and set $c_i \leftarrow (-1)^{\gamma_i} \cdot g_i^r$ for every $i \in [\ell]$. The distribution of c is statistically close to the uniform distribution over $\mathcal{V}$. Moreover, r is a witness of $c \in \mathcal{V}$. We can sample a random element from $\mathcal{C}$ in a similar fashion.

For $(\mathcal{C}, \mathcal{V})$ defined above, we construct two projective hash functions $\mathcal{H} = (\mathcal{C}, \mathcal{V}, \mathcal{K}, \mathcal{SK}, \mathcal{PK}, \Lambda, \mu)$ and $\hat{\mathcal{H}} = \left(\mathcal{C}, \mathcal{V}, \hat{\mathcal{K}}, \hat{\mathcal{SK}}, \hat{\mathcal{PK}}, \hat{\Lambda}, \hat{\mu}\right)$. The construction of $\mathcal{H}$ is a slightly modified version of projective hash function based on the DCR assumption proposed by Wee [19] thus is a generalization of the KDM-CPA secure PKE scheme proposed by Brakerski and Goldwasser [5]. For the reason we need a modification, see Remark 3 after the constructions.

4.1 Construction of $\mathcal{H}$

We define $\mathbb{QR}_{N^s} = G_{N^{s-1}} \otimes G_n$ and $\mathbb{J}_{N^s} = G_{N^{s-1}} \otimes \langle -1 \rangle \otimes G_n = \langle -1 \rangle \otimes \mathbb{QR}_{N^s}$. We define $\mathcal{SK} = \{0,1\}^\ell$, $\mathcal{PK} = G_n$, and $\mathcal{K} = \mathbb{QR}_{N^s}$. For every $\mathsf{sk} = s_1 \cdots s_\ell \in \{0,1\}^\ell$ and $c = (c_1, \ldots, c_\ell) \in \mathcal{C}$, we also define μ and Λ as

$$\mu(\mathsf{sk}) = \prod_{i \in [\ell]} g_i^{2s_i} \text{ and } \Lambda_{\mathsf{sk}}(c) = \prod_{i \in [\ell]} c_i^{2s_i}.$$

Projective property. Let $\mathsf{sk} = s_1 \cdots s_\ell \in \{0,1\}^\ell$, $\mathsf{pk} = \prod_{i \in [\ell]} g_i^{2s_i}$, and $c = ((-1)^{\gamma_1} \cdot g_1^r, \ldots, (-1)^{\gamma_\ell} \cdot g_\ell^r)$, where $r \in \mathbb{Z}_n$ and $\gamma_i \in \mathbb{Z}_2$ for every $i \in [\ell]$. We define the public evaluation algorithm Pub as $\mathsf{Pub}(\mathsf{pk}, c, r) = \mathsf{pk}^r$. We see that

$$\mathsf{pk}^r = \left(\prod_{i \in [\ell]} g_i^{2s_i}\right)^r = \prod_{i \in [\ell]} (g_i^r)^{2s_i} = \prod_{i \in [\ell]} ((-1)^{\gamma_i} \cdot g_i^r)^{2s_i} = \Lambda_{\mathsf{sk}}(c)$$

and thus $\mathcal{H}$ satisfies projective property.

Homomorphism. For every $\mathsf{sk} = s_1 \cdots s_\ell \in \{0,1\}^\ell$, $c = (c_1, \ldots, c_\ell) \in \mathcal{C}$, and $c' = (c'_1, \ldots, c'_\ell) \in \mathcal{C}$, we have

$$\Lambda_{\mathsf{sk}}(c) \cdot \Lambda_{\mathsf{sk}}(c') = \prod_{i \in [\ell]} c_i^{2s_i} \cdot \prod_{i \in [\ell]} (c'_i)^{2s_i} = \prod_{i \in [\ell]} (c_i \cdot c'_i)^{2s_i} = \Lambda_{\mathsf{sk}}(c \cdot c')$$

and thus $\mathcal{H}$ is homomorphic.

Average-case smoothness. Similarly to Wee [19], we prove a weaker property that is sufficient for our construction.

For an element $e = T^d \cdot g^r \in \mathbb{QR}_{N^s}$, we define $e \bmod G_n = T^d$. Let $c = (c_1, \ldots, c_\ell) = (T^{d_1} \cdot (-1)^{\gamma_1} \cdot g_1^r, \ldots, T^{d_\ell} \cdot (-1)^{\gamma_\ell} \cdot g_\ell^r)$, where $d_1, \ldots, d_\ell \in \mathbb{Z}_N$, $\gamma_1, \ldots, \gamma_\ell \in \mathbb{Z}_2$, and $r \in \mathbb{Z}_n$. We have

$$\Lambda_{\mathsf{sk}}(c) \bmod G_n = \prod_{i\in[\ell]} \left(T^{d_i} \cdot g_i^r\right)^{2s_i} \bmod G_n = T^{2\sum_{i\in[\ell]} d_i s_i \bmod N}.$$

The leftover hash lemma implies that the following two distributions

$$\left(c, \sum_{i\in[\ell]} d_i s_i \bmod N, \prod_{i\in[\ell]} g_i^{2s_i}\right) \text{ and } \left(c, \mathsf{K}, \prod_{i\in[\ell]} g_i^{2s_i}\right)$$

are $\sqrt{\frac{N\cdot n}{4\cdot 2^\ell}}$-close, where $\mathsf{sk} = s_1 \cdots s_\ell \xleftarrow{\mathsf{r}} \{0,1\}^\ell$, $c = (c_1, \ldots, c_\ell) \xleftarrow{\mathsf{r}} \mathcal{C}$, and $\mathsf{K} \xleftarrow{\mathsf{r}} \mathbb{Z}_N$. Moreover, if K is uniformly at random over $\mathbb{Z}_N$, then so does $2\mathsf{K} \bmod N$. Therefore, by setting $\ell = 3\log N$, the distribution of $\Lambda_{\mathsf{sk}}(c) \bmod G_n$ is statistically close to uniform over G_N.

4.2 Construction of $\hat{\mathcal{H}}$

We define $\hat{\mathcal{SK}} = \mathbb{Z}_{Nn}^\ell$,[6] $\hat{\mathcal{PK}} = G_n$, and $\hat{\mathcal{K}} = \mathbb{QR}_{N^s}$. For every $\hat{\mathsf{sk}} = (x_1, \ldots, x_\ell) \in \hat{\mathcal{SK}}$ and $c = (c_1, \ldots, c_\ell) \in \mathcal{C}$, we also define $\hat{\mu}$ and $\hat{\Lambda}$ as

$$\hat{\mu}\left(\hat{\mathsf{sk}}\right) = \prod_{i\in[\ell]} g_i^{2x_i} \text{ and } \hat{\Lambda}_{\hat{\mathsf{sk}}}(c) = \prod_{i\in[\ell]} c_i^{2x_i}.$$

Projective property. For every $\hat{\mathsf{sk}} = (x_1, \ldots, x_\ell) \in \hat{\mathcal{SK}}$, $\hat{\mathsf{pk}} = \prod_{i\in[\ell]} g_i^{2x_i}$, and $c = ((-1)^{\gamma_1} \cdot g_1^r, \ldots, (-1)^{\gamma_\ell} \cdot g_\ell^r)$, where $r \in \mathbb{Z}_n$ and $\gamma_i \in \mathbb{Z}_2$ for every $i \in [\ell]$, we define the public evaluation algorithm $\hat{\mathsf{Pub}}$ as $\hat{\mathsf{Pub}}\left(\hat{\mathsf{pk}}, c, r\right) = \hat{\mathsf{pk}}^r$. Similarly to $\mathcal{H}$, we see that $\hat{\mathcal{H}}$ satisfies projective property.

Universal property. We need to prove that the universal property holds not only for all $c \in \mathcal{C} \setminus \mathcal{V}$ but also all $c \in \mathbb{J}_{N^s}^\ell \setminus \mathcal{C}$. This is because we cannot efficiently check the membership of $\mathcal{C}$. Note that we can check the membership of $\mathbb{J}_{N^s}$ by computing Jacobi symbol with respect to N, and Jacobi symbol with respect to N can be computed without factorizations of N, that is P and Q [18, Sect. 12.3].

For every $c \in \mathbb{J}_{N^s}^\ell \setminus \mathcal{C}$, we define $\hat{\Lambda}_{\hat{\mathsf{sk}}}(c)$ in the same way as above. For every $\hat{\mathsf{pk}} \in \hat{\mathcal{PK}}$, $c = (c_1, \ldots, c_\ell) \in \mathbb{J}_{N^s}^\ell$, and $\pi \in \hat{\mathcal{K}}$, we consider the following probability

[6] In the actual construction, we sample $\hat{\mathsf{sk}}$ from $\mathbb{Z}_{\frac{N(N-1)}{4}}^{\lambda\times\ell}$ to sample $\hat{\mathsf{sk}}$ without knowing n. The uniform distributions over $\mathbb{Z}_{Nn}^{\lambda\times\ell}$ and $\mathbb{Z}_{\frac{N(N-1)}{4}}^{\lambda\times\ell}$ are statistically close.

$$\Pr_{x_i \xleftarrow{r} \mathbb{Z}_{Nn}}\left[\prod_{i\in[\ell]} c_i^{2x_i} = \pi \,\middle|\, \prod_{i\in[\ell]} g_i^{2x_i} = \hat{\mathsf{pk}}\right]$$

$$= \Pr_{x_i \xleftarrow{r} \mathbb{Z}_{Nn}}\left[\prod_{i\in[\ell]} c_i^{2x_i} = \pi \,\middle|\, \prod_{i\in[\ell]} g_i^{2(x_i \bmod n)} = \hat{\mathsf{pk}}\right]. \quad (1)$$

We first consider the case where at least one element of $c = (c_1, \ldots, c_\ell)$ is not in $\langle -1 \rangle \otimes G_n$. Suppose that $c_{i^*} \in \mathbb{J}_{N^s} \setminus \langle -1 \rangle \otimes G_n$ for some $i^* \in [\ell]$.

For two elements $e_0, e_1 \in \mathbb{QR}_{N^s}$, we write $e_0 \equiv e_1 \bmod G_n$ to denote that $e_0 \bmod G_n = e_1 \bmod G_n$. For two elements $e_0, e_1 \in \mathbb{QR}_{N^s}$, if $e_0 = e_1$ holds, then so does $e_0 \equiv e_1 \bmod G_n$. Thus, the probability of Eq. 1 is bounded by

$$\Pr_{x_i \xleftarrow{r} \mathbb{Z}_{Nn}}\left[\prod_{i\in[\ell]} c_i^{2x_i} \equiv \pi \bmod G_n \,\middle|\, \prod_{i\in[\ell]} g_i^{2(x_i \bmod n)} = \hat{\mathsf{pk}}\right].$$

For every $i \in [\ell]$, $c_i^{2x_i} \bmod G_n$ is determined by only $x_i \bmod N$ and independent of $x_i \bmod n$ from the Chinese Remainder Theorem since $N = PQ$ and $n = pq$ are relatively prime. Therefore, the above probability is

$$\Pr_{x_i \xleftarrow{r} \mathbb{Z}_{Nn}}\left[\prod_{i\in[\ell]} c_i^{2x_i} \equiv \pi \bmod G_n\right].$$

Since $c_{i^*} \notin \langle -1 \rangle \otimes G_n$, we can write $c_{i^*} = T^{d_{i^*}} \cdot (-1)^{\gamma_{i^*}} \cdot g^{r_{i^*}}$, where $d_{i^*} \in \mathbb{Z}_N$ such that $d_{i^*} \neq 0$, $\gamma_{i^*} \in \mathbb{Z}_2$, and $r_{i^*} \in \mathbb{Z}_n$. We have

$$c_{i^*}^{2x_{i^*}} = T^{2d_{i^*}(x_{i^*} \bmod N)} \cdot g^{2r_{i^*}(x_{i^*} \bmod n)}.$$

Then, the above probability is the same as

$$\Pr_{x_i \xleftarrow{r} \mathbb{Z}_{Nn}}\left[T^{2d_{i^*}(x_{i^*} \bmod N)} \equiv \pi \cdot \left(\prod_{i\in[\ell], i\neq i^*} c_i^{2x_i}\right)^{-1} \bmod G_n\right].$$

This probability is smaller than $\frac{1}{P}$ or $\frac{1}{Q}$. Thus, in this case, the probability of Eq. 1 is negligible in λ.

We next consider the case where all elements of $c = (c_1, \ldots, c_\ell) \notin \mathcal{V}$ are in $\langle -1 \rangle \otimes G_n$. In this case, we can write $c_i = (-1)^{\gamma_i} \cdot g_i^{r_i}$, where $\gamma_i \in \mathbb{Z}_2$ and $r_i \in \mathbb{Z}_n$ for every $i \in [\ell]$. Since $c \notin \mathcal{V}$, there exist $i_1, i_2 \in [\ell]$ such that $r_{i_1} \neq r_{i_2}$. Let g be a generator of G_n. Since g_i is a generator of G_n, there exists $\alpha_i \in \mathbb{Z}_n^*$ such that $g_i = g^{\alpha_i}$ for every $i \in [\ell]$. The probability of Eq. 1 is 0 if $\pi \notin G_n$, and thus we consider cases of $\pi \in G_n$. Then, the probability of Eq. 1 is the same as

$$\Pr_{x_i \xleftarrow{r} \mathbb{Z}_n}\left[2\sum_{i\in[\ell]} \alpha_i r_i x_i \equiv \log_g \pi \bmod n \,\middle|\, 2\sum_{i\in[\ell]} \alpha_i x_i \equiv \log_g \hat{\mathsf{pk}} \bmod n\right].$$

Since $r_1 \not\equiv r_2 \bmod n$, either $r_{i_1} \not\equiv r_{i_2} \bmod p$ or $r_{i_1} \not\equiv r_{i_2} \bmod q$ holds. Without loss of generality, we assume that $r_{i_1} \not\equiv r_{i_2} \bmod p$. Since p and q are primes, the above probability is bounded by

$$\Pr_{x_i \xleftarrow{r} \mathbb{Z}_n}\left[\sum_{i\in[\ell]} \alpha_i r_i x_i \equiv 2^{-1}\cdot \log_g \pi \bmod p \,\middle|\, \sum_{i\in[\ell]} \alpha_i x_i \equiv 2^{-1}\cdot \log_g \hat{\mathsf{pk}} \bmod p\right].$$

Since $r_{i_1} \not\equiv r_{i_2} \bmod p$, two equations

$$\sum_{i\in[\ell]} \alpha_i r_i x_i \equiv 2^{-1}\cdot \log_g \pi \bmod p, \text{ and } \sum_{i\in[\ell]} \alpha_i x_i \equiv 2^{-1}\cdot \log_g \hat{\mathsf{pk}} \bmod p$$

are linearly independent. Therefore, the above probability is $\frac{1}{p}$.

Thus, for every $c \in \mathbb{J}_{N^s}^{\ell} \setminus \mathcal{V}$, the probability of Eq. 1 is negligible in λ.

Remark 3 (*Difference with previous works* [5,19]). The difference between our construction and previous works is that when we compute a hash value of c, we first square each element of c. By this operation, the ranges of $\mathcal{H}$ and $\hat{\mathcal{H}}$ are $\mathbb{QR}_{N^s} = G_N \cdot G_n$.

If we do not perform squaring, the ranges will be $\mathbb{J}_{N^s} = G_N \cdot \langle -1 \rangle \cdot G_n$ and hash values of some elements can be predicted with high probability since the order of $\langle -1 \rangle$ is 2. In fact, we can correctly guess the hash value of $(-1, \ldots, -1) \in \langle -1 \rangle^{\ell}$ with probability at least $\frac{1}{2}$. In this case, to achieve universal property of $\hat{\mathcal{H}}$, we need parallelization similarly to the QR based construction.

One might think we have another option where $\mathcal{C}$ and $\mathcal{V}$ are defined as subgroups of $\mathbb{QR}_{N^s}$ and G_n, respectively. This option is not working. The reason is that we cannot efficiently check the membership of $\mathbb{QR}_{N^s}$. Therefore, if we use such $\mathcal{C}$ and $\mathcal{V}$, we still need to take elements of $\mathbb{J}_{N^s}$ into account, and thus we need squaring.

4.3 Associated Function Class

The message space of the DCR based construction is $\mathbb{Z}_N$. We define $\phi(m \in \mathbb{Z}_N) = T^m$. Let $\mathcal{F}_{\mathsf{dcr}}$ be a family of functions described as

$$\begin{aligned} f_e\left(\mathsf{sk}, \hat{\mathsf{sk}}, c^*, d^*\right) &= \phi^{-1}\left(\Lambda_{\mathsf{sk}}\left(T^{e_1/2}, \ldots, T^{e_\ell/2}\right) + \phi\left(f\left(\hat{\mathsf{sk}}, c^*, d^*\right)\right)\right) \\ &= \phi^{-1}\left(T^{\sum_{i\in[\ell]} e_i s_i + f\left(\hat{\mathsf{sk}}, c^*, d^*\right)}\right) \\ &= \left(\sum_{i\in[\ell]} e_i s_i + f\left(\hat{\mathsf{sk}}, c^*, d^*\right)\right) \bmod N, \end{aligned}$$

where $\frac{1}{2}$ denotes the inverse of 2 modulo N, $e_i \in \mathbb{Z}_N$ for every $i \in [\ell]$, and f is a function whose range is $\mathbb{Z}_N$. The DCR based construction is $\mathcal{F}_{\mathsf{dcr}}$-KDM$^{(1)}$-CCA secure. In the construction, we can maintain $\hat{\mathsf{sk}}$, c^*, and d^* as bit strings. In this case, the above function class includes affine functions and projection functions.

5 KDM-CCA Secure PKE from the DDH Assumption

Although our framework shown in Sect. 3 captures only $\mathrm{KDM}^{(1)}$-CCA security, we can prove the KDM-CCA security of concrete instantiations. In this section, we prove that our concrete instantiation based on the DDH assumption is KDM-CCA secure. We also briefly explain how to prove the multi user security of our QR and DCR based schemes in Remark 5 at the end of this section. We first introduce the DDH assumption, and then provide the construction.

Definition 7 (DDH assumption). *Let $\mathbb{G}$ be a cyclic group of order p and g a random generator of $\mathbb{G}$. We say that the DDH assumption holds if for any PPT algorithm $\mathcal{A}$, $|\Pr[\mathcal{A}(p, g, g^x, g^y, g^{xy}) = 1] - \Pr[\mathcal{A}(p, g, g^x, g^y, g^z) = 1] = \mathsf{negl}(\lambda)|$ holds, where $x, y, z \xleftarrow{r} \mathbb{Z}_p$.*

Let $\mathbb{G}$ be a cyclic group of prime order p and g a random generator of $\mathbb{G}$. Let $\Pi_{\mathsf{cca}} = (\mathsf{KG}_{\mathsf{cca}}, \mathsf{Enc}_{\mathsf{cca}}, \mathsf{Dec}_{\mathsf{cca}})$ be a PKE scheme. We assume that the secret-key space of Π_{cca} is $\mathbb{G}$ for simplicity. We construct the following PKE scheme $\Pi_{\mathsf{ddh}} = (\mathsf{KG}_{\mathsf{ddh}}, \mathsf{Enc}_{\mathsf{ddh}}, \mathsf{Dec}_{\mathsf{ddh}})$. The message space of Π_{ddh} is $\{0, 1\}$.

$\mathsf{KG}_{\mathsf{ddh}}(1^\lambda)$:
- Generate $g_1, \ldots, g_\ell \xleftarrow{r} \mathbb{G}$.
- Generate $s = s_1 \cdots s_\ell \xleftarrow{r} \{0, 1\}^\ell$ and $x_1, \ldots, x_\ell \xleftarrow{r} \mathbb{Z}_p$.
- Compute $g_0 \leftarrow \prod_{i \in [\ell]} g_i^{s_i}$ and $\hat{g}_0 \leftarrow \prod_{i \in [\ell]} g_i^{x_i}$.
- Generate $(\mathsf{cpk}, \mathsf{csk}) \leftarrow \mathsf{KG}_{\mathsf{cca}}(1^\lambda)$.
- Generate $w_i \xleftarrow{r} \mathbb{Z}_p$ and set $e_i \leftarrow g_i^{w_i}$ for every $i \in [\ell]$.
- Compute $e_0 \leftarrow \prod_{i \in [\ell]} e_i^{s_i}$ and $u \leftarrow e_0 \cdot \mathsf{csk}$.
- Set $v := \{x_i\}_{i \in [\ell]} \| \{e_i\}_{i \in [\ell]} \| u$.
- Return $\mathsf{PK} := \left(\{g_i\}_{i \in [\ell]}, g_0, \hat{g}_0, \mathsf{cpk}\right)$ and $\mathsf{SK} := (s, v)$.

$\mathsf{Enc}_{\mathsf{ddh}}(\mathsf{PK}, m)$:
- Parse $\left(\{g_i\}_{i \in [\ell]}, g_0, \hat{g}_0, \mathsf{cpk}\right) \leftarrow \mathsf{PK}$.
- Generate $r \xleftarrow{r} \mathbb{Z}_p$ and compute $c_i \leftarrow g_i^r$ for every $i \in [\ell]$.
- Compute $d \leftarrow g^m \cdot g_0^r$ and $\pi \leftarrow \hat{g}_0^r$.
- Return $\mathsf{CT} \leftarrow \mathsf{Enc}_{\mathsf{cca}}\left(\mathsf{cpk}, \left(\{c_i\}_{i \in [\ell]}, d, \pi\right)\right)$.

$\mathsf{Dec}_{\mathsf{ddh}}(\mathsf{SK}, \mathsf{CT})$:
- Parse $\left(s, \{x_i\}_{i \in [\ell]} \| \{e_i\}_{i \in [\ell]} \| u\right) \leftarrow \mathsf{SK}$.
- Compute $\mathsf{csk} \leftarrow u \cdot \left(\prod_{i \in [\ell]} e_i^{s_i}\right)^{-1}$.
- Compute $\left(\{c_i\}_{i \in [\ell]}, d, \pi\right) \leftarrow \mathsf{Dec}_{\mathsf{cca}}(\mathsf{csk}, \mathsf{CT})$. If the decryption result is not in $\mathbb{G}^{\ell+2}$, returns $\perp$. Otherwise, compute as follows.
- Return $\perp$ if $\pi \neq \prod_{i \in [\ell]} c_i^{x_i}$ and $m \leftarrow \log_g \left(d \cdot \left(\prod_{i \in [\ell]} c_i^{s_i}\right)^{-1}\right)$ otherwise.

Correctness. In the decryption algorithm, we need to compute discrete logarithm on $\mathbb{G}$. We can efficiently perform this operation since we restrict the message space to $\{0,1\}$. The decryption algorithm returns $\perp$ if $d \cdot \left(\prod_{i\in[\ell]} c_i^{s_i}\right)^{-1} \notin \{1, g\}$. Then, the correctness of Π_{ddh} follows from that of Π_{cca}.

Let n be the number of key pairs in the security game. We define $\mathcal{F}_{\mathsf{ddh}}$ as a function family consisting of functions described as

$$f'\left(\{s_k, v_k\}_{k\in[n]}\right) = \sum_{k\in[n]} \langle a_k, s_k\rangle + f\left(\{v_k\}_{k\in[n]}\right),$$

where $\langle\cdot,\cdot\rangle$ denotes inner product over $\mathbb{Z}$, $a_k \in \{0,1\}^\ell$, and f is a function such that $\sum_{k\in[n]} \langle a_k, s_k\rangle + f\left(\{v_k\}_{k\in[n]}\right) \in \{0,1\}$ for every $\{s_k\}_{k\in[n]}$ and $\{v_k\}_{k\in[n]}$. By maintaining $\{v_k\}_{k\in[n]}$ as bit strings, $\mathcal{F}_{\mathsf{ddh}}$ includes projection functions of single-bit output. Π_{kdm} is KDM-CCA secure with respect to $\mathcal{F}_{\mathsf{ddh}}$. Formally, we prove the following theorem.

Theorem 4. *Let Π_{cca} be IND-CCA secure. Assuming the DDH problem is hard on $\mathbb{G}$, Π_{ddh} is $\mathcal{F}_{\mathsf{ddh}}$-KDM-CCA secure.*

Remark 4 (Extension to affine functions). We can construct a DDH based PKE scheme that is KDM-CCA secure with respect to affine functions by applying the following modifications to the above construction. We set the message space as $\mathbb{G}$. Let $\mathsf{SK} \in \{0,1\}^L$ be a bit string that is a concatenation of s and bit representation of v. We maintain a secret-key $\mathsf{SK} = s_1 \cdots s_L$ as $(g^{s_1}, \ldots, g^{s_L})$. Then, the construction is $\mathcal{F}_{\mathsf{aff}}$-KDM-CCA secure, where $\mathcal{F}_{\mathsf{aff}}$ is a function class consisting of functions described as

$$f(\mathsf{SK}_1, \ldots, \mathsf{SK}_n) = \left(\prod_{i\in[L]} (g^{s_{ki}})^{a_{ki}}\right) \cdot a_0,$$

where $\mathsf{SK}_k = s_{k1} \cdots s_{kL}$ for every $k \in [n]$, $a_0 \in \mathbb{G}$ and $a_{ki} \in \mathbb{Z}_p$ for every $i \in [\ell]$ and $k \in [n]$. This is exactly the affine functions defined by Boneh et al. [4].

Proof of Theorem 4. Let n be the number of keys. Let $\mathcal{A}$ be an adversary that attacks the $\mathcal{F}_{\mathsf{ddh}}$-KDM-CCA security of Π_{ddh}. We proceed the proof via a sequence of games. For every $t \in \{0, \ldots, 11\}$, let $\mathtt{SUC}_t$ be the event that $\mathcal{A}$ succeeds in guessing the challenge bit b in Game t.

Game 0: This is the original $\mathcal{F}_{\mathsf{ddh}}$-KDM$^{(n)}$-CCA game regarding Π_{ddh}. We have $\mathsf{Adv}^{\mathsf{kdmcca}}_{\Pi_{\mathsf{ddh}},\mathcal{F}_{\mathsf{ddh}},\mathcal{A},n}(\lambda) = \left|\Pr[\mathtt{SUC}_0] - \frac{1}{2}\right|$.

1. The challenger chooses $b \xleftarrow{r} \{0,1\}$ and generates $(\mathsf{PK}_k, \mathsf{SK}_k)$ for every $k \in [n]$ as follows.
   (a) Generate $g_{k1}, \ldots, g_{k\ell} \xleftarrow{r} \mathbb{G}$.
   (b) Generate $s_k = s_{k1} \cdots s_{k\ell} \xleftarrow{r} \{0,1\}^\ell$ and $x_{k1}, \ldots, x_{k\ell} \xleftarrow{r} \mathbb{Z}_p$.

(c) Compute $g_{k0} \leftarrow \prod_{i\in[\ell]} (g_{ki})^{s_{ki}}$ and $\hat{g}_{k0} \leftarrow \prod_{i\in[\ell]} (g_{ki})^{x_{ki}}$.
(d) Generate $(\mathsf{cpk}_k, \mathsf{csk}_k) \leftarrow \mathsf{KG}_{\mathsf{cca}}(1^\lambda)$.
(e) Generate $w_{ki} \xleftarrow{r} \mathbb{Z}_p$ and set $e_{ki} \leftarrow (g_{ki})^{w_{ki}}$ for every $i \in [\ell]$.
(f) Compute $e_{k0} \leftarrow \prod_{i\in[\ell]} (e_{ki})^{s_{ki}}$ and $u_k \leftarrow e_{k0} \cdot \mathsf{csk}_k$.
(g) Set $v_k := \{x_{ki}\}_{i\in[\ell]} \| \{e_{ki}\}_{i\in[\ell]} \| u_k$.
(h) Set $\mathsf{PK}_k := \left(\mathsf{cpk}_k, \{g_{ki}\}_{i\in[\ell]}, g_{k0}, \hat{g}_{k0}\right)$ and $\mathsf{SK}_k := (s_k, v_k)$.
The challenger sends $\{\mathsf{PK}_k\}_{k\in[n]}$ to $\mathcal{A}$ and prepares a list L_{kdm}.

2. The challenger responds to queries made by $\mathcal{A}$.
For a KDM query $\left(j, \left(\{a_k^0\}_{k\in[n]}, f^0\right), \left(\{a_k^1\}_{k\in[n]}, f^1\right)\right)$ made by $\mathcal{A}$, the challenger responds as follows.
(a) Set $m := \sum_{k\in[n]} \langle a_k^b, s_k\rangle + f^b\left(\{v_k\}_{k\in[n]}\right)$.
(b) Generate $r \xleftarrow{r} \mathbb{Z}_p$ and compute $c_i \leftarrow (g_{ji})^r$ for every $i \in [\ell]$.
(c) Compute $d \leftarrow g^m \cdot (g_{j0})^r$ and $\pi \leftarrow (\hat{g}_{j0})^r$.
(d) Return $\mathsf{CT} \leftarrow \mathsf{Enc}_{\mathsf{cca}}\left(\mathsf{cpk}_j, \left(\{c_i\}_{i\in[\ell]}, d, \pi\right)\right)$ and add (j, CT) to L_{kdm}.
For a decryption query (j, CT) made by $\mathcal{A}$, the challenger returns $\perp$ to $\mathcal{A}$ if $(j, \mathsf{CT}) \in L_{\mathsf{kdm}}$, and otherwise responds as follows.
(a) Compute $\left(\{c_i\}_{i\in[\ell]}, d, \pi\right) \leftarrow \mathsf{Dec}_{\mathsf{cca}}(\mathsf{csk}_j, \mathsf{CT})$. If the decryption result is not in $\mathbb{G}^{\ell+2}$, return $\perp$ and otherwise respond as follows.
(b) Return $\perp$ if $\pi \neq \prod_{i\in[\ell]} c_i^{x_{ji}}$ and $m \leftarrow \log_g\left(d \cdot \left(\prod_{i\in[\ell]} c_i^{s_{ji}}\right)^{-1}\right)$ otherwise.

3. $\mathcal{A}$ outputs $b' \in \{0,1\}$.

Game 1: Same as Game 0 except how the challenger computes $\{e_{ki}\}_{i\in[\ell],k\in[n]}$. The challenger generates $w_i \xleftarrow{r} \mathbb{Z}_p$ for every $i \in [\ell]$ and computes $e_{ki} \leftarrow (g_{ki})^{w_i}$ for every $i \in [\ell]$ and $k \in [n]$.

We have $|\Pr[\mathtt{SUC}_0] - \Pr[\mathtt{SUC}_1]| = \mathsf{negl}(\lambda)$ since $((g_{1i})^{w_{1i}}, \ldots, (g_{ni})^{w_{ni}})$ and $((g_{1i})^{w_i}, \ldots, (g_{ni})^{w_i})$ are computationally indistinguishable by the DDH assumption for every $i \in [\ell]$.

Game 2: Same as Game 1 except how the challenger generates $\{s_k\}_{k\in[n]}$ and $\{g_{ki}\}_{i\in[\ell],k\in[n]}$. The challenger first generates $s = s_1 \cdots s_\ell \xleftarrow{r} \{0,1\}^\ell$ and $g_1, \ldots g_\ell \xleftarrow{r} \mathbb{G}$. Then, for every $k \in [n]$, the challenger generates $\Delta_k \xleftarrow{r} \{0,1\}^\ell$ and computes $s_k \leftarrow s \oplus \Delta_k$. In addition, for every $i \in [\ell]$ and $k \in [n]$, the challenger generates $\gamma_{ki} \xleftarrow{r} \mathbb{Z}_p$ and computes $g_{ki} \leftarrow g_i^{\gamma_{ki}}$.

$|\Pr[\mathtt{SUC}_1] - \Pr[\mathtt{SUC}_2]| = 0$ holds since the difference between Game 1 and 2 is only conceptual.

From Game 3 to 7, we change the game so that we do not need s to respond to KDM queries made by $\mathcal{A}$.

In Game 2, we have $g_{k0} = \prod_{i\in[\ell]} (g_{ki})^{s_{ki}} = \prod_{i\in[\ell]} (g_i^{\gamma_{ki}})^{s_i \oplus \Delta_{ki}}$, where Δ_{ki} is the i-th bit of Δ_k for every $i \in [\ell]$. For every $i \in [\ell]$ and $k \in [n]$, we have

$$s_i \oplus \Delta_{ki} = \begin{cases} s_i & (\Delta_{ki} = 0) \\ 1 - s_i & (\Delta_{ki} = 1) \end{cases}.$$

Thus, by defining

$$\delta_{ki} = \begin{cases} 1 & (\Delta_{ki} = 0) \\ -1 & (\Delta_{ki} = 1) \end{cases}, \tag{2}$$

for every $i \in [\ell]$ and $k \in [n]$, we have

$$g_{k0} = \prod_{i\in\Delta_k} g_i^{\gamma_{ki}} \cdot \prod_{i\in[\ell]} g_i^{\delta_{ki}\gamma_{ki}s_i} = \prod_{i\in\Delta_k} g_{ki} \cdot \prod_{i\in[\ell]} g_i^{\delta_{ki}\gamma_{ki}s_i}$$

for every $k \in [n]$, where $\prod_{i\in\Delta_k} X_i$ denotes $\prod_{i\in[\ell]} X_i^{\Delta_{ki}}$.[7]

Game 3: Same as Game 2 except that the challenger uses $\delta_{ki}\gamma_{ki}$ instead of γ_{ki} for every $i \in [\ell]$ and $k \in [n]$. More precisely, the challenger computes $g_{ki} \leftarrow g_i^{\delta_{ki}\gamma_{ki}}$ for every $i \in [\ell]$ and $k \in [n]$, and $g_{k0} \leftarrow \prod_{i\in\Delta_k} g_{ki} \cdot \prod_{i\in[\ell]} g_i^{\gamma_{ki}s_i}$ for every $k \in [n]$. Note that $\delta_{ki} \cdot \delta_{ki} = 1$ for every $i \in [\ell]$ and $k \in [n]$.

If γ_{ki} distributes uniformly at random, then so does $\delta_{ki}\gamma_{ki}$ for every $i \in [\ell]$ and $k \in [n]$. Therefore, we have $|\Pr[\mathsf{SUC}_2] - \Pr[\mathsf{SUC}_3]| = 0$.

Game 4: Same as Game 3 except how the challenger computes $g_{k0}, g_{k1}, \ldots, g_{k\ell}$ for every $k \in [n]$. The challenger generates γ_k for every $k \in [n]$ and computes $g_{ki} \leftarrow g_i^{\gamma_k\delta_{ki}}$ for every $i \in [\ell]$ and $k \in [n]$. Moreover, the challenger computes $g_{k0} \leftarrow \prod_{i\in\Delta_k} g_{ki} \cdot \prod_{i\in[\ell]} g_i^{\gamma_k s_i}$ for every $k \in [n]$.

$|\Pr[\mathsf{SUC}_3] - \Pr[\mathsf{SUC}_4]| = \mathsf{negl}(\lambda)$ holds since $(g_1^{\gamma_{k1}}, \ldots, g_\ell^{\gamma_{k\ell}})$ and $(g_1^{\gamma_k}, \ldots, g_\ell^{\gamma_k})$ are computationally indistinguishable by the DDH assumption for every $k \in [n]$.

Below, we let $g_0 = \prod_{i\in[\ell]} g_i^{s_i}$. In Game 4, for every $k \in [n]$, we have

$$g_{ki} = g_i^{\gamma_k\delta_{ki}} \ (i \in [\ell]) \ , \text{ and}$$

$$g_{k0} = \prod_{i\in\Delta_k} g_{ki} \cdot \prod_{i\in[\ell]} g_i^{\gamma_k s_i} = \left(\prod_{i\in\Delta_k} g_{ki}\right) \cdot g_0^{\gamma_k}.$$

Then, the answer to a KDM query $\left(j, \left(\left\{a_k^0\right\}_{k\in[n]}, f^0\right), \left(\left\{a_k^1\right\}_{k\in[n]}, f^1\right)\right)$ in Game 4 is $\mathsf{Enc_{cca}}\left(\mathsf{cpk}_j, \left(\left\{c_i\right\}_{i\in[\ell]}, d, \pi\right)\right)$, where

$$c_i = (g_{ji})^r = (g_i^r)^{\gamma_j\delta_{ji}} \ (i \in [\ell]) \ , \ d = g^{\sum_{k\in[k]}\langle a_k^b, s_k\rangle + f^b(\{v_k\}_{k\in[n]})} \cdot (g_{j0})^r \ ,$$
$$\pi = (\hat{g}_{j0})^r = \prod_{i\in[\ell]} c_i^{x_{ji}} \ , \text{ and } r \xleftarrow{\mathsf{r}} \mathbb{Z}_p.$$

[7] That is, $\prod_{i\in\Delta_k} X_i$ denotes the summation of X_i over positions i such that $\Delta_{ki} = 1$.

We also have

$$\sum_{k\in[n]} \langle a_k^b, s_k \rangle = \sum_{k\in[n]} \langle a_k^b, s \oplus \Delta_k \rangle = \sum_{k\in[n]} \sum_{i\in\Delta_k} a_{ki}^b + \sum_{k\in[n]} \sum_{i\in[\ell]} a_{ki}^b \delta_{ki} s_i,$$

where summation is done over $\mathbb{Z}$ and a_{ki}^b is the i-th bit of a_k^b for every $i \in [\ell]$. Thus, by defining

$$Y^b = \sum_{k\in[n]} \sum_{i\in\Delta_k} a_{ki}^b + f^b\left(\{v_k\}_{k\in[n]}\right) \text{ and } \mu_i^b = \sum_{k\in[n]} a_{ki}^b \delta_{ki} \ (i \in [\ell]) \ , \quad (3)$$

we have

$$\begin{aligned} d &= g^{Y^b + \sum_{i\in[\ell]} \mu_i^b s_i} \cdot \left(\prod_{i\in\Delta_j} g_{ji}\right)^r \cdot \left(\prod_{i\in[\ell]} g_i^{s_i}\right)^{\gamma_j r} \\ &= g^{Y^b} \cdot \prod_{i\in\Delta_j} c_i \cdot \prod_{i\in[\ell]} \left(g^{\mu_i^b} \cdot (g_i^r)^{\gamma_j}\right)^{s_i} . \end{aligned}$$

Note that Y^b and $\{\mu_i^b\}_{i\in[\ell]}$ are computed from $\left(\{a_k^b\}_{k\in[n]}, f^b\right)$ and $\{\delta_{ki}\}_{i\in[\ell],k\in[n]}$.

Hereafter, we show the difference from the previous game by colored parts.

Game 5: Same as Game 4 except how the challenger responds to KDM queries. For a KDM query $\left(j, \left(\{a_k^0\}_{k\in[n]}, f^0\right), \left(\{a_k^1\}_{k\in[n]}, f^1\right)\right)$ made by $\mathcal{A}$, the challenger responds as follows.

1. Compute Y^b and $\{\mu_i^b\}_{i\in[\ell]}$ as Eq. 3.
2. Generate $r_1, \ldots, r_\ell \xleftarrow{r} \mathbb{Z}_p$.
3. Compute $c_i \leftarrow (g_i^{r_i})^{\gamma_j \delta_{ji}}$ for every $i \in [\ell]$.
4. Compute $d \leftarrow g^{Y^b} \cdot \prod_{i\in\Delta_j} c_i \cdot \prod_{i\in[\ell]} \left(g^{\mu_i^b} \cdot (g_i^{r_i})^{\gamma_j}\right)^{s_i}$.
5. Compute $\pi \leftarrow \prod_{i\in[\ell]} c_i^{x_{ji}}$.
6. Return $\mathsf{CT} \leftarrow \mathsf{Enc_{cca}}\left(\mathsf{cpk}_j, \left(\{c_i\}_{i\in[\ell]}, d, \pi\right)\right)$ and add (j, CT) to L_{kdm}.

By the DDH assumption, $(g_1^r, \ldots, g_\ell^r)$ and $(g_1^{r_1}, \ldots, g_\ell^{r_\ell})$ are computationally indistinguishable. Thus, we have $|\Pr[\mathsf{SUC}_4] - \Pr[\mathsf{SUC}_5]| = \mathsf{negl}(\lambda)$.

Game 6: Same as Game 5 except how the challenger responds to KDM queries. For a KDM query $\left(j, \left(\{a_k^0\}_{k\in[n]}, f^0\right), \left(\{a_k^1\}_{k\in[n]}, f^1\right)\right)$ made by $\mathcal{A}$, the challenger responds as follows.

1. Compute Y^b and $\{\mu_i^b\}_{i\in[\ell]}$ as Eq. 3.
2. Generate $r_1, \ldots, r_\ell \xleftarrow{r} \mathbb{Z}_p$.
3. Compute $c_i \leftarrow \left(g^{-\mu_i^b} \cdot g_i^{r_i}\right)^{\delta_{ji}}$ for every $i \in [\ell]$.

4. Compute $d \leftarrow g^{Y^b} \cdot \prod_{i \in \Delta_j} c_i \cdot \prod_{i \in [\ell]} g_i^{r_i s_i}$.
5. Compute $\pi \leftarrow \prod_{i \in [\ell]} c_i^{x_{ji}}$.
6. Return $\mathsf{CT} \leftarrow \mathsf{Enc_{cca}}\left(\mathsf{cpk}_j, \left(\{c_i\}_{i \in [\ell]}, d, \pi\right)\right)$ and add (j, CT) to L_{kdm}.

We can make this change in two steps. We first replace $g_i^{r_i \gamma_j}$ with $g_i^{r_i}$. We then replace $g_i^{r_i}$ with $g^{-\mu_i^b} \cdot g_i^{r_i}$. Since r_i is uniformly at random for every $i \in [\ell]$, the answer to a KDM query made by $\mathcal{A}$ identically distributes between Game 5 and 6. Thus, we have $|\Pr[\mathtt{SUC}_5] - \Pr[\mathtt{SUC}_6]| = 0$.

Game 7: Same as Game 6 except how the challenger responds to KDM queries. For a KDM query $\left(j, \left(\{a_k^0\}_{k \in [n]}, f^0\right), \left(\{a_k^1\}_{k \in [n]}, f^1\right)\right)$ made by $\mathcal{A}$, the challenger responds as follows.

1. Compute Y^b and $\{\mu_i^b\}_{i \in [\ell]}$ as Eq. 3.
2. Generate $r \xleftarrow{\mathsf{r}} \mathbb{Z}_p$.
3. Compute $c_i \leftarrow \left(g^{-\mu_i^b} \cdot g_i^r\right)^{\delta_{ji}}$ for every $i \in [\ell]$.
4. Compute $d \leftarrow g^{Y^b} \cdot \prod_{i \in \Delta_j} c_i \cdot \prod_{i \in [\ell]} g_i^{r s_i}$.
5. Compute $\pi \leftarrow \prod_{i \in [\ell]} c_i^{x_{ji}}$.
6. Return $\mathsf{CT} \leftarrow \mathsf{Enc_{cca}}\left(\mathsf{cpk}_j, \left(\{c_i\}_{i \in [\ell]}, d, \pi\right)\right)$ and add (j, CT) to L_{kdm}.

By the DDH assumption, $(g_1^r, \ldots, g_\ell^r)$ and $(g_1^{r_1}, \ldots, g_\ell^{r_\ell})$ are computationally indistinguishable. Thus, $|\Pr[\mathtt{SUC}_6] - \Pr[\mathtt{SUC}_7]| = \mathsf{negl}(\lambda)$ holds.

In Game 7, d generated to respond to a KDM query is of the form

$$d = g^{Y^b} \cdot \prod_{i \in \Delta_j} c_i \cdot \prod_{i \in [\ell]} g_i^{r s_i} = g^{Y^b} \cdot \left(\prod_{i \in \Delta_j} c_i\right) \cdot g_0^r.$$

Thus, we can reply to a KDM query made by $\mathcal{A}$ using g_0 instead of s in Game 7.

Next, we eliminate secret keys of Π_{cca} from the view of $\mathcal{A}$. For this aim, we make e_{k0} that is used to mask csk_k uniformly at random for every $k \in [n]$. We first change how the challenger responds to decryption queries made by $\mathcal{A}$.

Game 8: Same as Game 7 except how the challenger responds to decryption queries.

For a decryption query (j, CT) made by $\mathcal{A}$, the challenger returns $\perp$ to $\mathcal{A}$ if $(j, \mathsf{CT}) \in L_{\mathsf{kdm}}$, and otherwise responds as follows.

1. Compute $\left(\{c_i\}_{i \in [\ell]}, d, \pi\right) \leftarrow \mathsf{Dec_{cca}}(\mathsf{csk}_j, \mathsf{CT})$. If the decryption result is not in $\mathbb{G}^{\ell+2}$, return $\perp$. Otherwise, compute as follows.
2. Let $c_i = (g_{ji})^{r_i}$ for every $i \in [\ell]$.[8] If there exists $i' \in \{2, \ldots, \ell\}$ such that $r_1 \neq r_{i'}$, return $\perp$. Otherwise, respond as follows.

[8] Note that such r_i exists unless g_{ji} is the identity element since $c_i \in \mathbb{G}$ for every $i \in [\ell]$. The probability that g_{ji} is the identity element is negligible. Thus, we ignore this issue for simplicity.

3. Return $\perp$ if $\pi \neq \prod_{i\in[\ell]} c_i^{x_{ji}}$ and otherwise $m \leftarrow \log_g \left(d \cdot \left(\prod_{i\in[\ell]} c_i^{s_{ji}}\right)^{-1}\right)$.

We define the following event in Game i ($i = 7, \ldots, 11$).

BDQ_i: $\mathcal{A}$ makes a decryption query $(j, \mathsf{CT}) \notin L_{\mathsf{kdm}}$ which satisfies the following conditions, where $\left(\{c_i\}_{i\in[\ell]}, d, \pi\right) \leftarrow \mathsf{Dec}_{\mathsf{cca}}(\mathsf{csk}_j, \mathsf{CT})$.

- $\left(\{c_i\}_{i\in[\ell]}, d, \pi\right) \in \mathbb{G}^{\ell+2}$. Then, let $c_i = g_{ji}^{r_i}$, where $r_i \in \mathbb{Z}_p$ for every $i \in [\ell]$.
- There exists $i' \in \{2, \ldots, \ell\}$ such that $r_1 \neq r_{i'}$.
- $\pi = \prod_{i\in[\ell]} c_i^{x_{ji}}$.

We call such a decryption query a "**bad decryption query**".

Games 7 and 8 are identical games unless $\mathcal{A}$ make a bad decryption query in each game. Therefore, we have $|\Pr[\mathsf{SUC}_7] - \Pr[\mathsf{SUC}_8]| \leq \Pr[\mathsf{BDQ}_8]$.

For every $k \in [n]$, we have

$$e_{ki} = (g_{ki})^{w_i} = (g_i^{w_i})^{\gamma_k \delta_{ki}} \ (i \in [\ell])$$

$$e_{k0} = \prod_{i\in[\ell]} (e_{ki})^{s_{ki}} = \left(\prod_{i\in\Delta_k} e_{ki}\right) \prod_{i\in[\ell]} (e_{ki})^{\delta_{ki} s_i} = \left(\prod_{i\in\Delta_k} e_{ki}\right) \left(\prod_{i\in[\ell]} g_i^{w_i s_i}\right)^{\gamma_k}.$$

Note that $\delta_{ki} \cdot \delta_{ki} = 1$ for every $i \in [\ell]$ and $k \in [n]$.

Game 9: Same as Game 8 except that $e_0 \xleftarrow{r} \mathbb{G}$ is used instead of $\prod_{i\in[\ell]} g_i^{w_i s_i}$.

The view of $\mathcal{A}$ in Games 8 and 9 can be perfectly simulated by

$$\left(g_1, \ldots, g_\ell, g_1^{w_1}, \ldots, g_\ell^{w_\ell}, \prod_{i\in[\ell]} g_i^{w_i s_i}, g_0\right) \text{ and } (g_1, \ldots, g_\ell, g_1^{w_1}, \ldots, g_\ell^{w_\ell}, e_0, g_0),$$

respectively, where $g_i \xleftarrow{r} \mathbb{G}$ and $w_i \xleftarrow{r} \mathbb{Z}_p$ for every $i \in [\ell]$, $s = s_1 \cdots s_\ell \xleftarrow{r} \{0,1\}^\ell$, $e_0 \xleftarrow{r} \mathbb{G}$, and $g_0 = \prod_{i\in[\ell]} g_i^{s_i}$. By the leftover hash lemma, the view of $\mathcal{A}$ in Game 8 is $2^{-\frac{\ell-2\lambda}{2}}$-close to that in Game 9. Thus, by setting $\ell = 3\lambda$, $|\Pr[\mathsf{SUC}_8] - \Pr[\mathsf{SUC}_9]| = \mathsf{negl}(\lambda)$ and $|\Pr[\mathsf{BDQ}_8] - \Pr[\mathsf{BDQ}_9]| = \mathsf{negl}(\lambda)$ hold.

There exists $\alpha_i \in \mathbb{Z}_p$ such that $g^{\alpha_i} = g_i$ for every $i \in [\ell]$. Then, for every $k \in [n]$, we have

$$g_{ki} = g^{\alpha_i \gamma_k \delta_{ki}} = (g^{\gamma_k})^{\alpha_i \delta_{ki}} \ (i \in [\ell]), \ g_{k0} = \prod_{i\in[\ell]} (g_{ki})^{s_{ki}}$$

$$e_{ki} = (g_{ki})^{w_i} \ (i \in [\ell]), \text{ and } e_{k0} = \left(\prod_{i\in\Delta_k} e_{ki}\right) e_0^{\gamma_k}.$$

Game 10: Same as Game 9 except that for every $k \in [n]$, the challenger generates $e_{k0} \leftarrow \left(\prod_{i\in\Delta_k} e_{ki}\right) e_0^{z_k}$, where $z_k \xleftarrow{r} \mathbb{Z}_p$.

$|\Pr[\mathtt{SUC}_9] - \Pr[\mathtt{SUC}_{10}]| = \mathsf{negl}(\lambda)$ holds since $(g, e_0, g^{\gamma_k}, e_0^{\gamma_k})$ and $(g, e_0, g^{\gamma_k}, e_0^{z_k})$ are computationally indistinguishable by the DDH assumption for every $k \in [n]$.

Moreover, we can efficiently check whether $\mathcal{A}$ makes a bad decryption query or not by using $\{\mathsf{csk}_k\}_{k\in[n]}$, $\{\alpha_i\}_{i\in[\ell]}$, and $\{x_{ki}\}_{i\in[\ell],k\in[n]}$. Therefore, we also have $|\Pr[\mathtt{BDQ}_9] - \Pr[\mathtt{BDQ}_{10}]| = \mathsf{negl}(\lambda)$ by the DDH assumption.

In Game 10, e_{k0} distributes uniformly at random for every $k \in [n]$. Therefore, $\mathcal{A}$ cannot obtain any information of csk_k from $u_k = e_{k0} \cdot \mathsf{csk}_k$ for every $k \in [n]$, and thus we can use IND-CCA security of Π_{cca}.

Game 11: Same as Game 10 except that the challenger responds to KDM queries made by $\mathcal{A}$ with $\mathsf{CT} \leftarrow \mathsf{Enc}_{\mathsf{cca}}\left(\mathsf{cpk}_j, 0^{(\ell+2)\cdot|g|}\right)$.

By the IND-CCA security of Π_{cca}, we obtain $|\Pr[\mathtt{SUC}_{10}] - \Pr[\mathtt{SUC}_{11}]| = \mathsf{negl}(\lambda)$.

Moreover, we can efficiently check whether $\mathcal{A}$ makes a bad decryption query or not by using decryption queries for Π_{cca}, $\{\alpha_i\}_{i\in[\ell]}$, and $\{x_{ki}\}_{i\in[\ell],k\in[n]}$. Thus, $|\Pr[\mathtt{BDQ}_{10}] - \Pr[\mathtt{BDQ}_{11}]| = \mathsf{negl}(\lambda)$ also holds by the IND-CCA security of Π_{cca}.

The value of b is information theoretically hidden from the view of $\mathcal{A}$ in Game 11. Thus, we have $\left|\Pr[\mathtt{SUC}_{11}] - \frac{1}{2}\right| = 0$.

In Game 11, $x_{k1}, \ldots, x_{k\ell}$ are hidden from the view of $\mathcal{A}$ except $\hat{g}_{k0} = \prod_{i\in[\ell]} (g_{ki})^{x_{ki}}$ for every $k \in [n]$. Note that $\mathcal{A}$ cannot obtain information of $x_{k1}, \ldots, x_{k\ell}$ other than $\hat{g}_{k0}$ through decryption queries for every $k \in [n]$. The reason is as follows. If a decryption query (j, CT) made by $\mathcal{A}$ is not a bad decryption query, there exists $r_1 \in \mathbb{Z}_p$ such that $c_i = (g_{ji})^{r_1}$ for every $i \in [\ell]$, where $\left(\{c_i\}_{i\in[\ell]}, d, \pi\right) \leftarrow \mathsf{Dec}_{\mathsf{cca}}(\mathsf{csk}_j, \mathsf{CT})$. Then, we have

$$\prod_{i\in[\ell]} c_i^{x_{ji}} = \prod_{i\in[\ell]} (g_{ji})^{r_1 x_{ji}} = \left(\prod_{i\in[\ell]} (g_{ji})^{x_{ji}}\right)^{r_1} = (\hat{g}_{j0})^{r_1}.$$

In addition, bad decryption queries made by $\mathcal{A}$ are replied with $\perp$ in Game 11. This means that for every $k \in [n]$, $\mathcal{A}$ cannot obtain information of $x_{k1}, \ldots, x_{k\ell}$ other than $\hat{g}_{k0}$ through decryption queries.

We estimate $\Pr[\mathtt{BDQ}_{11}]$. Let (j, CT) be a decryption query made by $\mathcal{A}$ and let $\left(\{c_i\}_{i\in[\ell]}, d, \pi\right) \leftarrow \mathsf{Dec}_{\mathsf{cca}}(\mathsf{csk}_j, \mathsf{CT})$. Suppose that $\left(\{c_i\}_{i\in[\ell]}, d, \pi\right) \in \mathbb{G}^{\ell+2}$, $c_i = (g_{ji})^{r_i}$ for every $i \in [\ell]$, and there exists $i' \in \{2, \ldots, \ell\}$ such that $r_1 \neq r_{i'}$. The probability that this query is a bad decryption query is

$$\Pr_{x_{ji} \xleftarrow{r} \mathbb{Z}_p}\left[\prod_{i\in[\ell]} c_i^{x_{ji}} = \pi \,\middle|\, \prod_{i\in[\ell]} (g_{ji})^{x_{ji}} = \hat{g}_{j0}\right]. \tag{4}$$

This probability is the same as

$$\Pr_{x_{ji} \xleftarrow{r} \mathbb{Z}_p}\left[\sum_{i\in[\ell]} \alpha_i \gamma_j \delta_{ji} r_i x_{ji} = \log_g \pi \bmod p \,\middle|\, \sum_{i\in[\ell]} \alpha_i \gamma_j \delta_{ji} x_{ji} = \log_g \hat{g}_{j0} \bmod p\right].$$

$\alpha_i \neq 0$ and $\gamma_j \neq 0$ holds for every $i \in [\ell]$ and $j \in [n]$ with high probability and thus we assume so. Then, two equations

$$\sum_{i\in[\ell]} \alpha_i\gamma_j\delta_{ji}r_ix_{ji} = \log_g \pi \bmod p \text{ and } \sum_{i\in[\ell]} \alpha_i\gamma_j\delta_{ji}x_{ji} = \log_g \hat{g}_{j0} \bmod p$$

are linearly independent, and thus the probability shown in Eq. 4 is $\frac{1}{p}$. Therefore, we obtain $\Pr[\mathsf{BDQ}_{11}] = \mathsf{negl}(\lambda)$.

From the above arguments, we have $\mathsf{Adv}^{\mathsf{kdmcca}}_{\Pi_{\mathsf{ddh}},\mathcal{F}_{\mathsf{ddh}},\mathcal{A},n}(\lambda) = \mathsf{negl}(\lambda)$. Since the choice of $\mathcal{A}$ and n is arbitrary, Π_{ddh} is $\mathcal{F}_{\mathsf{ddh}}$-KDM-CCA secure. □ (**Theorem** 4)

Remark 5 (The multi user security of the QR and DCR based schemes). Our QR and DCR based constructions are based on those proposed by Brakerski and Goldwasser [5]. If we allow the length of secret keys to depend on the number of users n, we can prove that our QR and DCR based constructions are KDM$^{(n)}$-CCA secure using a technique similar to Brakerski and Goldwasser.

To prove KDM$^{(n)}$-CCA security, we need to eliminate encrypted n secret keys of the outer IND-CCA secure PKE scheme contained in secret keys of the KDM-CCA secure scheme. In the above proof of DDH based scheme, by using the self reducibility of the DDH problem, we complete such a task by making a single group element $\prod_{i\in[\ell]} g_i^{w_i s_i}$ random using the leftover hash lemma.

However, when proving the KDM$^{(n)}$-CCA security of the QR and DCR based constructions, to complete such a task, we need to make n group elements random using the leftover hash lemma. Therefore, in that case, we need to set the length of secret keys depending on n similarly to the proof of KDM$^{(n)}$-CPA security by Brakerski and Goldwasser.

Acknowledgement. A part of this work was supported by Input Output Hong Kong, Nomura Research Institute, NTT Secure Platform Laboratories, Mitsubishi Electric, JST CREST JPMJCR14D6, JST OPERA, JSPS KAKENHI JP16H01705, JP16J10322, JP17H01695.

References

1. Alperin-Sheriff, J., Peikert, C.: Circular and KDM security for identity-based encryption. In: Fischlin, M., Buchmann, J., Manulis, M. (eds.) PKC 2012. LNCS, vol. 7293, pp. 334–352. Springer, Heidelberg (2012). https://doi.org/10.1007/978-3-642-30057-8_20
2. Applebaum, B.: Key-dependent message security: generic amplification and completeness. In: Paterson, K.G. (ed.) EUROCRYPT 2011. LNCS, vol. 6632, pp. 527–546. Springer, Heidelberg (2011). https://doi.org/10.1007/978-3-642-20465-4_29
3. Black, J., Rogaway, P., Shrimpton, T.: Encryption-scheme security in the presence of key-dependent messages. In: Nyberg, K., Heys, H. (eds.) SAC 2002. LNCS, vol. 2595, pp. 62–75. Springer, Heidelberg (2003). https://doi.org/10.1007/3-540-36492-7_6

4. Boneh, D., Halevi, S., Hamburg, M., Ostrovsky, R.: Circular-secure encryption from decision Diffie-Hellman. In: Wagner, D. (ed.) CRYPTO 2008. LNCS, vol. 5157, pp. 108–125. Springer, Heidelberg (2008). https://doi.org/10.1007/978-3-540-85174-5_7
5. Brakerski, Z., Goldwasser, S.: Circular and leakage resilient public-key encryption under subgroup indistinguishability (or: Quadratic residuosity strikes back). In: Rabin, T. (ed.) CRYPTO 2010. LNCS, vol. 6223, pp. 1–20. Springer, Heidelberg (2010). https://doi.org/10.1007/978-3-642-14623-7_1
6. Camenisch, J., Chandran, N., Shoup, V.: A public key encryption scheme secure against key dependent chosen plaintext and adaptive chosen ciphertext attacks. In: Joux, A. (ed.) EUROCRYPT 2009. LNCS, vol. 5479, pp. 351–368. Springer, Heidelberg (2009). https://doi.org/10.1007/978-3-642-01001-9_20
7. Camenisch, J., Lysyanskaya, A.: An efficient system for non-transferable anonymous credentials with optional anonymity revocation. In: Pfitzmann, B. (ed.) EUROCRYPT 2001. LNCS, vol. 2045, pp. 93–118. Springer, Heidelberg (2001). https://doi.org/10.1007/3-540-44987-6_7
8. Cramer, R., Shoup, V.: Universal hash proofs and a paradigm for adaptive chosen ciphertext secure public-key encryption. In: Knudsen, L.R. (ed.) EUROCRYPT 2002. LNCS, vol. 2332, pp. 45–64. Springer, Heidelberg (2002). https://doi.org/10.1007/3-540-46035-7_4
9. Han, S., Liu, S., Lyu, L.: Efficient KDM-CCA secure public-key encryption for polynomial functions. In: Cheon, J.H., Takagi, T. (eds.) ASIACRYPT 2016. LNCS, vol. 10032, pp. 307–338. Springer, Heidelberg (2016). https://doi.org/10.1007/978-3-662-53890-6_11
10. Hofheinz, D.: Circular chosen-ciphertext security with compact ciphertexts. In: Johansson, T., Nguyen, P.Q. (eds.) EUROCRYPT 2013. LNCS, vol. 7881, pp. 520–536. Springer, Heidelberg (2013). https://doi.org/10.1007/978-3-642-38348-9_31
11. Hohenberger, S., Lewko, A., Waters, B.: Detecting dangerous queries: a new approach for chosen ciphertext security. In: Pointcheval, D., Johansson, T. (eds.) EUROCRYPT 2012. LNCS, vol. 7237, pp. 663–681. Springer, Heidelberg (2012). https://doi.org/10.1007/978-3-642-29011-4_39
12. Kitagawa, F., Matsuda, T., Hanaoka, G., Tanaka, K.: Completeness of single-bit projection-KDM security for public key encryption. In: Nyberg, K. (ed.) CT-RSA 2015. LNCS, vol. 9048, pp. 201–219. Springer, Cham (2015). https://doi.org/10.1007/978-3-319-16715-2_11
13. Kurosawa, K., Desmedt, Y.: A new paradigm of hybrid encryption scheme. In: Franklin, M. (ed.) CRYPTO 2004. LNCS, vol. 3152, pp. 426–442. Springer, Heidelberg (2004). https://doi.org/10.1007/978-3-540-28628-8_26
14. Lu, X., Li, B., Jia, D.: KDM-CCA security from RKA secure authenticated encryption. In: Oswald, E., Fischlin, M. (eds.) EUROCRYPT 2015, Part I. LNCS, vol. 9056, pp. 559–583. Springer, Heidelberg (2015). https://doi.org/10.1007/978-3-662-46800-5_22
15. Myers, S., Shelat, A.: Bit encryption is complete. In: 50th FOCS, pp. 607–616 (2009)
16. Naor, M., Yung, M.: Public-key cryptosystems provably secure against chosen ciphertext attacks. In: 22nd ACM STOC, pp. 427–437 (1990)
17. Shoup, V.: Using hash functions as a hedge against chosen ciphertext attack. In: Preneel, B. (ed.) EUROCRYPT 2000. LNCS, vol. 1807, pp. 275–288. Springer, Heidelberg (2000). https://doi.org/10.1007/3-540-45539-6_19

18. Shoup, V.: A Computational Introduction to Number Theory and Algebra. Cambridge University Press, Cambridge (2006)
19. Wee, H.: KDM-security via homomorphic smooth projective hashing. In: Cheng, C.-M., Chung, K.-M., Persiano, G., Yang, B.-Y. (eds.) PKC 2016, Part II. LNCS, vol. 9615, pp. 159–179. Springer, Heidelberg (2016). https://doi.org/10.1007/978-3-662-49387-8_7

Understanding and Constructing AKE via Double-Key Key Encapsulation Mechanism

Haiyang Xue[1,2,3], Xianhui Lu[1,2,3](✉), Bao Li[1,2,3], Bei Liang[4], and Jingnan He[1,2]

[1] State Key Laboratory of Information Security, Institute of Information Engineering, Chinese Academy of Sciences, Beijing, China
{hyxue12,xhlu}@is.ac.cn
[2] Data Assurance and Communication Security Research Center, Chinese Academy of Sciences, Beijing, China
[3] School of Cyber Security, University of Chinese Academy of Sciences, Beijing, China
[4] Chalmers University of Technology, Gothenburg, Sweden

Abstract. Motivated by abstracting the common idea behind several implicitly authenticated key exchange (AKE) protocols, we introduce a primitive that we call double-key key encapsulation mechanism (2-key KEM). It is a special type of KEM involving two pairs of secret-public keys and satisfying some function and security property. Such 2-key KEM serves as the core building block and provides alternative approaches to simplify the constructions of AKE. To see the usefulness of 2-key KEM, we show how several existing constructions of AKE can be captured as 2-key KEM and understood in a unified framework, including widely used HMQV, NAXOS, Okamoto-AKE, and FSXY12-13 schemes. Then, we show (1) how to construct 2-key KEM from concrete assumptions, (2) how to adapt the classical Fujisaki-Okamoto transformation and KEM combiner to achieve the security requirement of 2-key KEM, (3) an elegant Kyber-AKE over lattice using the improved Fujisaki-Okamoto technique.

Keywords: Authenticated key exchange · CK model
Key encapsulation mechanism

1 Introduction

Key exchange (KE), which enables two parties to securely establish a common session key while communicating over an insecure channel, is one of the most important and fundamental primitives in cryptography. After the introduction of Diffie-Hellman key exchange in [12], cryptographers have devised a wide selection of the KE with various use-cases. One important direction is authenticated key exchange (AKE). The main problems that the following works focus on are

T. Peyrin and S. Galbraith (Eds.): ASIACRYPT 2018, LNCS 11273, pp. 158–189, 2018.
https://doi.org/10.1007/978-3-030-03329-3_6

specified as security models [5–7, 15, 24], efficient and provably-secure realizations [1–3, 7, 15, 16, 22, 24–27, 29, 34, 35].

In an AKE protocol, each party has a pair of secret-public keys, a *static/long-term public key* and the corresponding *static/long-term secret key*. The static public key is interrelated with a party's identity, which enables the other parties to verify the authentic binding between them. A party who wants to share information with another party generates ephemeral one-time randomness which is known as *ephemeral secret keys*, computes *session state* (which is originally not explicitly defined [7], but nowadays it is generally agreed [15, 24] that the session state should at least contain ephemeral secret keys) from ephemeral and static secret keys and incoming message, then outputs corresponding *ephemeral public outgoing message*. Then each party uses their static secret keys and the ephemeral secret keys along with the transcripts of the session to compute a shared *session key*.

Many studies have investigated the security notion of AKE including BR model and Canetti-Krawczyk (CK) model [7]. Fujioka *et al.* [15] re-formulated the *desirable* security notion of AKE in [23], including resistance to KCI (key compromise impersonation attack), wPFS (weak perfect forward attack) and MEX (maximal exposure attack), as well as provable security in the CK model, and called it the CK^+ security model. LaMacchia *et al.* [24] also proposed a very strong security model, called the eCK model. The CK model and the eCK model are incomparable [6], and the eCK model is not stronger than the CK model while the CK^+ model is [15]. However, each of these two models, eCK and CK^+ can be theoretically seen as a strong version of the AKE security model.

To achieve a secure AKE in one of the above security models (CK, CK^+, eCK), the solutions are divided into two classes: explicit AKE and implicit AKE. The solution of explicit AKE is to explicitly authenticate the exchanged messages between the involved parties by generally using additional primitives *i.e.*, signature or MAC to combine with the underlying KE, such as IKE [8], SIGMA [22], TLS [2, 21] etc.; while the solution of implicit AKE initiated by [25], is to implicitly authenticate each party by its unique ability so as to compute the resulted session key. These kinds of implicit AKE schemes include (H)MQV [23, 26], Okamoto [27, 28], NAXOS [24], OAKE [34], FSXY variants [1, 15, 16, 33], and AKE from lattice assumptions [3, 35].

Motivation. In this paper, we focus on the second class, *i.e.*, constructions of *implicit AKE*. Based on different techniques and assumptions, many implicit AKE protocols have been proposed in recent years [15, 16, 23, 24, 27, 28, 34].

However, the constructing techniques and methods of the existing implicit AKE protocols are somewhat separate and the study on the highly accurate analysis of AKE's requirement for the building block is critically in a shortage, especially for the exact underlying primitives that serve as fundamental building blocks and capture the common idea and technique behind the constructions and security proofs of AKE. On the contrary, with respect to explicit AKE Canetti and Krawcayk [8, 22] gave the frame of "SIGin-and-MAc" (later extended by [29]) which provides a good guideline for designing explicit AKE.

In fact, Boyd *et al.* [1] and Fujioka *et al.* [15,16] initiated the research on studying frameworks of implicit AKE. Boyd *et al.* firstly noticed the connection between AKE and key encapsulation mechanism (KEM), then Fujioka *et al.* provided CK^+ secure AKE protocols from chosen ciphertext (CCA) secure KEM in the random oracle and standard models. Although the paradigm of connecting the AKE with KEM is of great significance, it can not be applied to explain many widely-used and well-known constructions of AKE such as HMQV and its variant [23,34] which are built on the challenge-respond signature; AKE protocol in [27] which results from universal hash proof [10]; as well as NAXOS [24].

Hence, one of the important problems on AKE is to give an even more general framework for constructing AKE that is able to not only unify the existing structures of AKE protocol as much as possible, but also to systemize and simplify the construction and analysis methods of AKE protocol. It will be useful and helpful for understanding the existing works and future studying on formalization of the AKE construction under a unified framework with some well-studied and simple cryptographic primitive as building block.

1.1 Our Contributions

- Based on the above motivations and observations, we introduce *double-key key encapsulation mechanism* (2-key KEM) and its secure notions, *i.e.*, [IND/OW-CCA, IND/OW-CPA] security. We also show its distinction with previous similar notions.
- Based on the [IND/OW-CCA, IND/OW-CPA] secure 2-key KEM, we present unified frames of CK^+ secure AKE, which in turn conceptually capture the common pattern for the existing constructions and security proof of AKE, including well-known HMQV [23], NAXOS [24], Okamoto-AKE [27,28], and FSXY12 [15], FSXY13 [16].
- We investigate the constructions of 2-key KEM based on concrete assumptions. We also show the failure of implying [IND/OW-CCA, IND/OW-CPA] secure 2-key KEM from KEM combiner and the classical Fujisaki-Okamoto (FO) transformation. Hence, with a slight but vital modification by taking public key as input to the hash step we provide improved KEM combiner and improved FO to adapt them in our 2-key KEM setting.
- Equipped with 2-key KEM and our frame above, we propose a post-quantum AKE based on Module-LWE assumption, which consumes less communications than Kyber [3] using frame of FSXY13 [16].

2-Key Key Encapsulation Mechanism. Generally, the 2-key KEM scheme is a public key encapsulation with two pairs of public and secret keys, but the main distinctions are the functionality and security.

The encapsulation and decapsulation algorithms: instead of taking as input single public key to generate a random key K and a ciphertext C and single secret key to decapsulate ciphertext C, each algorithm takes two public keys (pk_1, pk_0) to generate (C, K) and only with both two secret keys (sk_1, sk_0) the decapsulation algorithm can decapsulate C.

We define the security notion of 2-key KEM/PKE in the attacking model [IND/OW-CCA, IND/OW-CPA] which captures the idea that the 2-key KEM is secure under one secret-public key pair even if another pair of secret-public key is generated by the adversary. Informally, the [IND/OW-CCA, ·] denotes the security model where adversary $\mathcal{A}$ aims to attack the ciphertext under pk_1 and pk_0^* (with its control over the generation of pk_0^*), and it is allowed to query a strong decapsulation oracle that will decapsulate the ciphertext under pk_1 and arbitrary pk_0' (generated by challenger); while [·, IND/OW-CPA] denotes the security model where adversary $\mathcal{B}$ aims to attack the ciphertext under pk_0 and pk_1^* (with its control over the generation of pk_1^*). We say a 2-key KEM is [IND/OW-CCA, IND/OW-CPA] secure if it is both [IND/OW-CCA, ·] and [·, IND/OW-CPA] secure.

Compared with classical definition of CCA security, the [CCA, ·] adversary of 2-key KEM has two main enhancements: (1) one of the challenge public keys pk_0^*, under which the challenge ciphertext is computed, is generated by the adversary; (2) the adversary is allowed to query a strong decryption oracle, and get decapsulation of the ciphertext under arbitrary public keys (pk_1^*, pk_0') where pk_0' is generated by the challenger.

AKE from 2-Key KEM. Equipped with [IND/OW-CCA, IND/OW-CPA] 2-key KEM, by taking pk_1 as static public key and pk_0 as ephemeral public key, we give several general frames of CK$^+$ secure AKE, AKE, $\mathsf{AKE}_{\mathsf{ro\text{-}pkic\text{-}lr}}$ and $\mathsf{AKE}_{\mathsf{std}}$, depending on different tricks. The CK$^+$ security of our AKE is decomposed to the [IND/OW-CCA, ·] security (corresponding to KCI and MEX security) and [·, IND/OW-CPA] security (corresponding to wPFS) of 2-key KEM. Furthermore, to resist the leakage of partial randomness, a function $f(ssk_B, esk_B)$ is required so that if one of ssk_B and esk_B is leaked $f(ssk_B, esk_B)$ is still computationally indistinguishable with a random string.

In Table 1 we summarize which one of our general frames is used to explain which one of the existing AKE protocols by employing the specific tricks and assumptions. Our general protocols capture the common idea of constructing CK$^+$ secure AKE. And depending on 2-key KEM and different tricks, it facilitates a number of instantiations, including HMQV [23], NAXOS [24], Okamoto [27], FSXY12 [15], and FSXY13 [16].

By considering an AKE protocol in such a framework based on 2-key KEM, the complicated security proofs of existing AKE is decomposed into several smaller cases each of which is easier to work with. Moreover, this general scheme not only explains previous constructions, but also yields efficient AKE from lattice problems. After giving [IND-CPA, IND-CPA] twin-kyber under Module-LWE assumption, we obtain a *post-quantum AKE* with less communications.

Constructions of 2-Key KEM. In addition to show that existing AKEs imply [CCA, CPA] secure 2-key KEM, we investigate the general constructions.

Putting Public Key in the Hashing or PRF step. The Fujisaki-Okamoto (FO) [14,18] transformation and KEM combiner are general techniques of classical CCA security for one-key KEM. We show the failure of implying [IND/OW-

Table 1. The unification of AKEs. Comb. is the abbreviation for combiner. GDH is the Gap-DH assumption. RO is the notion of random oracle. Std is the shortened form of standard model. πPRF means the pairwise-independent random source PRF [28]

Frameworks	Models	Concrete AKEs	Assumptions	Tricks
AKE	RO	FSXY13 [16], Kyber [3]	OW-CCA	Modified KEM Comb.
	RO	AKE-2Kyber (Sect.7)	M-LWE	Modified FO
$\mathsf{AKE}_{\mathsf{ro\text{-}pkic\text{-}lr}}$	RO	HMQV [23] OAKE [34]	GDH, KEA1	Remarks 1–3
	RO	NAXOS [24]	GDH	Remarks 1, 2
$\mathsf{AKE}_{\mathsf{std}}$	Std	FSXY12 [15]	IND-CCA	Modified KEM Comb.
	Std	Okamoto [28]	DDH, πPRF	Twisted PRF

CCA, IND/OW-CPA] secure 2-key KEM from KEM combiner and the classical FO transformation by giving particular attacks on concrete schemes. Hence, we show that with a slight but vital modification, when extracting encapsulated key, by taking public key as input to the hash or PRF step, the modified KEM combiner and FO transformation work for 2-key KEM.

1.2 Strong Point of the AKE via 2-Key KEM

The main advantage of our contributions is that we use a non-interactive primitive to handle the complex requirement of interactive protocols. The functionality and security requirements of [CCA, CPA] secure 2-key KEM are relatively easier to work with and understand. As it is known, in AKE we have to consider complex and diverse adversaries. However, when considering the AKE under our unified framework based on 2-key KEM, all the attacking strategies in CK^+ model can be simplified to the singular security of 2-key KEM.

The non-interactive 2-key KEM helps us to highly simplify the constructions for AKE as well as to understand the essential working mechanism. In fact, KEM is relatively well-studied and intensively analyzed. Following the first practical CCA secure PKE [9], there have been a number of CCA secure PKE/KEM schemes based on both concrete assumptions [3,9,30,31] and general cryptographic primitives [11,19,30]. Therefore, it is possible for us to employ the established and nature technique of classical KEM to construct 2-key KEM, and further AKE.

2 Preliminary

For a variable x, if x is a bit string, denote $[x]_i$ as the i-th bit of x; if x is a polynomial, denote $[x]_i$ as the i-th coefficient of x; if x is a sets of vectors (with string or number) denote $[x]_i$ as the sets of all i-th element of vectors in x;

2.1 CK$^+$ Security Model

We recall the CK$^+$ model introduced by [23] and later refined by [15,16], which is a CK [7] model integrated with the weak PFS, resistance to KCI and MEX properties. Since we focus on **two-pass protocols** in this paper, for simplicity, we show the model specified to two pass protocols.

In AKE protocol, U_i denotes a party indexed by i, who is modeled as probabilistic polynomial time (PPT) interactive Turing machines. We assume that each party U_i owns a static pair of secret-public keys (ssk_i, spk_i), where the static public key is linked to U_i's identity, using some systems i.e. PKI, such that the other parties can verify the authentic binding between them. We do not require the well-formness of static public key, in particular, a corrupted party can adaptively register any static public key of its choice.

Session. Each party can be activated to run an instance called a *session*. A party can be activated to initiate the session by an incoming message of the forms $(\Pi, \mathcal{I}, U_A, U_B)$ or respond to an incoming message of the forms $(\Pi, \mathcal{R}, U_B, U_A, X_A)$, where Π is a protocol identifier, $\mathcal{I}$ and $\mathcal{R}$ are role identifiers corresponding to *initiator* and *responder*. Activated with $(\Pi, \mathcal{I}, U_A, U_B)$, U_A is called the session *initiator*. Activated with $(\Pi, \mathcal{R}, U_B, U_A, X_A)$, U_B is called the session *responder*.

According to the specification of AKE, the party creates randomness which is called *ephemeral secret key*, computes and maintains a *session state*, and completes the session by outputting a session key and erasing the session state. Note that Canetti-Krawczyk [7] defines session state as session-specific secret information but leaves it up to a protocol to specify which information is included in session state; LaMacchia et al. [24] explicitly set all random coins used by a party in a session as session-specific secret information and call it *ephemeral secret key*. We require that the session state at least contains the ephemeral secret key.

A session may also be aborted without generating a session key. The initiator U_A creates a session state and outputs X_A, then may receive an incoming message of the forms $(\Pi, \mathcal{I}, U_A, U_B, X_A, X_B)$ from the responder U_B, then may computes the session key SK. On the contrary, the responder U_B outputs X_B, and may compute the session key SK. We say that a session is *completed* if its owner computes the session key.

A session is associated with its owner, a peer, and a session identifier. If U_A is the initiator, the session identifier is $\mathsf{sid} = (\Pi, \mathcal{I}, U_A, U_B, X_A)$ or $\mathsf{sid} = (\Pi, \mathcal{I}, U_A, U_B, X_A, X_B)$, which denotes U_A as an owner and U_B as a peer. If U_B is the responder, the session is identified by $\mathsf{sid} = (\Pi, \mathcal{R}, U_B, U_A, X_A, X_B)$, which denotes U_B as an owner and U_A as a peer. The *matching session* of $(\Pi, \mathcal{I}, U_A, U_B, X_A, X_B)$ is $(\Pi, \mathcal{R}, U_B, U_A, X_A, X_B)$ and vice versa.

Adversary. The adversary $\mathcal{A}$ is modeled in the following to capture real attacks in open networks.

- Send(message): $\mathcal{A}$ could send message in one of the forms: $(\Pi, \mathcal{I}, U_A, U_B)$, $(\Pi, \mathcal{R}, U_B, U_A, X_A)$, or $(\Pi, \mathcal{I}, U_A, U_B, X_A, X_B)$, and obtains the response.

- $\mathsf{SessionKeyReveal(sid)}$: if the session sid is completed, $\mathcal{A}$ obtains the session key SK for sid.
- $\mathsf{SessionStateReveal(sid)}$: The adversary $\mathcal{A}$ obtains the session state of the owner of sid if the session is not completed. The session state includes all ephemeral secret keys and intermediate computation results except for immediately erased information but does not include the static secret key.
- $\mathsf{Corrupt}(U_i)$: By this query, $\mathcal{A}$ learns all information of U_A (including the static secret, session states and session keys stored at U_A); in addition, from the moment U_A is corrupted all its actions may be controlled by $\mathcal{A}$.

Freshness. Let $\mathsf{sid}^* = (\Pi, \mathcal{I}, U_A, U_B, X_A, X_B)$ or $(\Pi, \mathcal{I}, U_A, U_B, X_A, X_B)$ be a completed session between honest users U_A and U_B. If the matching session of sid^* exists, denote it by $\overline{\mathsf{sid}^*}$. We say session sid^* is fresh if $\mathcal{A}$ does not queries: (1) $\mathsf{SessionStateReveal}(\mathsf{sid}^*)$, $\mathsf{SessionKeyReveal}(\mathsf{sid}^*)$, and $\mathsf{SessionStateReveal}(\overline{\mathsf{sid}^*})$, $\mathsf{SessionKeyReveal}(\overline{\mathsf{sid}^*})$ if $\overline{\mathsf{sid}^*}$ exists; (2) $\mathsf{SessionStateReveal}(\mathsf{sid}^*)$ and $\mathsf{SessionKeyReveal}(\mathsf{sid}^*)$ if $\overline{\mathsf{sid}^*}$ does not exist.

Security Experiment. The adversary $\mathcal{A}$ could make a sequence of the queries described above. During the experiment, $\mathcal{A}$ makes the query of $\mathsf{Test}(\mathsf{sid}^*)$, where sid^* must be a fresh session. $\mathsf{Test}(\mathsf{sid}^*)$ select random bit $b \in_U \{0, 1\}$, and return the session key held by sid^* if $b = 0$; and return a random key if $b = 1$.

The experiment continues until $\mathcal{A}$ returns b' as a guess of b. The adversary $\mathcal{A}$ wins the game if the test session sid^* is still fresh and $b' = b$. The advantage of the adversary $\mathcal{A}$ is defined as $\mathsf{Adv}_{\Pi}^{ck+}(\mathcal{A}) = \Pr[\mathcal{A} \text{ wins}] - \frac{1}{2}$.

Definition 1. *We say that a AKE protocol Π is secure in the CK^+ model if the following conditions hold:*
(Correctness:) if two honest parties complete matching sessions, then they both compute the same session key except with negligible probability.
(Soundness:) for any PPT $\mathcal{A}$, $\mathsf{Adv}_{\Pi}^{ck+}(\mathcal{A})$ is negligible for the test session sid^*,

1. *the static secret key of the owner of sid^* is given to $\mathcal{A}$, if $\overline{\mathsf{sid}^*}$ does not exist.*
2. *the ephemeral secret key of the owner of sid^* is given to $\mathcal{A}$, if $\overline{\mathsf{sid}^*}$ does not exist.*
3. *the static secret key of the owner of sid^* and the ephemeral secret key of $\overline{\mathsf{sid}^*}$ are given to $\mathcal{A}$, if $\overline{\mathsf{sid}^*}$ exists.*
4. *the ephemeral secret key of sid^* and the ephemeral secret key of $\overline{\mathsf{sid}^*}$ are given to $\mathcal{A}$, if $\overline{\mathsf{sid}^*}$ exists.*
5. *the static secret key of the owner of sid^* and the static secret key of the peer of sid^* are given to $\mathcal{A}$, if $\overline{\mathsf{sid}^*}$ exists.*
6. *the ephemeral secret key of sid^* and the static secret key of the peer of sid^* are given to $\mathcal{A}$, if $\overline{\mathsf{sid}^*}$ exists.*

As indicated in Table 2, the CK^+ model captures all non-trivial patterns of exposure of static and ephemeral secret keys listed in Definition 1, and these ten cases cover wPFS, resistance to KCI, and MEX.

Table 2. The behavior of AKE adversary in CK$^+$ model. $\overline{\mathsf{sid}^*}$ is the matching session of sid^*, if it exists. "Yes" means that there exists $\overline{\mathsf{sid}^*}$, "No" means do not. $ssk_A(ssk_B)$ means the static secret key of $A(B)$. $esk_A(esk_B)$ is the ephemeral secret key of $A(B)$ in sid^* or $\overline{\mathsf{sid}^*}$ if there exists. "$\surd$" means the secret key may be revealed to adversary, "$\times$" means is not. "-" means the secret key does not exist

Event	Case	sid^*	$\overline{\mathsf{sid}^*}$	ssk_A	esk_A	esk_B	ssk_B	Security
E_1	1	A	No	$\surd$	$\times$	-	$\times$	KCI
E_2	2	A	No	$\times$	$\surd$	-	$\times$	MEX
E_3	2	B	No	$\times$	-	$\surd$	$\times$	MEX
E_4	1	B	No	$\times$	-	$\times$	$\surd$	KCI
E_5	5	A or B	Yes	$\surd$	$\times$	$\times$	$\surd$	wPFS
E_6	4	A or B	Yes	$\times$	$\surd$	$\surd$	$\times$	MEX
$E_{7\text{-}1}$	3	A	Yes	$\surd$	$\times$	$\surd$	$\times$	KCI
$E_{7\text{-}2}$	3	B	Yes	$\times$	$\surd$	$\times$	$\surd$	KCI
$E_{8\text{-}1}$	6	A	Yes	$\times$	$\surd$	$\times$	$\surd$	KCI
$E_{8\text{-}2}$	6	B	Yes	$\surd$	$\times$	$\surd$	$\times$	KCI

3 2-Key Key Encapsulation Mechanism and Basic Results

3.1 2-Key Key Encapsulation Mechanism

Generally, a double-key (2-key) KEM is a public key encapsulation with two pairs of public and secret keys. Formally, a 2-key KEM $\mathsf{2KEM} = (\mathsf{KeyGen1}, \mathsf{KeyGen0}, \mathsf{Encaps}, \mathsf{Decaps})$ is a quadruple of PPT algorithms together with a key space $\mathcal{K}$.

- $\mathsf{KeyGen1}(\lambda, pp)$: on inputs security parameter λ, and public parameters pp, output a pair of public-secret keys (pk_1, sk_1). In order to show the randomness that is used, we denote key generation algorithm as $\mathsf{KeyGen1}(\lambda, pp; r)$. For simplicity, sometimes we omit the input security parameter λ and public parameter pp and denote it as $\mathsf{KeyGen1}(r)$ directly.
- $\mathsf{KeyGen0}(\lambda)$: on inputs security parameter λ output a pair of public and secret keys (pk_0, sk_0).
- $\mathsf{Encaps}(pk_1, pk_0; \mathsf{aux_e})$: on input public keys pk_1, pk_0 and auxiliary input $\mathsf{aux_e}$ (if there is), output ciphertext c and encapsulated key k in key space $\mathcal{K}$. Sometimes, we explicitly add the randomness r and denote it as $\mathsf{Encaps}(pk_1, pk_0, r; \mathsf{aux_e})$.
- $\mathsf{Decaps}(sk_1, sk_0, c; \mathsf{aux_d})$: on input secret keys sk_0, sk_1, auxiliary input $\mathsf{aux_d}$ (if there is) and c, output key k.

Correctness. For $(pk_1, sk_1) \leftarrow \mathsf{KeyGen1}(\lambda, pp)$, $(pk_0, sk_0) \leftarrow \mathsf{KeyGen0}(\lambda, pp)$ and $(c, k) \leftarrow \mathsf{Encaps}(pk_1, pk_0)$, we require that $\mathsf{Decaps}(sk_1, sk_0, c) = k$ holds with all but negligible probability.

Security. We consider two kinds of security *i.e.*, indistinguishability and one-wayness in the attacking model $[\mathsf{ATK}_1, \mathsf{ATK}_0]$. More precisely, in our $[\mathsf{ATK}_1, \mathsf{ATK}_0]$ security model for 2KEM, we consider two adversaries, *i.e.*, $\mathcal{A} = (\mathcal{A}_1, \mathcal{A}_2)$ attacking pk_1 (controlling the generation of pk_0^*) and $\mathcal{B} = (\mathcal{B}_1, \mathcal{B}_2)$ attacking pk_0 (controlling the generation of pk_1^*). In Fig. 1 below we show the security games of one-wayness and indistinguishable security corresponding to $[\mathsf{IND/OW\text{-}ATK}_1, \cdot]$ and $[\cdot, \mathsf{IND/OW\text{-}ATK}_0]$ respectively.

To be clear, the auxiliary inputs $\mathsf{aux_e}$ and $\mathsf{aux_d}$ may contain public part, called public auxiliary input, and secret part, called secret auxiliary input. In the security games, both the challenger and adversary have public auxiliary input, while only the challenger has the secret auxiliary input. For simplicity, we do not explicitly show $\mathsf{aux_e}$ and $\mathsf{aux_d}$ in the security games.

Game [IND-ATK1, ·] on pk_1	**Game [·, IND-ATK0] on** pk_0
$(pk_1, sk_1) \leftarrow \mathsf{KeyGen1}(pp)$;	$(pk_0, sk_0) \leftarrow \mathsf{KeyGen0}(pp)$
$L_0 = \{(-,-,-)\}$	$L_1 = \{(-,-,-)\}$
$(state, pk_0^*) \leftarrow \mathcal{A}_1^{\mathcal{O}_{\mathsf{ATK}_1}, \mathcal{O}_{\mathsf{leak}_0}}(pk_1)$	$(state, pk_1^*) \leftarrow \mathcal{B}_1^{\mathcal{O}_{\mathsf{ATK}_0}, \mathcal{O}_{\mathsf{leak}_1}}(pk_0)$;
$b \leftarrow \{0,1\}$;	$b \leftarrow \{0,1\}$;
$(c^*, k_0^*) \leftarrow \mathsf{Encaps}(pk_1, pk_0^*), k_1^* \leftarrow \mathcal{K}$;	$(c^*, k_0^*) \leftarrow \mathsf{Encaps}(pk_1^*, pk_0), k_1^* \leftarrow \mathcal{K}$;
$b' \leftarrow \mathcal{A}_2^{\mathcal{O}_{\mathsf{ATK}_1}, \mathcal{O}_{\mathsf{leak}_0}}(state, c^*, k_b^*)$;	$b' \leftarrow \mathcal{B}_2^{\mathcal{O}_{\mathsf{ATK}_0}, \mathcal{O}_{\mathsf{leak}_1}}(state, c^*, k_b^*)$;
return $b' \stackrel{?}{=} b$	return $b' \stackrel{?}{=} b$
Game [OW-ATK1, ·] on pk_1	**Game [·, OW-ATK0] on** pk_0
$(pk_1, sk_1) \leftarrow \mathsf{KeyGen1}(pp)$;	$(pk_0, sk_0) \leftarrow \mathsf{KeyGen0}(pp)$
$L_0 = \{(-,-,-)\}$	$L_1 = \{(-,-,-)\}$
$(state, pk_0^*) \leftarrow \mathcal{A}_1^{\mathcal{O}_{\mathsf{ATK}_1}, \mathcal{O}_{\mathsf{leak}_0}}(pk_1)$	$(state, pk_1^*) \leftarrow \mathcal{B}_1^{\mathcal{O}_{\mathsf{ATK}_0}, \mathcal{O}_{\mathsf{leak}_1}}(pk_0)$;
$(c^*, k^*) \leftarrow \mathsf{Encaps}(pk_1, pk_0^*)$;	$(c^*, k^*) \leftarrow \mathsf{Encaps}(pk_1^*, pk_0)$;
$k' \leftarrow \mathcal{A}_2^{\mathcal{O}_{\mathsf{ATK}_1}, \mathcal{O}_{\mathsf{leak}_0}}(state, c^*)$;	$k' \leftarrow \mathcal{B}_2^{\mathcal{O}_{\mathsf{ATK}_0}, \mathcal{O}_{\mathsf{leak}_1}}(state, c^*)$;
return $k' \stackrel{?}{=} k^*$	return $k' \stackrel{?}{=} k^*$

Fig. 1. The $[\mathsf{ATK1}, \cdot]$, and $[\cdot, \mathsf{ATK0}]$ games of 2KEM for adversaries $\mathcal{A}$ and $\mathcal{B}$. The oracles $\mathcal{O}_{\mathsf{leak}_0}$, $\mathcal{O}_{\mathsf{ATK}_1}$, $\mathcal{O}_{\mathsf{leak}_1}$, and $\mathcal{O}_{\mathsf{ATK}_0}$ are defined in the following

On the i-th query of $\mathcal{O}_{\mathsf{leak}_0}$, the challenger generates $(pk_0^i, sk_0^i) \leftarrow \mathsf{KeyGen0}(r_0^i)$, sets $L_0 = L_0 \cup \{(pk_0^i, sk_0^i, r_0^i)\}$ and returns (pk_0^i, sk_0^i, r_0^i) to adversary $\mathcal{A}$. On the i-th query of $\mathcal{O}_{\mathsf{leak}_1}$, the challenger generates $(pk_1^i, sk_1^i) \leftarrow \mathsf{KeyGen1}(r_1^i)$, sets $L_1 = L_1 \cup \{(pk_1^i, sk_1^i, r_1^i)\}$ and returns (pk_1^i, sk_1^i, r_1^i) to adversary $\mathcal{B}$.

Depending on the definition of oracle $\mathcal{O}_{\mathsf{ATK}_1}$ the adversary $\mathcal{A}$ accesses, and $\mathcal{O}_{\mathsf{ATK}_0}$ that the adversary $\mathcal{B}$ accesses, we get CPA and CCA notions respectively.

- if $\mathcal{O}_{\mathsf{ATK}_1(pk_0', c')} = -$, it implies CPA notion;
- if $\mathcal{O}_{\mathsf{ATK}_1(pk_0', c')} \neq -$, it works as following: If $pk_0' \in [L_0]_1 \wedge (c' \neq c^* \vee pk_0' \neq pk_0^*)$, compute $k' \leftarrow \mathsf{Decaps}(sk_1, sk_0', c')$, and return the corresponding k', otherwise return $\perp$. This case implies CCA notion.

- if $\mathcal{O}_{\mathsf{ATK}_0(pk'_1,c')} = -$, it implies CPA notion;
- if $\mathcal{O}_{\mathsf{ATK}_0(pk'_1,c')} \neq -$, it works as following: If $pk'_1 \in [L_1]_1 \wedge (c' \neq c^* \vee pk'_1 \neq pk^*_1)$, compute $k' \leftarrow \mathsf{Decaps}(sk'_1, sk_0, c')$, and return the corresponding k', otherwise return $\perp$. This case implies CCA notion.

Let $\mathcal{A} = (\mathcal{A}_1, \mathcal{A}_2)$ be an adversary against pk_1 of 2KEM. We define the advantage of $\mathcal{A}$ winning in the game IND-ATK1 and OW-ATK1 respectively as: $\mathrm{Adv}^{[\mathsf{IND\text{-}ATK1},\cdot]}_{\mathsf{2KEM}}(\mathcal{A}) = \left|\Pr[\mathsf{IND\text{-}ATK1}^{\mathcal{A}} \Rightarrow 1] - \frac{1}{2}\right|$, and $\mathrm{Adv}^{[\mathsf{OW\text{-}ATK1},\cdot]}_{\mathsf{2KEM}}(\mathcal{A}) = \Pr[\mathsf{OW\text{-}ATK1}^{\mathcal{A}} \Rightarrow 1]$, where game [IND-ATK1, ·] and [OW-ATK1, ·] are described in Fig. 1.

We say that 2KEM is [IND-ATK1, ·] secure, if $\mathrm{Adv}^{[\mathsf{IND\text{-}ATK1},\cdot]}_{\mathsf{2KEM}}(\mathcal{A})$ is negligible; that 2KEM is [OW-ATK1, ·] secure, if $\mathrm{Adv}^{[\mathsf{OW\text{-}ATK1},\cdot]}_{\mathsf{2KEM}}(\mathcal{A})$ is negligible, for any PPT adversary $\mathcal{A}$. The [·, IND-ATK0] and [·, OW-ATK0] security can be defined in the same way. Here to avoid repetition we omit their description.

[ATK1, ATK0] Security. The scheme 2KEM is called [ATK1, ATK0] secure if it is both [ATK1, ·] and [·, ATK0] secure for any PPT algorithms $\mathcal{A}$ and $\mathcal{B}$. By the combination of adversaries $\mathcal{A}$ and $\mathcal{B}$ attacking different security (*i.e.*, indistinguishability and one-wayness), we could get 16 different definitions of security for 2-key KEM. What we concern in this paper is the [CCA, CPA] security in both indistinguishability and one-wayness setting. For simplicity, we abbreviate the security model as [IND/OW-CCA, IND/OW-CPA].

3.2 Differences Between [CCA, ·] Security and Previous Definitions

In order to avoid confusion, we re-clarify the definition of [IND/OW-CCA, ·] security and analyze its difference with previous similar notions, including classical CCA security, KEM combiner [17], and completely non-malleable scheme [13].

Compared with classical CCA adversary, the [CCA, ·] adversary of 2-key KEM (1) has the capability of choosing one of the challenge public key pk^*_0; (2) could query a strong decryption oracle, which decapsulates the ciphertext under several public keys (pk^*_1, pk'_0) where pk'_0 is generated by the challenger. While in the classical definition of decapsulation oracle the adversary could only query decapsulation oracle with ciphertext under the challenge public keys (pk^*_1, pk^*_0).

Very recently, Giacon *et. al* [17] study combiners for KEMs. That is, given a set of KEMs, an unknown subset of which might be arbitrarily insecure, Giacon *et. al* investigate how they can be combined to form a single KEM that is secure if at least one ingredient KEM is. The KEM combiners treated by Giacon *et al.* have a parallel structure: If the number of KEMs to be combined is n, a public key of the resulting KEM consists of a vector of n public keys; likewise for secret keys. The encapsulation procedure performs n independent encapsulations, one for each combined KEM. The ciphertext of the resulting KEM is simply the concatenation of all generated ciphertexts. The session key is obtained as a function of keys and ciphertexts. Although from the literature our 2-key KEM looks like the two KEM combiner, the security requirement and concrete constructions between them are completely different. Since the two KEM combiner considers the problem that if one of two KEMs is insecure and the other one is CCA secure, how to combine them to obtain a CCA secure single KEM. In fact, the adversary of KEM combiner security model is the classical CCA adversary (it can only query the decryption oracle under certain public keys). Actually, in Sect. 6.1, we show there exists [CCA, ·] adversary to attack a CCA secure two KEM combiner.

Aiming to construct non-malleable commitments, Fischlin [13] considered completely non-malleable (NM) schemes. The complete NM scheme is later extended to indistinguishability setting by Barbosa and Farshim [4] with a strong decryption oracle, which allows the adversary to queries with ciphertext under *arbitrary public key of its choice.* Note that our [CCA, ·] is also modeled to allow the adversary to query a strong (but weaker than complete NM) decapsulation oracle with ciphertext under several public keys that are chosen by challenger instead of by adversary. On the other hand, the complete NM adversary is not allowed to choose part of challenge public key, while [CCA, ·] is.

Based on the above observations, we give comparison among these different definitions by considering two public keys in Table 3. For convenience, we consider classical CCA and complete NM schemes in which public keys are expressed as two public keys (pk_1, pk_0) and let KEM combiner be two combiner of KEM. The differences among security requirements are the capability of adversary, namely, whether the adversary is allowed to choose part of the challenge public keys, or under which public keys the ciphertexts that adversary is allowed to query decryption oracle with are computed.

Table 3. The differences of related definitions. "Cha." is the abbreviation of "challenge". $\mathcal{C}$ denote the challenger and $\mathcal{A}$ denote the adversary. We use $\mathcal{A}(sk_0^*)$ to denote that $\mathcal{A}$ breaks the KEM under pk_0^*. In both Classical CCA and KEM combiner the decapsulation oracle only returns when $(pk_1, pk_0) = (pk_1^*, pk_0^*)$, while in Complete NM (pk_1, pk_0) could be arbitrary public keys chosen by adversary, and in [CCA, ·], pk_0 could be arbitrary public key chosen by challenger.

Definitions	Cha. PK (pk_1^*, pk_0^*)	Cha. ciphertext c^*	$\mathcal{O}_{\mathsf{Dec}}((pk_1, pk_0), c')$
Classical CCA	$(pk_1^*, pk_0^*) \leftarrow \mathcal{C}$	c^* under (pk_1^*, pk_0^*)	$(pk_1, pk_0) = (pk_1^*, pk_0^*)$
KEM Combiner [17]	$(pk_1^*, pk_0^*) \leftarrow \mathcal{C}$, $\mathcal{A}(sk_0^*)$	$c_1^* \Vert c_0^*$, c_i^* under pk_i^*	$(pk_1, pk_0) = (pk_1^*, pk_0^*)$
Complete NM [13]	$(pk_1^*, pk_0^*) \leftarrow \mathcal{C}$	c^* under (pk_1^*, pk_0^*)	$(pk_1, pk_0) \leftarrow \mathcal{A}$
[CCA, ·]	$pk_1^* \leftarrow \mathcal{C}, pk_0^* \leftarrow \mathcal{A}$	c^* under (pk_1^*, pk_0^*)	$pk_1 = pk_1^*$, $pk_0 \leftarrow \mathcal{C}$

3.3 Basic Definitions and Results Related to 2-Key KEM

[CCA, ·] Security with Non-adaptive Adversary. We can define a weak [CCA, ·] adversary, who is not able to adaptively choose the challenge public key. In this case, taking the adversary $\mathcal{A}$ attacking pk_1 as an example, the challenge public key pk_0^* is generated by challenger instead of $\mathcal{A}$, which means $pk_0^* \in [L_0]_1$.

Public Key Independent Ciphertext. The concept of public-key-independent-ciphertext (PKIC) was first proposed in [33]. We extend it to 2-key

KEM setting. The PKIC 2-key KEM allows a ciphertext to be generated independently from one of two public keys, while the encapsulated key underlay in such ciphertext to be generated with the randomness and both two public keys. More precisely, algorithm $(c, k) \leftarrow \mathsf{Encaps}(pk_1, pk_0, r)$ can be realized in two steps: in step 1, ciphertex c is generated from pk_1 and randomness r. We precisely denote it as $c \leftarrow \mathsf{Encaps0}(pk_1, \text{-}, r)$; in step 2, the encapsulated key k in c is generated from r, pk_1, and pk_0. We precisely denote it as $k \leftarrow \mathsf{Encaps1}(pk_1, pk_0, r)$.

Classical One-Key KEM and 2-Key KEM. Note that given a concrete 2-key KEM, usually it is not obvious and natural to regress to one-key KEM by setting $pk_0 = \text{-}$. However given any classical one-key KEM, it can be seen as a 2-key KEM with KeyGen0 not in use and $pk_0 = \text{-}$. At that time, the [OW/IND-CCA, ·] security of this 2-key KEM return to the classical OW/IND-CCA security of the underlying KEM.

Min-Entropy. In case of 2-key KEM with PPT adversary $\mathcal{A}$, for $(pk_1, sk_1) \leftarrow \mathsf{KeyGen1}$ and $pk_0 \leftarrow \mathcal{A}$ or $(pk_0, sk_0) \leftarrow \mathsf{KeyGen0}$ and $pk_1 \leftarrow \mathcal{A}$, we define the *min-entropy* of $\mathsf{Encaps}(pk_1, pk_0)$ by $\gamma(pk_1, pk_0, \mathcal{A}) = -\log \max_{c \in \mathcal{C}} \Pr[c = \mathsf{Encaps}(pk_1, pk_0)]$. We say that KEM is *$\gamma$-spread* if for every $(pk_1, sk_1) \leftarrow \mathsf{KeyGen1}$ and $pk_0 \leftarrow \mathcal{A}$ or $(pk_0, sk_0) \leftarrow \mathsf{KeyGen0}$ and $pk_1 \leftarrow \mathcal{A}$, $\gamma(pk_1, pk_0, \mathcal{A}) \geq \gamma$, which means for every ciphertext $c \in \mathcal{C}$, it has $\Pr[c = \mathsf{Encaps}(pk_1, pk_0)] \leq 2^{-\gamma}$.

4 Authenticated Key Exchange from 2-Key KEM

In this section, we propose CK$^+$ secure AKEs from [CCA, CPA] secure 2-key KEM in both random oracle and standard models. Before showing our AKEs, we need a primitive of random function with half of leakage, that is used by several existing AKEs.

Definition 2 (Random Function with half of leakage (hl-RF)). *Let $f : D_{sk} \times D_b \rightarrow R$ be a function from domain $D_{sk} \times D_b$ to R. Denote $\mathsf{KeyGen} \rightarrow D_{sk} \times D_{pk}$ as key generation algorithm for some KEM. Let $\mathcal{D}_b, \mathcal{R}$ be the uniformly distributions over D_b, R. It is called $(\varepsilon_1, \varepsilon_2)$ hl-RF with respect to KeyGen, if for $(pk, sk) \leftarrow \mathsf{KeyGen}$, the following distributions are computational indistinguishable with advantage $\varepsilon_1, \varepsilon_2$.*

$$\{(pk, sk, f(sk, b)) | b \leftarrow \mathcal{D}_b\} =_{\varepsilon_1} \{(pk, sk, U) | U \leftarrow \mathcal{R}\};$$
$$\{(pk, b, f(sk, b)) | b \leftarrow \mathcal{D}_b\} =_{\varepsilon_2} \{(pk, b, U) | b \leftarrow \mathcal{D}_b, U \leftarrow \mathcal{R}\}.$$

The hk-RF can be achieved in both random oracle model and standard model.

- In the random oracle model, if f is a hash function, without the knowledge of b, the output of f is totally random; if KEM with respect to KeyGen is secure, without the knowledge of sk the output of f is computational indistinguishable with a random string (otherwise the adversary must query random oracle with sk which against the security of KEM) given pk. Then Eq. 2 holds. This structure is known as NAXOS trick [24].

- Let $F' : D_b \times \{0,1\}^\lambda \to R$ and $F'' : D_{sk} \times D_b \to R$ be two pseudo random functions (PRFs). If assume KeyGen outputs an additional string $s \leftarrow \{0,1\}^\lambda$, after obtaining (pk, sk), set $sk = (sk||s)$. If $f(sk, b) = F'_b(1^\lambda) \oplus F''_s(b)$, then even given pk, without the knowledge of s or b, $f(sk, b)$ is computational indistinguishable with random distribution over R. This is known as twisted PRF trick [15,27].

4.1 AKE from 2-Key KEM in Random Oracle Model

Roadmap: We first give a basic AKE from two [OW-CCA, OW-CPA] secure 2-key KEMs. Utilizing extra properties of 2-key KEM, like PKIC or resistance of leakage of partial randomness, we then present two elegant AKEs based on 2-key KEM with different property.

Let 2KEM = (KeyGen1, KeyGen0, Encaps, Decaps) be a [OW-CCA, OW-CPA] secure 2-key KEM with secret key space $D_{sk_1} \times D_{sk_0}$, random space R. Let $H : \{0,1\}^* \to \{0,1\}^\lambda$ be hash function, $f_A : D_{sk_1} \times \{0,1\}^* \to R$ and $f_B : D_{sk_1} \times \{0,1\}^* \to R$ be hl-RFs. The CK$^+$ secure AKE is presented in Fig. 2.

Stage 0: static secret-public key pair and public parameters. Each user's static secret-public key pair is generated using KeyGen1. Sample one pair of key $(cpk_0, csk_0) \leftarrow$ KeyGen0 (which need not to be randomly generated). Set cpk_0 as the predetermined ephemeral public key which will be used by initiator afterwards and csk_0 as the predetermined ephemeral secret key that will be used by responder. Let (cpk_0, csk_0) be parts of public parameters.

Stage 1: Initiator U_A generates two randomness r_A, r_{A0}; it computes (C_B, K_B) under public key pk_B and predetermined cpk_0 with randomness $f_A(sk_A, r_A)$, and generates ephemeral secret-public key $(pk_{A0}, sk_{A0}) \leftarrow$ KeyGen0(r_{A0}). Then it sends C_B, pk_{A0} to U_B.

Stage 2: Responder U_B generates randomness r_B; it computes (C_A, K_A) under public keys pk_A and pk_{A0} with randomness $f_B(sk_B, r_B)$; U_B sends C_A to U_A and de-encapsulates C_B using sk_B and predetermined csk_0 to obtain K'_B; it then computes $SK = H(U_A, U_B, pk_A, pk_B, C_B, pk_{A0}, C_A, K_A, K'_B)$, and erases K'_B.

Stage 3: U_A de-encapsulates C_A using sk_A and sk_{A0} to obtain K'_A and computes $SK = H(U_A, U_B, pk_A, pk_B, C_B, pk_{A0}, C_A, K'_A, K_B)$.

The session state of sid owned by U_A consists of ephemeral secret key r_{A0}, r_A, decapsulated key K'_A and encapsulated key K_B; The session state of sid owned by U_B consists of ephemeral secrete key r_B and encapsulated key K_A.

Theorem 1. *If the underlying 2KEM is [OW-CCA, OW-CPA] secure and γ-spread, f_A, f_B are $(\varepsilon_1, \varepsilon_2)$ hl-RFs, and there are N users in the AKE protocol and the upbound of sessions between two users is l, for any PPT adversary $\mathcal{A}$ against AKE with totally q times of CK$^+$ queries, there exists $\mathcal{S}$ s.t.,*

$$Adv_{\mathsf{AKE}}^{ck+}(\mathcal{A}) \leq \frac{1}{2} + \min \left\{ \begin{array}{l} N^2 l \cdot Adv_{\mathsf{2KEM}}^{[\mathsf{OW\text{-}CCA},\cdot]}(\mathcal{S}) + N^2 lq \cdot (\varepsilon_1 + \varepsilon_2 + 2^{-\gamma}), \\ N^2 l \cdot Adv_{\mathsf{2KEM}}^{[\cdot,\mathsf{OW\text{-}CPA}]}(\mathcal{S}) + N^2 lq \cdot \varepsilon_2 \end{array} \right\}.$$

U_A		U_B
$(pk_A, sk_A) \leftarrow \mathsf{KeyGen1}$		$(pk_B, sk_B) \leftarrow \mathsf{KeyGen1}$
$r_A \leftarrow \{0,1\}^*, r_{A0} \leftarrow \{0,1\}^*$		$r_B \leftarrow \{0,1\}^*$
$R_A := f_A(sk_A, r_A)$		
$(C_B, K_B) \leftarrow \mathsf{Encaps}(pk_B, cpk_0, R_A)$		$R_B := f_B(sk_B, r_B)$
$(pk_{A0}, sk_{A0}) \leftarrow \mathsf{KeyGen0}(r_{A0})$	$\xrightarrow{C_B, pk_{A0}}$	$(C_A, K_A) \leftarrow \mathsf{Encaps}(pk_A, pk_{A0}, R_B)$
$K'_A \leftarrow \mathsf{Decaps}(sk_A, sk_{A0}, C_A)$	$\xleftarrow{C_A}$	$K'_B \leftarrow \mathsf{Decaps}(sk_B, csk_0, C_B)$
$SK = H(si, K'_A, K_B)$		$SK = H(si, K_A, K'_B)$

Fig. 2. AKE from [OW-CCA, OW-CPA] secure 2KEM in random oracle model. cpk_0, csk_0 are predetermined and default ephemeral keys and they are part of the public parameters. si here is $(U_A, U_B, pk_A, pk_B, C_B, pk_{A0}, C_A)$

Proof of Theorem 1. Let Succ be the event that the guess of $\mathcal{A}$ against freshed test session is correct. Let AskH be the event that $\mathcal{A}$ poses $(U_A, U_B, pk_A, pk_B, C_B, pk_{A0}, C_A, K_A, K_B)$ to H, where C_B, pk_{A0}, C_A are the views of the test session and K_A, K_B are the keys encapsulated in the test session. Let $\overline{\mathsf{AskH}}$ be the complement of AskH. Then,

$$\Pr[\mathsf{Succ}] = \Pr[\mathsf{Succ} \wedge \overline{\mathsf{AskH}}] + \Pr[\mathsf{Succ} \wedge \mathsf{AskH}] \leq \Pr[\mathsf{Succ} \wedge \overline{\mathsf{AskH}}] + \Pr[\mathsf{AskH}],$$

where the probability is taken over the randomness used in CK^+ experiment.

We then show that $\Pr[\mathsf{Succ} \wedge \overline{\mathsf{AskH}}] \leq 1/2$ (as in Lemma 1) and $\Pr[\mathsf{AskH}]$ is negligible (as in Lemma 2) in all the events (listed in Table 2) of CK^+ model. Followed by Lemmas 1 and 2, we acheive the security of AKE in CK^+ model. Thus, we only need to prove Lemmas 1 and 2.

Lemma 1. *If H is modeled as a random oracle, we have* $Pr[\mathsf{Succ} \wedge \overline{\mathsf{AskH}}] \leq 1/2$.

Proof of Lemma 1. If $\Pr[\overline{\mathsf{AskH}}] = 0$ then the claim is straightforward, otherwise we have $\Pr[\mathsf{Succ} \wedge \overline{\mathsf{AskH}}] = \Pr[\mathsf{Succ}|\overline{\mathsf{AskH}}]\Pr[\overline{\mathsf{AskH}}] \leq \Pr[\mathsf{Succ}|\overline{\mathsf{AskH}}]$. Let sid be any completed session owned by an honest party such that $\mathsf{sid} \neq \mathsf{sid}^*$ and sid is not matching sid^*. The inputs to sid are different from those to sid^* and $\overline{\mathsf{sid}^*}$ (if there exists the matching session of sid^*). If $\mathcal{A}$ does not explicitly query the view and keys to oracle, then $H(U_A, U_B, pk_A, pk_B, C_B, pk_{A0}, C_A, K_A, K_B)$ is completely random from $\mathcal{A}$'s point of view. Therefore, the probability that $\mathcal{A}$ wins when AskH does not occur is exactly 1/2.

Lemma 2. *If the underlying 2KEM is [OW-CCA, OW-CPA] secure, the probability of event AskH defined above is negligible. Precisely,*

$$\Pr[\mathit{AskH}] \leq \min \left\{ \begin{array}{l} N^2 l \cdot Adv_{\mathit{2KEM}}^{[\mathit{OW\text{-}CCA}, \cdot]}(\mathcal{S}) + N^2 lq \cdot (\varepsilon_1 + \varepsilon_2 + 2^{-\gamma}), \\ N^2 l \cdot Adv_{\mathit{2KEM}}^{[\cdot, \mathit{OW\text{-}CPA}]}(\mathcal{S}) + N^2 lq \cdot \varepsilon_2 \end{array} \right\}.$$

Please refer the full version [32] for the formal proof. we give a sketch of proof here. In the following, to bound $\Pr[\mathsf{AskH}]$, we work with the events in Table 4.

Table 4. The bounds of $\mathsf{AskH} \wedge \overline{\mathsf{Askh}}$ in the proof of Lemma 2. Refer Table 2 for the meanings of notions.

Events	sid*	$\overline{\text{sid}^*}$	ssk_A	esk_A	esk_B	ssk_B	Bounds
$\mathsf{AskH} \wedge E_1$	A	No	√	×	-	×	$\mathrm{Adv}_{\mathsf{2KEM}}^{[\mathsf{OW\text{-}CCA},\cdot]}$, $pk_1 = pk_B$, $pk_0^* = cpk_0$
$\mathsf{AskH} \wedge E_2$	A	No	×	√	-	×	$\mathrm{Adv}_{\mathsf{2KEM}}^{[\mathsf{OW\text{-}CCA},\cdot]}$, $pk_1 = pk_B$, $pk_0^* = cpk_0$
$\mathsf{AskH} \wedge E_3$	B	No	×	-	√	×	$\mathrm{Adv}_{\mathsf{2KEM}}^{[\mathsf{OW\text{-}CCA},\cdot]}$, $pk_1 = pk_A$, $pk_0^* \leftarrow \mathcal{A}$
$\mathsf{AskH} \wedge E_4$	B	No	×	-	×	√	$\mathrm{Adv}_{\mathsf{2KEM}}^{[\mathsf{OW\text{-}CCA},\cdot]}$, $pk_1 = pk_A$, $pk_0^* \leftarrow \mathcal{A}$
$\mathsf{AskH} \wedge E_5$	A/B	Yes	√	×	×	√	$\mathrm{Adv}_{\mathsf{2KEM}}^{[\cdot,\mathsf{OW\text{-}CPA}]}$, $pk_0 = pk_0(\mathsf{sid}^*)$ $pk_1^* \in [L_1]_1$
$\mathsf{AskH} \wedge E_6$	A/B	Yes	×	√	√	×	$\mathrm{Adv}_{\mathsf{2KEM}}^{[\mathsf{OW\text{-}CCA},\cdot]}$, $pk_1 = pk_A, pk_0^* \in [L_0]_1$
$\mathsf{AskH} \wedge E_{7\text{-}1}$	A	Yes	√	×	√	×	$\mathrm{Adv}_{\mathsf{2KEM}}^{[\mathsf{OW\text{-}CCA},\cdot]}$, $pk_1 = pk_B$ $pk_0^* = cpk_0$
$\mathsf{AskH} \wedge E_{7\text{-}2}$	B	Yes	×	√	×	√	$\mathrm{Adv}_{\mathsf{2KEM}}^{[\mathsf{OW\text{-}CCA},\cdot]}$, $pk_1 = pk_A$, $pk_0^* \in [L_0]_1$
$\mathsf{AskH} \wedge E_{8\text{-}1}$	A	Yes	×	√	×	√	$\mathrm{Adv}_{\mathsf{2KEM}}^{[\mathsf{OW\text{-}CCA},\cdot]}$, $pk_1 = pk_A$, $pk_0^* \in [L_0]_1$
$\mathsf{AskH} \wedge E_{8\text{-}2}$	B	Yes	√	×	√	×	$\mathrm{Adv}_{\mathsf{2KEM}}^{[\mathsf{OW\text{-}CCA},\cdot]}$, $pk_1 = pk_B$, $pk_0^* = cpk_0$

Due to the [OW-CCA, ·] security of 2KEM with $pk_1 = pk_A$ and pk_0^* generated by $\mathcal{A}$, the probability of events $\mathsf{AskH} \wedge E_3$ and $\mathsf{AskH} \wedge E_4$ is negligible; Due to the [OW-CCA, ·] security of KEM with $pk_1 = pk_B$ and $pk_0^* = cpk_0$, the probability of events $\mathsf{AskH} \wedge E_1$, $\mathsf{AskH} \wedge E_2$, $\mathsf{AskH} \wedge E_{7\text{-}1}$ and $\mathsf{AskH} \wedge E_{8\text{-}2}$ is negligible; Due to the [OW-CCA, ·] security of 2KEM with $pk_1 = pk_A$ and $pk_0^* \in [L_0]_1$, the probability of events $\mathsf{AskH} \wedge E_6$, $\mathsf{AskH} \wedge E_{7\text{-}2}$ and $\mathsf{AskH} \wedge E_{8\text{-}1}$ is negligible. Due to the [·, OW-CPA] security with $pk_1^* \in [L_1]_1$, the probability of event $\mathsf{AskH} \wedge E_5$ is negligible.

Here, we only take $\mathsf{AskH} \wedge E_3$ as an example to explain in detail. For the other cases we can deal with them in a similar way. In the event E_3, the test session sid* has no matching session, and the ephemeral secret keys r_B of U_B is given to $\mathcal{A}$. In case of $\mathsf{AskH} \wedge E_3$, the [OW-CCA, ·] adversary $\mathcal{S}$ performs as follows. It simulates the CK$^+$ games, and transfers the probability that the event AskH performed by $\mathcal{A}$ occurs to the advantage of attacking [OW-CCA, ·] security.

In order to simulate the random oracles, $\mathcal{S}$ maintains two lists for H oracle and SessionKeyReveal respectively. H-oracle and SessionKeyReveal are related, which means the adversary may ask SessionKeyReveal without the encapsulated keys at first, and then may ask H-oracle with the encapsulated keys. Thus, the reduction must ensure consistency with the random oracle queries to H and SessionKeyReveal. The decryption oracle for [OW-CCA, ·] game would help to maintain the consistency of H-oracle and SessionKeyReveal.

On receiving the public key pk_1 from the [OW-CCA, ·] challenger, to simulate the CK$^+$ game, $\mathcal{S}$ randomly chooses two parties U_A, U_B and the i-th session as a guess of the test session with success probability $1/N^2 l$. $\mathcal{S}$, picks one preset $(cpk_0, csk_0) \leftarrow$ KeyGen0 as public parameters, runs KeyGen1 to set all the static secret and public key pairs (pk_P, sk_P) for all N users U_P except for U_A. Specially, $\mathcal{S}$ sets the static secret and public key pairs (pk_B, sk_B) for U_B, and sets $pk_A = pk_1$.

Without knowing the secret key of U_A, $\mathcal{S}$ chooses totally random r_A as part of ephemeral secret key and totally random R_A for Encaps. Since f_A is $(\varepsilon_1, \varepsilon_2)$ hl-RF, the difference between simulation with modification of r_A and real game is bounded by ε_1. When a ephemeral public key pk_{P0} is needed, $\mathcal{S}$ queries $(pk_0^i, sk_0^i, r_0^i) \leftarrow \mathcal{O}_{\mathsf{leak}_0}$ and sets $pk_{P0} = pk_0^i$. When a session state revealed to a session owned by U_A, is queried, $\mathcal{S}$ returns r_A and r_0^i of this session as part of ephemeral secret key.

On receiving the i-th session (C'_B, pk_0^*) from U_A (that is sent by $\mathcal{A}$ in the CK$^+$ games), $\mathcal{S}$ returns pk_0^* to the [OW-CCA, $\cdot$] challenger and receives the challenge ciphertext C^* under public key pk_1 and pk_0^*. Then $\mathcal{S}$ returns C^* to U_A as the response of i-th session from U_B. $\mathcal{S}$ chooses a totally independent randomness r_B as the ephemeral secret key of U_B for C^* and leaks it to adversary $\mathcal{A}$. Since f_B is $(\varepsilon_1, \varepsilon_2)$ hl-RF, the difference between simulation with modification of r_B and real game is bounded by ε_2.

$\mathcal{S}$ simulates the oracle queries of $\mathcal{A}$ and maintains the hash lists. Specially, when AskH happens, which means $\mathcal{A}$ poses $(U_A, U_B, pk_A, pk_B, C'_B, pk_0^*, C^*, K_A, K_B)$ to H, where C'_B, pk_0^*, C^* are the views of the test session and K_B is the key encapsulated in C'_B, $\mathcal{S}$ returns K_A as the guess of K^* encapsulated in C^*, which contradicts with the [OW-CCA, $\cdot$] security for $pk_1 = pk_A$, $pk_0^* \leftarrow \mathcal{A}$. □

4.1.1 If 2-Key KEM Is PKIC

As we notice in AKE, the session state of sid owned by U_B does not contain decapsulated key K'_B. If the underlying 2-key KEM is PKIC (which is defined in Sect. 3.3), and U_B also sends ephemeral public key pk_{B0} out in every session, K'_B is encapsulated under two public keys pk_B and pk_{B0}, then K'_B could be included in session state, and the predetermined ephemeral public key cpk_0 can be omitted. Let $\mathsf{2KEM_{pkic}}$ = (KeyGen1, KeyGen0, Encaps0, Encaps1, Decaps) be PKIC and [OW-CCA, OW-CPA] secure 2-key KEM. The AKE can be modified to include K'_B as session state by (1) replacing 2KEM with $\mathsf{2KEM_{pkic}}$; (2) requiring U_B to generate a fresh $(pk_{B0}, sk_{B0}) \leftarrow$ KeyGen0 and send out ephemeral public key pk_{B0}; (3) encapsulating and separating $(C_B, K_B) \leftarrow \mathsf{Encaps}(pk_B, pk_{B0}, R_A)$ in two steps and computing $C_B \leftarrow \mathsf{Encaps0}(pk_B, \text{-}, R_A)$ and $K_B \leftarrow \mathsf{Encaps1}(pk_B, pk_{B0}, R_A)$. The modified protocol $\mathsf{AKE_{ro\text{-}pkic}}$ is shown in Fig. 3.

Note that the encapsulation algorithm of PKIC 2-key KEM can be split into two steps. Since the generation of ciphertext C_B does not require pk_{B0}, we denote it as $C_B \leftarrow \mathsf{Encaps0}(pk_B, \text{-}, R_A)$. The computation of encapsulated key K_B requires pk_{B0}, and we denote it as $K_B \leftarrow \mathsf{Encaps1}(pk_B, pk_{B0}, R_A)$.

Since the proof mainly follows that of Theorem 1, we only show the difference here. The main difference is the analysis of Pr[AskH] in Lemma 2. Now, the probability of events AskH $\wedge E_1$, AskH $\wedge E_2$, AskH $\wedge E_{7\text{-}1}$, AskH $\wedge E_{8\text{-}2}$ is bounded by the [OW-CCA, $\cdot$] security of $\mathsf{2KEM_{pkic}}$ with pk_0^* chosen by $\mathcal{A}$ rather than the predetermined cpk_0. Precisely, in those events, when the adversary queries the session state of U_B whose secret key is unknown to simulator $\mathcal{S}$, in AKE, $\mathcal{S}$ queries the decryption oracle of 2KEM with cpk_0 and C_B (when adversary queries $\mathsf{Send}(\Pi, R, U_B, U_P, C_B, pk_{A0})$), while in $\mathsf{AKE_{pkic}}$, $\mathcal{S}$ queries the decryption oracle of $\mathsf{2KEM_{pkic}}$ with (pk_{B0}, C_B) chosen by $\mathcal{A}$. This modification does not affect the proof of security.

U_A		U_B
$(pk_A, sk_A) \leftarrow \mathsf{KeyGen1}$		$(pk_B, sk_B) \leftarrow \mathsf{KeyGen1}$
$r_A \leftarrow \{0,1\}^*, r_{A0} \leftarrow \{0,1\}^*$		$r_B \leftarrow \{0,1\}^*, r_{B0} \leftarrow \{0,1\}^*$
$R_A := f_A(sk_A, r_A)$		
$\boxed{C_B \leftarrow \mathsf{Encaps0}(pk_B, -, R_A)}$		$R_B := f_B(sk_B, r_B)$
$(pk_{A0}, sk_{A0}) \leftarrow \mathsf{KeyGen0}(r_{A0})$	$\xrightarrow{C_B, pk_{A0}}$	$(C_A, K_A) \leftarrow \mathsf{Encaps}(pk_A, pk_{A0}, R_B)$
	$\xleftarrow{C_A, \boxed{pk_{B0}}}$	$\boxed{(pk_{B0}, sk_{B0}) \leftarrow \mathsf{KeyGen0}(r_{B0})}$
$K'_A \leftarrow \mathsf{Decaps}(sk_A, sk_{A0}, C_A)$		
$\boxed{K_B \leftarrow \mathsf{Encaps1}(pk_B, pk_{B0}, R_A)}$		$\boxed{K'_B \leftarrow \mathsf{Decaps}(sk_B, sk_{B0}, C_B)}$
$SK \leftarrow H(si, K'_A, K_B)$		$SK \leftarrow H(si, K_A, K'_B)$

Fig. 3. $\mathsf{AKE}_{\mathsf{ro\text{-}pkic}}$ from PKIC [OW-CCA, OW-CPA] secure 2KEM. Here $si = (U_A, U_B, pk_A, pk_B, C_B, pk_{A0}, C_A, pk_{B0})$. The boxed argument is the difference with AKE

4.1.2 If PKIC 2-Key KEM Is Even Secure with Leakage of Partial Randomness

We can further refine the framework $\mathsf{AKE}_{\mathsf{ro\text{-}pkic}}$ based on two observations: (1) From the proof of Theorem 1 (especially Lemma 2), we can see that the only purpose of f_A and f_B is to preserve the [OW-CCA, $\cdot$] security with $pk_1 = pk_A$ and the [$\cdot$, OW-CPA] security with $pk_0 = pk_{A0}$ even if part of randomness, r_B or sk_B is leaked to the adversary. If the underlying 2-key KEM itself is strong enough to preserve the [OW-CCA, OW-CPA] security with respect to *some* function $f_A(sk_A, r_A)$ (resp. $f_B(sk_B, r_A)$), and leakage of sk_A or r_A for fixed pk_A (resp. sk_B or r_B for fixed pk_B), the functions f_A and f_B don't have to be hl-RFs. (2) if the 2-key KEM is strong enough to preserve security even when the randomness r_{B0} used to generate pk_{B0} is generated from $f_{B0}(sk_B, r_B)$ for some function f_{B0}, then we could regard $f_{B0}(sk_B, r_B)$ as a random string using to compute pk_{B0}. The same holds when $(pk_{A0}, sk_{A0}) \leftarrow \mathsf{KeyGen0}(r_{A0})$ where $r_{A0} = f_{A0}(sk_A, r_A)$ for some function f_{A0}.

Therefore, the problem comes down to study the security of 2-key KEM when C_A (under public keys pk_A and pk_{A0}) shares the randomness of pk_B and pk_{B0}.

Definition 3. *We say 2-key KEM is leakage resistant of partial randomness with respect to f_B and f_{B0} (they need not to be hl-RFs), if the following property holds. Under public key pk_A and pk_{A0}, the [OW-CCA, OW-CPA] security still holds where the ciphertext is computed as $\mathsf{Encaps}(pk_A, pk_{A0}, f_B(sk_B, r_B))$ for some fixed pk_B (where $(pk_B, sk_B) \leftarrow \mathsf{KeyGen1}$), when either r_B and pk_{B0} or sk_B and pk_{B0} are given to adversary, where $(pk_{B0}, sk_{B0}) \leftarrow \mathsf{KeyGen0}(f_{B0}(sk_B, r_B))$.*

Equipped with PKIC 2-key KEM that resists to the leakage of partial randomness with respect to f_B and f_{B0}, we set $f_{A0}(sk_A, r_A)$ and $f_{B0}(sk_B, r_B)$ as the randomness for KeyGen0, and denote the result AKE as $\mathsf{AKE}_{\mathsf{ro\text{-}pkic\text{-}lr}}$ in Fig. 4. The session state of sid owned by U_A consists of r_A, K'_A and K_B, the session state of sid owned by U_B consists of r_B, K_A and K'_B.

U_A		U_B
$(pk_A, sk_A) \leftarrow \mathsf{KeyGen1}$		$(pk_B, sk_B) \leftarrow \mathsf{KeyGen1}$
$r_A \leftarrow \{0,1\}^*$, $\boxed{r_{A0} = f_{A0}(sk_A, r_A)}$		$r_B \leftarrow \{0,1\}^*$, $\boxed{r_{B0} = f_{B0}(sk_B, r_B)}$
$R_A := f_A(sk_A, r_A)$		
$C_B \leftarrow \mathsf{Encaps0}(pk_B, -, R_A)$		$R_B := f_B(sk_B, r_B)$
$(pk_{A0}, sk_{A0}) \leftarrow \mathsf{KeyGen0}(r_{A0})$	$\xrightarrow{(C_B), pk_{A0}}$	$(C_A, K_A) \leftarrow \mathsf{Encaps}(pk_A, pk_{A0}, R_B)$
	$\xleftarrow{(C_A), pk_{B0}}$	$(pk_{B0}, sk_{B0}) \leftarrow \mathsf{KeyGen0}(r_{B0})$
$K'_A \leftarrow \mathsf{Decaps}(sk_A, sk_{A0}, C_A)$		
$K_B \leftarrow \mathsf{Encaps1}(pk_B, pk_{B0}, R_A)$		$K'_B \leftarrow \mathsf{Decaps}(sk_B, sk_{B0}, C_B)$
$SK \leftarrow H(si, K'_A, K_B)$		$SK \leftarrow H(si, K_A, K'_B)$

Fig. 4. $\mathsf{AKE}_{\text{ro-pkic-lr}}$. Here $si = (U_A, U_B, pk_A, pk_B, C_B, pk_{A0}, C_A, pk_{B0})$. The boxed argument is the main difference with $\mathsf{AKE}_{\text{ro-pkic}}$

Remark 1. As in the definition of 2-key KEM, both Encaps and Decaps allow to have auxiliary input $\mathsf{aux_e}$ or $\mathsf{aux_d}$. In $\mathsf{AKE}_{\text{ro-pkic-lr}}$ (AKE and $\mathsf{AKE}_{\text{ro-pkic}}$), the static public keys are generated by KeyGen1 during the registration phase (i.e., Stage 0) and publicly available. Thus, in the protocol, it makes sense that Encaps and Decaps algorithms take the static public keys as public auxiliary input. And for user U_A (resp. U_B), it is also reasonable that Encaps executed by U_A (resp. U_B) takes his static secret key sk_A (resp. sk_B) as auxiliary input. In this sense, one couple of 2KEM is really "coupled" with each other.

Remark 2. Since C_A share the randomness of pk_{B0} and secret key of pk_B, if the 2-key KEM and function f_B/f_{B0} further satisfy that C_A is publicly computable from pk_B and pk_{B0}, we can omit C_A in the communications. The same holds for C_B, if it is publicly computable from pk_A and pk_{A0}, we can omit C_B.

Remark 3. Note that the computation of f_B is part of $\mathsf{Encaps}(pk_A, pk_{A0}, R_B)$ algorithm. f_B may take pk_A as input. At that time, to be clear, we denote $f_B(sk_B, r_B)$ as $f_B(sk_B, r_B, pk_A)$. It is similar in the case of f_A.

With these modifications, we should handle the proof more carefully. The main challenge is that the ciphertext C_A, static public key pk_B, ephemeral public key pk_{B0} are correlated (the same holds for C_B, pk_A, and pk_{A0}). We should handle the problem that, since C_A shares the randomness with pk_{B0} and secret key of pk_B, when applying the [OW-CCA, $\cdot$] security of 2-key KEM with $pk_1 = pk_A$ in event $\mathsf{AskH} \wedge E_3$, $\mathsf{AskH} \wedge E_6$, not only sk_A but also sk_B is unknown to simulator $\mathcal{S}$. (The same situation occurs when applying [OW-CCA, $\cdot$] security of 2-key KEM with $pk_1 = pk_B$ in event $\mathsf{AskH} \wedge E_2$).

The way to solving this problem is to bring in another [OW-CCA, $\cdot$] challenge. As an example, we sketch the proof of event $\mathsf{AskH} \wedge E_3$ to show how this resolves the above problem. The main modification is for the proof of Lemma 2. In case of $\mathsf{AskH} \wedge E_3$, the [OW-CCA, $\cdot$] adversary $\mathcal{S}$ performs as follows. On receiving the public key pk_1 from the [OW-CCA, $\cdot$] challenger, to simulate the CK^+ game, $\mathcal{S}$

randomly chooses two parties U_A, U_B and the i-th session as a guess of the test session. $\mathcal{S}$ runs KeyGen1 to generate all static public keys except U_A and U_B. $\mathcal{S}$ queries the first [OW-CCA, $\cdot$] challenger to get pk_1, and sets $pk_A = pk_1$. $\mathcal{S}$ queries the second [OW-CCA, $\cdot$] challenger again to get another pk_1' and sets $pk_B = pk_1'$.

Note that now $\mathcal{S}$ does not know the secret key of both pk_A and pk_B. Here $\mathcal{S}$ generates (pk_{B0}^*, sk_{B0}^*) by itself. $\mathcal{S}$ sends pk_{B0}^* to the second challenge to get challenge ciphertext C_B^* and keeps both pk_{B0}^* and C_B^* secret to CK$^+$ adversary $\mathcal{A}$. On receiving the i-th session (C_B', pk_{A0}^*) from U_A (that is sent by $\mathcal{A}$ in the CK$^+$ games), $\mathcal{S}$ queries the first [OW-CCA, $\cdot$] challenger with pk_{A0}^* and obtains C_A^*, pk_{B0} and its randomness r_{B0}. $\mathcal{S}$ returns C_A^* and pk_{B0} to U_A as the response of i-th session from U_B, and sets pk_{A0}^* as the public key under which C_A^* is encrypted. $\mathcal{S}$ also leaks r_{B0} to adversary as the ephemeral secret key.

With the first [OW-CCA, $\cdot$] challenge, $\mathcal{S}$ could partially maintain the hash list and SessionStateReveal and SessionKeyReveal with strong decapsulation oracle when U_B is not involved. When U_B is involved, the second [OW-CCA, $\cdot$] challenge is needed. Note that since 2-key KEM is γ-spread, the probability that $\mathcal{A}$ queries a message with $C_B = C_B^*$ is bounded by $q \times 2^{-\gamma}$. The simulation is perfect and the other part of proof proceeds the same with Lemma 2.

4.2 AKE from 2-Key KEM in Standard Model

The protocol $\mathsf{AKE}/\mathsf{AKE}_{\mathsf{ro\text{-}pkic}}$ in random oracle model can be easily extended to one that is secure in the standard model, denoted by $\mathsf{AKE}_{\mathsf{std}}/\mathsf{AKE}_{\mathsf{std\text{-}pkic}}$, via the following steps:

1. replacing the [OW-CCA, OW-CPA] secure 2-key KEM in random oracle model with the [IND-CCA, IND-CPA] secure 2-key KEM in standard model;
2. instantiating the hl-RF functions f_A, f_B in standard model instead of the random oracle model. As noted after the definition, the instantiation of hl-RF in standard model require PRF and extra randomness. Thus every user holds extra random secret $s_P \leftarrow \{0,1\}^\lambda$ as part of the static secret key and $R_A = f_A(sk_A||s_A, r_A)$, $R_B = f_B(sk_B||s_B, r_B)$.
3. replacing the random oracle $H(si, K_A, K_B)$ with $F_{K_A}(si) \oplus \hat{F}_{K_B}(si)$, to extract session key, where F and $\hat{F}$ are PRFs.

Actually, converting a scheme in the random oracle model into that in the standard model is generally not trivial, and there are many negative results. However, without taking advantage of strong property of random oracle, our step 2 and 3 just use the property that if the input is unknown then the output is totally random. The difficult part is step 1. Once the 2-key KEM in random oracle model is replaced by [IND-CCA, IND-CPA] secure 2-key KEM in standard model, the proof of security for AKE in standard model is straightforward.

5 Unification of Prior Works

In this section, we show that existing AKEs, HMQV [23], NAXOS [24], Okamoto [27], and FSXY framework [15,16], can be explained in our unified frameworks.

5.1 HMQV-AKE

In HMQV [23], the 2-key KEM is initiated by $\mathsf{2KEM_{HMQV}}$ in Fig. 5. Let h and $\hat{H}$ be hash functions. Let G be a group of prime order p with g as a generator. Both Encaps and Decaps algorithms have auxiliary input $\mathsf{aux_e} = (B, b)$ where $B = g^b$ and $\mathsf{aux_d} = B$. Note that, here, B is the public auxiliary input and b is the secret auxiliary input. By applying $\mathsf{AKE_{ro\text{-}pkic\text{-}lr}}$, Remarks 1–3, we present how the HMQV scheme is integrated in our unified framework of AKE and how it is built from the view of 2-key KEM in Fig. 6.

KeyGen1(λ)	KeyGen0(λ)	Encaps(pk_1, pk_0; $\mathsf{aux}_e(B, b)$)	Decaps(sk_1, sk_0, c; $\mathsf{aux}_d(B)$)
$a \leftarrow \mathbb{Z}_p$;	$x \leftarrow \mathbb{Z}_p$	$y \leftarrow \mathbb{Z}_p$, $Y = g^y$,	$YB^e \leftarrow c$;
$A = g^a$	$X = g^x$	$e = h(Y, A), d = h(X, B)$	$e = h(Y, A), d = h(X, B)$
$pk_1 = A$	$pk_0 = X$;	$k = \hat{H}((XA^d)^{y+eb})$	$k' = \hat{H}((YB^e)^{x+da})$
$sk_1 = a$	$sk_0 = x$.	Return $k, c = YB^e$.	Return k'

Fig. 5. The [OW-CCA, OW-CCA] secure $\mathsf{2KEM_{HMQV}}$ implied by HMQV.

Theorem 2. *Under the Gap-DH and KEA1 assumptions*[1], $\mathsf{2KEM_{HMQV}}$ *in Fig. 5 is [OW-CCA, OW-CCA] secure with the resistance to the leakage of partial randomness with respect to* $f_B(b, y, A) = y + b \cdot h(g^y, A)$ *and* $f_{B0}(b, y) = y$ *in the random oracle model.*

Please refer the full version [32] for the proof of Theorem 2.

As said in Remark 3, f_B takes A as input and $f_B(b, y, A) = y + b \cdot h(g^y, A)$. By Theorem 2, $\mathsf{2KEM_{HMQV}}$ is [OW-CCA, OW-CCA] secure even if partial randomness (b or y) is leaked with respect to $f_B(b, y, A) = y + b \cdot h(g^y, A)$ and $f_{B0}(b, y) = y$. By changing the role of A and B, X and Y, we also get a dual scheme of $\mathsf{2KEM_{HMQV}}$, with respect to $f_A(a, x, B) = x + a \cdot h(g^x, B)$ and $f_{A0}(a, x) = x$. Obviously, $\mathsf{2KEM_{HMQV}}$ is PKIC, which means that the ciphertext is independent of the public key pk_0. Thus the Encaps algorithm can be split into two steps Encaps0 and Encaps1. However, when integrating $\mathsf{2KEM_{HMQV}}$ into $\mathsf{AKE_{ro\text{-}pkic\text{-}lr}}$ to reproduce HMQV, one may doubt that whether $\mathsf{aux}_e = (B, b)$ or (A, a) required by Encaps and $\mathsf{aux}_d = B$ or A required by Decaps influence the reconstruction. As explained in Remark 2, since B and A are the static public keys and generated during the registration phase, they can be used as the public auxiliary input by any user during the execution phase. As a static secret key, b can be used by U_B as secret auxiliary input during the execution phase. Based on the above analysis, applying $\mathsf{AKE_{ro\text{-}pkic\text{-}lr}}$ and Remarks 1–3 to $\mathsf{2KEM_{HMQV}}$, HMQV is reconstructed in Fig. 6.

Moreover, A, B are static public keys, and d, e are publicly computable, C_A, C_B can be publicly computed from $pk_{B0} = Y$ and $pk_{A0} = X$. Thus, we can apply Remark 1 to omit $C_B = XA^d$ and $C_A = YB^d$ in the communications.

[1] For formal definitions of Gap-DH and KEA1 assumptions, please refer HMQV.

$U_A : A = g^a, a$		$U_B : B = g^b, b$
$x \leftarrow \mathbb{Z}_p, X = g^x$		$y \leftarrow \mathbb{Z}_p, Y = g^y$
$d = h(X,B), C_B = XA^d$	$(C_B = XA^d,)pk_{A0} = X$ $\longrightarrow$	$e = h(Y,A), C_A = YB^e$
$e = h(Y,A)$	$\longleftarrow$ $(C_A = YB^e,)pk_{B0} = Y$	$d = h(X,B)$
$K_B = K'_A = \hat{H}\left((YB^e)^{x+ad}\right)$		$K_A = K'_B = \hat{H}\left((XA^d)^{y+be}\right)$
$SK \leftarrow H(si, K_B)$		$SK \leftarrow H(si, K_A)$

Fig. 6. Understanding HMQV with $\mathsf{2KEM}_{\mathsf{HMQV}}$ in the frame $\mathsf{AKE}_{\mathsf{ro\text{-}pkic\text{-}lr}}$ where $si = (U_A, U_B, A, B, C_B, X, C_A, Y)$.

5.2 NAXOS-AKE

In [24], the 2-key KEM is initiated by $\mathsf{2KEM}_{\mathsf{NAXOS}}$ in Fig. 7. Let G be a group of prime order p with g as a generator. Let $h : \mathbb{Z}_p \times \mathbb{Z}_p \rightarrow \mathbb{Z}_p$ and $\hat{H} : \mathbb{Z}_p \times \mathbb{Z}_p \rightarrow \{0,1\}^\lambda$ be hash functions. By applying $\mathsf{AKE}_{\mathsf{ro\text{-}pkic\text{-}lr}}$ and Remarks 1–2, in Fig. 8, we present how the NAXOS scheme is integrated in our unified framework of AKE and how it is built from the view of 2-key KEM.

$\mathsf{KeyGen1}(\lambda)$	$\mathsf{KeyGen0}(\lambda)$	$\mathsf{Encaps}(pk_1, pk_0; \mathsf{aux}_e(B,b))$;	$\mathsf{Decaps}(sk_1, sk_0, c)$
$a \leftarrow \mathbb{Z}_p$;	$x \leftarrow \mathbb{Z}_p$	$y_0 \leftarrow \mathbb{Z}_p$, $y = h(y_0, b)$	$Y \leftarrow c$;
$A = g^a$	$X = g^x$	$Y = g^y$	$x = h(x_0, a)$
$pk_1 = A$	$pk_0 = X$;	$k = \hat{H}(A^y, X^y)$	$k' = \hat{H}(Y^a, Y^x)$
$sk_1 = a$	$sk_0 = x$.	Return $k, c = Y$.	Return k'

Fig. 7. The [OW-CCA, OW-CCA] secure $\mathsf{2KEM}_{\mathsf{NAXOS}}$ implied by NAXOS

Theorem 3. *Under the Gap-DH assumption,* $\mathsf{2KEM}_{\mathsf{NAXOS}}$ *is [OW-CCA, OW-CCA] secure even with the leakage of one of* y_0 *and* b *where* $f_B(b, y_0) = h(b, y_0)$ *and* $f_{B0}(b, y_0) = h(b, y_0)$ *in the random oracle model.*

By Theorem 3, $\mathsf{2KEM}_{\mathsf{NAXOS}}$ is [OW-CCA, OW-CCA] secure even if partial randomness (b or y_0) is leaked with respect to $f_B(b, y_0) = h(b, y_0)$ and $f_{B0}(b, y_0) = h(b, y_0)$. Obviously, $\mathsf{2KEM}_{\mathsf{NAXOS}}$ is PKIC. We split Encaps algorithm into two steps Encaps0 and Encaps1. As explained in Remark 2, since b is static secret key and generated by U_B, in the execution phase U_B takes it as secret auxiliary input. Based on the above analysis, applying $\mathsf{AKE}_{\mathsf{ro\text{-}pkic\text{-}lr}}$ and Remarks 1–2 to $\mathsf{2KEM}_{\mathsf{NAXOS}}$, NAXOS is reconstructed in Fig. 8.

Moreover, C_A is equal to $pk_{B0} = Y$ and C_B is equal to $pk_{A0} = X$. Thus we can apply Remark 2 to omit $C_B = X$ and $C_A = Y$ in the communications.

5.3 Okamoto-AKE

In Okamoto-AKE [27], the 2-key KEM is initiated by $\mathsf{2KEM}_{\mathsf{Oka}}$ in Fig. 9. In $\mathsf{2KEM}_{\mathsf{Oka}}$, the computation is proceeded over group G of prime order p with

$U_A : A = g^a, a$		$U_B : B = g^b, b$
$x_0 \leftarrow \mathbb{Z}_p, x = h(x_0, a)$		$y_0 \leftarrow \mathbb{Z}_p, y = h(y_0, b)$
$C_B = pk_{A0} = X = g^x$	$\xrightarrow{(C_B = X), pk_{A0} = X}$	$C_A = pk_{B0} = Y = g^y$
$K_B = \hat{H}(B^x, Y^x)$	$\xleftarrow{(C_A = Y), pk_{B0} = Y}$	$K_A = \hat{H}(A^y, X^y)$
$K'_A = \hat{H}(Y^a, Y^x)$		$K'_B = \hat{H}(X^b, X^y)$
$SK \leftarrow H(si, K'_A, K_B)$		$SK \leftarrow H(si, K_A, K'_B)$

Fig. 8. Understanding NAXOS with $2\mathsf{KEM}_{\mathsf{naxos}}$ in the frame $\mathsf{AKE}_{\mathsf{ro\text{-}pkic\text{-}lr}}$ where $si = (U_A, U_B, A, B, X, Y)$.

generator g, h_{tcr} is a target-collision resistant (TCR) hash function and $\bar{F}$ is a pairwise-independent random source PRF. (Please refer [27] for the formal definition of pairwise-independent random source PRFs.)

$2\mathsf{KEM}_{\mathsf{Oka}}.\mathsf{KeyGen1}(\lambda)$	$2\mathsf{KEM}_{\mathsf{Oka}}.\mathsf{KeyGen0}(\lambda)$
$a_1, a_2, a_3, a_4 \leftarrow \mathbb{Z}_p^4$, $A_1 = g_1^{a_1} g_2^{a_2}$, $A_2 = g_1^{a_3} g_2^{a_4}$ $pk_1 = (A_1, A_2)$, $sk_1 = (a_1, a_2, a_3, a_4)$	$x_3 \leftarrow \mathbb{Z}_p$, $X_3 = g_1^{x_3}$ $pk_0 = X_3$, $sk_0 = x_3$
$2\mathsf{KEM}_{\mathsf{Oka}}.\mathsf{Encaps}(pk_0, pk_1)$;	$2\mathsf{KEM}_{\mathsf{Oka}}.\mathsf{Decaps}(sk_0, sk_1, C)$
$y, y_3 \leftarrow \mathbb{Z}_p^2$, $Y_1 = g_1^y, Y_2 = g_2^y$, $Y_3 = g_1^{y_3}$ $C = (Y_1, Y_2, Y_3), c = h_{tcr}(A_1, A_2, C)$ $\sigma = X_3^{y_3}(A_1 A_2^c)^y$ $K = \bar{F}_\sigma(pk_0, C)$	$C \in G^3$, $(Y_1, Y_2, Y_3) \leftarrow C$; $c = h_{tcr}(A_1, A_2, C)$ $\sigma' = Y_3^{x_3} Y_1^{a_1 + ca_3} Y_2^{a_2 + ca_4}$ $K' = \bar{F}_{\sigma'}(pk_0, C)$

Fig. 9. The [IND-CCA, IND-CPA] secure $2\mathsf{KEM}_{\mathsf{Oka}}$ implied by Okamato-AKE.

Let G be a group of order p with the generator g. Let $1_G = g^p$ be the identity element. The DDH assumption states that $\{(G, g^a, g^b, g^{ab})\}_\lambda$ is computationally indistinguishable from $\{(G, g^a, g^b, g^c)\}_\lambda$, where a, b, c are randomly and independently chosen in $\mathbb{Z}_p$. If $c = ab$, (g, g^a, g^b, g^c) is called a DDH tuple, otherwise it's called a non-DDH tuple. Denote the advantage of any PPT algorithm $\mathcal{B}$ solving DDH problem as $\mathrm{Adv}_{\mathcal{B}}^{\mathsf{ddh}} = |\Pr[\mathcal{B}(g^a, g^b, g^{ab}) = 1] - \Pr[\mathcal{B}(g^a, g^b, g^c) = 1]|$.

Theorem 4. *Under the DDH assumption, if h_{tcr} is a TCR hash function and $\bar{F}$ is a pairwise-independent random source PRF, then $2\mathsf{KEM}_{\mathsf{Oka}}$ in Fig. 9 is [IND-CCA, IND-CPA] secure in the standard model.*

Please refer the full version [32] for the formal proof of Theorem 4.

By applying $\mathsf{AKE}_{\mathsf{std}}$, in Fig. 10, we present how the Okamato scheme is integrated in our unified framework of AKE and how it is built from the view of 2-key KEM. Let $F' : \{0,1\}^\lambda \times \{0,1\}^\lambda \to \mathbb{Z}_p$ and $F'' : \mathbb{Z}_p \times \{0,1\}^\lambda \to \mathbb{Z}_p$ be PRFs. In the frame of $\mathsf{AKE}_{\mathsf{std}}$, by setting $s_A = a_0, s_B = b_0, r_A = x'_1 || x'_2, r_{A0} = x_3, r_B = y'_1 || y'_2$, choosing $cpk_0 = 1_G, csk_0 = p$, initiating f_A and f_B as $F'_{x'_1}(1^k) \oplus F''_{\sum_0^4 a_i}(x'_2)$ and $F'_{y'_1}(1^k) \oplus F''_{\sum_0^4 b_i}(y'_2)$, and applying $2\mathsf{KEM}_{\mathsf{Oka}}$ as 2-key KEM, we will get Okamoto AKE in Fig. 10.

$U_A : A_1, A_2, a_1, a_2, a_3, a_4, a_0 \leftarrow \mathbb{Z}_p$		$U_B : B_1, B_2, b_1, b_2, b_3, b_4, b_0 \leftarrow \mathbb{Z}_p$
$x_1', x_2' \leftarrow \{0,1\}^\lambda$		$y_1', y_2' \leftarrow \{0,1\}^\lambda$
$(x, x_3) = F'_{x_1'}(1^k) + F''_{\sum_0^4 a_i}(x_2')$		$(y, y_3) = F'_{y_1'}(1^k) + F''_{\sum_0^4 b_i}(y_2')$
$X_1 = g_1^x, X_2 = g_2^x, X_3 = g_1^{x_3}$		$Y_1 = g_1^y, Y_2 = g_2^y, Y_3 = g_1^{y_3}$
$C_B = (X_1, X_2, 1_G), pk_{A0} = X_3$	$\xrightarrow{C_B, X_3}$	$C_A = (Y_1, Y_2, Y_3)$
$d = h_{tcr}(U_B, X_1, X_2)$	$\xleftarrow{C_A}$	$c = h_{tcr}(U_A, Y_1, Y_2, Y_3)$
$\sigma_B = (B_1 B_2^d)^x, K_B = \bar{F}_{\sigma_B}(1_G, C_B)$		$\sigma_A = X_3^{y_3}(A_1 A_2^c)^y, K_A = \bar{F}_{\sigma_A}(X_3, C_A)$
$c = h_{tcr}(U_A, C_A)$		$d = h_{tcr}(U_B, C_B)$
$\sigma_A' = X_3^{y_3} Y_1^{a_1 + ca_3} Y_2^{a_2 + ca_4}$		$\sigma_B' = X_1^{b_1 + db_3} X_2^{b_2 + db_4}$
$K_A' = \bar{F}_{\sigma_A'}(X_3, C_A)$		$K_A' = \bar{F}_{\sigma_B'}(1_G, C_B)$
$SK \leftarrow F_{K_B}(si) \oplus \hat{F}_{K_A'}(si)$		$SK \leftarrow F_{K_B'}(si) \oplus \hat{F}_{K_A}(si)$

Fig. 10. Understanding Okamoto-AKE from $\mathsf{2KEM_{Oka}}$ where $si = (U_A, U_B, C_B, X_3, C_A)$ in frame $\mathsf{AKE_{std}}$. Some notions are borrowed from $\mathsf{2KEM_{Oka}}$

5.4 FSXY12-AKE and FSXY13-AKE

Fujioka *et al.* in PKC 12 (called FSXY12 [15]) proposed a construction of AKE from IND-CCA secure KEM and IND-CPA secure KEM in the standard model. In FSXY12 [15], U_B sends a ciphertext of IND-CCA secure KEM and a ciphertext of IND-CPA secure KEM, and the session key is computed from these two encapsulated keys, public key of IND-CPA secure KEM, and ciphertext in the PRF functions. As we point out in Sect. 6.1, the FSXY12 scheme implies a trivial [IND-CCA, IND-CPA] secure 2-key KEM from the improved KEM combiner in the standard model. More precisely, in $\mathsf{AKE_{std}}$, cpk_0 and csk_0 is set to be empty; C_B is just $c_{B1}||$-, where c_{B1} is the ciphertext of IND-CCA secure one-key KEM under pk_B; C_A is replaced by the concatenation of $c_{A1}||c_{A0}$, where c_{A1} is the ciphertext of IND-CCA secure one-key KEM under pk_A with encapsulated key k_{A1} and c_{A0} is the ciphertext of IND-CPA secure one-key KEM under pk_{A0} with encapsulated key k_{A0}; and K_A is replaced by $F_{k_{A1}}(pk_{A0}, c_{A1}||c_{A0}) \oplus F_{k_{A0}}(pk_{A0}, c_{A1}||c_{A0})$. To make it clearer, in Sect. 6.1 we explain why we should put public key in PRFs when combining two KEMs. Note that FSXY12 implicitly did it in the same way by putting sid in PRF. Thus, due to this observation, our frame of $\mathsf{AKE_{std}}$ with improved KEM combiner can be used to explain the FSXY12 scheme.

Considering efficiency, Fujioka *et al.* in AsiaCCS 13 (called FSXY13 [16]) proposed AKE from OW-CCA secure KEM and OW-CPA secure KEM in the random oracle model. In FSXY13 [16], U_B sends a ciphertext of OW-CCA secure KEM and a ciphertext of OW-CPA secure KEM. The session key is computed from these two encapsulated keys, public key of CPA secure KEM, and ciphertext in the hashing step. As we point out in Sect. 6.1, the FSXY13 scheme implies a trivial [OW-CCA, OW-CPA] secure 2-key KEM from the improved KEM combiner in the random oracle model. Precisely, in AKE, cpk_0 and csk_0 is set to be empty; C_B is just $c_{B1}||$-, where c_{B1} is the ciphertext of OW-CCA secure one-key KEM under pk_B; C_A is replaced by the concatenation of $c_{A1}||c_{A0}$, where c_{A1} is the ciphertext of OW-CCA secure one-key KEM under pk_A with encapsulated key k_{A1} and c_{A0} is the ciphertext of OW-CPA secure one-key KEM under pk_{A0} with encapsulated key k_{A0}; and K_A is replaced by $\hat{H}(pk_{A0}, k_1||k_{A0}, c_{A1}||c_{A0})$. In Sect. 6.1 we explain why we should put public key in hashing step when combining two KEMs. Note that FSXY13 implicitly did it in the same way by putting sid in hashing step. Thus, our frame of AKE with improved KEM combiner works for explaining the FSXY13 scheme.

6 More General Constructions for 2-Key KEM

In this section we investigate how to improve the KEM combiner [17] and Fujisaki-Okamoto transformation [14,18] so as to yield more general constructions of 2-key KEM, which are much more well-suited for lattice assumptions.

6.1 Improved Combiner of Two KEMs

Giacon *et al.* [17] propose two KEM combiner and yield a new single KEM that is classical CCA secure as long as one of the ingredient KEMs is. We show that the simple KEM combiner does not work for our 2-key KEM. Furthermore, we show that with a slight but vital modification the combiner could work.

6.1.1 The Failure to Imply [OW-CCA, ·] Secure 2key KEM from KEM Combiner

We give a scheme that is a CCA secure two KEM combiner but is not [OW-CCA, ·] secure.

Let h and H be hash functions. Let $G =< g >$ be a group with prime order p. Let $pk_1 = (g_1, g_2 = g_1^a), sk_1 = a$, the ciphertext be $c_1 = (g_1^r, g_2^r \cdot m)$ where $r = h(m)$ and the encapsulated key be $k_1 = H(m)$. By the FO transformation [14] and DDH assumption, the first KEM is one-way-CCA secure. Let $pk_0 = (h_1, h_2 = h_1^b), sk_0 = b$, the ciphertext be $c_0 = h_1^x$ and the encapsulated key be $k_0 = H(h_2^x)$; and obviously the second KEM is IND-CPA secure.

Let the combined ciphertext be $(c_1||c_0)$ and combined encapsulated key be $K = \hat{H}(k_1||k_0, c_1||c_0)$, by the KEM combiner [17] (Lemma 6 and Example 3 in [17]), the combined KEM is CCA secure. However, such combined KEM is not [OW-CCA, ·] secure which means there exists an adversary $\mathcal{A}$ that can break [OW-CCA, ·] game.

Note that $c_0 = h_1^x$ encapsulates the key $k_0^* = H(h_2^x)$ under public key $pk_0 = (h_1, h_2)$ while it encapsulates the same key $k_0^* = H(h_2^x)$ under public key $pk_0 = (h_1^c, h_2^c)$ for some $c \in \mathbb{Z}_p$. The [OW-CCA, ·] adversary $\mathcal{A}$ first queries the $\mathcal{O}_{\mathsf{leak}}$ oracle and gets $pk_0 = (h_1, h_2)$. Then it randomly chooses $c \in \mathbb{Z}_p$ and sets $pk_0^* = (h_1^c, h_2^c)$. After receiving $c_1^*||c_0^*$ under public keys pk_1 and pk_0^*, $\mathcal{A}$ queries the decryption oracle with $(pk_1, pk_0, c_1^*||c_0^*)$, and would receive exactly $K^* = \hat{H}(k_1^*||k_0^*, c_1^*||c_0^*)$.

6.1.2 Improvement on KEM Combiner to Achieve [CCA, CPA] Secure 2-Key KEM

Inspired by the attacks above, we propose a improved combiner of CCA secure and CPA secure KEMs to achieve [CCA, CPA] secure 2-key KEM. Let $\mathsf{KEM_{cca}} = (\mathsf{KeyGen_{cca}}, \mathsf{Encaps_{cpa}}, \mathsf{Decaps_{cca}})$ be IND-CCA secure KEM, $\mathsf{KEM_{cpa}} = (\mathsf{KeyGen_{cpa}}, \mathsf{Encaps_{cpa}}, \mathsf{Decaps_{cpa}})$ be IND-CPA secure KEM. Let $\hat{H}$ be a hash function and F be a PRF. The improved combiner is shown in Fig. 11, where function $f(pk_0, k_1||k_0, c)$ can be initiated by $\hat{H}(pk_0, k_1||k_0, c)$ or $F_{k_1}(pk_0, c) \oplus F_{k_0}(pk_0, c)$. Our main modification is to take public key as input to the hash function or PRF when generating encapsulated key.

$\mathsf{KeyGen1}(\lambda)$	$\mathsf{KeyGen0}(\lambda)$	$\mathsf{Enc}(pk_1, pk_0);$	$\mathsf{Dec}(sk_1, sk_0, c_1\|\|c_0)$
$(pk_1, sk_1) \leftarrow$ $\mathsf{KeyGen_{cca}}$	$(pk_0, sk_0) \leftarrow$ $\mathsf{KeyGen_{cpa}}$	$(c_1, k_1) \leftarrow \mathsf{Encaps_{cca}}(pk_1)$	$k_1 \leftarrow \mathsf{Decaps_{cca}}(sk_1, c_1)$
		$(c_0, k_0) \leftarrow \mathsf{Encaps_{cpa}}(pk_0)$	$k_0 \leftarrow \mathsf{Decaps_{cpa}}(sk_0, c_0)$
		$c = c_1\|\|c_0,\ k = f(pk_0, k_1\|\|k_0, c)$	$k = f(pk_0, k_1\|\|k_0, c)$

Fig. 11. The [CCA, CPA] secure $\mathsf{2KEM}_f$ in random oracle or standard model depending on the instantiation of $f(pk_0, k_1||k_0, c)$.

Theorem 5. *Let the underlying two KEMs be IND-CCA and IND-CPA secure. If $f(pk_0, k_1||k_0, c) = \hat{H}(pk_0, k_1||k_0, c)$ for a hash function $\hat{H}$, $\mathsf{2KEM}_f$ in Fig. 11 is [OW-CCA, OW-CCA] secure in random oracle model; if $f(pk_0, k_1||k_0, c) = F_{k_1}(pk_0, c) \oplus F_{k_0}(pk_0, c)$ for PRF F, $\mathsf{2KEM}_f$ in Fig. 11 is [IND-CCA, IND-CPA] secure in standard model.*

Please refer the full version [32] for the proof.

6.2 Modified FO Transformation

In this section, we investigate the constructions of passively 2-key PKE and give a modified FO transformation which can be used to transform a passively secure 2-key PKE to an adaptively secure 2-key KEM.

6.2.1 Passively Secure 2-Key PKE

As the preparation for realizing adaptively secure 2-key KEM and the modified FO transformation, similar to the notion of 2-key KEM, we can also provide the notion of 2-key (public key encryption) PKE.

Informally, a 2-key PKE 2PKE=(KeyGen0, KeyGen1, Enc, Dec) is a quadruple of PPT algorithms together with a plaintext space $\mathcal{M}$ and a ciphertext space $\mathcal{C}$, where KeyGen1 outputs a pair of public and secret keys (pk_1, sk_1), KeyGen0 outputs a pair of keys (pk_0, sk_0), $\mathsf{Enc}(pk_1, pk_0, m)$ outputs the ciphertext $C \in \mathcal{C}$, and $\mathsf{Dec}(sk_1, sk_0, C)$ outputs a plaintext m. Sometimes, we explicitly add the randomness r to Enc and denote it as $\mathsf{Enc}(pk_1, pk_0, m, r)$. Here we only describe

Game IND-CPA on pk_1	Game IND-CPA on pk_0
01 $(pk_1, sk_1) \leftarrow \mathsf{KeyGen1}(pp)$	15 $(pk_0, sk_0) \leftarrow \mathsf{KeyGen0}(pp)$
02 $L_0 = \{(-,-,-)\}$	16 $L_1 = \{(-,-,-)\}$
03 $(state, pk_0^*, m_1, m_1) \leftarrow \mathcal{A}_1^{\mathcal{O}_{\mathsf{leak0}}}(pk_1)$	17 $(state, pk_1^*, m_0, m_1) \leftarrow \mathcal{B}_1^{\mathcal{O}_{\mathsf{leak1}}}(pk_0)$
04 $b \leftarrow \{0,1\};$	18 $b \leftarrow \{0,1\}$
05 $c^* \leftarrow \mathsf{Enc}(pk_1, pk_0^*, m_b);$	19 $c^* \leftarrow \mathsf{Enc}(pk_1^*, pk_0, m_b);$
06 $b' \leftarrow \mathcal{A}_2^{\mathcal{O}_{\mathsf{leak0}}}(state, c^*)$	20 $b' \leftarrow \mathcal{B}_2^{\mathcal{O}_{\mathsf{leak1}}}(state, c^*)$
07 return $b' \stackrel{?}{=} b$	21 return $b' \stackrel{?}{=} b$

Fig. 12. The [IND-CPA, ·], and [·, IND-CPA] games of 2PKE for adversaries $\mathcal{A}$ and $\mathcal{B}$.

the [IND-CPA, IND-CPA] security game in Fig. 12. For more concrete and full definition of 2-key PKE please refer the full version [32].

Passively Secure Twin-ElGamal from DDH Assumption. Our construction is actually a conjoined ElGamal encryption. Let's call it twin-ElGamal. The [IND-CPA, IND-CPA] secure twin-ElGamal $2\mathsf{PKE}_{\mathsf{cpaddh}}$ = $(\mathsf{KeyGen1}, \mathsf{KeyGen0}, \mathsf{Enc}, \mathsf{Dec})$ is presented in detail in Fig. 13.

$\mathsf{KeyGen1}(\lambda)$	$\mathsf{KeyGen0}(\lambda)$	$\mathsf{Enc}(pk_1, pk_0, m);$	$\mathsf{Dec}(sk_0, sk_1, C)$
$a_1 \leftarrow \mathbb{Z}_p, h_1 = g^{a_1};$	$a_0 \leftarrow \mathbb{Z}_p, h_0 = g^{a_0};$	$r_1, r_0 \leftarrow \mathbb{Z}_p$	$(c_1, c_2, c_3) \leftarrow C$
$pk_1 = (g, h_1), sk_1 = a_1$	$pk_0 = (g, h_0), sk_0 = a_0$	$c = g^{r_1}, g^{r_0}, h_1^{r_1} h_0^{r_0} \cdot m$	$m' = c_3/c_1^{a_1} c_2^{a_0}$

Fig. 13. The [IND-CPA, IND-CPA] secure $2\mathsf{PKE}_{\mathsf{cpaddh}}$ under DDII assumption

Theorem 6. *Under the DDH assumption, the twin-ElGamal* $2\mathsf{PKE}_{\mathsf{cpaddh}}$ *scheme shown in Fig. 13 is* [*IND-CPA, IND-CPA*] *secure.*

Please refer the full version [32] for the proof.

6.2.2 Modified FO Transformation from Passive to Adaptive Security

In the random oracle model, the FO [14,18] technique is able to transform a passively secure one-key encryption scheme to an adaptively secure scheme. We show that the classical FO transformation does not work for our 2-key encryption scheme. Then we show that with a slight but vital modification the FO transformation could work.

The Failure of Classical FO Transform on 2-key KEM. We give a novel twin-ElGamal scheme by injecting redundant public keys, and show that such twin-ElGamal scheme after FO transformation is still OW-CCA secure, but not [OW-CCA, ·] secure.

The $\mathsf{KeyGen0}$ algorithm of $2\mathsf{PKE}_{\mathsf{cpaddh}}$ chooses a random $z \leftarrow \mathbb{Z}_p$, and sets $pk_0 = (g, h_0, g_0 = g^z), sk_0 = (a_0, z)$. The algorithm $\mathsf{KeyGen1}, \mathsf{Enc}, \mathsf{Dec}$ are the same as in $\mathsf{2PKE_{cpaddh}}$. Obviously this novel twin-ElGamal scheme is IND-CPA secure under DDH assumption. Let $\mathsf{2PKE^{fo}_{cpaddh}}$ be the scheme by applying classical FO transform on the novel twin-Elgamal. It is OW-CCA secure. Note that the encapsulated key is $K = H(m, c)$ where H is a hash function.

However, there exists an $[\mathsf{IND\text{-}CCA}, \cdot]$ attacker $\mathcal{A}$ of $\mathsf{2PKE^{fo}_{cpaddh}}$ that works as follows: $\mathcal{A}$ first queries the $\mathcal{O}_{\mathsf{leak_0}}$ and gets $pk_0^1 = (g, h_0, g_0 = g^z), sk_0^1 = (a_0, z)$. Then $\mathcal{A}$ chooses $g_0' \neq g_0 \in \mathbb{G}$, and sets $pk_0^* = (g, h_0, g_0')$ as challenge public key. On receiving challenge ciphertext c^* under (pk_1, pk_0^*), $\mathcal{A}$ queries $\mathcal{O}_{\mathsf{ow\text{-}cca}}$ with (pk_0^1, c^*). Since $pk_0^1 \neq pk_0^*$, $\mathcal{O}_{\mathsf{ow\text{-}cca}}$ would return K'. $\mathcal{A}$ just outputs K'. Since c^* encapsulated the same key $K^* = H(m, c^*)$ under both public keys (pk_1, pk_0^1) and (pk_1, pk_0^*). $\mathcal{A}$ will succeed with probability 1.

Modification on FO Transform to Achieve [IND-CCA, IND-CCA] Secure 2-Key KEM from 2-Key PKE. Motivated by the above attacks, we give a modified FO transform by a slight but vital modification from "*Hashing*" in [18] to "*Hashing with public key as input*". Actually, taking the public keys as input to hash function is also motivated by the fact that: from the perspective of proof, "Hashing with public key as input" would help to preserve the consistency of strong decryption oracle and hashing list.

Since we take the decryption failure into account, let's firstly recall and adapt the definition of correctness for decryption in [18] to our 2-key setting. When $\mathsf{2PKE} = \mathsf{2PKE}^G$ is defined with respect to a random oracle G, it is said to be δ_{q_G}-correct if for adversary $\mathcal{A}$ making at most q_G queries to random oracle G, it holds that $\Pr[\mathsf{COR\text{-}RO}^{\mathcal{A}_{\mathsf{2PKE}}} \Rightarrow 1] \leq \delta_{q_G}$, where the correctness game COR-RO is defined as following: $(pk_1, sk_1) \leftarrow \mathsf{KeyGen1}(pp)$, $(pk_0, sk_0) \leftarrow \mathsf{KeyGen0}(pp)$, $m \leftarrow \mathcal{A}^{G(\cdot)}(pk_1, sk_1, pk_0, sk_0)$, $c \leftarrow \mathsf{Enc}(pk_1, pk_0, m)$. Return $\mathsf{Dec}(sk_1, sk_0, c) \stackrel{?}{=} m$.

Let $\mathsf{2PKE} = (\mathsf{KeyGen1', KeyGen0', Enc, Dec})$ be a [IND-CPA, IND-CPA] secure 2-key PKE with message space $\mathcal{M}$. The [IND-CCA, IND-CCA] secure $\mathsf{2KEM} = (\mathsf{KeyGen1, KeyGen0, Encaps, Decaps})$ are described as in Fig. 14.

$\mathsf{KeyGen1}(\lambda)$	$\mathsf{KeyGen0}(\lambda)$
$(pk_1', sk_1') \leftarrow \mathsf{KeyGen1'}$, $s_1 \leftarrow \{0,1\}^l$; $sk_1 = (sk_1', s_1)$, $pk_1 = pk_1'$	$(pk_0', sk_0') \leftarrow \mathsf{KeyGen0'}$, $s_0 \leftarrow \{0,1\}^l$ $sk_0 = (sk_0', s_0)$, $pk_0 = pk_0'$;
$\mathsf{Encaps}(pk_1, pk_0)$;	$\mathsf{Decaps}(sk_1, sk_0, c)$
$m \leftarrow \mathcal{M}$ $c \leftarrow \mathsf{Enc}(pk_1, pk_0, m; G(m))$ $K = H(pk_1, pk_0, m, c)$; return (K, c)	$sk_1 = (sk_1', s_1)$, $sk_0 = (sk_0', s_0)$ $m' = \mathsf{Dec}(sk_1', sk_0', c)$ $c' = \mathsf{Enc}(pk_1, pk_0, m'; G(m'))$ if $m' = \perp$ or $c \neq c'$, let $m' = s_1 \| s_0$ return $K = H(pk_1, pk_0, m', c)$

Fig. 14. The [IND-CCA, IND-CCA] secure 2-key KEM 2KEM by modified FO

Theorem 7. *For any [IND-CCA, $\cdot$] adversary $\mathcal{C}$, or [$\cdot$, IND-CCA] adversary $\mathcal{D}$ against 2KEM with at most q_D queries to decapsulation oracle DECAPS, q_H*

(resp. q_G) queries to random oracle H (resp. G), there are [IND-CPA, $\cdot$] adversary $\mathcal{A}$, or [$\cdot$, IND-CPA] adversary $\mathcal{B}$ against 2PKE, that make at most q_H (resp. q_G) queries to random oracle H (resp. G) s.t.

$$Adv_{\mathsf{2KEM}}^{[\mathsf{IND\text{-}CCA},\cdot]}(\mathcal{C}) \leq \frac{q_H}{2^l} + \frac{q_H+1}{|M|} + q_G \cdot \delta + 4Adv_{\mathsf{2PKE}}^{[\mathsf{IND\text{-}CPA},\cdot]}(\mathcal{A}).$$

Please refer the full version [32] for the proof.

7 Efficient Post-quantum AKE from Module-LWE

With the above analysis and tools, we give a more compact AKE from Module-LWE assumption with less communications than Kyber [3]. The roadmap is that we first give a [IND-CPA, IND-CPA] secure 2-key PKE from Module-LWE, by applying the modified FO transform in Sect. 6.2.2 and the AKE in Sect. 4.1 step by step, and we finally obtain a AKE scheme.

Let q be a prime and R_q denote the ring $\mathbb{Z}_q[x]/(x^n+1)$. Define the centered binomial distribution B_η for positive integer η as: sample $(a_1, \cdots, a_\eta, b_1, \cdots, b_\eta)$ uniformly from $\{0,1\}$, and output $\sum_{i=1}^{\eta}(a_i - b_i)$. Denote $\mathbf{s} \leftarrow \beta_\eta$ as that each of $\mathbf{s}$'s coefficient is generated according to B_η. Let k, m be a positive integer parameter. For PPT adversary $\mathcal{A}$, the advantage $\mathbf{Adv}_{m,k,\eta}^{mlwe}(\mathcal{A})$ of solving Module-LWE problem is the advantage of distinguishing two distributions $\{(\mathbf{A} \leftarrow R_q^{m\times k}, \mathbf{As}+\mathbf{e})|(\mathbf{s},\mathbf{e}) \leftarrow \beta_\eta^k \times \beta_\eta^k\}$ and $\{(\mathbf{A} \leftarrow R_q^{m\times k}, \mathbf{b} \leftarrow R_q^m)\}$.

Let $d_{t_1}, d_{t_0}, d_{u_1}, d_{u_0}, d_v$ be positive numbers, depending on the special choice of the parameters settings, and $n = 256$. Every message in $\mathcal{M} = \{0,1\}^n$ can be seen as a polynomial in R_q with coefficients in $\{0,1\}$. Let $\mathbf{A}$ be a random $k \times k$ matrix in R_q. Let $\lceil x \rfloor$ be the rounding of x to the closest integer. For distribution X, let $\sim X = \mathsf{Samp}(r)$ be sample algorithm with randomness r according to distribution X.

For an even (resp. odd) positive integer α, we define $r' = r \mod {}^{\pm}\alpha$ to be the unique element r' in the range $-\frac{\alpha}{2} < r' \leq \frac{\alpha}{2}$ (resp. $-\frac{\alpha-1}{2} \leq r' \leq \frac{\alpha-1}{2}$) such that $r' = r \mod \alpha$. For any positive integer α, define $r' = r \mod {}^{+}\alpha$ to be the unique element r' in the range $0 < r' < \alpha$ such that $r' = r \mod \alpha$. When the exact representation is not important, we simplify it as $r \mod \alpha$. For $x \in \mathbb{Q}$, $d \leq \log_2 q$, define the compress function as $\mathsf{Comp}_q(x,d) = \lceil (2^d)/q \cdot x \rfloor \mod {}^{+}2^d$, and the decompress function as $\mathsf{Decomp}_q(x,d) = \lceil q/(2^d) \cdot x \rfloor$. And when applying the Comp and Decomp function to $\mathbf{x}$, the procedure is applied to coefficient.

Twin-Kyber. Our construction, called twin-kyber, is an extension of kyber scheme [3] in the same conjoined way for our twin-ElGamal scheme. With the parameters above, twin-kyber $\mathsf{2PKE_{mlwe}}$ = (KeyGen1, KeyGen0, Enc, Dec) is shown in Fig. 15.

Theorem 8. *If there is a PPT adversary $\mathcal{A}$ against [IND-CPA, IND-CPA] security of $\mathsf{2PKE}_{mlwe}$, there exists $\mathcal{B}$ such that, $\boldsymbol{Adv}_{\mathsf{2PKE}_{mlwe}}^{[\mathsf{IND\text{-}CPA},\mathsf{IND\text{-}CPA}]}(\mathcal{A}) \leq 2\boldsymbol{Adv}_{k+1,k,\eta}^{mlwe}(\mathcal{B})$.*

$\mathsf{KeyGen1}(\lambda)$	$\mathsf{KeyGen0}(\lambda)$
$\sigma_1 \leftarrow \{0,1\}^{256}$	$\sigma_0 \leftarrow \{0,1\}^{256}$
$(\mathbf{s_1}, \mathbf{e_1}) \sim \beta_\eta^k \times \beta_\eta^k = \mathsf{Sam}(\sigma_1)$	$(\mathbf{s_0}, \mathbf{e_0}) \sim \beta_\eta^k \times \beta_\eta^k = \mathsf{Sam}(\sigma_0)$
$\boldsymbol{t_1} = \mathsf{Comp}_q(\mathbf{A}\mathbf{s_1} + \mathbf{e_1}, d_{t_1} = \lceil \log q \rceil)$	$\boldsymbol{t_0} = \mathsf{Comp}_q(\mathbf{A}\mathbf{s_0} + \mathbf{e_0}, d_{t_0} = \lceil \log q \rceil)$
$(pk_1 = \mathbf{t_1}, sk_1 = \mathbf{s_1})$	$(pk_0 = \mathbf{t_0}, sk_0 = \mathbf{s_0})$
$\mathsf{Enc}(pk_1 = \mathbf{t_1}, pk_0 = \mathbf{t_0}, m \in \mathcal{M})$	$\mathsf{Dec}(sk_1 = \mathbf{s_1}, sk_0 = \mathbf{s_0}, c = (\mathbf{u_1}, \mathbf{u_0}, v)$
$r', r \leftarrow \{0,1\}^{256}$	$\mathbf{u_1} = \mathsf{Decomp}_q(\mathbf{u_1}, d_{u_1})$
$(\mathbf{r_1}, \mathbf{r_0}, \mathbf{e_3}, \mathbf{e_4}, e) \sim (\beta_\eta^k)^4 \times \beta_\eta = \mathsf{Sam}(r)$	$\mathbf{u_0} = \mathsf{Decomp}_q(\mathbf{u_0}, d_{u_0})$
$\mathbf{u_1} = \mathsf{Comp}_q(\mathbf{A}^T\mathbf{r_1} + \mathbf{e_3}, d_{u_1})$	$v = \mathsf{Decomp}_q(v, d_v)$
$\mathbf{u_0} = \mathsf{Comp}_q(\mathbf{A}^T\mathbf{r_0} + \mathbf{e_4}, d_{u_0})$	$m' = \mathsf{Comp}_q(v - \mathbf{s_1}^T\mathbf{u_1} - \mathbf{s_0}^T\mathbf{u_0}, 1)$
$v = \mathsf{Comp}_q(\mathbf{t_1}^T\mathbf{r_1} + \mathbf{t_0}^T\mathbf{r_0} + e + \lceil \frac{q}{2} \rfloor m, d_v)$	
$c = (\mathbf{u_1}, \mathbf{u_0}, v)$	

Fig. 15. The [IND-CPA, IND-CPA] secure $\mathsf{2PKE_{mlwe}}$ under Module-LWE assumption.

Please refer the full version [32] for the analysis of decryption failure and proof. By applying the modified FO transformation to $\mathsf{2PKE_{mlwe}}$, we obtain a [OW-CCA, OW-CCA] secure $\mathsf{2KEM_{mlwe}}$. Then by setting $cpk_0 = (0)^k$ and $csk_0 = (0)^k$, and integrating $\mathsf{2KEM_{mlwe}}$ to AKE in Sect. 4, a novel and efficient post-quantum AKE from Module-LWE assumption is constructed.

The parameter setting and comparison are given in Tables 5 and 6. Note that by setting $d_{t_1} = d_{t_0} = \lceil \log q \rceil$ we actually do not apply compress on public keys. (which fix one bug of the security proof in [3]). One may doubt that with $q = 3329$ we can not apply NTT technique to accelerate the multiplications of two polynomials $f(x) \times g(x)$ over R_q, since $512 \nmid 3328$. Actually, we can fix this gap. Separate $f(x) = f_B(x^2) + x f_A(x^2)$, $g(x) = g_2(x^2) + x g_1(x^2)$ into a series of odd power and a series of even power, then $f(x) \times g(x) = f_B(x^2) g_2(x^2) + (f_A(x^2) g_2(x^2) + f_B(x^2) g_1(x^2)) x + f_A(x^2) g_1(x^2) x^2$. Then we can apply NTT to $f_i(y) g_j(y)$ over $Z_q[y]/(y^{128} + 1)$ by setting $y = x^2$ since $256 | 3328$.

Table 5. The parameters for $\mathsf{2KEM_{mlwe}}$. δ is the decryption failure.

Scheme	n	k	q	η	$(d_{t_1}, d_{t_0}, d_{u_1}, d_{u_0}, d_v)$	δ	Security Level
$\mathsf{2KEM_{mlwe}}$	256	4	3329	1	$(12, 12, 9, 9, 5)$	$2^{-174.3}$	256

Table 6. The message size for Kyber in frame of FSXY13 and ours in frame of AKE.

AKEs	Assumptions	Sec	$U_A \rightarrow U_B$ (Bytes)	$U_B \rightarrow U_A$ (Bytes)
Kyber.AKE	$\mathbf{Adv}_{5,4,5}^{mlwe}$	256	2912	3008
AKE from $\mathsf{2KEM_{mlwe}}$	$\mathbf{Adv}_{5,4,5}^{mlwe}$	256	2838	2464

Acknowledgments. Haiyang Xue was supported by the National Natural Science Foundation of China 61602473, 61672019, 61772522, and the National Cryptography Development Fund MMJJ20170116. Xianhui Lu was supported by the National Natural Science Foundation of China 61572495. Bao Li was supported by the National Natural Science Foundation of China 61772515. Jingnan He was supported by the National Natural Science Foundation of China 61672030. Bei Liang was partially supported by the STINT grant (no 3720596). This work was supported by the National 973 Program of China under Grant 2014CB340603 and the Fundamental theory and cutting edge technologyResearch Program of Institute of Information Engineering, CAS (Grant No. Y7Z0291103).

References

1. Boyd, C., Cliff, Y., Gonzalez Nieto, J., Paterson, K.G.: Efficient one-round key exchange in the standard model. In: Mu, Y., Susilo, W., Seberry, J. (eds.) ACISP 2008. LNCS, vol. 5107, pp. 69–83. Springer, Heidelberg (2008). https://doi.org/10.1007/978-3-540-70500-0_6
2. Bos, J.W., Costello, C., Naehrig, M., Stebila, D.: Post-quantum key exchange for the TLS protocol from the ring learning with errors problem. In: 2015 IEEE Symposium on Security and Privacy, pp. 553–570 (2015)
3. Bos, J., et al.: CRYSTALS - Kyber: a CCA secure module-lattice-based KEM. In: 2018 IEEE Symposium on Security and Privacy, pp. 353–367. Code is available in https://github.com/pq-crystals/kyber
4. Barbosa, M., Farshim, P.: Relations among notions of complete non-malleability: indistinguishability characterisation and efficient construction without random oracles. In: Steinfeld, R., Hawkes, P. (eds.) ACISP 2010. LNCS, vol. 6168, pp. 145–163. Springer, Heidelberg (2010). https://doi.org/10.1007/978-3-642-14081-5_10
5. Bellare, M., Rogaway, P.: Entity authentication and key distribution. In: Stinson, D.R. (ed.) CRYPTO 1993. LNCS, vol. 773, pp. 232–249. Springer, Heidelberg (1994). https://doi.org/10.1007/3-540-48329-2_21
6. Cremers, C.J.F.: Session-state reveal is stronger than ephemeral key reveal: attacking the NAXOS authenticated key exchange protocol. In: Abdalla, M., Pointcheval, D., Fouque, P.-A., Vergnaud, D. (eds.) ACNS 2009. LNCS, vol. 5536, pp. 20–33. Springer, Heidelberg (2009). https://doi.org/10.1007/978-3-642-01957-9_2
7. Canetti, R., Krawczyk, H.: Analysis of key-exchange protocols and their use for building secure channels. In: Pfitzmann, B. (ed.) EUROCRYPT 2001. LNCS, vol. 2045, pp. 453–474. Springer, Heidelberg (2001). https://doi.org/10.1007/3-540-44987-6_28
8. Canetti, R., Krawczyk, H.: Security analysis of IKE's signature-based key-exchange protocol. In: Yung, M. (ed.) CRYPTO 2002. LNCS, vol. 2442, pp. 143–161. Springer, Heidelberg (2002). https://doi.org/10.1007/3-540-45708-9_10
9. Cramer, R., Shoup, V.: A practical public key cryptosystem provably secure against adaptive chosen ciphertext attack. In: Krawczyk, H. (ed.) CRYPTO 1998. LNCS, vol. 1462, pp. 13–25. Springer, Heidelberg (1998). https://doi.org/10.1007/BFb0055717
10. Cramer, R., Shoup, V.: Universal hash proofs and a paradigm for adaptive chosen ciphertext secure public-key encryption. In: Knudsen, L.R. (ed.) EUROCRYPT 2002. LNCS, vol. 2332, pp. 45–64. Springer, Heidelberg (2002). https://doi.org/10.1007/3-540-46035-7_4

11. Dolev, D., Dwork, C., Naor, M.: Non-malleable cryptography. SIAM J. Comput. **30**, 391–437 (2000)
12. Diffie, W., Hellman, M.: New directions in cryptography. IEEE Trans. Inf. Theory **22**(6), 644–654 (1976)
13. Fischlin, M.: Completely non-malleable schemes. In: Caires, L., Italiano, G.F., Monteiro, L., Palamidessi, C., Yung, M. (eds.) ICALP 2005. LNCS, vol. 3580, pp. 779–790. Springer, Heidelberg (2005). https://doi.org/10.1007/11523468_63
14. Fujisaki, E., Okamoto, T.: Secure integration of asymmetric and symmetric encryption schemes. In: Wiener, M. (ed.) CRYPTO 1999. LNCS, vol. 1666, pp. 537–554. Springer, Heidelberg (1999). https://doi.org/10.1007/3-540-48405-1_34
15. Fujioka, A., Suzuki, K., Xagawa, K., Yoneyama, K.: Strongly secure authenticated key exchange from factoring, codes, and lattices. In: Fischlin, M., Buchmann, J., Manulis, M. (eds.) PKC 2012. LNCS, vol. 7293, pp. 467–484. Springer, Heidelberg (2012). https://doi.org/10.1007/978-3-642-30057-8_28
16. Fujioka, A., Suzuki, K., Xagawa, K., Yoneyama, K.: Practical and post-quantum authenticated key exchange from one-way secure key encapsulation mechanism. In: AsiaCCS, pp. 83–94 (2013)
17. Giacon, F., Heuer, F., Poettering, B.: KEM combiners. In: Abdalla, M., Dahab, R. (eds.) PKC 2018. LNCS, vol. 10769, pp. 190–218. Springer, Cham (2018). https://doi.org/10.1007/978-3-319-76578-5_7
18. Hofheinz, D., Hövelmanns, K., Kiltz, E.: A modular analysis of the Fujisaki-Okamoto transformation. In: Kalai, Y., Reyzin, L. (eds.) TCC 2017. LNCS, vol. 10677, pp. 341–371. Springer, Cham (2017). https://doi.org/10.1007/978-3-319-70500-2_12
19. Kiltz, E.: Chosen-ciphertext security from tag-based encryption. In: Halevi, S., Rabin, T. (eds.) TCC 2006. LNCS, vol. 3876, pp. 581–600. Springer, Heidelberg (2006). https://doi.org/10.1007/11681878_30
20. Kiltz, E., Pietrzak, K., Stam, M., Yung, M.: A new randomness extraction paradigm for hybrid encryption. In: Joux, A. (ed.) EUROCRYPT 2009. LNCS, vol. 5479, pp. 590–609. Springer, Heidelberg (2009). https://doi.org/10.1007/978-3-642-01001-9_34
21. Krawczyk, H.: The order of encryption and authentication for protecting communications (or: How secure is SSL?). In: Kilian, J. (ed.) CRYPTO 2001. LNCS, vol. 2139, pp. 310–331. Springer, Heidelberg (2001). https://doi.org/10.1007/3-540-44647-8_19
22. Krawczyk, H.: SIGMA: the 'SIGn-and-MAc' approach to authenticated Diffie-Hellman and its use in the IKE protocols. In: Boneh, D. (ed.) CRYPTO 2003. LNCS, vol. 2729, pp. 400–425. Springer, Heidelberg (2003). https://doi.org/10.1007/978-3-540-45146-4_24
23. Krawczyk, H.: HMQV: a high-performance secure Diffie-Hellman protocol. In: Shoup, V. (ed.) CRYPTO 2005. LNCS, vol. 3621, pp. 546–566. Springer, Heidelberg (2005). https://doi.org/10.1007/11535218_33
24. LaMacchia, B., Lauter, K., Mityagin, A.: Stronger security of authenticated key exchange. In: Susilo, W., Liu, J.K., Mu, Y. (eds.) ProvSec 2007. LNCS, vol. 4784, pp. 1–16. Springer, Heidelberg (2007). https://doi.org/10.1007/978-3-540-75670-5_1
25. Matsumoto, T., Takashima, Y., Imai, H.: On seeking smart public-key distribution systems. Trans. IECE Jpn. **E69**(2), 99–106 (1986)
26. Menezes, A., Qu, M., Vanstone, S.: Some new key agreement protocols providing mutual implicit authentication. In: SAC 1995, pp. 22–32 (1995)

27. Okamoto, T.: Authenticated Key Exchange and Key Encapsulation Without Random Oracles. IACR ePrint report 2007/473, full version of [28]
28. Okamoto, T.: Authenticated key exchange and key encapsulation in the standard model. In: Kurosawa, K. (ed.) ASIACRYPT 2007. LNCS, vol. 4833, pp. 474–484. Springer, Heidelberg (2007). https://doi.org/10.1007/978-3-540-76900-2_29
29. Peikert, C.: Lattice cryptography for the internet. In: Mosca, M. (ed.) PQCrypto 2014. LNCS, vol. 8772, pp. 197–219. Springer, Cham (2014). https://doi.org/10.1007/978-3-319-11659-4_12
30. Peikert, C., Waters, B.: Lossy trapdoor functions and their applications. In: STOC 2008, pp. 187–196 (2008)
31. Wee, H.: Efficient chosen-ciphertext security via extractable hash proofs. In: Rabin, T. (ed.) CRYPTO 2010. LNCS, vol. 6223, pp. 314–332. Springer, Heidelberg (2010). https://doi.org/10.1007/978-3-642-14623-7_17
32. Xue, H., Lu, X., Li, B., Liang, B., He, J.: Understanding and Constructing AKE via Double-key Key Encapsulation Mechanism IACR ePrint report 2018/817
33. Yoneyama, K.: One-round authenticated key exchange with strong forward secrecy in the standard model against constrained adversary. In: Hanaoka, G., Yamauchi, T. (eds.) IWSEC 2012. LNCS, vol. 7631, pp. 69–86. Springer, Heidelberg (2012). https://doi.org/10.1007/978-3-642-34117-5_5
34. Yao, A.C.C., Zhao, Y.: OAKE: a new family of implicitly authenticated Diffie-Hellman protocols. In: CCS 2013, pp. 1113–1128 (2013)
35. Zhang, J., Zhang, Z., Ding, J., Snook, M., Dagdelen, Ö.: Authenticated key exchange from ideal lattices. In: Oswald, E., Fischlin, M. (eds.) EUROCRYPT 2015. LNCS, vol. 9057, pp. 719–751. Springer, Heidelberg (2015). https://doi.org/10.1007/978-3-662-46803-6_24

Identity-Based Encryption Tightly Secure Under Chosen-Ciphertext Attacks

Dennis Hofheinz[1], Dingding Jia[2,3,4](✉), and Jiaxin Pan[1]

[1] Karlsruhe Institute of Technology, Karlsruhe, Germany
{Dennis.Hofheinz,Jiaxin.Pan}@kit.edu

[2] State Key Laboratory of Information Security, Institute of Information Engineering, CAS, Beijing, China
jiadingding@iie.ac.cn

[3] Data Assurance and Communication Security Research Center, IIE, CAS, Beijing, China

[4] School of Cyber Security, University of Chinese Academy of Sciences, Beijing, China

Abstract. We propose the first identity-based encryption (IBE) scheme that is (almost) tightly secure against chosen-ciphertext attacks. Our scheme is efficient, in the sense that its ciphertext overhead is only seven group elements, three group elements more than that of the state-of-the-art passively (almost) tightly secure IBE scheme. Our scheme is secure in a multi-challenge setting, i.e., in face of an arbitrary number of challenge ciphertexts. The security of our scheme is based upon the standard symmetric external Diffie-Hellman assumption in pairing-friendly groups, but we also consider (less efficient) generalizations under weaker assumptions.

Keywords: Identity-based encryption · Chosen-ciphertext security Tight security reductions

1 Introduction

Tight Security. Usually, security reductions are used to argue the security of a cryptographic scheme S. A reduction reduces any attack on S to an attack on a suitable computational problem P. More specifically, a reduction constructs a successful P-solver $\mathcal{A}_P$ out of any given successful adversary $\mathcal{A}_S$ on S. Intuitively, a reduction thus shows that S is at least as hard to break/solve as P.

Ideally, we would like a reduction to be *tight*, in the sense that the constructed $\mathcal{A}_P$ has the same complexity and success probability as the given $\mathcal{A}_S$. A tight security reduction implies that the security of S is tightly coupled with the hardness of P. From a more practical perspective, a tight security reduction allows for more efficient parameter choices for S, when deriving those parameters from the best known attacks on P.

T. Peyrin and S. Galbraith (Eds.): ASIACRYPT 2018, LNCS 11273, pp. 190–220, 2018.
https://doi.org/10.1007/978-3-030-03329-3_7

Current State of the Art. Tight reductions have been studied for a variety of cryptographic primitives, such as public-key encryption [6,17,27–29,37,38], signature schemes [1,2,4,8,10,12,13,18,27,29,32,37,43], identity-based encryption (IBE) [3,8,11,12,21,22,31], non-interactive zero-knowledge proofs [17,29,37], and key exchange [5,26].

Existing tight reductions and corresponding schemes differ in the type and quality of tightness, and in the incurred cost of tightness. For instance, most of the referenced works provide only what is usually called "almost tight" reductions. In an almost tight reduction, the success probability of $\mathcal{A}_P$ may be smaller than $\mathcal{A}_S$, but only by a factor depends only on the security parameter (but not, e.g., on the size of $\mathcal{A}_S$). Furthermore, some reductions consider the scheme only in a somewhat restricted setting, such as an IBE setting in which only one challenge ciphertext is considered.

Our Goal: (Almost) Tightly CCA-Secure IBE Schemes in the Multi-challenge Setting. In this work, we are interested in (almost) tight reductions for IBE schemes. As remarked above, there already exist a variety of (almost) tightly secure IBE schemes. However, most of these schemes only provide security of one challenge ciphertext, and none of them provide security against chosen-ciphertext attacks. Security of many challenge ciphertexts is of course a more realistic notion; and while this notion is polynomially equivalent to the one-challenge notion, the corresponding reduction is far from tight, and defeats the purpose of tight security of the overall scheme in a realistic setting. Furthermore, chosen-ciphertext security guarantees security even against active adversaries [42].

On the Difficulty of Achieving Our Goal. Achieving many-challenge IBE security and chosen-ciphertext security appears to be technically challenging. First, with the exception of [21,22], all known IBE constructions that achieve (almost) tight many-challenge security rely on composite-order groups, and are thus comparatively inefficient. The exception [22] (like its predecessor [21]) constructs an efficient (almost) tightly secure IBE scheme in the many-challenge setting by adapting and implementing the "(extended) nested dual system groups" framework [12,31] in prime-order groups. Since this work is closest to ours, we will take a closer look at it after we have described our technical contribution. We stress, however, that also [22] does not achieve chosen-ciphertext security.

Second, canonical approaches to obtain chosen-ciphertext security do not appear to apply to existing tightly secure IBE schemes. For instance, it is known that *hierarchical* identity-based encryption (HIBE) implies chosen-ciphertext secure IBE [9]. However, currently no tightly secure HIBE schemes are known, and in fact there are lower bounds on the quality of (a large class of) security reductions for HIBE schemes [36].

Another natural approach to achieve chosen-ciphertext security is to equip ciphertexts with a non-interactive zero-knowledge (NIZK) proof of knowledge of the corresponding plaintext. Intuitively, a security reduction can use this NIZK proof to extract the plaintext message from any adversarially generated decryption query. Highly optimized variants of this outline are responsible for highly efficient public-key encryption schemes (e.g., [14,15,35,41]).

It is plausible that this approach can be used to turn, e.g., the tightly secure schemes of [21,22] into chosen-ciphertext secure schemes. However, this requires a NIZK proof system which is tightly secure and sound even in the presence of many simulated proofs. While such proof systems are constructible by combining Groth-Sahai proofs [24] with a tightly secure structure-preserving signature scheme [18] (see also [23,29]), the resulting NIZK and IBE schemes would not be very efficient. In fact, efficient suitable NIZK schemes are only known for simple languages [17], which do not appear compatible with the complex IBE schemes of [21,22].

Our Results. We provide a tightly chosen-ciphertext secure IBE scheme in the multi-challenge setting. Our scheme builds upon a new tightly chosen-plaintext secure IBE scheme whose efficiency is comparable with that of the state-of-the-art scheme of [22]. However, unlike [22], our scheme *is* compatible with the highly efficient NIZK proof system of [17]. This allows to upgrade our scheme to chosen-ciphertext security by adding an efficient consistency proof (that consists of only three group elements) to ciphertexts. We briefly remark that, similar to previous schemes [3,8,21,22], our scheme also achieves a (somewhat weak) form of anonymity. We compare the efficiency of our scheme with existing state-of-the-art schemes in Table 1.

Table 1. Comparison between known (almost) tightly and adaptively secure IBEs in prime-order groups from standard assumptions. We count the number of group elements in $\mathbb{G}$ (for symmetric pairings), $\mathbb{G}_1, \mathbb{G}_2$, and $\mathbb{G}_T$. $|\mathsf{pk}|$ denotes the size of the (master) public key, and $|\mathsf{C}|$ denotes the ciphertext overhead (on top of the message size).'MC' denotes many-challenge security, and 'CCA' chosen-ciphertext security. 'Loss' denotes the reduction loss, and 'Assump.' the assumption reduced to. $\mathsf{H} : \mathbb{G} \times \mathbb{G}_T \times \mathbb{G}_T \to \mathbb{Z}_q$ is a universal one-way hash function and $|\mathsf{H}|$ denotes the size of the representation of H. $|\mathsf{CH}|$ is the size of the hash key of a chameleon hash $\mathsf{CH} : \mathbb{G}_1^{k+1} \to \{0,1\}^L$ and $|\mathsf{R}|$ is the size of its randomness.

Scheme	$\lvert\mathsf{pk}\rvert$	$\lvert\mathsf{C}\rvert$	MC	CCA	Loss	Assump
Gen06 [19]	$5\lvert\mathbb{G}_1\rvert + \lvert\mathsf{H}\rvert$	$\lvert\mathbb{G}\rvert + 2\lvert\mathbb{G}_T\rvert$	–	✓	$O(1)$	q-ABDHE
CW13 [12]	$2k^2(2\lambda+1)\lvert\mathbb{G}_1\rvert + k\lvert\mathbb{G}_T\rvert$	$4k\lvert\mathbb{G}_1\rvert$	–	–	$O(\lambda)$	k-LIN
BKP14 [8]	$(2\lambda k^2 + 2k)\lvert\mathbb{G}_1\rvert$	$(2k+1)\lvert\mathbb{G}_1\rvert$	–	–	$O(\lambda)$	k-LIN
AHY15 [3]	$(16\lambda + 8)\lvert\mathbb{G}_1\rvert + 2\lvert\mathbb{G}_T\rvert$	$8\lvert\mathbb{G}_1\rvert$	✓	–	$O(\lambda)$	k-LIN
GCD+16 [21]	$(6\lambda k^2 + 3k^2)\lvert\mathbb{G}_1\rvert + k\lvert\mathbb{G}_T\rvert$	$6k\lvert\mathbb{G}_1\rvert$	✓	–	$O(\lambda)$	k-LIN
GCD+16 [21]	$(4\lambda k^2 + 2k^2)\lvert\mathbb{G}_1\rvert + k\lvert\mathbb{G}_T\rvert$	$4k\lvert\mathbb{G}_1\rvert$	✓	–	$O(\lambda)$	k-LINAI
GDCC16 [22]	$(2\lambda k^2 + 3k^2)\lvert\mathbb{G}_1\rvert + k\lvert\mathbb{G}_T\rvert$	$4k\lvert\mathbb{G}_1\rvert$	✓	–	$O(\lambda)$	k-LIN
HLQG18 [25]	$(4\lambda k^2 + k^2 + 2k)\lvert\mathbb{G}_1\rvert + \lvert\mathsf{CH}\rvert$	$(2k+1)\lvert\mathbb{G}_1\rvert + \lvert\mathsf{R}\rvert$	–	✓	$O(\lambda)$	k-LIN
Ours	$((5+4\lambda)k^2 + (2+2\lambda)k)\lvert\mathbb{G}_1\rvert$ $+(2\lambda k^2 + 4k^2 + k)\lvert\mathbb{G}_2\rvert$	$(6k+1)\lvert\mathbb{G}_1\rvert$	✓	✓	$O(\lambda)$	k-LIN

1.1 Technical Overview

The Approach of Blazy, Kiltz, and Pan (BKP). Our starting point is the MAC→IBE transformation of Blazy, Kiltz, and Pan (BKP) [8], which in turn abstracts the IBE construction of Chen and Wee [12], and generalizes the PRF→signatures transformation of Bellare and Goldwasser [7]. The BKP transformation assumes an "affine message authentication code" (affine MAC), i.e., a MAC in which verification consists in checking a system of affine equations. The variables in these affine equations comprise the MAC secret key, and the (public) coefficients are derived from the message to be signed.

This affine MAC is turned into an IBE scheme as follows: the IBE master public key $\mathsf{pk} = \mathsf{Com}(\mathsf{K})$ consists of a commitment to the MAC secret key K. An IBE user secret key $\mathsf{usk}[\mathsf{id}]$ for an identity id consists of a MAC tag τ_{id} on the message id, along with a NIZK proof that τ_{id} indeed verifies correctly relative to pk. The key observation of BKP is now that we can implement commitments and NIZK proof using the Groth-Sahai proof system [24]. Since the used MAC is affine, the corresponding verification involves only linear equations, which makes the corresponding proofs rerandomizable.

Now an IBE ciphertext C essentially contains a rerandomized version of the public, say, left-hand side of the NIZK equations for verifying the validity of τ_{id}. The corresponding right-hand side can be computed either from the randomization information (known to the sender), or using the NIZK proof for τ_{id} (known to the receiver through $\mathsf{usk}[\mathsf{id}]$). Of course, this technique relies on subtleties of the Groth-Sahai proof system that our high-level overview cannot cover.

Advantages and Limitations of the BKP Approach. The BKP approach has the nice property that the (one-challenge, chosen-plaintext) security of the resulting IBE scheme can be tightly reduced to the (one-challenge) security of the MAC scheme. In particular, BKP also gave a MAC scheme which is tightly secure in a one-challenge setting under a standard computational assumption. At the same time, BKP only consider one IBE challenge ciphertext, and chosen-plaintext security. In particular in large-scale scenarios with huge amounts of ciphertexts and active adversaries, this again defeats the purpose of a tight reduction.

First Modification: Achieving Many-Challenge Security. We will first show that the BKP reduction can be easily extended to the many-challenge case, assuming of course that the underlying MAC scheme is secure in the many-challenge setting. In this, the actual difficulty lies in constructing a suitable MAC scheme. We do so by adapting the affine MAC $\mathsf{MAC}_{\mathsf{BKP}}$ of BKP, using ideas from the recent (almost) tightly secure PKE scheme of Gay et al. [17].

More specifically, $\mathsf{MAC}_{\mathsf{BKP}}$ operates in a group $\mathbb{G} = \langle g \rangle$ of order q. We use the implicit notation $[x] := g^x$ for group elements. $\mathsf{MAC}_{\mathsf{BKP}}$ assumes a public matrix $[\mathbf{B}] \in \mathbb{G}^{n \times n}$ of a dimension n that depends on the underlying computational assumption. Its secret key is of the form

$$\mathsf{sk}_{\mathsf{MAC}} = ((\mathbf{x}_{i,b})_{i,b}, x_0') \in (\mathbb{Z}_q^n)^{\ell \cdot 2} \times \mathbb{Z}_q,$$

and a tag for a message $\mathsf{m} \in \{0,1\}^\ell$ is of the form

$$\tau = ([\mathbf{t}], [u]) \in \mathbb{G}^n \times \mathbb{G} \quad \text{with} \quad \begin{array}{l} \mathbf{t} = \mathbf{B}\mathbf{s} \in \mathbb{Z}_q^n \quad \text{for} \quad \mathbf{s} \xleftarrow{\$} \mathbb{Z}_q^{n'} \\ u = \sum_i \mathbf{x}_{i,\mathsf{m}_i}^\top \mathbf{t} + x_0' \in \mathbb{Z}_q \end{array}. \tag{1}$$

Verification checks that u is of the form from (1).

We sketch now a bit more specifically how $\mathsf{MAC}_{\mathsf{BKP}}$'s security proof proceeds, assuming an adversary $\mathcal{A}$ in the EUF-CMA security game. The overall strategy is to gradually randomize all u values issued in $\mathcal{A}$'s tag queries. This is equivalent to using different and independent "virtual" secret keys for each message. Hence, once this is done, $\mathcal{A}$ cannot be successful by an information-theoretic argument.

The main difficulty in randomizing all u is that a reduction must be able to still evaluate $\mathcal{A}$'s success in forging a tag for fresh message. In particular, the reduction must be able to compute $u^* = \sum \mathbf{x}_{i,\mathsf{m}_i^*}^\top \mathbf{t}^* + x_0'$ for a message m^* and value $\mathbf{t}^*$ adaptively selected by $\mathcal{A}$. The solution chosen by BKP, following Chen and Wee [12], is to iterate over all bit indices i. For each i, the reduction guesses the i-th bit m_i^* of $\mathcal{A}$'s forgery message, and embeds a computational challenge into $\mathbf{x}_{i,1-\mathsf{m}_i^*}$. This allows to randomize all u in issued tags with $\mathsf{m}_i \neq \mathsf{m}_i^*$, and still be able to evaluate u^*. The corresponding reduction loses a multiplicative factor of only $O(\ell)$. However, note that this strategy would not work with multiple challenges (i.e., potential forgeries (m^*, τ^*)) from $\mathcal{A}$. For instance, the simulation above is always only able to verify a given τ^* for exactly one of the two messages $\mathsf{m}_0^* = 0^\ell$ and $\mathsf{m}_1^* = 1^\ell$.

Our solution here is to instead employ the randomization strategy used by Gay et al. [17] in the context of public-key encryption. Namely, we first increase the dimension of $\mathbf{x}$. This allows us to essentially randomize both tags for messages with $\mathsf{m}_i = 0$ *and* $\mathsf{m}_i = 1$ simultaneously, using different parts of the $\mathbf{x}_{i,b}$ independently. In particular, we will embed computational challenges in different parts of both $\mathbf{x}_{i,0}$ and $\mathbf{x}_{i,1}$. This allows to adapt the argument of Gay et al. to the case of MACs, and hence to prove a slight variant of the BKP MAC secure even under many-challenge attacks.

Second Modification: Achieving Chosen-Ciphertext Security. So far, we could almost completely follow the BKP approach, with only a slight twist to the BKP MAC, and by adapting the proof strategy of Gay et al. However, the resulting scheme is still not chosen-ciphertext secure. To achieve chosen-ciphertext security, we will follow one of the generic approaches outlined above. In this, the modular structure of the BKP IBE, and the simplicity of the used MAC will pay off.

More concretely, following Naor and Yung [41], we will add a NIZK proof to each ciphertext. Unlike in the generic paradigm of achieving chosen-ciphertext security via NIZK proofs, we do not explicitly prove knowledge of the corresponding plaintext. Instead, following Cramer and Shoup [14,15], we prove only consistency of the ciphertext, in the sense that the ciphertext is a possible output of the encryption algorithm. Compared to a NIZK proof of knowledge (of plaintext), this yields a much more efficient scheme, but also requires more subtle proof of security.

Our security argument is reminiscent of that of Cramer and Shoup, but of course adapted to the IBE setting. Our reduction will be able to generate user decryption keys for all identities. These decryption keys will function perfectly well on consistent (in the above sense) ciphertexts at all times in the proof, but their action on inconsistent ciphertexts will be gradually randomized. Hence, adversarial decryption queries, whose consistency is guaranteed by the attached NIZK proof, will be decrypted correctly at all times. On the other hand, all generated challenge ciphertexts will be made inconsistent and will be equipped with simulated NIZK proofs early on.

Unlike Cramer and Shoup, who considered only one challenge ciphertext (for a PKE scheme), we need a very powerful NIZK scheme which enjoys (almost) tight unbounded simulation-soundness. Fortunately, the language for which we require this scheme is linear (due to the restriction to affine MACs), and hence we can use (a slight variant of) the highly efficient NIZK scheme from [17].

We stress that this proof blueprint is compatible with the proof of the BKP transformation, even when adapted to many challenges as explained above. In particular, we are able to extend the BKP transformation not only to many challenges, but also (and additionally) to chosen-ciphertext security. The resulting transformation is black-box and works for any given affine MAC that is secure in a many-challenge setting.

1.2 More on Related Work

We are not aware of any (almost) tightly chosen-ciphertext secure IBE scheme in the many-challenge setting. A natural idea is of course to adapt existing (almost) tightly chosen-plaintext secure schemes to chosen-ciphertext security. As we have explained in Sect. 1 above, straightforward generic approaches fail. However, another natural approach is to look at concrete state-of-the-art IBE schemes, and try to use their specific properties. Since we are interested in schemes in prime-order groups for efficiency reasons, the scheme to consider here is that of Gong et al. [22] (cf. also Table 1).

Remark About and Comparison to the Work of Gong et al. Interestingly, Gong et al. also take the BKP scheme as a basis, and extend it to (chosen-plaintext) many-challenge security, even in a setting with many instances of the IBE scheme itself. However, they first interpret and then extend the BKP scheme in the framework of (extended) nested dual system groups [12,31]. Remarkably, the resulting IBE scheme looks similar to the chosen-plaintext secure, many-challenge scheme that we use as a stepping stone towards many-challenge chosen-ciphertext security. In particular, the efficiency characteristics of those two schemes are comparable.

Still, for the express purpose of achieving chosen-ciphertext security, we found it easier to stick to (an extension of) the original BKP transformation and strategy, for two reasons. First, the modularity of BKP allows us to give an abstract

MAC→IBE transformation that achieves chosen-ciphertext security. This allows to isolate the intricate many-challenge security argument for the MAC from the orthogonal argument to achieve chosen-ciphertext security. Since the argument for tight security is directly woven into the notion of (extended) nested dual systems groups, it does not seem clear how to similarly isolate arguments (and proof complexity) for the scheme and strategy of Gong et al.

Second, as hinted above, our strategy to obtain chosen-ciphertext security requires a NIZK proof to show consistency of a ciphertext. With the BKP construction, consistency translates to a statement from a linear language, which allows to employ very efficient NIZK proof systems. For the construction of Gong et al., it is not clear how exactly such a consistency language would look like. In particular, it is not clear at all if highly efficient NIZK proofs for linear languages can be used.[1]

2 Basic Preliminaries

2.1 Notations

We use $x \xleftarrow{\$} \mathcal{S}$ to denote the process of sampling an element x from $\mathcal{S}$ uniformly at random if $\mathcal{S}$ is a set. For positive integers $k > 1, \eta \in \mathbb{Z}^+$ and a matrix $\mathbf{A} \in \mathbb{Z}_q^{(k+\eta)\times k}$, we denote the upper square matrix of $\mathbf{A}$ by $\overline{\mathbf{A}} \in \mathbb{Z}_q^{k\times k}$ and the lower η rows of $\mathbf{A}$ by $\underline{\mathbf{A}} \in \mathbb{Z}_q^{\eta\times k}$. Similarly, for a column vector $\mathbf{v} \in \mathbb{Z}_q^{k+\eta}$, we denote the upper k elements by $\overline{\mathbf{v}} \in \mathbb{Z}_q^k$ and the lower η elements of $\mathbf{v}$ by $\underline{\mathbf{v}} \in \mathbb{Z}_q^\eta$. For a bit string $\mathsf{m} \in \{0,1\}^n$, m_i denotes the ith bit of m ($i \leq n$) and $\mathsf{m}_{|i}$ denotes the first i bits of m.

All our algorithms are probabilistic polynomial time unless we stated otherwise. If $\mathcal{A}$ is an algorithm, then we write $a \xleftarrow{\$} \mathcal{A}(b)$ to denote the random variable that outputted by $\mathcal{A}$ on input b.

GAMES. We follow [8] to use code-based games for defining and proving security. A game G contains procedures INIT and FINALIZE, and some additional procedures $\mathrm{P}_1, \ldots, \mathrm{P}_n$, which are defined in pseudo-code. Initially all variables in a game are undefined (denoted by $\perp$), and all sets are empty (denote by $\emptyset$). An adversary $\mathcal{A}$ is executed in game G (denote by $\mathsf{G}^{\mathcal{A}}$) if it first calls INIT, obtaining its output. Next, it may make arbitrary queries to P_i (according to their specification), again obtaining their output. Finally, it makes one single call to FINALIZE$(\cdot)$ and stops. We use $\mathsf{G}^{\mathcal{A}} \Rightarrow d$ to denote that G outputs d after interacting with $\mathcal{A}$, and d is the output of FINALIZE.

2.2 Collision Resistant Hash Functions

Let $\mathcal{H}$ be a family of hash functions $H : \{0,1\}^* \to \{0,1\}^\lambda$. We assume that it is efficient to sample a function from $\mathcal{H}$, which is denoted by $H \xleftarrow{\$} \mathcal{H}$.

[1] To be clear: we do not claim that the scheme of Gong et al. cannot be upgraded to chosen-ciphertext security. However, it seems that such an upgrade would require a more complex restructuring of their proof strategy.

Definition 1 (Collision resistance). *We say a family of hash functions $\mathcal{H}$ is (t, ε)-collision-resistant (CR) if for all adversaries $\mathcal{A}$ that run in time t,*

$$\Pr[x \neq x' \wedge H(x) = H(x') \mid H \xleftarrow{\$} \mathcal{H}, (x, x') \xleftarrow{\$} \mathcal{A}(1^\lambda, H)] \leq \varepsilon.$$

2.3 Pairing Groups and Matrix Diffie-Hellman Assumptions

Let GGen be a probabilistic polynomial time (PPT) algorithm that on input 1^λ returns a description $\mathcal{G} := (\mathbb{G}_1, \mathbb{G}_2, \mathbb{G}_T, q, P_1, P_2, e)$ of asymmetric pairing groups where $\mathbb{G}_1$, $\mathbb{G}_2$, $\mathbb{G}_T$ are cyclic groups of order q for a λ-bit prime q, P_1 and P_2 are generators of $\mathbb{G}_1$ and $\mathbb{G}_2$, respectively, and $e : \mathbb{G}_1 \times \mathbb{G}_2$ is an efficient computable (non-degenerated) bilinear map. Define $P_T := e(P_1, P_2)$, which is a generator in $\mathbb{G}_T$. In this paper, we only consider Type III pairings, where $\mathbb{G}_1 \neq \mathbb{G}_2$ and there is no efficient homomorphism between them. All our constructions can be easily instantiated with Type I pairings by setting $\mathbb{G}_1 = \mathbb{G}_2$ and defining the dimension k to be greater than 1.

We use implicit representation of group elements as in [16]. For $s \in \{1, 2, T\}$ and $a \in \mathbb{Z}_q$ define $[a]_s = aP_s \in \mathbb{G}_s$ as the implicit representation of a in $\mathbb{G}_s$. Similarly, for a matrix $\mathbf{A} = (a_{ij}) \in \mathbb{Z}_q^{n \times m}$ we define $[\mathbf{A}]_s$ as the implicit representation of $\mathbf{A}$ in $\mathbb{G}_s$. $\mathsf{Span}(\mathbf{A}) := \{\mathbf{Ar} | \mathbf{r} \in \mathbb{Z}_q^m\} \subset \mathbb{Z}_q^n$ denotes the linear span of $\mathbf{A}$, and similarly $\mathsf{Span}([\mathbf{A}]_s) := \{[\mathbf{Ar}]_s | \mathbf{r} \in \mathbb{Z}_q^m\} \subset \mathbb{G}_s^n$. Note that it is efficient to compute $[\mathbf{AB}]_s$ given $([\mathbf{A}]_s, \mathbf{B})$ or $(\mathbf{A}, [\mathbf{B}]_s)$ with matching dimensions. We define $[\mathbf{A}]_1 \circ [\mathbf{B}]_2 := e([\mathbf{A}]_1, [\mathbf{B}]_2) = [\mathbf{AB}]_T$, which can be efficiently computed given $[\mathbf{A}]_1$ and $[\mathbf{B}]_2$.

Next we recall the definition of the matrix Diffie-Hellman (MDDH) and related assumptions [16].

Definition 2 (Matrix distribution). *Let $k, \ell \in \mathbb{N}$ with $\ell > k$. We call $\mathcal{D}_{\ell,k}$ a matrix distribution if it outputs matrices in $\mathbb{Z}_q^{\ell \times k}$ of full rank k in polynomial time. Let $\mathcal{D}_k := \mathcal{D}_{k+1,k}$.*

Without loss of generality, we assume the first k rows of $\mathbf{A} \xleftarrow{\$} \mathcal{D}_{\ell,k}$ form an invertible matrix. The $\mathcal{D}_{\ell,k}$-Matrix Diffie-Hellman problem is to distinguish the two distributions $([\mathbf{A}], [\mathbf{Aw}])$ and $([\mathbf{A}], [\mathbf{u}])$ where $\mathbf{A} \xleftarrow{\$} \mathcal{D}_{\ell,k}$, $\mathbf{w} \xleftarrow{\$} \mathbb{Z}_q^k$ and $\mathbf{u} \xleftarrow{\$} \mathbb{Z}_q^\ell$.

Definition 3 ($\mathcal{D}_{\ell,k}$-Matrix Diffie-Hellman assumption). *Let $\mathcal{D}_{\ell,k}$ be a matrix distribution and $s \in \{1, 2, T\}$. We say that the $\mathcal{D}_{\ell,k}$-Matrix Diffie-Hellman ($\mathcal{D}_{\ell,k}$-MDDH) is (t, ε)-hard relative to GGen in group $\mathbb{G}_s$ if for all adversaries $\mathcal{A}$ with running time t, it holds that*

$$|\Pr[\mathcal{A}(\mathcal{G}, [\mathbf{A}]_s, [\mathbf{Aw}]_s) = 1] - \Pr[\mathcal{A}(\mathcal{G}, [\mathbf{A}]_s, [\mathbf{u}]_s) = 1]| \leq \varepsilon,$$

where the probability is taken over $\mathcal{G} \xleftarrow{\$} \mathsf{GGen}(1^\lambda)$, $\mathbf{A} \xleftarrow{\$} \mathcal{D}_{\ell,k}, \mathbf{w} \xleftarrow{\$} \mathbb{Z}_q^k$ and $\mathbf{u} \xleftarrow{\$} \mathbb{Z}_q^\ell$.

We define the $\mathcal{D}_k$-Kernel Diffie-Hellman ($\mathcal{D}_k$-KerMDH) assumption [39] which is a natural search variant of the $\mathcal{D}_k$-MDDH assumption.

Definition 4 ($\mathcal{D}_k$-Kernel Diffie-Hellman assumption). *Let $\mathcal{D}_k$ be a matrix distribution and $s \in \{1,2\}$. We say that the $\mathcal{D}_k$-kernel Matrix Diffie-Hellman ($\mathcal{D}_k$-KerMDH) is (t,ε)-hard relative to GGen in group $\mathbb{G}_s$ if for all adversaries $\mathcal{A}$ that runs in time t, it holds that*

$$\Pr[\mathbf{c}^\top \mathbf{A} = \mathbf{0} \wedge \mathbf{c} \neq \mathbf{0} | [\mathbf{c}]_{3-s} \xleftarrow{\$} \mathcal{A}(\mathcal{G}, [\mathbf{A}]_s)] \leq \varepsilon,$$

where the probability is taken over $\mathcal{G} \xleftarrow{\$} \mathsf{GGen}(1^\lambda)$, $\mathbf{A} \xleftarrow{\$} \mathcal{D}_k$.

The following lemma shows that the $\mathcal{D}_k$-KerMDH assumption is a relaxation of the $\mathcal{D}_k$-MDDH assumption since one can use a non-zero vector in the kernel of $\mathbf{A}$ to test membership in the column space of $\mathbf{A}$.

Lemma 1 ($\mathcal{D}_k$-MDDH $\Rightarrow$ $\mathcal{D}_k$-KerMDH [39]). *For any matrix distribution $\mathcal{D}_k$, if $\mathcal{D}_k$-MDDH is (t,ε)-hard in $\mathbb{G}_s$, then $\mathcal{D}_k$-KerMDH is (t',ε)-hard in $\mathbb{G}_s$, where $t' \approx t$.*

The uniform distribution is a particular matrix distribution that deserves special attention, as an adversary breaking the $\mathcal{U}_{\ell,k}$ assumption can also distinguish between real MDDH tuples and random tuples for all other possible matrix distributions. For uniform distributions, they stated in [17] that $\mathcal{U}_k$-MDDH and $\mathcal{U}_{\ell,k}$-MDDH assumptions are equivalent.

Definition 5 (Uniform distribution). *Let $k, \ell \in \mathbb{N}$ with $\ell > k$. We call $\mathcal{U}_{\ell,k}$ a uniform distribution if it outputs uniformly random matrices in $\mathbb{Z}_q^{\ell \times k}$ of rank k in polynomial time.*

Lemma 2 ($\mathcal{D}_{\ell,k}$-MDDH $\Rightarrow$ $\mathcal{U}_{\ell,k}$-MDDH $\Leftrightarrow$ $\mathcal{U}_k$-MDDH [16,17]). *For $\ell > k$, let $\mathcal{D}_{\ell,k}$ be a matrix distribution, then if $\mathcal{D}_{\ell,k}$-MDDH is (t,ε)-hard in $\mathbb{G}_s$, $\mathcal{U}_{\ell,k}$-MDDH is (t',ε)-hard in $\mathbb{G}_s$, where $t' \approx t$. If $\mathcal{U}_k$-MDDH is (t,ε)-hard in $\mathbb{G}_s$, $\mathcal{U}_{\ell,k}$-MDDH is (t',ε)-hard in $\mathbb{G}_s$, where $t' \approx t$, vice versa.*

For $Q \in \mathbb{N}$, $\mathbf{W} \xleftarrow{\$} \mathbb{Z}_q^{k \times Q}$, $\mathbf{U} \xleftarrow{\$} \mathbb{Z}_q^{\ell \times Q}$, consider the Q-fold $\mathcal{D}_{\ell,k}$-MDDH problem which is distinguishing the distributions $([\mathbf{A}], [\mathbf{AW}])$ and $([\mathbf{A}], [\mathbf{U}])$. That is, the Q-fold $\mathcal{D}_{\ell,k}$-MDDH problem contains Q independent instances of the $\mathcal{D}_{\ell,k}$-MDDH problem (with the same $\mathbf{A}$ but different $\mathbf{w}_i$). The following lemma shows that the two problems are tightly equivalent. The reduction quality is tighter for uniform distribution.

Lemma 3 (Random self-reducibility [16]). *For $\ell > k$ and any matrix distribution $\mathcal{D}_{\ell,k}$, $\mathcal{D}_{\ell,k}$-MDDH is random self-reducible. In particular, for any $Q \geq 1$, if $\mathcal{D}_{\ell,k}$-MDDH is (t,ε)-hard relative to GGen in group $\mathbb{G}_s$, then Q-fold $\mathcal{D}_{\ell,k}$-MDDH is (t',ε')-hard relative to GGen in group $\mathbb{G}_s$, where $t \approx t' + Q \cdot \mathsf{poly}(\lambda)$, $\varepsilon' \leq (\ell - k)\varepsilon + \frac{1}{q-1}$, and for $\mathcal{D}_{\ell,k} = \mathcal{U}_{\ell,k}$, $\varepsilon' \leq \varepsilon + \frac{1}{q-1}$.*

3 Affine MACs in the Multi-Challenge Setting

3.1 Definition

We recall the definition of affine MACs from [8] and extend its security requirements of pseudorandomness to the multi-challenge setting.

Definition 6 (Affine MACs). *Let* par *be system parameters which contain a pairing group description* $\mathcal{G} = (\mathbb{G}_1, \mathbb{G}_2, \mathbb{G}_T, q, P_1, P_2, e)$ *of prime order* q*, and let* n *be a positive integer,* $\mathsf{MAC} = (\mathsf{Gen}_{\mathsf{MAC}}, \mathsf{Tag}, \mathsf{Ver}_{\mathsf{MAC}})$ *is an affine MAC over* $\mathbb{Z}_q^n$ *if the following conditions hold:*

1. $\mathsf{sk}_{\mathsf{MAC}} \xleftarrow{\$} \mathsf{Gen}_{\mathsf{MAC}}(\mathsf{par})$*, where* $\mathsf{sk}_{\mathsf{MAC}} = (\mathbf{B}, \mathbf{X}_0, ..., \mathbf{X}_\ell, \mathbf{x}'_0, ..., \mathbf{x}'_{\ell'}) \in \mathbb{Z}_q^{n \times n'} \times (\mathbb{Z}_q^{\eta \times n})^{\ell+1} \times (\mathbb{Z}_q^{\eta})^{\ell'+1}$*,* n', ℓ, ℓ' *and* η *are positive integers and the rank of* $\mathbf{B}$ *is at least 1.*
2. $\tau \xleftarrow{\$} \mathsf{Tag}(\mathsf{sk}_{\mathsf{MAC}}, \mathsf{m})$*, where* $\tau := ([\mathbf{t}]_2, [\mathbf{u}]_2) \in \mathbb{G}_2^n \times \mathbb{G}_2^\eta$ *is computed as*
$$\mathbf{t} := \mathbf{B}\mathbf{s} \in \mathbb{Z}_q^n \quad \textit{for} \quad \mathbf{s} \xleftarrow{\$} \mathbb{Z}_q^{n'} \tag{2}$$
$$\mathbf{u} := \sum_{i=0}^{\ell} f_i(\mathsf{m})\mathbf{X}_i\mathbf{t} + \sum_{i=0}^{\ell'} f'_i(\mathsf{m})\mathbf{x}'_i \in \mathbb{Z}_q^\eta \tag{3}$$
for some public defining functions $f_i : \mathcal{M} \to \mathbb{Z}_q$ *and* $f'_i : \mathcal{M} \to \mathbb{Z}_q$*. Note that only* $\mathbf{u}$ *is the message dependent part.*
3. $\mathsf{Ver}_{\mathsf{MAC}}(\mathsf{sk}_{\mathsf{MAC}}, \mathsf{m}, \tau = ([\mathbf{t}]_2, [\mathbf{u}]_2))$ *output 1 iff* (3) *holds, 0 otherwise.*

Definition 7. *An affine* MAC *over* $\mathbb{Z}_q^n$ *is* $(Q_e, Q_c, t, \varepsilon)$*-*mPR-CMA *(pseudorandom against chosen-message and multi-challenge attacks) if for all* $\mathcal{A}$ *that runs in time* t*, makes at most* Q_e *queries to the evaluation oracle,* Eval*, and at most* Q_c *queries to the challenge oracle,* Chal*, the following holds*

$$|\Pr[\mathsf{mPR\text{-}CMA}_0^{\mathcal{A}} \Rightarrow 1] - \Pr[\mathsf{mPR\text{-}CMA}_1^{\mathcal{A}} \Rightarrow 1]| \le \varepsilon,$$

where experiments $\mathsf{mPR\text{-}CMA}_0$ *and* $\mathsf{mPR\text{-}CMA}_1$ *are defined in Fig. 1.*

Init:
$\mathsf{sk}_{\mathsf{MAC}} \xleftarrow{\$} \mathsf{Gen}_{\mathsf{MAC}}(\mathsf{par})$
Return ϵ
 	
Eval(m): // at most Q_e queries
$\mathcal{Q}_{\mathcal{M}} = \mathcal{Q}_{\mathcal{M}} \cup \{\mathsf{m}\}$
If $(\mathbf{t}_{\mathsf{m}}, \mathbf{u}_{\mathsf{m}}) = (\bot, \bot)$ then
$([\mathbf{t}_{\mathsf{m}}]_2, [\mathbf{u}_{\mathsf{m}}]_2) \xleftarrow{\$} \mathsf{Tag}(\mathsf{sk}_{\mathsf{MAC}}, \mathsf{m})$
Return $([\mathbf{t}_{\mathsf{m}}]_2, [\mathbf{u}_{\mathsf{m}}]_2)$
	Chal(m*): // at most Q_c queries
	$\mathcal{C}_{\mathcal{M}} = \mathcal{C}_{\mathcal{M}} \cup \{\mathsf{m}^*\}$
	$\mathbf{h} \xleftarrow{\$} \mathbb{Z}_q^\eta$;
	$\mathbf{h}_0 = \sum f_i(\mathsf{m}^*)\mathbf{X}_i{}^\top \mathbf{h} \in \mathbb{Z}_q^n$
	$h_1 = \sum f'_i(\mathsf{m}^*)\mathbf{x}'_i{}^\top \mathbf{h} \in \mathbb{Z}_q$
	$\mathbf{h}_0 \xleftarrow{\$} \mathbb{Z}_q^n, \quad h_1 \xleftarrow{\$} \mathbb{Z}_q$
	Return $([\mathbf{h}]_1, [\mathbf{h}_0]_1, [h_1]_T)$
	
	Finalize($d \in \{0,1\}$):
	Return $d \wedge (\mathcal{Q}_{\mathcal{M}} \cap \mathcal{C}_{\mathcal{M}} = \emptyset)$

Fig. 1. Games $\mathsf{mPR\text{-}CMA}_0$ and $\mathsf{mPR\text{-}CMA}_1$ for defining mPR-CMA security.

Our notion is a generalization of the PR-CMA security in [8]. In [8] an adversary $\mathcal{A}$ can only query the challenge oracle CHAL at most once, while here $\mathcal{A}$ can ask multiple times.

3.2 Instantiation

We extend the tightly secure affine MAC $\mathsf{MAC}_{\mathsf{NR}}[\mathcal{D}_k]$ from [8] to the multi-challenge setting. Instead of choosing random vectors $\mathbf{x}_{i,b} \in \mathbb{Z}_q^k$ as the MAC secret keys in the original, here we choose random matrices $\mathbf{X}_{i,b} \in \mathbb{Z}_q^{2k \times k}$ such that in the security proof we can randomize all the tags and at the same time answer multiple challenge queries in a tight way.

Let $\mathcal{G} := (\mathbb{G}_1, \mathbb{G}_2, \mathbb{G}_T, q, P_1, P_2, e)$ be an asymmetric pairing group and $\mathsf{par} := \mathcal{G}$. Our affine MAC $\mathsf{MAC}_{\mathsf{NR}}^{\mathsf{mc}} := (\mathsf{Gen}_{\mathsf{MAC}}, \mathsf{Tag}, \mathsf{Ver}_{\mathsf{MAC}})$ for message space $\{0,1\}^L$ is defined as follows.

$\mathsf{Gen}_{\mathsf{MAC}}(\mathsf{par})$:	$\mathsf{Tag}(\mathsf{sk}_{\mathsf{MAC}}, \mathsf{m} \in \{0,1\}^L)$:	$\mathsf{Ver}_{\mathsf{MAC}}(\mathsf{sk}_{\mathsf{MAC}}, \tau, \mathsf{m})$:
$\mathbf{A} \xleftarrow{\$} \mathcal{U}_{2k,k}$	$\mathbf{s} \xleftarrow{\$} \mathbb{Z}_q^k, \mathbf{t} := \mathbf{B}\mathbf{s} \in \mathbb{Z}_q^k$	Parse $\tau := ([\mathbf{t}]_2, [\mathbf{u}]_2)$
$\mathbf{B} := \overline{\mathbf{A}} \in \mathbb{Z}_q^{k \times k}$	$\mathbf{X}_{\mathsf{m}} := \sum_{i=1}^L \mathbf{X}_{i,\mathsf{m}_i}$	$\mathbf{X}_{\mathsf{m}} := \sum_{i=1}^L \mathbf{X}_{i,\mathsf{m}_i}$
For $1 \le i \le L$ and $b = 0, 1$:	$\mathbf{u} := \mathbf{X}_{\mathsf{m}}\mathbf{t} + \mathbf{x}' \in \mathbb{Z}_q^{2k}$	If $[\mathbf{u}]_2 = [\mathbf{X}_{\mathsf{m}}\mathbf{t} + \mathbf{x}']_2$ then
$\quad \mathbf{X}_{i,b} \xleftarrow{\$} \mathbb{Z}_q^{2k \times k}$	Return $\tau = ([\mathbf{t}]_2, [\mathbf{u}]_2)$	$\quad$ return 1
$\mathbf{x}' \xleftarrow{\$} \mathbb{Z}_q^{2k}$		Else return 0.
$\mathsf{sk}_{\mathsf{MAC}} := (\mathbf{B}, \mathbf{X}_{1,0}, \dots, \mathbf{X}_{L,1}, \mathbf{x}')$		
Return $\mathsf{sk}_{\mathsf{MAC}}$		

Our scheme can be present by using any $\mathcal{D}_{2k,k}$ distribution and some of them have compact representation and give more efficient scheme. For simplicity of presentation, we present our scheme based on the $\mathcal{U}_{2k,k}$ distribution.

INIT:
$\mathbf{A} \xleftarrow{\$} \mathcal{U}_{2k,k}$, $\mathbf{B} := \overline{\mathbf{A}}$
For $j = 1, \dots, L$: $\mathbf{X}_{j,0}, \mathbf{X}_{j,1} \xleftarrow{\$} \mathbb{Z}_q^{2k \times k}$
$\mathbf{x}' \xleftarrow{\$} \mathbb{Z}_q^{2k}$
Return ϵ

CHAL(m^*): // G_0, $\boxed{\mathsf{G}_{1,i}}$, $\fbox{$\mathsf{G}_2, \mathsf{G}_3$}$
$\mathcal{C}_{\mathcal{M}} := \mathcal{C}_{\mathcal{M}} \cup \{\mathsf{m}^*\}$; $\mathbf{x}'_{\mathsf{m}^*} := \mathbf{x}'$
$\mathbf{h} \xleftarrow{\$} \mathbb{Z}_q^{2k}$; $\boxed{\mathbf{x}'_{\mathsf{m}^*} := \mathsf{RF}_i(\mathsf{m}^*_{|i})}$
$\mathbf{h}_0 := (\sum_{j=1}^L \mathbf{X}_{j,\mathsf{m}^*_j})^\top \mathbf{h}$; $\fbox{$\mathbf{h}_0 \xleftarrow{\$} \mathbb{Z}_q^k$}$
$h_1 := \mathbf{x}'^{\top}_{\mathsf{m}^*} \mathbf{h} \in \mathbb{Z}_q$; $\fbox{$h_1 \xleftarrow{\$} \mathbb{Z}_q$}$
Return $([\mathbf{h}]_1, [\mathbf{h}_0]_1, [h_1]_T)$

EVAL(m): // G_0, G_3, $\boxed{\mathsf{G}_{1,i}}$, $\fbox{$\mathsf{G}_2$}$
$\mathcal{Q}_{\mathcal{M}} := \mathcal{Q}_{\mathcal{M}} \cup \{\mathsf{m}\}$
If $([\mathbf{t}_{\mathsf{m}}]_2, [\mathbf{u}_{\mathsf{m}}]_2) = (\perp, \perp)$ then
$\quad \mathbf{s}_{\mathsf{m}} \xleftarrow{\$} \mathbb{Z}_q^k$; $\mathbf{t}_{\mathsf{m}} := \mathbf{B}\mathbf{s}_{\mathsf{m}}$
$\quad \mathbf{x}'_{\mathsf{m}} := \mathbf{x}'$
$\quad \boxed{\mathbf{x}'_{\mathsf{m}} := \mathsf{RF}_i(\mathsf{m}_{|i})}$
$\quad \fbox{$\mathbf{x}'_{\mathsf{m}} \xleftarrow{\$} \mathbb{Z}_q^{2k}$}$
$\quad \mathbf{u}_{\mathsf{m}} := \sum_{j=1}^L \mathbf{X}_{j,\mathsf{m}_j} \mathbf{t}_{\mathsf{m}} + \mathbf{x}'_{\mathsf{m}}$
Return $([\mathbf{t}_{\mathsf{m}}]_2, [\mathbf{u}_{\mathsf{m}}]_2)$

FINALIZE($d \in \{0,1\}$):
Return $d \wedge (\mathcal{Q}_{\mathcal{M}} \cap \mathcal{C}_{\mathcal{M}} = \emptyset)$

Fig. 2. Games G_0, $\mathsf{G}_{1,i}$ $(0 \le i \le L)$, G_2, G_3 for the proof of Theorem 1. $\mathsf{RF}_i : \{0,1\}^i \rightarrow \mathbb{Z}_q^{2k}$ is a random function. Boxed codes are only executed in the games marked in the same box style at the top right of every procedure. Non-boxed codes are always run.

$\underline{\text{INIT:}}$ // $\mathsf{G}_{1,i}$, $\mathsf{H}_{i,1}$, $\boxed{\mathsf{H}_{i,2}}$, $\mathsf{H}_{i,3}$, $\mathsf{H}_{i,4}$, $\mathsf{H}_{i,5}, \mathsf{G}_{1,i+1}$

$\mathbf{A} \xleftarrow{\$} \mathcal{U}_{2k,k}$; $\mathbf{B} := \overline{\mathbf{A}}$

For $j = 1, \ldots, L : \mathbf{X}_{j,0}, \mathbf{X}_{j,1} \xleftarrow{\$} \mathbb{Z}_q^{2k \times k}$

$\mathbf{A}_0, \mathbf{A}_1 \xleftarrow{\$} \mathcal{U}_{2k,k}$

Compute $\mathbf{A}_0^{\perp}, \mathbf{A}_1^{\perp} \in \mathbb{Z}_q^{2k \times k}$ s.t.

$\mathbf{A}_0^{\top} \mathbf{A}_0^{\perp} = \mathbf{A}_1^{\top} \mathbf{A}_1^{\perp} = \mathbf{0}$

For all $\mathsf{m} \in \{0,1\}^L$:

$\quad \mathbf{X}_{\mathsf{m}} := \sum_{j=1}^{L} \mathbf{X}_{j,\mathsf{m}_j}$

$\quad \mathbf{x}'_{\mathsf{m}} := \mathsf{RF}_i(\mathsf{m}_{|i})$

$\quad \boxed{\mathbf{x}'_{\mathsf{m}} := \mathbf{A}_0^{\perp} \mathsf{ZF}_i(\mathsf{m}_{|i}) + \mathbf{A}_1^{\perp} \mathsf{OF}_i(\mathsf{m}_{|i})}$

$\quad \mathbf{x}'_{\mathsf{m}} := \mathbf{A}_0^{\perp} \mathsf{ZF}_{i+1}(\mathsf{m}_{|i+1}) + \mathbf{A}_1^{\perp} \mathsf{OF}_i(\mathsf{m}_{|i})$

$\quad \mathbf{x}'_{\mathsf{m}} := \mathbf{A}_0^{\perp} \mathsf{ZF}_{i+1}(\mathsf{m}_{|i+1}) + \mathbf{A}_1^{\perp} \mathsf{OF}_{i+1}(\mathsf{m}_{|i+1})$

$\quad \mathbf{x}'_{\mathsf{m}} := \mathsf{RF}_{i+1}(\mathsf{m}_{|i+1})$

Return ϵ

$\underline{\text{CHAL}(\mathsf{m}^*)\text{:}}$ // $\boxed{\mathsf{G}_{1,i}, \mathsf{G}_{1,i+1}}$, $\mathsf{H}_{i,1}$-$\mathsf{H}_{i,5}$

$\mathcal{C}_{\mathcal{M}} := \mathcal{C}_{\mathcal{M}} \cup \{\mathsf{m}^*\}$

$\boxed{\mathbf{h} \xleftarrow{\$} \mathbb{Z}_q^{2k}}$

$\mathbf{r} \xleftarrow{\$} \mathbb{Z}_q^{k}, \mathbf{h} := \mathbf{A}_{\mathsf{m}^*_{i+1}} \mathbf{r}$

$\mathbf{h}_0 := \mathbf{X}_{\mathsf{m}^*}^{\top} \mathbf{h}$; $h_1 = \mathbf{x}'^{\top}_{\mathsf{m}^*} \mathbf{h}$

Return $([\mathbf{h}]_1, [\mathbf{h}_0]_1, [h_1]_T)$

$\underline{\text{EVAL}(\mathsf{m})\text{:}}$ // $\mathsf{G}_{1,i}, \mathsf{G}_{1,i+1}, \mathsf{H}_{i,1}$-$\mathsf{H}_{i,5}$

$\mathcal{Q}_{\mathcal{M}} := \mathcal{Q}_{\mathcal{M}} \cup \{\mathsf{m}\}$

If $([\mathbf{t}_{\mathsf{m}}]_2, [\mathbf{u}_{\mathsf{m}}]_2) = (\perp, \perp)$ then

$\quad \mathbf{s}_{\mathsf{m}} \xleftarrow{\$} \mathbb{Z}_q^{k}$; $\mathbf{t}_{\mathsf{m}} := \mathbf{B}\mathbf{s}_{\mathsf{m}}$

$\quad \mathbf{u}_{\mathsf{m}} := \mathbf{X}_{\mathsf{m}} \mathbf{t}_{\mathsf{m}} + \mathbf{x}'_{\mathsf{m}}$

Return $([\mathbf{t}_{\mathsf{m}}]_2, [\mathbf{u}_{\mathsf{m}}]_2)$

$\underline{\text{FINALIZE}(d \in \{0,1\})\text{:}}$

Return $d \wedge (\mathcal{Q}_{\mathcal{M}} \cap \mathcal{C}_{\mathcal{M}} = \emptyset)$

Fig. 3. Games $\mathsf{G}_{1,i}$, $\mathsf{G}_{1,i+1}$, $\mathsf{H}_{i,1}$,..., $\mathsf{H}_{i,5}$ $(0 \le i \le L)$ for the proof of Lemma 5. $\mathsf{RF}_i : \{0,1\}^i \to \mathbb{Z}_q^{2k}$, $\mathsf{ZF}_i, \mathsf{OF}_i : \{0,1\}^i \to \mathbb{Z}_q^{k}$ are three independent random functions.

Theorem 1. *If the* $\mathcal{U}_{2k,k}$-MDDH *problem is* (t_1, ε_1)*-hard in* $\mathbb{G}_1$ *and* (t_2, ε_2)*-hard in* $\mathbb{G}_2$*, the* $\mathcal{U}_{2k}$-MDDH *problem is* (t_3, ε_3)*-hard in* $\mathbb{G}_1$*, then* $\mathsf{MAC}_{\mathsf{NR}}^{\mathsf{mc}}$ *is* $(Q_{\mathsf{e}}, Q_{\mathsf{c}}, t_{\mathcal{A}}, \varepsilon)$-mPR-CMA*-secure with* $t_1 \approx t_2 \approx t_3 \approx t_{\mathcal{A}} + (Q_{\mathsf{e}} + Q_{\mathsf{c}})\mathsf{poly}(\lambda)$*, and* $\varepsilon \le 4L\varepsilon_1 + 3L\varepsilon_2 + 3\varepsilon_3 + 2^{-\Omega(\lambda)}$*, where* $\mathsf{poly}(\lambda)$ *is independent of* $t_{\mathcal{A}}$.

Proof. We prove the theorem via a sequence of games as shown in Fig. 2.

Lemma 4 **(G_0 to $\mathsf{G}_{1,0}$).** $\Pr[\mathsf{mPR\text{-}CMA}_0^{\mathcal{A}} \Rightarrow 1] = \Pr[\mathsf{G}_0^{\mathcal{A}} \Rightarrow 1] = \Pr[\mathsf{G}_{1,0}^{\mathcal{A}} \Rightarrow 1]$.

Proof. G_0 is the original game and it is the same as $\mathsf{mPR\text{-}CMA}_0$. In $\mathsf{G}_{1,0}$, we define $\mathsf{RF}_0(\epsilon)$ as a fix random vector $\mathbf{x}' \xleftarrow{\$} \mathbb{Z}_q^{2k}$ and then have Lemma 4. □

Lemma 5 **($\mathsf{G}_{1,i}$ to $\mathsf{G}_{1,i+1}$).** *If the* $\mathcal{U}_{2k,k}$-MDDH *problem is* (t_1, ε_1)*-hard in* $\mathbb{G}_1$ *and* (t_2, ε_2)*-hard in* $\mathbb{G}_2$*, then* $|\Pr[\mathsf{G}_{1,i}^{\mathcal{A}} \Rightarrow 1] - \Pr[\mathsf{G}_{1,i+1}^{\mathcal{A}} \Rightarrow 1]| \le 4\varepsilon_1 + 2\varepsilon_2 + 2^{-\Omega(\lambda)}$ *and* $t_1 \approx t_2 \approx t_{\mathcal{A}} + (Q_{\mathsf{e}} + Q_{\mathsf{c}})\mathsf{poly}(\lambda)$*, where* $\mathsf{poly}(\lambda)$ *is independent of* $t_{\mathcal{A}}$.

Proof (of Lemma 5). To bound the difference between $\mathsf{G}_{1,i}$ and $\mathsf{G}_{1,i+1}$, we introduce a series of intermediate games $\mathsf{H}_{i,1}$ to $\mathsf{H}_{i,5}$ as in Fig. 3. An overview of the transitions is given in Fig. 4.

Lemma 6 **($\mathsf{G}_{1,i}$ to $\mathsf{H}_{i,1}$).** *If the* $\mathcal{U}_{2k,k}$-MDDH *problem is* (t_1, ε_1)*-hard in* $\mathbb{G}_1$*, then* $|\Pr[\mathsf{G}_{1,i}^{\mathcal{A}} \Rightarrow 1] - \Pr[\mathsf{H}_{i,1}^{\mathcal{A}} \Rightarrow 1]| \le 2\varepsilon_1 + 2/(q-1)$ *and* $t_1 \approx t_{\mathcal{A}} + (Q_{\mathsf{e}} + Q_{\mathsf{c}})\mathsf{poly}(\lambda)$*, where* $\mathsf{poly}(\lambda)$ *is independent of* $t_{\mathcal{A}}$.

#	h in CHAL	$\mathbf{x}'_{\mathsf{m}}$ in CHAL and EVAL	game knows	remark
$\mathsf{G}_{1,i}$	random	$\mathsf{RF}_i(\mathsf{m}_{\mid i})$	-	-
$\mathsf{H}_{i,1}$	$\mathbf{A}_{\mathsf{m}^*_{i+1}}\mathbf{r}$	$\mathsf{RF}_i(\mathsf{m}_{\mid i})$	-	$\mathcal{U}_{2k,k}$-MDDH in $\mathbb{G}_1$
$\mathsf{H}_{i,2}$	$\mathbf{A}_{\mathsf{m}^*_{i+1}}\mathbf{r}$	$\mathbf{A}_0^\perp\mathsf{ZF}_i(\mathsf{m}_{\mid i}) + \mathbf{A}_1^\perp\mathsf{OF}_i(\mathsf{m}_{\mid i})$	$\mathbf{A}_0^\perp, \mathbf{A}_1^\perp$	-
$\mathsf{H}_{i,3}$	$\mathbf{A}_{\mathsf{m}^*_{i+1}}\mathbf{r}$	$\mathbf{A}_0^\perp\mathsf{ZF}_{i+1}(\mathsf{m}_{\mid i+1}) + \mathbf{A}_1^\perp\mathsf{OF}_i(\mathsf{m}_{\mid i})$	$\mathbf{A}_0^\perp, \mathbf{A}_1^\perp$	$\mathcal{U}_{2k,k}$-MDDH in $\mathbb{G}_2$
$\mathsf{H}_{i,4}$	$\mathbf{A}_{\mathsf{m}^*_{i+1}}\mathbf{r}$	$\mathbf{A}_0^\perp\mathsf{ZF}_{i+1}(\mathsf{m}_{\mid i+1}) + \mathbf{A}_1^\perp\mathsf{OF}_{i+1}(\mathsf{m}_{\mid i+1})$	$\mathbf{A}_0^\perp, \mathbf{A}_1^\perp$	$\mathcal{U}_{2k,k}$-MDDH in $\mathbb{G}_2$
$\mathsf{H}_{i,5}$	$\mathbf{A}_{\mathsf{m}^*_{i+1}}\mathbf{r}$	$\mathsf{RF}_{i+1}(\mathsf{m}_{\mid i+1})$	$\mathbf{A}_0^\perp, \mathbf{A}_1^\perp$	-
$\mathsf{G}_{1,i+1}$	random	$\mathsf{RF}_{i+1}(\mathsf{m}_{\mid i+1})$	-	$\mathcal{U}_{2k,k}$-MDDH in $\mathbb{G}_1$

Fig. 4. Overview of the transitions in the proof of Lemma 5. We highlight the respective changes between the games in gray. $\mathsf{RF}_i : \{0,1\}^i \to \mathbb{Z}_q^{2k}$, and $\mathsf{ZF}_i, \mathsf{OF}_i : \{0,1\}^i \to \mathbb{Z}_q^k$ are three independent random functions.

Proof. Let $\mathbf{A}_0, \mathbf{A}_1 \xleftarrow{\$} \mathcal{U}_{2k,k}$. We define an intermediate game $\mathsf{H}'_{i,1}$ which is the same as $\mathsf{G}_{1,i}$ except for CHAL: precisely, if $\mathsf{m}^*_{i+1} = 0$ then we pick $\mathbf{h}$ uniformly random from $\mathsf{Span}(\mathbf{A}_0)$; otherwise, $\mathbf{h} \xleftarrow{\$} \mathbb{Z}_q^{2k}$. Oracles INIT, EVAL and FINALIZE are simulated as in $\mathsf{G}_{1,i}$.

The difference between $\mathsf{G}_{1,i}$ and $\mathsf{H}'_{i,1}$ is bounded by a straightforward reduction to break the Q_{c}-fold $\mathcal{U}_{2k,k}$-MDDH problem in $\mathbb{G}_1$ with $[\mathbf{A}_0]_1$ as the challenge matrix. Thus, by Lemma 3 we have

$$|\Pr[\mathsf{G}_{1,i}^{\mathcal{A}} \Rightarrow 1] - \Pr[\mathsf{H}_{i,1}^{\prime\mathcal{A}} \Rightarrow 1]| \leq \varepsilon_1 + \frac{1}{q-1}.$$

Similarly, we can bound $\mathsf{H}'_{i,1}$ and $\mathsf{H}_{i,1}$ with the $\mathcal{U}_{2k,k}$-MDDH assumption in $\mathbb{G}_1$, namely,

$$|\Pr[\mathsf{H}_{i,1}^{\prime\mathcal{A}} \Rightarrow 1] - \Pr[\mathsf{H}_{i,1}^{\mathcal{A}} \Rightarrow 1]| \leq \varepsilon_1 + \frac{1}{q-1}.$$

Here we have $t_1 \approx t_{\mathcal{A}} + (Q_{\mathsf{e}} + Q_{\mathsf{c}})\mathsf{poly}(\lambda)$, where $\mathsf{poly}(\lambda)$ is independent of $t_{\mathcal{A}}$. □

After switching $[\mathbf{h}]_1$ in CHAL to the right span, the following reductions can have $\mathbf{A}_0$ and $\mathbf{A}_1$ over $\mathbb{Z}_q$. Since the rank of $\mathbf{A}_0$ and that of $\mathbf{A}_1$ are both k, we can efficiently compute the kernel matrix $\mathbf{A}_0^\perp \in \mathbb{Z}_q^{2k\times k}$ (resp. $\mathbf{A}_1^\perp$) of $\mathbf{A}_0$ (resp. $\mathbf{A}_1$). We note that $\mathbf{A}_0^\top\mathbf{A}_0^\perp = \mathbf{0} = \mathbf{A}_1^\top\mathbf{A}_1^\perp$ and $(\mathbf{A}_0^\perp \mid \mathbf{A}_1^\perp) \in \mathbb{Z}_q^{2k\times 2k}$ is a full-rank matrix with overwhelming probability $1 - 2^{-\Omega(\lambda)}$, since $\mathbf{A}_0$ and $\mathbf{A}_1$ are two random matrices.

Let ZF_i and OF_i be two independent random functions mapping from $\{0,1\}^i$ to $\mathbb{Z}_q^k$.

Lemma 7 **($\mathsf{H}_{i,1}$ to $\mathsf{H}_{i,2}$).** $|\Pr[\mathsf{H}_{i,1}^{\mathcal{A}} \Rightarrow 1] - \Pr[\mathsf{H}_{i,2}^{\mathcal{A}} \Rightarrow 1]| \leq 2^{-\Omega(\lambda)}$.

Proof. The difference between these two games is statistically bounded. In $\mathsf{H}_{i,2}$, we just rewrite $\mathsf{RF}_i(\mathsf{m}_{\mid i})$ as

$$\mathsf{RF}_i(\mathsf{m}_{\mid i}) := (\mathbf{A}_0^\perp \mid \mathbf{A}_1^\perp)\begin{pmatrix}\mathsf{ZF}_i(\mathsf{m}_{\mid i})\\ \mathsf{OF}_i(\mathsf{m}_{\mid i})\end{pmatrix} \tag{4}$$

Since $(\mathbf{A}_0^\perp \mid \mathbf{A}_1^\perp)$ is a full-rank matrix with overwhelming probability $1 - \frac{k}{q}$ and ZF_i, $\mathsf{OF}_i : \{0,1\}^i \to \mathbb{Z}_q^k$ are two independent random functions, $\mathsf{RF}_i : \{0,1\}^i \to \mathbb{Z}_q^{2k}$ in (4) is a random function as well. Thus, $\mathsf{H}_{i,1}$ and $\mathsf{H}_{i,2}$ are distributed the same except with probability $2^{-\Omega(\lambda)}$. □

The following step is a main difference to $\mathsf{MAC}_{\mathsf{NR}}[\mathcal{D}_k]$ in the original BKP framework [8]. Here our reduction can randomize EVAL queries with the MDDH assumption and at the same time it can answer multiple CHAL queries, while the original $\mathsf{MAC}_{\mathsf{NR}}[\mathcal{D}_k]$ can not. Precisely, to be able to go from RF_i to RF_{i+1}, the security reduction of $\mathsf{MAC}_{\mathsf{NR}}[\mathcal{D}_k]$ (cf. Lemma 3.6 in [8]) guesses $b \xleftarrow{\$} \{0,1\}$ which stands for the $(i+1)$-th bit of m^* and implicitly embeds $\mathbf{T_D} := \underline{\mathbf{D}}\overline{\mathbf{D}}^{-1}$ in the secret key $\mathbf{x}_{i+1,1-b}$. Note that the reduction does not know $\mathbf{x}_{i+1,1-b}$, but, since the adversary $\mathcal{A}$ only has at most *one* query to CHAL and b is hidden from $\mathcal{A}$, the reduction can hope $\mathsf{m}^*_{i+1} \neq 1-b$ (with probability 1/2) and it can simulate the experiment. However, this proof strategy does not work in the multi-challenge setting, since $\mathcal{A}$ can ask two challenge queries with one query which has b in the $(i+1)$-th position and $1-b$ in the other.

By increasing the dimension of $\mathbf{X}_{j,\beta}$, our strategy is first embedding $\mathbf{A}_0^\perp \mathbf{T_D}$ in $\mathbf{X}_{i+1,0}$ such that we can add entropy to $\mathbf{x}'_{\mathsf{m}}$ in the span of $\mathbf{A}_0^\perp$ and at the same time upon CHAL queries with 0 in the $(i+1)$-th position $\mathbf{T_D}$ will be canceled out, and then add entropy to $\mathbf{x}'_{\mathsf{m}}$ in the span of $\mathbf{A}_1^\perp$ in the similar way.

Lemma 8 **($\mathsf{H}_{i,2}$ to $\mathsf{H}_{i,3}$).** *If the $\mathcal{U}_{2k,k}$-MDDH problem is (t_2, ε_2)-hard in $\mathbb{G}_2$, then $|\Pr[\mathsf{H}_{i,2}^{\mathcal{A}} \Rightarrow 1] - \Pr[\mathsf{H}_{i,3}^{\mathcal{A}} \Rightarrow 1]| \leq \varepsilon_2 + 2^{-\Omega(\lambda)}$ and $t_2 \approx t_{\mathcal{A}} + (Q_e + Q_c)\mathsf{poly}(\lambda)$, where $\mathsf{poly}(\lambda)$ is independent of $t_{\mathcal{A}}$.*

Proof. We bound the difference between $\mathsf{H}_{i,2}$ and $\mathsf{H}_{i,3}$ by the Q_e-fold $\mathcal{U}_{2k,k}$-MDDH assumption in $\mathbb{G}_2$. Formally, on receiving a Q_e-fold $\mathcal{U}_{2k,k}$-MDDH challenge $([\mathbf{D}]_2, [\mathbf{F}]_2 := ([\mathbf{f}_1, \cdots, \mathbf{f}_{Q_e}]_2)) \in \mathbb{G}_2^{2k \times k} \times \mathbb{G}_2^{2k \times Q_e}$, where Q_e denotes the number of evaluation queries, we construct a reduction $\mathcal{B}_2$ as in Fig. 5. Let $\mathsf{ZF}_i, \mathsf{ZF}'_i$ be two independent random functions, we define ZF_{i+1} as

$$\mathsf{ZF}_{i+1}(\mathsf{m}_{|i+1}) := \begin{cases} \mathsf{ZF}_i(\mathsf{m}_{|i}) + \mathsf{ZF}'_i(\mathsf{m}_{|i}) & \text{if } \mathsf{m}_{i+1} = 0 \\ \mathsf{ZF}_i(\mathsf{m}_{|i}) & \text{if } \mathsf{m}_{i+1} = 1 \end{cases}$$

Note that ZF_{i+1} is a random function, given ZF_i and ZF'_i are two independent random functions. If an adversary $\mathcal{A}$ queries messages m with $\mathsf{m}_{i+1} = 1$ to EVAL and CHAL, then $\mathcal{A}$'s view in $\mathsf{H}_{i,2}$ is the same as that in $\mathsf{H}_{i,3}$. Thus, we only focus on messages with $\mathsf{m}_{i+1} = 0$.

For queries with CHAL, if $\mathsf{m}^*_{i+1} = 0$, $\mathcal{B}_2$ does not have $\mathbf{X}_{i+1,0} = \hat{\mathbf{X}} + \mathbf{A}_0^\perp \underline{\mathbf{D}}\overline{\mathbf{D}}^{-1}$, since $\mathcal{B}_2$ does not know $\underline{\mathbf{D}}\overline{\mathbf{D}}^{-1}$ either over $\mathbb{Z}_q$ or $\mathbb{G}_2$, but, since $\mathbf{h} \in \mathsf{Span}(\mathbf{A}_0)$ for such m^*, $(\mathbf{A}_0^\perp \underline{\mathbf{D}}\overline{\mathbf{D}}^{-1})^\top \mathbf{h} = \mathbf{0}$ and thus $\mathcal{B}_2$ computes

$$\mathbf{h}_0 = (\mathbf{X}_{\mathsf{m}\setminus i+1} + \hat{\mathbf{X}} + \mathbf{A}_0^\perp \underline{\mathbf{D}}\overline{\mathbf{D}}^{-1})^\top \mathbf{h} = (\mathbf{X}_{\mathsf{m}\setminus i+1} + \hat{\mathbf{X}})^\top \mathbf{h}.$$

Init:
$\mathbf{A}_0, \mathbf{A}_1 \xleftarrow{\$} \mathcal{U}_{2k,k}$
Compute $\mathbf{A}_0^\perp, \mathbf{A}_1^\perp \in \mathbb{Z}_q^{2k \times k}$ s.t.
$\mathbf{A}_0^\top \mathbf{A}_0^\perp = \mathbf{A}_1^\top \mathbf{A}_1^\perp = \mathbf{0}$
For $j = 1, ..., L$ and $\beta = 0, 1$:
  If $j \neq i+1$ or $\beta \neq 0$ then
    $\mathbf{X}_{j,\beta} \xleftarrow{\$} \mathbb{Z}_q^{2k \times k}$
$\widehat{\mathbf{X}} \xleftarrow{\$} \mathbb{Z}_q^{2k \times k}$
// $\mathbf{T}_\mathbf{D} := \underline{\mathbf{D}}\overline{\mathbf{D}}^{-1}$
// implicitly $\mathbf{X}_{i+1,0} := \widehat{\mathbf{X}} + \mathbf{A}_0^\perp \mathbf{T}_\mathbf{D}$
For all $\mathsf{m} \in \{0,1\}^L$:
  $\mathbf{X}_\mathsf{m} := \sum_{j=1}^{L} \mathbf{X}_{j,\mathsf{m}_j}$
  $\mathbf{X}_{\mathsf{m}\setminus(i+1)} := \sum_{j=1, j\neq i+1}^{L} \mathbf{X}_{j,\mathsf{m}_j}$
  $\mathbf{x}'_\mathsf{m} := \mathbf{A}_0^\perp \mathsf{ZF}_i(\mathsf{m}_{|i}) + \mathbf{A}_1^\perp \mathsf{OF}_i(\mathsf{m}_{|i})$
Return ϵ

Finalize($d \in \{0,1\}$):
Return $d \wedge (\mathcal{Q}_\mathcal{M} \cap \mathcal{C}_\mathcal{M} = \emptyset)$.

Eval(m): // c-th $\mathsf{m}_{|i}$
$\mathcal{Q}_\mathcal{M} := \mathcal{Q}_\mathcal{M} \cup \{\mathsf{m}\}$
If $([\mathbf{t}_\mathsf{m}]_2, [\mathbf{u}_\mathsf{m}]_2) = (\perp, \perp)$ then
  $\mathbf{s} \xleftarrow{\$} \mathbb{Z}_q^k$, $[\mathbf{t}_\mathsf{m}]_2 := [\overline{\mathbf{D}}\mathbf{s}]_2 + [\overline{\mathbf{f}_c}]_2$
  If $\mathsf{m}_{i+1} = 0$ then
    $[\delta]_2 := [\mathbf{A}_0^\perp \underline{\mathbf{f}_c}]_2 \in \mathbb{Z}_q^{2k}$
    $[\mathbf{u}_\mathsf{m}]_2 := [\mathbf{x}'_\mathsf{m} + (\mathbf{X}_{\mathsf{m}\setminus(i+1)} + \hat{\mathbf{X}})\mathbf{t}_\mathsf{m} + \mathbf{A}_0^\perp \underline{\mathbf{D}}\mathbf{s} + \delta]_2$
  If $\mathsf{m}_{i+1} = 1$ then
    $[\mathbf{u}_\mathsf{m}]_2 := [\mathbf{x}'_\mathsf{m} + \mathbf{X}_\mathsf{m}\mathbf{t}_\mathsf{m}]_2$
Return $([\mathbf{t}_\mathsf{m}]_2, [\mathbf{u}_\mathsf{m}]_2)$

Chal(m^*):
$\mathcal{C}_\mathcal{M} := \mathcal{C}_\mathcal{M} \cup \{\mathsf{m}^*\}$
$\mathbf{r} \xleftarrow{\$} \mathbb{Z}_q^k$; $\mathbf{h} := \mathbf{A}_{\mathsf{m}^*_{i+1}}\mathbf{r}$;
If $\mathsf{m}^*_{i+1} = 0$ then $\mathbf{h}_0 := (\mathbf{X}_{\mathsf{m}^*\setminus(i+1)} + \hat{\mathbf{X}})^\top \mathbf{h}$
If $\mathsf{m}^*_{i+1} = 1$ then $\mathbf{h}_0 := \mathbf{X}_{\mathsf{m}^*}^\top \mathbf{h}$
$h_1 := {\mathbf{x}'_{\mathsf{m}^*}}^\top \mathbf{h}$
Return $([\mathbf{h}]_1, [\mathbf{h}_0]_1, [h_1]_T)$

Fig. 5. Description of $\mathcal{B}_2(\mathsf{par}, ([\mathbf{D}]_2, [\mathbf{F}]_2))$ for proving Lemma 8.

For queries with Eval, if $\mathsf{m}_{i+1} = 0$, we write $\mathbf{f}_c := \begin{pmatrix} \overline{\mathbf{D}}\mathbf{w}_c \\ \underline{\mathbf{D}}\mathbf{w}_c + \mathbf{r}_c \end{pmatrix}$ for some $\mathbf{w}_c \in \mathbb{Z}_q^k$, where $\mathbf{r}_c \in \mathbb{Z}_q^k$ is $\mathbf{0}$ if $[\mathbf{F}]_2$ is from the real $\mathcal{U}_{2k,k}$-MDDH distribution, or $\mathbf{r}_c$ is random otherwise. Then, we have

$$\begin{aligned}
\mathbf{u}_\mathsf{m} &:= \mathbf{x}'_\mathsf{m} + \mathbf{X}_{\mathsf{m}\setminus(i+1)}\mathbf{t}_\mathsf{m} + \hat{\mathbf{X}}\mathbf{t}_\mathsf{m} + \mathbf{A}_0^\perp\underline{\mathbf{D}}\mathbf{s} + \mathbf{A}_0^\perp\underline{\mathbf{f}_c} \\
&= \mathbf{x}'_\mathsf{m} + \mathbf{X}_{\mathsf{m}\setminus(i+1)}\mathbf{t}_\mathsf{m} + \hat{\mathbf{X}}\mathbf{t}_\mathsf{m} + \mathbf{A}_0^\perp\underline{\mathbf{D}}\mathbf{s} + \mathbf{A}_0^\perp(\underline{\mathbf{D}}\mathbf{w}_c + \mathbf{r}_c) \\
&= \mathbf{x}'_\mathsf{m} + \mathbf{X}_{\mathsf{m}\setminus(i+1)}\mathbf{t}_\mathsf{m} + \hat{\mathbf{X}}\mathbf{t}_\mathsf{m} + \mathbf{A}_0^\perp\underline{\mathbf{D}}(\mathbf{s} + \mathbf{w}_c) + \mathbf{A}_0^\perp\mathbf{r}_c \\
&= \mathbf{x}'_\mathsf{m} + \mathbf{X}_{\mathsf{m}\setminus(i+1)}\mathbf{t}_\mathsf{m} + \hat{\mathbf{X}}\mathbf{t}_\mathsf{m} + \mathbf{A}_0^\perp\underline{\mathbf{D}}\overline{\mathbf{D}}^{-1}\underbrace{\overline{\mathbf{D}}(\mathbf{s} + \mathbf{w}_c)}_{\mathbf{t}_\mathsf{m}} + \mathbf{A}_0^\perp\mathbf{r}_c \\
&= \mathbf{X}_\mathsf{m}\mathbf{t}_\mathsf{m} + \underbrace{\mathbf{A}_1^\perp\mathsf{OF}_i(\mathsf{m}_{|i}) + \mathbf{A}_0^\perp\mathsf{ZF}_i(\mathsf{m}_{|i})}_{\mathbf{x}'_\mathsf{m}} + \mathbf{A}_0^\perp\mathbf{r}_c
\end{aligned}$$

Now it is clear that if $\mathbf{r}_c = \mathbf{0}$ then $\mathbf{u}_\mathsf{m}$ is distributed as in $\mathsf{H}_{i,2}$; if $\mathbf{r}_c$ is random, then we define $\mathsf{ZF}'_i(\mathsf{m}_{|i}) := \mathbf{r}_c$ and $\mathbf{u}_\mathsf{m}$ is distributed as in $\mathsf{H}_{i,3}$. □

The proof of Lemma 9 is very similar to that of Lemma 8 except that it handles cases with $\mathsf{m}_{i+1} = 1$. More precisely, we define

$$\mathsf{OF}_{i+1}(\mathsf{m}_{|i+1}) := \begin{cases} \mathsf{OF}_i(\mathsf{m}_{|i}) & \text{if } \mathsf{m}_{i+1} = 0 \\ \mathsf{OF}_i(\mathsf{m}_{|i}) + \mathsf{OF}'_i(\mathsf{m}_{|i}) & \text{if } \mathsf{m}_{i+1} = 1 \end{cases},$$

where $\mathsf{OF}_i, \mathsf{OF}'_i$ are two independent random functions mapping from $\{0,1\}^i$ to $\mathbb{Z}_q^k$. By the similar arguments of Lemma 8, we have the following lemma.

Lemma 9 **($\mathsf{H}_{i,3}$ to $\mathsf{H}_{i,4}$).** *If the $\mathcal{U}_{2k,k}$-MDDH problem is (t_2, ε_2)-hard in $\mathbb{G}_2$, then* $|\Pr[\mathsf{H}_{i,3}^{\mathcal{A}} \Rightarrow 1] - \Pr[\mathsf{H}_{i,4}^{\mathcal{A}} \Rightarrow 1]| \le \varepsilon_2 + 2^{-\Omega(\lambda)}$ *and* $t_2 \approx t_{\mathcal{A}}$.

Lemmata 10 and 11 are the reverse of Lemmata 6 and 7, and we omit the detailed proofs.

Lemma 10 **($\mathsf{H}_{i,4}$ to $\mathsf{H}_{i,5}$).** $|\Pr[\mathsf{H}_{i,4}^{\mathcal{A}} \Rightarrow 1] - \Pr[\mathsf{H}_{i,5}^{\mathcal{A}} \Rightarrow 1]| \le 2^{-\Omega(\lambda)}$.

Lemma 11 **($\mathsf{H}_{i,5}$ to $\mathsf{G}_{1,i+1}$).** *If the $\mathcal{U}_{2k,k}$-MDDH problem is (t_1, ε_1)-hard in $\mathbb{G}_1$, then* $|\Pr[\mathsf{H}_{i,5}^{\mathcal{A}} \Rightarrow 1] - \Pr[\mathsf{G}_{1,i+1}^{\mathcal{A}} \Rightarrow 1]| \le 2\varepsilon_1 + 2^{-\Omega(\lambda)}$ *and* $t_2 \approx t_{\mathcal{A}} + (Q_{\mathsf{e}} + Q_{\mathsf{c}})\mathsf{poly}(\lambda)$, *where* $\mathsf{poly}(\lambda)$ *is independent of* $t_{\mathcal{A}}$.

Lemma 12 **($\mathsf{G}_{1,L}$ to G_2).** *If the $\mathcal{U}_{2k}$-MDDH problem is (t_3, ε_3)-hard in $\mathbb{G}_1$, then*

$$|\Pr[\mathsf{G}_{1,L}^{\mathcal{A}} \Rightarrow 1] - \Pr[\mathsf{G}_2^{\mathcal{A}} \Rightarrow 1]| \le 3\varepsilon_3 + 2^{-\Omega(\lambda)} \text{ and } t_3 \approx t_{\mathcal{A}} + (Q_{\mathsf{e}} + Q_{\mathsf{c}})\mathsf{poly}(\lambda),$$

where $\mathsf{poly}(\lambda)$ *is independent of* $t_{\mathcal{A}}$.

Proof. Firstly we bound the difference between $\mathsf{G}_{1,L}$ and $\mathsf{G}_{2'}$ by the Q_{c}-fold $\mathcal{U}_{2k}$-MDDH assumption in $\mathbb{G}_1$, where G'_2 is the same as $\mathsf{G}_{1,L}$ except that on a challenge query, we pick a random $h_1 \xleftarrow{\$} \mathbb{Z}_q$ for each query in G'_2.

Formally, on receiving a Q_{c}-fold $\mathcal{U}_{2k}$-MDDH challenge $([\mathbf{D}]_1, [\mathbf{F}]_1 := ([\mathbf{f}_1, \cdots, \mathbf{f}_{Q_{\mathsf{c}}}]_1)) \in \mathbb{G}_1^{(2k+1)\times 2k} \times \mathbb{G}_1^{(2k+1)\times Q_{\mathsf{c}}}$, where Q_{c} denotes the number of challenge queries, we construct a reduction $\mathcal{B}_2$ as in Fig. 6.

For Eval queries, since $\mathbf{u}_{\mathsf{m}}$ is information-theoretically hidden by $\mathsf{RF}(\mathsf{m})$, we can just pick $\mathbf{u}_{\mathsf{m}}$ uniformly random. For Chal queries, we write $\mathbf{f}_c :=$

Init:	**Chal(m^*):** // c-th query
$\mathbf{A} \xleftarrow{\$} \mathcal{U}_{2k,k}$; $\mathbf{B} := \overline{\mathbf{A}}$	$\mathcal{C}_{\mathcal{M}} := \mathcal{C}_{\mathcal{M}} \cup \{\mathsf{m}^*\}$
For $(j, \beta) \in ([L], \{0,1\})$:	If $\mathsf{RF}'(\mathsf{m}^*) = \perp$, then
$\quad \mathbf{X}_{j,\beta} \xleftarrow{\$} \mathbb{Z}_q^{2k \times k}$	$\quad \mathsf{RF}'(\mathsf{m}^*) \xleftarrow{\$} \mathbb{Z}_q^{2k}$
For all $\mathsf{m} \in \{0,1\}^L$:	$\quad \mathcal{RL} := \mathcal{RL} \cup \{(\mathsf{m}^*, \mathsf{RF}'(\mathsf{m}^*))\}$
$\quad \mathbf{X}_{\mathsf{m}} := \sum_{j=1}^{L} \mathbf{X}_{j,\mathsf{m}_j}$	$[\mathbf{h}]_1 := [\overline{\mathbf{f}_c}]_1$; $[\mathbf{h}_0]_1 := [\mathbf{X}_{\mathsf{m}^*}^{\top}\mathbf{h}]_1$;
Return ϵ	$[h_1]_1 := [\mathsf{RF}'(\mathsf{m}^*)^{\top}\overline{\mathbf{f}_c} + \underline{\mathbf{f}_c}]_1$;
	// implicitly set $\mathsf{RF}(\mathsf{m}^*) := \mathsf{RF}'(\mathsf{m}^*) + (\underline{\mathbf{D}}\overline{\mathbf{D}}^{-1})^{\top}$
Eval(m):	Return $([\mathbf{h}]_1, [\mathbf{h}_0]_1, [h_1]_T)$
$\mathcal{Q}_{\mathcal{M}} := \mathcal{Q}_{\mathcal{M}} \cup \{\mathsf{m}\}$	
If $([\mathbf{t}_{\mathsf{m}}]_2, [\mathbf{u}_{\mathsf{m}}]_2) = (\perp, \perp)$ then	**Finalize($d \in \{0,1\}$):**
$\quad \mathbf{t}_{\mathsf{m}} \xleftarrow{\$} \mathbb{Z}_q^k$; $\mathbf{u}_{\mathsf{m}} \xleftarrow{\$} \mathbb{Z}_q^{2k}$	Return $d \wedge (\mathcal{Q}_{\mathcal{M}} \cap \mathcal{C}_{\mathcal{M}} = \emptyset)$.
Return $([\mathbf{t}_{\mathsf{m}}]_2, [\mathbf{u}_{\mathsf{m}}]_2)$	

Fig. 6. Description of $\mathcal{B}'(\mathcal{G}_1, ([\mathbf{D}]_1, [\mathbf{F}]_1)$ interpolating between G'_2 and $\mathsf{G}_{1,L}$.

<u>INIT:</u> for $(j,\beta) \neq (1,0)$: $\mathbf{X}_{j,\beta} \xleftarrow{\$} \mathbb{Z}_q^{2k \times k}$ For all $\mathsf{m} \in \{0,1\}^L$: $\quad \mathbf{X}_{\mathsf{m}} := \sum_{j=1}^{m} \mathbf{X}_{j,\mathsf{m}_j}$ $\quad \mathbf{X}_{\mathsf{m}\backslash 1} := \sum_{j=2}^{m} \mathbf{X}_{j,\mathsf{m}_j}$ Return ϵ <u>EVAL(m):</u> $\mathcal{Q}_{\mathcal{M}} := \mathcal{Q}_{\mathcal{M}} \cup \{\mathsf{m}\}$ If $([\mathbf{t}_{\mathsf{m}}]_2, [\mathbf{u}_{\mathsf{m}}]_2) = (\perp, \perp)$ then $\quad \mathbf{t}_{\mathsf{m}} \xleftarrow{\$} \mathbb{Z}_q^k, \quad \mathbf{u}_{\mathsf{m}} \xleftarrow{\$} \mathbb{Z}_q^{2k}$ Return $([\mathbf{t}_{\mathsf{m}}]_2, [\mathbf{u}_{\mathsf{m}}]_2)$	<u>CHAL(m*):</u> // c-th query $\mathcal{C}_{\mathcal{M}} := \mathcal{C}_{\mathcal{M}} \cup \{\mathsf{m}^*\}$; $[\mathbf{h}]_1 := [\overline{\mathbf{f}_c}]_1$; If $\mathsf{m}_1^* = 1$ then $[\mathbf{h}_0]_1 := [\mathbf{X}_{\mathsf{m}^*}^\top \mathbf{h}]_1$ If $\mathsf{m}_1^* = 0$ then $[\mathbf{h}_0]_1 := [\mathbf{X}_{\mathsf{m}^*\backslash 1}^\top \mathbf{h}]_1 + [\underline{\mathbf{f}_c}]_1$; $h_1 \xleftarrow{\$} \mathbb{Z}_q$; // here we implicitly set $\mathbf{X}_{1,0} := (\underline{\mathbf{D}}\overline{\mathbf{D}}^{-1})^\top$; Return $([\mathbf{h}]_1, [\mathbf{h}_0]_1, [h_1]_T)$ <u>FINALIZE($d \in \{0,1\}$):</u> Return $d \wedge (\mathcal{Q}_{\mathcal{M}} \cap \mathcal{C}_{\mathcal{M}} = \emptyset)$

Fig. 7. Description of $\mathcal{B}'(\mathcal{G}_1, ([\mathbf{D}]_1, [\mathbf{F}]_1)$ interpolating between G_2'' and G_2'.

$\begin{pmatrix} \overline{\mathbf{D}}\mathbf{w}_c \\ \underline{\mathbf{D}}\mathbf{w}_c + r_c \end{pmatrix}$ for some $\mathbf{w}_c \in \mathbb{Z}_q^{2k}$, where $r_c \in \mathbb{Z}_q$ is 0 if $[\mathbf{F}]_2$ is from the real $\mathcal{U}_{2k}$-MDDH distribution, and r_c is random otherwise. Then, we have

$$\begin{aligned} h_1 &:= \mathsf{RF}'(\mathsf{m}^*)^\top \overline{\mathbf{f}_c} + \underline{\mathbf{f}_c} = \mathsf{RF}'(\mathsf{m}^*)^\top \overline{\mathbf{f}_c} + \underline{\mathbf{D}}\mathbf{w}_c + r_c \\ &= \mathsf{RF}'(\mathsf{m}^*)^\top \overline{\mathbf{f}_c} + \underline{\mathbf{D}}\overline{\mathbf{D}}^{-1}\overline{\mathbf{f}_c} + r_c = \underbrace{(\mathsf{RF}'(\mathsf{m}^*)^\top + \underline{\mathbf{D}}\overline{\mathbf{D}}^{-1})}_{\mathsf{RF}(\mathsf{m}^*)^\top} \overline{\mathbf{f}_c} + r_c. \end{aligned}$$

If $r_c = 0$ then h_1 is distributed as in $\mathsf{G}_{1,L}$; if r_c is random then h_1 is distributed as in G_2'.

Next we bound the difference between G_2' and G_2'' by the Q_c-fold $\mathcal{U}_{3k,2k}$-MDDH assumption in $\mathbb{G}_1$, where G_2'' is the same as G_2' except that when answering CHAL with $\mathsf{m}_1^* = 0$, one picks a random $\mathbf{h}_0 \xleftarrow{\$} \mathbb{Z}_q^k$ for each query. And the difference between G_2' and G_2'' can be bounded by the Q_c-fold $\mathcal{U}_{3k,2k}$-MDDH assumption in $\mathbb{G}_1$. Formally, on receiving a Q_c-fold $\mathcal{U}_{3k,2k}$-MDDH challenge $([\mathbf{D}]_1, [\mathbf{F}]_1 := ([\mathbf{f}_1, \cdots, \mathbf{f}_{Q_c}]_1)) \in \mathbb{G}_1^{3k \times 2k} \times \mathbb{G}_1^{3k \times Q_c}$, where Q_c denotes the number of challenge queries, we construct a reduction $\mathcal{B}_2$ as in Fig. 7.

For EVAL(m) queries, since $\mathbf{u}_{\mathsf{m}}$ is information-theoretically hidden by $\mathsf{RF}(\mathsf{m})$, here we just pick $\mathbf{u}_{\mathsf{m}}$ uniformly random.

For CHAL(m*) queries, if $\mathsf{m}_1^* = 1$, G_2'' and G_2' are the same, if $\mathsf{m}_1^* = 0$, we write $\mathbf{f}_c := \begin{pmatrix} \overline{\mathbf{D}}\mathbf{w}_c \\ \underline{\mathbf{D}}\mathbf{w}_c + \mathbf{r}_c \end{pmatrix}$ for some $\mathbf{w}_c \in \mathbb{Z}_q^{2k}$, where $\mathbf{r}_c \in \mathbb{Z}_q^k$ is $\mathbf{0}$ if $[\mathbf{F}]_2$ is from the real $\mathcal{U}_{3k,2k}$-MDDH distribution, and $\mathbf{r}_c$ is random otherwise. Then, we have

$$\begin{aligned} \mathbf{h}_0 &:= \mathbf{X}_{\mathsf{m}^*\backslash 1}^\top \mathbf{h} + \underline{\mathbf{f}_c} = \mathbf{X}_{\mathsf{m}^*\backslash 1}^\top \mathbf{h} + \underline{\mathbf{D}}\mathbf{w}_c + \mathbf{r}_c = \mathbf{X}_{\mathsf{m}^*\backslash 1}^\top \mathbf{h} + \underline{\mathbf{D}}\overline{\mathbf{D}}^{-1}\overline{\mathbf{f}_c} + \mathbf{r}_c \\ &= \underbrace{(\mathbf{X}_{\mathsf{m}^*\backslash 1}^\top + \underline{\mathbf{D}}\overline{\mathbf{D}}^{-1})}_{\mathbf{X}_{\mathsf{m}^*}^\top} \overline{\mathbf{f}_c} + \mathbf{r}_c. \end{aligned}$$

If $\mathbf{r}_c = \mathbf{0}$ then $\mathbf{h}_0$ is distributed as in G_2'; if $\mathbf{r}_c$ is random then $\mathbf{h}_0$ is distributed as in G_2''. The difference between G_2'' and G_2 can be bounded by the Q_c-fold $\mathcal{U}_{3k,2k}$-MDDH assumption in a similar way. □

□

We perform all the previous changes of Fig. 2 in a reverse order without changing the simulation of CHAL. Then we have the following lemma.

Lemma 13 (G_2 **to** G_3)**.** *If the* $\mathcal{U}_{3k,k}$-MDDH *problem is* (t_2, ε_2)*-hard in* $\mathbb{G}_2$*, then* $|\Pr[\mathsf{G}_2^{\mathcal{A}} \Rightarrow 1] - \Pr[\mathsf{mPR\text{-}CMA}_1^{\mathcal{A}} \Rightarrow 1]| \leq L\varepsilon_2 + 2^{-\Omega(\lambda)}$ *and* $t_1 \approx t_2 \approx t_{\mathcal{A}} + (Q_e + Q_c)\mathsf{poly}(\lambda)$*, where* $\mathsf{poly}(\lambda)$ *is independent of* $t_{\mathcal{A}}$.

By observing G_3 is the same as $\mathsf{mPR\text{-}CMA}_1$, we sum up Lemmata 4 to 13 and conclude Theorem 1. □

4 Quasi-adaptive Zero-Knowledge Arguments for Linear Subspaces

4.1 Definition

The notion of quasi-adaptive non-interactive zero knowledge arguments (QANIZK) is proposed by Jutla and Roy [33], where the common reference string CRS depends on the specific language for which proofs are generated. In the following we define a tag-based variant of QANIZK [17,34]. For simplicity, we only consider arguments for linear subspaces.

Let par be the public parameters for QANIZK and $\mathcal{D}_{\mathsf{par}}$ be a probability distribution over a collection of relations $R = \{R_{[\mathbf{M}]_1}\}$ parametrized by a matrix $[\mathbf{M}]_1 \in \mathbb{G}_1^{n \times t}$ $(n > t)$ with associated language $\mathcal{L}_{[\mathbf{M}]_1} = \{[\mathbf{c}_0]_1 : \exists \mathbf{r} \in \mathbb{Z}_q^t, \text{ s.t. } [\mathbf{c}_0]_1 = [\mathbf{Mr}]_1\}$. We consider witness sampleable distributions [33] where there is an efficiently sampleable distribution $\mathcal{D}'_{\mathsf{par}}$ outputs $\mathbf{M}' \in \mathbb{Z}_q^{n \times t}$ such that $[\mathbf{M}']_1$ distributes the same as $[\mathbf{M}]_1$. We note that the matrix distribution in Definition 2 is sampleable.

Definition 8 (Tag-based QANIZK**).** *A tag-based quasi-adaptive non-interactive zero-knowledge argument (*QANIZK*) for a language distribution* $\mathcal{D}_{\mathsf{par}}$ *consists of four PPT algorithms* $\Pi = (\mathsf{Gen}_{\mathsf{NIZK}}, \mathsf{Prove}, \mathsf{Ver}_{\mathsf{NIZK}}, \mathsf{Sim})$.

- *The key generation algorithm* $\mathsf{Gen}_{\mathsf{NIZK}}(\mathsf{par}, [\mathbf{M}]_1)$ *returns a common reference string* crs *and the trapdoor* td*, where* crs *defines a tag space* $\mathcal{T}$.
- *The proving algorithm* $\mathsf{Prove}(\mathsf{crs}, \mathsf{tag}, [\mathbf{c}_0]_1, \mathbf{r})$ *returns a proof* π.
- *The deterministic verification algorithm* $\mathsf{Ver}_{\mathsf{NIZK}}(\mathsf{crs}, \mathsf{tag}, [\mathbf{c}_0]_1, \pi)$ *returns 1 or 0, where* 1 *indicates that* π *is a valid proof for* $[\mathbf{c}_0]_1 \in \mathcal{L}_{[\mathbf{M}]_1}$.
- *The simulation algorithm* $\mathsf{Sim}(\mathsf{crs}, \mathsf{td}, \mathsf{tag}, [\mathbf{c}_0]_1)$ *returns a proof* π *for* $[\mathbf{c}_0]_1 \in \mathcal{L}_{[\mathbf{M}]_1}$.

(Perfect Completeness.) For all λ*, all* $[\mathbf{M}]_1$*, all* $([\mathbf{c}_0]_1, \mathbf{r})$ *with* $[\mathbf{c}_0]_1 = [\mathbf{Mr}]_1$*, all* $(\mathsf{crs}, \mathsf{td}) \in \mathsf{Gen}_{\mathsf{NIZK}}(\mathsf{par}, [\mathbf{M}]_1)$*, and all* $\pi \in \mathsf{Prove}(\mathsf{crs}, \mathsf{tag}, [\mathbf{c}_0]_1, \mathbf{r})$*, we have* $\mathsf{Ver}_{\mathsf{NIZK}}(\mathsf{crs}, \mathsf{tag}, [\mathbf{c}_0]_1, \pi) = 1$.

$\textsc{Init}(\mathbf{M})$:	$\textsc{Finalize}(\mathsf{tag}^*, [\mathbf{c}_0^*]_1, \pi^*)$:
$(\mathsf{crs}, \mathsf{td}) \xleftarrow{\$} \mathsf{Gen}_{\mathsf{NIZK}}(\mathsf{par}, [\mathbf{M}]_1)$	If $\mathsf{Ver}_{\mathsf{NIZK}}(\mathsf{crs}, \mathsf{tag}^*, [\mathbf{c}_0^*]_1, \pi^*) = 1 \wedge [\mathbf{c}_0^*]_1 \notin \mathcal{L}_{[\mathbf{M}]_1} \wedge (\mathsf{tag}^*, [\mathbf{c}_0^*]_1, \pi^*) \notin \mathcal{P}$ then
Return crs.	return 1
$\textsc{Sim}(\mathsf{tag}, [\mathbf{c}_0]_1)$: // Q_{s} queries	Else return 0
$\pi \xleftarrow{\$} \mathsf{Sim}(\mathsf{crs}, \mathsf{td}, \mathsf{tag}, [\mathbf{c}_0]_1)$;	
$\mathcal{P} := \mathcal{P} \cup (\mathsf{tag}, [\mathbf{c}_0]_1, \pi)$;	
Return π	

Fig. 8. USS security game for QANIZK

We require Π to have the following security. Here we require a stronger version of unbounded simulation soundness than the usual one in [17,34], where an adversary is allowed to submit a forgery with a reused tag.

Definition 9 (Perfect Zero-Knowledge). *A tag-based* QANIZK Π *is perfectly zero-knowledge if for all* λ, *all* $[\mathbf{M}]_1$, *all* $([\mathbf{c}_0]_1, \mathbf{r})$ *with* $[\mathbf{c}_0]_1 = [\mathbf{Mr}]_1$, *and all* $(\mathsf{crs}, \mathsf{td}) \in \mathsf{Gen}_{\mathsf{NIZK}}(\mathsf{par}, [\mathbf{M}]_1)$, *the following two distributions are identical:*

$$\mathsf{Prove}(\mathsf{crs}, \mathsf{tag}, [\mathbf{c}_0]_1, \mathbf{r}) \ \textit{and}\ \mathsf{Sim}(\mathsf{crs}, \mathsf{td}, \mathsf{tag}, [\mathbf{c}_0]_1).$$

Definition 10 (Unbounded Simulation Soundness). *A tag-based* QANIZK Π *is* $(Q_{\mathsf{s}}, t, \varepsilon)$*-unbounded simulation sound* (USS) *if for any adversary* $\mathcal{A}$ *that runs in time* t, *it holds that* $\Pr[\mathsf{USS}^{\mathcal{A}} \Rightarrow 1] \leq \varepsilon$, *where Game* USS *is defined in Fig. 8.*

4.2 Construction: QANIZK with Unbounded Simulation Soundness

We (slightly) modify the QANIZK scheme in [17] to achieve our stronger unbounded simulation soundness (as in Definition 10). Let $\mathsf{par} := (\mathbb{G}_1, \mathbb{G}_2, \mathbb{G}_T, q, P_1, P_2, e, H)$ be the system parameter, where $H : \mathcal{T} \times \mathbb{G}_1^{n+k} \to \{0,1\}^{\lambda}$ is chosen uniformly from a collision-resistant hash function family $\mathcal{H}$. Our QANIZK scheme Π is defined as in Figure 9.

Theorem 2. *The QANIZK system* Π_{uss} *defined in Fig. 9 has perfect completeness and perfect zero-knowledge. Suppose in addition that the distribution of matrix* $\mathbf{M}$ *is witness sampleable, the* $\mathcal{D}_k$-MDDH *is* (t_1, ε_1)*-hard in* $\mathbb{G}_1$, *the* $\mathcal{D}_k$-KerMDH *is* (t_2, ε_2)*-hard in* $\mathbb{G}_2$, $\mathcal{H}$ *is a* (t_3, ε_3)*-collision resistant hash function family, then* Π_{uss} *is* (t, ε)-USS, *where* $t_1 \approx t_2 \approx t_3 \approx t + Q_{\mathsf{s}}\mathsf{poly}(\lambda)$, *and* $\varepsilon \leq \varepsilon_2 + 4\lambda\varepsilon_1 + \varepsilon_3 + 2^{-\Omega(\lambda)}$, $\mathsf{poly}(\lambda)$ *is a polynomial independent of* t.

The proof is similar to that of [17] and we give the formal proof in the full version.

$\mathsf{Gen}_{\mathsf{NIZK}}(\mathsf{par}, [\mathbf{M}]_1 \in \mathbb{G}_1^{n \times t})$:
$\mathbf{A}, \mathbf{B} \xleftarrow{\$} \mathcal{D}_k, \mathbf{K} \xleftarrow{\$} \mathbb{Z}_q^{n \times (k+1)}\ H \xleftarrow{\$} \mathcal{H}$
For $j = 1, .., \lambda$ and $b = 0, 1$:
$\quad \mathbf{K}_{j,b} \xleftarrow{\$} \mathbb{Z}_q^{k \times (k+1)}$
$\mathsf{crs} := ([\mathbf{A}]_2, [\mathbf{KA}]_2, [\overline{\mathbf{B}}]_1, [\mathbf{M}^\top \mathbf{K}]_1,$
$([\mathbf{K}_{j,b}\mathbf{A}]_2, [\overline{\mathbf{B}}\mathbf{K}_{j,b}]_1)_{1 \le j \le \lambda, 0 \le b \le 1}, H)$
$\mathsf{td} := \mathbf{K}$
Return $(\mathsf{crs}, \mathsf{td})$

$\mathsf{Ver}_{\mathsf{NIZK}}(\mathsf{crs}, \mathsf{tag}, [\mathbf{c}_0]_1, \pi)$:
Parse $\pi = ([\mathbf{t}]_1, [\mathbf{u}]_1)$
$\tau := H(\mathsf{tag}, [\mathbf{c}_0]_1, [\mathbf{t}]_1)$
$\mathbf{K}_\tau := \sum_{j=1}^{\lambda} \mathbf{K}_{j,\tau_j}$
If $[\mathbf{u}]_1 \circ [\mathbf{A}]_2 = [\mathbf{c}_0^\top]_1 \circ [\mathbf{KA}]_2 + [\mathbf{t}^\top]_1 \circ [\mathbf{K}_\tau \mathbf{A}]_2$, then
$\quad$ return 1
Else return 0

$\mathsf{Prove}(\mathsf{crs}, \mathsf{tag}, [\mathbf{c}_0]_1, \mathbf{r})$: // $\mathbf{c}_0 = \mathbf{Mr} \in \mathbb{Z}_q^n$
$\mathbf{s} \xleftarrow{\$} \mathbb{Z}_q^k, [\mathbf{t}]_1 := [\overline{\mathbf{B}}\mathbf{s}]_1 \in \mathbb{G}_1^k$
$\tau := H(\mathsf{tag}, [\mathbf{c}_0]_1, [\mathbf{t}]_1)$
$[\overline{\mathbf{B}}^\top \mathbf{K}_\tau]_1 := [\sum_{j=1}^{\lambda} \overline{\mathbf{B}}^\top \mathbf{K}_{j,\tau_j}]_1$
$[\mathbf{u}]_1 := [\mathbf{r}^\top \cdot \mathbf{M}^\top \mathbf{K}]_1 + [\mathbf{s}^\top \cdot (\overline{\mathbf{B}}^\top \mathbf{K}_\tau)]_1$
Return $\pi := ([\mathbf{t}]_1, [\mathbf{u}]_1) \in \mathbb{G}_1^k \times \mathbb{G}_1^{1 \times (k+1)}$

$\mathsf{Sim}(\mathsf{crs}, \mathsf{td}, \mathsf{tag}, [\mathbf{c}_0]_1)$:
$\mathbf{s} \xleftarrow{\$} \mathbb{Z}_q^k, [\mathbf{t}]_1 := [\overline{\mathbf{B}}\mathbf{s}]_1 \in \mathbb{G}_1^k$
$\tau := H(\mathsf{tag}, [\mathbf{c}_0]_1, [\mathbf{t}]_1)$
$[\overline{\mathbf{B}}^\top \mathbf{K}_\tau]_1 := [\sum_{j=1}^{\lambda} \overline{\mathbf{B}}^\top \mathbf{K}_{j,\tau_j}]_1$
$[\mathbf{u}]_1 := [\mathbf{c}_0^\top \cdot \mathbf{K}]_1 + [\mathbf{s}^\top (\overline{\mathbf{B}}^\top \mathbf{K}_\tau)]_1$
Return $\pi := ([\mathbf{t}]_1, [\mathbf{u}]_1) \in \mathbb{G}_1^k \times \mathbb{G}_1^{1 \times (k+1)}$

Fig. 9. Construction of Π_{uss}.

5 Identity-Based Key Encapsulation Mechanism

We give our generic construction of an identity-based key encapsulation mechanism (IBKEM) from an affine MAC. Here we only focus on IBKEMs, since, even in the multi-instance, multi-challenge setting, a constrained CCA (resp. CPA) secure IBKEM can be transformed to a CCA (resp. CPA) secure identity-based encryption (IBE) in an efficient and tightly secure way by using an authenticated symmetric encryption scheme. One can prove this by adapting the known techniques from [20, 30] in a straightforward way.

5.1 Definition

Let par be a set of system parameters.

Definition 11 (Identity-based key encapsulation mechanism). *An identity-based key encapsulation mechanism (IBKEM) has four algorithms* $\mathsf{IBKEM} := (\mathsf{Setup}, \mathsf{Ext}, \mathsf{Enc}, \mathsf{Dec})$ *with the following properties:*

- *The key generation algorithm* $\mathsf{Setup}(\mathsf{par})$ *returns the (master) public/secret key* $(\mathsf{pk}, \mathsf{sk})$. *We assume that* pk *implicitly defines an identity space* $\mathcal{ID}$, *a symmetric key space* $\mathcal{K}$, *and a ciphertext space* $\mathcal{C}$.
- *The user secret-key generation algorithm* $\mathsf{Ext}(\mathsf{sk}, \mathsf{id})$ *returns a user secret key* $\mathsf{usk}[\mathsf{id}]$ *for an identity* $\mathsf{id} \in \mathcal{ID}$.
- *The encapsulation algorithm* $\mathsf{Enc}(\mathsf{pk}, \mathsf{id})$ *returns a symmetric key* $\mathsf{K} \in \mathcal{K}$ *together with a ciphertext* $\mathsf{C} \in \mathcal{C}$ *with respect to identity* id.
- *The deterministic decapsulation algorithm* $\mathsf{Dec}(\mathsf{usk}[\mathsf{id}], \mathsf{id}, \mathsf{C})$ *returns the decapsulated key* $\mathsf{K} \in \mathcal{K}$ *or the rejection symbol* $\perp$.

(Perfect correctness). *We require that for all pairs* $(\mathsf{pk},\mathsf{sk}) \xleftarrow{\$} \mathsf{Setup}(\mathsf{par})$, *all identities* $\mathsf{id} \in \mathcal{ID}$, *all* $\mathsf{usk}[\mathsf{id}] \xleftarrow{\$} \mathsf{Ext}(\mathsf{sk},\mathsf{id})$ *and all* $(\mathsf{K},\mathsf{C}) \xleftarrow{\$} \mathsf{Enc}(\mathsf{pk},\mathsf{id})$, $\Pr[\mathsf{Dec}(\mathsf{usk}[\mathsf{id}],\mathsf{id},\mathsf{C}) = \mathsf{K}] = 1$.

We define indistinguishability against constrained chosen-ciphertext and chosen-identity attacks for IBKEM in the multi-challenge setting.

Definition 12 **(mID-CCCA security).** *An identity-based key encapsulation scheme* IBKEM *is* $(Q_{\mathsf{ext}}, Q_{\mathsf{enc}}, Q_{\mathsf{dec}}, t, \varepsilon)$*-mID-CCCA-secure if for all* $\mathcal{A}$ *with negligible* $\mathsf{uncert}(\mathcal{A})$ *that runs in time* t*, makes at most* Q_{ext} *user secret-key queries,* Q_{enc} *encryption queries and* Q_{dec} *decryption queries,*

$$|\Pr[\mathsf{mID\text{-}CCCA}_0^{\mathcal{A}} \Rightarrow 1] - \Pr[\mathsf{mID\text{-}CCCA}_1^{\mathcal{A}} \Rightarrow 1]| \leq \varepsilon,$$

where the security game is defined as in Fig. 10, here $\mathsf{pred}_i : \mathcal{K} \to \{0,1\}$ *denotes the predicate sent in the* i*th decryption query, the* uncertainty of knowledge about keys *corresponding to decryption queries is defined as*

$$\mathsf{uncert}(\mathcal{A}) := \frac{1}{Q_{\mathsf{dec}}} \sum_{i=1}^{Q_{\mathsf{dec}}} \Pr_{\mathsf{K} \xleftarrow{\$} \mathcal{K}}[\mathsf{pred}_i(\mathsf{K}) = 1].$$

If an adversary is not allowed to query Dec, then we get the security notion of indistinguishability against chosen-plaintext and chosen-identity attacks.

Definition 13 **(mID-CPA security).** *An identity-based key encapsulation scheme* IBKEM *is* $(Q_{\mathsf{ext}}, Q_{\mathsf{enc}}, t, \varepsilon)$*-mID-CPA-secure if* IBKEM *is* $(Q_{\mathsf{ext}}, Q_{\mathsf{enc}}, 0, t, \varepsilon)$*-mID-CCCA-secure.*

*Remark 1 (*Ext *queries with the same identity).* For simplicity, we assume that an adversary can query Ext with the same identity at most once. This is without

<u>Init:</u>
$(\mathsf{pk},\mathsf{sk}) \xleftarrow{\$} \mathsf{Setup}(\mathsf{par})$
Return pk
 	
<u>Dec$(\mathsf{id}_i, \mathsf{C}_i, \mathsf{pred}_i)$:</u> // at most Q_{dec} queries
$\mathsf{usk}[\mathsf{id}_i] \xleftarrow{\$} \mathsf{Ext}(\mathsf{sk},\mathsf{id}_i)$
$\mathsf{K}_i \leftarrow \mathsf{Dec}(\mathsf{usk}[\mathsf{id}_i], \mathsf{id}_i, \mathsf{C}_i)$
If $(\mathsf{id}_i, \mathsf{C}_i) \notin \mathcal{C}_{\mathsf{enc}}$ and $\mathsf{pred}_i(\mathsf{K}_i) = 1$ then
  return K_i
Else return $\perp$
 	
<u>Finalize(d):</u>
Return $d \wedge (\mathcal{Q}_{\mathsf{usk}} \cap \mathcal{Q}_{\mathsf{enc}} = \emptyset)$
	<u>Enc(id^*):</u> // at most Q_{enc} queries
	$\mathcal{Q}_{\mathsf{enc}} := \mathcal{Q}_{\mathsf{enc}} \cup \{\mathsf{id}^*\}$
	$(\mathsf{C},\mathsf{K}) \xleftarrow{\$} \mathsf{Enc}(\mathsf{pk},\mathsf{id}^*)$
	$\mathsf{K} \xleftarrow{\$} \mathcal{K}$
	Return (C,K)
	
	<u>Ext(id):</u> // at most Q_{ext} queries
	$\mathcal{Q}_{\mathsf{usk}} := \mathcal{Q}_{\mathsf{usk}} \cup \{\mathsf{id}\}$
	If $\mathsf{usk}[\mathsf{id}] = \perp$ then
	  $\mathsf{usk}[\mathsf{id}] \xleftarrow{\$} \mathsf{Ext}(\mathsf{sk},\mathsf{id})$
	Return $\mathsf{usk}[\mathsf{id}]$

Fig. 10. Games $\mathsf{mID\text{-}CCCA}_0$ and $\mathsf{mID\text{-}CCCA}_1$ for defining mID-CCCA-security.

loss of generality when assuming that the scheme is made deterministic, e.g., by generating the randomness in EXT with a (tightly secure) pseudorandom function such as the Naor-Reingold PRF [40]. Thus the anonymity we achieve here is usually called weak anonymity [22].

Remark 2 (On $\mathsf{uncert}(\mathcal{A})$*).* When we prove the IND-CCA security of the hybrid IBE scheme by combining an IND-CCCA secure ID-KEM together with an unconditionally one-time secure authenticated encryption scheme AE, the term $(Q_{\mathsf{dec}} + Q_{\mathsf{enc}})\mathsf{uncert}(\mathcal{A})$ is related to the one-time integrity of AE and can be made exponentially small (since it does not necessarily rely on any computational assumption). Hence, in line with previous works (e.g., [17]), we still call our reduction (almost) tight.

5.2 Two Transformations

We construct two generic transformations of IBKEM from affine MACs, IBKEM_1 and IBKEM_2. Let $\mathsf{par} := (\mathbb{G}_1, \mathbb{G}_2, \mathbb{G}_T, q, P_1, P_2, e)$, $\mathsf{MAC} := (\mathsf{Gen}_{\mathsf{MAC}}, \mathsf{Tag}, \mathsf{Ver}_{\mathsf{MAC}})$ be an affine MAC and $\Pi := (\mathsf{Gen}_{\mathsf{NIZK}}, \mathsf{Prove}, \mathsf{Ver}_{\mathsf{NIZK}}, \mathsf{Sim})$ be a QANIZK system for linear language $\mathcal{L}_{[\mathbf{M}]_1} := \{[\mathbf{c}_0]_1 : \exists \mathbf{r} \in \mathbb{Z}_q^k \text{ s.t. } \mathbf{c}_0 = \mathbf{M}\mathbf{r}\}$, where $\mathbf{M} \in \mathcal{U}_{k+\eta,k}$. Our IBKEMs IBKEM_1 and IBKEM_2 are defined in Fig. 11.

It is worth mentioning that if we instantiate our schemes with the SXDH assumption then we have: 4 elements in user secret keys, 4 elements in ciphertexts, and $(2\lambda + 4)$ elements in master public keys for IBKEM_1 (which is denoted by $(|\mathsf{usk}|, |\mathsf{C}|, |\mathsf{pk}|) = (4, 4, 2\lambda + 4)$); and $(|\mathsf{usk}|, |\mathsf{C}|, |\mathsf{pk}|) = (4, 7, 8\lambda + 12)$ for IBKEM_2. We give concrete instantiations in the full version based on the MDDH and SXDH assumptions, respectively.

IBKEM_1 is mID-CPA-secure and it follows the same idea as $\mathsf{IBE}[\mathsf{MAC}, \mathcal{D}_k]$ in [8]. Since our underlying MAC is secure in the multi-challenge setting, IBKEM_1 is ID-CPA-secure in the multi-challenge setting, and it can be also viewed as an alternative abstraction of [22] in the BKP framework.

The difficulty for IBKEM_1 to achieve mID-CCCA security is that decryption answers may leak information about $\mathsf{usk}[\mathsf{id}]$ for challenge id. We observe that if ciphertexts satisfy that $(\mathbf{c}_0 = \mathbf{M}\mathbf{r}) \wedge (\mathbf{c}_1 = (\sum_{i=0}^{\ell} f_i(\mathsf{id})\mathbf{Z}_i) \cdot \mathbf{r})$ for some $\mathbf{r}$ (we call such ciphertexts as "well-formed"), then the decrypted K reveals no more information about $\mathsf{usk}[\mathsf{id}]$ than pk. Since "$\mathbf{c}_0 \in \mathsf{Span}(\mathbf{M})$" is a linear statement, we can introduce the efficient unbounded simulation-sound QANIZK from Section 4 to reject DEC queries with $[\mathbf{c}_0]_1 \notin \mathsf{Span}([\mathbf{M}]_1)$. Furthermore, due to the randomness contained in $\mathsf{usk}[\mathsf{id}]$, if $\mathbf{c}_0 \in \mathsf{Span}(\mathbf{M})$ but $\mathbf{c}_1$ is not "well-formed", the decrypted K will be randomly distributed and thus it will be rejected by the decryption oracle. Note that $[\mathbf{c}_1]_1$ works as the tag for QANIZK argument. We refer the proof of Theorem 4 for technical details.

Theorem 3 (mID-CPA **Security of** IBKEM_1)**.** *If the* $\mathcal{U}_k$-MDDH *is* (t_1, ε_1)*-hard in* $\mathbb{G}_1$*, and* MAC *is a* $(Q_{\mathsf{e}}, Q_{\mathsf{c}}, t_2, \varepsilon_2)$-mPR-CMA*-secure affine MAC, then* IBKEM_1 *is* $(Q_{\mathsf{ext}}, Q_{\mathsf{enc}}, t, \varepsilon)$-mID-CPA*-secure, where* $Q_{\mathsf{ext}} \leq Q_{\mathsf{e}}, Q_{\mathsf{enc}} \leq Q_{\mathsf{c}}$, $t_1 \approx t_2 \approx t + (Q_{\mathsf{ext}} + Q_{\mathsf{enc}})\mathsf{poly}(\lambda)$ *and* $\varepsilon \leq 2(\varepsilon_1 + \varepsilon_2 + 2^{-\Omega(\lambda)})$.

Setup(par):
$\mathbf{M} \stackrel{\$}{\leftarrow} \mathcal{U}_{k+\eta,k}$
$\mathsf{sk}_{\mathsf{MAC}} \stackrel{\$}{\leftarrow} \mathsf{Gen}_{\mathsf{MAC}}(\mathsf{par})$
Parse $\mathsf{sk}_{\mathsf{MAC}} := (\mathbf{B}, \mathbf{X}_0, \dots, \mathbf{X}_\ell, \mathbf{x}'_0, \dots, \mathbf{x}'_{\ell'})$
$(\mathsf{crs}, \mathsf{td}) \stackrel{\$}{\leftarrow} \mathsf{Gen}_{\mathsf{NIZK}}(\mathsf{par}, [\mathbf{M}]_1)$
For $i = 0, \dots, \ell$:
$\quad \mathbf{Y}_i \stackrel{\$}{\leftarrow} \mathbb{Z}_q^{k \times n}$; $\mathbf{Z}_i = (\mathbf{Y}_i^\top \mid \mathbf{X}_i^\top) \cdot \mathbf{M} \in \mathbb{Z}_q^{n \times k}$
For $i = 0, \dots, \ell'$:
$\quad \mathbf{y}'_i \stackrel{\$}{\leftarrow} \mathbb{Z}_q^{k}$; $\mathbf{z}'_i = (\mathbf{y}'^\top_i \mid \mathbf{x}'^\top_i) \cdot \mathbf{M} \in \mathbb{Z}_q^{1 \times k}$
$\mathsf{pk} := ($ crs $, [\mathbf{M}]_1, ([\mathbf{Z}_i]_1)_{0 \le i \le \ell}, ([\mathbf{z}'_i]_1)_{0 \le i \le \ell'})$
$\mathsf{sk} := (\mathsf{sk}_{\mathsf{MAC}}, (\mathbf{Y}_i)_{0 \le i \le \ell}, (\mathbf{y}'_i)_{0 \le i \le \ell'})$
Return $(\mathsf{pk}, \mathsf{sk})$

Ext(sk, id):
$([\mathbf{t}]_2, [\mathbf{u}]_2) \stackrel{\$}{\leftarrow} \mathsf{Tag}(\mathsf{sk}_{\mathsf{MAC}}, \mathsf{id})$
$/\!/\ \mathbf{u} = \sum_{i=0}^{\ell} f_i(\mathsf{id}) \mathbf{X}_i \mathbf{t} + \sum_{i=0}^{\ell'} f'_i(\mathsf{id}) \mathbf{x}'_i$
$\mathbf{v} = \sum_{i=0}^{\ell} f_i(\mathsf{id}) \mathbf{Y}_i \mathbf{t} + \sum_{i=0}^{\ell'} f'_i(\mathsf{id}) \mathbf{y}'_i \in \mathbb{Z}_q^k$
Return $\mathsf{usk}[\mathsf{id}] := ([\mathbf{t}]_2, [\mathbf{u}]_2, [\mathbf{v}]_2) \in \mathbb{G}_2^{n+\eta+k}$

Enc(pk, id):
$\mathbf{r} \stackrel{\$}{\leftarrow} \mathbb{Z}_q^k$; $\mathbf{c}_0 = \mathbf{M}\mathbf{r} \in \mathbb{Z}_q^{k+\eta}$
$\mathbf{c}_1 = (\sum_{i=0}^{\ell} f_i(\mathsf{id}) \mathbf{Z}_i) \cdot \mathbf{r} \in \mathbb{Z}_q^n$
$\pi = \mathsf{Prove}(\mathsf{crs}, [\mathbf{c}_1]_1, [\mathbf{c}_0]_1, \mathbf{r})$
$K = (\sum_{i=0}^{\ell'} f'_i(\mathsf{id}) \mathbf{z}'_i) \cdot \mathbf{r} \in \mathbb{Z}_q$
$\mathsf{C} := ([\mathbf{c}_0]_1, [\mathbf{c}_1]_1, \pi)$
Return $(\mathsf{C}, \mathsf{K} := [K]_T)$.

Dec(usk[id], id, C):
Parse $\mathsf{usk}[\mathsf{id}] = ([\mathbf{t}]_2, [\mathbf{u}]_2, [\mathbf{v}]_2)$
Parse $\mathsf{C} = ([\mathbf{c}_0]_1, [\mathbf{c}_1]_1, \pi)$
If $\mathsf{Ver}_{\mathsf{NIZK}}(\mathsf{crs}, [\mathbf{c}_1]_1, [\mathbf{c}_0]_1, \pi) = 0$ then
$\quad$ return $\perp$
$\mathbf{w}^\top := (\mathbf{v}^\top \mid \mathbf{u}^\top)$
$\mathsf{K} = [\mathbf{c}_0^\top]_1 \circ [\mathbf{w}]_2 - [\mathbf{c}_1^\top]_1 \circ [\mathbf{t}]_2$
Return $\mathsf{K} \in \mathbb{G}_T$

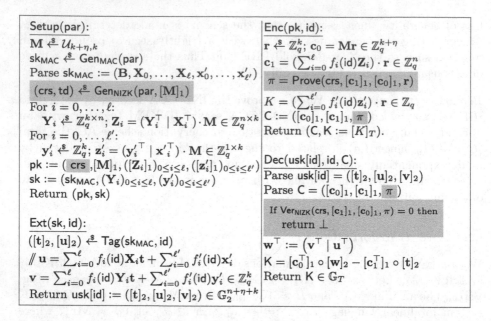

Fig. 11. IBKEM_1 and IBKEM_2. Gray instructions are only executed in IBKEM_2.

The proof of Theorem 3 is an extension of Theorem 4.3 in [8] in the multi-challenge setting. We leave the proof in the full version.

Theorem 4 (mID-CCCA **Security of** IBKEM_2)**.** *If the* $\mathcal{U}_k$-MDDH *is* (t_1, ε_1)-*hard in* $\mathbb{G}_1$, MAC *is a* $(Q_{\mathsf{e}}, Q_{\mathsf{c}}, t_2, \varepsilon_2)$-mPR-CMA-*secure affine MAC,* Π *is a* $(Q_{\mathsf{s}}, t_3, \varepsilon_3)$-USS *QANIZK, then* IBKEM_2 *is* $(Q_{\mathsf{ext}}, Q_{\mathsf{enc}}, Q_{\mathsf{dec}}, t, \varepsilon)$-mID-CCCA-*secure, where* $Q_{\mathsf{ext}} \le Q_{\mathsf{e}}$, $Q_{\mathsf{enc}} \le Q_{\mathsf{c}} \approx Q_{\mathsf{s}}$, $t_3 \approx t_1 \approx t_2 \approx t + (Q_{\mathsf{dec}} + Q_{\mathsf{enc}} + Q_{\mathsf{ext}})\mathsf{poly}(\lambda)$ *and* $\varepsilon \le 2(\varepsilon_1 + \varepsilon_2 + \varepsilon_3 + 2Q_{\mathsf{dec}} \cdot \mathsf{uncert}(\mathcal{A}) + 2^{-\Omega(\lambda)})$.

It is easy to verify the correctness of IBKEM_1 and IBKEM_2.

Proof (of Theorem 4). We define a series of games in Fig. 12 to prove the mID-CCCA security of IBKEM_2. A brief overview of game changes is described as in Fig. 13. For a simple presentation of Fig. 12, we define $\mathbf{X}_{\mathsf{id}} := \sum_{i=0}^{\ell} f_i(\mathsf{id})\mathbf{X}_i$, $\mathbf{Y}_{\mathsf{id}} := \sum_{i=0}^{\ell} f_i(\mathsf{id})\mathbf{Y}_i$, $\mathbf{Z}_{\mathsf{id}} := \sum_{i=0}^{\ell} f_i(\mathsf{id})\mathbf{Z}_i$, $\mathbf{x}'_{\mathsf{id}} := \sum_{i=0}^{\ell'} f'_i(\mathsf{id})\mathbf{x}'_i$, $\mathbf{y}'_{\mathsf{id}} := \sum_{i=0}^{\ell'} f'_i(\mathsf{id})\mathbf{y}'_i$, $\mathbf{z}'_{\mathsf{id}} := \sum_{i=0}^{\ell'} f'_i(\mathsf{id})\mathbf{z}'_i$ for an $\mathsf{id} \in \{0,1\}^L$.

Lemma 14 (G_0 **to** G_1)**.** $\Pr[\text{mID-CCCA}_0^{\mathcal{A}} \Rightarrow 1] = \Pr[\mathsf{G}_0^{\mathcal{A}} \Rightarrow 1] = \Pr[\mathsf{G}_1^{\mathcal{A}} \Rightarrow 1]$

Proof. G_0 is the real attack game. In G_1, we change the simulation of $\mathbf{c}_1$ and K in $\textsc{Enc}(\mathsf{id}^*)$ by substituting $\mathbf{Z}_i$ and $\mathbf{z}'_i$ with their respective definitions:

$$\mathbf{c}_1 = \mathbf{Z}_{\mathsf{id}^*}\mathbf{r} = (\mathbf{Y}_{\mathsf{id}^*}^\top \mid \mathbf{X}_{\mathsf{id}^*}^\top)\mathbf{M}\mathbf{r} = (\mathbf{Y}_{\mathsf{id}^*}^\top \mid \mathbf{X}_{\mathsf{id}^*}^\top)\mathbf{c}_0$$

<u>INIT:</u>
$\mathbf{M} \stackrel{\$}{\leftarrow} \mathcal{U}_{k+\eta,k}$, $\mathsf{sk_{MAC}} \stackrel{\$}{\leftarrow} \mathsf{Gen_{MAC}}(\mathsf{par})$
Parse $\mathsf{sk_{MAC}} := (\mathbf{B}, \mathbf{X}_0, \ldots, \mathbf{X}_\ell, \mathbf{x}'_0, \ldots, \mathbf{x}'_{\ell'})$
$(\mathsf{crs}, \mathsf{td}) \stackrel{\$}{\leftarrow} \mathsf{Gen_{NIZK}}(\mathsf{par}, [\mathbf{M}]_1)$
For $i = 0, \ldots, \ell$:
  $\mathbf{Y}_i \stackrel{\$}{\leftarrow} \mathbb{Z}_q^{k \times n}$;
  $\mathbf{Z}_i = (\mathbf{Y}_i^\top \mid \mathbf{X}_i^\top) \cdot \mathbf{M} \in \mathbb{Z}_q^{n \times k}$
For $i = 0, \ldots, \ell'$:
  $\mathbf{y}'_i \stackrel{\$}{\leftarrow} \mathbb{Z}_q^k$; $\mathbf{z}'_i = (\mathbf{y}'^\top_i \mid \mathbf{x}'^\top_i) \cdot \mathbf{M} \in \mathbb{Z}_q^{1 \times k}$
$\mathsf{pk} := (\mathsf{crs}, [\mathbf{M}]_1, ([\mathbf{Z}_i]_1)_{0 \le i \le \ell}, ([\mathbf{z}'_i]_1)_{0 \le i \le \ell'})$
$\mathsf{sk} := (\mathsf{sk_{MAC}}, (\mathbf{Y}_i)_{0 \le i \le \ell}, (\mathbf{y}'_i)_{0 \le i \le \ell'})$
Return pk

<u>DEC(id, C, pred):</u> // $\mathsf{G}_{0\text{-}7}$, $\boxed{\mathsf{G}_3}$, $\mathsf{G}_{4\text{-}6}$ (dashed box)
If $(\mathsf{id}, \mathsf{C}) \in \mathcal{C}_{\mathsf{enc}}$ then return $\perp$
Parse $\mathsf{C} = ([\mathbf{c}_0]_1, [\mathbf{c}_1]_1, \pi)$
If $\mathsf{Ver_{NIZK}}(\mathsf{crs}, [\mathbf{c}_1]_1, [\mathbf{c}_0]_1, \pi) = 0$ then return $\perp$
[box] If $\mathsf{id} \notin \mathcal{Q}_{\mathsf{usk}}$ then
  if $\mathbf{c}_0 \notin \mathsf{Span}(\mathbf{M})$ then return $\perp$
[dashed box]
  if $(\mathbf{c}_1 \neq \mathbf{Z}_{\mathsf{id}} \overline{\mathbf{M}}^{-1} \overline{\mathbf{c}_0})$ then
    return $\perp$
  else
    $\mathsf{K} := [(\mathbf{z}'_{\mathsf{id}} \overline{\mathbf{M}}^{-1} \overline{\mathbf{c}_0})]_T$
    if $\mathsf{pred}(\mathsf{K}) = 1$ then return K
    else return $\perp$
$\mathsf{usk}[\mathsf{id}] = ([\mathbf{t}]_2, [\mathbf{u}]_2, [\mathbf{v}]_2) \stackrel{\$}{\leftarrow} \mathrm{EXT}'(\mathsf{id})$
$\mathbf{w}^\top := (\mathbf{v}^\top \mid \mathbf{u}^\top)$
$\mathsf{K} = [\mathbf{c}_0^\top]_1 \circ [\mathbf{w}]_2 - [\mathbf{c}_1^\top]_1 \circ [\mathbf{t}]_2$
If $\mathsf{pred}(\mathsf{K}) = 1$ then return K
Else return $\perp$

<u>FINALIZE(d):</u>
Return $d \wedge (\mathcal{Q}_{\mathsf{enc}} \cap \mathcal{Q}_{\mathsf{usk}} = \emptyset)$

<u>ENC(id*):</u> // G_0, $\boxed{\mathsf{G}_1}$, $\mathsf{G}_{2\text{-}4}$ (dashed box), G_5 (grey), $\boxed{\mathsf{G}_6}$
$\mathcal{Q}_{\mathsf{enc}} := \mathcal{Q}_{\mathsf{enc}} \cup \{\mathsf{id}^*\}$
$\mathbf{r} \stackrel{\$}{\leftarrow} \mathbb{Z}_q^k$, $\mathbf{c}_0 = \mathbf{M}\mathbf{r} \in \mathbb{Z}_q^{k+\eta}$
[dashed box] $\mathbf{c}_0 \stackrel{\$}{\leftarrow} \mathbb{Z}_q^{k+\eta}$
[grey] $\mathbf{h} \stackrel{\$}{\leftarrow} \mathbb{Z}_q^\eta$, $\mathbf{h}_0 := \mathbf{X}_{\mathsf{id}^*}^\top \mathbf{h}$, $h_1 := \mathbf{x}'^\top_{\mathsf{id}^*} \mathbf{h}$
[box] $\mathbf{h} \stackrel{\$}{\leftarrow} \mathbb{Z}_q^\eta$, $\mathbf{h}_0 \stackrel{\$}{\leftarrow} \mathbb{Z}_q^k$, $h_1 \stackrel{\$}{\leftarrow} \mathbb{Z}_q$;
[grey] $\overline{\mathbf{c}_0} \stackrel{\$}{\leftarrow} \mathbb{Z}_q^k$, $\underline{\mathbf{c}_0} := \mathbf{h} + \underline{\mathbf{M}}\overline{\mathbf{M}}^{-1}\overline{\mathbf{c}_0}$
$\pi = \mathsf{Prove}(\mathsf{crs}, [\mathbf{c}_1]_1, [\mathbf{c}_0]_1, \mathbf{r})$
$\mathbf{c}_1 = \mathbf{Z}_{\mathsf{id}^*} \cdot \mathbf{r} \in \mathbb{Z}_q^n$; $K = \mathbf{z}'_{\mathsf{id}^*} \cdot \mathbf{r} \in \mathbb{Z}_q$
[box] $\mathbf{c}_1 = (\mathbf{Y}_{\mathsf{id}^*}^\top \mid \mathbf{X}_{\mathsf{id}^*}^\top)\mathbf{c}_0 \in \mathbb{Z}_q^n$
  $K = (\mathbf{y}'^\top_{\mathsf{id}^*} \mid \mathbf{x}'^\top_{\mathsf{id}^*})\mathbf{c}_0 \in \mathbb{Z}_q$
[grey] $[\mathbf{c}_1]_1 = [\mathbf{Z}_{\mathsf{id}^*} \overline{\mathbf{M}}^{-1} \overline{\mathbf{c}_0}]_1 + [\mathbf{h}_0]_1$
  $\mathsf{K} = [\mathbf{z}'_{\mathsf{id}^*} \overline{\mathbf{M}}^{-1} \overline{\mathbf{c}_0}]_T + [h_1]_T$
[box] $\pi = \mathsf{Sim}(\mathsf{crs}, \mathsf{td}, [\mathbf{c}_1]_1, [\mathbf{c}_0]_1)$
$\mathcal{C}_{\mathsf{enc}} := \mathcal{C}_{\mathsf{enc}} \cup \{(\mathsf{id}^*, ([\mathbf{c}_0]_1, [\mathbf{c}_1]_1, \pi))\}$
Return $\mathsf{C} = ([\mathbf{c}_0]_1, [\mathbf{c}_1]_1, \pi) \in \mathbb{G}_1^{n+k+\eta}$ and $\mathsf{K} = [K]_T$.

<u>EXT(id)</u>
$\mathcal{Q}_{\mathsf{usk}} := \mathcal{Q}_{\mathsf{usk}} \cup \{\mathsf{id}\}$
$\mathsf{usk}[\mathsf{id}] := ([\mathbf{t}]_2, [\mathbf{u}]_2, [\mathbf{v}]_2) \stackrel{\$}{\leftarrow} \mathrm{EXT}'(\mathsf{id})$
Return $\mathsf{usk}[\mathsf{id}]$

<u>EXT′(id):</u> // $\mathsf{G}_{0\text{-}4}$, $\boxed{\mathsf{G}_{5\text{-}6}}$
$([\mathbf{t}]_2, [\mathbf{u}]_2) \stackrel{\$}{\leftarrow} \mathsf{Tag}(\mathsf{sk_{MAC}}, \mathsf{id})$
$\mathbf{v} := \mathbf{Y}_{\mathsf{id}}\mathbf{t} + \mathbf{y}'_{\mathsf{id}} \in \mathbb{Z}_q^k$
[box] $\mathbf{v}^\top := (\mathbf{t}^\top \mathbf{Z}_{\mathsf{id}} + \mathbf{z}'_{\mathsf{id}} - \mathbf{u}^\top \underline{\mathbf{M}})\overline{\mathbf{M}}^{-1}$
$\mathsf{usk}[\mathsf{id}] := ([\mathbf{t}]_2, [\mathbf{u}]_2, [\mathbf{v}]_2) \in \mathbb{G}_2^{n+\eta+k}$
$\mathsf{Key} := \mathsf{Key} \cup \{(\mathsf{id}, \mathsf{usk}[\mathsf{id}])\}$
Return $\mathsf{usk}[\mathsf{id}] \in \mathbb{G}_2^{n+\eta+k}$

Fig. 12. Games G_0-G_6 for the proof of Theorem 4.

and $K = (\mathbf{y}'^\top_{\mathsf{id}^*} \mid \mathbf{x}'^\top_{\mathsf{id}^*})\mathbf{M}\mathbf{r} = (\mathbf{y}'_{\mathsf{id}^*}{}^\top \mid \mathbf{x}'_{\mathsf{id}^*}{}^\top)\mathbf{c}_0$. This change is only conceptual. Moreover, we simulate the QANIZK proof π in ENC(id*) by using Π's zero-knowledge simulator. By the perfect zero-knowledge property of Π, G_1 is identical to G_0. □

Lemma 15 (G_1 **to** G_2). *If the* $\mathcal{U}_{k+\eta,k}$-MDDH *problem is* (t_1, ε_1)*-hard in* $\mathbb{G}_1$*, then* $|\Pr[\mathsf{G}_1^{\mathcal{A}} \Rightarrow 1] - \Pr[\mathsf{G}_2^{\mathcal{A}} \Rightarrow 1]| \le \varepsilon_1 + 2^{-\Omega(\lambda)}$ *and* $t_1 \approx t_{\mathcal{A}} + (Q_{\mathsf{dec}} + Q_{\mathsf{enc}} + Q_{\mathsf{ext}})\mathsf{poly}(\lambda)$*, where* poly *is a polynomial independent of* $t_{\mathcal{A}}$.

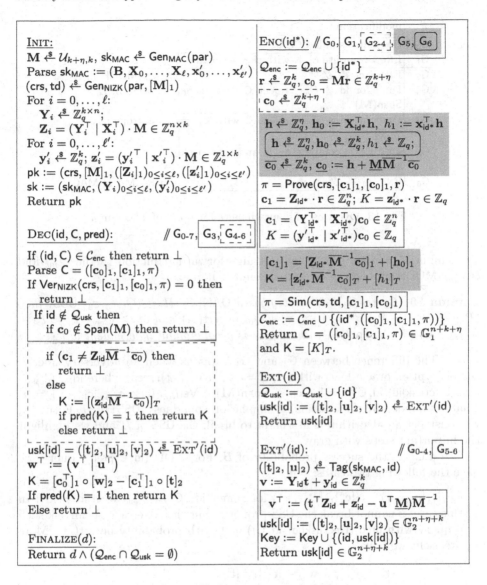

#	modification	remarks
G_0	the same as $\mathsf{mID\text{-}CCCA}_0$	-
G_1	$\textsc{Enc}$: compute $\mathbf{c}_1, \mathsf{K}$ with sk, π with td	ZK of Π
G_2	$\textsc{Enc}$: $\mathbf{c}_0 \xleftarrow{\$} \mathbb{Z}_q^{k+\eta}$	$\mathcal{U}_{k+\eta,k}$-MDDH in $\mathbb{G}_1$
G_3	$\textsc{Dec}$: for $\mathsf{id} \notin \mathcal{Q}_{\mathsf{usk}}$, reject C with $\mathbf{c}_0 \notin \mathsf{Span}(\mathbf{M})$	USS of Π
G_4	$\textsc{Dec}$: for $\mathsf{id} \notin \mathcal{Q}_{\mathsf{usk}}$, reject C with $\mathbf{c}_1 \neq \mathbf{Z}_{\mathsf{id}}\overline{\mathbf{M}}^{-1}\overline{\mathbf{c}_0}$	entropy of $\mathbf{t}$
G_5	$\textsc{Ext}, \textsc{Enc}$: compute $\mathbf{c}_1, K$ and $\mathbf{v}$ with pk and $\mathsf{sk}_{\mathsf{MAC}}$	-
G_6	$\textsc{Enc}$: $\mathbf{c}_1 \xleftarrow{\$} \mathbb{Z}_q^k, K \xleftarrow{\$} \mathbb{Z}_q$	mPR-CMA of MAC

Fig. 13. Overview of game changes for proof of Theorem 4

Lemma 15 can be proved by a straightforward reduction to the $\mathcal{Q}_{\mathsf{enc}}$-fold $\mathcal{U}_{k+\eta,k}$-MDDH problem in $\mathbb{G}_1$ and we omit it here.

Lemma 16 (G_2 **to** G_3). *If the tag-based* QANIZK Π *is* $(Q_{\mathsf{s}}, t_3, \varepsilon_3)$-USS, *then* $|\Pr[\mathsf{G}_2^{\mathcal{A}} \Rightarrow 1] - \Pr[\mathsf{G}_3^{\mathcal{A}} \Rightarrow 1]| \leq \varepsilon_3 + \mathcal{Q}_{\mathsf{dec}}\mathsf{uncert}(\mathcal{A})$ *and* $Q_{\mathsf{s}} \geq \mathcal{Q}_{\mathsf{enc}}$, $t_3 \approx t_{\mathcal{A}} + (\mathcal{Q}_{\mathsf{dec}} + \mathcal{Q}_{\mathsf{ext}} + \mathcal{Q}_{\mathsf{enc}})\mathsf{poly}(\lambda)$, *where* poly *is a polynomial independent of* $t_{\mathcal{A}}$.

Proof. The difference between G_2 and G_3 happens when an adversary queries the decryption oracle $\textsc{Dec}$ with $(\mathsf{id}, \mathsf{C} = ([\mathbf{c}_0]_1, [\mathbf{c}_1]_1, \pi), \mathsf{pred})$ where $\mathsf{id} \notin \mathcal{Q}_{\mathsf{usk}} \wedge \mathsf{pred}(\mathsf{Dec}(\mathsf{usk}[\mathsf{id}], \mathsf{id}, \mathsf{C})) = 1 \wedge \mathbf{c}_0 \notin \mathsf{Span}(\mathbf{M}) \wedge \mathsf{Ver}_{\mathsf{NIZK}}(\mathsf{crs}, [\mathbf{c}_1]_1, [\mathbf{c}_0]_1, \pi) = 1$. That is bounded by the unbounded simulation soundness (USS) of Π. Formally, we construct an algorithm $\mathcal{B}$ in Fig. 14 to break the USS of Π and we highlight the important steps with gray.

We analyze the success probability of $\mathcal{B}$. For a $\textsc{Dec}(\mathsf{id}, \mathsf{C}, \mathsf{pred}_i)$ query, we have the following two cases:

- $([\mathbf{c}_1]_1, [\mathbf{c}_0]_1, \pi) = ([\mathbf{c}_1^*]_1, [\mathbf{c}_0^*]_1, \pi^*)$ for some $(\mathsf{id}^*, \mathsf{C}^*) \in \mathcal{C}_{\mathsf{enc}}$ with $\mathsf{id} \neq \mathsf{id}^*$. In this case, $\mathcal{B}$ cannot break the USS property, but the adversary $\mathcal{A}$ can ask such a query with $\mathsf{pred}_i(\mathsf{Dec}(\mathsf{usk}[\mathsf{id}], \mathsf{id}, \mathsf{C})) = 1$ with probability $\mathsf{uncert}(\mathcal{A})$. More precisely, we have

$$\begin{aligned}
\mathsf{K} &= [\mathbf{c}_0^\top]_1 \circ [\mathbf{w}]_2 - [\mathbf{c}_1^\top]_1 \circ [\mathbf{t}]_2 \\
&= [\mathbf{c}_0^\top]_1 \circ [\mathbf{w}]_2 - [\mathbf{c}_0^\top(\mathbf{Y}_{\mathsf{id}^*} \mid \mathbf{X}_{\mathsf{id}^*})]_1 \circ [\mathbf{t}]_2 \\
&= [\mathbf{c}_0^\top]_1 \circ [(\mathbf{Y}_{\mathsf{id}} \mid \mathbf{X}_{\mathsf{id}})\mathbf{t}]_2 - [\mathbf{c}_0^\top(\mathbf{Y}_{\mathsf{id}^*} \mid \mathbf{X}_{\mathsf{id}^*})]_1 \circ [\mathbf{t}]_2 \\
&= [\mathbf{c}_0^\top]_1 \circ [(\mathbf{Y}_\Delta \mid \mathbf{X}_\Delta)\mathbf{t}]_2,
\end{aligned}$$

  where $\mathbf{Y}_\Delta := \mathbf{Y}_{\mathsf{id}} - \mathbf{Y}_{\mathsf{id}^*}$ and $\mathbf{X}_\Delta := \mathbf{X}_{\mathsf{id}} - \mathbf{X}_{\mathsf{id}^*}$. By $\mathsf{id} \notin \mathcal{Q}_{\mathsf{usk}}$, the corresponding $\mathbf{t}$ is randomly distributed in the adversary's view. Clearly, $(\mathbf{Y}_\Delta \mid \mathbf{X}_\Delta) \neq \mathbf{0}$, since $\mathsf{id} \neq \mathsf{id}^*$. Thus, K is randomly distributed and $\mathcal{A}$ can output a pred_i such that $\mathsf{pred}_i(\mathsf{K}) = 1$ with probability $\mathsf{uncert}(\mathcal{A})$.
- $([\mathbf{c}_1]_1, [\mathbf{c}_0]_1, \pi) \neq ([\mathbf{c}_1^*]_1, [\mathbf{c}_0^*]_1, \pi^*)$ for all $(\mathsf{id}^*, \mathsf{C}^*) \in \mathcal{C}_{\mathsf{enc}}$. In this case, $([\mathbf{c}_1]_1, [\mathbf{c}_0]_1, \pi)$ is a valid proof to break the USS of Π.

INIT:
$\mathbf{M} \xleftarrow{\$} \mathcal{U}_{k+\eta,k}$
Compute $\mathbf{M}^{\perp} \in \mathbb{Z}_q^{(k+\eta)\times\eta}$ s.t. $\mathbf{M}^{\top}\mathbf{M}^{\perp} = \mathbf{0}$
$\mathsf{sk}_{\mathsf{MAC}} \xleftarrow{\$} \mathsf{Gen}_{\mathsf{MAC}}(\mathsf{par})$
Parse $\mathsf{sk}_{\mathsf{MAC}} := (\mathbf{B}, \mathbf{X}_0, \dots, \mathbf{X}_\ell, \mathbf{x}'_0, \dots, \mathbf{x}'_{\ell'})$
$\mathsf{crs} \xleftarrow{\$} \text{INIT}_{\mathsf{NIZK}}(\mathbf{M})$
For $i = 0, \dots, \ell$:
  $\mathbf{Y}_i \xleftarrow{\$} \mathbb{Z}_q^{k\times n}$;
  $[\mathbf{Z}_i]_1 = [(\mathbf{Y}_i^{\top} \mid \mathbf{X}_i^{\top}) \cdot \mathbf{M}]_1 \in \mathbb{Z}_q^{n\times k}$
For $i = 0, \dots, \ell'$:
  $\mathbf{y}'_i \xleftarrow{\$} \mathbb{Z}_q^{k}$,
  $[\mathbf{z}'_i]_1 = [(\mathbf{y}'^{\top}_i \mid \mathbf{x}'^{\top}_i) \cdot \mathbf{M}]_1 \in \mathbb{Z}_q^{1\times k}$
$\mathsf{pk} := (\mathsf{crs}, [\mathbf{M}]_1, ([\mathbf{Z}_i]_1)_{0\le i\le \ell}, ([\mathbf{z}'_i]_1)_{0\le i\le \ell'})$
$\mathsf{sk} := (\mathsf{sk}_{\mathsf{MAC}}, (\mathbf{Y}_i)_{0\le i\le \ell}, (\mathbf{y}'_i)_{0\le i\le \ell'})$
Return pk

EXT(id):
$\mathcal{Q}_{\mathsf{usk}} := \mathcal{Q}_{\mathsf{usk}} \cup \{\mathsf{id}\}$
$([\mathbf{t}]_2, [\mathbf{u}]_2) \xleftarrow{\$} \mathsf{Tag}(\mathsf{sk}_{\mathsf{MAC}}, \mathsf{id})$
$\mathbf{v} := \mathbf{Y}_{\mathsf{id}}\mathbf{t} + \mathbf{y}'_{\mathsf{id}} \in \mathbb{Z}_q^{k}$
Return $\mathsf{usk}[\mathsf{id}] := ([\mathbf{t}]_2, [\mathbf{u}]_2, [\mathbf{v}]_2) \in \mathbb{G}_2^{n+\eta+k}$

FINALIZE(d):
Return $d \wedge (\mathcal{Q}_{\mathsf{enc}} \cap \mathcal{Q}_{\mathsf{usk}} = \emptyset)$

ENC(id*):
$\mathcal{Q}_{\mathsf{enc}} := \mathcal{Q}_{\mathsf{enc}} \cup \{\mathsf{id}^*\}$
$\mathbf{c}_0 \xleftarrow{\$} \mathbb{Z}_q^{k+\eta}$
$\mathbf{c}_1 = (\mathbf{Y}_{\mathsf{id}^*}^{\top} \mid \mathbf{X}_{\mathsf{id}^*}^{\top})\mathbf{c}_0 \in \mathbb{Z}_q^{n}$
$K = (\mathbf{y}'^{\top}_{\mathsf{id}^*} \mid \mathbf{x}'^{\top}_{\mathsf{id}^*})\mathbf{c}_0 \in \mathbb{Z}_q$
$\pi = \text{SIM}([\mathbf{c}_1]_1, [\mathbf{c}_0]_1)$
$\mathcal{P} := \mathcal{P} \cup \{([\mathbf{c}_1]_1, [\mathbf{c}_0]_1, \pi)\}$
$\mathcal{C}_{\mathsf{enc}} := \mathcal{C}_{\mathsf{enc}} \cup \{(\mathsf{id}^*, ([\mathbf{c}_0]_1, [\mathbf{c}_1]_1, \pi))\}$
$\mathsf{C} = ([\mathbf{c}_0]_1, [\mathbf{c}_1]_1, \pi)$ and $\mathsf{K} = [K]_T$.
Return (C, K)

DEC(id, C, pred):
If $(\mathsf{id}, \mathsf{C}) \in \mathcal{C}_{\mathsf{enc}}$ then return $\perp$
Parse $\mathsf{C} = ([\mathbf{c}_0]_1, [\mathbf{c}_1]_1, \pi)$
If $\mathsf{Ver}_{\mathsf{NIZK}}(\mathsf{crs}, [\mathbf{c}_1]_1, [\mathbf{c}_0]_1, \pi) = 1$ then
  if $\mathsf{id} \notin \mathcal{Q}_{\mathsf{usk}} \wedge ([\mathbf{c}_1]_1, [\mathbf{c}_0]_1, \pi) \notin \mathcal{P} \wedge$ $[\mathbf{c}_0^{\top}\mathbf{M}^{\perp}]_1 \neq [\mathbf{0}]_1$ then
    Call $\text{FINALIZE}_{\mathsf{NIZK}}([\mathbf{c}_1]_1, [\mathbf{c}_0]_1, \pi)$
  $\mathsf{usk}[\mathsf{id}] \xleftarrow{\$} \mathsf{Ext}(\mathsf{sk}, \mathsf{id})$
  Parse $\mathsf{usk}[\mathsf{id}] := ([\mathbf{t}]_2, [\mathbf{u}]_2, [\mathbf{v}]_2)$
  $\mathbf{w}^{\top} := (\mathbf{v}^{\top} \mid \mathbf{u}^{\top})$
  $\mathsf{K} = [\mathbf{c}_0^{\top}]_1 \circ [\mathbf{w}]_2 - [\mathbf{c}_1^{\top}]_1 \circ [\mathbf{t}]_2$
  If $\mathsf{pred}(\mathsf{K}) = 1$ then return K
Else return $\perp$.

Fig. 14. Description of $\mathcal{B}$ with oracle access to $\text{INIT}_{\mathsf{NIZK}}, \text{SIM}, \text{FINALIZE}_{\mathsf{NIZK}}$ of the USS games of Fig. 8 for the proof of Lemma 16.

To sum up, the success probability of $\mathcal{B}$ is at least $|\Pr[\mathsf{G}_2^{\mathcal{A}} \Rightarrow 1] - \Pr[\mathsf{G}_3^{\mathcal{A}} \Rightarrow 1]| - Q_{\mathsf{dec}} \cdot \mathsf{uncert}(\mathcal{A})$. □

Lemma 17 (G_3 **to** G_4)**.** $|\Pr[\mathsf{G}_3^{\mathcal{A}} \Rightarrow 1] - \Pr[\mathsf{G}_4^{\mathcal{A}} \Rightarrow 1]| \le Q_{\mathsf{dec}} \cdot \mathsf{uncert}(\mathcal{A})$.

Proof. An adversary $\mathcal{A}$ can distinguish G_4 from G_3 if $\mathcal{A}$ asks the decryption oracle DEC with $(\mathsf{id}, \mathsf{C} = ([\mathbf{c}_0]_1, [\mathbf{c}_1]_1, \pi), \mathsf{pred})$ where $\mathbf{c}_1 \neq \mathbf{Z}_{\mathsf{id}}\overline{\mathbf{M}}^{-1} \cdot \overline{\mathbf{c}_0}$ but $\mathsf{pred}(\mathsf{Dec}(\mathsf{usk}[\mathsf{id}], \mathsf{id}, \mathsf{C})) = 1$.

We show that, before an identity id is queried to EXT, for any $(\mathbf{c}_0, \mathbf{c}_1)$, the value $K = \mathbf{c}_0^{\top}\begin{pmatrix}\mathbf{v}_{\mathsf{id}}\\ \mathbf{u}_{\mathsf{id}}\end{pmatrix} - \mathbf{c}_1^{\top}\mathbf{t}_{\mathsf{id}}$ is uniformly random from the adversary's view, where $([\mathbf{t}_{\mathsf{id}}]_2, [\mathbf{u}_{\mathsf{id}}]_2, [\mathbf{v}_{\mathsf{id}}]_2) \in \text{EXT}(\mathsf{id})$:

$$K = \mathbf{c}_0^{\top}\begin{pmatrix}\mathbf{v}_{\mathsf{id}}\\ \mathbf{u}_{\mathsf{id}}\end{pmatrix} - \mathbf{c}_1^{\top}\mathbf{t}_{\mathsf{id}} = \mathbf{c}_0^{\top}\begin{pmatrix}((\mathbf{t}_{\mathsf{id}}^{\top}\mathbf{Z}_{\mathsf{id}} + \mathbf{z}'_{\mathsf{id}} - \mathbf{u}_{\mathsf{id}}^{\top} \cdot \underline{\mathbf{M}}) \cdot \overline{\mathbf{M}}^{-1})^{\top}\\ \mathbf{u}_{\mathsf{id}}\end{pmatrix} - \mathbf{c}_1^{\top}\mathbf{t}_{\mathsf{id}}$$

$$= \overline{\mathbf{c}}_0^{\top}(\overline{\mathbf{M}}^{-1})^{\top}\mathbf{z}'^{\top}_{\mathsf{id}} + \underbrace{(\underline{\mathbf{c}}_0^{\top} - (\underline{\mathbf{M}}\overline{\mathbf{M}}^{-1}\overline{\mathbf{c}_0})^{\top})}_{\Delta_1}\mathbf{u}_{\mathsf{id}} + \underbrace{((\mathbf{Z}_{\mathsf{id}} \cdot \overline{\mathbf{M}}^{-1} \cdot \overline{\mathbf{c}}_0)^{\top} - \mathbf{c}_1^{\top})}_{\Delta_2}\mathbf{t}_{\mathsf{id}}$$

In G_3 and G_4, a DEC query with $\mathbf{c}_0 \notin \mathsf{Span}(\mathbf{M})$ and $\mathsf{id} \notin \mathcal{Q}_{\mathsf{usk}}$ will be rejected, and thus we have $\Delta_1 = \mathbf{0}$. As id has never been queried to EXT, $\mathbf{t}_{\mathsf{id}}$ is uniformly random to the adversary. Thus, if $\mathbf{c}_1 \neq \mathbf{Z}_{\mathsf{id}}\overline{\mathbf{M}}^{-1}\overline{\mathbf{c}_0}$ (namely, $\Delta_2 \neq \mathbf{0}$) then K is random and a query of this form will be rejected except with probability $\mathsf{uncert}(\mathcal{A})$. By the union bound, the difference between G_3 and G_4 is bounded by $\mathcal{Q}_{\mathsf{dec}} \cdot \mathsf{uncert}(\mathcal{A})$. □

Lemma 18 (G_4 **to** G_5)**.** $\Pr[\mathsf{G}_4^{\mathcal{A}} \Rightarrow 1] = \Pr[\mathsf{G}_5^{\mathcal{A}} \Rightarrow 1]$.

Proof. The change from G_4 to G_5 is only conceptual. By $\mathbf{Z}_i = (\mathbf{Y}_i^\top \mid \mathbf{X}_i^\top)\mathbf{M}$, we have $\mathbf{Y}_i^\top = (\mathbf{Z}_i - \mathbf{X}_i^\top \cdot \underline{\mathbf{M}}) \cdot (\overline{\mathbf{M}})^{-1}$, and similarly we have $\mathbf{y}_i'^\top = (\mathbf{z}_i' - \mathbf{x}_i'^\top \cdot \underline{\mathbf{M}}) \cdot \overline{\mathbf{M}}^{-1}$. For EXT(id), by substituting $\mathbf{Y}_i^\top$ and $\mathbf{y}_i'^\top$, we obtain

$$\mathbf{v}^\top = \left(\mathbf{t}^\top(\mathbf{Z}_{\mathsf{id}} - \mathbf{X}_{\mathsf{id}}^\top \cdot \underline{\mathbf{M}}) + (\mathbf{z}_{\mathsf{id}}' - \mathbf{x}_{\mathsf{id}}'^\top \cdot \underline{\mathbf{M}})\right)\overline{\mathbf{M}}^{-1}$$

$$= \left(\mathbf{t}^\top \mathbf{Z}_{\mathsf{id}} + \mathbf{z}_{\mathsf{id}}' - \underbrace{(\mathbf{t}^\top \mathbf{X}_{\mathsf{id}}^\top + \mathbf{x}_{\mathsf{id}}'^\top) \cdot \underline{\mathbf{M}}}_{\mathbf{u}^\top}\right) \cdot \overline{\mathbf{M}}^{-1}$$

Note that we can compute $[\mathbf{v}]_2$ in G_5, since $\mathbf{A}$, $\mathbf{z}_i'$ and $\mathbf{Z}_i$ are known explicitly over $\mathbb{Z}_q$ and $[\mathbf{t}]_2$ and $[\mathbf{u}]_2$ are known.

$\mathbf{c}_0$ from ENC(id*) is uniformly random in G_4 and G_5. By $\mathbf{h} = \underline{\mathbf{c}_0} - \underline{\mathbf{M}} \cdot \overline{\mathbf{M}}^{-1}\overline{\mathbf{c}_0}$, we have

$$\begin{aligned}\mathbf{c}_1 &= \mathbf{Z}_{\mathsf{id}^*} \cdot \overline{\mathbf{M}}^{-1}\overline{\mathbf{c}_0} + \mathbf{X}_{\mathsf{id}^*}^\top \cdot (\underline{\mathbf{c}_0} - \underline{\mathbf{M}} \cdot \overline{\mathbf{M}}^{-1}\overline{\mathbf{c}_0}) \\ &= (\mathbf{Y}_{\mathsf{id}^*}^\top \overline{\mathbf{M}} + \mathbf{X}_{\mathsf{id}^*}^\top \underline{\mathbf{M}}) \cdot \overline{\mathbf{M}}^{-1}\overline{\mathbf{c}_0} + \mathbf{X}_{\mathsf{id}^*}^\top \cdot (\underline{\mathbf{c}_0} - \underline{\mathbf{M}} \cdot \overline{\mathbf{M}}^{-1}\overline{\mathbf{c}_0}) \\ &= (\mathbf{Y}_{\mathsf{id}^*}^\top \mid \mathbf{X}_{\mathsf{id}^*}^\top)\mathbf{c}_0\end{aligned}$$

and $\mathbf{c}_1$ is distributed as in G_4. The distribution of K can be proved by a similar argument. □

Lemma 19 (G_5 **to** G_6)**.** *If* MAC *is* $(Q_{\mathsf{e}}, Q_{\mathsf{c}}, t_2, \varepsilon_2)$-mPR-CMA-*secure, then* $|\Pr[\mathsf{G}_5^{\mathcal{A}} \Rightarrow 1] - \Pr[\mathsf{G}_6^{\mathcal{A}} \Rightarrow 1]| \leq \varepsilon_2$ *with* $\mathcal{Q}_{\mathsf{ext}} \leq Q_{\mathsf{e}}$, $\mathcal{Q}_{\mathsf{enc}} \leq Q_{\mathsf{c}}$, $t_2 \approx t_{\mathcal{A}} + (\mathcal{Q}_{\mathsf{dec}} + \mathcal{Q}_{\mathsf{ext}} + \mathcal{Q}_{\mathsf{enc}})\mathsf{poly}(\lambda)$, *where* poly *is a polynomial independent of* $t_{\mathcal{A}}$.

Proof. In G_6, we answer the ENC(id) query by choosing random K and $([\mathbf{c}_0]_1, [\mathbf{c}_1]_1)$. We construct an adversary $\mathcal{D}$ in Fig. 15 to bound the differences between G_5 and G_6 with the mPR-CMA security of MAC. The decryption oracle DEC is simulated as in G_5 and G_6. Now if $\mathcal{D}$ is in $\mathsf{mPR\text{-}CMA}_1$ then the simulated distribution is identical to G_6; otherwise, it is identical to G_5. □

We observe that G_6 is computationally indistinguishable from $\mathsf{mID\text{-}CCCA}_{\mathsf{rand}}$ by a reverse arguments of Lemmata 14 to 19 without changing the distribution of K in ENC. More precisely, we can argue this by switching the ciphertexts from random to real and removing all the additional rejection rules in DEC. Thus, we conclude Theorem 4. □

<u>INIT:</u>
$\mathbf{M} \xleftarrow{\$} \mathcal{U}_{k+\eta,k}$
Compute $\mathbf{M}^{\perp} \in \mathbb{Z}_q^{(k+\eta)\times\eta}$ s.t. $\mathbf{M}^{\top}\mathbf{M}^{\perp} = \mathbf{0}$
$\epsilon \xleftarrow{\$} \textsc{Init}_{\mathsf{MAC}}$
$(\mathsf{crs}, \mathsf{td}) \xleftarrow{\$} \mathsf{Gen}_{\mathsf{NIZK}}(\mathsf{par}, [\mathbf{M}]_1)$
For $i = 0, \ldots, \ell$: $\mathbf{Z}_i \xleftarrow{\$} \mathbb{Z}_q^{n\times k}$
For $i = 0, \ldots, \ell'$: $\mathbf{z}'_i \xleftarrow{\$} \mathbb{Z}_q^{1\times k}$
$\mathsf{pk} := (\mathsf{crs}, [\mathbf{M}]_1, ([\mathbf{Z}_i]_1)_{0\le i\le \ell}, ([\mathbf{z}'_i]_1)_{0\le i\le \ell'})$
Return pk

<u>EXT(id):</u>
$\mathcal{Q}_{\mathsf{usk}} := \mathcal{Q}_{\mathsf{usk}} \cup \{\mathsf{id}\}$
$([\mathbf{t}]_2, [u]_2) \xleftarrow{\$} \textsc{Eval}(\mathsf{id})$
$\mathbf{v}^{\top} := (\mathbf{t}^{\top}\mathbf{Z}_{\mathsf{id}} + \mathbf{z}'_{\mathsf{id}} - \mathbf{u}^{\top} \cdot \underline{\mathbf{M}}) \cdot (\overline{\mathbf{M}})^{-1}$
Return $\mathsf{usk}[\mathsf{id}] := ([\mathbf{t}]_2, [\mathbf{u}]_2, [\mathbf{v}]_2) \in \mathbb{G}_2^{n+\eta+k}$

<u>ENC(id*):</u>
$\mathcal{Q}_{\mathsf{enc}} := \mathcal{Q}_{\mathsf{enc}} \cup \{\mathsf{id}^*\}$
$([\mathbf{h}]_1, [\mathbf{h}_0]_1, [h_1]_T) \xleftarrow{\$} \textsc{Chal}(\mathsf{id}^*)$
$\overline{\mathbf{c}_0} \xleftarrow{\$} \mathbb{Z}_q^k$
$\underline{\mathbf{c}_0} := \mathbf{h} + \underline{\mathbf{M}} \cdot \overline{\mathbf{M}}^{-1}\overline{\mathbf{c}_0} \in \mathbb{Z}_q^{\eta}$
$\mathbf{c}_1 := \mathbf{Z}_{\mathsf{id}^*} \cdot \overline{\mathbf{M}}^{-1}\overline{\mathbf{c}_0} + \mathbf{h}_0$
$K := \mathbf{z}'_{\mathsf{id}^*} \cdot \overline{\mathbf{M}}^{-1}\overline{\mathbf{c}_0} + h_1$
$\pi := \mathsf{Sim}(\mathsf{crs}, \mathsf{td}, [\mathbf{c}_1]_1, [\mathbf{c}_0]_1)$
$\mathcal{C}_{\mathsf{enc}} := \mathcal{C}_{\mathsf{enc}} \cup \{(\mathsf{id}, ([\mathbf{c}_0]_1, [\mathbf{c}_1]_1, \pi))\}$
$\mathsf{C} := ([\mathbf{c}_0]_1, [\mathbf{c}_1]_1, \pi)$ and $\mathsf{K} := [K]_T$.
Return (C, K)

<u>FINALIZE(*d*):</u>
Return $\textsc{Finalize}_{\mathsf{MAC}}(d) \wedge (\mathcal{Q}_{\mathsf{enc}} \cap \mathcal{Q}_{\mathsf{usk}} = \emptyset)$

Fig. 15. Description of $\mathcal{D}$ (with access to oracles $\textsc{Init}_{\mathsf{MAC}}$, $\textsc{Eval}$, $\textsc{Chal}$, $\textsc{Finalize}_{\mathsf{MAC}}$ of the $\mathsf{mPR\text{-}CMA}_0/\mathsf{mPR\text{-}CMA}_1$ games of Fig. 1) for the proof of Lemma 19.

Remark 3 (Anonymity). In G_0 all the challenge ciphertexts are independent of the challenge identity id^*: $[\mathbf{c}_1]_1$ is uniform and $[\mathbf{c}_0]_1$ and π are independent of id^*. Thus, our scheme is trivially anonymous.

Acknowledgments. We thank the anonymous reviewers for their comments and, in particular, for pointing a problem in our definition of unbounded simulation soundness, and one in the proof of Theorem 4 in a previous version of this paper. The first author was supported by ERC Project PREP-CRYPTO (724307) and DFG grants (HO 4534/4-1, HO 4534/2-2), the second author was supported by the National Nature Science Foundation of China (Nos. 61502484, 61572495, 61772515), the Fundamental theory and cutting edge technology Research Program of Institute of Information Engineering, CAS (Grant No. Y7Z0291103) and the National Cryptography Development Fund (No. MMJJ20170116), and the third author was supported by the DFG grant (HO 4534/4-1). This work was done while the second author was visiting KIT. The visit was supported by China Scholarship Council.

References

1. Abe, M., David, B., Kohlweiss, M., Nishimaki, R., Ohkubo, M.: Tagged one-time signatures: tight security and optimal tag size. In: Kurosawa, K., Hanaoka, G. (eds.) PKC 2013. LNCS, vol. 7778, pp. 312–331. Springer, Heidelberg (2013). https://doi.org/10.1007/978-3-642-36362-7_20
2. Abe, M., Hofheinz, D., Nishimaki, R., Ohkubo, M., Pan, J.: Compact structure-preserving signatures with almost tight security. In: Katz, J., Shacham, H. (eds.) CRYPTO 2017. LNCS, vol. 10402, pp. 548–580. Springer, Cham (2017). https://doi.org/10.1007/978-3-319-63715-0_19

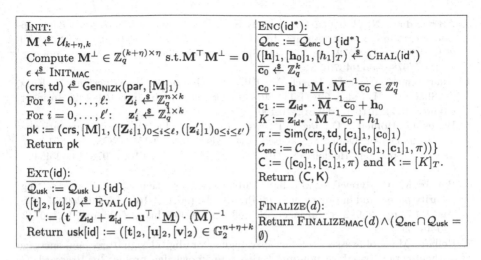

3. Attrapadung, N., Hanaoka, G., Yamada, S.: A framework for identity-based encryption with almost tight security. In: Iwata, T., Cheon, J.H. (eds.) ASIACRYPT 2015. LNCS, vol. 9452, pp. 521–549. Springer, Heidelberg (2015). https://doi.org/10.1007/978-3-662-48797-6_22
4. Auerbach, B., Cash, D., Fersch, M., Kiltz, E.: Memory-tight reductions. In: Katz, J., Shacham, H. (eds.) CRYPTO 2017. LNCS, vol. 10401, pp. 101–132. Springer, Cham (2017). https://doi.org/10.1007/978-3-319-63688-7_4
5. Bader, C., Hofheinz, D., Jager, T., Kiltz, E., Li, Y.: Tightly-secure authenticated key exchange. In: Dodis, Y., Nielsen, J.B. (eds.) TCC 2015. LNCS, vol. 9014, pp. 629–658. Springer, Heidelberg (2015). https://doi.org/10.1007/978-3-662-46494-6_26
6. Bellare, M., Boldyreva, A., Micali, S.: Public-key encryption in a multi-user setting: security proofs and improvements. In: Preneel, B. (ed.) EUROCRYPT 2000. LNCS, vol. 1807, pp. 259–274. Springer, Heidelberg (2000). https://doi.org/10.1007/3-540-45539-6_18
7. Bellare, M., Goldwasser, S.: New paradigms for digital signatures and message authentication based on non-interactive zero knowledge proofs. In: Brassard, G. (ed.) CRYPTO 1989. LNCS, vol. 435, pp. 194–211. Springer, New York (1990). https://doi.org/10.1007/0-387-34805-0_19
8. Blazy, O., Kiltz, E., Pan, J.: (Hierarchical) identity-based encryption from affine message authentication. In: Garay, J.A., Gennaro, R. (eds.) CRYPTO 2014. LNCS, vol. 8616, pp. 408–425. Springer, Heidelberg (2014). https://doi.org/10.1007/978-3-662-44371-2_23
9. Boneh, D., Canetti, R., Halevi, S., Katz, J.: Chosen-ciphertext security from identity-based encryption. SIAM J. Comput. **36**(5), 1301–1328 (2007)
10. Boneh, D., Mironov, I., Shoup, V.: A secure signature scheme from bilinear maps. In: Joye, M. (ed.) CT-RSA 2003. LNCS, vol. 2612, pp. 98–110. Springer, Heidelberg (2003). https://doi.org/10.1007/3-540-36563-X_7
11. Chen, J., Gong, J., Weng, J.: Tightly secure IBE under constant-size master public key. In: Fehr, S. (ed.) PKC 2017. LNCS, vol. 10174, pp. 207–231. Springer, Heidelberg (2017). https://doi.org/10.1007/978-3-662-54365-8_9
12. Chen, J., Wee, H.: Fully, (almost) tightly secure ibe and dual system groups. In: Canetti, R., Garay, J.A. (eds.) CRYPTO 2013. LNCS, vol. 8043, pp. 435–460. Springer, Heidelberg (2013). https://doi.org/10.1007/978-3-642-40084-1_25
13. Chevallier-Mames, B., Joye, M.: A practical and tightly secure signature scheme without hash function. In: Abe, M. (ed.) CT-RSA 2007. LNCS, vol. 4377, pp. 339–356. Springer, Heidelberg (2006). https://doi.org/10.1007/11967668_22
14. Cramer, R., Shoup, V.: Universal hash proofs and a paradigm for adaptive chosen ciphertext secure public-key encryption. In: Knudsen, L.R. (ed.) EUROCRYPT 2002. LNCS, vol. 2332, pp. 45–64. Springer, Heidelberg (2002). https://doi.org/10.1007/3-540-46035-7_4
15. Cramer, R., Shoup, V.: Design and analysis of practical public-key encryption schemes secure against adaptive chosen ciphertext attack. SIAM J. Comput. **33**(1), 167–226 (2003)
16. Escala, A., Herold, G., Kiltz, E., Ràfols, C., Villar, J.: An algebraic framework for diffie-hellman assumptions. In: Canetti, R., Garay, J.A. (eds.) CRYPTO 2013. LNCS, vol. 8043, pp. 129–147. Springer, Heidelberg (2013). https://doi.org/10.1007/978-3-642-40084-1_8

17. Gay, R., Hofheinz, D., Kiltz, E., Wee, H.: Tightly CCA-secure encryption without pairings. In: Fischlin, M., Coron, J.-S. (eds.) EUROCRYPT 2016. LNCS, vol. 9665, pp. 1–27. Springer, Heidelberg (2016). https://doi.org/10.1007/978-3-662-49890-3_1
18. Gay, R., Hofheinz, D., Kohl, L., Pan, J.: More efficient (almost) tightly secure structure-preserving signatures. In: Nielsen, J.B., Rijmen, V. (eds.) EUROCRYPT 2018. LNCS, vol. 10821, pp. 230–258. Springer, Cham (2018). https://doi.org/10.1007/978-3-319-78375-8_8
19. Gentry, C.: Practical identity-based encryption without random oracles. In: Vaudenay, S. (ed.) EUROCRYPT 2006. LNCS, vol. 4004, pp. 445–464. Springer, Heidelberg (2006). https://doi.org/10.1007/11761679_27
20. Giacon, F., Kiltz, E., Poettering, B.: Hybrid encryption in a multi-user setting, revisited. In: Abdalla, M., Dahab, R. (eds.) PKC 2018. LNCS, vol. 10769, pp. 159–189. Springer, Cham (2018). https://doi.org/10.1007/978-3-319-76578-5_6
21. Gong, J., Chen, J., Dong, X., Cao, Z., Tang, S.: Extended nested dual system groups, revisited. In: Cheng, C.-M., Chung, K.-M., Persiano, G., Yang, B.-Y. (eds.) PKC 2016. LNCS, vol. 9614, pp. 133–163. Springer, Heidelberg (2016). https://doi.org/10.1007/978-3-662-49384-7_6
22. Gong, J., Dong, X., Chen, J., Cao, Z.: Efficient IBE with tight reduction to standard assumption in the multi-challenge setting. In: Cheon, J.H., Takagi, T. (eds.) ASIACRYPT 2016. LNCS, vol. 10032, pp. 624–654. Springer, Heidelberg (2016). https://doi.org/10.1007/978-3-662-53890-6_21
23. Groth, J.: Simulation-sound NIZK proofs for a practical language and constant size group signatures. In: Lai, X., Chen, K. (eds.) ASIACRYPT 2006. LNCS, vol. 4284, pp. 444–459. Springer, Heidelberg (2006). https://doi.org/10.1007/11935230_29
24. Groth, J., Sahai, A.: Efficient noninteractive proof systems for bilinear groups. SIAM J. Comput. **41**(5), 1193–1232 (2012)
25. Han, S., Liu, S., Qin, B., Gu, D.: Tightly CCA-secure identity-based encryption with ciphertext pseudorandomness. Designs, Codes and Cryptography **86**(3), 517–554 (2018). https://doi.org/10.1007/s10623-017-0339-3
26. Hesse, J., Hofheinz, D., Kohl, L.: On tightly secure non-interactive key exchange. In: Shacham, H., Boldyreva, A. (eds.) CRYPTO 2018. LNCS, vol. 10992, pp. 65–94. Springer, Cham (2018). https://doi.org/10.1007/978-3-319-96881-0_3
27. Hofheinz, D.: Algebraic partitioning: fully compact and (almost) tightly secure cryptography. In: Kushilevitz, E., Malkin, T. (eds.) TCC 2016. LNCS, vol. 9562, pp. 251–281. Springer, Heidelberg (2016). https://doi.org/10.1007/978-3-662-49096-9_11
28. Hofheinz, D.: Adaptive partitioning. In: Coron, J.-S., Nielsen, J.B. (eds.) EUROCRYPT 2017. LNCS, vol. 10212, pp. 489–518. Springer, Cham (2017). https://doi.org/10.1007/978-3-319-56617-7_17
29. Hofheinz, D., Jager, T.: Tightly secure signatures and public-key encryption. In: Safavi-Naini, R., Canetti, R. (eds.) CRYPTO 2012. LNCS, vol. 7417, pp. 590–607. Springer, Heidelberg (2012). https://doi.org/10.1007/978-3-642-32009-5_35
30. Hofheinz, D., Kiltz, E.: Secure hybrid encryption from weakened key encapsulation. In: Menezes, A. (ed.) CRYPTO 2007. LNCS, vol. 4622, pp. 553–571. Springer, Heidelberg (2007). https://doi.org/10.1007/978-3-540-74143-5_31
31. Hofheinz, D., Koch, J., Striecks, C.: Identity-based encryption with (almost) tight security in the multi-instance, multi-ciphertext setting. In: Katz, J. (ed.) PKC 2015. LNCS, vol. 9020, pp. 799–822. Springer, Heidelberg (2015). https://doi.org/10.1007/978-3-662-46447-2_36

32. Jutla, C.S., Ohkubo, M., Roy, A.: Improved (almost) tightly-secure structure-preserving signatures. In: Abdalla, M., Dahab, R. (eds.) PKC 2018. LNCS, vol. 10770, pp. 123–152. Springer, Cham (2018). https://doi.org/10.1007/978-3-319-76581-5_5
33. Jutla, C.S., Roy, A.: Shorter quasi-adaptive NIZK proofs for linear subspaces. In: Sako, K., Sarkar, P. (eds.) ASIACRYPT 2013. LNCS, vol. 8269, pp. 1–20. Springer, Heidelberg (2013). https://doi.org/10.1007/978-3-642-42033-7_1
34. Kiltz, E., Wee, H.: Quasi-adaptive NIZK for linear subspaces revisited. In: Oswald, E., Fischlin, M. (eds.) EUROCRYPT 2015. LNCS, vol. 9057, pp. 101–128. Springer, Heidelberg (2015). https://doi.org/10.1007/978-3-662-46803-6_4
35. Kurosawa, K., Desmedt, Y.: A new paradigm of hybrid encryption scheme. In: Franklin, M. (ed.) CRYPTO 2004. LNCS, vol. 3152, pp. 426–442. Springer, Heidelberg (2004). https://doi.org/10.1007/978-3-540-28628-8_26
36. Lewko, A., Waters, B.: Why proving HIBE systems secure is difficult. In: Nguyen, P.Q., Oswald, E. (eds.) EUROCRYPT 2014. LNCS, vol. 8441, pp. 58–76. Springer, Heidelberg (2014). https://doi.org/10.1007/978-3-642-55220-5_4
37. Libert, B., Joye, M., Yung, M., Peters, T.: Concise multi-challenge CCA-secure encryption and signatures with almost tight security. In: Sarkar, P., Iwata, T. (eds.) ASIACRYPT 2014. LNCS, vol. 8874, pp. 1–21. Springer, Heidelberg (2014). https://doi.org/10.1007/978-3-662-45608-8_1
38. Libert, B., Peters, T., Joye, M., Yung, M.: Compactly hiding linear spans. In: Iwata, T., Cheon, J.H. (eds.) ASIACRYPT 2015. LNCS, vol. 9452, pp. 681–707. Springer, Heidelberg (2015). https://doi.org/10.1007/978-3-662-48797-6_28
39. Morillo, P., Ràfols, C., Villar, J.L.: The kernel matrix Diffie-Hellman assumption. In: Cheon, J.H., Takagi, T. (eds.) ASIACRYPT 2016. LNCS, vol. 10031, pp. 729–758. Springer, Heidelberg (2016). https://doi.org/10.1007/978-3-662-53887-6_27
40. Naor, M., Reingold, O.: Number-theoretic constructions of efficient pseudo-random functions. In: 38th FOCS, pp. 458–467. IEEE Computer Society Press, October 1997
41. Naor, M., Yung, M.: Public-key cryptosystems provably secure against chosen ciphertext attacks. In: 22nd ACM STOC, pp. 427–437. ACM Press, May 1990
42. Shoup, V., Shoup, V.: Why chosen ciphertext security matters. IBM research report RZ 3076 (1998)
43. Wang, Y., Matsuda, T., Hanaoka, G., Tanaka, K.: Memory lower bounds of reductions revisited. In: Nielsen, J.B., Rijmen, V. (eds.) EUROCRYPT 2018. LNCS, vol. 10820, pp. 61–90. Springer, Cham (2018). https://doi.org/10.1007/978-3-319-78381-9_3

Short Digital Signatures and ID-KEMs via Truncation Collision Resistance

Tibor Jager(✉) and Rafael Kurek

Paderborn University, Paderborn, Germany
{tibor.jager,rafael.kurek}@upb.de

Abstract. *Truncation collision resistance* is a simple non-interactive complexity assumption that seems very plausible for standard cryptographic hash functions like SHA-3. We describe how this assumption can be leveraged to obtain standard-model constructions of public-key cryptosystems that previously seemed to require a programmable random oracle. This includes the first constructions of identity-based key encapsulation mechanisms (ID-KEMs) and digital signatures over bilinear groups with full adaptive security and without random oracles, where a ciphertext or signature consists of only a single element of a prime-order group. We also describe a generic construction of ID-KEMs with full adaptive security from a scheme with very weak security ("selective and non-adaptive chosen-ID security"), and a similar generic construction for digital signatures.

Keywords: Identity-based encryption · Digital signatures
Random oracle model · Extremely lossy functions · Provable security

1 Introduction

The random oracle model (ROM) [BR93] is often used to analyze the security of cryptosystems in a hypothetical setting, where a cryptographic hash function is modeled as an oracle that implements a truly random function. This provides a very strong handle for formal security proofs. For example, an adversary in this model has to explicitly query the oracle to evaluate the hash function, and it is possible to adaptively "program" the hash function to map certain input values to specific output values in the security proof. The random oracle is a hypothetical concept, used only in a security proof, but instantiated in practice with a standard cryptographic hash function, like SHA-3. This incurs the additional assumption that this hash function is "secure enough" for the given application.

Besides the well-known difficulty of instantiating random oracles [CGH98], the major drawback of this approach is that the random oracle essentially is a "perfect" hash function, which provides not only standard security properties, like onewayness and collision resistance, but essentially all imaginable security properties simultaneously. Therefore a security proof in the random oracle model

T. Peyrin and S. Galbraith (Eds.): ASIACRYPT 2018, LNCS 11273, pp. 221–250, 2018.
https://doi.org/10.1007/978-3-030-03329-3_8

does not explain which precise security properties of a hash function are actually necessary or sufficient for a given application. This is very undesirable, as we want to understand the required security properties and we want to provide cryptanalysts with clearly-defined cryptanalytic goals to attack the "security" of cryptographic hash functions. Therefore the ROM is often seen as only a first step towards achieving provably-secure constructions in the standard model.

The only known security proofs for many important cryptographic constructions seem to inherently require an adaptively programmable random oracle [Nie02, FLR+10, HMS12, FF13]. There are many primitives for which it is still unknown whether and how they can be instantiated without random oracles, and where no standard-model security proofs based on classical complexity assumptions on cryptographic hash functions are known so far. Several previous works isolated specific properties of random oracles, such as programmability [HK08, HJK11, FHPS13, CFN15] or extreme lossyness [Zha16], and realized these with standard-model constructions of special-purpose functions and based on algebraic public-key techniques, which are relatively inefficient in comparison to standard cryptographic hash functions. In the instead, we ask:

Which reasonable, simple, and non-interactive complexity assumptions for standard cryptographic hash functions are sufficient to obtain instantiations of cryptographic tools that currently require the ROM?

Hence, we do not ask for new non-standard hash functions that realize specific properties of a random oracle, but for reasonable assumptions on *standard* hash functions that are sufficient to avoid the random oracle. In this sense, we follow a line of research initiated by Canetti in 1997 [Can97], and continued by the UCE approach introduced by Bellare *et al.* [BHK13] and continued by Farshim and Mittelbach [FM16].

Truncation collision resistance. Truncation collision resistance (TruCR) basically demands that there is no algorithm that finds collisions significantly faster than the standard birthday collision algorithm, even when (short) *prefixes* of hash values are considered. More precisely, let $H : \{0,1\}^* \rightarrow \{0,1\}^k$ be a cryptographic hash function, and write $H_j(x)$ to denote the first j bits of $H(x)$. Truncation collision resistance requires that two input values x, x' with $x \neq x'$ and $H_j(x) = H_j(x')$ cannot be found for *any* value of j with significantly better time-to-success ratio than the standard birthday collision algorithm.

In contrast to the ROM, this assumption provides an explicit and well-defined goal for the cryptanalysis of hash functions. It is a single simple assumption, rather than a complex family of UCE assumptions of [BHK13], and based on simple "symmetric-key techniques" (i.e., standard cryptographic hash functions).

Contributions. We show that truncation collision resistance enables several interesting applications that previously required a random oracle. This includes:

- Identity-based key encapsulation schemes (ID-KEMs) with very short ciphertexts (only a single group element) and full adaptive security.

- Short digital signatures over bilinear groups with very short signatures (only a single group element) and full adaptive security.
- Generic constructions of ID-KEMs and digital signatures with full adaptive security from ID-KEMs and signatures with extremely weak "selective and non-adaptive" security.

Due to the relatively large (but polynomially-bounded) security loss of our security proofs, the practical value of our constructions is limited, if tightness is taken into account. However, we see truncation collision resistance as a step towards avoiding the random oracle for cryptosystems with minimal overhead.

Leveraging truncation collision resistance. In order to sketch how truncation collision resistance can be used in a security proof, let us consider the case of short digital signatures as an example. We work in the bilinear group setting, where we have groups $\mathbb{G}_1, \mathbb{G}_2, \mathbb{G}_T$ of prime order p, and an efficiently computable bilinear map $e : \mathbb{G}_1 \times \mathbb{G}_2 \to \mathbb{G}_T$. Signatures consist of only one element of $\mathbb{G}_1$. A secret key consist of $\ell = \log 4(k+1)$ elements $x_1, \ldots, x_\ell \in \mathbb{Z}_p$, where k is the security parameter. The corresponding public key consists of one element of $\mathbb{G}_1$ plus $4(k+1)$ elements of $\mathbb{G}_2$. Thus, public and secret keys are larger than for the random-oracle-based short signature scheme of Boneh, Lynn, and Shacham [BLS04], but the signature size is identical.

Computing a signature on a message m works as follows. For a cryptographic hash function $H : \{0,1\}^* \to \{0,1\}^{4(k+1)}$, let us write $H_{2^j}(m)$ to denote the first 2^j bits of $H(m)$. In order to sign a message m, we first compute

$$G(m) = \prod_{j=1}^{\ell} (x_j + H_{2^j}(m)) \bmod p.$$

Note that one can perform this computation very efficiently, as it involves only elementary operations over $\mathbb{Z}_p$. Finally, the signature for m is

$$\sigma = g_1^{1/G(m)} \in \mathbb{G}_1,$$

where $g_1 \in \mathbb{G}_1$ is a generator. Thus, computing a signature requires to perform only a *single* exponentiation in $\mathbb{G}_1$, plus a small number of additional operations in $\mathbb{Z}_p$.

A signature can be verified by first computing $g_2^{G(m)} \in \mathbb{G}_2$ from the group elements contained in the public key, which involves $\mathcal{O}(k)$ operations in $\mathbb{Z}_p$, $\mathcal{O}(k)$ multiplications in $\mathbb{G}_2$, and then testing whether

$$e(\sigma, g_2^{G(m)}) \stackrel{?}{=} e(g_1, g_2).$$

Note that this test requires only a single application of the bilinear map e to compute $e(\sigma, g_2^{G(m)})$, because the term $e(g_1, g_2)$ is independent of the given message and signature, and can thus be precomputed.

In order to sketch how truncation collision resistance is used in the security proof, note that a signature has the form

$$\sigma = g_1^{1/\prod_{j=1}^{\ell}(x_j + H_{2^j}(m))}, \tag{1}$$

which can be viewed as an aggregation of ℓ signatures of the form

$$\sigma_j = g_1^{1/(x_j + H_{2^j}(m))}. \tag{2}$$

Let us view a signature σ as an ℓ-tuple $\sigma = (\sigma_1, \ldots, \sigma_\ell)$, where σ_j is as in (2). We describe later how these signatures can be aggregated to obtain our actual scheme. Note that each σ_j is a Boneh-Boyen signature [BB04c] over the first 2^j bits of $H(m)$. In the security proof, we will choose j such that it simultaneously achieves the following two properties.

1. The index j is *sufficiently small*. Let m^* be the message for which the assumed adversary $\mathcal{A}$ forges a signature. We want that j is small enough, such that we can guess $H_{2^j}(m^*) \in \{0,1\}^{2^j}$ with reasonable success probability, even *before* the security experiment starts, and we are able to prepare signatures for *all other* values $\{0,1\}^{2^j} \setminus H_{2^j}(m^*)$.
2. At the same time, we will make sure that the index j is *sufficiently large*, such that it is "sufficiently unlikely" that the adversary finds a collision for H_{2^j}. More precisely, we want that it is "sufficiently unlikely" that the adversary ever requests a signature for a message m_i and then outputs a forgery for message m^* with $H_{2^j}(m_i) = H_{2^j}(m^*)$.

The main difficulty of our security analysis lies in the second property, therefore let us consider this one more closely. Truncation collision resistance basically guarantees that there is no algorithm that finds collisions with significantly better time-to-success ratio than the standard birthday collision algorithm, even when prefixes $H_{2^j}(x)$ of hash values $H(x)$ are considered. Of course we will not be able to choose j such that the probability that $\mathcal{A}$ finds a collision is *negligibly* small – at least not without sacrificing the first condition, which we cannot afford. However, we will be able to choose j such that we can argue that the probability that $\mathcal{A}$ finds a collision for H_{2^j} is at most $\epsilon/2$, where ϵ is the success probability of $\mathcal{A}$ in breaking our signature scheme. This is "sufficiently unlikely", because it means: while *sometimes* $\mathcal{A}$ may break the security of the signature scheme by finding a collision, at least *sometimes* (more precisely: with probability at least $\epsilon/2$) the adversary will also be able to break the signature scheme *without* finding a collision. This allows us to reduce the full EUF-CMA-security of our scheme to the SUF-naCMA-security of the underlying Boneh-Boyen scheme.

Since Boneh-Boyen signatures are not known to be efficiently aggregable in the sense of [BGLS03,LOS+06], we have to overcome another hurdle to obtain a short signature scheme. Note that computing a signature that satisfies (1) essentially yields a "polynomial in the exponent" in unknowns $x_1, \ldots, x_\ell$ of degree ℓ. In order to verify whether a given value σ indeed satisfies (1) using a bilinear map, we therefore must to be able to compute group elements of the form

$$g^{x_1^{b_1} \cdots x_\ell^{b_\ell}}. \tag{3}$$

for all possible values of $b_1, \ldots, b_\ell \in \{0,1\}$. Note that these are 2^ℓ different values, but we have $\ell = \mathcal{O}(\log k)$ This allows us to include all required values of the form (3) in the public key, which yields a public key of size $\mathcal{O}(k)$.

On the necessity of using ℓ parallel copies. A signature σ in the construction described above essentially consists of ℓ aggregated copies of signatures σ_j, $j \in [\ell]$. The purpose of j is to find a balance the two properties described above, but the "right" choice of j depends on the given adversary: different adversaries may require a different value of j to achieve the right balance.

The fact that we essentially run several copies of the scheme in parallel may appear artificial, but it is the only way that we currently know to guarantee a suitable value of j for any possible adversary, and thus the only way we know to prove security against any efficient adversary. There are other schemes that essentially run many copies of an underlying scheme in parallel "only" to achieve provable security. This includes, for instance, pseudorandom functions [DS15, BH15] and digital signatures [BHJ+13, HW09a, BK10].

Comparison to other prefix-guessing techniques. The main difference between our approach and the prefix-guessing technique of [HW09b, BK10] is that we essentially guess a short prefix of the hash of the "target message" *directly*, exploiting the truncation collision resistance to argue that this hash cannot be equal to the hash of any chosen-message query. We do not have to know any chosen-message queries of the adversary to do this, which makes the technique also applicable to identity-based schemes like ID-KEMs. In contrast, the prefix-guessing technique of [HW09b, BK10] guesses the shortest prefix of the target message that is not equal to a prefix of a chosen-message query, which depends on the chosen-message queries made by the adversary and therefore can only be used to construct non-adaptively secure signatures (adaptive security is then achieved in a second step, e.g. using [EGM96]).

2 Truncation Collision-Resistant Hashing

Intuitively, truncation collision resistance (TruCR) means that there exists no algorithm which finds collisions with significantly better *work factor* [BR09] than the trivial birthday collision algorithm. This must hold even if the output of the hash function is truncated. This notion is strongly related to standard collision resistance [RS04], but to our best knowledge has not yet been formally defined or used as a basis for formal security proofs of cryptosystems.

Computational model. We consider algorithms as Turing machines, which operate on a binary alphabet and write their output bit-by-bit to an output tape, where each written bit takes one elementary machine operation.[1] The *running time* of

[1] We explain below how our results can be extended to models of computation where an algorithm is able to output multiple bits per elementary machine operation.

an algorithm is defined as the number of elementary operations performed by this machine.

Truncation collision resistance. Let $\mathcal{H} = \{H : \{0,1\}^* \to \{0,1\}^\alpha\}$ be a family of keyed hash functions and let H_i denote the function obtained by evaluating H and truncating its output to the first i bits. Thus, $H_1(x)$ consists of the first bit of $H(x)$, and $H_\alpha(x) = H(x)$ for all $x \in \{0,1\}^*$.

Definition 1. *We say that adversary $\mathcal{B}$ i-breaks the truncation collision resistance of $\mathcal{H}$, if it runs in time $t_\mathcal{B}$ and*

$$\Pr_{H \xleftarrow{\$} \mathcal{H}} \left[\begin{matrix} (x_0, \ldots, x_q) \xleftarrow{\$} \mathcal{B}(H) : \\ \exists u, v \text{ s.t. } H_i(x_u) = H_i(x_v) \land x_u \neq x_v \end{matrix} \right] > \frac{t_\mathcal{B}(t_\mathcal{B} - 1)}{2^{i+1}}.$$

The bound $t_\mathcal{B}(t_\mathcal{B} - 1)/2^{i+1}$ in the above definition stems from the birthday bound, which states that an adversary which evaluates a random function with range $\{0,1\}^i$ at most q times will find a collision with probability at most $q(q-1)/2^{i+1}$. Observe here that an adversary in our computational model must perform at least $q \cdot \log_2 q$ computational operations in order to output q pairwise distinct bit strings. Hence, in order to break TruCR, an algorithm must be better than the trivial birthday attack algorithm by a factor larger than $\log_2 q$.

Constructing hash families from standard hash functions. Let H' be any standard cryptographic hash function, such as SHA-3, for example. We can construct a hash function family $\mathcal{H}$ as

$$\mathcal{H} := \{H : H(x) := H'(r||x), r \in \{0,1\}^k\}.$$

A uniformly random hash function H from the family is chosen by selecting a uniformly random bit string $r \in \{0,1\}^k$. $H(x)$ is evaluated by computing $H'(r||x)$.

Strength of the TruCR assumption. We view truncation collision resistance as a very natural security property for cryptographic hash functions. Note that truncated versions of SHA-256 (to 224 bits) and SHA-512 (to 384 bits) have been standardized by NIST [Nat15a]. Also the SHA-3 standard [Nat15b] defines two extendable-output-functions (XOFs), in which the output length can be adapted to any desired length.

Furthermore, recall that the standard way to determine the size of the output of a hash function in practice is to fix a security parameter k, and to take a hash function of output size $2k$. For example, choosing SHA-256 (which has 256-bit hash values) for $k = 128$ is considered an adequate choice in practice, if collision-resistance at "128-bit security level" is required. Note that one essentially assumes here already that there is no significantly better collision attack than the generic birthday algorithm. TruCR generalizes this assumption to *prefixes* of the hash function output.

We also note that our applications will require hash functions with output length $4(k+1)$, rather than the "minimal" $2k$. For example, for $k = 127$ we would use SHA-512.

In the full version [JK17], we also sketch how TruCR hash functions can be constructed from standard assumptions.

Choice of computational model and weakening the TruCR assumption. Assume a computational model where an algorithm is able to output many pairwise distinct values $x_0, \ldots, x_q$ in a *single* elementary machine operation, and thus within a single time unit. Note that such an algorithm would be able to trivially break the TruCR assumption with a simple birthday attack. To overcome this technical obstacle, we are working in a computational model where algorithms are assumed to write their output bit-by-bit to an output tape.

In order to generalize this to a computational model where algorithms are able to output any constant number of bits in parallel in a single step, we can weaken Definition 1 by increasing the size of the prefix for which the adversary has to find a collision. To this end, one would replace the requirement

$$H_i(x_u) = H_i(x_v).$$

in Definition 1 with $H_{i+c}(x_u) = H_{i+c}(x_v)$ for some small constant value c (e.g., $c \in \{1, ..., 10\}$). This also allows to add some additional "safety margin" to the assumption, if desired, at the cost of an additional constant tightness loss factor of 2^c in the security proofs of our constructions. In the remainder of the paper, we will work with the original Definition 1, as it simplifies the exposition of our main results.

Relation to ELFs. From a high-level perspective, truncation collision-resistant hash functions are related to *extremely lossy functions* (ELFs), which were introduced by Zhandry [Zha16]. In some applications, TruCR and ELFs can be used in a very similar way to argue in a security proof, and it seems that some of our applications can also be achieved by using an ELF instead. ELFs furthermore allow for some additional applications, like the construction of *output-intractable* hash functions or a standard-model instantiation of full-domain hash (the latter in combination with indistinguishability obfuscation).

The main difference between Zhandry's work and ours is that [Zha16] gives new constructions of hash functions based on public-key techniques and the reasonable exponential hardness assumption of the decisional Diffie-Hellman problem in algebraic groups. Instead, following [Can97, BHK13, FM16], we use standard cryptographic hash functions that are already widely-used in practice, and a similarly reasonable complexity assumption for such functions. This partially resolves the open problem posed in [Zha16] of constructing ELFs using symmetric-key techniques: while we do not construct full ELFs, we show how certain potential applications of ELFs can be realized based on standard hash functions. We furthermore show how TruCR can be used to obtain interesting new constructions: the first ID-KEM with full adaptive security and very short ciphertexts (only a single element from a bilinear group), and the first digital signature scheme with full adaptive security and very short signatures (again, only single element from a bilinear group). One can also show that ELFs and TruCR hash functions do not imply each other. Due to space limitations, this is deferred to the full version of this paper [JK17].

On assuming exponential hardness. Both the work of Zhandry [Zha16] and ours assume exponential hardness of the underlying computational problems. The construction of ELFs from [Zha16] assumes the exponential hardness of the DDH assumption in suitable algebraic groups. This is a strong assumption, but it appears reasonable, e.g., in certain elliptic curve groups, where the best known algorithms for solving the DDH problem have exponential complexity. Furthermore, note that this matches the choice of elliptic curve groups in practice, where typically a group of prime order $\approx 2^{2k}$ is expected to achieve "k-bit security". Similarly, we assume that for a cryptographic hash function there exists no significantly better collision attack than the generic birthday collision algorithm, which also has exponential complexity.

Useful technical lemma. To conclude our discussion of TruCR, we state a technical lemma, which will be useful to leverage truncation collision resistance in security proofs. Intuitively, the lemma will provide bounds to ensure in our security proofs that for each adversary with some running time t and success probability ϵ there always exists a "good" index j such that H_{2^j} is "sufficiently collision-resistant", but at the same time the range $\{0,1\}^{2^j}$ of H_{2^j} is "sufficiently small". As usual, all logarithms are to base 2 in the sequel.

Lemma 1. *Let $t \in \mathbb{N}$ and $\epsilon \in (0,1]$ with $t/\epsilon < 2^k$, and $j := \lfloor \log\log(4t^2/\epsilon) \rfloor + 1$. Then it holds that*

$$j \in \{1, \dots, \log 4(k+1)\}, \qquad \frac{4t^2}{2^{2^j+1}} < \frac{\epsilon}{2} \qquad \textit{and} \qquad 2^{2^j} \leq \left(\frac{4t^2}{\epsilon}\right)^2.$$

Proof. We first show that $j \in \{1, \dots, \log 4(k+1)\}$. Since $\epsilon > 0$, we trivially have $j \geq 1$. Additionally using that $t/\epsilon < 2^k$, we obtain

$$\begin{aligned} j &= \lfloor \log\log(4t^2/\epsilon) \rfloor + 1 \leq \log\log(4t^2/\epsilon) + 1 \\ &< \log\log(2^{2k+2}) + 1 = \log 4(k+1). \end{aligned}$$

To show $4t^2/2^{2^j+1} < \epsilon/2$, we compute

$$\frac{4t^2}{2 \cdot 2^{2^j}} = \frac{4t^2}{2 \cdot 2^{2^{\lfloor \log\log(4t^2/\epsilon) \rfloor + 1}}} < \frac{4t^2}{2 \cdot 2^{2^{\log\log(4t^2/\epsilon)}}} = \frac{4t^2}{2 \cdot (4t^2/\epsilon)} = \frac{\epsilon}{2}.$$

Finally, we get $2^{2^j} \leq \left(4t^2/\epsilon\right)^2$ from

$$2^{2^j} = 2^{2^{\lfloor \log\log(4t^2/\epsilon) \rfloor + 1}} \leq 2^{2 \cdot 2^{\log\log(4t^2/\epsilon)}} = (4t^2/\epsilon)^2.$$

□

3 Identity-Based Key Encapsulation

Recall that the commonly accepted standard security notion for identity-based key encapsulation (ID-KEM) is *adaptive chosen-ID* security (IND-ID-CPA), as introduced in [BFMLS08]. Here, the adversary in the security experiment may adaptively choose *both* the "challenge identity" (i.e., the identity for which it receives a challenge ciphertext) and the "key-query identities" (i.e., the identities for which it requests a user secret key). A much weaker common standard security notion is *selective challenge-ID security* (IND-sID-CPA) [CHK03, CHK04], where the adversary has to announce the challenge identity and at the very beginning of the security experiment, even before seeing the master public key, but may adaptively query for user secret keys. In this work, we consider the even weaker notion with *selective* challenge-identity and *non-adaptive* key-queries (IND-snaID-CPA), where the adversary has to announce *both* the challenge identity and all key-query identities at the very beginning of the security experiment, even before seeing the master public key (see Sect. 3.1 for formal definitions).

As a first application of TruCR, we describe a simple generic construction of a fully adaptively IND-ID-CPA-secure ID-KEM from any ID-KEM which is only IND-snaID-CPA-secure. This shows that if TruCR hash functions exist, then ID-KEMs with full IND-ID-CPA-security are implied by IND-snaID-CPA-secure ID-KEMs. The latter are usually significantly easier to construct. This result also introduces a technique for leveraging truncation collision-resistance in security proofs. The generic conversion is relatively efficient: it increases the size of public parameters, user secret keys, and ciphertexts by a factor of only $\mathcal{O}(\log k)$, where k is the security parameter. The security reduction is non-tight, but polynomial-time. Previous standard techniques to build an adaptively secure ID-KEM from a selectively-secure one, e.g. by using admissible [BB04b] or programmable [HK08, Wat05] hash functions, work only non-generically for certain schemes with specific properties. The only previously known *generic* way to turn an IND-snaID-CPA-secure scheme into a fully IND-ID-CPA-secure one is to use the programmable ROM.

Then we show how TruCR can be used to obtain the first ID-KEM with full IND-ID-CPA-security without random oracles and with very short ciphertexts, where the ciphertext overhead is only a single element from a prime-order group. The only previously known ID-KEM with such short ciphertexts and adaptive security is the construction of Boneh and Franklin [BF01], which only has a security proof in the ROM. The adaptively secure standard-model scheme of Wee [Wee16] requires significantly larger composite-order groups. Our scheme is based on the selectively-secure Boneh-Boyen IBE scheme [BB04a] and proven secure under a q-type assumption, but it shows that adaptively secure ID-KEMs with such short ciphertext overhead can be constructed without random oracles.

On using complexity leveraging. Achieving adaptive security from selective security is sometimes also possible by directly assuming exponential hardness of breaking the underlying selectively-secure scheme, and then using complexity leveraging. For instance, in order to convert an IND-sID-CPA-secure ID-KEM into an IND-ID-CPA-secure one, we can simply guess the challenge identity id^* chosen by the IND-ID-CPA adversary up front at the beginning of the security experiment, and use this to implement a straightforward reduction to the IND-sID-CPA of the considered scheme. Since the identity space usually has exponential size 2^k where k is the security parameter, then this incurs an exponential security loss of 2^k, which must be compensated by choosing larger parameters for the underlying scheme. If the underlying scheme is exponentially secure, then doubling the size of parameters, such as underlying algebraic groups for instance, usually suffices in this case.

However, note that this complexity leveraging approach is *not* useful if one starts from the weaker IND-snaID-CPA-security, as we do in this work. This is because here we would have to guess not only the challenge identity id^*, but also *all* q identities $id_1, \ldots, id_q$ of key-queries made by the IND-ID-CPA adversary up front, which yields a security loss of $\binom{2^k}{q+1} \geq 2^{kq - \log q} \approx 2^{kq}$. This cannot be easily compensated with larger parameters, because even if the underlying scheme is exponentially secure, then this would still require to increase the parameters by a factor of about q, which is completely impractical.

Relation to a result by Döttling and Garg. There exists several (semi-)generic constructions of strongly-secure signatures from signatures with weaker security [EGM96,BSW06,SPW07,HW09b,BK10]. All these works have in common that they can be applied only to signature scheme, but not to identity-based schemes like ID-KEMs, because they are either probabilistic (e.g., based on ephemeral one-time signatures or chameleon hash functions), or consider a setting with a non-adaptive adversary, which is forced to output all chosen-message queries before seeing the public key.

Döttling and Garg [DG17a] describe a generic construction of adaptively secure IBE from selectively-secure IBE. Their approach is completely different from ours, as it is based on the techniques introduced in [DG17b]. A ciphertext of the adaptively secure scheme consists of $n+1$ garbled circuits, ℓ corresponding labels, and ℓ ciphertexts of a specific type of encryption scheme called *one-time signature with encryption (OTSE)*, plus a few additional values. Here, n is the bit-length of identities and ℓ denotes the length of encrypted messages. A ciphertext of the OTSE scheme in turn consist of $2k$ ciphertexts of the underlying selectively-secure scheme, where k is the security parameter. The size of public and secret keys is similarly large.

In contrast, our generic construction is much more direct, and shows how to construct an adaptively secure scheme that requires only $\log k$ copies of the underlying scheme (with similarly short public and secret keys), but based on an additional security assumption on the hash function. Our approach also enables the construction of an adaptively secure scheme where a ciphertext consists only of a single group element, which currently seems out of reach of the approach of Döttling and Garg.

Another difference is that they start from the IND-sID-CPA security notion, while we start from the even weaker IND-snaID-CPA notion. It is unclear whether their results can be adopted to the same setting.

In summary, the construction of Döttling and Garg has the advantage of not requiring an additional complexity assumption, but also seems rather far away from practical applicability and is therefore currently mostly of theoretical interest. In contrast, our construction requires an additional assumption, but is more direct and incurs significantly less overhead, such that it already yields very efficient schemes. Thus, both approaches achieve different goals.

3.1 Definitions and Security Notions

Definition 2. *An ID-KEM consists of the following four PPT algorithms:*

$\mathsf{Setup}(1^k)$ *returns the public parameters* PP *and the master secret key* MSK*. We assume that* PP *defines (implicitly or explicitly) an identity space* $\mathcal{I}$*, a key space* $\mathcal{K}$ *and a ciphertext space* $\mathcal{C}$*.*
$\mathsf{KeyGen}(MSK, id)$ *returns the user secret key* USK_{id} *for identity* $id \in \mathcal{I}$*.*
$\mathsf{Encap}(PP, id)$ *returns a tuple* (C, K)*, where* $K \in \mathcal{K}$ *is a key and* $C \in \mathcal{C}$ *is a ciphertext encapsulating* K *with respect to identity* id*.*
$\mathsf{Decap}(USK_{id}, C, id)$ *returns the decapsulated key* $K \in \mathcal{K}$ *or an error symbol* $\perp$*.*

For perfect correctness we require that for all $k \in \mathbb{N}$*, all pairs* (PP, MSK) *generated by* $\mathsf{Setup}(1^k)$*, all identities* $id \in \mathcal{I}$*, all* (K, C) *output by* $\mathsf{Encap}(PP, id)$ *and all* USK_{id} *generated by* $\mathsf{KeyGen}(MSK, id)$*:*

$$\Pr[\mathsf{Decap}(USK_{id}, C, id) = K] = 1.$$

Adaptive security. Let us first recall the standard IND-CPA-security notion for ID-KEMs from [BFMLS08]. To this end, consider the IND-ID-CPA security experiment depicted in Fig. 1.

$\mathsf{IND\text{-}snaID\text{-}CPA}_{\Pi}^{q,\mathcal{A}}(k)$	$\mathsf{IND\text{-}ID\text{-}CPA}_{\Pi}^{q,\mathcal{A}}(k)$
$b \stackrel{\$}{\leftarrow} \{0,1\}$	$b \stackrel{\$}{\leftarrow} \{0,1\}$
$(id^*, id_1, ..., id_q, st_1) \leftarrow \mathcal{A}_1(1^k)$	$(PP, MSK) \stackrel{\$}{\leftarrow} \mathsf{Setup}(1^k)$
$(PP, MSK) \stackrel{\$}{\leftarrow} \mathsf{Setup}(1^k)$	$(id^*, st) \leftarrow \mathcal{A}_1^{\mathsf{KeyGen}(MSK,\cdot)}(1^k, PP)$
$USK_{id_i} \stackrel{\$}{\leftarrow} \mathsf{KeyGen}(MSK, id_i)\ \forall i \in [q]$	$K_0 \stackrel{\$}{\leftarrow} \mathcal{K}$; $(C, K_1) \stackrel{\$}{\leftarrow} \mathsf{Encap}(PP, id^*)$
$K_0 \stackrel{\$}{\leftarrow} \mathcal{K}$; $(C, K_1) \stackrel{\$}{\leftarrow} \mathsf{Encap}(PP, id^*)$	$b' \leftarrow \mathcal{A}_2^{\mathsf{KeyGen}(MSK,\cdot)}(st, C, K_b)$
$b' \leftarrow \mathcal{A}_2(st_1, (USK_{id_i})_{i\in[q]}, C, K_b)$	Return $(b' == b)$
Return $(b' == b)$	

Fig. 1. The security experiments for ID-KEMs, executed with scheme $\Pi = (\mathsf{Setup}, \mathsf{KeyGen}, \mathsf{Encap}, \mathsf{Decap})$ and adversary $\mathcal{A} = (\mathcal{A}_1, \mathcal{A}_2)$. The oracle $\mathsf{KeyGen}(MSK, id)$ returns $USK_{id} \stackrel{\$}{\leftarrow} \mathsf{KeyGen}(MSK, id)$ with the restriction that $\mathcal{A}$ is not allowed to query oracle $\mathsf{KeyGen}(MSK, \cdot)$ for the target identity id^*.

Definition 3. *We say that adversary* $\mathcal{A}$ $(t_{\mathcal{A}}, q, \epsilon_{\mathcal{A}})$*-breaks the* IND-ID-CPA *security of* Π*, if* $\Pr[\mathsf{IND\text{-}ID\text{-}CPA}_{\Pi}^{q,\mathcal{A}}(k) = 1] - \frac{1}{2} \geq \epsilon_{\mathcal{A}}$ *and* $t_{\mathcal{A}}$ *is the running time of* $\mathcal{A}$*, including the security experiment.*

Remark 1. Including the running time of the security experiment into $t_{\mathcal{A}}$ will later allow us to simplify our security analysis and the statement of theorems significantly.

Selective and non-adaptive security. We also define a very weak security notion for ID-KEMs. Consider the IND-snaID-CPA security experiment depicted in Fig. 1, where the attacker has to commit to both the challenge-ID id^* the key-query identities $id_1, \ldots, id_q$ non-adaptively and even before receiving the master public key PP.

Definition 4. *We say that $\mathcal{A}$ $(t_{\mathcal{A}}, q, \epsilon_{\mathcal{A}})$-breaks the* IND-snaID-CPA *security of Π, if it runs in time $t_{\mathcal{A}}$ and*

$$\Pr[\mathsf{IND\text{-}snaID\text{-}CPA}_{\Pi}^{q,\mathcal{A}}(k) = 1] - \frac{1}{2} \geq \epsilon_{\mathcal{A}}.$$

3.2 From Weak Security to Adaptive Security

Construction. Let $\mathcal{H} = \{H | \{0,1\}^* \to \{0,1\}^{4(k+1)}\}$ be a family of keyed hash functions and define

$$\ell := \log 4(k+1).$$

Let $\Pi' = (\mathsf{Setup}', \mathsf{KeyGen}', \mathsf{Encap}', \mathsf{Decap}')$ be an ID-KEM. We construct our ID-KEM scheme $\Pi = (\mathsf{Setup}, \mathsf{KeyGen}, \mathsf{Encap}, \mathsf{Decap})$ as follows.

Setup. Compute $(PP_i, MPK_i) \xleftarrow{\$} \mathsf{Setup}'(1^k)$ for all $i \in \{1, \ldots, \ell\}$ and $H \leftarrow \mathcal{H}$ and define

$$PP = (H, PP_1, \ldots, PP_\ell) \qquad \text{and} \qquad MSK = (MSK_1, \ldots, MSK_\ell).$$

and output (PP, MSK).

User Key Generation. To create a private key for the identity id, compute $USK_i \xleftarrow{\$} \mathsf{KeyGen}'(MSK_i, H_{2^i}(id))$ for all $i \in \{1, \ldots, \ell\}$. Define

$$USK_{id} := (USK_1, \ldots, USK_\ell)$$

and output USK_{id}.

Encapsulation. On input $PP = (H, PP_1, \ldots, PP_\ell)$ and id, compute $(K_i, C_i) \xleftarrow{\$} \mathsf{Encap}'(PP_i, H_{2^i}(id))$ for all $i \in \{1, \ldots, \ell\}$. Then define $K := \bigoplus_{i=1}^{\ell} K_i$, where $\bigoplus$ denotes the XOR-operation and output $(C, K) = ((C_1, ..., C_\ell), K)$.

Decapsulation. On input $C = (C_1, ... C_\ell)$ and USK_{id}, compute

$$K_i = \mathsf{Decap}'(USK_i, C_i)$$

for all $i \in \{1, \ldots, \ell\}$ and output $K := \bigoplus_{i=1}^{\ell} K_i$.

The correctness of Π follows immediately from the correctness of Π'.

Security analysis. Recall that we have $\ell := \log 4(k+1)$, and that Lemma 1 shows that for each adversary $\mathcal{A}$ with $t_\mathcal{A}/\epsilon_\mathcal{A} < 2^k$, there exists an index $j \in \{1, \ldots, \ell\}$ such that

$$j = \lfloor \log\log 4t_\mathcal{A}^2/\epsilon_\mathcal{A} \rfloor + 1. \tag{4}$$

Theorem 1. *Let $\mathcal{A}$ be an adversary that $(t_\mathcal{A}, q_\mathcal{A}, \epsilon_\mathcal{A})$-breaks the* IND-ID-CPA-*security of Π such that $t_\mathcal{A}/\epsilon_\mathcal{A} < 2^k$ and let j be an index such that (4) is satisfied. Given $\mathcal{A}$ and j, we can either construct an adversary $\mathcal{B}_j$ that $(t_\mathcal{B}, q_\mathcal{B}, \epsilon_\mathcal{B})$-breaks the* IND-snaID-CPA-*security of Π' with*

$$t_\mathcal{B} = \mathcal{O}(t_\mathcal{A}^4/\epsilon_\mathcal{A}^2), \qquad q_\mathcal{B} < 4t_\mathcal{A}^4/\epsilon_\mathcal{A}^2 \quad and \quad \epsilon_\mathcal{B} \geq \frac{\epsilon_\mathcal{A}^3}{32t_\mathcal{A}^4}$$

or an adversary $\mathcal{C}$ that 2^j-breaks the truncation collision resistance of $\mathcal{H}$.

Note that the theorem considers adversaries that for a given security parameter k have "work factor" $t_\mathcal{A}/\epsilon_\mathcal{A}$ below 2^k. This deviates slightly from the common asymptotic definition, where it is required that $t_\mathcal{A}$ is polynomially-bounded and $\epsilon_\mathcal{A}$ is non-negligible. Assuming $t_\mathcal{A}/\epsilon_\mathcal{A} < 2^k$ is an alternative way of expressing that a cryptosystem is secure with respect to a given security parameter k that originates from the "concrete security" approach of Bellare and Ristenpart [BR09]. Note also that the security loss of reduction $\mathcal{B}$ is polynomially-bounded, but relatively large.

Proof. We say that event coll_j occurs in the $\mathsf{IND\text{-}ID\text{-}CPA}_\Pi^{q,\mathcal{A}}(k)$ security experiment, when $\mathcal{A}$ ever queries a user secret key for identity id_z such that $H_{2^j}(id_z) = H_{2^j}(id^*)$, where id^* is the challenge identity. We distinguish between two cases.

Case 1: $\Pr[\mathsf{coll}_j] > \epsilon_\mathcal{A}/2$. In this case we are able to construct an adversary $\mathcal{C}$ on the truncation collision resistance of H.

Construction of $\mathcal{C}$. $\mathcal{C}$ runs the $\mathsf{IND\text{-}ID\text{-}CPA}_\Pi^{q,\mathcal{A}}(k)$ experiment. Whenever $\mathcal{A}$ issues a query id_i to KeyGen, then $\mathcal{C}$ additionally outputs id_i. When $\mathcal{A}$ outputs the challenge identity id^*, then $\mathcal{C}$ outputs id^*. When $\mathcal{A}$ terminates, then $\mathcal{C}$ terminates, too.

Running time of $\mathcal{C}$. To bound the running time of $\mathcal{C}$, note that it consists of the time required to run $\mathcal{A}$, plus the time required to simulate the experiment, plus the time required to output the queries $id_1, \ldots, id_q, id^*$ made by $\mathcal{A}$. Thus, since $t_\mathcal{A}$ already includes the running time of the experiment, the total running time of $\mathcal{C}$ is bounded by $t_\mathcal{C} \leq 2 \cdot t_\mathcal{A}$.

Success probability of $\mathcal{C}$. To analyze the success probability of $\mathcal{C}$, let $i := 2^j$. Note that the success probability of $\mathcal{C}$ is equal to $\Pr[\mathsf{coll}_j]$, and by definition of j and Lemma 1 we have

$$\Pr[\mathsf{coll}_j] > \epsilon_\mathcal{A}/2 > 4t_\mathcal{A}^2/2^{i+1} \geq 2t_\mathcal{A}(2t_\mathcal{A} - 1)/2^{i+1} \geq t_\mathcal{C}(t_\mathcal{C} - 1)/2^{i+1}$$

so that indeed $\mathcal{C}$ breaks the truncation collision resistance of H.

Case 2: $\Pr[\mathsf{coll}_j] \leq \epsilon_{\mathcal{A}}/2$. In this case we construct an algorithm $\mathcal{B}_j$ on the IND-snaID-CPA security of Π'. Before we are able to describe $\mathcal{B}_j$, we will describe a short sequence of games, which gradually modifies the original $\mathsf{IND\text{-}ID\text{-}CPA}_{\Pi}^{q,\mathcal{A}}(k)$ experiment. In the sequel let G_i denote the event that Game i outputs 1.

Game 0. This is the original $\mathsf{IND\text{-}ID\text{-}CPA}_{\Pi}^{q,\mathcal{A}}(k)$ security experiment. By definition, we have

$$\Pr[G_0] = \frac{1}{2} + \epsilon_{\mathcal{A}}.$$

Game 1. Game 1 is identical to Game 0, except that if coll_j occurs, then Game 1 outputs a random bit and aborts.

Using that $G_1 \wedge \neg\mathsf{coll}_j \iff G_0 \wedge \neg\mathsf{coll}_j$ and that $\Pr[\mathsf{coll}_j] \leq \epsilon_{\mathcal{A}}/2$, we obtain

$$\Pr[G_1] \geq \Pr[G_1 \wedge \neg\mathsf{coll}_j] = \Pr[G_0 \wedge \neg\mathsf{coll}_j] \geq \Pr[G_0] - \Pr[\mathsf{coll}_j] \geq \frac{1}{2} + \frac{\epsilon_{\mathcal{A}}}{2}.$$

Game 2. In Game 2, we additionally guess a string $ID^* \stackrel{\$}{\leftarrow} \{0,1\}^{2^j}$ uniformly random. We raise event $\mathsf{abort_{chal}}$ if adversary $\mathcal{A}$ requests a challenge ciphertext for identity id^* with $H_{2^j}(id^*) \neq ID^*$.

We stress that this game merely *defines* event $\mathsf{abort_{chal}}$, as a preparation for the analysis in the following game, but we do not make any changes to the experiment. Thus, we have

$$\Pr[G_2] = \Pr[G_1].$$

Note also that $\mathcal{A}$ receives no information about ID^* and thus the events G_2 and $\mathsf{abort_{chal}}$ are independent.

Game 3. This game is identical to Game 2, except that we output a random bit and abort the game, if $\mathsf{abort_{chal}}$ occurs.

Using that $G_3 \wedge \neg\mathsf{abort_{chal}} \iff G_2 \wedge \neg\mathsf{abort_{chal}}$ we first get

$$\begin{aligned}
\Pr[G_3] &= \Pr[G_3 \mid \mathsf{abort_{chal}}] \cdot (1 - \Pr[\neg\mathsf{abort_{chal}}]) + \Pr[G_3 \wedge \neg\mathsf{abort_{chal}}] \\
&= \frac{1}{2} \cdot (1 - \Pr[\neg\mathsf{abort_{chal}}]) + \Pr[G_2 \wedge \neg\mathsf{abort_{chal}}] \\
&= \frac{1}{2} \cdot (1 - \Pr[\neg\mathsf{abort_{chal}}]) + \Pr[G_2 \mid \neg\mathsf{abort_{chal}}] \cdot \Pr[\neg\mathsf{abort_{chal}}] \\
&= \frac{1}{2} + \Pr[\neg\mathsf{abort_{chal}}] \cdot \left(\Pr[G_2 \mid \neg\mathsf{abort_{chal}}] - \frac{1}{2}\right).
\end{aligned}$$

Using now that $\Pr[G_2 \mid \neg\mathsf{abort_{chal}}] = \Pr[G_2]$, since G_2 and $\mathsf{abort_{chal}}$ are independent, the bound on $\Pr[G_2]$ from Game 2, and finally using that our choice of j and Lemma 1 yield that $2^{2^j} \leq 16t_{\mathcal{A}}^4/\epsilon_{\mathcal{A}}^2$, we obtain

$$\begin{aligned}\Pr[G_3] &= \frac{1}{2} + \Pr[\neg\mathsf{abort}_{\mathsf{chal}}] \cdot \left(\Pr[G_2 \mid \neg\mathsf{abort}_{\mathsf{chal}}] - \frac{1}{2}\right) \\ &= \frac{1}{2} + \Pr[\neg\mathsf{abort}_{\mathsf{chal}}] \cdot \left(\Pr[G_2] - \frac{1}{2}\right) \\ &\geq \frac{1}{2} + \frac{1}{2^{2^j}} \cdot \frac{\epsilon_{\mathcal{A}}}{2} \geq \frac{1}{2} + \frac{\epsilon_{\mathcal{A}}^3}{32t_{\mathcal{A}}^4}.\end{aligned}$$

Construction of $\mathcal{B}_j$. Now we are ready to construct $\mathcal{B}_j$, which simulates Game 3 as follows.

Initialization. At the beginning of the experiment, $\mathcal{B}_j$ samples a random bit string $ID^* \leftarrow \{0,1\}^{2^j}$ and defines $2^{2^j}-1$ identities $ID_1, \ldots, ID_{2^{2^j}-1}$, consisting of all values in $\{0,1\}^{2^j} \setminus \{ID^*\}$. It outputs these values to the IND-snaID-CPA experiment, which then generates and responds with a key pair $(PP', MSK') \xleftarrow{\$} \mathsf{Setup}'(1^k)$, user secret keys USK'_{ID_s}, $s \in \{1, \ldots, 2^{2^j}-1\}$, for the requested identities, and a challenge ciphertext (C', K'), where $(C', K) \xleftarrow{\$} \mathsf{Encap}'(PP', ID^*)$ and either $K' = K$ or K' is uniformly random.

Simulation of the public key. In order to simulate the public key, $\mathcal{B}_j$ generates $H \leftarrow \mathcal{H}$ and $\ell - 1$ additional key pairs by running $(PP_i, MPK_i) \xleftarrow{\$} \mathsf{Setup}'$ for all $i \in \{1, \ldots, \ell\} \setminus \{j\}$. Then it sets

$$PP = (H, PP_1, ..., PP_{j-1}, PP', PP_{j+1}, ..., PP_l).$$

Finally, $\mathcal{B}_j$ outputs PP to $\mathcal{A}$. Note that this is a correctly distributed master public key for scheme Π.

Simulation of key queries. Note that the two abort conditions introduced in Games 1 and 3 together imply in particular that $\mathcal{B}_j$ aborts and outputs a random bit, if $\mathcal{A}$ ever issues a key query for identity id_z with $H_{2^j}(id_z) = ID^*$. This is because in this case either it holds that $H_{2^j}(id_z) = ID^* \neq H_{2^j}(id^*)$, in which case $\mathsf{abort}_{\mathsf{chal}}$ occurs, or it holds that $H_{2^j}(id_z) = ID^* = H_{2^j}(id^*)$, which means that coll_j occurs. Thus, we only have to consider the case $H_{2^j}(id_z) \neq ID^*$ in the sequel. Note also that $\mathcal{B}_j$ knows MSK_i for all $i \neq j$ and user secret keys for USK'_{ID_s} for all $ID_s \in \{0,1\}^{2^j} \setminus \{ID^*\}$. Therefore it is able to compute and return valid user secret keys to $\mathcal{A}$ for all identities id_z with $H_{2^j}(id_z) \neq ID^*$.

Whenever $\mathcal{A}$ requests a user secret key for an identity $id_z \in \{0,1\}^*$, $\mathcal{B}_j$ proceeds as follows. If there is no abort, then $\mathcal{B}_j$ computes

$$(USK_i) \xleftarrow{\$} \mathsf{KeyGen}'(MSK_i, H_{2^i}(id_z))$$

for all $i \in \{1, \ldots, \ell\} \setminus \{j\}$. Recall that $\mathcal{B}_j$ has requested user secret keys for all values $H_{2^j}(id_z) \in \{0,1\}^{2^j}$ with $H_{2^j}(id_z) \neq ID^*$, in particular for $ID_s \in \{0,1\}^{2^j}$ such that $ID_s = H_{2^j}(id_z)$. Therefore it is able to efficiently determine and output

$$USK_{id_z} = (USK_1, ..., USK_{j-1}, USK'_{ID_s}, USK_{j+1}, ..., USK_l).$$

Computing the challenge ciphertext. Recall that we only have to consider the case $H_{2^j}(id^*) = ID^*$, as otherwise $\mathcal{B}_j$ outputs a random bit and aborts. Thus, when adversary $\mathcal{A}$ outputs a challenge identity id^* with $H_{2^j}(id^*) = ID^*$, then $\mathcal{B}_j$ computes $(C_i, K_i) \xleftarrow{\$} \mathsf{Encap}'(PP_i, H_{2^i}(id^*))$ for all $i \in \{1, \ldots, \ell\} \setminus \{j\}$, and then

$$K := \bigoplus_{i=1, i \neq j}^{\ell} K_i \oplus K' \text{ and } C := (C_1, \ldots, C_{j-1}, C', C_{j+1}, \ldots, C_\ell),$$

where (C', K') is the tuple received from the IND-snaID-CPA-experiment. $\mathcal{B}_j$ returns (C, K) to $\mathcal{A}$ and outputs whatever $\mathcal{A}$ outputs. Note that if K' is a "real" key, then so is K, while if K' is "random", then so is K.

Success probability of $\mathcal{B}_j$. Since $\mathcal{B}_j$ provides a perfect simulation of Game 3 for $\mathcal{A}$, we have

$$\Pr\left[\mathsf{IND\text{-}snaID\text{-}CPA}_{\Pi'}^{q,\mathcal{B}}(k) = 1\right] = \Pr[G_3] \geq 1/2 + \frac{\epsilon_{\mathcal{A}}^3}{32 t_{\mathcal{A}}^4}.$$

Running time of $\mathcal{B}_j$. The running time $t_{\mathcal{B}}$ of $\mathcal{B}_j$ consists of the time needed to execute $\mathcal{A}$, the time required to simulate the IND-ID-CPA security experiment, and the time required to request the $2^{2^j} - 1$ user secret keys from the IND-snaID-CPA experiment, plus a minor number of additional operations. Making use of Lemma 1, we get

$$t_{\mathcal{B}} \approx t_{\mathcal{A}} + \mathcal{O}(2^{2^j} - 1) \approx t_{\mathcal{A}} + \mathcal{O}\left(\frac{t_{\mathcal{A}}^4}{\epsilon_{\mathcal{A}}^2}\right) = \mathcal{O}\left(\frac{t_{\mathcal{A}}^4}{\epsilon_{\mathcal{A}}^2}\right).$$

Remark 2. We remark also that $t_{\mathcal{B}} \approx t_{\mathcal{A}}$ if we instead consider the generic construction of an IND-ID-CPA-secure ID-KEM from an IND-sID-CPA-secure one. This is because in this case the reduction $\mathcal{B}_j$ does not have to issue all KeyGen queries at the beginning of the experiment. Instead, it can make all queries "on demand", whenever $\mathcal{A}$ issues such a query. Their number is identical to the number q of KeyGen made by $\mathcal{A}$, so that we get a reduction which runs in strict polynomial time.

Note also that $\mathcal{B}_j$ issues $q_{\mathcal{B}} = 2^{2^j} - 1 < 4t_{\mathcal{A}}^4/\epsilon_{\mathcal{A}}^2$ user key queries. This completes the proof of Theorem 1.

□

3.3 Adaptively Secure ID-KEM with Short Ciphertexts

Now we show that it is possible to construct an ID-KEM with full adaptive security, where a ciphertext consists of only a *single* element of a bilinear group. A comparison to previous IBE-schemes, viewed as ID-KEMs, is given in Fig. 2.

Scheme	$\lvert\mathbb{G}\rvert$	$\lvert pk\rvert$	$\lvert C\rvert$	Security	Assumption	ROM	Security Loss
[BF01]	Prime	2	1	Full	BDDH	Yes	$\mathcal{O}(q_{key})$
[BB04a]	Prime	4	2	Selective	strong q-DH	No	$\mathcal{O}(1)$
[Wat05]	Prime	$n+3$	2	Full	BDDH	No	$\tilde{\mathcal{O}}(t^2 + (n \cdot q_{key} \cdot \epsilon^{-1})^2)$
[Wee16]	Comp.	3	1	Full	Dec. Subgrp.	No	$\mathcal{O}(q_{key})$
Ours	Prime	$\mathcal{O}(k)$	1	Full	q-DH	No	$\mathcal{O}(t_{\mathcal{A}}^7/\epsilon_{\mathcal{A}}^4)$

Fig. 2. Comparison of ID-based encryption schemes with short ciphertexts. The column $\lvert\mathbb{G}\rvert$ refers to the order of the underlying group (prime or composite), $\lvert pk\rvert$ is the number of group elements in public keys (common descriptions of groups and hash functions not included), where n is the length of identities and k the security parameter. All public keys include one element from the target group of the pairing, except for [BF01]. $\lvert C\rvert$ is the number of group elements in the ciphertexts when viewed as a KEM. "Full" security means IND-ID-CPA security as defined below, "selective" security is from [BB04a]. The remaining columns state the hardness assumption in the security proof, whether the Random Oracle Model is used, and the security loss of the reduction, where q_{key} is the number of identity key queries, $t_{\mathcal{A}}$ and $\epsilon_{\mathcal{A}}$ the running time and advantage of the adversary, and the loss is the value L that satisfies $t_{\mathcal{B}}/\epsilon_{\mathcal{B}} = L \cdot t_{\mathcal{A}}/\epsilon_{\mathcal{A}}$, where $t_{\mathcal{B}}$ and $\epsilon_{\mathcal{B}}$ are the success probability and running time of the reduction.

Building Block: Simplified Boneh-Boyen ID-KEM. The following ID-KEM is based on the IBE scheme of Boneh and Boyen [BB04a]. Let $\mathbb{G}_1, \mathbb{G}_2, \mathbb{G}_T$ be groups of prime order p with generators g_1, g_2, g_T, respectively, and let $e : \mathbb{G}_1 \times \mathbb{G}_2 \to \mathbb{G}_T$ be an efficiently computable pairing. We will use the implicit notation of Escala *et al.* [EHK+13], and write $[x]_s$ shorthand for g_s^x for all $s \in \{1, 2, T\}$.

Simple ID-KEM based on the Boneh-Boyen IBE scheme. We use the following scheme as a building block for our adaptively secure ID-KEM.

Setup. Choose two random elements $x, y \xleftarrow{\$} \mathbb{Z}_p$. Then define $\nu = e([1]_1, [y]_2)$. The public parameters PP and the master secret key MSK are defined as $PP = ([1]_1, [x]_1, \nu)$ *and* $MSK = (x, y)$.

Key Generation. To create a private key for identity $id \in \mathbb{Z}_p$, compute and return $USK_{id} = [y/(id + x)]_2$.

Encapsulation. To encapsulate a key $K \in \mathbb{G}_T$ under public key $id \in \mathbb{Z}_p$, pick a random $r \in \mathbb{Z}_p$ and output $(C, K) = ([id + x]_1^r, \nu^r) \in \mathbb{G}_1 \times \mathbb{G}_T$.

Decapsulation. To decapsulate C using the private key USK_{id}, compute and output $e(C, USK_{id})$.

Proving security of the simplified Boneh Boyen IBE. Consider the following experiment q-BDDHI(1^k), which was generalized to asymmetric bilinear groups in [BB11]. With regard to the security parameter k, the challenger generates an asymmetric pairing group and chooses $x \in \mathbb{Z}_p$ uniformly at random. Then it chooses $T \xleftarrow{\$} \mathbb{G}_T$ and defines

$$T_0 := ([1]_1, [x]_1, [1]_2, [x]_2, \dots [x^q]_2, T),$$
$$T_1 := ([1]_1, [x]_1, [1]_2, [x]_2, \dots [x^q]_2, e([1]_1, [1]_2)^{\frac{1}{x}}).$$

Finally, it flips a fair coin $\beta \xleftarrow{\$} \{0,1\}$ and outputs T_β to the adversary. The task of adversary $\mathcal{B}$ is to determine β.

Definition 5. *We say that adversary $\mathcal{B}$ (t, ϵ)-solves the q-BDDHI problem, if it runs in time t and*

$$|\Pr[\mathcal{B}(T_0)] - \Pr[\mathcal{B}(T_1)]| \geq \epsilon.$$

It is straightforward to prove the IND-snaID-CPA-security of our simplified Boneh-Boyen scheme using standard techniques from [BB04a, BB11], therefore we state the following theorem without proof.

Theorem 2. *From an adversary $\mathcal{A}$ that $(t_\mathcal{A}, q_s, \epsilon_\mathcal{A})$-breaks the* IND-snaID-CPA-*security of the simplified Boneh-Boyen ID-KEM one can construct an algorithm $\mathcal{B}$ that $(t_\mathcal{B}, \epsilon_\mathcal{B})$-solves the q-BDDHI problem with $q = q_s + 1$ such that*

$$t_\mathcal{B} \approx t_\mathcal{A} \quad and \quad \epsilon_\mathcal{B} = \epsilon_\mathcal{A}.$$

Adaptively Secure Construction. *Encoding elements of $\{0,1\}^{4(k+1)}$ as $\mathbb{Z}_p$-elements.* In order to simplify the notation and description of the construction and its security analysis, we will henceforth make the implicit assumption that elements of $\{0,1\}^{4(k+1)}$ can be injectively encoded as elements of $\mathbb{Z}_p$. This is of course easily possible by choosing p large enough, such that $p > 4(k+1)$. However, this would yield an unnaturally large group order (a typical choice in practice is $2k$). In practice, one would map elements of $\{0,1\}^{4(k+1)}$ to elements in $\mathbb{Z}_p$ by using a collision-resistant hash function $h : \{0,1\}^{4(k+1)} \to \mathbb{Z}_p$, which for our purposes is as good as an injective map. However, to simplify the description of our scheme and its security proof we do not make h explicit in the sequel.

The construction. In the sequel, let $\mathcal{H} = \{H | \{0,1\}^* \to \{0,1\}^{4(k+1)}\}$ be a family of keyed hash functions and define $\ell := \log 4(k+1)$. We construct ID-KEM scheme $\Pi =$ (Setup, KeyGen, Encap, Decap) as follows.

Setup. Sample random generators $[1]_1 \in \mathbb{G}_1$, $[1]_2 \in \mathbb{G}_2$, elements $y, x_1, \dots, x_\ell \in \mathbb{Z}_p$ and a hash function $H \leftarrow \mathcal{H}$ and define the master secret key MSK as

$$MSK = (y, x_1, \dots, x_\ell) \in \mathbb{Z}_p^{\ell+1}.$$

Define $b_i(n)$ for positive integers i as the function that, on input of integer $n \geq 0$, outputs the i-th bit of the binary representation of n. Let $F(MSK, n)$ be the function that on input of $MSK = (x_1, \dots, x_\ell)$ and an integer $n \geq 0$ outputs

$$F(MSK, n) = \prod_{i=1}^{\ell} x_i^{b_i(n)}.$$

The public parameters are defined as

$$PP = (H, [F(MSK, 0)]_1, \ldots, [F(MSK, 2^\ell - 1]_1, [1]_2, \nu),$$

where $\nu = e([1]_1, [y]_2)$.

Key Generation. The private key for identity id is computed as

$$USK_{id} = [y/u(id)]_2,$$

where

$$u(id) = \prod_{i=1}^{\ell}(H_{2^i}(id) + x_i) \in \mathbb{Z}_p. \tag{5}$$

Encapsulation. Observe that

$$u(id) = \prod_{i=1}^{\ell}(H_{2^i}(id) + x_i) = d_0 + \sum_{n=1}^{2^\ell - 1}\left(d_n \prod_{i=1}^{\ell} x_i^{b_i(n)}\right),$$

where the constants d_i are efficiently computable from $H(id)$.
To encapsulate a key, first $[u(id)]_1$ is computed. Note that this is possible from $H(id)$ and the values $F(MSK, n)$ contained in the public parameters (in particular, without knowing $x_1, \ldots, x_\ell$ explicitly), by computing

$$[u(id)]_1 = \left[d_0 + \sum_{n=1}^{2^\ell - 1}\left(d_n \prod_{i=1}^{\ell} x_i^{b_i(n)}\right)\right]_1 = [d_0]_1 \cdot \prod_{n=1}^{2^\ell - 1}[F(MSK, n)]_1^{d_n}.$$

Finally, the ciphertext and key are computed as

$$(C, K) = ([u(id)]_1^r, \nu^r) \in \mathbb{G}_T^2$$

for uniformly random $r \stackrel{\$}{\leftarrow} \mathbb{Z}_p$.

Decapsulation. To recover K from a ciphertext C for identity id and a matching user secret key $[y/(u(id))]_2$, compute and output $e(C, USK_{id})$.

Correctness. The correctness follows from

$$e(C, USK_{id}) = e([u(id)]_1^r, [y/u(id)]_2) = e([1]_1, [y]_2)^r = \nu^r.$$

Note that the scheme described above has extremely short ciphertexts, consisting of only one element of $\mathbb{G}_1$, and also very efficient decapsulation, which takes only a single pairing evaluation.

Theorem 3. *Let $\mathcal{A}$ be an adversary that $(t_\mathcal{A}, q_\mathcal{A}, \epsilon_\mathcal{A})$-breaks the* IND-ID-CPA-*security of Π such that $t_\mathcal{A}/\epsilon_\mathcal{A} < 2^k$ and let j be an index such that (4) is satisfied. Given $\mathcal{A}$ and j, we can either construct an adversary $\mathcal{B}_j$ that $(t_\mathcal{B}, q_\mathcal{B}, \epsilon_\mathcal{B})$-breaks the* IND-snaID-CPA-*security of Π' with*

$$t_\mathcal{B} = \mathcal{O}(t_\mathcal{A}^4/\epsilon_\mathcal{A}^2), \quad q_\mathcal{B} < 4t_\mathcal{A}^4/\epsilon_\mathcal{A}^2 \quad \text{and} \quad \epsilon_\mathcal{B} \geq \frac{\epsilon_\mathcal{A}^3}{32t_\mathcal{A}^4}$$

or an adversary $\mathcal{C}$ that 2^j-breaks the truncation collision resistance of $\mathcal{H}$.

Proof. The proof of Theorem 3 is almost identical to the proof of Theorem 1. The main difference is that we additionally use the algebraic structure of the underlying Boneh-Boyen ID-KEM to achieve short ciphertexts.

Setup and initial input. Just like in the proof of Theorem 1, $\mathcal{B}$ picks a random value $ID^* \xleftarrow{\$} \{0,1\}^{2^j}$ and requests a challenge ciphertext for identity ID^* and user secret keys for all $2^{2^j} - 1$ identities in the set $\{0,1\}^{2^j} \setminus \{\}$. In response, $\mathcal{B}$ receives public parameters $PP' = ([1]_1, [x_j]_1, \nu)$ from the IND-snaID-CPA experiment, as well as user secret keys $[y/(ID + x_j)]_2$ for all $ID \neq ID^*$ and a challenge ciphertext (C', K').

Additionally, $\mathcal{B}$ chooses $\ell - 1$ integers x_i for all $i \in \{1, \dots, \ell\} \setminus \{j\}$ and a hash function $H \leftarrow \mathcal{H}$.

Simulation of the public parameters. Note that $\mathcal{B}$ is not able to compute the function $F((x_1, \dots, x_\ell), n) = \prod_{i=1}^{\ell} x_i^{b_i(n)}$ for all values of n efficiently, since it does not know x_j. However, $\mathcal{B}$ is able to efficiently compute

$$[F((x_1, \dots, x_\ell), n)]_1 = \left[\prod_{i=1}^{\ell} x_i^{b_i(n)}\right]_1$$

for all values of n from $[x_j]_1$ and the x_i, $i \in \{1, \dots, \ell\} \setminus \{j\}$. This is sufficient to properly simulate a public key of scheme Π.

Simulation of user secret keys. Using the user secret keys received from the IND-snaID-CPA challenger, $\mathcal{B}$ is able to answer all secret key queries for all identities id with $H_{2^j}(id) \neq ID^*$. To this end, it computes

$$USK_{id} = \left[y/\prod_{i=1}^{\ell}(H_{2^i}(id) + x_i)\right]_2 = [y/(H_{2^j}(id) + x_j)]_2^{1/u_j(id)},$$

where

$$u_j(id) = \prod_{i=1, i \neq j}^{\ell} (H_{2^i}(id) + x_i)).$$

Creating the challenge ciphertext. $\mathcal{B}$ creates the challenge ciphertext as follows. If $\mathcal{A}$ has selected a target identity id^* with $H_{2^j}(id^*) = ID^*$, then $\mathcal{B}$ computes $C := (C')^{u_j(id^*)}$ and outputs (C, K). Note that

$$C = [(H_{2^j}(id^*) + x_j)]^{r \prod_{i=1, i \neq j}^{\ell}(H_{2^i}(id^*) + x_i)} = \left[\prod_{i=1}^{\ell}(H_{2^i}(id^*) + x_i)\right]_1^r$$

such that C is a correctly distributed challenge ciphertext, and K is either "real" or "random", depending on the choice of the IND-snaID-CPA security experiment.

Analysis. The analysis of the success probability of $\mathcal{B}$ is identical to the analysis from the proof of Theorem 1, and yields identical bounds. □

4 Digital Signatures

Recall that the commonly accepted security notion for digital signatures is *existential unforgeability under adaptive chosen-message attacks*, as introduced by Goldwasser, Micali, and Rivest [GMR88] (EUF-CMA, see Sect. 4.1 for formal definitions). There are several different ways to turn signatures schemes with weaker security properties into ones with full EUF-CMA-security, even without random oracles. These are either based on one-time signatures [EGM96] or chameleon hash functions [KR00, BSW06, SPW07], and work generically for any signature scheme. However, all these generic constructions start from an *existentially-unforgeable* scheme, where the adversary has to select the "chosen-message queries", for which it requests a signature, even before seeing the public key, but is able to choose the "target-message" for which it forges a signatures adaptively (EUF-naCMA-security).

We consider the even weaker notion of *selective unforgeability under non-adaptive chosen-message attacks* (SUF-naCMA) [HW09b, BK10], where the adversary has to select both the "target-message" for which it forges a signatures and the chosen-message queries for which it requests a signature already before seeing the public key. We describe a generic construction of EUF-CMA-secure digital signatures from signatures that are only SUF-naCMA-secure. This construction is also relatively efficient: it increases the size of public keys, secret keys, and signatures by a factor of only $\mathcal{O}(\log k)$, where k is the security parameter. Again, the security reduction is non-tight, but polynomial-time.

4.1 Definitions and Security Notions

Definition 6. *A digital signature scheme consists of three PPT algorithms with the following syntax.*

$\mathsf{Gen}(1^k)$ *outputs a key pair* (pk, sk). *We assume that* pk *implicitly or explicitly defines a message space* $\mathcal{M}$.

$\mathsf{Sign}(sk, m)$ *on input of* sk *and message* $m \in \mathcal{M}$ *outputs a signature* σ.

$\mathsf{Vfy}(pk, m, \sigma)$ *outputs* 1 *if* σ *is a valid signature for* m *with respect to* pk *and else* 0.

Adaptive security. We recall the standard security notion *existential unforgeability under adaptive chosen message attack* (EUF-CMA) depicted in Fig. 3. Note that the adversary may choose the challenge-message m^* after it has received the public key pk and may adaptively query signatures for messages $m_i \neq m^*$.

Definition 7. *We say that adversary* $\mathcal{A}$ $(t_\mathcal{A}, q, \epsilon_\mathcal{A})$*-breaks the* EUF-CMA *security of* $\Sigma = (\mathsf{Gen}, \mathsf{Sign}, \mathsf{Vfy})$, *if* $\Pr[\mathsf{EUF\text{-}CMA}_\Sigma^{q,\mathcal{A}}(k) = 1] \geq \epsilon_\mathcal{A}$ *and* $t_\mathcal{A}$ *is the running time of* $\mathcal{A}$ including *the* EUF-CMA *security experiment.*

Selective and non-adaptive security. We also define a very weak security notion for digital signature schemes. Consider the SUF-naCMA security experiment depicted in Fig. 3, where the attacker has to commit to both the challenge-message m^* the signing-query messages $m_1, \ldots, m_q$ non-adaptively and even before receiving the public key pk.

$\mathsf{SUF\text{-}naCMA}_{\Sigma}^{q,\mathcal{A}}(k)$	$\mathsf{EUF\text{-}CMA}_{\Sigma}^{q,\mathcal{A}}(k)$
$(m^*, m_1, ..., m_q, st_1) \leftarrow \mathcal{A}_1(1^k)$	$(pk, sk) \xleftarrow{\$} \mathsf{Gen}(1^k)$
$(pk, sk) \xleftarrow{\$} \mathsf{Gen}(1^k)$	$(m^*, \sigma^*) \leftarrow \mathcal{A}^{\mathsf{Sign}(sk,\cdot)}(1^k, pk)$
$\sigma_i \xleftarrow{\$} \mathsf{Sign}(sk, m_i)\ \forall i \in [q]$	If $(\exists i \in [q] : m^* == m_i)$ return 0
$(m^*, \sigma^*) \leftarrow \mathcal{A}_2(st_1, (\sigma_i)_{i\in[q]})$	else return $\mathsf{Vfy}(pk, m^*, \sigma^*)$
If $(\exists i \in [q] : m^* == m_i)$ return 0	
else return $\mathsf{Vfy}(pk, m^*, \sigma^*)$	

Fig. 3. The security experiments for digital signature schemes, executed with scheme $\Sigma = (\mathsf{Gen}, \mathsf{Sign}, \mathsf{Vfy})$ and adversary $\mathcal{A} = (\mathcal{A}_1, \mathcal{A}_2)$. The oracle $\mathsf{Sign}(sk, m)$ returns $\sigma \xleftarrow{\$} \mathsf{Sign}(sk, m)$ with the restriction that $\mathcal{A}$ is not allowed to query oracle $\mathsf{Sign}(sk, m^*)$ for m^*.

Definition 8. *We say that $\mathcal{A}$ $(t_{\mathcal{A}}, q, \epsilon_{\mathcal{A}})$-breaks the* SUF-naCMA *security of Σ, if it runs in time $t_{\mathcal{A}}$ and* $\Pr[\mathsf{SUF\text{-}naCMA}_{\Sigma}^{q,\mathcal{A}}(k) = 1] \geq \epsilon_{\mathcal{A}}$.

4.2 From Weak Security to Adaptive Security

Construction. Let $\mathcal{H} = \{H | \{0,1\}^* \to \{0,1\}^{4(k+1)}\}$ be a family of keyed hash functions and $\Sigma' = (\mathsf{Gen}', \mathsf{Sign}', \mathsf{Vfy}')$ a digital signature scheme. In the sequel, let $\ell := \log 4(k+1)$. We construct our digital signature scheme $\Sigma = (\mathsf{Gen}, \mathsf{Sign}, \mathsf{Vfy})$ as follows.

- **Key Generation.** Algorithm Gen computes $(pk_i, sk_i) \xleftarrow{\$} \mathsf{Gen}'(1^k)$ for all $i \in \{1, \ldots, \ell\}$ and $H \leftarrow \mathcal{H}$, defines
$$pk := (H, pk_1, \ldots, pk_\ell) \text{ and } sk = (sk_1, \ldots, sk_\ell)$$
and outputs (pk, sk).
- **Signing.** To sign a message m, compute $\sigma_i \xleftarrow{\$} \mathsf{Sign}'(sk_i, H_{2^i}(m))$ for all $i \in \{1, \ldots, \ell\}$, and return the signature $\sigma = (\sigma_1, \ldots, \sigma_\ell)$.
- **Verification.** To verify a signature $\sigma = (\sigma_1, \ldots, \sigma_\ell)$, return 1 if and only if $\mathsf{Vfy}'(pk_i, H_{2^i}(m)) = 1$ for all $i \in [\ell]$.

Theorem 4. *Let $\mathcal{A}$ be an adversary that $(t_{\mathcal{A}}, q_{\mathcal{A}}, \epsilon_{\mathcal{A}})$-breaks the* EUF-CMA-*security of $\Sigma = (\mathsf{Gen}, \mathsf{Sign}, \mathsf{Vfy})$ such that $t_{\mathcal{A}}/\epsilon_{\mathcal{A}} < 2^k$ and let j be an index such that (4) is satisfied. Given $\mathcal{A}$ and j, we can either construct an adversary $\mathcal{B}_j$ that $(t_{\mathcal{B}}, q_{\mathcal{B}}, \epsilon_{\mathcal{B}})$-breaks the* SUF-naCMA-*security of $\Sigma' = (\mathsf{Gen}', \mathsf{Sign}', \mathsf{Vfy}')$ with*

$$t_{\mathcal{B}} = \mathcal{O}(t_{\mathcal{A}}^4/\epsilon_{\mathcal{A}}^2), \quad q_{\mathcal{B}} < 4t_{\mathcal{A}}^4/\epsilon_{\mathcal{A}}^2 \quad \text{and} \quad \epsilon_{\mathcal{B}} \geq \frac{\epsilon_{\mathcal{A}}^3}{32t_{\mathcal{A}}^4}$$

or an adversary $\mathcal{C}$ that 2^j- breaks the truncation collision resistance of $\mathcal{H}$.

The proof of Theorem 4 is nearly identical to the proof of Theorem 1, except that some arguments and computing some bounds works *slightly* differently, because in the ID-KEM setting from Theorem 1 we are considering an "indistinguishability" security experiment, while in the digital signature setting of Theorem 4 we consider a "search problem". The full proof is contained in the full version [JK17].

4.3 Very Short Signatures with Adaptive Security

The generic construction of adaptively secure digital signature schemes described in Sect. 4.2 increases the size of keys and signatures by a factor of $\mathcal{O}(\log k)$. Again it is possible to obtain a more efficient scheme based on specific, number-theoretic constructions. In this section we describe a variant of the Boneh-Boyen signature scheme [BB04c] that applies a truncation collision resistant hash function to achieve adaptive security without random oracles, and where a signature consists of only a *single* group element. A comparison to previous short signature schemes is given in Fig. 4.

Scheme	$\lvert\mathbb{G}\rvert$	$\lvert pk\rvert$	$\lvert\sigma\rvert$	Security	Assumption	ROM	Security Loss
[BLS04]	Prime	2	1	Full	CDH	Yes	$\mathcal{O}(q_{Sig})$
[BB04c]	Prime	5	2	Selective	strong q-DH	No	$\mathcal{O}(1)$
[Wat05]	Prime	$n+3$	2	Full	CDH	No	$\mathcal{O}(n \cdot q_{Sig})$
[HJK11]	Prime	$n+k+3$	2	Full	q-DH	No	$\mathcal{O}(n^2 \cdot q_{Sig})$
[BHJ+13]	Prime	$\mathcal{O}(\log k)$	3	Full	CDH	No	$\mathcal{O}((\epsilon^{-1} \cdot q_{Sig}^{m+1})^{c/m})$
[Wee16]	Comp.	3	1	Full	Dec. Subgrp.	No	$\mathcal{O}(q_{Sig})$
Ours	Prime	$\mathcal{O}(k)$	1	Full	q-DH	No	$\mathcal{O}(t_{\mathcal{A}}^7/\epsilon_{\mathcal{A}}^4)$

Fig. 4. Comparison of short signature schemes, instantiated with asymmetric pairings. The column $\lvert\mathbb{G}\rvert$ refers to the order of the underlying groups (prime or composite), $\lvert pk\rvert$ is the number of group elements in public keys, where common descriptions of groups and hash functions are not included, n is the length of messages, and k the security parameter. All public keys include one element from the target group of the pairing, except for [BLS04,HJK11,BHJ+13]. The column $\lvert\sigma\rvert$ refers to the number of group elements in the signature. "Full" security means EUF-CMA security as defined below, "selective" security is from [BB04c]. The remaining columns state the assumption the proof is based on, whether the Random Oracle Model is used, and the security loss of the reduction, where q_{Sig} is the number of signing queries, $t_{\mathcal{A}}$ and $\epsilon_{\mathcal{A}}$ the running time and advantage of the adversary, and the loss is computed as explained in Fig. 2. The values m and c are system parameters influencing keys and signature sizes. Note that [HJK11] present also other trade-offs with larger public keys consisting and shorter signatures, but always strictly larger than one group element.

Building Block: Simplified Boneh-Boyen Signatures. Again we let $\mathbb{G}_1$, $\mathbb{G}_2$, $\mathbb{G}_T$ be groups of prime order p with generators g_1, g_2, g_T, respectively, and $e : \mathbb{G}_1 \times \mathbb{G}_2 \rightarrow \mathbb{G}_T$ be an efficiently computable pairing. Recall that write $[x]_s$ shorthand for g_s^x for all $s \in \{1, 2, T\}$, following [EHK+13]. The Boneh-Boyen signature scheme [BB04c] consists of the following algorithms $\Sigma' = (\mathsf{Gen}', \mathsf{Sign}', \mathsf{Vfy}')$.

Key generation. Algorithm $\mathsf{Gen}'(k)$ chooses a random integer $x \stackrel{\$}{\leftarrow} \mathbb{Z}_p$ and defines $\nu = e([1]_1, [1]_2)$. The public keys and the secret key are defined as $pk := ([1]_1, [x]_1, [1]_2, \nu)$ and $sk := x$.

Signing. Algorithm Sign' receives as input $sk = x$ and message $m \in \mathbb{Z}_p$, and computes and returns $\sigma := [1/(x+m)]_2 \in \mathbb{G}_2$.

Verification. Algorithm Vfy' takes as input a public key $pk = ([1]_1, [x]_1, \nu) \in \mathbb{G}_1^2 \times \mathbb{G}_2$, message $m \in \mathbb{Z}_p$, and $\sigma \in \mathbb{G}_2$. It returns 1 iff $e([x]_1 \cdot [1]_1^m, \sigma) = \nu$.

Security. The original paper by Boneh and Boyen [BB04c] proves security of this scheme in the sense of *existential unforgeability under non-adaptive chosen-message attacks* (EUF-naCMA), under the *strong* (or "flexible") q-Diffie-Hellman assumption. We will require only a weaker notion of security, in the sense of *selective unforgeability against non-adaptive chosen message attacks* (SUF-naCMA), which is achievable under a weaker, "non-flexible" q-type assumption.

Definition 9. *We say that adversary* $\mathcal{A}$ $(\epsilon_{\mathcal{A}}, t_{\mathcal{A}})$*-breaks the* q-Diffie-Hellman assumption *in group* $\mathbb{G}$ *of order* p*, if it runs in time* $t_{\mathcal{A}}$ *and*

$$\Pr\left[x \stackrel{\$}{\leftarrow} \mathbb{Z}_p; h \stackrel{\$}{\leftarrow} \mathcal{A}([1], [x], [x^2], \ldots, [x^q]) : h = [1/x]\right] \geq \epsilon_{\mathcal{A}}.$$

The above assumption is also known as the q-Diffie-Hellman Inversion assumption [ZSS04]. By using the "generator-shifting" technique of [HJK11], one can prove the following theorem along the lines of the original proof of Boneh and Boyen [BB04c].

Theorem 5. *From an adversary* $\mathcal{A}$ *that* $(t_{\mathcal{A}}, q_s, \epsilon_{\mathcal{A}})$*-breaks the* SUF-naCMA*-security of* Σ' *chosen-message queries, one can construct an adversary* $\mathcal{B}$ *that* $(t_{\mathcal{B}}, \epsilon_{\mathcal{B}})$*-breaks the q-Diffie-Hellman assumption with* $q = q_s + 1$*,* $t_{\mathcal{B}} \approx t_{\mathcal{A}}$ *and* $\epsilon_{\mathcal{B}} = \epsilon_{\mathcal{A}}$.

Encoding elements of $\{0,1\}^{4(k+1)}$ *as* $\mathbb{Z}_p$*-elements.* In order to simplify the notation and description of the construction and its security analysis, we will henceforth make the implicit assumption that elements of $\{0,1\}^{4(k+1)}$ can be injectively encoded as elements in $\mathbb{Z}_p$ (see also the corresponding, more detailed comment in Sect. 3.3).

Construction. Let $\mathcal{H} = \{H | \{0,1\}^* \rightarrow \{0,1\}^{4(k+1)}\}$ be a family of keyed hash functions and $\ell := \log 4(k+1)$. We construct signature scheme $\Sigma = (\mathsf{Gen}, \mathsf{Sign}, \mathsf{Vfy})$ as follows.

Key generation. Algorithm $\mathsf{Gen}(k)$ chooses ℓ random integers $x_1, \ldots, x_\ell \stackrel{\$}{\leftarrow} \mathbb{Z}_p$ and $H \leftarrow \mathcal{H}$. It defines the secret key as $sk := (x_1, \ldots, x_\ell) \in \mathbb{Z}_p^\ell$. Note that sk contains only $\ell = \log 4(k+1)$ elements of $\mathbb{Z}_p$.

The public key is computed as follows. For a positive integer $i \geq 1$, let $b_i(n)$ be the function that, on input of integer $n \geq 0$, outputs the i-th bit of the (canonical) binary representation of n. Let $F(sk, n)$ be the function that, on input of $sk = (x_1, \ldots, x_\ell)$ and integer $n \geq 0$, outputs

$$F(sk, n) := \prod_{i=1}^{\ell} x_i^{b_i(n)}.$$

The public key is defined as $pk := (H, [F(sk, 0)]_1, \ldots, [F(sk, 2^\ell - 1)]_1, [1]_2, \nu)$, where $\nu = e([1]_1, [1]_2)$.

Signing. Algorithm Sign receives as input $sk = (x_1, \ldots, x_\ell)$ and message $m \in \{0,1\}^*$. Let $u(m)$ be the function

$$u(m) := \prod_{i=1}^{\ell} (x_i + H_{2^i}(m)) \in \mathbb{Z}_p, \tag{6}$$

where bit strings $H_{2^i}(m)$ are interpreted canonically as integers in $\mathbb{Z}_p$. Recall here that by our assumption on p this is injective for all $i \in \{1, \ldots, \ell\}$.

The signing algorithm computes and returns $\sigma := [1/u(m)]_2 \in \mathbb{G}_1$.

Note that computing signatures is *extremely* efficient. It involves only the computation of $1/u(m) \in \mathbb{Z}_p$, which can be performed over the integers modulo p, where p is the group order, and then a *single* exponentiation in $\mathbb{G}_1$ to compute $g_1^{1/u(m)} \in \mathbb{G}_1$.

Verification. Algorithm Vfy takes as input a public key

$$pk = ([F(sk, 0)]_1, \ldots, [F(sk, 2^\ell - 1)]_1, [1]_2, \nu),$$

message $m \in \{0,1\}^*$ and $\sigma \in \mathbb{G}_2$. Note here that $[F(sk, 0)]_1 = [1]_1$. The algorithm returns 1 if and only if

$$e([u(m)]_1, \sigma) = \nu. \tag{7}$$

Here $[u(m)]_1$ is computed as follows. Viewing $u(m) = \prod_{i=1}^{\ell}(x_i + H_{2^i}(m))$ as a polynomial in ℓ unknowns $x_1, \ldots, x_\ell$, we can expand the product from (6) to obtain the equation

$$u(m) = \prod_{i=1}^{\ell} (x_i + H_{2^i}(m)) = d_0 + \sum_{n=1}^{2^\ell - 1} \left(d_n \prod_{i=1}^{\ell} x_i^{b_i(n)} \right) \tag{8}$$

for integers d_i, which are efficiently computable from $H(m)$. This yields the equation

$$[u(m)]_1 = \left[d_0 + \sum_{n=1}^{2^\ell - 1} \left(d_n \prod_{i=1}^{\ell} x_i^{b_i(n)} \right) \right]_2 = [d_0]_2 \cdot \prod_{n=0}^{2^\ell - 1} [F(sk, n)]_2^{d_n}. \tag{9}$$

Therefore the verification algorithms proceeds as follows:

1. From $H(m)$ it computes the integers d_i as in (8).
2. Then it computes $[u(m)]_1$ as in (9) from the group elements $[F(sk, n)]_1$ contained in the public key.
3. Finally, it outputs 1 if and only if Eq. (7) holds.

Theorem 6. *Let $\mathcal{A}$ be an adversary that $(t_\mathcal{A}, q_\mathcal{A}, \epsilon_\mathcal{A})$-breaks the* EUF-CMA-*security of Σ such that $t_\mathcal{A}/\epsilon_\mathcal{A} < 2^k$ and let j be an integer that such that (4) is satisfied. Given $\mathcal{A}$ and j we can either construct an adversary $\mathcal{B}_j$ that $(t_\mathcal{B}, q_\mathcal{B}, \epsilon_\mathcal{B})$-breaks the* SUF-naCMA *security of the Boneh-Boyen signature scheme $\Sigma' = (\mathsf{Gen}', \mathsf{Sign}', \mathsf{Vfy}')$ with*

$$t_\mathcal{B} = \mathcal{O}(t_\mathcal{A}^4/\epsilon_\mathcal{A}^2), \qquad q_\mathcal{B} < 4t_\mathcal{A}^4/\epsilon_\mathcal{A}^2 \qquad \text{and} \qquad \epsilon_\mathcal{B} \geq \frac{\epsilon_\mathcal{A}^3}{32t_\mathcal{A}^4}$$

or and adversary $\mathcal{C}$ that 2^j-breaks the truncation collision resistance of $\mathcal{H}$.

The proof of Theorem 6 is almost identical to the proofs of Theorems 3 and 4. It is contained in the full version [JK17].

5 Conclusion

Truncation collision resistance enables very efficient generic constructions of adaptively-secure cryptographic primitives from building blocks with very weak selective and non-adaptive security. We showed this for identity-based encryption and digital signatures, but expect further useful applications to other cryptographic primitives.

Two particularly interesting applications are the first standard-model constructions of an ID-KEM where a ciphertext consist of only a single group element of a prime-order group, and a digital signature scheme where signatures consist of only a single prime-order group element. Both achieve full adaptive security. Previously, it was not clear that this is possible without random oracles and based on simple, non-interactive hardness assumptions.

Acknowledgements. We would like to thank all anonymous reviewers for their helpful comments.

References

[BB04a] Boneh, D., Boyen, X.: Efficient selective-ID secure identity-based encryption without random oracles. In: Cachin, C., Camenisch, J.L. (eds.) EUROCRYPT 2004. LNCS, vol. 3027, pp. 223–238. Springer, Heidelberg (2004). https://doi.org/10.1007/978-3-540-24676-3_14

[BB04b] Boneh, D., Boyen, X.: Secure identity based encryption without random oracles. In: Franklin, M. (ed.) CRYPTO 2004. LNCS, vol. 3152, pp. 443–459. Springer, Heidelberg (2004). https://doi.org/10.1007/978-3-540-28628-8_27

[BB04c] Boneh, D., Boyen, X.: Short signatures without random oracles. In: Cachin, C., Camenisch, J.L. (eds.) EUROCRYPT 2004. LNCS, vol. 3027, pp. 56–73. Springer, Heidelberg (2004). https://doi.org/10.1007/978-3-540-24676-3_4

[BB11] Boneh, D., Boyen, X.: Efficient selective identity-based encryption without random oracles. J. Cryptol. **24**(4), 659–693 (2011). October

[BF01] Boneh, D., Franklin, M.: Identity-based encryption from the Weil pairing. In: Kilian, J. (ed.) CRYPTO 2001. LNCS, vol. 2139, pp. 213–229. Springer, Heidelberg (2001). https://doi.org/10.1007/3-540-44647-8_13

[BFMLS08] Bentahar, K., Farshim, P., Malone-Lee, J., Smart, N.P.: Generic constructions of identity-based and certificateless KEMs. J. Cryptol. **21**(2), 178–199 (2008)

[BGLS03] Boneh, D., Gentry, C., Lynn, B., Shacham, H.: Aggregate and verifiably encrypted signatures from bilinear maps. In: Biham, E. (ed.) EUROCRYPT 2003. LNCS, vol. 2656, pp. 416–432. Springer, Heidelberg (2003). https://doi.org/10.1007/3-540-39200-9_26

[BH15] Berman, I., Haitner, I.: From non-adaptive to adaptive pseudorandom functions. J. Cryptol. **28**(2), 297–311 (2015)

[BHJ+13] Böhl, F., Hofheinz, D., Jager, T., Koch, J., Seo, J.H., Striecks, C.: Practical signatures from standard assumptions. In: Johansson, T., Nguyen, P.Q. (eds.) EUROCRYPT 2013. LNCS, vol. 7881, pp. 461–485. Springer, Heidelberg (2013). https://doi.org/10.1007/978-3-642-38348-9_28

[BHK13] Bellare, M., Hoang, V.T., Keelveedhi, S.: Instantiating random oracles via UCEs. In: Canetti, R., Garay, J.A. (eds.) CRYPTO 2013. LNCS, vol. 8043, pp. 398–415. Springer, Heidelberg (2013). https://doi.org/10.1007/978-3-642-40084-1_23

[BK10] Brakerski, Z., Kalai, Y.T.: A framework for efficient signatures, ring signatures and identity based encryption in the standard model. Cryptology ePrint Archive, Report 2010/086 (2010). http://eprint.iacr.org/2010/086

[BLS04] Boneh, D., Lynn, B., Shacham, H.: Short signatures from the Weil pairing. J. Cryptol. **17**(4), 297–319 (2004)

[BR93] Bellare, M., Rogaway, P.: Random oracles are practical: a paradigm for designing efficient protocols. In: Ashby, V., (eds.), ACM CCS 1993, pp. 62–73, Fairfax, Virginia, USA, November 3–5, 1993. ACM Press, New York (1993)

[BR09] Bellare, M., Ristenpart, T.: Simulation without the artificial abort: simplified proof and improved concrete security for Waters' IBE scheme. In: Joux, A. (ed.) EUROCRYPT 2009. LNCS, vol. 5479, pp. 407–424. Springer, Heidelberg (2009). https://doi.org/10.1007/978-3-642-01001-9_24

[BSW06] Boneh, D., Shen, E., Waters, B.: Strongly unforgeable signatures based on computational Diffie-Hellman. In: Yung, M., Dodis, Y., Kiayias, A., Malkin, T. (eds.) PKC 2006. LNCS, vol. 3958, pp. 229–240. Springer, Heidelberg (2006). https://doi.org/10.1007/11745853_15

[Can97] Canetti, R.: Towards realizing random oracles: hash functions that hide all partial information. In: Kaliski, B.S. (ed.) CRYPTO 1997. LNCS, vol. 1294, pp. 455–469. Springer, Heidelberg (1997). https://doi.org/10.1007/BFb0052255

[CFN15] Catalano, D., Fiore, D., Nizzardo, L.: Programmable hash functions go private: constructions and applications to (homomorphic) signatures with shorter public keys. In: Gennaro, R., Robshaw, M. (eds.) CRYPTO 2015. LNCS, vol. 9216, pp. 254–274. Springer, Heidelberg (2015). https://doi.org/10.1007/978-3-662-48000-7_13

[CGH98] Canetti, R., Goldreich, O., Halevi, S.: The random oracle methodology, revisited (preliminary version). In: 30th ACM STOC, May 23–26, 1998, pp. 209–218. ACM Press, Dallas (1998)

[CHK03] Canetti, R., Halevi, S., Katz, J.: A forward-secure public-key encryption scheme. In: Biham, E. (ed.) EUROCRYPT 2003. LNCS, vol. 2656, pp. 255–271. Springer, Heidelberg (2003). https://doi.org/10.1007/3-540-39200-9_16

[CHK04] Canetti, R., Halevi, S., Katz, J.: Chosen-ciphertext security from identity-based encryption. In: Cachin, C., Camenisch, J.L. (eds.) EUROCRYPT 2004. LNCS, vol. 3027, pp. 207–222. Springer, Heidelberg (2004). https://doi.org/10.1007/978-3-540-24676-3_13

[DG17a] Döttling, N., Garg, S.: From selective IBE to Full IBE and selective HIBE. In: Kalai, Y., Reyzin, L. (eds.) TCC 2017. LNCS, vol. 10677, pp. 372–408. Springer, Cham (2017). https://doi.org/10.1007/978-3-319-70500-2_13

[DG17b] Döttling, N., Garg, S.: Identity-based encryption from the Diffie-Hellman assumption. In: Katz, J., Shacham, H. (eds.) CRYPTO 2017. LNCS, vol. 10401, pp. 537–569. Springer, Cham (2017). https://doi.org/10.1007/978-3-319-63688-7_18

[DS15] Döttling, N., Schröder, D.: Efficient pseudorandom functions via on-the-fly adaptation. In: Gennaro, R., Robshaw, M. (eds.) CRYPTO 2015. LNCS, vol. 9215, pp. 329–350. Springer, Heidelberg (2015). https://doi.org/10.1007/978-3-662-47989-6_16

[EGM96] Even, S., Goldreich, O., Micali, S.: On-line/off-line digital signatures. J. Cryptol. **9**(1), 35–67 (1996)

[EHK+13] Escala, A., Herold, G., Kiltz, E., Ràfols, C., Villar, J.: An algebraic framework for Diffie-Hellman assumptions. In: Canetti, R., Garay, J.A. (eds.) CRYPTO 2013. LNCS, vol. 8043, pp. 129–147. Springer, Heidelberg (2013). https://doi.org/10.1007/978-3-642-40084-1_8

[FF13] Fischlin, M., Fleischhacker, N.: Limitations of the meta-reduction technique: the case of schnorr signatures. In: Johansson, T., Nguyen, P.Q. (eds.) EUROCRYPT 2013. LNCS, vol. 7881, pp. 444–460. Springer, Heidelberg (2013). https://doi.org/10.1007/978-3-642-38348-9_27

[FHPS13] Freire, E.S.V., Hofheinz, D., Paterson, K.G., Striecks, C.: Programmable hash functions in the multilinear setting. In: Canetti, R., Garay, J.A. (eds.) CRYPTO 2013. LNCS, vol. 8042, pp. 513–530. Springer, Heidelberg (2013). https://doi.org/10.1007/978-3-642-40041-4_28

[FLR+10] Fischlin, M., Lehmann, A., Ristenpart, T., Shrimpton, T., Stam, M., Tessaro, S.: Random oracles with(out) programmability. In: Abe, M. (ed.) ASIACRYPT 2010. LNCS, vol. 6477, pp. 303–320. Springer, Heidelberg (2010). https://doi.org/10.1007/978-3-642-17373-8_18

[FM16] Farshim, P., Mittelbach, A.: Modeling random oracles under unpredictable queries. In: Peyrin, T. (ed.) FSE 2016. LNCS, vol. 9783, pp. 453–473. Springer, Heidelberg (2016). https://doi.org/10.1007/978-3-662-52993-5_23

[GMR88] Goldwasser, S., Micali, S., Rivest, R.L.: A digital signature scheme secure against adaptive chosen-message attacks. SIAM J. Comput. **17**(2), 281–308 (1988)

[HJK11] Hofheinz, D., Jager, T., Kiltz, E.: Short signatures from weaker assumptions. In: Lee, D.H., Wang, X. (eds.) ASIACRYPT 2011. LNCS, vol. 7073, pp. 647–666. Springer, Heidelberg (2011). https://doi.org/10.1007/978-3-642-25385-0_35

[HK08] Hofheinz, D., Kiltz, E.: Programmable hash functions and their applications. In: Wagner, D. (ed.) CRYPTO 2008. LNCS, vol. 5157, pp. 21–38. Springer, Heidelberg (2008). https://doi.org/10.1007/978-3-540-85174-5_2

[HMS12] Hanaoka, G., Matsuda, T., Schuldt, J.C.N.: On the impossibility of constructing efficient key encapsulation and programmable hash functions in prime order groups. In: Safavi-Naini, R., Canetti, R. (eds.) CRYPTO 2012. LNCS, vol. 7417, pp. 812–831. Springer, Heidelberg (2012). https://doi.org/10.1007/978-3-642-32009-5_47

[HW09a] Hohenberger, S., Waters, B.: Realizing hash-and-sign signatures under standard assumptions. In: Joux, A. (ed.) EUROCRYPT 2009. LNCS, vol. 5479, pp. 333–350. Springer, Heidelberg (2009). https://doi.org/10.1007/978-3-642-01001-9_19

[HW09b] Hohenberger, S., Waters, B.: Short and stateless signatures from the RSA assumption. In: Halevi, S. (ed.) CRYPTO 2009. LNCS, vol. 5677, pp. 654–670. Springer, Heidelberg (2009). https://doi.org/10.1007/978-3-642-03356-8_38

[JK17] Jager, T., Kurek, R.: Short digital signatures and ID-based KEMs via truncation collision resistance. Cryptology ePrint Archive, Report 2017/061 (2017). Full version of an ASIACRYPT 2018 paper. https://eprint.iacr.org/2017/061

[KR00] Krawczyk, H., Rabin, T.: Chameleon signatures. In: NDSS 2000, San Diego, CA, USA, February 2–4, 2000. The Internet Society (2000)

[LOS+06] Lu, S., Ostrovsky, R., Sahai, A., Shacham, H., Waters, B.: Sequential aggregate signatures and multisignatures without random oracles. In: Vaudenay, S. (ed.) EUROCRYPT 2006. LNCS, vol. 4004, pp. 465–485. Springer, Heidelberg (2006). https://doi.org/10.1007/11761679_28

[Nat15a] National Institute of Standards and Technology. FIPS PUB 180–4: Secure Hash Standard. August 2015. https://nvlpubs.nist.gov/nistpubs/FIPS/NIST.FIPS.180-4.pdf

[Nat15b] National Institute of Standards and Technology. FIPS PUB 202: SHA-3 Standard: Permutation-Based Hash and Extendable-Output Functions. August 2015. https://nvlpubs.nist.gov/nistpubs/fips/nist.fips.202.pdf

[Nie02] Nielsen, J.B.: Separating random oracle proofs from complexity theoretic proofs: the non-committing encryption case. In: Yung, M. (ed.) CRYPTO 2002. LNCS, vol. 2442, pp. 111–126. Springer, Heidelberg (2002). https://doi.org/10.1007/3-540-45708-9_8

[RS04] Rogaway, P., Shrimpton, T.: Cryptographic hash-function basics: definitions, implications, and separations for preimage resistance, second-preimage resistance, and collision resistance. In: Roy, B., Meier, W. (eds.) FSE 2004. LNCS, vol. 3017, pp. 371–388. Springer, Heidelberg (2004). https://doi.org/10.1007/978-3-540-25937-4_24

[SPW07] Steinfeld, R., Pieprzyk, J., Wang, H.: How to strengthen any weakly unforgeable signature into a strongly unforgeable signature. In: Abe, M. (ed.) CT-RSA 2007. LNCS, vol. 4377, pp. 357–371. Springer, Heidelberg (2006). https://doi.org/10.1007/11967668_23

[Wat05] Waters, B.: Efficient identity-based encryption without random oracles. In: Cramer, R. (ed.) EUROCRYPT 2005. LNCS, vol. 3494, pp. 114–127. Springer, Heidelberg (2005). https://doi.org/10.1007/11426639_7

[Wee16] Wee, H.: Déjà Q: Encore! Un Petit IBE. In: Kushilevitz, E., Malkin, T. (eds.) TCC 2016. LNCS, vol. 9563, pp. 237–258. Springer, Heidelberg (2016). https://doi.org/10.1007/978-3-662-49099-0_9

[Zha16] Zhandry, M.: The magic of ELFs. In: Robshaw, M., Katz, J. (eds.) CRYPTO 2016. LNCS, vol. 9814, pp. 479–508. Springer, Heidelberg (2016). https://doi.org/10.1007/978-3-662-53018-4_18

[ZSS04] Zhang, F., Safavi-Naini, R., Susilo, W.: An efficient signature scheme from bilinear pairings and its applications. In: Bao, F., Deng, R., Zhou, J. (eds.) PKC 2004. LNCS, vol. 2947, pp. 277–290. Springer, Heidelberg (2004). https://doi.org/10.1007/978-3-540-24632-9_20

Asiacrypt 2018 Award Paper I

Tighter Security Proofs for GPV-IBE in the Quantum Random Oracle Model

Shuichi Katsumata[1,2](✉), Shota Yamada[2](✉), and Takashi Yamakawa[3](✉)

[1] The University of Tokyo, Tokyo, Japan
shuichi_katsumata@it.k.u-tokyo.ac.jp
[2] National Institute of Advanced Industrial Science, Tokyo, Japan
yamada-shota@aist.go.jp
[3] NTT Secure Platform Laboratories, Tokyo, Japan
yamakawa.takashi@lab.ntt.co.jp

Abstract. In (STOC, 2008), Gentry, Peikert, and Vaikuntanathan proposed the first identity-based encryption (GPV-IBE) scheme based on a post-quantum assumption, namely, the learning with errors (LWE) assumption. Since their proof was only made in the random oracle model (ROM) instead of the *quantum* random oracle model (QROM), it remained unclear whether the scheme was truly post-quantum or not. In (CRYPTO, 2012), Zhandry developed new techniques to be used in the QROM and proved security of GPV-IBE in the QROM, hence answering in the affirmative that GPV-IBE is indeed post-quantum. However, since the general technique developed by Zhandry incurred a large reduction loss, there was a wide gap between the concrete efficiency and security level provided by GPV-IBE in the ROM and QROM. Furthermore, regardless of being in the ROM or QROM, GPV-IBE is not known to have a tight reduction in the multi-challenge setting. Considering that in the real-world an adversary can obtain many ciphertexts, it is desirable to have a security proof that does not degrade with the number of challenge ciphertext.

In this paper, we provide a much tighter proof for the GPV-IBE in the QROM in the single-challenge setting. In addition, we also show that a slight variant of the GPV-IBE has an almost tight reduction in the multi-challenge setting both in the ROM and QROM, where the reduction loss is independent of the number of challenge ciphertext. Our proof departs from the traditional partitioning technique and resembles the approach used in the public key encryption scheme of Cramer and Shoup (CRYPTO, 1998). Our proof strategy allows the reduction algorithm to program the random oracle the same way for all identities and naturally fits the QROM setting where an adversary may query a superposition of all identities in one random oracle query. Notably, our proofs are much simpler than the one by Zhandry and conceptually much easier to follow for cryptographers not familiar with quantum computation. Although at a high level, the techniques used for the single and multi-challenge setting are similar, the technical details are quite different. For the multi-challenge setting, we rely on the Katz-Wang technique (CCS, 2003) to overcome some obstacles regarding the leftover hash lemma.

T. Peyrin and S. Galbraith (Eds.): ASIACRYPT 2018, LNCS 11273, pp. 253–282, 2018.
https://doi.org/10.1007/978-3-030-03329-3_9

Keywords: Identity-Based Encryption
Quantum random oracle models · LWE assumption
Tight security reduction · Multi-challenge security

1 Introduction

1.1 Background

Shor [Sho94] in his breakthrough result showed that if a quantum computer is realized, then almost all cryptosystems used in the real world will be broken. Since then, a significant amount of studies have been done in the area of post-quantum cryptography, whose motivation is constructing cryptosystems secure against quantum adversaries. Recently in 2016, the National Institute of Standards and Technology (NIST) initiated the Post-Quantum Cryptography Standardization, and since then post-quantum cryptography has been gathering increasingly more attention.

Random Oracles in Quantum World. In general, security proofs of practical cryptographic schemes are given in the random oracle model (ROM) [BR93], which is an idealized model where a hash function is modeled as a publicly accessible oracle that computes a random function. Boneh et al. [BDF+11] pointed out that the ROM as in the classical setting is not reasonable when considering security against quantum adversaries, since quantum adversaries may compute hash functions over quantum superpositions of many inputs. Considering this fact, as a reasonable model against quantum adversaries, they proposed a new model called the quantum random oracle model (QROM), where a hash function is modeled as a *quantumly accessible* random oracle. As discussed in [BDF+11], many commonly-used proof techniques in the ROM do not work in the QROM. Therefore even if we have a security proof in the ROM, we often require new techniques to obtain similar results in the QROM.

Identity-Based Encryption in QROM. Identity-Based Encryption (IBE) is a generalization of a public key encryption scheme where the public key of a user can be any arbitrary string such as an e-mail address. The first IBE scheme based on a post-quantum assumption is the one proposed by Gentry et al. (GPV-IBE) [GPV08], which is based on the learning with errors (LWE) assumption [Reg05]. To this date, GPV-IBE is still arguably the most efficient IBE scheme that is based on a hardness assumption that resists quantum attacks. However, since their original security proof was made in the ROM instead of the QROM, it was unclear if we could say the scheme is truly post-quantum. Zhandry [Zha12b] answered this in the affirmative by proving that the GPV-IBE is indeed secure in the QROM under the LWE assumption, hence truly post-quantum, by developing new techniques in the QROM.

Tight Security of GPV-IBE. However, if we consider the tightness of the reduction, the security proof of the GPV-IBE by Zhandry [Zha12b] does not provide a satisfactory security. Specifically, GPV-IBE may be efficient in the

ROM, but it is no longer efficient in the QROM. In general, a cryptographic scheme is said to be tightly secure under some assumption if breaking the security of the scheme is as hard as solving the assumption. More precisely, suppose that we proved that if there exists an adversary breaking the security of the scheme with advantage ϵ and running time T, we can break the underlying assumption with advantage ϵ' and running time T'. We say that the scheme is tightly-secure if we have $\epsilon'/T' \approx \epsilon/T$. By using this notation, Zhandry gave a reduction from the security of GPV-IBE to the LWE assumption with $\epsilon' \approx \epsilon^2/(Q_{\mathsf{H}}+Q_{\mathsf{ID}})^4$ and $T' \approx T + (Q_{\mathsf{H}} + Q_{\mathsf{ID}})^2 \cdot \mathsf{poly}(\lambda)$ where Q_{H} denotes the number of hash queries, Q_{ID} denotes the number of secret key queries, λ denotes the security parameter, and poly denotes some fixed polynomial. Though the reduction is theoretically interesting, the meaning of the resulting security bound in a realistic setting is unclear. For example, if we want to obtain 128-bit security for the resulting IBE, and say we had $\epsilon = 2^{-128}$, $Q_{\mathsf{H}} = 2^{100}$, $Q_{\mathsf{ID}} = 2^{20}$, then even if we ignore the blowup for the running time, we would have to start from at least a 656-bit secure LWE assumption, which incurs a significant blowup of the parameters. Indeed, Zhandry left it as an open problem to give a tighter reduction for the GPV-IBE.

Multi-challenge Tightness. The standard security notion of IBE considers the setting where an adversary obtains only one challenge ciphertext. This is because security against adversaries obtaining many challenge ciphertexts can be reduced to the security in the above simplified setting. However, as pointed out by Hofheinz and Jager [HJ12], tightness is not preserved in the above reduction since the security degrades by the number of ciphertexts. Therefore tightly secure IBE in the single-challenge setting does not imply tightly secure IBE in the multi-challenge setting. On the other hand, in the real world, it is natural to assume that an adversary obtains many ciphertexts, and thus tight security in the multi-challenge setting is desirable. However, there is no known security proof for the GPV-IBE or its variant that does not degrade with the number of challenge ciphertexts even in the classical setting.

1.2 Our Contribution

We provide much tighter security proofs for the GPV-IBE in the QROM in the single-challenge setting. Furthermore, we provide a multi-challenge tight variant of GPV-IBE that is secure both in the ROM and QROM. In the following, we describe the tightness of our security proofs by using the same notation as in the previous section.

- In the single-challenge setting, we give a reduction from the security of GPV-IBE to the LWE assumption with $\epsilon' \approx \epsilon$ and $T' = T+(Q_{\mathsf{H}}+Q_{\mathsf{ID}})^2 \cdot \mathsf{poly}(\lambda)$. If we additionally assume quantumly secure pseudorandom functions (PRFs), then we further obtain a tighter reduction, which gives $\epsilon' \approx \epsilon$ and $T' = T + (Q_{\mathsf{H}} + Q_{\mathsf{ID}}) \cdot \mathsf{poly}(\lambda)$. This is the first security proof for GPV-IBE whose security bound does not degrade with Q_{H} or Q_{ID} even in the classical setting.

We note that the same security bound can be achieved without assuming PRFs in the classical ROM.
- We give a slight variant of GPV-IBE scheme whose multi-challenge security is reduced to the LWE assumption with $\epsilon' = \epsilon/\mathsf{poly}(\lambda)$ and $T' \approx T + (Q_{\mathsf{H}} + Q_{\mathsf{ID}} + Q_{\mathsf{ch}})^2 \cdot \mathsf{poly}(\lambda)$ where Q_{ch} denotes the number of challenge queries. If we additionally assume quantumly secure PRFs, then we further obtain a tighter reduction. Namely, ϵ' is the same as the above, and $T' = T + (Q_{\mathsf{H}} + Q_{\mathsf{ID}} + Q_{\mathsf{ch}}) \cdot \mathsf{poly}(\lambda)$. This is the first variant of the GPV-IBE scheme whose security bound does not degrade with Q_{ch} even in the classical setting. We note that the same security bound can be achieved without assuming PRFs in the classical ROM.

Moreover, our security proofs are much simpler than the one by Zhandry [Zha12b]. In his work, he introduced new techniques regarding indistinguishability of oracles against quantum adversaries. Though his techniques are general and also useful in other settings (e.g., [Zha12a]), it involves some arguments on quantum computation, and they are hard to follow for cryptographers who are not familiar with quantum computation. On the other hand, our proofs involve a minimal amount of discussions about quantum computation, and our proofs are done almost similar to the counterparts in the classical ROM.

1.3 Technical Overview

GPV-IBE. First, we briefly describe the GPV-IBE [GPV08], which is the main target of this paper. A master public key is a matrix $\mathbf{A} \in \mathbb{Z}_q^{n \times m}$ and a master secret key is its trapdoor $\mathbf{T_A} \in \mathbb{Z}^{m \times m}$, which enables one to compute a short vector $\mathbf{e} \in \mathbb{Z}_q^m$ such that $\mathbf{Ae} = \mathbf{u}$ given an arbitrary vector $\mathbf{u} \in \mathbb{Z}_q^n$. A private key $\mathsf{sk_{ID}}$ for an identity $\mathsf{ID} \in \mathcal{ID}$ is a short vector $\mathbf{e} \in \mathbb{Z}_q^m$ such that $\mathbf{Ae} = \mathbf{u}_{\mathsf{ID}}$ where $\mathbf{u}_{\mathsf{ID}} = \mathsf{H}(\mathsf{ID})$ for a hash function $\mathsf{H} : \mathcal{ID} \rightarrow \mathbb{Z}_q^n$, which is modeled as a random oracle. A ciphertext for a message $\mathsf{M} \in \{0,1\}$ consists of $c_0 = \mathbf{u}_{\mathsf{ID}}^\top \mathbf{s} + x + \mathsf{M}\lfloor q/2 \rceil$ and $\mathbf{c}_1 = \mathbf{A}^\top \mathbf{s} + \mathbf{x}$. Here $\mathbf{s}$ is a uniformly random vector over $\mathbb{Z}_q^n$ and $x, \mathbf{x}$ are small "noise" terms where each entries are sampled from some specific Gaussian distribution χ. Decryption can be done by computing $w = c_0 - \mathbf{c}_1^\top \mathbf{e}_{\mathsf{ID}} \in \mathbb{Z}_q$ and deciding if w is closer to 0 or to $\lfloor q/2 \rceil$ modulo q.

Security Proof in Classical ROM. The above IBE relies its security on the LWE assumption, which informally states the following: given a uniformly random matrix $[\mathbf{A}|\mathbf{u}] \leftarrow \mathbb{Z}_q^{n \times (m+1)}$ and some vector $\mathbf{b} \in \mathbb{Z}_q^{m+1}$, there is no PPT algorithm that can decide with non-negligible probability whether $\mathbf{b}$ is of the form $[\mathbf{A}|\mathbf{u}]^\top \mathbf{s} + \mathbf{x}'$ for some $\mathbf{s} \leftarrow \mathbb{Z}_q^n$ and $\mathbf{x}' \leftarrow \chi^{m+1}$, or a uniformly random vector over $\mathbb{Z}_q^{m+1}$, i.e., $\mathbf{b} \leftarrow \mathbb{Z}_q^{m+1}$. Below, we briefly recall the original security proof in the classical ROM given by Gentry et al. [GPV08] and see how the random oracle is used by the reduction algorithm. The proof relies on a key lemma which states that we can set $\mathsf{H}(\mathsf{ID})$ and $\mathbf{e}$ in the "reverse order" from the real scheme. That is, we can first sample $\mathbf{e}$ from some distribution and program $\mathsf{H}(\mathsf{ID}) := \mathbf{Ae}$ so that their distributions are close to uniformly random as in the real scheme. In the security proof, a reduction algorithm guesses $i \in [Q]$ such that the adversary's i-th hash query is the challenge identity ID^* where Q denotes the number of hash queries made by the adversary. Then for all but the i-th hash query, the reduction algorithm programs $\mathsf{H}(\mathsf{ID})$ in the above manner, and for the i-th query, it programs the output of $\mathsf{H}(\mathsf{ID}^*)$ to be the vector $\mathbf{u}$ contained in the LWE instance that is given as the challenge. Specifically, the reduction algorithm sets the challenge user's identity vector $\mathbf{u}_{\mathsf{ID}^*}$ as the random vector $\mathbf{u}$ contained in the LWE instance. If the guess is correct, then it can embed the LWE instance into the challenge ciphertexts c_0^* and $\mathbf{c}_1^*$; in case it is a valid LWE instance, then $(c_0^*, \mathbf{c}_1^*)$ is properly set to $(\mathbf{u}_{\mathsf{ID}^*}^\top \mathbf{s} + x + \mathsf{M}\lfloor q/2 \rceil, \mathbf{A}^\top \mathbf{s} + \mathbf{x})$ as in the real scheme. Therefore, the challenge ciphertext can be switched to random due to the LWE assumption. After this switch, M is perfectly hidden and thus the security of GPV-IBE is reduced to the LWE assumption. Since the reduction algorithm programs the random oracle in the same way except for the challenge identity, this type of proof methodology is often times referred to as the "all-but-one programming".

Security Proof in QROM in [Zha12b]**.** Unfortunately, the above proof cannot be simply extended to a proof in the QROM. The reason is that in the QROM, even a single hash query can be a superposition of *all* the identities. In such a case, to proceed with the above all-but-one programming approach, the reduction algorithm would have to guess a single identity out of all the possible identities which he hopes that would be used as the challenge identity ID^* by the adversary. Obviously, the probability of the reduction algorithm being right is negligible, since the number of possible identities is exponentially large. This is in sharp contrast with the ROM setting, where the reduction algorithm was allowed to guess the single identity out of the polynomially many (classical) random oracle queries made by the adversary. Therefore, the all-but-one programming as in the classical case cannot be used in the quantum case. To overcome this barrier, Zhandry [Zha12b] introduced a useful lemma regarding what he calls the semi-constant distribution. The semi-constant distribution with parameter $0 < p < 1$ is a distribution over functions from $\mathcal{X}$ to $\mathcal{Y}$ such that a function chosen according to the distribution gives the same fixed value for random p-fraction of all inputs, and behaves as a random function for the rest of the inputs. He proved that a function according to the semi-constant distribution with parameter p and a random function cannot be distinguished by an adversary that makes Q oracle queries with advantage greater than $\frac{8}{3}Q^4p^2$. In the security proof, the reduction algorithm partitions the set of identities into controlled and uncontrolled sets. The uncontrolled set consists of randomly chosen p-fraction of all identities, and the controlled set is the complement of it. The reduction algorithm embeds an LWE instance into the uncontrolled set, and programs the hash values for the controlled set so that the decryption keys for identities in the controlled set can be extracted efficiently. Then the reduction algorithm works as long as the challenge identity falls inside the uncontrolled set and all identities for secret key queries fall inside the controlled set (otherwise it aborts). By appropriately setting p, we can argue that the probability that the reduction algorithm does not abort is non-negligible, and thus the security proof is completed. Though this technique is very general and useful, a huge reduction loss is inherent as long as we take the above strategy because the reduction algorithm has to abort with high probability. It may be useful to point out for readers who are familiar with IBE schemes in the standard model that the above technique is conceptually very similar to the partitioning technique which is often used in the context of adaptively secure IBE scheme in the standard model [Wat05, ABB10, CHKP10]. The reason why we cannot make the proof tight is exactly the same as that for the counterparts in the standard model.

Our Tight Security Proof in QROM. As discussed above, we cannot obtain a tight reduction as long as we use a partitioning-like technique. Therefore we take a completely different approach, which is rather similar to that used in the public key encryption scheme of Cramer and Shoup [CS98], which has also been applied to the pairing-based IBE construction of Gentry [Gen06]. The idea is that we simulate in a way so that we can create exactly one valid secret key for every identity. Note that this is opposed to the partitioning technique (and the all-but-one programming technique) where the simulator cannot create a secret key for an identity in the uncontrolled set. To create the challenge ciphertext, we use the one secret key we know for that challenge identity. If the adversary can not tell which secret key the ciphertext was created from and if there are potentially many candidates for the secret key, we can take advantage of the entropy of the secret key to statistically hide the message.

In more detail, the main observation is that the secret key $\mathbf{e}$, i.e. a short vector $\mathbf{e}$ such that $\mathbf{Ae} = \mathbf{u}$, retains plenty of entropy even after fixing the public values $\mathbf{A}$ and $\mathbf{u}$. Therefore, by programming the hash value $\mathbf{u}$ of an identity, we can easily create a situation where the simulator knows exactly one secret key out of the many possible candidates. Furthermore, the simulator knowing a secret key $\mathbf{e}_{\mathsf{ID}^*}$ such that $\mathbf{A}\mathbf{e}_{\mathsf{ID}^*} = \mathbf{u}_{\mathsf{ID}^*}$, can simulate the challenge ciphertext by creating $c_0^* = \mathbf{e}_{\mathsf{ID}^*}^\top \mathbf{c}_1^* + \mathsf{M}\lfloor q/2 \rceil$ and $\mathbf{c}_1^* = \mathbf{A}^\top \mathbf{s} + \mathbf{x}$. Here, the key observation is that we no longer require the LWE instance $(\mathbf{u}_{\mathsf{ID}^*}, \mathbf{u}_{\mathsf{ID}^*}^\top \mathbf{s} + x)$ to simulate the challenge ciphertext. Though the distribution of c_0^* simulated as above is slightly different from that of the real ciphertext due to the difference in the noise distributions, we ignore it in this overview. In the real proof, we overcome this problem by using the noise rerandomization technique by Katsumata and Yamada [KY16]. Then we use the LWE assumption to switch $\mathbf{c}_1^*$ to random. Finally, we argue that $\mathbf{e}_{\mathsf{ID}^*}^\top \mathbf{c}_1^*$ is almost uniform if the min-entropy of $\mathbf{e}_{\mathsf{ID}^*}$ is high and $\mathbf{c}_1^*$ is uniformly random due to the leftover hash lemma. Therefore, all information of the message M is hidden and thus the proof is completed.

Finally, we observe that the above proof naturally fits in the QROM setting. The crucial difference from the partitioning technique is that in our security proof we program the random oracle in the same way for all identities. Therefore even if an adversary queries a superposition of all identities, the simulator can simply quantumly perform the programming procedure for the superposition. Thus the proof in the classical ROM can be almost automatically converted into the one in the QROM in this case.

Tight Security in Multi-challenge Setting. Unfortunately, the above idea does not extend naturally to the tightly-secure multi-challenge setting. One can always prove security in the multi-challenge setting starting from a scheme that is single-challenge secure via a hybrid argument, however, as mentioned by Hofheinz and Jager [HJ12], this type of reduction does not preserve tightness. A careful reader may think that the above programming technique can be extended to the multi-challenge setting, hence bypassing the hybrid argument. We briefly explain why this is not the case. Informally, in the above proof, the reduction algorithm embeds its given LWE instance $(\mathbf{A}, \mathbf{A}^\top \mathbf{s} + \mathbf{x})$ into the challenge ciphertext by creating $(c_0^* = \mathbf{e}_{\mathsf{ID}^*}^\top \mathbf{c}_1^* + \mathsf{M}\lfloor q/2 \rceil, \mathbf{c}_1^* = \mathbf{A}^\top \mathbf{s} + \mathbf{x})$, where $\mathbf{e}_{\mathsf{ID}^*}$ is the secret key of the challenge user $\mathbf{u}_{\mathsf{ID}^*}$. Therefore, since the $\mathbf{c}_1^*$ component of every ciphertext is an LWE instance for the same public matrix $\mathbf{A}$, to simulate multiple challenge ciphertexts in the above manner, the reduction algorithm must be able to prepare a special type of LWE instance $(\mathbf{A}, \{\mathbf{A}^\top \mathbf{s}^{(k)} + \mathbf{x}^{(k)}\}_{k \in [N]})$, where $N = \mathsf{poly}(\lambda)$ is the number of challenge ciphertext queried by the adversary. It can be easily seen that this construction is tightly-secure in the multi-challenge setting with the same efficiency as the single-challenge setting, *if* we assume that this special type of LWE problem is provided to the reduction algorithm as the challenge. However, unfortunately, we still end up losing a factor of N in the reduction when reducing the standard LWE problem to this special LWE problem. In particular, we only shifted the burden of having to go through the N hybrid arguments to the assumption rather than to the scheme. As one may have noticed, there is a way to bypass the problem of going through the N hybrid arguments by using conventional techniques (See [Reg05, Reg10]) of constructing an unlimited number of fresh LWE instances given a fixed number of LWE instances. However, this techniques requires the noise of the newly created LWE instances to grow proportionally to the number of created instances. In particular, to create the above special LWE instance from a standard LWE instance, we require the size of the noise $\mathbf{x}^{(k)}$ to grow polynomially with N, where recall that N can be an arbitrary polynomial. Hence, although we can show a tightly secure reduction in the multi-challenge setting, for the concrete parameters of the scheme to be independent of N, we need to assume the super-polynomial LWE assumption to cope with the super-polynomial noise blow up. This is far more inefficient than in the single-challenge setting where we only require a polynomial LWE assumption.

To overcome this problem, we use the "lossy mode" of the LWE problem. It is well known that the secret vector $\mathbf{s}$ is uniquely defined given an LWE instance $(\mathbf{A}, \mathbf{A}^\top \mathbf{s} + \mathbf{x})$ for large enough samples. A series of works, e.g., [GKPV10, BKPW12, AKPW13, LSSS17] have observed that if we instead sample $\mathbf{A}$ from a special distribution that is computationally indistinguishable from the uniform distribution, then $(\mathbf{A}, \mathbf{A}^\top \mathbf{s} + \mathbf{x})$ leaks almost no information of the secret $\mathbf{s}$, hence the term "lossy mode". This idea can be leveraged to prove (almost) tight security of the above single-challenge construction, where the reduction loss is independent of the number of challenge ciphertext. A first attempt of using this idea is as follows: During the security proof of the GPV-IBE, we first change the public matrix $\mathbf{A}$ to a lossy matrix $\tilde{\mathbf{A}}$ and generate the secret keys and program the random oracle in the same way as before. To create the challenge ciphertexts, the reduction algorithm honestly samples $\mathbf{s}^{(k)}$, $x^{(k)}$, $\mathbf{x}^{(k)}$ and sets $(c_0^* = \mathbf{u}_{\mathsf{ID}^*}^\top \mathbf{s}^{(k)} + x^{(k)} + \mathsf{M}^{(k)}\lfloor q/2 \rceil, \mathbf{c}_1^* = \mathbf{A}^\top \mathbf{s}^{(k)} + \mathbf{x}^{(k)})$. Now, it may seem that owing to the lossy mode of LWE, we can rely on the entropy of the secret vector $\mathbf{s}^{(k)}$ to argue that c_0^* is distributed uniformly random via the leftover hash lemma. The main difference between the previous single-challenge setting is that we can rely on the entropy of the secret vector $\mathbf{s}^{(k)}$ rather than on the entropy of the secret key $\mathbf{e}_{\mathsf{ID}^*}$. Since each challenge ciphertext is injected with fresh entropy and we can argue statistically that a single challenge ciphertext is not leaking any information on the message, the reduction loss will be independent of the number of challenge ciphertext query N.

Although the above argument may seem correct at first glance, it incurs a subtle but a fatal flaw, thus bringing us to our proposed construction. The problem of the above argument is how we use the leftover hash lemma. To use the lemma correctly, the vector $\mathbf{u}_{\mathsf{ID}^*}$ viewed as a hash function is required to be universal. This is true in case $\mathbf{u}_{\mathsf{ID}^*}$ is set as $\mathbf{A}\mathbf{e}_{\mathsf{ID}^*}$, where $\mathbf{A} \leftarrow \mathbb{Z}_q^{n \times m}$ and $\mathbf{e}_{\mathsf{ID}^*}$ is sampled from some appropriate distribution. However, this is *not* true anymore once we change $\mathbf{A}$ to a lossy matrix $\tilde{\mathbf{A}}$, since $\tilde{\mathbf{A}}$ now lives in an exponentially small subset of $\mathbb{Z}_q^{n \times m}$, hence, we can no longer rely on the entropy of $\mathbf{s}^{(k)}$ to statistically hide the message. To overcome this problem, our final idea is to use the Katz-Wang [KW03] technique. Specifically, we slightly alter the encryption algorithm of GPV-IBE to output the following instead:

$$c_0 = \mathbf{u}_{\mathsf{ID}||0}^\top \mathbf{s} + x_0 + \mathsf{M}\lfloor q/2 \rceil, \quad c_1 = \mathbf{u}_{\mathsf{ID}||1}^\top \mathbf{s} + x_1 + \mathsf{M}\lfloor q/2 \rceil, \quad \text{and} \quad \mathbf{c}_2 = \mathbf{A}^\top \mathbf{s} + \mathbf{x},$$

where $\mathbf{u}_{\mathsf{ID}||b} = H(\mathsf{ID}||b)$ for $b \in \{0, 1\}$. During the security proof, the reduction algorithm sets $\mathbf{u}_{\mathsf{ID}||0}$ and $\mathbf{u}_{\mathsf{ID}||1}$ so that one of them is uniformly random over $\mathbb{Z}_q^n$ and the other is constructed as $\mathbf{A}\mathbf{e}_{\mathsf{ID}}$. Then, for the ciphertext c_b corresponding to the uniformly random vector $\mathbf{u}_{\mathsf{ID}||b}$, we can correctly use the leftover hash lemma to argue that c_b statistically hides the message M. By going through one more hybrid argument, we can change both c_0, c_1 into random values that are independent of the message M. Note that instead of naively using the Katz-Wang technique, by reusing the $\mathbf{c}_2$ component, the above GPV-IBE variant only requires one additional element in $\mathbb{Z}_q$ compared to the original GPV-IBE. Furthermore, in the actual construction, we do not require the noise terms x_0, x_1 in c_0, c_1 since we no longer rely on the LWE assumption to change c_0, c_1 into random values. Our construction and security reduction does not depend on the number of challenge ciphertext query N and in particular, can be proven under the polynomial LWE assumption, which is only slightly worse than the single-challenge construction. In addition, due to the same reason as the single-challenge setting, our classical ROM proof can be naturally converted to a QROM proof.

1.4 Discussion

Similar Techniques in Other Works. The idea to simulate GPV-IBE in a way so that we can create exactly one valid secret key for every secret key query is not new. We are aware of few works that are based on this idea. Gentry et al. [GPV08] mentioned that by using this technique, they can prove the security of the GPV-IBE in the standard model based on a non-standard interactive variant of the LWE (I-LWE) assumption which requires a hash function to define. Here since the hash function is given to the adversary, a quantum adversary may query quantum states to the hash functions on its own. Therefore, in addition with the fact that the I-LWE assumption is made in the standard model, the statement made by [GPV08] would hold in the QROM as well. However, they only gave a sketch of the proof, and did not give a formal proof. Alwen et al. [ADN+10] use the idea to construct an identity-based hash proof system (IB-HPS) based on the mechanism of GPV-IBE. We note that they assume the modulus q to be super-polynomial. Outside the context of identity-based primitives, Applebaum et al. [ACPS09] and Bourse et al. [BDPMW16] provide an analysis of rerandomizing LWE samples which can be seen as a refinement of the idea mentioned in [GPV08]. [ACPS09] constructs a KDM-secure cryptosystem based on the LWE problem and [BDPMW16] shows a simple method for constructing circuit private fully homomorphic encryption schemes (FHE) based on the lattice-based FHE scheme of Gentry et al. [GSW13]. Both of their analysis only requires the modulus q to be polynomial. In summary, though similar ideas have been used, all of the previous works are irrelevant to tight security or the security in the QROM.

On Parameter-Tightness of Our Schemes. In the above overview, we focused on the tightness of the security proof. Here, we provide some discussions on how the parameters compare to the original GPV-IBE scheme [GPV08]. For the single challenge setting, our parameters are only a small factor worse than the GPV-IBE scheme. This is because the only difference is using the noise rerandomization technique of [KY16], which only slightly degrades the noise-level.[1] For the multi-challenge setting, the situation is more different. In this case, the parameters are much worse than the original (single-challenge secure) GPV-IBE scheme. This is because we have to go through the lossy-mode of LWE which requires for larger parameters. The concrete parameters are provided in Sect. 4.2.

Relation to CCA-Secure PKE. By applying the Canetti-Halevi-Katz transformation [CHK04] to our single-challenge-secure IBE scheme, we obtain a public key encryption (PKE) scheme secure against chosen ciphertext attacks (CCA) that is tightly secure in the single-challenge setting under the LWE assumption in the QROM. We note that Saito et al. [SXY18] already proposed such a PKE

[1] Our parameter selection in the main body may seem much worse compared to GPV-IBE, but this is only because we choose the parameters conservatively. Specifically, we can set the parameters to be only slightly worse than GPV-IBE by setting them less conservatively as in [GPV08]. Please, see end of Sect. 3.2 for more details.

scheme in the single-challenge setting that is more efficient than the scheme obtained by the above transformation.

On Running Time of Reductions. In the above overview, we ignore the running time of reductions. Though it seems that the above described reductions run in nearly the same time as the adversaries, due to a subtle problem of simulating random oracles against quantum adversaries, there is a significant blowup by a square factor of the number of queries the adversaries make. In the classical ROM, when we simulate a random oracle in security proofs, we usually sample a random function in a lazy manner. That is, whenever an adversary queries a point that has not been queried before, a reduction algorithm samples a fresh randomness and assigns it as a hash value for that point. However, this cannot be done in the QROM because an adversary may query a superposition of all the inputs in a single query. Therefore a reduction algorithm has to somehow commit to the hash values of all inputs at the beginning of the simulation.

Zhandry [Zha12b] proved that an adversary that makes Q queries cannot distinguish a random function and a $2Q$-wise independent hash function via quantum oracle accesses. Therefore we can use a $2Q$-wise independent hash to simulate a random oracle. However, if we take this method, the simulator has to evaluate a $2Q$-wise independent hash function for each hash query, and this is the reason why the running time blowups by $\Omega(Q^2)$.

One possible way to avoid this huge blowup is to simulate a random oracle by a PRF secure against quantum accessible adversaries. Since the time needed to evaluate a PRF is some fixed polynomial in the security parameter, the blowup for the running time can be made $Q \cdot \mathsf{poly}(\lambda)$ which is significantly better than $\Omega(Q^2)$. However, in order to use this method, we have to additionally assume the existence of quantumly secure PRFs. Such PRFs can be constructed based on any quantumly-secure one-way function [Zha12a], and thus they exist if the LWE assumption holds against quantum adversaries. However, the reduction for such PRFs are non-tight and thus we cannot rely on them in the context of tight security. Our suggestion is to use a real hash function to implement PRFs and to assume that it is a quantumly secure PRF. We believe this to be a natural assumption if we are willing to idealize a hash function as a random oracle. (See also the discussion in Sect. 2.2.)

1.5 Related Work

Schemes in QROM. Boneh et al. [BDF+11] introduced the QROM, and gave security proofs for the GPV-signature [GPV08] and a hybrid variant of the Bellare-Rogaway encryption [BR93] in the QROM. We note that their security proof for the GPV-signature is tight. Zhandry [Zha12b] proved that GPV-IBE and full-domain hash signatures are secure in the QROM. Targhi and Unruh [TU16] proposed variants of Fujisaki-Okamoto transformation and OAEP that are secure in the QROM. Some researchers studied the security of the Fiat-Shamir transform in the QROM [ARU14, Unr15, Unr17]. Unruh [Unr14b] proposed a revocable quantum timed-release encryption scheme in the QROM.

Unruh [Unr14a] proposed a position verification scheme in the QROM. Recently, some researchers studied tight securities in the QROM. Alkim et al. [ABB+17] proved that the signature scheme known as TESLA [BG14] is tightly secure under the LWE assumption. Saito et al. [SXY18] proposed a tightly CCA secure variant of the Bellare-Rogaway encryption. Kiltz et al. [KLS18] gave a tight reduction for the Fiat-Shamir transform in the QROM.

Tightly Secure IBEs. The first tightly secure IBE scheme from lattices in the single challenge setting and in the standard model was proposed by Boyen and Li [BL16]. While the construction is theoretically interesting and elegant, it is very inefficient and requires LWE assumption with super-polynomial approximation factors. As for the construction from bilinear maps, the first tightly secure IBE from standard assumptions in the single challenge setting and in the random oracle model was proposed by Katz and Wang [KW03]. Coron [Cor09] gave a tight reduction for a variant of the original Boneh-Franklin IBE [BF01]. Later, the first realization in the standard model was proposed by Chen and Wee [CW13]. In the subsequent works, it is further extended to the multi-challenge setting [HKS15, AHY15, GDCC16]. They are efficient but are not secure against quantum computers.

2 Preliminaries

Notations. For $n \in \mathbb{N}$, denote $[n]$ as the set $\{1, \cdots, n\}$. For a finite set S, we let $U(S)$ denote the uniform distribution over S. For a distribution D and integer $k > 0$, define $(D)^k$ as the distribution $\prod_{i\in[k]} D$. For a distribution or random variable X we write $x \leftarrow X$ to denote the operation of sampling a random x according to X. For a set S, we write $s \leftarrow S$ as a shorthand for $s \leftarrow U(S)$. Let X and Y be two random variables over some finite set S_X, S_Y, respectively. The *statistical distance* $\Delta(X,Y)$ between X and Y is defined as $\Delta(X,Y) = \frac{1}{2}\Sigma_{s\in S_X \cup S_Y} |\Pr[X = s] - \Pr[Y = s]|$. The *min-entropy* of a random variable X is defined as $\mathbf{H}_\infty(X) = -\log(\max_x \Pr[X = x])$, where the base of the logarithm is taken to be 2 throughout the paper. For a bit $b \in \{0,1\}$, $\bar{b}$ denotes $1-b$. For sets $\mathcal{X}$ and $\mathcal{Y}$, $\mathsf{Func}(\mathcal{X},\mathcal{Y})$ denotes the set of all functions from $\mathcal{X}$ to $\mathcal{Y}$. For a vector $\mathbf{v} \in \mathbb{R}^n$, denote $\|\mathbf{v}\|$ as the standard Euclidean norm. For a matrix $\mathbf{R} \in \mathbb{R}^{n\times n}$, denote $\|\mathbf{R}\|$ as the length of the longest column and $\|\mathbf{R}\|_{\mathsf{GS}}$ as the longest column of the Gram-Schmidt orthogonalization of $\mathbf{R}$.

2.1 Quantum Computation

We briefly give some backgrounds on quantum computation. We refer to [NC00] for more details. A state $|\psi\rangle$ of n qubits is expressed as $\sum_{x\in\{0,1\}^n} \alpha_x |x\rangle \in \mathbb{C}^{2^n}$ where $\{\alpha_x\}_{x\in\{0,1\}^n}$ is a set of complex numbers such that $\sum_{x\in\{0,1\}^n} |\alpha_x|^2 = 1$ and $\{|x\rangle\}_{x\in\{0,1\}^n}$ is an orthonormal basis on $\mathbb{C}^{2^n}$ (which is called a computational basis). If we measure $|\psi\rangle$ in the computational basis, then the outcome is a classical bit string $x \in \{0,1\}^n$ with probability $|\alpha_x|^2$, and the state becomes

$|x\rangle$. An evolution of quantum state can be described by a unitary matrix U, which transforms $|x\rangle$ to $U|x\rangle$. A quantum algorithm is composed of quantum evolutions described by unitary matrices and measurements. We also consider a quantum oracle algorithm, which can quantumly access to certain oracles. The running time $\mathsf{Time}(\mathcal{A})$ of a quantum algorithm $\mathcal{A}$ is defined to be the number of universal gates (e.g., Hadamard, phase, CNOT, and $\pi/8$ gates) and measurements required for running $\mathcal{A}$. (An oracle query is counted as a unit time if $\mathcal{A}$ is an oracle algorithm.) Any efficient classical computation can be realized by a quantum computation efficiently. That is, for any function f that is classically computable, there exists a unitary matrix U_f such that $U_f|x, y\rangle = |x, f(x) \oplus y\rangle$, and the number of universal gates to express U_f is linear in the size of a classical circuit that computes f.

Quantum Random Oracle Model. Boneh et al. [BDF+11] introduced the quantum random oracle model (QROM), which is an extension of the usual random oracle model to the quantum setting. Roughly speaking, the QROM is an idealized model where a hash function is idealized to be a quantumly accessible oracle that simulates a random function. More precisely, in security proofs in the QROM, a random function $\mathsf{H} : \mathcal{X} \to \mathcal{Y}$ is uniformly chosen at the beginning of the experiment, and every entity involved in the system is allowed to access to an oracle that is given $\sum_{x,y} \alpha_{x,y} |x, y\rangle$ and returns $\sum_{x,y} \alpha_{x,y} |x, \mathsf{H}(x) \oplus y\rangle$. We denote a quantum algorithm $\mathcal{A}$ that accesses to the oracle defined as above by $\mathcal{A}^{|\mathsf{H}\rangle}$. In the QROM, one query to the random oracle is counted as one unit time. As in the classical case, we can implement two random oracles H_0 and H_1 from one random oracle H by defining $\mathsf{H}_0(x) := \mathsf{H}(0||x)$ and $\mathsf{H}_1(x) := \mathsf{H}(1||x)$. More generally, we can implement n random oracles from one random oracle by using $\lfloor \log n \rfloor$-bit prefix of an input as index of random oracles.

As shown by Zhandry [Zha12b], a quantum random oracle can be simulated by a family of $2Q$-wise independent hash functions against an adversary that quantumly accesses to the oracle at most Q times. As a result, he obtained the following lemma.

Lemma 1 *([Zha12b, Theorem 6.1]). Any quantum algorithm $\mathcal{A}$ making quantum queries to random oracles can be efficiently simulated by a quantum algorithm $\mathcal{B}$, which has the same output distribution, but makes no queries. Especially, if $\mathcal{A}$ makes at most Q queries to a random oracle $\mathsf{H} : \{0,1\}^a \to \{0,1\}^b$, then $\mathsf{Time}(\mathcal{B}) \approx \mathsf{Time}(\mathcal{A}) + Q \cdot T_{a,b}^{2Q\text{-wise}}$ where $T_{a,b}^{2Q\text{-wise}}$ denotes the time to evaluate a $2Q$-wise independent hash function from $\{0,1\}^a$ to $\{0,1\}^b$.*

The following lemma was shown by Boneh et al. [BDF+11]. Roughly speaking, this lemma states that if an oracle outputs independent and almost uniform value for all inputs, then it is indistinguishable from a random oracle even with quantum oracle accesses.

Lemma 2 *([BDF+11, Lemma 3]). Let $\mathcal{A}$ be a quantum algorithm that makes at most Q oracle queries, and $\mathcal{X}$ and $\mathcal{Y}$ be arrbitrary sets. Let $\mathcal{H}$ be a distribution over $\mathsf{Func}(\mathcal{X}, \mathcal{Y})$ such that when we take $\mathsf{H} \xleftarrow{\$} \mathcal{H}$, for each $x \in \mathcal{X}$, $\mathsf{H}(x)$ is* *identically and independently distributed according to a distribution D whose statistical distance is within ϵ from uniform. Then for any input z. We have*

$$\Delta(\mathcal{A}^{|\mathsf{RF}\rangle}(z), \mathcal{A}^{|\mathsf{H}\rangle}(z)) \leq 4Q^2\sqrt{\epsilon}$$

where $\mathsf{RF} \leftarrow \mathsf{Func}(\mathcal{X}, \mathcal{Y})$ *and* $\mathsf{H} \leftarrow \mathcal{H}$.

2.2 Pseudorandom Function

We review the definition of quantum-accessible pseudorandom functions (PRFs) [BDF+11].

Definition 1 (Quantum-accessible PRF). *We say that a function $F: \mathcal{K} \times \mathcal{X} \rightarrow \mathcal{Y}$ is a quantum-accessible pseudorandom function if for all PPT adversaries $\mathcal{A}$, its advantage defined below is negligible:*

$$\mathsf{Adv}^{\mathsf{PRF}}_{\mathcal{A},F}(\lambda) := \left| \Pr\left[\mathcal{A}^{|\mathsf{RF}\rangle}(1^\lambda) = 1\right] - \Pr\left[\mathcal{A}^{|F(K,\cdot)\rangle}(1^\lambda) = 1\right] \right|$$

where $\mathsf{RF} \leftarrow \mathsf{Func}(\mathcal{X}, \mathcal{Y})$ *and* $K \leftarrow \mathcal{K}$.

Zhandry [Zha12a] proved that some known constructions of classical PRFs including the tree-based construction [GGM86] and lattice-based construction [BPR12] are also quantum-accessible PRFs. However, these reductions are non-tight, and thus we cannot rely on these results when aiming for tight security. Fortunately, we can use the following lemma which states that we can use a quantum random oracle as a PRF similarly to the classical case.

Lemma 3 *([SXY18, Lemma 2.2]). Let ℓ be an integer. Let $\mathsf{H}: \{0,1\}^\ell \times \mathcal{X} \rightarrow \mathcal{Y}$ and $\mathsf{H}': \mathcal{X} \rightarrow \mathcal{Y}$ be two independent random functions. If an unbounded time quantum adversary $\mathcal{A}$ makes a query to H at most Q_H times, then we have*

$$\left| \Pr[\mathcal{A}^{|\mathsf{H}\rangle, |\mathsf{H}(K,\cdot)\rangle}(1^\lambda) = 1 \mid K \leftarrow \{0,1\}^\ell] - \Pr[\mathcal{A}^{|\mathsf{H}\rangle, |\mathsf{H}'\rangle}(1^\lambda) = 1] \right| \leq Q_\mathsf{H} \cdot 2^{\frac{-\ell+1}{2}}.$$

2.3 Identity-Based Encryption

Syntax. We use the standard syntax of IBE [BF01]. Let $\mathcal{ID}$ be the ID space of the scheme. If a collision resistant hash function $CRH : \{0,1\}^* \rightarrow \mathcal{ID}$ is available, one can use an arbitrary string as an identity. An IBE scheme is defined by the following four algorithms.

$\mathsf{Setup}(1^\lambda) \rightarrow (\mathsf{mpk}, \mathsf{msk})$: The setup algorithm takes as input a security parameter 1^λ and outputs a master public key mpk and a master secret key msk.

$\mathsf{KeyGen}(\mathsf{mpk}, \mathsf{msk}, \mathsf{ID}) \rightarrow \mathsf{sk}_\mathsf{ID}$: The key generation algorithm takes as input the master public key mpk, the master secret key msk, and an identity $\mathsf{ID} \in \mathcal{ID}$. It outputs a private key sk_ID. We assume that ID is implicitly included in sk_ID.

$\mathsf{Encrypt}(\mathsf{mpk}, \mathsf{ID}, \mathsf{M}) \rightarrow C$: The encryption algorithm takes as input a master public key mpk, an identity $\mathsf{ID} \in \mathcal{ID}$, and a message M. It outputs a ciphertext C.

$\mathsf{Decrypt}(\mathsf{mpk}, \mathsf{sk}_{\mathsf{ID}}, C) \to \mathsf{M}$ or $\perp$: The decryption algorithm takes as input the master public key mpk, a private key $\mathsf{sk}_{\mathsf{ID}}$, and a ciphertext C. It outputs the message M or $\perp$, which means that the ciphertext is not in a valid form.

Correctness. We require correctness of decryption: that is, for all λ, all $\mathsf{ID} \in \mathcal{ID}$, and all M in the specified message space,

$$\Pr[\mathsf{Decrypt}(\mathsf{mpk}, \mathsf{sk}_{\mathsf{ID}}, \mathsf{Encrypt}(\mathsf{mpk}, \mathsf{ID}, \mathsf{M})) = \mathsf{M}] = 1 - \mathsf{negl}(\lambda)$$

holds, where the probability is taken over the randomness used in $(\mathsf{mpk}, \mathsf{msk}) \leftarrow \mathsf{Setup}(1^\lambda)$, $\mathsf{sk}_{\mathsf{ID}} \leftarrow \mathsf{KeyGen}(\mathsf{mpk}, \mathsf{msk}, \mathsf{ID})$, and $\mathsf{Encrypt}(\mathsf{mpk}, \mathsf{ID}, \mathsf{M})$.

Security. We now define the security for an IBE scheme Π. This security notion is defined by the following game between a challenger and an adversary $\mathcal{A}$. Let $\mathsf{CTSam}(\cdot)$ be a sampling algorithm that takes as input a master public key of the scheme and outputs an element in the ciphertext space.

- Setup. At the outset of the game, the challenger runs $\mathsf{Setup}(1^\lambda) \to (\mathsf{mpk}, \mathsf{msk})$ and gives mpk to $\mathcal{A}$. The challenger also picks a random coin $\mathsf{coin} \leftarrow \{0, 1\}$ and keeps it secretly. After given mpk, $\mathcal{A}$ can adaptively make the following two types of queries to the challenger. These queries can be made in any order and arbitrarily many times.

Secret Key Queries. If $\mathcal{A}$ submits $\mathsf{ID} \in \mathcal{ID}$ to the challenger, the challenger returns $\mathsf{sk}_{\mathsf{ID}} \leftarrow \mathsf{KeyGen}(\mathsf{mpk}, \mathsf{msk}, \mathsf{ID})$.

Challenge Queries. If $\mathcal{A}$ submits a message M^* and an identity $\mathsf{ID}^* \in \mathcal{ID}$ to the challenger, the challenger proceeds as follows. If $\mathsf{coin} = 0$, it runs $\mathsf{Encrypt}(\mathsf{mpk}, \mathsf{ID}^*, \mathsf{M}^*) \to C^*$ and gives the challenge ciphertext C^* to $\mathcal{A}$. If $\mathsf{coin} = 1$, it chooses the challenge ciphertext C^* from the distribution $\mathsf{CTSam}(\mathsf{mpk})$ as $C^* \xleftarrow{\$} \mathsf{CTSam}(\mathsf{mpk})$ at random and gives it to $\mathcal{A}$.

We prohibit $\mathcal{A}$ from making a challenge query for an identity ID^* such that it has already made a secret key query for the same $\mathsf{ID} = \mathsf{ID}^*$ and vice versa.

- Guess. Finally, $\mathcal{A}$ outputs a guess $\widehat{\mathsf{coin}}$ for coin. The advantage of $\mathcal{A}$ is defined as

$$\mathsf{Adv}^{\mathsf{IBE}}_{\mathcal{A},\Pi}(\lambda) = \left| \Pr[\widehat{\mathsf{coin}} = \mathsf{coin}] - \frac{1}{2} \right|.$$

We say that Π is adaptively-anonymous secure, if there exists efficiently sampleable distribution $\mathsf{CTSam}(\mathsf{mpk})$ and the advantage of any PPT $\mathcal{A}$ is negligible in the above game. The term anonymous captures the fact that the ciphertext does not reveal the identity for which it was sent to. (Observe that $\mathsf{CTSam}(\mathsf{mpk})$ depends on neither of ID^* nor M^*.)

Single Challenge Security. We can also consider a variant of the above security definition where we restrict the adversary to make the challenge query only once during the game. We call this security notion "single challenge adaptive anonymity", and call the notion without the restriction "multi challenge security". By a simple hybrid argument, we can show that these definitions are in fact equivalent in the sense that one implies another. However, the proof that the former implies the latter incurs a huge security reduction loss that is linear in the number of challenge queries. Since the focus of this paper is on tight security reductions, we typically differentiate these two notions.

Remark 1. We say that an IBE scheme is stateful if the key generation algorithm has to record all previously issued secret keys, and always outputs the same secret key for the same identity. By the technique by Goldreich [Gol86], a stateful scheme can be converted to a stateless one (in which the key generation algorithm need not remember previous executions) by using PRFs. Since PRFs exist in the QROM without assuming any computational assumption as shown in Lemma 3, if we make the key size of PRFs sufficiently large, this conversion hardly affects the tightness. Therefore in this paper, we concentrate on constructing tightly secure stateful IBE scheme for simplicity.

2.4 Background on Lattices

A (full-rank-integer) m-dimensional lattice Λ in $\mathbb{Z}^m$ is a set of the form $\{\sum_{i\in[m]} x_i \mathbf{b}_i | x_i \in \mathbb{Z}\}$, where $\mathbf{B} = \{\mathbf{b}_1, \cdots, \mathbf{b}_m\}$ are m linearly independent vectors in $\mathbb{Z}^m$. We call $\mathbf{B}$ the basis of the lattice Λ. For any positive integers n, m and $q \geq 2$, a matrix $\mathbf{A} \in \mathbb{Z}_q^{n\times m}$ and a vector $\mathbf{u} \in \mathbb{Z}_q^n$, we define $\Lambda^\perp(\mathbf{A}) = \{\mathbf{z} \in \mathbb{Z}^m | \mathbf{A}\mathbf{z} = \mathbf{0} \mod q\}$, and $\Lambda_\mathbf{u}^\perp(\mathbf{A}) = \{\mathbf{z} \in \mathbb{Z}^m | \mathbf{A}\mathbf{z} = \mathbf{u} \mod q\}$.

Gaussian Measures. For an m-dimensional lattice Λ, the discrete Gaussian distribution over Λ with center $\mathbf{c}$ and parameter σ is defined as $D_{\Lambda,\sigma,\mathbf{c}}(\mathbf{x}) = \rho_{\sigma,\mathbf{c}}(\mathbf{x})/\rho_{\sigma,\mathbf{c}}(\Lambda)$ for all $\mathbf{x} \in \Lambda$, where $\rho_{\sigma,\mathbf{c}}(\mathbf{x})$ is a Gaussian function defined as $\exp(-\pi\|\mathbf{x}-\mathbf{c}\|^2/\sigma^2)$ and $\rho_{\sigma,\mathbf{c}}(\Lambda) = \sum_{\mathbf{x}\in\Lambda} \rho_{\sigma,\mathbf{c}}(\mathbf{x})$. Further for an m-dimensional shifted lattice $\Lambda + \mathbf{t}$, we define the Gaussian distribution $D_{\Lambda+\mathbf{t},\sigma}$ with parameter σ as the process of adding the vector $\mathbf{t}$ to a sample from $D_{\Lambda,\sigma,-\mathbf{t}}$. Finally, we call D a B-bounded distribution, if all the elements in the support of D have absolute value smaller than B.

Discrete Gaussian Lemmas. The following lemmas are used to manipulate and obtain meaningful bounds on discrete Gaussian vectors.

Lemma 4 (Adopted from [GPV08], **Lemma 5.2).** *Let n, m, q be positive integers such that $m \geq 2n \log q$ and q a prime. Let σ be any positive real such that $\sigma \geq \sqrt{n + \log m}$. Then for all but $2^{-\Omega(n)}$ fraction of $\mathbf{A} \in \mathbb{Z}_q^{n\times m}$, we have that the distribution of $\mathbf{u} = \mathbf{A}\mathbf{e} \mod q$ for $\mathbf{e} \leftarrow D_{\mathbb{Z}^m,\sigma}$ is $2^{-\Omega(n)}$-close to uniform distribution over $\mathbb{Z}_q^n$. Furthermore, for a fixed $\mathbf{u} \in \mathbb{Z}_q^n$, the conditional distribution of $\mathbf{e} \leftarrow D_{\mathbb{Z}^m,\sigma}$, given $\mathbf{A}\mathbf{e} = \mathbf{u} \mod q$ is $D_{\Lambda_\mathbf{u}^\perp(\mathbf{A}),\sigma}$.*

The following lemma is obtained by combining Lemma 4.4 in [MR07] and Lemma 5.3 in [GPV08].

Lemma 5 ([MR07], [GPV08])**.** *Let $\sigma > 16\sqrt{\log 2m/\pi}$ and $\mathbf{u}$ be any vector in $\mathbb{Z}_q^n$. Then, for all but q^{-n} fraction of $\mathbf{A} \in \mathbb{Z}_q^{n\times m}$, we have that*

$$\Pr_{\mathbf{x}\leftarrow D_{\Lambda_\mathbf{u}^\perp,\sigma}(\mathbf{A})}[\|\mathbf{x}\| > \sigma\sqrt{m}] < 2^{-(m-1)}.$$

The following lemma can be obtained by a straightforward combination of Lemma 2.6, Lemma 2.10 and Lemma 5.3 in [GPV08] (See also [PR06, Pei07]).

Lemma 6 ([PR06, Pei07, GPV08]). *Let* $\sigma > 16\sqrt{\log 2m/\pi}$ *and* $\mathbf{u}$ *be any vector in* $\mathbb{Z}_q^n$. *Then, for all but* q^{-n} *fraction of* $\mathbf{A} \in \mathbb{Z}_q^{n\times m}$, *we have*

$$\mathbf{H}_\infty(D_{\Lambda_\mathbf{u}^\perp(\mathbf{A}),\sigma}) \geq m-1.$$

The following is a useful lemma used during the security proof. It allows the simulator to create new LWE samples from a given set of LWE samples (i.e., the LWE challenge provided to the simulator) for which it does not know the associating secret vector.[2] We would like to note that the following lemma is built on top of many previous results [Reg05, Pei10, BLP+13] and is formatted in a specific way to be useful in the security proof for LWE-based cryptosystems.

Lemma 7 (Noise Rerandomization, [KY16], Lemma 1). *Let* q, ℓ, m *be positive integers and* r *a positive real satisfying* $r > \Omega(\sqrt{n})$. *Let* $\mathbf{b} \in \mathbb{Z}_q^m$ *be arbitrary and* $\mathbf{z}$ *chosen from* $D_{\mathbb{Z}^m,r}$. *Then there exists a PPT algorithm* ReRand *such that for any* $\mathbf{V} \in \mathbb{Z}^{m\times\ell}$ *and positive real* $\sigma > s_1(\mathbf{V})$, *the output of* $\mathsf{ReRand}(\mathbf{V}, \mathbf{b}+\mathbf{z}, r, \sigma)$ *is distributed as* $\mathbf{b}' = \mathbf{V}^\top\mathbf{b}+\mathbf{z}' \in \mathbb{Z}_q^\ell$ *where the distribution of* $\mathbf{z}'$ *is within* $2^{-\Omega(n)}$ *statistical distance of* $D_{\mathbb{Z}^\ell,2r\sigma}$.

Sampling Algorithms. The following lemma states useful algorithms for sampling short vectors from lattices. In particular, the second preimage sampler is the exact gaussian sampler of [BLP+13], Lemma 2.3.

Lemma 8. ([GPV08, MP12, BLP+13]) *Let* $n, m, q > 0$ *be integers with* $m > 3n\lceil\log q\rceil$.

- $\mathsf{TrapGen}(1^n, 1^m, q) \to (\mathbf{A}, \mathbf{T_A})$: *a randomized algorithm that outputs a matrix* $\mathbf{A} \in \mathbb{Z}_q^{n\times m}$ *and a full-rank matrix* $\mathbf{T_A} \in \mathbb{Z}^{m\times m}$, *where* $\mathbf{T_A}$ *is a basis for* $\Lambda^\perp(\mathbf{A})$, *the distribution of* $\mathbf{A}$ *is* $2^{-\Omega(n)}$*-close to uniform and* $\|\mathbf{T_A}\|_{\mathrm{GS}} = O(\sqrt{n\log q})$.
- $\mathsf{SamplePre}(\mathbf{A}, \mathbf{T_A}, \mathbf{u}, \sigma)$: *a randomized algorithm that, given a matrix* $\mathbf{A} \in \mathbb{Z}_q^{n\times m}$, *a basis* $\mathbf{T_A} \in \mathbb{Z}^{m\times m}$ *for* $\Lambda^\perp(\mathbf{A})$, *a vector* $\mathbf{u} \in \mathbb{Z}_q^n$ *and a Gaussian parameter* $\sigma > \|\mathbf{T_A}\|_{\mathrm{GS}} \cdot \sqrt{\log(2m+4)/\pi}$, *outputs a vector* $\mathbf{e} \in \mathbb{Z}^m$ *sampled from a distribution* $2^{-\Omega(n)}$*-close to* $D_{\Lambda_\mathbf{u}^\perp(\mathbf{A}),\sigma}$.
- $\mathsf{Sample}\mathbb{Z}(\sigma)$: *a randomized algorithm that, given a Gaussian parameter* $\sigma > 16(\sqrt{\log 2m/\pi})$, *outputs a vector* $\mathbf{e} \in \mathbb{Z}^m$ *sampled from a distribution* $2^{-\Omega(n)}$*-close to* $D_{\mathbb{Z}^m,\sigma}$.

Hardness Assumptions. We define the Learning with Errors (LWE) problem introduced by Regev [Reg05].

[2] Compared to [KY16] our choice of parameter is more conservative since we consider $2^{-\Omega(n)}$ statistical distance rather than $2^{-\omega(\log n)}$.

Definition 2 (Learning with Errors). *For integers $n = n(\lambda), m = m(n)$, a prime $q = q(n) > 2$, an error distribution over $\chi = \chi(n)$ over $\mathbb{Z}$, and a PPT algorithm $\mathcal{A}$, the advantage for the* learning with errors problem $\mathsf{LWE}_{n,m,q,\chi}$ *of $\mathcal{A}$ is defined as follows:*

$$\mathsf{Adv}_{\mathcal{A}}^{\mathsf{LWE}_{n,m,q,\chi}} = \left| \Pr\left[\mathcal{A}(\mathbf{A}, \mathbf{A}^\top \mathbf{s} + \mathbf{z}) = 1\right] - \Pr\left[\mathcal{A}(\mathbf{A}, \mathbf{w} + \mathbf{z}) = 1\right] \right|$$

where $\mathbf{A} \leftarrow \mathbb{Z}_q^{n\times m}$, $\mathbf{s} \leftarrow \mathbb{Z}_q^n$, $\mathbf{w} \leftarrow \mathbb{Z}_q^m$, $\mathbf{z} \leftarrow \chi^m$. We say that the LWE *assumption holds if $\mathsf{Adv}_{\mathcal{A}}^{\mathsf{LWE}_{n,m,q,\chi}}$ is negligible for all PPT $\mathcal{A}$.*

The (decisional) $\mathsf{LWE}_{n,m,q,D_{\mathbb{Z},\alpha q}}$ for $\alpha q > 2\sqrt{n}$ has been shown by Regev [Reg05] to be as hard as approximating the worst-case SIVP and GapSVP problems to within $\tilde{O}(n/\alpha)$ factors in the ℓ_2-norm in the worst case. In the subsequent works, (partial) dequantumization of the reduction were achieved [Pei09, BLP+13].

We also define the LWE assumption against adversaries that can access to a quantum random oracle as is done by Boneh et al. [BDF+11].

Definition 3 (Learning with Errors relative to Quantum Random Oracle). *Let n, m, q and χ be the same as in Definition 2, and a, b be some positive integers. For a PPT algorithm $\mathcal{A}$, the advantage for the* learning with errors problem $\mathsf{LWE}_{n,m,q,\chi}$ *of $\mathcal{A}$ relative to a quantum random oracle is defined as follows:*

$$\mathsf{Adv}_{\mathcal{A},\mathsf{QRO}_{a,b}}^{\mathsf{LWE}_{n,m,q,\chi}}(\lambda) = \left| \Pr\left[\mathcal{A}^{|\mathsf{H}\rangle}(\mathbf{A}, \mathbf{A}^\top \mathbf{s} + \mathbf{z}) = 1\right] - \Pr\left[\mathcal{A}^{|\mathsf{H}\rangle}(\mathbf{A}, \mathbf{w} + \mathbf{z}) = 1\right] \right|$$

where $\mathbf{A} \leftarrow \mathbb{Z}_q^{n\times m}$, $\mathbf{s} \leftarrow \mathbb{Z}_q^n$, $\mathbf{w} \leftarrow \mathbb{Z}_q^m$, $\mathbf{z} \leftarrow \chi^m$, $\mathsf{H} \xleftarrow{\$} \mathsf{Func}(\{0,1\}^a, \{0,1\}^b)$. We say that the LWE *assumption relative to an (a,b)-quantum random oracle holds if $\mathsf{Adv}_{\mathcal{A},\mathsf{QRO}_{a,b}}^{\mathsf{LWE}_{n,m,q,\chi}}(\lambda)$ is negligible for all PPT $\mathcal{A}$.*

It is easy to see that the LWE assumption relative to a quantum random oracle can be reduced to the LWE assumption with a certain loss of the time for the reduction by Lemma 1. Alternatively, if we assume the existence of a quantumly-accessible PRF, then the reduction loss can be made smaller. Namely, we have the following lemmas.

Lemma 9. *For any n, m, q, χ, a, b, and an algorithm $\mathcal{A}$ making at most Q oracle queries, there exists an algorithm $\mathcal{B}$ such that*

$$\mathsf{Adv}_{\mathcal{A},\mathsf{QRO}_{a,b}}^{\mathsf{LWE}_{n,m,q,\chi}}(\lambda) = \mathsf{Adv}_{\mathcal{B}}^{\mathsf{LWE}_{n,m,q,\chi}}(\lambda)$$

and $\mathsf{Time}(\mathcal{B}) \approx \mathsf{Time}(\mathcal{A}) + Q \cdot T_{a,b}^{2Q\text{-wise}}$ where $T_{a,b}^{2Q\text{-wise}}$ denotes the time to evaluate a $2Q$-wise independent hash function from $\{0,1\}^a$ to $\{0,1\}^b$.

Lemma 10. *Let $F : \mathcal{K} \times \{0,1\}^a \to \{0,1\}^b$ be a quantumly-accessible PRF. For any n, m, q, χ, a, b and an algorithm $\mathcal{A}$ making at most Q oracle queries, there exist algorithms $\mathcal{B}$ and $\mathcal{C}$ such that*

$$\mathsf{Adv}_{\mathcal{A},\mathsf{QRO}_{a,b}}^{\mathsf{LWE}_{n,m,q,\chi}}(\lambda) \le \mathsf{Adv}_{\mathcal{B}}^{\mathsf{LWE}_{n,m,q,\chi}}(\lambda) + \mathsf{Adv}_{\mathcal{C},F}^{\mathsf{PRF}}(\lambda)$$

and $\mathsf{Time}(\mathcal{B}) \approx \mathsf{Time}(\mathcal{A}) + Q \cdot T_F$ *and* $\mathsf{Time}(\mathcal{C}) \approx \mathsf{Time}(\mathcal{A})$ *where* T_F *denotes the time to evaluate* F.

In this paper, we give reductions from the security of IBE schemes to the LWE assumption relative to a quantrum random oracle. Given such reductions, we can also reduce them to the LWE assumption or to the LWE assumption plus the security of quantumly-accessible PRFs by Lemma 9 or 10, respectively. The latter is tighter than the former at the cost of assuming the existence of quantumly-accessible PRFs.

Remark 2. A keen reader may wonder why we have to require the extra assumption on the existence of PRFs when we are working in the QROM, since as we mentioned earlier in Sect. 2.2, it seems that we can use a QRO as a PRF. The point here is that during the security reduction, the simulator (which is given the classical LWE instance) must simulate the QRO query to the adversary against the LWE problem relative to a quantum random oracle query, hence, the simulator is not in possession of the QRO. Note that the reason why we are able to use the QRO as a PRF as mentioned in Remark 1 is because the simulator is aiming to reduce the LWE problem relative to a quantum random oracle query to the IBE scheme. Specifically, in this case the simulator can use the QRO provided by its challenge to simulate a PRF.

3 Tightly Secure Single Challenge GPV-IBE

In this section, we show that we can give a tight security proof for the original GPV-IBE [GPV08] in the single-challenge setting if we set the parameters appropriately. Such proofs can be given in both the classical ROM and QROM settings.

3.1 Construction

Let the identity space $\mathcal{ID}$ of the scheme be $\mathcal{ID} = \{0,1\}^{\ell_{\mathsf{ID}}}$, where $\ell_{\mathsf{ID}}(\lambda)$ denotes the identity-length. Let also $\mathsf{H} : \{0,1\}^{\ell_{\mathsf{ID}}} \to \mathbb{Z}_q^n$ be a hash function treated as a random oracle during security analysis. The IBE scheme GPV is given as follows. For simplicity, we describe the scheme as a stateful one. As remarked in Remark 1, we can make the scheme stateless without any additional assumption in the QROM.

$\mathsf{Setup}(1^\lambda)$: On input 1^λ, it first chooses a prime q, positive integers n, m, and Gaussian parameters α', σ, where all these values are implicitly a function of the security parameter λ. The precise parameter selection is specified in the following section. It then runs $(\mathbf{A}, \mathbf{T_A}) \leftarrow \mathsf{TrapGen}(1^n, 1^m, q)$ to generate a matrix $\mathbf{A} \in \mathbb{Z}_q^{n\times m}$ with a trapdoor $\mathbf{T_A} \in \mathbb{Z}^{m\times m}$ such that $\|\mathbf{T_A}\|_{\mathrm{GS}} \leq O(n \log q)$. Then it outputs

$$\mathsf{mpk} = \mathbf{A} \quad \text{and} \quad \mathsf{msk} = \mathbf{T_A}$$

$\mathsf{KeyGen}(\mathsf{mpk}, \mathsf{msk}, \mathsf{ID})$: If $\mathsf{sk}_{\mathsf{ID}}$ is already generated, then this algorithm returns it. Otherwise it computes $\mathbf{u}_{\mathsf{ID}} = \mathsf{H}(\mathsf{ID})$ and samples $\mathbf{e}_{\mathsf{ID}} \in \mathbb{Z}^m$ such that

$$\mathbf{A}\mathbf{e}_{\mathsf{ID}} = \mathbf{u}_{\mathsf{ID}} \mod q$$

using $\mathbf{e}_{\mathsf{ID}} \leftarrow \mathsf{SamplePre}(\mathbf{A}, \mathbf{T_A}, \mathbf{u}_{\mathsf{ID}}, \sigma)$. It returns $\mathsf{sk}_{\mathsf{ID}} = \mathbf{e}_{\mathsf{ID}}$ as the secret key.

$\mathsf{Enc}(\mathsf{mpk}, \mathsf{ID}, \mathsf{M})$: To encrypt a message $\mathsf{M} \in \{0,1\}$, it first samples $\mathbf{s} \leftarrow \mathbb{Z}_q^n$, $\mathbf{x} \leftarrow D_{\mathbb{Z}^m,\alpha' q}$ and $x \leftarrow D_{\mathbb{Z},\alpha' q}$. Then it sets $\mathbf{u}_{\mathsf{ID}} = \mathsf{H}(\mathsf{ID})$ and computes

$$c_0 = \mathbf{u}_{\mathsf{ID}}^\top \mathbf{s} + x + \mathsf{M}\lfloor q/2 \rceil, \quad \mathbf{c}_1 = \mathbf{A}^\top \mathbf{s} + \mathbf{x}.$$

Finally, it outputs the ciphertext $C = (c_0, \mathbf{c}_1) \in \mathbb{Z}_q \times \mathbb{Z}_q^m$.

$\mathsf{Dec}(\mathsf{mpk}, \mathsf{sk}_{\mathsf{ID}}, C)$: To decrypt a ciphertext $C = (c_0, \mathbf{c}_1)$ with a secret key $\mathsf{sk}_{\mathsf{ID}}$, it computes $w = c_0 - \mathbf{c}_1^\top \mathbf{e}_{\mathsf{ID}} \in \mathbb{Z}_q$ and outputs 0 if w is closer to 0 than to $\lfloor q/2 \rceil$ modulo q. Otherwise it outputs 1.

3.2 Correctness and Parameter Selection

The following shows correctness of the above IBE scheme.

Lemma 11 (Correctness). *Suppose the parameters q, σ, and α' are such that*

$$\sigma > \|\mathbf{T_A}\|_{\mathrm{GS}} \cdot \sqrt{\log(2m+4)/\pi}, \qquad \alpha' < 1/8\sigma m.$$

Let $\mathbf{e}_{\mathsf{ID}} \leftarrow \mathsf{KeyGen}(\mathbf{A}, \mathbf{T_A}, \mathsf{ID}), C \leftarrow \mathsf{Enc}(\mathbf{A}, \mathsf{ID}', \mathsf{M} \in \{0,1\})$ *and* $\mathsf{M}' \leftarrow \mathsf{Dec}(\mathbf{A}, \mathbf{e}_{\mathsf{ID}}, C)$. *If* $\mathsf{ID} = \mathsf{ID}'$, *then with overwhelming probability we have* $\mathsf{M}' = \mathsf{M}$.

Proof. When the Dec algorithm operates as specified, we have

$$w = c_0 - \mathbf{e}_{\mathsf{ID}}^\top \mathbf{c}_1 = \mathsf{M}\lfloor q/2 \rceil + \underbrace{x + \mathbf{e}_{\mathsf{ID}}^\top \mathbf{x}}_{\text{error term}}.$$

By Lemma 8 and the condition posed on the choice of σ, we have that the distribution of $\mathbf{e}_{\mathsf{ID}}$ is $2^{-\Omega(n)}$ close to $D_{\Lambda_{\mathbf{u}}^{\perp}(\mathbf{A}),\sigma}$. Therefore, by Lemma 5, we have $x \leq \alpha' q\sqrt{m}$, $\|\mathbf{x}\| \leq \alpha' q\sqrt{m}$, and $\|\mathbf{e}_{\mathsf{ID}}\| \leq \sigma \cdot \sqrt{m}$ except for $2^{-\Omega(n)}$ probability. Then, the error term is bounded by

$$|\mathbf{h}^\top \mathbf{x} - \mathbf{e}_{\mathsf{ID}}^\top \mathbf{x}| \leq x + |\mathbf{e}_{\mathsf{ID}}^\top \mathbf{x}| \leq 2\alpha' q\sigma m.$$

Hence, for the error term to have absolute value less than $q/4$, it suffices to choose q and α' as in the statement of the lemma.

Parameter Selection. For the system to satisfy correctness and make the security proof work, we need the following restrictions. Note that we will prove the security of the scheme under the LWE assumption whose noise rate is α, which is lower than α' that is used in the encryption algorithm.

- The error term is less than $q/4$ (i.e., $\alpha' < 1/8m\sigma$ by Lemma 11)
- $\mathsf{TrapGen}$ operates properly (i.e., $m > 3n \log q$ by Lemma 8)

- Samplable from $D_{\Lambda^{\perp}_{\mathbf{u}}(\mathbf{A}),\sigma}$ (i.e., $\sigma > \|\mathbf{T}_{\mathbf{A}}\|_{\mathrm{GS}} \cdot \sqrt{\log(2m+4)/\pi} = O(\sqrt{n \log m \log q})$ by Lemma 8),
- σ is sufficiently large so that we can apply Lemmas 4 and 6 (i.e., $\sigma > \sqrt{n + \log m}, 16\sqrt{\log 2m/\pi}$),
- We can apply Lemma 7 (i.e., $\alpha'/2\alpha > \sqrt{n(\sigma^2 m + 1)}$),
- $\mathsf{LWE}_{n,m,q,D_{\mathbb{Z},\alpha q}}$ is hard (i.e., $\alpha q > 2\sqrt{n}$).

To satisfy these requirements, for example, we can set the parameters $m, q, \sigma, \alpha, \alpha'$ as follows:

$$m = n^{1+\kappa}, \qquad q = 10n^{3.5+4\kappa}, \qquad \sigma = n^{0.5+\kappa},$$
$$\alpha' q = n^{2+2\kappa}, \qquad \alpha q = 2\sqrt{n},$$

where $\kappa > 0$ is a constant that can be set arbitrarily small. To withstand attacks running in time 2^{λ}, we may set $n = \tilde{\Omega}(\lambda)$. In the above, we round up m to the nearest integer and q to the nearest largest prime. We remark that though the above parameter is worse compared to the original GPV-IBE scheme, this is due to our conservative choice of making the statistical error terms appearing in the reduction cost $2^{-\Omega(n)}$ rather than the standard negligible notion $2^{-\omega(\log \lambda)}$. The latter choice of parameters will lead to better parameters, which may be as efficient as the original GPV-IBE.

3.3 Security Proof in QROM

The following theorem addresses the security of GPV in the classical ROM setting. Our analysis departs from the original one [GPV08] and as a consequence much tighter. The proof can be found in the full version.

Theorem 1. *The IBE scheme* GPV *is adaptively-anonymous single-challenge secure in the random oracle model assuming the hardness of* $\mathsf{LWE}_{n,m,q,D_{\mathbb{Z},\alpha q}}$. *Namely, for any classical adversary* $\mathcal{A}$ *making at most* Q_{H} *random oracle queries to* H *and* Q_{ID} *secret key queries, there exists an algorithm* $\mathcal{B}$ *such that*

$$\mathsf{Adv}^{\mathsf{IBE}}_{\mathcal{A},\mathsf{GPV}}(\lambda) \le \mathsf{Adv}^{\mathsf{LWE}_{n,m,q,D_{\mathbb{Z},\alpha q}}}_{\mathcal{B}}(\lambda) + (Q_{\mathsf{H}} + Q_{\mathsf{ID}}) \cdot 2^{-\Omega(n)}$$

and

$$\mathsf{Time}(\mathcal{B}) = \mathsf{Time}(\mathcal{A}) + (Q_{\mathsf{H}} + Q_{\mathsf{ID}}) \cdot \mathsf{poly}(\lambda).$$

As we explained in the introduction, our analysis in the ROM can be easily be extended to the QROM setting. We can prove the following theorem that addresses the security of the GPV-IBE scheme in the QROM setting. The analysis here is different from that by Zhandry [Zha12b], who gave the first security proof for the GPV-IBE scheme in the QROM setting and our analysis here is much tighter.

Theorem 2. *The IBE scheme* GPV *is adaptively-anonymous single-challenge secure assuming the hardness of* $\mathsf{LWE}_{n,m,q,D_{\mathbb{Z},\alpha q}}$ *in the quantum random oracle* *model. Namely, for any quantum adversary $\mathcal{A}$ making at most Q_{H} queries to $|\mathsf{H}\rangle$ and Q_{ID} secret key queries, there exists a quantum algorithm $\mathcal{B}$ making $Q_{\mathsf{H}}+Q_{\mathsf{ID}}$ quantum random oracle queries such that*

$$\mathsf{Adv}^{\mathsf{IBE}}_{\mathcal{A},\mathsf{GPV}}(\lambda) \leq \mathsf{Adv}^{\mathsf{LWE}_{n,m,q,D_{\mathbb{Z},\alpha q}}}_{\mathcal{B},\mathsf{QRO}_{\ell_{\mathsf{ID}},\ell_r}}(\lambda) + (Q_{\mathsf{H}}^2 + Q_{\mathsf{ID}}) \cdot 2^{-\Omega(n)}$$

and

$$\mathsf{Time}(\mathcal{B}) = \mathsf{Time}(\mathcal{A}) + (Q_{\mathsf{H}} + Q_{\mathsf{ID}}) \cdot \mathsf{poly}(\lambda)$$

where ℓ_r denotes the length of the randomness for $\mathsf{Sample}\mathbb{Z}$.

Proof (Proof of Theorem 2). Let $\mathsf{CTSam}(\mathsf{mpk})$ be an algorithm that outputs a random element from $\mathbb{Z}_q \times \mathbb{Z}_q^m$ and $\mathcal{A}$ be a quantum adversary that attacks the adaptively-anonymous security of the IBE scheme. Without loss of generality, we can assume that $\mathcal{A}$ makes secret key queries on the same identity at most once. We show the security of the scheme via the following games. In each game, we define X_i as the event that the adversary $\mathcal{A}$ wins in Game_i.

Game_0: This is the real security game for the adaptively-anonymous security. At the beginning of the game, the challenger chooses a random function $\mathsf{H} : \{0,1\}^{\ell_{\mathsf{ID}}} \to \mathbb{Z}_q^n$. Then it generates $(\mathbf{A}, \mathbf{T_A}) \xleftarrow{\$} \mathsf{TrapGen}(1^n, 1^m, q)$ and gives $\mathbf{A}$ to $\mathcal{A}$. Then it samples $\mathsf{coin} \xleftarrow{\$} \{0,1\}$ and keeps it secret. During the game, $\mathcal{A}$ may make (quantum) random oracle queries, secret key queries, and a challenge query. These queries are handled as follows:

- When $\mathcal{A}$ makes a random oracle query on a quantum state $\sum_{\mathsf{ID},y} \alpha_{\mathsf{ID},y} |\mathsf{ID}\rangle |y\rangle$, the challenger returns $\sum_{\mathsf{ID},y} \alpha_{\mathsf{ID},y} |\mathsf{ID}\rangle |\mathsf{H}(\mathsf{ID}) \oplus y\rangle$.
- When $\mathcal{A}$ makes a secret key query on ID, the challenger samples $\mathbf{e}_{\mathsf{ID}} = \mathsf{SamplePre}(\mathbf{A}, \mathbf{T_A}, \mathbf{u}_{\mathsf{ID}}, \sigma)$ and returns $\mathbf{e}_{\mathsf{ID}}$ to $\mathcal{A}$.
- When $\mathcal{A}$ makes a challenge query for ID^* and a message M^*, the challenger returns $(c_0, \mathbf{c}_1) \xleftarrow{\$} \mathsf{Encrypt}(\mathsf{mpk}, \mathsf{ID}, \mathsf{M})$ if $\mathsf{coin} = 0$ and $(c_0, \mathbf{c}_1) \xleftarrow{\$} \mathsf{CTSam}(\mathsf{mpk})$ if $\mathsf{coin} = 1$.

At the end of the game, $\mathcal{A}$ outputs a guess $\widehat{\mathsf{coin}}$ for coin. Finally, the challenger outputs $\widehat{\mathsf{coin}}$. By definition, we have $\left|\Pr[X_0] - \frac{1}{2}\right| = \left|\Pr[\widehat{\mathsf{coin}} = \mathsf{coin}] - \frac{1}{2}\right| = \mathsf{Adv}^{\mathsf{IBE}}_{\mathcal{A},\mathsf{GPV}}(\lambda)$.

Game_1: In this game, we change the way the random oracle H is simulated. Namely, the challenger first chooses another random function $\widehat{\mathsf{H}} \xleftarrow{\$} \mathsf{Func}(\{0,1\}^{\ell_{\mathsf{ID}}}, \{0,1\}^{\ell_r})$. Then we define $\mathsf{H}(\mathsf{ID}) := \mathbf{A}\mathbf{e}_{\mathsf{ID}}$ where $\mathbf{e}_{\mathsf{ID}} := \mathsf{Sample}\mathbb{Z}(\sigma; \widehat{\mathsf{H}}(\mathsf{ID}))$, and use this H throughout the game. For any fixed ID, the distribution of $\mathsf{H}(\mathsf{ID})$ is identical and its statistical distance from the uniform distribution is $2^{-\Omega(n)}$ for all but $2^{-\Omega(n)}$ fraction of $\mathbf{A}$ due to Lemma 4 since we choose $\sigma > \sqrt{n + \log m}$. Note that in this game, we only change the distribution of $\mathbf{u}_{\mathsf{ID}}$ for each identity, and the way we create secret keys are unchanged. Then due to Lemma 2, we have $\left|\Pr[X_0] - \Pr[X_1]\right| = 2^{-\Omega(n)} + 4Q_{\mathsf{H}}^2\sqrt{2^{-\Omega(n)}} = Q_{\mathsf{H}}^2 \cdot 2^{-\Omega(n)}$.

Game_2: In this game, we change the way secret key queries are answered. By the end of this game, the challenger will no longer require the trapdoor $\mathbf{T_A}$ to generate the secret keys. When $\mathcal{A}$ queries a secret key for ID, the challenger returns $\mathbf{e}_{\mathsf{ID}} := \mathsf{Sample}\mathbb{Z}(\sigma; \widehat{\mathsf{H}}(\mathsf{ID}))$. For any fixed $\mathbf{u}_{\mathsf{ID}} \in \mathbb{Z}_q^n$, let $\mathbf{e}^{(1)}_{\mathsf{ID},\mathbf{u}_{\mathsf{ID}}}$ and $\mathbf{e}^{(2)}_{\mathsf{ID},\mathbf{u}_{\mathsf{ID}}}$ be random variables that are distributed according to the distributions of $\mathbf{e}_{\mathsf{ID}}$ conditioning on $\mathsf{H}(\mathsf{ID}) = \mathbf{u}_{\mathsf{ID}}$ in Game_1 and Game_2, respectively. Due to Lemma 8, we have $\Delta(\mathbf{e}^{(1)}_{\mathsf{ID},\mathbf{u}_{\mathsf{ID}}}, D_{\Lambda^{\perp}_{\mathbf{u}_{\mathsf{ID}}}(\mathbf{A}),\sigma}) \leq 2^{-\Omega(n)}$. On the other hand, due to Lemma 4, we have $\Delta(\mathbf{e}^{(2)}_{\mathsf{ID},\mathbf{u}_{\mathsf{ID}}}, D_{\Lambda^{\perp}_{\mathbf{u}_{\mathsf{ID}}}(\mathbf{A}),\sigma}) \leq 2^{-\Omega(n)}$. Since $\mathcal{A}$ obtains at most Q_{ID} user secret keys $\mathbf{e}_{\mathsf{ID}}$, we have $\left|\Pr[X_1] - \Pr[X_2]\right| = Q_{\mathsf{ID}} \cdot 2^{-\Omega(n)}$.

Game_3: In this game, we change the way the matrix $\mathbf{A}$ is generated. Concretely, the challenger chooses $\mathbf{A} \leftarrow \mathbb{Z}_q^{n\times m}$ without generating the associated trapdoor $\mathbf{T}_{\mathbf{A}}$. By Lemma 8, the distribution of $\mathbf{A}$ differs at most by $2^{-\Omega(n)}$. Since the challenger can answer all the secret key queries without the trapdoor due to the change we made in the previous game, the view of $\mathcal{A}$ is altered only by $2^{-\Omega(n)}$. Therefore, we have $\left|\Pr[X_2] - \Pr[X_3]\right| = 2^{-\Omega(n)}$.

Game_4: In this game, we change the way the challenge ciphertext is created when $\mathsf{coin} = 0$. Recall in the previous games when $\mathsf{coin} = 0$, the challenger created a valid challenge ciphertext as in the real scheme. In this game, to create the challenge ciphertext for identity ID^* and message bit M^*, the challenger first computes $\mathbf{e}_{\mathsf{ID}^*} := \mathsf{Sample}\mathbb{Z}(\sigma; \widehat{\mathsf{H}}(\mathsf{ID}^*))$ and $\mathbf{u}_{\mathsf{ID}^*} := \mathbf{A}\mathbf{e}_{\mathsf{ID}^*}$. Then the challenger picks $\mathbf{s} \leftarrow \mathbb{Z}_q^n$, $\bar{\mathbf{x}} \leftarrow D_{\mathbb{Z}^m,\alpha q}$ and computes $\mathbf{v} = \mathbf{A}^\top \mathbf{s} + \bar{\mathbf{x}} \in \mathbb{Z}_q^m$. It then runs

$$\mathsf{ReRand}([\mathbf{e}_{\mathsf{ID}^*}|\mathbf{I}_m], \mathbf{v}, \alpha q, \frac{\alpha'}{2\alpha}) \to \mathbf{c}' \in \mathbb{Z}_q^{m+1}$$

from Lemma 7, where $\mathbf{I}_m$ is the identity matrix with size m. Let $c_0' \in \mathbb{Z}_q$ denote the first entry of $\mathbf{c}'$ and $\mathbf{c}_1 \in \mathbb{Z}_q^m$ denote the remaining entries of $\mathbf{c}'$. Finally, the challenger outputs the challenge ciphertext as

$$C^* = (c_0 = c_0' + \mathsf{M}^* \lfloor q/2 \rceil, \ \ \mathbf{c}_1). \tag{1}$$

We now proceed to bound $|\Pr[X_3] - \Pr[X_4]|$. We apply the noise rerandomization lemma (Lemma 7) with $\mathbf{V} = [\mathbf{e}_{\mathsf{ID}^*}|\mathbf{I}_m]$, $\mathbf{b} = \mathbf{A}^\top\mathbf{s}$ and $\mathbf{z} = \bar{\mathbf{x}}$ to see that the following equation holds:

$$\mathbf{c}' = \mathbf{V}^\top \mathbf{b} + \mathbf{x}' = \left(\mathbf{A} \cdot [\mathbf{e}_{\mathsf{ID}^*}|\mathbf{I}_m]\right)^\top \mathbf{s} + \mathbf{x}' = [\mathbf{u}_{\mathsf{ID}^*}|\mathbf{A}]^\top \mathbf{s} + \mathbf{x}'$$

where $\mathbf{x}'$ is distributed according to a distribution whose statistical distance is at most $2^{-\Omega(n)}$ from $D_{\mathbb{Z}^{m+1},\alpha' q}$. Here, the last equality follows from $\mathbf{A}\mathbf{e}_{\mathsf{ID}^*} = \mathbf{u}_{\mathsf{ID}^*}$ and we can appropriately apply the noise rerandomization lemma since we have the following for our parameter selection:

$$\alpha'/2\alpha > \sqrt{n(\sigma^2 m + 1)} \geq \sqrt{n(\|\mathbf{e}_{\mathsf{ID}^*}\|^2 + 1)} \geq \sqrt{n} \cdot s_1([\mathbf{e}_{\mathsf{ID}^*}|\mathbf{I}_m]),$$

where the second inequality holds with $1 - 2^{-\Omega(n)}$ probability. It therefore follows that the statistical distance between the distributions of the challenge ciphertext in Game_3 and Game_4 is at most $2^{-\Omega(n)}$. Therefore, we may conclude that $\left|\Pr[X_3] - \Pr[X_4]\right| = 2^{-\Omega(n)}$.

Game_5: In this game, we further change the way the challenge ciphertext is created when $\mathsf{coin} = 0$. If $\mathsf{coin} = 0$, to create the challenge ciphertext the challenger first picks $\mathbf{b} \leftarrow \mathbb{Z}_q^m$, $\bar{\mathbf{x}} \leftarrow D_{\mathbb{Z}^m,\alpha q}$ and computes $\mathbf{v} = \mathbf{b} + \bar{\mathbf{x}} \in \mathbb{Z}_q^m$. It then runs the ReRand algorithm as in Game_4. Finally, it sets the challenge ciphertext as in Eq. (1). We claim that $\left|\Pr[X_4] - \Pr[X_5]\right|$ is negligible assuming the hardness of the $\mathsf{LWE}_{n,m,q,D_{\mathbb{Z},\alpha q}}$ problem relative to a quantum random oracle $|\widehat{\mathsf{H}}\rangle : \{0,1\}^{\ell_{\mathsf{ID}}} \to \{0,1\}^{\ell_r}$. To show this, we use $\mathcal{A}$ to construct an adversary $\mathcal{B}$ that breaks the LWE assumption relative to $|\widehat{\mathsf{H}}\rangle$.

$\mathcal{B}$ is given a problem instance of LWE as $(\mathbf{A}, \mathbf{v} = \mathbf{b} + \bar{\mathbf{x}}) \in \mathbb{Z}_q^{n\times m} \times \mathbb{Z}_q^m$ where $\bar{\mathbf{x}} \leftarrow D_{\mathbb{Z}^m,\alpha q}$. The task of $\mathcal{B}$ is to distinguish whether $\mathbf{b} = \mathbf{A}^\top\mathbf{s}$ for some $\mathbf{s} \leftarrow \mathbb{Z}_q^n$ or $\mathbf{b} \leftarrow \mathbb{Z}_q^m$. First, we remark that $\mathcal{B}$ can simulate the quantum random oracle $|\mathsf{H}\rangle$ for $\mathcal{A}$ by using its own random oracle $|\widehat{\mathsf{H}}\rangle$ because H is programmed as $\mathsf{H}(\mathsf{ID}) := \mathbf{A}\mathbf{e}_{\mathsf{ID}}$ where $\mathbf{e}_{\mathsf{ID}} := \mathsf{Sample}\mathbb{Z}(\sigma; \widehat{\mathsf{H}}(\mathsf{ID}))$ by the modification we made in Game_1. $\mathcal{B}$ sets the master public key mpk to be the LWE matrix $\mathbf{A}$. Note that unlike the real IBE scheme, $\mathcal{B}$ does not require the master secret key $\mathbf{T}_\mathbf{A}$ due to the modification we made in Game_3. Namely, when $\mathcal{A}$ queries ID for the key oracle, $\mathcal{B}$ just returns $\mathbf{e}_{\mathsf{ID}} := \mathsf{Sample}\mathbb{Z}(\sigma; \widehat{\mathsf{H}}(\mathsf{ID}))$. To generate the challenge ciphertext, $\mathcal{B}$ first picks $\mathsf{coin} \leftarrow \{0,1\}$. If $\mathsf{coin} = 0$, it generates the challenge ciphertext as in Eq. (1) using $\mathbf{v}$, and returns it to $\mathcal{A}$. We emphasize that all $\mathcal{B}$ needs to do to generate the ciphertext is to run the ReRand algorithm, which it can do without the knowledge of the secret randomness $\mathbf{s}$ and $\bar{\mathbf{x}}$. If $\mathsf{coin} = 1$, $\mathcal{B}$ returns a random ciphertext using $\mathsf{CTSam}(\mathsf{mpk})$. At the end of the game, $\mathcal{A}$ outputs $\widehat{\mathsf{coin}}$. Finally, $\mathcal{B}$ outputs 1 if $\widehat{\mathsf{coin}} = \mathsf{coin}$ and 0 otherwise.

It can be seen that if $\mathbf{A}, \mathbf{v}$ is a valid LWE sample (i.e., $\mathbf{v} = \mathbf{A}^\top\mathbf{s}$), the view of the adversary corresponds to Game_4. Otherwise (i.e., $\mathbf{v} \leftarrow \mathbb{Z}_q^m$), it corresponds to Game_5. Therefore we have $\left|\Pr[X_4] - \Pr[X_5]\right| = \mathsf{Adv}_{\mathcal{B},\mathsf{QRO}_{\ell_{\mathsf{ID}},\ell_r}}^{\mathsf{LWE}_{n,m,q,D_{\mathbb{Z},\alpha q}}}(\lambda)$. As for the running time, we have $\mathsf{Time}(\mathcal{B}) = \mathsf{Time}(\mathcal{A}) + (Q_{\mathsf{H}} + Q_{\mathsf{ID}}) \cdot \mathsf{poly}(\lambda)$ since all $\mathcal{B}$ has to do is to run $\mathcal{A}$ once plus to compute some additional computations that can be done in a fixed polynomial time whenever $\mathcal{A}$ makes a quantum random oracle or secret key query.

Game_6: In this game, we further change the way the challenge ciphertext is created. If $\mathsf{coin} = 0$, to create the challenge ciphertext the challenger first picks $\mathbf{b} \leftarrow \mathbb{Z}_q^m$, $\mathbf{x}' \leftarrow D_{\mathbb{Z}^m,\alpha' q}$ and computes

$$\mathbf{c}' = [\mathbf{e}_{\mathsf{ID}^*}|\mathbf{I}_m]^\top\mathbf{b} + \mathbf{x}'.$$

It then parses $\mathbf{c}'$ into c_0' and $\mathbf{c}_1$ (as in Game_4) and sets the challenge ciphertext as Eq. (1). Similarly to the change from Game_3 to Game_4, we have $\left|\Pr[X_5] - \Pr[X_6]\right| = 2^{-\Omega(n)}$ by Lemma 7.

It remains to show that no adversary has non-negligible chance in winning Game_6. Notice that when $\mathsf{coin} = 0$, the challenge ciphertext can be written as

$$c_0 = \mathbf{e}_{\mathsf{ID}^*}^\top\mathbf{b} + x_0' + \mathsf{M}\lfloor q/2\rceil, \mathbf{c}_1 = \mathbf{b} + \mathbf{x}_1',$$

where x'_0 is the first entry of $\mathbf{x}'$ and $\mathbf{x}'_1$ is the remaining entries. It suffices to show that the joint distribution of $(\mathbf{b}, \mathbf{e}_{\mathsf{ID}^*}^\top \mathbf{b})$ is statistically close to the uniform distribution over $\mathbb{Z}_q^m \times \mathbb{Z}_q$, conditioned on $\mathbf{u}_{\mathsf{ID}^*}$. From the view of $\mathcal{A}$, $\mathbf{e}_{\mathsf{ID}^*}$ is distributed as $D_{\Lambda^\perp_{\mathbf{u}(\mathsf{ID}^*)}(\mathbf{A}),\sigma}$ because all information of $\mathbf{e}_{\mathsf{ID}^*}$ revealed to $\mathcal{A}$ is $\mathsf{H}(\mathsf{ID}^*) = \mathbf{A}\mathbf{e}_{\mathsf{ID}^*}$ where $\mathbf{e}_{\mathsf{ID}^*} = \mathsf{SampleZ}(\sigma; \widehat{\mathsf{H}}(\mathsf{ID}^*))$ and $\widehat{\mathsf{H}}(\mathsf{ID}^*)$ is completely random from the view of $\mathcal{A}$. (Remark that $\widehat{\mathsf{H}}(\mathsf{ID}^*)$ is used in the game only when $\mathcal{A}$ queries ID^* to the key generation oracle, which is prohibited in the adaptively-anonymous security game.) By Lemma 6, we have

$$\mathbf{H}_\infty(\mathbf{e}_{\mathsf{ID}^*}) \geq m - 1$$

for all but $2^{-\Omega(n)}$ fraction of $\mathbf{A}$. Now we can apply the leftover hash lemma since $\mathbf{b}$ is distributed uniformly at random over $\mathbb{Z}_q^m$ and conclude that $(\mathbf{b}, \mathbf{e}_{\mathsf{ID}^*}^\top \mathbf{b})$ is $\sqrt{q/2^{m-1}}$-close to the uniform distribution by the leftover hash lemma. Hence, we have $\Pr[X_6] \leq 2^{-\Omega(n)} + \sqrt{q/2^{m-1}} < 2^{-\Omega(n)}$.

Therefore, combining everything together, the theorem is proven.

4 (Almost) Tightly Secure Multi-challenge IBE

In this section, we propose an IBE scheme that is (almost) tightly secure in the multi-challenge setting. The security of the scheme is proven both in the classical ROM and QROM settings. Our construction is obtained by applying the Katz-Wang [KW03] technique to the original GPV-IBE scheme.

4.1 Construction

Let the identity space $\mathcal{ID}$ of the scheme be $\mathcal{ID} = \{0,1\}^{\ell_{\mathsf{ID}}}$, where $\ell_{\mathsf{ID}}(\lambda)$ denotes the identity-length. Let also $\mathsf{H} : \{0,1\}^{\ell_{\mathsf{ID}}+1} \rightarrow \mathbb{Z}_q^n$ be a hash function treated as a random oracle during the security analysis where ℓ_{ID} denotes the identity-length. The IBE scheme $\mathsf{GPV}_{\mathsf{mult}}$ is given as follows. For simplicity, we describe the scheme as a stateful one. As remarked in Remark 1, we can make the scheme stateless without any additional assumption in the QROM.

$\mathsf{Setup}(1^\lambda)$: On input 1^λ, it first chooses a prime q, positive integers n, m, γ, and Gaussian parameters α, σ, where all these values are implicitly a function of the security parameter λ. The precise parameter selection is specified in the following section. It then runs $(\mathbf{A}, \mathbf{T}_\mathbf{A}) \leftarrow \mathsf{TrapGen}(1^n, 1^m, q)$ to generate a matrix $\mathbf{A} \in \mathbb{Z}_q^{n \times m}$ with a trapdoor $\mathbf{T}_\mathbf{A} \in \mathbb{Z}^{m \times m}$ such that $\|\mathbf{T}_\mathbf{A}\|_{\mathrm{GS}} \leq O(n \log q)$. Then it outputs

$$\mathsf{mpk} = \mathbf{A} \quad \text{and} \quad \mathsf{msk} = \mathbf{T}_\mathbf{A}$$

$\mathsf{KeyGen}(\mathsf{mpk}, \mathsf{msk}, \mathsf{ID})$: If $\mathsf{sk}_{\mathsf{ID}}$ is already generated, then this algorithm returns it. Otherwise it picks $b_{\mathsf{ID}} \xleftarrow{\$} \{0,1\}$, computes $\mathbf{u}_{\mathsf{ID}\|b_{\mathsf{ID}}} = \mathsf{H}(\mathsf{ID}\|b_{\mathsf{ID}})$, and samples $\mathbf{e}_{\mathsf{ID}\|b_{\mathsf{ID}}} \in \mathbb{Z}^m$ such that

$$\mathbf{A}\mathbf{e}_{\mathsf{ID}\|b_{\mathsf{ID}}} = \mathbf{u}_{\mathsf{ID}\|b_{\mathsf{ID}}} \mod q$$

as $\mathbf{e}_{\mathsf{ID}\|b_{\mathsf{ID}}} \leftarrow \mathsf{SamplePre}(\mathbf{A}, \mathbf{T_A}, \mathbf{u}_{\mathsf{ID}\|b_{\mathsf{ID}}}, \sigma)$. It returns $\mathsf{sk}_{\mathsf{ID}} = (b_{\mathsf{ID}}, \mathbf{e}_{\mathsf{ID}\|b_{\mathsf{ID}}})$ as the secret key.

$\mathsf{Enc}(\mathsf{mpk}, \mathsf{ID}, \mathsf{M})$: To encrypt a message $\mathsf{M} \in \{0,1\}$, it first samples $\mathbf{s} \xleftarrow{\$} U([-\gamma,\gamma])$, $\mathbf{x} \leftarrow D_{\mathbb{Z}^m,\alpha q}$. Then it computes $\mathbf{u}_{\mathsf{ID}\|0} = \mathsf{H}(\mathsf{ID}\|0)$ and $\mathbf{u}_{\mathsf{ID}\|1} = \mathsf{H}(\mathsf{ID}\|1)$ and sets the ciphertext as

$$c_0 = \mathbf{u}_{\mathsf{ID}\|0}^\top \mathbf{s} + \mathsf{M}\lfloor q/2 \rceil, \quad c_1 = \mathbf{u}_{\mathsf{ID}\|1}^\top \mathbf{s} + \mathsf{M}\lfloor q/2 \rceil, \quad \mathbf{c}_2 = \mathbf{A}^\top \mathbf{s} + \mathbf{x}.$$

Finally, it outputs the ciphertext $C = (c_0, c_1, \mathbf{c}_2) \in \mathbb{Z}_q \times \mathbb{Z}_q \times \mathbb{Z}_q^m$.

$\mathsf{Dec}(\mathsf{mpk}, \mathsf{sk}_{\mathsf{ID}}, C)$: To decrypt a ciphertext $C = (c_0, c_1, \mathbf{c}_2)$ with a secret key $\mathsf{sk}_{\mathsf{ID}}$, it computes $w = c_{b_{\mathsf{ID}}} - \mathbf{c}_2^\top \mathbf{e}_{\mathsf{ID}\|b_{\mathsf{ID}}} \in \mathbb{Z}_q$ and outputs 0 if w is closer to 0 than to $\lfloor q/2 \rceil$ modulo q. Otherwise it outputs 1.

4.2 Correctness and Parameter Selection

The following shows correctness of the above IBE scheme.

Lemma 12 (Correctness). *Suppose the parameters q, σ, and α are such that*

$$\sigma > \|\mathbf{T_A}\|_{\mathrm{GS}} \cdot \sqrt{\log(2m+4)/\pi}, \qquad \alpha < 1/4\sigma m.$$

Let $\mathbf{e}_{\mathsf{ID}\|b_{\mathsf{ID}}} \leftarrow \mathsf{KeyGen}(\mathbf{A}, \mathbf{T_A}, \mathsf{ID}), C \leftarrow \mathsf{Enc}(\mathbf{A}, \mathsf{ID}', \mathsf{M} \in \{0,1\})$ *and* $\mathsf{M}' \leftarrow \mathsf{Dec}(\mathbf{A}, \mathbf{e}_{\mathsf{ID}\|b_{\mathsf{ID}}}, C)$. *If* $\mathsf{ID} = \mathsf{ID}'$, *then with overwhelming probability we have* $\mathsf{M}' = \mathsf{M}$.

Proof. When the Dec algorithm operates as specified, we have

$$w = c_{b_{\mathsf{ID}}} - \mathbf{e}_{\mathsf{ID}\|b_{\mathsf{ID}}}^\top \mathbf{c}_2 = \mathsf{M}\lfloor q/2 \rceil + \underbrace{\mathbf{e}_{\mathsf{ID}\|b_{\mathsf{ID}}}^\top \mathbf{x}}_{\text{error term}}.$$

By Lemma 8 and the condition posed on the choice of σ, we have that the distribution of $\mathbf{e}_{\mathsf{ID}\|b_{\mathsf{ID}}}$ is $2^{-\Omega(n)}$ close to $D_{\Lambda^{\perp}_{\mathbf{u}_{\mathsf{ID}\|b_{\mathsf{ID}}}}(\mathbf{A}),\sigma}$. Therefore, by Lemma 5, we have $\|\mathbf{x}\| \leq \alpha q \sqrt{m}$, and $\|\mathbf{e}_{\mathsf{ID}\|b_{\mathsf{ID}}}\| \leq \sigma \cdot \sqrt{m}$ except for $2^{-\Omega(n)}$ probability. Then, the error term is bounded by

$$|\mathbf{h}^\top \mathbf{x} - \mathbf{e}_{\mathsf{ID}}^\top \mathbf{x}| \leq |\mathbf{e}_{\mathsf{ID}}^\top \mathbf{x}| \leq \alpha q \sigma m.$$

Hence, for the error term to have absolute value less than $q/4$, it suffices to choose q and α as in the statement of the lemma.

Parameter Selection. For example, we can set the parameters $\ell, n, m, q, \sigma, \alpha, \beta, \gamma$ as follows:

$$n = 25\ell, \qquad m = n^{1+\kappa}, \qquad \sigma = n^{0.5+\kappa}, \qquad q = 5n^{5.5+3\kappa},$$
$$\alpha q = n^{4+\kappa}, \qquad \beta q = n, \qquad \gamma = n,$$

where $\kappa > 0$ is a constant that can be set arbitrarily small. To withstand attacks running in time 2^λ, we may set $\ell = \tilde{\Omega}(\lambda)$. In the above, we round up m to the nearest integer and q to the nearest largest prime. As the case with the single-challenge setting, if we make the more aggressive choice of using the negligible notion $2^{-\omega(\log \lambda)}$, we will be able to obtain better parameter selections. More detailed discussion on the parameter selection can be found in the full version.

4.3 Security

We can (almost) tightly prove the security of our IBE scheme $\mathsf{GPV}_{\mathsf{mult}}$ both in the classical ROM and QROM settings. The following theorem addresses the security of $\mathsf{GPV}_{\mathsf{mult}}$ in the classical ROM setting. The proof of the theorem can be found in the full version.

Theorem 3. *The IBE scheme* $\mathsf{GPV}_{\mathsf{mult}}$ *is adaptively-anonymous multi-challenge secure assuming the hardness of* $\mathsf{LWE}_{\ell,m,q,\chi}$ *in the random oracle model, where* $\chi = D_{\mathbb{Z},\alpha q}$. *Namely, for any classical adversary* $\mathcal{A}$ *making at most* Q_{H} *queries to* H, Q_{ch} *challenge queries, and* Q_{ID} *secret key queries, there exists an algorithm* $\mathcal{B}$ *such that*

$$\mathsf{Adv}^{\mathsf{IBE}}_{\mathcal{A},\mathsf{GPV}_{\mathsf{mult}}}(\lambda) \leq 3n \cdot \mathsf{Adv}^{\mathsf{LWE}_{\ell,m,q,D_{\mathbb{Z},\alpha q}}}_{\mathcal{B}}(\lambda) + (Q_{\mathsf{H}} + Q_{\mathsf{ID}} + Q_{\mathsf{ch}}) \cdot 2^{-\Omega(n)}$$

and

$$\mathsf{Time}(\mathcal{B}) = \mathsf{Time}(\mathcal{A}) + (Q_{\mathsf{H}} + Q_{\mathsf{ID}} + Q_{\mathsf{ch}}) \cdot \mathsf{poly}(\lambda).$$

As we explained in the introduction, our analysis in the ROM can be easily extended to the QROM setting. We can prove the following theorem that addresses the security of $\mathsf{GPV}_{\mathsf{mult}}$ in the QROM. The proof can be found in the full version.

Theorem 4. *The IBE scheme* $\mathsf{GPV}_{\mathsf{mult}}$ *is adaptively-anonymous multi-challenge secure assuming the hardness of* $\mathsf{LWE}_{\ell,m,q,\chi}$ *in the quantum random oracle model, where* $\chi = D_{\mathbb{Z},\alpha q}$. *Namely, for any classical adversary* $\mathcal{A}$ *making at most* Q_{H} *quantum random oracle queries,* Q_{ch} *challenge queries, and* Q_{ID} *secret key queries, there exists an algorithm* $\mathcal{B}$ *making at most* $3Q_{\mathsf{H}} + 2Q_{\mathsf{ID}} + 6Q_{\mathsf{ch}}$ *quantum random oracle queries such that*

$$\mathsf{Adv}^{\mathsf{IBE}}_{\mathcal{A},\mathsf{GPV}_{\mathsf{mult}}}(\lambda) \leq 3n \cdot \mathsf{Adv}^{\mathsf{LWE}_{\ell,m,q,D_{\mathbb{Z},\alpha q}}}_{\mathcal{B},\mathsf{QRO}_{\ell_{\mathsf{ID}}+2,\max\{\ell_r,(\lfloor \log q \rfloor + 2\lambda)\times n\}}}(\lambda) + (Q_{\mathsf{H}} + Q_{\mathsf{ID}} + Q_{\mathsf{ch}}) \cdot 2^{-\Omega(n)}$$

and

$$\mathsf{Time}(\mathcal{B}) = \mathsf{Time}(\mathcal{A}) + (Q_{\mathsf{H}} + Q_{\mathsf{ID}} + Q_{\mathsf{ch}}) \cdot \mathsf{poly}(\lambda)$$

where ℓ_r *denotes the length of the randomness for* $\mathsf{Sample}\mathbb{Z}$.

These proofs are similar and obtained by combining the idea of using the lossy mode for LWE with the Katz-Wang technique as we explained in Sect. 1.3. We need some results on randomness extraction and lossy mode LWE during the proof. The details can be found in the full version.

Acknowledgement. The first author was partially supported by JST CREST Grant Number JPMJCR1302 and JSPS KAKENHI Grant Number 17J05603. The second author was supported by JST CREST Grant No. JPMJCR1688 and JSPS KAKENHI Grant Number 16K16068.

References

[ABB10] Agrawal, S., Boneh, D., Boyen, X.: Efficient lattice (H)IBE in the standard model. In: Gilbert, H. (ed.) EUROCRYPT 2010. LNCS, vol. 6110, pp. 553–572. Springer, Heidelberg (2010). https://doi.org/10.1007/978-3-642-13190-5_28

[ABB+17] Alkim, E., et al.: Revisiting TESLA in the quantum random oracle model. In: Lange, T., Takagi, T. (eds.) PQCrypto 2017. LNCS, vol. 10346, pp. 143–162. Springer, Cham (2017). https://doi.org/10.1007/978-3-319-59879-6_9

[ACPS09] Applebaum, B., Cash, D., Peikert, C., Sahai, A.: Fast cryptographic primitives and circular-secure encryption based on hard learning problems. In: Halevi, S. (ed.) CRYPTO 2009. LNCS, vol. 5677, pp. 595–618. Springer, Heidelberg (2009). https://doi.org/10.1007/978-3-642-03356-8_35

[ADN+10] Alwen, J., Dodis, Y., Naor, M., Segev, G., Walfish, S., Wichs, D.: Public-key encryption in the bounded-retrieval model. In: Gilbert, H. (ed.) EUROCRYPT 2010. LNCS, vol. 6110, pp. 113–134. Springer, Heidelberg (2010). https://doi.org/10.1007/978-3-642-13190-5_6

[AHY15] Attrapadung, N., Hanaoka, G., Yamada, S.: A framework for identity-based encryption with almost tight security. In: Iwata, T., Cheon, J.H. (eds.) ASIACRYPT 2015, Part I. LNCS, vol. 9452, pp. 521–549. Springer, Heidelberg (2015). https://doi.org/10.1007/978-3-662-48797-6_22

[AKPW13] Alwen, J., Krenn, S., Pietrzak, K., Wichs, D.: Learning with rounding, revisited. In: Canetti, R., Garay, J.A. (eds.) CRYPTO 2013, Part I. LNCS, vol. 8042, pp. 57–74. Springer, Heidelberg (2013). https://doi.org/10.1007/978-3-642-40041-4_4

[ARU14] Ambainis, A., Rosmanis, A., Unruh, D.: Quantum attacks on classical proof systems: The hardness of quantum rewinding. In: FOCS, pp. 474–483. IEEE (2014)

[BDF+11] Boneh, D., Dagdelen, Ö., Fischlin, M., Lehmann, A., Schaffner, C., Zhandry, M.: Random oracles in a quantum world. In: Lee, D.H., Wang, X. (eds.) ASIACRYPT 2011. LNCS, vol. 7073, pp. 41–69. Springer, Heidelberg (2011). https://doi.org/10.1007/978-3-642-25385-0_3

[BDPMW16] Bourse, F., Del Pino, R., Minelli, M., Wee, H.: FHE circuit privacy almost for free. In: Robshaw, M., Katz, J. (eds.) CRYPTO 2016, Part II. LNCS, vol. 9815, pp. 62–89. Springer, Heidelberg (2016). https://doi.org/10.1007/978-3-662-53008-5_3

[BF01] Boneh, D., Franklin, M.: Identity-based encryption from the weil pairing. In: Kilian, J. (ed.) CRYPTO 2001. LNCS, vol. 2139, pp. 213–229. Springer, Heidelberg (2001). https://doi.org/10.1007/3-540-44647-8_13

[BG14] Bai, S., Galbraith, S.D.: An improved compression technique for signatures based on learning with errors. In: Benaloh, J. (ed.) CT-RSA 2014. LNCS, vol. 8366, pp. 28–47. Springer, Cham (2014). https://doi.org/10.1007/978-3-319-04852-9_2

[BKPW12] Bellare, M., Kiltz, E., Peikert, C., Waters, B.: Identity-based (lossy) trapdoor functions and applications. In: Pointcheval, D., Johansson, T. (eds.) EUROCRYPT 2012. LNCS, vol. 7237, pp. 228–245. Springer, Heidelberg (2012). https://doi.org/10.1007/978-3-642-29011-4_15

[BL16] Boyen, X., Li, Q.: Towards tightly secure lattice short signature and Id-based encryption. In: Cheon, J.H., Takagi, T. (eds.) ASIACRYPT 2016, Part II. LNCS, vol. 10032, pp. 404–434. Springer, Heidelberg (2016). https://doi.org/10.1007/978-3-662-53890-6_14

[BLP+13] Brakerski, Z., Langlois, A., Peikert, C., Regev, O., Stehlé, D.: Classical hardness of learning with errors. In: STOC, pp. 575–584 (2013)

[BPR12] Banerjee, A., Peikert, C., Rosen, A.: Pseudorandom functions and lattices. In: Pointcheval, D., Johansson, T. (eds.) EUROCRYPT 2012. LNCS, vol. 7237, pp. 719–737. Springer, Heidelberg (2012). https://doi.org/10.1007/978-3-642-29011-4_42

[BR93] Bellare, M., Rogaway, P.: Random oracles are practical: a paradigm for designing efficient protocols. In: CCS, pp. 62–73. ACM (1993)

[CHK04] Canetti, R., Halevi, S., Katz, J.: Chosen-ciphertext security from identity-based encryption. In: Cachin, C., Camenisch, J.L. (eds.) EUROCRYPT 2004. LNCS, vol. 3027, pp. 207–222. Springer, Heidelberg (2004). https://doi.org/10.1007/978-3-540-24676-3_13

[CHKP10] Cash, D., Hofheinz, D., Kiltz, E., Peikert, C.: Bonsai trees, or how to delegate a lattice basis. In: Gilbert, H. (ed.) EUROCRYPT 2010. LNCS, vol. 6110, pp. 523–552. Springer, Heidelberg (2010). https://doi.org/10.1007/978-3-642-13190-5_27

[Cor09] Coron, J.-S.: A variant of Boneh-Franklin IBE with a tight reduction in the random oracle model. Des. Codes Cryptogr. **50**(1), 115–133 (2009)

[CS98] Cramer, R., Shoup, V.: A practical public key cryptosystem provably secure against adaptive chosen ciphertext attack. In: Krawczyk, H. (ed.) CRYPTO 1998. LNCS, vol. 1462, pp. 13–25. Springer, Heidelberg (1998). https://doi.org/10.1007/BFb0055717

[CW13] Chen, J., Wee, H.: Fully, (Almost) tightly secure IBE and dual system groups. In: Canetti, R., Garay, J.A. (eds.) CRYPTO 2013, Part II. LNCS, vol. 8043, pp. 435–460. Springer, Heidelberg (2013). https://doi.org/10.1007/978-3-642-40084-1_25

[GDCC16] Gong, J., Dong, X., Chen, J., Cao, Z.: Efficient IBE with tight reduction to standard assumption in the multi-challenge setting. In: Cheon, J.H., Takagi, T. (eds.) ASIACRYPT 2016, Part II. LNCS, vol. 10032, pp. 624–654. Springer, Heidelberg (2016). https://doi.org/10.1007/978-3-662-53890-6_21

[Gen06] Gentry, C.: Practical identity-based encryption without random oracles. In: Vaudenay, S. (ed.) EUROCRYPT 2006. LNCS, vol. 4004, pp. 445–464. Springer, Heidelberg (2006). https://doi.org/10.1007/11761679_27

[GGM86] Goldreich, O., Goldwasser, S., Micali, S.: How to construct random functions. J. ACM **33**(4), 792–807 (1986)

[GKPV10] Goldwasser, S., Kalai, Y., Peikert, C., Vaikuntanathan, V.: Robustness of the learning with errors assumption. In: ICS, pp. 230–240 (2010)

[Gol86] Goldreich, O.: Two remarks concerning the goldwasser-micali-rivest signature scheme. In: Odlyzko, A.M. (ed.) CRYPTO 1986. LNCS, vol. 263, pp. 104–110. Springer, Heidelberg (1987). https://doi.org/10.1007/3-540-47721-7_8

[GPV08] Gentry, C., Peikert, C., Vaikuntanathan, V.: Trapdoors for hard lattices and new cryptographic constructions. In: STOC, pp. 197–206. ACM (2008)

[GSW13] Gentry, C., Sahai, A., Waters, B.: Homomorphic encryption from learning with errors: conceptually-simpler, asymptotically-faster, attribute-based. In: Canetti, R., Garay, J.A. (eds.) CRYPTO 2013, Part I. LNCS, vol. 8042, pp. 75–92. Springer, Heidelberg (2013). https://doi.org/10.1007/978-3-642-40041-4_5

[HJ12] Hofheinz, D., Jager, T.: Tightly secure signatures and public-key encryption. In: Safavi-Naini, R., Canetti, R. (eds.) CRYPTO 2012. LNCS, vol. 7417, pp. 590–607. Springer, Heidelberg (2012). https://doi.org/10.1007/978-3-642-32009-5_35

[HKS15] Hofheinz, D., Koch, J., Striecks, C.: Identity-based encryption with (almost) tight security in the multi-instance, multi-ciphertext setting. In: Katz, J. (ed.) PKC 2015. LNCS, vol. 9020, pp. 799–822. Springer, Heidelberg (2015). https://doi.org/10.1007/978-3-662-46447-2_36

[KLS18] Kiltz, E., Lyubashevsky, V., Schaffner, C.: A concrete treatment of fiat-shamir signatures in the quantum random-oracle model. In: Nielsen, J.B., Rijmen, V. (eds.) EUROCRYPT 2018, Part III. LNCS, vol. 10822, pp. 552–586. Springer, Cham (2018). https://doi.org/10.1007/978-3-319-78372-7_18

[KW03] Katz, J., Wang, N.: Efficiency improvements for signature schemes with tight security reductions. In: Computer and Communications Security, pp. 155–164. ACM (2003)

[KY16] Katsumata, S., Yamada, S.: Partitioning via non-linear polynomial functions: more compact IBEs from ideal lattices and bilinear maps. In: Cheon, J.H., Takagi, T. (eds.) ASIACRYPT 2016, Part II. LNCS, vol. 10032, pp. 682–712. Springer, Heidelberg (2016). https://doi.org/10.1007/978-3-662-53890-6_23

[LSSS17] Libert, B., Sakzad, A., Stehlé, D., Steinfeld, R.: All-but-many lossy trapdoor functions and selective opening chosen-ciphertext security from LWE. In: Katz, J., Shacham, H. (eds.) CRYPTO 2017, Part III. LNCS, vol. 10403, pp. 332–364. Springer, Cham (2017). https://doi.org/10.1007/978-3-319-63697-9_12

[MP12] Micciancio, D., Peikert, C.: Trapdoors for lattices: simpler, tighter, faster, smaller. In: Pointcheval, D., Johansson, T. (eds.) EUROCRYPT 2012. LNCS, vol. 7237, pp. 700–718. Springer, Heidelberg (2012). https://doi.org/10.1007/978-3-642-29011-4_41

[MR07] Micciancio, D., Regev, O.: Worst-case to average-case reductions based on gaussian measures. SIAM J. Comput. **37**(1), 267–302 (2007)

[NC00] Nielsen, M.A., Isaac, L.: Quantum Computation and Quantum Information. Cambridge University Press, Chuang (2000)

[Pei07] Peikert, C.: Limits on the hardness of lattice problems in ell _p norms. In: Conference on Computational Complexity, pp. 333–346. IEEE (2007)

[Pei09] Peikert, C.: Public-key cryptosystems from the worst-case shortest vector problem. In: STOC, pp. 333–342. ACM (2009)

[Pei10] Peikert, C.: An efficient and parallel gaussian sampler for lattices. In: Rabin, T. (ed.) CRYPTO 2010. LNCS, vol. 6223, pp. 80–97. Springer, Heidelberg (2010). https://doi.org/10.1007/978-3-642-14623-7_5

[PR06] Peikert, C., Rosen, A.: Efficient collision-resistant hashing from worst-case assumptions on cyclic lattices. In: Halevi, S., Rabin, T. (eds.) TCC 2006. LNCS, vol. 3876, pp. 145–166. Springer, Heidelberg (2006). https://doi.org/10.1007/11681878_8

[Reg05] Regev, O.: On lattices, learning with errors, random linear codes, and cryptography. In: STOC, pp. 84–93. ACM Press (2005)
[Reg10] Regev, O.: The learning with errors problem. Invited survey in CCC (2010)
[Sho94] Shor, P.W.: Algorithms for quantum computation: discrete logarithms and factoring. In: FOCS, pp. 124–134. IEEE (1994)
[SXY18] Saito, T., Xagawa, K., Yamakawa, T.: Tightly-secure key-encapsulation mechanism in the quantum random oracle model. In: Nielsen, J.B., Rijmen, V. (eds.) EUROCRYPT 2018, Part III. LNCS, vol. 10822, pp. 520–551. Springer, Cham (2018). https://doi.org/10.1007/978-3-319-78372-7_17
[TU16] Targhi, E.E., Unruh, D.: Post-quantum security of the fujisaki-okamoto and OAEP transforms. In: Hirt, M., Smith, A. (eds.) TCC 2016, Part II. LNCS, vol. 9986, pp. 192–216. Springer, Heidelberg (2016). https://doi.org/10.1007/978-3-662-53644-5_8
[Unr14a] Unruh, D.: Quantum position verification in the random oracle model. In: Garay, J.A., Gennaro, R. (eds.) CRYPTO 2014, Part II. LNCS, vol. 8617, pp. 1–18. Springer, Heidelberg (2014). https://doi.org/10.1007/978-3-662-44381-1_1
[Unr14b] Unruh, D.: Revocable quantum timed-release encryption. In: Nguyen, P.Q., Oswald, E. (eds.) EUROCRYPT 2014. LNCS, vol. 8441, pp. 129–146. Springer, Heidelberg (2014). https://doi.org/10.1007/978-3-642-55220-5_8
[Unr15] Unruh, D.: Non-interactive zero-knowledge proofs in the quantum random oracle model. In: Oswald, E., Fischlin, M. (eds.) EUROCRYPT 2015, Part II. LNCS, vol. 9057, pp. 755–784. Springer, Heidelberg (2015). https://doi.org/10.1007/978-3-662-46803-6_25
[Unr17] Unruh, D.: Post-quantum security of fiat-shamir. In: Takagi, T., Peyrin, T. (eds.) ASIACRYPT 2017, Part I. LNCS, vol. 10624, pp. 65–95. Springer, Cham (2017). https://doi.org/10.1007/978-3-319-70694-8_3
[Wat05] Waters, B.: Efficient identity-based encryption without random oracles. In: Cramer, R. (ed.) EUROCRYPT 2005. LNCS, vol. 3494, pp. 114–127. Springer, Heidelberg (2005). https://doi.org/10.1007/11426639_7
[Zha12a] Zhandry, M.: How to construct quantum random functions. In: FOCS, pp. 679–687. IEEE (2012)
[Zha12b] Zhandry, M.: Secure identity-based encryption in the quantum random oracle model. In: Safavi-Naini, R., Canetti, R. (eds.) CRYPTO 2012. LNCS, vol. 7417, pp. 758–775. Springer, Heidelberg (2012). https://doi.org/10.1007/978-3-642-32009-5_44

Side-Channels

New Instantiations of the CRYPTO 2017 Masking Schemes

Pierre Karpman[1,2(✉)] and Daniel S. Roche[3(✉)]

[1] Univ. Grenoble Alpes, CNRS, 38000 Grenoble, France
pierre.karpman@univ-grenoble-alpes.fr
[2] INP, Institute of Engineering Univ. Grenoble Alpes, LJK, 38000 Grenoble, France
[3] United States Naval Academy, Annapolis, USA
roche@usna.edu

Abstract. At CRYPTO 2017, Belaïd *et al.* presented two new private multiplication algorithms over finite fields, to be used in secure masking schemes. To date, these algorithms have the lowest known complexity in terms of *bilinear* multiplication and random masks respectively, both being linear in the number of shares $d+1$. Yet, a practical drawback of both algorithms is that their safe *instantiation* relies on finding matrices satisfying certain conditions. In their work, Belaïd *et al.* only address these up to $d = 2$ and 3 for the first and second algorithm respectively, limiting so far the practical usefulness of their constructions.

In this paper, we use in turn an algebraic, heuristic, and experimental approach to find many more safe instances of Belaïd *et al.*'s algorithms. This results in explicit instantiations up to order $d = 6$ over large fields, and up to $d = 4$ over practically relevant fields such as $\mathbb{F}_{2^8}$.

Keywords: Masking · Linear algebra · MDS matrices

1 Introduction

It has become a well-accepted fact that the black-box security of a cryptographic scheme and the security of one of its real-life implementations may be two quite different matters. In the latter case, numerous side-channels or fault injection techniques may be used to aid in the cryptanalysis of what could otherwise be a very sensible design (for instance a provably-secure mode of operation on top of a block cipher with no known dedicated attacks).

A successful line of side-channel attacks is based on the idea of differential power analysis (DPA), which was introduced by Kocher, Jaffe and Jun at CRYPTO'99 [KJJ99]. The practical importance of this threat immediately triggered an effort from cryptographers to find adequate protections. One of the notable resulting counter-measures is the *masking* approach from Chari *et al.* and Goubin and Patarin [CJRR99,GP99]. The central idea of this counter-measure is to add a "mask" to sensitive variables whose observation through a side-channel could otherwise leak secret information; such variables are for instance intermediate values in a block cipher computation that depend on a

T. Peyrin and S. Galbraith (Eds.): ASIACRYPT 2018, LNCS 11273, pp. 285–314, 2018.
https://doi.org/10.1007/978-3-030-03329-3_10

known plaintext and a round key. Masking schemes apply a secret-sharing technique to several masked instances of every sensitive variable: a legitimate user knowing all the shares can easily compute the original value, while an adversary is now forced to observe more than one value in order to learn anything secret. The utility of this overall approach is that it is experimentally the case that the work required to observe n values accurately through DPA increases exponentially with n.

The challenge in masking countermeasures is to find efficient ways to compute with shared masked data while maintaining the property that the observation of n intermediate values is necessary to learn a secret (for some parameter n). When computations are specified as arithmetic circuits over a finite field $\mathbb{F}_q$, this task reduces mostly to the specification of secure shared addition and multiplication in that field. A simple and commonly used secret sharing scheme used in masking is the linear mapping $x \mapsto \left(r_1, \ldots, r_d, x + \sum_{i=1}^{d} r_i\right)$ which makes addition trivial; the problem then becomes how to *multiply* shared values. At CRYPTO 2003, Ishai, Sahai and Wagner introduced exactly such a shared multiplication over $\mathbb{F}_2$, proven secure in a *d-probing model* that they introduced [ISW03]. Their scheme requires $d(d+1)/2$ random field elements (*i.e.* bits) and $(d+1)^2$ field multiplications to protect against an adversary able to observe d intermediate values. This relatively high quadratic complexity in the *order* d of the scheme lead to an effort to decrease the theoretical and/or practical cost of masking.

At EUROCRYPT 2016, Belaïd *et al.* presented a masking scheme over $\mathbb{F}_2$ with *randomness complexity* decreased to $d + d^2/4$; implementations at low but practically relevant orders $d \leq 4$ confirmed the gain offered by their new algorithm [BBP+16]. At CRYPTO 2017, the same authors presented two new private multiplication algorithms over arbitrary finite fields [BBP+17]. The first, *Algorithm 4*, decreases the number of *bilinear* multiplications to $2d + 1$ at the cost of additional constant multiplications and increased randomness complexity; the second, *Algorithm 5*, decreases the randomness complexity to only d, at the cost of $d(d+1)$ constant multiplications. Furthermore, both algorithms are proven secure w.r.t. the strong, composable notions of d-(strong) non-interference from Barthe *et al.* [BBD+16]. Yet a practical drawback of these last two algorithms is that their safe instantiation depends on finding matrices satisfying a certain number of conditions. Namely, Algorithm 4 uses two (related) matrices in $\mathbb{F}_q^{d \times d}$ for an instantiation at order $d+1$ over $\mathbb{F}_q$, while Algorithm 5 uses a single matrix in $\mathbb{F}_q^{d+1 \times d}$ for the same setting. In their paper, Belaïd *et al.* only succeed in providing "safe matrices" for the small cases $d = 2$ and $d = 2, 3$ for Algorithms 4 and 5 respectively, and in giving a non-constructive existence theorem for safe matrices when $q \geq O(d)^{d+1}$ (resp. $q \geq O(d)^{d+2}$).

1.1 Our Contribution

In this work, we focus on the problem of safely instantiating the two algorithms of Belaïd *et al.* from CRYPTO 2017. We first develop equivalent matrix conditions which are in some sense simpler and much more efficient to check computationally. We use this reformulation to develop useful *preconditions* based on MDS matrices that increase the likelihood that a given matrix is safe. We show how to generate matrices that satisfy our preconditions by construction, which then allows to give an explicit sufficient condition, as well as a construction of safe matrices for both schemes at order $d \leq 3$. Our simplification of the conditions also naturally transforms into a testing algorithm, an efficient implementation of which is used to perform an extensive experimental search. We provide explicit matrices for safe instantiations in all of the following cases:

- For $d = 3$, fields $\mathbb{F}_{2^k}$ with $k \geq 3$
- For $d = 4$, fields $\mathbb{F}_{2^k}$ with $5 \leq k \leq 16$
- For $d = 5$, fields $\mathbb{F}_{2^k}$ with $10 \leq k \leq 16$, and additionally $k = 9$ for Algorithm 5.
- For $d = 6$, fields $\mathbb{F}_{2^k}$ with $15 \leq k \leq 16$

These are the first known instantiations for $d \geq 4$ or for $d = 3$ over $\mathbb{F}_{2^3}$. We also gather detailed statistics about the proportion of safe matrices in all of these cases.

1.2 Roadmap

We recall the two masking schemes of CRYPTO 2017 and the associated matrix conditions in Sect. 3. We give our simplifications of the latter in Sect. 4 and state our preconditions in Sect. 5. A formal analysis of the case of order up to 3 is given in Sect. 6, where explicit conditions and instantiations for these orders are also developed. We present our algorithms and discuss their implementations in Sect. 7, and conclude with experimental results in Sect. 8.

2 Preliminaries

2.1 Notation

We use $\mathbb{K}^{m \times n}$ to denote the set of matrices with m rows and n columns over the field $\mathbb{K}$. We write $m = \operatorname{rowdim} A$ and $n = \operatorname{coldim} \boldsymbol{A}$. For any vector $\boldsymbol{v}$, $\operatorname{wt}(\boldsymbol{v})$ denotes the *Hamming weight* of $\boldsymbol{v}$, *i.e.*, the number of non-zero entries.

We use $\mathbf{0}_{m \times n}$ (resp. $\mathbf{1}_{m \times n}$) to denote the all-zero (resp. all-one) matrix in $\mathbb{K}^{m \times n}$ for any fixed $\mathbb{K}$ (which will always be clear from the context). Similarly, $\boldsymbol{I}_d$ is the identity matrix of dimension d.

We generally use bold upper-case to denote matrices and bold lower-case to denote vectors. (The exception is some lower-case Greek letters for matrices that have been already defined in the literature, notably $\boldsymbol{\gamma}$.) For a matrix $\boldsymbol{M}$, $\boldsymbol{M}_{i,j}$ is the coefficient at the ith row and jth column, with numbering (usually) starting from one. (Again, γ will be an exception as its row numbering starts at 0.) Similarly, a matrix may be directly defined from its coefficients as $(\boldsymbol{M}_{i,j})$.

We use "hexadecimal notation" for binary field elements. This means that $a = \sum_{i=0}^{n-1} a_i X^i \in \mathbb{F}_{2^n} \cong \mathbb{F}_2[X]/\langle I(X) \rangle$ (where $I(X)$ is a degree-n irreducible polynomial) is equated to the integer $\tilde{a} = \sum_{i=0}^{n-1} a_i 2^i$, which is then written in base 16. The specific field representations we use throughout are:

$\mathbb{F}_{2^2} \cong \mathbb{F}_2[x]/\langle X^2+X+1\rangle$	$\mathbb{F}_{2^3} \cong \mathbb{F}_2[x]/\langle X^3+X+1\rangle$
$\mathbb{F}_{2^4} \cong \mathbb{F}_2[x]/\langle X^4+X+1\rangle$	$\mathbb{F}_{2^5} \cong \mathbb{F}_2[x]/\langle X^5+X^2+1\rangle$
$\mathbb{F}_{2^6} \cong \mathbb{F}_2[X]/\langle X^6+X+1\rangle$	$\mathbb{F}_{2^7} \cong \mathbb{F}_2[X]/\langle X^7+X+1\rangle$
$\mathbb{F}_{2^8} \cong \mathbb{F}_2[X]/\langle X^8+X^4+X^3+X+1\rangle$	$\mathbb{F}_{2^9} \cong \mathbb{F}_2[X]/\langle X^9+X+1\rangle$
$\mathbb{F}_{2^{10}} \cong \mathbb{F}_2[X]/\langle X^{10}+X^3+1\rangle$	$\mathbb{F}_{2^{11}} \cong \mathbb{F}_2[X]/\langle X^{11}+X^2+1\rangle$
$\mathbb{F}_{2^{12}} \cong \mathbb{F}_2[X]/\langle X^{12}+X^3+1\rangle$	$\mathbb{F}_{2^{13}} \cong \mathbb{F}_2[X]/\langle X^{13}+X^4+X^3+X+1\rangle$
$\mathbb{F}_{2^{14}} \cong \mathbb{F}_2[X]/\langle X^{14}+X^5+1\rangle$	$\mathbb{F}_{2^{15}} \cong \mathbb{F}_2[X]/\langle X^{15}+X+1\rangle$
$\mathbb{F}_{2^{16}} \cong \mathbb{F}_2[X]/\langle X^{16}+X^5+X^3+X+1\rangle$	

Additional notation is introduced on first use.

2.2 MDS and Cauchy Matrices

An $[n,k,d]_{\mathbb{K}}$ linear code of length n, dimension k, minimum distance d over the field $\mathbb{K}$ is *maximum-distance separable* (MDS) if it reaches the Singleton bound, *i.e.* if $d = n-k+1$. An *MDS matrix* is the redundancy part $\boldsymbol{A}$ of a systematic generating matrix $\boldsymbol{G} = \begin{pmatrix}\boldsymbol{I}_k & \boldsymbol{A}\end{pmatrix}$ of a (linear) MDS code of length double its dimension.

A useful characterization of MDS matrices of particular interest in our case is stated in the following theorem (see *e.g.* [MS06, Chap. 11, Theorem 8]):

Theorem 1. *A matrix is MDS if and only if all its minors are non-zero,* i.e. *all its square sub-matrices are invertible.*

Square *Cauchy matrices* satisfy the above condition by construction, and are thence MDS. A (non-necessarily square) matrix $\boldsymbol{A} \in \mathbb{K}^{n\times m}$ is a Cauchy matrix if $\boldsymbol{A}_{i,j} = (x_i - y_j)^{-1}$, where $\{x_1,\ldots,x_n,y_1,\ldots,y_m\}$ are $n+m$ distinct elements of $\mathbb{K}$.

A Cauchy matrix $\boldsymbol{A}$ may be *extended* to a matrix $\widetilde{\boldsymbol{A}}$ by adding a row or a column of ones. It can be shown that all square submatrices of $\widetilde{\boldsymbol{A}}$ are invertible, and thus themselves MDS [RS85]. By analogy and by a slight abuse of terminology, we will say of a square matrix $\boldsymbol{A}$ that it is *extended MDS* (XMDS) if all square submatrices of $\boldsymbol{A}$ extended by one row or column of ones are MDS. Further depending on the context, we may only require this property to hold for row (or column) extension to call a matrix XMDS.

A (possibly extended) Cauchy matrix $\boldsymbol{A}$ may be *generalized* to a matrix $\boldsymbol{A}'$ by multiplying it with (non-zero) row and column scaling: one has $\boldsymbol{A}'_{i,j} = c_i d_j \cdot (x_i - y_j)^{-1}$, $c_i d_j \neq 0$. All square submatrices of generalized (extended) Cauchy matrices are MDS [RS85], but not necessarily XMDS, as one may already use the scaling to set any row or column of $\boldsymbol{A}'$ to an arbitrary value.

2.3 Security Notions for Masking Schemes

We recall the security notions under which the masking schemes studied in this paper were analysed. These are namely *d-non-interference* (d-NI) and *d-strong non-interference* (d-SNI), which were both introduced by Barthe *et al.* [BBD+16] as stronger and composable alternatives to the original d-probing model of Ishai *et al.* [ISW03].

Note that none of the notions presented below are explicitly used in this paper, and we only present them for the sake of completeness. Our exposition is strongly based on the one of Belaïd *et al.* [BBP+17].

Definition 2 (Gadgets). *Let* $f : \mathbb{K}^n \to \mathbb{K}^m$, $u, v \in \mathbb{N}$; *a* (u,v)-gadget *for the function* f *is a randomized circuit* C *such that for every tuple* $(\boldsymbol{x}_1, \ldots, \boldsymbol{x}_n) \in (\mathbb{K}^u)^n$ *and every set of random coins* $\mathcal{R}$, $(\boldsymbol{y}_1, \ldots, \boldsymbol{y}_m) \leftarrow C(\boldsymbol{x}_1, \ldots, \boldsymbol{x}_n; \mathcal{R})$ *satisfies:*

$$\left(\sum_{j=1}^{v} y_{1,j}, \ldots, \sum_{j=1}^{v} y_{m,j}\right) = f\left(\sum_{j=1}^{u} x_{1,j}, \ldots, \sum_{j=1}^{u} x_{m,j}\right).$$

One further defines x_i *as* $\sum_{j=1}^{u} \boldsymbol{x}_{i,j}$, *and similarly for* y_i; $\boldsymbol{x}_{i,j}$ *is called the* j*th* share *of* x_i.

In the above, the randomized circuit C has access to random-scalar gates that generate elements of $\mathbb{K}$ independently and uniformly at random, and the variable $\mathcal{R}$ records the generated values for a given execution. Furthermore, one calls *probes* any subset of the wires of C (or equivalently edges of its associated graph).

Definition 3 (t-Simulability). *Let* C *be a* (u,v)*-gadget for* $f : \mathbb{K}^n \to \mathbb{K}^n$, *and* ℓ, $t \in \mathbb{N}$. *A set* $\{p_1, \ldots, p_\ell\}$ *of probes of* C *is said to be* t-simulable *if* $\exists I_1, \ldots, I_n \subseteq \{1, \ldots, u\}$; $\#I_i \leq t$ *and a randomized function* $\pi : (\mathbb{K}^t)^n \to \mathbb{K}^\ell$ *such that for any* $(\boldsymbol{x}_1, \ldots, \boldsymbol{x}_n) \in (\mathbb{K}^u)^n$, $\{p_1, \ldots, p_\ell\} \sim \{\pi(\{x_{1,i}, i \in I_1\}, \ldots, \{x_{n,i}, i \in I_n\})\}$.

This notion of simulability leads to the following.

Definition 4 (d-Non-interference). *A* (u,v)*-gadget* C *for a function over* $\mathbb{K}^n$ *is* d-non-interfering *(or d-NI) if and only if any set of at most d probes of* C *is* t*-simulable,* $t \leq d$.

Definition 5 (d-Strong non-interference). *A* (u,v)*-gadget* C *for a function over* $\mathbb{K}^n$ *is* d-strong non-interfering *(or d-SNI) if and only if for every set* P_1 *of at most* d_1 internal probes *(that do not depend on "output wires" or output shares* $y_{i,j}$*'s) and every set* P_2 *of* d_2 external probes *(on output wires or shares) such that* $d_1 + d_2 \leq d$, *then* $P_1 \cup P_2$ *is* d_1*-simulable.*

It is clear that a d-SNI gadget is also d-NI. Barthe *et al.* also showed that the two notions were not equivalent, but that the composition of a d-NI and a d-SNI gadget was d-SNI [BBD+16].

3 The Masking Schemes of CRYPTO 2017

We recall here the main ideas of the two masking schemes of Belaïd *et al.* introduced at CRYPTO 2017 [BBP+17] and their associated matrix conditions; we refer to that paper for a full description of the gadgets and algorithms.

3.1 Pseudo-Linear Multiplication Complexity [BBP+17, Sect. 4]

This scheme is the composition of two gadgets, only the first of which is of interest to us. In order to build a d-SNI multiplication gadget with $d+1$ input and output shares, Belaïd *et al.* first give a d-NI gadget with $d+1$ input and $2d+1$ output shares, and then compress its output into $d+1$ shares using a d-SNI gadget from Carlet *et al.* [CPRR16].

To implement d-NI multiplication over a field $\mathbb{K}$, the first gadget needs a certain matrix $\boldsymbol{\gamma} \in \mathbb{K}^{d\times d}$; in turn, this defines a related matrix $\boldsymbol{\delta} \in \mathbb{K}^{d\times d}$ as $\boldsymbol{\delta} = \mathbf{1}_{d\times d} - \boldsymbol{\gamma}$. The multiplication algorithm is then derived from the equality:

$$a \cdot b = \left(a_0 + \sum_{i=1}^{d}(r_i + a_i)\right) \cdot \left(b_0 + \sum_{i=1}^{d}(s_i + b_i)\right)$$
$$- \sum_{i=1}^{d} r_i \cdot \left(b_0 + \sum_{j=1}^{d}(\boldsymbol{\delta}_{i,j} s_j + b_j)\right) - \sum_{i=1}^{d} s_i \cdot \left(a_0 + \sum_{j=1}^{d}(\boldsymbol{\gamma}_{i,j} r_j + a_j)\right),$$

where $a = \sum_{i=0}^{d} a_i$, $b = \sum_{i=0}^{d} b_i$ are the shared multiplicands, and the r_is and s_is are arbitrary (*a priori* random) values. This equality leads to defining the output shares of this first gadget as:

- $c_0 := \left(a_0 + \sum_{i=1}^{d}(r_i + a_i)\right) \cdot \left(b_0 + \sum_{i=1}^{d}(s_i + b_i)\right)$;
- $c_i := -r_i \cdot \left(b_0 + \sum_{j=1}^{d}(\boldsymbol{\delta}_{i,j} s_j + b_j)\right)$, $1 \le i \le d$;
- $c_{i+d} := -s_i \cdot \left(a_0 + \sum_{j=1}^{d}(\boldsymbol{\gamma}_{i,j} r_j + a_j)\right)$, $1 \le i \le d$.

By considering a proper scheduling of the operations needed to compute the above shares and the probes that this makes available to the adversary, Belaïd *et al.* show that a necessary and sufficient condition for their resulting scheme to be d-SNI is that $\boldsymbol{\gamma}$ and $\boldsymbol{\delta}$ *both* satisfy a certain condition, stated below.

Condition 4.1 ([BBP+17]). *Let* $\boldsymbol{\gamma} \in \mathbb{K}^{d\times d}$; $\ell = 2d^2 + 4d + 1$; $\boldsymbol{D}_{\boldsymbol{\gamma},j} \in \mathbb{K}^{d\times d}$ *be the diagonal matrix whose non-zero entry at row* i *is equal to* $\boldsymbol{\gamma}_{j,i}$; $\boldsymbol{T}_d \in \mathbb{K}^{d\times d}$ *be the upper-triangular matrix whose non-zero entries are all one; and* $\boldsymbol{T}_{\boldsymbol{\gamma},j} \in \mathbb{K}^{d\times d} = \boldsymbol{D}_{\boldsymbol{\gamma},j}\boldsymbol{T}_d$. *Equivalently:*

$$\boldsymbol{I}_d = \begin{pmatrix} 1 & 0 & \cdots & 0 \\ 0 & 1 & & 0 \\ \vdots & & \ddots & \vdots \\ 0 & \cdots & 0 & 1 \end{pmatrix}, \quad \boldsymbol{D}_{\boldsymbol{\gamma},j} = \begin{pmatrix} \boldsymbol{\gamma}_{j,1} & 0 & \cdots & 0 \\ 0 & \boldsymbol{\gamma}_{j,2} & & 0 \\ \vdots & & \ddots & \vdots \\ 0 & \cdots & 0 & \boldsymbol{\gamma}_{j,d} \end{pmatrix},$$

$$\boldsymbol{T}_d = \begin{pmatrix} 1 & 1 & \cdots & 1 \\ 0 & 1 & \cdots & 1 \\ \vdots & & \ddots & \vdots \\ 0 & \cdots & 0 & 1 \end{pmatrix}, \quad \boldsymbol{T}_{\boldsymbol{\gamma},j} = \begin{pmatrix} \boldsymbol{\gamma}_{j,1} & \boldsymbol{\gamma}_{j,1} & \cdots & \boldsymbol{\gamma}_{j,1} \\ 0 & \boldsymbol{\gamma}_{j,2} & \cdots & \boldsymbol{\gamma}_{j,2} \\ \vdots & & \ddots & \vdots \\ 0 & \cdots & 0 & \boldsymbol{\gamma}_{j,d} \end{pmatrix}.$$

One then defines $\boldsymbol{L} \in \mathbb{K}^{(d+1)\times \ell}$ *and* $\boldsymbol{M}_\gamma \in \mathbb{K}^{d\times \ell}$ *as:*

$$\boldsymbol{L} = \begin{pmatrix} 1 & \mathbf{0}_{1\times d} & \mathbf{0}_{1\times d} & \mathbf{0}_{1\times d} & \mathbf{0}_{1\times d} & \cdots & \mathbf{0}_{1\times d} & \mathbf{1}_{1\times d} & \mathbf{1}_{1\times d} & \cdots & \mathbf{1}_{1\times d} \\ \mathbf{0}_{d\times 1} & \boldsymbol{I}_d & \mathbf{0}_{d\times d} & \boldsymbol{I}_d & \boldsymbol{I}_d & \cdots & \boldsymbol{I}_d & \boldsymbol{T}_d & \boldsymbol{T}_d & \cdots & \boldsymbol{T}_d \end{pmatrix},$$

$$\boldsymbol{M}_\gamma = (\mathbf{0}_{d\times 1} \quad \mathbf{0}_{d\times d} \quad \boldsymbol{I}_d \quad \boldsymbol{I}_d \quad \boldsymbol{D}_{\gamma,1} \quad \cdots \quad \boldsymbol{D}_{\gamma,d} \quad \boldsymbol{T}_d \quad \boldsymbol{T}_{\gamma,1} \quad \cdots \quad \boldsymbol{T}_{\gamma,d}).$$

Finally, γ *is said to satisfy Condition 4.1 if for any vector* $\boldsymbol{v} \in \mathbb{K}^\ell$ *of Hamming weight* $\mathrm{wt}(\boldsymbol{v}) \leq d$ *such that* $\boldsymbol{L}\boldsymbol{v}$ *contains no zero coefficient (*i.e. *is of maximum Hamming weight* $d+1$*), then* $\boldsymbol{M}_\gamma \boldsymbol{v} \neq \mathbf{0}_{d\times 1}$.

An equivalent, somewhat more convenient formulation of Condition 4.1 can be obtained by contraposition; γ satisfies Condition 4.1 if:

$$\boldsymbol{v} \in \ker(\boldsymbol{M}_\gamma) \wedge \mathrm{wt}(\boldsymbol{v}) \leq d \Rightarrow \mathrm{wt}(\boldsymbol{L}\boldsymbol{v}) < d+1. \tag{1}$$

Whichever formulation is adopted, the logic behind this condition is that a violation of the implication means that there exists a linear combination of at most d probes that depends on all the input shares (as $\boldsymbol{L}\boldsymbol{v}$ is of full weight) and on no random mask (as $\boldsymbol{M}_\gamma \boldsymbol{v} = \mathbf{0}_{d\times 1}$). In that respect, $\boldsymbol{L}$ and $\boldsymbol{M}$ behave as "indicator matrices" for the shares and masks on which depend individual probes.

3.2 Linear Randomness Complexity [BBP+17, Sect. 5]

The second scheme that we consider is defined by a single d-NI multiplication gadget over $\mathbb{K}$ that has $(d+1)$ input and output shares. An instantiation depends on a matrix $\gamma \in \mathbb{K}^{(d+1)\times d}$ whose rows sum to zero, *i.e.*, such that $\sum_{i=0}^{d} \gamma_i = \mathbf{0}_{1\times d}$.[1] This lets us defining the output shares as:

- $c_i = a_0 b_i + \sum_{j=1}^{d} (\gamma_{i,j} r_j + a_j b_i)$, $0 \leq i \leq d$,

where again $a = \sum_{i=0}^{d} a_i$, $b = \sum_{i=0}^{d} b_i$ are the shared multiplicands and the r_is are arbitrary values.

Belaïd *et al.* show that a necessary and sufficient condition for their resulting gadget to be d-NI is that γ satisfies a condition similar to Condition 4.1, stated below.

Condition 5.1 ([BBP+17]). *Let* $\gamma \in \mathbb{K}^{(d+1)\times d}$ ℓ, $\boldsymbol{D}_{\gamma,j}$, $\boldsymbol{T}_d$, $\boldsymbol{T}_{\gamma,j}$ *be as in Condition 4.1 and* $\mathbb{K}(\omega_0, \ldots, \omega_d)$ *be the field of rational fractions over indeterminates* $\omega_0, \ldots, \omega_d$*; define* $\boldsymbol{L}' \in \mathbb{K}(\omega_0, \ldots, \omega_d)^{(d+1)\times \ell}$ *and* $\boldsymbol{M}'_\gamma \in \mathbb{K}^{d\times \ell}$ *as:*

$$\boldsymbol{L}' = \begin{pmatrix} 1 & \mathbf{0}_{1\times d} & \mathbf{0}_{1\times d} & \mathbf{0}_{1\times d} & \mathbf{0}_{1\times d} & \cdots & \mathbf{0}_{1\times d} & \omega_0 \mathbf{1}_{1\times d} & \omega_1 \mathbf{1}_{1\times d} & \cdots & \omega_d \mathbf{1}_{1\times d} \\ \mathbf{0}_{d\times 1} & \boldsymbol{I}_d & \mathbf{0}_{d\times d} & \omega_0 \boldsymbol{I}_d & \omega_1 \boldsymbol{I}_d & \cdots & \omega_d \boldsymbol{I}_d & \omega_0 \boldsymbol{T}_d & \omega_1 \boldsymbol{T}_d & \cdots & \omega_d \boldsymbol{T}_d \end{pmatrix},$$

$$\boldsymbol{M}'_\gamma = (\mathbf{0}_{d\times 1} \quad \mathbf{0}_{d\times d} \quad \boldsymbol{I}_d \quad \boldsymbol{D}_{\gamma,0} \quad \boldsymbol{D}_{\gamma,1} \quad \cdots \quad \boldsymbol{D}_{\gamma,d} \quad \boldsymbol{T}_{\gamma,0} \quad \boldsymbol{T}_{\gamma,1} \quad \cdots \quad \boldsymbol{T}_{\gamma,d}).$$

Then γ *is said to satisfy Condition 5.1 if for any vector* $\boldsymbol{v} \in \mathbb{K}^\ell$ *of Hamming weight* $\mathrm{wt}(\boldsymbol{v}) \leq d$ *such that* $\boldsymbol{L}'\boldsymbol{v}$ *contains no zero coefficient, then* $\boldsymbol{M}'_\gamma \boldsymbol{v} \neq \mathbf{0}_{d\times 1}$.

[1] Note that for convenience in the subsequent share definitions and consistency with the notation of [BBP+17], the row index of γ starts from zero and not one.

Note that as $\mathbb{K}$ is a subfield of $\mathbb{K}(\omega_0, \ldots, \omega_d)$ (*viz.*the field of its constants), the product $\boldsymbol{L}'\boldsymbol{v}$ is well-defined. Also, again by contraposition, Condition 5.1 can be expressed as:

$$\boldsymbol{v} \in \ker(\boldsymbol{M}'_\gamma) \wedge \mathrm{wt}(\boldsymbol{v}) \leq d \Rightarrow \mathrm{wt}(\boldsymbol{L}'\boldsymbol{v}) < d+1. \tag{2}$$

4 Simplifying and Unifying the Conditions

In this section, we describe a few simplifications and consolidations of the correctness and safety for the two schemes described in the previous section. These simplifications are important for our analytical and algorithmic results, and the consolidations of the two schemes allow for ease in presentation.

Specifically, we develop three related conditions $\mathcal{C}$, $\mathcal{C}'$, and $\mathcal{C}''$, on the matrices $\boldsymbol{M}_\gamma$, $\boldsymbol{L}_d$, $\boldsymbol{M}'_\gamma$, and $\boldsymbol{L}'_d$ defined in Conditions 4.1 and 5.1, such that the safety of the masking schemes is guaranteed when these conditions are true. We prove that the first condition $\mathcal{C}$ and the third condition $\mathcal{C}''$ are both exactly equivalent to the requirements of Conditions 4.1 and 5.1. The second condition $\mathcal{C}'$ is always a *sufficient* condition as it implies the other two, and it is also *necessary* under a very mild condition on the cardinality of $\mathbb{K}$.

4.1 Unifying $\boldsymbol{M}_\gamma$ and $\boldsymbol{M}'_\gamma$

Recall the definitions of matrices $\boldsymbol{M}_\gamma$ from Condition 4.1 and $\boldsymbol{M}'_\gamma$ from Condition 5.1. These are both $d \times \ell$ matrices (where $\ell = 2d^2 + 4d + 1$) consisting of zeros, ones, and entries from $\boldsymbol{\gamma}$. Moreover, $\boldsymbol{M}_\gamma$ and $\boldsymbol{M}'_\gamma$ are exactly the same except for in one submatrix of d columns: this submatrix is $\boldsymbol{T}_d$ in $\boldsymbol{M}_\gamma$ and $\boldsymbol{T}_{\gamma,0}$ in $\boldsymbol{M}'_\gamma$.

We can unify these two matrices by considering, in the case of Condition 4.1, augmenting the $\boldsymbol{\gamma}$ matrix with an additional row of 1's at index 0. Then $\boldsymbol{T}_d = \boldsymbol{T}_{\gamma,0}$ and we can consider only the second form of the matrix $\boldsymbol{M}'_\gamma$.

Note that the corresponding matrices $\boldsymbol{L}_\gamma$ and $\boldsymbol{L}'_\gamma$ from Conditions 4.1 and 5.1 respectively are still not identical, but the locations of non-zero entries (*i.e.*, the *support*) in $\boldsymbol{L}_\gamma$ and $\boldsymbol{L}'_\gamma$ are the same.

Now for both schemes, there is a single matrix $\boldsymbol{\gamma} \in \mathbb{K}^{(d+1)\times d}$ which determines their *correctness* (do the output shares always correspond to the multiplication of the input value) and *safety* (is it possible for an attacker to learn any secret with at most d probes).

To succinctly state the unified condition, we first define a simple predicate $\mathcal{Z}$ for when a matrix $\boldsymbol{X} \in \mathbb{K}^{m\times n}$ (or column vector $\boldsymbol{x} \in \mathbb{K}^m$) has at least one row of zeros:

$$\mathcal{Z}(\boldsymbol{X}) := \exists i \in \{1, \ldots, m\} \text{ s.t. } \forall j \in \{1, \ldots, n\}, \boldsymbol{X}_{i,j} = 0.$$

Based on the above discussion, we define the following crucial predicate for the safety definition for two arbitrary matrices $\boldsymbol{A}$ and $\boldsymbol{B}$ with the same number of columns:

$$\mathcal{C}(\boldsymbol{A},\boldsymbol{B}) := \forall\, \boldsymbol{v} \in \ker(\boldsymbol{A}) \text{ s.t. } \mathrm{wt}(\boldsymbol{v}) \leq \mathrm{rowdim}(\boldsymbol{A}), \text{ then } \mathcal{Z}(\boldsymbol{B}\boldsymbol{v}). \tag{3}$$

Typically we will have $\boldsymbol{A} = \boldsymbol{M}'_\gamma$ and $\boldsymbol{B}$ is either $\boldsymbol{L}$ or $\boldsymbol{L}'$.

Now we can restate the correctness and safety conditions for the two schemes. The following propositions follow directly from the definitions and discussions so far.

Proposition 6. *For $\gamma \in \mathbb{K}^{(d+1)\times d}$, the scheme of Sect. 3.1 is correct and safe if and only if the following conditions are met, where $\boldsymbol{\delta} = \begin{pmatrix} \mathbf{2}_{1\times d} \\ \mathbf{1}_{d\times d} \end{pmatrix} - \gamma$:*[2]

(1) $\gamma_{0,j} = 1$ for all $j \in \{1,\ldots,d\}$
(2) $\mathcal{C}(\boldsymbol{M}'_\gamma, \boldsymbol{L})$
(3) $\mathcal{C}(\boldsymbol{M}'_\delta, \boldsymbol{L})$

Proposition 7. *For $\gamma \in \mathbb{K}^{(d+1)\times d}$, the scheme of Sect. 3.2 is correct and safe if and only if the following conditions are met:*

(1) $\sum_{i=0}^{d} \gamma_i = \mathbf{0}_{1\times d}$

(2) $\mathcal{C}(\boldsymbol{M}'_\gamma, \boldsymbol{L}')$

4.2 Equivalent Condition With Kernel Bases

Next we develop a condition similar to the definition of $\mathcal{C}(\boldsymbol{A},\boldsymbol{B})$ as defined in (3) above, but in terms of kernel bases rather than individual vectors. This modified condition is equivalent under a mild requirement on the size of the field $\mathbb{K}$.

The general idea is that rather than considering all matrix-vector products $\boldsymbol{B}\boldsymbol{v}$, where $\boldsymbol{v}$ is a d-sparse vector in the right kernel of $\boldsymbol{A}$, we consider instead the kernel basis for a size-d subset of $\boldsymbol{A}$'s columns, and multiply the corresponding columns in $\boldsymbol{B}$ times this basis. Specifying this condition requires some additional notation which will also be useful later on.

Let $\mathrm{kerb}(\boldsymbol{X})$ denote a basis of the right kernel of $\boldsymbol{X}$. That is, any vector $\boldsymbol{v} \in \ker(\boldsymbol{X})$ is a linear combination of the columns of $\mathrm{kerb}(\boldsymbol{X})$.

Let $[c_1,\ldots,c_k]$ be a list of k distinct column indices, where each $1 \leq c_i \leq \ell$. Selecting only these columns from any matrix with ℓ columns is a linear operator corresponding to a *selection matrix* $\boldsymbol{P} \in \{0,1\}^{\ell\times k}$, where $\boldsymbol{P}_{i,j} = 1$ iff $c_j = i$. Define S^ℓ_m as the set of all $\ell \times m$ selection matrices. That is, S^ℓ_m consists of all $\{0,1\}$-matrices with ℓ rows and at most m columns, where there is a single 1 in each column and no two 1s in the same row.

[2] In fields of characteristic 2, the matrix $\mathbf{2}_{1\times d}$ is actually $\mathbf{0}_{1\times d}$.

Note that the product of a selection matrix and its transpose is an identity matrix with some rows and columns set to zero. For any matrix (or vector) $\boldsymbol{X} \in \mathbb{K}^{m\times n}$ with at most k non-zero rows, there is a selection matrix $\boldsymbol{P} \in S_m^k$ such that $\boldsymbol{P}\boldsymbol{P}^T\boldsymbol{X} = \boldsymbol{X}$.

The equivalent condition to (3) that we consider now is formed by multiplying some subset of $\boldsymbol{B}$'s columns times a kernel basis of the same subset of $\boldsymbol{A}$'s columns:

$$\mathcal{C}'(\boldsymbol{A},\boldsymbol{B}) := \forall\, \boldsymbol{P} \in S^{\ell}_{\mathrm{rowdim}(\boldsymbol{A})},\ \mathcal{Z}(\boldsymbol{B}\boldsymbol{P}\cdot \mathrm{kerb}(\boldsymbol{A}\boldsymbol{P})). \tag{4}$$

One direction of the equivalence is straightforward, and the other depends on the Schwartz-Zippel lemma and therefore on the size of the field. Even so, the field size requirement here is very mild; indeed the field is sufficiently large in all cases where we are aware of any valid constructions of the schemes.

Theorem 8. *For any $\boldsymbol{A} \in \mathbb{K}^{n\times\ell}$ and $\boldsymbol{B} \in \mathbb{K}^{m\times\ell}$, we have $\mathcal{C}'(\boldsymbol{A},\boldsymbol{B}) \Rightarrow \mathcal{C}(\boldsymbol{A},\boldsymbol{B})$. If $\mathbb{K}$ has at least $m+1$ distinct elements, then $\mathcal{C}'(\boldsymbol{A},\boldsymbol{B}) \Leftarrow \mathcal{C}(\boldsymbol{A},\boldsymbol{B})$ also.*

Proof. We begin with the "⇒" direction.

Let $\boldsymbol{v}$ be a vector satisfying the conditions of $\mathcal{C}(\boldsymbol{A},\boldsymbol{B})$; that is, $\boldsymbol{v} \in \ker \boldsymbol{A}$ and $\mathrm{wt}(\boldsymbol{v}) \le \mathrm{rowdim}(\boldsymbol{A})$. The latter fact means that there exists $\boldsymbol{P} \in S^{\ell}_{\mathrm{rowdim}(\boldsymbol{A})}$ such that $\boldsymbol{P}\boldsymbol{P}^T\boldsymbol{v} = \boldsymbol{v}$.

Because $\boldsymbol{A}\boldsymbol{v} = \boldsymbol{0}$, we then have $(\boldsymbol{A}\boldsymbol{P})(\boldsymbol{P}^T\boldsymbol{v}) = \boldsymbol{0}$, which means that the vector $\boldsymbol{P}^T\boldsymbol{v}$ is a linear combination of the columns of $\mathrm{kerb}(\boldsymbol{A}\boldsymbol{P})$.

The condition $\mathcal{C}(\boldsymbol{A},\boldsymbol{B})$ concerns the matrix-vector product $\boldsymbol{B}\boldsymbol{v}$, which equals $\boldsymbol{B}\boldsymbol{P}\boldsymbol{P}^T\boldsymbol{v}$. From above, we know that this is a linear combination of the columns in the matrix $\boldsymbol{B}\boldsymbol{P}\cdot\mathrm{kerb}(\boldsymbol{A}\boldsymbol{P})$. By the assumption that $\mathcal{C}'(\boldsymbol{A},\boldsymbol{B})$, this matrix contains a zero row, and therefore any linear combination of its columns also contains a zero row; hence $\mathcal{Z}(\boldsymbol{B}\boldsymbol{v})$.

For the "⇐" direction, we prove using the contrapositive. Assume there exists some selection of columns $\boldsymbol{P} \in S^{\ell}_n$ such that $\neg\,\mathcal{Z}(\boldsymbol{B}\boldsymbol{P}\cdot\mathrm{kerb}(\boldsymbol{A}\boldsymbol{P}))$. We need to show that $\neg\,\mathcal{C}(\boldsymbol{A},\boldsymbol{B})$.

Suppose the column dimension of $\mathrm{kerb}(\boldsymbol{A}\boldsymbol{P})$ (*i.e.*, the nullity of $\boldsymbol{A}\boldsymbol{P}$) is k, and let $\boldsymbol{x}$ be a column vector of k indeterminates $x_1,\ldots,x_k$. Now consider the matrix-vector product $\boldsymbol{B}\boldsymbol{P}\cdot\mathrm{kerb}(\boldsymbol{A}\boldsymbol{P})\cdot\boldsymbol{x}$. This is a column vector of dimension m consisting of degree-1 polynomials in the k indeterminates. Furthermore, none of these polynomials is zero because of the assumption $\neg\,\mathcal{Z}(\boldsymbol{B}\boldsymbol{P}\cdot\mathrm{kerb}(\boldsymbol{A}\boldsymbol{P}))$.

The product of the m polynomials in $\boldsymbol{B}\boldsymbol{P}\cdot\mathrm{kerb}(\boldsymbol{A}\boldsymbol{P})\cdot\boldsymbol{x}$ is a single non-zero polynomial in k variables with total degree m. By the Schwartz-Zippel-DeMillo-Lipton lemma [Sch80, Corollary 1], and because $\#\mathbb{K} > m$, there must exist some assignment of the k variables to values in $\mathbb{K}$ such that this product polynomial is non-zero. That is, there exists some column vector $\boldsymbol{w} \in \mathbb{K}^k$ such that $\mathrm{wt}(\boldsymbol{B}\boldsymbol{P}\cdot\mathrm{kerb}(\boldsymbol{A}\boldsymbol{P})\cdot\boldsymbol{w}) = m$.

Because $\mathrm{kerb}(\boldsymbol{A}\boldsymbol{P})\cdot\boldsymbol{w} \in \mathbb{K}^n$, there is an n-sparse vector $\boldsymbol{v} \in \mathbb{K}^{\ell}$ such that $\boldsymbol{P}^T\boldsymbol{v} = \mathrm{kerb}(\boldsymbol{A}\boldsymbol{P})\cdot\boldsymbol{w}$. This vector $\boldsymbol{v}$ shows that $\mathcal{C}(\boldsymbol{A},\boldsymbol{B})$ is false. Namely, $\boldsymbol{v} \in \ker(\boldsymbol{A})$ because $\boldsymbol{A}\boldsymbol{v} = (\boldsymbol{A}\boldsymbol{P})(\boldsymbol{P}^T\boldsymbol{v}) = \boldsymbol{0}$; it has low weight $\mathrm{wt}(\boldsymbol{v}) \le n$; and $\boldsymbol{B}\boldsymbol{v} = (\boldsymbol{B}\boldsymbol{P})(\boldsymbol{P}^T\boldsymbol{v})$ is of full weight m from the previous paragraph. □

4.3 Eliminating Rows and Columns

The third simplification to the correctness and safety conditions of the two masking schemes that we develop is an equivalent condition to $\mathcal{C}(\boldsymbol{A}, \boldsymbol{B})$ that depends on less than half of the columns in the original matrices. The intuition is that most of the columns of these matrices have weight 1, and thus those probes in the masking scheme do not gain the attacker any real advantage. So we can focus on only the parts of $\boldsymbol{A}$ and $\boldsymbol{B}$ whose columns have weight greater than 1. We first develop some new terminology to talk about these submatrices, then prove a lemma which shows how to eliminate columns from γ corresponding to the weight-one probes, and finally state and prove the equivalent condition $\mathcal{C}''$.

So far the schemes are both defined by a matrix γ with $d+1$ rows and d columns. In fact, the definitions of matrices $\boldsymbol{M}_\gamma$, $\boldsymbol{M}'_\gamma$, $\boldsymbol{L}$, and $\boldsymbol{L}'$ from Conditions 4.1 and 5.1 generalize to any rectangular matrix $\gamma \in \mathbb{K}^{(d+1)\times n}$. If γ has $d+1$ rows and n columns, then $\boldsymbol{M}_\gamma$ and $\boldsymbol{M}'_\gamma$ both have n rows, while $\boldsymbol{L}_n$ and $\boldsymbol{L}'_n$ have $n+1$ rows, and all four matrices have $\ell_n = 2dn + 4n + 1$ columns.

We focus on the bottom-right $n \times (dn+n)$ submatrix of each $\boldsymbol{M}'_\gamma$, $\boldsymbol{L}_n$ and $\boldsymbol{L}'_n$, which we call the "triangular part" of each. Formally, we define a linear operator $\boldsymbol{\Delta}$ such that, for any matrix $\boldsymbol{A}$ with n or $n+1$ rows and $2dn+4n+1$ columns, $\boldsymbol{\Delta}(\boldsymbol{A})$ consists of the bottom-right $n \times (dn+n)$ submatrix of $\boldsymbol{A}$.

In summary, we have:

$$\boldsymbol{L}_n = \Bigg(\underbrace{\begin{matrix} 1 & \boldsymbol{0}_{1\times n} & \boldsymbol{0}_{1\times n} & \boldsymbol{0}_{1\times n} & \boldsymbol{0}_{1\times n} & \cdots & \boldsymbol{0}_{1\times n} & \boldsymbol{1}_{1\times n} & \boldsymbol{1}_{1\times n} & \cdots & \boldsymbol{1}_{1\times n} \\ \boldsymbol{0}_{n\times 1} & \boldsymbol{I}_n & \boldsymbol{0}_{n\times n} & \boldsymbol{I}_n & \boldsymbol{I}_n & & \boldsymbol{I}_n & \boldsymbol{T}_n & \boldsymbol{T}_n & & \boldsymbol{T}_n \end{matrix}}_{\boldsymbol{\Delta}(\boldsymbol{L}_n)} \Bigg),$$

$$\boldsymbol{L}'_n = \Bigg(\underbrace{\begin{matrix} 1 & \boldsymbol{0}_{1\times n} & \boldsymbol{0}_{1\times n} & \boldsymbol{0}_{1\times n} & \boldsymbol{0}_{1\times n} & \cdots & \boldsymbol{0}_{1\times n} & \omega_0\boldsymbol{1}_{1\times n} & \omega_1\boldsymbol{1}_{1\times n} & \cdots & \omega_d\boldsymbol{1}_{1\times n} \\ \boldsymbol{0}_{n\times 1} & \boldsymbol{I}_n & \boldsymbol{0}_{n\times n} & \omega_0\boldsymbol{I}_n & \omega_1\boldsymbol{I}_n & & \omega_d\boldsymbol{I}_n & \omega_0\boldsymbol{T}_n & \omega_1\boldsymbol{T}_n & & \omega_d\boldsymbol{T}_n \end{matrix}}_{\boldsymbol{\Delta}(\boldsymbol{L}'_n)} \Bigg),$$

$$\boldsymbol{M}'_\gamma = \big(\boldsymbol{0}_{n\times 1}\ \boldsymbol{0}_{n\times n}\ \ \boldsymbol{I}_n\ \ \boldsymbol{D}_{\gamma,0}\ \boldsymbol{D}_{\gamma,1} \cdots \boldsymbol{D}_{\gamma,d}\ \underbrace{\boldsymbol{T}_{\gamma,0}\ \ \boldsymbol{T}_{\gamma,1}\ \cdots\ \boldsymbol{T}_{\gamma,d}}_{\boldsymbol{\Delta}(\boldsymbol{M}'_\gamma)} \big).$$

Notice that the matrices $\boldsymbol{L}_n$ and $\boldsymbol{L}'_n$ have some different entries but the same support; for convenience we denote by $\boldsymbol{N}_n$ any matrix with this same dimension and support.

Inspecting the definition of $\boldsymbol{M}'_\gamma$, we see that rows of this matrix correspond to columns of γ, and removing one column of γ corresponds to removing a single row and $2d+4$ columns from each of $\boldsymbol{M}'_\gamma$ and $\boldsymbol{N}$.

Notice also that the columns of $\boldsymbol{M}'_\gamma$ and of $\boldsymbol{L}_n$ which are not in the triangular parts all have weight at most one. This means, as we show in the following technical lemma, that the effect of any such column choice (as a probe) can be eliminated by removing one row each from $\boldsymbol{M}'_\gamma$ and $\boldsymbol{L}_n$. In terms of masking schemes, this means that a single probe corresponding to these non-triangular parts allows the adversary to cancel at most one random value and to learn at most one share. Because the number of shares is $d+1$ in a scheme allowing d probes, this results in no advantage for the adversary.

Lemma 9. *Let* $\gamma \in \mathbb{K}^{(d+1)\times n}$, $\boldsymbol{M}'_\gamma$ *and* $\boldsymbol{N}_n$ *be as above. Suppose* $\boldsymbol{u} \in \mathbb{K}^{\ell_n}$ *is a vector with* $\mathrm{wt}(\boldsymbol{u}) = 1$ *whose single non-zero entry is between index* 2 *and* $dn+3n+1$ *inclusive, and* $\boldsymbol{v} \in \mathbb{K}^{\ell_n}$ *is any other vector. Then there exists a selection matrix* $\boldsymbol{P} \in S^n_{n-1}$ *and another vector* $\boldsymbol{w} \in \mathbb{K}^{\ell_{n-1}}$ *with* $\mathrm{wt}(\boldsymbol{w}) \leq \mathrm{wt}(\boldsymbol{v})$ *such that*

$$\mathrm{wt}(\boldsymbol{M}'_{\gamma\boldsymbol{P}}\boldsymbol{w}) \leq \mathrm{wt}(\boldsymbol{M}'_\gamma(\boldsymbol{u}+\boldsymbol{v})) \quad \textit{and} \quad \mathrm{wt}(\boldsymbol{N}_{n-1}\boldsymbol{w}) \geq \mathrm{wt}(\boldsymbol{N}_n(\boldsymbol{u}+\boldsymbol{v})) - 1.$$

Proof. Write i for the index of the non-zero entry in $\boldsymbol{u}$. We can see that the ith column of $\boldsymbol{M}'_\gamma$ and $\boldsymbol{N}_n$ both have weight at most one. Indeed, for each $i \in \{2,\ldots,dn+3n+1\}$, there is a corresponding index $j \in \{1,\ldots,n\}$ such that the ith columns of $\boldsymbol{M}'_\gamma$ and $\boldsymbol{N}_n$ are zero everywhere except possibly in row j (provided that we continue to index the rows of $\boldsymbol{N}_n$ starting at 0).

Removing the jth row from $\boldsymbol{M}'_\gamma$ and $\boldsymbol{N}_n$ results in two new matrices $\boldsymbol{A}, \boldsymbol{B}$ (respectively) whose ith columns are both zero, and hence $\boldsymbol{Au} = \boldsymbol{0}$ and $\boldsymbol{Bu} = \boldsymbol{0}$. This means that

$$\mathrm{wt}(\boldsymbol{Av}) = \mathrm{wt}(\boldsymbol{A}(\boldsymbol{u}+\boldsymbol{v})) \leq \mathrm{wt}(\boldsymbol{M}'_\gamma(\boldsymbol{u}+\boldsymbol{v}))$$
$$\mathrm{wt}(\boldsymbol{Bv}) = \mathrm{wt}(\boldsymbol{B}(\boldsymbol{u}+\boldsymbol{v})) \geq \mathrm{wt}(\boldsymbol{N}_n(\boldsymbol{u}+\boldsymbol{v})) - 1.$$

Write $\boldsymbol{P} \in S^n_{n-1}$ as the matrix which selects all n columns of $\boldsymbol{\gamma}$ except for the jth column. Now $\boldsymbol{A}$ and $\boldsymbol{B}$ are the same as $\boldsymbol{M}'_{\gamma\boldsymbol{P}}$ and $\boldsymbol{N}_{n-1}$ respectively, except that they each have $2d+4$ extra columns. The remaining task is to modify $\boldsymbol{v}$ so that it is zero at all the indices corresponding to these extra columns, without changing $\mathrm{wt}(\boldsymbol{Av})$ or $\mathrm{wt}(\boldsymbol{Bv})$.

We can see that $d+3$ of these extra columns come from the first $dn+3n+1$ columns of $\boldsymbol{M}'_\gamma$ and $\boldsymbol{N}_n$ and, since the jth row has been removed, they are in fact now zero columns. So letting $\boldsymbol{v}'$ be the same as $\boldsymbol{v}$ with any such entries set to zero, we do not change the products $\boldsymbol{Av}'$ or $\boldsymbol{Bv}'$ at all.

The $d+1$ remaining extra columns come from the triangular parts $\boldsymbol{\Delta}(\boldsymbol{M}'_\gamma)$ and $\boldsymbol{\Delta}(\boldsymbol{N}_n)$. There are now two cases to consider. First, if $j=1$, *i.e.*, we have removed the second row of $\boldsymbol{N}_n$ and the first row of $\boldsymbol{M}'_\gamma$. Then these extra columns from the triangular part of $\boldsymbol{A}$ are all zero columns, and from $\boldsymbol{B}$ they have the form $(a\ 0\ \cdots\ 0)^T$ for some non-zero entry a in the first row of $\boldsymbol{N}_n$. Upon inspection, we see that these columns are exactly a times the very first columns of $\boldsymbol{A}$ and $\boldsymbol{B}$ respectively. Therefore we can modify the vector $\boldsymbol{v}'$ to a new vector $\boldsymbol{v}''$, where any non-zero entries in such positions are divided by a and added to the first entry, then set to zero. This does not change the value of $\boldsymbol{Av}''$ or $\boldsymbol{Bv}''$.

The second case is that $j \geq 2$, *i.e.*, we have removed a later row. Then the extra columns in $\boldsymbol{A}$ and $\boldsymbol{B}$ are exactly identical to the columns immediately to their left in the respective matrices. So we can form $\boldsymbol{v}''$ in this case by adding any non-zero entry of $\boldsymbol{v}'$ in such positions to the adjacent position and then setting it to zero, without changing $\boldsymbol{Av}''$ or $\boldsymbol{Bv}''$.

After this, we have a vector $\boldsymbol{v}''$ with $\text{wt}(\boldsymbol{v}'') \leq \text{wt}(\boldsymbol{v})$, and with zeros in all of the "extra column" indices of $\boldsymbol{A}$ and $\boldsymbol{B}$, such that $\text{wt}(\boldsymbol{A}\boldsymbol{v}'') \leq \text{wt}(\boldsymbol{M}'_\gamma(\boldsymbol{u}+\boldsymbol{v}))$ and $\text{wt}(\boldsymbol{B}\boldsymbol{v}'') \geq \text{wt}(\boldsymbol{N}_n(\boldsymbol{u}+\boldsymbol{v})) - 1$. Finally, setting $\boldsymbol{w}$ to be the sub-vector of $\boldsymbol{v}''$ with these extra column entries removed completes the proof. □

Repeated application of the previous lemma allows us to completely eliminate all of the columns in $\boldsymbol{M}'_\gamma$ and $\boldsymbol{N}_n$ other than the triangular parts, at the cost of having to consider all possible column-subsets of γ itself. This leads to the following condition:

$$\mathcal{C}''(\boldsymbol{M}'_\gamma, \boldsymbol{N}_n) := \ \forall k \in \{1, \ldots, n\}, \forall \boldsymbol{P} \in S^n_k,\ \mathcal{C}(\boldsymbol{\Delta}(\boldsymbol{M}'_{\gamma\boldsymbol{P}}), \boldsymbol{\Delta}(\boldsymbol{N}_k)). \qquad (5)$$

In other words, we restrict our attention to only square submatrices of the triangular parts of $\boldsymbol{M}'_\gamma$ and $\boldsymbol{N}_n$. As it turns out, this condition is exactly equivalent to the original one.

Theorem 10. *For any field $\mathbb{K}$, matrix $\gamma \in \mathbb{K}^{(d+1)\times n}$ where $n \geq 1$, and matrix $\boldsymbol{N}_n \in \{\boldsymbol{L}_n, \boldsymbol{L}'_n\}$, we have $\mathcal{C}''(\boldsymbol{M}'_\gamma, \boldsymbol{N}_n) \Leftrightarrow \mathcal{C}(\boldsymbol{M}'_\gamma, \boldsymbol{N}_n)$.*

Proof. We prove the equivalent double negation $\neg\mathcal{C}(\boldsymbol{M}'_\gamma, \boldsymbol{N}_n) \Leftrightarrow \neg\mathcal{C}''(\boldsymbol{M}'_\gamma, \boldsymbol{N}_n)$.

First we prove the "$\Rightarrow$" direction by induction on n. Assuming that $\neg\mathcal{C}(\boldsymbol{M}'_\gamma, \boldsymbol{N}_n)$ means there exists a vector $\boldsymbol{v} \in \mathbb{K}^{\ell_n}$ such that $\text{wt}(\boldsymbol{v}) \leq n$, $\boldsymbol{M}'_\gamma \boldsymbol{v} = \boldsymbol{0}$, and $\boldsymbol{N}_n \boldsymbol{v}$ has full weight $n+1$.

For the base case, let $n = 1$. Because $\text{wt}(\boldsymbol{v}) = 1$ and $\text{wt}(\boldsymbol{N}_n \boldsymbol{v}) = 2$, the lone non-zero entry of $\boldsymbol{v}$ must correspond to a weight-2 column in $\boldsymbol{N}_n$, and the only such columns are in the triangular part. So considering the vector formed from the last $d+1$ entries of $\boldsymbol{v}$ shows that $\neg\mathcal{C}(\boldsymbol{\Delta}(\boldsymbol{M}'_\gamma), \boldsymbol{\Delta}(\boldsymbol{N}_n))$, which is equivalent to $\neg\mathcal{C}''(\boldsymbol{M}'_\gamma, \boldsymbol{N}_n)$ when $n = 1$.

Now for the induction case, let $n \geq 2$ and assume the $\Rightarrow$ direction is true for all size-$(n-1)$ subsets of columns of γ.

Again we start with a vector $\boldsymbol{v}$ which is a counterexample to $\mathcal{C}(\boldsymbol{M}'_\gamma, \boldsymbol{N}_n)$. If $\boldsymbol{v}$ has any non-zero entry in indices 2 through $dn+3n+1$, then we can isolate that entry in its own vector $\boldsymbol{u}$ and write $\boldsymbol{v} = \boldsymbol{u}+\boldsymbol{v}^*$, where $\text{wt}(\boldsymbol{v}^*) = \text{wt}(\boldsymbol{v})-1 \leq n-1$. Now apply Lemma 9 to obtain a vector $\boldsymbol{w} \in \mathbb{K}^{\ell_{n-1}}$ and a selection matrix $\boldsymbol{P} \in S^n_{n-1}$ such that $\text{wt}(\boldsymbol{w}) \leq n-1$, $\boldsymbol{M}'_{\gamma\boldsymbol{P}}\boldsymbol{w} = \boldsymbol{0}$, and $\text{wt}(\boldsymbol{N}_{n-1}\boldsymbol{w}) = n-1$. Therefore $\neg\mathcal{C}(\boldsymbol{M}'_{\gamma\boldsymbol{P}}, \boldsymbol{N}_{n-1})$, so we can apply the induction hypothesis to complete this sub-case.

Otherwise, the non-zero entries of $\boldsymbol{v}$ are in the very first index, or in the last $(d+1)n$ indices which correspond to the triangular parts. But the first columns of $\boldsymbol{N}_n$ and $\boldsymbol{M}'_\gamma$ are all zeros except for the first row in $\boldsymbol{N}_n$, which is eliminated in the triangular part $\boldsymbol{\Delta}(\boldsymbol{N}_n)$. Therefore, if this entry of $\boldsymbol{v}$ is non-zero, we can change it to zero without affecting $\boldsymbol{M}'_\gamma \boldsymbol{v}$, which must equal $\boldsymbol{0}$, or the last n rows of $\boldsymbol{N}_n \boldsymbol{v}$, which must be all non-zero. Hence the vector consisting of the last $(d+1)n$ entries of $\boldsymbol{v}$ is a counterexample to $\mathcal{C}(\boldsymbol{\Delta}(\boldsymbol{M}'_\gamma), \boldsymbol{\Delta}(\boldsymbol{N}_n))$. This completes the $\Rightarrow$ direction of the proof.

For the $\Leftarrow$ direction, assume that $\neg\mathcal{C}''(\boldsymbol{M}'_\gamma, \boldsymbol{N}_n)$. This means there is some $k \in \{1, \ldots, n\}$, some selection of columns from γ defined by $\boldsymbol{P} \in S_k^n$, and some $\boldsymbol{v} \in \mathbb{K}^{\ell_k}$ such that $\mathrm{wt}(\boldsymbol{v}) \le k$, $\boldsymbol{\Delta}(\boldsymbol{M}'_{\gamma\boldsymbol{P}})\boldsymbol{v} = \boldsymbol{0}$, and $\boldsymbol{\Delta}(\boldsymbol{N}_k)\boldsymbol{v}$ has full weight k.

Because the triangular part is a subset of the whole, we can prepend $\boldsymbol{v}$ with $dk + 3k + 1$ zeros to obtain a vector $\boldsymbol{v}'$ such that $\boldsymbol{M}'_{\gamma\boldsymbol{P}}\boldsymbol{v}' = \boldsymbol{0}$ and $\boldsymbol{N}_k\boldsymbol{v}'$ is non-zero everywhere except possibly in the first row. Observe that the row of $\boldsymbol{N}_k$ immediately above the triangular part is exactly identical to the top row of $\boldsymbol{\Delta}(\boldsymbol{N}_k)$, so in fact $\boldsymbol{N}_k\boldsymbol{v}'$ has full weight $k+1$.

This shows that there exists at least one $k \ge 1$ such that there exists a selection $\boldsymbol{P} \in S_k^n$ and a vector $\boldsymbol{v}'$ which is a counterexample to $\mathcal{C}(\boldsymbol{M}'_{\gamma\boldsymbol{P}}, \boldsymbol{N}_k)$. Assume now that k is the *largest* such integer.

If $k = n$, then $\boldsymbol{M}'_{\gamma\boldsymbol{P}} = \boldsymbol{M}'_\gamma$, and $\boldsymbol{v}'$ is a counterexample to $\mathcal{C}(\boldsymbol{M}'_\gamma, \boldsymbol{N}_n)$ already.

Otherwise, if $k < n$, we show that we can construct a larger selection matrix $\boldsymbol{Q}$ and corresponding vector $\boldsymbol{w}$ satisfying the conditions above, which is a contradiction to the assumption that k is the largest such value.

Construct another selection matrix $\boldsymbol{Q} \in S_{k+1}^n$ consisting of the columns selected by $\boldsymbol{P}$ plus some additional column i; for convenience write $\zeta = \gamma\boldsymbol{Q}$. Note that $\boldsymbol{M}'_{\gamma\boldsymbol{P}}$ and $\boldsymbol{N}_k$ are submatrices of $\boldsymbol{M}'_\zeta$ and $\boldsymbol{N}_{k+1}$ respectively, the latter both having exactly one more row and some number of extra columns. Therefore by extending $\boldsymbol{v}'$ to a larger vector $\boldsymbol{v}''$ by inserting zeros in the locations of these extra columns, we have that $\boldsymbol{M}'_\zeta\boldsymbol{v}''$ is zero everywhere except possibly at index i, and $\boldsymbol{N}_{k+1}\boldsymbol{v}''$ is non-zero everywhere except at index i. Let a be the ith entry of $\boldsymbol{M}'_\zeta\boldsymbol{v}''$ and b be the ith entry of $\boldsymbol{N}_{k+1}\boldsymbol{v}''$.

Finally, we show how to add one more entry to $\boldsymbol{v}''$ to "fix" the exceptions at index i in the previous sentence, making $a = 0$ and $b \ne 0$. There are four cases to consider:

1. If $a = 0$ and $b \ne 0$, then we are done.
2. If $a = 0$ and $b = 0$, then set the $(i+1)$th entry of $\boldsymbol{v}$ to 1; this corresponds to a column of zeros in $\boldsymbol{M}'_\zeta$ and a column of the identity matrix in $\boldsymbol{N}_{k+1}$. So adding that column keeps $a = 0$ but sets b to 1.
3. If $a \ne 0$ and $b \ne 0$, then set the $(k+i+1)$th entry of $\boldsymbol{v}$ to $-a$. This entry corresponds to a column of the identity matrix in $\boldsymbol{M}'_\zeta$ and a column of zeros in $\boldsymbol{N}_{k+1}$, so adding it keeps $b \ne 0$ but cancels the value of a.
4. If $a \ne 0$ and $b = 0$, then set the $(2k+i+2)$th entry of $\boldsymbol{v}$ to $-a/\zeta_{0,i}$. This entry corresponds to a column of $\boldsymbol{D}_{\zeta,0}$ in $\boldsymbol{M}'_\zeta$, and a column of either $\boldsymbol{I}_{k+1}$ or $\omega_0\boldsymbol{I}_{k+1}$ within $\boldsymbol{N}_{k+1}$, and therefore the change to $\boldsymbol{v}$ cancels out a and sets b to some non-zero value.

This newly constructed vector has weight at most $\mathrm{wt}(\boldsymbol{v}'') + 1 \le k + 1$, and is therefore a counterexample to $\mathcal{C}(\boldsymbol{M}'_\zeta, \boldsymbol{N}_{k+1})$. This is a contradiction to the assumption that k was maximal, which completes the $\Leftarrow$ direction and the entire proof. $\square$

5 A Matrix Precondition

We use the results of the previous two sections to develop a useful precondition for generating γ matrices which satisfy the safety and correctness conditions of the two schemes. This precondition guarantees the correctness conditions, and (as we will see in later sections) seems to increase the probability that a matrix satisfies the safety condition. We then show how to explicitly generate matrices which satisfy these preconditions.

5.1 Definitions

As in the previous section, let $\gamma \in \mathbb{K}^{(d+1)\times d}$ be a matrix whose entries determine the correctness and safety of one of the two masking schemes according to Proposition 6 or Proposition 7. (Either γ must have a row equal to $\mathbf{1}$, or they must sum to $\mathbf{0}$.)

Then Theorems 8 and 10 tell us that a sufficient condition for safety is that for every square submatrix of $\boldsymbol{\Delta}(\boldsymbol{M}'_\gamma)$, all vectors in its right kernel have at least one joint zero entry when multiplied with the corresponding submatrix of $\boldsymbol{\Delta}(\boldsymbol{N}_d)$. The general idea of the preconditions developed in this section is to *minimize the rank of this right kernel*, effectively limiting the number of possible "unsafe" vectors. In particular, when a square submatrix of $\boldsymbol{\Delta}(\boldsymbol{M}'_\gamma)$ is non-singular, then its nullity is zero and the scheme is safe with respect to that subset of rows and columns.

This suggests a strategy to increase the likelihood of a matrix leading to a safe scheme: one may try to choose γ in a way that ensures that $\boldsymbol{\Delta}(\boldsymbol{M}'_{\gamma\boldsymbol{P}})\boldsymbol{Q}$ has a trivial kernel for as many selection matrices $\boldsymbol{P} \in S^d_k$ and $\boldsymbol{Q} \in S^{\ell_k}_k$ as possible. That is, square submatrices of the triangular part of $\boldsymbol{M}'_\gamma$ should be non-singular as often as possible.

A good such choice for γ is to take it to be such that all its square submatrices are MDS. To justify this claim, recall from Sect. 2 that any square submatrix of an MDS matrix is invertible, *i.e.*, has a trivial kernel. Further, from the definition of $\boldsymbol{\Delta}(\boldsymbol{M}'_\gamma)$, its columns consist of (partial) rows of γ; therefore many of its submatrices are in fact (transposed) submatrices of γ itself.

Example 11. Consider for the case $d = 3$, the submatrix of $\boldsymbol{\Delta}(\boldsymbol{M}'_\gamma)$ given by:

$$\boldsymbol{X} = \begin{pmatrix} \gamma_{0,1} & \gamma_{1,1} & \gamma_{2,1} \\ 0 & \gamma_{1,2} & \gamma_{2,2} \\ 0 & \gamma_{1,3} & \gamma_{2,3} \end{pmatrix}.$$

(Note that in the case of Condition 4.1, $\gamma_{0,1}$ must equal 1.) If all square submatrices of γ are MDS, the bottom-right 2×2 submatrix of $\boldsymbol{X}$ is necessarily non-singular, and $\gamma_{0,1} \neq 0$, so therefore this entire submatrix is non-singular. This would not be the case for an arbitrary matrix γ, even if say, one takes it to be full-rank.

We now state our two *preconditions* on the matrices used to instantiate either masking scheme. As will be clear in the remainder of this paper, these preconditions are by no means sufficient, nor necessary. Yet we will also see, both formally (in Sect. 6) and experimentally (in Sect. 8) how they may be useful.

Precondition 4.1. *A matrix* $\gamma \in \mathbb{K}^{(d+1)\times d}$ satisfies Precondition *4.1 for Condition 4.1 if it can be written as* $\gamma = \begin{pmatrix} \mathbf{1}_{1\times d} \\ \boldsymbol{A} \end{pmatrix}$, *and both matrices* $\boldsymbol{A}$ *and* $\mathbf{1}_{d\times d} - \boldsymbol{A}$ *are row XMDS.*

Any such matrix $\boldsymbol{\gamma}$ clearly satisfies the correctness condition, which is item (1) in Proposition 6. The XMDS property also ensures that all square submatrices of $\boldsymbol{\gamma}$ and $\boldsymbol{\delta}$ are non-singular, which (we expect) will make the safety conditions (2) and (3) from Proposition 6 more likely satisfied.

Precondition 5.1. *A matrix* $\gamma \in \mathbb{K}^{(d+1)\times d}$ satisfies Precondition *5.1 for Condition 5.1 if* $\sum_{i=0}^{d} \gamma_i = \mathbf{0}_{1\times d}$ *and all of its square submatrices are MDS.*

Again, this precondition guarantees the correctness of the scheme, corresponding to item (1) of Proposition 7, and the non-singular submatrices make it (we expect) more likely that the safety condition, item (2), is also true.

5.2 Explicit constructions

It is relatively easy to check if a given matrix satisfies either of the above preconditions. Here we do even better, providing a direct construction for families of matrices that satisfy each of them.

Theorem 12 (Satisfying Precondition 4.1). *Let* $\{x_1, \ldots, x_d, y_1, \ldots, y_d\} \in \mathbb{K}\backslash\{0\}$ *be* $2d$ *distinct non-zero elements of* $\mathbb{K}$*, and define matrix* $\boldsymbol{A} \in \mathbb{K}^{d\times d}$ *by* $\boldsymbol{A}_{i,j} = x_i/(x_i - y_j)$. *Then the corresponding* $\gamma \in \mathbb{K}^{(d+1)\times d}$ *satisfies Precondition 4.1.*

Proof. Define the row-extended Cauchy matrix $\boldsymbol{B}$ as $\boldsymbol{B}_{0,j} = 1, 1 \le j \le d$; $\boldsymbol{B}_{i,j} = (x_i - y_j)^{-1}, 1 \le i,j \le d$. The generalized extended matrix obtained from $\boldsymbol{B}$ by the row scaling $\boldsymbol{c} = \begin{pmatrix} 1 \; x_1 \cdots x_d \end{pmatrix}$ is equal to $\boldsymbol{\gamma}$, and all its square submatrices are invertible by construction, hence $\boldsymbol{A}$ is row XMDS.

The matrix $\boldsymbol{C} = \mathbf{1}_{d\times d} - \boldsymbol{A}$ is given by $\left((x_i - y_j - x_i)\cdot(x_i - y_j)^{-1}\right) = \left(-y_j \cdot (x_i - y_j)^{-1}\right)$. It is a generalized Cauchy matrix with column scaling given by $\begin{pmatrix} -y_1 \ldots -y_d \end{pmatrix}^T$, and is then MDS. Because $0 \notin \{x_1, \ldots, x_d, y_1, \ldots, y_d\}$, one may extend $\boldsymbol{C}$ by one row on top using $x_0 = 0$, resulting in $\boldsymbol{C}'$ s.t. $\boldsymbol{C}'_{0,j} = -y_j \cdot (0 - y_j)^{-1} = 1, 1 \le j \le d$; $\boldsymbol{C}'_{i,j} = \boldsymbol{C}_{i,j}, 1 \le i,j \le d$. In other words,

$$\boldsymbol{C}' = \begin{pmatrix} \mathbf{1}_{1\times d} \\ \boldsymbol{C} \end{pmatrix}$$

is a generalized Cauchy matrix, whose square submatrices are all invertible by construction, hence $\boldsymbol{C} = \mathbf{1}_{d\times d} - \boldsymbol{A}$ is row XMDS. □

Theorem 13 (Satisfying Precondition 5.1**).** *Let* $\{x_1, \ldots, x_d, x_{d+1}, y_1, \ldots, y_d\} \in \mathbb{K}$ *be* $2d+1$ *distinct elements of* $\mathbb{K}$*; let* $\boldsymbol{A} = \left((x_i - y_j)^{-1}\right)$*; and let* $\boldsymbol{c} = \begin{pmatrix} c_1 \cdots c_{d+1} \end{pmatrix}$ *be a non-zero vector in the left kernel of* $\boldsymbol{A}$*. Then* $\gamma = \left(c_i \cdot (x_i - y_j)^{-1}\right)$ *satisfies Precondition 5.1.*

Proof. By construction, the $d+1 \times d$ Cauchy matrix $\boldsymbol{A}$ has a left kernel of dimension one. Furthermore, any vector of this kernel that is not the null vector is of full Hamming weight, as being otherwise would imply the existence of $k \leq d$ linearly-dependent rows of $\boldsymbol{A}$. The row scaling coefficients $\begin{pmatrix} c_1 \cdots c_{d+1} \end{pmatrix}$ are thus all non-zero, and the generalized Cauchy matrix $\boldsymbol{A}'$ is such that its rows sum to the null vector and all its square submatrices are invertible. □

6 Analytic Construction for Order up to 3

In this section, we develop explicit polynomial conditions on the entries of generalized Cauchy matrices that are sufficient to ensure both the correctness and safety of the two masking schemes described in Sect. 3.

The results are explicit constructions for many field sizes. For order $d = 1$, Corollary 15 proves that any non-zero γ matrix makes the scheme secure. For order $d = 2$, Corollary 16 proves that our MDS preconditions of the previous section always produce safe constructions without the need for any further checks. Finally, for order $d = 3$, Theorems 19 and 21 provide x_i and y_i values to use in order to generate safe Cauchy matrices for any field of characteristic 2 with $q \geq 4$.

The idea behind our preconditions in Sect. 5 was to ensure that all square submatrices of γ are non-singular, and therefore *many* square submatrices of the matrix $\boldsymbol{\Delta}(\boldsymbol{M}'_\gamma)$ have nullity zero. For small dimensions, we can go further and actually require that *all* submatrices of $\boldsymbol{\Delta}(\boldsymbol{M}'_\gamma)$ which could possibly violate the condition $\mathcal{C}''$ from (5) are non-singular. This will in turn guarantee a safe and correct construction by Theorem 10 and Propositions 6 and 7.

6.1 Columns Which Must be Selected

Let $\gamma \in \mathbb{K}^{(d+1)\times n}$ and recall the definitions of $\boldsymbol{\Delta}(\boldsymbol{N}_n)$ and $\boldsymbol{\Delta}(\boldsymbol{M}'_\gamma)$; in the former case we show only the positions of the non-zero entries, which are the same whether $\boldsymbol{N}_n = \boldsymbol{L}_n$ or $\boldsymbol{N}_n = \boldsymbol{L}'_n$.

$$\boldsymbol{\Delta}(\boldsymbol{N}_n) = \begin{pmatrix} * & * & \cdots & * & * & * & \cdots & * & & * & * & \cdots & * \\ & * & \cdots & * & & * & \cdots & * & & & * & \cdots & * \\ & & \ddots & \vdots & & & \ddots & \vdots & \cdots & & & \ddots & \vdots \\ & & & * & & & & * & & & & & * \end{pmatrix},$$

$$\boldsymbol{\Delta}(\boldsymbol{M}'_\gamma) = \begin{pmatrix} \gamma_{0,1} & \gamma_{0,1} & \cdots & \gamma_{0,1} & \gamma_{1,1} & \gamma_{1,1} & \cdots & \gamma_{1,1} & & \gamma_{d,1} & \gamma_{d,1} & \cdots & \gamma_{d,1} \\ & \gamma_{0,2} & \cdots & \gamma_{0,2} & & \gamma_{1,2} & \cdots & \gamma_{1,2} & & & \gamma_{d,2} & \cdots & \gamma_{d,2} \\ & & \ddots & \vdots & & & \ddots & \vdots & \cdots & & & \ddots & \vdots \\ & & & \gamma_{0,n} & & & & \gamma_{1,n} & & & & & \gamma_{d,n} \end{pmatrix}.$$

Notice that all pairs of columns in $\boldsymbol{M}'_\gamma$ and $\boldsymbol{N}_n$ with the same index (hence corresponding to the same probe in the masking scheme) have the same weight. The next lemma shows that any unsafe set of probes from among these columns must include at least two of the full-weight columns.

Lemma 14. *Let* $\gamma \in \mathbb{K}^{(d+1)\times n}, \boldsymbol{M}'_\gamma, \boldsymbol{L}_n$ *be as above. If* γ *has no zero entries, then any column selection* $\boldsymbol{P} \in S_n^{\ell_n}$ *which is a counterexample to* $\mathcal{C}'(\boldsymbol{\Delta}(\boldsymbol{M}'_\gamma), \boldsymbol{\Delta}(\boldsymbol{N}_n))$ *must include at least two columns of full weight* n *from* $\boldsymbol{\Delta}(\boldsymbol{M}'_\gamma)$ *and* $\boldsymbol{\Delta}(\boldsymbol{N}_n)$.

Proof. A counterexample to $\mathcal{C}'(\boldsymbol{\Delta}(\boldsymbol{M}'_\gamma), \boldsymbol{\Delta}(\boldsymbol{N}_n))$ is a selection matrix $\boldsymbol{P} \in S_n^{\ell_n}$ such that the matrix product $\boldsymbol{\Delta}(\boldsymbol{N}_n)\boldsymbol{P} \cdot \mathrm{kerb}(\boldsymbol{\Delta}(\boldsymbol{M}'_\gamma)\boldsymbol{P})$ has no zero rows.

The only columns of $\boldsymbol{\Delta}(\boldsymbol{N}_n)$ which are non-zero in the last row are those columns of full weight, so at least one must be included in $\boldsymbol{P}$ for the product to have no zero rows. But in order for $\boldsymbol{\Delta}(\boldsymbol{M}'_\gamma)\boldsymbol{P}$ to have a non-trivial kernel, it must have a *second* column with a non-zero in the last row. □

6.2 Dimensions 1 and 2

Combined with the results of the prior sections, this leads immediately to solutions for orders $n = 1$ or $n = 2$.

Corollary 15. *For any* $\gamma \in \mathbb{K}^{(d+1)\times 1}$ *that contains no zero entries, we have* $\mathcal{C}(\boldsymbol{M}'_\gamma, \boldsymbol{N}_1)$.

Proof. Clearly there is no way to include two full-weight columns in a selection $\boldsymbol{P} \in S_1^{\ell_1}$ of a single column. Therefore from Lemma 14, we have $\neg\mathcal{C}'(\boldsymbol{\Delta}(\boldsymbol{M}'_\gamma), \boldsymbol{\Delta}(\boldsymbol{N}_1))$. By Theorems 8 and 10 this implies the statement above. □

Corollary 16. *For any* $\gamma \in \mathbb{K}^{(d+1)\times 2}$ *such that all square submatrices of* γ *are MDS, we have* $\mathcal{C}(\boldsymbol{M}'_\gamma, \boldsymbol{N}_2)$.

Proof. Any selection of 2 columns of $\boldsymbol{\Delta}(\boldsymbol{M}'_\gamma)$ that includes at least 2 full-weight columns is simply a transposed submatrix of γ of dimension 2. By Theorem 1, any such submatrix is non-singular, and thus has a trivial kernel. Therefore by Lemma 14 there are no counterexamples to $\mathcal{C}'(\boldsymbol{\Delta}(\boldsymbol{M}'_\gamma), \boldsymbol{\Delta}(\boldsymbol{N}_2))$, and by Theorems 8 and 10 again the stated result follows. □

Most notably, these corollaries guarantee that *any* matrix with column dimension 1 or 2 which satisfies Precondition 4.1 or Precondition 5.1 is an instantiation of the respective masking scheme that is correct and safe. Because we have explicit constructions for these preconditions in Theorems 12 and 13 over any field $\mathbb{F}_q$ with $q > 2d + 1$, we also have explicit instantiations for the masking schemes secure against 1 or 2 probes.

6.3 Dimension 3

Next we turn to the case of $n = 3$. It is no longer possible to construct safe instances of γ based on the MDS preconditions alone, but there is only one other shape of square submatrices that need be considered.

Lemma 17. *Let $\gamma \in \mathbb{K}^{(d+1)\times 3}$, M'_γ, L_n be as above. If every square submatrix of γ is MDS, and for all distinct triples of indices $\{i, j, k\} \subseteq \{0, 1, \ldots, d+1\}$ the matrix*

$$\begin{pmatrix} \gamma_{i,1} & \gamma_{j,1} & \gamma_{k,1} \\ \gamma_{i,2} & \gamma_{j,2} & \gamma_{k,2} \\ \gamma_{i,3} & \gamma_{j,3} & 0 \end{pmatrix}$$

is non-singular, then we have $\mathcal{C}(M'_\gamma, N_3)$.

Proof. The goal is to ensure that no square submatrix of $\boldsymbol{\Delta}(M'_\gamma)$ which could possibly be part of a counterexample to $\mathcal{C}'(\boldsymbol{\Delta}(M'_\gamma), \boldsymbol{\Delta}(N_3))$ has a non-trivial kernel. Already we know from Lemma 14 that any such submatrix must include two distinct full-weight columns. Because all square submatrices of γ are MDS, these two columns have a trivial kernel, meaning a third column must be added if one hopes to find a counterexample. This leads to three cases, depending on the weight of this third column.

If the third column has weight 1, the situation is analogous to that of Example 11. The corresponding matrix is non-singular if and only if some 2×2 submatrix of γ is non-singular, which it must be by the MDS assumption.

Next, if the third column has full weight 3, then we have a 3×3 submatrix of γ, which again must be non-singular.

The remaining case is that the third column has weight 2, as in the statement of the lemma. All that remains is to prove that this index k must be distinct from i and j. By way of contradiction, and without loss of generality, suppose $i = k$. Then after subtracting the third column from the first, we obtain the matrix

$$\begin{pmatrix} 0 & \gamma_{j,1} & \gamma_{i,1} \\ 0 & \gamma_{j,2} & \gamma_{i,2} \\ \gamma_{i,3} & \gamma_{j,3} & 0 \end{pmatrix},$$

which is non-singular if and only if the original matrix is non-singular. And indeed, this matrix must be non-singular because the upper-right 2×2 matrix is a submatrix of γ.

Therefore the only remaining case of a submatrix which could be a counterexample to $\mathcal{C}'(\boldsymbol{\Delta}(M'_\gamma), \boldsymbol{\Delta}(N_3))$ is one of the form given in the statement of the lemma. Applying once again Theorems 8 and 10 completes the proof. □

This finally leads to a way to construct safe instances for the schemes when $d = 3$ based only on polynomial conditions, via the following steps:

1. Write down a symbolic 4×3 matrix γ satisfying Precondition 4.1 or Precondition 5.1 according to the constructions of Theorem 12 or Theorem 13, leaving all the x_i's and y_i's as indeterminates.

2. Extract all 3×3 matrices from γ that match the form of Lemma 17 and compute their determinants, which are rational functions in the x_is and y_is.
3. Factor the numerators of all determinants, removing duplicate factors and factors such as $x_i - y_i$ which must be non-zero by construction.
4. A common non-root to the resulting list of polynomials corresponds to a γ matrix which is safe for the given scheme.

Next we show the results of these computations for each of the two schemes. We used the Sage [Sag16] computer algebra system to compute the lists of polynomials according to the procedure above, which takes about 1 s on a modern laptop computer.

Proposition 18. *If $x_1, x_2, x_3, y_1, y_2, y_3 \in \mathbb{F}_q$ are distinct non-zero elements so that the list of polynomials in Fig. 1 all evaluate to non-zero values, then the matrix γ constructed according to Theorem 12 generates a safe masking scheme according to Condition 4.1.*

From the degrees of these polynomials, and by the Schwartz-Zippel lemma [Sch80] and applying the union bound, a safe construction for Condition 4.1 exists over any field $\mathbb{F}_q$ with $q > 54$.

In fact, we have an explicit construction for any binary field $\mathbb{F}_q$ with $q \geq 16$.

Theorem 19. *Let $(x_1, x_2, x_3) = (1, 3, 5)$ and $(y_1, y_2, y_3) = (6, 4, a)$. Then for any $k \geq 4$, the matrix γ constructed according to Theorem 12 generates a safe masking scheme over $\mathbb{F}_{2^k}$ according to Condition 4.1.*

Proof. Small cases with $4 \leq k \leq 8$ are checked computationally by making the appropriate substitutions into the polynomials of Fig. 1.

For $k \geq 9$, consider the degrees of the x_is and y_is when treated as polynomials over $\mathbb{F}_2$. The highest degree is $\deg y_3 = 3$, and all other elements have degree at most 2. Inspecting the polynomials in Fig. 1, we see that they are all sums of products of at most three distinct variables. Therefore, when evaluated at these x_is and y_is, the degree of any resulting polynomial is at most 7. Over $\mathbb{F}_{2^k}$ where $k \geq 8$ there is therefore no reduction, and the polynomials are guaranteed to be non-zero in all cases because they are non-zero over $\mathbb{F}_{2^8}$. □

Next we do the same for the masking scheme with linear randomness complexity, namely that of Condition 5.1.

Proposition 20. *If $x_1, x_2, x_3, x_4, y_1, y_2, y_3 \in \mathbb{F}_q$ are distinct non-zero elements so that the list of polynomials in Fig. 2 all evaluate to non-zero values, then the matrix constructed according to Theorem 13 generates a safe masking scheme according to Condition 5.1.*

Applying the Schwartz-Zippel lemma and union bound in this context guarantees a safe construction for Condition 5.1 over any field $\mathbb{F}_q$ with $q > 36$. Again, we have an explicit construction for binary fields of order at least 16.

$$
\begin{gathered}
x_2x_3 - y_1y_2 - x_2y_3 - x_3y_3 + y_1y_3 + y_2y_3 \\
x_2x_3 - x_3y_1 - x_3y_2 + y_1y_2 - x_2y_3 + x_3y_3 \\
x_2x_3 - x_2y_1 - x_2y_2 + y_1y_2 + x_2y_3 - x_3y_3 \\
x_1x_3 - y_1y_2 - x_1y_3 - x_3y_3 + y_1y_3 + y_2y_3 \\
x_1x_3 - x_3y_1 - x_3y_2 + y_1y_2 - x_1y_3 + x_3y_3 \\
x_1x_3 - x_1y_1 - x_1y_2 + y_1y_2 + x_1y_3 - x_3y_3 \\
x_1x_2 - y_1y_2 - x_1y_3 - x_2y_3 + y_1y_3 + y_2y_3 \\
x_1x_2 - x_2y_1 - x_2y_2 + y_1y_2 - x_1y_3 + x_2y_3 \\
x_1x_2 - x_1y_1 - x_1y_2 + y_1y_2 + x_1y_3 - x_2y_3 \\
x_2y_1y_2 - x_3y_1y_2 - x_2x_3y_3 + x_3y_1y_3 + x_3y_2y_3 - y_1y_2y_3 \\
x_2y_1y_2 - x_3y_1y_2 + x_2x_3y_3 - x_2y_1y_3 - x_2y_2y_3 + y_1y_2y_3 \\
x_1y_1y_2 - x_3y_1y_2 - x_1x_3y_3 + x_3y_1y_3 + x_3y_2y_3 - y_1y_2y_3 \\
x_1y_1y_2 - x_3y_1y_2 + x_1x_3y_3 - x_1y_1y_3 - x_1y_2y_3 + y_1y_2y_3 \\
x_1y_1y_2 - x_2y_1y_2 - x_1x_2y_3 + x_2y_1y_3 + x_2y_2y_3 - y_1y_2y_3 \\
x_1y_1y_2 - x_2y_1y_2 + x_1x_2y_3 - x_1y_1y_3 - x_1y_2y_3 + y_1y_2y_3 \\
x_2x_3y_1 + x_2x_3y_2 - x_2y_1y_2 - x_3y_1y_2 - x_2x_3y_3 + y_1y_2y_3 \\
x_1x_3y_1 + x_1x_3y_2 - x_1y_1y_2 - x_3y_1y_2 - x_1x_3y_3 + y_1y_2y_3 \\
x_1x_2y_1 + x_1x_2y_2 - x_1y_1y_2 - x_2y_1y_2 - x_1x_2y_3 + y_1y_2y_3 \\
x_1x_2x_3 - x_2x_3y_1 - x_2x_3y_2 - x_1y_1y_2 + x_2y_1y_2 + x_3y_1y_2 - x_1x_2y_3 - x_1x_3y_3 + x_2x_3y_3 + x_1y_1y_3 + x_1y_2y_3 - y_1y_2y_3 \\
x_1x_2x_3 - x_1x_3y_1 - x_1x_3y_2 + x_1y_1y_2 - x_2y_1y_2 + x_3y_1y_2 - x_1x_2y_3 + x_1x_3y_3 - x_2x_3y_3 + x_2y_1y_3 + x_2y_2y_3 - y_1y_2y_3 \\
x_1x_2x_3 - x_1x_2y_1 - x_1x_2y_2 + x_1y_1y_2 + x_2y_1y_2 - x_3y_1y_2 + x_1x_2y_3 - x_1x_3y_3 - x_2x_3y_3 + x_3y_1y_3 + x_3y_2y_3 - y_1y_2y_3
\end{gathered}
$$

Fig. 1. Polynomials which should be non-zero to generate a safe construction according to Condition 4.1. There are 9 degree-2 polynomials with 6 terms, 9 degree-3 polynomials with 6 terms, and 3 degree-3 polynomials with 12 terms.

Theorem 21. *Let* $(x_1, x_2, x_3, x_4) = (1, 2, 5, 6)$ *and* $(y_1, y_2, y_3) = (4, 7, f)$. *Then for any* $k \geq 4$, *the matrix* γ *constructed according to Theorem 13 generates a safe masking scheme over* $\mathbb{F}_{2^k}$ *according to Condition 5.1.*

The proof is the same as Theorem 19, consisting of computational checks for $4 \leq k \leq 8$ and then an argument for all $k \geq 9$ based on the degrees of the x_i and y_i polynomials.

7 Efficient Algorithms to Test Safeness

We now turn to a computational approach, in order to deal with the schemes at order $d > 3$ that were not treated in the previous section.

$$
\begin{gathered}
x_2x_3x_4 - x_3x_4y_1 - x_3x_4y_2 - x_2y_1y_2 + x_3y_1y_2 + x_4y_1y_2 - x_2x_3y_3 - x_2x_4y_3 + x_3x_4y_3 + x_2y_1y_3 + x_2y_2y_3 - y_1y_2y_3 \\
x_2x_3x_4 - x_2x_4y_1 - x_2x_4y_2 + x_2y_1y_2 - x_3y_1y_2 + x_4y_1y_2 - x_2x_3y_3 + x_2x_4y_3 - x_3x_4y_3 + x_3y_1y_3 + x_3y_2y_3 - y_1y_2y_3 \\
x_2x_3x_4 - x_2x_3y_1 - x_2x_3y_2 + x_2y_1y_2 + x_3y_1y_2 - x_4y_1y_2 + x_2x_3y_3 - x_2x_4y_3 - x_3x_4y_3 + x_4y_1y_3 + x_4y_2y_3 - y_1y_2y_3 \\
x_1x_3x_4 - x_3x_4y_1 - x_3x_4y_2 - x_1y_1y_2 + x_3y_1y_2 + x_4y_1y_2 - x_1x_3y_3 - x_1x_4y_3 + x_3x_4y_3 + x_1y_1y_3 + x_1y_2y_3 - y_1y_2y_3 \\
x_1x_3x_4 - x_1x_4y_1 - x_1x_4y_2 + x_1y_1y_2 - x_3y_1y_2 + x_4y_1y_2 - x_1x_3y_3 + x_1x_4y_3 - x_3x_4y_3 + x_3y_1y_3 + x_3y_2y_3 - y_1y_2y_3 \\
x_1x_3x_4 - x_1x_3y_1 - x_1x_3y_2 + x_1y_1y_2 + x_3y_1y_2 - x_4y_1y_2 + x_1x_3y_3 - x_1x_4y_3 - x_3x_4y_3 + x_4y_1y_3 + x_4y_2y_3 - y_1y_2y_3 \\
x_1x_2x_4 - x_2x_4y_1 - x_2x_4y_2 - x_1y_1y_2 + x_2y_1y_2 + x_4y_1y_2 - x_1x_2y_3 - x_1x_4y_3 + x_2x_4y_3 + x_1y_1y_3 + x_1y_2y_3 - y_1y_2y_3 \\
x_1x_2x_4 - x_1x_4y_1 - x_1x_4y_2 + x_1y_1y_2 - x_2y_1y_2 + x_4y_1y_2 - x_1x_2y_3 + x_1x_4y_3 - x_2x_4y_3 + x_2y_1y_3 + x_2y_2y_3 - y_1y_2y_3 \\
x_1x_2x_4 - x_1x_2y_1 - x_1x_2y_2 + x_1y_1y_2 + x_2y_1y_2 - x_4y_1y_2 + x_1x_2y_3 - x_1x_4y_3 - x_2x_4y_3 + x_4y_1y_3 + x_4y_2y_3 - y_1y_2y_3 \\
x_1x_2x_3 - x_2x_3y_1 - x_2x_3y_2 - x_1y_1y_2 + x_2y_1y_2 + x_3y_1y_2 - x_1x_2y_3 - x_1x_3y_3 + x_2x_3y_3 + x_1y_1y_3 + x_1y_2y_3 - y_1y_2y_3 \\
x_1x_2x_3 - x_1x_3y_1 - x_1x_3y_2 + x_1y_1y_2 - x_2y_1y_2 + x_3y_1y_2 - x_1x_2y_3 + x_1x_3y_3 - x_2x_3y_3 + x_2y_1y_3 + x_2y_2y_3 - y_1y_2y_3 \\
x_1x_2x_3 - x_1x_2y_1 - x_1x_2y_2 + x_1y_1y_2 + x_2y_1y_2 - x_3y_1y_2 + x_1x_2y_3 - x_1x_3y_3 - x_2x_3y_3 + x_3y_1y_3 + x_3y_2y_3 - y_1y_2y_3
\end{gathered}
$$

Fig. 2. Polynomials which should be non-zero to generate a safe construction according to Condition 5.1. There are 12 degree-3 polynomials with 12 terms each.

To test whether a matrix may be used to safely instantiate either of the masking schemes of Belaïd *et al.*, we use the condition $\mathcal{C}'(\boldsymbol{M}'_\gamma, \boldsymbol{N}_d)$ defined in (4), which according to Theorem 8 is a sufficient condition for the scheme under consideration to be safe. The definition of this condition immediately indicates an algorithm, which we have implemented with some optimizations, using M4RIE [Alb13] for the finite field arithmetic.

7.1 The Algorithm

To test whether a matrix $\gamma \in \mathbb{K}^{(d+1)\times d}$ satisfies the conditions of Proposition 6 or Proposition 7, simply construct $\boldsymbol{M}'_\gamma$ and $\boldsymbol{N}_d$ and for all d-subsets of columns $\boldsymbol{P} \in S^\ell_d$, check if $\mathcal{Z}(\boldsymbol{N}_d\boldsymbol{P} \cdot \mathrm{kerb}(\boldsymbol{M}'_\gamma\boldsymbol{P}))$.

This algorithm is much more efficient than the one directly suggested by Condition 4.1: instead of testing all $\sum_{i=1}^{d}\binom{\ell}{i}q^i$ vectors of $\mathbb{F}_q^\ell$ of weight d or less, it is enough to do $\binom{\ell}{d}$ easy linear algebra computations. While this remains exponential in d, it removes the practically insuperable factor q^d and gives a complexity that does not depend on the field size (save for the cost of arithmetic).

(Note that we could have used the condition $\mathcal{C}''$ as in Theorem 10 instead, but this turns out to be more complicated in practice due to the need to take arbitrary subsets of the rows and columns of $\boldsymbol{M}'_\gamma$ and $\boldsymbol{N}_d$.)

We now describe two implementation strategies for this algorithm.

7.2 Straightforward Implementation with Optimizations

Two simple optimizations may be used to make a straightforward implementation of the above algorithm more efficient in practice.

Skipping Bad Column Picks. We can see already from the support of $\boldsymbol{N}_d$ that some subsets of columns $\boldsymbol{P} \in S^\ell_d$ never need to be checked because $\mathcal{Z}(\boldsymbol{N}_d\boldsymbol{P})$ is already true, independent of the actual choice of γ. This is the case for example when the columns selected by $\boldsymbol{P}$ are all of weight 1.

For the specific cases of $d = 4$, this reduces the number of supports to be considered from $\binom{49}{4} = 211\,876$ to $103\,030$, saving roughly a factor 2. A similar behaviour is observed for $d = 5$, when one only has to consider $6\,448\,239$ supports among the $\binom{71}{5} = 13\,019\,909$ possible ones. Note that the same optimization could be applied to the naïve algorithm that exhaustively enumerates low-weight vectors of $\mathbb{F}_q^\ell$.

Testing Critical Cases First. Looking again at how $\boldsymbol{M}'_\gamma$ is defined, it is easy to see that for some column selections $\boldsymbol{P}$, $\boldsymbol{M}'_\gamma\boldsymbol{P}$ does not in fact depend on γ. For these, it is enough to check once and for all that $\mathcal{Z}(\boldsymbol{N}_\gamma\boldsymbol{P} \cdot \mathrm{kerb}(\boldsymbol{M}'_\gamma\boldsymbol{P}))$ indeed holds (if it does not, the scheme would be generically broken). Going further, even some column subsets such that $\boldsymbol{M}_\gamma\boldsymbol{P}$ actually depends on γ may always be "safe" provided that γ satisfies a certain precondition, such as for instance being MDS, as suggested in Sect. 5.

Conversely, it may be the case that for some $\boldsymbol{P}$, $\mathcal{Z}(\boldsymbol{N}_d\boldsymbol{P}\cdot\mathrm{kerb}(\boldsymbol{M}'_\gamma\boldsymbol{P}))$ often does *not* hold. It may then be beneficial to test this subset $\boldsymbol{P}$ before others that are less likely to make the condition fail. We have experimentally observed that such subsets do exist. For instance, in the case $d = 5$ for Condition 4.1, only ≈320 000 column subsets seem to determine whether a matrix satisfies the condition or not.[3] There, checking these supports first and using an early-abort strategy, verifying that a matrix *does not* satisfy the condition is at least ≈20 times faster than enumerating all possible column subsets.

7.3 Batch Implementation

Especially when the matrix γ under consideration actually satisfies the required conditions, checking these using the straightforward strategy entails considerable redundant computation due to the overlap between subsets of columns.

To avoid this, we also implemented a way to check the condition $\mathcal{C}'(\boldsymbol{M}'_\gamma, \boldsymbol{N}_d)$ that operates over the entire matrix simultaneously, effectively considering many subsets of columns in a single batch.

Recall that the algorithm needs to (1) extract a subset of columns of $\boldsymbol{M}'_\gamma$, (2) compute a right kernel basis for this subset, (3) multiply $\boldsymbol{N}_d$ times this kernel basis, and (4) check for zero rows in the resulting product.

Steps (2) and (3) would typically be performed via Gaussian elimination: For each column of $\boldsymbol{M}'_\gamma$ that is in the selection, we search for a pivot row, permute rows if necessary to move the pivot up, then eliminate above and below the pivot and move on. If there is no pivot in some column, this means a new null vector has been found; we use the previous pivots to compute the null vector and add it to the basis. Finally, we multiply this null space basis by the corresponding columns in $\boldsymbol{N}_d$ and check for zero rows.

The key observation for this algorithm is that we can perform these steps (2) and (3) *in parallel* to add one more column to an existing column selection. That is, starting with some subset of columns, we consider the effect on the null space basis and the following multiplication by $\boldsymbol{N}_d$ simultaneously for all other columns in the matrices. Adding columns with pivots does not change the null space basis or the product with $\boldsymbol{N}_d$. Columns with no pivots add one additional column to the null space basis, which results in a new column in the product with $\boldsymbol{N}_d$. This new column of $\boldsymbol{N}_d\boldsymbol{P}\cdot\mathrm{kerb}(\boldsymbol{M}'_\gamma\boldsymbol{P})$ may be checked for non-zero entries and then immediately discarded as the search continues; in later steps, the *rows* of this product which already have a non-zero entry no longer need to be considered.

All of this effectively reduces the cost of the check by a factor of ℓ compared to the prior version, replacing the search over all size-d subsets with a search over size-$(d-1)$ subsets and some matrix computations. This strategy is especially effective when the γ matrix under consideration is (nearly or actually) safe, meaning that the early termination techniques above will not be very useful.

[3] This figure was found experimentally by regrouping the supports in clusters of 10 000, independently of q. A more careful analysis may lead to a more precise result.

8 Experimental Results and Explicit Instantiations

We implemented both algorithms of the previous section in the practically-useful case of binary fields, using M4RIE for the underlying linear algebra [Alb13], and searched for matrices fulfilling Conditions 4.1 and 5.1 in various settings, leading to instantiations of the masking schemes of Belaïd *et al.* up to $d = 6$ and $\mathbb{F}_{2^{16}}$.[4] We also collected statistics about the fraction of matrices satisfying the conditions, notably in function of the field over which they are defined, and experimentally verified the usefulness of Precondition 4.1.

8.1 Statistics

We give detailed statistics about the proportion of preconditioned matrices allowing to instantiate either masking scheme up to order 6; this is presented in Tables 1 and 2. The data was collected by drawing at random matrices satisfying Precondition 4.1 or Precondition 5.1 and checking if they satisfied the safety conditions or not for the respective scheme.

For combinations of field size and order where no safe matrix was found, we give the result as an upper bound.

Notice that the probability for Condition 5.1 appears to be consistently a bit higher than that for Condition 4.1. The combinations of field size q and order d where safe instances are found were almost the same for both schemes, except for order 5 and $q = 2^9$, where a safe preconditioned matrix was found for Condition 5.1 but not for Condition 4.1. This difference between the schemes may be explained by the fact that Condition 4.1 places conditions on two matrices $\boldsymbol{\gamma}$ and $\mathbf{1}_{d\times d} - \boldsymbol{\gamma}$, whereas Condition 5.1 depends only on the single matrix $\boldsymbol{\gamma}$.

An important remark is that for the smallest field $\mathbb{F}_{2^5}$, the statistics do not include results about the *non-preconditioned safe matrices*, which were the only safe ones we found, see the further discussion below.

We indicate the sample sizes used to obtain each result, as they may vary by several orders of magnitude due to the exponentially-increasing cost of our algorithm with the order. As an illustration, our batch implementation is able to check 1 000 000 dimension-4 matrices over $\mathbb{F}_{2^6}$ in 12 400 seconds on one core of a 2 GHz Sandy Bridge CPU, which increases to 590 000 and 740 000 s for $\mathbb{F}_{2^{12}}$ and $\mathbb{F}_{2^{16}}$ respectively because of more expensive field operations; 1 600 000 s allowed to test ≈145 000 and ≈25 000 dimension-5 matrices for these last two fields, and ≈2 400 dimension-6 matrices for $\mathbb{F}_{2^{16}}$.

Usefulness of the Preconditions. We now address the question of the usefulness of the preconditions of Sect. 5. Our goal is to determine with what probability randomly-generated matrices in fact already satisfy the preconditions, and whether doing so for a matrix $\boldsymbol{\gamma}$ has a positive impact on its satisfying Condition 4.1 or Condition 5.1.

[4] $\mathbb{F}_{2^{16}}$ is the largest field size implemented in M4RIE, and $d = 6$ the maximum dimension for which safe instantiations (seem to) exist below this field size limitation.

Table 1. Instantiations over $\mathbb{F}_{2^5} \sim \mathbb{F}_{2^{10}}$. Sample sizes (as indicated by symbols in the exponents) were as follows: $* \approx 400\,000$; $\ddagger = 1\,000\,000$; $\star \approx 4\,000\,000$; $\dagger \approx 11\,000\,000$.

q	2^5	2^6	2^7	2^8	2^9	2^{10}
d	Condition 4.1 and Precondition 4.1					
4	$\leq 2^{-28.8}$	$2^{-15.25\dagger}$	$0.009^{\dagger}$	$0.11^{\ddagger}$	$0.34^{\ddagger}$	$0.59^{\ddagger}$
5	–	–	–	–	$\leq 2^{-27.5}$	$2^{-18.9\star}$
d	Condition 5.1 and Precondition 5.1					
4	$\leq 2^{-33.5}$	$2^{-9.10\ddagger}$	$0.062^{\ddagger}$	$0.27^{\ddagger}$	$0.53^{\ddagger}$	$0.73^{\ddagger}$
5	–	–	–	–	$2^{-18.6*}$	$2^{-11.0*}$

Table 2. Instantiations over $\mathbb{F}_{2^{11}} \sim \mathbb{F}_{2^{16}}$. Sample sizes (as indicated by symbols in the exponents) were as follows: $\ddagger = 1\,000\,000$; $* \approx 400\,000$; $\diamond \approx 145\,000$; $\bullet \approx 65\,000$; $\lhd \approx 40\,000$; $\oslash \approx 30\,000$; $\ltimes \approx 25\,000$; $\wr \approx 560\,000$; $\curlywedge \approx 12\,700$.

q	2^{11}	2^{12}	2^{13}	2^{14}	2^{15}	2^{16}
d	Condition 4.1 and Precondition 4.1					
4	$0.77^{\ddagger}$	$0.88^{\ddagger}$	$0.94^{\ddagger}$	$0.97^{\ddagger}$	$0.98^{\ddagger}$	$0.99^{\ddagger}$
5	0.0015^{*}	$0.04^{\diamond}$	$0.2^{\bullet}$	$0.45^{\lhd}$	$0.67^{\oslash}$	$0.82^{\ltimes}$
6	–	–	–	–	$2^{-16.8\wr}$	$0.003^{\curlywedge}$
d	Condition 5.1 and Precondition 5.1					
4	$0.86^{\ddagger}$	$0.92^{\ddagger}$	$0.96^{\ddagger}$	$0.98^{\ddagger}$	$0.99^{\ddagger}$	$1.00^{\ddagger}$
5	0.021^{*}	0.14^{*}	0.39^{*}	0.62^{*}	0.78^{*}	0.89^{*}
6	–	–	–	–	$2^{-12.7\lhd}$	$0.002^{\lhd}$

We did this experimentally in two settings, both for the first scheme corresponding to Condition 4.1: order $d = 4$ over $\mathbb{F}_{2^8}$ and order $d = 5$ over $\mathbb{F}_{2^{13}}$. We generated enough random matrices γ in order to obtain respectively 20 000 and 2 000 of them satisfying Condition 4.1, and counted how many of the corresponding safe pairs $(\gamma, \mathbf{1}_{d\times d} - \gamma)$ had at least one or both elements that were MDS and XMDS. The same statistics were gathered for all the generated matrices, including the ones that were not safe. The results are respectively summarized in Tables 3 and 4.

Table 3. Case $d = 4$ over $\mathbb{F}_{2^8}$, for Condition 4.1.

	Total	One+ MDS	Both MDS	One+ XMDS	Both XMDS
#Random	672 625	634 096	389 504	515 840	315 273
#Safe	20 000	19 981	19 981	19 981	19 981
Ratio	0.030	0.032	0.051	0.039	0.063

Table 4. Case $d = 5$ over $\mathbb{F}_{2^{13}}$, for Condition 4.1.

	Total	One+ MDS	Both MDS	One+ XMDS	Both XMDS
#Random	15 877	15 867	14 978	15 486	14 623
#Safe	2 000	2 000	2 000	2 000	2 000
Ratio	0.13	0.13	0.13	0.13	0.14

A first comment on the results is that as already remarked in Sect. 5, the preconditions are not necessary to find safe instantiations. Indeed, for a few of the smallest cases $d = 3, q = 2^3$ and $d = 4, q = 2^5$, we were only able to find safe instantiations that did *not* meet the preconditions. For example, one can clearly see that the leading 2×2 submatrix of the following matrix is singular, and hence the matrix is not MDS:

$$\gamma = \begin{pmatrix} 4 & 2 & 6 \\ 4 & 2 & 3 \\ 4 & 2 & 3 \end{pmatrix}.$$

Yet (surprisingly), γ and $\mathbf{1} - \gamma$ satisfy all requirements of Condition 4.1 over $\mathbb{F}_{2^3}$.

Nonetheless, the precondition is clearly helpful in the vast majority of cases. From our experiments, *in cases where any preconditioned safe matrix exists*, then nearly all safe matrices satisfy the precondition, while a significant fraction of random matrices do not. Enforcing the precondition by construction or as a first check is then indeed a way to improve the performance of a random search of a safe matrix. This is especially true for larger orders; for example, we did not find any safe matrices for order $d = 6$ over $\mathbb{F}_{2^{15}}$ by random search, but only by imposing Precondition 4.1.

Lastly, one should notice that specifically considering Cauchy matrices seems to further increase the odds of a matrix being safe, beyond the fact that it satisfies Condition 4.1: in the case $d = 4$, $\mathbb{F}_{2^8}$, Table 1 gives a success probability of 0.11, which is significantly larger than the 0.063 of Table 3, and in the case $d = 5$, $\mathbb{F}_{2^{13}}$, Table 2 gives 0.2, also quite higher than the 0.14 of Table 4. As of yet, we do not have an explanation for this observation.

8.2 Instantiations of [BBP+17, Sect. 4]

We conclude by giving explicit matrices allowing to safely instantiate the scheme of [BBP+17, Sect. 4] over various binary fields from order 3 up to 6; the case of order at most 2 is treated in Sect. 6 (Belaïd *et al.* also provided examples for $d = 2$). Our examples include practically-relevant instances with $d = 3, 4$ over $\mathbb{F}_{2^8}$.

We only give one matrix γ for every case we list, but we emphasise that as is required by the masking scheme, this means that both γ and $\boldsymbol{\delta} = \mathbf{1}_{d \times d} - \gamma$ satisfy Condition 4.1. We list instances only for the smallest field size we know of, and for $\mathbb{F}_{2^8}$ (when applicable), but have computed explicit instances for all field sizes up to $\mathbb{F}_{2^{16}}$. These are given in the full version of this paper [KR18, Appendix A].

Instantiations at Order 3. The smallest field for which we could find an instantiation at order 3 was $\mathbb{F}_{2^3}$. Recall that we also have an explicit construction in Sect. 6 for any 2^k with $k \geq 4$.

$$\gamma(\mathbb{F}_{2^3}) = \begin{pmatrix} \texttt{3} & \texttt{5} & \texttt{4} \\ \texttt{3} & \texttt{6} & \texttt{7} \\ \texttt{3} & \texttt{5} & \texttt{4} \end{pmatrix} \qquad \gamma(\mathbb{F}_{2^8}) = \begin{pmatrix} \texttt{e3} & \texttt{b7} & \texttt{50} \\ \texttt{bd} & \texttt{e8} & \texttt{8b} \\ \texttt{53} & \texttt{25} & \texttt{a0} \end{pmatrix}$$

Instantiations at Order 4. The smallest field for which we could find an instantiation at order 4 was $\mathbb{F}_{2^5}$. The following matrices $\gamma(\mathbb{F}_q)$ may be used to instantiate the scheme over $\mathbb{F}_q$.

$$\gamma(\mathbb{F}_{2^5}) = \begin{pmatrix} \texttt{1c} & \texttt{c} & \texttt{1e} & \texttt{b} \\ \texttt{1c} & \texttt{c} & \texttt{1e} & \texttt{12} \\ \texttt{10} & \texttt{18} & \texttt{17} & \texttt{14} \\ \texttt{1c} & \texttt{c} & \texttt{1e} & \texttt{10} \end{pmatrix} \quad \gamma(\mathbb{F}_{2^8}) = \begin{pmatrix} \texttt{56} & \texttt{5e} & \texttt{a1} & \texttt{3d} \\ \texttt{97} & \texttt{27} & \texttt{71} & \texttt{c7} \\ \texttt{f5} & \texttt{ae} & \texttt{68} & \texttt{88} \\ \texttt{1c} & \texttt{3} & \texttt{9c} & \texttt{8e} \end{pmatrix}$$

Instantiations at Order 5. The smallest field for which we could find an instantiation at order 5 was $\mathbb{F}_{2^{10}}$. The following matrix may be used to instantiate the scheme over $\mathbb{F}_{2^{10}}$.

$$\gamma(\mathbb{F}_{2^{10}}) = \begin{pmatrix} \texttt{276} & \texttt{13e} & \texttt{64} & \texttt{1ab} & \texttt{120} \\ \texttt{189} & \texttt{181} & \texttt{195} & \texttt{30f} & \texttt{3fe} \\ \texttt{20a} & \texttt{3a1} & \texttt{199} & \texttt{30} & \texttt{2db} \\ \texttt{156} & \texttt{1ab} & \texttt{2f8} & \texttt{e5} & \texttt{2a8} \\ \texttt{303} & \texttt{321} & \texttt{265} & \texttt{d8} & \texttt{3a} \end{pmatrix}$$

Instantiations at Order 6. The smallest field for which we could find an instantiation at order 6 was $\mathbb{F}_{2^{15}}$. The following matrix may be used to instantiate the scheme over $\mathbb{F}_{2^{15}}$.

$$\gamma(\mathbb{F}_{2^{15}}) = \begin{pmatrix} \texttt{151d} & \texttt{5895} & \texttt{5414} & \texttt{392b} & \texttt{2092} & \texttt{29a6} \\ \texttt{5c69} & \texttt{2f9e} & \texttt{241d} & \texttt{2ef7} & \texttt{baa} & \texttt{6f40} \\ \texttt{6e0d} & \texttt{8cf} & \texttt{7ca1} & \texttt{6503} & \texttt{23dc} & \texttt{6b3b} \\ \texttt{10d7} & \texttt{588e} & \texttt{2c22} & \texttt{1245} & \texttt{6a38} & \texttt{6484} \\ \texttt{1637} & \texttt{7062} & \texttt{2ae0} & \texttt{d1b} & \texttt{5305} & \texttt{381f} \\ \texttt{23f6} & \texttt{7d5} & \texttt{21bf} & \texttt{2879} & \texttt{2033} & \texttt{4377} \end{pmatrix}$$

8.3 Instantiations of [BBP+17, Sect. 5]

We now give similar instantiation results for the scheme with linear randomness complexity. This time, only a single matrix of dimension $(d+1) \times d$ is necessary to obtain a d-NI scheme. As in the previous case, we only focus here on the cases where $3 \leq d \leq 6$, and only list the matrices over the smallest binary field we have as well as $\mathbb{F}_{2^8}$ (where possible). We refer to [KR18] for all other cases.

Instantiations at Order 3. The smallest field for which we could find an instantiation at order 3 was $\mathbb{F}_{2^3}$. Recall that we also have an explicit construction in Sect. 6 for any 2^k with $k \geq 4$.

$$\gamma(\mathbb{F}_{2^3}) = \begin{pmatrix} 1 & 7 & 4 \\ 4 & 4 & 4 \\ 2 & 1 & 4 \\ 7 & 2 & 4 \end{pmatrix} \qquad \gamma(\mathbb{F}_{2^8}) = \begin{pmatrix} \mathtt{da} & \mathtt{d5} & \mathtt{e6} \\ \mathtt{e8} & \mathtt{1d} & \mathtt{44} \\ \mathtt{ad} & \mathtt{b3} & \mathtt{ce} \\ \mathtt{9f} & \mathtt{7b} & \mathtt{6c} \end{pmatrix}$$

Instantiations at Order 4. The smallest field for which we could find an instantiation at order 4 was $\mathbb{F}_{2^5}$. The following matrices $\gamma(\mathbb{F}_q)$ may be used $\mathbb{F}_q$.

$$\gamma(\mathbb{F}_{2^5}) = \begin{pmatrix} \mathtt{17} & \mathtt{f} & \mathtt{13} & \mathtt{16} \\ \mathtt{b} & \mathtt{7} & \mathtt{1a} & \mathtt{11} \\ \mathtt{1} & \mathtt{1e} & \mathtt{19} & \mathtt{3} \\ \mathtt{1b} & \mathtt{10} & \mathtt{2} & \mathtt{a} \\ \mathtt{6} & \mathtt{6} & \mathtt{12} & \mathtt{e} \end{pmatrix} \quad \gamma(\mathbb{F}_{2^8}) = \begin{pmatrix} \mathtt{ac} & \mathtt{39} & \mathtt{c0} & \mathtt{36} \\ \mathtt{79} & \mathtt{5f} & \mathtt{d9} & \mathtt{51} \\ \mathtt{9d} & \mathtt{16} & \mathtt{ca} & \mathtt{63} \\ \mathtt{a3} & \mathtt{cb} & \mathtt{6} & \mathtt{81} \\ \mathtt{eb} & \mathtt{bb} & \mathtt{d5} & \mathtt{85} \end{pmatrix}$$

Instantiations at Order 5. The smallest field for which we could find an instantiation at order 5 was $\mathbb{F}_{2^9}$. The following matrix may be used to instantiate the scheme over $\mathbb{F}_{2^9}$.

$$\gamma(\mathbb{F}_{2^9}) = \begin{pmatrix} \mathtt{7d} & \mathtt{12c} & \mathtt{18} & \mathtt{1a3} & \mathtt{da} \\ \mathtt{121} & \mathtt{131} & \mathtt{109} & \mathtt{1a7} & \mathtt{3b} \\ \mathtt{4a} & \mathtt{131} & \mathtt{91} & \mathtt{a4} & \mathtt{1c4} \\ \mathtt{17c} & \mathtt{cb} & \mathtt{14b} & \mathtt{41} & \mathtt{57} \\ \mathtt{fd} & \mathtt{87} & \mathtt{ac} & \mathtt{17a} & \mathtt{149} \\ \mathtt{97} & \mathtt{160} & \mathtt{67} & \mathtt{19b} & \mathtt{3b} \end{pmatrix}$$

Instantiations at Order 6. The smallest field for which we could find an instantiation at order 6 was $\mathbb{F}_{2^{15}}$. The following matrix may be used to instantiate the scheme over $\mathbb{F}_{2^{15}}$.

$$\gamma(\mathbb{F}_{2^{15}}) = \begin{pmatrix} \mathtt{475c} & \mathtt{77e7} & \mathtt{64ef} & \mathtt{7893} & \mathtt{4cd1} & \mathtt{6e20} \\ \mathtt{63dd} & \mathtt{71f} & \mathtt{29da} & \mathtt{600e} & \mathtt{36be} & \mathtt{1db7} \\ \mathtt{5511} & \mathtt{d63} & \mathtt{3719} & \mathtt{4874} & \mathtt{664} & \mathtt{5014} \\ \mathtt{410e} & \mathtt{7cf2} & \mathtt{9d9} & \mathtt{10a1} & \mathtt{7525} & \mathtt{6098} \\ \mathtt{7bfe} & \mathtt{2998} & \mathtt{7e20} & \mathtt{1438} & \mathtt{35e6} & \mathtt{51e} \\ \mathtt{7564} & \mathtt{75d3} & \mathtt{221a} & \mathtt{67c7} & \mathtt{56f1} & \mathtt{18d5} \\ \mathtt{3e04} & \mathtt{5d22} & \mathtt{2fcf} & \mathtt{33b7} & \mathtt{6a39} & \mathtt{5ed0} \end{pmatrix}$$

8.4 Minimum Field Sizes for Safe Instantiations

We conclude by briefly comparing the minimum field sizes for which we could find safe instantiations of Conditions 4.1 and 5.1 with the ones given by the non-constructive existence theorems of Belaïd *et al.* Namely, [BBP+17, Theorem 4.5] guarantees the existence of a pair of safe matrices for Condition 4.1 in dimension d over $\mathbb{F}_q$ as long as $q > 2d \cdot (12d)^d$, and [BBP+17, Theorem 5.4] of a safe matrix for Condition 5.1 as long as $q > d \cdot (d+1) \cdot (12d)^d$. We give in Table 5 the explicit values provided by these two theorems for $2 \leq d \leq 6$ and q a power of two, along with the experimental minima that we found. From these, it seems that the sufficient condition of Belaïd *et al.* is in fact rather pessimistic.

Table 5. Sufficient field sizes for safe instantiations in characteristic two. Sizes are given as $\log(q)$.

d/min(log(q))	[BBP+17, Theorem 4.5]	Section 8.2	[BBP+17, Theorem 5.4]	Section 8.3
2	11	3	12	3
3	19	3	20	3
4	26	5	27	5
5	33	10	35	9
6	41	15	43	15

Acknowledgements. We thank Daniel Augot for the interesting discussions we had in the early stages of this work.

This work was performed while the second author was graciously hosted by the Laboratoire Jean Kuntzmann at the Université Grenoble Alpes.

The first author was supported in part by the French National Research Agency through the framework of the "Investissements d'avenir" program (ANR-15-IDEX-02).

The second author was supported in part by the National Science Foundation under grants #1319994 and #1618269, and in part by the Office of Naval Research award #N0001417WX01516.

Some of the computations were performed using the Grace supercomputer hosted by the U.S. Naval Academy Center for High Performance Computing, with funding from the DoD HPC Modernization Program.

References

[Alb13] Albrecht, M.: The M4RIE library, The M4RIE Team (2013)

[BBD+16] Barthe, G., et al.: Strong non-interference and type-directed higher-order masking. In: Weippl, E.R., Katzenbeisser, S., Kruegel, C., Myers, A.C., Halevi, S. (eds.) ACM CCS 2016, pp. 116–129. ACM (2016)

[BBP+16] Belaïd, S., Benhamouda, F., Passelègue, A., Prouff, E., Thillard, A., Vergnaud, D.: Randomness complexity of private circuits for multiplication. In: Fischlin, M., Coron, J.-S. (eds.) EUROCRYPT 2016. LNCS, vol. 9666, pp. 616–648. Springer, Heidelberg (2016). https://doi.org/10.1007/978-3-662-49896-5_22

[BBP+17] Belaïd, S., Benhamouda, F., Passelègue, A., Prouff, E., Thillard, A., Vergnaud, D.: Private multiplication over finite fields. In: Katz, J., Shacham, H. (eds.) CRYPTO 2017. LNCS, vol. 10403, pp. 397–426. Springer, Cham (2017). https://doi.org/10.1007/978-3-319-63697-9_14

[CJRR99] Chari, S., Jutla, C.S., Rao, J.R., Rohatgi, P.: Towards Sound Approaches to Counteract Power-Analysis Attacks, in Wiener [Wie99], pp. 398–412
[CPRR16] Carlet, C., Prouff, E., Rivain, M., Roche, T.: Algebraic Decomposition for Probing Security. IACR Cryptology ePrint Archive 2016, 321 (2016)
[GP99] Goubin, L., Patarin, J.: DES and differential power analysis the "Duplication" method. In: Koç, Ç.K., Paar, C. (eds.) CHES 1999. LNCS, vol. 1717, pp. 158–172. Springer, Heidelberg (1999). https://doi.org/10.1007/3-540-48059-5_15
[ISW03] Ishai, Y., Sahai, A., Wagner, D.: Private circuits: securing hardware against probing attacks. In: Boneh, D. (ed.) CRYPTO 2003. LNCS, vol. 2729, pp. 463–481. Springer, Heidelberg (2003). https://doi.org/10.1007/978-3-540-45146-4_27
[KJJ99] Kocher, P.C., Jaffe, J., Jun, B.: Differential Power Analysis, in Wiener [Wie99], pp. 388–397
[KR18] Karpman, P., Roche, D.S.: New Instantiations of the CRYPTO 2017 Masking Schemes. IACR Cryptology ePrint Archive 2018, 492 (2018)
[MS06] MacWilliams, F.J., Sloane, N.J.A.: The Theory of Error-Correcting Codes, 12th edn. North-Holland Mathematical Library, North-Holland (2006)
[RS85] Roth, R.M., Seroussi, G.: On generator matrices of MDS codes. IEEE Trans. Inf. Theor. **31**(6), 826–830 (1985)
[Sag16] The Sage Developers: Sagemath, the Sage Mathematics Software System (Version 7.4) (2016)
[Sch80] Schwartz, J.T.: Fast probabilistic algorithms for verification of polynomial identities. J. ACM **27**(4), 701–717 (1980)
[Wie99] Wiener, Michael (ed.): CRYPTO 1999. LNCS, vol. 1666. Springer, Heidelberg (1999). https://doi.org/10.1007/3-540-48405-1

Statistical Ineffective Fault Attacks on Masked AES with Fault Countermeasures

Christoph Dobraunig[1], Maria Eichlseder[1], Hannes Gross[1], Stefan Mangard[1], Florian Mendel[2], and Robert Primas[1(✉)]

[1] Graz University of Technology, Graz, Austria
robert.primas@iaik.tugraz.at
[2] Infineon Technologies AG, Neubiberg, Germany

Abstract. Implementation attacks like side-channel and fault attacks are a threat to deployed devices especially if an attacker has physical access. As a consequence, devices like smart cards and IoT devices usually provide countermeasures against implementation attacks, such as masking against side-channel attacks and detection-based countermeasures like temporal or spacial redundancy against fault attacks. In this paper, we show how to attack implementations protected with both masking and detection-based fault countermeasures by using statistical ineffective fault attacks using a single fault induction per execution. Our attacks are largely unaffected by the deployed protection order of masking and the level of redundancy of the detection-based countermeasure. These observations show that the combination of masking plus error detection alone may not provide sufficient protection against implementation attacks.

Keywords: Implementation attack · Fault attack · SFA · SIFA

1 Introduction

Fault attacks and passive side-channel attacks, like power [17] or EM analysis [21], are very powerful attacks on implementations of cryptographic algorithms. Therefore, devices like smart cards and IoT devices implement corresponding countermeasures, especially if they are potentially physically accessible by an attacker. In the case of symmetric cryptography, the typical approach to protecting an implementation against these attacks is to use masking and redundancy mechanisms. Masking is the most prominent and widely deployed countermeasure against passive side-channel attacks. There exists a wide range of masking schemes for software and hardware [15,22,23] providing protection up to a given protection order.

The list of authors is in alphabetical order (https://www.ams.org/profession/leaders/culture/CultureStatement04.pdf).

T. Peyrin and S. Galbraith (Eds.): ASIACRYPT 2018, LNCS 11273, pp. 315–342, 2018.
https://doi.org/10.1007/978-3-030-03329-3_11

For redundancy mechanisms against fault attacks, there has been less research compared to masking. A standard approach to counteract fault attacks is to use temporal or spacial redundancy mechanisms to detect errors. The basic idea is to compute critical operations multiple times and to release the output only if all redundant computations match. There are also works that directly combine masking and redundant encoding techniques for error detection [24]. The standard reasoning when combining masking and error-detection mechanisms is that their effects add up. For example, assume an implementation of AES protected by a masking scheme of protection order d and all encryption/decryption operations are always computed d times, compared, and the output is only released if the outputs of all d operations match. In this case, the typical assumption is that this implementation is secured against up to d fault inductions in one execution/encryption, because this is detected by the redundant computations, as well as secured against side-channel attacks of up to order d due to the masking scheme.

This reasoning is valid for fault attacks that exploit faulty outputs of a cryptographic algorithm to reveal the key. The most prominent attacks of this type are Differential Fault Attacks (DFA) [2] and Statistical Fault Attacks (SFA) [13]. However, some variants of fault attacks are based on a different approach. Ineffective fault attacks (IFA) [5] and Statistical Ineffective Fault Attacks (SIFA) [10] exploit those outputs of a cipher that are correct although a fault induction has been performed. While IFA requires exact knowledge about the location and effect of a fault, SIFA has much more relaxed requirements, thus allowing to exploit noisy faults whose exact effect is unknown to the attacker. The basic idea of SIFA is to repeatedly execute a cryptographic operation with a fixed key for different inputs and to apply a fault induction for each execution. The attacker then collects those outputs of the cryptographic operation where the fault induction has not changed any intermediate value. Given that the implementation is protected by an error-detection scheme, such as a redundant execution of the cipher, this corresponds exactly to the valid outputs of the system. In fact, the error detection that is implemented against DFA provides exactly the filtering of the outputs which is needed to apply SIFA or IFA.

Our Contribution. So far, implementations combing masking and error-detection schemes were typically thought to be secure against attacks exploiting single ineffective faults due to masking, as discussed for example by Clavier for IFA [5]. It was typically assumed that all shares representing an intermediate value would need to be faulted for exploiting ineffective faults and it was an open question whether this can be done efficiently in practice.

In this work, we show that SIFA attacks are much more powerful than expected so far. Our central contribution is to show that SIFA is not only independent of the degree of redundancy but also essentially independent of the degree of masking for typical masked implementations and hence a suitable choice against implementations with countermeasures against both power analysis and fault attacks. Additionally, we show that SIFA is not restricted to

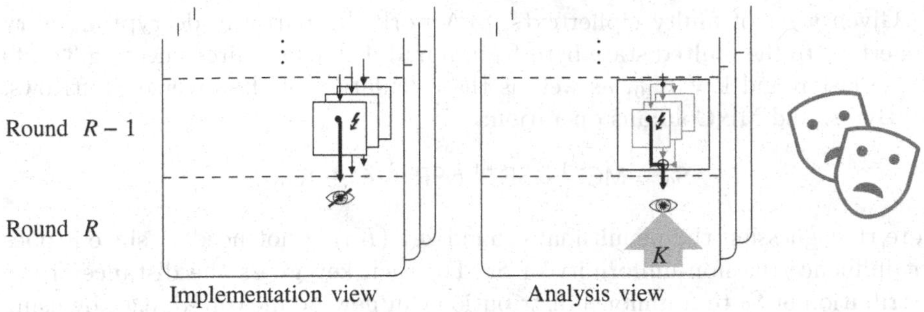

Fig. 1. Biased fault attacks on masked, redundant implementations: high-level view.

biased faults. Instead, any type of fault might be suitable to mount this kind of attack. In order to better explain why, we introduce a change of perspective by separating the fault location and the logical attack location. To back up our claims we provide a broad evaluation based on multiple (masked) S-boxes and two real AES implementations.

More concretely, we demonstrate that faulting a single share during the computation of an S-box is often sufficient to induce a bias in an unshared intermediate value, which can then be exploited with a statistical analysis based on SIFA. Unlike classical fault attacks, attackers cannot directly use this fault as a distinguisher for the key recovery attack: they cannot recover this intermediate value from observing the ciphertext and guessing parts of the key, but can only recover the unshared output of the S-box (Fig. 1). We analyze the impact of the local fault on the unshared output for several different S-boxes (including the AES S-box), fault distributions, masking schemes, and protection orders, as well as other fault countermeasures like dummy rounds. We conclude that in all analyzed cases, a simple fault setup with a single fault attempt per encryption is sufficient to recover part of the key, given a suitable number of faulted encryptions. This number depends on the precision of the fault and the deployed countermeasures; for example, 1000 encryptions with a cheap clock glitching setup are sufficient for an 8-bit AES software implementation protected with 10th-order masking and arbitrary temporal redundancy on block cipher level running on a standard 8-bit microcontroller.

2 Background on Statistical Faults

2.1 Statistical Fault Attacks

Statistical Fault Attacks (SFA), originally proposed by Fuhr et al. [13], present a way to recover an AES key with quite relaxed assumptions on the fault induction. In fact, SFA solely requires the attacker to let one AES state byte in round 9 follow any (possibly unknown) non-uniform distribution. This can be achieved in practice, e.g., by using several types of stuck-at faults or instruction skips.

Given a set of faulty ciphertexts, SFA works by partially decrypting every ciphertext to the faulted state byte S_9 in round 9. This requires guessing 32 bits of the last round key K_{10}, as well as the calculation of the inverse ShiftRows, SubBytes, and MixColumns operation:

$$S_9 = \mathsf{MC}^{-1} \circ \mathsf{SB}^{-1} \circ \mathsf{SR}^{-1}(C \oplus K_{10}).$$

Note that guessing the penultimate round key (K_9) is not needed, since it does not influence the non-uniformity of S_9. For each key guess the distance of the distribution of S_9 to a uniform distribution can now be measured, e.g., by using the χ^2-statistic (CHI) or the closely related Squared Euclidean Imbalance (SEI). For a sufficient number of evaluated ciphertexts, the key guess corresponding to the highest CHI or SEI statistic is most likely correct. The necessary number of ciphertexts depends on the strength of the bias, i.e., the distance of the biased distribution p from the uniform distribution, which is quantified by the capacity $C(p)$. If the bias is small, then the necessary number of faulted ciphertexts is inverse proportional to $C(p)$; we refer to [10] for a more detailed discussion.

One obvious downside of SFA, from a practical perspective, is that it relies on exploiting faulty ciphertexts. This is problematic, since most cryptographic implementations that operate with critical data can be expected to have various countermeasures against implementation attacks in place. A fault countermeasure like temporal or spacial redundancy would already prevent SFA using single fault inductions. While an adoption of SFA to some fault countermeasures is possible, a significantly more powerful attacker would be required. Hence, the threat of SFA to such protected implementations is limited.

2.2 Statistical Ineffective Fault Attacks

Statistical Ineffective Fault Attacks (SIFA) [10] allow an attacker to circumvent many popular fault countermeasures. As the name suggests, and in contrast to SFA, SIFA solely relies on exploiting faulted encryptions where the induced faults are ineffective and the obtained (filtered) ciphertexts are hence always correct. The basic observation of SIFA is that induced faults can lead to a non-uniform distribution of intermediate values for the cases where the fault has been ineffective, which in turn can be exploited in a key-recovery attack. The data complexity of the attack then depends on the strength of the bias in the targeted intermediate variable and the necessary number of faulted encryptions to obtain sufficiently many ineffective samples.

SIFA is applicable just as easily for more than two redundant computations, since only one computation needs to be faulted. In fact, it has been shown in [10] that SIFA is not only applicable against redundancy countermeasures, but also against infective countermeasures [27]. Although in the latter case more faulted encryptions are necessary, the presented attacks are still efficient.

Consider an AES with simple temporal redundancy and an attacker that is able to fault a certain byte in round 9 such that the faulted value follows some non-uniform distribution, which is not known to the attacker. If the attacker is faulting only one of the redundant computations, the attacker will eventually observe correct ciphertexts where the induced fault was ineffective. This filtered set of correct ciphertexts will, when partially decrypted using a correct key guess, typically also show some non-uniform, biased distribution in the faulted byte, related to the non-uniform distribution after fault induction. Now, the attacker can perform the same key recovery attack as in SFA. The basic intuition here is that certain values of the faulted byte lead to ineffective faults and hence correct ciphertexts more often than others. As a consequence, when decrypting this filtered set of correct ciphertexts using a correct key guess, certain values in the faulted byte will show up more frequently than others. Still, knowledge about the exact effect of the fault induction (and the resulting non-uniformity) is not required, since the SEI or CHI metric measures the distance of any distribution to a uniform distribution.

This fact will be important when SIFA is performed against masked implementations (cf. Sect. 3). Here it is practically impossible to predict the actual effect of a fault induction if the attacked implementation is unknown. At the same time it is still comparably easy to cause a joint non-uniform distribution over all shares of an intermediate variable as discussed in the upcoming sections. However, as we will see, it is beneficial to change the usual view that faults just manipulate values. Instead, to better understand the underlying principles exploited in our attack, it is more useful to see the faults as changes to the actual function that is computed.

3 Faults on Masking

In this section, we study the influence of single faults on masked AND gates and subsequently on masked S-boxes. To do so, we first briefly recapitulate the fundamentals of masking. Then, we discuss how faults influence the distribution of unmasked values by taking masked AND gates as an example. After that, we evaluate how single faults influence masked implementations of some S-boxes. Finally, we take a closer look at the internal activities in a faulted masked S-box that allow an SFA and SIFA and argue that it is probably always possible to influence the distribution of input and output values of masked S-boxes, so that an attacker can exploit this behavior using techniques introduced for SFA and SIFA.

For an easier understanding of why single faults on a single share can cause a bias in unshared values, we consider very simple fault models such as stuck-at faults in the following exposition. However, it is important to note that the attack approach generalizes efficiently to noisy, unpredictable and imprecise faults. For a discussion of how the attack complexity scales under the influence of noise, we refer to Sect. 5 and the SIFA analysis in [10].

3.1 Concept of Masking

The goal of masking is to randomize the representation of security-sensitive data in each execution to counteract side-channel analysis by making the resulting side-channel leakage, such as power consumption or electromagnetic emanation, independent of the underlying data. The most popular masking approaches are Boolean masking schemes, which are formed over finite field arithmetic in GF(2^n).

In Boolean masking, a sensitive variable x is split into a number of so-called shares (denoted x_i) which, when considered on their own or in conjunction of up to d shares, are statistically independent of the unshared variable x. This degree of independence is usually referred to as the protection order d and requires to split each variable with sensitive information into at least $d+1$ shares. The shares are uniformly random in each execution, but at any time, it is ensured that the sum over all shares again results in the unshared variable x:

$$x = x_0 \oplus x_1 \oplus x_2 \oplus \cdots \oplus x_d.$$

In a similar manner, functions over shared variables are split into component functions $\mathrm{f}_i(\dots)$ such that again a correct and secure sharing of the original function is established:

$$\mathrm{f}(x, y) = \mathrm{f}_0(\dots) \oplus \mathrm{f}_1(\dots) \oplus \mathrm{f}_2(\dots) \oplus \cdots \oplus \mathrm{f}_d(\dots).$$

Throughout the entire implementation, a proper separation of shares and of the output of the component functions needs to be ensured in order to not violate the dth-order independence, which is commonly expressed in the probing model of Ishai et al. [16]. In the probing model, an attacker is modeled with the ability to probe up to d intermediate results of the masked implementation. An implementation is said to be secure if the probing attacker cannot gain any statistical advantage in guessing any secret variable by combining the probed results in an arbitrary manner. While this share separation can be easily ensured for functions which are linear over GF(2^n) – for example, the masked calculation of $x \oplus y$ can be performed share-wise ($x_i \oplus y_i$) –, the secure implementation of nonlinear functions usually requires the introduction of fresh randomness.

As an example for a shared implementation of a nonlinear function, we consider the generic masked multiplication algorithm by Ishai et al. [16]. In order to securely calculate $q = x \cdot y$, each of the $d+1$ shares of x is multiplied with each of the shares of y, resulting in $(d+1)^2$ multiplication terms. Subsequently, the multiplication terms are summed up together with fresh random variables denoted $r_{i,j}$, and distributed to the output shares q_i (Algorithm 1).

A first-order masked GF(2) multiplication, which corresponds to the calculation of an AND gate, is given in (1):

$$\begin{aligned} q_0 &= x_0 y_0 \oplus r_{0,1} \\ q_1 &= x_1 y_1 \oplus (r_{0,1} \oplus x_0 y_1 \oplus x_1 y_0). \end{aligned} \tag{1}$$

A uniform distribution of each of the shares of q is ensured by the random r shares. In general, the joint distribution of any d shares of q in the masked multiplication algorithm is uniform, or in other words, any d shares are independently and identically (uniformly) distributed. It thus appears as if in order to insert a bias in the underlying unshared value, an attacker would need to insert a biased fault in either each share of x or y, or to insert a bias in each of the component functions in the calculation of q. However, in the following, we show that this intuition is not true.

Algorithm 1. Masked GF(2^n) multiplication according to Ishai et al. [16] (ISW)

Input: $x_0, \dots x_d$, $y_0, \dots y_d \in \mathrm{GF}(2^n)$
Output: $q_0, \dots q_d \in \mathrm{GF}(2^n)$
for $i = 0$ to d **do**
  for $j = i + 1$ to d **do**
    $r_{i,j} \xleftarrow{?} \mathrm{GF}(2^n)$
    $t_{i,j} \leftarrow r_{i,j}$
    $t_{j,i} \leftarrow r_{i,j} \oplus x_i y_j \oplus x_j y_i$
for $i = 0$ to d **do**
  $q_i \leftarrow x_i y_i$
  for $j = 0$ to d **do**
    if $i \neq j$ **then**
      $q_i \leftarrow q_i \oplus t_{i,j}$

3.2 Faulting Masked AND Gates

We first note that the calculation of the AND $q = x \cdot y$ itself has a probability of 25% for q to be 1. An attacker therefore successfully biases the masked AND gate if the probability of q to be 1 is more or less likely than 25%. As an example, we consider an attacker who can skip any AND calculation in Eq. 1, for instance the first AND calculating $x_0 y_0$ in q_0. The shared function then effectively calculates q $(= q_0 \oplus q_1)$ to be $x_1 y_1 \oplus x_0 y_1 \oplus x_1 y_0$, which has a probability of 37.5% to be 1. If the attacker instead introduced a fault that skips the addition of the uniformly random bit $r_{0,1}$ in q_0, then the distribution of q would again be biased, since the probability of observing a 1 changes from 25% to 50%.

We observe the same biases when looking at single faults for other masked AND gates, like the one used in the CMS scheme of Reparaz et al. [22] or in the Domain-Oriented Masking scheme by Gross et al. [14,15]. This same bias behavior results from the fact that these masked ANDs calculate the same terms $x_i y_j$. The masked ANDs only differ in the arrangement of $x_i y_j$ in q_0 and q_1, and the amount of used fresh randomness. Since q is equal to $q_0 \oplus q_1$, the arrangement of the terms has no influence on the bias behavior of q, and a fault of an addition of a single random r bit has the same impact on all masked ANDs.

Another prominent protection mechanism falling in the category of masking schemes are threshold implementations [20]. Threshold implementations use an increased number of shares to achieve first-order side-channel resistance without requiring fresh randomness. In order to explore the impact on threshold implementations, we look at a four-share realization of a first-order masked AND gate by Nikova et al. [20]:

$$\begin{aligned} q_0 &= (x_2 \oplus x_3)(y_1 \oplus y_2) \oplus y_1 \oplus y_2 \oplus y_3 \oplus x_1 \oplus x_2 \oplus x_3 \\ q_1 &= (x_0 \oplus x_2)(y_0 \oplus y_3) \oplus y_0 \oplus y_2 \oplus y_3 \oplus x_0 \oplus x_2 \oplus x_3 \\ q_2 &= (x_1 \oplus x_3)(y_0 \oplus y_3) \oplus y_1 \oplus x_1 \\ q_3 &= (x_0 \oplus x_1)(y_1 \oplus y_2) \oplus y_0 \oplus x_0 \end{aligned} \quad (2)$$

For this shared AND gate, we perform two experiments. In the first experiment, we have a look at the distribution of the output $q = q_0 \oplus q_1 \oplus q_2 \oplus q_3$ assuming an instruction skip. In the second, we fix one input share x_0 to zero and look what happens.

For the instruction skip, we assume that in q_0 one instruction is skipped and so $q_0 = (x_2)(y_1 \oplus y_2) \oplus y_1 \oplus y_2 \oplus y_3 \oplus x_1 \oplus x_2 \oplus x_3$ is calculated, the other shares are processed correctly. In this case, we observe that for all 256 possible values of the shared input, the unshared output is 160 times (62.5%) 0 and 96 (37.5%) times 1, a clear deviation of the value an unfaulted AND should have.

Next, we fix x_0 to zero and perform the computations according to Eq. 2 for all 256 possible values the shared input can take. If we now look at q, we see that 192 times a 0 (75%) appears and 64 times a 1 (25%), which corresponds to the distribution of a correct AND gate. However, if we only consider correct computations of $q = x \cdot y$, we observe that only 192 out of 256 computations are performed correctly. For those correct computations q is 160 times a 0 (83.3%) and 32 times a 1 (16.6%). This "filtered" distribution is the one an attacker can potentially exploit in the case of SIFA [10]. In the next section, we will discuss the consequences of our observations with respect to S-boxes.

3.3 Faulting Masked S-Boxes

In this section, we discuss how single faults influence the behavior of S-boxes. It is worth mentioning that our selection of masked S-boxes is arbitrary and does not imply that those S-boxes are weaker or more susceptible to SFA and SIFA than others. We have selected those S-boxes, because they have a simple and compact description. We will start with a compact 4-bit S-box called Sbox13 [28] shown in Fig. 2. We have implemented a masked implementation of this S-box in software by using a four-shared threshold implementation of AND (see Eq. 2), OR and XOR. We target exclusively the AND labeled with q, x, and y in Fig. 2.

For the first experiment, we assume an instruction skip that alters the execution of the first AND of the S-box, changing the calculation of one share q_0 to $q_0 = (x_2)(y_1 \oplus y_2) \oplus y_1 \oplus y_2 \oplus y_3 \oplus x_1 \oplus x_2 \oplus x_3$. In Fig. 3a, we record the

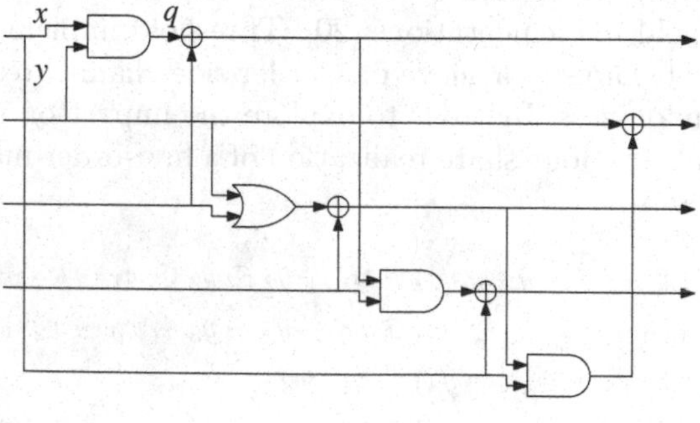

Fig. 2. Schematic of the 4 × 4 S-box: Sbox13 [28].

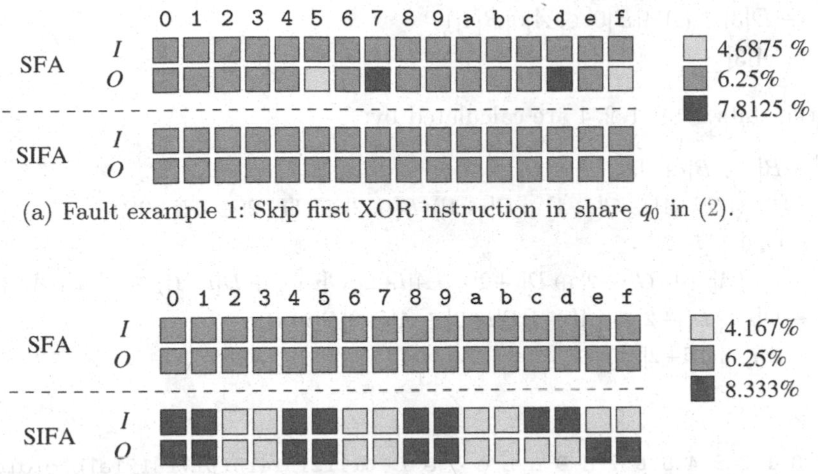

(a) Fault example 1: Skip first XOR instruction in share q_0 in (2).

(b) Fault example 2: Set input share x_0 of the first AND to zero in (2).

Fig. 3. Distribution of input I and output O for faulted 4×4 Sbox13.

distribution of each unshared input value and each unshared output value for each of the $2^{4 \cdot 4} = 65536$ shared input combinations, which can be exploited by an SFA [13], as well as the "filtered" distribution for ineffectively faulted S-box transitions, which can be exploited by SIFA [10]. This "filtered" distribution stems from the subset of transitions, for which the induction of the fault has no influence on the output of the S-box.

As we can see in Fig. 3a, in the unfiltered case, we see a clearly non-uniform distribution, which can be possibly exploited by an SFA. However, we observe a uniform distribution in the SIFA case. So does this mean this S-box is secure against SIFA? Let us consider the distributions we obtain when setting one share x_0 at the input of the first AND permanently to 0. The corresponding distributions we get in this experiment are shown in Figure 3b.

As we can see in Fig. 3b, the situation for this fault changes, so that now, the ineffective faults can be exploited, whereas the distribution without filtering cannot be exploited. Until now, we have exploited the sequential sharing of instructions, especially that we can change the distribution of an AND gate. So one might wonder what happens if an S-box is directly shared, so that the output shares are uniformly distributed.

To explore the case of directly shared S-boxes, let us take a closer look at the uniform 4-share threshold implementation of the Keccak S-box proposed by Bilgin et al. [3]. Here, $A[i]$, $B[i]$, $C[i]$, and $D[i]$ represent the 4 shares of bit i with $i = 0, \ldots, 4$. While the bit $i = 3$ is calculated by:

$$A'[3] \leftarrow B[3] \oplus B[0] \oplus C[0] \oplus D[0] \oplus ((B[4] \oplus C[4] \oplus D[4])(B[0] \oplus C[0] \oplus D[0]))$$
$$B'[3] \leftarrow C[3] \oplus A[0] \oplus (A[4](C[0] \oplus D[0]) \oplus A[0](C[4] \oplus D[4]) \oplus A[0]A[4])$$

$$C'[3] \leftarrow D[3] \oplus (A[4]B[0] \oplus A[0]B[4])$$
$$D'[3] \leftarrow A[3]$$

the other bits $i = 0, 1, 2, 4$ are calculated by:

$$\begin{aligned} A'[i] \leftarrow & B[i] \oplus B[i{+}2] \\ & \oplus\ ((B[i{+}1] \oplus C[i{+}1] \oplus D[i{+}1])(B[i{+}2] \oplus C[i{+}2] \oplus D[i{+}2])) \\ B'[i] \leftarrow & C_i \oplus C[i{+}2] \\ & \oplus\ (A[i{+}1](C[i{+}2] \oplus D[i{+}2]) \oplus A[i{+}2](C[i{+}1] \oplus D[i{+}1]) \oplus A[i{+}1]A[i{+}2]) \\ C'[i] \leftarrow & D[i] \oplus D[i{+}2] \oplus (A[i{+}1]B[i{+}2] \oplus A[i{+}2]B[i{+}1]) \\ D'[i] \leftarrow & A[i] \oplus A[i{+}2] \end{aligned}$$

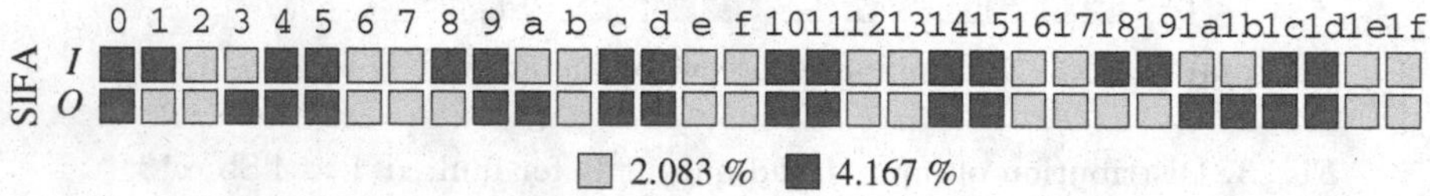

Fig. 4. Distribution of I, O for faulted 4-shared Keccak S-box.

Now, in our simple experiment, let us consider that bits 0 to 3 are calculated correctly and an attacker changes the value of one input share $A[0]$ always to 0 before the calculation of the 4 shares for output bit $i = 4$. Then an attacker is able to mount SIFA as indicated by the distributions of Fig. 4. This leads again to an exploitable bias of the distribution of unmasked values at the output of the S-box and the attacker can mount SIFA.

The aim of this section was to give reproducible, easy-to-follow examples of inducing a bias in the unshared variable of masked S-boxes by just faulting one share of the S-box. We want to mention that the given ways and locations of introducing the faults are not exhaustive and that there are many more locations and various types of faults that make an attack successful. In the next section, we give a closer view on the problem of protecting an S-box against these attacks and get more insight into the effect allowing statistical attacks with the help of a 3-bit S-box as an example.

3.4 A Closer Look

In general, fault attacks exploit knowledge about intermediate values of cryptographic primitives, which are gained by disturbing the computation or intermediate values directly by the means of faults. In the case of DFA [2], this knowledge is that in certain intermediate bits or bytes a difference is induced, while others remain fault-free. In the case of SFA and SIFA, this knowledge is that the distribution of certain intermediate values is changed from a uniform to a non-uniform distribution. This allows an attacker to guess parts of the round key and calculate backwards to these influenced intermediate values from collected ciphertexts. If a key guess is wrong, an attacker expects to see a distribution of intermediate values, which is closer to uniform compared to the guess of the right key.

Getting such a non-uniform distribution of intermediate values can be achieved in many ways. For ciphers following the SPN structure, where every S-box and the linear layer is a bijective function (permutation), non-uniform distribution of intermediate value can be achieved, for instance, by disturbing the computation of a single S-box, so that this S-box does not act as a permutation anymore. While such a behavior can be expected from an unmasked S-box in the case of a fault induction, this seems quite counterintuitive for masked implementations at first glance. Thus, we will first discuss the unmasked case to get more insight in which cases SFA and SIFA will work. Then we will take a closer look on masked S-box implementations.

Influencing Unmasked S-Boxes. First, we will explore the case of SFA. We consider a bijective S-box, as illustrated in Fig. 5. For the sake of simplicity, let us assume that the S-box is implemented in a bit-sliced manner (as a sequence of instructions), or as a Boolean circuit in hardware. Let us further assume that an attacker influences the correct computation by the means of faults. By faulting this computation, it is very likely that the faulted S-box does not behave as a bijection, but rather becomes a general function, which is non-surjective. This leads to a non-uniform distribution of intermediate values, which can be exploited with SFA. In the case of SIFA, transitions where a fault induction has an effect and causes a change in the output of the S-box are filtered. This filtering can happen by using the fact that detection-based countermeasures do not deliver an output in the case the fault has an effect, or by comparing the obtained output with an output where no fault was injected. So in SIFA, we observe a function where a reduced set of transitions remains compared to the unfaulted S-box.

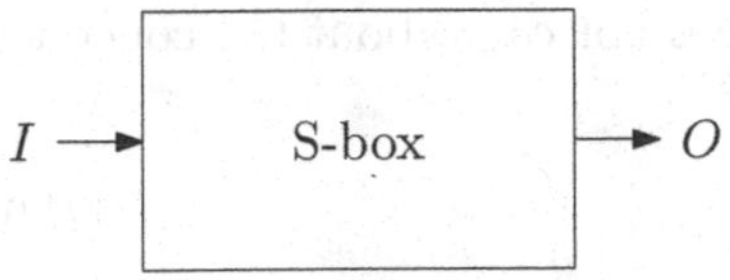

Fig. 5. An unmasked S-box.

To get more insight into the behavior of a faulted S-box, we will use the 3×3 S-box χ based on Daemen's χ-layer [7,8] as an illustrative example. Figure 6a shows the 3-bit S-box χ, where the red cross represents a fault that sets the input of the subsequent inversion to zero and hence the input of the AND gate to 1. Please note that this is only one example of many how to fault an S-box to apply an SFA or SIFA.

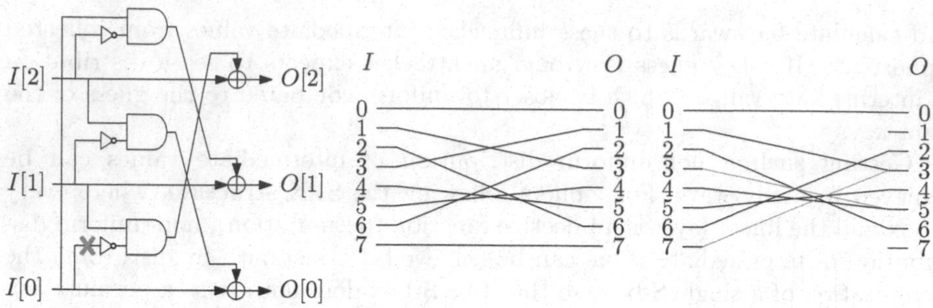

(a) Circuit with single fault (b) Unfaulted mapping (c) Faulted mapping

Fig. 6. 3-bit S-box χ with a single fault. (Color figure online)

The fault depicted in Fig. 6a changes the behavior of the χ S-box, which is not bijective anymore. Figure 6c shows the transition graph for the faulted S-box. The fault just changes the transitions depicted in red.

In our case, the transitions mapping from $3 \rightarrow 1$ and $7 \rightarrow 7$ in the unfaulted S-box (Fig. 6b), now map from $3 \rightarrow 5$ and $7 \rightarrow 3$ (considering $I[0]$ and $O[0]$ being the LSB). This means that the output values 1 and 7 never appear, but 3 and 5 appear twice, leading to a non-surjective behavior. In the case of SIFA, the red edges represent fault inductions that show an effect on the output. When applying SIFA, those edges are filtered (e.g. by detection-based countermeasure) and just the black edges remain. Hence, when performing SIFA, the correct transitions $3 \rightarrow 1$ and $7 \rightarrow 7$ do not appear and an attacker can observe an exploitable non-uniform distribution of intermediates.

Influencing Masked S-Boxes. Now let us have a look at a shared bijective S-box. For instance, consider the masked S-box shown in Fig. 7a that takes two shares as input and returns two output shares. Here, the goal for an attacker is also to influence the distribution or transitions of the unshared values $I = I_0 \oplus I_1$ and $O = O_0 \oplus O_1$, but does not care about the concrete values of the shares.

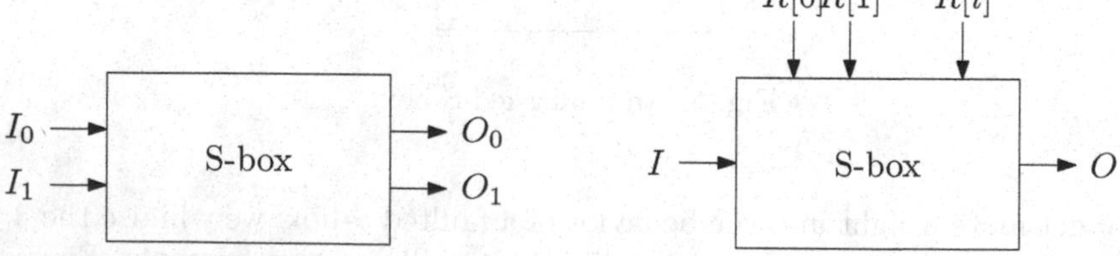

(a) Implementation with 2 shares (b) Functional equivalent view

Fig. 7. A masked S-box.

For this reason, it is easier to work with the functional equivalent model shown in Fig. 7b. In this model, we see a masked S-box as a function, which takes an unshared input I and some randomness $R[i]$ and produces an unshared output O. Here, some of the random bits symbolize all values a shared input can take in a real implementation, e.g., $I_0 = I \oplus R[0]$, and $I_1 = R[0]$, while others represent randomness used in the masked implementation. Now, we can see masking as a very special and complicated function, which takes the inputs I, $R[0]$, $R[1]$, ... $R[i]$ and produces an output O, so that the same I always leads to the same O for all possible choices of $R[0]$, $R[1]$, ... $R[i]$. It seems very unlikely that a shared S-box behaves in the same manner in the presence of faults.

To apply SFA successfully, we need that not all values for O (iterating over all values of I) appear the exact same number of times when counting for all possible assignments of $R[0]$, $R[1]$, and $R[2]$. This prerequisite is very likely to hold considering an attacker that can tamper with the intermediate calculation performed, even when restricting the attacker to just manipulate one share used in an intermediate calculation. Similarly, to apply SIFA successfully, we need a fault such that among the ineffectively faulted computations, not all values for I or O appear the exact same number of times over all values of $R[0]$, $R[1]$,... $R[i]$. This condition is similarly very likely to happen in practice when introducing just single faults, as we will show with our practical experiments in Sect. 4.

As an example, consider again the 3-bit Keccak χ S-box, now with the following masked implementation:

$$O_0[i] \leftarrow (I_0[i+1] \oplus 1) I_0[i+2] \oplus ((I_0[i+1] \oplus 1) I_1[i+2] \oplus I_0[i])$$
$$O_1[i] \leftarrow I_1[i+1] I_0[i+2] \oplus (I_1[i+1] I_1[i+2] \oplus I_1[i])$$

This masked S-box just serves us as an illustrative example of the effect of faults on an S-box, hence, we do not care about potential positioning of registers or additional randomness at the output for re-sharing. Figure 8 shows the equivalent circuit of the S-box, where again we just set a single value to 0. The result of this fault is that the value of $O_0[2]$ equals $I_0[2]$. Everything else is calculated correctly.

For our example depicted in Fig. 8, we list all possible assignments of $I[0]$, $I[1]$, $I[2]$, $R[0]$, $R[1]$, and $R[2]$ in Table 1. The entries marked in red in Table 1 are entries where the fault depicted in Fig. 8 has an effect. Due to the more complex calculations that happen for masked S-boxes, we get a more complex relation between masks and actual values of bits. For instance, the transition $2 \rightarrow 6$ is only valid if $R[0] = 1$ and wrong $(2 \rightarrow 2)$ if $R[0] = 0$.

Again, we can represent all possible transitions from inputs I, to the outputs O in a graph shown in Fig. 9 (in a similar way as in Fig. 6c). However, due to the 2^3 possible ways of masking our input values, each transition from input to output will happen 8 times for an *unfaulted* masked 3-bit S-box χ. In the faulted case, this condition does not hold anymore as shown in Table 1. Hence, we have additional transitions shown in red in Fig. 9. These "wrong" transitions also reduce the number of times the "correct" transition happens.

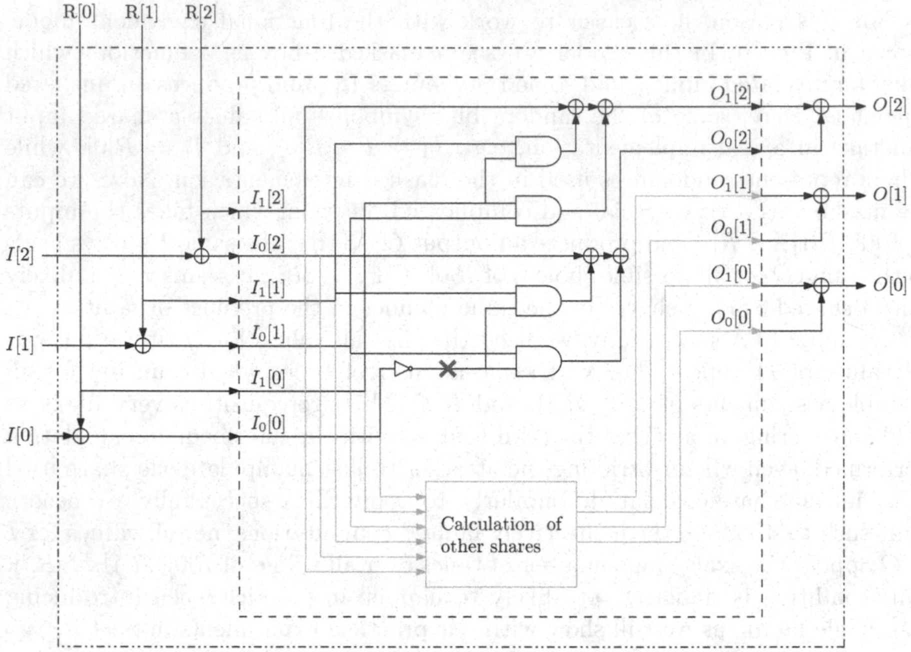

Fig. 8. Single fault on masked 3-bit χ S-box.

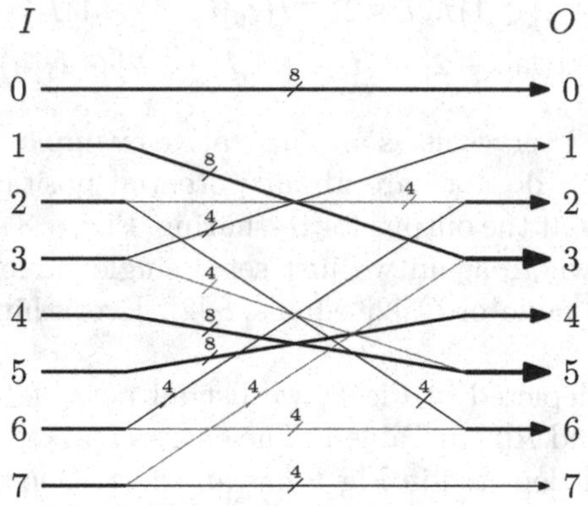

Fig. 9. Transition graph of faulted masked 3-bit S-box χ. (Color figure online)

If we now count the number of transitions in Fig. 9 that lead to a certain value O, we see that 12 transitions lead to values 3 and 5, whereas only 4 lead to 1 and 7. This means that an attacker faulting a device can apply an SFA, since the attacker can expect a non-uniform distribution of the value after the S-box for correct key guesses. If we apply SIFA, the transitions marked in red in Fig. 9, will be filtered. As an effect, the transitions $2 \rightarrow 6$, $3 \rightarrow 1$, $5 \rightarrow 2$, and

Table 1. Transitions of faulted masked 3-bit S-box χ.

$I[2]$	$R[2]$	$I[1]$	$R[1]$	$I[0]$	$R[0]$	$O[2]$	$O[1]$	$O[0]$	$I[2]$	$R[2]$	$I[1]$	$R[1]$	$I[0]$	$R[0]$	$O[2]$	$O[1]$	$O[0]$
0	0	0	0	0	0	0	0	0	1	0	0	0	0	0	1	0	1
0	0	0	0	0	1	0	0	0	1	0	0	0	0	1	1	0	1
0	0	0	0	1	0	0	1	1	1	0	0	0	1	0	1	0	0
0	0	0	0	1	1	0	1	1	1	0	0	0	1	1	1	0	0
0	0	0	1	0	0	0	0	0	1	0	0	1	0	0	1	0	1
0	0	0	1	0	1	0	0	0	1	0	0	1	0	1	1	0	1
0	0	0	1	1	0	0	1	1	1	0	0	1	1	0	1	0	0
0	0	0	1	1	1	0	1	1	1	0	0	1	1	1	1	0	0
0	0	1	0	0	0	0	1	0	1	0	1	0	0	0	1	1	0
0	0	1	0	0	1	1	1	0	1	0	1	0	0	1	0	1	0
0	0	1	0	1	0	0	0	1	1	0	1	0	1	0	1	1	1
0	0	1	0	1	1	1	0	1	1	0	1	0	1	1	0	1	1
0	0	1	1	0	0	0	1	0	1	0	1	1	0	0	1	1	0
0	0	1	1	0	1	1	1	0	1	0	1	1	0	1	0	1	0
0	0	1	1	1	0	0	0	1	1	0	1	1	1	0	1	1	1
0	0	1	1	1	1	1	0	1	1	0	1	1	1	1	0	1	1
0	1	0	0	0	0	0	0	0	1	1	0	0	0	0	1	0	1
0	1	0	0	0	1	0	0	0	1	1	0	0	0	1	1	0	1
0	1	0	0	1	0	0	1	1	1	1	0	0	1	0	1	0	0
0	1	0	0	1	1	0	1	1	1	1	0	0	1	1	1	0	0
0	1	0	1	0	0	0	0	0	1	1	0	1	0	0	1	0	1
0	1	0	1	0	1	0	0	0	1	1	0	1	0	1	1	0	1
0	1	0	1	1	0	0	1	1	1	1	0	1	1	0	1	0	0
0	1	0	1	1	1	0	1	1	1	1	0	1	1	1	1	0	0
0	1	1	0	0	0	0	1	0	1	1	1	0	0	0	1	1	0
0	1	1	0	0	1	1	1	0	1	1	1	0	0	1	0	1	0
0	1	1	0	1	0	0	0	1	1	1	1	0	1	0	1	1	1
0	1	1	0	1	1	1	0	1	1	1	1	0	1	1	0	1	1
0	1	1	1	0	0	0	1	0	1	1	1	1	0	0	1	1	0
0	1	1	1	0	1	1	1	0	1	1	1	1	0	1	0	1	0
0	1	1	1	1	0	0	0	1	1	1	1	1	1	0	1	1	1
0	1	1	1	1	1	1	0	1	1	1	1	1	1	1	0	1	1

$7 \rightarrow 7$ appear with reduced frequency for uniformly distributed $R[0]$, $R[1]$, and $R[2]$. Again, this can be exploited in a key recovery attack.

4 Attack Evaluation

In this section, we demonstrate the applicability of Statistically Ineffective Fault Analysis (SIFA) for two very different publicly available masked AES implementations. First, we perform a practical attack evaluation for the provable secure, higher-order masked AES implementation from Rivain et al. [23] on a standard 8-bit microcontroller (ATXmega 128D4). We then present a comprehensive evaluation of simulated faults for the 32-bit, bitsliced, first-order masked AES implementation of Schwabe and Stoffelen [25]. Since both implementations do not originally have additional fault countermeasures in place, we added temporal redundancy, meaning that the block cipher is executed multiple times and the ciphertexts are compared. The number of redundant computations was set to two, since more redundancy does not affect the effectiveness of SIFA.

Our experiments require multiple faulted encryptions, but only one fault induction per encryption. The precise location as well as the actual effect of the induced fault does not need to be known by the attacker. Indeed, inducing a fault anywhere in the shared S-box in round 9 likely leads to a situation that is similar as described in Sect. 3.4. The resulting joint non-uniform (biased) distribution over all shares of an intermediate variable can then be used to distinguish correct and wrong key candidates (cf. Sect. 2).

4.1 Practical Attack on AES from Rivain et al.

The higher-order masked AES from Rivain et al. [23] consists of a generic dth-order masked S-box that is combined with a linear layer for the $d+1$ shares of the AES state. The target of our fault induction is the shared S-box implementation in round 9. First, we briefly describe the implementation of the masked S-box. Then we present the attack setup that was used for fault induction. The results of this practical evaluation are stated at the end of this section.

Generic Higher-Order Masked S-Box. The algebraic description of the 8-bit AES S-box consists of determining the multiplicative inverse of a number in $\mathbb{F}_{2^8} = \mathbb{F}_2[x]/(x^8 + x^4 + x^3 + x + 1)$, followed by an affine transformation over $\mathbb{F}_2^8$. While masking the affine transformation is trivial, since it can be calculated separately for each share, the calculation of the masked multiplicative inverse requires more work. In the design of Rivain et al. the inversion is calculated via the power function $x \rightarrow x^{254}$ over $\mathbb{F}_{2^8}$ which is in return calculated via the square-and-multiply algorithm. The squaring operation in $\mathbb{F}_{2^8}$ is a linear function which leaves the masking of the field multiplication as the only non-trivial task. The used algorithm for dth-order masked field multiplication is based on the ISW scheme (cf. Algorithm 1). For a more detailed description we refer to the original paper [23].

Attack Setup. In the practical evaluation, we perform fault inductions on an ATXmega 128D4 via clock glitching. More precisely, we insert an additional fast clock cycle in between two ordinary clock cycles during the execution of one of the redundant encryptions. The width of the induced clock cycle is chosen such that it is recognized by the microprocessor but too short to allow a correct execution of the current instruction. The target of our fault is one of the higher-order masked field multiplication operations (`SecMult`) that occur multiple times (1st-order: 64 times, 10th-order: 2880 times) during the computation of the masked S-box in round 9. We neither require to fault one specific `SecMult` invocation nor to fault one specific instruction within any of the `SecMult` invocations. In fact, any fault that causes a joint non-uniform distribution over all shares (cf. Sect. 3.3) is sufficient for our attack. For this reason, finding a suitable fault location might actually be easier for higher-order masked implementations since the runtime of masked S-boxes grows faster than the runtime of the masked linear layer for increasing masking orders.

The implementation of the higher-order masked AES by Coron et al. [6] has a configurable masking order d. Our experiments were performed up to 10th-order masking, with temporal redundancy as an additional fault countermeasure. In order to attack such a protected implementation we exploit statistically ineffective faults. The restriction to ineffective faults is required, since we want to circumvent the redundancy countermeasure and the subsequent statistical fault analysis is required, since the effect of a fault is almost impossible to predict, in particular if masked and/or unknown implementations are attacked.

If the induced fault results in a faulty computation we do not observe any ciphertext, because of the redundancy countermeasure. However, we do observe correct ciphertexts stemming from faulted encryptions where the induced fault was ineffective. This filtered set of correct ciphertexts can then again be used to perform key recovery. Since our attacks work comparably well for any masking order d we only state concrete results for $d = 10$ in this section.

Results. In Fig. 10, we show the distribution of the AES state bytes in round 9 from the 48 collected correct ciphertexts. For a correct partial key guess, we can observe a strong biased distribution in one of the state bytes in round 9 and thus can perform key recovery (cf. Sect. 2.1). Note that in the attack we only exploit correct ciphertexts and thus successfully circumvent the redundancy countermeasure. Already 20 (of the 48) collected correct ciphertexts stemming from about 1000 faulted encryptions the SEI of the observed distributions is the highest for the correct partial key guess. The time required for collecting the correct ciphertexts was about 3 min, and key recovery was performed in about 2 min with negligible memory requirements. Repetitions of the experiment lead to very similar results.

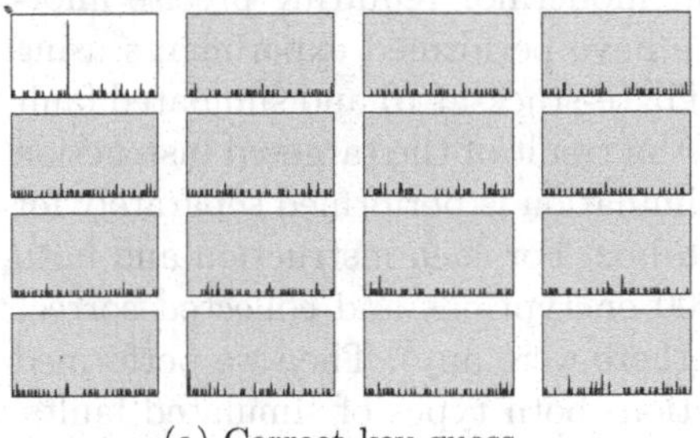

(a) Correct key guess.

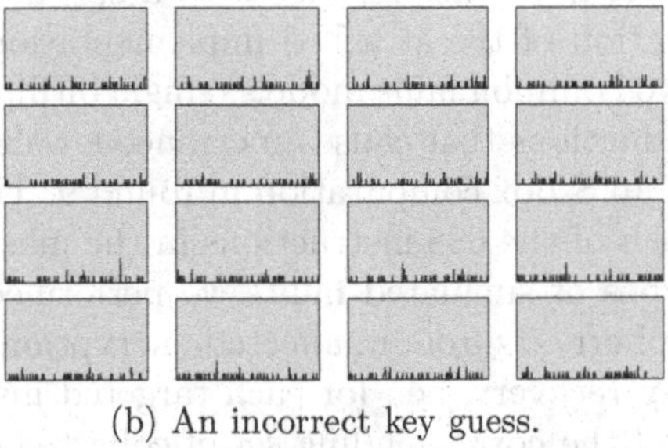

(b) An incorrect key guess.

Fig. 10. 10th-order masked AES with temporal redundancy. One clock glitch was performed during the calculation of the masked Sbox in round 9. Distribution of AES state bytes after S-box in round 9 after collecting a sufficient amount of correct ciphertexts. 32 key bits can be recovered.

4.2 Simulated Attacks on AES from Schwabe and Stoffelen

In this section, we present a comprehensive analysis of simulated faults for an assembler-optimized, masked AES implementation for the 32-bit Cortex-M4 platform with high practical relevance of Schwabe and Stoffelen [25]. This implementation can encrypt two 128-bit inputs per block cipher call in CTR mode and is fully unrolled. For our purposes, we add temporal redundancy but only encrypt one 128-bit input per block cipher call in ECB mode to have the same scenario as in the previous section. We briefly describe the masked S-box implementation of Schwabe and Stoffelen and then we discuss the results of our evaluation that is split into three parts:

First, we analyse how many instructions in the masked S-box in round 9 are "*susceptible*" to faults considering two common fault models, i.e., would allow an attacker to mount SIFA. Then we pick one susceptible instruction and discuss the required effort of mounting SIFA considering 7 common fault models. For each fault model we give the required amount of faulted encryptions and the amount of recoverable key bits. Finally, we present a figure that illustrates the effect of faulting the masked Sbox on the unmasked AES state bytes (that are observed during key recovery).

Optimized, Bitsliced, 1st-Order Masked S-Box. One shared S-box computation consists of 688 instructions and is executed in parallel for the entire AES state. The implementation is based on the efficient bitsliced, S-box implementation from Boyar et al. [4]. Masking via Trichina gates [26] as well as efficient platform-specific scheduling was added by Schwabe and Stoffelen [25].

Results – Susceptible Instructions. In this section, we demonstrate that SIFA is neither restricted to a specific fault model nor requiring precise information of the attacked implementation. We have performed experiments using two common fault models (single bitflip and byte-stuck-at-0) and simulated fault inductions that cause an erroneous value in the result of the targeted instruction of an S-box computation in round 9. This simulation is performed separately for each of the 688 instructions in the masked S-box. For each instruction and both types of simulated faults we performed 2000 encryptions and collected correct ciphertexts from unaffected encryptions (if there were any). Then we performed key recovery, i.e., for each targeted instruction, both types of simulated faults, and the corresponding set of collected ciphertexts we guessed 32 bits of the last round key, calculated back to round 9 and checked if some bytes follow a non-uniform distribution (using the SEI distinguisher). To reduce the runtime of the evaluation we took one shortcut by always fixing 16-bit of the 32-bit partial key guess to the correct value. While this significantly reduced the runtime of our exhaustive analysis, it does not affect the results.

The results of our analysis are presented in Fig. 11. Figure 11a shows for each of the 688 instructions within the masked S-box whether or not single bitflips in this specific instruction allow an attacker to mount SIFA, i.e., recover bits of the key. Note that black lines represent susceptible instructions while white lines represent the other instructions. An instruction is not susceptible, e.g., if a bitflip is never ineffective, always ineffective, or does not lead to a non-uniform distribution that is distinguishable from uniform after observing 2 000 faulted encryptions. In total, 359 out of 688 (52%) of the instructions are susceptible to single bitflips. In Fig. 11b, we show the same analysis using byte-stuck-at-0 faults instead. Here, 483 (70%) of the instructions are susceptible. If we oppose these results with the fact that the masked linear layer in round 9 only consists of 290 instructions, it is fairly safe to say that finding a suitable fault location should be easy in practice.

(a) Bitflips: 359 (52%) of the S-box instructions are susceptible.

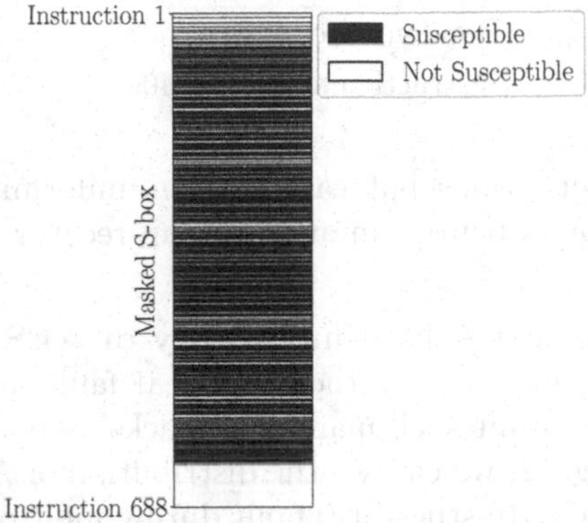

(b) Byte-stuck-at-0: 483 (70%) of the S-box instructions are susceptible.

Fig. 11. Instructions in the masked S-box in round 9 that are susceptible to faults and allow to mount SIFA.

Results – Attack Performance for Various Fault Models. After determining that large parts of the masked S-box are susceptible to single fault inductions in the previous section, we now discuss the effort of key recovery when targeting one of these susceptible instructions. This time we consider 7 different fault models and the results are presented in Table 2. For each of the 7 fault models we give the number of faulted encryptions, the number of resulting ineffective fault inductions (i.e., correct ciphertexts), and the number of key bits that can be recovered from those correct ciphertexts. Each experiment was repeated 3 to 5 times, and the averaged values are presented. The relative position of the affected bytes/bits within the targeted 32-bit register is not important for the analysis.

From the results we can see that faults with fine granularity (only affecting single bits) allow an attacker to recover key bits faster (= using less faulted encryptions). However, only 32 key bits can be recovered in these scenarios since only a small portion of the AES state is affected by those fault inductions. On the other side, faults that affect whole bytes/registers require more faulted

Table 2. 32-bit Cortex-M4: Attack evaluation when targeting one of the instructions in the masked S-box in round 9. Each experiment was repeated 3 to 5 times, the resulting numbers were averaged.

Fault effect	# Ineffective faults	# Faulted encryptions	# Recoverable key bits
Flip one bit	194	386	32
Set one bit to zero	214	428	32
Randomize one bit	574	763	32
Flip one byte	192	2 940	128
Set one byte to zero	192	3 129	128
Randomize one byte	602	1 808	128
Instruction skip	400	45 527	128

encryptions but cause a non-uniformity in bigger portions of the AES state. Consequently, an attacker can recover more key bits.

Results – Non-uniformity of AES State Bytes. Finally, we present more arguments why the statistical fault analysis (SFA) portion of SIFA is crucial to mount such manifold attacks as presented in this work. If we take a look at Fig. 12, we can see the distribution of AES state bytes in round 9 after inducing one byte-stuck-at-0 fault during multiple encryptions and performing key recovery using unaffected, correct ciphertexts. Even though our simulated faults are noise-free, i.e., they have the same effect on each faulted instruction, there is no meaningful way (other than having precise knowledge of the attacked implementation and the induced fault) for the attacker to predict the resulting non-uniformity in the state bytes which would allow for faster key recovery than in SIFA (or SFA). In fact, the observed distributions have some relations with the pen-and-paper examples given in Sect. 3.3 and can be expected to vary significantly depending on the attacked implementation, the fault location, and the actual fault effect. This motivates our choice of simply using a metric of non-uniformity to distinguish the key candidates.

5 Discussion

5.1 On the Nature and Number of Faults

In Sect. 3, we explored the behavior of masked building blocks using deterministic stuck-at-0 faults or instruction skips. The reason for this is to make the processes leading to a bias easier to understand. However, it is easy to see that making the fault probabilistic, e.g., assuming a more realistic setup, where an instruction skip does not work all the time, or that a bit is only set to 0 with a certain probability, just affects the bias an attacker observes and hence, the amount of ciphertext the attacker has to collect, but the attack still works (see [10] for more details).

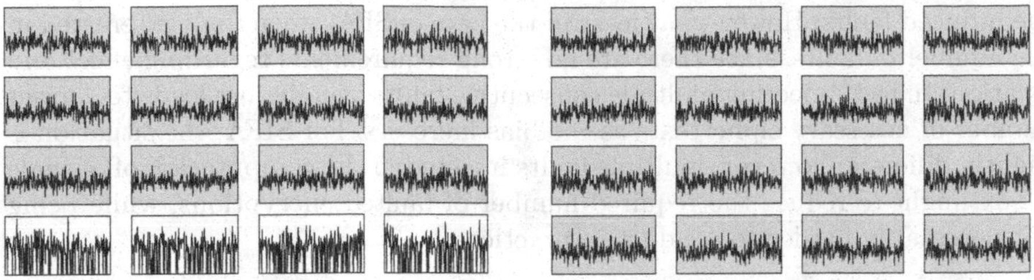

(a) Correct key guess. (b) An incorrect key guess.

Fig. 12. 1st-order masked, bitsliced AES with temporal redundancy. Byte-stuck-at-0 fault model. Distribution of AES state bytes after S-box in round 9 after collecting a sufficient amount of correct ciphertexts. The whole 128-bit key can be recovered.

Furthermore, clock glitches and setting values to zero are not an exhaustive list of effects that a fault could have in order to make the attack work. For instance, in Sect. 4.2 we show that attacks are possible even for random faults and bitflips. All in all, the only requirement we have on the fault is that it leads to a biased distribution of the real (unmasked) value at a suitable place in the primitive among the filtered encryptions. In general, a fault can have a more complex nature than only the cases discussed in Sect. 3 or 4.2. For instance, in software implementations of masked ciphers, a large number of instructions are LOAD instructions from memory since all shares might not fit in the registers. We have observed in experiments that skipping a LOAD can also lead to biased S-box distributions, but having a quite complex effect depending on previous calculations. However, the big benefit of SIFA is the fact that an attacker does not have to know or model the effect of a fault.

This fact also comes into play when dealing with the location of a fault. The examples for the location (e.g. skipped instruction) of the fault given in Sect. 3 just show one out of many different locations, where a fault targeting the S-box leads to a biased distribution that can be exploited in SFA or SIFA. In Sect. 4.2, we evaluated the number of instructions that can be faulted and in turn, can be exploited in an attack for one particular implementation. However, how many such locations exist crucially depends on how the S-box is implemented. In a similar manner as for the effect of a fault, an attacker does not have to know, or to aim for just one specific instruction or location to fault. The only requirement for the attack to work in practice is that the faulted location leads to a bias. All these points make the attack to be executed in practice quite easily, even with a rather cheap setup using clock glitches as demonstrated in Sect. 4.

The last point, we want to discuss regarding faults is the number of faults per execution. We have opted for a single fault per execution, since inserting multiple faults per execution is usually considered to be harder. This is probably related to the prominence of fault attack techniques where attacks requiring multiple faults per execution have high requirements of the exact location and effects of the induced faults. However, at least in the case of SFA, we are not interested in the number of faults, since there are no strong requirements regarding effect and location. In fact, injecting multiple consecutive faults usually just leads to a lower number of necessary ciphertexts as the bias increases. For SIFA, the situation is slightly different; however, multiple faults injected in the computation of a single S-box might to reduce the required number of faulted encryptions, while being not necessarily harder to conduct in practice.

5.2 Countermeasures

In the following, we discuss the effectivity and practicability of well-known countermeasures against our attacks. Since most fault countermeasures prevent the SFA variants of our attack using a single fault per execution, we focus on the SIFA variants and show that it is not easy to prevent these attacks. In fact, some countermeasures (e.g. detection) even facilitate certain aspects of SIFA in practice.

Self-destruct. The most radical approach of destroying the device as soon as a fault is detected is a valid countermeasure against any fault attack. However, this technique has a few downsides and limitations, including false positives and additional effort to reliably destroy a circuit.

A lot of cryptographic devices deployed in the field like smart cards and RFID tags have to function and operate under rather tough conditions. They typically have to deal with abrupt loss of power, for instance if a smart card is withdrawn from the terminal while working. Furthermore, they have to handle power spikes from electrostatic discharges or electromagnetic fields. Hence, deciding between an active fault attack and interference due to normal usage is not a trivial task and would potentially lead to detection of a huge amount of false positives that render such an approach useless for a wide range of applications.

One way to compensate some false positives is to destruct a device only once a certain amount of faults was detected. Such a fault counter could be considered an effective countermeasure, yet is still not used by a large portion of embedded devices, since it is challenging to implement appropriately tamper-resistant, especially in hardware.

Correction. A different approach to make use of redundancy is to correct the effect of a fault, for instance using error-correcting codes or simple majority voting. However, correction-based countermeasures usually can be reduced to the detection-based case using additional faults. How hard this is and which requirements this might have on the precision of the fault crucially depends on the implementation of the countermeasure. As an example let us assume a simple majority voting between the result of 3 block cipher calls. To do this, the 3 block cipher calls take the same inputs and hence, perform redundant computations. An attacker can now use an additional fault to just ensure that the computations performed on one redundant block cipher call will always be incorrect. This usually does not require a precise fault. This reduces the majority voting of 3 block cipher calls to a construction which essentially behaves as a detection-based countermeasure (or infection-like countermeasure if the majority voting happens at bit-level of the ciphertext). Then, an attacker can proceed with the same attacks as before, using a second targeted fault.

Infection. In [10], the application of SIFA on an infective countermeasure [27] has been demonstrated. The employed dummy rounds in this countermeasure increase the needed number of faulted encryptions until the key can be recovered. However, when aiming to prevent SIFA, dummy rounds that do not infect the state in the case of a fault should provide even more protection. Hence, we explore this countermeasure next.

Hiding. The goal of hiding countermeasures is to reduce the attacker's knowledge of what is currently computed, and thus effectively decrease his precision when placing the fault. Examples include adding dummy rounds randomly between the relevant rounds, or shuffling the order of execution, for example the order in which the 16 AES S-boxes per round are executed. In the following, we analyze the case of dummy AES rounds in more detail, and show that the noise introduced this way quadratically increases the necessary number of faulty encryptions for the analysis.

Dummy Rounds. We consider a protected AES implementation and make the following assumptions for our model:

- The attacker needs to fault round 9 out of 10 (identical) AES rounds.
- The protected implementation executes 10 real AES rounds and $(k-1)\cdot 10$ ineffective dummy rounds in a uniformly random ordering, labeled $1,\ldots,R$ with $R = 10k$.
- The attacker targets round $R-t$. Three outcomes are possible:
  1. Hit: It is the real round 9 with probability σ, resulting in a distribution with ineffectivity rate π_{fault} and ineffective distribution p_{fault}.
  2. Miss: It is a dummy round with ineffectivity rate π_1 and uniform ineffective distribution θ
  3. Miss: It is a real round, but not round 9, with ineffectivity rate π_{fault} and uniform ineffective distribution θ. For simplicity, we assume an ineffectivity rate of π_1, so this case can be merged with item 2.

With these assumptions, the success probability that round $R-t$ of R is a hit (signal) is

$$\sigma_{\mathsf{fault}}[R,t] = \mathbb{P}[\text{Hit in round } R-t] = \frac{t\cdot\binom{R-t-1}{8}}{\binom{R}{10}} = \frac{90\cdot t}{R(R-1)}\prod_{s=2}^{9}\left[1-\frac{t-1}{R-s}\right].$$

This parametrized function is plotted in Fig. 13 and attains its maximum near $t = k = \frac{R}{10}$. The resulting function $\sigma_{\mathsf{fault}}[10k,k]$ for the optimized success probability is also plotted in Fig. 13 (dashed, with x-axis $t = k$), and can be approximated as

$$\sigma_{\mathsf{fault}}[10k, k] = \mathbb{P}[\text{Hit in round } 9k \text{ of } 10k] = \frac{90k}{10k \cdot (10k-1)} \cdot \prod_{s=2}^{9} \left[1 - \frac{k-1}{10k-s}\right]$$

$$= \frac{1}{k} \cdot \prod_{s=1}^{9} \frac{9k-s+1}{10k-s} \xrightarrow{k\to\infty} \frac{1}{k} \cdot \left(\frac{9}{10}\right)^9 \approx \frac{1}{k} \cdot 0.387 \qquad \text{for large } k\,.$$

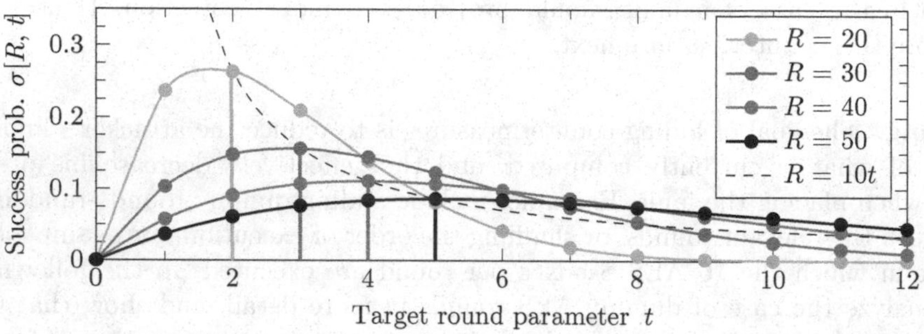

Fig. 13. Success probability $\sigma[R, t]$ when targeting round $R - t$, for different $R = 10k$. For the choice $t = k$ (dashed line), $\sigma[10k, k] \approx \frac{0.387}{k}$ for $k \gg 2$.

A SIFA attacker samples the resulting distribution p_{total} among the ineffective faults, with a total ineffectivity rate of π_{total} and a signal of σ_{total}:

$$\pi_{\mathsf{total}} = \sigma_{\mathsf{fault}} \cdot \pi_{\mathsf{fault}} + (1 - \sigma_{\mathsf{fault}}) \cdot 1 = 1 - (1 - \pi_{\mathsf{fault}}) \cdot \sigma_{\mathsf{fault}}$$

$$\sigma_{\mathsf{total}} = \frac{\sigma_{\mathsf{fault}} \cdot \pi_{\mathsf{fault}}}{\pi_{\mathsf{total}}}$$

$$p_{\mathsf{total}}(x) = \sigma_{\mathsf{total}} \cdot p_{\mathsf{fault}}(x) + (1 - \sigma_{\mathsf{total}}) \cdot \theta(x)$$

The necessary sample size to distinguish p_{total} is inverse proportional to the capacity

$$C(p_{\mathsf{total}}) = \sigma_{\mathsf{total}}^2 \cdot C(p_{\mathsf{fault}})\,,$$

which corresponds to a data complexity proportional to $(\pi_{\mathsf{total}} \cdot \sigma_{\mathsf{total}}^2 \cdot C(p_{\mathsf{fault}}))^{-1}$.

Thus, for a fixed fault setup with $p_{\mathsf{fault}}, \pi_{\mathsf{fault}}$, increasing the dummy factor k increases the data complexity of the attack quadratically (Fig. 14):

$$(\pi_{\mathsf{total}} \cdot \sigma_{\mathsf{total}}^2)^{-1} = \frac{1 - (1 - \pi_{\mathsf{fault}}) \cdot \sigma_{\mathsf{fault}}}{\sigma_{\mathsf{fault}}^2 \cdot \pi_{\mathsf{fault}}^2} \approx k^2 \frac{1}{(0.387 \cdot \pi_{\mathsf{fault}})^2} - k \frac{1 - \pi_{\mathsf{fault}}}{0.387 \cdot \pi_{\mathsf{fault}}^2}\,.$$

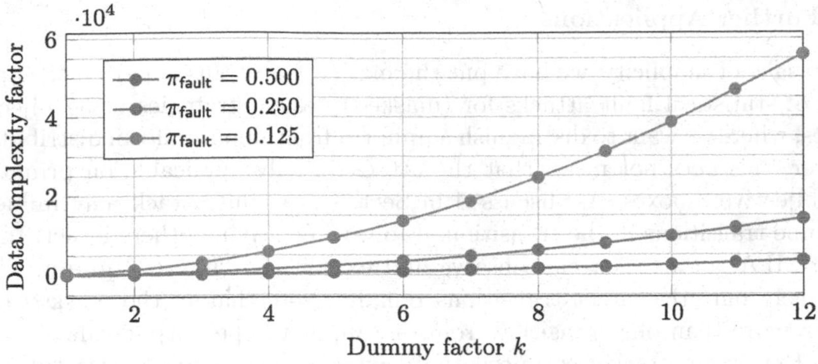

Fig. 14. Increasing data complexity with dummy factor k, for different π_{fault}.

Shuffling. Similar to dummy rounds, shuffling operations reduces the attacker's precision and success probability in hitting the right S-box and thus induces noise in the distribution. However, in the case of SIFA, there is an important difference due to the ineffectivity rate in case of misses, which we assume is the same as in case of hits. For this reason, the data complexity will also grow quadratically in the number of shuffled operations in the relevant scope (e.g., 16 S-boxes), but only linearly instead of quadratically in the inverse ineffectivity rate π_{fault}^{-1}.

Limiting the Data Complexity. For our attacks to work, we usually need several faulted encryptions per key to retrieve it. Therefore, methods that restrict the usage of the key and hence, put a limit on the data complexity can be a viable strategy for providing protection against this type of attack. Existing re-keying strategies can be roughly split into two groups, one where the used key is derived via a re-keying function from a static master key [1,11,12,18] and the other group being methods where a secret internal state is maintained and constantly updated. In the first group, the problem of protection against the attack is basically shifted to the re-keying function and has to be solved there.

5.3 Choice of the Target and Attack Setup

It is important to note that we have not chosen the S-boxes in Sect. 3 or AES in Sect. 4 as targets of our attacks because we have found them to be weaker than others. In fact, we chose them, because many masked implementations for them are publicly available.

Furthermore, we performed the practical experiments using clock glitches because the equipment is cheap and we do not have easy access to other, more sophisticated equipment at the moment. Obviously, the attack is not limited to a specific fault injection method; quite on the contrary, we expect other methods of inserting faults, such as Lasers, needle probes, etc., to be far superior compared to our cheap setup using clock glitches [9].

5.4 Further Applications

For the sake of simplicity, we have put the main focus of this paper on the application of statistical fault attacks for (masked) design strategies using bijective S-boxes, where we want to distinguish a uniform from a non-uniform distribution. However, this does not mean that the attack in only applicable on primitives using bijective S-boxes. As discussed in Sect. 3.4, a fault attack may influence only some transitions in the transition graph, while leaving others intact. In the case of SIFA, an attacker can observe and exploit the "filtered" graph, where most likely only the intact transitions remain. Note that in the masked case, there is more than one transition from one input to one output value, due to masks. Hence, an attacker can potentially exploit all cases where this "filtered" transition graph shows a differently distributed occurrence of input and output transitions.

As another narrative restriction, we have restricted our focus on block ciphers. One potential countermeasure one could come up with against our attack is the use of a PRF like the AES-PRF [19] instead of a block cipher. Such a PRF prevents an attacker from observing ciphertexts and decrypting backwards under guessing the key. However, SIFA remains possible by targeting the input of the AES-PRF since here, a known input like a nonce is usually processed. In general, the presented attacks are almost always applicable whenever some known input is mixed with a secret, which covers most stateless symmetric cryptographic primitives. However, it is an interesting future research topic to evaluate how well such attacks will work.

6 Conclusion

This paper demonstrates that SIFA is a very powerful attack. We show that state-of-the-art countermeasures against implementation attacks, redundancy against faults and masking against side-channels, are not as effective against SIFA as expected. In particular, SIFA is still possible using just a single fault per execution, contradicting the common folklore that masking plus a detection-based countermeasure provides sufficient protection against fault attacks.

We presented a comprehensive analysis of simulated faults for an assembler-optimized, masked AES implementation for the 32-bit Cortex-M4 platform that might be of high practical relevance. We showed that most of the instructions of the masked S-box implementation are "susceptible" to faults and can be exploited in SIFA using any of the common fault models.

Moreover, the practical feasibility of the attack was shown by attacking a 10th-order masked AES software implementation with arbitrary temporal redundancy on block cipher level on a standard 8-bit microcontroller without specific security features using a cheap clock glitch setup. Even with such a cheap setup, we are able to recover 32 bits of the key after collecting 20 ciphertexts where the fault is ineffective, needing approximately a total of 1000 encryptions where a single fault induction is performed.

Acknowledgments. This project has received funding in part from the European Research Council (ERC) under the European Union's Horizon 2020 research and innovation programme (grant agreement No 681402) and by the Austrian Research Promotion Agency (FFG) via the project ESPRESSO, which is funded by the province of Styria and the Business Promotion Agencies of Styria and Carinthia.

References

1. Berti, F., Pereira, O., Peters, T., Standaert, F.X.: On leakage-resilient authenticated encryption with decryption leakages. IACR Trans. Symmetric Cryptol. **2017**(3), 271–293 (2017)
2. Biham, E., Shamir, A.: Differential fault analysis of secret key cryptosystems. In: Kaliski, B.S. (ed.) CRYPTO 1997. LNCS, vol. 1294, pp. 513–525. Springer, Heidelberg (1997). https://doi.org/10.1007/BFb0052259
3. Bilgin, B., Daemen, J., Nikov, V., Nikova, S., Rijmen, V., Van Assche, G.: Efficient and first-order DPA resistant implementations of Keccak. In: Francillon, A., Rohatgi, P. (eds.) CARDIS 2013. LNCS, vol. 8419, pp. 187–199. Springer, Cham (2014). https://doi.org/10.1007/978-3-319-08302-5_13
4. Boyar, J., Peralta, R.: A depth-16 circuit for the AES S-box. IACR Cryptology ePrint Archive, Report 2011/332 (2011). https://eprint.iacr.org/2011/332
5. Clavier, C.: Secret external encodings do not prevent transient fault analysis. In: Paillier, P., Verbauwhede, I. (eds.) CHES 2007. LNCS, vol. 4727, pp. 181–194. Springer, Heidelberg (2007). https://doi.org/10.1007/978-3-540-74735-2_13
6. Coron, J.S.: Higher order countermeasures for AES and DES (2017). https://github.com/coron/htable#higher-order-countermeasures-for-aes-and-des
7. Daemen, J.: Cipher and hash function design, strategies based on linear and differential cryptanalysis. Ph.D. thesis, KU Leuven (1995). http://jda.noekeon.org/
8. Daemen, J., Govaerts, R., Vandewalle, J.: An efficient nonlinear shift-invariant transformation. In: Macq, B. (ed.) Information Theory in the Benelux. pp. 108–115. Werkgemeenschap voor Informatie- en Communicatietheorie (1994)
9. Dobraunig, C., Eichlseder, M., Korak, T., Lomné, V., Mendel, F.: Statistical fault attacks on nonce-based authenticated encryption schemes. In: Cheon, J.H., Takagi, T. (eds.) ASIACRYPT 2016, Part I. LNCS, vol. 10031, pp. 369–395. Springer, Heidelberg (2016). https://doi.org/10.1007/978-3-662-53887-6_14
10. Dobraunig, C., Eichlseder, M., Korak, T., Mangard, S., Mendel, F., Primas, R.: SIFA: exploiting ineffective fault inductions on symmetric cryptography. IACR Trans. Cryptogr. Hardw. Embed. Syst. **2018**(3), 547–572 (2018)
11. Dobraunig, C., Eichlseder, M., Mangard, S., Mendel, F., Unterluggauer, T.: ISAP - towards side-channel secure authenticated encryption. IACR Trans. Symmetric Cryptol. **2017**(1), 80–105 (2017)
12. Dobraunig, C., Koeune, F., Mangard, S., Mendel, F., Standaert, F.-X.: Towards fresh and hybrid re-keying schemes with beyond birthday security. In: Homma, N., Medwed, M. (eds.) CARDIS 2015. LNCS, vol. 9514, pp. 225–241. Springer, Cham (2016). https://doi.org/10.1007/978-3-319-31271-2_14
13. Fuhr, T., Jaulmes, É., Lomné, V., Thillard, A.: Fault attacks on AES with faulty ciphertexts only. In: Fischer, W., Schmidt, J.M. (eds.) FDTC 2013, pp. 108–118. IEEE Computer Society, Los Alamitos (2013)
14. Groß, H., Mangard, S., Korak, T.: Domain-oriented masking: Compact masked hardware implementations with arbitrary protection order. IACR Cryptology ePrint Archive, Report 2016/486 (2016). https://eprint.iacr.org/2016/486

15. Gross, H., Mangard, S., Korak, T.: An efficient side-channel protected AES implementation with arbitrary protection order. In: Handschuh, H. (ed.) CT-RSA 2017. LNCS, vol. 10159, pp. 95–112. Springer, Cham (2017). https://doi.org/10.1007/978-3-319-52153-4_6
16. Ishai, Y., Sahai, A., Wagner, D.: Private circuits: securing hardware against probing attacks. In: Boneh, D. (ed.) CRYPTO 2003. LNCS, vol. 2729, pp. 463–481. Springer, Heidelberg (2003). https://doi.org/10.1007/978-3-540-45146-4_27
17. Kocher, P., Jaffe, J., Jun, B.: Differential power analysis. In: Wiener, M. (ed.) CRYPTO 1999. LNCS, vol. 1666, pp. 388–397. Springer, Heidelberg (1999). https://doi.org/10.1007/3-540-48405-1_25
18. Medwed, M., Standaert, F.-X., Großschädl, J., Regazzoni, F.: Fresh re-keying: security against side-channel and fault attacks for low-cost devices. In: Bernstein, D.J., Lange, T. (eds.) AFRICACRYPT 2010. LNCS, vol. 6055, pp. 279–296. Springer, Heidelberg (2010). https://doi.org/10.1007/978-3-642-12678-9_17
19. Mennink, B., Neves, S.: Optimal PRFs from blockcipher designs. IACR Trans. Symmetric Cryptol. **2017**(3), 228–252 (2017)
20. Nikova, S., Rechberger, C., Rijmen, V.: Threshold implementations against side-channel attacks and glitches. In: Ning, P., Qing, S., Li, N. (eds.) ICICS 2006. LNCS, vol. 4307, pp. 529–545. Springer, Heidelberg (2006). https://doi.org/10.1007/11935308_38
21. Quisquater, J.-J., Samyde, D.: ElectroMagnetic Analysis (EMA): measures and counter-measures for smart cards. In: Attali, I., Jensen, T. (eds.) E-smart 2001. LNCS, vol. 2140, pp. 200–210. Springer, Heidelberg (2001). https://doi.org/10.1007/3-540-45418-7_17
22. Reparaz, O., Bilgin, B., Nikova, S., Gierlichs, B., Verbauwhede, I.: Consolidating masking schemes. In: Gennaro, R., Robshaw, M. (eds.) CRYPTO 2015, Part I. LNCS, vol. 9215, pp. 764–783. Springer, Heidelberg (2015). https://doi.org/10.1007/978-3-662-47989-6_37
23. Rivain, M., Prouff, E.: Provably secure higher-order masking of AES. In: Mangard, S., Standaert, F.-X. (eds.) CHES 2010. LNCS, vol. 6225, pp. 413–427. Springer, Heidelberg (2010). https://doi.org/10.1007/978-3-642-15031-9_28
24. Schneider, T., Moradi, A., Güneysu, T.: ParTI – towards combined hardware countermeasures against side-channel and fault-injection attacks. In: Robshaw, M., Katz, J. (eds.) CRYPTO 2016, Part II. LNCS, vol. 9815, pp. 302–332. Springer, Heidelberg (2016). https://doi.org/10.1007/978-3-662-53008-5_11
25. Schwabe, P., Stoffelen, K.: All the aes you need on Cortex-M3 and M4. In: Avanzi, R., Heys, H. (eds.) SAC 2016. LNCS, vol. 10532, pp. 180–194. Springer, Cham (2017). https://doi.org/10.1007/978-3-319-69453-5_10
26. Trichina, E.: Combinational logic design for AES SubByte transformation on masked data. IACR Cryptology ePrint Archive, Report 2003/236 (2003). https://eprint.iacr.org/2003/236
27. Tupsamudre, H., Bisht, S., Mukhopadhyay, D.: Destroying fault invariant with randomization. In: Batina, L., Robshaw, M. (eds.) CHES 2014. LNCS, vol. 8731, pp. 93–111. Springer, Heidelberg (2014). https://doi.org/10.1007/978-3-662-44709-3_6
28. Ullrich, M., De Cannière, C., Indesteege, S., Küçük, Ö., Mouha, N., Preneel, B.: Finding optimal bitsliced implementations of 4 × 4-bit S-boxes. In: ECRYPT Symmetric Key Encryption Workshop - SKEW 2011, pp. 16–17 (2011)

Tight Private Circuits: Achieving Probing Security with the Least Refreshing

Sonia Belaïd[1(✉)], Dahmun Goudarzi[1,2(✉)], and Matthieu Rivain[1(✉)]

[1] CryptoExperts, Paris, France
[2] ENS CNRS INRIA and PSL Research University, Paris, France
{sonia.belaid,dahmun.goudarzi,matthieu.rivain}@cryptoexperts.com

Abstract. Masking is a common countermeasure to secure implementations against side-channel attacks. In 2003, Ishai, Sahai, and Wagner introduced a formal security model, named t-probing model, which is now widely used to theoretically reason on the security of masked implementations. While many works have provided security proofs for small masked components, called *gadgets*, within this model, no formal method allowed to securely compose gadgets with a tight number of shares (namely, $t+1$) until recently. In 2016, Barthe *et al.* filled this gap with `maskComp`, a tool checking the security of masking schemes composed of several gadgets. This tool can achieve provable security with tight number of shares by inserting mask-refreshing gadgets at carefully selected locations. However the method is not tight in the sense that there exists some compositions of gadgets for which it cannot exhibit a flaw nor prove the security. As a result, it is overconservative and might insert more refresh gadgets than actually needed to ensure t-probing security. In this paper, we exhibit the first tool, referred to as `tightPROVE`, able to clearly state whether a shared circuit composed of standard gadgets (addition, multiplication, and refresh) is t-probing secure or not. Given such a composition, our tool either produces a probing-security proof (valid at any order) or exhibits a security flaw that directly implies a probing attack at a given order. Compared to `maskComp`, `tightPROVE` can drastically reduce the number of required refresh gadgets to get a probing security proof, and thus the randomness requirement for some secure shared circuits. We apply our method to a recent AES implementation secured with higher-order masking in bitslice and we show that we can save all the refresh gadgets involved in the s-box layer, which results in an significant performance gain.

Keywords: Side-channel · Masking · Composition · Private circuits

1 Introduction

Most cryptographic algorithms are assumed to be secure against the so-called *black-box* attacks, where the adversary is restricted to the knowledge of inputs and outputs to recover the secret key. However, the late nineties revealed a new

T. Peyrin and S. Galbraith (Eds.): ASIACRYPT 2018, LNCS 11273, pp. 343–372, 2018.
https://doi.org/10.1007/978-3-030-03329-3_12

class of attacks, referred to as *side-channel attacks*, that exploit the physical leakages (*e.g.* temperature, power consumption) of components which execute implementations of cryptographic algorithms. Many implementations of symmetric cryptographic algorithms have been broken so far [7,17], raising the need for concrete and efficient protection.

A sound and widely deployed approach to counteract side-channel attacks is the so-called *masking* countermeasure that was simultaneously introduced in 1999 by Chari *et al.* [8] and by Goubin and Patarin [13]. The idea is to split each key-dependent variable x of the implementation into d *shares* $(x_i)_{0 \leq i \leq d-1}$ such that $x = x_0 * \cdots * x_{d-1}$ for some law $*$ and any strict subset of shares is uniformly distributed. The number of degrees-of-freedom $d-1$ of such a sharing is referred to as the *masking order*. When $*$ is the addition on a finite field of characteristic two, the approach is referred to as *Boolean masking*, and when d is additionally strictly greater than 2, the approach is referred to as *higher-order Boolean masking*. Chari *et al.* showed that recombining d noisy shares to recover the secret is then exponentially complex in d which makes the masking order a sound security parameter with respect to side-channel attacks.

In order to design masking schemes and theoretically reason on their security, the community has defined several leakage models. In the most realistic one, the *noisy leakage model* introduced by Rivain and Prouff [19] as a specialization of the *only computation leaks* model [18], the adversary gets a noisy function of each intermediate variable of the cryptographic computation. Unfortunately, this model is not very convenient to build security proofs as it requires complex mutual information computations. A second and widely used leakage model is the *t-probing model* introduced by Ishai, Sahai, and Wagner [15] in which the adversary gets the exact values of t chosen intermediate variables. As it manipulates exact values in a limited quantity, this model is advantageously much more convenient for security proofs. In order to benefit from the advantages of both models, Duc, Dziembowski, and Faust demonstrated in [12] a reduction from the noisy leakage model to the t-probing model. In a nutshell, an implementation that is secure in the t-probing model is also secure in the more realistic noisy leakage model for some level of noise.

In their seminal work [15], Ishai *et al.* proposed a t-probing secure masking scheme for any circuit based on $d = 2t + 1$ shares. This scheme was extended by Rivain and Prouff in [20] with the aim to derive a tight t-probing secure implementation of AES, where *tightness* means that the t-probing security is obtained with the optimal number of $d = t + 1$ shares. In particular, they show that the so-called ISW multiplication gadget actually achieves tight probing security provided that the two input sharings are mutually independent. In order to obtain tight security for the full AES circuit, Rivain and Prouff suggested to insert *refresh gadgets* that renew the randomness of sharings at carefully chosen locations [20]. But the proposed refresh gadget was shown to introduce a flaw in the composition [10]. In 2016, Barthe *et al.* introduced new security notions to fill this gap, namely the *t-non interference* and the *t-strong non interference* [2]. When these notions are met by a set of gadgets, one can easily reason on the probing security of their composition. Informally, a gadget is t-non interfering (or t-NI) if and only if any set of at most t intermediate variables can be perfectly simulated with at most t shares of each input. Since t input shares are trivially independent from the input itself as long as $t < d$, non-interference trivially implies probing security. While this notion was first defined in [2], it was actually already met by most existing gadgets. One step further, a gadget is t-strong non interfering (or t-SNI) if and only if any set of t intermediate variables among which t_{out} are output variables can be perfectly simulated with $t_{int} = t - t_{out}$ shares of each input sharing. This property makes it possible to compose any set of SNI gadgets since it stops the propagation of dependencies. A concrete tool to build probing secure implementations from unprotected implementations is provided [2] which was later called `maskComp`. Following this work, numerous examples of globally probing secure schemes were proposed with a decomposition in identified NI and SNI gadgets [3,11,21]. While these schemes achieve their security goals, each inserted SNI refresh gadget increase the requirement of fresh randomness which is generally expensive to generate. And up to now, no efficient method exists to check the probing security of any given composition of gadgets. As a result, existing tools such as `maskComp` are overconservative and might insert more refresh gadgets than necessary.

Nevertheless, some formal tools have been recently developed to evaluate the probing security of implementations at a given masking order. Among the most efficient ones, Barthe *et al.* developed `maskVerif` [1] and Coron developed `CheckMasks` [9]. Both tools take as input a shared circuit and return a formal security proof when no attack is found. But here again, this evaluation is not tight and false negatives may occur and hence imply the addition of unnecessary refresh gadgets. Moreover, while such tools are very convenient to evaluate the security of concrete implementations, they suffer from an important limitation which is their exponential complexity in the size of the circuit and consequently in the masking order. As a result, these tools are impractical beyond a small number of shares (typically $d = 5$). In a recent work, Bloem *et al.* [5] further developed a new tool to verify the security of masked implementations subject to *glitches*, which is an important step towards provable and practical security of hardware implementations. However this tool still suffers from the same efficiency limitations as the previous ones.

Motivation and Contributions. The method of Barthe *et al.* [2] allows one to safely compose t-NI and t-SNI gadgets and get probing security at any order. Nevertheless, it is not tight and makes use of more refresh gadgets than required. In many contexts, randomness generation is expensive and might be the bottleneck for masked implementations. For instance, Journault Standaert describe an AES encryption shared at the order $d = 32$ for which up to 92% of the running time is spent on randomness generation [16]. In such a context, it is fundamental to figure out whether the number of t-SNI refresh gadgets inserted by Barthe *et al.*'s tool `maskComp` is actually minimal to achieve t-probing security. In this paper, we find out that it is not and we provide a new method which *exactly* identifies the concrete probing attacks in a Boolean shared circuit.

Let us take a simple example. We consider the small randomized circuit referred to as Circuit 1 and illustrated in Fig. 1 with $[\oplus]$ a t-NI sharewise addition, $[\otimes]$ a t-SNI multiplication, and two Boolean sharings $[x_1]$ and $[x_2]$. Applying Barthe *et al.*'s tool `maskComp` on this circuit automatically inserts a t-SNI refresh gadget in the cycle formed by gates $[x_1]$, $[\oplus]$, and $[\otimes]$ as represented in Fig. 2. However, it can be verified that for any masking order t, the initial circuit is t-probing secure without any additional refresh gadget. Therefore, in the following, this paper aims to refine the state-of-the-art method [2] to only insert refresh gadgets when absolutely mandatory for the t-probing security.

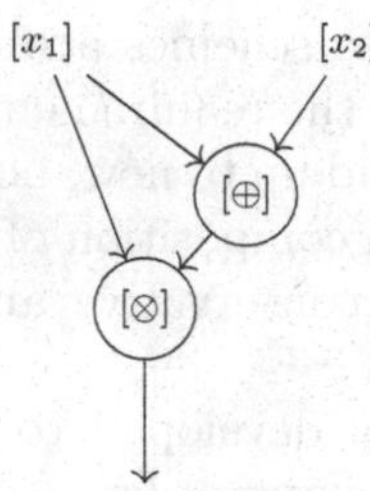

Fig. 1. Graph representation of Circuit 1.

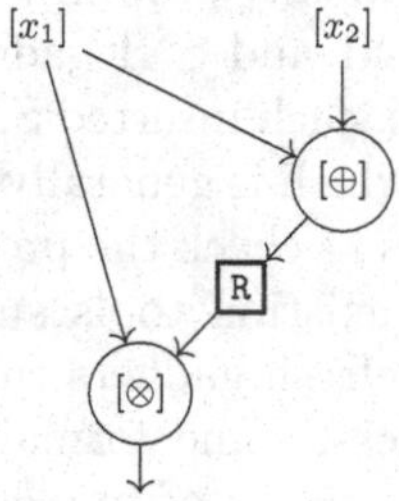

Fig. 2. Graph representation of Circuit 1 after `maskComp`.

More specifically, our contributions can be summarized as follows:

(1) We introduce formal definitions of the probing, non-interfering, and strong-non-interfering security notions for shared circuits based on concrete security games. Although these definitions are no more than a reformulation of existing security notions, we believe that they provide a simple and precise framework to reason about probing security.
(2) From the introduced game-based definitions, we provide a reduction of the probing security of a given *standard shared circuit* –*i.e.* a shared circuit composed of ISW multiplication gadgets, sharewise addition gadgets and SNI refresh gadgets– to the probing security of a simpler circuit of multiplicative depth 1 and for which the adversary is restricted to probe the multiplication inputs (which are linear combinations of the circuit inputs).
(3) We give an algebraic characterization of the final security game, which allows us to express the probing security of any standard shared circuit in terms of linear algebra.
(4) We show how to solve the latter problem with a new exact and proven method. Our method takes the description of any standard shared circuit and either produces a probing-security proof (valid at any order) or exhibits a probing attack (*i.e.* a set of $t < d$ probes that reveal information on the circuit d-shared input for some d). We provide a concrete tool, named

tightPROVE (for tight PRObing VErification), implementing our method in Sage.

(5) We apply tightPROVE to the efficient implementation of the AES s-box developed by Goudarzi and Rivain in [14]. Based on the previous state of the art, this s-box was implemented using one SNI refresh gadget per multiplication gadget (to refresh one of the operands), hence requiring a total of 32 refresh gadgets (which was later on confirmed by the maskComp tool). Our new method formally demonstrates that the same d-shared implementation is actually t-probing secure with *no* refresh gadget for any $d = t + 1$. We provide implementation results and a performance analysis: this new implementation achieves an asymptotic gain up to 43%. The code is provided at https://github.com/CryptoExperts/tightPROVE.

(6) We extend our results to larger circuits by establishing new compositional properties on t-probing secure gadgets. In particular, these new composition properties well apply to the case of SPN-based block ciphers. We also show that they apply to a wide range of Boolean circuits with common gadgets and input sets.

Paper Organization. In Sect. 2, useful notions are introduced, security definitions for composition are formalized through concrete security games, and some useful security results are provided. Section 3 provides our security reduction for standard shared circuits. Section 4 then details our new method to exactly determine the probing security of a standard shared circuit. It also gives an upper bound on the number of required refresh gadgets together with an exhaustive method to make a standard shared circuit achieve tight probing security. In Sect. 5, our new method is extended to apply to larger circuits, and in particular to SPN-based block ciphers, with new compositional properties. Finally, Sect. 6 describes the new tool tightPROVE we implemented to experiment our method on concrete circuits.

2 Formal Security Notions

2.1 Notations

In this paper, we denote by $\mathbb{F}_2$ the finite field with two elements and by $[\![i, j]\!]$ the integer interval $\mathbb{Z} \cap [i, j]$ for any two integers i and j. For a finite set $\mathcal{X}$, we denote by $|\mathcal{X}|$ the cardinality of $\mathcal{X}$ and by $x \leftarrow \mathcal{X}$ the action of picking x from $\mathcal{X}$ independently and uniformly at random. For some (probabilistic) algorithm $\mathcal{A}$, we further denote $x \leftarrow \mathcal{A}(in)$ the action of running algorithm $\mathcal{A}$ on some inputs in (with fresh uniform random tape) and setting x to the value returned by $\mathcal{A}$.

2.2 Basic Notions

A *Boolean circuit* is a directed acyclic graph whose vertices are input gates, output gates, constant gates of fan-in 0 that output constant values, and operation gates of fan-in at most 2 and fan-out at most 1 and whose edges are wires. In this paper we consider Boolean circuits with two types of operation gates: addition gates (computing an addition on $\mathbb{F}_2$) and multiplication gates (computing a multiplication on $\mathbb{F}_2$). A *randomized circuit* is a Boolean circuit augmented with random-bit gates of fan-in 0 that outputs a uniformly random bit.

A *d-Boolean sharing* of $x \in \mathbb{F}_2$ is a random tuple $(x_0, x_1, \ldots, x_{d-1}) \in \mathbb{F}_2^d$ satisfying $x = \sum_{i=0}^{d-1} x_i$. The sharing is said to be *uniform* if, for a given x, it is uniformly distributed over the subspace of tuples satisfying $x = \sum_{i=0}^{d-1} x_i$. A uniform sharing of x is such that any m-tuple of its *shares* x_i is uniformly distributed over $\mathbb{F}_2^m$ for any $m \leq d-1$. In the following, a d-Boolean sharing of a given variable x is denoted by $[x]$ when the sharing order d is clear from the context. We further denote by Enc a probabilistic *encoding* algorithm that maps $x \in \mathbb{F}_2$ to a fresh uniform sharing $[x]$.

A *d-shared circuit* C is a randomized circuit working on d-shared variables. More specifically, a d-shared circuit takes a set of n input sharings $[x_1], \ldots, [x_n]$ and computes a set of m output sharings $[y_1], \ldots, [y_m]$ such that $(y_1, \ldots, y_m) = f(x_1, \ldots, x_n)$ for some deterministic function f. A *probe* on C refers to a wire index (for some given indexing of C's wires). An *evaluation* of C on input $[x_1]$, $\ldots$, $[x_n]$ under a set of probes $\mathcal{P}$ refers to the distribution of the tuple of wires pointed by the probes in $\mathcal{P}$ when the circuit is evaluated on $[x_1], \ldots, [x_n]$, which is denoted by $C([x_1], \ldots, [x_n])_{\mathcal{P}}$.

We consider a special kind of shared circuits which are composed of *gadgets*. A gadget is a simple building block of a shared circuit that performs a given operation on its input sharing(s). For instance, for some two-input operation $*$, a $*$-gadget takes two input sharings $[x_1]$ and $[x_2]$ and it outputs a sharing $[y]$ such that $y = x_1 * x_2$. In the paper, we specifically consider three types of gadgets, namely ISW-multiplication gadgets ($[\otimes]$), ISW-refresh gadgets ($[\mathtt{R}]$) and sharewise addition gadgets ($[\oplus]$). The ISW-multiplication gadget, introduced in [15], takes two d-sharings $[a]$ and $[b]$ as inputs and computes the output d-sharing $[c]$ such that $c = a \cdot b$ as follows:

1. for every $0 \leq i < j \leq d-1$, pick uniformly at random a value $r_{i,j}$ over $\mathbb{F}_2$;
2. for every $0 \leq i < j \leq d-1$, compute $r_{j,i} \leftarrow (r_{i,j} + a_i \cdot b_j) + a_j \cdot b_i$;
3. for every $0 \leq i \leq d-1$, compute $c_i \leftarrow a_i \cdot b_i + \sum_{j \neq i} r_{i,j}$.

The ISW-refresh gadget is actually the ISW-multiplication gadget in which the second operand $[b]$ is set to the constant Boolean sharing $(1, 0, \ldots, 0)$. The output $[c]$ is thus a fresh independent sharing of a. Finally, a sharewise addition gadget computes a d-sharing $[c]$ such that $c = a + b$ by letting $c_i \leftarrow a_i + b_i$ for every $0 \leq i \leq d-1$. When called with a second operand equal to the constant Boolean sharing $(1, 0, \ldots, 0)$, such a sharewise addition gadget computes the complementary of its first operand $c = \overline{a}$.

Definition 1. *A standard shared circuit is a shared circuit exclusively composed of ISW-multiplication gadgets, ISW-refresh gadgets, and sharewise addition gadgets as described above.*

2.3 Game-Based Security Definitions

In the following, we recall the *probing*, *non-interfering*, and *strong non-interfering* security notions introduced in [2,15] and we formalize them through concrete security games. Each of these games is defined for a given n-input d-shared circuit C and it opposes an *adversary* $\mathcal{A}$, which is a deterministic algorithm outputting a set of (plain) inputs $x_1, \ldots, x_n$ and a set of probes $\mathcal{P}$, to a simulator $\mathcal{S}$, which aims at simulating the distribution $C([x_1], \ldots, [x_n])_{\mathcal{P}}$.

Probing Security. We first recall the definition from [15]. Our game-based definition is then given with a proposition to state the equivalence of both notions.

Definition 2 (from [15]). *A circuit is t-probing secure if and only if any set of at most t intermediate variables is independent from the secret.*

Probing Security Game. The t-probing security game is built based on two experiments as described in Fig. 3. In both experiments, an adversary $\mathcal{A}$ outputs a set of probes $\mathcal{P}$ (indices of circuit's wires) such that $|\mathcal{P}| = t$ and n input values $x_1, \ldots, x_n \in \mathbb{F}_2$.

In the first (real) experiment, referred to as ExpReal, the chosen input values $x_1, \ldots, x_n$ are mapped into n sharings $[x_1], \ldots, [x_n]$ with encoding algorithm Enc. The resulting encodings are given as inputs to the shared circuit C. The real experiment then outputs a random evaluation $C([x_1], \ldots, [x_n])_{\mathcal{P}}$ of the chosen gates through a t-uple $(v_1, \ldots, v_t)$.

<u>$\mathsf{ExpReal}(\mathcal{A}, C)$:</u>
1. $(\mathcal{P}, x_1, \ldots, x_n) \leftarrow \mathcal{A}()$
2. $[x_1] \leftarrow \mathsf{Enc}(x_1), \ldots, [x_n] \leftarrow \mathsf{Enc}(x_n)$
3. $(v_1, \ldots, v_t) \leftarrow C([x_1], \ldots, [x_n])_{\mathcal{P}}$
4. Return $(v_1, \ldots, v_t)$

<u>$\mathsf{ExpSim}(\mathcal{A}, \mathcal{S}, C)$:</u>
1. $(\mathcal{P}, x_1, \ldots, x_n) \leftarrow \mathcal{A}()$
2. $(v_1, \ldots, v_t) \leftarrow \mathcal{S}(\mathcal{P})$
3. Return $(v_1, \ldots, v_t)$

Fig. 3. t-probing security game.

In the second experiment, referred to as ExpSim, the probing simulator $\mathcal{S}$ takes the (adversary chosen) set of probes $\mathcal{P}$ and outputs a simulation of the evaluation $C([x_1], \ldots, [x_n])_{\mathcal{P}}$, which is returned by the simulation experiment. The simulator wins the game if and only if the two experiments return identical distributions.

Proposition 1. *A shared circuit C is t-probing secure if and only if for every adversary $\mathcal{A}$, there exists a simulator $\mathcal{S}$ that wins the t-probing security game defined in Fig. 3, i.e. the random experiments* $\mathsf{ExpReal}(\mathcal{A}, C)$ *and* $\mathsf{ExpSim}(\mathcal{A}, \mathcal{S}, C)$ *output identical distributions.*

Proof. From right to left, if for every adversary $\mathcal{A}$, there exists a simulator $\mathcal{S}$ that wins the t-probing security game defined in Fig. 3, then any set of probes is independent from the secret as $\mathcal{S}$ has no knowledge of the secret inputs. Thus C is trivially t-probing secure by Definition 2. From left to right, if the random experiments $\mathsf{ExpReal}(\mathcal{A}, C)$ and $\mathsf{ExpSim}(\mathcal{A}, \mathcal{S}, C)$ do not output identical distributions, then there exists a set of at most t intermediate variables which cannot be perfectly simulated without the knowledge of the input secrets. As a consequence, the circuit is not t-probing secure from Definition 2. □

A shared circuit C which is t-probing secure is referred to as a *t-private circuit.* It is not hard to see that a d-shared circuit can only achieve t-probing security for $d > t$. When a d-shared circuit achieves t-probing security with $d = t + 1$, we call it a *tight private circuit.*

Non-Interfering Security. The non-interfering security notion is a little bit stronger ([2]). Compared to the probing security notion, it additionally benefits from making the security evaluation of composition of circuits easier. We recall its original definition from [2] before we give an equivalent formal game-based definition.

Definition 3 (from [2]**).** *A circuit is t-non-interfering (t-NI) if and only if any set of at most t intermediate variables can be perfectly simulated from at most t shares of each input.*

Non-Interfering Security Game. The t-non-interfering (t-NI) security game is built based on two experiments as described in Fig. 4. In both experiments, an adversary $\mathcal{A}$ outputs a set of probes $\mathcal{P}$ (indices of circuit's wires) such that $|\mathcal{P}| = t$ and n input sharings $[x_1], \ldots, [x_n] \in \mathbb{F}_2^d$.

The first (real) experiment, referred to as $\mathsf{ExpReal}$, simply returns an evaluation of C on input sharings $[x_1], \ldots, [x_n]$ under the set of probes $\mathcal{P}$.

The second experiment, referred to as ExpSim, is defined for a two-round simulator $\mathcal{S} = (\mathcal{S}^1, \mathcal{S}^2)$. In the first round, the simulator $\mathcal{S}^1$ takes the (adversary chosen) set of probes $\mathcal{P}$ and outputs n sets of indices $\mathcal{I}_1, \ldots, \mathcal{I}_n \subseteq \{1, \ldots, d\}$, such that $|\mathcal{I}_1| = \cdots = |\mathcal{I}_n| = t$. In the second round, in addition to the set of probes $\mathcal{P}$, the simulator $\mathcal{S}^2$ receives the (adversary chosen) input sharings restricted to the shares indexed by the sets $\mathcal{I}_1, \ldots, \mathcal{I}_n$, denoted $[x_1]_{\mathcal{I}_1}, \ldots, [x_n]_{\mathcal{I}_n}$, and outputs a simulation of $C([x_1], \ldots, [x_n])_{\mathcal{P}}$, which is returned by the simulation experiment. The simulator wins the game if and only if the two experiments return identical distributions.

Proposition 2. *A shared circuit C is* t-non-interfering secure *if and only if for every adversary $\mathcal{A}$, there exists a simulator $\mathcal{S}$ that wins the t-non-interfering security game defined in Fig. 4, i.e. the random experiments* $\mathsf{ExpReal}(\mathcal{A}, C)$ *and* $\mathsf{ExpSim}(\mathcal{A}, \mathcal{S}, C)$ *output identical distributions.*

ExpReal($\mathcal{A}, C$):

1. $(\mathcal{P}, [x_1], \ldots, [x_n]) \leftarrow \mathcal{A}()$
2. $(v_1, \ldots, v_t) \leftarrow C([x_1], \ldots, [x_n])_{\mathcal{P}}$
3. Return $(v_1, \ldots, v_t)$

ExpSim($\mathcal{A}, \mathcal{S}, C$): *

1. $(\mathcal{P}, [x_1], \ldots, [x_n]) \leftarrow \mathcal{A}()$
2. $\mathcal{I}_1, \ldots, \mathcal{I}_n \leftarrow \mathcal{S}^1(\mathcal{P})$
3. $(v_1, \ldots, v_t) \leftarrow \mathcal{S}^2(\mathcal{P}, [x_1]_{\mathcal{I}_1}, \ldots, [x_n]_{\mathcal{I}_n})$
4. Return $(v_1, \ldots, v_t)$

* For t-NI: $|\mathcal{I}_1| = \cdots = |\mathcal{I}_n| = t$.
For t-SNI: $|\mathcal{I}_1| = \cdots = |\mathcal{I}_n| = |\mathcal{P}_{int}| \leq t$.

Fig. 4. t-(S)NI security game.

Proof. From right to left, if for every adversary $\mathcal{A}$, there exists a simulator $\mathcal{S}$ that wins the t-non interfering security game defined in Fig. 3, then any set of probes can be perfectly simulated from sets of at most t shares of each input. Thus C is trivially t-non-interfering from Definition 3. From left to right, if the random experiments ExpReal($\mathcal{A}, C$) and ExpSim($\mathcal{A}, \mathcal{S}, C$) do not output identical distributions, then there exists a set of at most t intermediate variables which cannot be perfectly simulated from sets $\mathcal{I}_j$ of input shares whose cardinalities are less than t. As a consequence, the circuit is not t-non interfering secure from Definition 3. □

Strong Non-Interfering Security. The strong non-interfering security is a stronger notion than non-interfering security as it additionally guarantees the independence between input and output sharings. The latter property is very convenient to securely compose gadgets with related inputs.

Definition 4 (Strong non-interfering security from [2]). *A circuit is t-strong non-interfering (t-SNI) if and only if any set of at most t intermediate variables whose t_1 on the internal variables (i.e. intermediate variables except the output's ones) and t_2 on output variables can be perfectly simulated from at most t_1 shares of each input.*

Strong Non-Interfering Security Game. The t-strong-non-interfering (t-SNI) security game is similar to the t-NI security game depicted in Fig. 4. The only difference relies in the fact that the first-round simulator $\mathcal{S}^1$ outputs n sets of indices $\mathcal{I}_1, \ldots, \mathcal{I}_n \subseteq \{1, \ldots, d\}$, such that $|\mathcal{I}_1| = \cdots = |\mathcal{I}_n| = |\mathcal{P}_{int}| \leq t$ where $\mathcal{P}_{int} \subseteq \mathcal{P}$ refers to the probes on internal wires, *i.e.* the probes in $\mathcal{P}$ which do not point to outputs of C.

Proposition 3. *A shared circuit C is* t-strong-non-interfering secure *if and only if for every adversary $\mathcal{A}$, there exists a simulator $\mathcal{S}$ that wins the t-SNI security game defined in Fig. 4, i.e. the random experiments* ExpReal($\mathcal{A}, C$) *and* ExpSim($\mathcal{A}, \mathcal{S}, C$) *output identical distributions.*

Proof. From right to left, if for every adversary $\mathcal{A}$, there exists a simulator $\mathcal{S}$ that wins the t-non interfering security game defined in Fig. 3, then any set of probes can be perfectly simulated from sets of at most $|\mathcal{P}_{int}| = t_1$ shares of each input. Thus C is trivially t-strong non-interfering from Definition 4. From left to right, if the random experiments $\mathsf{ExpReal}(\mathcal{A}, C)$ and $\mathsf{ExpSim}(\mathcal{A}, \mathcal{S}, C)$ do not output identical distributions, then there exists a set of at most t intermediate variables which cannot be perfectly simulated from sets $\mathcal{I}_j$ of input shares whose cardinalities are less than t_1. As a consequence, the circuit is not t-strong non interfering secure from Definition 4. □

2.4 Useful Security Results

This section states a few useful security results. From the above definitions, it is not hard to see that for any shared circuit C we have the following implications:

$$C \text{ is } t\text{-SNI} \Rightarrow C \text{ is } t\text{-NI} \Rightarrow C \text{ is } t - \text{probing secure}$$

while the converses are not true. While the ISW-multiplication (and refresh) gadget defined above was originally shown to achieve probing security, it actually achieves the more general notion of strong non-interfering security as formally stated in the following theorem:

Theorem 1 ([2]). *For any integers d and t such that $t < d$, the d-shared ISW-multiplication gadget $[\otimes]$ and the d-shared ISW-refresh gadget $[R]$ are both t-SNI.*

The next lemma states a simple implication of the t-SNI notion (which up to our knowledge has never been stated in the literature):

Lemma 1. *Let C be a n-input $(t+1)$-shared t-SNI circuit. Then for every $(x_1, \ldots, x_n) \in \mathbb{F}_2^n$, an evaluation of C taking n uniform and independent $(t+1)$-Boolean sharings $[x_1], \ldots, [x_n]$ as input produces a sharing $[y]$ (of some value $y \in \mathbb{F}_2$ function of $x_1, \ldots, x_n$) which is uniform and mutually independent of $[x_1], \ldots, [x_n]$.*

Proof of Lemma 1 is available in the full version of this paper [4].

3 A Security Reduction

This section provides a reduction for the t-probing security of a standard $(t+1)$-shared circuit C as defined in Sect. 2. Through a sequence of games we obtain a broad simplification of the problem of verifying whether C is probing secure or not. At each step of our reduction, a new game is introduced which is shown to be equivalent to the previous one, implying that for any adversary $\mathcal{A}$, there exists a simulator $\mathcal{S}$ that wins the new game if and only if the circuit C is t-probing secure. We get a final game (see Game 3 hereafter) in which only the inputs of the multiplication gadgets can be probed by the adversary and the circuit is *flattened* into an (equivalent) circuit of multiplicative depth one. This allows us to express the probing security property as a linear algebra problem, which can then be solved efficiently as we show in Sect. 4.

In a nutshell, our Game 0 exactly fits the game-based definition of t-probing security given in the previous section. Then, with Game 1, we prove that verifying the t-probing security of a standard shared circuit C is exactly equivalent to verifying the t-probing security of the same circuit C where the attacker $\mathcal{A}$ is restricted to probe inputs of refresh gadgets, pairs of inputs of multiplication gadgets, and inputs and outputs of sharewise additions (i.e., no internal gadgets variables). Game 2 then shows that verifying the t-probing security of a standard shared circuit C with a restricted attacker $\mathcal{A}$ is equivalent to verifying the t-probing security of a functionally equivalent circuit C' of multiplicative depth one where all the outputs of multiplication and refresh gadgets in C are replaced by fresh input sharings of the same values in the rest of the circuit. Finally, with Game 3, we show that we can even restrict the adversary to probe only pairs (x_i, y_j) where x_i (resp. y_j) is the ith share of x (resp. the jth share of y) and such that x and y are operands of the same multiplication in C. These three games are deeply detailed hereafter and proofs of their consecutive equivalence are provided at each step. An overview is displayed on Fig. 5.

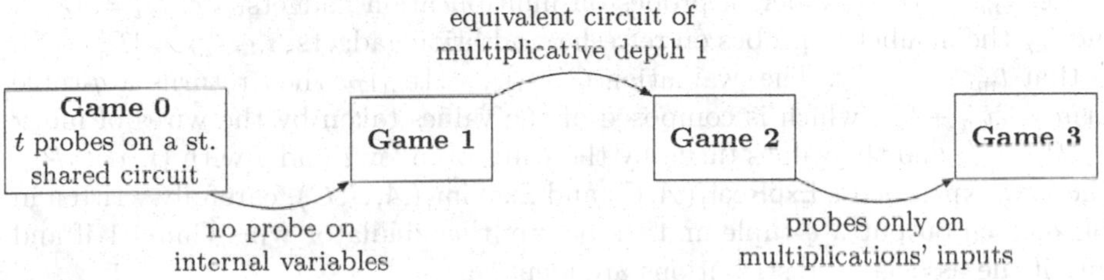

Fig. 5. Overview of the sequence of games.

Game 1. In a nutshell, our first game transition relies on the fact that each probe in a t-SNI gadget can be replaced by 1 or 2 probes on the input sharing(s) of the gadget. In particular, one probe on a refresh gadget is equivalent to revealing one input share, one probe on a multiplication gadget is equivalent to revealing two input shares (one share per input sharings). Formally, in the random experiments $\mathsf{ExpReal}(\mathcal{A}, C)$ and $\mathsf{ExpSim}(\mathcal{A}, \mathcal{S}, C)$, the set of probes $\mathcal{P}$ returned by $\mathcal{A}$, noted $\mathcal{P}'$ in the following, has a different form explicitly defined below.

Let us associate an index g to each gadget in the standard shared circuit and denote by $\mathcal{G}$ the set of gadget indices. Let us further denote by $\mathcal{G}_r$, $\mathcal{G}_m$ and $\mathcal{G}_a$ the index sets of refresh gadgets, multiplication gadgets and addition gadgets, such that $\mathcal{G} = \mathcal{G}_r \cup \mathcal{G}_m \cup \mathcal{G}_a$. Then we can denote by $\mathcal{I}_g$ and $\mathcal{J}_g$ the indices of circuit wires which are the shares of the (right and left) input operands of gadget

$g \in \mathcal{G}$ (where $\mathcal{J}_g = \emptyset$ if gadget g is a refresh). Similarly, we denote by $\mathcal{O}_g$ the indices of circuit wires which represent the output of gadget $g \in \mathcal{G}$. From these notations, an admissible set of probes $\mathcal{P}'$ from the adversary in the new game is of the form

$$\mathcal{P}' = \mathcal{P}'_r \cup \mathcal{P}'_m \cup \mathcal{P}'_a$$

where

$$\mathcal{P}'_r \subseteq \bigcup_{g \in \mathcal{G}_r} \mathcal{I}_g$$

$$\mathcal{P}'_m \subseteq \bigcup_{g \in \mathcal{G}_m} \mathcal{I}_g \times \mathcal{J}_g$$

$$\mathcal{P}'_a \subseteq \bigcup_{g \in \mathcal{G}_a} \mathcal{I}_g \bigcup_{g \in \mathcal{G}_a} \mathcal{J}_g \bigcup_{g \in \mathcal{G}_a} \mathcal{O}_g$$

and $|\mathcal{P}'| = t$. That is, each of the t elements of $\mathcal{P}'$ either is a pair of index in $\mathcal{I}_g \times \mathcal{J}_g$ for a multiplication gadget g, or a single index in $\mathcal{I}_g$ for a refresh gadget g, or a single index in $\mathcal{I}_g \cup \mathcal{J}_g \cup \mathcal{O}_g$ for an addition gadget. Note that in the latter case, the index can correspond to any wire in the addition gadget (which is simply composed of $t+1$ addition gates).

Let t_m be the number of probes on multiplication gadgets, *i.e.* $t_m = |\mathcal{P}'_m|$, and t_{ar} the number of probes on refresh or addition gadgets, *i.e.* $t_{ar} = |\mathcal{P}'_a \cup \mathcal{P}'_r|$, so that $t_m + t_{ar} = t$. The evaluation $C([x_1], \ldots, [x_n])_{\mathcal{P}'}$ then returns a q-tuple for $q = 2t_m + t_{ar}$, which is composed of the values taken by the wires of index $i \in \mathcal{P}'_a \cup \mathcal{P}'_r$, and the values taken by the wires of index i and j with $(i, j) \in \mathcal{P}'_m$. The new experiments $\mathsf{ExpReal}_1(\mathcal{A}, C)$ and $\mathsf{ExpSim}_1(\mathcal{A}, \mathcal{S}, C)$, carefully written in Fig. 6, each output a q-tuple and, as before, the simulator wins Game 1 if and only if the associated distributions are identical.

$\mathsf{ExpReal}_1(\mathcal{A}, C)$:
1. $(\mathcal{P}', x_1, \ldots, x_n) \leftarrow \mathcal{A}()$
2. $[x_1] \leftarrow \mathsf{Enc}(x_1), \ldots, [x_n] \leftarrow \mathsf{Enc}(x_n)$
3. $(v_1, \ldots, v_q) \leftarrow C([x_1], \ldots, [x_n])_{\mathcal{P}'}$
4. Return $(v_1, \ldots, v_q)$

$\mathsf{ExpSim}_1(\mathcal{A}, \mathcal{S}, C)$:
1. $(\mathcal{P}', x_1, \ldots, x_n) \leftarrow \mathcal{A}()$
2. $(v_1, \ldots, v_q) \leftarrow \mathcal{S}(\mathcal{P}')$
3. Return $(v_1, \ldots, v_q)$

Fig. 6. Game 1.

Proposition 4. *A standard shared circuit C is t-probing secure if and only if for every adversary $\mathcal{A}$, there exists a simulator $\mathcal{S}$ that wins Game 1 defined above, i.e. the random experiments* $\mathsf{ExpReal}_1(\mathcal{A}, C)$ *and* $\mathsf{ExpSim}_1(\mathcal{A}, \mathcal{S}, C)$ *output identical distributions.*

Proof. Basically, the proof is based on the fact that with the SNI property on the gadgets in our circuit, each probe in a t-SNI gadget can be replaced by 1 or 2 probes on the input sharing(s) of the gadget. The complete proof can be found in the full version of this paper [4].

Game 2. Our second game transition consists in replacing the circuit C by a functionally equivalent circuit C' of multiplicative depth one and with an extended input. In a nutshell, each output of a multiplication or a refresh gadget in C is replaced by a fresh new input sharing of the same value in the rest of the circuit. The new circuit hence takes N input sharings $[x_1], \ldots, [x_n], [x_{n+1}], \ldots, [x_N]$, with $N = n + |\mathcal{G}_m| + |\mathcal{G}_r|$. The two circuits are functionally equivalent in the sense that for every input $(x_1, \ldots, x_n)$ there exists an extension $(x_{n+1}, \ldots, x_N)$ such that $C([x_1], \ldots, [x_n])$ and $C'([x_1], \ldots, [x_N])$ have output sharings encoding the same values. This transformation is further referred to as Flatten in the following, and is illustrated on Fig. 7.

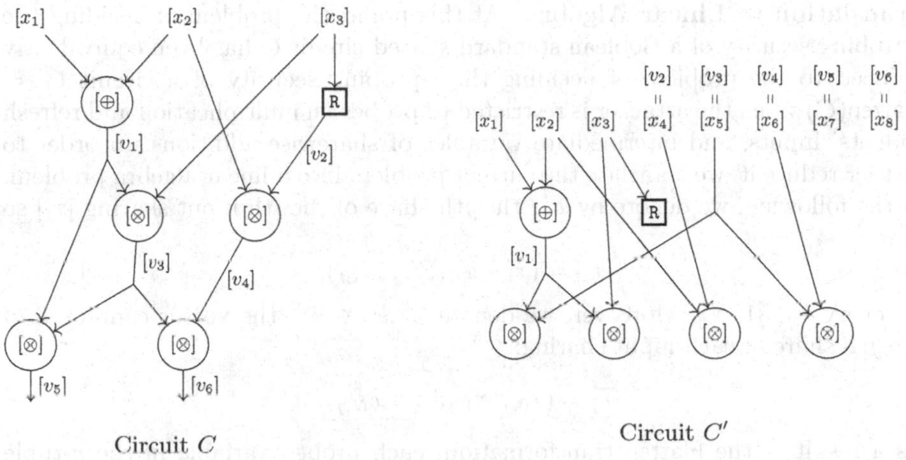

Fig. 7. Illustration of the Flatten transformation.

The resulting Game 2 is illustrated on Fig. 8. Although the additional inputs $x_{n+1}, \ldots, x_N$ are deterministic functions of the original inputs $x_1, \ldots, x_n$, we allow the adversary to select the full extended input $x_1, \ldots, x_N$ for the sake of simplicity. This slight adversarial power overhead does not affect the equivalence between the games.

$\mathsf{ExpReal}_2(\mathcal{A}, C)$:

1. $C' \leftarrow \mathsf{Flatten}(C)$
2. $(\mathcal{P}', x_1, \ldots, x_N) \leftarrow \mathcal{A}()$
3. $[x_1] \leftarrow \mathsf{Enc}(x_1), \ldots, [x_N] \leftarrow \mathsf{Enc}(x_N)$
4. $(v_1, \ldots, v_q) \leftarrow C'([x_1], \ldots, [x_N])_{\mathcal{P}'}$
5. Return $(v_1, \ldots, v_q)$

$\mathsf{ExpSim}_2(\mathcal{A}, \mathcal{S}, C)$:

1. $C' \leftarrow \mathsf{Flatten}(C)$
2. $(\mathcal{P}', x_1, \ldots, x_N) \leftarrow \mathcal{A}()$
3. $(v_1, \ldots, v_q) \leftarrow \mathcal{S}(\mathcal{P}')$
4. Return $(v_1, \ldots, v_q)$

Fig. 8. Game 2.

Proposition 5. *A standard shared circuit C is t-probing secure if and only if for every adversary $\mathcal{A}$, there exists a simulator $\mathcal{S}$ that wins Game 2 defined above, i.e. the random experiments* $\mathsf{ExpReal}_2(\mathcal{A}, C)$ *and* $\mathsf{ExpSim}_2(\mathcal{A}, \mathcal{S}, C)$ *output identical distributions.*

Proof. Basically, the proof is based on the fact that the output encodings of a ISW multiplication are completely independent of its inputs encodings. The complete proof can be found in the full version of this paper [4].

Corollary 1. *A standard shared circuit C is t-probing secure if and only if the standard shared circuit* $\mathsf{Flatten}(C)$ *is t-probing secure.*

Translation to Linear Algebra. At this point, the problem of deciding the t-probing security of a Boolean standard shared circuit C has been equivalently reduced to the problem of deciding the t-probing security of a circuit $C' = \mathsf{Flatten}(C)$ when the attacker is restricted to probes on multiplication and refresh gadgets' inputs, and intermediate variables of sharewise additions. In order to further reduce it, we translate the current problem into a linear algebra problem. In the following, we denote by $x_{i,j}$ the jth share of the ith input sharing $[x_i]$ so that

$$[x_i] = (x_{i,0}, x_{i,1}, \ldots, x_{i,t}),$$

for every $i \in [\![1, N]\!]$. Moreover, we denote by $\overrightarrow{x_j} \in \mathbb{F}_2^N$ the vector composed of the jth share of each input sharing:

$$\overrightarrow{x_j} = (x_{0,j}, x_{1,j}, \ldots, x_{N,j}).$$

As a result of the $\mathsf{Flatten}$ transformation, each probed variable in the q-tuple $(v_1, \ldots, v_q) = C([x_1], \ldots, [x_N])_{\mathcal{P}'}$ is a linear combination of the input sharings $[x_1], \ldots, [x_N]$. Moreover, since the addition gadgets are sharewise, for every $k \in [\![1, q]\!]$, there is a single share index j such that the probed variable v_k only depends of the jth shares of the input sharings, giving:

$$v_k = \overrightarrow{a_k} \cdot \overrightarrow{x_j}, \tag{1}$$

for some constant coefficient vector $\overrightarrow{a_k} \in \mathbb{F}_2^N$. Without loss of generality, we assume that the tuple of probed variables is ordered w.r.t. the share index j corresponding to each v_k (*i.e.* starting from $j = 0$ up to $j = t$). Specifically, the q-tuple $(v_1, \ldots, v_q)$ is the concatenation of $t + 1$ vectors

$$\overrightarrow{v_0} = M_0 \cdot \overrightarrow{x_0}\ ,\quad \overrightarrow{v_1} = M_1 \cdot \overrightarrow{x_1}\ ,\quad \ldots\quad \overrightarrow{v_t} = M_t \cdot \overrightarrow{x_t}, \tag{2}$$

where the matrix M_j is composed of the row coefficient vectors $\overrightarrow{a_k}$ for the probed variable indices k corresponding to the share index j.

Lemma 2. *For any $(x_1, \ldots, x_N) \in \mathbb{F}_2^N$, the q-tuple of probed variables $(v_1, \ldots, v_q) = C([x_1], \ldots, [x_N])_{\mathcal{P}'}$ can be perfectly simulated if and only if the M_j matrices satisfy*

$$\mathrm{Im}(M_0^T) \cap \mathrm{Im}(M_1^T) \cap \cdots \cap \mathrm{Im}(M_t^T) = \emptyset.$$

Moreover, if the M_j matrices are full-rank (which can be assumed without loss of generality), then the above equation implies that $(v_1, \ldots, v_q)$ is uniformly distributed.

Proof. Without loss of generality we can assume that the M_j matrices are full-rank since otherwise the probed variables $v_1, \ldots, v_q$ would be mutually linearly dependent and simulating them would be equivalent to simulating any subset $(v_k)_{k \in \mathcal{K} \subseteq [\![1,q]\!]}$ defining a free basis of $(v_1, \ldots, v_q)$, and which would then induce full-rank matrices M_j.

Throughout this proof, we denote $\overrightarrow{x} = (x_1, \ldots, x_N)$. We first show that a non-null intersection implies a non-uniform distribution of $(v_1, \ldots, v_q)$ which is statistically dependent on $\overrightarrow{x}$. Indeed, a non-null intersection implies that there exist a non-null vector $\overrightarrow{w} \in \mathbb{F}_2^N$ satisfying

$$\overrightarrow{w} = \overrightarrow{u_0} \cdot M_0 = \overrightarrow{u_1} \cdot M_1 = \cdots = \overrightarrow{u_t} \cdot M_t. \tag{3}$$

for some (constant) vectors $\overrightarrow{u_0}$, …, $\overrightarrow{u_t}$. It follows that

$$\sum_{j=0}^{t} \overrightarrow{u_j} \cdot \overrightarrow{v_j} = \sum_{j=0}^{t} \overrightarrow{w} \cdot \overrightarrow{x_j} = \overrightarrow{w} \cdot \overrightarrow{x},$$

which implies that the distribution of the q-tuple $(v_1, \ldots, v_q) = (\overrightarrow{v_0} \parallel \cdots \parallel \overrightarrow{v_t})$ is non-uniform and dependent on $\overrightarrow{x}$.

We now show that a null intersection implies a uniform distribution (which can then be easily simulated). The uniformity and mutual independence between the sharings $[x_1]$, …, $[x_N]$ implies that we can see $\overrightarrow{x_1}$, …, $\overrightarrow{x_t}$ as t uniform and independent vectors on $\mathbb{F}_2^N$, and $\overrightarrow{x_0}$ as

$$\overrightarrow{x_0} = \overrightarrow{x} + \overrightarrow{x_1} + \cdots + \overrightarrow{x_t}.$$

The joint distribution of $\overrightarrow{v_1}$, …, $\overrightarrow{v_t}$ is hence clearly uniform. Then each coordinate of $\overrightarrow{v_0}$ is the result of the inner product $\overrightarrow{r} \cdot \overrightarrow{x_0}$ where $\overrightarrow{r}$ is a row of M_0. By assumption, there exists at least one matrix M_j such that $\overrightarrow{r} \notin \operatorname{Im}(M_j^T)$. It results that $\overrightarrow{r} \cdot \overrightarrow{x_j}$ is a uniform random variable independent of $\overrightarrow{v_1}$, …, $\overrightarrow{v_t}$ and the other coordinates of $\overrightarrow{v_0}$ (since M_0 is full-rank). Since the latter holds for all the coordinates of $\overrightarrow{x_0}$ we get overall uniformity of $(\overrightarrow{v_0} \parallel \cdots \parallel \overrightarrow{v_t})$ which concludes the proof. □

Lemma 2 allows us to reduce the t-probing security of a standard shared circuit to a linear algebra problem. If an adversary exists that can choose the set of probes $\mathcal{P}'$ such that the transposes of induced matrices M_1, …, M_t have intersecting images, then the distribution of $(v_1, \ldots, v_q)$ depends on $(x_1, \ldots, x_N)$ and a perfect simulation is impossible (which means that the circuit is not probing secure). Otherwise, the tuple $(v_1, \ldots, v_q)$ can always be simulated by a uniform distribution and the circuit is probing secure. This statement is the basis of our verification method depicted in the next section. But before introducing our verification method, we can still simplify the probing security game as shown hereafter by using Lemma 2.

Game 3. In this last game, the adversary is restricted to probe the multiplication gadgets only. Formally, $\mathcal{A}$ returns a set of probes $\mathcal{P}' = \mathcal{P}'_r \cup \mathcal{P}'_m \cup \mathcal{P}'_a$ such that $\mathcal{P}'_r = \emptyset$ and $\mathcal{P}'_a = \emptyset$. Such a set, denoted $\mathcal{P}''$ is hence composed of t pairs of inputs from $\bigcup_{g \in \mathcal{G}_m} \mathcal{I}_g \times \mathcal{J}_g$. The evaluation $C([x_1], \ldots, [x_n])_{\mathcal{P}''}$ then returns a q-tuple for $q = 2t$. The new experiments $\mathsf{ExpReal}_3(\mathcal{A}, C)$ and $\mathsf{ExpSim}_3(\mathcal{A}, \mathcal{S}, C)$, displayed in Fig. 6, each output a q-tuple and, as before, the simulator wins Game 3 if and only if the associated distributions are identical.

$\mathsf{ExpReal}_3(\mathcal{A}, C)$:
1. $C' \leftarrow \mathsf{Flatten}(C)$
2. $(\mathcal{P}'', x_1, \ldots, x_N) \leftarrow \mathcal{A}()$
3. $[x_1] \leftarrow \mathsf{Enc}(x_1), \ldots, [x_N] \leftarrow \mathsf{Enc}(x_N)$
4. $(v_1, \ldots, v_q) \leftarrow C'([x_1], \ldots, [x_N])_{\mathcal{P}''}$
5. Return $(v_1, \ldots, v_q)$

$\mathsf{ExpSim}_3(\mathcal{A}, \mathcal{S}, C)$:
1. $C' \leftarrow \mathsf{Flatten}(C)$
2. $(\mathcal{P}'', x_1, \ldots, x_N) \leftarrow \mathcal{A}()$
3. $(v_1, \ldots, v_q) \leftarrow \mathcal{S}(\mathcal{P}'')$
4. Return $(v_1, \ldots, v_q)$

Fig. 9. Game 3.

Proposition 6. *A standard shared circuit C is t-probing secure if and only if for every adversary $\mathcal{A}$, there exists a simulator $\mathcal{S}$ that wins Game 3 defined above, i.e. the random experiments* $\mathsf{ExpReal}_3(\mathcal{A}, C)$ *and* $\mathsf{ExpSim}_3(\mathcal{A}, \mathcal{S}, C)$ *output identical distributions.*

Proof. Basically, the proof is based on the fact that probing a cross products $a_i \cdot b_j$ allows you to gain informations on the two shares a_i and b_j. The complete proof can be found in the full version of this paper [4].

4 Probing-Security Verification for Standard Shared Circuits

In this section, we describe a formal verification method that checks for any $t \in \mathbb{N}$ whether a standard $(t + 1)$-shared circuit C achieves t-probing security for every $t \in \mathbb{N}$. Specifically, our tool `tightPROVE` either provides a formal proof that C is t-probing secure (where C is a standard shared circuit with sharing order $t + 1$), or it exhibits a *probing attack* against C for the given t, namely it finds a set of probes $\mathcal{P}$ (indices of wires) in the $(t+1)$-shared instance of C, such that $|\mathcal{P}| = t$, for which the evaluation $C([x_1], \ldots, [x_n])_{\mathcal{P}}$ cannot be simulated without some knowledge on the plain input $(x_1, \ldots, x_n)$.

4.1 Linear Algebra Formulation

As demonstrated in the previous section, the t-probing security game for a standard $(t+1)$-shared circuit C can be reduced to a game where an adversary selects a set of probes $\mathcal{P}''$ solely pointing to input shares of the multiplication gadgets of a *flattened* circuit C'. In the following, we will denote by m the number of multiplication gadgets in C (or equivalently in C') and by $g \in [\![1, m]\!]$ the index of a multiplication gadget of C. We will further denote by $[a_g]$ and $[b_g]$ the input sharings of the g-th multiplication gadget so that we have

$$[a_g] = (\overrightarrow{a_g} \cdot \overrightarrow{x_0}, \ldots, \overrightarrow{a_g} \cdot \overrightarrow{x_t}) \text{ and } [b_g] = (\overrightarrow{b_g} \cdot \overrightarrow{x_0}, \ldots, \overrightarrow{b_g} \cdot \overrightarrow{x_t}), \tag{4}$$

for some constant coefficient vectors $\overrightarrow{a_g}, \overrightarrow{b_g} \in \mathbb{F}_2^N$, recalling that $\overrightarrow{x_j}$ denotes the vector with the jth share of each input sharing $[x_1]$, ..., $[x_N]$. In the following, the vectors $\{\overrightarrow{a_g}, \overrightarrow{b_g}\}_g$ are called the *operand vectors*.

In Game 3, the adversary chooses t pairs of probes such that each pair points to one share of $[a_g]$ and one share of $[b_g]$ for a multiplication gadget g. Without loss of generality, the set of pairs output by the adversary can be relabeled as a set of triplet $\mathcal{P} = \{(g, j_1, j_2)\}$ where $g \in [\![1, m]\!]$ is the index of a multiplication gadget, j_1 and j_2 are share indices. For any triplet $(g, j_1, j_2) \in \mathcal{P}$ the two input shares $\overrightarrow{a_g} \cdot \overrightarrow{x_{j_1}}$ and $\overrightarrow{b_g} \cdot \overrightarrow{x_{j_2}}$ are added to the $(2t)$-tuple of probed variables to be simulated. This set of triplets exactly defines a sequence of $t+1$ matrices M_0, ..., M_t, defined iteratively by adding $\overrightarrow{a_g}$ to the rows of M_{j_1} and $\overrightarrow{b_g}$ to the rows of M_{j_2} for each $(g, j_1, j_2) \in \mathcal{P}$. Equivalently, the matrix M_j is defined as

$$M_j = \mathsf{rows}(\{\overrightarrow{a_g}\ ;\ (g, j, *) \in \mathcal{P}\} \cup \{\overrightarrow{b_g}\ ;\ (g, *, j) \in \mathcal{P}\}), \tag{5}$$

for every $j \in [\![0, t]\!]$ where rows maps a set of vectors to the matrix with rows from this set.

Lemma 2 then implies that a probing attack on C consists of a set of probes $\mathcal{P} = \{(g, j_1, j_2)\}$ such that the transposes of the induced M_j have intersecting images. Moreover, since the total number of rows in these matrices is $2t$, at least one of them has a single row $\overrightarrow{w}$. In particular, the image intersection can only be the span of this vector (which must match the row of all single-row matrices) and this vector belongs to the set of operand vectors $\{\overrightarrow{a_g}, \overrightarrow{b_g}\}_g$. In other words, there exists a probing attack on C if and only if a choice of probes $\mathcal{P} = \{(g, j_1, j_2)\}$ implies

$$\mathrm{Im}(M_0^T) \cap \mathrm{Im}(M_1^T) \cap \cdots \cap \mathrm{Im}(M_t^T) = \langle \overrightarrow{w} \rangle. \tag{6}$$

for some vector $\overrightarrow{w} \in \{\overrightarrow{a_g}, \overrightarrow{b_g}\}_g$. In that case we further say that there is a probing attack on the operand vector $\overrightarrow{w}$.

In the remainder of this section, we describe an efficient method that given a set of vector operands $\{\overrightarrow{a_g}, \overrightarrow{b_g}\}_g$ (directly defined from a target circuit C) determines whether there exists a parameter t and a set $\mathcal{P} = \{(g, j_1, j_2)\}$ (of cardinality t) for which (6) can be satisfied. We prove that (1) if such sets $\mathcal{P}$ exist, our method returns one of these sets, (2) if no set is returned by our method then the underlying circuit is t-probing secure for any sharing order $(t+1)$.

4.2 Method Description

The proposed method loops over all the vector operands $\overrightarrow{w} \in \{\overrightarrow{a_g}, \overrightarrow{b_g}\}_g$ and checks whether there exists a probing attack on $\overrightarrow{w}$ (*i.e.* whether a set $\mathcal{P}$ can be constructed that satisfies (6)).

For each $\overrightarrow{w} \in \{\overrightarrow{a_g}, \overrightarrow{b_g}\}_g$ the verification method is iterative. It starts from a set $\mathcal{G}_1 \subseteq [\![1, m]\!]$ defined as

$$\mathcal{G}_1 = \{g \; ; \; \overrightarrow{a_g} = \overrightarrow{w}\} \cup \{g \; ; \; \overrightarrow{b_g} = \overrightarrow{w}\}. \tag{7}$$

Namely $\mathcal{G}_1$ contains the indices of all the multiplication gadgets that have $\overrightarrow{w}$ as vector operand. Then the set of *free vector operands* $\mathcal{O}_1$ is defined as

$$\mathcal{O}_1 = \{\overrightarrow{b_g} \; ; \; \overrightarrow{a_g} = \overrightarrow{w}\} \cup \{\overrightarrow{a_g} \; ; \; \overrightarrow{b_g} = \overrightarrow{w}\}. \tag{8}$$

The terminology of *free* vector operand comes from the following intuition: if a probing adversary spends one probe on gadget $g \in \mathcal{G}_1$ such that $\overrightarrow{a_g} = \overrightarrow{w}$ to add $\overrightarrow{w}$ to a matrix M_j (or equivalently to get the share $\overrightarrow{w} \cdot \overrightarrow{x_j}$), then she can also add $\overrightarrow{b_g}$ to another matrix $M_{j'}$ (or equivalently get the share $\overrightarrow{b_g} \cdot \overrightarrow{x_{j'}}$) for *free*. The adversary can then combine several free vector operands to make $\overrightarrow{w} \in \mathrm{Im}(M_{j'}^T)$ occur without directly adding $\overrightarrow{w}$ to $M_{j'}$ (or equivalently without directly probing $\overrightarrow{w} \cdot \overrightarrow{x_{j'}}$). This is possible if and only if $\overrightarrow{w} \in \langle \mathcal{O}_1 \rangle$.

The free vector operands can also be combined with the operands of further multiplications to generate a probing attack on $\overrightarrow{w}$. To capture such higher-degree combinations, we define the sequences of sets $(\mathcal{G}_i)_i$ and $(\mathcal{O}_i)_i$ as follows:

$$\mathcal{G}_{i+1} = \{g \; ; \; \overrightarrow{a_g} \in \overrightarrow{w} + \langle \mathcal{O}_i \rangle\} \cup \{g \; ; \; \overrightarrow{b_g} \in \overrightarrow{w} + \langle \mathcal{O}_i \rangle\}, \tag{9}$$

and

$$\mathcal{O}_{i+1} = \{\overrightarrow{b_g} \; ; \; \overrightarrow{a_g} \in \overrightarrow{w} + \langle \mathcal{O}_i \rangle\} \cup \{\overrightarrow{a_g} \; ; \; \overrightarrow{b_g} \in \overrightarrow{w} + \langle \mathcal{O}_i \rangle\}. \tag{10}$$

for every $i \geq 1$. The rough idea of this iterative construction is the following: if at step $i+1$ a probing adversary spends one probe on gadget $g \in \mathcal{G}_{i+1}$ such that $\overrightarrow{a_g} \in \overrightarrow{w} + \langle \mathcal{O}_i \rangle$, then she can add $\overrightarrow{a_g}$ together with some free vector operands of previous steps to M_j in order to get $\overrightarrow{w} \in \mathrm{Im}(M_j^T)$. Then she can also add $\overrightarrow{b_g}$ to another matrix $M_{j'}$, making $\overrightarrow{b_g}$ a new free vector operand of step $i+1$.

Based on these definitions, our method iterates the construction of the sets $\mathcal{G}_i$ and $\mathcal{O}_i$. At setp i, two possible stop conditions are tested:

1. if $\mathcal{G}_i = \mathcal{G}_{i-1}$, then there is no probing attack on $\overrightarrow{w}$, the method stops the iteration on $\overrightarrow{w}$ and continues with the next element in the set of vector operands;
2. if $\overrightarrow{w} \in \langle \mathcal{O}_i \rangle$, then there is a probing attack on $\overrightarrow{w}$, the method stops and returns `True` (with $\overrightarrow{w}$ and the sequence of sets $(\mathcal{G}_i, \mathcal{O}_i)_i$ as proof);

The method returns `True` if there exists a concrete probing attack on a vector $\overrightarrow{w} \in \{\overrightarrow{a_g}, \overrightarrow{b_g}\}_g$ for a certain sharing order $t+1$. Otherwise, it will eventually stop with vector operand $\overrightarrow{w}$ since the number of multiplications is finite and since $\mathcal{G}_i \subseteq \mathcal{G}_{i+1}$ for every $i \geq 1$. When all the possible vector operands have been tested without finding a probing attack, the method returns `False`. Algorithm 1 hereafter gives a pseudocode of our method where NextSets denotes the procedure that computes $(\mathcal{G}_{i+1}, \mathcal{O}_{i+1})$ from $(\mathcal{G}_i, \mathcal{O}_i)$ and is implemented in Sect. 6.

Algorithm 1. Search probing attack

Input: A set of vector operands $\{\overrightarrow{a_g}, \overrightarrow{b_g}\}_g$
Output: True if there is probing attack on some $\overrightarrow{w} \in \{\overrightarrow{a_g}, \overrightarrow{b_g}\}_g$ and False otherwise

```
for all w ∈ {a_g, b_g}_g do
    (G_1, O_1) ← NextSets(∅, ∅, {a_g, b_g}_g, w)
    if w ∈ ⟨O_1⟩ then return True
    for i = 1 to m do
        (G_{i+1}, O_{i+1}) ← NextSets(G_i, O_i, {a_g, b_g}_g, w)
        if G_{i+1} = G_i then break
        if w ∈ ⟨O_i⟩ then return True
    end for
end for
return False
```

In the rest of the section we first give some toy examples to illustrate our methods and then provides a proof of its correctness.

4.3 Toy Examples

Two examples are provided hereafter to illustrate our iterative method in the absence then in the presence of a probing attack.

In the very simple example of Fig. 1, two variables are manipulated in multiplications in the circuit C: $\overrightarrow{w}_1 = \overrightarrow{x_1}$ and $\overrightarrow{w}_2 = \overrightarrow{x_1} + \overrightarrow{x_2}$. The set of multiplications $\mathcal{G}$ is of cardinality one since it only contains one multiplication $(\overrightarrow{w}_1, \overrightarrow{w}_2)$. Following the number of variables, the method proceeds at most in two steps:

1. As depicted in Algorithm 1, the method first determines whether there exists a probing attack on $\overrightarrow{w}_1$. In this purpose, a first set $\mathcal{G}_1$ is built, such that $\mathcal{G}_1 = (\overrightarrow{w}_1, \overrightarrow{w}_2)$ and $\mathcal{O}_1 = \overrightarrow{w}_2$. Since $\mathcal{G}_1 \neq \emptyset$ and $\overrightarrow{w}_1 \neq \overrightarrow{w}_2$, then a second set must be built. However, there is no multiplication left, that is $\mathcal{G}_2 = \mathcal{G}_1$ and so there is no attack on $\overrightarrow{w}_1$.
2. The method then focuses on $\overrightarrow{w}_2$. In this purpose, a dedicated set $\mathcal{G}_1$ is built, such that $\mathcal{G}_1 = (\overrightarrow{w}_2, \overrightarrow{w}_1)$ and $\mathcal{O}_1 = \overrightarrow{w}_1$. Since $\mathcal{G}_1 \neq \emptyset$ and $\overrightarrow{w}_2 \neq \overrightarrow{w}_1$, then a second set must be built. However, there is no multiplication left, that is $\mathcal{G}_2 = \mathcal{G}_1$ and so there is no attack on $\overrightarrow{w}_2$ either. Since there is no input variable left, the method returns False, which means that there is no possible probing attack on this circuit.

Figure 10 provides a second Boolean circuit. It manipulates five variables $\overrightarrow{w}_i$ as operands of multiplication gadgets: $\overrightarrow{w}_1 = \overrightarrow{x_1}$, $\overrightarrow{w}_2 = \overrightarrow{x_2}$, $\overrightarrow{w}_3 = \overrightarrow{x_3}$, $\overrightarrow{w}_4 = \overrightarrow{x_1} + \overrightarrow{x_2}$, and $\overrightarrow{w}_5 = \overrightarrow{x_2} + \overrightarrow{x_3}$. The set of multiplications $\mathcal{G}$ is of cardinality three with $(\overrightarrow{w}_1, \overrightarrow{w}_2)$, $(\overrightarrow{w}_4, \overrightarrow{w}_5)$, and $(\overrightarrow{w}_3, \overrightarrow{w}_4)$. Following the number of variables, the method proceeds at most in five steps:

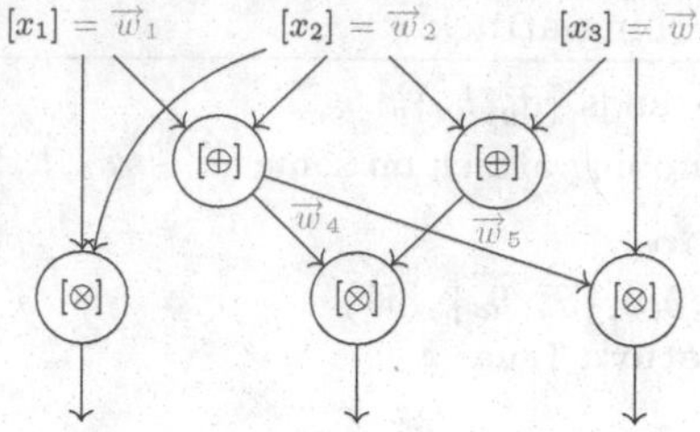

Fig. 10. Graph representation of a second Boolean circuit.

1. The method first determines whether there exists a probing attack on $\overrightarrow{w}_1$. In this purpose, a first set $\mathcal{G}_1$ is built, such that $\mathcal{G}_1 = (\overrightarrow{w}_1, \overrightarrow{w}_2)$ and $\mathcal{O}_1 = \overrightarrow{w}_2$. Since $\mathcal{G}_1 \neq \emptyset$ and $\overrightarrow{w}_1 \neq \overrightarrow{w}_2$, then a second set must be built. $\mathcal{G}_2 = \mathcal{G}_1 \cup \{(\overrightarrow{w}_4, \overrightarrow{w}_5), (\overrightarrow{w}_4, \overrightarrow{w}_3)\}$ since $\overrightarrow{w}_4 = \overrightarrow{w}_1 + \overrightarrow{w}_2$. However, $\overrightarrow{w}_1 \notin \mathcal{O}_2 (=< \overrightarrow{w}_2, \overrightarrow{w}_3, \overrightarrow{w}_5 >)$, so a third set must be built. Since there is no multiplication left, that is $\mathcal{G}_3 = \mathcal{G}_2$, there is no attack on $\overrightarrow{w}_1$.
2. The method then focuses on $\overrightarrow{w}_2$. In this purpose, a dedicated set $\mathcal{G}_1$ is built, such that $\mathcal{G}_1 = (\overrightarrow{w}_2, \overrightarrow{w}_1)$ and $\mathcal{O}_1 = \overrightarrow{w}_1$. Since $\mathcal{G}_1 \neq \emptyset$ and $\overrightarrow{w}_2 \neq \overrightarrow{w}_1$, then a second set must be built. $\mathcal{G}_2 = \mathcal{G}_1 \cup \{(\overrightarrow{w}_4, \overrightarrow{w}_5), (\overrightarrow{w}_4, \overrightarrow{w}_3)\}$ since $\overrightarrow{w}_4 = \overrightarrow{w}_2 + \overrightarrow{w}_1$. And in that case, $\overrightarrow{w}_2 \in \mathcal{O}_2 (=< \overrightarrow{w}_1, \overrightarrow{w}_3, \overrightarrow{w}_5 >)$ since $\overrightarrow{w}_2 = \overrightarrow{w}_3 + \overrightarrow{w}_5$. Thus the method returns `True` and there exists an attack on $\overrightarrow{w}_2 = \overrightarrow{x_2}$ for some masking order t.

4.4 Proof of Correctness

This section provides a proof of correctness of the method. This proof is organized in two propositions which are based on some invariants in Algorithm 1. The first proposition shows that if the method returns `True` for some operand vector $\overrightarrow{w}$ and corresponding sets $(\mathcal{G}_i, \mathcal{O}_i)$ then there exists a probing attack on $\overrightarrow{w}$ (*i.e.* a set $\mathcal{P}$ can be constructed that satisfies (6)). The second proposition shows that if the method returns `False` then there exists no probing attack for any $\overrightarrow{w}$, namely the underlying circuit is t-probing secure as soon as masked variables are masked with $t+1$ shares.

Proposition 7. *For every $i \in \mathbb{N}$, if $\overrightarrow{w} \in \langle \mathcal{O}_i \rangle$ then there exists $t \in \mathbb{N}$ and $\mathcal{P} = \{(g, j_1, j_2)\}$ with $|\mathcal{P}| = t$ implying $\bigcap_{j=0}^{t} \mathrm{Im}(M_j^T) = \overrightarrow{w}$.*

Proposition 8. *Let $i > 1$ such that $\mathcal{G}_1 \subset \cdots \subset \mathcal{G}_{i-1} = \mathcal{G}_i$ and $\overrightarrow{w} \notin \langle \mathcal{O}_i \rangle$. Then for any $t \in \mathbb{N}$ and $\mathcal{P} = \{(g, j_1, j_2)\}$ with $|\mathcal{P}| = t$ we have $\overrightarrow{w} \notin \bigcap_{j=0}^{t} \mathrm{Im}(M_j^T)$.*

Proofs of Propositions 7 and 8 are available in the full version of this paper [4].

4.5 Towards Efficient Construction of Tight *t*-Private Circuits

Our formal verification method exactly reveals all the t-probing attacks on standard shared circuits. A sound countermeasure to counteract these attacks is the use of refresh gadgets. We discuss here how to transform a flawed standard shared circuit into a t-private circuit with exactly the minimum number of refresh gadgets.

In a first attempt, we easily show that refreshing the left operands of each multiplication in C is enough to provide t-probing security.

Proposition 9. *A standard shared circuit C augmented with t-SNI refresh gadgets operating on the left operand of each multiplication gadget is t-probing secure.*

In a second attempt, we need to slightly modify Algorithm 1 so that it conducts an analysis on all the possible operands in order to return a complete list of the flawed ones. So far, it stops at the first flaw. With such a list for a standard shared circuit, we can show that refreshing only the flawed operands is enough to provide t-probing security.

Proposition 10. *A standard shared circuit C augmented with t-SNI refresh gadgets operating on each flawed operand, as revealed by our method, of its multiplication gadgets is t-probing secure.*

Proofs of these propositions are available in the full version of this paper [4].

Propositions 9 and 10 provide an upper bound of the required number of refresh gadgets in a standard shared circuit to achieve probing security at any order t. If we denote by m the number of multiplications in a standard shared circuit C and by o the number of flawed operands returned by our method, then C is to be augmented of at most $r = \min(m, o)$ refresh gadgets to achieve probing security at any order t. Given this upper bound, an iterative number of refresh gadgets from 1 to r can be inserted at each location in C in order to exhibit a tight private circuit with a minimum number of refresh gadgets.

5 Further Steps

Now that we are able to exactly determine the t-probing security of standard shared circuits, a natural follow-up consists in studying the t-probing security of their composition. In a first part, we establish several compositional properties, and then we show how they apply to the widely deployed SPN-based block ciphers. We eventually discuss the extension of our results to generic shared circuits.

5.1 Generic Composition

This section is dedicated to the statement of new compositional properties on tight private circuits. In a first attempt, we show that the composition of a t-private circuit whose outputs coincide with the outputs of t-SNI gadgets with another t-private circuit is still a t-private circuit.

Proposition 11. *Let us consider a standard shared circuit C composed of two sequential circuits:*

- *a t-probing secure circuit C_1 whose outputs are all outputs of t-SNI gadgets,*
- *a t-probing secure circuit C_2 whose inputs are C_1's outputs.*

Then, $C = C_2 \circ C_1$ is t-probing secure.

Proof. As the outputs of the first circuit C_1 are the outputs t-SNI gadgets, we get from Lemma 1 that the input encodings of C_1 and the input encodings of C_2 are independent and uniformly distributed. Then, the proof is straightforward from Proposition 5. Basically, the analysis of C's t-probing security can be equivalently reduced to the analysis of the t-probing security of $C' = \mathsf{Flatten}(C)$ in which each output of a t-SNI gadget is replaced by a fresh new input sharing of the corresponding value in the rest of the circuit, *i.e.* C_2. As a consequence, C is t-probing secure if and only if both C_1 and C_2 are t-probing secure, which is correct by assumption. □

In a second attempt, we establish the secure composition of a standard shared circuit that implements a (shared) linear surjective transformation through several sharewise addition gadgets, that we refer to as a t-linear surjective circuit, and a standard t-probing circuit.

Proposition 12. *Let us consider a standard shared circuit C composed of two sequential circuits:*

- *a t-linear surjective circuit C_1, exclusively composed of sharewise additions,*
- *a t-probing secure circuit C_2 whose inputs are C_1's outputs.*

Then, $C = C_2 \circ C_1$ is t-probing secure.

Proof. We consider a standard shared circuit C with input $\overrightarrow{x} = (x_1, \ldots, x_n)$ composed of a t-linear surjective circuit C_1 as input to a t-probing secure circuit C_2. We denote by $\overrightarrow{y} = (y_1, \ldots, y_{n'})$ the set of C_1's outputs, or equivalently the set of C_2's inputs. From Proposition 6, the t-probing security of C can be reduced to the t-probing security of circuit $C' = \mathsf{Flatten}(C)$ for probes restricted to the multiplications' operands. In our context, C_1 is exclusively composed of sharewise additions, so the probes are restricted to C_2. From Lemma 2, any set of probed variables on C_2's multiplications operands $(v_1, \ldots, v_q)$ can be written as the concatenation of the $t+1$ vectors

$$\overrightarrow{v_0} = M_0 \cdot \overrightarrow{y_0}\ , \quad \overrightarrow{v_1} = M_1 \cdot \overrightarrow{y_1}\ , \quad \ldots \quad \overrightarrow{v_t} = M_t \cdot \overrightarrow{y_t},$$

where

$$\mathrm{Im}(M_0^T) \cap \mathrm{Im}(M_1^T) \cap \cdots \cap \mathrm{Im}(M_t^T) = \emptyset. \tag{11}$$

To achieve global t-probing security for C, we need to achieve a null intersection for matrices that apply on C's inputs instead of C_2's inputs. As C_1 implements a linear surjective transformation f, there exists a matrix M_f of rank n' such that

$$\forall\, 0 \leq i \leq t, \quad \overrightarrow{y_i} = M_f \cdot \overrightarrow{x_i}.$$

As a consequence, any set of probes $(v_1, \ldots, v_q)$ in C' as defined in Game 3 can equivalently be rewritten as the concatenation of the $t+1$ vectors

$$\overrightarrow{v_0} = M_0 \cdot M_f \cdot \overrightarrow{x_0}\ , \quad \overrightarrow{v_1} = M_1 \cdot M_f \cdot \overrightarrow{x_1}\ , \quad \ldots \quad \overrightarrow{v_t} = M_t \cdot M_f \cdot \overrightarrow{x_t}.$$

By contradiction, let us assume that

$$\mathrm{Im}(M_f^T \cdot M_0^T) \cap \mathrm{Im}(M_f^T \cdot M_1^T) \cap \cdots \cap \mathrm{Im}(M_f^T \cdot M_t^T) \neq \emptyset,$$

that is, there exists a non-null vector $\overrightarrow{w}$ such that

$$\overrightarrow{w} \in \mathrm{Im}(M_f^T \cdot M_0^T) \cap \mathrm{Im}(M_f^T \cdot M_1^T) \cap \cdots \cap \mathrm{Im}(M_f^T \cdot M_t^T).$$

Equivalently, there exists $\overrightarrow{z_0}, \overrightarrow{z_1}, \ldots, \overrightarrow{z_t}$ such that

$$\overrightarrow{w} = M_f^T \cdot M_0^T \cdot \overrightarrow{z_0} = M_f^T \cdot M_1^T \cdot \overrightarrow{z_1} = \ldots = M_f^T \cdot M_1^T \cdot \overrightarrow{z_t}.$$

From Eq. (11), there exist at least two distinct indices i and j in $\{0, \ldots, t\}$, such that

$$M_i^T \cdot \overrightarrow{z_i} \neq M_j^T \cdot \overrightarrow{z_j}.$$

As $\overrightarrow{w} = M_f^T \cdot M_i^T \cdot \overrightarrow{z_i} = M_f^T \cdot M_j^T \cdot \overrightarrow{z_j}$, the difference $M_i^T \cdot \overrightarrow{z_i} - M_j^T \cdot \overrightarrow{z_j}$ belongs to M_f^T's kernel. But from the surjective property of M_f, M_f^T has full column rank n', and thus a null kernel:

$$\dim(\mathrm{Ker}(M_f^T)) = n' - \dim(\mathrm{Im}(M_f^T)) = 0.$$

As a consequence, $M_i^T \cdot \overrightarrow{z_i} - M_j^T \cdot \overrightarrow{z_j} = 0$ and since $M_i^T \cdot \overrightarrow{z_i} \neq M_j^T \cdot \overrightarrow{z_j}$ we have a contradiction which completes the proof. □

Eventually, we claim that two t-private circuits on independent encodings form a t-private circuit as well.

Proposition 13. *Let us consider a standard shared circuit C composed of two parallel t-probing secure circuits which operate on independent input sharings. Then, $C = C_1 \| C_2$ is t-probing secure.*

Proof. As the input sharings are independent, the result is straightforward from Lemma 2. □

5.2 Application to SPN-Based Block Ciphers

An SPN-based block cipher is a permutation which takes as inputs a key k in $\{0,1\}^\kappa$ and a plaintext p in $\{0,1\}^n$ and outputs a ciphertext c in $\{0,1\}^n$, where n and κ are integers. It is defined by successive calls to a round function and by an optional expansion algorithm KS. The round function is a combination of a non linear permutation S and a linear permutation L.

Proposition 14. *Let C be a standard shared circuit implementing an SPN block cipher. And let C_S and C_{KS} be the standard shared (sub-)circuits implementing S and KS respectively. If both conditions*

1. *C_S's and C_{KS}'s outputs are t-SNI gadgets' outputs,*
2. *C_S and C_{KS} are t-probing secure (for any sharing order $t+1$),*

are fulfilled, then C is also t-probing secure.

Note that if S's and KS's outputs are not t-SNI gadgets' outputs, then the linear surjective circuit can be extended to the last t-SNI gadgets' outputs of these circuits without loss of generality.

Proof. As S and KS are t-probing secure, it follows from Proposition 13, that when implemented in parallel on independent input encodings, their composition is t-probing secure as well. Then, as the output of their composition matches the outputs of t-SNI gadgets, then they can be sequentially composed with a t-probing secure circuit from Proposition 11. Finally, the composition of linear surjective circuits with t-probing secure circuits is ensured by Proposition 12, which completes the proof. □

5.3 Extension to Generic Shared Circuits

We discuss hereafter two straightforward extensions of our work. Namely some constraints on gadgets that compose the standard shared circuits can be relaxed, and the considered circuit can easily be extended to work on larger finite fields.

On Standard Shared Circuits. The method presented in this paper through Sects. 3 and 4 aims to accurately establish the t-probing security of a *standard shared circuit* for any sharing order $t+1$. Namely, it is restricted to Boolean shared circuits exclusively composed of ISW-multiplication gadgets, ISW-refresh gadgets, and sharewise addition gadgets. While the assumption on addition gadgets is quite natural, the restrictions made on the multiplication and refresh gadgets can be relaxed. The reduction demonstrated in Sect. 3 only expects the refresh gadgets to be t-SNI secure to ensure the equivalence between Game 1 and the initial t-probing security game. Afterwards, t-probing security is equivalently evaluated on a corresponding *flattened* circuit with probes on multiplications' operands only. Therefore, there is no restriction on the choice of refresh gadgets but their t-SNI security. While multiplication gadgets are also expected to be t-SNI secure for the equivalence between Game 1 and the initial t-probing security game to hold, this feature is not enough. To prove this equivalence, multiplication gadgets are also expected to compute intermediate products between every share of their first operand and every share of their second operand. Otherwise, our method could still establish the probing security of a circuit, but not in a tight manner, meaning that security under Game 3 would imply probing security but insecurity under Game 3 would not imply insecurity w.r.t. the original probing insecurity notion. Our method would hence allowed false negatives, as state-of-the-art methods currently do. Beyond the advantages of providing an exact method, this restriction is not very constraining since not only the widely deployed ISW-multiplication gadgets but also the large majority of existing multiplication gadgets achieve this property.

On Circuits on Larger Fields. Since ISW-multiplication gadgets and ISW-refresh gadgets can straightforwardly be extended to larger fields our reduction and verification method could easily be extended to circuits working on larger fields.

6 Application

Following the results presented in previous sections, we developed a tool in sage, `tightPROVE`, that takes as input a standard shared circuit and determines whether or not it is t-probing secure with Algorithm 1. Specifically, the standard shared circuit given as input to `tightPROVE` is expressed as a set of instructions (`XOR`, `AND`, `NOT`, `REFRESH`) with operands as indices of either shared input values or shared outputs of previous instructions. Namely, the `XOR` instructions are interpreted as sharewise addition gadgets of fan-in 2, the `NOT` instructions as sharewise addition gadgets of fan-in 1 with the constant shared input $(1, 0, \ldots, 0)$, the `AND` instructions as ISW-multiplication gadgets of fan-in 2, and the `REFRESH` instructions as ISW-refresh gadgets of fan-in 1. As an application, we experimented `tightPROVE` on several standard shared circuits. First, we analyzed the t-probing security of the small examples of Sect. 4 as a sanity check. Then, we investigated the t-probing security of the AES s-box circuit from [6] and compared the result with what the `maskComp` tool produces. Additionally, we studied the impact of our tool to practical implementations (for both the randomness usage and the performance implications).

6.1 Application to Section 4 Examples

In order to have some sanity checks of our new method on simple standard shared circuits, we applied `tightPROVE` to the examples given in Sect. 4, namely the standard shared circuits depicted in Figs. 1 and 10. Specifically, we first translated the two standard shared circuits into a list of instructions that is given to our tool. For each circuit, the first instruction gives the number of shared inputs. Then, each of the following instruction matches one of the four possible operations among `XOR`, `AND`, `NOT`, and `REFRESH` together with the indices of the corresponding one or two operands. The output of each such operation is then represented by the first unused index. At the end, from the generated list of instructions the tool derives a list of pairs of operands, namely the inputs to the multiplications in the circuit. Finally, Algorithm 1 is evaluated on the obtained list of operands.

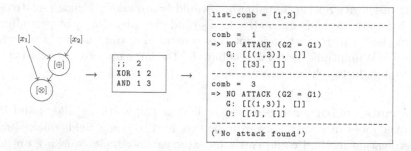

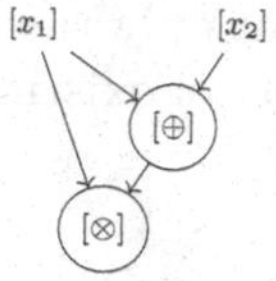


```
;;  2
XOR 1 2
AND 1 3
```

```
list_comb = [1,3]
------------------------------
comb =  1
=> NO ATTACK (G2 = G1)
   G: [[(1,3)], []]
   O: [[3], []]
------------------------------
comb =  3
=> NO ATTACK (G2 = G1)
   G: [[(1,3)], []]
   O: [[1], []]
------------------------------
('No attack found')
```

Fig. 11. New method applied on example 1.

The first example is based on a standard shared circuit that takes 2 shared inputs and then performs two operations, namely a sharewise addition (XOR) and an ISW-multiplication (AND). The AND instruction takes two inputs, namely the output of the XOR and one of the two inputs of the circuit, which means that there is only two possible target vectors for an attack to be mounted. They are displayed in the list `list_comb`. For both these two vectors successively displayed with variable `comb`, the tool generates their respective sets $\mathcal{G}_1$ and $\mathcal{O}_1$, as defined in Sect. 4. Then since $\mathcal{G}_2$ is equal to $\mathcal{G}_1$ for both vectors, the tool outputs that no attack could be found. The circuit is thus t-probing secure. The complete process is described in Fig. 11.

The second example is based on a standard shared circuit that takes 3 shared inputs and then performs 5 operations, namely 2 sharewise additions (XOR) and 3 ISW-multiplications (AND). The three AND instructions take five distinct inputs, which means that there are five possible target vectors for an attack to be mounted. For the two first target vectors, no attack could be found as the tool expressed all the multiplications in the circuit with two sets $\mathcal{G}_1$ and $\mathcal{G}_2$ without finding any attack. For the third target vector, after the construction of $\mathcal{G}_2$ an attack was found as the target vector belonged to the span of the set $\mathcal{O}_2$. The complete process is described in Fig. 12. Moreover, we verified that by adding a refresh gadget on the operand for which our tool finds an attack prior to the multiplication where it is used, the tool is not able any more to find an attack on the new circuit for this example. The results can be found in the full version of this paper [4].

6.2 Application to AES s-box

At Eurocrypt 2017, Goudarzi and Rivain [14] proposed an efficient software implementation of the s-box of the AES for higher-order masking. Based on

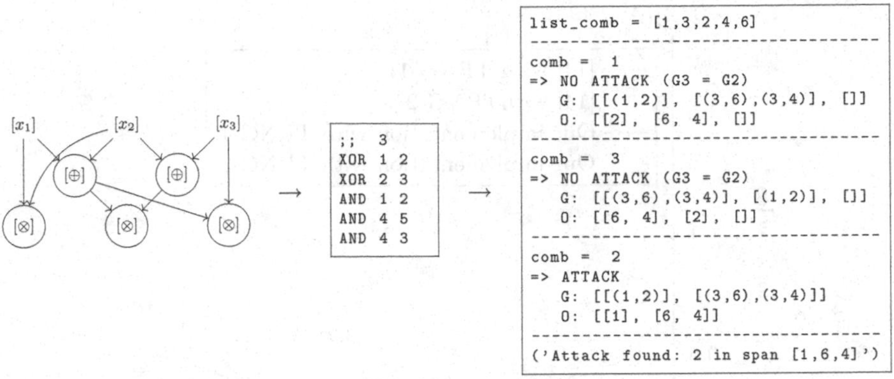

[x1]
[x2]
[x3]
[⊕]
[⊕]
[⊗]
[⊗]
[⊗]
;; 3
XOR 1 2
XOR 2 3
AND 1 2
AND 4 5
AND 4 3
list_comb = [1,3,2,4,6]
comb = 1
=> NO ATTACK (G3 = G2)
G: [[(1,2)], [(3,6),(3,4)], []]
O: [[2], [6, 4], []]
comb = 3
=> NO ATTACK (G3 = G2)
G: [[(3,6),(3,4)], [(1,2)], []]
O: [[6, 4], [2], []]
comb = 2
=> ATTACK
G: [[(1,2)], [(3,6),(3,4)]]
O: [[1], [6, 4]]
('Attack found: 2 in span [1,6,4]')

Fig. 12. New method applied on example 2.

the Boolean circuit of Boyar *et al.* [6], their implementation evaluates the s-box on a state under bitsliced representation with only 32 AND gates. In order to be t-probing secure without doubling the number of shares in the encoding of sensitive variables, a conservative choice was made to add a refresh gadget prior to each multiplication. As explained in Sect. 1, a major drawback of such a conservative approach is the performance overhead induced by the number of calls to refresh gadgets due to the randomness usage.

In order to obtain efficient implementations of the AES s-box and to be tight on the number of randomness requirement, we have applied our tool to the circuit of the s-box reordered by Goudarzi and Rivain without any refreshing gadget. Interestingly, we obtained that no attack can be found for any masking order. More precisely, the tool first identified 36 distinct target vectors out of the 64 possible operands of multiplication gadgets (it can be easily checked on the circuit found in Sect. 6 of [14]). For each of the 36 target vectors, the corresponding set $\mathcal{G}_1$ is constructed. Then, for every variable the algorithm stops as the respective sets $\mathcal{G}_2$ are always equal to the respective sets $\mathcal{G}_1$. The complete report of the tool results can be found in the full version of this paper [4].

To prove the security of the AES s-box circuit, our tool took only 427 ms. This speed is mainly due to the fact that for each possible target variable, only the set $\mathcal{G}_1$ is computed. For comparison, we looked at the time taken by the `maskVerif` tool of [1]. For a masking order $t = 2$, `maskVerif` found no attack in 35.9 s and for $t = 3$ in approximately 10 h.

For the sake of comparison, we also applied the `maskComp` tool on the same circuit. We obtained that `maskComp` adds refresh gadgets prior to each multiplication in the circuit, transforming it into a new t-NI secure circuit. Since our tool has shown that the circuit is t-probing secure with no refresh gadgets, adding those refresh gadgets implies an overhead in the t-probing security that can lead to less efficient practical implementations. As an illustration, we have implemented the AES s-box circuit in bitslice for a generic masking order to see the impact in performances between a full refresh approach (*i.e.* the conservative

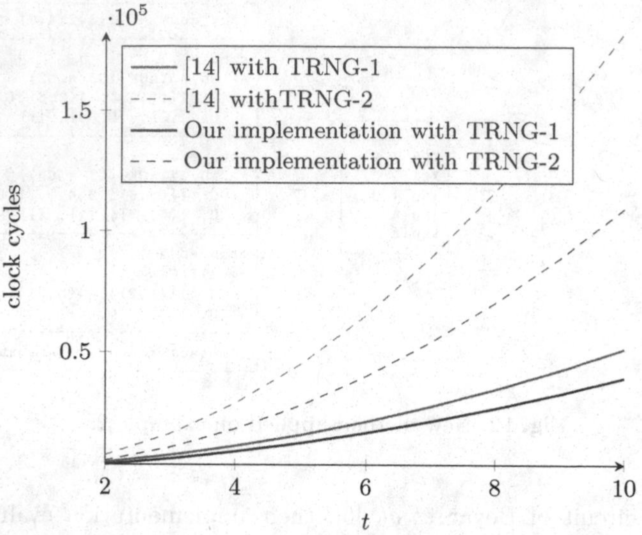

Fig. 13. Timings of a t-probing secure AES s-box implementation.

choice of Goudarzi and Rivain and the result of `maskComp`) and a no refresh approach (our new tool). Each of this two approaches produces a circuit that is at least t-probing secure for any masking order t. Both produced circuit are securely composable with other circuits (for `maskComp` from the proofs given in [2] and for our tool from the result of Sect. 5). To be consistent with the state of the art, the randomness in our implementations can be obtained from a TRNG with two different settings: a first setting with a *free* TRNG that outputs 32-bit of fresh randomness every 10 clock cycles (as in [14]) and a second setting with a constrained TRNG that outputs 32-bit of fresh randomness every 80 clock cycles (as in [16]). The performance results can be found in Table 1. For both approaches, the number of refresh gadgets used and the number of randomness needed are displayed. Then, the timing in clock cycles for both settings are shown. We can see that our tool allows to divide by 2 the number of required randomness and benefits from an asymptotic gain of up to 43% in speed. The comparison of the timings for several masking orders are depicted in Fig. 13.

Table 1. Performance results of the implementation AES s-box depending on the number of refresh gadgets

	Nb. of refresh	Nb. of random	Timing (Set. 1)	Timing (Set. 2)
[14]	32	$32\,t(t-1)$	$408\,t^2 + 928\,t + 1262$	$1864\,t^2 - 528\,t + 1262$
this paper	0	$16\,t(t-1)$	$295.5\,t^2 + 905.5\,t + 872$	$1069\,t^2 + 132\,t + 872$

Acknowledgments. We would like to thank François-Xavier Standaert and Gaëtan Cassiers for their in-depth review and helpful comments.

References

1. Barthe, G., Belaïd, S., Dupressoir, F., Fouque, P.-A., Grégoire, B., Strub, P.-Y.: Verified proofs of higher-order masking. In: Oswald, E., Fischlin, M. (eds.) EUROCRYPT 2015. LNCS, vol. 9056, pp. 457–485. Springer, Heidelberg (2015). https://doi.org/10.1007/978-3-662-46800-5_18
2. Barthe, G., et al.: Strong non-interference and type-directed higher-order masking. In: Weippl, E.R., Katzenbeisser, S., Kruegel, C., Myers, A.C., Halevi, S. (eds.) ACM CCS 2016, pp. 116–129. ACM Press, New York, October 2016
3. Barthe, G., et al.: Masking the GLP lattice-based signature scheme at any order. In: Nielsen, J.B., Rijmen, V. (eds.) EUROCRYPT 2018. LNCS, vol. 10821, pp. 354–384. Springer, Cham (2018). https://doi.org/10.1007/978-3-319-78375-8_12
4. Belaïd, S., Goudarzi, D., Rivain, M.: Tight private circuits: achieving probing security with the least refreshing. IACR Cryptol. ePrint Arch. **2018**, 439 (2018)
5. Bloem, R., Gross, H., Iusupov, R., Könighofer, B., Mangard, S., Winter, J.: Formal verification of masked hardware implementations in the presence of glitches. In: Nielsen, J.B., Rijmen, V. (eds.) EUROCRYPT 2018. LNCS, vol. 10821, pp. 321–353. Springer, Cham (2018). https://doi.org/10.1007/978-3-319-78375-8_11
6. Boyar, J., Matthews, P., Peralta, R.: Logic minimization techniques with applications to cryptology. J. Cryptol. **26**(2), 280–312 (2013)
7. Brier, E., Clavier, C., Olivier, F.: Correlation power analysis with a leakage model. In: Joye, M., Quisquater, J.-J. (eds.) CHES 2004. LNCS, vol. 3156, pp. 16–29. Springer, Heidelberg (2004). https://doi.org/10.1007/978-3-540-28632-5_2
8. Chari, S., Jutla, C.S., Rao, J.R., Rohatgi, P.: Towards sound approaches to counteract power-analysis attacks. In: Wiener, M. (ed.) CRYPTO 1999. LNCS, vol. 1666, pp. 398–412. Springer, Heidelberg (1999). https://doi.org/10.1007/3-540-48405-1_26
9. Coron, J.-S.: Formal verification of side-channel countermeasures via elementary circuit transformations. Cryptology ePrint Archive, Report 2017/879 (2017). http://eprint.iacr.org/2017/879
10. Coron, J.-S., Prouff, E., Rivain, M., Roche, T.: Higher-order side channel security and mask refreshing. In: Moriai, S. (ed.) FSE 2013. LNCS, vol. 8424, pp. 410–424. Springer, Heidelberg (2014). https://doi.org/10.1007/978-3-662-43933-3_21
11. Coron, J.-S., Rondepierre, F., Zeitoun, R.: High order masking of look-up tables with common shares. Cryptology ePrint Archive, Report 2017/271 (2017). http://eprint.iacr.org/2017/271
12. Duc, A., Dziembowski, S., Faust, S.: Unifying leakage models: from probing attacks to noisy leakage. In: Nguyen, P.Q., Oswald, E. (eds.) EUROCRYPT 2014. LNCS, vol. 8441, pp. 423–440. Springer, Heidelberg (2014). https://doi.org/10.1007/978-3-642-55220-5_24
13. Goubin, L., Patarin, J.: DES and differential power analysis the "Duplication" method. In: Koç, Ç.K., Paar, C. (eds.) CHES 1999. LNCS, vol. 1717, pp. 158–172. Springer, Heidelberg (1999). https://doi.org/10.1007/3-540-48059-5_15
14. Goudarzi, D., Rivain, M.: How fast can higher-order masking be in software? In: Coron, J.-S., Nielsen, J.B. (eds.) EUROCRYPT 2017. LNCS, vol. 10210, pp. 567–597. Springer, Cham (2017). https://doi.org/10.1007/978-3-319-56620-7_20

15. Ishai, Y., Sahai, A., Wagner, D.: Private circuits: securing hardware against probing attacks. In: Boneh, D. (ed.) CRYPTO 2003. LNCS, vol. 2729, pp. 463–481. Springer, Heidelberg (2003). https://doi.org/10.1007/978-3-540-45146-4_27
16. Journault, A., Standaert, F.-X.: Very high order masking: efficient implementation and security evaluation. In: Fischer, W., Homma, N. (eds.) CHES 2017. LNCS, vol. 10529, pp. 623–643. Springer, Cham (2017). https://doi.org/10.1007/978-3-319-66787-4_30
17. Messerges, T.S.: Using second-order power analysis to attack DPA resistant software. In: Koç, Ç.K., Paar, C. (eds.) CHES 2000. LNCS, vol. 1965, pp. 238–251. Springer, Heidelberg (2000). https://doi.org/10.1007/3-540-44499-8_19
18. Micali, S., Reyzin, L.: Physically observable cryptography. In: Naor, M. (ed.) TCC 2004. LNCS, vol. 2951, pp. 278–296. Springer, Heidelberg (2004). https://doi.org/10.1007/978-3-540-24638-1_16
19. Prouff, E., Rivain, M.: Masking against side-channel attacks: a formal security proof. In: Johansson, T., Nguyen, P.Q. (eds.) EUROCRYPT 2013. LNCS, vol. 7881, pp. 142–159. Springer, Heidelberg (2013). https://doi.org/10.1007/978-3-642-38348-9_9
20. Rivain, M., Prouff, E.: Provably secure higher-order masking of AES. In: Mangard, S., Standaert, F.-X. (eds.) CHES 2010. LNCS, vol. 6225, pp. 413–427. Springer, Heidelberg (2010). https://doi.org/10.1007/978-3-642-15031-9_28
21. Zhang, R., Qiu, S., Zhou, Y.: Further improving efficiency of higher order masking schemes by decreasing randomness complexity. IEEE Trans. Inf. Forensics Secur. **12**(11), 2590–2598 (2017)

Attacks and Countermeasures for White-box Designs

Alex Biryukov[1(✉)] and Aleksei Udovenko[2(✉)]

[1] SnT and CSC, University of Luxembourg, Esch-sur-Alzette, Luxembourg
alex.biryukov@uni.lu
[2] SnT, University of Luxembourg, Esch-sur-Alzette, Luxembourg
aleksei.udovenko@uni.lu

Abstract. In traditional symmetric cryptography, the adversary has access only to the inputs and outputs of a cryptographic primitive. In the *white-box* model the adversary is given full access to the implementation. He can use both static and dynamic analysis as well as fault analysis in order to break the cryptosystem, e.g. to extract the embedded secret key. Implementations secure in such model have many applications in industry. However, creating such implementations turns out to be a very challenging if not an impossible task.

Recently, Bos *et al.* [7] proposed a generic attack on white-box primitives called differential computation analysis (DCA). This attack was applied to many white-box implementations both from academia and industry. The attack comes from the area of side-channel analysis and the most common method protecting against such attacks is masking, which in turn is a form of secret sharing. In this paper we present multiple generic attacks against masked white-box implementations. We use the term "masking" in a very broad sense. As a result, we deduce new constraints that any secure white-box implementation must satisfy.

Based on the new constraints, we develop a general method for protecting white-box implementations. We split the protection into two independent components: value hiding and structure hiding. Value hiding must provide protection against passive DCA-style attacks that rely on analysis of computation traces. Structure hiding must provide protection against circuit analysis attacks. In this paper we focus on developing the value hiding component. It includes protection against the DCA attack by Bos *et al.* and protection against a new attack called algebraic attack.

We present a provably secure first-order protection against the new algebraic attack. The protection is based on small gadgets implementing secure masked XOR and AND operations. Furthermore, we give a proof of compositional security allowing to freely combine secure gadgets. We derive concrete security bounds for circuits built using our construction.

Keywords: White-box · Obfuscation · Cryptanalysis Provable security · Masking

The work of Aleksei Udovenko is supported by the *Fonds National de la Recherche*, Luxembourg (project reference 9037104).

T. Peyrin and S. Galbraith (Eds.): ASIACRYPT 2018, LNCS 11273, pp. 373–402, 2018.
https://doi.org/10.1007/978-3-030-03329-3_13

1 Introduction

White-box cryptography aims to develop cryptographic primitives that can withstand attacks of very powerful adversaries. Those adversaries have full access to the implementations, either in the form of source code or in the form of compiled programs. They can perform both static and dynamic analysis, including debugging, tracing the execution, injecting faults, modifying the program parts, etc. Cryptographic implementation resistant to such attacks is also called *strong white-box* since it is essentially equivalent to a public key scheme achieved by code-obfuscation means.

In 2002, Chow *et al.* [14,15] proposed the first white-box implementations of the AES and DES block ciphers. The main idea was to represent small parts of a block cipher as look-up tables and compose them with randomized invertible mappings to hide the secret key information. Each such look-up table by itself does not give any information about the key. In order to attack such scheme, multiple tables must be considered. Another approach was proposed by Bringer *et al.* [10]. Instead of look-up tables, the cipher is represented as a sequence of functions over $\mathbb{F}_{2^n}$ for some n, with some additional computations as noise. These functions are then composed with random linear mappings to hide the secret key, similarly to the Chow *et al.* approach.

Unfortunately, both approaches fell to practical attacks [2,16,28]. Consequent attempts to fix them were not successful [27,33]. Moreover, Michiels *et al.* generalized the attack by Billet *et al.* [2] and showed that the approach of Chow *et al.* is not secure for any SPN cipher with MDS matrices. This follows from the efficient cryptanalysis of any SASAS structure [5]. Recently several white-box schemes based on the ASASA structure were proposed [3]. However the strong white-box scheme from that paper was broken [4,21,29] (which also broadens the white-box attacker's arsenal even further). Another recent approach consists in obfuscating a block cipher implementation using candidates for indistinguishability obfuscation (e.g. [20]).

Besides academia, there are commercial white-box solutions which are used in real products. The design behind those implementations is kept secret, thus adding *security-by-obscurity* protection. Nevertheless, Bos *et al.* [7] proposed a framework for attacks on white-box implementations which can automatically break many white-box implementations. The idea is to apply techniques from grey-box analysis (i.e. side-channel attacks) but using more precise data traces obtained from the implementation. The attack is called *differential computation analysis* (DCA). Sasdrich *et al.* [30] pointed out that the weakness against the DCA attack can be explained using the Walsh transform of the encoding functions. Banik *et al.* [1] analyzed software countermeasures against the DCA attack and proposed another automated attack called Zero Difference Enumeration attack.

In light of such powerful automated attack the question arises: how to create a whitebox scheme secure against the DCA attack? The most common countermeasure against side-channel attacks is masking, which is a form of secret sharing. It is therefore natural to apply masking to protect white-box implementations. We define masking to be any obfuscation method that encodes each original bit by a relatively small amount of bits. Such masking-based obfuscation may be more practical in contrast to cryptographic obfuscation built from current indistinguishability obfuscation candidates [13,20].

In this paper we investigate the possibility of using masking schemes in the white-box setting. We restrict our analysis to implementations in the form of Boolean circuits. Our contribution splits into three parts:

1. **Attacks on Masked White-Box Implementations.** In Sect. 3 we develop a more generic DCA framework and describe multiple generic attacks against masked implementations. The attacks show that the classic Boolean masking (XOR-sharing) is inherently weak. Previous and new attacks are summarized in Table 1. We remark that conditions for different attacks vary significantly and the attacks should not be compared solely by time complexity. For example, the fault-based attacks are quite powerful, but it is relatively easy to protect an implementation from these attacks. From our attacks we conclude that more general nonlinear encodings are needed and we deduce constraints that a secure implementation must satisfy. We believe that our results provide new insights on the design of white-box implementations. We note that a basic variant of the (generalized) linear algebra attack was independently discovered by Goubin *et al.* [23].
2. **Components of Protection.** We propose in Sect. 4 a general method for designing a secure white-box implementation. The idea is to split the protection into two independent components: *value hiding* and *structure hiding*. The value hiding component must provide protection against passive DCA-style attacks - attacks that rely solely on analysis of computed values. In particular, it must provide security against the correlation attack and the algebraic attack. We suggest that security against these two attacks can be achieved by applying a classic linear masking scheme on top of a nonlinear masking scheme protecting against the algebraic attack. The structure hiding component must secure the implementation against circuit analysis attacks. The component must protect against circuit minimization, pattern recognition, pseudorandomness removal, fault injections, etc. Possibly this component may be splitted into more sub-components (e.g. an integrity protection). Development of a structure hiding protection is left as a future work.
3. **Provably Secure Construction.** Classic t-th order masking schemes protect against adversaries that are allowed to probe t intermediate values computed by the implementation. The complexity of the attack grows fast when t increases. In the new algebraic attack the adversary is allowed to probe all intermediate values but she can combine them only with a function of low algebraic degree d. Similarly, the attack complexity grows fast when d increases and also when the circuit size increases. We develop a framework for securing an implementation against the algebraic attack. We describe a formal security model and prove composability of first-order secure circuits. Finally, we propose a first-order secure masking scheme implementing XOR and AND operations. As a result, our framework provides provable security

Table 1. Attacks on masked white-box implementations.

Attack	Ref.	Data	Time
Correlation	[7], Sect. 3.1	$\mathcal{O}(2^t)$	$\mathcal{O}(n^t k 2^{2t})$
Time-Memory Tradeoff	Sect. 3.1	$\mathcal{O}(1)$	$\mathcal{O}(n^{\lceil s/2 \rceil} + n^{\lfloor s/2 \rfloor} k)$
Linear Algebra	[23], Sect. 3.2	$\mathcal{O}(n)$	$\mathcal{O}(n^\omega + n^2 k)$
Generalized Lin. Alg.	[23], Sect. 3.2	$\mathcal{O}(\sigma(n,d)))$	$\mathcal{O}(\sigma(n,d)^\omega + \sigma(n,d)^2 k)$
LPN-based Gen. Lin. Alg.	Sect. 3.2	$D_{LPN}(r, \sigma(n,d))$	$T_{LPN}(r, \sigma(n,d))$
1-Share Fault Injection	Sect. 3.3	$\mathcal{O}(n)$	$\mathcal{O}(n^2)$
2-Share Fault Injection	Sect. 3.3	$\mathcal{O}(n^2)$	$\mathcal{O}(n^3)$

Notations: n denotes size of the obfuscated circuit or its part selected for the attack; s is the number of shares in the masking scheme; k is the number of key candidates required to compute a particular intermediate value in the circuit; t denotes the correlation order ($t \le s$); ω is the matrix multiplication exponent (e.g. $\omega = 2.8074$ for Strassen algorithm); d is the algebraic degree of the masking decoder (see Sect. 3); $\sigma(n, d) = \sum_{i=0}^{d} \binom{n}{i}$ is the number of monomials of n bit variables of degree at most d; r is the noise ratio in the system of equations, $T_{LPN}(r, m), D_{LPN}(r, m)$ are time and data complexities of solving an LPN instance with noise ratio r and m variables.

against the first-order algebraic attack. We derive concrete security bounds for our construction. Finally, we implement the AES-128 block cipher protected using our new masking scheme.

A code implementing the described attacks, verification of the algebraic masking schemes and the masked AES-128 implementation is publicly available at [6]:

https://github.com/cryptolu/whitebox

Outline. We provide the notations in Sect. 2. The general attack setting and attacks are described in Sect. 3. We discuss a general method for securing a white-box design in Sect. 4. In Sect. 5 we develop countermeasures against the algebraic attack. Finally, we conclude and suggest future work in Sect. 6.

2 Notations and Definitions

Throughout the paper, we use the following notations and definitions.

- $\wedge, \vee, \oplus$ denote Boolean AND, OR and XOR respectively.
- $\mathbb{F}_2$ is the finite field of size 2 and $\mathbb{F}_2^n$ is the vector space over $\mathbb{F}_2$ of dimension n.
- Elements in vectors are indexed starting from 1. For a vector v from $\mathbb{F}_2^n$ we write $v = (v_1, \ldots, v_n)$.
- $|X|$ denotes the size of the vector/set X. If X is a circuit, $|X|$ denotes the number of nodes in it.
- The *Weight* of a vector v is the number or nonzero entries in it and is denoted $wt(v)$. Weight of a Boolean function is the weight of its truth table.

- The *Bias* of a Boolean function $f : \mathbb{F}_2^n \to \mathbb{F}_2$ is denoted $\mathcal{E}(f)$ and is equal to $|1/2 - wt(f)/2^n|$.
- The *Correlation* of two n-bit vectors v_1 and v_2 is defined as

$$cor(v_1, v_2) = \frac{n_{11}n_{00} - n_{01}n_{10}}{\sqrt{(n_{00}+n_{01})(n_{00}+n_{10})(n_{11}+n_{01})(n_{11}+n_{10})}},$$

  where n_{ij} denotes the number of positions where v_1 equals to i and v_2 equals to j. If the denominator is zero then the correlation is set to zero. cor is the sample Pearson correlation coefficient of two binary variables, also known as the Phi coefficient. Other correlation coefficients may be used, see e.g. [32].
- $\mathbf{0}, \mathbf{1}$ denote the two constant functions.
- Any Boolean function f with n-bit input has unique representation of the form $f(x) = \bigoplus_{u \in \mathbb{F}_2^n} a_u x^u$ called the *algebraic normal form (ANF)*. Here x^u is a shorthand for $x_1^{u_1} \dots x_n^{u_n}$ and such products are called *monomials*.
- The *algebraic degree* of a Boolean function f is the maximum Hamming weight of all u such that $a_u = 1$. Equivalently, it is the maximum degree of a monomial in the ANF of f. It is denoted $\deg f$.
- $\sigma(n, d) = \sum_{i=0}^{d} \binom{n}{i}$ is the number of monomials of n bit variables from $\mathbb{F}_2$ of degree at most d.
- Let $\mathcal{V}$ be a set of Boolean functions with the same domain $\mathbb{F}_2^n$. Define the *d-th order closure of* $\mathcal{V}$ (denoted $\mathcal{V}^{(d)}$) to be the vector space of all functions obtained by composing any function of degree at most d with functions from $\mathcal{V}$:

$$\mathcal{V}^{(d)} = \{f \circ (g_1, \dots, g_{|\mathcal{V}|}) \mid \forall f : \mathbb{F}_2^{|\mathcal{V}|} \to \mathbb{F}_2, \deg f \le d, g_i \in \mathcal{V}\},$$

  where $g_i : \mathbb{F}_2^n \to \mathbb{F}_2$ and $h = f \circ (g_1, \dots, g_{|\mathcal{V}|})$, $h : \mathbb{F}_2^n \to \mathbb{F}_2$ is such that $h(x) = f(g_1(x), \dots, g_{|\mathcal{V}|}(x))$. For example,
  - $\mathcal{V}^{(1)}$ is spanned by $\{\mathbf{1}\} \cup \{g_i \mid g_i \in \mathcal{V}\}$,
  - $\mathcal{V}^{(2)}$ is spanned by $\{\mathbf{1}\} \cup \{g_i g_j \mid g_i, g_j \in \mathcal{V}\}$, etc. (includes $\mathcal{V}^{(1)}$ as $i = j$ is allowed).

3 Attacks On Masked Implementations

We describe the general setting for our attacks. We consider *a keyed symmetric primitive*, e.g. a block cipher. A *white-box designer* takes a naive implementation with a hardcoded secret key and obfuscates it producing *a white-box implementation*. An adversary receives the white-box implementation and her goal is to recover the secret key or a part of it. We restrict our analysis to implementations in the form of *Boolean circuits*.

Definition 1. A Boolean circuit C is a directed acyclic graph where each node with the indegree $k > 0$ has an associated k-ary symmetric Boolean function. Nodes with the indegree equal to zero are called inputs of C and nodes with the outdegree equal to zero are called outputs of C.

Let $x = (x_1, \dots, x_n)$ (resp. $y = (y_1, \dots, y_m)$) be a vector of input (resp. output) nodes in some fixed order. For each node v in C we say that it computes a Boolean function $f_v : \mathbb{F}_2^n \to \mathbb{F}_2$ defined as follows:

- for all $1 \leq i \leq n$ set $f_{x_i}(z) = z_i$,
- for all non-input nodes v in C set $f_v(z) = g(f_{c_1}(z), \ldots, f_{c_k}(z))$, where $c_1, \ldots, c_k$ are nodes having an outgoing edge to v.

The set of f_v for all nodes v in C is denoted $\mathcal{F}(C)$ and the set of f_{x_i} for all input nodes x_i is denoted $\mathcal{X}(C)$. By an abuse of notation we also define the function $C : \mathbb{F}_2^n \to \mathbb{F}_2^m$ as $C = (f_{y_1}, \ldots, f_{y_m})$.

Masking. We assume that the white-box designer uses masking in some form, but we do not restrict him from using other obfuscation techniques. The only requirement is that there exists a relatively small set of nodes in the obfuscated circuit (called *shares*) such that during a legitimate computation the values computed in these nodes sum to *a predictable value*. We at least expect this to happen with overwhelming probability. In a more general case, we allow arbitrary functions to be used to compute the predictable value from the shares instead of plain XOR. We call these functions *decoders*. The classic Boolean masking technique is based on the XOR decoder. The number of shares is denoted by s.

A predictable value typically is a value computed in the beginning or in the end of the reference algorithm such that it depends only on a few key bits and on the plaintexts/ciphertexts. In such case the adversary makes a guess for the key bits and computes the corresponding candidate for the predictable value. The total number of candidates is denoted by k.

The obfuscation method may require random bits e.g. for splitting the secret value into random shares. Even if the circuit may have input nodes for random bits in order to achieve non-deterministic encryption, the adversary can easily manipulate them. Therefore, the obfuscation method has to rely on pseudorandomness computed solely from the input. Locating and manipulating the pseudorandomness generation is a possible attack direction. However, as we aim to study the applicability of masking schemes, we assume that the adversary can not directly locate the pseudorandomness computations and remove the corresponding nodes. Moreover, the adversary can not predict the generated pseudorandom values with high probability, i.e. such values are not predictable values.

Window coverage. In a typical case shares of a predictable value will be relatively close in the circuit (for example, at the same circuit level or at a short distance in the circuit graph). This fact can be exploited to improve efficiency of the attacks. We cover the circuit by sets of closely located nodes. Any such set is called *a window* (as in power analysis attack terminology e.g. from [9]). The described attacks can be applied to each window instead of the full circuit. By varying the window size the attacks may become more efficient. Here we do not investigate methods of choosing windows to cover a given circuit. One possible approach is to assign each level or a sequence of adjacent levels in the circuit to a window. Choosing the full circuit as a single window is also allowed. In our attacks we assume that a coverage is already chosen. For simplicity, we describe how each attack is applied to a single window. In case when multiple windows are chosen, the attack has to be repeated for each window. The window size is denoted by n. It is equal to the circuit size in the case of the single window coverage.

General DCA attack. We would like to note that the term "differential computation analysis" (DCA) is very general. In [7] the authors introduced it mainly for the correlation-based attack. In fact our new attacks fit the term well and provide new tools for the "analysis" stage of the attack. The first stage remains the same except that we adapt the terminology for the case of Boolean circuits instead of recording the memory access traces. Our view of the procedure of the DCA attack on a white-box implementation C is given in Algorithm 1.

Algorithm 1. General procedure of DCA attacks on Boolean circuits.

1. Generate a random tuple of plaintexts $P = (p_1, p_2, \ldots)$.
2. For each plaintext p_i from P:
   (a) Compute the circuit C on input p_i: $c_i = C(p_i)$.
   (b) For each node indexed j in the circuit:
      i. Record the computed value as $v_{j,i}$.
   (c) For each predictable value indexed j:
      i. Record the predictable value computed using plaintext p_i (or ciphertext c_i) as $\tilde{v}_{j,i}$.
3. Generate the bit-vector $v_j = (v_{j,1}, \ldots, v_{j,|P|})$ of computed bits for each node j in the circuit. Denote by V the set of all vectors v_j: $V = \{v_1, \ldots, v_{|C|}\}$.
4. Generate the bit-vector $\tilde{v}_j = (\tilde{v}_{j,1}, \ldots, \tilde{v}_{j,|P|})$ for each predictable value j. Denote by $\tilde{V}$ the set of all predictable vectors $\tilde{v}_j$: $\tilde{V} = \{\tilde{v}_1, \ldots, \tilde{v}_k\}$.
5. Choose a coverage of V by windows of size n.
6. For each window in the coverage:
   (a) Perform analysis on the window $W \subseteq V$ using the set of predictable vectors $\tilde{V}$.

We remark that the correlation-based DCA attack from [7] can be implemented on-the-fly, without computing the full vectors v_j. In contrast, most of our attacks require full vectors.

In the following two sections we describe two classes of DCA attacks: combinatorial and algebraic. They both follow the procedure described above and differ only in the analysis part (Step 6a). Afterwards, we describe two fault-injection attacks which allow to find locations of shares efficiently.

3.1 Combinatorial DCA attacks

The most straightforward way to attack a masked implementation is to guess location of shares inside the current window. For each guess we need to check if the shares match the predictable value. In the basic case of classic Boolean masking where the decoder function is simply XOR of the shares the check is trivial. If an unknown general decoder function has to be considered, the attack becomes more difficult. One particularly interesting case is a basic XOR decoder with added noise. The main attack method in such cases is correlation.

Correlation attack. The correlation DCA attack from [7] is based on correlation between single bits. However, in the case of classic Boolean masking with strong pseudorandom masks all s shares are required to perform a successful correlation attack. In the case of a nonlinear decoder less shares may be enough: even a single share correlation can break many schemes as demonstrated in [7]. Existing higher-order power analysis attacks are directly applicable to memory or value traces of white-box implementations. However, the values leaked in the white-box setting are exact in contrast to side-channel setting and the attack may be described in a simpler way. We reformulate the higher-order correlation attack in our DCA framework.

Assume that locations of t shares are guessed and t vectors v_j are selected. For simplicity, we denote them by $(v_1, \ldots, v_t)$. For each t-bit vector m we compute the t-bit u_m where

$$u_{m,i} = (v_{1,i} = m_1) \wedge \ldots \wedge (v_{t,i} = m_t).$$

In other words, $u_{m,i}$ is equal to 1 if and only if during encryption of the i-th plaintext the shares took the value described by m . For each predictable vector $\tilde{v}$ we compute the correlation $cor(u_m, \tilde{v})$. If its absolute value is above a predefined threshold, we conclude that the attack succeeded and possibly recover part of the key from the predictable value $\tilde{v}$. Furthermore, the entire vector of correlations $(cor(u_{(0,\ldots,0)}, \tilde{v}), cor(u_{(0,\ldots,1)}, \tilde{v}), \ldots)$ may be used in analysis, e.g. the average or the maximum value of its absolute entries.

We assume that the predictable value is not highly unbalanced. Then for the attack to succeed we need the correlated shares to hit at least one combination m a constant number of times (that is obtain $wt(u_m) \geq const$). Therefore the data complexity is $|P| = \mathcal{O}(2^t)$. However, with larger number of shares the noise increases and more data may be required. We estimate the time complexity of the attack as $\mathcal{O}(n^t k 2^t |P|) = \mathcal{O}(n^t k 2^{2t})$. Here n^t corresponds to guessing location of shares inside each window (we assume $t \ll n$); k corresponds to iterating over all predictable values; 2^{2t} corresponds to iterating over all t-bit vectors m and computing the correlations.

The main advantage of this attack is its generality. It works against general decoder functions even with additional observable noise. In fact, the attack may work even if we correlate less shares than the actual encoding requires. Indeed, the attack from [7] relied on single-bit correlations and still was successfully applied to break multiple whitebox designs. The generality of the attack makes it inefficient for some special cases, in particular for the classic Boolean masking. We investigate this special case and describe more efficient attacks.

Time-Memory Trade-off. We now consider the case of XOR decoder and absence of observable noise. That is, the decoder function must map the shares to the correct predictable value for all recorded plaintexts. In such case we can use extra memory to improve the attack. Consider two simple cases by the number of shares:

1. Assume that the decoder uses a single share (i.e. unprotected implementation). We precompute all the predictable vectors and put them in a table.

Then we simply sweep through the circuit nodes and for each vector v_i check if it is in the table. For the right predictable vector $\tilde{v}$ we will have a match.
2. Assume that the decoder uses two shares (i.e. first-order protected implementation). We are looking for indices i, j such that $v_i \oplus v_j = \tilde{v}$ for some predictable vector $\tilde{v}$. Equivalently, $v_i = \tilde{v} \oplus v_j$. We sweep through the window's nodes and put all the node vectors in a table. Then we sweep again and for each vector v_j in the window and for each predictable vector $\tilde{v}$ we check if $v_j \oplus \tilde{v}$ is in the table. For the right $\tilde{v}$ we will have a match and it will reveal both shares.

This method easily generalizes for arbitrary number of shares. We put the larger half of shares on the left side of the equation and put the corresponding tuples of vectors in the table. Then we compute the tuples of vectors for the smaller half of shares and look-up them in the table. We remark that this attack's complexity still has combinatorial explosion. However the time-memory trade-off essentially allows to half the exponent in the complexity.

The attack effectively checks $n^s k$ sums of vectors to be equal to zero. To avoid false positives, the data complexity should be set to $O(s \log_2 n + \log_2 k)$. We consider this data complexity negligible, especially because for large number of shares the attack quickly becomes infeasible. For simplicity, we assume the data complexity is $O(1)$ and then the time complexity of the attack is $\mathcal{O}(n^{\lceil s/2 \rceil} + n^{\lfloor s/2 \rfloor} k)$.

The described attack is very efficient for unprotected or first-order masked implementations. For small windows it can also be practical for higher-order protections. In the following section we describe a more powerful attack whose complexity is independent of the number of shares.

3.2 Algebraic DCA attacks

For the classic Boolean masking the problem of finding shares consists in finding a subset of the window's vectors which sums to one of predictable vectors. Clearly, this is a basic linear algebra problem. Let M be the matrix that has as columns vectors from the current window. For each predictable vector $\tilde{v}$ we solve the equation $M \times x = \tilde{v}$. A solution vector x reveals shares locations. To avoid false-positive solutions the number $|P|$ of encryptions should be increased proportionally to the window size. For the same matrix M we need to check all predictable vectors. Instead of solving the entire system each time, we precompute the LU decomposition of the matrix and then use it for checking each predictable vector much faster. We estimate the data complexity $|P| = \mathcal{O}(n)$ and the time complexity $\mathcal{O}(n^\omega + n^2 k)$, where ω is the matrix multiplication exponent. This attack was independently discovered by the CryptoExperts team in [23] and among other techniques was successfully applied [22] during the WhibOx 2017 competition [17] in order to break the winning challenge "Adoring Poitras".

We conclude that classic Boolean masking is insecure regardless of the number of shares. The attack complexity is polynomial in the circuit size. Even though it may not be highly practical to apply the attack to entire circuits containing millions of nodes, good window coverage makes the attack much more efficient. The attack becomes especially dangerous if a window containing all shares may be located by analyzing the circuit. Indeed, this is how team CryptoExperts attacked the main circuit of the winning challenge of the WhibOx competition. They obtained a minimized circuit containing around 300000 nodes; they draw the data dependency graph (DDG) of the top 5% nodes and visually located several groups of 50 nodes and successfully mounted the described linear attack on each of the groups.

Generalization through linearization. The described linear attack suggests that a nonlinear masking scheme has to be used. We show that the attack can be generalized to nonlinear masking schemes as well. Of course, the complexity grows faster. Still, the attack can be used to estimate the security of such implementations.

The generalization is based on the linearization technique. The idea is to compute products of vectors (with bitwise AND) and include them as possible shares of the predictable vector. Each such product corresponds to a possible monomial in the algebraic normal form of the decoder function. The correct linear combination of monomials equals to the decoder function. The corresponding linear combination of products of vectors equals to the correct predictable vector.

The set of products may be filtered. If a bound on the degree of the decoder function is known, products with higher degrees are not included. For example, for a quadratic decoder function only the vectors v_i and all pairwise products $v_i v_j$ should be included.

The data complexity is dependent on the number of possible monomials in the decoder function. For simplicity, we consider an upper bound d on the algebraic degree. Then the number of possible monomials is equal to $\sigma(n,d) = \sum_{i=0}^{d} \binom{n}{i}$. This generalized attack has the data complexity $\mathcal{O}(\sigma(n,d))$ and the time complexity $\mathcal{O}(\sigma(n,d)^{\omega} + \sigma(n,d)^2 k)$.

We remark that it is enough to consider only nonlinear (e.g. AND, OR) and input nodes inside the current window. All other nodes are affine combinations of these and are redundant. We formalize this fact in the following proposition.

Proposition 1. *Let C be a Boolean circuit. Let $\mathcal{N}(C)$ be the set of all functions computed in the circuit's nonlinear nodes (i.e. any node except XOR, NOT, NXOR) together with functions returning input bits. Then for any integer $d \geq 1$ the sets $\mathcal{F}^{(d)}(C)$ and $\mathcal{N}^{(d)}(C)$ are the equal.*

Proof. Note that for any set $\mathcal{V}$ we have $\mathcal{V}^{(d)} = (\mathcal{V}^{(1)})^{(d)}$. Therefore, we only need to prove that $\mathcal{F}^{(1)}(C) = \mathcal{N}^{(1)}(C)$. It is sufficient to show that any function from $\mathcal{F}$ belongs to $\mathcal{N}^{(1)}(C)$. This can be easily proved by induction on circuit levels. □

We describe an interesting scenario where this generalized attack is highly relevant. Assume that a white-box designer first applies classic Boolean masking to the reference circuit. Afterwards, each intermediate bit is encoded by e.g. 8 bits using a random nonlinear encoding. The masked circuit then is transformed into a network of lookup tables which perform operations on the encoded bits without explicitly decoding them. The motivation for such scheme is that there will be no correlation between a single 8-bit encoding and any predictable vector because of the linear masking applied under the hood. For the generalized linear attack the degree bound is equal to 8 and normally, the time complexity would be impractical. However, in this case the lookup tables reveal the locations of encodings, i.e. the 8-bit groups. Therefore, we include only 2^8 products from each group and no products across the groups. The attack works because the predictable value is a linear combination of XOR-shares which in turn are linear combinations of products (monomials) from each group.

Value-restriction analysis. The described algebraic attack can be modified to cover a broader range of masking schemes. Consider a low-degree combination of vectors from the current window and assume that the function it computes can be expressed as $s \wedge r$, where s is the correct predictable value and r is some uniform pseudorandom (unrelated) value. The basic algebraic attack will not succeed because $s \wedge r$ is not always equal to the predictable value s. However, it is possible to extend the attack to exploit the leakage of $s \wedge r$. The adversary chooses a set of inputs for which the predictable value s is equal to 0 and adds a single random input for which the predictable value is equal to 1 (the adversary may need to guess a part of the key to compute the predictable value). Then with probability 1/2 he is expected to find a vector with all bits equal to 0 except the last bit equal to 1. In case the predictable value is wrong, the chance of finding such vector is exponentially small in the size of the plaintext set. The same approach works for more complex leaked functions. In particular, the leaked function may depend on multiple predictable values, e.g. on all output bits of an S-Box. The only requirement is that the leaked function must be constant for at least one assignment of the predictable values (except of course the case when the leaked function is constant on all inputs). Note that the adversary must be able to find the correct assignment of predictable values. As a conclusion, this attack variant reveals a stronger constraint that a masking scheme must satisfy in order to be secure.

Algebraic attack in the presence of noise. In spirit of the value-restriction analysis, we continue to explore classes of exploitable leaking functions. Assume that a low-degree combination of vectors from the current window corresponds to a function $s \oplus e$, where s is the correct predictable vector and e is a function with a low Hamming weight. The function e may be unpredictable and we consider it as noise. The problem of solving a noisy system of linear equations is well known as Learning Parity with Noise (LPN). It is equivalent to the problem of decoding random linear codes. The best known algorithms have exponential running time. We refer to a recent result by Both *et al.* [8] where the authors propose an algorithm with approximated complexity $2^{1.3nr}$, where n is the number of unknown variables and r is the noise ratio. Several algorithms with low memory consumption were recently proposed by Esser *et al.* [18]. The best algorithm for the problem depends on the exact instance parameters. The number of variables in our case corresponds to the number of monomials considered, i.e. the window size n in the linear attack and $\sigma(n, d)$ in the generalized attack. For example, if a linear combination of vectors from a 100-node window leaks s with noise ratio 1/4 then the LPN-based attack will take time $2^{32.5}$ using the algorithm from [8].

3.3 Fault Attacks

Initially, we assumed that the adversary knows the obfuscated circuit and can analyze it in an arbitrary way. Still, the attacks described in previous sections were passive: they relied on analysis of computed intermediate values during encryptions of random plaintexts. In this section we show that active attacks (fault injections) can also be used to attack masked white-box implementations. We assume that the classic Boolean masking is used. We also allow any form of integrity protection which protects the values but does not protect the shares.

Two-Share Fault Injection. The main goal of a fault attack against masking is to locate shares of the masked values. Observe that flipping two XOR-shares of a value does not change the value. The attack follows:

1. Encrypt a random plaintext p and save the ciphertext $E(p)$.
2. Choose two intermediate nodes c_i, c_j and flip them during encryption of p. Denote the ciphertext by $E'(p)$.
3. If $E(p) = E'(p)$, conclude that c_i, c_j are shares of the same value (possibly repeat check for other plaintexts). Otherwise try another two intermediate nodes.

As shares of the same value should be placed closely in the circuit, a window coverage can be used to improve efficiency of this attack too. The idea is to choose two shares only inside each window and not across the windows.

The described attack allows to locate all shares of each value, independently of the sharing degree. The attack performs $\mathcal{O}(n^2)$ encryptions and has time complexity $\mathcal{O}(|C|n^2)$.

One-Share Fault Injection. Recall that we allow an integrity protection on the values but not on the shares. One possible way an integrity protection may be implemented is to perform the computations twice and spread the difference between the two results across the output in some deterministic way. In such way small errors are amplified into random ciphertext differences. In case of such protection or absence of any protection we can improve the efficiency of the fault attack.

The main idea for improvements comes from the following observation: if we flip any single share of the same value, the masked value will be flipped as well. This results in a fault injected in the unmasked circuit. We assume that the circuit output does not depend on which share was faulted. This observation allows to split the two-share fault attack and perform fault injection only for each node instead of each pair of nodes, at the cost of additional storage:

1. Encrypt a random plaintext p and save the ciphertext $E(p)$.

2. For each intermediate node c_i:
   (a) Flip the value of c_i during encryption of p. Denote the ciphertext by $E'_i(p)$.
   (b) Store $E'_i(p)$ in a table.
   (c) If $E'_i(p)$ was already stored in the table as $E'_j(p)$ we learn that nodes c_i and c_j are shares of the same value.

The attack performs $\mathcal{O}(n)$ encryptions, which requires $\mathcal{O}(|C|n)$ time. It provides substantial improvement over previous attack, though it requires stronger assumption about the implementation. The most relevant counter-example is when the integrity protection does not amplify the error but simply returns a fixed output for any detected error. In a sense, such protection does not reveal in the output any information about the fault. On the other hand, it may be possible to locate the error checking part in the circuit and remove the protection.

The attacks can be adapted for nonlinear masking as well. In such case the injected fault may leave the masked value unflipped. When a zero difference is observed in the output, the fault injection should be repeated for other plaintexts. As plaintext is the only source of pseudorandomness, changing the plaintext should result in different values of shares. Flipping a share would result in flipping the masked value with nonzero probability. The exact probability depends on the decoder function.

Remark. The two described attacks perform faults on *nodes* of the circuit. In some cases, a node value may be used as a share of multiple different values, for example, if the same pseudorandom value is used to mask several values. A more general variant of attacks would inject faults on *wires*. However, multiple wires may need to be faulted in order to succeed. The goal is to get the same faulted output by flipping different nodes or wires as such an event uncovers important structural information about the white-box design (if the space of faulted outputs is large enough).

4 Countermeasures

The attacks described in the previous section significantly narrow down the space of masking schemes useful for white-box obfuscation. We deduce the following main constraints:

1. The number of shares should be high enough to avoid combinatorial attacks. Moreover, the minimum number of shares that correlate with the reference circuit values should be high as well.
2. There should be no low-degree decoders in order to prevent the algebraic attack.
3. The circuit must not admit analysis that allows to locate shares of the same values.
4. The integrity of pseudorandom shares must be protected.

The aim of this paper is to analyze the possibility of using masking schemes with *relatively small* number of shares for white-box cryptography. The complexity of combinatorial attacks splits into two parts: locating the shares and correlating them. If the number of shares is very high then the correlation part becomes infeasible. Possibly, in such case it is not even necessary to hide the location of shares. The downside is that designing such masking schemes is quite challenging and this direction leads into rather theoretical constructions like indistinguishability obfuscation [20] from fully homomorphic encryption and other cryptographic primitives. We aim to find more practical obfuscation techniques. Therefore, we study obfuscation methods relying on hardness of locating shares inside the obfuscated circuit. Such obfuscation is a challenging problem. In the light of described attacks, we suggest a modular approach to solve this problem. We split the problem into two components:

1. *(Value Hiding)* Protection against generic passive attacks that do not rely on the analysis of the circuit.
2. *(Structure Hiding)* Protection against circuit analysis and fault injections.

Value Hiding. The first component basically requires designing a proper masking scheme. As we have shown, the requirements are much stronger than for the usual masking in the side-channel setting (e.g. the provably secure masking by Ishai *et al.* [26]). To the best of our knowledge, this direction was not studied in the literature. However, there is a closely related notion: fully homomorphic encryption (FHE). Indeed, it can be seen as an extreme class of masking schemes. FHE encryption is a process of creating shares of a secret value and the FHE's evaluation functions allow to perform arbitrary computations on the ciphertexts (shares) without leaking the secret value. In fact, any secure FHE scheme would solve the "Value Hiding" problem (even though the adversary may learn the key from the decryption phase, the locations of intermediate shares are unknown and the scheme may remain secure). However, this direction leads to very inefficient schemes: typical FHE schemes have very large ciphertexts and complex circuits. This contradicts our goal to investigate schemes with reasonable number of shares.

We suggest to further split the first component into two parts. The first part is protection against algebraic attacks. It is a nonlinear masking scheme without low-degree decoders. However, we allow the scheme to be imperfect: the computed values may correlate with the secret values. Though one has to be careful and avoid very strong correlation, otherwise the LPN-based variant of the algebraic attack may be applicable. The second part is protection against correlation attacks. It can be implemented using a provably secure linear masking scheme on top of the nonlinear masking from the first part. The two parts may be composed in the following way: the algebraically secure nonlinear masking scheme is applied to the reference circuit and afterwards the linear masking scheme is applied to the transformed circuit. We investigate possibilities for the algebraically secure nonlinear masking in the next section.

Structure Hiding. The second component resembles what is usually understood by *software obfuscation*. Indeed, the usual software obfuscation aims to obfuscate the control flow graph and hide important operations. Often such obfuscation includes integrity protections to avoid patching. The computed values are not hidden but merely blended among redundant values computed by dummy instructions. For circuits the problem is less obscure and ad hoc. In particular, an integrity protection scheme for circuits was proposed by Ishai *et al.* in [25]. Though, formalizing the "protection against analysis" is not trivial. Applying structure hiding protection on top of value hiding protection should secure the implementation from attacks described in Sect. 3. We do not investigate structure hiding further in this paper and leave it as future work.

We note that it is not possible to formally separate value hiding from structure hiding. If we give the adversary computed vectors of values even in shuffled order, she can reconstruct the circuit in reasonable time and then analyze it. One possible direction is to mix the value vectors linearly by a random linear mapping before giving to the adversary. It may be a difficult problem for the adversary to recover the circuit or its parts from such input. However, such model makes the correlation DCA attack almost inapplicable, since a lot of values are unnaturally mixed up and the correlations are not predictable, even though it is perfectly possible that the original unmixed values have strong correlations with secret variables.

5 Algebraically Secure Masking Schemes

The algebraic attack is very powerful and the classic XOR-sharing masking schemes can not withstand it. Therefore, it is important to develop new masking schemes which are secure against the algebraic attack. In this section we formalize security against the algebraic attack and propose a provably first-order secure construction.

We start by describing the attack model and formalizing security against the algebraic attack in Sect. 5.1. Ways of proving security in the new model are developed in Sect. 5.2. Next, we analyze composability in Sect. 5.3. An algorithm for checking security of gadgets is proposed in Sect. 5.4. Finally, we propose a concrete secure gadget in Sect. 5.5.

5.1 Security Model

We extract a subproblem from the whitebox design problem. Recall that during the algebraic attack, the adversary tries to find a function f of low degree d such that when applied to values computed in the nodes of the obfuscated circuit it would produce some predictable value. Typically, predictable value is a value computed using the *reference circuit* and it depends on a small fraction of the key. Our aim is to "hide" predictable values among unpredictable values. The unpredictability of computed functions may only come from the secret key/randomness used during the obfuscation process. In order to develop a formal attack model we allow the obfuscated circuit to use *random* bits. We underline that randomness here is merely an abstraction required for provable security arguments.

In the real whitebox implementation the random bits may be implemented as *pseudorandom* values computed from the input. Of course the pseudorandom generation part has to be protected as well. However, the white-box designer is free to choose arbitrary pseudorandom generator and its protection is an easier task then obfuscating a general circuit. For example, the designer can choose a random circuit satisfying some basic properties like computing a balanced function. The resulting circuit protected against the algebraic attack using pseudorandomly generated bits must further be obfuscated and protected from *removal* of the pseudorandomness. This is type of protection that we called *structure hiding* in Sect. 4 and it is out of scope of this paper.

We note a strong similarity between the algebraic attack and the side channel probing attack. In the t-th order probing attack the adversary may observe t intermediate values computed in the circuit. In the d-th order algebraic attack the adversary may observe all intermediate values but she can combine them only with a function of degree at most d.

The main idea of masking schemes is to *hide the values* computed in the reference circuit using (pseudo)random masks. We assume that the adversary knows the reference circuit. Given the inputs (e.g. a plaintext and a key) she can compute all intermediate values. The final goal of the adversary is to recover the key of an obfuscated implementation or, at least, learn some partial information about it. To formalize this, we adapt classic semantic security and indistinguishability ideas. The adversary may ask to encrypt two different vectors of inputs. The challenger chooses randomly one of the vectors and provides an oracle modelling the algebraic attack to the adversary. The goal of the adversary is to decide which of the vectors was encrypted. If she can not do this, then she can not learn any information about the hidden inputs (e.g. the plaintext and the key). Note that in this model the adversary may choose many different keys which is not possible in the white-box scenario. However, it leads to simpler definitions since we do not have to distinguish plaintext and key and we just treat them as one input. It is possible to add a constraint allowing to choose only a single key per input vector, but this would not lead to any improvement.

The oracle modelling the algebraic attack should not reveal too much information about computed values. Otherwise, it may be possible for the adversary to reconstruct the obfuscated circuit and then we would arrive in the general white-box scenario. We model the attack as follows: the adversary chooses the target function among linear (or higher-order) combinations of the intermediate functions in the circuit and she tries to guess its values during encryptions of the inputs from one of the two vectors. Note that some functions may have strong correlation with some function of the input. For a small vector of inputs the adversary may simply guess the value, ask the oracle a few times until the guess is correct and then compute the correlations. However, in the real algebraic attack this is not possible due to presence of "noise" in the circuit. For a small number of plaintexts there will be a lot of false matches for any "predicted" value, because there are many different functions computed in the circuit and it is highly probable that there is a linear combination of them matching an arbitrary value. We take this into account and require that only the function chosen by the adversary has to match the predicted value. As a result, the adversary can not accurately predict values of any *single* function in the d-th order closure of the circuit functions in order to run the linear algebra attack.

The circuit in the model can not take the input as it is, because these values allow for a simple distinguisher. Since we are developing a masking scheme, we assume that the inputs are already masked using random shares. This goes in parallel with the classic Boolean masking scenarios. We would like to stress that this is necessary in order to formally analyze the security of masked computations. Therefore, we do not consider the initial masking and the final un-masking processes. Indeed, these procedures are not relevant for the algebraic attack since they are not related to the reference circuit.

Taking into account the above discussions, we propose the following game-based security definition:

Definition 2. (Prediction Security (d-PS)) Let $C : \mathbb{F}_2^{N'} \times \mathbb{F}_2^{R_C} \to \mathbb{F}_2^M$ be a Boolean circuit, $E : \mathbb{F}_2^N \times \mathbb{F}_2^{R_E} \to \mathbb{F}_2^{N'}$ an arbitrary function, $d \geq 1$ an integer and $\mathcal{A}$ an adversary. Consider the following security game:

Experiment $\mathsf{PS}^{C,E,d}(\mathcal{A}, b)$:
$(\tilde{f}, x^{[0]}, x^{[1]}, \tilde{y}) \leftarrow \mathcal{A}(C, E, d)$, where
$\tilde{f} \in \mathcal{F}^{(d)}(C), x^{[l]} = (x_1^{[l]}, \ldots, x_Q^{[l]}), x_i^{[l]} \in \mathbb{F}_2^N, \tilde{y} \in \mathbb{F}_2^Q$
$(r_1, \ldots, r_Q) \xleftarrow{\$} (\mathbb{F}_2^{R_E})^Q$
$(\tilde{r}_1, \ldots, \tilde{r}_Q) \xleftarrow{\$} (\mathbb{F}_2^{R_C})^Q$
For any $f \in \mathcal{F}^{(d)}(C)$ define
$y(f) = \left(f(E(x_1^{[b]}, r_1), \tilde{r}_1), \ldots, f(E(x_Q^{[b]}, r_Q), \tilde{r}_Q)\right)$
$F \leftarrow \{f \in \mathcal{F}^{(d)}(C) \mid y(f) = \tilde{y}\}$
return $F = \{\tilde{f}\}$

In the above experiment, $\xleftarrow{\$}$ means sampling uniformly at random. Define the advantage of an adversary $\mathcal{A}$ as

$$\mathsf{Adv}_{C,E,d}^{\mathsf{PS}}[\mathcal{A}] = \left|\Pr[\mathsf{PS}^{C,E,d}(\mathcal{A}, 0) = 1] - \Pr[\mathsf{PS}^{C,E,d}(\mathcal{A}, 1) = 1]\right|.$$

The pair (C, E) is said to be d-th order prediction-secure (d-PS) if for any adversary $\mathcal{A}$ the advantage is negligible.

Example. Consider a white-box AES implementation with a first-order Boolean masking protection. Assume that there are two nodes in the circuit computing two masks of an output bit of an S-Box in the first round. Denote the functions computed by masks as f_1, f_2. The adversary finds these nodes and chooses $\tilde{f} = f_1 \oplus f_2 \in \mathcal{F}^{(1)}(C)$. She also chooses sufficiently large Q and random vectors $x^{[0]}$ and $x^{[1]}$ of Q (plaintext, key) pairs. For example, the same key may be used for all pairs in $x^{[0]}$ and another key for all pairs in $x^{[1]}$. The adversary computes $\tilde{y} = (s(x_1^{[0]}), ..., s(x_Q^{[0]}))$ (where function s computes the output bit of the attacked S-Box in the first round from the plaintext and the key). In this case the adversary succeeds in the game with advantage close to 1 and the implementation is not prediction-secure (indeed, the adversary easily distinguishes the two keys). Note that we required the adversary to find the nodes in order to choose the right function $\tilde{f}$. Since the adversary is unbounded, this is just a technical requirement. In the real attack the adversary does not need to guess the function.

The function E in the definition should be referred to as *an encoding function*. Though the definition allows the encoding function to be arbitrary, we are mainly interested in the encodings with useful semantics, i.e. masking. Moreover, we expect the encoding to be lightweight and universal: main computations should be performed in the circuit C.

The circuit C can be completely unobfuscated but still prediction-secure, because the adversary is forced to consider the whole vector space $\mathcal{F}^{(d)}(C)$. In a real white-box implementation this restriction is expected to be enforced by the structure-hiding protection.

We now discuss possible attacks that are not covered by this definition. The definition ensures that any single function from $\mathcal{F}^{(d)}(C)$ is unpredictable. However, it may be possible that multiple functions jointly exhibit a behaviour that leads to an attack. For example, the dimension of $\mathcal{F}^{(d)}(C)$ may differ depending on the input being encoded. The definition also does not cover the LPN-based attack.

5.2 Security Analysis

In the experiment both the encoding function E and the circuit C use randomness. However, the d-th order closure is computed only using functions from $\mathcal{F}(C)$. Still, the inputs of C include the outputs of E and that is how the randomness used in E affects the computations in C. In other words, E generates some distribution in the inputs of C. Therefore, in order to study functions from $\mathcal{F}^{(d)}(C)$ we need to compose them with E.

It is crucial to study how functions from $\mathcal{F}^{(d)}(C)$ composed with E behave with a fixed input x. Consider a function $f \in \mathcal{F}^{(d)}(C)$. If the function $f(E(x, \cdot), \cdot)$ is constant for some x and the function $f(E(x', \cdot), \cdot)$ is non-constant for some $x' \neq x$ (or is constant but $f(E(x, \cdot), \cdot) \neq f(E(x', \cdot), \cdot)$, then these inputs are distinguishable and the pair (C, E) is insecure[1]. More generally, if for some $f \in \mathcal{F}^{(d)}(C) \setminus \{\mathbf{0}, \mathbf{1}\}$ and for some $x \in \mathbb{F}_2^N$ the function $f(E(x, \cdot), \cdot)$ is non-constant but has a high bias (i.e. it has very low or very high weight), then the adversary still may have high chances to predict its output. We conclude that for all functions $f \in \mathcal{F}^{(d)}(C) \setminus \{\mathbf{0}, \mathbf{1}\}$ and for all $x \in \mathbb{F}_2^N$ the function $f(E(x, \cdot), \cdot)$ should have a low bias.

[1] Unless $f(E(x', \cdot), \cdot)$ has extremely high bias and is indistinguishable from the constant function on practice.

We now show that this requirement is enough to achieve d-th order prediction security if there are enough random bits used in the main circuit. The following proposition gives an upper bound on d-PS advantage from the maximum bias and the number of random bits.

Definition 3. Let C, E be defined as above. For any function $f \in \mathcal{F}^{(d)}(C) \setminus \{\mathbf{0}, \mathbf{1}\}$ and for any $x \in \mathbb{F}_2^N$ define $f_x : \mathbb{F}_2^{R_E} \times \mathbb{F}_2^{R_C} \to \mathbb{F}_2$ given by $f_x(r_e, r_c) = f(E(x, r_e), r_c)$ and denote the set of all such functions $\mathcal{R}$:

$$\mathcal{R} = \{f(E(x,\cdot),\cdot) \mid f \in \mathcal{F}^{(d)}(C) \setminus \{\mathbf{0},\mathbf{1}\}, x \in \mathbb{F}_2^N\}.$$

Proposition 2. *Let ε be the maximum bias among all functions from $\mathcal{R}$:*

$$\varepsilon = \max_{f_x \in \mathcal{R}} \mathcal{E}(f_x).$$

Let $e = -\log_2(1/2 + \varepsilon)$. Then for any adversary $\mathcal{A}$ choosing vectors of size Q

$$\mathsf{Adv}^{\mathsf{PS}}_{C,E,d}[\mathcal{A}] \le min(2^{Q-R_C}, 2^{-eQ}). \tag{1}$$

Proof. First, we prove that $\mathsf{Adv}^{\mathsf{PS}}_{C,E,d}[\mathcal{A}] \le 2^{Q-R_C}$. If $\tilde{f}$ chosen by the adversary is an affine function of random bits r (independent of x), then it is clear that the advantage is zero. Otherwise, we compute the probability of the event when the predicted value $\tilde{y}$ matches some linear function of random bits r. There are R_C independent uniformly distributed random vectors $r_1, \ldots, r_{R_C}$ from $\mathbb{F}_2^Q$. Let p be the probability of the event that they span the whole space $\mathbb{F}_2^Q$. In this case the experiment returns 0, because any $\tilde{y}$ matches a function different from the one chosen by the adversary. The following holds (see e.g. [19]):

$$p = \prod_{i=0}^{Q-1}(1 - 2^{i-R_C}), \quad \log_2(1-p) \le Q - R_C.$$

We conclude that $p \ge 1 - 2^{Q-R_C}$ and the advantage is upper bounded by 2^{Q-R_C}.

Now we prove that $\mathsf{Adv}^{\mathsf{PS}}_{C,E,d}[\mathcal{A}] \le 2^{-eQ}$. We simply bound the probability that the adversary submits $\tilde{f}, \tilde{y}$ such that $y(\tilde{f}) = \tilde{y}$ in the experiment. Since elements of $y(\tilde{f})$ are independent, the probability to have $y(\tilde{f}) = \tilde{y}$ is maximized when each bit of $\tilde{y}$ equals to the most probable value of the respective bit of $y(\tilde{f})$ (the adversary would also need to use the least probable value at least once to avoid matching with the constant functions). For each bit the probability is bounded by $1/2 + \varepsilon$, therefore for Q bits the bound is $(1/2+\varepsilon)^Q = 2^{-eQ}$. □

Note that the bounds are quite loose. The randomness-based term takes into account only single random bits from r_c. The randomness in the inputs of C (generated from r_e in the encoding process) as well as all intermediate values computed in the circuit add much more noise (note that we can not directly include r_e since it is used in the encoding process and not in the main circuit). The bias-based term bounds only the probability of predicting the output for a single vector of inputs. It does not include the cost of distinguishing the two vectors. We stick to these bounds as our current goal is to provide a simple and sound provably secure protection.

Assume that we know the maximum bias ε in $\mathcal{R}$ and we want to achieve a better security bound. We can always add "dummy" random bits to the circuit. Note that this leads to stronger requirements for the structure-hiding protection. It follows that given the maximum bias, we can compute how many "dummy" random bits are needed to achieve any required security level:

Corollary 1. *Let k be a positive integer. Then for any adversary $\mathcal{A}$*

$$\mathsf{Adv}^{\mathsf{PS}}_{C,E,d}[\mathcal{A}] \leq 2^{-k} \text{ if}$$

$$e > 0 \text{ and } R_C \geq k \cdot (1 + \frac{1}{e}).$$

Proof. Consider each term of the bound from Proposition 2:

$$Q - R_C \leq -k \text{ or } -eQ \leq -k.$$

The result follows from the second term if $Q \geq \frac{k}{e}$. To cover all other Q we need $R_C \geq Q + k \geq k \cdot (1 + \frac{1}{e})$. □

We remark that the advantage bound is information-theoretic as we do not constraint the adversary's powers. This is an effect of the attack formalization given in Definition 2: the attack requires that the adversary predicts the chosen function precisely. An unbounded adversary could simply iterate over all functions $f \in \mathcal{F}^{(d)}(C)$ and e.g. compute the bias. We argue that this kind of attack is not the linear algebra attack that we consider. Furthermore, the attack model restricts the adversary to use the full circuit C. Without this restriction it would be possible to choose a part of the circuit (a *window*) to reduce the noise. In our model we expect that a structure-hiding protection is used to prevent this.

5.3 First-order Secure Construction

Given the notion of prediction security we are now interested in developing secure constructions. A common strategy is to develop small secure circuits (called *gadgets*) and compose them in a provably secure way. Our definition does not immediately lead to composability, because it includes the encoding step which is not expected to be present in the intermediate gadgets. In order to proceed, we split up the prediction security into circuit security and encoding security. The new notions are stronger in order to get proofs of secure composability. Note that they are limited to the first-order security ($d = 1$) and it is not obvious how to extend them to higher orders.

Definition 4. (Circuit Algebraic Security (ε-1-AS)) Let $C(x, r) : \mathbb{F}_2^{N'} \times \mathbb{F}_2^{R_C} \to \mathbb{F}_2^M$ be a Boolean circuit. Then C is called first-order algebraically ε-secure (ε-1-AS) if for any $f \in \mathcal{F}^{(1)}(C) \setminus \{\mathbf{0}, \mathbf{1}\}$ one of the following conditions holds:

1. f is an affine function of x,
2. for any $x \in \mathbb{F}_2^{N'}$ $\mathcal{E}(f(x,\cdot)) \le \varepsilon$, where $f(x,\cdot) : \mathbb{F}_2^{R_C} \to \mathbb{F}_2$

Definition 5. (Encoding Algebraic Security (ε-1-AS)) Let $E(x,r) : \mathbb{F}_2^N \times \mathbb{F}_2^{R_E} \to \mathbb{F}_2^{N'}$ be an arbitrary encoding function. Let $\mathcal{Y}$ be the set of the coordinate functions of E (i.e. functions given by the outputs bits of E). The function E is called a first-order algebraically ε-secure encoding (ε-1-AS) if for any function $f \in \mathcal{Y}^{(1)} \setminus \{\mathbf{0},\mathbf{1}\}$ and any $x \in \mathbb{F}_2^N$ the bias of the function $f(x,\cdot) : \mathbb{F}_2^{R_E} \to \mathbb{F}_2$ is not greater than ε:

$$\max_{f \in \mathcal{Y}^{(1)} \setminus \{\mathbf{0},\mathbf{1}\}, x \in \mathbb{F}_2^N} \mathcal{E}(f(x,\cdot)) \le \varepsilon.$$

The following proposition shows that if both an encoding and a circuit are algebraically secure, then their combination is prediction-secure:

Proposition 3. *Let $C : \mathbb{F}_2^{N'} \times \mathbb{F}_2^{R_C} \to \mathbb{F}_2^M$ be a Boolean circuit and let $E : \mathbb{F}_2^N \times \mathbb{F}_2^{R_E} \to \mathbb{F}_2^{N'}$ be an arbitrary encoding function.*

If C is ε_C-1-AS circuit and E is ε_E-1-AS encoding, then

$$\mathsf{Adv}^{\mathsf{PS}}_{C,E,d}[\mathcal{A}] \le min(2^{Q-R_C}, 2^{-eQ}),$$

where $e = -\log_2(1/2 + max(\varepsilon_C, \varepsilon_E))$.

Proof. If the function $\tilde{f}$ chosen by the adversary is an affine combination of the input x of C, then the encoding security of E applies leading to the bound with $e = -\log_2(1/2 + \varepsilon_E)$. Otherwise, ε_C-1-AS security of C provides the bound with $e = -\log_2(1/2 + \varepsilon_C)$ (the bias bound applies for any fixed input x of C, therefore it applies for any distribution of x generated by E as well). □

Finally, we show that ε-1-AS circuits are composable, i.e. are secure gadgets. We can compose gadgets in arbitrary ways and then join the final circuit with a secure encoding function to obtain a prediction-secure construction.

Proposition 4. *(ε-1-AS Composability) Consider ε-1-AS circuits $C_1(x_1,r_1)$ and $C_2(x_2,r_2)$. Let C be the circuit obtained by connecting the output of C_1 to the input x_2 of C_2 and letting the input r_2 of C_2 be the extra input of C:*

$$C(x_1,(r_1,r_2)) = C_2(C_1(x_1,r_1),r_2).$$

Then $C(x_1,(r_1,r_2))$ is also a ε-1-AS circuit.

Proof. Consider an arbitrary function $\tilde{f}(x_1,r_1,r_2) \in \mathcal{F}^{(1)}(C)$. By linearity, it can be written as $u \oplus v$, where $u \in \mathcal{F}^{(1)}(C_1)$ and v is a function from $\mathcal{F}^{(1)}(C_2)$ composed with C_1 (by connecting the output of C_1 to the input x_2 of C_2). Since C_2 is ε-1-AS, v is either an affine function of x_2 (which belongs to $\mathcal{F}^{(1)}(C_1)$) or has a bias not greater than ε when x_2 is fixed (i.e. when x_1, r_1 are fixed). In the first case, we get that $\tilde{f}$ belongs to $\mathcal{F}^{(1)}(C_1)$ and security follows from ε-1-AS security of C_1. In the second case, observe that the bias of v can not exceed ε for any fixed x_2 and, therefore, it can not exceed ε for any distribution of x_2. Moreover, u is independent from r_2. Therefore, the bias of $\tilde{f} = u \oplus v$ is not greater than the bias of v which is bounded by ε since C_2 is a ε-1-AS circuit. □

This result shows that due to frequent use of fresh randomness it is guaranteed that the maximum bias does not grow when we build large algebraically secure circuits from smaller ones. It means that ε-1-AS circuits offer a solid protection against the LPN-based variant of the algebraic attack as well. The complexity of LPN algorithms grows exponentially with the number of unknowns. Therefore, increasing the number of random nodes as suggested by the Corollary 1 allows to reach any required level of security against LPN attacks at the same time. Exact required number of random nodes depends on the maximum bias ε and chosen LPN algorithm.

5.4 Verifying Algebraic Security

Proposition 4 shows that we can compose algebraically secure circuits. Large circuits can be constructed from a set of *gadgets* - small algebraically secure circuits with some useful semantics. In order to design new gadgets we need to be able to check their algebraic security. The simplest way to get a bound on bias is based on looking at the algebraic degree of computed functions: the minimum weight of a nonzero function of n bits of degree d is equal to 2^{n-d} (see e.g. [12]). Therefore, we can think about the following algorithm for checking a circuit $C(x, r_C)$: for any fixed input x compute the ANFs of the functions computed in $C(x, \cdot)$ (functions of r_C) and return the maximum observed degree. The degree can not grow when functions are combined linearly. Therefore, the bias bound can not grow as well, except when the resulting function is constant in which case the bias is maximal and the gadget may be insecure. As a result, our method for verifying algebraic security splits into two parts:

1. verify that there is no bias equal to 1/2 among restrictions of functions from $\mathcal{F}^{(1)}(C)$ except the constant functions and affine functions of x;
2. compute the maximum degree among all restrictions of the intermediate functions and compute the corresponding bias bound.

The second step is straight-forward. We describe an algorithm that solves the first step.

Consider a circuit $C(x, r) : \mathbb{F}_2^N \times \mathbb{F}_2^R \to \mathbb{F}_2^M$. For all $c \in \mathbb{F}_2^N$ let L_c be the linear map that returns the restriction $x = c$ of a function f from $\mathcal{F}^{(1)}(C)$ (e.g. if functions are represented as truth table vectors then L_c returns the truth table entries corresponding to the case $x = c$). Note that the domain of L_c is defined to be the subspace $\mathcal{F}^{(1)}(C)$.

We now give an equivalent condition for the first part of the verification. It serves as a basis for the verification algorithm given in Algorithm 2.

Proposition 5. *The circuit C is ε-1-AS for some $\varepsilon < 1/2$ if and only if for all c the following holds:*

$$\dim \ker L_c = N. \tag{2}$$

Proof. For any $c \in \mathbb{F}_2^N$ let F_c be the subspace of $\mathcal{F}^{(1)}(C)$ containing functions that are constant when x is fixed to c. Also let $F = \bigcup_c F_c$. $\varepsilon < 1/2$ requires that any $f \in \mathcal{F}^{(1)}(C)$ either belongs to $\mathcal{X}^{(1)}(C)$ or is non-constant for any fixed x. It is equivalent to require that F is equal to $\mathcal{X}^{(1)}(C)$. Note that each F_c includes $\mathcal{X}^{(1)}(C)$ as a subset. Therefore, $F = \bigcup_c F_c$ is equal to $\mathcal{X}^{(1)}(C)$ if and only if for all c $F_c = \mathcal{X}^{(1)}(C)$. Since these are linear subspaces then we can compare their dimensions.

$\mathcal{X}^{(1)}(C)$ is spanned by all x_i and the constant-1 function:

$$\dim \mathcal{X}^{(1)}(C) = N + 1; \tag{3}$$

The constant-1 function always belongs to $\mathcal{F}^{(1)}(C)$ and to any of the F_c. The subspace of functions that are constant on the restriction can be obtained by adding the constant-1 function to the subspace of functions that are equal to zero on the restriction:

$$F_c = \ker L_c \oplus \{\mathbf{0}, \mathbf{1}\}, \tag{4}$$

$$\dim F_c = \dim \ker L_c + 1. \tag{5}$$

By comparing the dimensions obtained in Eqs. 3 and 5 we prove the proposition. □

The algorithm operates on functions using their truth tables. The truth tables are obtained by evaluating the circuit on all possible inputs and recording the values computed in each node. The set of computed truth tables corresponds to $\mathcal{F}(C)$. By removing redundant vectors we can compute a basis $\mathcal{B}$ of $\mathcal{F}^{(1)}(C)$ (and also ensure presence of the constant-1 vector). Then, for each c we take the part of each basis vector that corresponds to the fixed $x = c$ (and r taking all possible values). These parts form the subspace $\operatorname{Im} L_c$. We compute a basis $\mathcal{B}_c$ of these parts. Finally, we verify that

$$\dim \ker L_c = \dim \mathcal{F}^{(1)}(C) - \dim \operatorname{Im} L_c = |\mathcal{B}| - |\mathcal{B}_c| = N. \tag{6}$$

The algorithm is implemented in SageMath [31] and publicly available in [6].

Complexity analysis. The truth tables have size 2^{N+R} bits. Computing the basis of $\mathcal{F}^{(1)}(C)$ takes time $\mathcal{O}(min(2^{N+R}, |C|)^{\omega})$. The same holds for $\operatorname{Im} L_c$ except that the vectors have size 2^R and for small R this can be done more efficiently. The total complexity is $\mathcal{O}(min(2^{N+R}, |C|)^{\omega} + 2^N min(2^R, |C|)^{\omega})$. Recall that by Proposition 1 we should consider only the nonlinear nodes of the circuit.

5.5 Algebraically Secure Gadgets

In this section we develop an algebraically secure masking scheme. First we give a broad definition of a masking scheme which we will use further. Then we describe concrete circuits which can be verified to be first-order algebraically secure gadgets using Algorithm 2.

Definition 6. (Masking Scheme) An N-bit masking scheme is defined by an encoding function $Encode : \mathbb{F}_2 \times \mathbb{F}_2^R \to \mathbb{F}_2^N$, a decoding function $Decode : \mathbb{F}_2^N \to \mathbb{F}_2$ and a set of triplets $\{(\diamond, Eval_\diamond, C_\diamond), \ldots\}$ where each triplet consists of:

Algorithm 2. Verification of Algebraic Security

Input: a Boolean circuit $C(x, r) : \mathbb{F}_2^N \times \mathbb{F}_2^R \to \mathbb{F}_2^M$;
Output: `Secure` if the circuit C is ε-1-AS for some $\varepsilon < 0.5$,
`Insecure` otherwise.

evaluate C on all possible inputs;
associate the vector of computed values to each node of C;
let $\mathcal{V}$ be the set of all associated vectors;
let $\mathcal{B}$ be a basis of $\mathcal{V}^{(1)}$;
for all $c \in \mathbb{F}_2^N$ **do**
  let $\mathcal{V}_c$ be the set of all vectors from $\mathcal{B}$ restricted to the case of $x = c$;
  let $\mathcal{B}_c$ be a basis of $\mathcal{V}_c^{(1)}$;
  if $|\mathcal{B}| - |\mathcal{B}_c| \neq N$ **then**
    return `Insecure`;
return `Secure`.

1. a Boolean operator $\diamond : \mathbb{F}_2 \times \mathbb{F}_2 \to \mathbb{F}_2$,
2. a circuit $Eval_\diamond : \mathbb{F}_2^N \times \mathbb{F}_2^N \times \mathbb{F}_2^{R'} \to \mathbb{F}_2^N$.

For any $r \in \mathbb{F}_2^R$ and any $x \in \mathbb{F}_2$ it must hold that $Decode(Encode(x, r)) = x$. Moreover, the following equation must be satisfied for all operators $\diamond$ and all values $r' \in \mathbb{F}_2^{R'}, x_1 \in \mathbb{F}_2^N, x_2 \in \mathbb{F}_2^N$:

$$Decode(Eval_\diamond(x_1, x_2, r')) = Decode(x_1) \diamond Decode(x_2).$$

The degree of the masking scheme is the algebraic degree of the *Decode* function. The masking scheme is called nonlinear if its degree is greater than 1.

Note that $Eval_\diamond$ takes three arguments in our definition. The first two are shares of the secret values and the third one is optional randomness that must not change the secret values.

Minimalist Quadratic Masking. Since the decoding function has to be at least quadratic, we need at least two bits to encode a single bit. For two bits all nonlinear decoding functions are linear equivalent to a quadratic monomial being simply the product of the two input bits. Unfortunately, this decoding function is vulnerable to the linear algebra attack. Any quadratic function with 2-bit input is unbalanced. Therefore, one of the reference bit values can be encoded by 3 different values and the other value has only 1 possible encoding. For example, if the value is equal to 1 and the decoding function is simply AND, the input has to be equal to (1, 1). In this case there is no randomness involved and the hidden value is leaked. The conclusion is that any value of the original bit should include randomness in its encoding. In particular, the decoding function can not be a point function.

We move on to 3-bit encodings. The simplest quadratic function using all 3 input bits a, b, c is $ab \oplus c$. Note the similarity with the broken 2-bit scheme: the

$$\begin{aligned} Encode(x, r_a, r_b) &= (r_a, r_b, r_a r_b \oplus x), && (7)\\ Decode(a, b, c) &= ab \oplus c, && (8)\\ Eval_{XOR}((a,b,c),(d,e,f)) &= (a \oplus d,\ b \oplus e,\ ae \oplus bd \oplus c \oplus f), && (9)\\ Eval_{AND}((a,b,c),(d,e,f)) &= (ae,\ bd,\ (cd)e \oplus a(bf) \oplus cf), && (10)\\ Refresh((a,b,c),(r_a,r_b)) &= (a \oplus r_a,\ b \oplus r_b,\ c \oplus r_a b \oplus r_b a \oplus r_a r_b). && (11) \end{aligned}$$

Fig. 1. An insecure quadratic masking scheme.

quadratic monomial ab is simply linearly masked by c. However, this linear mask is enough to prevent the attack: in this case $Decode(a, b, c) = 1$ does not imply $a = 1$ or $b = 1$. In fact, such $Decode$ is balanced: both 0 and 1 have exactly 4 preimages. We first describe an insecure yet simple masking scheme based on this decoding function in Fig. 1. It is easy to verify that $Eval_{XOR}$ and $Eval_{AND}$ satisfy the requirements from Definition 6. In addition, $Refresh(a, r)$ returns fresh random encoding of a, meaning that $Decode(a) = Decode(Refresh(a, r))$ for any r and new encoding reveals no information about the old encoding.

$$\begin{aligned} Encode(x, r_a, r_b) &= (r_a, r_b, r_a r_b \oplus x), && (7)\\ Decode(a, b, c) &= ab \oplus c, && (8)\\ Eval_{XOR}((a,b,c),(d,e,f)) &= (a \oplus d,\ b \oplus e,\ ae \oplus bd \oplus c \oplus f), && (9)\\ Eval_{AND}((a,b,c),(d,e,f)) &= (ae,\ bd,\ (cd)c \oplus a(bf) \oplus cf), && (10)\\ Refresh((a,b,c),(r_a,r_b)) &= (a \oplus r_a,\ b \oplus r_b,\ c \oplus r_a b \oplus r_b a \oplus r_a r_b). && (11) \end{aligned}$$

We now observe that $Refresh$ is not ε-1-AS for any $\varepsilon < 1/2$: the computed term $r_a b$ is constant when b is fixed to 0 and equals to r_a otherwise (leading to $\varepsilon = 1/2$). This can be fixed by using an extra random bit r_c to mask a, b through the computations:

$$Refresh((a,b,c),(r_a,r_b,r_c)) = \\ (a \oplus r_a,\ b \oplus r_b,\ c \oplus r_a(b \oplus r_c) \oplus r_b(a \oplus r_c) \oplus (r_a \oplus r_c)(r_b \oplus r_c) \oplus r_c).$$

The new $Refresh$ function can be verified to be secure using the algorithm from Sect. 5.4. Moreover, the circuit computing $Eval_{XOR}$ applied to refreshed inputs is secure as well. However, $Eval_{AND}$ is not secure even if composed with the fixed $Refresh$ gadget. Consider the linear combination of computed terms $a(bf) \oplus cf = (ab \oplus c)f$. Here the variables are refreshed masks and can not be fixed by the adversary. However, the refreshing function does not change the hidden value. Therefore, $ab \oplus c$ would be equal to the value hidden by initial non-refreshed shares which can be fixed. Fixing the hidden value to 0 makes the combination $f(ab \oplus c)$ equal to 0 and be equal to the random share f when the hidden value is fixed to 1. We observe that it is possible to use a trick similar to the one used to fix the $Refresh$ function. In fact, the extra random shares added to fix the $Refresh$ function may be reused to fix the $Eval_{AND}$ function.

As a result, we obtain a fully secure masking scheme. The complete description is given in Algorithm 3.

Algorithm 3. Minimalist Quadratic Masking Scheme.

1: **function** ENCODE(x, r_a, r_b)
2:     **return** $(r_a, r_b, r_a r_b \oplus x)$

3: **function** DECODE(a, b, c)
4:     **return** $ab \oplus c$

5: **function** EVALXOR$((a, b, c), (d, e, f), (r_a, r_b, r_c), (r_d, r_e, r_f))$
6:     $(a, b, c) \leftarrow$ REFRESH$((a, b, c), (r_a, r_b, r_c))$
7:     $(d, e, f) \leftarrow$ REFRESH$((d, e, f), (r_d, r_e, r_f))$
8:     $x \leftarrow a \oplus d$
9:     $y \leftarrow b \oplus e$
10:     $z \leftarrow c \oplus f \oplus ae \oplus bd$
11:     **return** (x, y, z)

12: **function** EVALAND$((a, b, c), (d, e, f), (r_a, r_b, r_c), (r_d, r_e, r_f))$
13:     $(a, b, c) \leftarrow$ REFRESH$((a, b, c), (r_a, r_b, r_c))$
14:     $(d, e, f) \leftarrow$ REFRESH$((d, e, f), (r_d, r_e, r_f))$
15:     $m_a \leftarrow bf \oplus r_c e$
16:     $m_d \leftarrow ce \oplus r_f b$
17:     $x \leftarrow ae \oplus r_f$
18:     $y \leftarrow bd \oplus r_c$
19:     $z \leftarrow am_a \oplus dm_d \oplus r_c r_f \oplus cf$
20:     **return** (x, y, z)

21: **function** REFRESH$((a, b, c), (r_a, r_b, r_c))$
22:     $m_a \leftarrow r_a \cdot (b \oplus r_c)$
23:     $m_b \leftarrow r_b \cdot (a \oplus r_c)$
24:     $r_c \leftarrow m_a \oplus m_b \oplus (r_a \oplus r_c)(r_b \oplus r_c) \oplus r_c$
25:     $a \leftarrow a \oplus r_a$
26:     $b \leftarrow b \oplus r_b$
27:     $c \leftarrow c \oplus r_c$
28:     **return** (a, b, c)

Security. First, we verify $Eval_{XOR}$ and $Eval_{AND}$ gadgets using Algorithm 2. We obtain that they are ε-1-AS circuits for some $\varepsilon < 1/2$. Then we construct the ANFs of intermediate functions. The maximum degree is equal to 4. It is achieved for example in the term cf in the gadget $Eval_{AND}$: its ANF contains the term $r_a r_b r_d r_e$. Therefore, $Eval_{AND}$ is ε-1-AS with $\varepsilon \leq 1/2 - 2^{-4} = 7/16$. The gadget $Eval_{XOR}$ has degree 2 and is 1/4-1-AS. Unfortunately, we do not have a pen-and-paper proof for security of the gadgets and rely solely on the verification algorithm (which is able to spot the described weaknesses in the insecure versions of the gadgets).

Verifying security of the encoding function *Encode* can be done in the same way. Clearly, no linear combination of $r_a, r_b, r_a r_b \oplus x$ is constant for any fixed x. The coordinate $r_a r_b \oplus x$ has degree 2 and its weight and bias are equal to 1/4. Therefore, *Encode* is an ε-1-AS encoding with $\varepsilon = 1/4$.

By applying Proposition 3, we obtain that for any adversary $\mathcal{A}$, for any circuit C build from the gadgets $Eval_{XOR}, Eval_{AND}$ and for the described *Encode* encoding we have:

$$\mathsf{Adv}^{\mathsf{PS}}_{C,E,d}[\mathcal{A}] \leq min(2^{Q-R_C}, 2^{-eQ}), \tag{12}$$

where $e = -\log_2(1/2 + 7/16) \approx 0.093$. According to Corollary 1, in order to achieve provable 80-bit security we need to have $R_C \geq 80(1 + 1/e) \approx 940$ random bits in the circuit. Note that it does not depend on the actual size of the circuit, i.e. 940 random bits are enough for an arbitrary-sized circuit. However, the adversary should not be able to shrink the window so that it contains less than 940 random bits. This is expected to be guaranteed by a structure hiding protection. Finally, we remark that the bounds are rather loose and more fine-grained analysis should improve the bound significantly.

5.6 Implementation

We applied our masking scheme to an AES-128 implementation to estimate the overhead. Our reference AES circuit contains 31,783 gates. It is based on Canright's S-Box implementation [11] and naive implementation of MixColumns. After applying our nonlinear masking scheme and a first-order linear masking scheme on top the circuit expands to 2,588,743 gates of which 409,664 gates are special gates modeling external random bits. The circuit can be encoded in 16.5 MB. Extra RAM needed for computations is less than 1 KB. On a common laptop it takes 0.05 s to encrypt 1 block. Since the implementation is bitwise, 64 blocks can be done in parallel at the same time on 64-bit platforms. There is still a large room for optimizations. We used the Daredevil CPA tool [24] to test our implementation. Due to the first-order linear masking on top we did not detect any leakage. Pure nonlinear masking scheme does leak the key so the combination of both is needed as we suggested in Sect. 4. The implementation code is publicly available [6]. We remark that it is a proof-of-concept and not a secure white-box implementation; it can be broken in various ways.

6 Conclusions

In this paper we investigated the possibility of using masking techniques for white-box implementations. We presented several attacks applicable in different scenarios. As a result we obtained requirements for a masking scheme to be useful. We divided the requirements into value hiding and structure hiding protections. Furthermore, we suggested that value hiding may be achieved using an algebraically secure nonlinear masking scheme and a classic linear masking scheme. We developed a framework for provable security against the algebraic attack and proposed a concrete provably secure first-order masking scheme. Therefore, a value hiding protection can be implemented.

We believe that our work opens new promising directions in obfuscation and white-box design. In this paper we focused on value hiding protection and developed a first-order protection against the algebraic attack. The natural open question is developing higher-order countermeasures for the algebraic attack. Another direction is to study structure hiding countermeasures. Finally, it seems that pseudorandom generators play an important role in white-box obfuscation and are useful at all layers of protection. Randomness helps to develop formal security models and pseudorandom generators bridge the gap between theoretical constructions and real world implementations. Therefore, designing an easy-to-obfuscate pseudorandom generators is another important open problem.

References

1. Banik, S., Bogdanov, A., Isobe, T., Jepsen, M.: Analysis of software countermeasures for Whitebox encryption. IACR Trans. Symmetric Cryptol. **2017**(1), 307–328 (2017). Mar
2. Billet, O., Gilbert, H., Ech-Chatbi, C.: Cryptanalysis of a White Box AES implementation. In: Handschuh, H., Hasan, M.A. (eds.) SAC 2004. LNCS, vol. 3357, pp. 227–240. Springer, Heidelberg (2004). https://doi.org/10.1007/978-3-540-30564-4_16
3. Biryukov, A., Bouillaguet, C., Khovratovich, D.: Cryptographic schemes based on the ASASA structure: Black-Box, White-Box, and public-key (Extended Abstract). In: Sarkar, P., Iwata, T. (eds.) ASIACRYPT 2014. LNCS, vol. 8873, pp. 63–84. Springer, Heidelberg (2014). https://doi.org/10.1007/978-3-662-45611-8_4
4. Biryukov, A., Khovratovich, D., Perrin, L.: Multiset-algebraic cryptanalysis of reduced Kuznyechik, Khazad, and secret SPNs. IACR Trans. Symmetric Cryptol. **2016**(2), 226–247 (2017)
5. Biryukov, A., Shamir, A.: Structural Cryptanalysis of SASAS. In: Pfitzmann, B. (ed.) EUROCRYPT 2001. LNCS, vol. 2045, pp. 395–405. Springer, Heidelberg (2001). https://doi.org/10.1007/3-540-44987-6_24
6. Biryukov, A., Udovenko, A.: White-box Tools (2018). https://github.com/cryptolu/whitebox
7. Bos, J.W., Hubain, C., Michiels, W., Teuwen, P.: Differential computation analysis: hiding your White-Box designs is not enough. In: Gierlichs, B., Poschmann, A.Y. (eds.) CHES 2016. LNCS, vol. 9813, pp. 215–236. Springer, Heidelberg (2016). https://doi.org/10.1007/978-3-662-53140-2_11
8. Both, Leif, May, Alexander: Decoding linear codes with high error rate and its impact for LPN security. In: Lange, Tanja, Steinwandt, Rainer (eds.) PQCrypto 2018. LNCS, vol. 10786, pp. 25–46. Springer, Cham (2018). https://doi.org/10.1007/978-3-319-79063-3_2
9. Bottinelli, P., Bos, J.W.: Computational aspects of correlation power analysis. J. Cryptogr. Eng. **7**(3), 167–181 (2017). Sep
10. Bringer, J., Chabanne, H., Dottax, E.: White Box Cryptography: Another Attempt. Cryptology ePrint Archive, Report 2006/468 (2006). http://eprint.iacr.org/2006/468

11. Canright, D.: A very compact S-Box for AES. In: Rao, J.R., Sunar, B. (eds.) CHES 2005. LNCS, vol. 3659, pp. 441–455. Springer, Heidelberg (2005). https://doi.org/10.1007/11545262_32
12. Carlet, C.: Boolean functions for cryptography and error-correcting codes, Encyclopedia of Mathematics and its Applications. pp. 257–397. Cambridge University Press, Cambridge (2010)
13. Carmer, B., Malozemoff, A.J., Raykova, M.: 5Gen-C: Multi-input Functional Encryption and Program Obfuscation for Arithmetic Circuits. In: Proceedings of the 2017 ACM SIGSAC Conference on Computer and Communications Security, CCS 2017, pp. 747–764. ACM, New York (2017)
14. Chow, S., Eisen, P., Johnson, H., van Oorschot, P.C.: A White-Box DES implementation for DRM applications. In: Feigenbaum, J. (ed.) DRM 2002. LNCS, vol. 2696, pp. 1–15. Springer, Heidelberg (2003). https://doi.org/10.1007/978-3-540-44993-5_1
15. Chow, S., Eisen, P., Johnson, H., Van Oorschot, P.C.: White-Box cryptography and an AES implementation. In: Nyberg, K., Heys, H. (eds.) SAC 2002. LNCS, vol. 2595, pp. 250–270. Springer, Heidelberg (2003). https://doi.org/10.1007/3-540-36492-7_17
16. De Mulder, Y., Wyseur, B., Preneel, B.: Cryptanalysis of a perturbated White-Box AES implementation. In: Gong, G., Gupta, K.C. (eds.) INDOCRYPT 2010. LNCS, vol. 6498, pp. 292–310. Springer, Heidelberg (2010). https://doi.org/10.1007/978-3-642-17401-8_21
17. ECRYPT-CSA Consortium: CHES 2017 Capture The Flag Challenge. The WhibOx Contest (2017). http://whibox.cr.yp.to/
18. Esser, A., Kübler, R., May, A.: LPN decoded. In: Katz, J., Shacham, H. (eds.) CRYPTO 2017. LNCS, vol. 10402, pp. 486–514. Springer, Cham (2017). https://doi.org/10.1007/978-3-319-63715-0_17
19. Ferreira, P.J.S.G., Jesus, B., Vieira, J., Pinho, A.J.: The rank of random binary matrices and distributed storage applications. IEEE Commun. Lett. **17**(1), 151–154 (2013). January
20. Garg, S., Gentry, C., Halevi, S., Raykova, M., Sahai, A., Waters, B.: Candidate indistinguishability obfuscation and functional encryption for all circuits. In: 2013 IEEE 54th Annual Symposium on Foundations of Computer Science, pp. 40–49, October 2013
21. Gilbert, H., Plût, J., Treger, J.: Key-Recovery attack on the ASASA cryptosystem with expanding S-Boxes. In: Gennaro, R., Robshaw, M. (eds.) CRYPTO 2015. LNCS, vol. 9215, pp. 475–490. Springer, Heidelberg (2015). https://doi.org/10.1007/978-3-662-47989-6_23
22. L. Goubin, P. Paillier, M. Rivain, and J. Wang. Reveal Secrets in Adoring Poitras. A victory of reverse engineering and cryptanalysis over challenge 777, CHES 2017 Rump Session, slides (2017). https://ches.2017.rump.cr.yp.to/a905c99d1845f2cf373aad564ac7b5e4.pdf
23. Goubin, L., Paillier, P., Rivain, M., Wang, J.: How to reveal the secrets of an obscure white-box implementation. Cryptology ePrint Archive, Report 2018/098 (2018). https://eprint.iacr.org/2018/098
24. Hubain, C., et al.: Side-Channel Marvels (2016). https://github.com/SideChannelMarvels
25. Ishai, Y., Prabhakaran, M., Sahai, A., Wagner, D.: Private circuits II: keeping secrets in tamperable circuits. In: Vaudenay, S. (ed.) EUROCRYPT 2006. LNCS, vol. 4004, pp. 308–327. Springer, Heidelberg (2006). https://doi.org/10.1007/11761679_19

26. Ishai, Y., Sahai, A., Wagner, D.: Private circuits: securing hardware against probing attacks. In: Boneh, D. (ed.) CRYPTO 2003. LNCS, vol. 2729, pp. 463–481. Springer, Heidelberg (2003). https://doi.org/10.1007/978-3-540-45146-4_27
27. Karroumi, M.: Protecting White-Box AES with dual ciphers. In: Rhee, K.-H., Nyang, D.H. (eds.) ICISC 2010. LNCS, vol. 6829, pp. 278–291. Springer, Heidelberg (2011). https://doi.org/10.1007/978-3-642-24209-0_19
28. Lepoint, T., Rivain, M.: Another Nail in the Coffin of White-Box AES Implementations. Cryptology ePrint Archive, Report 2013/455 (2013). http://eprint.iacr.org/2013/455
29. Minaud, B., Derbez, P., Fouque, P.-A., Karpman, P.: Key-Recovery attacks on ASASA. In: Iwata, T., Cheon, J.H. (eds.) ASIACRYPT 2015. LNCS, vol. 9453, pp. 3–27. Springer, Heidelberg (2015). https://doi.org/10.1007/978-3-662-48800-3_1
30. Sasdrich, P., Moradi, A., Güneysu, T.: White-Box cryptography in the gray box. In: Peyrin, T. (ed.) FSE 2016. LNCS, vol. 9783, pp. 185–203. Springer, Heidelberg (2016). https://doi.org/10.1007/978-3-662-52993-5_10
31. The Sage Developers: SageMath, the Sage Mathematics Software System (Version 7.3) (2016). http://www.sagemath.org
32. Warrens, M.J., et al.: Similarity coefficients for binary data: properties of coefficients, coefficient matrices, multi-way metrics and multivariate coefficients. Psychometrics and Research Methodology Group, Leiden University Institute for Psychological Research, Faculty of Social Sciences, Leiden University (2008)
33. Xiao, Y., Lai, X.: A secure implementation of White-Box AES. In: 2009 2nd International Conference on Computer Science and its Applications, pp. 1–6, December 2009

Signatures

Signatures with Flexible Public Key: Introducing Equivalence Classes for Public Keys

Michael Backes[1,3], Lucjan Hanzlik[2,3], Kamil Kluczniak[1,3,4], and Jonas Schneider[2,3](✉)

[1] CISPA Helmholtz Center (i.G.) GmbH, Saarbrücken, Germany
{backes,kamil.kluczniak}@cispa.saarland
[2] CISPA, Saarland University, Saarbrücken, Germany
{hanzlik,jonas.schneider}@cispa.saarland
[3] Saarland Informatics Campus, Saarbrücken, Germany
[4] Department of Computing, The Hong Kong Polytechnic University, Kowloon, Hong Kong

Abstract. We introduce a new cryptographic primitive called signatures with flexible public key (SFPK). We divide the key space into equivalence classes induced by a relation $\mathcal{R}$. A signer can efficiently change his or her key pair to a different representatives of the same class, but without a trapdoor it is hard to distinguish if two public keys are related. Our primitive is motivated by structure-preserving signatures on equivalence classes (SPS-EQ), where the partitioning is done on the message space. Therefore, both definitions are complementary and their combination has various applications.

We first show how to efficiently construct static group signatures and self-blindable certificates by combining the two primitives. When properly instantiated, the result is a group signature scheme that has a shorter signature size than the current state-of-the-art scheme by Libert, Peters, and Yung from Crypto'15, but is secure in the same setting.

In its own right, our primitive has stand-alone applications in the cryptocurrency domain, where it can be seen as a straightforward formalization of so-called stealth addresses. Finally, it can be used to build the first efficient ring signature scheme in the plain model without trusted setup, where signature size depends only sub-linearly on the number of ring members. Thus, we solve an open problem stated by Malavolta and Schröder at ASIACRYPT'2017.

Keywords: Flexible Public Key · Equivalence classes
Stealth addresses · Ring signatures · Group signatures

1 Introduction

Digital signatures aim to achieve two security goals: integrity of the signed message and authenticity of the signature. A great number of proposals relax these

T. Peyrin and S. Galbraith (Eds.): ASIACRYPT 2018, LNCS 11273, pp. 405–434, 2018.
https://doi.org/10.1007/978-3-030-03329-3_14

goals or introduce new ones to accommodate the requirements of specific applications. As one example, consider sanitizable signatures [1] where the goal of preserving the integrity of the message is relaxed to allow for authorized modification and redactions of the signed message.

The primitive we introduce in this work allows for a relaxed characterization of authenticity instead. The goal is not complete relaxation, such that an impostor could sign messages on behalf of a legitimate signer, but rather that authenticity holds with respect to *some established legitimate signer*, but who it is exactly remains hidden.

The new primitive, called *signatures with flexible public key* (SFPK) formalizes a signature scheme, where verification and signing keys live in a system of equivalence classes induced by a relation $\mathcal{R}$. Given a signing or verification key it is possible to transform the key into a different representative of the same equivalence class, i.e., the pair of old key and new key are related via $\mathcal{R}$. Thus, we extend the requirement of unforgeability of signatures to the whole equivalence class of the given key under attack.

Additionally, it should be infeasible, without a trapdoor, to check whether two keys are in the same class. This property, which we call computational *class-hiding*, ensures that given an old verification key, a signature under a fresh representative is indistinguishable from a signature under a different newly generated key, which lives in a different class altogether with overwhelming probability. Intuitively this means that signers can produce signatures for their whole class of keys, but they cannot sign for a different class (because of unforgeability) and they are able to hide class to which the signature belongs to, i.e., to hide their own identity in the signature (because of class-hiding). This primitive is motivated by (structure-preserving) signatures on equivalence classes [29] (SPS-EQ), where relations are defined for the message space, instead of the key space. Both notions are complementary, in the sense that we can use SPS-EQ to *certify* the public key of an SFPK scheme if the respective equivalence relations are compatible, which immediately gives so called signatures with self-blindable certificates [40].

Signatures with flexible public key are especially useful in applications where there is a (possibly pre-defined) set of known verification keys and a verifier only needs to know that the originator of a given signature was part of that set. Indeed, upon reading the first description of the scheme's properties, what should come to mind immediately is the setting of group signatures [18] and to some extent ring signatures [36] where the group is chosen at signing time and considered a part of the signature. Our primitive yields highly efficient, cleanly constructed group and ring signature schemes, but it should be noted, that SFPK on its own is neither of the two.

The basic idea to build a group signature scheme from signatures with flexible public key is to combine them with an equally re-randomizable certificate on the signing key. Such a certificate is easily created through structure-preserving signatures on equivalence classes by the group manager on the members' verification key. A group signature is then produced by signing the message under a fresh representative of the flexible public key and tying that signature to the group by also providing a blinded certificate corresponding to the fresh flexible key. This fresh certificate can be generated from the one provided by the group manager. Opening of group signatures is done using the trapdoor that can be used to distinguish if public keys belong to the same equivalence class. In the case of ring signatures with n signers, the certification of keys becomes slightly more complex, since we cannot make any assumption on the presence of a trusted group manager. Therefore, the membership certificate is realized through a perfectly sound proof of membership, which has a size of $\mathcal{O}(\sqrt{n})$ if we use general proofs and the square matrix idea for membership proofs due to Chandran et al. [15].

Our Contributions. This paper develops a new cryptographic building block from the ground up, presenting security definitions, concrete instantiations and applications. The main contributions are as follows:

Signatures with flexible public key and their applications. Our new primitive is a natural counterpart of structure-preserving signatures on equivalence classes, but for the public key space. We demonstrate how SFPK can be used to build group and ring signatures in a modularized fashion. For each construction, we give an efficient standard model SFPK instantiation which takes into account the differences in setting between group and ring signatures. The resulting group and ring signature schemes have smaller (asymptotic and concrete) signature sizes than the previous state of the art schemes also secure in the strongest attacker model, including schemes with non-standard assumptions.

For instance, the static group signature scheme due to Libert, Peters, and Yung achieves fully anonymous signatures secure under standard non-interactive assumptions at a size of 8448 bits per signature. Our scheme, based on comparable assumptions, achieves the same security using 7680 bits per signature. Another variant of our scheme under an interactive assumption achieves signature sizes of only 3072 bits per signature, thus more than halving the size achieved in [32] and not exceeding by more than factor 3 the size of signatures in the scheme due to Bichsel et al. [7] which produces signatures of size 1280 bits but only offers a weaker form of anonymity under an interactive assumption in the random oracle model. A comprehensive comparison between our scheme and known group signature constructions can be found in Sect. 5.3. Our ring signature construction is the first to achieve signature sizes in $\mathcal{O}(\sqrt{N})$ without trusted setup and with security under standard assumptions in the strongest security model by Bender et al. [6]. We also show how to efficiently instantiate the scheme using Groth-Sahai proofs and thereby we solve an open problem stated in the ASIACRYPT'2017 presentation of [34], namely: *Are there efficient ring signature schemes without trusted setup provably secure under falsifiable assumptions?*

Applications of independent interest. We also show that signatures with flexible public key which also implement a key recovery property contribute to the field of cryptocurrencies. In particular, our definitions can be seen as a formalization of the informal requirements for a technique called stealth addresses [35,37,39], which allows a party to transfer currency to an anonymous address that the sender has generated from the receivers long-term public key. No interaction with the receiver is necessary for this transaction and the receiver can recover and subsequently spend the funds without linking them to their long-term identity. Moreover, existing schemes implementing stealth addresses are based on a variant of the Diffie-Hellman protocol and inherently bound to cryptography based on the discrete logarithm problem. On the other hand, our definition is generic and SFPK can potentially be instantiated from e.g. lattice assumptions.

1.1 Related Work

At first glance, signatures with flexible public keys are syntactically reminiscent of structure-preserving signatures on equivalence classes [29]. While both primitives are similar in spirit, the former considers equivalence classes of key pairs while the latter only considers equivalence classes on messages.

There exist many primitives that allow for a limited malleability of the signed message. Homomorphic signatures [10] allow to sign any subspace of a vector space. In particular, given a number of signatures σ_i for vectors $\boldsymbol{v}_i$, everyone can compute a signature of $\sum_i \beta_i \cdot \boldsymbol{v}_i$ for scalars β_i.

Chase et al. [16] discussed malleable signatures, which allow any party knowing a signature of message m to construct a signature of message $m' = T(m)$ for some defined transformation T. One can consider malleable signatures as a generalization of quotable [2] and redactable signatures [31].

Signatures on randomized ciphertexts by Blazy et al. [8] allow any party that is given a signature on a ciphertext to randomize the ciphertext and adapt the signature to maintain public verifiability.

Verheul [40] introduces so-called self-blindable certificates. The idea is to use the same scalar to randomize the signature and corresponding message. Verheul proposed that one can view the message as a public key, which allows to preserve the validity of this "certificate" under randomization/blinding. However, the construction does not yield a secure signature scheme. We will show that combining our primitive with signatures on equivalence classes [29] can be used to instantiate self-blindable certificates.

As noted above, all the mentioned works consider malleability of the message space. In our case we consider malleability of the key space. A related primitive are signatures with re-randomizable keys introduced by Fleischhacker et al. [22]. It allows a re-randomization of signing and verification keys such that re-randomized keys share the same distribution as freshly generated keys and a signature created under a randomized key can be verified using an analogously randomized verification key.

They also define a notion of unforgeability under re-randomized keys, which allows an adversary to learn signatures under the adversaries' choice of randomization of the signing key under attack. The goal of the adversary is to output a forgery under the original key or under one of its randomizations. Regular existential unforgeability for signature schemes is a special case of this notion, where the attacker does not make use of the re-randomization oracle.

The difference to signatures with flexible public keys is that re-randomization in [22] is akin to sampling a fresh key from the space of all public keys, while changing the representative in our case is restricted to the particular key's equivalence class. Note that one might intuitively think that signatures under re-randomizable keys are just signatures with flexible keys where there is only one class of keys since re-randomizing is indistinguishable from fresh sampling. In this case class-hiding would be perfect. However, such a scheme cannot achieve unforgeability under flexible keys, since it would be enough for an attacker to sample a fresh key pair and use a signature under that key as the forgery.

2 Preliminaries

We denote by $y \leftarrow \mathcal{A}(x, \omega)$ the execution of algorithm $\mathcal{A}$ outputting y, on input x with randomness ω, writing just $y \xleftarrow{\$} \mathcal{A}(x)$ if the specific randomness used is not important. We will sometimes omit the use of random coins in the description of algorithms if it is obvious from the context (e.g. sampling group elements). The superscript $\mathcal{O}$ in $\mathcal{A}^{\mathcal{O}}$ means that algorithm $\mathcal{A}$ has access to oracle $\mathcal{O}$. Moreover, we say that $\mathcal{A}$ is probabilistic polynomial-time (PPT) if $\mathcal{A}$ uses internal random coins and the computation for any input $x \in \{0,1\}^*$ terminates in polynomial time. By $r \xleftarrow{\$} S$ we mean that r is chosen uniformly at random from the set S. We will use $1_{\mathbb{G}}$ to denote the identity element in group $\mathbb{G}$, $[n]$ to denote the set $\{1, \ldots, n\}$, $\boldsymbol{u}$ to denote a vector and $(x_0 \ldots x_{|x|})_{\mathsf{bin}}$ to denote the binary representation of x.

Remark 1. Due to space limitations, we omit full formal definitions of the syntax and security properties of ring and group signatures as well as some proofs. These omitted materials may be found in the full version of this work [3].

Definition 1 (Bilinear map). *Let us consider cyclic groups $\mathbb{G}_1$, $\mathbb{G}_2$, $\mathbb{G}_T$ of prime order p. Let g_1, g_2 be generators of respectively $\mathbb{G}_1$ and $\mathbb{G}_2$. We call $e : \mathbb{G}_1 \times \mathbb{G}_2 \to \mathbb{G}_T$ a* bilinear map *(pairing) if it is efficiently computable and the following conditions hold:*

Bilinearity: $\forall (S,T) \in \mathbb{G}_1 \times \mathbb{G}_2$, $\forall a, b \in \mathbb{Z}_p$, *we have* $e(S^a, T^b) = e(S,T)^{a \cdot b}$,
Non-degeneracy: $e(g_1, g_2) \neq 1$ *is a generator of group* $\mathbb{G}_T$,

Definition 2 (Bilinear-group generator). *A bilinear-group generator is a deterministic polynomial-time algorithm* BGGen *that on input a security parameter λ returns a bilinear group* $\mathsf{BG} = (p, \mathbb{G}_1, \mathbb{G}_2, \mathbb{G}_T, e, g_1, g_2)$ *such that $\mathbb{G}_1 = \langle g_1 \rangle$, $\mathbb{G}_2 = \langle g_2 \rangle$ and $\mathbb{G}_T$ are groups of order p and $e : \mathbb{G}_1 \times \mathbb{G}_2 \to \mathbb{G}_T$ is a bilinear map.*

Bilinear map groups with an efficient bilinear-group generator are known to be instantiable with ordinary elliptic curves introduced by Barreto and Naehrig [4] (in short BN-curves).

Invertible Sampling. We use a technique due to Damgård and Nielsen [21]:

- A standard sampler returns a group element X on input coins ω.
- A "trapdoor" sampler returns coins ω' on input a group element X.

Invertible sampling requires that (X, ω) and (X, ω') are indistinguishably distributed.

This technique was also used by Bender et al. [6] to prove full anonymity (where the adversary receives the random coins used by honest users to generate their keys) of their ring signature scheme.

2.1 Number Theoretical Assumptions

In this section we recall assumptions relevant to our schemes. They are stated relative to bilinear group parameters $\mathsf{BG} := (p, \mathbb{G}_1, \mathbb{G}_2, \mathbb{G}_T, e, g_1, g_2) \leftarrow_{\$} \mathsf{BGGen}(\lambda)$.

Definition 3 (Decisional Diffie-Hellman Assumption in $\mathbb{G}_i$). *Given* BG *and elements* $g_i^a, g_i^b, g_i^z \in \mathbb{G}_i$ *it is hard for all PPT adversaries* $\mathcal{A}$ *to decide whether* $z = a \cdot b \mod p$ *or* $z \leftarrow_{\$} \mathbb{Z}_p^*$. *We will use* $\mathsf{Adv}_{\mathcal{A}}^{\mathsf{ddh}}(\lambda)$ *to denote the advantage of the adversary in solving this problem.*

We now state the bilateral variant of the well known decisional linear assumption, where the problem instance is given in both $\mathbb{G}_1$ and $\mathbb{G}_2$. This definition was also used by Ghadafi et al. [26].

Definition 4 (Symmetric Decisional Linear Assumption). *Given* BG, *elements* $f_1 = g_1^f, h_1 = g_1^h, f_1^a, h_1^b, g_1^z \in \mathbb{G}_1$ *and elements* $f_2 = g_2^f, h_2 = g_2^h, f_2^a, h_2^b, g_2^z \in \mathbb{G}_2$ *for uniformly random* $f, h, a, b \in \mathbb{Z}_p^*$ *it is hard for all PPT adversaries* $\mathcal{A}$ *to decide whether* $z = a + b \mod p$ *or* $z \leftarrow_{\$} \mathbb{Z}_p^*$. *We will use* $\mathsf{Adv}_{\mathcal{A}}^{\mathsf{linear}}(\lambda)$ *to denote the advantage of the adversary in solving this problem.*

In this paper we use a variant of the 1-Flexible Diffie-Hellman assumption [33]. We show that this new assumption, which we call the co-Flexible Diffie-Hellman (co-Flex) assumption, holds if the decisional linear assumption holds.

Definition 5 (co-Flexible Diffie-Hellman Assumption). *Given* BG, *elements* $g_1^a, g_1^b, g_1^c, g_1^d \in \mathbb{G}_1$ *and* $g_2^a, g_2^b, g_2^c, g_2^d \in \mathbb{G}_2$ *for uniformly random* $a, b, c, d \in \mathbb{Z}_p^*$, *it is hard for all PPT adversaries* $\mathcal{A}$ *to output* $(g_1^c)^r, (g_1^d)^r, g_1^{r \cdot a \cdot b}$. *We will use* $\mathsf{Adv}_{\mathcal{A}}^{\mathsf{co\text{-}flexdh}}(\lambda)$ *to denote the advantage of the adversary in solving this problem.*

Lemma 1. *The co-Flexible Diffie-Hellman assumption holds for* BG *if the decisional linear assumption holds for* BG.

Proof. Suppose we have an efficient algorithm $\mathcal{A}$ that solves the co-Flexible Diffie-Hellman problem with non-negligible probability. We will show how to build algorithm $\mathcal{R}$ that solves the decision linear problem. Let $(\mathsf{BG}, f_1, f_2, h_1, h_2, f_1^a, f_2^a, h_1^b, h_2^b, g_1^z, g_2^z)$ be an instance of the decision linear problem. The algorithm

$\mathcal{R}$ first runs algorithm $\mathcal{A}$ on input $(\mathsf{BG}, f_1, f_2, g_1^z, g_2^z, f_1^a, f_2^a, h_1^b, h_2^b)$. With non-negligible probability $\mathcal{A}$ outputs a solution to the co-Flexible Diffie-Hellman problem, i.e. it outputs the tuple $((f_1^a)^r, (h_1^b)^r, (f_1^z)^r)$. Then $\mathcal{R}$ computes

$$\begin{aligned} T_1 =& e((f_1^z)^r, h_2) = e(f_1, h_2^r)^z, \\ T_2 =& e((f_1^a)^r, h_2) = e(f_1, h_2^r)^a, \\ T_3 =& e((h_1^b)^r, f_2) = e(h_1, f_2^r)^b = e(f_1^r, h_2)^b, \end{aligned}$$

and outputs 1 if $T_1 = T_2 \cdot T_3$ and 0 otherwise.

2.2 Programmable Hash Functions

Programmable hash functions presented at Crypto'08 by Hofheinz and Kiltz [30] introduce a way to create hash functions with limited programmability. In particular, they show that the function introduced by Waters [41] is a programmable hash function. To formally define such function we first define so called *group hash functions* for a group $\mathbb{G}$, which consists of two polynomial time algorithms $\mathsf{PHF.Gen}$, $\mathsf{PHF.Eval}$ and has an output length of $\ell = \ell(\lambda)$. For a security parameter λ the generation algorithm $\mathsf{PHF.Gen}(\lambda)$ outputs a key K_{PHF}, which can be used in the deterministic algorithm $\mathsf{PHF.Eval}$ to evaluate the hash function via $y \overset{\$}{\leftarrow} \mathsf{PHF.Eval}(K_{\mathsf{PHF}}, X) \in \mathbb{G}$. We will use $\mathcal{H}_{K_{\mathsf{PHF}}}(X)$ to denote the evaluation of the function $\mathsf{PHF.Eval}(K_{\mathsf{PHF}}, X)$ on $X \in \{0,1\}^\ell$. We can now recall the definition of programmable has functions.

Definition 6. *A group hash function is an (m, n, γ, δ)-programmable hash function if there are polynomial time algorithms* $\mathsf{PHF.TrapGen}$ *and* $\mathsf{PHF.TrapEval}$ *such that:*

- *For any $g, h \in \mathbb{G}$ the trapdoor algorithm $(K'_{\mathsf{PHF}}, t) \overset{\$}{\leftarrow} \mathsf{PHF.TrapGen}(\lambda, g, h)$ outputs a key K' and trapdoor t. Moreover, for every $X \in \{0,1\}^\ell$ we have $(a_X, b_X) \overset{\$}{\leftarrow} \mathsf{PHF.TrapEval}(t, X)$, where $\mathsf{PHF.Eval}(K'_{\mathsf{PHF}}, X) = g^{a_X} h^{b_X}$.*
- *For all $g, h \in \mathbb{G}$ and for $(K'_{\mathsf{PHF}}, t) \overset{\$}{\leftarrow} \mathsf{PHF.TrapGen}(\lambda, g, h)$ and $K_{\mathsf{PHF}} \overset{\$}{\leftarrow} \mathsf{PHF.Gen}(\lambda)$, the keys K_{PHF} and K'_{PHF} are statistically γ-close.*
- *For all $g, h \in \mathbb{G}$ and all possible keys K'_{PHF} from the range of $\mathsf{PHF.TrapGen}(\lambda, g, h)$, for all $X_1, \ldots, X_m, Z_1, \ldots, Z_n \in \{0,1\}^\ell$ such that $X_i \neq Z_j$ for any i, j and for the corresponding $(a_{X_i}, b_{X_i}) \overset{\$}{\leftarrow} \mathsf{PHF.TrapEval}(t, X_i)$ and $(a_{Z_i}, b_{Z_i}) \overset{\$}{\leftarrow} \mathsf{PHF.TrapEval}(t, Z_i)$ we have*

$$\Pr[a_{X_1} = \cdots = a_{X_m} = 0 \;\wedge\; a_{Z_1} = \cdots = a_{Z_n} \neq 0] \geq \delta,$$

where the probability is over trapdoor t that was generated with key K'_{PHF}.

Note that using this definition we can define the Waters hash function, with key $K_{\mathsf{PHF}} = (h_0, \ldots, h_\ell) \in \mathbb{G}^{\ell+1}$ and message $X = (x_1, \ldots, x_\ell) \in \{0,1\}^\ell$ as $h_0 \cdot \prod_{i=1}^{\ell} h_i^{x_i}$. Hofheinz and Kiltz prove that for any fixed $q = q(\lambda)$ this is a $(1, q, 0, 1/8 \cdot (\ell+1) \cdot q)$-programmable hash function. Unless mentioned otherwise, we will always instantiate the programmable hash function using the Waters function and use $\ell = \lambda$.

2.3 Non-Interactive Proof Systems

In this paper we make use of non-interactive proof systems. Although we define the proof system for arbitrarily languages, in our schemes we use the efficient Groth-Sahai (GS) proof system for pairing product equations [28]. Let $\mathcal{R}$ be an efficiently computable binary relation, where for $(x, w) \in \mathcal{R}$ we call x a statement and w a witness. Moreover, we denote by $L_{\mathcal{R}}$ the language consisting of statements in $\mathcal{R}$, i.e. $L_{\mathcal{R}} = \{x | \exists w : (x, w) \in \mathcal{R}\}$.

Definition 7 (Non-Interactive Proof System). *A non-interactive proof system Π consists of the following three algorithms* (Setup, Prove, Verify)*:*

Setup(λ)**:** *on input security parameter λ, this algorithm outputs a common reference string ρ.*
Prove(ρ, x, w)**:** *on input common reference string ρ, statement x and witness w, this algorithm outputs a proof π.*
Verify(ρ, x, π)**:** *on input common reference string ρ, statement x and proof π, this algorithm outputs either* accept(1) *or* reject(0)*.*

Some proof systems do not need a common reference string. In such case, we omit the first argument to Prove *and* Verify*.*

Definition 8 (Soundness). *A proof system Π is called* sound*, if for all PPT algorithms $\mathcal{A}$ the following probability, denoted by $\mathsf{Adv}^{\mathsf{sound}}_{\Pi,\mathcal{A}}(\lambda)$, is negligible in the security parameter λ:*

$$\Pr[\rho \leftarrow \mathsf{Setup}(\lambda); (x, \pi) \leftarrow \mathcal{A}(\rho) : \quad \mathsf{Verify}(\rho, x, \pi) = \mathtt{accept} \wedge x \notin L_{\mathcal{R}}].$$

We say that the proof system is perfectly sound if $\mathsf{Adv}^{\mathsf{sound}}_{\Pi,\mathcal{A}}(\lambda) = 0$.

Definition 9 (Witness Indistinguishability (WI)). *A proof system Π is* witness indistinguishable*, if for all PPT algorithms $\mathcal{A}$ we have that the advantage $\mathsf{Adv}^{\mathsf{wi}}_{\Pi,\mathcal{A}}(\lambda)$ computed as:*

$$\begin{aligned} |\Pr[\rho \leftarrow \mathsf{Setup}(\lambda); (x, w_0, w_1) \leftarrow \mathcal{A}(\lambda, \rho); \pi \leftarrow \mathsf{Prove}(\rho, x, w_0) : \ \mathcal{A}(\pi) = 1] - \\ \Pr[\rho \leftarrow \mathsf{Setup}(\lambda); (x, w_0, w_1) \leftarrow \mathcal{A}(\lambda, \rho); \pi \leftarrow \mathsf{Prove}(\rho, x, w_1) : \ \mathcal{A}(\pi) = 1]|, \end{aligned}$$

where $(x, w_0), (x, w_1) \in \mathcal{R}$, is at most negligible in λ. We say that the proof system if perfectly witness indistinguishable if $\mathsf{Adv}^{\mathsf{wi}}_{\Pi,\mathcal{A}}(\lambda) = 0$.

Perfectly Sound Proof System for Pairing Product Equations. We briefly recall the framework of pairing product equations that is used for the languages of the Groth-Sahai proof system [28]. For constants $A_i \in \mathbb{G}_1$, $B_i \in \mathbb{G}_2$, $t_T \in \mathbb{G}_T$, $\gamma_{ij} \in \mathbb{Z}_p$ which are either publicly known or part of the statement, and witnesses $X_i \in \mathbb{G}_1$, $Y_i \in \mathbb{G}_2$ given as commitments, we can prove that:

$$\prod_{i=1}^{n} e(A_i, Y_i) \cdot \prod_{i=1}^{m} e(X_i, B_i) \cdot \prod_{j=1}^{m} \prod_{i=1}^{n} e(X_i, Y_i)^{\gamma_{ij}} = t_T.$$

$\mathsf{Prove}(x, w)$

$\rho_1 := (f_1, f_2, h_1, h_2, \ldots) \xleftarrow{\$} \mathsf{Setup}_{\mathsf{PPE}}(\lambda); r, s \xleftarrow{\$} \mathbb{Z}_p^*$

$\rho_2 := (f_1, f_2, h_1, h_2, f_1^r, f_2^r, h_1^s, h_2^s, g_1^{r+s}, g_2^{r+s})$

$\pi_{\text{Linear}} \xleftarrow{\$} \mathsf{Prove}_{\mathsf{Linear}}((\rho_1, \rho_2), (r, s))$

$\pi_1 \xleftarrow{\$} \mathsf{Prove}_{\mathsf{PPE}}(\rho_1, x, w);\ \pi_2 \xleftarrow{\$} \mathsf{Prove}_{\mathsf{PPE}}(\rho_2, x, w)$

return $\pi := (\rho_1, \rho_2, \pi_{\text{Linear}}, \pi_1, \pi_2)$

$\mathsf{Verify}(x, \pi)$

parse $\pi = (\rho_1, \rho_2, \pi_{\text{Linear}}, \pi_1, \pi_2)$

return $\mathsf{Verify}_{\mathsf{PPE}}(\rho_1, x, \pi_1) = 1 \wedge$

$\mathsf{Verify}_{\mathsf{PPE}}(\rho_2, x, \pi_2) = 1 \wedge$

$\mathsf{Verify}_{\mathsf{Linear}}((\rho_1, \rho_2), \pi_{\text{Linear}}) = 1$

Scheme 1. Perfectly Sound Proof System for Pairing Product Equations

The system $(\mathsf{Setup}_{\mathsf{PPE}}, \mathsf{Prove}_{\mathsf{PPE}}, \mathsf{Verify}_{\mathsf{PPE}})$ has several instantiations based on different assumptions. In this paper we only consider the instantiation based on the symmetric linear assumption given by Ghadafi et al. [26].

For soundness it must be ensured, that $\mathsf{Setup}_{\mathsf{PPE}}$ outputs a valid DLIN tuple. This can be enforced by requiring a trusted party perform the setup. However, our schemes require a proof system which is perfectly sound, even if a malicious prover executes the $\mathsf{Setup}_{\mathsf{PPE}}$ algorithm.

To achieve this we use the ideas by Groth et al. [27]. They propose a perfectly sound and perfectly witness indistinguishable proof system $(\mathsf{Prove}_{\mathsf{Linear}}, \mathsf{Verify}_{\mathsf{Linear}})$ which does not require a trusted setup. Using it one can show that given tuples T_1, T_2 as a statement, at least one of T_1 and T_2 is a DLIN tuple. The results were shown for type 1 pairing but the proof itself is only given as elements in $\mathbb{G}_2$. Moreover, our variant of the DLIN assumption gives the elements in both groups. Thus, we can apply the same steps as in [27]. The size of such a proof is 6 elements in $\mathbb{G}_2$.

Next is the observation that the tuples T_1 and T_2 can each be used as common reference strings for the pairing product equation proof system. Since at least one of the tuples is a valid DLIN tuple, at least one of the resulting proofs will be perfectly sound. Witness-indistinguishability will be only computational, since we have to provide T_1 and T_2 to the verifier but that is sufficient in our case. The full scheme is presented in Scheme 1.

Theorem 1. *Scheme 1 is a perfectly sound proof system for pairing product equations if the system* $(\mathsf{Setup}_{\mathsf{PPE}}, \mathsf{Prove}_{\mathsf{PPE}}, \mathsf{Verify}_{\mathsf{PPE}})$ *is perfectly sound in the common reference string model.*

Theorem 2. *Scheme 1 is a computational witness-indistinguishable proof system if the system* $(\mathsf{Setup}_{\mathsf{PPE}}, \mathsf{Prove}_{\mathsf{PPE}}, \mathsf{Verify}_{\mathsf{PPE}})$ *is perfectly witness-indistinguishable in the common reference string model.*

2.4 Structure-Preserving Signatures on Equivalence Classes

Hanser and Slamanig introduced a cryptographic primitive called structure-preserving signatures on equivalence classes [29]. Their work was further extended by Fuchsbauer et al. in [24,25]. The idea is simple but provides a powerful functionality. The signing $\mathsf{Sign}_{\mathsf{SPS}}(M, \mathsf{sk}_{\mathsf{SPS}})$ algorithm defines an equivalence relation $\mathcal{R}$ that induces a partition on the message space. By signing one representative of a partition, the signer in fact provides a signature for all elements in it. Moreover, there exists a procedure $\mathsf{ChgRep}_{\mathsf{SPS}}(M, \sigma_{\mathsf{SPS}}, r, \mathsf{pk}_{\mathsf{SPS}})$ that can be used to change the signature to a different representative without knowledge of the secret key. Existing instantiations allow to sign messages from the space $(\mathbb{G}_i^*)^\ell$, for $\ell > 1$, and for the following relation $\mathcal{R}_{exp}$: given two messages $M = (M_1, \ldots, M_\ell)$ and $M' = (M'_1, \ldots, M'_\ell)$, we say that M and M' are from the same equivalence class (denoted by $[M]_\mathcal{R}$) if there exists a scalar $r \in \mathbb{Z}_p^*$, such that $\forall_{i \in [\ell]} (M_i)^r = M'_i$.

The original paper defines two properties of SPS-EQ namely unforgeability under chosen-message attacks and class-hiding. Fuchsbauer and Gay [23] recently introduced a weaker version of unforgeability called unforgeability under chosen-open-message attacks, which restricts the adversary's signing queries to messages where it knows all exponents.

Definition 10 (Signing Oracles). *A signing oracle is an oracle* $\mathcal{O}_{\mathsf{SPS}}(\mathsf{sk}_{\mathsf{SPS}}, \cdot)$ *(resp.* $\mathcal{O}_{\mathsf{op}}(\mathsf{sk}_{\mathsf{SPS}}, \cdot)$*), which accepts messages* $(M_1, \ldots, M_\ell) \in (\mathbb{G}_i^*)^\ell$ *(resp. vectors* $(e_1, \ldots, e_\ell) \in (\mathbb{Z}_p^*)^\ell$*) and returns a signature under* $\mathsf{sk}_{\mathsf{SPS}}$ *on those messages (resp. on messages* $(g_1^{e_1}, \ldots, g_1^{e_\ell}) \in (\mathbb{G}_i^*)^\ell$*).*

Definition 11 (EUF-CMA (resp. EUF-CoMA)). *A* SPS-EQ *scheme* $(\mathsf{BGGen}_{\mathsf{SPS}}, \mathsf{KGen}_{\mathsf{SPS}}, \mathsf{Sign}_{\mathsf{SPS}}, \mathsf{ChgRep}_{\mathsf{SPS}}, \mathsf{Verify}_{\mathsf{SPS}}, \mathsf{VKey}_{\mathsf{SPS}})$ *on* $(\mathbb{G}_i^*)^\ell$ *is called existentially unforgeable under chosen message attacks (resp. adaptive chosen-open-message attacks), if for all PPT algorithms* $\mathcal{A}$ *with access to an open signing oracle* $\mathcal{O}_{\mathsf{SPS}}(\mathsf{sk}_{\mathsf{SPS}}, \cdot)$ *(resp.* $\mathcal{O}_{\mathsf{op}}(\mathsf{sk}_{\mathsf{SPS}}, \cdot)$*) the following advantage (with templates* T_1, T_2 *defined below) is negligible in the security parameter* λ*:*

$$\mathbf{Adv}^{\ell, T_1}_{\mathsf{SPS\text{-}EQ}, \mathcal{A}}(\lambda) = \Pr\left[\begin{array}{l}\mathsf{BG} \leftarrow \mathsf{BGGen}_{\mathsf{SPS}}(\lambda);\\ (\mathsf{sk}_{\mathsf{SPS}}, \mathsf{pk}_{\mathsf{SPS}}) \xleftarrow{\$} \mathsf{KGen}_{\mathsf{SPS}}(\mathsf{BG}, \ell);\\ (M^*, \sigma^*_{\mathsf{SPS}}) \xleftarrow{\$} \mathcal{A}^{\mathcal{O}_{T_2}(\mathsf{sk}_{\mathsf{SPS}}, \cdot)}(\mathsf{pk}_{\mathsf{SPS}})\end{array} : \begin{array}{l}\forall M \in Q.\ [M^*]_\mathcal{R} \neq [M]_\mathcal{R} \quad \wedge\\ \mathsf{Verify}_{\mathsf{SPS}}(M^*, \sigma^*_{\mathsf{SPS}}, \mathsf{pk}_{\mathsf{SPS}}) = 1\end{array}\right],$$

where Q *is the set of messages signed by the signing oracle* $\mathcal{O}_{T_2}$ *and for* $T_1 =$ $\mathsf{euf\text{-}cma}$ *we have* $T_2 = \mathsf{SPS}$*, and for* $T_1 = \mathsf{euf\text{-}coma}$ *we have* $T_2 = \mathsf{op}$*.*

A stronger notion of class hiding, called perfect adaptation of signatures, was proposed by Fuchsbauer et al. in [25]. Informally, this definition states that signatures received by changing the representative of the class and new signatures for the representative are identically distributed. In our schemes we will only use this stronger notion.

Definition 12 (Perfect Adaptation of Signatures). *A* SPS-EQ *scheme on* $(\mathbb{G}_i^*)^\ell$ *perfectly adapts signatures if for all* $(\mathsf{sk}_{\mathsf{SPS}}, \mathsf{pk}_{\mathsf{SPS}}, M, \sigma, r)$*, where* $\mathsf{VKey}_{\mathsf{SPS}}(\mathsf{sk}_{\mathsf{SPS}}, \mathsf{pk}_{\mathsf{SPS}}) = 1$*,* $M \in (\mathbb{G}_1^*)^\ell$*,* $r \in \mathbb{Z}_p^*$ *and* $\mathsf{Verify}_{\mathsf{SPS}}(M, \sigma, \mathsf{pk}_{\mathsf{SPS}}) = 1$*, the distribution of*

$$((M)^r, \mathsf{Sign}_{\mathsf{SPS}}(M^r, \mathsf{sk}_{\mathsf{SPS}})) \text{ and } \mathsf{ChgRep}_{\mathsf{SPS}}(M, \sigma, r, \mathsf{pk}_{\mathsf{SPS}})$$

are identical.

3 Signatures with Flexible Public Key

We begin by motivating the idea behind our primitive. In the notion of existential unforgeability of digital signatures, the adversary must return a signature valid under the public key given to him by the challenger. Imagine now that we allow a more flexible forgery. The adversary can return a signature that is valid under a public key that is in some relation $\mathcal{R}$ to the public key chosen by the challenger. Similar to the message space of SPS-EQ signatures, this relation induces a system of equivalence classes on the set of possible public keys. A given public key, along with the corresponding secret key can be transformed to a different representative in the same class using an efficient, randomized algorithm. Since there may be other ways of obtaining a new representative, the forgery on the challenge equivalence class is valid as long as the relation holds, even without knowledge of the explicit randomness that leads to the given transformation.

Note, that because of this the challenger needs a way to efficiently ascertain whether the forgery is valid, even if no transformation randomness is given. Indeed, for the full definition of our schemes' security we will require that it should not be feasible, in absence of the concrete transformation randomness, to determine whether a given public key belongs to one class or another. This property —called *class-hiding* in the style of a similar property for SPS-EQ signatures— should hold even for an adversary who has access to the randomness used to create the key pairs in question.

The apparent conflict is resolved by introducing a trapdoor key generation algorithm $\mathsf{TKeyGen}$ which outputs a key pair $(\mathsf{sk}, \mathsf{pk})$ and a class trapdoor τ for the class the key pair is in. The trapdoor allows the challenger to reveal whether a given key is in the same class as pk, even if doing so efficiently is otherwise assumed difficult. Since we require that the keys generated using the trapdoor key generation and the regular key generation are distributed identically, unforgeability results with respect to the former also hold with respect to the latter.

Definition 13 (Signature with Flexible Public Key). *A signature scheme with flexible public key* (SFPK) *is a tuple of* PPT *algorithms* ($\mathsf{KeyGen}, \mathsf{TKeyGen}, \mathsf{Sign}, \mathsf{ChkRep}, \mathsf{ChgPK}, \mathsf{ChgSK}, \mathsf{Verify}$) *such that:*

$\mathsf{KeyGen}(\lambda, \omega)$: *takes as input a security parameter* λ, *random coins* $\omega \in \mathsf{coin}$ *and outputs a pair* $(\mathsf{sk}, \mathsf{pk})$ *of secret and public keys,*

$\mathsf{TKeyGen}(\lambda, \omega)$: *a trapdoor key generation that takes as input a security parameter* λ, *random coins* $\omega \in \mathsf{coin}$ *and outputs a pair* $(\mathsf{sk}, \mathsf{pk})$ *of secret and public keys, and a trapdoor* τ.

$\mathsf{Sign}(\mathsf{sk}, m)$: *takes as input a message* $m \in \{0,1\}^\lambda$ *and a signing key* sk, *and outputs a signature* σ,

$\mathsf{ChkRep}(\tau, \mathsf{pk})$: *takes as input a trapdoor* τ *for some equivalence class* $[\mathsf{pk}']_{\mathcal{R}}$ *and public key* pk, *the algorithm outputs* 1 *if* $\mathsf{pk} \in [\mathsf{pk}']_{\mathcal{R}}$ *and* 0 *otherwise,*

$\mathsf{ChgPK}(\mathsf{pk}, r)$: *on input a representative public key* pk *of an equivalence class* $[\mathsf{pk}]_{\mathcal{R}}$ *and random coins* r, *this algorithm returns a different representative* pk', *where* $\mathsf{pk}' \in [\mathsf{pk}]_{\mathcal{R}}$.

$\mathsf{ChgSK}(\mathsf{sk}, r)$: *on input a secret key* sk *and random coins* r, *this algorithm returns an updated secret key* sk'.

$\mathsf{Verify}(\mathsf{pk}, m, \sigma)$: *takes as input a message* m, *signature* σ, *public verification key* pk *and outputs 1 if the signature is valid and 0 otherwise.*

A signature scheme with flexible public key is correct *if for all* $\lambda \in \mathbb{N}$, *all random coins* $\omega, r \in \mathsf{coin}$ *the following conditions hold:*

1. *The distribution of key pairs produced by* KeyGen *and* $\mathsf{TKeyGen}$ *is identical.*
2. *For all key pairs* $(\mathsf{sk}, \mathsf{pk}) \xleftarrow{\$} \mathsf{KeyGen}(\lambda, \omega)$ *and all messages* m *we have* $\mathsf{Verify}(\mathsf{pk}, m, \mathsf{Sign}(\mathsf{sk}, m)) = 1$ *and* $\mathsf{Verify}(\mathsf{pk}', m, \mathsf{Sign}(\mathsf{sk}', m)) = 1$, *where* $\mathsf{ChgPK}(\mathsf{pk}, r) = \mathsf{pk}'$ *and* $\mathsf{ChgSK}(\mathsf{sk}, r) = \mathsf{sk}'$.
3. *For all* $(\mathsf{sk}, \mathsf{pk}, \tau) \xleftarrow{\$} \mathsf{TKeyGen}(\lambda, \omega)$ *and all* pk' *we have* $\mathsf{ChkRep}(\tau, \mathsf{pk}') = 1$ *if and only if* $\mathsf{pk}' \in [\mathsf{pk}]_{\mathcal{R}}$.

Definition 14 (Class-hiding). *For scheme* SFPK *with relation* $\mathcal{R}$ *and adversary* $\mathcal{A}$ *we define the following experiment:*

$$
\begin{array}{l}
\underline{\mathsf{C\text{-}H}^{\mathcal{A}}_{\mathsf{SFPK},\mathcal{R}}(\lambda)} \\
\omega_0, \omega_1 \xleftarrow{\$} \mathsf{coin} \\
(\mathsf{sk}_i, \mathsf{pk}_i) \xleftarrow{\$} \mathsf{KeyGen}(\lambda, \omega_i) \text{ for } i \in \{0,1\} \\
b \xleftarrow{\$} \{0,1\}; r \xleftarrow{\$} \mathsf{coin} \\
\mathsf{sk}' \xleftarrow{\$} \mathsf{ChgSK}(\mathsf{sk}_b, r); \mathsf{pk}' \xleftarrow{\$} \mathsf{ChgPK}(\mathsf{pk}_b, r) \\
\hat{b} \xleftarrow{\$} \mathcal{A}^{\mathsf{Sign}(\mathsf{sk}', \cdot)}(\omega_0, \omega_1, \mathsf{pk}') \\
\textbf{return } b = \hat{b}
\end{array}
$$

A SFPK *is* class-hiding *if for all* PPT *adversaries* $\mathcal{A}$, *its advantage in the above experiment is negligible:*

$$
\mathsf{Adv}^{\mathsf{c\text{-}h}}_{\mathcal{A},\mathsf{SFPK}}(\lambda) = \left| \Pr\left[\mathsf{C\text{-}H}^{\mathcal{A}}_{\mathsf{SFPK},\mathcal{R}}(\lambda) = 1 \right] - \frac{1}{2} \right| = \mathsf{negl}(\lambda).
$$

Definition 15 (Existential Unforgeability under Flexible Public Key). *For scheme* SFPK *with relation* $\mathcal{R}$ *and adversary* $\mathcal{A}$ *we define the following experiment:*

$\underline{\mathsf{EUF\text{-}CMA}^{\mathcal{A}}_{\mathsf{SFPK},\mathcal{R}}(\lambda)}$

$\omega \xleftarrow{\$} \mathsf{coin}$

$(\mathsf{sk}, \mathsf{pk}, \tau) \xleftarrow{\$} \mathsf{TKeyGen}(\lambda, \omega); Q := \emptyset$

$(\mathsf{pk}', m^*, \sigma^*) \xleftarrow{\$} \mathcal{A}^{\mathcal{O}^1(\mathsf{sk},\cdot),\mathcal{O}^2(\mathsf{sk},\cdot,\cdot)}(\mathsf{pk}, \tau)$

return $(m^*, \cdot) \notin Q \wedge$

$\quad \mathsf{ChkRep}(\tau, \mathsf{pk}') = 1 \wedge$

$\quad \mathsf{Verify}(\mathsf{pk}', m^*, \sigma^*) = 1$

$\underline{\mathcal{O}^1(\mathsf{sk}, m)}$

$\sigma \xleftarrow{\$} \mathsf{Sign}(\mathsf{sk}, m)$

$Q := Q \cup \{(m, \sigma)\}$

return σ

$\underline{\mathcal{O}^2(\mathsf{sk}, m, r)}$

$\mathsf{sk}' \xleftarrow{\$} \mathsf{ChgSK}(\mathsf{sk}, r)$

$\sigma \xleftarrow{\$} \mathsf{Sign}(\mathsf{sk}', m)$

$Q := Q \cup \{(m, \sigma)\}$

return σ

A SFPK *is* existentially unforgeable with flexible public key under chosen message attack *if for all* PPT *adversaries* $\mathcal{A}$ *the advantage in the above experiment is negligible:*

$$\mathsf{Adv}^{\mathsf{euf-cma}}_{\mathcal{A},\mathsf{SFPK}}(\lambda) = \Pr\left[\mathsf{EUF-CMA}^{\mathcal{A}}_{\mathsf{SFPK}}(\lambda) = 1\right] = \mathsf{negl}(\lambda).$$

Definition 16 (Strong Existential Unforgeability under Flexible Public Key). *A* SFPK *is* strongly existentially unforgeable with flexible public key under chosen message attack *if for all* PPT *adversaries* $\mathcal{A}$ *the advantage* $\mathsf{Adv}^{\mathsf{seuf-cma}}_{\mathcal{A},\mathsf{SFPK}}(\lambda)$ *in the above experiment, where we replace the line* $(m^*, \cdot) \notin Q$ *with* $(m^*, \sigma^*) \notin Q$*, is negligible.*

In a standard application, the public key and secret key are jointly randomized by the signer using the same randomness in ChgPK and ChgSK. However, the ChgPK algorithm alone can be executed by a third party given only the public key and random coins r. Revealing r to the signer allows them to compute the corresponding secret key. For some applications we want to avoid interaction during this recovery of the secret key. Allowing the user to extract the new secret key only using their old secret key would break class-hiding, since the attacker in this case has access to the pre-transformed secret keys. Fortunately, we can instead use the additional trapdoor returned by the TKeyGen algorithm. More formally, we define this optional property as follows.

Definition 17 (Key Recovery). *A* SFPK *has* recoverable signing keys *if there exists an efficient algorithm* Recover *such that for all security parameters* $\lambda \in \mathbb{N}$*, random coins* ω, r *and all* $(\mathsf{sk}, \mathsf{pk}, \tau) \xleftarrow{\$} \mathsf{TKeyGen}(\lambda, \omega)$ *and* $\mathsf{pk}' \xleftarrow{\$} \mathsf{ChgPK}(\mathsf{pk}, r)$ *we have* $\mathsf{ChgSK}(\mathsf{sk}, r) = \mathsf{Recover}(\mathsf{sk}, \tau, \mathsf{pk}')$.

3.1 Flexible Public Key in the Multi-user Setting

In this subsection, we address applications where part of each user's public key is shared with all the other public keys and is precomputed by a trusted third party in a setup phase, e.g. the key used in a programmable hash function. We therefore define an additional algorithm CRSGen that, given a security parameter, outputs a common reference string ρ. We assume that this string is an implicit input to all algorithms. If the KeyGen is independent from ρ, we say that such a scheme supports *key generation without setup*.

We will now discuss the implication of this new algorithm on the security definitions. Usually, we require that the common reference string is generated by an honest and trusted party (i.e. by the challenger in Definitions 14 and 15). We additionally define those notions under maliciously generated ρ. We call a scheme *class-hiding under malicious reference string* if the class-hiding definition holds even if in Definition 14 the adversary is allowed to generate the string ρ. Similarly, we call a SFPK scheme *unforgeable under malicious reference string* if the unforgeability Definition 15 holds if ρ is generated by the adversary.

4 Applications

In this section we present natural applications of signatures with flexible public key. First we show how to implement cryptocurrency stealth addresses from schemes which have the additional key recovery property.

Then follow generic constructions of group and ring signature schemes. As we will see in Sect. 5, each of the schemes presented in this section can be instantiated with an SFPK scheme such that it improves on the respective state-of-the-art in terms of concrete efficiency, necessary assumptions or both.

4.1 Cryptocurrency Stealth Addresses

In cryptocurrency systems transactions are confirmed through digital signatures from the spending party on, among other things, the public key of the receiving party. Using a technique called stealth addresses [37,39], it is possible for the sender to create a fresh public key (address) for the receiving party from their known public key such that these two keys cannot be linked. The receiving party can recognize the fresh key as its own and generate a corresponding private key, subsequently enabling it to spend any funds send to the fresh unlinkable key. Crucially, there is no interaction necessary between sender and receiver to establish the fresh key and only the receiver can recover the right secret key.

Informally, a sender can take a recipient's public address and transform it to a one-time address such that:

- The new one is unlinkable to the original one and other one-time addresses,
- only the recipient (or a party given the view key) can link all payments,
- only the recipient can derive the spending key for the one-time address.

In existing schemes, stealth addresses are implemented using a variant of the Diffie-Hellman protocol [20,37]. Let g^a be the public key of the sender and g^b the recipient's public address. The sender computes the secret $s = \mathsf{H}(g^{a \cdot b})$ and to finish the transaction sends the funds to the address g^s. Note that this requires the recipient to immediately spend the coins, because the sender also knows s. To protect against this type of misuse, an asymmetric Diffie-Hellman was introduced, i.e. the funds are sent to the address $g^{s+b} = (g)^s \cdot g^b$. Note that since only the recipient knows both s and b, only he can spend the money.

In practice, the sender's public key g^a is ephemeral and unique for each transaction. Moreover, to increase efficiency a 2-key stealth address scheme was introduced. The recipient still holds the key for spending the coin, but gives a view key g^v to a third party for checking incoming transactions. Therefore, the recipient is not required to download all transactions and check if they correspond to their identity. However, the party holding the view key can break the anonymity of the recipient. To enable this feature, the sender also publishes $(g^v)^a$, as part of this transaction.

It is worth noting that the technique was introduced without a formal model and as an add-on for existing cryptocurrencies. In particular, as shown in [20] there exist many security pitfalls, which are exhibited by some of the schemes. Moreover, all existing schemes inherently rely on the Diffie-Hellman protocol, which is defined for groups in which the discrete logarithm is hard.

We will now show that signatures with flexible public keys that additionally implement the Recover algorithm can be seen as a formalization of 2-key stealth addresses. Let us consider the following scenario. A sender wants to send funds to a recipient identified by an address pk, where $(\mathsf{sk}, \mathsf{pk}, \tau) \xleftarrow{\$} \mathsf{TKeyGen}(\lambda, \omega)$. In order to send the coins, the sender first chooses randomness r and computes the one-time address $\mathsf{pk}' \xleftarrow{\$} \mathsf{ChgPK}(\mathsf{pk}, r)$. The trapdoor τ can be used as the view key to identify an incoming transaction using $\mathsf{ChkRep}(\tau, \mathsf{pk}')$. Finally, the recipient can use $\mathsf{Recover}(\mathsf{sk}, \tau, \mathsf{pk}')$ to compute the secret key sk' that can be used to spend funds sent to address pk'.

The main advantage of instantiating 2-key stealth addresses using SFPK is that we can use the security arguments of the latter. In particular, unforgeability of SFPK means that there cannot exist an efficient adversary that can spend the recipient's coins. Note that this holds even if the adversary knows the view key τ. Privacy of the recipient is protected by class-hiding. Since the distributions of TKeyGen and KeyGen are identical, it follows that any adversary breaking privacy would break class-hiding. The party holding the view key τ can distinguish transactions by definition, hence class-hiding does not hold for this party.

It is worth noting, that all previous descriptions of stealth addresses did not consider any formal model and rigorous proofs. As we have argued above, our definition of SFPK with key recovery seems to directly address the requirements set before stealth addresses. Thus, our schemes are provable secure realizations of a stealth address scheme. Moreover, since we do not use a particular group structure, our construction could be instantiated using e.g. lattice-based cryptography. We leave an instantiation of SFPK from lattices as an open problem.

Finally, note that Scheme 4 is an instance of signatures with flexible public key which has the required recovery algorithm. We also show how to extend Schemes 5 and 6 to support it.

```
KeyGen_GS(1^λ, n)
  BG ←$ BGGen_SPS(1^λ); (pk_SPS, sk_SPS) ←$ KGen_SPS(BG, ℓ)
  ρ ←$ CRSGen(1^λ) // optional
  foreach user i ∈ [n] :
    (pk^i, sk^i, τ^i) ←$ TKeyGen(1^λ, ω_i)
    σ^i_SPS ←$ Sign_SPS(pk^i, sk_SPS)
  return (gpk := (BG, pk_SPS, ρ), gmsk := ([(τ^i, pk^i)]^n_{i=1}),
          gski := (pk^i, sk^i, σ^i_SPS))
```

```
Sign_GS(gski, m)
  parse gski = (pk, sk, σ_SPS)
  r ←$ Z*_p; pk' ← ChgPK(pk, r); sk' ← ChgSK(sk, r)
  (pk', σ'_SPS) ← ChgRep_SPS(pk, σ_SPS, r, pk_SPS)
  M := m||σ'_SPS||pk'
  σ ←$ Sign(sk', M)
  return σ_GS := (pk', σ, σ'_SPS)
```

Scheme 2. Generic Group Signature Scheme

4.2 Group Signatures/Self-Blindable Certificates

We now present an efficient generic construction of static group signatures that uses SFPK as a building block and which is secure in the model by Bellare et al. [5]. The idea is to generate a SFPK secret/public key pair and "certify" the public part with a SPS-EQ signature. To sign a message, the signer changes the representation of their SFPK key, and changes the representation of the SPS-EQ certificate. The resulting signature is the SFPK signature, the randomized public key and the SPS-EQ certificate.

To enable subsequent opening, the group manager generates the SFPK keys using TKeyGen and stores their trapdoors. Opening is then performed using the stored trapdoors with the ChkRep algorithm. The group manager can also generate $\rho \xleftarrow{\$}$ CRSGen for the SFPK signatures and use it as part of the group public key. This allows us to use schemes which are secure in the multi-user setting, e.g. Scheme 5. If the KeyGen algorithm is used instead of TKeyGen to compute the SFPK key pairs, there is no efficient opening procedure and the combination of SFPK and SPS-EQ signature scheme yields a self-blindable certificate scheme [40].

Due to space limitations, we only present the setup and signing algorithm for Scheme 2. Verification and opening procedures should be clear from the context.

Theorem 3. *Scheme 2 is fully traceable if the* SPS-EQ *and the* SFPK *signature schemes are existentially unforgeable under chosen-message attack.*

Proof (Sketch). The proof relies on the fact that the only way for an adversary to win the full traceability game is by either creating a new group member (thus directly breaking the unforgeability of the SPS-EQ scheme) or by creating a forged signature for an existing group member (thus breaking the unforgeability of the SFPK scheme).

Theorem 4. *Scheme 2 is fully anonymous if the* SPS-EQ *signature scheme perfectly adapts signatures and is existentially unforgeable under chosen-message attacks, the* SFPK *scheme is class-hiding and strongly existentially unforgeable.*

Proof (Sketch). We first use the perfect adaptation of SPS-EQ signatures to re-sign the public key pk′ used in the challenge signature. Then we exclude the case that the adversary issues an open query that cannot be opened. This means that the adversary created a new group member and can be used to break the unforgeability of the SPS-EQ scheme. In the next step we choose one of the users (and abort if he is not part of the query issued by the adversary to the challenge oracle) for which we change the way we generate the secret key. Instead of using TKeyGen, we use the standard key generation algorithm KeyGen. Note that in such a case, the open oracle cannot identify signatures created by this user. However, since signatures cannot be opened by the oracle for this user we can identify such a case and return his identifier. Finally, we replace the SFPK public key and signature in the challenged group signature by a random one (which is indistinguishable by class-hiding). In the end the challenged signature is independent from the bit $\hat{b}$. However, the adversary still has non-zero advantage. This follows from the fact that it can randomize the challenged signature and our oracle will output $i_{\hat{b}}$ (because the SFPK public key is random in the signature, the oracle will fail to open and return the user's identifier). However, if the adversary is able to submit such a query we can break the strong existential unforgeability of the SFPK scheme.

4.3 Ring Signatures

In ring signatures there is no trusted entity such as a group manager and groups are chosen ad hoc by the signers themselves. Thus, to certify ring members we use a membership proof instead of a SPS-EQ signature. This proof is perfectly sound even if the common reference string is generated by the signer. In other words, the actual ring signature is a SFPK signature (pk', σ) and a proof Π that there exists a public key $\mathsf{pk} \in \mathtt{Ring}$ that is in relation to the public key pk', i.e. the signer proves knowledge of the random coins used to get pk'. The signature's anonymity relies on the class-hiding property of SFPK. Unfortunately, in the proof, the reduction does not know a valid witness for proof Π, since it does not choose the random coins for the challenged signature. Thus, we extend the signer's public keys by a tuple of three group elements (A, B, C) and prove an OR statement which allows the reduction to compute a valid proof Π if (A, B, C) is a non-DDH tuple (cf. Scheme 3). We can instantiate this scheme with a membership proof based on the $\mathcal{O}(\sqrt{n})$ size ring signatures by Chandran et al. [15] and the perfectly sound proof system for NP languages by Groth et al. [27]. The resulting membership proof is perfectly sound and of sub-linear size in the size of the set. It follows, that our ring signature construction yields the first sub-linear ring signature from standard assumptions without a trusted setup.

Theorem 5. *The generic construction of ring signatures presented in Scheme 3 is unforgeable w.r.t. insider corruption assuming the* SFPK *scheme is existentially unforgeable, the proof system used is perfectly sound and the decisional Diffie-Hellman assumption holds.*

Proof (Sketch). We first fix all public keys of honest users to contain only DDH tuples. This ensures that the forgery $\Sigma^* = (\mathsf{pk}^*, \sigma^*, \Pi^*, \rho^*_\Pi)$ includes a perfectly

$\mathsf{RKeyGen}(1^\lambda)$

$(\mathsf{sk}, \mathsf{pk}) \xleftarrow{\$} \mathsf{KeyGen}(\lambda, \omega)$
$I := (A, B, C) \xleftarrow{\$} \mathbb{G}_1^3$
return $(\mathsf{pk}_{\mathsf{RS}} := (\mathsf{pk}, I), \mathsf{sk}_{\mathsf{RS}} := \mathsf{sk})$

$\mathsf{RVerify}(m, \Sigma, \mathtt{Ring})$

parse $\Sigma = (\mathsf{pk}', \sigma, \Pi, \rho_\Pi)$
return $\mathsf{Verify}(x, \Pi) \wedge$
$\mathsf{Verify}(\mathsf{pk}', m, \sigma)$

$\mathsf{RSign}(m, \mathsf{sk}_{\mathsf{RS}}, \mathtt{Ring})$

$r \xleftarrow{\$} \mathbb{Z}_p^*$; $\mathsf{sk}' \xleftarrow{\$} \mathsf{ChgSK}(\mathsf{sk}, r)$; $\mathsf{pk}' \xleftarrow{\$} \mathsf{ChgPK}(\mathsf{pk}, r)$
$\sigma \xleftarrow{\$} \mathsf{Sign}(\mathsf{sk}', m||\mathtt{Ring})$
$\Pi \xleftarrow{\$}$ $\mathsf{Prove}(x, (\mathsf{pk}, r))$ where x is statement
$\exists_{i,\mathsf{pk},r} ((i, \mathsf{pk}, \cdot) \in \mathtt{Ring} \wedge \mathsf{ChgPK}(\mathsf{pk}, r) = \mathsf{pk}') \vee$
$\exists_{i,I} ((i, \cdot, I) \in \mathtt{Ring} \wedge I$ is not a DDH tuple$)$
return $\Sigma := (\mathsf{pk}', \sigma, \Pi)$

Scheme 3. Generic Ring Signature Scheme

sound proof for the first clause of the statement, i.e. there exists a public key $\mathsf{pk} \in \mathtt{Ring}$, which is in relation to pk^* (all users in $\mathtt{Ring}$ must be honest). This enables us to break existential unforgeability of the SFPK scheme. Note that we have to guess the correct user to execute a successful reduction.

Theorem 6. *The generic construction of ring signatures presented in Scheme 3 is anonymous against full key exposure assuming the* SFPK *scheme is class-hiding and the used proof system is computationally witness-indistinguishable.*

Proof (Sketch). We first fix all public keys of honest users to contain only non-DDH tuples I. In the next step we randomly choose a fresh bit $\hat{b} \xleftarrow{\$} \{0,1\}$ and use the witness for the tuple $I_{i_{\hat{b}}}$ in the challenged signature. Note that the proof is valid for both values of $\hat{b}$ but now the proof part is independent from the bit b. Next we change the SFPK scheme public key pk' and signature σ returned as part of the challenged signature $\Sigma = (\mathsf{pk}', \sigma', \Pi)$. Again we choose a fresh bit $\hat{b} \xleftarrow{\$} \{0,1\}$ and compute them using $\mathsf{pk}' \xleftarrow{\$} \mathsf{ChgPK}(\mathsf{pk}_{i_{\hat{b}}}, r)$, $\mathsf{sk}' \xleftarrow{\$} \mathsf{ChgSK}(\mathsf{sk}_{i_{\hat{b}}}, r)$ and $\sigma \xleftarrow{\$} \mathsf{Sign}(\mathsf{sk}', m||\mathtt{Ring})$. Any adversary distinguishing this change can be used to break the class-hiding property of the SFPK scheme. Finally, all elements of Σ are independent from b and the adversary's advantage is zero.

5 Efficient Instantiation from Standard Assumptions

In this section we present two efficient instantiations of signatures with flexible public key. All schemes support the same exponentiation relation $\mathcal{R}_{exp}$. We say that public keys $\mathsf{pk}_1 = (\mathsf{pk}_{1,1}, \ldots, \mathsf{pk}_{1,k})$ and $\mathsf{pk}_2 = (\mathsf{pk}_{2,1}, \ldots, \mathsf{pk}_{2,k})$ are in this relation, denoted $(\mathsf{pk}_1, \mathsf{pk}_2) \in \mathcal{R}_{exp}$, if and only if there exists a value $r \in \mathbb{Z}_p^*$ such that $\forall_{i\in[k]} (\mathsf{pk}_{1,i})^r = \mathsf{pk}_{2,i}$. We assume that in the plain model scheme (i.e.

$\mathsf{KeyGen_{FW}}(\lambda, \omega)$

$K_{\mathsf{PHF}} \xleftarrow{\$} \mathsf{PHF.Gen}(\lambda) \in \mathbb{G}_1^{\lambda+1}$
$A, B, C, D, X \xleftarrow{\$} \mathbb{G}_1 \; y \xleftarrow{\$} \mathbb{Z}_p^*$
$t \leftarrow e(X^y, g_2)$
$\textbf{return } (\mathsf{pk_{FW}} := (A, B, C, D, t, K_{\mathsf{PHF}}),$
$\quad \mathsf{sk_{FW}} := (y, X, \mathsf{pk_{FW}}))$

$\mathsf{TKeyGen_{FW}}(\lambda, \omega)$

$K_{\mathsf{PHF}} \xleftarrow{\$} (g_1^{\mu_i} \mid i \in \{0, \ldots, \lambda\}, \mu_i \xleftarrow{\$} \mathbb{Z}_p)$
$a, b, c, d, x \xleftarrow{\$} \mathbb{Z}_p^* \; y \xleftarrow{\$} \mathbb{Z}_p^*$
$t \leftarrow e(g_1^{x \cdot y}, g_2)$
$\textbf{return } (\mathsf{pk_{FW}} := (g_1^a, g_1^b, g_1^c, g_1^{x \cdot d}, t, K_{\mathsf{PHF}})$
$\quad \mathsf{sk_{FW}} := (y, g_1^x, \mathsf{pk_{FW}}),$
$\quad \tau := (d, g_2^y, g_2^a, g_2^b, g_2^c, g_2^{\mu_0}, g_2^{\mu_1}, \ldots, g_2^{\mu_\lambda}))$

$\mathsf{Sign_{FW}}(\mathsf{sk_{FW}}, m)$

$\textbf{parse } \mathsf{sk_{FW}} = (y, X, \mathsf{pk_{FW}})$
$r \xleftarrow{\$} \mathbb{Z}_p^*$
$\textbf{return}$
$\quad \sigma_{\mathsf{FW}} := (X^y \cdot (\mathcal{H}_{K_{\mathsf{PHF}}}(m))^r, g_1^r, g_2^r)$

$\mathsf{Verify_{FW}}(\mathsf{pk_{FW}}, m, \sigma_{\mathsf{FW}})$

$\textbf{parse } \sigma_{\mathsf{FW}} = (\sigma_{\mathsf{FW}}^1, \sigma_{\mathsf{FW}}^2, \sigma_{\mathsf{FW}}^3)$
$\quad \mathsf{pk_{FW}} = (A, B, C, D, t, K_{\mathsf{PHF}})$
$\textbf{return } e(\sigma_{\mathsf{W}}^2, g_2) = e(g_1, \sigma_{\mathsf{W}}^3) \wedge$
$\quad e(\sigma_{\mathsf{FW}}^1, g_2) = t \cdot e\left(\mathcal{H}_{K_{\mathsf{PHF}}}(m), \sigma_{\mathsf{FW}}^3\right)$

$\mathsf{ChgSK_{FW}}(\mathsf{sk_{FW}}, r)$

$\textbf{parse } \mathsf{sk_{FW}} = (y, X, \mathsf{pk_{FW}})$
$\mathsf{pk_{FW}}' \leftarrow \mathsf{ChgPK_{FW}}(\mathsf{pk_{FW}}, r)$
$\textbf{return } \mathsf{sk_{FW}}' := (y, (X^r), \mathsf{pk_{FW}}')$

$\mathsf{ChgPK_{FW}}(\mathsf{pk_{FW}}, r)$

$\textbf{parse } \mathsf{pk_{FW}} = (A, B, C, D, t, K_{\mathsf{PHF}})$
$\textbf{return } \mathsf{pk_{FW}}' := (A^r, B^r, C^r, D^r, t^r, (K_{\mathsf{PHF}})^r)$

$\mathsf{ChkRep_{FW}}(\tau, \mathsf{pk_{FW}}, \mathsf{pk_{FW}}')$

$\textbf{parse } \mathsf{pk_{FW}}' = (\mathsf{pk}_1, \mathsf{pk}_2, \mathsf{pk}_3, X, t, \mathsf{pk}_4, \ldots, \mathsf{pk}_{\lambda+4})$
$\quad \tau = (d, Y_2, \tau_1, \ldots, \tau_{\lambda+4})$
$\textbf{return } e(X^{d^{-1}}, Y_2) = t \wedge$
$\quad \bigwedge_{i=1}^{\lambda+4} \bigwedge_{j=1}^{\lambda+4} e(\mathsf{pk}_i, \tau_j) = e(\mathsf{pk}_j, \tau_i)$

$\mathsf{Recover}(\mathsf{sk}, \tau, \mathsf{pk}')$

$\textbf{parse } \mathsf{sk} = (y, g_1^x, \mathsf{pk})$
$\quad \tau = (d, g_2^y, g_2^a, g_2^b, g_2^c, g_2^{\mu_0}, \ldots g_2^{\mu_\lambda})$
$\quad \mathsf{pk}' = (A^r, B^r, C^r, D^r, t^r, (K_{\mathsf{PHF}})^r)$
$X' \leftarrow (D^r)^{1/d}$
$\textbf{return } \mathsf{sk}' := (y, X', \mathsf{pk}')$

Scheme 4. Warm-up Scheme for Waters Signatures

without a common reference string) the public key contains the implicit security parameter λ and parameters BG. Since the bilinear-group generation algorithm $\mathsf{BGGen}(\lambda)$ is deterministic, it follows that this does not influence the class-hiding property or the unforgeability property. Therefore, for readability we omit those parameters.

The first instantiation is based on a modified version of Waters signatures [41] for type-2 and type-3 pairings due to Chatterjee and Menezes [17]. The scheme has the key recovery property and can hence be used to implement stealth addresses and instantiate our ring signature construction.

The second scheme works in the multi-user setting and features small public key size, independent of the security parameter λ. It is also based on the modified version of Waters signatures. A strongly unforgeable variant of this scheme is ideal for instantiating the group signature scheme presented in Sect. 4. In combination with the SPS-EQ from [23] it results in the shortest static group signature scheme under standard assumptions. Further, using type-2 pairing and the random oracle model allows to use this scheme without a trusted party.

5.1 Warm-Up Scheme

Theorem 7. *Scheme 4 is existentially unforgeable under flexible public key, assuming the decisional linear assumption holds and that* PHF *is* $(1, \mathsf{poly}(\lambda))$

Proof. In this particular proof we assume that we can re-run $\mathsf{PHF.TrapGen}$ using the same random coins on a different group, i.e. that we can generate key $K_{\mathsf{PHF}} = (g_1^{\mu_0}, \ldots, g_1^{\mu_\lambda}) \in \mathbb{G}_1^{\lambda+1}$ and a corresponding key $K'_{\mathsf{PHF}} = (g_2^{\mu_0}, \ldots, g_2^{\mu_\lambda}) \in \mathbb{G}_2^{\lambda+1}$. Note that this means that we make non-blackbox use of the underlying programmable hash function, but this re-running is possible for the hash function we use, i.e. the Waters hash function.

Let $(f_1, f_2, h_1, h_2, f_1^\alpha, f_2^\alpha, h_1^\beta, h_2^\beta, g_1^\gamma, g_2^\gamma)$ be an instance of the decisional linear problem and let $\mathcal{A}$ be an PPT adversary that has non-negligible advantage $\mathsf{Adv}^{\mathsf{euf-cma}}_{\mathcal{A},\mathsf{SFPK}}(\lambda)$. We will show an algorithm $\mathcal{R}$ that uses $\mathcal{A}$ to break the above problem instance.

In the first step, the reduction $\mathcal{R}$ prepares the public key $\mathsf{pk_{FW}} = (A, B, C, D, t, K_{\mathsf{PHF}})$ as follows. It sets:

$$X = g_1^\gamma \qquad A = f_1^\alpha \qquad B = h_1^\beta$$
$$C = h_1 \qquad t = e(X, f_2) = e(X^\phi, g_2) \qquad D = X^d$$

and $(K_{\mathsf{PHF}}, \tau_{\mathsf{PHF}}) \overset{\$}{\leftarrow} \mathsf{PHF.TrapGen}(\lambda, g_1^\gamma, g_1)$. The reduction also prepares the trapdoor $\tau = (d, f_2, f_2^\alpha, h_2^\beta, h_2, K'_{\mathsf{PHF}})$, where to generate K'_{PHF} we re-run the algorithm $\mathsf{PHF.TrapGen}(\lambda, g_2^\gamma, g_2)$.

Let (m, l) be one of $\mathcal{A}'s$ signing queries. To answer it, $\mathcal{R}$

- chooses random values $t \overset{\$}{\leftarrow} \mathbb{Z}_p^*$,
- it computes $(a_m, b_m) \overset{\$}{\leftarrow} \mathsf{PHF.TrapEval}(\tau_{\mathsf{PHF}}, m)$ and aborts if $a_m = 0$,
- it computes $\mathsf{pk_{FW}}' \overset{\$}{\leftarrow} \mathsf{ChgPK_{SFPK}}(\mathsf{pk_{SFPK}}, l)$,
- it computes:

$$\sigma^1_{\mathsf{FW}} = (g_1^\gamma)^{t \cdot l \cdot a_m} \cdot ((f_1)^{(-a_m^{-1})} \cdot g_1^t))^{l \cdot b_m},$$
$$\sigma^2_{\mathsf{FW}} = (f_1)^{-a_m^{-1}} \cdot g_1^t, \qquad \sigma^3_{\mathsf{FW}} = (f_1)^{-a_m^{-1}} \cdot g_2^t,$$

- it returns the signature $\sigma_{\mathsf{FW}} = (\sigma^1_{\mathsf{FW}}, \sigma^2_{\mathsf{FW}}, \sigma^3_{\mathsf{FW}})$.

Let $f_1 = g_1^\phi$. We will now show that this is a valid signature. Note that the a valid signature is of the form $(f_1^{\gamma \cdot l} \cdot ((g_1^\gamma)^{a_m} \cdot g_1^{b_m})^{l \cdot r}, g_1^r, g_2^r)$. In this case, the reduction has set $r = -a_m^{-1} \cdot \phi + t$ and this means that the $f_1^{\gamma \cdot l}$ cancels out and the reduction does not need to compute f_1^γ.

Finally, $\mathcal{A}$ will output a valid signature under message m^*: $\sigma_{\hat{\mathsf{FW}}} = ({\sigma_{\hat{\mathsf{FW}}}}^1, {\sigma_{\hat{\mathsf{FW}}}}^2, {\sigma_{\hat{\mathsf{FW}}}}^3) = ((g_1^{\gamma \cdot \phi} \mathcal{H}_{K_{\mathsf{PHF}}}(m^*)^{r^*})^{l^*}, g_1^{r^*}, g_2^{r^*})$, for which we hope that $a_{m^*} = 0$, where $(a_{m^*}, b_{m^*}) \overset{\$}{\leftarrow} \mathsf{PHF.TrapEval}(\tau_{\mathsf{PHF}}, m^*)$. Moreover, since this should be a valid forgery then we have that this signature is under a public key $\mathsf{pk}_{\hat{\mathsf{FW}}}$ for which $(\mathsf{pk_{FW}}, \mathsf{pk}_{\hat{\mathsf{FW}}}) \in \mathcal{R}$. Thus, we have $\sigma_{\hat{\mathsf{FW}}} = ((f_1^\gamma (g_1^{r^*})^{b_{m^*}})^{l^*}, g_1^{r^*}, g_2^{r^*})$, for some unknown r^* but known b_{m^*}. Since $(\mathsf{pk_{FW}}, \mathsf{pk}_{\hat{\mathsf{FW}}}) \in \mathcal{R}$. This means that $\mathsf{pk}_{\hat{\mathsf{FW}}} = (A^{l^*}, B^{l^*}, C^{l^*}, D^{l^*}, t^{l^*}, K^{l^*}_{\mathsf{PHF}}) = ((f_1^\alpha)^{l^*}, (h_1^\beta)^{l^*}, (h_1)^{l^*}, (g_1^{\gamma \cdot d})^{l^*}, t^{l^*}, K^{l^*}_{\mathsf{PHF}})$. We now compute

$$T_1 = e({\sigma_{\hat{\mathsf{FW}}}}^1, h_2) = e(f_1^\gamma (g_1^{r^*})^{b_{m^*}}, h_2^{l^*}) \quad T_2 = e(h_1^{l^*}, g_2^{r^*})^{b_{m^*}} = e(g_1^{r^* \cdot b_{m^*}}, h_2^{l^*})$$
$$T_3 = e((f_1^\alpha)^{l^*}, h_2) = e(f_1^\alpha, h_2^{l^*}) \qquad T_4 = e((h_1^\beta)^{l^*}, f_2) = e(f_1^\beta, h_2^{l^*})$$

Finally, the reduction $\mathcal{R}$ returns 1 if $T_1 \cdot T_2^{-1} = T_3 \cdot T_4$ and 0, otherwise. Note that $T_1 \cdot T_2^{-1} = e(f_1^\gamma, h_2^{l^*})$ and the above equation is correct only if $\gamma = \alpha + \beta$.

The success probability of the reduction $\mathcal{R}$ depends on whether it can answer all signing queries of $\mathcal{A}$ and on the returned forgery (i.e. for which we must have

$a_{m^*} = 0$). However, since we assume that the used hash function is a $(1, \mathsf{poly}(\lambda))$-programmable hash function, it follows that $\mathcal{R}$ has a non-negligible advantage in solving the decisional linear problem.

Theorem 8. *Scheme 4 is class-hiding, assuming the decisional Diffie-Hellman assumption in* $\mathbb{G}_1$ *holds.*

Proof. In this proof we will use the game based approach. We start with $\mathbf{GAME}_0$ which is the original class-hiding experiment and let S_0 be an event that the experiment evaluates to 1, i.e. the adversary wins. We then make small changes and show in the end that the adversary's advantage is zero. We will use S_i to denote the event that the adversary wins the class-hiding experiment in $\mathbf{GAME}_i$. We will also use the vector $\boldsymbol{u}$ to denote the key for the programmable hash function K_{PHF}. Let $\mathsf{pk_{FW}}' = (A', B', C', D', t', \boldsymbol{u}')$ be the public key given to the adversary as part of the challenge. Moreover, let $\mathsf{pk_{FW}}_0 = (A_0, B_0, C_0, D_0, t_0, \boldsymbol{u}_0)$ and $\mathsf{pk_{FW}}_1 = (A_1, B_1, C_1, D_1, t_1, \boldsymbol{u}_1)$ be the public keys that are returned by the KeyGen algorithm on input of random coins ω_0 and ω_1 given to the adversary and $\hat{b}$ be the bit chosen by the challenger.

$\mathbf{GAME}_1$: In this game we change the way we sample $\mathsf{pk_{FW}}_0$ and $\mathsf{pk_{FW}}_1$. Instead of sampling directly from $\mathbb{G}_1$, we sample $a, b, c, d, x, \nu_1, \ldots, \nu_\lambda \xleftarrow{\$} \mathbb{Z}_p^*$ and set $A = g_1^a$, $B = g_1^b$, $C = g_1^c$, $D = g_1^d$, $X = g_1^x$ and $\boldsymbol{u} = (g_1^{\nu_0}, \ldots, g_1^{\nu_\lambda})$. Moreover, we change the way $\mathsf{sk_{FW}}'$ and $\mathsf{pk_{FW}}'$ are computed from $\mathsf{sk_{FW}}_{\hat{b}}$ $\mathsf{pk_{FW}}_{\hat{b}}$, i.e. $\mathsf{pk_{FW}}' = (Q^a, Q^b, Q^c, Q^d, e(Q^x, g_2^y), (Q^{\nu_0}, \ldots, Q^{\nu_\lambda}))$, and $\mathsf{sk_{FW}}' = (y, Q^x, \mathsf{pk_{FW}}')$. In other words, instead of using the value r to randomize the public key and secret key, we use a group element Q to do it.
Because we can use the invertible sampling algorithm to retrieve the random coins ω_0 and ω_1 and since the distribution of the keys does not change, it follows that $\Pr[S_1] = \Pr[S_0]$. Note that since the secret key $\mathsf{sk_{FW}}'$ is known, the signing oracle $\mathsf{Sign}(\mathsf{sk_{FW}}', \cdot)$ can be properly simulated for any adversary.

$\mathbf{GAME}_2$: In this game instead of computing $\mathsf{pk_{FW}}' = (Q^a, Q^b, Q^c, Q^d, e(Q^{x_{\hat{b}}}, g_2^{y_{\hat{b}}}), (Q^{\nu_0}, \ldots, Q^{\nu_\lambda}))$ as in $\mathbf{GAME}_1$, we sample $A' \xleftarrow{\$} \mathbb{G}_1$ set $\mathsf{pk_{FW}}' = (A', Q^b, Q^c, Q^d, e(Q^{x_{\hat{b}}}, g_2^{y_{\hat{b}}}), (Q^{\nu_0}, \ldots, Q^{\nu_\lambda}))$.

We will show that this transition only lowers the adversary's advantage by a negligible fraction. In particular, we will show a reduction $\mathcal{R}$ that uses an adversary $\mathcal{A}$ that can distinguish between those two games to break the decisional Diffie-Hellman assumption in $\mathbb{G}_1$. Let $(g_1^\alpha, g_1^\beta, g_1^\gamma)$ be a instance of this problem in $\mathbb{G}_1$. $\mathcal{R}$ samples $r_{0,A}, r_{1,A} \xleftarrow{\$} \mathbb{Z}_p^*$ and sets $A_0 = (g_1^\alpha)^{r_{0,A}}$, $A_1 = (g_1^\alpha)^{r_{1,A}}$.

Additionally, the reduction uses $Q = g_1^\beta$ and the public key

$$\mathsf{pk_{FW}}' = ((g_1^\gamma)^{r_{\hat{b},A}}, Q^b, Q^c, Q^d, e(Q^{x_{\hat{b}}}, g_2^{y_{\hat{b}}}), (Q^{\nu_0}, \ldots, Q^{\nu_\lambda})).$$

Note that since $\mathcal{R}$ knows the secret key $\mathsf{sk_{FW}}'$ it can answer signing queries.

$\mathsf{CRSGen}(\lambda, \omega)$

$\mathsf{BG} \xleftarrow{\$} \mathsf{BGGen}(\lambda)$
$K_{\mathsf{PHF}} \xleftarrow{\$} \mathsf{PHF.Gen}(\lambda) \in \mathbb{G}_1^{\lambda+1}$
$y \xleftarrow{\$} \mathbb{Z}_p^*; Y_1 \leftarrow g_1^y; Y_2 \leftarrow g_2^y$
return $\rho := (\mathsf{BG}, Y_1, Y_2, K_{\mathsf{PHF}})$

$\mathsf{KeyGen}_{\mathsf{FW}}(\lambda, \omega)$

$A, B \xleftarrow{\$} \mathbb{G}_1; x \xleftarrow{\$} \mathbb{Z}_p^*$
return $(\mathsf{pk}_{\mathsf{FW}} := (A, B, g_1^x)$
$\quad \mathsf{sk}_{\mathsf{FW}} := (Y_1^x, \mathsf{pk}_{\mathsf{FW}}))$

$\mathsf{TKeyGen}_{\mathsf{FW}}(\lambda, \omega)$

$a, b, x \xleftarrow{\$} \mathbb{Z}_p^*$
return $(\mathsf{pk}_{\mathsf{FW}} := (g_1^a, g_1^b, g_1^x),$
$\quad \mathsf{sk}_{\mathsf{FW}} := (Y_1^x, \mathsf{pk}_{\mathsf{FW}}),$
$\quad \tau := (g_2^a, g_2^b, g_2^x))$

$\mathsf{Sign}_{\mathsf{FW}}(\mathsf{sk}_{\mathsf{FW}}, m)$

parse $\mathsf{sk}_{\mathsf{FW}} = (Z, \mathsf{pk}_{\mathsf{FW}})$
$r \xleftarrow{\$} \mathbb{Z}_p^*$
return
$\quad \sigma_{\mathsf{FW}} := (Z \cdot (\mathcal{H}_{K_{\mathsf{PHF}}}(m))^r, g_1^r, g_2^r)$

$\mathsf{Verify}_{\mathsf{FW}}(\mathsf{pk}_{\mathsf{FW}}, m, \sigma_{\mathsf{FW}})$

parse $\mathsf{pk}_{\mathsf{FW}} = (A, B, X)$
$\quad \sigma_{\mathsf{FW}} = (\sigma_{\mathsf{FW}}^1, \sigma_{\mathsf{FW}}^2, \sigma_{\mathsf{FW}}^3)$
return $e(\sigma_{\mathsf{W}}^2, \hat{g}_2) = e(\hat{g}_1, \sigma_{\mathsf{W}}^3) \wedge$
$\quad e(\sigma_{\mathsf{FW}}^1, \hat{g}_2) = e(X, Y_2) \cdot e(\mathcal{H}_{K_{\mathsf{PHF}}}(m), \sigma_{\mathsf{FW}}^3)$

$\mathsf{ChgSK}_{\mathsf{FW}}(\mathsf{sk}_{\mathsf{FW}}, r)$

parse $\mathsf{sk}_{\mathsf{FW}} = (Z, \mathsf{pk}_{\mathsf{FW}})$
$\mathsf{pk}_{\mathsf{FW}}' \leftarrow \mathsf{ChgPK}_{\mathsf{FW}}(\mathsf{pk}_{\mathsf{FW}}, r)$
return
$\quad \mathsf{sk}_{\mathsf{FW}}' := ((Z)^r, \mathsf{pk}_{\mathsf{FW}}')$

$\mathsf{ChgPK}_{\mathsf{FW}}(\mathsf{pk}_{\mathsf{FW}}, r)$

parse $\mathsf{pk}_{\mathsf{FW}} = (A, B, X)$
return $\mathsf{pk}_{\mathsf{FW}}' := (A^r, B^r, X^r)$

$\mathsf{ChkRep}_{\mathsf{FW}}(\tau, \mathsf{pk}_{\mathsf{FW}}')$

parse $\tau = (\tau_1, \tau_2, \tau_3)$
$\quad \mathsf{pk}_{\mathsf{FW}}' = (\mathsf{pk}_1, \mathsf{pk}_2, \mathsf{pk}_3)$
return
$\quad \bigwedge_{i \in [3]} \bigwedge_{j \in [3]} e(\mathsf{pk}_i, \tau_j) = e(\mathsf{pk}_j, \tau_i)$

Scheme 5. Multi-user Flexible Public Key

Finally notice, that if $\gamma = \alpha \cdot \beta$ then $(\mathsf{pk}_{\mathsf{FW}}', \sigma_{\mathsf{FW}})$ have the same distribution as in $\mathbf{GAME}_1$ and otherwise as in $\mathbf{GAME}_2$. Thus, we have $|\Pr[S_2] - \Pr[S_1]| \leq \mathsf{Adv}_{\mathcal{A}}^{\mathsf{ddh}}(\lambda)$.

$\mathbf{GAME}_3$ (series of sub-games): In this game instead of computing $\mathsf{pk}_{\mathsf{FW}}' = (A', Q^b, Q^c, Q^d, e(Q^{x_{\hat{b}}}, g_2^{y_{\hat{b}}}), (Q^{\nu_1}, \ldots, Q^{\nu_\lambda}))$ as in $\mathbf{GAME}_2$, we sample $B', C', D', u_0', \ldots, u_\lambda' \xleftarrow{\$} \mathbb{G}_1$ and set $\mathsf{pk}_{\mathsf{FW}}' = (A', B', C', D', e(Q^{x_{\hat{b}}}, g_2^{y_{\hat{b}}}), (u_0', \ldots, u_\lambda'))$.

This transition is composed of a number of sub-games, in which we change each element of the public key $\mathsf{pk}_{\mathsf{FW}}'$ separately. Obviously, we can use the same reduction as above and show that each change lowers the adversary's advantage by at most $\mathsf{Adv}_{\mathcal{A}}^{\mathsf{ddh}}(\lambda)$. It is worth noting, that the reduction can always create a valid signature, since the secret key $\mathsf{sk}_{\mathsf{FW}}' = (y_{\hat{b}}, Q^{x_{\hat{b}}}, \mathsf{pk}_{\mathsf{FW}}')$ can be computed by $\mathcal{R}$. Thus, we have $|\Pr[S_3] - \Pr[S_2]| \leq (4 + \lambda) \cdot \mathsf{Adv}_{\mathcal{A}}^{\mathsf{ddh}}(\lambda)$.

Let us now take a look at the randomized public key and signature given to the adversary. Because of all the changes, we have: $\mathsf{pk}_{\mathsf{FW}}' = (A', B', C' e(Q^{x_{\hat{b}} \cdot y_{\hat{b}}}, g_2), \boldsymbol{u}')$ and signatures from the oracle are of the form $(Q^{x_{\hat{b}} \cdot y_{\hat{b}}}(\mathcal{H}_{K_{\mathsf{PHF}}}(m))^r, g_1^r, g_2^r)$ for some $r \in \mathbb{Z}_p^*$ and $A', B', C', \boldsymbol{u}'(= K_{\mathsf{PHF}}), Q$, which are independent from the bit $\hat{b}$ and the original public keys. Since the value Q is random and only appears as part of the term $Q^{x_{\hat{b}} \cdot y_{\hat{b}}}$, we can always restate this term to $Q'^{x_{1-\hat{b}} \cdot y_{1-\hat{b}}}$ where $Q' = Q^{(x_{1-\hat{b}} \cdot y_{1-\hat{b}}) \cdot (x_{\hat{b}} \cdot y_{\hat{b}})^{-1}}$ and Q' is a random value. It follows that the adversaries advantage is zero, i.e. $\Pr[S_3] = 0$.

Finally, we have $\mathsf{Adv}_{\mathcal{A},\mathsf{SFPK}}^{\mathsf{c\text{-}h}}(\lambda) = \Pr[S_0] \leq (5 + \lambda) \cdot \mathsf{Adv}_{\mathcal{A}}^{\mathsf{ddh}}(\lambda)$.

5.2 Flexible Public Key Scheme in the Multi-user Setting

Theorem 9. *Scheme 5 is existentially unforgeable under flexible public key in the common reference string model, assuming the co-Flexible Diffie-Hellman assumption holds and that* PHF *is a* $(1, \mathsf{poly}(\lambda))$*-programmable hash function.*

Proof (Sketch). The proof follows the same idea as the proof of Theorem 7. The only difference is that in this case we will use a reduction directly to the co-Flexible Diffie-Hellman assumption. Let $(g_1^\alpha, g_2^\alpha, g_1^\beta, g_2^\beta, g_1^\gamma, g_2^\gamma, g_1^\theta, g_2^\theta)$ be an instance of this problem. The reduction $\mathcal{R}$ prepares the common reference string $\rho = (\mathsf{BG}, Y_1, Y_2, K_{\mathsf{PHF}})$ and the public key $\mathsf{pk}_{\mathsf{FW}} = (A, B, X)$ as follows. It sets $X = g_1^\beta, Y_1 = g_1^\alpha, Y_2 = g_2^\alpha, A = g_1^\gamma, B = g_1^\theta$ and $(K_{\mathsf{PHF}}, \tau_{\mathsf{PHF}}) \xleftarrow{\$} \mathsf{PHF.TrapGen}(\lambda, g_1^\beta, g_1)$. Moreover, $\mathcal{R}$ sets $\tau = (g_2^\gamma, g_2^\theta, g_2^\beta)$. Finally, the adversary $\mathcal{A}$ will output a public key $\hat{\mathsf{pk}_{\mathsf{FW}}} = (A^{l^*}, B^{l^*}, X^{l^*})$ and a valid signature under message m^*: $\hat{\sigma_{\mathsf{FW}}} = ((g_1^{\alpha \cdot \beta})^{l^*} (g_1^{r^*})^{b_{m^*}}, g_1^{r^*}, g_2^{r^*})$, for some unknown r^* but known b_{m^*}. The reduction can compute $S = (g_1^{\alpha \cdot \beta})^{l^*}$ and return (A^{l^*}, B^{l^*}, S) as a solution to the co-Flexible Diffie-Hellman problem.

Theorem 10. *Scheme 5 is class-hiding under the DDH assumption in* $\mathbb{G}_1$.

Proof (Sketch). The proof is analogous to the proof of Theorem 8.

Remark 2 (Key Recovery). To support key recovery, the public key must be extended to the form (A, B, C, X) for $C = Y_1^c$. The value c is then part of τ and can be used to restore the value Y_1^r, where r is the randomness used to change the public key. Given Y_1^r we need to compute $Z^r = Y_1^{xr}$, therefore we also have to include x as part of the original secret key $\mathsf{sk}_{\mathsf{FW}} = (x, Y_1^x) = (x, Z)$.

Transformation to Strong Existential Unforgeability. Scheme 5 is only existentially unforgeable under flexible public key and this directly follows from the fact that given a signature $(g_1^{x \cdot y \cdot l} \mathcal{H}_{K_{\mathsf{PHF}}}(m)^r, g_1^r, g_2^r)$ on message m, we can compute a randomized signature $(\sigma_{\mathsf{FW}}^1, \sigma_{\mathsf{FW}}^2, \sigma_{\mathsf{FW}}^3) = (g_1^{x \cdot y \cdot l} \mathcal{H}_{K_{\mathsf{PHF}}}(m)^r \cdot \mathcal{H}_{K_{\mathsf{PHF}}}(m)^{r'}, g_1^r g_1^{r'}, g_2^r g_2^{r'})$ for a fresh value $r' \xleftarrow{\$} \mathbb{Z}_p^*$.

A generic transformation from existentially unforgeable to strongly unforgeable signatures was proposed by Boneh et al. [11]. In particular, they use Waters signatures as a case study. It works for all schemes for which there exist two algorithms F_1 and F_2 with the following properties: (1) the output signature is (σ_1, σ_2), where $\sigma_1 \xleftarrow{\$} F_1(m, r, \mathsf{sk})$ and $\sigma_2 \xleftarrow{\$} F_2(r, \mathsf{sk})$, (2) given m and σ_2 there exists at most one σ_1 so that (σ_1, σ_2) is a valid signature under pk. It is easy to see that these properties hold for standard Waters signatures and for Scheme 5, since we can compute $\sigma_{\mathsf{FW}}^2, \sigma_{\mathsf{FW}}^3$ in algorithm F_2 and σ_{FW}^1 in F_1. What is more, once the random value r is set, there exists exactly one value σ_{FW}^1, for which $(\sigma_{\mathsf{FW}}^1, \sigma_{\mathsf{FW}}^2, \sigma_{\mathsf{FW}}^3)$ is valid under a *given* public key.

The high level idea of the solution is to bind the part computed by F_2 using a hash function, i.e. the output of F_2 is hashed together with the actual message m and the output is signed. In a scenario where we consider a given public key,

$\mathsf{Sign}_{\mathsf{FW}}(\mathsf{sk}_{\mathsf{FW}}, m)$

$\textbf{parse } \mathsf{sk}_{\mathsf{FW}} = (Z, \mathsf{pk}_{\mathsf{FW}})$
$r \xleftarrow{\$} \mathbb{Z}_p^*; s \xleftarrow{\$} \mathbb{Z}_p^*$
$v \leftarrow \mathsf{H}(m, g_1^r, g_2^r, \mathsf{pk}_{\mathsf{FW}}) \in \mathbb{Z}_p^*$
$M \leftarrow g_1^v h^s$
$\textbf{return } \sigma_{\mathsf{FW}} := (Z \cdot (\mathcal{H}_{K_{\mathsf{PHF}}}(M))^r, g_1^r, g_2^r, s)$

$\mathsf{Verify}_{\mathsf{FW}}(\mathsf{pk}_{\mathsf{FW}}, m, \sigma_{\mathsf{FW}})$

$\textbf{parse } \mathsf{pk}_{\mathsf{FW}} = (A, B, X)$
$\sigma_{\mathsf{FW}} = (\sigma_{\mathsf{FW}}^1, \sigma_{\mathsf{FW}}^2, \sigma_{\mathsf{FW}}^3, s)$
$v \leftarrow \mathsf{H}(m, g_1^r, g_2^r, \mathsf{pk}_{\mathsf{FW}})$
$M \leftarrow g_1^v h^s$
$\textbf{return } e(\sigma_{\mathsf{W}}^2, \hat{g}_2) = e(\hat{g}_1, \sigma_{\mathsf{W}}^3) \wedge$
$e(\sigma_{\mathsf{FW}}^1, \hat{g}_2) = e(X, Y_2) \cdot e(\mathcal{H}_{K_{\mathsf{PHF}}}(M), \sigma_{\mathsf{FW}}^3)$

Scheme 6. Strong Existential Unforgeable Variant of Scheme 5

this means that the signature cannot be randomized. Any manipulation of the values $(\sigma_{\mathsf{FW}}^2, \sigma_{\mathsf{FW}}^3)$ would result in a different signed message, which would lead to an attack against existential unforgeability of the underlying scheme. Fixing $(\sigma_{\mathsf{FW}}^2, \sigma_{\mathsf{FW}}^3)$ fixes σ_{FW}^1, as required by the properties above. Unfortunately, the second argument does not hold for strong unforgeability under flexible public key. Note that the adversary can still change σ_{FW}^1 by randomizing the public key. We can overcome this by simply including the public key in the hash computation.

This idea prevents the randomization of the signature but breaks the security proof of the underlying scheme. To allow the security reduction to bypass this protection Boneh, Shen and Waters propose to sign a Pedersen commitment to this hash value, instead of the value itself. The reduction can use a trapdoor to bypass this protection using equivocation of the commitment. At the same time the binding property still makes it impossible for the adversary to randomize the signature. To apply this idea in our case, we first extend the common reference string ρ by an element $h \xleftarrow{\$} \mathbb{G}_1$. This element is part of the commitment key for the Pedersen scheme. More details are given in Scheme 6.

Theorem 11. *Scheme 6 is strongly existentially unforgeable under flexible public key in the CRS model, assuming the co-Flexible Diffie-Hellman assumption holds and the hash function* H *is collision-resistant.*

Proof (Sketch). The proof follows directly from the proof given in [11].

Theorem 12. *Scheme 6 is class-hiding under the DDH assumption in* $\mathbb{G}_1$.

Proof (Sketch). We can apply the same reasoning as in the proof of Theorem 10.

5.3 Discussion

In this we instantiate the generic group signature Scheme 2 and the generic ring signature Scheme 3 with our SFPK instantiations.

Note that in the case of group signatures we can use a SFPK scheme that is strongly existentially unforgeable in the multi-user setting, since the group manager can be trusted to perform a proper setup of public parameters. Thus, a natural candidate is Scheme 6. We also require a SPS-EQ signature scheme, which

Scheme	Public Key Size		Signature Size				CRS		Assumption	Key Recovery
	$[\mathbb{G}_1]$	$[\mathbb{G}_T]$	$[\mathbb{G}_1]$	$[\mathbb{G}_2]$	$[\mathbb{G}_T]$	$[\mathbb{Z}_p^*]$	$[\mathbb{G}_1]$	$[\mathbb{G}_2]$		
4	$(\lambda+5)$	1	2	1	-	-	-	-	DLIN + DDH	✓
5	3	-	2	1	-	-	$(\lambda+2)$	1	co-Flex (or DLIN) + DDH	✗/✓†
6	3	-	2	1	-	1	$(\lambda+3)$	1	co-Flex + DDH + CRHF	✗/✓†

† Can support key recovery at an expense of a larger public key (one element in $\mathbb{G}_1$).

Fig. 1. Comparison of presented instantiations

we instantiate using the scheme presented in [23]. A caveat to this scheme is that it only supports a one-time adaptation of signatures to a different representative. This does not impact our use of the scheme since in our application the group member performs the adaptation only once per signing. Further, the scheme is only unforgeable under adaptive chosen-*open*-message attacks, hence we require the following lemma.

Lemma 2. *Let the public key of the* SFPK *scheme consist only of elements sampled directly from* $\mathbb{G}_1$ *or computed as* g_1^x*, where* $x \xleftarrow{\$} \mathbb{Z}_p^*$*. Theorems 3 and 4 still hold if the* SPS-EQ *scheme is only existential unforgeable under adaptive chosen-open-message attacks.*

Proof (Sketch). In the proof of Theorem 3, instead of excluding the case where the adversary creates a new user, we can toss a coin and chose the adversary's strategy (forging the SPS-EQ or SFPK signature). In case we end up choosing the SPS-EQ, we can freely choose the SFPK public keys and issue signing oracles to get all σ_{SPS}^i. In the proof of Theorem 4 we use the unforgeability of SPS-EQ to exclude the case that the adversary issues an open query for a new user. Because this is the first change, we can again freely choose the SFPK public keys and issue signing oracles to get all σ_{SPS}^i. Finally, we note that in such proofs we make a non-blackbox use of the SFPK scheme.

For message space $(\mathbb{G}_1^*)^\ell$ the size of the SPS-EQ signature is $(4 \cdot \ell + 2)$ elements in $\mathbb{G}_1$ and 4 elements in $\mathbb{G}_2$. The security of the SPS-EQ scheme relies on the decisional linear assumption and the decisional Diffie-Hellman assumption in $\mathbb{G}_2$, while the security of our SFPK relies on the co-Flexible Diffie-Hellman assumption. All in all, the proposed instantiation yields a static group signature scheme that is secure under standard assumptions and has a signature size of 20 elements in $\mathbb{G}_1$ (counting elements in $\mathbb{Z}_q^*$ as $\mathbb{G}_1$) and 5 elements in $\mathbb{G}_2$. It therefore has shorter signatures than the current state-of-the-art scheme in [32].

Even shorter signatures can be achieved at the expense of introducing stronger assumptions without relying on Lemma 2, by using the scheme found in [24], which is unforgeable in the generic group model and has signatures of size 2 elements in $\mathbb{G}_1$ and 1 element in $\mathbb{G}_2$. More details are given in Fig. 2.

We now focus on instantiating our ring signatures construction. Combining any scheme from Sect. 5 with a generic perfectly sound proof system would result

	Scheme	Signature size* [bits]	Key size* [bits gpk + bits gmsk]	Anonymity	Assumptions
Random Oracle	Camenisch-Groth [14]	13 568	26 112 + $\mathcal{O}(\lambda)$	full	standard
	Boneh-Boyen-Shacham [9]	2 304	2 048 + 512	CPA-full	q-type
	Bichsel et al. [7]†	1 280	1 024 + 512	no key exposure	interactive
No Random Oracle	Boyen-Waters [13]	18 432	$\mathcal{O}(\lambda) + 6144$	CPA-full	q-type
	Boyen-Waters [13]‡	6 656	$\mathcal{O}(\lambda) + 512$	CPA-full	q-type
	Libert-Peters-Yung [32]	8 448	18 688¶ + 256	full	standard
	Ours with [24]	3 072	$\mathcal{O}(\lambda) + \mathcal{O}(n)$	full	interactive
	Ours with [23]	7 680	$\mathcal{O}(\lambda) + \mathcal{O}(n)$	full	standard

* At a 256-bit (resp. 512-bit) representation of $\mathbb{Z}_q, \mathbb{G}_1$ (resp. $\mathbb{G}_2$) for Type 3 pairings and at a 3072-bit factoring and DL modulus with 256-bit key

† The scheme defines additionally a join↔issue procedure

‡ Adapted from type 1 to type 3 pairings as in [32]; ¶ A chameleon hash key excluded.

Fig. 2. Comparison of static group signature schemes

in a ring signature scheme that is unlikely to be of interest, as there are already more efficient schemes with/without a trusted setup (see Fig. 3 for a comprehensive comparison). However, using the results presented by Chandran et al. [15] we can make the membership proof efficient. They propose a perfectly sound proof of size $\mathcal{O}(\sqrt{n})$ that a public key $\mathsf{pk} \in \mathbb{G}_1$ (or $\mathsf{pk} \in \mathbb{G}_2$), is in a $\mathtt{Ring}$ of size n. This idea can be applied to arbitrary public keys (i.e. consisting of group elements in different groups) in combination with a perfectly sound proof system for NP languages. Thus, we must use a compatible SFPK instantiation, leaving as the only scheme without a trusted party assumption Scheme 4. A public key of Scheme 4 contains an element in $\mathbb{G}_T$ and therefore cannot be used with the proof system from Subsect. 2.3, which is based on the efficient Groth-Sahai proofs for pairing product equations. We solve this problem in the following way:

Lemma 3. *Scheme 4 is unforgeable and class-hiding even if $X = g_1^x$, $Y = g_2^y$ are publicly known, where $t = e(X^y, g_2) = e(X, Y)$ is part of the signer's public key. Moreover, knowing the secret key one can compute such values.*

Proof. Class-hiding still holds, because the adversary is given the secret keys sk_i for $i \in \{0, 1\}$, which contain X_i and y_i so it can compute X_i and Y_i by itself already. To show that unforgeability still holds, we first have to note that Y is part of the trapdoor τ and does not provide new information for the adversary. Finally, in the proof of unforgeability of Scheme 4 X is set to be g_1^γ, where g_1^γ is part of the decisional linear problem instance. This element is not given to the adversary directly but the same proof works if this value would be given to the adversary.

The idea is that instead of putting the public key $\mathsf{pk}_{\mathsf{FW}} = (A, B, C, D, t, K_{\mathsf{PHF}})$ into the ring, we put $(A, B, C, D, X, Y, K_{\mathsf{PHF}})$. Finally, we modify the first part of the statement proven during signing, i.e. we use

	Scheme	Signature size	Assumptions
Trusted Setup	Shacham-Waters [39]	$\mathcal{O}(n)$	standard
	Boyen [12]	$\mathcal{O}(n)$	q-type
	Chandran-Groth-Sahai [15]	$\mathcal{O}(\sqrt{n})$	q-type
	Malavolta-Schröder [34]	$\mathcal{O}(1)$	q-type + GGM
No Trusted Setup	Chow et al. [19]	$\mathcal{O}(n)$	q-type
	Bender-Katz-Morselli [6]	$\mathcal{O}(n)$	ENC + ZAP
	Malavolta-Schröder [34]	$\mathcal{O}(n)$	q-type + knowledge
	Our scheme	$\mathcal{O}(n)$	standard
	Our scheme with [15]	$\mathcal{O}(\sqrt{n})$	standard

Fig. 3. Comparison of ring signature schemes without random oracles and secure in the strongest model from [6]

$$\begin{aligned}\exists_{A,B,C,D,X,X',Y,K_{\mathsf{PHF}},r}\ (i,(A,B,C,D,X,Y,K_{\mathsf{PHF}}),\cdot) \in \texttt{Ring} \wedge e(X,g_2^r) = e(X',g_2) \wedge \\ e(X',Y) = t' \wedge e(A,g_2^r) = e(A',g_2) \wedge \\ e(B,g_2^r) = e(B',g_2) \wedge e(C,g_2^r) = e(C',g_2) \wedge \\ e(D,g_2^r) = e(D',g_2) \wedge e(K_{\mathsf{PHF}},g_2^r) = e(K'_{\mathsf{PHF}},g_2),\end{aligned}$$

instead of $\exists_{\mathsf{pk},r}\left((i,\mathsf{pk},\cdot) \in \texttt{Ring} \wedge \mathsf{ChgPK}(\mathsf{pk},r) = \mathsf{pk}'\right)$, where $\mathsf{pk_{FW}}' = (A', B', C', D', t', K'_{\mathsf{PHF}})$ is the randomized SFPK public key used as part of the ring signature. Since all elements in the ring are now elements in $\mathbb{G}_1$ or $\mathbb{G}_2$, we can use the proof system from Subsect. 2.3 to efficiently instantiate the proof used in our ring signature construction. What is more, we can also apply the trick from [15] and create a membership proof of length only $\mathcal{O}(\sqrt{n})$. The resulting ring signature scheme is the first efficient scheme that is secure under falsifiable assumptions, without a trusted party and with signature size that does not depend linearly on the number of ring members. This solves the open problem stated by Malavolta and Schröder [34].

Acknowledgments. This work was supported by the German Federal Ministry of Education and Research (BMBF) through funding for CISPA and the CISPA-Stanford Center for Cybersecurity (FKZ: 16KIS0762).

References

1. Ateniese, G., Chou, D.H., de Medeiros, B., Tsudik, G.: Sanitizable signatures. In: di Vimercati, S.C., Syverson, P., Gollmann, D. (eds.) ESORICS 2005. LNCS, vol. 3679, pp. 159–177. Springer, Heidelberg (2005). https://doi.org/10.1007/11555827_10
2. Attrapadung, N., Libert, B., Peters, T.: Efficient completely context-hiding quotable and linearly homomorphic signatures. In: Kurosawa, K., Hanaoka, G. (eds.) PKC 2013. LNCS, vol. 7778, pp. 386–404. Springer, Heidelberg (2013). https://doi.org/10.1007/978-3-642-36362-7_24
3. Backes, M., Hanzlik, L., Kluczniak, K., Schneider, J.: Signatures with Flexible Public Key: Introducing Equivalence Classes for Public Keys. Cryptology ePrint Archive, Report 2018/191 (2018)
4. Barreto, P.S.L.M., Naehrig, M.: Pairing-friendly elliptic curves of prime order. In: Preneel, B., Tavares, S. (eds.) SAC 2005. LNCS, vol. 3897, pp. 319–331. Springer, Heidelberg (2006). https://doi.org/10.1007/11693383_22
5. Bellare, M., Micciancio, D., Warinschi, B.: Foundations of group signatures: formal definitions, simplified requirements, and a construction based on general assumptions. In: Biham, E. (ed.) EUROCRYPT 2003. LNCS, vol. 2656, pp. 614–629. Springer, Heidelberg (2003). https://doi.org/10.1007/3-540-39200-9_38
6. Bender, A., Katz, J., Morselli, R.: Ring signatures: stronger definitions, and constructions without random oracles. In: Halevi, S., Rabin, T. (eds.) TCC 2006. LNCS, vol. 3876, pp. 60–79. Springer, Heidelberg (2006). https://doi.org/10.1007/11681878_4
7. Bichsel, P., Camenisch, J., Neven, G., Smart, N.P., Warinschi, B.: Get shorty via group signatures without encryption. In: Garay, J.A., De Prisco, R. (eds.) SCN 2010. LNCS, vol. 6280, pp. 381–398. Springer, Heidelberg (2010). https://doi.org/10.1007/978-3-642-15317-4_24
8. Blazy, O., Fuchsbauer, G., Pointcheval, D., Vergnaud, D.: Signatures on randomizable ciphertexts. In: Catalano, D., Fazio, N., Gennaro, R., Nicolosi, A. (eds.) PKC 2011. LNCS, vol. 6571, pp. 403–422. Springer, Heidelberg (2011). https://doi.org/10.1007/978-3-642-19379-8_25
9. Boneh, D., Boyen, X., Shacham, H.: Short group signatures. In: Franklin, M. (ed.) CRYPTO 2004. LNCS, vol. 3152, pp. 41–55. Springer, Heidelberg (2004). https://doi.org/10.1007/978-3-540-28628-8_3
10. Boneh, D., Freeman, D., Katz, J., Waters, B.: Signing a linear subspace: signature schemes for network coding. In: Jarecki, S., Tsudik, G. (eds.) PKC 2009. LNCS, vol. 5443, pp. 68–87. Springer, Heidelberg (2009). https://doi.org/10.1007/978-3-642-00468-1_5
11. Boneh, D., Shen, E., Waters, B.: Strongly unforgeable signatures based on computational Diffie-Hellman. In: Yung, M., Dodis, Y., Kiayias, A., Malkin, T. (eds.) PKC 2006. LNCS, vol. 3958, pp. 229–240. Springer, Heidelberg (2006). https://doi.org/10.1007/11745853_15
12. Boyen, X.: Mesh signatures. In: Naor, M. (ed.) EUROCRYPT 2007. LNCS, vol. 4515, pp. 210–227. Springer, Heidelberg (2007). https://doi.org/10.1007/978-3-540-72540-4_12
13. Boyen, X., Waters, B.: Full-domain subgroup hiding and constant-size group signatures. In: Okamoto, T., Wang, X. (eds.) PKC 2007. LNCS, vol. 4450, pp. 1–15. Springer, Heidelberg (2007). https://doi.org/10.1007/978-3-540-71677-8_1

14. Camenisch, J., Groth, J.: Group signatures: better efficiency and new theoretical aspects. In: Blundo, C., Cimato, S. (eds.) SCN 2004. LNCS, vol. 3352, pp. 120–133. Springer, Heidelberg (2005). https://doi.org/10.1007/978-3-540-30598-9_9
15. Chandran, N., Groth, J., Sahai, A.: Ring signatures of sub-linear size without random oracles. In: Arge, L., Cachin, C., Jurdziński, T., Tarlecki, A. (eds.) ICALP 2007. LNCS, vol. 4596, pp. 423–434. Springer, Heidelberg (2007). https://doi.org/10.1007/978-3-540-73420-8_38
16. Chase, M., Kohlweiss, M., Lysyanskaya, A., Meiklejohn, S.: Malleable signatures: new Definitions and delegatable anonymous credentials. In: CSF 2014. IEEE Computer Society (2014)
17. Chatterjee, S., Menezes, A.: On cryptographic protocols employing asymmetric pairings - the role of revisited. Discret. Appl. Math. **159**(13), 1311–1322 (2011)
18. Chaum, D., van Heyst, E.: Group signatures. In: Davies, D.W. (ed.) EUROCRYPT 1991. LNCS, vol. 547, pp. 257–265. Springer, Heidelberg (1991). https://doi.org/10.1007/3-540-46416-6_22
19. Chow, S.S.M., Wei, V.K.-W., Liu, J.K., Yuen, T.H.: Ring signatures without random oracles. In: Lin, F.-C., Lee, D.-T., Paul, B.-S.P., Lin, Shieh, S., Jajodia, S. (eds.) ASIACCS 2006. ACM (2006)
20. Courtois, N.T., Mercer, R.: Stealth address and key management techniques in blockchain systems. In: Mori, P., Furnell, S., Camp, O. (eds.) ICISSP 2017. SciTePress (2017)
21. Damgård, I., Nielsen, J.B.: Improved non-committing encryption schemes based on a general complexity assumption. In: Bellare, M. (ed.) CRYPTO 2000. LNCS, vol. 1880, pp. 432–450. Springer, Heidelberg (2000). https://doi.org/10.1007/3-540-44598-6_27
22. Fleischhacker, N., Krupp, J., Malavolta, G., Schneider, J., Schröder, D., Simkin, M.: Efficient unlinkable sanitizable signatures from signatures with re-randomizable keys. In: Cheng, C.-M., Chung, K.-M., Persiano, G., Yang, B.-Y. (eds.) PKC 2016. LNCS, vol. 9614, pp. 301–330. Springer, Heidelberg (2016). https://doi.org/10.1007/978-3-662-49384-7_12
23. Fuchsbauer, G., Gay, R.: Weakly Secure Equivalence-Class Signatures from Standard Assumptions. Cryptology ePrint Archive, Report 2018/037 (2018)
24. Fuchsbauer, G., Hanser, C., Slamanig, D.: EUF-CMA- Secure Structure-Preserving Signatures on Equivalence Classes. Cryptology ePrint Archive, Report 2014/944 (2014)
25. Fuchsbauer, G., Hanser, C., Slamanig, D.: Practical round-optimal blind signatures in the standard model. In: Gennaro, R., Robshaw, M. (eds.) CRYPTO 2015. LNCS, vol. 9216, pp. 233–253. Springer, Heidelberg (2015). https://doi.org/10.1007/978-3-662-48000-7_12
26. Ghadafi, E., Smart, N.P., Warinschi, B.: Groth–Sahai proofs revisited. In: Nguyen, P.Q., Pointcheval, D. (eds.) PKC 2010. LNCS, vol. 6056, pp. 177–192. Springer, Heidelberg (2010). https://doi.org/10.1007/978-3-642-13013-7_11
27. Groth, J., Ostrovsky, R., Sahai, A.: Non-interactive zaps and new techniques for NIZK. In: Dwork, C. (ed.) CRYPTO 2006. LNCS, vol. 4117, pp. 97–111. Springer, Heidelberg (2006). https://doi.org/10.1007/11818175_6
28. Groth, J., Sahai, A.: Efficient non-interactive proof systems for bilinear groups. In: Smart, N. (ed.) EUROCRYPT 2008. LNCS, vol. 4965, pp. 415–432. Springer, Heidelberg (2008). https://doi.org/10.1007/978-3-540-78967-3_24

29. Hanser, C., Slamanig, D.: Structure-preserving signatures on equivalence classes and their application to anonymous credentials. In: Sarkar, P., Iwata, T. (eds.) ASIACRYPT 2014. LNCS, vol. 8873, pp. 491–511. Springer, Heidelberg (2014). https://doi.org/10.1007/978-3-662-45611-8_26
30. Hofheinz, D., Kiltz, E.: Programmable hash functions and their applications. In: Wagner, D. (ed.) CRYPTO 2008. LNCS, vol. 5157, pp. 21–38. Springer, Heidelberg (2008). https://doi.org/10.1007/978-3-540-85174-5_2
31. Johnson, R., Molnar, D., Song, D., Wagner, D.: Homomorphic signature schemes. In: Preneel, B. (ed.) CT-RSA 2002. LNCS, vol. 2271, pp. 244–262. Springer, Heidelberg (2002). https://doi.org/10.1007/3-540-45760-7_17
32. Libert, B., Peters, T., Yung, M.: Short group signatures via structure-preserving signatures: standard model security from simple assumptions. In: Gennaro, R., Robshaw, M. (eds.) CRYPTO 2015. LNCS, vol. 9216, pp. 296–316. Springer, Heidelberg (2015). https://doi.org/10.1007/978-3-662-48000-7_15
33. Libert, B., Vergnaud, D.: Multi-use unidirectional proxy resignatures. In: Ning, P., Syverson, P.F., Jha, S.: CCS 2008. ACM (2008)
34. Malavolta, G., Schröder, D.: Efficient ring signatures in the standard model. In: Takagi, T., Peyrin, T. (eds.) ASIACRYPT 2017. LNCS, vol. 10625, pp. 128–157. Springer, Cham (2017). https://doi.org/10.1007/978-3-319-70697-9_5
35. Nakamoto, S.: Bitcoin: a peer-to-peer electronic cash system. http://bitcoin.org/bitcoin.pdf
36. Rivest, R.L., Shamir, A., Tauman, Y.: How to leak a secret. In: Boyd, C. (ed.) ASIACRYPT 2001. LNCS, vol. 2248, pp. 552–565. Springer, Heidelberg (2001). https://doi.org/10.1007/3-540-45682-1_32
37. van Saberhagen, N.: CryptoNote v 2.0., October 2013. https://cryptonote.org/whitepaper.pdf
38. Shacham, H., Waters, B.: Efficient ring signatures without random oracles. In: Okamoto, T., Wang, X. (eds.) PKC 2007. LNCS, vol. 4450, pp. 166–180. Springer, Heidelberg (2007). https://doi.org/10.1007/978-3-540-71677-8_12
39. Todd, P.: Stealth Addresses. https://lists.linuxfoundation.org/pipermail/bitcoin-dev/2014-January/004020.html
40. Verheul, E.R.: Self-blindable credential certificates from the weil pairing. In: Boyd, C. (ed.) ASIACRYPT 2001. LNCS, vol. 2248, pp. 533–551. Springer, Heidelberg (2001). https://doi.org/10.1007/3-540-45682-1_31
41. Waters, B.: Efficient identity-based encryption without random oracles. In: Cramer, R. (ed.) EUROCRYPT 2005. LNCS, vol. 3494, pp. 114–127. Springer, Heidelberg (2005). https://doi.org/10.1007/11426639_7

Compact Multi-signatures for Smaller Blockchains

Dan Boneh[1(✉)], Manu Drijvers[2,3(✉)], and Gregory Neven[2(✉)]

[1] Stanford University, Stanford, USA
dabo@cs.stanford.edu
[2] DFINITY, Zurich, Switzerland
{manu,gregory}@dfinity.org
[3] ETH Zurich, Zurich, Switzerland

Abstract. We construct new multi-signature schemes that provide new functionality. Our schemes are designed to reduce the size of the Bitcoin blockchain, but are useful in many other settings where multi-signatures are needed. All our constructions support both signature compression and public-key aggregation. Hence, to verify that a number of parties signed a common message m, the verifier only needs a short multi-signature, a short aggregation of their public keys, and the message m. We give new constructions that are derived from Schnorr signatures and from BLS signatures. Our constructions are in the plain public key model, meaning that users do not need to prove knowledge or possession of their secret key.

In addition, we construct the first short accountable-subgroup multi-signature (ASM) scheme. An ASM scheme enables any subset S of a set of n parties to sign a message m so that a valid signature discloses which subset generated the signature (hence the subset S is *accountable* for signing m). We construct the first ASM scheme where signature size is only $O(\kappa)$ bits over the description of S, where κ is the security parameter. Similarly, the aggregate public key is only $O(\kappa)$ bits, independent of n. The signing process is non-interactive. Our ASM scheme is very practical and well suited for compressing the data needed to spend funds from a t-of-n Multisig Bitcoin address, for any (polynomial size) t and n.

1 Introduction

Consider n parties where each party independently generates a key pair for a signature scheme. Some time later all n parties want to sign the same message m. A *multi-signature scheme* [29,39] is a protocol that enables the n signers to jointly generate a short signature σ on m so that σ convinces a verifier that all n parties signed m. Specifically, the verification algorithm is given as input the n public keys, the message m, and the multi-signature σ. The algorithm either accepts or rejects σ. The multi-signature σ should be short – its length should be independent of the number of signers n. We define this concept more precisely in

M. Drijvers and G. Neven—Work partially done at IBM Research – Zurich.

T. Peyrin and S. Galbraith (Eds.): ASIACRYPT 2018, LNCS 11273, pp. 435–464, 2018.
https://doi.org/10.1007/978-3-030-03329-3_15

the next section, where we also present the standard security model for such schemes [39]. Secure multi-signatures have been constructed from Schnorr signatures (e.g. [9]), from BLS signatures (e.g. [10]), and from many other schemes as discussed in Sect. 1.4.

A more general concept called an *aggregate signature scheme* [13] lets each of the n parties sign a *different* message, but all these signatures can be aggregated into a single short signature σ. As before, this short signature should convince the verifier that all signers signed their designated message.

Applications to Bitcoin. Multi-signatures and aggregate signatures can be used to shrink the size of the Bitcoin blockchain [41]. In recent work, Maxwell, Poelstra, Seurin, and Wuille [36] suggest using multi-signatures to shrink the transaction data associated with Bitcoin Multisig addresses. Conceptually, a Multisig address is the hash of n public keys $pk_1, \ldots, pk_n$ along with some number $t \in \{1, \ldots, n\}$ called a threshold (see [2,36] for details). To spend funds associated with this address, one creates a transaction containing all n public keys $pk_1, \ldots, pk_n$ followed by t valid signatures from t of the n public keys, and writes this transaction to the blockchain. The message being signed is the same in all t signatures, namely the transaction data.

In practice, Multisig addresses often use $t = n$, so that signatures from all n public keys are needed to spend funds from this address. In this case, all n signatures can be compressed using a multi-signature scheme into a single short signature. This shrinks the overall transaction size and reduces the amount of data written to the blockchain. This approach can also be made to work for $t < n$, when $\binom{n}{t}$ is small, by enumerating all t-size subsets [36, Sect. 5.2]. Multi-signatures can also be used to compress multi-input transactions, but for simplicity we will focus on Multisig addresses.

Notice that we still need to write all n public keys to the blockchain, so compressing the signatures does not save too much. Fortunately, there is a solution to this as well. Maxwell et al. [36], building on the work on Bellare and Neven [9], construct a Schnorr-based multi-signature scheme that also supports public key aggregation; the verifier only needs a short aggregate public key instead of an explicit list of all n public keys. With this approach, an n-of-n Multisig address is simply the hash of the short aggregate public key, and the data written to the blockchain in a spending transaction is this single short aggregated public key, a single short compressed signature, and the message. This data is sufficient to convince the verifier that all n signers signed the transaction. It shrinks the amount of data written to the blockchain by a factor of n.

Maxwell et al. call this primitive a multi-signature scheme with public key aggregation. Their signing protocol requires two rounds of communication among the signing parties, and they prove security of their scheme assuming the one-more discrete-log assumption (as assumption introduced in [8]). However, recent work [22] has shown that there is a gap in the security proof, and that security cannot be proven under this assumption. Whether their scheme can be proved secure under a different assumption or in a generic group model is currently an open problem.

In Sect. 5, we present a modification of the scheme by Maxwell et al. that we prove secure under the standard discrete-log assumption. Our $\mathcal{MSDL}$ scheme retains all the benefits of the original scheme, and in particular uses the same key aggregation technique, but we add one round to the signing protocol. Independently from our work, Maxwell et al. [37] revised their work to use the same protocol we present here.

1.1 Better Constructions Using Pairings

Our main results show that we can do much better by replacing the Schnorr signature scheme in [36] by BLS signatures [14]. The resulting schemes are an extremely good fit for Bitcoin, but are also very useful wherever multi-signatures are needed.

To describe our new constructions, we first briefly review the BLS signature scheme and its aggregation mechanism. Recall that the scheme needs: (1) An efficiently computable non-degenerate pairing $e : \mathbb{G}_1 \times \mathbb{G}_2 \rightarrow \mathbb{G}_t$ in groups $\mathbb{G}_1, \mathbb{G}_2, \mathbb{G}_t$ of prime order q. We let g_1 and g_2 be generators of $\mathbb{G}_1$ and $\mathbb{G}_2$ respectively. (2) A hash function $\mathsf{H}_0 : \mathcal{M} \rightarrow \mathbb{G}_1$. Now the BLS signature scheme works as follows:

- Key generation: choose a random $sk \xleftarrow{\$} \mathbb{Z}_q$ and output (pk, sk) where $pk \leftarrow g_2^{sk} \in \mathbb{G}_2$.
- $\mathsf{Sign}(sk, m)$: output $\sigma \leftarrow \mathsf{H}_0(m)^{sk} \in \mathbb{G}_1$.
- $\mathsf{Verify}(pk, m, \sigma)$: if $e(\sigma, g_2) \stackrel{?}{=} e\big(\mathsf{H}_0(m), pk\big)$ output "accept", otherwise output "reject".

This signature scheme supports a simple signature aggregation procedure. Given triples $(pk_i,\ m_i,\ \sigma_i)$ for $i = 1, \ldots, n$, anyone can aggregate the signatures $\sigma_1, \ldots, \sigma_n \in \mathbb{G}_1$ into a short convincing aggregate signature σ by computing

$$\sigma \leftarrow \sigma_1 \cdots \sigma_n \in \mathbb{G}_1. \tag{1}$$

To verify this aggregate signature $\sigma \in \mathbb{G}_1$ one checks that:

$$e(\sigma, g_2) = e\big(\mathsf{H}_0(m_1), pk_1\big) \cdots e\big(\mathsf{H}_0(m_n), pk_n\big). \tag{2}$$

Note that verification requires all $(pk_i,\ m_i)$ for $i = 1, \ldots, n$. When all the messages being signed are the same (i.e., $m_1 = \ldots = m_n$) the verification relation (2) reduces to a simpler test that requires only two pairings:

$$e(\sigma, g_2) \stackrel{?}{=} e\Big(\mathsf{H}_0(m_1),\ pk_1 \cdots pk_n\Big). \tag{3}$$

Observe that the verifier only needs to be given a short aggregate public-key $apk := pk_1 \cdots pk_n \in \mathbb{G}_2$.

The Rogue Public-Key Attack. The simple signature aggregation method in (1) is insecure on its own, and needs to be enhanced. To see why, consider the following rogue public-key attack: an attacker registers a rogue public key

$pk_2 := g_2^\alpha \cdot (pk_1)^{-1} \in \mathbb{G}_2$, where $pk_1 \in \mathbb{G}_2$ is a public key of some unsuspecting user Bob, and $\alpha \xleftarrow{\$} \mathbb{Z}_q$ is chosen by the attacker. The attacker can then claim that both it and Bob signed some message $m \in \mathcal{M}$ by presenting the aggregate signature $\sigma := \mathsf{H}_0(m)^\alpha$. This signature verifies as an aggregate of two signatures, one from pk_1 and one from pk_2, because

$$e(\sigma, g_2) = e\big(\mathsf{H}_0(m)^\alpha, g_2\big) = e\big(\mathsf{H}_0(m), g_2^\alpha\big) = e\big(\mathsf{H}_0(m), pk_1 \cdot pk_2\big).$$

Hence, this σ satisfies (3). In effect, the attacker committed Bob to the message m, without Bob ever signing m.

Defenses. There are two standard defenses against the rogue public-key attack:

- Require every user to prove knowledge or possession of the corresponding secret key [10,33,47]. However, this is difficult to enforce in practice, as argued in [7,47], and does not fit well with applications to crypto currencies, as explained in [36].
- Require that the messages being aggregated are distinct [7,13], namely the verifier rejects an aggregate signature on non-distinct messages. This is sufficient to prevent the rogue key attack. Moreover, message distinctness can be enforced by always prepending the public key to every message prior to signing. However, because now all messages are distinct, we cannot take advantage of fast verification and public-key aggregation as in (3) when aggregating signatures on a common message m.

1.2 Our Pairing-Based Results

In Sect. 3 we propose a different defense against the rogue public-key attack that retains all the benefits of both defenses above without the drawbacks. Our multi-signature scheme, called $\mathcal{MSP}$, supports public key aggregation and fast verification as in (3). Moreover, the scheme is secure in the plain public-key model, which means that users do not need to prove knowledge or possession of their secret key. The scheme has two additional useful properties:

- The scheme supports batch verification where a set of multi-signatures can be verified as a batch faster than verifying them one by one.
- We show in Sect. 3.3 that given several multi-signatures on different messages, it is possible to aggregate all them using (1) into a single short signature. This can be used to aggregate signatures across many transactions and further shrink the data on the blockchain.

Our construction is based on the approach developed in [9] and [36] for securing Schnorr multi-signatures against the rogue public key attack.

Our BLS-based multi-signature scheme $\mathcal{MSP}$ is much easier to use than Schnorr multi-signatures. Recall that aggregation in Schnorr can only take place at the time of signing and requires a multi-round protocol between the signers. In our new scheme, aggregation can take place publicly by a simple multiplication, even long after all the signatures have been generated and the signers are no longer available. Concretely, in the context of Bitcoin this means that all the signers behind a Multisig address can simply send their signatures to one party who aggregates all of them into a single signature. No interaction is needed, and the parties do not all need to be online at the same time.

Accountable-Subgroup Multi-signatures. Consider again n parties where each party generates an independent signing key pair. An ASM enables any subset S of the n parties to jointly sign a message m, so that a valid signature implicates the subset S that generated the signature; hence S is accountable for signing m. The verifier in an ASM is given as input the (aggregate) ASM public key representing all n parties, the set $S \subseteq \{1, \ldots, n\}$, the signature generated by the set S, and the message m. It accepts or rejects the signature. Security should ensure that a set of signers $S' \not\supseteq S$ cannot issue a signature that will be accepted as if it were generated by S. We define ASMs and their security properties precisely in Sect. 4. This concept was previously studied by Micali et al. [39].

Any secure signature scheme gives a trivial ASM: every party generates an independent signing key pair. A signature by a set S on message m is simply the concatenation of all the signatures by the members of S. For a security parameter κ, the public key size in this trivial ASM is $O(n \times \kappa)$ bits. The signature size is $O(|S| \times \kappa)$ bits.

Our new ASM scheme, called $\mathcal{ASM}$, is presented in Sect. 4.2. It is the first ASM where signature size is only $O(\kappa)$ bits beyond the description of the set S, independent of n. The public key is only $O(\kappa)$ bits. Concretely, the signature is only two group elements, along with the description of S, and the public key is a single group element. The signing process is non-interactive, but initial key generation requires a simple one-round protocol between the all n signers. We also present an aggregate ASM, called $\mathcal{AASM}$, that partially aggregates w $\mathcal{ASM}$ signatures into a single signature that is considerably smaller than w separate $\mathcal{ASM}$ signatures.

To see how all this can be used, consider again a Bitcoin n-of-n Multisig address. We already saw that multi-signatures with public key aggregation reduce the amount of data written to the blockchain to only $O(\kappa)$ bits when spending funds from this address (as opposed to $O(\kappa \times n)$ bits as currently done in Bitcoin). The challenge is to do the same for a t-of-n Multisig address where $t < n$. Our ASM gives a complete solution; the only information that is written to the blockchain is a description of S plus three additional group elements: one for the public key and two for the signature, even when $\binom{n}{t}$ is exponential. When a block contains w such transactions, our aggregate ASM in Sect. 4.4 can reduce this further to two (amortized) group elements per transaction. This is significantly better than the trivial linear size ASM scheme currently employed by Bitcoin.

Proofs of Possession. We further observe that all our schemes, both BLS-based and Schnorr-based, can be adapted to a setting where all users are required to provide a proof of possession (PoP) of their secret key. Proofs of possession increase the size of individual public keys, but there are applications where

Table 1. Comparison of the space required to authorize a block in the Bitcoin blockchain containing tx transactions, each containing inp inputs, all from n-out-of-n multisig wallets. Here, $|\mathbb{G}|$ denotes the space required to represent an element of a group. The fourth column shows the concrete number of bytes taken in a bitcoin block by choosing some sample parameters ($tx = 1500$, $inp = 3$, $n = 3$), using secp256k1 [19] for Bitcoin, MuSig, and $\mathcal{MSDL}$ schemes ($|\mathbb{G}| = 32B$, $|\mathbb{Z}_q| = 32B$), and BLS381 [6] for the pairing-based $\mathcal{MSP}, \mathcal{AMSP}, \mathcal{ASM}$, and $\mathcal{AASM}$ schemes ($|\mathbb{G}_1| = 96B$, $|\mathbb{G}_2| = 48B$, $|\mathbb{Z}_q| = 32B$). In the right-most column, "linear" denotes that t-of-n thresholds are supported with key and signature sizes linear in n and t, "small" denotes that support is limited to $\binom{n}{t}$ being small, and "any" denotes support for arbitrary (polynomial size) t and n.

	Combined public key size	**Combined signature size**	**Total size (KB)**	**Threshold support**
Bitcoin	$tx \cdot inp \cdot n \cdot \|\mathbb{G}\|$	$tx \cdot inp \cdot n \cdot 2 \cdot \|\mathbb{Z}_q\|$	1296	linear
MuSig ([36])	$tx \cdot inp \cdot \|\mathbb{G}\|$	$tx \cdot (\|\mathbb{G}\| + \|\mathbb{Z}_q\|)$	240	small
$\mathcal{MSDL}$ (Sec. 5)	$tx \cdot inp \cdot \|\mathbb{G}\|$	$tx \cdot (\|\mathbb{G}\| + \|\mathbb{Z}_q\|)$	240	small
$\mathcal{MSP}$ (Sec. 3.1)	$tx \cdot inp \cdot \|\mathbb{G}_2\|$	$tx \cdot \|\mathbb{G}_1\|$	360	small
$\mathcal{AMSP}$ (Sec. 3.3)	$tx \cdot inp \cdot \|\mathbb{G}_2\|$	$\|\mathbb{G}_1\|$	216	small
$\mathcal{ASM}$ (Sec. 4)	$tx \cdot inp \cdot \|\mathbb{G}_2\|$	$tx \cdot inp \cdot (\|\mathbb{G}_1\| + \|\mathbb{G}_2\|)$	864	any
$\mathcal{AASM}$ (Sec. 4.4)	$tx \cdot inp \cdot \|\mathbb{G}_2\|$	$tx \cdot inp \cdot \|\mathbb{G}_2\| + \|\mathbb{G}_1\|$	432	any

the size of individual keys is less relevant. For example, Multisig addresses in Bitcoin only need to store the aggregate public key on the blockchain, whereas the individual public keys are only relevant to the signers and can be kept off-chain, or verified once and then discarded. Other applications may involve a more or less static set of signing nodes whose keys can be verified once and used in arbitrary combinations thereafter.

The PoP variants offer some advantages over our main schemes, such as simply using the product or hash of the public keys as the aggregate public key (as opposed to a multi-exponentiation), and having tighter security proofs to the underlying security assumption. Due to space constraints, the PoP variants are only presented in the full version of this work [12].

1.3 Efficiency Comparison

Table 1 shows to what extent our constructions reduce the size of the Bitcoin blockchain. Our pairing-based scheme and $\mathcal{AMSP}$ and our discrete logarithm-based scheme $\mathcal{MSDL}$ both require less than 20% of the space to authenticate all transactions in a Bitcoin block compared to the currently deployed solution, assuming realistic parameters. While not immediately visible from the table, accountable-subgroup multi-signature schemes $\mathcal{AASM}$ is most useful for t-of-n signatures when $\binom{n}{t}$ is very large. For instance, for a 50-out-of-100 multisig wallets, the currently deployed bitcoin solution would require almost 60 times more space than our $\mathcal{ASM}$ scheme. The other schemes support threshold signatures using Merkle trees [38] as outlined in [36, Sect. 5.2], but only when $\binom{n}{t}$ is small enough to generate the tree. This method would for example be infeasible for a 50-of-100 threshold scheme.

1.4 Related Work

Multi-signatures have been studied extensively based on RSA [29,30,43,45], discrete logarithms [3,4,9,17,18,20,22,26–28,32,35,36,39,44], pairings [10,11,31, 33,47], and lattices [5]. Defending against rogue public-key attacks has always been a primary concern in the context of multi-signature schemes based on discrete-log and pairings [7,9,13,28,39,40,47], and is the main reason for the added complexity in discrete-log-based multi-signature systems. Aggregate signatures [1,13,25] are a closely related concept where signatures by different signers on different messages can be compressed together. Sequential aggregate signatures [15,24,33,34,42] are a variant where signers take turns adding their own signature onto the aggregate. The concept of public-key aggregation in addition to signature compression has not been explicitly discussed in the plain public key model until [36] and this work. This concept greatly reduces the combined length of the data needed to verify a multi-signature.

2 Preliminaries

2.1 Bilinear Groups

Let $\mathcal{G}$ be a bilinear group generator that takes as an input a security parameter κ and outputs the descriptions of multiplicative groups $(q, \mathbb{G}_1, \mathbb{G}_2, \mathbb{G}_t, e, g_1, g_2)$ where $\mathbb{G}_1$, $\mathbb{G}_2$, and $\mathbb{G}_t$ are groups of prime order q, e is an efficient, non-degenerating bilinear map $e : \mathbb{G}_1 \times \mathbb{G}_2 \rightarrow \mathbb{G}_t$, and g_1 and g_2 are generators of the groups $\mathbb{G}_1$ and $\mathbb{G}_2$, respectively.

2.2 Computational Problems

Definition 1 (Discrete Log Problem). *For a group $\mathbb{G} = \langle g \rangle$ of prime order q, we define $\mathsf{Adv}^{\mathsf{dl}}_{\mathbb{G}}$ of an adversary $\mathcal{A}$ as*

$$\Pr\left[y = g^x : y \xleftarrow{\$} \mathbb{G}, x \xleftarrow{\$} \mathcal{A}(y)\right],$$

where the probability is taken over the random choices of $\mathcal{A}$ and the random selection of y. $\mathcal{A}$ (τ, ϵ)-breaks the discrete log problem if it runs in time at most τ and has $\mathsf{Adv}^{\mathsf{dl}}_{\mathbb{G}} \geq \epsilon$. Discrete log is (τ, ϵ)-hard if no such adversary exists.

Definition 2 (Computational co-Diffie-Hellman Problem). *For a groups $\mathbb{G}_1 = \langle g_1 \rangle, \mathbb{G}_2 = \langle g_2 \rangle$ of prime order q, define $\mathsf{Adv}^{\mathsf{co\text{-}CDH}}_{\mathbb{G}_1,\mathbb{G}_2}$ of an adversary $\mathcal{A}$ as*

$$\Pr\left[y = g_1^{\alpha\beta} : (\alpha, \beta) \xleftarrow{\$} \mathbb{Z}_q^2, y \leftarrow \mathcal{A}(g_1^{\alpha}, g_1^{\beta}, g_2^{\beta})\right],$$

where the probability is taken over the random choices of $\mathcal{A}$ and the random selection of (α, β). $\mathcal{A}$ (τ, ϵ)-breaks the co-CDH *problem if it runs in time at most τ and has $\mathsf{Adv}^{\mathsf{co\text{-}CDH}}_{\mathbb{G}_1,\mathbb{G}_2} \geq \epsilon$.* co-CDH *is (τ, ϵ)-hard if no such adversary exists.*

Definition 3 (Computational ψ-co-Diffie-Hellman Problem). *For groups $\mathbb{G}_1 = \langle g_1 \rangle, \mathbb{G}_2 = \langle g_2 \rangle$ of prime order q, let $\mathcal{O}^{\psi}(\cdot)$ be an oracle that on input $g_2^x \in \mathbb{G}_2$ returns $g_1^x \in \mathbb{G}_1$. Define $\mathsf{Adv}^{\psi\text{-co-CDH}}_{\mathbb{G}_1,\mathbb{G}_2}$ of an adversary $\mathcal{A}$ as*

$$\Pr\left[y = g_1^{\alpha\beta} : (\alpha, \beta) \xleftarrow{\$} \mathbb{Z}_q^2, y \leftarrow \mathcal{A}^{\mathcal{O}^{\psi}(\cdot)}(g_1^{\alpha}, g_1^{\beta}, g_2^{\beta})\right],$$

where the probability is taken over the random choices of $\mathcal{A}$ and the random selection of (α, β). $\mathcal{A}$ (τ, ϵ)-breaks the ψ-co-CDH problem if it runs in time at most τ and has $\mathsf{Adv}^{\psi\text{-co-CDH}}_{\mathbb{G}_1,\mathbb{G}_2} \geq \epsilon$. ψ-co-CDH is (τ, ϵ)-hard if no such adversary exists.

2.3 Generalized Forking Lemma

The forking lemma of Pointcheval and Stern [46] is commonly used to prove the security of schemes based on Schnorr signatures [48] in the random-oracle model. Their lemma was later generalized to apply to a wider class of schemes [3,9]. We recall the version due to Bagherzandi, Cheon, and Jarecki [3] here.

Let $\mathcal{A}$ be an algorithm that on input *in* interacts with a random oracle $\mathsf{H} : \{0,1\}^* \rightarrow \mathbb{Z}_q$. Let $f = (\rho, h_1, \ldots, h_{q_\mathsf{H}})$ be the randomness involved in an execution of $\mathcal{A}$, where ρ is $\mathcal{A}$'s random tape, h_i is the response to $\mathcal{A}$'s i-th query to H, and q_H is its maximal number of random-oracle queries. Let Ω be the space of all such vectors f and let $f|_i = (\rho, h_1, \ldots, h_{i-1})$. We consider an execution of $\mathcal{A}$ on input *in* and randomness f, denoted $\mathcal{A}(in, f)$, as *successful* if it outputs a pair $(J, \{out_j\}_{j \in J})$, where J is a multi-set that is a non-empty subset of $\{1, \ldots, q_\mathsf{H}\}$ and $\{out_j\}_{j \in J}$ is a multi-set of side outputs. We say that $\mathcal{A}$ failed if it outputs $J = \emptyset$. Let ϵ be the probability that $\mathcal{A}(in, f)$ is successful for fresh randomness $f \xleftarrow{\$} \Omega$ and for an input $in \xleftarrow{\$} \mathsf{IG}$ generated by an input generator IG.

For a given input *in*, the generalized forking algorithm $\mathcal{GF}_\mathcal{A}$ is defined as follows:

$\mathcal{GF}_\mathcal{A}(in)$:
  $f = (\rho, h_1, \ldots, h_{q_\mathsf{H}}) \xleftarrow{\$} \Omega$
  $(J, \{out_j\}_{j \in J}) \leftarrow \mathcal{A}(in, f)$
  If $J = \emptyset$ then output `fail`
  Let $J = \{j_1, \ldots, j_n\}$ such that $j_1 \leq \ldots \leq j_n$
  For $i = 1, \ldots, n$ do
    $succ_i \leftarrow 0$; $k_i \leftarrow 0$; $k_{\max} \leftarrow 8nq_\mathsf{H}/\epsilon \cdot \ln(8n/\epsilon)$
    Repeat until $succ_i = 1$ or $k_i > k_{\max}$
      $f'' \xleftarrow{\$} \Omega$ such that $f'|_{j_i} = f|_{j_i}$
      Let $f'' = (\rho, h_1, \ldots, h_{j_i - 1}, h''_{j_i}, \ldots, h''_{q_\mathsf{H}})$
      $(J'', \{out''_j\}_{j \in J''}) \leftarrow \mathcal{A}(in, f'')$
      If $h''_{j_i} \neq h_{j_i}$ and $J'' \neq \emptyset$ and $j_i \in J''$ then
        $out'_{j_i} \leftarrow out''_{j_i}$; $succ_i \leftarrow 1$
  If $succ_i = 1$ for all $i = 1, \ldots, n$
  Then output $(J, \{out_j\}_{j \in J}, \{out'_j\}_{j \in J})$ else output `fail`

We say that $\mathcal{GF}_{\mathcal{A}}$ succeeds if it doesn't output fail. Bagherzandi et al. proved the following lemma for this forking algorithm.

Lemma 1 (Generalized Forking Lemma [3]). *Let* IG *be a randomized algorithm and* $\mathcal{A}$ *be a randomized algorithm running in time* τ *making at most* q_{H} *random-oracle queries that succeeds with probability* ϵ. *If* $q > 8nq_{\mathrm{H}}/\epsilon$, *then* $\mathcal{GF}_{\mathcal{A}}(in)$ *runs in time at most* $\tau \cdot 8n^2 q_{\mathrm{H}}/\epsilon \cdot \ln(8n/\epsilon)$ *and succeeds with probability at least* $\epsilon/8$, *where the probability is over the choice of* $in \xleftarrow{\$} \mathsf{IG}$ *and over the coins of* $\mathcal{GF}_{\mathcal{A}}$.

2.4 Multi-signatures and Aggregate Multi-signatures

We follow the definition of Bellare and Neven [9] and define a multisignature scheme as algorithms Pg, Kg, Sign, KAg, and Vf. A trusted party generates the system parameters $par \leftarrow \mathsf{Pg}$. Every signer generates a key pair $(pk, sk) \xleftarrow{\$} \mathsf{Kg}(par)$, and signers can collectively sign a message m by each calling the interactive algorithm $\mathsf{Sign}(par, \mathcal{PK}, sk, m)$, where $\mathcal{PK}$ is the set of the public keys of the signers, and sk is the signer's individual secret key. At the end of the protocol, every signer outputs a signature σ. Algorithm KAg on input a set of public keys $\mathcal{PK}$ outputs a single aggregate public key apk. A verifier can check the validity of a signature σ on message m under an aggregate public key apk by running $\mathsf{Vf}(par, apk, m, \sigma)$ which outputs 0 or 1 indicating that the signatures is invalid or valid, respectively.

A multisignature scheme should satisfy completeness, meaning that for any n, if we have $(pk_i, sk_i) \leftarrow \mathsf{Kg}(par)$ for $i = 1, \ldots, n$, and for any message m, if all signers input $\mathsf{Sign}(par, \{pk_1, \ldots, pk_n\} sk_i, m)$, then every signer will output a signature σ such that $\mathsf{Vf}(par, \mathsf{KAg}(par, \{pk_i\}_{i=1}^n), m, \sigma) = 1$. Second, a multisignature scheme should satisfy unforgeability. Unforgeability of a multisignature scheme $\mathcal{MS} = (\mathsf{Pg}, \mathsf{Kg}, \mathsf{Sign}, \mathsf{KAg}, \mathsf{Vf})$ is defined by a three-stage game.

Setup. The challenger generates the parameters $par \leftarrow \mathsf{Pg}$ and a challenge key pair $(pk^*, sk^*) \xleftarrow{\$} \mathsf{Kg}(par)$. It runs the adversary on the public key $\mathcal{A}(par, pk^*)$.

Signature queries. $\mathcal{A}$ is allowed to make signature queries on any message m for any set of signer public keys $\mathcal{PK}$ with $pk^* \in \mathcal{PK}$, meaning that it has access to oracle $\mathcal{O}^{\mathsf{Sign}(par,\cdot,sk^*,\cdot)}$ that will simulate the honest signer interacting in a signing protocol with the other signers of $\mathcal{PK}$ to sign message m. Note that $\mathcal{A}$ may make any number of such queries concurrently.

Output. Finally, the adversary outputs a multisignature forgery σ, a message m, and a set of public keys $\mathcal{PK}$. The adversary wins if $pk^* \in \mathcal{PK}$, $\mathcal{A}$ made no signing queries on m^*, and $\mathsf{Vf}(par, \mathsf{KAg}(par, \mathcal{PK}), m)\}, \sigma) = 1$.

Definition 4. *We say* $\mathcal{A}$ *is a* $(\tau, q_{\mathrm{S}}, q_{\mathrm{H}}, \epsilon)$*-forger for multisignature scheme* $\mathcal{MS} = (\mathsf{Pg}, \mathsf{Kg}, \mathsf{Sign}, \mathsf{KAg}, \mathsf{Vf})$ *if it runs in time* τ, *makes* q_{S} *signing queries, makes* q_{H} *random oracle queries, and wins the above game with probability at least* ϵ. $\mathcal{MS}$ *is* $(\tau, q_{\mathrm{S}}, q_{\mathrm{H}}, \epsilon)$*-unforgeable if no* $(\tau, q_{\mathrm{S}}, q_{\mathrm{H}}, \epsilon)$*-forger exists.*

2.5 Aggregate Multi-signatures

We now introduce aggregate multi-signatures, combining the concepts of aggregate signatures and multisignatures, allowing for multiple multisignatures to be aggregated into one. More precisely, we extend the definition of multisignatures with two algorithms. SAg takes input a set of tuples, each tuple containing an aggregate public key apk, a message m, and a multisignature σ, and outputs a single aggregate multisignature Σ. AVf takes input a set of tuples, each tuple containing an aggregate public key apk and a message m, and an aggregate multisignature Σ, and outputs 0 or 1 indicating that the aggregate multisignatures is invalid or valid, respectively. Observe that any multisignature scheme can be transformed into an aggregate multisignature scheme in a trivial manner, by implementing $\mathsf{SAg}(par, \{apk_i, m_i, \sigma_i\})$ to output $\Sigma \leftarrow (\sigma_1, \ldots, \sigma_n)$, and $\mathsf{AVf}(par, \{apk_i, m_i\}, (\sigma_1, \ldots, \sigma_n))$ to output 1 if all individual multisignatures are valid. The goal however is to have Σ much smaller than the concatenation of the individual multisignatures, and ideally of constant size.

The security of aggregate multisignatures is very similar to the security of multisignatures. First, an aggregate multisignature scheme should satisfy completeness, meaning that 1) for any n, if we have $(pk_i, sk_i) \leftarrow \mathsf{Kg}(par)$ for $i = 1, \ldots, n$, and for any message m, if all signers input $\mathsf{Sign}(par, \{pk_1, \ldots, pk_n\} sk_i, m)$, then every signer will output a signature σ such that $\mathsf{Vf}(par, \mathsf{KAg}(par, \{pk_i\}_{i=1}^n), m, \sigma) = 1$, and 2) for any set of valid multisignatures $\{(apk_i, m_i, \sigma_i)\}$ (with $\mathsf{Vf}(par, apk_i, m_i, \sigma_i) = 1$), the aggregated multisignature is also valid: $\mathsf{AVf}(par, \{apk_i, m_i\}, \mathsf{SAg}(par, \{(apk_i, m_i, \sigma_i)\})) = 1$. Second, an aggregate multisignature scheme should satisfy unforgeability. Unforgeability of an aggregate multisignature scheme $\mathcal{AMS} = (\mathsf{Pg}, \mathsf{Kg}, \mathsf{Sign}, \mathsf{KAg}, \mathsf{Vf}, \mathsf{SAg}, \mathsf{AVf})$ is defined by a three-stage game, where the setup stage and the signature queries stage are the same as in the multisignature unforgeability game. The output stage is changed as follows:

Output. Finally, the adversary halts by outputting an aggregate multisignature forgery Σ, set of aggregate public keys a message pairs $\{apk_i, m_i\}$, a set of public keys $\mathcal{PK}$, and a message m^*. The adversary wins if $pk^* \in \mathcal{PK}$, $\mathcal{A}$ made no signing queries on m^*, and $\mathsf{AVf}(par, \{(apk_i, m_i)\} \cup \{(\mathsf{KAg}(par, \mathcal{PK}), m^*)\}, \Sigma) = 1$.

Definition 5. *We say $\mathcal{A}$ is a $(\tau, q_S, q_H, \epsilon)$-forger for aggregate multisignature scheme $\mathcal{AMS} = (\mathsf{Pg}, \mathsf{Kg}, \mathsf{Sign}, \mathsf{KAg}, \mathsf{Vf}, \mathsf{SAg}, \mathsf{AVf})$ if it runs in time τ, makes q_S signing queries, makes q_H random oracle queries, and wins the above game with probability at least ϵ. $\mathcal{AMS}$ is $(\tau, q_S, q_H, \epsilon)$-unforgeable if no $(\tau, q_S, q_H, \epsilon)$-forger exists.*

3 Multi-signatures with Key Aggregation from Pairings

We begin by presenting our new pairing-based multi-signature scheme that supports public-key aggregation. Bilinear groups are typically asymmetric, in the sense that one of the two groups has a more compact representation.

The pairing-based schemes below require public keys and signatures to live in different groups. For standard signatures, a single public key is used to sign many messages, so it would make sense to use the more compact group for signatures. Because our schemes below enable aggregation of both signatures and public keys, however, this may no longer be true, and the best choice of groups may depend strongly on the concrete application. We describe our schemes below placing signatures in $\mathbb{G}_1$ and public keys in $\mathbb{G}_2$, but leave it open which of those two groups has the more compact representation. Note that efficient hash functions exist mapping into either of the groups [16,23,49].

3.1 Description of Our Pairing-Based Scheme

Our pairing-based multi-signature with public-key aggregation $\mathcal{MSP}$ is built from the BLS signature scheme [14]. The scheme is secure in the plain public key model, and assumes hash functions $\mathsf{H}_0 : \{0,1\}^* \to \mathbb{G}_1$ and $\mathsf{H}_1 : \{0,1\}^* \to \mathbb{Z}_q$.

Parameters Generation. $\mathsf{Pg}(\kappa)$ sets up bilinear group $(q, \mathbb{G}_1, \mathbb{G}_2, \mathbb{G}_t, e, g_1, g_2) \leftarrow \mathcal{G}(\kappa)$ and outputs $par \leftarrow (q, \mathbb{G}_1, \mathbb{G}_2, \mathbb{G}_t, e, g_1, g_2)$.

Key Generation. The key generation algorithm $\mathsf{Kg}(par)$ chooses $sk \xleftarrow{\$} \mathbb{Z}_q$, computes $pk \leftarrow g_2^{sk}$, and outputs (pk, sk).

Key Aggregation. $\mathsf{KAg}(\{pk_1, \ldots, pk_n\})$ outputs

$$apk \leftarrow \prod_{i=1}^{n} pk_i^{\mathsf{H}_1(pk_i, \{pk_1, \ldots, pk_n\})} .$$

Signing. Signing is a single round protocol. $\mathsf{Sign}(par, \{pk_1, \ldots, pk_n\}, sk_i, m)$ computes $s_i \leftarrow \mathsf{H}_0(m)^{a_i \cdot sk_i}$, where $a_i \leftarrow \mathsf{H}_1(pk_i, \{pk_1, \ldots, pk_n\})$. Send s_i to a designated combiner who computes the final signature as $\sigma \leftarrow \prod_{j=1}^{n} s_j$. This designated combiner can be one of the signers or it can be an external party.

Multi-signature Verification. $\mathsf{Vf}(par, apk, m, \sigma)$ outputs 1 iff

$$e(\sigma, g_2^{-1}) \cdot e(\mathsf{H}_0(m), apk) \stackrel{?}{=} 1_{\mathbb{G}_t} .$$

Batch Verification. We note that a set of b multi-signatures can be verified as a batch faster than verifying them one by one. To see how, suppose we are given triples (m_i, σ_i, apk_i) for $i = 1, \ldots, b$, where apk_i is the aggregated public-key used to verify the multi-signature σ_i on m_i. If all the messages $m_1, \ldots, m_b$ are distinct then we can use signature aggregation as in (1) to verify all these triples as a batch:

– Compute an aggregate signature $\tilde{\sigma} = \sigma_1 \cdots \sigma_b \in \mathbb{G}_1$,
– Accept all b multi-signature tuples as valid iff

$$e(\tilde{\sigma}, g_2) \stackrel{?}{=} e\big(\mathsf{H}_0(m_1), apk_1\big) \cdots e\big(\mathsf{H}_0(m_b), apk_b\big).$$

This way, verifying the b multi-signatures requires only $b+1$ pairings instead of $2b$ pairings to verify them one by one. This simple batching procedure can only be used when all the messages $m_1, \ldots, m_b$ are distinct. If some messages are repeated then batch verification can be done by first choosing random exponents $\rho_1, \ldots, \rho_b \stackrel{\$}{\leftarrow} \{1, \ldots, 2^\kappa\}$, where κ is a security parameter, computing $\tilde{\sigma} = \sigma_1^{\rho_1} \cdots \sigma_b^{\rho_b} \in \mathbb{G}_2$, and checking that

$$e(\tilde{\sigma}, g_2) \stackrel{?}{=} e\big(\mathsf{H}_0(m_1), apk_1^{\rho_1}\big) \cdots e\big(\mathsf{H}_0(m_b), apk_b^{\rho_b}\big).$$

Of course the pairings on the right hand side can be coalesced for repeated messages.

3.2 Security Proof

Theorem 1. *$\mathcal{MSP}$ is an unforgeable multisignature scheme under the computational co-Diffie-Hellman problem in the random-oracle model. More precisely, $\mathcal{MSP}$ is $(\tau, q_S, q_H, \epsilon)$-unforgeable in the random-oracle model if $q > 8q_H/\epsilon$ and if* co-CDH *is $((\tau + q_H\tau_{\mathrm{exp}_1} + q_S(\tau_{\mathrm{exp}_2^l} + \tau_{\mathrm{exp}_1}) + \tau_{\mathrm{exp}_2^l}) \cdot 8q_H^2/\epsilon \cdot \ln(8q_H/\epsilon), \epsilon/(8q_H))$-hard, where l is the maximum number of signers involved in a single multisignature, τ_{exp_1} and τ_{exp_2} denote the time required to compute exponentiations in $\mathbb{G}_1$ and $\mathbb{G}_2$ respectively, and $\tau_{\mathrm{exp}_1^i}$ and $\tau_{\mathrm{exp}_2^i}$ denote the time required to compute i-multiexponentiations in $\mathbb{G}_1$ and $\mathbb{G}_2$ respectively.*

Proof. Suppose we have a $(\tau, q_S, q_H, \epsilon)$ forger $\mathcal{F}$ against the $\mathcal{MSP}$ multisignature scheme. Then consider an input generator IG that generates random tuples $(A, B_1, B_2) = (g_1^\alpha, g_1^\beta, g_2^\beta)$ where $\alpha, \beta \stackrel{\$}{\leftarrow} \mathbb{Z}_q$, and an algorithm $\mathcal{A}$ that on input (A, B_1, B_2) and randomness $f = (\rho, h_1, \ldots, h_{q_S})$ proceeds as follows.

Algorithm $\mathcal{A}$ picks an index $k \stackrel{\$}{\leftarrow} \{1, \ldots, q_H\}$ and runs the forger $\mathcal{F}$ on input $pk^* \leftarrow B_2$ with random tape ρ. It responds to $\mathcal{F}$'s i-th H_0 query by choosing $r_i \stackrel{\$}{\leftarrow} \mathbb{Z}_q$ and returning $g_1^{r_i}$ if $i \neq k$. The k-th H_0 query is answered by returning A. We assume w.l.o.g. that $\mathcal{F}$ makes no repeated H_0 queries. $\mathcal{A}$ responds to $\mathcal{F}$'s H_1 queries as follows. We distinguish three types of H_1 queries:

1. A query on $(pk, \mathcal{PK})$ with $pk \in \mathcal{PK}$ and $pk^* \in \mathcal{PK}$, and this is the first such query with $\mathcal{PK}$.
2. A query on $(pk, \mathcal{PK})$ with $pk \in \mathcal{PK}$ and $pk^* \in \mathcal{PK}$, and and a prior query of this form with $\mathcal{PK}$ has been made.
3. Queries of any other form.

$\mathcal{A}$ handles the i-th query of type (1) by choosing a random value for $\mathsf{H}_1(pk_i, \mathcal{PK})$ for every $pk_i \neq pk^* \in \mathcal{PK}$. It fixes $\mathsf{H}_1(pk^*, \mathcal{PK})$ to h_i, and returns the

$\mathsf{H}_1(pk, \mathcal{PK})$. $\mathcal{A}$ handles a type (2) query by returning the values chosen earlier when the type (1) query for $\mathcal{PK}$ was made. $\mathcal{A}$ handles a type (3) query by simply returning a random value in $\mathbb{Z}_q$.

When $\mathcal{F}$ makes a signing query on message m, with signers $\mathcal{PK}$, $\mathcal{A}$ computes $apk \leftarrow \mathsf{KAg}(par, \mathcal{PK})$ and looks up $\mathsf{H}_0(m)$. If this is A, then $\mathcal{A}$ aborts with output $(0, \bot)$. Else, it must be of form g_1^r, and $\mathcal{A}$ can simulate the honest signer by computing $s_i \leftarrow B_1^r$. When $\mathcal{F}$ fails to output a successful forgery, then $\mathcal{A}$ outputs $(0, \bot)$. If $\mathcal{F}$ successfully outputs a forgery for a message m so that $\mathsf{H}_0(m) \neq A$), then $\mathcal{A}$ also outputs $(0, \bot)$. Otherwise, $\mathcal{F}$ has output a forgery $(\sigma, \mathcal{PK}, m)$ such that

$$e(\sigma, g_2) = e(A, \mathsf{KAg}(par, \mathcal{PK})).$$

Let j_f be the index such that $\mathsf{H}_1(pk^*, \mathcal{PK}) = h_{j_f}$, let $apk \leftarrow \mathsf{KAg}(par, \mathcal{PK})$, and let $a_j \leftarrow \mathsf{H}_1(pk_j, \mathcal{PK})$ for $\mathcal{PK} = \{pk_1, \dots, pk_n\}$. Then $\mathcal{A}$ outputs $(J = \{j_f\}, \{(\sigma, \mathcal{PK}, apk, a_1, \dots, a_n)\})$.

The running time of $\mathcal{A}$ is that of $\mathcal{F}$ plus the additional computation $\mathcal{A}$ makes. Let q_{H} denote the total hash queries $\mathcal{F}$ makes, i.e., the queries to H_0 and H_1 combined. $\mathcal{A}$ needs one exponentiation in $\mathbb{G}_1$ to answer H_0 queries, so it spends at most $q_{\mathrm{H}} \cdot \tau_{\mathrm{exp}_1}$ to answer the hash queries. For signing queries with a $\mathcal{PK}$ of size at most l, $\mathcal{A}$ computes one multi-exponentiation costing time $\tau_{\mathrm{exp}_2^l}$, and one exponentiation in $\mathbb{G}_1$ costing τ_{exp_1}, giving a total of $q_{\mathrm{S}} \cdot (\tau_{\mathrm{exp}_2^l} + \tau_{\mathrm{exp}_1})$. Finally, $\mathcal{A}$ computes the output values, which costs an additional $\tau_{\mathrm{exp}_2^l}$ to compute apk. $\mathcal{A}$'s runtime is therefore $\tau + q_{\mathrm{H}}\tau_{\mathrm{exp}_1} + q_{\mathrm{S}}(\tau_{\mathrm{exp}_2^l} + \tau_{\mathrm{exp}_1}) + \tau_{\mathrm{exp}_2^l}$. The success probability of $\mathcal{A}$ is the probability that $\mathcal{F}$ succeeds and that it guessed the hash index of $\mathcal{F}$'s forgery correctly, which happens with probability at least $1/q_{\mathrm{H}}$, making $\mathcal{A}$'s overall success probability $\epsilon_{\mathcal{A}} = \epsilon / q_{\mathrm{H}}$.

We prove the theorem by constructing an algorithm $\mathcal{B}$ that, on input a co-CDH instance $(A, B_1, B_2) \in \mathbb{G}_1 \times \mathbb{G}_1 \times \mathbb{G}_2$ and a forger $\mathcal{F}$, solves the co-CDH problem in $(\mathbb{G}_1, \mathbb{G}_2)$. Namely, $\mathcal{B}$ runs the generalized forking algorithm $\mathcal{GF}_{\mathcal{A}}$ from Lemma 1 on input (A, B_1, B_2) with the algorithm $\mathcal{A}$ described above. Observe that the co-CDH-instance is distributed indentically to the output of IG. If $\mathcal{GF}_{\mathcal{A}}$ outputs $(0, \bot)$, then $\mathcal{B}$ outputs `fail`. If $\mathcal{GF}_{\mathcal{A}}$ outputs $(\{j_f\}, \{out\}, \{out'\})$, then $\mathcal{B}$ proceeds as follows. $\mathcal{B}$ parses out as $(\sigma, \mathcal{PK}, apk, a_1, \dots, a_n)$ and out' as $(\sigma', \mathcal{PK}', apk', a'_1, \dots, a'_{n'})$. From the construction of $\mathcal{GF}_{\mathcal{A}}$, we know that out and out' were obtained from two executions of $\mathcal{A}$ with randomness f and f' such that $f|_{j_f} = f'|_{j_f}$, meaning that these executions are identical up to the j_f-th H_1 query of type (1). In particular, this means that the arguments of this query are identical, i.e., $\mathcal{PK} = \mathcal{PK}'$ and $n = n'$. If i is the index of pk^* in $\mathcal{PK}$, then again by construction of $\mathcal{GF}_{\mathcal{A}}$, we have $a_i = h_{j_f}$ and $a'_i = h'_{j_f}$, and by the forking lemma it holds that $a_i \neq a'_i$. By construction of $\mathcal{A}$, we know that $apk = \prod_{j=1}^{n} pk_j^{a_j}$ and $apk' = \prod_{j=1}^{n} pk_j^{a'_j}$. Since $\mathcal{A}$ assigned $\mathsf{H}_1(pk_j, \mathcal{PK}) \leftarrow a_j$ for all $j \neq i$ *before* the forking point, we have that $a_j = a'_j$ for $j \neq i$, and therefore that $apk/apk' = {pk^*}^{a_i - a'_i}$. We know that $\mathcal{A}$'s output satisfies $e(\sigma, g_2) = e(A, apk)$ and $e(\sigma', g_2) = e(A, apk')$, so that $e(\sigma/\sigma', g_2) = e(A, {B_2}^{a_i - a'_i})$, showing that $(\sigma/\sigma')^{1/(a_i - a'_i)}$ is a solution to the co-CDH instance.

Using Lemma 1, we know that if $q > 8q_{\mathrm{H}}/\epsilon$, then $\mathcal{B}$ runs in time at most $(\tau + q_{\mathrm{H}}\tau_{\exp_1} + q_{\mathrm{S}}(\tau_{\exp_2^l} + \tau_{\exp_1}) + \tau_{\exp_2^l}) \cdot 8q_{\mathrm{H}}^2/\epsilon \cdot \ln(8q_{\mathrm{H}}/\epsilon)$ and succeeds with probability $\epsilon' \geq \epsilon/(8q_{\mathrm{H}})$.

3.3 Aggregating Multi-signatures

It is possible to further aggregate the multi-signatures of the $\mathcal{MSP}$ scheme by multiplying them together, as long as the messages of the aggregated multi-signatures are different. The easiest way to guarantee that messages are different is by including the aggregate public key in the message to be signed, which is how we define the aggregate multisignature scheme $\mathcal{AMSP}$ here. That is, $\mathcal{AMSP}$ and $\mathcal{MSP}$ share the Pg, Kg, and KAg, algorithms, but $\mathcal{AMSP}$ has slightly modified Sign and Vf algorithms that include *apk* in the signed message, and has additional algorithms SAg and AVf to aggregate signatures and verify aggregate signatures, respectively.

Signing. $\mathsf{Sign}(par, \mathcal{PK}, sk_i, m)$ computes $s_i \leftarrow \mathsf{H}_0(apk, m)^{a_i \cdot sk_i}$, where $apk \leftarrow \mathsf{KAg}(par, \mathcal{PK})$ and $a_i \leftarrow \mathsf{H}_1(pk_i, \{pk_1, \ldots, pk_n\})$. The designated combiner collect all signatures s_i and computes the final signature $\sigma \leftarrow \prod_{j=1}^{n} s_j$.

Multi-signature Verification. $\mathsf{Vf}(par, apk, m, \sigma)$ outputs 1 if and only if $e(\sigma, g_2^{-1}) \cdot e(\mathsf{H}_0(apk, m), apk) \stackrel{?}{=} 1_{\mathbb{G}_t}$.

Signature Aggregation. $\mathsf{SAg}(par, \{(apk_i, m_i, \sigma_i)\}_{i=1}^{n})$ outputs $\Sigma \leftarrow \prod_{i=1}^{n} \sigma_i$.

Aggregate Signature Verification. $\mathsf{AVf}(\{(apk_i, m_i)\}_{i=1}^{n}, \Sigma)$ outputs 1 if and only if $e(\Sigma, g_2^{-1}) \cdot \prod_{i=1}^{n} e(\mathsf{H}_0(apk_i, m_i), apk_i) \stackrel{?}{=} 1_{\mathbb{G}_t}$.

The security proof is almost identical to that of $\mathcal{MSP}$, but now requires an isomorphism ψ between $\mathbb{G}_1$ and $\mathbb{G}_2$. We therefore prove security under the stronger ψ-co-CDH assumption, which is equivalent to co-CDH but offers this isomorphism as an oracle to the adversary.

Theorem 2. *$\mathcal{AMSP}$ is a secure aggregate multisignature scheme under the computational ψ-co-Diffie-Hellman problem in the random-oracle model. More precisely, $\mathcal{AMSP}$ is $(\tau, q_{\mathrm{S}}, q_{\mathrm{H}}, \epsilon)$-unforgeable in the random-oracle model if $q > 8q_{\mathrm{H}}/\epsilon$ and if the computational ψ-co-Diffie-Hellman problem is $((\tau + q_{\mathrm{H}}\tau_{\exp_1} + q_{\mathrm{S}}(\tau_{\exp_2^l} + \tau_{\exp_1}) + \tau_{\exp_2^l} + \tau_{\exp_1^n}) \cdot 8q_{\mathrm{H}}^2/\epsilon \cdot \ln(8q_{\mathrm{H}}/\epsilon), \epsilon/(8q_{\mathrm{H}}))$-hard, where l is the maximum number of signers involved in a single multisignature, n is the amount of multisignatures aggregated into the forgery, $\tau_{\exp_1}$ and $\tau_{\exp_2}$ denote the time required to compute exponentiations in $\mathbb{G}_1$ and $\mathbb{G}_2$ respectively, and $\tau_{\exp_1^i}$ and $\tau_{\exp_2^i}$ denote the time required to compute i-multiexponentiations in $\mathbb{G}_1$ and $\mathbb{G}_2$ respectively.*

Proof. Suppose we have a $(\tau, q_{\mathrm{S}}, q_{\mathrm{H}}, \epsilon)$ forger $\mathcal{F}$ against the $\mathcal{AMSP}$ multisignature scheme. We construct $\mathcal{A}$ exactly as in the proof of Theorem 1, except that $\mathcal{F}$ now outputs an aggregate multisignature signature forgery instead of a plain multisignature forgery. That is, $\mathcal{F}$ outputs an aggregate multisignature Σ, a set of aggregate public keys and message pairs $\{(apk_1, m_1), \ldots, (apk_n, m_n)\}$, a set of public keys $\mathcal{PK}$, and a message m^*. Let $apk^* \leftarrow \mathsf{KAg}(par, \mathcal{PK})$. If $\mathcal{A}$ correctly guessed that the k-th H_0 query is $\mathsf{H}_0(apk^*, m^*)$, then we have that

$$e(\Sigma, g_2^{-1}) \cdot e(A, apk^*) \cdot \prod_{i=1}^{n} e(\mathsf{H}_0(apk_i, m_i), apk_i) = 1_{\mathbb{G}_t}.$$

$\mathcal{A}$ looks up r_i for every (apk_i, m_i) such that $\mathsf{H}_0(apk_i, m_i) = g_1^{r_i}$. It computes $\sigma \leftarrow \Sigma \cdot \prod_{i=1}^{n} \mathcal{O}^{\psi}(apk_i^{-r_i})$, so that

$$e(\sigma, g_2) = e(y, apk^*).$$

Note that $\mathcal{A}$ has now extracted a $\mathcal{MSP}$ forgery, meaning that the rest of the reduction is exactly as in the proof of Theorem 1. The success probability of the reduction is therefore the same, and the runtime is only increased by the extra steps required to compute σ, which costs $\tau_{\mathrm{exp}_1^n}$.

4 Accountable-Subgroup Multisignatures

Micali, Ohta, and Reyzin [39] defined an accountable-subgroup multisignature scheme as a multisignature scheme where any subset S of a group of signers $\mathcal{PK}$ can create a valid multisignature that can be verified against the public keys of signers in the subset. An ASM scheme can be combined with an arbitrary access structure over $\mathcal{PK}$ to determine whether the subset S is authorized to sign on behalf of $\mathcal{PK}$. For example, requiring that $|S| \geq t$ turns the ASM scheme into a type of threshold signature scheme whereby the signature also authenticates the set of signers that participated.

Verification of an ASM scheme obviously requires a description of the set S of signers which can be described by their indices in the group $\mathcal{PK}$ using $\min(|\mathcal{PK}|, |S| \times \lceil \log_2 |\mathcal{PK}| \rceil)$ bits. We describe the first ASM scheme that, apart from the description of S, requires no data items with sizes depending on $|S|$ or $|\mathcal{PK}|$. Verification is performed based on a compact aggregate public key and signature. The aggregate public key is publicly computable from the individual signers' public keys, but we do require all members of $\mathcal{PK}$ to engage in a one-time group setup after which each signer obtains a group-specific membership key that it needs to sign messages for the group $\mathcal{PK}$.

4.1 Definition of ASM Schemes

We adapt the original syntax and security definition of ASM schemes [39] to support public-key aggregation and an interactive group setup procedure.

An ASM scheme consists of algorithms Pg, Kg, GSetup, Sign, KAg, and Vf. The common system parameters are generated as $par \xleftarrow{\$} \mathsf{Pg}$. Each signer generates a key pair $(pk, sk) \xleftarrow{\$} \mathsf{Kg}(par)$. To paricipate in a group of signers $\mathcal{PK} = \{pk_1, \ldots, pk_n\}$, each signer in $\mathcal{PK}$ runs the interactive algorithm $\mathsf{GSetup}(sk, \mathcal{PK})$ to obtain a membership key mk. We assume that each signer in

$\mathcal{PK}$ is assigned a publicly computable index $i \in \{1, \ldots, |\mathcal{PK}|\}$, e.g., the index of pk in a sorted list of $\mathcal{PK}$. Any subgroup of signers $S \subseteq \{1, \ldots, |\mathcal{PK}|\}$ of $\mathcal{PK}$ can then collectively sign a message m by each calling the interactive algorithm $\mathsf{Sign}(par, \mathcal{PK}, S, sk, mk, m)$, where mk is the signer's membership key for this group of signers, to obtain a signature σ. The key aggregation algorithm, on input the public keys of a group of signers $\mathcal{PK}$, outputs an aggregate public key apk. A signature σ is verified by running $\mathsf{Vf}(par, apk, S, m, \sigma)$ which outputs 0 or 1.

Correctness requires that for all $n > 0$, for all $S \subseteq \{1, \ldots, n\}$, and for all $m \in \{0,1\}^*$ it holds that $\mathsf{Vf}(par, apk, S, m, \sigma) = 1$ with probability one when $par \stackrel{\$}{\leftarrow} \mathsf{Pg}$, $(pk_i, sk_i) \stackrel{\$}{\leftarrow} \mathsf{Kg}(par)$, $mk_i \stackrel{\$}{\leftarrow} \mathsf{GSetup}(sk_i, \{pk_1, \ldots, pk_n\})$, and $\sigma \stackrel{\$}{\leftarrow} \mathsf{Sign}(par, \{pk_1, \ldots, pk_n\}, S, sk_i, mk_i, m)$, where GSetup is executed by all signers $1, \ldots, n$ while Sign is only executed by the members of S.

Security. Unforgeability is described by the following game.

Setup. The challenger generates $par \leftarrow \mathsf{Pg}$ and $(pk^*, sk^*) \stackrel{\$}{\leftarrow} \mathsf{Kg}(par)$, and runs the adversary $\mathcal{A}(par, pk^*)$.

Group Setup. The adversary can perform the group setup protocol $\mathsf{GSetup}(sk^*, \mathcal{PK})$ for any set of public keys $\mathcal{PK}$ so that $pk^* \in \mathcal{PK}$, where the challenger plays the role of the target signer pk^*. The challenger stores the resulting membership key $mk^*_{\mathcal{PK}}$, but doesn't hand it to $\mathcal{A}$.

Signature queries. The adversary can also engage in arbitrarily many concurrent signing protocols for any message m, for any group of signers $\mathcal{PK}$ for which $pk^* \in \mathcal{PK}$ and $mk^*_{\mathcal{PK}}$ is defined, and for any $S \subseteq \{1, \ldots, |\mathcal{PK}|\}$ so that $i \in S$, where i is the index of pk^* in $\mathcal{PK}$. The challenger runs $\mathsf{Sign}(par, \mathcal{PK}, S, sk^*, mk^*, m)$ to play the role of the i-th signer and hands the resulting signature σ to $\mathcal{A}$.

Output. The adversary outputs a set of public keys $\mathcal{PK}$, a set $S \subseteq \{1, \ldots, |\mathcal{PK}|\}$, a message m and an ASM signature σ. It wins the game if $\mathsf{Vf}(par, apk, S, m, \sigma) = 1$, where $apk \leftarrow \mathsf{KAg}(\mathcal{PK})$, $pk^* \in \mathcal{PK}$ and i is the index of pk^* in $\mathcal{PK}$, $i \in S$, and $\mathcal{A}$ never submitted m as part of a signature query.

Definition 6. *We say that $\mathcal{A}$ is a $(\tau, q_{\mathrm{G}}, q_{\mathrm{S}}, q_{\mathrm{H}}, \epsilon)$-forger for accountable-subgroup multisignature scheme $\mathcal{ASM}$ if it runs in time τ, makes q_{G} group setup queries, q_{S} signing queries, q_{H} random-oracle queries, and wins the above game with probability at least ϵ. $\mathcal{ASM}$ is $(\tau, q_{\mathrm{G}}, q_{\mathrm{S}}, q_{\mathrm{H}}, \epsilon)$-unforgeable if no $(\tau, q_{\mathrm{G}}, q_{\mathrm{S}}, q_{\mathrm{H}}, \epsilon)$-forger exists.*

4.2 Our ASM Scheme

Key generation and key aggregation in our ASM scheme are the same as for our aggregatable multi-signature scheme in the previous section. We construct an ASM scheme by letting all signers, during group setup, contribute to multi-signatures on the aggregate public key and the index of every signer, such that the i-th signer in $\mathcal{PK}$ has a "membership key" which is a multi-signature on (apk, i). On a high level, an accountable-subgroup multi-siganture now consists of the aggregation of the individual signers' signatures and their membership keys and the aggregate public key of the subroup S. To verify whether a subgroup S signed a message, one checks that the signature is a valid aggregate signature where the aggregate public key of the subgroup signed the message and the membership keys corresponding to S.

The scheme uses hash functions $\mathsf{H}_0 : \{0,1\}^* \to \mathbb{G}_1$, $\mathsf{H}_1 : \{0,1\}^* \to \mathbb{Z}_q$, and $\mathsf{H}_2 : \{0,1\}^* \to \mathbb{G}_1$. Parameter generation, key generation, and key aggregation are the same as for the aggregate multi-signature scheme in Sect. 3.

Group Setup. $\mathsf{GSetup}(sk_i, \mathcal{PK} = \{pk_1, \ldots, pk_n\})$ checks that $pk_i \in \mathcal{PK}$ and that i is the index of pk_i in $\mathcal{PK}$. Signer i computes the aggregate public key $apk \leftarrow \mathsf{KAg}(\mathcal{PK})$ as well as $a_i \leftarrow \mathsf{H}_1(pk_i, \mathcal{PK})$. It then sends $\mu_{j,i} = \mathsf{H}_2(apk, j)^{a_i \cdot sk_i}$ to signer j for $j \neq i$, or simply publishes these values. After having received $\mu_{i,j}$ from all other signers $j \neq i$, it computes $\mu_{i,i} \leftarrow \mathsf{H}_2(apk, i)^{a_i \cdot sk_i}$ and returns the membership key $mk_i \leftarrow \prod_{j=1}^{n} \mu_{i,j}$. Note that if all signers behave honestly, we have that

$$e(mk_i, g_2) = e(\mathsf{H}_2(apk, i), apk).$$

In other words, this mk_i is a valid multi-signature on the message (apk, i) by all n parties, as defined in the scheme in Sect. 3.1.

Signing. $\mathsf{Sign}(par, \mathcal{PK}, S, sk_i, mk_i, m)$ computes $apk \leftarrow \mathsf{KAg}(\mathcal{PK})$ and

$$s_i \leftarrow \mathsf{H}_0(apk, m)^{sk_i} \cdot mk_i,$$

and sends (pk_i, s_i) to a designated combiner (either one of the members of S or an external party). The combiner computes

$$PK \leftarrow \prod_{j \in S} pk_j, \qquad s \leftarrow \prod_{j \in S} s_j,$$

and outputs the multisignature $\sigma := (PK, s)$. Note that the set S does not have to be fixed at the beginning of the protocol, but can be determined as partial signatures are collected.

Verification. $\mathsf{Vf}(par, apk, S, m, \sigma)$ parses σ as (PK, s) and outputs 1 iff

$$e(\mathsf{H}_0(apk, m), PK) \cdot e(\prod_{j \in S} \mathsf{H}_2(apk, j), apk) \stackrel{?}{=} e(s, g_2)$$

and S is a set authorized to sign.

The presented ASM scheme satisfies correctness. If parties honestly execute the group setup and and signing protocols, we have $PK = g_2^{\sum_{i \in S} sk_i}$, $apk = g_2^{\sum_{i=1,\ldots,n} a_i \cdot pk_i}$, and $s = \mathsf{H}_0(apk, m)^{\sum_{i \in S} sk_i} \cdot \prod_{i \in S} \mathsf{H}_2(apk, i)^{\sum_{j \in 1,\ldots,n} a_j \cdot sk_j}$, which passes verification:

$$
\begin{aligned}
e(s, g_2) &= e\big(\mathsf{H}_0(apk, m)^{\sum_{i\in S} sk_i} \cdot \prod_{i\in S} \mathsf{H}_2(apk, i)^{\sum_{j\in 1,\ldots,n} a_j \cdot sk_j}, g_2\big) \\
&= e\big(\mathsf{H}_0(apk, m), pk\big) \cdot e\big(\prod_{i\in S} \mathsf{H}_2(apk, i), g_2^{\sum_{j\in 1,\ldots,n} a_j \cdot sk_j}\big) \\
&= e\big(\mathsf{H}_0(apk, m), pk\big) \cdot e\big(\prod_{i\in S} \mathsf{H}_2(apk, i), apk\big)
\end{aligned}
$$

4.3 Security of Our ASM Scheme

Theorem 3. *Our ASM scheme is unforgeable under the hardness of the computational ψ-co-Diffie-Hellman problem in the random-oracle model. More precisely, it is $(\tau, q_{\mathrm{S}}, q_{\mathrm{H}}, \epsilon)$-unforgeable in the random-oracle model if $q > 8q_{\mathrm{H}}/\epsilon$ and if ψ-co-CDH is (τ', ϵ')-hard for*

$$
\begin{aligned}
\tau' &= (\tau + \tau'') \cdot \frac{8q_{\mathrm{H}}^2 q}{(q - q_{\mathrm{S}} - q_{\mathrm{H}}) \cdot \epsilon} \cdot \ln \frac{8q_{\mathrm{H}} q}{(q - q_{\mathrm{S}} - q_{\mathrm{H}}) \cdot \epsilon}, \\
\tau'' &= q_{\mathrm{H}} \cdot \max\left(\tau_{\mathrm{exp}_2^l}, \tau_{\mathrm{exp}_1^2}\right) + (l q_{\mathrm{G}} + q_{\mathrm{S}}) \cdot \tau_{\mathrm{exp}_1} + q_{\mathrm{S}} \cdot \tau_{\mathrm{exp}_2^l} + 2 \cdot \tau_{\mathrm{pair}} + \tau_{\mathrm{exp}_1^3}, \\
\epsilon' &= \frac{\epsilon}{8q_{\mathrm{H}}} - \frac{q_{\mathrm{S}} + q_{\mathrm{H}}}{8q q_{\mathrm{H}}},
\end{aligned}
$$

where l is the maximum number of signers involved in any group setup, τ_{exp_1} and τ_{exp_2} denote the time required to compute exponentiations in $\mathbb{G}_1$ and $\mathbb{G}_2$ respectively, and $\tau_{\mathrm{exp}_1^i}$ and $\tau_{\mathrm{exp}_2^i}$ denote the time required to compute i-multi-exponentiations in $\mathbb{G}_1$ and $\mathbb{G}_2$ respectively, and τ_{pair} denotes the time required to compute a pairing operation.

Proof. Given a forger $\mathcal{F}$ against the ASM scheme, we construct a wrapper algorithm $\mathcal{A}$ that can be used by the generalized forking algorithm $\mathcal{GF}_{\mathcal{A}}$. We then give an adversary $\mathcal{B}$ that can solve the ψ-co-CDH problem by running $\mathcal{GF}_{\mathcal{A}}$. The proof essentially combines techniques related to the non-extractability of BGLS aggregate signatures [13,21] with Maxwell et al.'s key aggregation technique [36].

Given a forger $\mathcal{F}$, consider the following algorithm $\mathcal{A}$. On input $in = (q, \mathbb{G}_1, \mathbb{G}_2, \mathbb{G}_t, e, g_1, g_2, A = g_1^{\alpha}, B_1 = g_1^{\beta}, B_2 = g_2^{\beta})$ and randomness $f = (\rho, h_1, \ldots, h_{q_{\mathrm{H}}})$, and given access to a homomorphism oracle $\mathcal{O}^{\psi}(\cdot)$, $\mathcal{A}$ proceeds as follows. It guesses a random index $k \xleftarrow{\$} \{1, \ldots, q_{\mathrm{H}}\}$ and runs $\mathcal{F}$ on input $par \leftarrow (q, \mathbb{G}_1, \mathbb{G}_2, \mathbb{G}_t, e, g_1, g_2)$ and $pk^* \leftarrow B_2$, answering its oracle queries using initially empty lists L_0, L_2 as follows:

- $\mathsf{H}_1(x)$: If x can be parsed as $(pk, \mathcal{PK})$ and $pk^* \in \mathcal{PK}$ and $\mathcal{F}$ did not make any previous query $\mathsf{H}_1(pk', \mathcal{PK})$, then it sets $\mathsf{H}_1(pk^*, \mathcal{PK})$ to the next unused value h_i and, for all $pk \in \mathcal{PK} \setminus \{pk^*\}$, assigns a random value in $\mathbb{Z}_q$ to $\mathsf{H}_1(pk, \mathcal{PK})$. Let $apk \leftarrow \prod_{pk\in\mathcal{PK}} pk^{\mathsf{H}_1(pk,\mathcal{PK})}$ and let i be the index of pk^* in $\mathcal{PK}$. If $\mathcal{F}$ previously made any random-oracle or signing queries involving apk, then we say that event **bad** happened and $\mathcal{A}$ gives up by outputting $(0, \perp)$. If $\mathsf{H}_1(x)$ did not yet get assigned a value, then $\mathcal{A}$ assigns a random value $\mathsf{H}_1(x) \xleftarrow{\$} \mathbb{Z}_q$.

- $\mathsf{H}_2(x)$: If x can be parsed as (apk, i) such that there exist defined entries for H_1 such that $apk = \prod_{pk \in \mathcal{PK}} pk^{\mathsf{H}_1(pk,\mathcal{PK})}$, $pk^* \in \mathcal{PK}$, and i is the index of pk^* in $\mathcal{PK}$, then $\mathcal{A}$ chooses $r \stackrel{\$}{\leftarrow} \mathbb{Z}_q$, adds $((apk, i), r, 1)$ to L_2 and assigns $\mathsf{H}_2(x) \leftarrow g_1^r A^{-1/a_i}$ where $a_i = \mathsf{H}_1(pk^*, \mathcal{PK})$. If not, then $\mathcal{A}$ chooses $r \stackrel{\$}{\leftarrow} \mathbb{Z}_q$, adds $(x, r, 0)$ to L_2 and assigns $\mathsf{H}_2(x) \leftarrow g_1^r$.
- $\mathsf{H}_0(x)$: If this is $\mathcal{F}$'s k-th random-oracle query, then $\mathcal{A}$ sets $m^* \leftarrow x$, hoping that $\mathcal{F}$ will forge on message m^*. It then chooses $r \stackrel{\$}{\leftarrow} \mathbb{Z}_q$, adds $(m^*, r, 1)$ to L_0 and assigns $\mathsf{H}_0(m^*) \leftarrow g_1^r$. If this is not $\mathcal{F}$'s k-th random-oracle query, then $\mathcal{A}$ chooses $r \stackrel{\$}{\leftarrow} \mathbb{Z}_q$, adds $(x, r, 0)$ to L_0 and assigns $\mathsf{H}_0(x) \leftarrow g_1^r A$.
- $\mathsf{GSetup}(\mathcal{PK})$: If $pk^* \notin \mathcal{PK}$, then $\mathcal{A}$ ignores this query. Otherwise, it computes $apk \leftarrow \prod_{pk \in \mathcal{PK}} pk^{\mathsf{H}_1(pk,\mathcal{PK})}$, internally simulating the random-oracle queries $\mathsf{H}_1(pk, \mathcal{PK})$ if needed. It also internally simulates queries $\mathsf{H}_2(apk, j)$ for $j = 1, \ldots, |\mathcal{PK}|, j \neq i$, to create entries $((apk, j), r_j, 0) \in L_2$, as well as $a_i \leftarrow \mathsf{H}_1(pk^*, \mathcal{PK})$, where i is the index of pk^* in $\mathcal{PK}$. Since $\mathsf{H}_2(apk, j) = g_1^{r_j}$, $\mathcal{A}$ can simulate the values $\mu_{j,i} = \mathsf{H}_2(apk, j)^{a_i \cdot sk^*} = \mathsf{H}_2(apk, j)^{a_i \cdot \beta}$ for $j \neq i$ as $\mu_{j,i} \leftarrow B_1^{a_i \cdot r_j}$.
  After having received $\mu_{i,j}$ from all other signers $j \neq i$, $\mathcal{A}$ internally stores $\mu_{apk} \leftarrow \prod_{j \neq i} \mu_{i,j}$.
- $\mathsf{Sign}(\mathcal{PK}, S, m)$: If $\mathcal{F}$ did not perform group setup for $\mathcal{PK}$, then $\mathcal{A}$ ignores this query. If $m = m^*$, then $\mathcal{A}$ gives up by outputting $(0, \perp)$. Otherwise, it recomputes $apk \leftarrow \mathsf{KAg}(\mathcal{PK})$ and looks up $((apk, m), r_0, 0) \in L_0$ and $((apk, i), r_2, 1) \in L_2$, internally simulating queries $\mathsf{H}_0(apk, m)$ and $\mathsf{H}_2(apk, i)$ to create them if needed, where i is the index of pk^* in $\mathcal{PK}$. Now $\mathcal{A}$ must simulate the partial signature $s_i = \mathsf{H}_0(apk, m)^{sk^*} \cdot \mu_{apk} \cdot \mathsf{H}_2(apk, i)^{a_i \cdot sk^*}$, where $a_i = \mathsf{H}_1(pk^*, \mathcal{PK})$. From the way $\mathcal{A}$ responded to random-oracle queries, we know that $\mathsf{H}_0(apk, m) = g_1^{r_0} A = g_1^{r_0 + \alpha}$ and $\mathsf{H}_2(apk, i) = g_1^{r_2} A^{-1/a_i} = g_1^{r_2 - \alpha/a_i}$, so that $\mathcal{A}$ has to simulate $s_i = g_1^{\beta(r_0+\alpha)} \cdot \mu_{apk} \cdot g_1^{\beta(a_i r_2 - \alpha)} = \mu_{apk} \cdot g_1^{\beta(r_0 + a_i r_2)}$, which it can easily compute as $s_i \leftarrow \mu_{apk} \cdot B_1^{r_0 + a_i r_2}$.

When $\mathcal{F}$ eventually outputs its forgery $(\mathcal{PK}, S, m, \sigma)$, $\mathcal{A}$ recomputes $apk^* \leftarrow \mathsf{KAg}(\mathcal{PK}) = \prod_{j=1}^{|\mathcal{PK}|} pk_j^{a_j}$, where pk_j is the j-th public key in $\mathcal{PK}$ and $a_j = \mathsf{H}_1(apk, j)$, and checks that the forgery is valid, i.e., $\mathsf{Vf}(par, apk, S, m, \sigma) = 1$, $pk^* \in \mathcal{PK}$, $i \in S$ where i is the index of $pk^* \in \mathcal{PK}$, and $\mathcal{F}$ never made a signing query for m. If any of these checks fails, $\mathcal{A}$ outputs $(0, \perp)$. If $m \neq m^*$, then $\mathcal{A}$ also outputs $(0, \perp)$. Else, observe that $\sigma = (PK, s)$ such that

$$s = \mathsf{H}_0(apk, m^*)^{\log PK} \cdot \prod_{j \in S} \mathsf{H}_2(apk, j)^{\log apk^*}.$$

Because of how $\mathcal{A}$ simulated $\mathcal{F}$'s random-oracle queries, it can look up $((apk^*, m^*), r_0, 1) \in L_0$, $((apk^*, j), r_{2,j}, 0) \in L_2$ for $j \in S \setminus \{i\}$, and $((apk^*, i), r_{2,i}, 1) \in L_2$, where i is the index of pk^* in $\mathcal{PK}$, such that

$$\begin{aligned} \mathsf{H}_0(apk, m^*) &= g_1^{r_0} \\ \mathsf{H}_2(apk, j) &= g_1^{r_{2,j}} \text{ for } j \in S \setminus \{i\} \\ \mathsf{H}_2(apk, i) &= g_1^{r_{2,i}} A^{-1/a_i} \end{aligned}$$

so that we have that

$$s = g_1^{\log PK \cdot r_0} \cdot g_1^{\log apk^* \cdot \sum_{j \in S} r_{2,j}} \cdot A^{-\log apk^*/a_i}$$

If we let

$$t \leftarrow (\mathcal{O}^{\psi}(PK)^{r_0} \cdot \mathcal{O}^{\psi}(apk^*)^{\sum_{j \in S} r_{2,j}} \cdot s^{-1})^{a_i}$$

then we have that

$$t = A^{\log apk^*} = A^{\sum_{j=1}^{|\mathcal{PK}|} a_j \log pk_j}.$$

If I is the index such that $\mathsf{H}(pk^*, \mathcal{PK}) = h_I$, then algorithm $\mathcal{A}$ outputs $(I, (t, \mathcal{PK}, a_1, \ldots, a_n))$.

$\mathcal{A}$'s runtime is $\mathcal{F}$'s runtime plus the additional computation $\mathcal{A}$ performs. Let q_{H} denote the total hash queries $\mathcal{F}$ makes, i.e., the queries to H_0, H_1, and H_2 combined. To answer a H_1 query, $\mathcal{A}$ computes *apk* which costs at most $\tau_{\mathrm{exp}_2^l}$ for groups consisting of up to l signers. To answer H_0 and H_2 queries, $\mathcal{A}$ performs at most $\tau_{\mathrm{exp}_1^2}$. $\mathcal{A}$ therefore spends at most $q_{\mathrm{H}} \cdot \max(\tau_{\mathrm{exp}_2^l}, \tau_{\mathrm{exp}_1^2})$ answering hash queries. For every group-setup query with l signers, $\mathcal{A}$ computes *apk* costing $\tau_{\mathrm{exp}_2^l}$, and $\mathcal{A}$ computes $\mu_{j,i}$ costing $(l-1)\tau_{\mathrm{exp}_1}$, meaning $\mathcal{A}$ spends $q_{\mathrm{G}} \cdot (l-1)\tau_{\mathrm{exp}_1}$ answering group setup queries. For signing queries with a $\mathcal{PK}$ of size at most l, $\mathcal{A}$ computes *apk* costing time $\tau_{\mathrm{exp}_2^l}$, and one exponentiation in $\mathbb{G}_1$ costing τ_{exp_1}, giving a total of $q_{\mathrm{S}} \cdot (\tau_{\mathrm{exp}_2^l} + \tau_{\mathrm{exp}_1})$. Finally, $\mathcal{A}$ computes the output values, which involves verifying the forgery (costing $2\tau_{\mathrm{pair}}$) and computing t (costing $\tau_{\mathrm{exp}_1^3}$), giving $\mathcal{A}$ a total runtime of $\tau + q_{\mathrm{H}} \cdot \max(\tau_{\mathrm{exp}_2^l}, \tau_{\mathrm{exp}_1^2}) + q_{\mathrm{G}} \cdot (l-1)\tau_{\mathrm{exp}_1} + q_{\mathrm{S}} \cdot (\tau_{\mathrm{exp}_2^l} + \tau_{\mathrm{exp}_1}) + 2\tau_{\mathrm{pair}} + \tau_{\mathrm{exp}_1^3}$.

$\mathcal{A}$ is successful if the **bad** event does not happen, if it guesses the index of the forgery correctly, and if $\mathcal{F}$ successfully forges. Event **bad** happens with probability at most $(q_{\mathrm{S}} + q_{\mathrm{H}})/q$ for every hash query, so it happens with probability $q_{\mathrm{H}}(q_{\mathrm{S}} + q_{\mathrm{H}})/q$. $\mathcal{A}$ guesses the forgery index correctly with probability $1/q_{\mathrm{H}}$, and $\mathcal{F}$ forges with probability ϵ, giving $\mathcal{A}$ success probability $(1 - (q_{\mathrm{S}} + q_{\mathrm{H}})/q) \cdot \epsilon / q_{\mathrm{H}}$.

Using the generalized forking lemma from Lemma 1, we can build an algorithm $\mathcal{B}$ that solves the ψ-co-CDH problem by, on input $(A = g_1^{\alpha}, B_1 = g_1^{\beta}, B_2 = g_2^{\beta})$, running $\mathcal{GF}_{\mathcal{A}}(q, \mathbb{G}_1, \mathbb{G}_2, \mathbb{G}_t, e, g_1, g_2, A, B_1, B_2)$ to obtain two outputs $(I, (t, \mathcal{PK}, a_1, \ldots, a_n))$ and $(I, (t', \mathcal{PK}', a_1', \ldots, a_n'))$, giving $\mathcal{GF}_{\mathcal{A}}$ access to the homomorphism oracle $\mathcal{O}^{\psi}(\cdot)$ offered by ψ-co-CDH. Since the two executions of $\mathcal{A}$ are identical up to the first query $\mathsf{H}_1(pk, \mathcal{PK})$ involving the forged set of signers $\mathcal{PK}$, we have that $\mathcal{PK} = \mathcal{PK}'$. Also, from the way $\mathcal{A}$ assigns values to outputs of H_1, one can see that $a_j = a_j'$ for $j \neq i$ and $a_i \neq a_i'$, where i is the index of pk^* in $\mathcal{PK}$. We therefore have that

$$t/t' = A^{(a_i - a_i') \log pk^*} = g_1^{\alpha\beta(a_i - a_i')},$$

so that $\mathcal{B}$ can output its solution $g_1^{\alpha \cdot \beta} = (t/t')^{1/(a_i - a_i')}$.

Using Lemma 1, we know that if $q > 8q_{\mathrm{H}}/\epsilon$, then $\mathcal{B}$ runs in time at most $(\tau + q_{\mathrm{H}} \cdot \max(\tau_{\mathrm{exp}_2^l}, \tau_{\mathrm{exp}_1^2}) + q_{\mathrm{G}} \cdot (l-1)\tau_{\mathrm{exp}_1} + q_{\mathrm{S}} \cdot (\tau_{\mathrm{exp}_2^l} + \tau_{\mathrm{exp}_1}) + 2\tau_{\mathrm{pair}} + \tau_{\mathrm{exp}_1^3}) \cdot 8q_{\mathrm{H}}^2/((1 - (q_{\mathrm{S}} + q_{\mathrm{H}})/q) \cdot \epsilon) \cdot \ln(8q_{\mathrm{H}}/((1 - (q_{\mathrm{S}} + q_{\mathrm{H}})/q) \cdot \epsilon))$ and succeeds with probability $(1 - (q_{\mathrm{S}} + q_{\mathrm{H}})/q) \cdot \epsilon/(8q_{\mathrm{H}})$, proving the bounds in the theorem.

4.4 Partial Aggregation of ASM Signatures

Looking at the description of the ASM scheme above, one would expect that one can further aggregate the second components when given several such ASM signatures. The first components are needed separately for verification, though, so even though we don't obtain full aggregation to constant-size signatures, we would shave a factor two off of the total signature length.

The straightforward way to partially aggregate ASM signatures is insecure, however, because the link between membership keys and signed messages is lost. For example, an aggregate ASM signature (PK_1, PK_2, s) for a set of tuples $\{(apk, S_1, m_1), (apk, S_2, m_2)\}$ would also be a valid signature for $\{(apk, S_1, m_2), (apk, S_2, m_1)\}$, leading to easy forgery attacks.

We show that a variation on Maxwell et al.'s key aggregation technique [36] can be used to create a provably secure scheme. We define an aggregate accountable-subgroup multi-signature (AASM) scheme as an ASM scheme with two additional algorithms SAg and AVf, where SAg takes as input a set of tuples $\{(apk_i, S_i, m_i, \sigma_i)_{i=1}^n\}$ where apk_i is an aggregate public key, S_i is a set of signers, m_i is a message, and σ_i is an accountable-subgroup multi-signature, and outputs an aggregate multi-signature Σ, while AVf takes a set of tuples (apk, S, m) and an AASM signature Σ, and outputs 0 or 1 indicating that the signature is invalid or valid, respectively.

Apart from satisfying the natural correctness definition, AASM schemes must satisfy an unforgeability notion that is similar to that of ASM schemes, but where the adversary outputs a signature Σ, a set of tuples $\{(apk_i, S_i, m_i)\}$, a set of public keys $\mathcal{PK}^*$, a set of signers S^*, and a message m^*. The adversary wins if $pk^* \in \mathcal{PK}^*$, $\mathcal{A}$ made no signing queries on m^*, and $\mathsf{AVf}(par, \{(apk_i, S_i, m_i)\} \cup \{(\mathsf{KAg}(par, \mathcal{PK}^*), S^*, m^*)\}, \Sigma) = 1$.

Our $\mathcal{AASM}$ scheme uses the Pg, Kg, GSetup, Sign, KAg, and Vf algorithms of $\mathcal{ASM}$, and adds the following two algorithms as well as a hash function $\mathsf{H}_3 : \{0,1\} \rightarrow \mathbb{Z}_q$.

Signature Aggregation. $\mathsf{SAg}(par, \{(apk_i, S_i, m_i, \sigma_i)_{i=1}^n\})$ parses σ_i as (PK_i, s_i) and for $i = 1, \ldots, n$ computes

$$b_i \leftarrow \mathsf{H}_3((apk_i, S_i, m_i, PK_i), \{(apk_j, S_j, m_j, PK_j)_{j=1}^n\}).$$

It aggregates the signatures by computing $s \leftarrow \prod_{i=1}^n s_i^{b_i}$, and outputs $\Sigma \leftarrow (PK_1, \ldots, PK_n, s)$.

Aggregate Signature Verification. $\mathsf{AVf}(\{(apk_i, S_i, m_i)_{i=1}^n\}, \Sigma)$ parses Σ as $(PK_1, \ldots, PK_n, s)$, computes

$$b_i \leftarrow \mathsf{H}_3((apk_i, S_i, m_i, PK_i), \{(apk_j, S_j, m_j, PK_j)_{j=1}^n\})$$

for $i = 1, \ldots, n$, and outputs 1 if and only if

$$\prod_{i=1}^n \left(e(\mathsf{H}_0(apk_i, m_i), PK_i^{b_i}) \cdot e(\prod_{j \in S_i} \mathsf{H}_2(apk_i, j), apk_i^{b_i}) \right) \stackrel{?}{=} e(s, g_2).$$

Theorem 4. *Our $\mathcal{AASM}$ scheme is unforgeable in the random-oracle model if $\mathcal{ASM}$ is unforgeable in the random-oracle model. More precisely, it is $(\tau, q_S, q_H, \epsilon)$-unforgeable in the random-oracle model if $q > 8lq_H/\epsilon$ and $\mathcal{ASM}$ is $((\tau + \tau_{\exp_1} + O(lq_H)) \cdot 8lq_H/\epsilon \cdot \ln(8l/\epsilon), q_S, q_H, \epsilon/8l)$-unforgeable in the random-oracle model, where l is the maximum number of multi-signatures that can be aggregated and $\tau_{\exp_1}$ denotes the time required to compute an exponentiation in $\mathbb{G}_1$.*

Proof. Given a forger $\mathcal{F}$ for $\mathcal{AASM}$, we construct a forger $\mathcal{G}$ for $\mathcal{ASM}$ as follows. We first build a wrapper algorithm $\mathcal{A}$ to be used in the forking lemma, and then construct $\mathcal{G}$ based on $\mathcal{GF}_{\mathcal{A}}$. We actually use a slight variation on the forking lemma (Lemma 1) by giving $\mathcal{A}$ access to oracles. To ensure that the executions of $\mathcal{A}$ are identical up to the forking points j_i, the forking algorithm $\mathcal{GF}_{\mathcal{A}}$ remembers the oracle responses during $\mathcal{A}$'s first run, and returns the same responses in all subsequent runs up to the respective forking points j_i. One can see that the same bounds hold as in Lemma 1.

Algorithm $\mathcal{A}$, on input a target public key pk^* and $f = (\rho, h_1, \ldots, h_{q_H})$ and given access to oracles H_0, H_1, H_2, GSetup, and Sign, runs the forger $\mathcal{F}$ on input pk^* by relaying queries and responses for the mentioned oracles, and responding to H_3 queries as:

- $\mathsf{H}_3(x)$: If x can be parsed as $(y, \mathcal{APK})$ with $\mathcal{APK} = \{(apk_i, S_i, m_i, PK_i)_{i=1}^n\}$ and $\mathcal{F}$ did not make any previous query $\mathsf{H}_1(y', \mathcal{APK})$, then $\mathcal{A}$ guesses an index $i^* \xleftarrow{\$} \{1, \ldots, n\}$ and sets $\mathsf{H}_3((apk_{i^*}, S_{i^*}, m_{i^*}, PK_{i^*}), \mathcal{APK})$ to the next unused value from $h_1, \ldots, h_{q_H}$. For all other indices $j \in \{1, \ldots, n\} \setminus \{i^*\}$, it assigns $\mathsf{H}_3((apk_j, S_j, m_j, PK_j), \mathcal{APK}) \xleftarrow{\$} \mathbb{Z}_q$. If $\mathsf{H}_3(x)$ did not yet get assigned a value, then $\mathcal{A}$ assigns a random value $\mathsf{H}_3(x) \xleftarrow{\$} \mathbb{Z}_q$. Finally, $\mathcal{A}$ makes queries $\mathsf{H}_0(apk_i, m_i)$ and $\mathsf{H}_2(apk_i, j)$ for all $i = 1, \ldots, n$ and $j \in S_i$, just to fix their values at this point.

When $\mathcal{F}$ outputs a valid forgery Σ, $\{(apk_i, S_i, m_i)_{i=1}^n\}$, $\mathcal{PK}^*$, S^*, and m^*, $\mathcal{A}$ looks up in its records for H_3 to check whether $\mathsf{H}_3((apk^*, S^*, m^*, PK*), \mathcal{APK}^*)$ was the random-oracle query for which $\mathcal{A}$ returned a value from $h_1, \ldots, h_{q_H}$, where $\mathcal{APK}^* = \{(apk_i, S_i, m_i)_{i=1}^n, (apk^*, S^*, m^*)\}$ and $apk^* \leftarrow \mathsf{KAg}(\mathcal{PK}^*)$. If so, then let j_f be the index of that query and let b^* be the response to that query, and let $\mathcal{A}$ return $(\{j_f\}, \{(\mathcal{PK}^*, S^*, m^*, PK^*, s, b^*)\})$. Otherwise, $\mathcal{A}$ returns $(\emptyset, \emptyset)$. The success probability of $\mathcal{A}$ is $\epsilon_{\mathcal{A}} \geq \epsilon/l$, while its running time is $\tau_{\mathcal{A}} = \tau + O(lq_H)$.

For the forgery to be valid, it must hold that

$$s = \mathsf{H}_0(apk^*, m^*)^{b^* \log PK^*} \cdot \prod_{j \in S^*} \mathsf{H}_2(apk^*, j)^{b^* \log apk^*} \cdot \prod_{i=1}^{n} \left(\mathsf{H}_0(apk_i, m_i)^{\log PK_i} \cdot \prod_{j \in S_i} \mathsf{H}_2(apk_i, j)^{\log apk_i} \right)^{b_i}, \tag{4}$$

where $b_i = \mathsf{H}_3((apk_i, S_i, m_i, PK_i), \mathcal{APK}^*)$.

Now consider the forger $\mathcal{G}$ against $\mathcal{ASM}$ that runs $\mathcal{GF}_{\mathcal{A}}$ to obtain two outputs $(\mathcal{PK}^*, S^*, m^*, PK^*, s, b^*)$ and $(\mathcal{PK}^*, S^*, m^*, PK^*, s', b^{*\prime})$. From the way $\mathcal{A}$

simulated $\mathcal{F}$'s oracle queries, one can see that all variables and random-oracle responses in Eq. (4) are the same in both executions of $\mathcal{A}$, except that $s \neq s'$ and $b^* \neq b^{*\prime}$. By dividing both equations, we have that

$$s/s' = \mathsf{H}_0(apk^*, m^*)^{(b^*-b^{*\prime})\log PK^*} \cdot \prod_{j \in S^*} \mathsf{H}_2(apk^*, j)^{(b^*-b^{*\prime})\log apk^*},$$

so that $\mathcal{G}$ can output $\mathcal{PK}^*, S^*, m^*, \sigma = (PK^*, (s/s')^{1/(b^*-b^{*\prime})})$ as its forgery against the $\mathcal{ASM}$ scheme. The bounds stated by the theorem follow from Lemma 1.

5 A Scheme from Discrete Logarithms

The basic key aggregation technique of our pairing-based schemes is due to Maxwell et al. [36], who presented a Schnorr-based multi-signature scheme that uses the same key aggregation technique and that also saves one round of interaction in the signing protocol with respect to Bellare-Neven's scheme [9]. Unfortunately, their security proof was found to be flawed due to a problem in the simulation of the signing protocol [22]. In the following, we recover Maxwell et al.'s key aggregation technique for ordinary (i.e., non-pairing-friendly) curves by combining it with Bellare-Neven's preliminary round of hashes. The resulting scheme achieves the same space savings as Maxwell et al.'s original scheme, but is provably secure under the hardness of the discrete-logarithm assumption. Independently from our work, Maxwell et al. [37] revised their work to use the same protocol we present here.

5.1 Description of Our Discrete-Logarithm Scheme

Our discrete-logarithm based multi-signature scheme $\mathcal{MSDL}$ uses hash functions $\mathsf{H}_0, \mathsf{H}_1, \mathsf{H}_2 : \{0,1\}^* \to \mathbb{Z}_q$, which can be instantiated from a single hash function using domain separation.

Parameters Generation. $\mathsf{Pg}(\kappa)$ sets up a group $\mathbb{G}$ of order q with generator g, where q is a κ-bit prime, and output $par \leftarrow (\mathbb{G}, g, q)$.

Key Generation. The key generation algorithm $\mathsf{Kg}(par)$ chooses $sk \xleftarrow{\$} \mathbb{Z}_q$ and computes $pk \leftarrow g^{sk}$. Output (pk, sk).

Key Aggregation. $\mathsf{KAg}(\{pk_1, \ldots, pk_n\})$ outputs

$$apk \leftarrow \prod_{i=1}^{n} pk_i^{\mathsf{H}_1(pk_i, \{pk_1, \ldots, pk_n\})}.$$

Signing. Signing is an interactive three-round protocol. On input $\mathsf{Sign}(par, \{pk_1, \ldots, pk_n\}, sk, m)$, signer i behaves as follows:

Round 1. Choose $r_i \xleftarrow{\$} \mathbb{Z}_q$ and compute $R_i \leftarrow g^{r_i}$. Let $t_i \leftarrow \mathsf{H}_2(R_i)$. Send t_i to all other signers corresponding to $pk_1, \ldots, pk_n$ and wait to receive t_j from all other signers $j \neq i$.

Round 2. Send R_i to all other signers corresponding to $pk_1, \ldots, pk_n$ and wait to receive R_j from all other signers $j \neq i$. Check that $t_j = \mathsf{H}_2(R_j)$ for all $j = 1, \ldots, n$.

Round 3. Compute $apk \leftarrow \mathsf{KAg}(\{pk_1, \ldots, pk_n\})$ and let $a_i \leftarrow \mathsf{H}_1(pk_i, \{pk_1, \ldots, pk_n\})$. Note that when multiple messages are signed with the same set of signers, apk and a_i can be stored rather than recomputed.

Compute $\bar{R} \leftarrow \prod_{j=1}^{n} R_j$ and $c \leftarrow \mathsf{H}_0(\bar{R}, apk, m)$. Compute $s_i \leftarrow r_i + c \cdot sk_i \cdot a_i \bmod q$. Send s_i to all other signers and wait to receive s_j from all other signers $j \neq i$. Compute $s \leftarrow \sum_{j=1}^{n} s_j$ and output $\sigma \leftarrow (\bar{R}, s)$ as the final signature.

Verification. $\mathsf{Vf}(par, apk, m, \sigma)$ parses σ as $(\bar{R}, s) \in \mathbb{G} \times \mathbb{Z}_q$, computes $c \leftarrow \mathsf{H}_0(\bar{R}, apk, m)$ and outputs 1 iff $g^s \cdot apk^{-c} \stackrel{?}{=} \bar{R}$.

The scheme allows for more efficient batch verification, which allows a verifier to check the validity of n signatures with one $3n$-multi-exponentiation instead of n 2-multi-exponentiations. To verify that every signature in a list of n signatures $\{(apk_i, m_i, (\bar{R}_i, s_i))\}_{i=1}^{n}$ is valid, compute $c_i \leftarrow \mathsf{H}_1(\bar{R}, apk_i, m_i)$, pick $\alpha_i \xleftarrow{\$} \mathbb{Z}_q$ for $i = 1, \ldots, n$, and accept iff

$$\prod_{i=1}^{n} g^{\alpha_i s_i} apk_i^{-\alpha_i c_i} \bar{R}_i^{-\alpha_i} \stackrel{?}{=} 1_{\mathbb{G}}.$$

5.2 Security Proof

The security proof follows that of [36] by applying the forking lemma twice: once by forking on a random-oracle query $\mathsf{H}_0(\bar{R}, apk, m)$ to obtain two forgeries from which the discrete logarithm w of apk can be extracted, and then once again by forking on a query $\mathsf{H}_1(pk_i, \{pk_1, \ldots, pk_n\}$ to obtain two such pairs (apk, w) and (apk', w') from which the discrete logarithm of the target public key can be extracted.

Theorem 5. *$\mathcal{MSDL}$ is an unforgeable multisignature scheme (as defined in Definition 4) in the random-oracle model if the discrete log problem is hard. More precisely, $\mathcal{MSDL}$ is $(\tau, q_{\mathrm{S}}, q_{\mathrm{H}}, \epsilon)$-unforgeable in the random-oracle model if $q > 8q_{\mathrm{H}}/\epsilon$ and if discrete log is $((\tau + 4lq_{\mathrm{T}} \cdot \tau_{\exp} + O(lq_{\mathrm{T}})) \cdot 512q_{\mathrm{T}}^2/(\epsilon - \delta) \cdot \ln^2(64/(\epsilon - \delta)), (\epsilon - \delta)/64)$-hard, where l is the maximum number of signers involved in a single multisignature, $q_{\mathrm{T}} = q_{\mathrm{H}} + q_{\mathrm{S}} + 1$, $\delta = 4lq_{\mathrm{T}}^2/q$, and $\tau_{\exp}$ is the time required to compute an exponentiation in $\mathbb{G}$.*

Proof. We first wrap the forger $\mathcal{F}$ into an algorithm $\mathcal{A}$ that can be used in the forking lemma. We then describe an algorithm $\mathcal{B}$ that runs $\mathcal{GF}_{\mathcal{A}}$ to obtain an aggregated public key apk and its discrete logarithm w. We finally describe a discrete-logarithm algorithm $\mathcal{D}$ that applies the forking lemma again to $\mathcal{B}$ by running $\mathcal{GF}_{\mathcal{B}}$ and using its output to compute the wanted discrete logarithm.

Algorithm $\mathcal{A}$, on input $in = (y, h_{1,1}, \ldots, h_{1,q_{\mathrm{H}}})$ and randomness $f = (\rho, h_{0,1}, \ldots, h_{0,q_{\mathrm{H}}})$ runs $\mathcal{F}$ on input $pk^* = y$ and random tape ρ, responding to its queries as follows:

- $\mathsf{H}_0(\bar{R}, apk, m)$: Algorithm $\mathcal{A}$ returns the next unused value $h_{0,i}$ from its randomness f.
- $\mathsf{H}_1(pk_i, \mathcal{PK})$: If $pk^* \in \mathcal{PK}$ and $\mathcal{F}$ did not make any previous query $\mathsf{H}_1(pk', \mathcal{PK})$, then $\mathcal{A}$ sets $\mathsf{H}_1(pk^*, \mathcal{PK})$ to the next unused value $h_{1,i}$ from its input and assigns $\mathsf{H}_1(pk, \mathcal{PK}) \xleftarrow{\$} \mathbb{Z}_q$ for all $pk \in \mathcal{PK} \setminus \{pk^*\}$. Let $apk \leftarrow \prod_{pk \in \mathcal{PK}} pk^{\mathsf{H}_1(pk, \mathcal{PK})}$. If $\mathcal{F}$ already made any random-oracle or signing queries involving apk, then we say that event $\mathbf{bad}_1$ happened and $\mathcal{A}$ gives up by outputting $(0, \perp)$.
- $\mathsf{H}_2(R)$: $\mathcal{A}$ simply chooses a random value $t \xleftarrow{\$} \mathbb{Z}_q$ and assigns $\mathsf{H}_2(R) \leftarrow t$. If there exists another $R' \neq R$ such that $\mathsf{H}_2(R') = t$, or if t has already been used (either by $\mathcal{F}$ or in $\mathcal{A}$'s simulation) in the first round of a signing query, then we say that event $\mathbf{bad}_2$ happened and $\mathcal{A}$ gives up by outputting $(0, \perp)$.
- $\mathsf{Sign}(\mathcal{PK}, m)$: Algorithm $\mathcal{A}$ first computes $apk \leftarrow \mathsf{KAg}(\mathcal{PK})$, simulating internal queries to H_1 as needed. In the first round of the protocol, $\mathcal{A}$ returns a random value $t_i \xleftarrow{\$} \mathbb{Z}_q$.
  After receiving values t_j from all other signers, it looks up the corresponding values R_j such that $\mathsf{H}_2(R_j) = t_j$. If not all such values can be found, then $\mathcal{A}$ sends $R_i \xleftarrow{\$} \mathbb{G}$ to all signers; unless $\mathbf{bad}_2$ happens, the signing protocol finishes in the next round. If all values R_j are found, then $\mathcal{A}$ chooses $s_i, c \xleftarrow{\$} \mathbb{Z}_q$, simulates an internal query $a_i \leftarrow \mathsf{H}_1(pk^*, \mathcal{PK})$, computes $R_i \leftarrow g^{s_i} pk^{*-a_i \cdot c}$ and $\bar{R} \leftarrow \prod_{j=1}^{n} R_j$, assigns $\mathsf{H}_2(R_i) \leftarrow t_i$ and $\mathsf{H}_0(\bar{R}, apk, m) \leftarrow c$, and sends R_i to all signers. If the latter assignment failed because the entry was taken, we say that event $\mathbf{bad}_3$ happened and $\mathcal{A}$ gives up by outputting $(0, \perp)$. (Note that the first assignment always succeeds, unless $\mathbf{bad}_2$ occurs.)
  After it received the values R_j from all other signers, $\mathcal{A}$ sends s_i.

When $\mathcal{F}$ outputs a valid forgery $(\bar{R}, s)$ on message m for a set of signers $\mathcal{PK} = \{pk_1, \ldots, pk_n\}$, $\mathcal{A}$ computes $apk \leftarrow \mathsf{KAg}(\mathcal{PK})$, $c \leftarrow \mathsf{H}_0(\bar{R}, apk, m)$, and $a_i \leftarrow \mathsf{H}_1(pk_i, \mathcal{PK})$ for $i = 1, \ldots, n$. If j is the index such that $c = h_{0,j}$, then $\mathcal{A}$ returns $(j, (\bar{R}, c, s, apk, \mathcal{PK}, a_1, \ldots, a_n))$.

Note that $apk = \prod_{i=1}^{n} pk_i^{a_i}$ and, because the forgery is valid, $g^s = \bar{R} \cdot apk^c$. If $\mathcal{F}$ is a $(\tau, q_{\mathrm{S}}, q_{\mathrm{H}}, \epsilon)$-forger, then $\mathcal{A}$ succeeds with probability

$$
\begin{aligned}
\epsilon_{\mathcal{A}} &= \Pr[\mathcal{F} \text{ succeeds} \wedge \overline{\mathbf{bad}_1} \wedge \overline{\mathbf{bad}_2} \wedge \overline{\mathbf{bad}_3}] \\
&\geq \Pr[\mathcal{F} \text{ succeeds}] - \Pr[\mathbf{bad}_1] - \Pr[\mathbf{bad}_2] - \Pr[\mathbf{bad}_3] \\
&\geq \epsilon - \frac{q_{\mathrm{H}}(q_{\mathrm{H}} + q_{\mathrm{S}} + 1)}{q} - \left(\frac{(q_{\mathrm{H}} + q_{\mathrm{S}})^2}{2q} + \frac{l q_{\mathrm{H}} q_{\mathrm{S}}}{q} \right) - \frac{q_{\mathrm{H}}(q_{\mathrm{H}} + q_{\mathrm{S}} + 1)}{q} \\
&\geq \epsilon - \frac{4 l q_{\mathrm{T}}^2}{q} = \epsilon - \delta
\end{aligned}
$$

where $q_T = q_H + q_S + 1$ and $\delta = 4l(q_H + q_S + 1)^2/q$. The running time of $\mathcal{A}$ is $\tau_{\mathcal{A}} = \tau + 4lq_T \cdot \tau_{\exp} + O(lq_T)$.

We now construct algorithm $\mathcal{B}$ that runs the forking algorithm $\mathcal{GF}_{\mathcal{A}}$ on algorithm $\mathcal{A}$, but that itself is a wrapper algorithm around $\mathcal{GF}_{\mathcal{A}}$ that can be used in the forking lemma. Algorithm $\mathcal{B}$, on input $in = y$ and randomness $f = (\rho, h_{1,1}, \ldots, h_{1,q_H})$, runs $\mathcal{GF}_{\mathcal{A}}$ on input $in' = (y, h_{1,1}, \ldots, h_{1,q_H})$ to obtain output

$$(j,\ (\bar{R}, c, s, apk, \mathcal{PK}, a_1, \ldots, a_n),\ (\bar{R}', c', s', apk', \mathcal{PK}', a_1', \ldots, a_n')).$$

In its two executions by $\mathcal{GF}_{\mathcal{A}}$, $\mathcal{F}$'s view is identical up to the j-th H_0 query $\mathsf{H}_0(\bar{R}, apk, m)$, meaning that also the arguments of that query are identical in both executions, and hence $\bar{R} = \bar{R}'$ and $apk = apk$. From the way $\mathcal{A}$ answers $\mathcal{F}$'s H_1 queries by aborting when $\mathbf{bad}_1$ happens, the fact that $apk = apk'$ also means that $\mathcal{PK} = \mathcal{PK}'$ and that $a_i = a_i'$ for $i = 1, \ldots, n$. The forking algorithm moreover guarantees that $c \neq c'$.

By dividing the two verification equations $g^s = \bar{R} \cdot apk^c$ and $g^{s'} = \bar{R}' \cdot {apk'}^{c'} = \bar{R} \cdot apk^{c'}$, one can see that $w \leftarrow (s - s')/(c - c') \bmod q$ is the discrete logarithm of apk. If i is the index such that $\mathsf{H}_1(pk^*, \mathcal{PK}) = h_{1,i}$, then $\mathcal{B}$ outputs $(i, (w, \mathcal{PK}, a_1, \ldots, a_n))$. It does so whenever $\mathcal{GF}_{\mathcal{A}}$ is successful, which according to Lemma 1 occurs with probability $\epsilon_{\mathcal{B}}$ and running time $\tau_{\mathcal{B}}$:

$$\begin{aligned}
\epsilon_{\mathcal{B}} &\geq \frac{\epsilon_{\mathcal{A}}}{8} \geq \frac{\epsilon - \delta}{8} \\
\tau_{\mathcal{B}} &= \tau_{\mathcal{A}} \cdot 8q_H/\epsilon_{\mathcal{A}} \cdot \ln(8/\epsilon_{\mathcal{A}}) \\
&\leq (\tau + 4lq_T \cdot \tau_{\exp} + O(lq_T)) \cdot \frac{8q_T}{\epsilon - \delta} \cdot \ln \frac{8}{\epsilon - \delta}.
\end{aligned}$$

Now consider the discrete-logarithm algorithm $\mathcal{D}$ that, on input y, runs $\mathcal{GF}_{\mathcal{B}}$ on input y to obtain output $(i, (w, \mathcal{PK}, a_1, \ldots, a_n), (w, \mathcal{PK}', a_1', \ldots, a_n'))$. Both executions of $\mathcal{B}$ in $\mathcal{GF}_{\mathcal{B}}$ are identical up to the i-th H_1 query $\mathsf{H}_1(pk, \mathcal{PK})$, so we have that $\mathcal{PK} = \mathcal{PK}'$. Because $\mathcal{A}$ immediately assigns outputs of H_1 for all public keys in $\mathcal{PK}$ as soon as the first query for $\mathcal{PK}$ is made, and because it uses $h_{1,i}$ to answer $\mathsf{H}_1(pk^*, \mathcal{PK})$, we also have that $a_i = a_i'$ for $pk_i \neq pk^*$ and $a_i \neq a_i'$ for $pk_i = pk^*$. By dividing the equations $apk = \prod_{i=1}^{n} pk_i^{a_i} = g^w$ and $apk' = \prod_{i=1}^{n} pk_i^{a_i'} = g^{w'}$, one can see that $\mathcal{D}$ can compute the discrete logarithm of $pk^* = y$ as $x \leftarrow (w - w')/(a_i - a_i') \bmod q$, where i is the index such that $pk_i = pk^*$. By Lemma 1, it can do so with the following success probability $\epsilon_{\mathcal{D}}$ and running time $\tau_{\mathcal{D}}$:

$$\begin{aligned}
\epsilon_{\mathcal{D}} &\geq \frac{\epsilon_{\mathcal{B}}}{8} \geq \frac{\epsilon - \delta}{64} \\
\tau_{\mathcal{D}} &= \tau_{\mathcal{B}} \cdot 8q_H/\epsilon_{\mathcal{B}} \cdot \ln(8/\epsilon_{\mathcal{B}}) \\
&\leq (\tau + 4lq_T \cdot \tau_{\exp} + O(lq_T)) \cdot \frac{512q_T^2}{\epsilon - \delta} \cdot \ln^2 \frac{64}{\epsilon - \delta}.
\end{aligned}$$

Acknowledgments. Boneh was supported by NSF, DARPA, a grant from ONR, the Simons Foundation, and a Google faculty fellowship. Drijvers and Neven were supported by the ERC under Grant PERCY #321310.

References

1. Ahn, J.H., Green, M., Hohenberger, S.: Synchronized aggregate signatures: new definitions, constructions and applications. In: Al-Shaer, E., Keromytis, A.D., Shmatikov, V. (eds.) ACM CCS 10: 17th Conference on Computer and Communications Security, Chicago, Illinois, USA, 4–8 Oct 2010, pp. 473–484. ACM Press (2010)
2. Andresen, G.: m-of-n standard transactions. Bitcoin improvement proposal (BIP) 0011 (2011)
3. Bagherzandi, A., Cheon, J.H., Jarecki, S.: Multisignatures secure under the discrete logarithm assumption and a generalized forking lemma. In: Ning, P., Syverson, P.F., Jha, S. (eds.) ACM CCS 08: 15th Conference on Computer and Communications Security, Alexandria, Virginia, USA, 27–31 Oct 2008, pp. 449–458. ACM Press (2008)
4. Bagherzandi, A., Jarecki, S.: Multisignatures using proofs of secret key possession, as secure as the Diffie-Hellman problem. In: Ostrovsky, R., De Prisco, R., Visconti, I. (eds.) SCN 2008. LNCS, vol. 5229, pp. 218–235. Springer, Heidelberg (2008). https://doi.org/10.1007/978-3-540-85855-3_15
5. El Bansarkhani, R., Sturm, J.: An efficient lattice-based multisignature scheme with applications to bitcoins. In: Foresti, S., Persiano, G. (eds.) CANS 2016. LNCS, vol. 10052, pp. 140–155. Springer, Cham (2016). https://doi.org/10.1007/978-3-319-48965-0_9
6. Barreto, P.S.L.M., Lynn, B., Scott, M.: On the selection of pairing-friendly groups. In: Matsui, M., Zuccherato, R.J. (eds.) SAC 2003. LNCS, vol. 3006, pp. 17–25. Springer, Heidelberg (2004). https://doi.org/10.1007/978-3-540-24654-1_2
7. Bellare, M., Namprempre, C., Neven, G.: Unrestricted aggregate signatures. In: Arge, L., Cachin, C., Jurdziński, T., Tarlecki, A. (eds.) ICALP 2007. LNCS, vol. 4596, pp. 411–422. Springer, Heidelberg (2007). https://doi.org/10.1007/978-3-540-73420-8_37
8. Bellare, M., Namprempre, C., Pointcheval, D., Semanko, M.: The one-more-RSA-inversion problems and the security of Chaum's blind signature scheme. J. Cryptol. **16**(3), 185–215 (2003)
9. Bellare, M., Neven, G.: Multi-signatures in the plain public-key model and a general forking lemma. In: Juels, A., Wright, R.N., Vimercati, S. (eds.) ACM CCS 06: 13th Conference on Computer and Communications Security, Alexandria, Virginia, USA, Oct 30–Nov 3 2006, pp. 390–399. ACM Press (2006)
10. Boldyreva, A.: Threshold signatures, multisignatures and blind signatures based on the Gap-Diffie-Hellman-Group signature scheme. In: Desmedt, Y.G. (ed.) PKC 2003. LNCS, vol. 2567, pp. 31–46. Springer, Heidelberg (2003). https://doi.org/10.1007/3-540-36288-6_3
11. Boldyreva, A., Gentry, C., O'Neill, A., Yum, D.H.: Ordered multisignatures and identity-based sequential aggregate signatures, with applications to secure routing. In: Ning, P., di Vimercati, S.D.C., Syverson, P.F. (eds.) ACM CCS 07: 14th Conference on Computer and Communications Security, Alexandria, Virginia, USA, 28–31 Oct 2007, pp. 276–285. ACM Press (2007)

12. Boneh, D., Drijvers, M., Neven, G.: Compact multi-signatures for smaller blockchains. Cryptology ePrint Archive, Report 2018/483 (2018). https://eprint.iacr.org/2018/483
13. Boneh, D., Gentry, C., Lynn, B., Shacham, H.: Aggregate and verifiably encrypted signatures from bilinear maps. In: Biham, E. (ed.) EUROCRYPT 2003. LNCS, vol. 2656, pp. 416–432. Springer, Heidelberg (2003). https://doi.org/10.1007/3-540-39200-9_26
14. Boneh, D., Lynn, B., Shacham, H.: Short signatures from the Weil pairing. In: Boyd, C. (ed.) ASIACRYPT 2001. LNCS, vol. 2248, pp. 514–532. Springer, Heidelberg (2001). https://doi.org/10.1007/3-540-45682-1_30
15. Brogle, K., Goldberg, S., Reyzin, L.: Sequential aggregate signatures with lazy verification from trapdoor permutations. In: Wang, X., Sako, K. (eds.) ASIACRYPT 2012. LNCS, vol. 7658, pp. 644–662. Springer, Heidelberg (2012). https://doi.org/10.1007/978-3-642-34961-4_39
16. Budroni, A., Pintore, F.: Efficient hash maps to $\mathbb{G}_2$ on BLS curves. Cryptology ePrint Archive, Report 2017/419 (2017). http://eprint.iacr.org/2017/419
17. Burmester, M., et al.: A Structured ElGamal-type multisignature scheme. In: Imai, H., Zheng, Y. (eds.) PKC 2000. LNCS, vol. 1751, pp. 466–483. Springer, Heidelberg (2000). https://doi.org/10.1007/978-3-540-46588-1_31
18. Castelluccia, C., Jarecki, S., Kim, J., Tsudik, G.: A robust multisignature scheme with applications to acknowledgement aggregation. In: Blundo, C., Cimato, S. (eds.) SCN 2004. LNCS, vol. 3352, pp. 193–207. Springer, Heidelberg (2005). https://doi.org/10.1007/978-3-540-30598-9_14
19. Certicom Research: Sec 2: Recommended elliptic curve domain parameters. Technical report, Certicom Research (2010)
20. Chang, C.-C., Leu, J.-J., Huang, P.-C., Lee, W.-B.: A scheme for obtaining a message from the digital multisignature. In: Imai, H., Zheng, Y. (eds.) PKC 1998. LNCS, vol. 1431, pp. 154–163. Springer, Heidelberg (1998). https://doi.org/10.1007/BFb0054022
21. Coron, J.-S., Naccache, D.: Boneh *et al.*'s k-element aggregate extraction assumption is equivalent to the Diffie-Hellman assumption. In: Laih, C.-S. (ed.) ASIACRYPT 2003. LNCS, vol. 2894, pp. 392–397. Springer, Heidelberg (2003). https://doi.org/10.1007/978-3-540-40061-5_25
22. Drijvers, M., Edalatnejad, K., Ford, B., Neven, G.: On the provable security of two-round multi-signatures. Cryptology ePrint Archive, Report 2018/417 (2018). https://eprint.iacr.org/2018/417
23. Fuentes-Castañeda, L., Knapp, E., Rodríguez-Henríquez, F.: Faster hashing to $\mathbb{G}_2$. In: Miri, A., Vaudenay, S. (eds.) SAC 2011. LNCS, vol. 7118, pp. 412–430. Springer, Heidelberg (2012). https://doi.org/10.1007/978-3-642-28496-0_25
24. Gentry, C., O'Neill, A., Reyzin, L.: A unified framework for trapdoor-permutation-based sequential aggregate signatures. In: Abdalla, M., Dahab, R. (eds.) PKC 2018. LNCS, vol. 10770, pp. 34–57. Springer, Cham (2018). https://doi.org/10.1007/978-3-319-76581-5_2
25. Gentry, C., Ramzan, Z.: Identity-based aggregate signatures. In: Yung, M., Dodis, Y., Kiayias, A., Malkin, T. (eds.) PKC 2006. LNCS, vol. 3958, pp. 257–273. Springer, Heidelberg (2006). https://doi.org/10.1007/11745853_17
26. Hardjono, T., Zheng, Y.: A practical digital multisignature scheme based on discrete logarithms (extended abstract). In: Seberry, J., Zheng, Y. (eds.) AUSCRYPT 1992. LNCS, vol. 718, pp. 122–132. Springer, Heidelberg (1993). https://doi.org/10.1007/3-540-57220-1_56

27. Harn, L.: Group-oriented (t, n) threshold digital signature scheme and digital multisignature. IEE Proc.-Comput. Digit. Tech. **141**(5), 307–313 (1994)
28. Horster, P., Michels, M., Petersen, H.: Meta-multisignature schemes based on the discrete logarithm problem. Information Security — the Next Decade. IFIP AICT, pp. 128–142. Springer, Boston (1995). https://doi.org/10.1007/978-0-387-34873-5_11
29. Itakura, K., Nakamura, K.: A public-key cryptosystem suitable for digital multisignatures. Technical report, NEC Research and Development (1983)
30. Komano, Y., Ohta, K., Shimbo, A., Kawamura, S.: Formal security model of multisignatures. In: Katsikas, S.K., López, J., Backes, M., Gritzalis, S., Preneel, B. (eds.) ISC 2006. LNCS, vol. 4176, pp. 146–160. Springer, Heidelberg (2006). https://doi.org/10.1007/11836810_11
31. Le, D.-P., Bonnecaze, A., Gabillon, A.: Multisignatures as secure as the Diffie-hellman problem in the plain public-key model. In: Shacham, H., Waters, B. (eds.) Pairing 2009. LNCS, vol. 5671, pp. 35–51. Springer, Heidelberg (2009). https://doi.org/10.1007/978-3-642-03298-1_3
32. Li, C.-M., Hwang, T., Lee, N.-Y.: Threshold-multisignature schemes where suspected forgery implies traceability of adversarial shareholders. In: De Santis, A. (ed.) EUROCRYPT 1994. LNCS, vol. 950, pp. 194–204. Springer, Heidelberg (1995). https://doi.org/10.1007/BFb0053435
33. Lu, S., Ostrovsky, R., Sahai, A., Shacham, H., Waters, B.: Sequential aggregate signatures and multisignatures without random oracles. In: Vaudenay, S. (ed.) EUROCRYPT 2006. LNCS, vol. 4004, pp. 465–485. Springer, Heidelberg (2006). https://doi.org/10.1007/11761679_28
34. Lysyanskaya, A., Micali, S., Reyzin, L., Shacham, H.: Sequential aggregate signatures from trapdoor permutations. In: Cachin, C., Camenisch, J.L. (eds.) EUROCRYPT 2004. LNCS, vol. 3027, pp. 74–90. Springer, Heidelberg (2004). https://doi.org/10.1007/978-3-540-24676-3_5
35. Ma, C., Weng, J., Li, Y., Deng, R.: Efficient discrete logarithm based multi-signature scheme in the plain public key model. Des. Codes Cryptogr. **54**(2), 121–133 (2010)
36. Maxwell, G., Poelstra, A., Seurin, Y., Wuille, P.: Simple Schnorr multi-signatures with applications to bitcoin. Cryptology ePrint Archive, Report 2018/068 (2018). https://eprint.iacr.org/2018/068/20180118:124757
37. Maxwell, G., Poelstra, A., Seurin, Y., Wuille, P.: Simple Schnorr multi-signatures with applications to bitcoin. Cryptology ePrint Archive, Report 2018/068 (2018). https://eprint.iacr.org/2018/068/20180520:191909
38. Merkle, R.C.: A digital signature based on a conventional encryption function. In: Pomerance, C. (ed.) CRYPTO 1987. LNCS, vol. 293, pp. 369–378. Springer, Heidelberg (1988). https://doi.org/10.1007/3-540-48184-2_32
39. Micali, S., Ohta, K., Reyzin, L.: Accountable-subgroup multisignatures: extended abstract. In: ACM CCS 01: 8th Conference on Computer and Communications Security, Philadelphia, PA, USA, 5–8 Nov 2001, pp. 245–254. ACM Press (2001)
40. Michels, M., Horster, P.: On the risk of disruption in several multiparty signature schemes. In: Kim, K., Matsumoto, T. (eds.) ASIACRYPT 1996. LNCS, vol. 1163, pp. 334–345. Springer, Heidelberg (1996). https://doi.org/10.1007/BFb0034859
41. Nakamoto, S.: Bitcoin: a peer-to-peer electronic cash system (2008). http://bitcoin.org/bitcoin.pdf
42. Neven, G.: Efficient sequential aggregate signed data. In: Smart, N. (ed.) EUROCRYPT 2008. LNCS, vol. 4965, pp. 52–69. Springer, Heidelberg (2008). https://doi.org/10.1007/978-3-540-78967-3_4

43. Ohta, K., Okamoto, T.: A digital multisignature scheme based on the Fiat-Shamir scheme. In: Imai, H., Rivest, R.L., Matsumoto, T. (eds.) ASIACRYPT 1991. LNCS, vol. 739, pp. 139–148. Springer, Heidelberg (1993). https://doi.org/10.1007/3-540-57332-1_11
44. Ohta, K., Okamoto, T.: Multi-signature schemes secure against active insider attacks. IEICE Trans. Fundam. Electron. Commun. Comput. Sci. **82**(1), 21–31 (1999)
45. Park, S., Park, S., Kim, K., Won, D.: Two efficient RSA multisignature schemes. In: Han, Y., Okamoto, T., Qing, S. (eds.) ICICS 1997. LNCS, vol. 1334, pp. 217–222. Springer, Heidelberg (1997). https://doi.org/10.1007/BFb0028477
46. Pointcheval, D., Stern, J.: Security arguments for digital signatures and blind signatures. J. Cryptol. **13**(3), 361–396 (2000)
47. Ristenpart, T., Yilek, S.: The power of proofs-of-possession: securing multiparty signatures against rogue-key attacks. In: Naor, M. (ed.) EUROCRYPT 2007. LNCS, vol. 4515, pp. 228–245. Springer, Heidelberg (2007). https://doi.org/10.1007/978-3-540-72540-4_13
48. Schnorr, C.P.: Efficient signature generation by smart cards. J. Cryptol. **4**(3), 161–174 (1991)
49. Scott, M., Benger, N., Charlemagne, M., Dominguez Perez, L.J., Kachisa, E.J.: Fast hashing to $\mathbb{G}_2$ on pairing-friendly curves. In: Shacham, H., Waters, B. (eds.) Pairing 2009. LNCS, vol. 5671, pp. 102–113. Springer, Heidelberg (2009). https://doi.org/10.1007/978-3-642-03298-1_8

Multi-key Homomorphic Signatures Unforgeable Under Insider Corruption

Russell W. F. Lai[1,2], Raymond K. H. Tai[1], Harry W. H. Wong[1], and Sherman S. M. Chow[1](✉)

[1] Chinese University of Hong Kong, Sha Tin, Hong Kong
{raymondtai,whwong,sherman}@ie.cuhk.edu.hk

[2] Friedrich-Alexander-Uiversität Erlangen-Nürnberg, Erlangen, Germany
russell.lai@cs.fau.de

Abstract. Homomorphic signatures (HS) allows the derivation of the signature of the message-function pair (m, g), where $m = g(m_1, \ldots, m_K)$, given the signatures of each of the input messages m_k signed under the same key. Multi-key HS (M-HS) introduced by Fiore *et al.* (ASIACRYPT'16) further enhances the utility by allowing evaluation of signatures under different keys. The unforgeability of existing M-HS notions assumes that all signers are honest. We consider a setting where an arbitrary number of signers can be corrupted, called unforgeability under corruption, which is typical for natural applications (*e.g.*, verifiable multi-party computation) of M-HS. Surprisingly, there is a huge gap between M-HS (for arbitrary circuits) with and without unforgeability under corruption: While the latter can be constructed from standard lattice assumptions (ASIACRYPT'16), we show that the former likely relies on non-falsifiable assumptions. Specifically, we propose a generic construction of M-HS with unforgeability under corruption from zero-knowledge succinct non-interactive argument of knowledge (ZK-SNARK) (and other standard assumptions), and then show that such M-HS implies zero-knowledge succinct non-interactive arguments (ZK-SNARG). Our results leave open the pressing question of what level of authenticity and utility can be achieved in the presence of corrupt signers under standard assumptions.

Keywords: Homomorphic Signatures · Multi-key · Insider ZK-SNARK

1 Introduction

In a basic signature scheme, a signer can use a secret key to sign messages which are verifiable using the corresponding public key. The signatures are required to be unforgeable, meaning that no efficient adversaries can forge a valid signature

A previous version of this paper is known as "A Zoo of Homomorphic Signatures: Multi-Key and Key-Homomorphism."

T. Peyrin and S. Galbraith (Eds.): ASIACRYPT 2018, LNCS 11273, pp. 465–492, 2018.
https://doi.org/10.1007/978-3-030-03329-3_16

on any message without the secret key. This requirement, however, limits the utility of the signed messages. For example, without the secret key, one cannot derive a signature of the result of a computation over the signed messages.

Homomorphic signature (HS) schemes [39] allow a third-party evaluator to compute any functions from a class of admissible functions over signed messages (from a single signer), and derive signatures of the computation results, without knowing the secret signing keys. HS is a handy tool for applications which require computation on authenticated data. For example, it is useful when computationally inferior data producers (*e.g.*, sensors in Internet-of-Things [23]) need to outsource expensive computations to a third-party (*e.g.*, the cloud) while assuring the authenticity of the computation result.

Since homomorphic evaluation of messages and signatures is allowed, the standard unforgeability notion can no longer be satisfied. There are two common meaningful relaxations. The first one is considered for linear homomorphic signatures [11], where only linear functions are admissible. Unforgeability of linear HS requires that no adversary can derive a signature of a vector which is not a linear combination of any honestly signed vectors. This relaxation is not suitable for fully homomorphic signatures [15,37] where all polynomials/circuits are admissible, as signatures for a wide range of messages can often be derived from just a single signed message. Thus, the second approach is to have the signature not only certify the message, but also the function that is used to compute the message. Unforgeability here means that no adversary can derive a signature of a message-function pair (m, g), such that m is not a function value of g evaluated over any honestly signed messages. This work considers HS for general functionality, hence we adopt the second approach.

1.1 Multi-key Homomorphic Signatures

To further extend the utility of HS, multi-key HS (M-HS) has recently received attention [28,29]. This extension of HS allows homomorphic evaluation of signatures signed under different keys. An evaluated signature is verifiable using a combined public key, *e.g.*, the ordered tuple consisting of all public keys of the signatures being evaluated. M-HS allows multiple data producers, who do not or should not share the same key, to contribute signed data for verifiable computation. Unfortunately, existing work [28,29] only considers weaker security models (see further discussion in Sect. 2.2), which do not capture insider attacks from malicious contributors. In fact, a malicious signer in the scheme of Fiore *et al.* [29] is able to create a signature on any message-function pairs (m, g) regardless of the honest signer inputs (see Appendix A). This problem seems to be inherent in all existing lattice-based signatures with trapdoors.

For certain classes of computation such as the majority vote, if the M-HS scheme is not secure against insider attacks, it might be possible that a compromised signer can manipulate the voting result. This limits the usefulness of existing M-HS solutions since it is often unrealistic to assume that all contributors to a multi-party computation are honest. We thus see a need for a stronger notion which provides unforgeability even in the presence of corrupt signers.

1.2 Our Results

Multi-key Homomorphic Signatures Unforgeable Under Insider Corruption. In Sect. 4, we revisit the notion of *multi-key homomorphic signatures* (M-HS). M-HS is a generalization of homomorphic signatures which allows a public evaluator to apply a function g to transform signatures of different messages $(m_1, \ldots, m_K)$ each signed under possibly different public keys to a signature of $(g(m_1, \ldots, m_K), g)$ signed under a combined public key. Existing work [28,29] assumes all signers are honest when defining and analyzing unforgeability. In contrast, we define a strong security notion of M-HS called *existential unforgeability under corruption and chosen message attack (cEUF-CMA)*, where the adversary controls a set of malicious signers. A signature of (m, g) is a valid forgery if the resulting message m is not in the range of g restricted by the input of the honest signer. Interestingly, cEUF-CMA-security also makes sense in the single-key setting, where we require that even the (possibly malicious) signer itself cannot produce a signature on (m, g) where m is not in the range of g.

Relations to Existing Notions. We study how cEUF-CMA-secure M-HS is related to other notions. First, we show in Sect. 5 that such M-HS can be constructed from zero-knowledge succinct non-interactive arguments of knowledge (ZK-SNARK) together with digital signatures. There are some impossibility results regarding the security of SNARKs in the presence of (signing) oracles (O-SNARK) [30]. In particular, there exists a secure signature scheme Σ such that no candidate construction of O-SNARK satisfies proof of knowledge with respect to the signing oracle of Σ. Fortunately, there are at least two ways to circumvent this impossibility result. The first approach is to use a ZK-SNARK with a "strong" proof of knowledge property [16,30], where the extractor takes as input an additional trapdoor and does not make use of the random tape of the adversary. In other words, the extractor does not need to simulate the signing oracle. The second approach is to use an underlying signature scheme for which there exists a secure O-SNARK [30, Sect. 5]. Either way, by a recursive witness extraction technique, we show that strong ZK-SNARKs implies a "poly-depth" M-HS, and O-SNARKs yields a "constant-depth" M-HS.

Then, in Sect. 6.1, we show that succinct functional signatures (FS) [16] can be constructed from a cEUF-CMA-secure two-key M-HS (2-HS). Since the existence of succinct functional signatures implies the existence of succinct non-interactive arguments (SNARG), we obtain as a corollary that the existence of cEUF-CMA-secure 2-HS implies the existence of SNARG.

The above implication is a bit unsatisfactory as it requires a 2-HS. We thus further show in Sect. 6.2 that the existence of cEUF-CMA-secure single-key HS is sufficient to imply that of SNARG. This makes cEUF-CMA-secure (M-)HS sits nicely between SNARK and SNARG, which only differ by the existence of the knowledge extractor.

Since it is known that the security of SNARGs cannot be based on falsifiable assumptions via black-box reductions [36], it follows that the cEUF-CMA-security of M-HS must also be based on non-falsifiable assumptions or proven via non-black-box techniques. This impossibility result puts us into an unfortunate situation where, either we rely on strong assumptions for our authenticity guarantee or we settle for some weaker authenticity guarantee. It would be interesting to construct M-HS schemes which can withstand a lower but still reasonable level of corruption from standard assumptions.

Note that the above implications concern about argument systems and HS schemes for the complexity class NP. Another direction of circumventing the impossibility would be to consider restricted classes of admissible functions.

Applications. Being such a powerful primitive, cEUF-CMA-secure M-HS implies most if not all other notions of signatures [23]. This paper describes two extensions in particular, namely, (multi-key) delegatable homomorphic signatures and (multi-key) attribute-message-homomorphic signatures. As these extensions mainly introduce more complicated syntax/functionalities without too much technicality, we only briefly describe them below but omit the details.

1.3 Extensions

We introduce two extensions, *multi-key delegatable homomorphic signatures* (M-DHS) and *multi-key attribute-message-homomorphic signatures* (M-AMHS), which are immediate applications of cEUF-CMA-secure M-HS but seem not to be realizable from non-corruption-resistant M-HS. M-DHS allows a group of signers to jointly fill in data according to a template. If it is not corruption-resistant, a signer may overwrite the template entries filled out by other signers. M-AMHS allows evaluation not only on data but also on attributes, *e.g.*, the trustworthiness of the data provider. If it is not corruption-resistant, a signer may fake its attributes. Here we consider M-HS schemes which support homomorphic evaluation of labeled-data [35] (to be explained in Sect. 4.1). In a nutshell, such schemes ensure that data with "incompatible" labels cannot be used for computation.

Delegation. M-DHS can be viewed as an extension to append-only signatures (AOS) [8,40]. It is motivated by the following scenario. Suppose that multiple data producers engage in a verifiable multi-party computation. Instead of contributing independently, these data producers are organized to form groups called delegation chains. Similar to AOS, in each of these chains, the first data producer contributes a template which is passed to each of the data producers along the chain, who fills out some of the entries in the template. The last data producer in each chain then passes the completed template to a third party evaluator, who performs computation over the collection of completed templates. M-DHS is easily realizable using cEUF-CMA-secure M-HS. To delegate, the delegator simply signs the (partially-filled) template labeled by the public key of the delegatee. By the corruption resistance of the M-HS, a delegatee cannot overwrite the template entries filled out by the delegators up the delegation chain.

Attribute-Homomorphism. M-AMHS allows "attribute-homomorphism" on top of the message-homomorphism of (M-)HS. Consider our running example of verifiable multi-party computation again. M-AMHS is useful when the computation not only depends on the data contributed by the data producers, but also their attributes such as trustworthiness, accuracy, and ranks [23]. For such a scenario, it is natural to have the authorities issue certificates to the data producers. A certificate is a signature on the attribute of the data producer labeled by its public key. The data producer signs its data as in M-HS, except that the evaluator now evaluates functions over both signatures produced by the data producers and the certificates. By the corruption resistance of the M-HS, it is infeasible for a data producer to fake its attributes.

2 Related Work

2.1 Existing Homomorphic Signatures

Homomorphic signatures have undergone great development, notably from supporting only addition or multiplication [9,11,19,32,34,44] to bounded-degree polynomials [10,20], and to (leveled) fully homomorphic operations which allow evaluation of general circuits of apriori bounded depth [15,37]. Beyond unforgeability, some works also consider privacy notions such as context hiding [1,3,4].

2.2 Existing Multi-key Homomorphic Signatures

The study of HS was restricted to the single-key setting until the recent works of Fiore *et al.* [29] and Derler and Slamanig [28], who defined multi-key homomorphic signatures with varying level of security. Independent of their work, we initiate the study of multi-key HS with *unforgeability under corruption.*

Fiore *et al.* [29] proposed the notion of multi-key homomorphic authenticators, which generalizes the multi-key homomorphic version of signatures and message authentication codes (MAC). They extended the HS by Gorbunov *et al.* [37] to an M-HS based on standard lattice assumptions, and introduce multi-key homomorphic MAC based on pseudorandom functions.

While the model of Fiore *et al.* allows the adversary to corrupt signers, a forgery is valid only if it passes verification under *non-corrupt keys.* In practice, it means that if any signer involved in the computation is corrupted, the authenticity of the derived result is no longer guaranteed. Indeed, as acknowledged [29], their construction is vulnerable to insider attacks. They claimed that preventing insider attacks is impossible, by arguing that, for general functions, controlling a few inputs implies controlling the function output. We find the claim inaccurate as there is a large class of functions which may not exhibit this property, *e.g.*, functions with majority gates and threshold gates. Our work, in contrast, constructs M-HS which prevent insider attacks, at the cost of stronger assumptions, *i.e.*, the existence of SNARKs.

Another independent work by Derler and Slamanig [28] also defined M-HS, with a stronger security model than that of Fiore *et al.* [29] but weaker than ours. Specifically, it allows corruption of all but one signer, and the forgery must pass verification under a set of public keys including the non-corrupted one.

In contrast, our model allows corruption of *all* signers, whose public keys are involved in the verification of the forgery.

Derler *et al.* [27] introduced homomorphic proxy re-authenticators, in which a proxy can evaluate functions over signed data and derive a corresponding MAC under a key of the receiver. To do so, the proxy needs to use some keys derived from the secrets of the signers and the MAC key. In contrast, homomorphic evaluation and verification of M-HS can be performed publicly without any secret.

2.3 Key-Homomorphism

Key-homomorphism has been studied in the context of threshold fully homomorphic encryption [2] and pseudorandom functions [13]. The main inspiration for considering attribute-homomorphism in M-AMHS comes from the study of key-homomorphic encryption (KHE) by Boneh *et al.* [12], who formulated KHE and constructed it based on lattice assumptions. Furthermore, they used KHE to construct attribute-based encryption for general circuits with short secret keys.

Although KHE is named with the term "key-homomorphic", the "public keys" in KHE are actually attributes possibly with semantic meaning. Unlike homomorphic encryption (HE) which allows homomorphic operations on the ciphertexts with respect to the plaintexts, KHE allows homomorphic operations on the ciphertexts with respect to the attributes. As the plaintexts are private while the attributes are public, KHE and HE are inherently different. For M-AMHS, both messages and attributes are public. We thus treat attributes as messages and have the authorities sign them using M-HS.

Derler and Slamanig [28] investigate key-homomorphic signatures in the more literal setting, *i.e.*, the homomorphism is over the randomly sampled keys. Their goal is to use a milder assumption to generalize more basic primitives such as ring signatures [17,25] and universal designated-verifier signatures [24,50].

Key-homomorphism in signatures is also considered in different extents in delegatable functional signatures (DFS) [6] and the operational signature scheme (OSS) [5]. In the former, the evaluator must use its secret key to derive signatures. The verification algorithm then takes as input both the public key of the original signature as well as the public key of the evaluator. In the latter, the evaluation algorithm takes as input tuples consisting of an identity, a message, and a signature. It outputs another tuple to a targeted identity. DFS is constructed generically from trapdoor permutations, while OSS is constructed from indistinguishability obfuscation and one-way functions. They thus serve as proof-of-concept without giving much intuition of how to achieve key-homomorphism in signatures. Other related notions include policy-based signatures [7], in which a policy-dependent signing key can only sign messages satisfying the policy, and functional signatures [16], in which a functional signing key can only sign messages in the range of the specified function.

3 Preliminaries

Let $\lambda \in \mathbb{N}$ be the security parameter. Let $\mathsf{negl}(\lambda)$ be functions which are negligible in λ. $[n] = \{1, \ldots, n\}$ denotes the set of positive integers at most n where $n \in \mathbb{N}$. For an algorithm $\mathcal{A}$, $x \in \mathcal{A}(\cdot)$ denotes that x is in the output range of $\mathcal{A}$. $x \leftarrow \mathcal{A}(\cdot)$ denotes assigning the output from the execution of algorithm $\mathcal{A}$ to the variable x. For a set S, $x \leftarrow S$ denotes sampling uniformly at random an element from S and naming it x. We use $:=$ to denote the assignment operation. The empty string and the empty set are denoted by ϵ and $\emptyset$ respectively.

3.1 Succinct Non-Interactive Arguments

Definition 1 (SNARG). *A tuple of* PPT *algorithms* $\Pi = (\mathsf{Gen}, \mathsf{Prove}, \mathsf{Vf})$ *is a* succinct non-interactive argument *(SNARG) for a language* $L \in \mathsf{NP}$ *with the witness relation* $\mathcal{R}$ *if it satisfies the following:*

- ***Completeness:*** *For all* x, w *such that* $\mathcal{R}(x, w) = 1$, *and for all common reference strings* $\mathsf{crs} \in \mathsf{Gen}(1^\lambda)$, *we have* $\mathsf{Vf}(\mathsf{crs}, x, \mathsf{Prove}(\mathsf{crs}, x, w)) = 1$.
- ***Soundness:*** *For all* PPT *adversaries* $\mathcal{A}$,

$$\Pr[\mathsf{Vf}(\mathsf{crs}, x, \pi) = 1 \wedge x \notin L : \mathsf{crs} \leftarrow \mathsf{Gen}(1^\lambda); (x, \pi) \leftarrow \mathcal{A}(\mathsf{crs})] \leq \mathsf{negl}(\lambda).$$

- ***Succinctness:*** *For all* x, w *such that* $\mathcal{R}(x, w) = 1$, $\mathsf{crs} \in \mathsf{Gen}(1^\lambda)$ *and* $\pi \in \mathsf{Prove}(\mathsf{crs}, x, w)$, *there exists a universal polynomial* $p(\cdot)$ *that does not depend on the relation* $\mathcal{R}$, *such that* $|\pi| \leq O(p(\lambda))$.

Definition 2 (ZK-SNARG). *A SNARG* $\Pi = (\mathsf{Gen}, \mathsf{Prove}, \mathsf{Vf})$ *is* zero-knowledge *(ZK) if there exists a* PPT *algorithm* $\mathcal{S} = (\mathcal{S}^{\mathsf{crs}}, \mathcal{S}^{\mathsf{Prove}})$ *such that, for all* PPT *adversaries* $\mathcal{A}$, *we have*

$$|\Pr[\mathcal{A}^{\mathsf{Prove}(\mathsf{crs},\cdot,\cdot)}(\mathsf{crs}) = 1 : \mathsf{crs} \leftarrow \mathsf{Gen}(1^\lambda)] - \Pr[\mathcal{A}^{\mathcal{S}'(\mathsf{crs},\mathsf{td},\cdot,\cdot)}(\mathsf{crs}) = 1 : (\mathsf{crs}, \mathsf{td}) \leftarrow \mathcal{S}^{\mathsf{crs}}(1^\lambda)]| \leq \mathsf{negl}(\lambda)$$

where $\mathcal{S}'(\mathsf{crs}, \mathsf{td}, x, w) = \mathcal{S}^{\mathsf{Prove}}(\mathsf{crs}, \mathsf{td}, x)$.

Definition 3 (Strong SNARK [16,30]). *A SNARG* $\Pi = (\mathsf{Gen}, \mathsf{Prove}, \mathsf{Vf})$ *is a strong* succinct non-interactive argument of knowledge *(SNARK) if there exists a* PPT *algorithm* $\mathsf{E} = (\mathsf{E}^1, \mathsf{E}^2)$ *such that for all* PPT *provers* $\mathcal{A}$, *and for* every *distinguisher* $\mathcal{D}$,

$$|\Pr[\mathcal{D}(\mathsf{crs}) = 1 : \mathsf{crs} \leftarrow \mathsf{Gen}(1^\lambda)] - \Pr[\mathcal{D}(\mathsf{crs}) = 1 : (\mathsf{crs}, \mathsf{td}) \leftarrow \mathsf{E}^1(1^\lambda)]| \leq \mathsf{negl}(\lambda).$$

Furthermore,

$$|\Pr[\mathsf{Vf}(\mathsf{crs}, x, \pi) = 1 \wedge (x, w^*) \notin \mathcal{R} : (\mathsf{crs}, \mathsf{td}) \leftarrow \mathsf{E}^1(1^\lambda), (x, \pi) \leftarrow \mathcal{A}(\mathsf{crs}), w^* \leftarrow \mathsf{E}^2(\mathsf{crs}, \mathsf{td}, x, \pi)]| \leq \mathsf{negl}(\lambda)$$

where the probabilities are taken over the random coins of E. *Here, the extractor is not required to take the random tape of the adversary as part of its input.*

Definition 4 (O-SNARK [30]**).** *A SNARG* $\Pi = (\mathsf{Gen}, \mathsf{Prove}, \mathsf{Vf})$ *is a* succinct non-interactive argument of knowledge in the presence of oracles for $\mathbb{O}$ *(O-SNARK) for the oracle family* $\mathbb{O}$ *if for all* PPT *provers* $\mathcal{A}$, *there exists a* PPT *algorithm* $\mathsf{E}_{\mathcal{A}}$ *such that*

$$|\Pr[\mathsf{Vf}(\mathsf{crs}, x, \pi) = 1 \wedge (x, w^*) \notin \mathcal{R} : \mathsf{crs} \leftarrow \mathsf{Gen}(1^\lambda),$$
$$\mathcal{O} \leftarrow \mathbb{O}; (x, \pi) \leftarrow \mathcal{A}^{\mathcal{O}}(\mathsf{crs}), w^* \leftarrow E_{\mathcal{A}}(\mathsf{crs}, \mathsf{qt})]| \leq \mathsf{negl}(\lambda)$$

where $\mathsf{qt} = \{q_i, \mathcal{O}(q_i)\}$ *is the transcript of all oracle queries and answers made and received by* $\mathcal{A}$ *during its execution.*

3.2 Signatures

Definition 5 (Digital Signatures). *A signature scheme for a message space* $\mathcal{M}$ *is a tuple of* PPT *algorithms* $\mathcal{DS}.(\mathsf{KGen}, \mathsf{Sig}, \mathsf{Vf})$ *defined as follows:*

- $(\mathsf{pk}, \mathsf{sk}) \leftarrow \mathsf{KGen}(1^\lambda)$: *The key generation algorithm takes as input the security parameter* λ *and generates a key pair* $(\mathsf{pk}, \mathsf{sk})$.
- $\sigma \leftarrow \mathsf{Sig}(\mathsf{sk}, m)$: *The signing algorithm takes as input a secret key* sk *and a message* $m \in \mathcal{M}$. *It outputs a signature* σ.
- $b \leftarrow \mathsf{Vf}(\mathsf{pk}, m, \sigma)$: *The verification algorithm takes as input a public key* pk, *a message* m, *and a signature* σ. *It outputs a bit* b.

Correctness. The scheme is correct if, for all $\lambda \in \mathbb{N}$, *all key pairs* $(\mathsf{pk}, \mathsf{sk}) \in \mathsf{KGen}(1^\lambda)$, *all messages* $m \in \mathcal{M}$, *and all signatures* $\sigma \in \mathsf{Sig}(\mathsf{sk}, m)$, *it holds that* $\mathsf{Vf}(\mathsf{pk}, m, \sigma) = 1$.

Definition 6 (Existential Unforgeability). *A signature scheme* $\mathcal{DS}$ *is* existentially unforgeable under chosen message attacks (EUF-CMA-secure) *if,*

$$\Pr[\mathsf{EUF\text{-}CMA}_{\mathcal{DS},\mathcal{A}}(1^\lambda) = 1] \leq \mathsf{negl}(\lambda)$$

for all PPT *adversaries* $\mathcal{A}$, *where the experiment* $\mathsf{EUF\text{-}CMA}_{\mathcal{DS},\mathcal{A}}$ *is as follows:*

- *The challenger* $\mathcal{C}$ *generates* $(\mathsf{pk}, \mathsf{sk}) \leftarrow \mathsf{KGen}(1^\lambda)$ *and gives* pk *to* $\mathcal{A}$.
- *The adversary* $\mathcal{A}$ *is given access to a signing oracle* $\mathcal{O}_{\mathsf{Sig}}(\mathsf{sk}, \cdot)$.
- *Eventually,* $\mathcal{A}$ *outputs a forgery* (m^*, σ^*).
- *If the signing oracle was not queried on* m^*, *the experiment outputs* $\mathsf{Vf}(\mathsf{pk}, m^*, \sigma^*)$. *Otherwise, the experiment outputs* 0.

3.3 Functional Signatures

Definition 7 (Functional Signatures [16]**).** *A functional signature (FS) scheme for a message space* $\mathcal{M}$ *and a function family* $\mathcal{F} = \{f : \mathcal{D}_f \rightarrow \mathcal{M}\}$ *consists of algorithms* $\mathcal{FS}.(\mathsf{Setup}, \mathsf{KGen}, \mathsf{Sig}, \mathsf{Vf})$.

- $(\mathsf{mpk}, \mathsf{msk}) \leftarrow \mathcal{FS}.\mathsf{Setup}(1^\lambda)$: *This algorithm takes in the security parameter* λ. *It outputs the master public key* mpk *and the master secret key* msk.

- $\mathsf{sk}_f \leftarrow \mathcal{FS}.\mathsf{KGen}(\mathsf{msk}, f)$: *This algorithm takes as input the master secret key* msk *and a function* $f \in \mathcal{F}$. *It outputs a secret key* sk_f *for* f.
- $(f(m), \sigma) \leftarrow \mathcal{FS}.\mathsf{Sig}(f, \mathsf{sk}_f, m)$: *This algorithm takes as input a function* $f \in \mathcal{F}$, *the secret key* sk_f *for the function* f, *and a message* $m \in \mathcal{D}_f$. *It outputs* $f(m)$ *and a signature of* $f(m)$.
- $b \leftarrow \mathcal{FS}.\mathsf{Vf}(\mathsf{mpk}, m, \sigma)$: *This algorithm takes as input the master public key* mpk, *a message* m, *and a signature* σ. *It outputs* 1 *for a valid signature.*

Correctness. We require that a signature signed under an honestly generated secret key to be valid. Formally, for any $\lambda \in \mathbb{N}$, *any* $(\mathsf{mpk}, \mathsf{msk}) \in \mathcal{FS}.\mathsf{Setup}(1^\lambda)$, *any* $f \in \mathcal{F}$, *any* $\mathsf{sk}_f \in \mathcal{FS}.\mathsf{KGen}(\mathsf{msk}, f)$, *any* $m \in \mathcal{D}_f$, *if* $(m^*, \sigma) \leftarrow \mathcal{FS}.\mathsf{Sig}(f, \mathsf{sk}_f, m)$, *then* $\mathcal{FS}.\mathsf{Vf}(\mathsf{mpk}, m^*, \sigma) = 1$.

With a secret key of a function, one can only produce new signatures on the range of that function.

Definition 8 (Unforgeability). *An FS scheme* $\mathcal{FS}$ *is unforgeable if for any* PPT *adversary* $\mathcal{A}$ *the probability that it wins in the following game is negligible:*

- *The challenger generates* $(\mathsf{mpk}, \mathsf{msk}) \leftarrow \mathcal{FS}.\mathsf{Setup}(1^\lambda)$, *and gives* mpk *to* $\mathcal{A}$.
- $\mathcal{A}$ *is allowed to query a key generation oracle* $\mathcal{O}_{\mathsf{key}}$ *and a signing oracle* $\mathcal{O}_{\mathsf{sign}}$ *defined as follows. These oracles share a dictionary indexed by tuples* $(f, i) \in \mathcal{F} \times \mathbb{N}$, *whose entries are signing keys:* $\mathsf{sk}_f \leftarrow \mathcal{FS}.\mathsf{KGen}(\mathsf{msk}, f)$. *This dictionary keeps track of the keys that have been previously generated.*
  - $\mathcal{O}_{\mathsf{key}}(f, i)$
    - *If there exists an entry for the key* (f, i) *in the dictionary, output the corresponding value* sk^i_f.
    - *Otherwise, sample a fresh key* $\mathsf{sk}^i_f \leftarrow \mathcal{FS}.\mathsf{KGen}(\mathsf{msk}, f)$, *then add an entry* $(f, i) \rightarrow \mathsf{sk}^i_f$ *to the dictionary and output* sk^i_f.
  - $\mathcal{O}_{\mathsf{sign}}(f, i, m)$
    - *If there exists an entry for the key* (f, i) *in the dictionary, output* $\sigma \leftarrow \mathcal{FS}.\mathsf{Sig}(f, \mathsf{sk}^i_f, m)$.
    - *Otherwise, sample a fresh key* $\mathsf{sk}^i_f \leftarrow \mathcal{FS}.\mathsf{KGen}(\mathsf{msk}, f)$, *then add it to the entry* (f, i) *of the dictionary, and output* $\sigma \leftarrow \mathcal{FS}.\mathsf{Sig}(f, \mathsf{sk}^i_f, m)$.
- $\mathcal{A}$ *wins if it can produce* (m^*, σ) *such that:*
  - $\mathcal{FS}.\mathsf{Vf}(\mathsf{mpk}, m^*, \sigma) = 1$;
  - *There does not exist* m *such that* $m^* = f(m)$ *for any* f *which was sent as a query to the* $\mathcal{O}_{\mathsf{key}}$ *oracle;*
  - *There does not exist a query* (f, m) *to* $\mathcal{O}_{\mathsf{sign}}$ *where* $m^* = f(m)$.

We require the signatures on a message generated by different secret keys to be indistinguishable even if the master signing key and the secret keys are given.

Definition 9 (Function-Privacy). *An FS scheme $\mathcal{FS}$ is function-private if for any* PPT *adversary $\mathcal{A}$ the probability that it wins in the following game is negligible:*

- *The challenger honestly generates* $(\mathsf{mpk}, \mathsf{msk}) \leftarrow \mathcal{FS}.\mathsf{Setup}(1^\lambda)$*, and gives* mpk *and* msk *(w.l.o.g. this includes the randomness used in* Setup*) to* $\mathcal{A}$*.*
- *$\mathcal{A}$ chooses a function f_0 and receives an honestly generated secret key* $\mathsf{sk}_{f_0} \leftarrow \mathcal{FS}.\mathsf{KGen}(\mathsf{msk}, f_0)$.
- *$\mathcal{A}$ chooses a second function f_1 for which $|f_0| = |f_1|$ (where padding can be useful if there is a known upper bound) and receives an honestly generated secret key* $\mathsf{sk}_{f_1} \leftarrow \mathcal{FS}.\mathsf{KGen}(\mathsf{msk}, f_1)$.
- *$\mathcal{A}$ chooses a pair of values m_0, m_1 s.t. $|m_0| = |m_1|$ and $f_0(m_0) = f_1(m_1)$.*
- *The challenger selects a random bit $b \leftarrow \{0,1\}$ and generates a signature on the image message $m' = f_0(m_0) = f_1(m_1)$ using secret key* sk_{f_b}*, and gives the resulting signature* $\sigma \leftarrow \mathcal{FS}.\mathsf{Sig}(f, \mathsf{sk}_{f_b}, m_b)$ *to* $\mathcal{A}$*.*
- *$\mathcal{A}$ outputs a bit b', and wins the game if $b' = b$.*

We require the signature size to be independent of the size $|m|$ of the input to the function, and the description size $|f|$ of the function f.

Definition 10 (Succinctness). *An FS scheme $\mathcal{FS}$ is succinct, if there exists a polynomial $s(\cdot)$ such that for every $\lambda \in \mathbb{N}$, $f \in \mathcal{F}$, $m \in \mathcal{D}_f$,* $(\mathsf{mpk}, \mathsf{msk}) \in \mathcal{FS}.\mathsf{Setup}(1^\lambda)$, $\mathsf{sk}_f \in \mathcal{FS}.\mathsf{KGen}(\mathsf{msk}, f)$, $(f(m), \sigma) \in \mathcal{FS}.\mathsf{Sig}(f, \mathsf{sk}_f, m)$*, it holds that the signature σ on $f(m)$ has size $|\sigma| \leq O(s(\lambda))$.*

4 Insider-Secure Multi-key Homomorphic Signatures

Our aim is to define and construct multi-key homomorphic signatures (M-HS) which is unforgeable under insider corruption and study its relation to existing notions. M-HS allows an arbitrary number of signers to generate keys and sign messages independently. In a simplified setting where messages are not labeled, suppose that each signer k signs a message m_k using its secret key sk_k, resulting in a set of signatures $\{\sigma_k\}$. An evaluator can then publicly evaluate a function g over the message-signature pairs (m_k, σ_k) to derive a signature of (m, g) where $m = g(m_1, \ldots, m_K)$. Syntactically, M-HS generalizes the normal homomorphic signatures (HS) since it reduces to HS when all the signatures are generated by the same secret key.

In the multi-signer setting, we must carefully analyze unforgeability when the adversary can corrupt some signers or even maliciously generate some key pairs. Such an insider attack is unnatural in HS since there is only one signer and hence one signing key involved with a signature. We formulate the unforgeability against insider corruption, which requires that such group of corrupt signers cannot produce signatures of (m, g), where the message m is outside the range of the function g restricted by the inputs of the non-corrupt signers. Security against insider attack is especially useful when the output of the function cannot be fully controlled by a few inputs, *e.g.*, functions with majority and threshold gates. To illustrate the meaning of a forgery, consider the following configuration: Let $g(m_1, \ldots, m_K) = \prod_{k=1}^{K} m_k$ be the product function and $m_k \in R$ for some ring R. As long as $m_k = 0$ for some non-corrupt signer k, the adversary should not be able to produce a signature of (m, g) where $m \neq 0$.

Interestingly, this requirement actually still makes sense even when there is only one signer who is also the adversary. In this case, unforgeability against insider corruption implies that even the only signer cannot produce a signature of (m, g) if there does not exist m' such that $m = g(m')$. Furthermore, if the signature scheme is context hiding, meaning that the signature of (m, g) reveals nothing more than the tuple (m, g) itself, then it can be regarded as an adaptive zero-knowledge succinct non-interactive argument (ZK-SNARG) of the NP language $\{(m, g) : \exists m' \text{ s.t. } m = g(m')\}$ as long as g is efficiently computable.

4.1 Notation

Labeled programs are (implicitly) used in various homomorphic signature schemes in which each message is signed under a label ℓ. A labeled program $\mathcal{P}$ consists of a function f and the input labels of the input to f. Formally, for a message space $\mathcal{M}$, a labeled program $\mathcal{P} = (f, \ell_1, \ldots, \ell_k)$ consists of a function $f : \mathcal{M}^k \rightarrow \mathcal{M}$ for some $k \in \mathbb{N}$, and a set of input labels $\ell_1, \ldots, \ell_k$, where ℓ_i is a label for the i-th input of f. An *identity program* $\mathcal{I}_\ell = (f_{id}, \ell)$ is defined as a labeled program with an identity function $f_{id} : \mathcal{M} \rightarrow \mathcal{M}$ and an input label ℓ.

Let $\mathcal{P}_i = (f_i, \ell_{i,1}, \ldots, \ell_{i,k_i})$ be some programs for $i \in [n]$ for some $n \in \mathbb{N}$. A *composed program* $\mathcal{P}^* = g(\mathcal{P}_1, \ldots, \mathcal{P}_n) = (g(f_1, \ldots, f_n), \ell_1, \ldots, \ell_{k^*})$ can be constructed by evaluating a function $g : \mathcal{M}^n \rightarrow \mathcal{M}$ on the outputs of a set of labeled programs $\mathcal{P}_1, \ldots, \mathcal{P}_n$. For such a composed program $\mathcal{P}^*$, we consider its labeled inputs $(\ell_1, \ldots, \ell_{k^*})$ only consist of all *distinct labeled inputs* of $\mathcal{P}_1, \ldots, \mathcal{P}_n$, where inputs with the same label are converted to a single input. In particular, a labeled program $\mathcal{P} = (f, \ell_1, \ldots, \ell_k)$ can be expressed as the composition of k identity programs $\mathcal{P} = f(\mathcal{I}_{\ell_1}, \ldots, \mathcal{I}_{\ell_k})$.

Following [29], we assume every user has an identity $\mathsf{id} \in \mathcal{ID}$ for some identity space $\mathcal{ID}$, and their keys are associated to id. To identify users in the multi-key setting using labeled programs, we associate a message to a label $\ell = (\mathsf{id}, \tau)$, where $\tau \in \mathcal{T}$ is a tag in some tag space $\mathcal{T}$.

For a labeled program $\mathcal{P} = (f, \ell_1, \ldots, \ell_n)$ with labels $\ell_i = (\mathsf{id}_i, \tau_i)$, we use $\mathsf{id} \in \mathcal{P}$ as a *compact notation for* $\mathsf{id} \in \{\mathsf{id}_1, \ldots, \mathsf{id}_n\}$.

4.2 Definitions

Syntax. A multi-key homomorphic signature scheme (M-HS) with N-hop evaluation consists of the PPT algorithms (Setup, KGen, Sig, Vf, Eval) defined as follows:

- $\mathsf{pp} \leftarrow \mathsf{Setup}(1^\lambda)$ inputs the security parameter λ. It outputs the public parameter pp which is an implicit input to all other M-HS algorithms. The public parameter defines the *maximum "hop" of evaluations* N, meaning it is not possible to apply Eval on signatures that have been evaluated for N times.

It also defines the message space $\mathcal{M}$, the class $\mathcal{G}$ of *admissible functions*, the identity space $\mathcal{ID}$, and the tag space $\mathcal{T}$. The label space $\mathcal{L} := \mathcal{ID} \times \mathcal{T}$ is defined as the Cartesian product of $\mathcal{ID}$ and $\mathcal{T}$.

- $(\mathsf{pk}, \mathsf{sk}) \leftarrow \mathsf{KGen}(\mathsf{pp})$ inputs the public parameter. It outputs the public key pk and the secret key sk. When an algorithm takes sk as input, we assume its corresponding pk is also taken as input implicitly.
- $\sigma \leftarrow \mathsf{Sig}(\mathsf{sk}, \ell, m)$ inputs the secret key sk, a label $\ell = (\mathsf{id}, \tau) \in \mathcal{L}$, and a message $m \in \mathcal{M}$. It outputs a signature σ. Without loss of generality, we assume σ is of the form $\sigma = (0, \sigma')$, where 0 indicates it is a fresh signature.
- $\sigma \leftarrow \mathsf{Eval}(g, (\mathcal{P}_k, \{\mathsf{pk}_{\mathsf{id}}\}_{\mathsf{id} \in \mathcal{P}_k}, m_k, \sigma_k)_{k \in [K]})$ inputs a function $g \in \mathcal{G}$ and, from each contributor, a labeled program[1] $\mathcal{P}_k$, the corresponding public keys $\{\mathsf{pk}_{\mathsf{id}}\}_{\mathsf{id} \in \mathcal{P}_k}$, a message m_k, and a signature σ_k, where $k \in [K]$.
  It outputs a signature σ, certifying that message m is the output of $\mathcal{P} = g(\mathcal{P}_1, \ldots, \mathcal{P}_K)$ over some signed labeled messages. Without loss of generality, we assume the signature takes the form $\sigma = (n, \sigma')$, where n indicates that the signature has undergone n hops of evaluation.
- $b \leftarrow \mathsf{Vf}(\mathcal{P}, \{\mathsf{pk}_{\mathsf{id}}\}_{\mathsf{id} \in \mathcal{P}}, m, \sigma)$ inputs a labeled program $\mathcal{P}$, the corresponding public keys $\{\mathsf{pk}_{\mathsf{id}}\}_{\mathsf{id} \in \mathcal{P}}$, a message $m \in \mathcal{M}$, and a signature σ.
  It outputs a bit $b \in \{0, 1\}$, indicating if message m is the output of evaluating $\mathcal{P}$ over some signed labeled messages.

Correctness. Roughly, we require that an honestly generated signature $\sigma \leftarrow \mathsf{Sig}(\mathsf{sk}, \ell, m)$ verifies for m as the output of the *identity program* $\mathcal{I}_\ell$.

In addition, we require that, if for all $i \in [K]$, σ_i verifies for m_i as the output of a labeled program $\mathcal{P}_i$, then the signature $\sigma \leftarrow \mathsf{Eval}(g, (\mathcal{P}_k, \{\mathsf{pk}_{\mathsf{id}}\}_{\mathsf{id} \in \mathcal{P}}, m_k, \sigma_k)_{k \in [K]})$ verifies for $g(m_1, \ldots, m_k)$ as the output of the composed program $g(\mathcal{P}_1, \cdots, \mathcal{P}_k)$.

Formally, the correctness of an M-HS scheme is defined as follows:

- Signing Correctness: For any $\mathsf{pp} \in \mathsf{Setup}(1^\lambda)$, $(\mathsf{pk}, \mathsf{sk}) \in \mathsf{KGen}(\mathsf{pp})$, $\ell = (\mathsf{id}, \tau) \in \mathcal{L}$, $m \in \mathcal{M}$, and $\sigma \in \mathsf{Sig}(\mathsf{sk}, \ell, m)$, it holds that $\mathsf{Vf}(\mathcal{I}_\ell, \mathsf{pk}_{\mathsf{id}}, m, \sigma) = 1$.
- Evaluation Correctness: Furthermore, for any $K \in \mathsf{poly}(\lambda)$, any $\mathcal{P}_k$, $\{\mathsf{pk}_{\mathsf{id}}\}_{\mathsf{id} \in \mathcal{P}_k}$, m_k, and $\sigma_k = (n_k, \sigma'_k)$ such that $\mathsf{Vf}(\mathcal{P}_k, \{\mathsf{pk}_{\mathsf{id}}\}_{\mathsf{id} \in \mathcal{P}_k}, m_k, \sigma_k) = 1$ where $k \in [K]$, $n_k \leq N - 1$, $\sigma \in \mathsf{Eval}(g, (\mathcal{P}_k, \{\mathsf{pk}_{\mathsf{id}}\}_{\mathsf{id} \in \mathcal{P}_k}, m_k, \sigma_k)_{k \in [K]})$, and $g \in \mathcal{G}$, it holds that $\mathsf{Vf}(\mathcal{P}, \{\mathsf{pk}_{\mathsf{id}}\}_{\mathsf{id} \in \mathcal{P}}, m, \sigma) = 1$, where $\mathcal{P} = g(\mathcal{P}_1, \ldots, \mathcal{P}_k)$.

[1] Our definition differs from [29] in that Eval takes previous labeled programs as input. The "recursive-proof"-style construction seems to make this unavoidable, as the evaluator needs to produce a proof for "I know some other proofs which satisfy some other statements". These other statements (containing the previous programs) are part of the new statement to be proven. We are not aware of any SNARK in which the prover does not need to take the statement to be proven as input. Another plausible approach to avoid proving the possession of other proofs is that the evaluator "updates" the input proofs. However, "updatable" SNARK is not known to exist. In practice, an evaluator would naturally verify the input signatures before proceeding with evaluations. Since an evaluator is also a verifier, it would need to know the "history" (the previous labeled programs) of the input messages anyway.

Unforgeability. For unforgeability against insider corruption, we require that if some signers are corrupted, they cannot produce a signature disrespecting the inputs of honest signers. For example, for a product function $g(m_1, \ldots, m_K) = \prod_{k=1}^{K} m_k$ and $m_k \in R$ for some ring R, as long as $m_k = 0$ for some honest signer k, no adversary can forge a signature of $(1, g)^2$. Even if all signers are corrupted, they cannot produce a signature on (m, g) such that m is outside the output range of the function g. For instance, if $g(m) = 0$ for all message m, then no adversary can produce a signature of $(1, g)$.

Formally, we consider the following security game cEUF-CMA (*existential unforgeability under corruption and chosen message attack*) between an adversary $\mathcal{A}$ and a challenger $\mathcal{C}$.

- The challenger $\mathcal{C}$ runs $\mathsf{pp} \leftarrow \mathsf{Setup}(1^\lambda)$ and gives pp to $\mathcal{A}$. $\mathcal{C}$ initializes a signing dictionary $D_{\mathsf{Sig}} = \emptyset$ and an honest user dictionary $D_{\mathsf{Honest}} = \emptyset$.
- The adversary $\mathcal{A}$ is given adaptive access to the signing oracle:
  - $\mathcal{A}$ queries (ℓ, m) where $\ell = (\mathsf{id}, \tau) \in \mathcal{L}$ is a label and $m \in \mathcal{M}$ is a message. If it is the first query with identity id, $\mathcal{C}$ generates keys $(\mathsf{pk}_{\mathsf{id}}, \mathsf{sk}_{\mathsf{id}}) \leftarrow \mathsf{KGen}(\mathsf{pp})$, updates $D_{\mathsf{Honest}} := D_{\mathsf{Honest}} \cup \{\mathsf{id}\}$, and gives $\mathsf{pk}_{\mathsf{id}}$ to $\mathcal{A}$.
    If $(\ell, m) \notin D_{\mathsf{Sig}}$, $\mathcal{C}$ computes $\sigma_\ell \leftarrow \mathsf{Sig}(\mathsf{sk}_{\mathsf{id}}, \ell, m)$, returns σ_ℓ to $\mathcal{A}$ and updates $D_{\mathsf{Sig}} \leftarrow D_{\mathsf{Sig}} \cup (\ell, m)$, else $\mathcal{C}$ just ignores the query.
- The adversary $\mathcal{A}$ outputs a labeled program $\mathcal{P}^* = (g^*, \ell_1^*, \ldots, \ell_K^*)$, a set of public keys $\{\mathsf{pk}_{\mathsf{id}}^*\}_{\mathsf{id} \in \mathcal{P}^*}$, a message m^*, and a signature σ^*.
- To describe the winning conditions, we *establish the following notations*:
  - Let $S = \{i : \mathsf{id}_i^* \in \mathcal{P}^* \cap D_{\mathsf{Honest}}\} \subseteq [K]$ denote the set collecting the indexes of inputs contributed from honest signers involved in $\mathcal{P}^*$.
  - Let $M_i = \{m : (\ell_i^*, m) \in D_{\mathsf{Sig}}\}$ denote the set collecting the messages which were queries to the signing oracle with label ℓ_i^*. Note that $\{\ell_i^*\}_{i \in S}$ are the labels of the inputs from the honest signers in the program $\mathcal{P}^*$.
  - Let $g^*(\{M_i\}_{i \in S})$ denote the set of all possible outputs of g^* when all the inputs of g^* with index $i \in S$ are restricted to the set M_i:
    When $S = \emptyset$, meaning there is no honest signer involved in $\mathcal{P}^*$, we define $g^*(\{M_i\}_{i \in S}) = g^*(\cdot)$.
    When $M_i = \emptyset$ for some $i \in S$, meaning that there exists $i \in S$ such that no query to the signing oracle was of the form $(\ell_i^*, \cdot)$,
    we define $g^*(\{M_i\}_{i \in S}) = \emptyset$.
- The experiment outputs 1 if all the following conditions are satisfied:
  - $\mathsf{Vf}(\mathcal{P}^*, \{\mathsf{pk}_{\mathsf{id}}^*\}_{\mathsf{id} \in \mathcal{P}^*}, m^*, \sigma^*) = 1$.
  - $\mathsf{pk}_{\mathsf{id}_i^*}^* = \mathsf{pk}_{\mathsf{id}_i^*}$ for all $i \in S$: The public keys for honest signers are consistent with those returned by the oracle.
  - $m^* \notin g^*(\{M_i\}_{i \in S})$: When there are honest signers involved in $\mathcal{P}^*$, it requires that m^* is not the correct output of $\mathcal{P}^*$ when executed over messages previously authenticated. When the signers involved in $\mathcal{P}^*$ are all corrupt, it requires that it is impossible to obtain m^* from $\mathcal{P}^*$.

---

[2] Formally, a forgery would be certifying $(1, \mathcal{P} = (g, \tau_1, \ldots, \tau_K))$ instead of $(1, g)$.

An M-HS scheme is unforgeable under corruption (cEUF-CMA-secure) if, for all PPT adversaries $\mathcal{A}$, we have $\Pr[\mathsf{cEUF\text{-}CMA}_{\mathcal{HS},\mathcal{A}} = 1] \leq \mathsf{negl}(\lambda)$.

We say that the scheme is unforgeable (EUF-CMA-secure) if $\mathcal{A}$ is not allowed to include maliciously generated public keys in the forgery, *i.e.*, for all $\mathsf{id} \in \mathcal{P}^*$, it holds that $\mathsf{id} \in D_{\mathsf{Honest}}$. Note that this recovers the definition of previous work [29] in the single dataset setting[3].

Context Hiding. We require an M-HS scheme to be weakly context hiding, such that the signature on an evaluated message does not reveal information about the function inputs. The property is "weak" since the functionality is not hidden. This is inherent to our notion as the symbolic labeled program is required for verification, as well as to existing homomorphic signatures supporting functionalities beyond linear functions. In the context of verifiable multi-party computation, function inputs should be hidden while the function itself should remain public. Therefore, in this context, weak context hiding is a more suitable property when compared to a variant which requires the fresh signature to be indistinguishable from the evaluated one, although the latter provides stronger privacy.

Formally, an M-HS scheme $\mathcal{HS}$ is said to be weakly context hiding, if there exists a simulator $\mathcal{S} = (\mathcal{S}^{\mathsf{Setup}}, \mathcal{S}^{\mathsf{Sig}})$ such that for any PPT adversaries $\mathcal{A}$, we have

$$\left|\Pr[\mathsf{ContextHiding}^0_{\mathcal{HS},\mathcal{S},\mathcal{A}}(1^\lambda) = 1] - \Pr[\mathsf{ContextHiding}^1_{\mathcal{HS},\mathcal{S},\mathcal{A}}(1^\lambda) = 1]\right| \leq \mathsf{negl}(\lambda)$$

$\mathsf{ContextHiding}^0_{\mathcal{HS},\mathcal{S},\mathcal{A}}(1^\lambda)$	$\mathsf{ContextHiding}^1_{\mathcal{HS},\mathcal{S},\mathcal{A}}(1^\lambda)$
$\mathsf{pp} \leftarrow \mathsf{Setup}(1^\lambda)$	$(\mathsf{pp}, \mathsf{td}) \leftarrow \mathcal{S}^{\mathsf{Setup}}(1^\lambda)$
$(g, (\mathcal{P}_k, \{\mathsf{pk}_{\mathsf{id}}\}_{\mathsf{id}\in\mathcal{P}_k}, m_k, \sigma_k)_{k=1}^K, \mathsf{st})$	$(g, (\mathcal{P}_k, \{\mathsf{pk}_{\mathsf{id}}\}_{\mathsf{id}\in\mathcal{P}_k}, m_k, \sigma_k)_{k=1}^K, \mathsf{st})$
$\quad \leftarrow \mathcal{A}(\mathsf{pp})$	$\quad \leftarrow \mathcal{A}(\mathsf{pp})$
foreach $k \in [K]$ **do**	**foreach** $k \in [K]$ **do**
$\quad b_k \leftarrow \mathsf{Vf}(\mathcal{P}_k, \{\mathsf{pk}_{\mathsf{id}}\}_{\mathsf{id}\in\mathcal{P}_k}, m_k, \sigma_k)$	$\quad b_k \leftarrow \mathsf{Vf}(\mathcal{P}_k, \{\mathsf{pk}_{\mathsf{id}}\}_{\mathsf{id}\in\mathcal{P}_k}, m_k, \sigma_k)$
	$\quad \mathcal{P} \leftarrow g(\mathcal{P}_1, \ldots, \mathcal{P}_K)$
	$\quad m \leftarrow g(m_1, \ldots, m_K)$
endfor	**endfor**
$\sigma \leftarrow \mathsf{Eval}(g, (\mathcal{P}_k, \{\mathsf{pk}_{\mathsf{id}}\}_{\mathsf{id}\in\mathcal{P}}, m_k, \sigma_k)_{k=1}^K)$	$\sigma \leftarrow \mathcal{S}^{\mathsf{Sig}}(\mathsf{td}, \mathcal{P}, \{\mathsf{pk}_{\mathsf{id}}\}_{\mathsf{id}\in\mathcal{P}}, m)$
$b' \leftarrow \mathcal{A}(\mathsf{st}, \sigma)$	$b' \leftarrow \mathcal{A}(\mathsf{st}, \sigma)$
return $\left(\bigwedge_k b_k\right) \wedge b'$	**return** $\left(\bigwedge_k b_k\right) \wedge b'$

Fig. 1. Context hiding experiments of M-HS

[3] To recover their definition in the multiple datasets setting, we need to add dataset identifiers to our definition. Since one can always include the dataset identifier in the label, and restrict a labeled program to be computed on inputs with the same dataset identifier, we just omit the dataset identifier in this paper.

where for $b \in \{0,1\}$ $\mathsf{ContextHiding}^b_{\mathcal{HS},\mathcal{S},\mathcal{A}}$ are experiments defined in Fig. 1.

Succinctness. We require the signature size to be independent of the sizes of the inputs to, the descriptions of, and the output of the labeled program.

Formally, an M-HS scheme is succinct if there exists a polynomial $s(\cdot)$, s.t. for any $\lambda \in \mathbb{N}$, $\mathsf{pp} \in \mathsf{Setup}(1^\lambda)$, positive integer $K \in \mathsf{poly}(\lambda)$, $\{\mathcal{P}_k, \{\mathsf{pk_{id}}\}_{\mathsf{id}\in\mathcal{P}_k}, m_k, \sigma_k\}_{k\in[K]}$, $g \in \mathcal{G}$, and $\sigma \in \mathsf{Eval}(g, (\mathcal{P}_k, \{\mathsf{pk_{id}}\}_{\mathsf{id}\in\mathcal{P}}, m_k, \sigma_k)_{k=1}^K)$, $|\sigma| \leq O(s(\lambda))$.

5 Construction

We construct M-HS with unforgeability under corruption generically from ordinary signatures and ZK-SNARKs, which can be seen as a multi-key generalization of the folklore construction of HS. We formalize the following idea. Signatures are produced freshly using an ordinary signature scheme. For evaluation, the evaluator proves that it possesses a set of signatures on messages, and the evaluation of a function on these messages produces the resulting message.

We use a family of argument systems recursively by using the proofs (the evaluated signatures) as witnesses to compute other proofs for further homomorphic evaluation.[4] The family of argument systems corresponds to a family of languages, which in turn is parameterized by the number of hops n the signature has been evaluated. A statement $(\mathcal{P}, \{\mathsf{pk_{id}}\}_{\mathsf{id}\in\mathcal{P}}, m)$ is contained in the n-th language denoted by L_n, if $\mathcal{P}$ is of hop n, and for some K such that, (1) for each $k \in [K]$, $(\mathcal{P}_k, \{\mathsf{pk_{id}}\}_{\mathsf{id}\in\mathcal{P}_k}, m_k)$ in the language L_{n_k} for some $n_k < n$, (2) $\mathcal{P} = g(\mathcal{P}_1, \ldots, \mathcal{P}_K)$ for some function g, (3) m is the output of g with inputs $m_1, \ldots, m_K$. If each proof is succinct, the recursively generated proofs, and hence the signatures, are also succinct.

Concretely, we define the family of argument systems and languages as follows. Let $\mathcal{DS}$ be a signature scheme for some message space $\mathcal{L} \times \mathcal{M}$, where $\mathcal{L} = \mathcal{ID} \times \mathcal{T}$ is a product of some identity space $\mathcal{ID}$ and tag space $\mathcal{T}$. Let $\mathcal{G} \subseteq \{g : \mathcal{M}^* \to \mathcal{M}\}$ be some set of admissible functions which are computable in polynomial time. For each $n \in [N]$, let Π_n be an argument system[5] for the following NP language L_n with witness relation $\mathcal{R}_n$:

$$L_n = \left\{ \begin{array}{l} (\mathcal{P}, \{\mathsf{pk_{id}}\}_{\mathsf{id}\in\mathcal{P}}, m) : \\ \exists\ (g, (\mathcal{P}_k, m_k, \sigma_k)_{k\in[K]})\ \text{ s.t.} \\ \mathcal{P} = g(\mathcal{P}_1, \ldots, \mathcal{P}_K)\ \wedge\ m = g(m_1, \ldots, m_K)\ \wedge \\ \forall k \in [K], \begin{array}{l} \sigma_k = (n_k, \sigma_k')\ \wedge\ n_k \in \{0, \ldots, n-1\}\ \wedge \\ \mathcal{R}_{n_k}((\mathcal{P}_k, \{\mathsf{pk_{id}}\}_{\mathsf{id}\in\mathcal{P}_k}, m_k), \sigma_k') = 1 \end{array} \end{array} \right\},$$

[4] Homomorphic encryption with targeted malleability [14] also used similar techniques.

[5] Defined in this way, our scheme produces N crs's. We see two plausible approaches for just using one crs: (1) Define a single "über language" which captures all N languages, so we only have statements in one language to be proven. (2) If an "updatable" SNARK is available, the evaluator does not need to produce new proofs.

except that L_n is defined by the following instead when $n = 1$:

$$L_1 = \left\{ \begin{array}{l} (\mathcal{P}, \{\mathsf{pk}_{\mathsf{id}}\}_{\mathsf{id} \in \mathcal{P}}, m) : \\ \exists\, (g, (\mathcal{I}_{\ell_k = (\mathsf{id}_k, \tau_k)}, m_k, \sigma_k)_{k \in [K]}) \text{ s.t.} \\ \mathcal{P} = g(\mathcal{I}_{\ell_1}, \ldots, \mathcal{I}_{\ell_K}) \wedge m = g(m_1, \ldots, m_K) \wedge \\ \forall k \in [K], \sigma_k = (0, \sigma'_k) \wedge \mathcal{DS}.\mathsf{Vf}(\mathsf{pk}_{\mathsf{id}_k}, (\ell_k, m_k), \sigma'_k) = 1 \end{array} \right\}.$$

Figure 2 formally shows our generic construction of multi-key homomorphic signature scheme $\mathcal{HS}$ from $\mathcal{DS}$ and $\Pi_1, \ldots, \Pi_N$. Its correctness follows directly from the correctness of $\mathcal{DS}$ and $\Pi_1, \ldots, \Pi_N$.

```
pp ← Setup(1^λ)
----------------------------------------
crs_n ← Π_n.Gen(1^λ) ∀n ∈ [N]
return pp = (1^λ, {crs_n}_{n∈[N]})

(pk, sk) ← KGen(pp)
----------------------------------------
(pk_DS, sk_DS) ← DS.KGen(1^λ)
return (pk, sk) := (pk_DS, sk_DS)

b ← Vf(P, {pk_id}_{id∈P}, m, σ)
----------------------------------------
parse σ = (n, σ')
b := 0
if n = 0 ∧ P = I_ℓ then
  parse ℓ = (id, τ)
  b ← DS.Vf(pk_id, (ℓ, m), σ')
elseif n ∈ [N] then
  x := (P, {pk_id}_{id∈P}, m)
  b ← Π_n.Vf(crs_n, x, σ')
endif
return b

σ ← Sig(sk, ℓ, m)
----------------------------------------
σ' ← DS.Sig(sk_DS, (ℓ, m))
return σ := (0, σ')

σ ← Eval(g, (P_k, {pk_id}_{id∈P_k}, m_k, σ_k)_{k∈[K]})
----------------------------------------
foreach k ∈ [K] do
  parse σ_k = (n_k, σ'_k)
endfor
n := max_{k∈[K]} (n_k)
P ← g(P_1, ..., P_K)
m = g(m_1, ..., m_K)
x := (P, {pk_id}_{id∈P}, m)
w := (g, (P_k, {pk_id}_{id∈P_k}, m_k, σ_k)_{k∈[K]})
σ' ← Π_{n+1}.Prove(crs_{n+1}, x, w)
return σ := (n + 1, σ')
```

Fig. 2. Construction of M-HS from ZK-SNARK

Next, we prove that $\mathcal{HS}$ is unforgeable against insider corruption. If the adversary outputs a signature (a proof) of a tuple $(\mathcal{P}^*, m^*)$ such that m^* is outside the range of the evaluation of $\mathcal{P}^*$ restricted by the inputs of the honest signer, either a proof can be extracted for a statement outside L_n for some n, which breaks the soundness of Π_n, or a forgery of $\mathcal{DS}$ verifiable under the public key of the honest signer can be extracted, which breaks the unforgeability of $\mathcal{DS}$.

Theorem 1. *If one-way functions exist, and Π_n is a strong SNARK (Definition 3) for all $n \in [N]$, $\mathcal{HS}$ is unforgeable under corruption.*

Proof. EUF-CMA-secure signatures can be constructed from one-way functions [43,49]. Thus, we suppose that $\mathcal{DS}$ is EUF-CMA-secure.

Suppose there exists an adversary $\mathcal{A}_{\mathcal{HS}}$ that produces a forgery in $\mathcal{HS}$ with non-negligible probability. We show how to construct an adversary $\mathcal{A}$ that uses $\mathcal{A}_{\mathcal{HS}}$ to break the soundness of Π_n for some n or produce a forgery of $\mathcal{DS}$. Without loss of generality, assume that $\mathcal{A}_{\mathcal{HS}}$ queries the signing oracle on at most $Q = \mathsf{poly}(\lambda)$ distinct identities.

$\mathcal{A}$ first guesses a number $n' \in \{0, \ldots, N\}$ denoting whether the forgery can be used to produce a forgery of $\mathcal{DS}$ (case $n' = 0$) or break the soundness of Π_n for some n (case $n' \in [N]$).

Case 1: Breaking the Unforgrability of $\mathcal{DS}$. Suppose $\mathcal{A}$ guesses $n' = 0$, *i.e.*, it attempts to use $\mathcal{A}_{\mathcal{HS}}$ to produce a forgery of $\mathcal{DS}$, we write $\mathcal{A}$ as $\mathcal{A}_{\mathcal{DS}}$. $\mathcal{A}_{\mathcal{DS}}$ acts as a challenger in the cEUF-CMA game of $\mathcal{HS}$. $\mathcal{A}_{\mathcal{DS}}$ obtains from its challenger the public key $\mathsf{pk}_{\mathcal{DS}}$. It generates, for each $n \in [N]$, $(\mathsf{crs}_n, \mathsf{td}_n) \leftarrow \Pi_n.\mathsf{E}^1(1^\lambda)$, a simulated crs_n for Π_n, together with a trapdoor td_n, and forwards $\mathsf{pp} = (1^\lambda, \mathsf{crs}_1, \ldots, \mathsf{crs}_N)$ to $\mathcal{A}_{\mathcal{HS}}$. Then $\mathcal{A}_{\mathcal{DS}}$ initializes an empty signing dictionary $D_{\mathsf{Sig}} = \emptyset$ and an empty honest user dictionary $D_{\mathsf{Honest}} = \emptyset$. $\mathcal{A}_{\mathcal{DS}}$ also randomly picks a value $q \in [Q]$.

Let $\hat{\mathsf{id}}$ be the q-th distinct identity on which $\mathcal{A}_{\mathcal{HS}}$ queries the signing oracle. $\mathcal{A}_{\mathcal{DS}}$ answers signing oracle queries as follows:

- $\mathcal{A}_{\mathcal{HS}}$ queries on (ℓ, m) where $\ell = (\mathsf{id}, \tau) \in \mathcal{L}$ and $m \in \mathcal{M}$.
  If this is the first query with identity id, $\mathcal{A}_{\mathcal{DS}}$ configures $\mathsf{pk}_{\mathsf{id}}$ as followings.
  If $\hat{\mathsf{id}} = \mathsf{id}$, $\mathcal{A}_{\mathcal{DS}}$ sets $\mathsf{pk}_{\hat{\mathsf{id}}} := \mathsf{pk}_{\mathcal{DS}}$ and gives it to $\mathcal{A}_{\mathcal{HS}}$, else $\mathcal{A}_{\mathcal{DS}}$ generates keys $(\mathsf{pk}_{\mathsf{id}}, \mathsf{sk}_{\mathsf{id}}) \leftarrow \mathsf{KGen}(\mathsf{pp})$ and gives $\mathsf{pk}_{\mathsf{id}}$ to $\mathcal{A}$.
  When $(\ell, m) \notin D_{\mathsf{Sig}}$, if $\ell = (\hat{\mathsf{id}}, \cdot)$, $\mathcal{A}_{\mathcal{DS}}$ forwards (ℓ, m) to its signing oracle to get σ'_ℓ, else $\mathcal{A}_{\mathcal{DS}}$ computes $\sigma'_\ell \leftarrow \mathsf{Sig}(\mathsf{sk}_{\mathsf{id}}, (\ell, m))$. In either case, $\mathcal{A}_{\mathcal{DS}}$ returns $\sigma_\ell = (0, \sigma'_\ell)$ to $\mathcal{A}_{\mathcal{HS}}$ and updates $D_{\mathsf{Sig}} \leftarrow D_{\mathsf{Sig}} \cup (\ell, m)$.
  If $(\ell, m) \in D_{\mathsf{Sig}}$, $\mathcal{A}_{\mathcal{DS}}$ just ignores the query.

$\mathcal{A}_{\mathcal{HS}}$ will output, as an alleged forgery of $\mathcal{HS}$, a labeled program $\mathcal{P}^* = (g^*, \ell_1^*, \ldots, \ell_K^*)$, a set of public keys $\{\mathsf{pk}^*_{\mathsf{id}}\}_{\mathsf{id} \in \mathcal{P}^*}$, a message m^*, and a signature $\sigma^* = (n^*, \sigma')$ such that $\mathsf{Vf}(\mathcal{P}^*, \{\mathsf{pk}^*_{\mathsf{id}}\}_{\mathsf{id} \in \mathcal{P}^*}, m^*, \sigma^*) = 1$, $\mathsf{pk}^*_{\mathsf{id}^*_i} = \mathsf{pk}_{\mathsf{id}^*_i}$ for all $i \in S$, and $m^* \notin g^*(\{M_i\}_{i \in S})$, where S is the set of indexes of inputs contributed by honest signers.

If $S = \emptyset$, meaning that all signers involved in $\mathcal{P}^*$ are corrupt, then $\mathcal{A}_{\mathcal{DS}}$ aborts (since the guess $n' = 0$ is wrong). Otherwise, there exists $i \in S$ and with probability at least $1/Q$ we have $\mathsf{id}^*_i = \hat{\mathsf{id}}$.

$\mathcal{A}_{\mathcal{DS}}$ greedily runs $\Pi_n.\mathsf{E}^2$, the extractor of ZK-SNARK for L_n, recursively from $n = n^*$ to $n = 1$, attempting to recover a set of label-message-signature tuples $\{((\ell^*_k, m^*_k), \sigma^*_k)\}$ such that all of which pass the verification of $\mathcal{DS}$. The only case when $\mathcal{A}_{\mathcal{DS}}$ is unable to do so is when there exists $n \in [N]$ such that a statement for which $\mathcal{A}_{\mathcal{DS}}$ possesses a valid proof is actually false. In this case, the guess $n' = 0$ is wrong, and $\mathcal{A}_{\mathcal{DS}}$ aborts.

Suppose $\mathcal{A}_{\mathcal{DS}}$ indeed successfully extracts such label-message-signature tuples. Since all statements for which proofs are extracted are true, *i.e.*, all evaluations are done faithfully, and $m^* \notin g^*(\{M_i\}_{i \in S})$, there must exists a tuple $((\ell' = (\hat{\mathsf{id}}, \tau'), m'), \sigma') \in \{((\ell_k^*, m_k^*), \sigma_k^*)\}_k$ such that $(\ell', m') \notin D_{\mathsf{Sig}}$. Since $\mathsf{pk}^*_{\mathsf{id}_i^*} = \mathsf{pk}_{\mathsf{id}_i^*}$ for all $i \in S$, and in particular $\mathsf{pk}^*_{\hat{\mathsf{id}}} = \mathsf{pk}_{\mathcal{DS}}$, $((\ell', m'), \sigma')$ is a valid forgery to $\mathcal{DS}$.

Note that by Definition 3, each extractor $\Pi_n.\mathsf{E}^2$ works for all provers and does not take as input the random tape of the prover, which is $\Pi_{n+1}.\mathsf{E}^2$ in our case. So, the extraction of each layer contributes an additive, instead of multiplicative, overhead to the runtime of the overall extraction. We can, therefore, afford the number of hops N to be polynomially large.

Case 2: Breaking the Soundness of Π_n. Suppose $\mathcal{A}$ guesses $n' \in [N]$, meaning that it attempts to use the forgery to break the soundness of $\Pi_{n'}$. We write $\mathcal{A}$ as $\mathcal{A}_{\Pi_{n'}}$, who acts as a challenger in the cEUF-CMA game of $\mathcal{HS}$.

$\mathcal{A}_{\Pi_{n'}}$ obtains from its challenger the common reference string crs. It sets $\mathsf{crs}_{n'} = \mathsf{crs}$. It generates for each $n \in [N] \backslash \{n'\}$, $(\mathsf{crs}_n, \mathsf{td}_n) \leftarrow \Pi_n.\mathsf{E}^1(1^\lambda)$, *i.e.*, a simulated crs_n for Π_n, together with a trapdoor td_n. It forwards the public parameters $\mathsf{pp} = (1^\lambda, \mathsf{crs}_1, \ldots, \mathsf{crs}_N)$ to $\mathcal{A}_{\mathcal{HS}}$. Then $\mathcal{A}_{\mathcal{DS}}$ initializes an empty signing dictionary $D_{\mathsf{Sig}} = \emptyset$ and an empty honest user dictionary $D_{\mathsf{Honest}} = \emptyset$.

$\mathcal{A}_{\Pi_{n'}}$ answers signing oracle queries as follows:

- $\mathcal{A}_{\mathcal{HS}}$ queries (ℓ, m) where $\ell = (\mathsf{id}, \tau) \in \mathcal{L}$ and $m \in \mathcal{M}$.
  If (ℓ, m) is the first query with identity id, $\mathcal{A}_{\Pi_i}$ generates keys $(\mathsf{pk}_{\mathsf{id}}, \mathsf{sk}_{\mathsf{id}}) \leftarrow \mathsf{KGen}(\mathsf{pp})$ and gives $\mathsf{pk}_{\mathsf{id}}$ to $\mathcal{A}_{\mathcal{HS}}$.
  If $(\ell, m) \notin D_{\mathsf{Sig}}$, $\mathcal{A}_{\Pi_i}$ computes $\sigma_\ell \leftarrow \mathsf{Sig}(\mathsf{sk}_{\mathsf{id}}, \ell, m)$, returns σ_ℓ to $\mathcal{A}_{\mathcal{HS}}$ and updates $D_{\mathsf{Sig}} \leftarrow D_{\mathsf{Sig}} \cup (\ell, m)$, else the query is ignored.

$\mathcal{A}_{\mathcal{HS}}$ will output, as an alleged forgery of $\mathcal{HS}$, a labeled program $\mathcal{P}^* = (g^*, \ell_1^*, \ldots, \ell_K^*)$, a set of public keys $\{\mathsf{pk}^*_{\mathsf{id}}\}_{\mathsf{id} \in \mathcal{P}^*}$, a message m^*, and a signature $\sigma^* = (n^*, \sigma')$ such that $\mathsf{Vf}(\mathcal{P}^*, \{\mathsf{pk}^*_{\mathsf{id}}\}_{\mathsf{id} \in \mathcal{P}^*}, m^*, \sigma^*) = 1$, and $m^* \notin g^*(\{M_i\}_{i \in S})$.

$\mathcal{A}_{\Pi_{n'}}$ greedily runs $\Pi_n.\mathsf{E}^2$, the extractor of ZK-SNARK for L_n, recursively from $n = n^*$ to n', attempting to recover all tuples $\{(\mathcal{P}_k^*, \{\mathsf{pk}^*_{\mathsf{id}}\}_{\mathsf{id} \in \mathcal{P}_k^*}, m_k^*, \sigma_k^*)\}$ such that all of which passes the verification of $\Pi_{n'}$. The only case when $\mathcal{A}_{\Pi_{n'}}$ is unable to do so is when there exists $n \in \{n^*, \ldots, n' + 1\}$ such that a statement in L_n induced by the forgery is false. In this case, the guess n' is wrong, and $\mathcal{A}_{\Pi_{n'}}$ aborts.

Suppose the above greedy extraction is successful, $\mathcal{A}_{\Pi_{n'}}$ checks if there exists an extracted tuple which does not satisfy the relation for $L_{n'}$. If so, then $\mathcal{A}_{\Pi_{n'}}$ successfully obtains a $\Pi_{n'}$ proof for a false statement and hence breaks the soundness of $\Pi_{n'}$. If not, then the guess n' is wrong and $\mathcal{A}_{\Pi_{n'}}$ aborts.

Summary. Overall, since the abort conditions of $\mathcal{A}$ for different choices of n' are disjoint, and n' is chosen randomly from $\{0, \ldots, N\}$, the probability that $\mathcal{A}$ does not abort is non-negligible. Therefore, we conclude that $\mathcal{A}$ can either break the unforgeability of $\mathcal{DS}$, or the soundness of Π_n for some $n \in [N]$.

Theorem 2. *Assume one-way function exists. If Π_n is an O-SNARK with respect to the signing oracle of $\mathcal{DS}$ (Definition 4) for all $n \in [N]$ where N is a constant, then $\mathcal{HS}$ is unforgeable under corruption. Note that in this case $\mathcal{HS}$ only supports constant-hop (N) evaluation.*

Proof. The proof is exactly the same as the proof of unforgeability from strong SNARK (Theorem 1), except that extractors with dependence on the provers are used. Specifically, $\mathcal{A} := \mathcal{A}_{n^*}$ acts as the prover for the extractor $\Pi_{n^*}.\mathsf{E}^2_{\mathcal{A}}$, and an extractor $\Pi_n.\mathsf{E}^2_{\mathcal{A}_n} := \mathcal{A}_{n-1}$ in the upper layer acts as the prover for the extractor $\Pi_{n-1}.\mathsf{E}^2_{\mathcal{A}_{n-1}}$ in the lower layer. Note that for all $n \in [N]$, the same signing oracle for $\mathcal{DS}$ is required. Therefore, with the transcript of signing oracle queries, the set of extractors $\Pi_n.\mathsf{E}^2_{\mathcal{A}_n}$ for the recursive language is able to extract the witnesses. Note that the runtime of $\Pi_n.\mathsf{E}^2_{\mathcal{A}_n}$ may depend on the runtime of $\mathcal{A}_n$. In general, $\Pi_n.\mathsf{E}^2_{\mathcal{A}_n}$ may run $\mathcal{A}_n$ as a black box polynomially-many times. In the worst case, suppose $n^* = N$. In this case, even if N is as small as logarithmic, the total runtime of recursively running the set of extractors $\Pi_n.\mathsf{E}^2_{\mathcal{A}_n}$ might become exponential, as the extractors need to take the provers (the extractor in the layer above) as input, each of which contributes a multiplicative polynomial overhead to the extraction time. We thus restrict N to be a constant.

Candidate Constructions of Strong SNARKs and O-SNARKs. As shown by Fiore *et al.* [30], there are a few candidates of O-SNARK. Computationally-sound proofs of Micali [47] can be used as O-SNARK without putting any restrictions on the underlying signature scheme in our construction. If we require the underlying signatures to be hash-and-sign signatures and model the hash as a random oracle, then all SNARKs can be used as O-SNARKs. In the standard model, if we require the message space of the signature scheme to be properly bounded and require the adversary to query almost the entire message space, or we require the adversary to issue oracle queries before seeing the common reference string, then all SNARKs can be used as O-SNARKs.

Yet, as far as we know, no strong SNARK candidate is known, although the notion has been used in the literature [16]. For example, in recent SNARK constructions [26,33,38,46] based on knowledge of exponents or certain extractability assumptions, the extractor needs to run the prover as a black box. This does not affect our overall results in the sense that, constant-hop M-HS constructed from O-SNARKs is sufficient to imply functional signatures and ZK-SNARGs.

Theorem 3. *If Π_n is zero knowledge for $n \in [N]$, $\mathcal{HS}$ is weakly context hiding.*

Proof. Π_n is zero-knowledge, so there exists a simulator $\mathcal{S}_{\Pi_n} = (\mathcal{S}^{\mathsf{crs}}_{\Pi_n}, \mathcal{S}^{\mathsf{Prove}}_{\Pi_n})$ which simulates a proof π_n for any instance in L_n. To construct a simulator $\mathcal{S}_{\mathcal{HS}}$ for $\mathcal{HS}$, we define $\mathcal{S}^{\mathsf{Setup}}_{\mathcal{HS}}$ which simulates the common reference strings crs_n using $\mathcal{S}^{\mathsf{crs}}_{\Pi_n}$, and $\mathcal{S}^{\mathsf{Sig}}_{\mathcal{HS}}$ which simulates the signatures using $\mathcal{S}^{\mathsf{Prove}}_{\Pi_n}$. The proofs simulated from $\mathcal{S}_{\Pi_n}$ are indistinguishable from the real proofs, so the simulated signatures from $\mathcal{S}_{\mathcal{HS}}$ are indistinguishable from the real signatures.

Theorem 4. *Let $N = \mathsf{poly}(\lambda)$ be a positive integer. If Π_n is succinct for all $n \in [N]$, then $\mathcal{HS}$ is succinct.*

Proof. The size of a signature produced by $\mathsf{Eval}(g, (\mathcal{P}_k, \{\mathsf{pk}_{\mathsf{id}}\}_{\mathsf{id}\in\mathcal{P}_k}, m_k, \sigma_k)_{k\in[K]})$ is the proof length of Π_n for some n plus the length of the binary representation of n. By the succinctness of Π_n, the proof length of Π_n is bounded by $O(p(\lambda))$ for some fixed polynomial p. Since $N \in \mathsf{poly}(\lambda)$ and $n \in [N]$, the binary representation of n is of size $O(\log \lambda)$. Therefore, $\mathcal{HS}$ is succinct.

6 Relation with Existing Notions

6.1 Functional Signatures from cEUF-CMA-Secure M-HS

To understand the relation of M-HS with existing notions, we begin by constructing functional signatures [16] (FS) using a 2-key HS. FS (Definition 7) allows an authority with a master secret key to derive function-specific signing keys. Given a signing key for function f, one can only sign messages in the range of f.

We construct FS using an M-HS supporting 1-hop evaluation of signatures signed under two different keys. For the setup, we generate two sets of M-HS keys, include both public keys and one secret key sk_1 in the master public key, and keep the other secret key sk_0 as the master secret key. The FS signing key consists of a signature σ_f of the function f signed under the master secret key. To sign a function output $f(m)$, the signer simply signs the input message m using sk_1, and evaluates the signatures σ_f and σ_m of the function and the message respectively using the universal circuit U, which is defined as $U(f, m) = f(m)$ for any function f and message m. The unforgeability under corruption of the M-HS scheme is crucial, for otherwise, the signer might be able to produce a signature (under the combined key $(\mathsf{pk}_0, \mathsf{pk}_1)$) on any message (possibly outside the range of f) using sk_1.

Formally, let U be the universal circuit which takes as input a circuit f and its input m, and computes $U(f, m) = f(m)$. We assume that the description size of f, the length of the input m, and the length of the output $f(m)$ are all bounded by some integer $n = \mathsf{poly}(\lambda)$. Let $\mathcal{F} = \{f : \{0,1\}^\ell \to \{0,1\}^k \text{ s.t. } |f|, \ell, k \le n\}$ denote the function family. Let $\mathcal{HS}.(\mathsf{KGen}, \mathsf{Sig}, \mathsf{Vf}, \mathsf{Eval})$ be a 1-hop 2-HS scheme, with label space $\mathcal{L} = \{0,1\} \times \{0,1\}^*$ and message space $\mathcal{M} = \{0,1\}^n$, for a labeled program family $\mathcal{G}$ such that $U \in \mathcal{G}$. We construct a functional signature scheme $\mathcal{FS}.(\mathsf{Setup}, \mathsf{KGen}, \mathsf{Sig}, \mathsf{Vf})$ for the function family $\mathcal{F}$ as shown in Fig. 3. The correctness follows straightforwardly from that of $\mathcal{HS}$.

Theorem 5. *If $\mathcal{HS}$ is cEUF-CMA-secure, $\mathcal{FS}$ is unforgeable.*

Proof. With an adversary $\mathcal{A}_{\mathcal{FS}}$ that produces a forgery of $\mathcal{FS}$ with non-negligible probability, we construct an adversary $\mathcal{A}_{\mathcal{HS}}$ that uses $\mathcal{A}_{\mathcal{FS}}$ to produce a forgery of $\mathcal{HS}$. $\mathcal{A}_{\mathcal{HS}}$ acts as a challenger in the unforgeability game of $\mathcal{FS}$.

$\mathcal{A}_{\mathcal{HS}}$ receives pp and $\mathsf{pk}_{\mathcal{HS}}$ from the EUF-CMA game of $\mathcal{HS}$. It sets $\mathsf{pk}_0 := \mathsf{pk}_{\mathcal{HS}}$ and generates $(\mathsf{pk}_1, \mathsf{sk}_1) \leftarrow \mathcal{HS}.\mathsf{KGen}(\mathsf{pp})$. It sets the master public key $\mathsf{mpk} = (\mathsf{pk}_0, \mathsf{pk}_1, \mathsf{sk}_1)$ and forwards mpk to $\mathcal{A}_{\mathcal{FS}}$. $\mathcal{A}_{\mathcal{HS}}$ simulates the two types of queries made by $\mathcal{A}_{\mathcal{FS}}$, namely, key generation oracle queries and signing oracle queries, as follows:

$(\mathsf{mpk}, \mathsf{msk}) \leftarrow \mathcal{FS}.\mathsf{Setup}(1^\lambda)$	$(f(m), \sigma) \leftarrow \mathcal{FS}.\mathsf{Sig}(f, \mathsf{sk}_f, m)$
$\mathsf{pp} \leftarrow \mathcal{HS}.\mathsf{Setup}(1^\lambda)$	**parse** sk_f **as** σ_f
$(\mathsf{pk}_0, \mathsf{sk}_0) \leftarrow \mathcal{HS}.\mathsf{KGen}(\mathsf{pp})$	// Pad f and m to length n.
$(\mathsf{pk}_1, \mathsf{sk}_1) \leftarrow \mathcal{HS}.\mathsf{KGen}(\mathsf{pp})$	$\tau \leftarrow \{0,1\}^\lambda$, $\sigma_m \leftarrow \mathcal{HS}.\mathsf{Sig}(\mathsf{sk}_1, (1, \tau), m)$
// Without loss of generality, assume pk_b is	$\eta_f := (\mathcal{I}_{0,\mathsf{pk}_1}, \mathsf{pk}_0, f, \sigma_f)$
// assigned to the identity b for $b \in \{0,1\}$.	$\eta_m := (\mathcal{I}_{1,\tau}, \mathsf{pk}_1, m, \sigma_m)$
$\mathsf{mpk} := (\mathsf{pk}_0, \mathsf{pk}_1, \mathsf{sk}_1)$	$\mathcal{P} = (U, (0, \mathsf{pk}_1), (1, \tau))$
$\mathsf{msk} := \mathsf{sk}_0$	$\sigma' \leftarrow \mathcal{HS}.\mathsf{Eval}(\mathcal{P}, (\eta_f, \eta_m))$
return $(\mathsf{mpk}, \mathsf{msk})$	// Pad $U(f, m)$ to length n.
	return $(U(f, m), \sigma := (\tau, \sigma'))$
$\mathsf{sk}_f \leftarrow \mathcal{FS}.\mathsf{KGen}(\mathsf{msk}, f)$	$b \leftarrow \mathcal{FS}.\mathsf{Vf}(\mathsf{mpk}, m, \sigma)$
$\sigma_f \leftarrow \mathcal{HS}.\mathsf{Sig}(\mathsf{sk}_0, (0, \mathsf{pk}_1), f)$	**parse** σ **as** (τ, σ')
return $\mathsf{sk}_f := \sigma_f$	$\mathcal{P} := (U, (0, \mathsf{pk}_1), (1, \tau))$
	$b \leftarrow \mathcal{HS}.\mathsf{Vf}(\mathcal{P}, \{\mathsf{pk}_0, \mathsf{pk}_1\}, m, \sigma')$
	return b

Fig. 3. Construction of FS from M-HS

- $\mathcal{O}_{\mathsf{key}}(f, i)$
  - If there exists an entry for (f, i) in the dictionary, output the corresponding value sk_f^i.
  - Otherwise, query the signing oracle of $\mathcal{HS}$ to get
  $$\sigma_f^i \leftarrow \mathcal{HS}.\mathsf{Sig}(\mathsf{sk}_{\mathcal{HS}}, (0, \mathsf{pk}_1), f).$$
  Then add $\mathsf{sk}_f^i = \sigma_f^i$ to the dictionary entry (f, i) and output sk_f^i.
- $\mathcal{O}_{\mathsf{sign}}(f, i, m)$
  - If there exists an entry for (f, i) in the dictionary, retrieve $\mathsf{sk}_f^i = \sigma_f^i$.
  - Otherwise, query the signing oracle of $\mathcal{HS}$ to get σ_f^i as above. Then add $\mathsf{sk}_f^i = \sigma_f^i$ to the dictionary entry (f, i).
  - Finally, sample $\tau \leftarrow \{0,1\}^\lambda$ and compute $\sigma_m \leftarrow \mathcal{HS}.\mathsf{Sig}(\mathsf{sk}_1, (1, \tau), m)$. Let $\mathcal{P} := (U, (0, \mathsf{pk}_1), (1, \tau))$, $\eta_f := (\mathcal{I}_{0,\mathsf{pk}_1}, \mathsf{pk}_0, f, \sigma_f^i)$ and $\eta_m := (\mathcal{I}_{1,\tau}, \mathsf{pk}_1, m, \sigma_m)$. Compute $\sigma' \leftarrow \mathcal{HS}.\mathsf{Eval}(\mathcal{P}, (\eta_f, \eta_m))$ and output $(U(f, m), (\tau, \sigma'))$.

After querying the oracles, $\mathcal{A}_{\mathcal{FS}}$ responds with forgery (m^*, σ^*), where $\sigma^* = (\tau^*, \sigma'^*)$. $\mathcal{A}_{\mathcal{HS}}$ returns $(\mathcal{P} = (U, (0, \mathsf{pk}_1), (1, \tau^*)), \{\mathsf{pk}_0, \mathsf{pk}_1\}, m^*, \sigma'^*)$. It is a valid forgery of $\mathcal{HS}$, since, by the definition of the unforgeability game of functional signatures, m^* is not in the range of any f queried to the $\mathcal{O}_{\mathsf{key}}$ oracle, and $m^* \neq f(m)$ for any (f, m) queried to the $\mathcal{O}_{\mathsf{sign}}$ oracle.

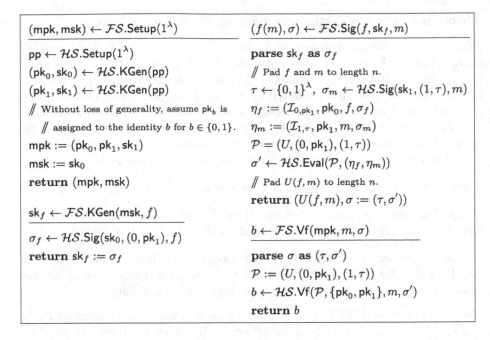

Theorem 6. *If $\mathcal{HS}$ is weakly context hiding, $\mathcal{FS}$ is function-private.*

Proof. Let $\mathcal{A}_{\mathcal{FS}}$ be an adversary of the function-privacy game. As $\mathcal{HS}$ is weakly context hiding, there exists a simulator $\mathcal{S}_{\mathcal{HS}}$ which, on input $(\mathcal{P} = (U, (0, \mathsf{pk}_1), (1, \tau)), \{\mathsf{pk}_0, \mathsf{pk}_1\}, f(m))$ for a random tag τ, outputs a signature of $f(m)$ which is indistinguishable from that produced by $\mathcal{FS}.\mathsf{Sig}(f, \mathsf{sk}_f, m)$. We can thus replace the challenger with the simulator $\mathcal{S}_{\mathcal{HS}}$, which is indistinguishable in the view of $\mathcal{A}_{\mathcal{FS}}$ except with negligible probability. The simulated signatures contain no information about the function f and input message m except for $f(m)$. The probability that $\mathcal{A}_{\mathcal{FS}}$ guesses correctly in the simulated game is $\frac{1}{2}$.

Theorem 7. *If $\mathcal{HS}$ is succinct, $\mathcal{FS}$ is succinct.*

Proof. The size of a signature produced by $\mathcal{FS}.\mathsf{Sig}(f, \mathsf{sk}_f, m)$ is the signature length of $\mathcal{HS}$. The succinctness of $\mathcal{FS}$ follows directly from that of $\mathcal{HS}$.

Since the existence of secure functional signatures implies that of SNARGs [16], for which security cannot be proven via a black-box reduction from falsifiable assumptions [36], we have the following corollary.

Corollary 1. *If cEUF-CMA-secure, weakly context hiding, and succinct* 1*-hop* 2*-HS for* NP *exists, then SNARG for* NP *exists. Moreover, the succinctness of M-HS must rely on either non-falsifiable assumptions or non-black-box techniques.*

6.2 ZK-SNARG from cEUF-CMA-Secure M-HS

We have shown that the existence of 2-HS implies that of FS, which in turn implies the existence of SNARGs. This implication is somewhat unsatisfactory since it relies on the existence of 2-HS, which might be more difficult to construct than (1-)HS (with unforgeability under corruption). Thus, in this section, we construct SNARGs directly from HS, making (M-)HS with unforgeability under corruption a notion sitting tightly and nicely in between SNARKs and SNARGs. This transformation also gives us zero-knowledge for free[6].

The direct construction is as follows. Let the public parameters of M-HS be the common reference string. The prover generates a fresh M-HS key and signs both the statement x and the witness w. Let $\ell_x = (\mathsf{id}, \tau_x)$ and $\ell_w = (\mathsf{id}, \tau_w)$ be labels for arbitrary identity id and tags τ_x and τ_w. It then evaluates the signatures using a labeled program $\mathcal{P} = (g, \ell_x, \ell_w)$ which, on input (x, w), outputs x if and only if w is a valid witness of x. It finally outputs the evaluated signature as the proof. Note that behavior of the program $\mathcal{P}$ with respect to the labels ℓ_x and ℓ_w is rather arbitrarily. We remark that Libert *et al.* [45] also use homomorphic signatures to construct proof systems, while the construction is quite different.

Formally, let $\mathcal{HS} = (\mathsf{Setup}, \mathsf{KGen}, \mathsf{Sig}, \mathsf{Vf}, \mathsf{Eval})$ be a 1-depth (1-)HS scheme for any label space $\mathcal{L} = \mathcal{ID} \times \mathcal{T}$ where $\log |\mathcal{ID}| = \mathsf{poly}(\lambda)$ and $\log |\mathcal{T}| = \mathsf{poly}(\lambda)$.

[6] Function privacy of FS is very similar to zero-knowledge, except that the former is defined in "indistinguishability-style" while the latter is defined in "simulation-style".

Let g be a function such that $g(x, w) = x$ if $R(x, w) = 1$, $\perp$ otherwise. Figure 4 shows our SNARG construction Π for NP language L with relation R. The completeness follows straightforwardly from the correctness of $\mathcal{HS}$.

$\mathsf{crs} \leftarrow \mathsf{Gen}(1^\lambda)$	$\pi \leftarrow \mathsf{Prove}(\mathsf{crs}, x, w)$
$\mathsf{pp} \leftarrow \mathcal{HS}.\mathsf{Setup}(1^\lambda)$	$(\mathsf{pk}, \mathsf{sk}) \leftarrow \mathcal{HS}.\mathsf{KGen}(\mathsf{pp})$
return $\mathsf{crs} := \mathsf{pp}$	$\mathsf{id} \leftarrow \mathcal{ID}$
	$\tau_x, \tau_w \leftarrow \mathcal{T}$
$b \leftarrow \mathsf{Vf}(\mathsf{crs}, x, \pi)$	$\sigma_x \leftarrow \mathcal{HS}.\mathsf{Sig}(\mathsf{sk}, (\mathsf{id}, \tau_x), x))$
parse π **as** $(\mathsf{pk}, \mathsf{id}, \tau_x, \tau_w, \sigma)$	$\sigma_w \leftarrow \mathcal{HS}.\mathsf{Sig}(\mathsf{sk}, (\mathsf{id}, \tau_w), w))$
$\mathcal{P} := (g, (\mathsf{id}, \tau_x), (\mathsf{id}, \tau_w))$	$\eta_x := (\mathcal{I}_{\mathsf{id}, \tau_x}, \mathsf{pk}, x, \sigma_x)$
return $b \leftarrow \mathcal{HS}.\mathsf{Vf}(\mathcal{P}, \mathsf{pk}, x, \pi)$	$\eta_w := (\mathcal{I}_{\mathsf{id}, \tau_w}, \mathsf{pk}, w, \sigma_w)$
	$\mathcal{P} := (g, (\mathsf{id}, \tau_x), (\mathsf{id}, \tau_w))$
	$\sigma \leftarrow \mathcal{HS}.\mathsf{Eval}(\mathcal{P}, (\eta_x, \eta_w))$
	return $\pi := (\mathsf{pk}, \mathsf{id}, \tau_x, \tau_w, \sigma)$

Fig. 4. Construction of SNARG from M-HS

Theorem 8. *If $\mathcal{HS}$ is cEUF-CMA-secure, then Π is sound.*

Proof. If there exists an adversary $\mathcal{A}_\Pi$ that breaks the soundness of Π with non-negligible probability, we can construct an adversary $\mathcal{A}_{\mathcal{HS}}$ that uses $\mathcal{A}_\Pi$ to produce a forgery of $\mathcal{HS}$. $\mathcal{A}_{\mathcal{HS}}$ acts as a challenger in the soundness game of Π.

$\mathcal{A}_{\mathcal{HS}}$ receives pp from the challenger of the cEUF-CMA game of $\mathcal{HS}$, and forwards the common reference string $\mathsf{crs} := \mathsf{pp}$ to $\mathcal{A}_\Pi$. Eventually, $\mathcal{A}_\Pi$ responds with (x^*, π^*) such that $\mathsf{Vf}(\mathsf{crs}, x^*, \pi^*) = 1$ but $x^* \notin L$. $\mathcal{A}_{\mathcal{HS}}$ then parses $\pi^* = (\mathsf{pk}^*, \mathsf{id}^*, \tau_x^*, \tau_w^*, \sigma^*)$, and answers $(\mathcal{P}^* = (g, (\mathsf{id}^*, \tau_x^*), (\mathsf{id}^*, \tau_w^*)), \mathsf{pk}^*, x^*, \sigma^*)$ to its cEUF-CMA game. Since $x^* \notin L$, we have $x^* \neq g(x, w)$ for all $(x, w) \in \mathcal{M}^2$.

Theorem 9. *If $\mathcal{HS}$ is weakly context hiding, then Π is zero-knowledge.*

Proof. Since $\mathcal{HS}$ is weakly context hiding, there exists a simulator $\mathcal{S}_{\mathcal{HS}} = (\mathcal{S}_{\mathcal{HS}}^{\mathsf{Setup}}, \mathcal{S}_{\mathcal{HS}}^{\mathsf{Sig}})$ such that, $\mathcal{S}_{\mathcal{HS}}^{\mathsf{Setup}}$ simulates the public parameter, and $\mathcal{S}_{\mathcal{HS}}^{\mathsf{Sig}}$ simulates on input $(\mathcal{P} = (g, (\mathsf{id}, \tau_x), (\mathsf{id}, \tau_w)), \{\mathsf{pk}_{\mathsf{id}}\}_{\mathsf{id} \in \mathcal{P}}, x)$, for some arbitrary id, τ_x, and τ_w, a signature on x which is statistically close to the real signatures. We can thus construct $\mathcal{S}_\Pi^{\mathsf{crs}}$ using $\mathcal{S}_{\mathcal{HS}}^{\mathsf{Setup}}$ and $\mathcal{S}_\Pi^{\mathsf{Prove}}$ using $\mathcal{S}_{\mathcal{HS}}^{\mathsf{Sig}}$, and conclude that Π is zero-knowledge.

Theorem 10. *If $\mathcal{HS}$ is succinct then Π is succinct.*

Proof. The proof produced by $\pi \leftarrow \mathsf{Prove}(\mathsf{crs}, x, w)$ consists of an HS public key, an identity, two tags, all of which has polynomial length, and a signature of $\mathcal{HS}$. By the succinctness of $\mathcal{HS}$, the signature size is also bounded by a polynomial.

If the underlying M-HS scheme is secure in the standard model (without a common reference string), *i.e.*, $\mathsf{pp} = \lambda$, the above construction would yield a ZK-SNARG in the standard model, which is impossible. Therefore, we can also rule out the possibility of constructing M-HS schemes which are unforgeable under corruption in the standard model. Interestingly, the only existing M-HS scheme [29] is unforgeable but without corruption in the standard model.

7 Conclusion and Open Problem

We study multi-key homomorphic signatures (M-HS) which are unforgeable under corruption and chosen message attacks (cEUF-CMA). We have constructed cEUF-CMA-secure M-HS from zero-knowledge succinct non-interactive argument of knowledge (ZK-SNARK), and shown that the existence of the former implies the existence of zero-knowledge succinct non-interactive argument (ZK-SNARG). Due to the known impossibility of SNARG from non-falsifiable assumptions, we pose it as an open problem to identify a weaker (but still reasonable) security model of M-HS, with constructions from standard assumptions.

Acknowledgments. Sherman S. M. Chow is supported by the General Research Fund (CUHK 14210217) of the Research Grants Council, University Grant Committee of Hong Kong.

We thank the anonymous reviewers for their detailed and helpful comments. We also thank Yvo Desmedt and Daniel Wichs for inspiring discussions.

A Insecurity of Existing Work against Insider Attack

We briefly explain why the existing construction of M-HS by Fiore *et al.* [29] suffers from insider attacks. Since their construction is a multi-key generalization of the (single-key) HS by Gorbunov *et al.* [37], we first demonstrate how the attack works in the single-key setting, then generalize it to the multi-key setting.

The HS construction by Gorbunov *et al.* [37] is based on the notion of homomorphic trapdoor functions. To recall, a homomorphic trapdoor function f maps a public key pk, an index x, and a preimage u to an image v. The function is homomorphic in the following sense: Given a function g and some preimages v_i for $i \in [N]$, one can efficiently compute an image v_g. If u_i where $v_i = f(\mathsf{pk}, x_i, u_i)$ for $i \in [N]$ are additionally given, then one can compute a preimage $u_{g(x_1,...,x_N)}$. The tuple $(v_g, u_{g(x_1,...,x_N)})$ "encodes" the computation $g(x_1, \ldots, x_N)$ in the sense that $v_g = f(\mathsf{pk}, g(x_1, \ldots, x_N), u_{g(x_1,...,x_N)})$. Note that these computations can be performed without the knowledge of the secret key. Furthermore, given the secret key sk corresponding to pk, *any* image v, and *any* index x, one can "invert" the function by sampling u such that $v = f(\mathsf{pk}, x, u)$. Given such homomorphic trapdoor functions, the construction of HS is almost apparent. Roughly speaking, the secret key corresponds to the signing key of the HS scheme, the public key and a set of images corresponds to the verification key, the indexes correspond to messages, and the preimages correspond to the signatures.

Note that the inversion capability of the trapdoor function is more than sufficient for signing. In particular, the signer who holds the secret trapdoor can choose to invert the function on an image-index tuple (v, x) which is otherwise impossible to obtain through homomorphic evaluations. While in a typical setting the signer is assumed to be honest and not to generate preimages for "invalid" image-index pairs, a malicious signer can sample a preimage/signature u^* such that $v_g = f(\mathsf{pk}, x, u^*)$ yet x is not in the range of g.

Generalizing, a multi-key homomorphic trapdoor function f (constructed implicitly in [29]) maps a set of public keys $\{\mathsf{pk}_i\}_{i \in [M]}$, an index x, and a preimage u to an image v. The knowledge of a secret key sk corresponding to any pk in $\{\mathsf{pk}_i\}_{i \in [M]}$ suffices to invert f on the tuple (v, x) with respect to $\{\mathsf{pk}_i\}_{i \in [M]}$. As a result, if any of the M signers is corrupt, an adversary can generate signatures that disrespect the messages signed by the other honest signers.

References

1. Ahn, J.H., Boneh, D., Camenisch, J., Hohenberger, S., Shelat, Waters, B.: Computing on authenticated data. In: Cramer, R. (ed.) TCC 2012. LNCS, vol. 7194, pp. 1–20. Springer, Heidelberg (2012). https://doi.org/10.1007/978-3-642-28914-9_1
2. Asharov, G., Jain, A., López-Alt, A., Tromer, E., Vaikuntanathan, V., Wichs, D.: Multiparty computation with low communication, computation and interaction via threshold FHE. In: Pointcheval, D., Johansson, T. (eds.) EUROCRYPT 2012. LNCS, vol. 7237, pp. 483–501. Springer, Heidelberg (2012). https://doi.org/10.1007/978-3-642-29011-4_29
3. Attrapadung, N., Libert, B., Peters, T.: Computing on authenticated data: new privacy definitions and constructions. In: Wang, X., Sako, K. (eds.) ASIACRYPT 2012. LNCS, vol. 7658, pp. 367–385. Springer, Heidelberg (2012). https://doi.org/10.1007/978-3-642-34961-4_23
4. Attrapadung, N., Libert, B., Peters, T.: Efficient completely context-hiding quotable and linearly homomorphic signatures. In: Kurosawa and Hanaoka [42], pp. 386–404
5. Backes, M., Dagdelen, Ö., Fischlin, M., Gajek, S., Meiser, S., Schröder, D.: Operational signature schemes. Cryptology ePrint Archive, Report 2014/820 (2014)
6. Backes, M., Meiser, S., Schröder, D.: Delegatable functional signatures. In: Cheng et al. [21], pp. 357–386
7. Bellare, M., Fuchsbauer, G.: Policy-based signatures. In: Krawczyk [41], pp. 520–537
8. Bethencourt, J., Boneh, D., Waters, B.: Cryptographic methods for storing ballots on a voting machine. In: ISOC Network and Distributed System Security Symposium - NDSS 2007. The Internet Society, February/March 2007
9. Boneh, D., Freeman, D., Katz, J., Waters, B.: Signing a linear subspace: signature schemes for network coding. In: Jarecki, S., Tsudik, G. (eds.) PKC 2009. LNCS, vol. 5443, pp. 68–87. Springer, Heidelberg (2009). https://doi.org/10.1007/978-3-642-00468-1_5
10. Boneh, D., Freeman, D.M.: Homomorphic signatures for polynomial functions. In: Paterson, K.G. (ed.) EUROCRYPT 2011. LNCS, vol. 6632, pp. 149–168. Springer, Heidelberg (2011). https://doi.org/10.1007/978-3-642-20465-4_10

11. Boneh, D., Freeman, D.M.: Linearly homomorphic signatures over binary fields and new tools for lattice-based signatures. In: Catalano et al. [18], pp. 1–16
12. Boneh, D., et al.: Fully key-homomorphic encryption, arithmetic circuit ABE and compact garbled circuits. In: Nguyen and Oswald [48], pp. 533–556
13. Boneh, D., Lewi, K., Montgomery, H., Raghunathan, A.: Key homomorphic PRFs and their applications. In: Canetti, R., Garay, J.A. (eds.) CRYPTO 2013. LNCS, vol. 8042, pp. 410–428. Springer, Heidelberg (2013). https://doi.org/10.1007/978-3-642-40041-4_23
14. Boneh, D., Segev, G., Waters, B.: Targeted malleability: homomorphic encryption for restricted computations. In: Goldwasser, S. (ed.) ITCS 2012: 3rd Innovations in Theoretical Computer Science, pp. 350–366. Association for Computing Machinery, January 2012
15. Boyen, X., Fan, X., Shi, E.: Adaptively secure fully homomorphic signatures based on lattices. Cryptology ePrint Archive, Report 2014/916 (2014)
16. Boyle, E., Goldwasser, S., Ivan, I.: Functional signatures and pseudorandom functions. In: Krawczyk [41], pp. 501–519
17. Brakerski, Z., Kalai, Y.T.: A framework for efficient signatures, ring signatures and identity based encryption in the standard model. Cryptology ePrint Archive, Report 2010/086 (2010)
18. Catalano, D., Fazio, N., Gennaro, R., Nicolosi, A. (eds.): PKC 2011. LNCS, vol. 6571. Springer, Heidelberg (2011). https://doi.org/10.1007/978-3-642-19379-8
19. Catalano, D., Fiore, D., Warinschi, B.: Efficient network coding signatures in the standard model. In: Fischlin et al. [31], pp. 680–696
20. Catalano, D., Fiore, D., Warinschi, B.: Homomorphic signatures with efficient verification for polynomial functions. In: Garay, J.A., Gennaro, R. (eds.) CRYPTO 2014. LNCS, vol. 8616, pp. 371–389. Springer, Heidelberg (2014). https://doi.org/10.1007/978-3-662-44371-2_21
21. Cheng, C.-M., Chung, K.-M., Persiano, G., Yang, B.-Y. (eds.): PKC 2016. LNCS, vol. 9614. Springer, Heidelberg (2016). https://doi.org/10.1007/978-3-662-49384-7
22. Cheon, J.H., Takagi, T. (eds.): ASIACRYPT 2016. LNCS, vol. 10032. Springer, Heidelberg (2016). https://doi.org/10.1007/978-3-662-53890-6
23. Chow, S.S.M.: Functional credentials for internet of things. In: Chow, R., Saldamli, G. (eds.) Proceedings of the 2nd ACM International Workshop on IoT Privacy, Trust, and Security, IoTPTS@AsiaCCS, Xi'an, China, 30 May 2016, p. 1. ACM (2016)
24. Chow, S.S.M., Haralambiev, K.: Non-interactive confirmer signatures. In: Kiayias, A. (ed.) CT-RSA 2011. LNCS, vol. 6558, pp. 49–64. Springer, Heidelberg (2011). https://doi.org/10.1007/978-3-642-19074-2_4
25. Chow, S.S.M., Wei, V.K.W., Liu, J.K., Yuen, T.H.: Ring signatures without random oracles. In: Lin, F.C., Lee, D.T., Lin, B.S., Shieh, S., Jajodia, S. (eds.) ASIACCS 06: 1st ACM Symposium on Information, Computer and Communications Security, pp. 297–302. ACM Press, March 2006
26. Danezis, G., Fournet, C., Groth, J., Kohlweiss, M.: Square span programs with applications to succinct NIZK arguments. In: Sarkar, P., Iwata, T. (eds.) ASIACRYPT 2014. LNCS, vol. 8873, pp. 532–550. Springer, Heidelberg (2014). https://doi.org/10.1007/978-3-662-45611-8_28
27. Derler, D., Ramacher, S., Slamanig, D.: Homomorphic proxy re-authenticators and applications to verifiable multi-user data aggregation. In: Kiayias, A. (ed.) FC 2017. LNCS, vol. 10322, pp. 124–142. Springer, Cham (2017). https://doi.org/10.1007/978-3-319-70972-7_7

28. Derler, D., Slamanig, D.: Key-homomorphic signatures and applications to multi-party signatures and non-interactive zero-knowledge. Cryptology ePrint Archive, Report 2016/792 (2016)
29. Fiore, D., Mitrokotsa, A., Nizzardo, L., Pagnin, E.: Multi-key homomorphic authenticators. In: Cheon and Takagi [22], pp. 499–530
30. Fiore, D., Nitulescu, A.: On the (in)security of SNARKs in the presence of oracles. In: Hirt, M., Smith, A. (eds.) TCC 2016. LNCS, vol. 9985, pp. 108–138. Springer, Heidelberg (2016). https://doi.org/10.1007/978-3-662-53641-4_5
31. Fischlin, M., Buchmann, J., Manulis, M. (eds.): PKC 2012. LNCS, vol. 7293. Springer, Heidelberg (2012). https://doi.org/10.1007/978-3-642-30057-8
32. Freeman, D.M.: Improved security for linearly homomorphic signatures: a generic framework. In: Fischlin et al. [31], pp. 697–714
33. Gennaro, R., Gentry, C., Parno, B., Raykova, M.: Quadratic span programs and succinct NIZKs without PCPs. In: Johansson, T., Nguyen, P.Q. (eds.) EUROCRYPT 2013. LNCS, vol. 7881, pp. 626–645. Springer, Heidelberg (2013). https://doi.org/10.1007/978-3-642-38348-9_37
34. Gennaro, R., Katz, J., Krawczyk, H., Rabin, T.: Secure network coding over the integers. In: Nguyen, P.Q., Pointcheval, D. (eds.) PKC 2010. LNCS, vol. 6056, pp. 142–160. Springer, Heidelberg (2010). https://doi.org/10.1007/978-3-642-13013-7_9
35. Gennaro, R., Wichs, D.: Fully homomorphic message authenticators. In: Sako, K., Sarkar, P. (eds.) ASIACRYPT 2013. LNCS, vol. 8270, pp. 301–320. Springer, Heidelberg (2013). https://doi.org/10.1007/978-3-642-42045-0_16
36. Gentry, C., Wichs, D.: Separating succinct non-interactive arguments from all falsifiable assumptions. In: Fortnow, L., Vadhan, S.P. (eds.) 43rd Annual ACM Symposium on Theory of Computing, pp. 99–108. ACM Press, June 2011
37. Gorbunov, S., Vaikuntanathan, V., Wichs, D.: Leveled fully homomorphic signatures from standard lattices. In: Servedio, R.A., Rubinfeld, R. (eds.) 47th Annual ACM Symposium on Theory of Computing, pp. 469–477. ACM Press, June 2015
38. Groth, J.: On the size of pairing-based non-interactive arguments. In: Fischlin, M., Coron, J.-S. (eds.) EUROCRYPT 2016. LNCS, vol. 9666, pp. 305–326. Springer, Heidelberg (2016). https://doi.org/10.1007/978-3-662-49896-5_11
39. Johnson, R., Molnar, D., Song, D., Wagner, D.: Homomorphic signature schemes. In: Preneel, B. (ed.) CT-RSA 2002. LNCS, vol. 2271, pp. 244–262. Springer, Heidelberg (2002). https://doi.org/10.1007/3-540-45760-7_17
40. Kiltz, E., Mityagin, A., Panjwani, S., Raghavan, B.: Append-only signatures. In: Caires, L., Italiano, G.F., Monteiro, L., Palamidessi, C., Yung, M. (eds.) ICALP 2005. LNCS, vol. 3580, pp. 434–445. Springer, Heidelberg (2005). https://doi.org/10.1007/11523468_36
41. Krawczyk, H. (ed.): PKC 2014. LNCS, vol. 8383. Springer, Heidelberg (2014). https://doi.org/10.1007/978-3-642-54631-0
42. Kurosawa, K., Hanaoka, G. (eds.): PKC 2013. LNCS, vol. 7778. Springer, Heidelberg (2013). https://doi.org/10.1007/978-3-642-36362-7
43. Lamport, L.: Constructing digital signatures from a one-way function. Technical report SRI-CSL-98, SRI International Computer Science Laboratory, October 1979
44. Libert, B., Peters, T., Joye, M., Yung, M.: Linearly homomorphic structure-preserving signatures and their applications. In: Canetti, R., Garay, J.A. (eds.) CRYPTO 2013. LNCS, vol. 8043, pp. 289–307. Springer, Heidelberg (2013). https://doi.org/10.1007/978-3-642-40084-1_17
45. Libert, B., Peters, T., Joye, M., Yung, M.: Non-malleability from malleability: simulation-sound quasi-adaptive NIZK proofs and CCA2-secure encryption from homomorphic signatures. In: Nguyen and Oswald [48], pp. 514–532

46. Lipmaa, H.: Succinct non-interactive zero knowledge arguments from span programs and linear error-correcting codes. In: Sako, K., Sarkar, P. (eds.) ASIACRYPT 2013. LNCS, vol. 8269, pp. 41–60. Springer, Heidelberg (2013). https://doi.org/10.1007/978-3-642-42033-7_3
47. Micali, S.: Computationally sound proofs. SIAM J. Comput. **30**(4), 1253–1298 (2000)
48. Nguyen, P.Q., Oswald, E. (eds.): EUROCRYPT 2014. LNCS, vol. 8441. Springer, Heidelberg (2014). https://doi.org/10.1007/978-3-642-55220-5
49. Rompel, J.: One-way functions are necessary and sufficient for secure signatures. In: 22nd Annual ACM Symposium on Theory of Computing, pp. 387–394. ACM Press, May 1990
50. Steinfeld, R., Bull, L., Wang, H., Pieprzyk, J.: Universal designated-verifier signatures. In: Laih, C.-S. (ed.) ASIACRYPT 2003. LNCS, vol. 2894, pp. 523–542. Springer, Heidelberg (2003). https://doi.org/10.1007/978-3-540-40061-5_33

Attribute-Based Signatures for Unbounded Languages from Standard Assumptions

Yusuke Sakai[1(✉)], Shuichi Katsumata[1,2], Nuttapong Attrapadung[1], and Goichiro Hanaoka[1]

[1] AIST, Tokyo, Japan
[2] The University of Tokyo, Tokyo, Japan
yusuke.sakai@aist.go.jp

Abstract. Attribute-based signature (ABS) schemes are advanced signature schemes that simultaneously provide fine-grained authentication while protecting privacy of the signer. Previously known expressive ABS schemes support either the class of deterministic finite automata and circuits from standard assumptions or Turing machines from the existence of indistinguishability obfuscations.

In this paper, we propose the first ABS scheme for a very general policy class, all deterministic *Turing machines*, from a standard assumption, namely, the Symmetric External Diffie-Hellman (SXDH) assumption. We also propose the first ABS scheme that allows *nondeterministic finite automata* (NFA) to be used as policies. Although the expressiveness of NFAs are more restricted than Turing machines, this is the first scheme that supports *nondeterministic* computations as policies.

Our main idea lies in abstracting ABS constructions and presenting the concept of *history of computations*; this allows a signer to prove possession of a policy that accepts the string associated to a message in zero-knowledge while also hiding the policy, regardless of the computational model being used. With this abstraction in hand, we are able to construct ABS for Turing machines and NFAs using a surprisingly weak NIZK proof system. Essentially we only require a NIZK proof system for proving that a (normal) signature is valid. Such a NIZK proof system together with a base signature scheme are, in turn, possible from bilinear groups under the SXDH assumption, and hence so are our ABS schemes.

Keywords: Attribute-based signatures · Groth-Sahai proofs
Structure-preserving signatures · Turing machines
Nondeterministic Finite Automata

1 Introduction

Attribute-based signature (ABS), initiated by Maji, Prabhakaran, and Rosulek [MPR11], is a cryptographic primitive that simultaneously allows fine-grained access control on user authentication and protection of users' privacy.

T. Peyrin and S. Galbraith (Eds.): ASIACRYPT 2018, LNCS 11273, pp. 493–522, 2018.
https://doi.org/10.1007/978-3-030-03329-3_17

In the so-called key-policy ABS[1], which is the focus of this work, each signer is associated with his/her own policy and obtains a signing key for this policy from an authority, who possesses the master key. Using the signing key, a signer can sign any message associated with any attribute subjected to the condition that the policy is satisfied by this attribute. ABS provides privacy in the sense that a signature hides the policy that is used to sign the message. That is, no information on the policy beyond the fact that it is satisfied by the associated attribute will be leaked to the verifier. ABS has many natural applications such as anonymous credential [SSN09], attribute-based messaging [MPR11], and secret leaking [MPR11].

One of the central research themes on ABS is to expand the expressiveness of policies that can be supported by the scheme. Results in this direction include the scheme by Okamoto and Takashima [OT11], which supports non-monotone span programs as policies. Tang, Li, and Liang [TLL14] proposed a scheme that supports bounded-depth circuits (albeit their scheme relies on strong tools, namely, multilinear maps). Nandi and Pandit [NP15] proposed several schemes including one that supports deterministic finite automata (DFA). One of the most expressive scheme to date is the ABS scheme proposed by Sakai, Attrapadung, and Hanaoka [SAH16]; their scheme supports unbounded-depth unbounded-size circuits and is based on bilinear maps under standard assumptions. On the other hand, recently, ABS schemes that support policies on the opposite end of the spectrum from circuits, namely Turing machines, were constructed by Datta, Dutta, and Mukhopadhyay [DDM17]. However, their scheme requires the strong assumption of the existence of indistinguishability obfuscations. Therefore, we still do not know of any ABS schemes achieving the ultimate goal of supporting Turing machines with unbounded-length inputs that rely on a well-established assumption such as a static assumption over bilinear groups. Considering the current situation that all the known encryption scheme counterparts of ABS (i.e., attribute-based encryption (ABE)) seem to require the power of indistinguishability obfuscation, one may think that it is simply out of our reach to construct ABS for Turing machines from standard assumptions.

Besides its theoretical interests, ABS for Turing machines, which naturally support unbounded languages, has a practical benefit. Here, by unbounded languages, we mean an ABS scheme where different signatures have attribute strings of different lengths. Policies are associated with signing keys, and thus the policy needs to accept variable-length attribute strings. To see the benefit of this primitive, let us suppose a company where the manager wants each employee to send an email on behalf of the company to the customers that are assigned to this employee. An ABS for unbounded languages provide a natural solution for this setting. In this solution, a manager of the company possesses a master secret key of an ABS scheme. Then the manager assigns to each employee a signing key with a policy. This policy describes what addresses the employee is allowed to submit an email. Then the employee signs an email using the destination

[1] The other type is called signature-policy, where the roles of policies and attributes are swapped.

address of a customer as an attribute string. The flexibility of ABS for Turing machines (or finite automata) is helpful in this scenario. The manager can specify the policy using a regular expression such as `*@division.example.com`, to restrict the employee to send an email to some division of a customer company. In this application, Turing machines or finite automata provide an expressive way to describe a policy. Moreover, unbounded attribute strings quite meet to this scenario, since attribute strings are set to be an email address, which has a variable length.

1.1 Our Contribution

In this paper, we present an attribute-based signature scheme over bilinear maps that allows us to use an arbitrary deterministic Turing machine as the policy from *standard assumptions*. In particular, unlike ABS schemes for policies such as non-uniform circuits, our scheme allows one to associate an *unbounded*-length string as an attribute to the message. Due to the uniform nature of Turing machines, we depart from the conventional ABS constructions and incorporate new ideas and techniques to cope with the unboundedness of the policies. Notably, we abstract ABS constructions, and use the concept of *history of computations* to prove that the signer is in possession of a Turing machine (or in general, some computational model) that accepts the string associated to the message. Furthermore, we build on the idea which we call the *locality of rewriting* to prove the above statement in zero-knowledge. These abstraction and ideas allow us to circumvent the standard intuition that we would require a strong NIZK proof system for proving a valid computation of a Turing machine to construct ABS schemes. Our scheme is reasonably efficient compared to other cryptographic schemes that support Turing machine type computations (e.g., ABE for Turing machines).

Our scheme satisfies perfect privacy and unforgeability. The scheme is proven secure under the symmetric external Diffie-Hellman (SXDH) assumption over bilinear groups. More precisely, our scheme is based on the Groth-Sahai proof system and a structure-preserving signature, both of which can be proven secure under the SXDH assumption. The signature size is $O(T^2)$ where T is an upper bound for the running time of a Turing machine, which is specified by the signer. The size of a signing key is $O(|Q| \cdot |\Gamma|^4)$ where $|Q|$ is the number of the states of the Turing machine and $|\Gamma|$ is the size of the tape alphabet. We emphasize that in spite of its expressiveness, our scheme only requires a standard static assumption (SXDH) over bilinear groups. This could be a striking contrast to the case of attribute-based encryption (ABE) for Turing machines, where available schemes [GKP+13, AS16] require much stronger tools, such as indistinguishability obfuscation.

In addition to the above main contribution, we also present another ABS scheme whose policy class is restricted to *nondeterministic finite automata*

(NFA).[2] This scheme is the first scheme that supports *nondeterministic* computation as a policy. The policy classes of all the previously known ABS schemes are only deterministic: (non-)monotone span programs, Boolean circuits, deterministic finite automata, and deterministic Turing machines. In addition, this scheme gains efficiency compared with the main scheme. Namely, it has the signature of size $O(|w|)$ where $|w|$ is the length of the input of the finite automaton. The size of a signing key is $O(|Q|^2 \cdot |\Sigma|)$ where $|Q|$ is the number of the states of the automaton, and $|\Sigma|$ is the size of the alphabet. In particular, the dependency on the alphabet size is down to $|\Sigma|$ from $|\Gamma|^4$.

1.2 Paper Organization

We dedicate the next section (Sect. 2) for describing the intuition of our schemes. We then begin with some preliminaries and formal definitions in Sect. 3 including the formal definition of Turing machines and related notions. Our main ABS scheme for Turing machines is then presented in Sect. 4, while its security proof is given in Sect. 5. The scheme for nondeterministic finite automata is given in Sect. 6.

2 Difficulties and Our Approach

2.1 Naive Ideas and Their Limitations

As a warm up, we provide some of the obstacles when trying to construct ABS schemes for Turing machines from previously known tools and techniques. One of the most naive approaches may be to base the construction on ABS schemes supporting circuits [SAH16], since theoretically, circuits are already quite powerful. However, this idea would not work because of the differences between the models of computations; circuits are non-uniform but Turing machines are uniform. Specifically, there is simply no easy way to embed a uniform computational model (i.e., Turing machine) into the signing key starting from an ABS scheme that only supports non-uniform computational models (i.e. circuits) as the key-policy. Another approach may be to base the scheme on expressive attribute-based encryption (ABE) schemes, however, the problem of this approach is that, at least in general, ABE schemes do not provide the anonymity property, which is an essential requirement for ABS schemes. Furthermore, no ABE schemes for Turing machines based on standard assumptions are known. One may also consider starting from policy-based signatures [BF14] or functional signatures [BGI14]. However, this does not provide a successful solution as well, since all the known policy-based signature schemes only support pairing-product equations for describing a policy, or if we want to support any NP relations, we

[2] In terms of languages that machines accept, NFA is equivalent to a subclass of Turing machines called read-only right-moving Turing machines. Both accept the class of regular languages.

need to employ general zero-knowledge. The same holds for functional signatures, namely, it supports any NP relations, at the cost of general zero-knowledge.

In a high level, all of the above obstacles seem to boil down to the problem of not having any efficient NIZK proof for proving correct computation of a Turing machine. As an example, ABS for circuits were achievable [SAH16], since Groth-Sahai proof systems can be used to prove correct circuit computation in zero-knowledge. Indeed, if we had an efficient NIZK proof for such an unbounded language, we could have taken another route and convert an ABE scheme for Turing machines into its ABS scheme counterpart by proving that the secret key associated with the Turing machine satisfies.

2.2 Our Approach

We now explain the technical overview of our ABS scheme for Turing machines and show how we circumvent the above problem. In particular, our construction does not rely on any strong NIZK proof system; essentially it only requires a NIZK proof system for proving that a signature is valid. In the following, we assume some familiarity on the standard notion of Turing machines and finite automata, which will be explained in Sects. 3 and 6.1, respectively. We first provide a high level approach to constructing ABS schemes using the concept of *history of computations*. Then, for simplicity, we explain how to use our idea for the case where the policies are "deterministic" finite automata, and provide an overview on how to further extend it to Turing machines via an idea we call the *locality of rewriting*.

Abstract Approach: Using a History of Computations. We first step back and give a high level background on how previous ABS schemes were constructed. One of the most standard ways of constructing an ABS scheme is the "certificate" method [MPR11,SAH16]. In this method, the authority issues each signer a digital signature signed on the user's policy, which will serve as a certificate for the user's signing privilege. When the signer decides to sign a message with some attribute, the signer proves in zero-knowledge that he possesses a valid signature on some policy in addition that the attribute satisfies that certain policy. Therefore, in theory, we can always use general NIZKs for NP languages to construct ABS schemes at the cost of a very inefficient scheme. In light of this, much of the efforts for constructing ABS schemes are centered around constructing an efficient NIZK proof system for proving that a policy embedded in the signature satisfies the attribute while also hiding the policy. In the following, we explain the abstract approach we take for constructing such NIZK proof systems.

As we have mentioned above, the central difficulty in constructing an ABS scheme for complex (unbounded) computational models, such as finite automata or Turing machines stems from the fact that we do not have sufficiently expressive and efficient NIZK proof systems. Toward this end, we take the approach of expressing a computation in a set of sufficiently simple formulae that can be handled by a simple and efficient NIZK proof system. In particular, our key idea is to use a *history of computations* to prove that the hidden policy satisfies the attribute. Here, by a history of computations, we mean a sequence $s_{\mathrm{init}}, s_1, \ldots, s_n$ of "snapshots" of a machine[3], which expresses how the computation proceeded in a step-by-step manner. For simplicity, for the time being, let us assume that the policy, i.e., the machine, is public. Then, the main advantage of the above approach is that even though it may be hard to express the actual computation of the policy into a simple formulae, once given a history of computations s_{init}, $s_1, \ldots, s_n$ and the policy, it may be much easier to express an algorithm that validates this sequence into a simple formulae. Note that this abstract idea can be used for any type of computational models (bounded or unbounded) as long as one can appropriately define the history of computations while being able to express them into simple formulae. For example, as we show later, it may be much easier to prove that, (s_{i-1}, s_i) for all i follow the (public) transition function of a machine, rather than writing out the automaton as a very large and complex formulae.

Now, taking into consideration that the policies must also be hidden, the following depicts our key idea on the whole.

$$s_{\mathrm{init}} \longrightarrow \boxed{s_1} \longrightarrow \boxed{s_2} \longrightarrow \cdots \longrightarrow \boxed{s_n} \in \boxed{F}$$

Here, consider the input w to the machine M to be implicitly included in the public state s_{init}. The gray box indicates that the snapshots s_i must be hidden and F indicates the set of accepting states of the machine M, which in some cases must be hidden since they may leak information on M. If the above can be proven in zero-knowledge, then a verifier would be convinced that the signer is in possession of a machine M which accepts the input w associated to the message. Now, we can break the problem of proving possession of a valid history of computations into three sub-problems: (i) prove that each hidden snapshots s_i are valid snapshots, (ii) prove that each transition of the snapshots s_i to s_{i+1} is consistent with the signer's policy and (iii) prove that the final snapshot s_n is in the accepting states F. Finally, to use this idea of a history of computations to construct an ABS scheme, we must make sure that the above policy and accepting states F showing up in the sub-problems (ii) and (iii), respectively, are certified by the authority. As one may think, the most difficult part of the sub-problems will turn out to be item (ii). In the following, we first provide a detailed explanation on how to use the above idea to construct an ABS scheme for deterministic automata. We then build on that idea to provide an explanation for the more complex Turing machine.

History of Computations for Finite Automata. Before getting into details, we define a finite automaton. Informally, a finite automaton M is defined by a set of states Q, a transition function $\delta\colon Q \times \Sigma \to Q$ and a set of accepting states

[3] Here, one can think of the "snapshot" as the state the algorithm is in. For example, a snapshot of a Turing machine is whatever written in the working tape, the state it is in, and the position of the head. Furthermore, we use the term machine loosely to express some computational model such as Turing machines or automata.

$F \subseteq Q$, where Σ denotes the input alphabet. Next, we define what a history of computations is for the case of finite automata. Since a history of computations is simply a sequence of snapshots of the finite automaton given an attribute string $w = w_1 \cdots w_n$, we can express this simply as a sequence of states $q_{\mathrm{init}}, q_1, \ldots, q_n$; the computation starts with the automaton being at the initial state q_{init}, then moving to state q_1 after reading w_1 (i.e., $q_1 \leftarrow \delta(q_{\mathrm{init}}, w_1)$), then moving to state q_2 after reading $w_2, \ldots$, and finally reading w_n and moving to q_n, which is an accepting state. Here, note that the states Q and the accepting states F are different for each automaton, and hence must be hidden. In particular, we use the following as the history of computations for finite automata:

$$\langle q_{\mathrm{init}}, w_1, \boxed{q_1} \rangle \longrightarrow \langle \boxed{q_1}, w_2, \boxed{q_2} \rangle \longrightarrow \cdots \longrightarrow \langle \boxed{q_{n-1}}, w_n, \boxed{q_n} \rangle,\ \boxed{q_n} \in \boxed{F}, \quad (1)$$

where once again the gray box indicates that they are to be hidden. Informally, the previous snapshot s_i now corresponds to $\langle q_i, w_{i+1}, q_{i+1} \rangle$.

Now that we have defined what the history of computations is, we must show how to solve the aforementioned problems: Below we look at first how to prove that each snapshot $\langle q_i, w_{i+1}, q_{i+1} \rangle$ are valid while hiding the automaton being used and how the authority certifies the automaton $M = (Q, \delta, F)$ to a signer. A naive approach would be to encode the transition function δ to a single large input-output table of size $|Q| \times |\Sigma|$ where the entries of the table is of the form $\langle q, w, q' \rangle$, sign this large table, and use this signature as a certificate for the signer. Then, the signer can prove sequentially in zero-knowledge that each snapshot is included in the table by using a NIZK proof system that supports simple vector-matrix multiplications.[4] However, this table-based approach cannot be secure because the table is variable-length. Namely, since each automaton may have different numbers of states $|Q|$, the size of the tables varies with the automata. Therefore if we use this variable-length table as a witness for the NIZK proof system, the length of the proof may also vary. Hence the signature (i.e., the zero-knowledge proof) leaks information on the automaton. We emphasize that the anonymity notion for ABS schemes requires that even when two automata have different numbers of the states, signatures produced by the two different automata as policies should be indistinguishable from each other, provided that these two automata accept the same string.

Instead, we let the authority issue the signer a signing key as the set of signatures on each entry of the table as follows:

$$\{\theta_{q,w} = \mathsf{Sign}(\mathsf{sk}, \langle q, w, \delta(q, w) \rangle)\}_{(q,w) \in Q \times \Sigma}, \quad \{\bar{\theta}_{\bar{q}} = \mathsf{Sign}(\mathsf{sk}, \bar{q})\}_{\bar{q} \in F}.$$

Here the number of signatures is roughly $|Q| \times |\Sigma|$. In particular, since Q and Γ are polynomial sizes in the security parameter, the total number of signatures is polynomial. Now, proving knowledge of a history of computations becomes

[4] In particular, it proves that the table includes an entry of the form $\langle q, w, q' \rangle$ while hiding which entry it is. This can be accomplished by viewing the table as a matrix and using unit vectors to indicate the row to pick up.

much simpler; the signer picks the respective signatures $\theta_{q_i,w_{i+1}}$ from the set of signatures $\{\theta_{q,w}\}$ and proves that they are valid signatures in zero-knowledge and proves that the final state q_n opens to some signature in $\{\bar{\theta}_{\bar{q}}\}$. The signer also shows that each transition of the snapshots are consistent with the signer's automaton by using the same commitments for each state $q \in Q$ and proving in zero knowledge that the committed signatures are valid. Since the number of steps it takes for an automaton to terminate is the same as the length of the input string, the aforementioned problem concerning the variable proof length is resolved. Finally, a subtle technical detail is that in the actual construction, the authority includes some nonce in the signatures $\theta_{q,w}$ and $\bar{\theta}_{\bar{q}}$ so that they are tied to a unique automaton to prevent collusion attacks.

An informal intuition on the security is as follows: let us consider for a moment a situation where a malicious signer wants to generate an attribute-based signature even though the automaton assigned to him does not accept the attribute string $w = w_1 \cdots w_n$. In this case, since the automaton does not accept the attribute string, we have that any sequence $q_{\text{init}}, q_1, \ldots, q_n$ leading to an accepting state must deviate from δ. Specifically, at least one adjacent pair (q_i, q_{i+1}) must satisfy $\delta(q_i, w_{i+1}) \neq q_{i+1}$. Since the signer is never issued a signature on this triple $\langle q_i, w_{i+1}, q_{i+1}\rangle$, he will not be able to execute the proof of knowledge.

Extending the Idea to Turing Machines. We now explain our history approach for the case of Turing machines. Again, the goal is to let the authority certify a signer's transition function in such a way that the signer can efficiently prove knowledge of a history of computations.

Firstly we briefly recapitulate the notion of Turing machines. A Turing machine is specified by a set of state Q, a transition function $\delta\colon Q \times \Gamma \rightarrow Q \times \Gamma \times \{\texttt{left}, \texttt{stay}, \texttt{right}\}$, an initial state $q_{\text{init}} \in Q$, and an accepting state q_{acc}, where Γ is the tape alphabet. In the following, we assume the initial state q_{init} and the accepting state q_{acc} are set to be special symbols that are common to all Turing machines. Specifically, the set of accepting states F can be made public. A Turing machine starts its computation with an input w on its working tape, the head at the leftmost cell. Then the machine moves the head left and right while rewriting the cells of the working tape one by one. We say the Turing machine accepts input w if the Turing machine reaches the accept state q_{acc}.

A snapshot of a Turing machine can be identified by specifying (1) the state, (2) the contents of the working tape, and (3) the position of the head. We encode this information by a string $uqv \in \Gamma^* \times Q \times \Gamma^*$ where $u, v \in \Gamma^*$ and $q \in Q$. This encoding specifies that the state is q, the contents of the working tape are uv, and the head is pointing at the leftmost symbol of v. For example, we encode a snapshot in which (1) the machine takes the state $q \in Q$, (2) the head is on the fourth symbol, and (3) the tape contents are $w_1w_2w_3w_4w_5w_6 \in \Gamma^*$ by the encoding

$$s = w_1w_2w_3\ q\ w_4w_5w_6.$$

Using this encoding, one way to define the history of computations of a Turing machine is as follows:

$$q_{\text{init}}\ w_1w_2w_3w_4w_5w_6 \longrightarrow \boxed{w'_1\ q_1\ w_2w_3w_4w_5w_6}$$
$$\longrightarrow \boxed{w'_1w'_2\ q_2\ w_3w_4w_5w_6} \longrightarrow \cdots \longrightarrow q_{\text{acc}}\ \boxed{w''_1w''_2w''_3w''_4w''_5w''_6} \in F.$$

With this history of computations in hand, we now must resolve the aforementioned three sub-problems (i), (ii), and (iii), of which the most difficult part is problem (ii), where we have to prove that adjacent snapshots $s_{i-1} \longrightarrow s_i$ are valid transitions. In the case of finite automata, the solution was to sign on all possible pairs of the form $\langle q, w, \delta(q, w)\rangle$, which specifies that the transition from q to $\delta(q, w)$ is valid. Unfortunately, the simple approach of signing on all possible valid pairs of snapshots $\langle s, t\rangle$ will not work for Turing machines. Due to the unboundedness of the model of computation, the length of a working tape is unbounded, and hence there are an unbounded, or even infinite, number of possible valid pairs of snapshots which the authority must sign.

"Locality of rewriting" is our key insight to overcome this difficulty. To explain this, let us consider a snapshot $s = abcdeqxfg$, i.e., the current state being q, the content written on the tape being $abcdexfg$, and the head pointing to x. For simplicity, in the following argument, we always use a, b, c, d, e, f, g to denote arbitrary symbols in Γ and use x to denote the symbol which the Turing machine reads next. Then, if the transition function satisfies $\delta(q, x) = (q', x', \texttt{left})$, the next snapshot would be $t = abcdq'ex'fg$, where q' is the next state and x' is the symbol written in place of x. Observe that the symbol x' and its position in t is determined by the two neighbors of the corresponding positions in s, namely, q and x, as the transition function directs the machine to rewrite x with x' and moves the head left. Similarly, the symbol b and its position in state t is determined by the three neighbors a, c, d in s. Namely, since none of its three neighbors are pointed by the head in s, the symbol b is unchanged. In general, any symbol in a succeeding snapshot is determined by the four neighbors in the current snapshot: the symbol in the same position, its left symbol, and the two symbols on its right. Figure 1 illustrates all the cases of the four neighbors determining the symbols in the succeeding snapshot, in the case that the head moves to left.[5] In this figure, the upper tapes denote the preceding snapshot, while the lower tapes denote its succeeding snapshot. The grayed boxes in the upper tapes denote the neighbors that determine the grayed box in the lower line. Although we included both cases 1 and 2 for completeness, the grayed boxes hold the same meaning since all the four neighbors in the preceding snapshot are constituted only from tape symbols. In particular, there are 5 cases depending on the position of the state q is in the four preceding neighbors.

Using this locality of rewriting, the authority signs all the possible occurring patterns of the above grey boxes, which consists of the four neighbors in the

[5] Similar illustrations can be obtained for the case that the head stays and moves to the right with the same idea.

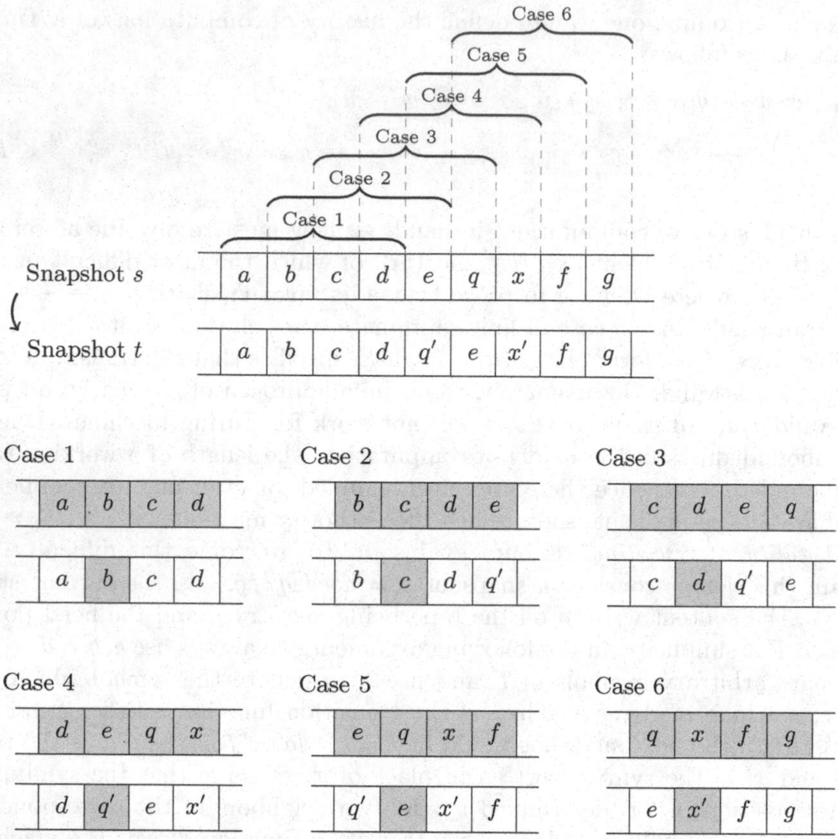

Fig. 1. All the patterns of "local" changes when a snapshot s becomes a snapshot t via a transition $\delta(q,x) = (q', x', \texttt{left})$.

preceding snapshot and the one symbol in the succeeding snapshot. In more detail, in the case that $\delta(q,x) = (q', x', \texttt{left})$, the authority signs on the following five types of tuples:

$$
\begin{array}{l}
(a,\ b,\ c,\ d,\ b\ ),\\
(c,\ d,\ e,\ q,\ d\ ),\\
(d,\ e,\ q,\ x,\ q'\ ),\\
(e,\ q,\ x,\ f,\ e\ ),\\
(q,\ x,\ f,\ g,\ x'\ )
\end{array}
\tag{2}
$$

for all possible choices of a, b, c, d, e, f, and $g \in \Gamma$.[6] Finally, the authority creates signatures for all possible choices of $(q, x) \in Q \times \Gamma$ and provides the set

[6] The other two cases **right** and **stay** are done similarly.

of these signatures to the signer as the signing key. Here, we did not need to consider the tuple (b, c, d, e, c), since this is captured by the first tuple of Eq. (2).

With this set of signatures, the signer can prove knowledge of a history of computations

$$s_{\text{init}} \longrightarrow s_1 \longrightarrow s_2 \longrightarrow \cdots \longrightarrow s_n$$

in the following way. For each adjacent snapshots $s_{i-1} = u_1 u_2 \cdots u_n$ and $s_i = v_1 v_2 \cdots v_n$ such that

$$u_1 u_2 \cdots u_n \longrightarrow v_1 v_2 \cdots v_n,$$

the signer proves knowledge of the possession of signatures for the following tuples:

$$\begin{array}{llllll}
\langle\, \llcorner, & u_1, & u_2, & u_3, & v_1 & \rangle, \\
\langle\, u_1, & u_2, & u_3, & u_4, & v_2 & \rangle, \\
\langle\, u_2, & u_3, & u_4, & u_5, & v_3 & \rangle, \\
 & & \vdots & & & , \\
\langle\, u_{n-3}, & u_{n-2}, & u_{n-1}, & u_n, & v_{n-2} & \rangle, \\
\langle\, u_{n-2}, & u_{n-1}, & u_n, & \llcorner, & v_{n-1} & \rangle, \\
\langle\, u_{n-1}, & u_n, & \llcorner, & \llcorner, & v_n, & \rangle.
\end{array}$$

where $\llcorner$ denotes the blank symbol included in Γ. This can be done if the transition $s_{i-1} \longrightarrow s_i$ follows the transition function, since the signer can pick the signature on each tuple from the signatures signed on the tuples in Eq. (2). This way, the signer can prove the consistency of transitions, namely, *both* the fact that the cells pointed at by the head are rewrote following the transition function and the fact that the cells not pointed at by the head are untouched. The blank symbols on the left and right sides of $u_1 u_2 \cdots u_n$ are included in order to also treat the corner cased where the header points to the leftmost or two rightmost cells. For a more formal discussion, we refer the readers to the AttrSign algorithm in Sect. 4.

An intuition on the security is similar to the case of finite automata. Let us suppose that a malicious signer whose Turing machine does not accept an attribute string tries to produce the above zero-knowledge proof. In this case, for any choice of a history of computations, at least one adjacent snapshots $s_{i-1} = u_1 \cdots u_n$ and $s_i = v_1 \cdots v_n$ deviate from the transition function. Informally, this would imply that, at least for some v_i, the tuple $\langle u_{i-1}, u_i, u_{i+1}, u_{i+2}, v_i \rangle$ does not match any of the tuples in Eq. (2). Therefore, the malicious signer is not issued a signature on such a tuple, hence he would not be able to execute the zero-knowledge proof. The actual proof will be more contrived since we add nonces in multiple places to prevent mix-and-match attacks.

Applying the Idea to Nondeterministic Finite Automata. Our approach can be extended to support nondeterministic finite automata (NFA). Before we explain how to do so, we first state some difficulty of obtaining ABS for NFA. A naive idea of converting an NFA into a *deterministic* finite automaton (DFA) and then using ABS for DFA (e.g., [NP15]) would not work since the equivalent DFA would suffer an exponential blowup in the number of states (see, for example, [Sip96]). Again we cannot rely on expressive zero-knowledge proofs that can express nondeterministic computation, because such proofs would be quite expensive, if possible at all.

Instead, we proceed with our idea of a history of computations. In our history approach, the authority issues a signature for each transition $q \longrightarrow \delta(q, w)$. Recall that in a nondeterministic finite automaton, there are multiple choices of transitions and the actual choice will be chosen nondeterministically. Let us consider a signer whose automaton has two choices of transition q' and q'' when the automaton is in state q and reading w. Nondeterminism means that if at least one choice of q' or q'' leads to an accepting state, the automaton accepts the input. Then, if the signer has two signatures on both $\langle q, w, q' \rangle$ and $\langle q, w, q'' \rangle$, then the signer can build a history of computations, together with a signature as in Eq. (1), by choosing either a signature on $\langle q, w, q' \rangle$ or a signature on $\langle q, w, q'' \rangle$ depending on which choice of the transition leads to an accepting state. Based on this idea, our scheme for nondeterministic finite automata lets the authority issue signatures on $\langle q, w, q' \rangle$ and $\langle q, w, q'' \rangle$ for both q' or q''. This way, to sign with a nondeterministic finite automata, the signer firstly computes a history of computations nondeterministically, then picks the signatures that correspond to the nondeterministic transition, and proves the knowledge of such signatures.

The size of signing key is $O(|Q|^2 \cdot |\Sigma|)$, where $|Q|$ is the number of the states of the automaton, and $|\Sigma|$ is the size of the alphabet. The factor $|Q| \cdot |\Sigma|$ corresponds to the fact that there are $|Q| \cdot |\Sigma|$ entries for the transition function, and the other factor $|Q|$ corresponds to the fact that there are at most $|Q|$ nondeterministic choices for each entry.

3 Preliminaries

We say that a function $f \colon \mathbb{N} \to \mathbb{R}$ is negligible if for any $c \in \mathbb{N}$ there exists x_0 satisfying that for any $x \leq x_0$ it holds that $f(x) \leq 1/x^c$. We denote by ϵ the empty string. For a string u we denote by $|u|$ the length of u. For two strings u and v we denote by uv the concatenation of u and v. For a set S, we denote by $\mathcal{P}(S)$ the powerset of S.

Turing Machines. We give the definition of Turing machines. We consider deterministic Turing machines in this paper, but will often omit the word 'deterministic'.

Definition 1. *A Turing machine over the input alphabet* $\{0, 1\}$ *is a tuple* $(Q, \Gamma, \delta, q_{\mathrm{init}}, q_{\mathrm{acc}}, q_{\mathrm{rej}})$ *where*

- *Q is a finite set of the states,*
- *Γ is a finite set of the tape alphabet which contains symbols 0 and 1, a left endmarker \$, and a blank symbol $\llcorner\!\lrcorner$.*
- *$\delta\colon Q \times \Gamma \rightarrow Q \times \Gamma \times \{\texttt{left}, \texttt{stay}, \texttt{right}\}$ is a transition function,*
- *$q_{\text{init}} \in Q$ is the initial state,*
- *$q_{\text{acc}} \in Q$ is the accept state, and*
- *$q_{\text{rej}} \in Q$ is the reject state, $q_{\text{rej}} \neq q_{\text{acc}}$.*

We require that the states and the tape alphabet do not intersect, namely, $Q \cap \Gamma = \emptyset$. We also require that all Turing machines do not rewrite the left endmarker \$ with another symbol and do not move the head beyond the endmarker. Formally, we require that the transition function satisfies $\delta(q, \$) = (q', \$, \texttt{right})$ or $\delta(q, \$) = (q', \$, \texttt{stay})$ for any q and some q'. Furthermore, we require that once the machine reaches to either the accept state q_{acc} or the reject state q_{rej}, the machine never moves to another state, namely, $\delta(q_{\text{acc}}, x) = (q_{\text{acc}}, x, \texttt{stay})$ and $\delta(q_{\text{rej}}, x) = (q_{\text{rej}}, x, \texttt{stay})$ for any $x \in \Gamma$.

We define the notion of a configuration. A configuration describes the entire snapshot of the machine and the tape, including the state $q \in Q$, the contents of the tape, and the position of the head. Formally, we say that a string $t \in \Gamma^* \times Q \times \Gamma^*$ is a configuration of a Turing machine. In a configuration t, the string obtained by removing the unique $q \in Q$ describes the contents of the tape. The occurrence of q simultaneously describes the state of the machine and the position of the head. The occurrence q specifies q as the current state of the machine, and also specifies the symbol at the right of q as the position of the head.

We then formally define the notion of transition.

Definition 2. *Let $M = (Q, \Gamma, \delta, q_{\text{init}}, q_{\text{acc}}, q_{\text{rej}})$ be a Turing machine and $s = uzqxv$ be a configuration for it, where u, $v \in \Gamma^*$, $z \in \Gamma \cup \{\epsilon\}$, and $q \in Q$. We denote $s \xrightarrow[M]{} t$ if one of the followings holds.*

1. *$\delta(q, x) = (q', x', \texttt{left})$ and $t = uq'zx'v$,*
2. *$\delta(q, x) = (q', x', \texttt{stay})$ and $t = uzq'x'v$,*
3. *$\delta(q, x) = (q', x', \texttt{right})$, and $t = uzx'q'v$.*

We denote by $\xrightarrow[M]{}^*$ the reflexive transitive closure of $\xrightarrow[M]{}$. We say that a Turing machine $M = (Q, \Gamma, \delta, q_{\text{init}}, q_{\text{acc}}, q_{\text{rej}})$ accepts $w \in \{0, 1\}^*$ if

$$q_{\text{init}}\$w\llcorner\!\lrcorner \cdots \llcorner\!\lrcorner \xrightarrow[M]{}^* q_{\text{acc}}v$$

for some $v \in \Gamma^*$ and sufficiently long $\llcorner\!\lrcorner \cdots \llcorner\!\lrcorner$.[7] Here we assume that all Turing machines halt after moving its head to the leftmost symbol.

During the computation of a Turing machine M, if the current configuration t is $uqxv$ where u, $v \in \Gamma^*$, $x \in \Gamma$, and $q \in Q$, we say that the machine *reads*

[7] Since our definition of transition does not automatically expand the tape with blank symbols, we need to explicitly pad with blank symbols. The length can be bounded by the number of the steps until the machine halts.

the symbol x, or the symbol x is *being read.* Furthermore, if the machine makes a transition $uqv \underset{M}{\longrightarrow} u'q'v'$, where $u, v, u', v' \in \Gamma^*$ and $q, q' \in Q$, then we say that the machine *moves* from the state q to the state q'.

Attribute-Based Signatures. We then define the syntax of attribute-based signatures for Turing machines. A formal treatment on Turing machines can be found in Sect. 3. An attribute-based signature scheme for Turing machines consists of the following four algorithms.

$\mathsf{AttrSetup}(1^k) \to (\mathsf{pp}, \mathsf{msk})$. The setup algorithm takes as an input a security parameter 1^k and outputs a public parameter pp and a master secret key msk.

$\mathsf{AttrGen}(\mathsf{pp}, \mathsf{msk}, M) \to \mathsf{sk}$. The key generation algorithm takes as inputs a public parameter pp, a master secret key msk, and a description of a Turing machine M and outputs a signing key sk.

$\mathsf{AttrSign}(\mathsf{pp}, \mathsf{sk}, T, w, m) \to \sigma$. The signing algorithm takes as inputs a public parameter pp, a signing key sk, an upper bound T for the running time of the Turing machine, a string $w \in \{0,1\}^*$, and a message $m \in \{0,1\}^*$ and outputs a signature σ.

$\mathsf{AttrVerify}(\mathsf{pp}, T, w, m, \sigma) \to 1/0$. The verification algorithm takes as inputs a public parameter pp, an upper bound T for the running time, a string w, and a message m and outputs a bit 1 or 0.

As the correctness condition, we require that for any $k \in \mathbb{N}$, any $(\mathsf{pp}, \mathsf{msk}) \leftarrow \mathsf{AttrSetup}(1^k)$, any Turing machine M, any $\mathsf{sk} \leftarrow \mathsf{AttrGen}(\mathsf{pp}, \mathsf{msk}, M)$, any $T \in \mathbb{N}$, any string $w \in \{0,1\}^*$ which is accepted by M within T steps, any message $m \in \{0,1\}^*$, and any $\sigma \leftarrow \mathsf{AttrSign}(\mathsf{pp}, \mathsf{sk}, T, w, m)$ it holds that $\mathsf{AttrVerify}(\mathsf{pp}, T, w, m, \sigma) = 1$.

We then define two security requirements for attribute-based signature schemes. The first requirement is anonymity, which requires that no information on the Turing machine used to generate a signature does leak. The other requirement is unforgeability. It requires that no collusion can generate a signature under attributes, if their policies do not accept the attributes.

Definition 3. *An attribute-based signature scheme is perfectly anonymous, if for any $k \in \mathbb{N}$, any $(\mathsf{pp}, \mathsf{msk}) \leftarrow \mathsf{AttrSetup}(1^k)$, any Turing machines M_0 and M_1, any $\mathsf{sk}_0 \leftarrow \mathsf{AttrGen}(\mathsf{pp}, \mathsf{msk}, M_0)$ and $\mathsf{sk}_1 \leftarrow \mathsf{AttrGen}(\mathsf{pp}, \mathsf{msk}, M_1)$, any $T \in \mathbb{N}$, any string $w \in \{0,1\}^*$ which is accepted within T steps by both M_0 and M_1, and any message $m \in \{0,1\}^*$, the distributions $\mathsf{AttrSign}(\mathsf{pp}, \mathsf{sk}_0, T, w, m)$ and $\mathsf{AttrSign}(\mathsf{pp}, \mathsf{sk}_1, T, w, m)$ are identical, where the probability is taken over the randomness of the $\mathsf{AttrSign}$ algorithm.*

Definition 4. *An attribute-based signature scheme is unforgeable if for any probabilistic polynomial-time adversary $\mathcal{A}$ the probability that the adversary $\mathcal{A}$ wins in the following game against a challenger is negligible in k.*

1. *The challenger generates a public parameter* pp *and a master secret key* msk *by running* $(\mathsf{pp}, \mathsf{msk}) \leftarrow \mathsf{AttrSetup}(1^k)$. *The challenger maintains a set of pairs of the form* (M, sk) *where* M *is a Turing machine and* sk *is a signing key. It is initially set to* $\emptyset$. *The challenger sends* pp *to the adversary* $\mathcal{A}$.
2. *Then the adversary* $\mathcal{A}$ *is allowed to issue key generation queries and signing queries.*
   - *For a key generation query* M, *the challenger searches for a tuple* (M, sk) *in the set. If it is not found, the challenger generates a signing key* sk *by running* $\mathsf{sk} \leftarrow \mathsf{AttrGen}(\mathsf{pp}, \mathsf{msk}, M)$ *and stores* (M, sk) *in the set. The challenger returns* sk *to the adversary* $\mathcal{A}$.
   - *For a signing query* (M, T, w, m), *the challenger verifies that* M *terminates within* T *steps on input* w. *If not, it returns* $\perp$. *Then the challenger searches for a tuple* (M, sk) *in the set. If it is not found, the challenger generates a signing key* sk *by running* $\mathsf{sk} \leftarrow \mathsf{AttrGen}(\mathsf{pp}, \mathsf{msk}, M)$ *and stores* (M, sk) *in the set. The challenger generates a signature by running* $\sigma \leftarrow \mathsf{AttrSign}(\mathsf{pp}, \mathsf{sk}, T, w, m)$ *and returns* σ *to the adversary* $\mathcal{A}$.
3. *The adversary* $\mathcal{A}$ *outputs* $(T^*, w^*, m^*, \sigma^*)$ *and halts.*
4. *The adversary* $\mathcal{A}$ *wins the game if the following conditions hold: (i)* $\mathsf{AttrVerify}(\mathsf{pp}, T^*, w^*, m^*, \sigma^*) = 1$; *(ii) the adversary* $\mathcal{A}$ *did not issue any key generation* M *which accepts* w^* *within time* T^*; *(iii) the adversary* $\mathcal{A}$ *did not issue a signing query* (M, T^*, w^*, m^*) *for any* M.

Bilinear Groups. A bilinear group parameter generation algorithm $\mathcal{G}$ takes a security parameter 1^k as an input and outputs a bilinear group parameter $\mathsf{gk} = (p, \mathbb{G}_1, \mathbb{G}_2, \mathbb{G}_T, e, g, \tilde{g})$ where p is a prime, $\mathbb{G}_1$, $\mathbb{G}_2$, and $\mathbb{G}_T$ are order-p multiplicative groups, $e\colon \mathbb{G}_1 \times \mathbb{G}_2 \to \mathbb{G}_T$ is a non-degenerate bilinear map, and g and $\tilde{g}$ is generators of $\mathbb{G}_1$ and $\mathbb{G}_2$. Our concrete scheme is based on the symmetric external Diffie-Hellman (SXDH) assumption. We omit the formal definitions of this assumption due to the page limitation.

Groth-Sahai Proofs. The Groth-Sahai proof system [GS12] is a non-interactive proof system which can prove the satisfiability of algebraic equations over bilinear groups called pairing product equations. A pairing product equation has a form of

$$\prod_{i=1}^{n} e(\mathcal{A}_i, \mathcal{Y}_i) \prod_{i=1}^{m} e(\mathcal{X}_j, \mathcal{B}_j) \prod_{i=1}^{n} \prod_{j=1}^{m} e(\mathcal{X}_i, \mathcal{Y}_j)^{\gamma_{i,j}} = T,$$

where $\mathcal{A}_i \in \mathbb{G}_1$, $\mathcal{B}_j \in \mathbb{G}_2$, $\gamma_{i,j} \in \mathbb{Z}_p$, and $T \in \mathbb{G}_T$ are public constants, and $\mathcal{X}_j \in \mathbb{G}_1$ and $\mathcal{Y}_i \in \mathbb{G}_2$ are secret assignments.

The Groth-Sahai proof system consists of the five algorithms $\mathsf{WISetup}$, $\mathsf{WIProve}$, $\mathsf{WIVerify}$, $\mathsf{ExtSetup}$, and $\mathsf{Extract}$. The common reference string generation algorithm $\mathsf{WISetup}$ takes as an input a bilinear group parameter gk and outputs a common reference string crs. The proof algorithm $\mathsf{WIProve}$ takes as inputs a common reference string crs, a statement (public constants) x, and a witness (secret assignments) w, and outputs a proof π. The verification algorithm WIVerify takes as inputs a common reference string crs, a statement x, and a proof π and outputs a bit 1 or 0. The extractable common reference string generation algorithm takes as an input a bilinear group parameter gk and outputs an extractable common reference string crs and an extraction key ek. The extraction algorithm Extract takes as inputs an extractable common reference string crs, an extraction key ek, a statement x, and a proof π and outputs a witness w. As the correctness condition, we require that for any $k \in \mathbb{N}$, any $\mathsf{gk} \leftarrow \mathcal{G}(1^k)$, any $\mathsf{crs} \leftarrow \mathsf{WISetup}(\mathsf{gk})$ any statement x and its witness w, it holds that $\mathsf{WIVerify}(\mathsf{crs}, x, \mathsf{WIProve}(\mathsf{crs}, x, w)) = 1$. The formal definitions of the security of proof systems are postponed to the full version.

The Groth-Sahai proof system proves the satisfiability of the pairing product equations in the following way. Firstly, the proof algorithm generates commitments to each element of the satisfying assignment. Secondly, it generates proof components which prove the satisfying assignments behind the commitments surely satisfies the statement in question. We call these commitments generated in the proving process Groth-Sahai commitments. The Groth-Sahai proof system can be instantiated from the SXDH assumption. In this case, a Groth-Sahai commitment is constituted by two source group elements for each witness element, and a proof component is constituted by eight group elements for each pairing product equation. See [GS12] for further details.

Structure-Preserving Signatures. A structure-preserving signature scheme consists of the three algorithms Kg, Sign, and Verify. The key generation algorithm takes as an input a bilinear group parameter gk and a message-length 1^n and outputs a verification key vk and a signing key sk. The signing algorithm Sign takes as inputs a signing key sk and a message $m \in \mathbb{G}_1{}^n$ and outputs a signature θ. The verification algorithm Verify takes as inputs a verification key vk, a message m, and a signature θ and outputs a bit 1 or 0. As the correctness condition, we require that for any $k \in \mathbb{N}$, any $n \in \mathbb{N}$, any $\mathsf{gk} \leftarrow \mathcal{G}(1^k)$, any $(\mathsf{vk}, \mathsf{sk}) \leftarrow \mathsf{Kg}(\mathsf{gk})$, and any $m \in \mathbb{G}_1{}^n$, it holds that $\mathsf{Verify}(\mathsf{vk}, m, \mathsf{Sign}(\mathsf{sk}, m)) = 1$. In addition, we require that the verification algorithm consist of the set of pairing-product equations, which enables us to prove the knowledge of signatures on either public or secret messages. Such a structure-preserving signature scheme can be instantiated from the SXDH assumption [KPW15]. The formal definition of unforgeability and an instantiation of a structure-preserving signature scheme from the SXDH assumption is postponed to the full version.

Collision-Resistant Hash Functions. A hash function family consists of the two algorithms $\mathcal{H}$ and Hash. The hashing key generation algorithm $\mathcal{H}$ takes as an input a security parameter 1^k and outputs a hashing key hk. The deterministic hashing algorithm Hash takes as inputs a hashing key hk and a message $m \in \{0,1\}^*$ and outputs a hash value h. We say that a hash function family is collision resistant if for any probabilistic polynomial-time algorithm $\mathcal{A}$ the probability $\Pr[\mathsf{hk} \leftarrow \mathcal{H}(1^k); (m, m') \leftarrow \mathcal{A}(\mathsf{hk}) : \mathsf{Hash}(\mathsf{hk}, m) = \mathsf{Hash}(\mathsf{hk}, m')]$ is negligible in k. We assume that the length of a hash value h is determined only from a security parameter k. We denote by ℓ this length of a hash value.

4 Attribute-Based Signatures for Turing Machines

Notations. In our scheme, given a Turing machine that describes a policy, we need to modify this Turing machine slightly in order to resist chosen-message attacks. The input of the modified Turing machine consists of two parts. The first is the hash value of the message to be signed, while the other is an actual input to the original (unmodified) Turing machine. The modified Turing machine ignores the first part and accepts the input if and only if the original Turing machine accepts the latter part of the input.

The formal definition is as follows. For a Turing machine M, we denote by $\overline{M}$ another Turing machine obtained by the following modifications to M. Let $h = h_1 \cdots h_\ell \in \{0,1\}^\ell$ be a string (a hash value) of length ℓ. Let w be the original input to M.

- $\overline{M}$ begins with the configuration $q_{\mathrm{init}}\$hw$.
- It skips the input h. More precisely, in the notation of configurations, it runs the computations in the following sequence:

$$q_{\mathrm{init}}\$h_1 \cdots h_\ell w \xrightarrow[\overline{M}]{} \$q_1 h_1 \cdots h_\ell w \xrightarrow[\overline{M}]{} \cdots \xrightarrow[\overline{M}]{} \$h_1 h_2 \cdots h_{\ell-1} q_\ell h_\ell w.$$

- It rewrites h_ℓ with \$. More formally,

$$\$h_1 h_2 \cdots h_{\ell-1} q_\ell h_\ell w \xrightarrow[\overline{M}]{} \$h_1 h_2 \cdots h_{\ell-1} q_{\ell+1} \$w$$

  where $q_{\ell+1}$ serves as a simulated M's initial state
- It starts the simulation of M using the new \$ as M's endmarker and w as M's input.
- If the simulated M accepts w, $\overline{M}$ moves the head to its endmarker \$ as

$$q_{\mathrm{acc}}\$h_1 \cdots h_{\ell-1}\$u.$$

  for some u and accepts hw. Otherwise $\overline{M}$ rejects hw.

Construction. In the construction of our scheme, we assume that the tape alphabet is a subset of $\{0, 1, \ldots, (p-1)/2\}$, and the set of states is a subset of $\{-1, -2, \ldots, -(p-1)/2\}$, where p is the order of the underlying bilinear groups. Furthermore, we assume that the initial state q_{init}, the accept state q_{acc}, and the reject state q_{rej} is respectively equal to -1, -2, and -3. For brevity, we denote a group element $[a]_1 \in \mathbb{G}_1$ as $[a]$. The description of our scheme is as follows.

$\mathsf{AttrSetup}(1^k)$. Given the security parameter 1^k, generate a bilinear group parameter $\mathsf{gk} \leftarrow \mathcal{G}(1^k)$, a witness-indistinguishable common reference string for Groth-Sahai proofs $\mathsf{crs} \leftarrow \mathsf{WISetup}(\mathsf{gk})$, two key pairs of the structure-preserving signature scheme $(\mathsf{vk}, \mathsf{sk}) \leftarrow \mathsf{Kg}(\mathsf{gk}, 1^6)$, and a hashing key $\mathsf{hk} \leftarrow \mathcal{H}(1^k)$. Set $\mathsf{pp} \leftarrow (\mathsf{gk}, \mathsf{crs}, \mathsf{vk}, \mathsf{hk})$ and $\mathsf{msk} \leftarrow \mathsf{sk}$, and output $(\mathsf{pp}, \mathsf{msk})$.

$\mathsf{AttrGen}(\mathsf{pp}, \mathsf{msk}, M)$. Given a public parameter pp, a master secret key msk, and a description M of a Turing machine, let $\overline{M} = (Q, \Gamma, \delta, q_{\mathrm{init}}, q_{\mathrm{acc}}, q_{\mathrm{rej}})$ be the modified Turing machine as defined above. Choose a random integer $\tau \leftarrow \mathbb{Z}_p$.[8] Then generate the following set of signatures.[9]

- For all a, b, c, and $d \in \Gamma$, generate

$$\theta[\![a, b, c, d]\!] \leftarrow \mathsf{Sign}(\mathsf{sk}, ([\tau], [a], [b], [c], [d], [b])). \tag{3}$$

- For all c, d, $e \in \Gamma$, and $q \in Q$, generate

$$\theta[\![c, d, e, q]\!] \leftarrow \mathsf{Sign}(\mathsf{sk}, ([\tau], [c], [d], [e], [q], [d])). \tag{4}$$

- For all $q \in Q$ and x, d, e, f, and $g \in \Gamma$, generate the following signatures.
  - If $\delta(q, x) = (q', x', \mathtt{left})$, generate

$$\theta[\![d, e, q, x]\!] \leftarrow \mathsf{Sign}(\mathsf{sk}, ([\tau], [d], [e], [q], [x], [q'])), \tag{5}$$

$$\theta[\![e, q, x, f]\!] \leftarrow \mathsf{Sign}(\mathsf{sk}, ([\tau], [e], [q], [x], [f], [e])), \tag{6}$$

$$\theta[\![q, x, f, g]\!] \leftarrow \mathsf{Sign}(\mathsf{sk}, ([\tau], [q], [x], [f], [g], [x'])). \tag{7}$$

  - If $\delta(q, x) = (q', x', \mathtt{stay})$, generate

$$\theta[\![d, e, q, x]\!] \leftarrow \mathsf{Sign}(\mathsf{sk}, ([\tau], [d], [e], [q], [x], [e])),$$
$$\theta[\![e, q, x, f]\!] \leftarrow \mathsf{Sign}(\mathsf{sk}, ([\tau], [e], [q], [x], [f], [q']),$$
$$\theta[\![q, x, f, g]\!] \leftarrow \mathsf{Sign}(\mathsf{sk}, ([\tau], [q], [x], [f], [g], [x']).$$

  - If $\delta(q, x) = (q', x', \mathtt{right})$, generate

$$\theta[\![d, e, q, x]\!] \leftarrow \mathsf{Sign}(\mathsf{sk}, ([\tau], [d], [e], [q], [x], [e]),$$
$$\theta[\![e, q, x, f]\!] \leftarrow \mathsf{Sign}(\mathsf{sk}, ([\tau], [e], [q], [x], [f], [x']),$$
$$\theta[\![q, x, f, g]\!] \leftarrow \mathsf{Sign}(\mathsf{sk}, ([\tau], [q], [x], [f], [g], [q']).$$

Output the signing key sk as

$$\begin{aligned}\mathsf{sk} = (M, \tau, (\theta[\![a, b, c, d]\!])_{(a,b,c,d) \in \Gamma\times\Gamma\times\Gamma\times\Gamma},\\ (\theta[\![c, d, e, q]\!])_{(c,d,e,q) \in \Gamma\times\Gamma\times\Gamma\times Q},\\ (\theta[\![d, e, q, x]\!])_{(d,e,q,x) \in \Gamma\times\Gamma\times Q\times\Gamma},\\ (\theta[\![e, q, x, f]\!])_{(e,q,x,f) \in \Gamma\times Q\times\Gamma\times\Gamma},\\ (\theta[\![q, x, f, g]\!])_{(q,x,f,g) \in Q\times\Gamma\times\Gamma\times\Gamma}).\end{aligned}$$

[8] This extra component of the messages is for resisting collusion attacks. Without this component, colluding signers may produce a forgery of the attribute-based signature scheme by mixing their certificates and forming a history of transitions that is not allowed to each of the signers.

[9] See Fig. 1 and Eq. (2) for intuition. The five tuples in Eq. (2) are implemented in Eqs. (3)–(7) for the case that the head moves to left. The other two cases are implemented similarly.

$\mathsf{AttrSign}(\mathsf{pp}, \mathsf{sk}, T, w, m)$. Let $\tilde{T}$ be the upper bound of $\overline{M}$'s required steps for simulating M's computation up to T steps.

1. Compute $h \leftarrow \mathsf{Hash}(hk, \langle T, w, m\rangle)$.
2. Let $t_0 = q_{\text{init}}\$hw(\_)^{\tilde{T}-|h|-|w|}$. Compute the sequence of configurations of $\overline{M}$ as
$$t_0 \xrightarrow[\overline{M}]{} t_1 \xrightarrow[\overline{M}]{} \cdots \xrightarrow[\overline{M}]{} t_{\tilde{T}}$$
that reaches to the accept state q_{acc}, where $t_{\tilde{T}} = q_{\text{acc}}u$ for some u. Let $t_i = t_{i,0} \cdots t_{i,\tilde{T}+1}$. Let $t_{i,-1} = t_{i,\tilde{T}+2} = t_{i,\tilde{T}+3} = \_$ for each $i \in \{0, \dots, \tilde{T}\}$.
3. Let
$$\theta_{i,j} \leftarrow \theta[\![t_{i,j-1}, t_{i,j}, t_{i,j+1}, t_{i,j+2}]\!]$$
for each $i \in \{0, \dots, \tilde{T}-1\}$ and each $j \in \{0, \dots, \tilde{T}+1\}$.
4. Compute
   - a Groth-Sahai commitment $\psi^{(\tau)}$ to $[\tau]$,
   - Groth-Sahai commitments $\psi^{(t)}_{i,j}$ to $[t_{i,j}]$ for all[10] $i \in \{1, \dots, \tilde{T}\}$ and $j \in \{0, \dots, \tilde{T}+1\}$ except for $t_{\tilde{T},0}$, which is equal to q_{acc} and thus treated as a public constant, and
   - Groth-Sahai commitments $\psi^{(\theta)}_{i,j}$ to $\theta_{i,j}$ for all[11] $i \in \{0, \dots, \tilde{T}-1\}$ and $j \in \{0, \dots, \tilde{T}+1\}$.
5. Generate a Groth-Sahai proof $\pi_{i,j}$ for the equation
$$\mathsf{Verify}(\mathsf{vk}, ([\tau], [t_{i,j-1}], [t_{i,j}], [t_{i,j+1}], [t_{i,j+2}], [t_{i+1,j}]), \theta_{i,j}) = 1$$
for each $i \in \{0, \dots, \tilde{T}-1\}$ and $j \in \{0, \dots, \tilde{T}+1\}$.
6. Output the signature σ as
$$\sigma = \Big(\psi^{(\tau)}, (\psi^{(t)}_{i,j})_{(i,j)\in\{1,\dots,\tilde{T}\}\times\{0,\dots,\tilde{T}+1\}\setminus\{(\tilde{T},0)\}},$$
$$(\psi^{(\theta)}_{i,j})_{(i,j)\in\{0,\dots,\tilde{T}-1\}\times\{0,\dots,\tilde{T}+1\}},$$
$$(\pi_{i,j})_{(i,j)\in\{0,\dots,\tilde{T}-1\}\times\{0,\dots,\tilde{T}+1\}}\Big).$$

$\mathsf{AttrVerify}(\mathsf{pp}, T, w, m, \sigma)$. Compute $h \leftarrow \mathsf{Hash}(\mathsf{hk}, \langle T, w, m\rangle)$ and verify all the proofs in σ under this T, w, m, and h. Here to verify that the initial configuration is valid and that the last state is q_{acc}, the initial configuration $t_0 = q_{\text{init}}\$hw(\_)^{\tilde{T}-|h|-|w|}$ and the state q_{acc} of the last configuration are treated as public constants in the proofs. If all the proofs are verified as valid, output 1. Otherwise output 0.

---

[10] We do not need $\psi^{(t)}_{i,j}$ for $i = 0$, since these cases correspond to the initial configuration, which is public.

[11] We do not need $\psi^{(\theta)}_{i,j}$ for $i = \tilde{T}$, since these commitments are used to bind a configuration t_i and the next configuration t_{i+1}, but $t_{\tilde{T}}$ is the last configuration.

5 Security of Our Scheme

In this section, we provide the security proof of our main scheme.

Before the proof of the main theorem, we introduce a notion of an authorized pair of configurations and present a lemma related to authorized pairs.

Definition 5. *Let $M = (Q, \Gamma, \delta, q_{\text{init}}, q_{\text{acc}}, q_{\text{rej}})$ be a Turing machine. Let $s = s_0 \cdots s_{\tilde{T}+1}$ and $t = t_0 \cdots t_{\tilde{T}+1}$ be strings of alphabets $Q \cup \Gamma$ such that $s \in \Gamma^* \times Q \times \Gamma^*$. Let $s_{-1} = s_{\tilde{T}+2} = s_{\tilde{T}+3} = t_{-1} = t_{\tilde{T}+2} = t_{\tilde{T}+3} = \text{␣}$. Let q be the state of s and let x be the symbols that the head is reading in s. We say that the pair (s, t) is authorized at position j with respect to M if*

- *It holds that $\delta(q, x) = (q', x', \texttt{left})$ and $(s_{j-1}, s_j, s_{j+1}, s_{j+2}, t_j)$ is equal to either of the following:*

$$(a, b, c, d, b), (c, d, e, q, d), (d, e, q, x, q'), (e, q, x, f, e) \text{ or } (q, x, f, g, x')$$

for some a, b, c, d, e, f, and $g \in \Gamma$.
- *It holds that $\delta(q, x) = (q', x', \texttt{stay})$ and $(s_{j-1}, s_j, s_{j+1}, s_{j+2}, t_j)$ is equal to either of the following:*

$$(a, b, c, d, b), (c, d, e, q, d), (d, e, q, x, e), (e, q, x, f, q'), \text{ or } (q, x, f, g, x')$$

for some a, b, c, d, e, f, and $g \in \Gamma$.
- *It holds that $\delta(q, x) = (q', x', \texttt{right})$ and $(s_{j-1}, s_j, s_{j+1}, s_{j+2}, t_j)$ is equal to either of the following:*

$$(a, b, c, d, b), (c, d, e, q, d), (d, e, q, x, e), (e, q, x, f, x'), \text{ or } (q, x, f, g, q')$$

for some a, b, c, d, e, f, and $g \in \Gamma$.

When (s, t) is authorized at position j with respect to M due to one of the tuples of the above forms, we also say that the symbol t_j is authorized by that tuple.

The following lemma plays an important role during the security proof. At a high level, it allows us to argue about valid transitions by only considering authorized configuration pairs.

Lemma 1. *Let M be a Turing machine and let $s = s_0 \cdots s_{\tilde{T}+1}$ and $t = t_0 \cdots t_{\tilde{T}+1}$ be strings in $(Q \cup \Gamma)^*$. If $s \underset{M}{\not\longrightarrow} t$ and $s \in \Gamma^* \times Q \times \Gamma^*$, then there is a position j such that (s, t) is not authorized at position j with respect to M.*

Proof. We prove the contraposition. Namely, assuming (s, t) is authorized at all positions $j \in \{0, \dots, \tilde{T}+1\}$ with respect to M, we will prove that either $s \underset{M}{\longrightarrow} t$ or $s \notin \Gamma^* \times Q \times \Gamma^*$ holds. Toward this end we assume that (s, t) is authorized at all positions $j \in \{0, \dots, \tilde{T}+1\}$ with respect to M and that $s \in \Gamma^* \times Q \times \Gamma^*$ and will prove that $s \underset{M}{\longrightarrow} t$.

Let us set

$$s = uzqxv$$

where $u \in \Gamma^*$, $z \in \Gamma \cup \{\epsilon\}$, $q \in Q$, $x \in \Gamma$, and $v \in \Gamma^*$. Without loss of generality we assume that if $u = \epsilon$, then $z = \epsilon$. Since (s, t) is authorized by M, we have that $|s| = |t|$. Thus we can set

$$t = u'\zeta\eta\chi v'$$

where $|u'| = |u|$, $|\zeta| = |z|$, $|\eta| = 1$, $|\chi| = 1$, $|v'| = |v|$. Similarly, we assume that if $\zeta = \epsilon$, then $u' = \epsilon$.

- Suppose $\delta(q, x) = (q', x', \texttt{left})$. Firstly it does not occur that $(u, z) = (\epsilon, \epsilon)$, since in this case the head does not move left. Hence we have that $z \neq \epsilon$.
  - All the symbols in u' are authorized by either (a, b, c, d, b) or (c, d, e, q, d), and hence $u' = u$.
  - The symbol ζ is authorized by (d, e, q, x, q'), and hence $\zeta = q'$.
  - The symbol η is authorized by (e, q, x, f, e), and hence $\eta = z$.
  - The symbol χ is authorized by (q, x, f, g, x'), and hence $\chi = x'$.
  - All the symbols in v' are authorized by (a, b, c, d, b), and hence $v' = v$.

  Therefore we have that $t = uq'zx'v$, and thus $s \underset{M}{\longrightarrow} t$.
- Suppose $\delta(q, x) = (q', x', \texttt{stay})$.
  - All symbols in u' are authorized by either (a, b, c, d, b) or (c, d, e, q, d), and hence $u' = u$.
  - The symbol ζ is authorized by (d, e, q, x, e), and hence $\zeta = z$.
  - The symbol η is authorized by (e, q, x, f, q'), and hence $\eta = q'$.
  - The symbol χ is authorized by (q, x, f, g, x'), and hence $\chi = x'$.
  - All the symbols in v' are authorized by (a, b, c, d, b), and hence $v' = v$.

  Therefore we have that $t = uzq'x'v$, and thus $s \underset{M}{\longrightarrow} t$.
- Suppose $\delta(q, x) = (q', x', \texttt{right})$.
  - All symbols in u' are authorized by either (a, b, c, d, b) or (c, d, e, q, d), and hence $u' = u$.
  - The symbol ζ is authorized by (d, e, q, x, e), and hence $\zeta = z$.
  - The symbol η is authorized by (e, q, x, f, x'), and hence $\eta = x'$.
  - The symbol χ is authorized by (q, x', f, g, q'), and hence $\chi = q'$.
  - All the symbols v' are authorized by (a, b, c, d, b), and hence $v' = v$.

  Therefore we have that $t = uzx'q'v$, and thus $s \underset{M}{\longrightarrow} t$.

Hence, since we have $s \underset{M}{\longrightarrow} t$ for all cases, the lemma holds. □

The main theorem is as follows.

Theorem 1. *Assuming the Groth-Sahai proof system is perfectly witness indistinguishable and computationally extractable, the structure-preserving signature scheme is existentially unforgeable, and the hash function family is collision resistant, the attribute-based signature scheme is perfectly anonymous and unforgeable.*

Instantiating all the primitives from the SXDH assumption, we have the following as a corollary.

Corollary 1. *If the SXDH assumption holds for $\mathcal{G}$, our instantiation is perfectly anonymous and unforgeable.*

We then prove the main theorem.

Theorem 2. *Assuming the Groth-Sahai proof system is perfectly witness indistinguishable, the attribute-based signature scheme is perfectly anonymous.*

Proof. The theorem immediately follows from the witness indistinguishability of the proof system. Fix two Turing machines M_0 and M_1 that accept a string $w \in \{0,1\}^*$ within T steps. Since both machines accept the same string, and both $\overline{M_0}$ and $\overline{M_1}$ halt with the same time $\tilde{T}$, we have two sequences of configurations

$$t_0 \xrightarrow[\overline{M_0}]{} t_1 \xrightarrow[\overline{M_0}]{} \cdots \xrightarrow[\overline{M_0}]{} t_{\tilde{T}}$$

for M_0 and

$$s_0 \xrightarrow[\overline{M_1}]{} s_1 \xrightarrow[\overline{M_1}]{} \cdots \xrightarrow[\overline{M_1}]{} s_{\tilde{T}}$$

for M_1, in which $t_0 = s_0$. Since the public constants in the proofs, in particular the initial configuration and the accept state q_{acc}, are determined by t_0 for M_0 and s_0 for M_1, the two proofs share the same public constants. Therefore, thanks to the witness indistinguishability of the proof system, both proofs are equally distributed. □

Theorem 3. *Assuming the Groth-Sahai proof system is perfectly witness indistinguishable and computationally extractable, the structure-preserving signature scheme is existentially unforgeable, and the hash function family is collision resistant, the attribute-based signature scheme is unforgeable.*

Proof. For a given hash value $h \in \{0,1\}^\ell$, we define a Turing machine $M[h]$ as follows: It compares the first ℓ symbols of the input with the hardwired hash value h; if they are identical, it moves its head to the endmarker and accepts the input, otherwise rejects the input.

Let us consider the following sequence of games.

Game 0. This is identical to the game in the definition of unforgeability.

Game 1. In the response to each signing query (M, T, w, m), the challenger uses the Turing machine $M[h]$ where $h \leftarrow \mathsf{Hash}(\mathsf{hk}, \langle T, w, m\rangle)$ instead of M. Namely, every time (M, T, w, m) is queried, the challenger generates a signing key for $M[h]$ and use this signing key to generate a signature to be returned to the adversary. The signing key for $M[h]$ will be generated every time a query is issued, and will not be reused.

Game 2. In this game, we add the following additional clause to the winning condition: *(iv) the adversary $\mathcal{A}$ did not issue any signing query (M, T, w, m) that satisfies* $\mathsf{Hash}(\mathsf{hk}, \langle T, w, m\rangle) = \mathsf{Hash}(\mathsf{hk}, \langle T^*, w^*, m^*\rangle)$.

Game 3. In the response to either key generation queries or signing queries, the random integer $\tau \leftarrow \mathbb{Z}_p$ is equal to any of the responses to the previous queries, the challenger returns $\perp$.

Game 4. In this game the challenger replaces the common reference string crs in the public parameter pp with the extractable one $\mathsf{crs} \leftarrow \mathsf{ExtSetup}(\mathsf{gk})$.

Let us denote by W_i the event that the winning conditions are satisfied in Game i. From the triangle inequality, we have that

$$\Pr[W_0] = \sum_{i=1}^{4}(\Pr[W_{i-1}] - \Pr[W_i]) + \Pr[W_4] \leq \sum_{i=1}^{4}|\Pr[W_{i-1}] - \Pr[W_i]| + \Pr[W_4]. \tag{8}$$

To complete the proof, we then need to bound each term in this inequality.

Lemma 2. *Assuming the witness indistinguishability of the Groth-Sahai proof system,* $|\Pr[W_0] - \Pr[W_1]| = 0$.

Proof (of Lemma 2). Observe that in both games the challenger proves the same set of equalities regardless of which Turing machine is used to generate a signing key. Therefore, due to the perfect witness indistinguishability of the proof system, the challenger's responses are equally distributed. Thus the lemma holds. □

Lemma 3. *Assuming the collision resistance of the hash function family, we have that* $|\Pr[W_1] - \Pr[W_2]|$ *is negligible.*

Proof (of Lemma 3). Let F_2 be the event that the winning conditions (i), (ii), and (iii) are satisfied but the condition (iv) is not satisfied. From the difference lemma we have that $|\Pr[W_1] - \Pr[W_2]| \leq \Pr[F_2]$. To bound this probability, we construct an algorithm which attacks the collision resistance of the hash function family. The construction is as follows: The algorithm takes as input a hashing key hk; using this hashing key, the algorithm sets up the rest of the components of pp and sends it to $\mathcal{A}$; the algorithm keeps the signing key of the structure-preserving signature scheme; key generation queries and signing queries are dealt with as in the description of the games using the signing key of the structure-preserving signature scheme; when the adversary halts with an output $(T^*, w^*, m^*, \sigma^*)$, the algorithm searches for a signing query (T, w, m) that satisfies $\mathsf{Hash}(\mathsf{hk}, \langle T, w, m\rangle) = \mathsf{Hash}(\mathsf{hk}, \langle T^*, w^*, m^*\rangle)$; if a query is found, the algorithms outputs $(\langle T, w, m\rangle, \langle T^*, w^*, m^*\rangle)$ as a collision. Let us argue that whenever F_2 occurs the algorithm breaks the collision resistance of the hash function family. Since we have that the winning condition (iv) is not met, the algorithm successfully finds a query (T, w, m) that satisfies $\mathsf{Hash}(\mathsf{hk}, \langle T, w, m\rangle) = \mathsf{Hash}(\mathsf{hk}, \langle T^*, w^*, m^*\rangle)$. Since we also have that the winning condition (iii) is met, we have that $\langle T, w, m\rangle \neq \langle T^*, w^*, m^*\rangle$. Therefore, we have that whenever F_2 occurs, the algorithm successfully breaks the collision resistance of the hash function family. This implies that the probability $\Pr[F_2]$ is negligible. □

Lemma 4. *The quantity* $|\Pr[W_2] - \Pr[W_3]|$ *is negligible.*

Proof (of Lemma 4). Let F_3 be the event that any of the integers τ generated in either key generation queries or signing queries is equal to any of the integers generated in the previous queries. From the difference lemma we have that $|\Pr[W_2] - \Pr[W_3]| \leq \Pr[F_3]$. Let $F_{3,i}$ be the event that the integer in the i-th (key generation or signing) query is equal to any of the integers in the previous queries. Hence $F_3 = F_{3,1} \vee \cdots \vee F_{3,q}$ where q is the total of the numbers of the key generation and signing queries. Then we have that $\Pr[F_3] \leq \sum_{i=1}^{q} \Pr[F_{3,i}] = \sum_{i=1}^{p} \frac{i-1}{p} = \frac{q(q-1)}{2p}$, which is negligible. □

Lemma 5. *Assuming the computational extractability of the Groth-Sahai proof system, we have that* $|\Pr[W_3] - \Pr[W_4]|$ *is negligible.*

Proof (of Lemma 5). Given an adversary $\mathcal{A}$ that plays either Game 3 or Game 4, we can construct an algorithm $\mathcal{B}$ that distinguishes a witness-indistinguishable common reference string from an extractable one. The construction of $\mathcal{B}$ is as follows: $\mathcal{B}$ is given a common reference string crs, and then it sets up all the other components of the public parameter pp; $\mathcal{B}$ runs the adversary $\mathcal{A}$ with its input pp; when $\mathcal{A}$ issues a key generation or a signing query, it responds as described in the games using the signing key of the structure-preserving signature, which was generated by $\mathcal{B}$ itself; when $\mathcal{A}$ halts, $\mathcal{B}$ outputs a bit 1 if the winning conditions are satisfied, otherwise outputs 0. Since the simulation of Game 3 and Game 4 is perfect, and then by the extractability of the Groth-Sahai proof system, $|\Pr[W_3] - \Pr[W_4]|$ is negligible. □

Finally, we bound the probability $\Pr[W_4]$.

Lemma 6. *Assuming the unforgeability of the structure-preserving signature scheme, we have that* $\Pr[W_4]$ *is negligible.*

Proof (of Lemma 6). In Game 4, let us consider having the challenger extract the witness behind the forgery $(T^*, w^*, m^*, \sigma^*)$. Let us denote this witness as

$$[\tau^*], ([t^*_{i,j}])_{(i,j)\in\{1,\ldots,\tilde{T}^*\}\times\{0,\ldots,\tilde{T}^*+1\}\setminus\{(\tilde{T}^*,0)\}},$$
$$([\theta^*_{i,j}])_{(i,j)\in\{0,\ldots,\tilde{T}^*-1\}\times\{0,\ldots,\tilde{T}^*+1\}}, \quad (9)$$

where $\tilde{T}^*$ is the upper bound for the running time determined by T^*.

Given this notion, let us consider the following algorithm $\mathcal{B}$ which internally simulates Game 4 and attacks the existential unforgeability of the structure-preserving signature scheme: Given a verification key vk of the signature scheme as an input, $\mathcal{B}$ sets up the rest of the public parameter pp of the attribute-based signature scheme as in Game 4; then $\mathcal{B}$ runs $\mathcal{A}$ providing pp as $\mathcal{A}$'s input; when $\mathcal{A}$ issues a key generation query or a signing query, $\mathcal{B}$ issues signing queries to its own challenger, and using the challenger's responses to answer $\mathcal{A}$'s query as described in Game 4; once $\mathcal{A}$ halts with a forgery $(T^*, w^*, m^*, \sigma^*)$, $\mathcal{B}$ extracts an entire witness from this forgery; finally, $\mathcal{B}$ searches the set of the witness for a forgery of the structure-preserving signature scheme; if a forgery is found, $\mathcal{B}$ outputs this forgery, otherwise outputs $\perp$.

Notice that in this construction of $\mathcal{B}$, due to the computational extractability of the Groth-Sahai proof system, whenever $\mathcal{A}$ satisfies the winning condition,

$\mathcal{B}$ successfully obtains a witness that satisfies the proved equations. Therefore, to complete the proof, we argue that whenever $\mathcal{B}$ successfully obtains a witness, $\mathcal{B}$ successfully outputs a forgery against the structure-preserving signature scheme. This implies that $\Pr[W_4]$ is negligible, which concludes the proof.

The argument proceeds with a case analysis. Let us consider the following conditions.

1. The extracted τ^* is equal to one of the random integer τ generated in a response to a key generation query.
2. The extracted τ^* is equal to one of the random integer τ generated in a response to a signing query.
3. The extracted τ^* is equal to none of the above two types of τ's.

These three cases are clearly comprehensive. In the last case, any of the witness $\theta^*_{i,j}$, that is a part of the extracted witness as above, serves as a valid forgery against the underlying signature scheme, since $\mathcal{B}$ only issues signing queries which do not include τ^* in the messages.

Next, we argue that in the first two cases $\mathcal{B}$ successfully outputs a forgery.

Let us set $h^* = \mathsf{Hash}(\mathsf{hk}, \langle T^*, w^*, m^* \rangle)$. Suppose the first case has occurred. Let M be the Turing machine that is used in the response to the key generation query whose random integer τ is equal to τ^*. Due to the change introduced in Game 3, there is a unique key generation query that satisfies this. Because of the winning condition (ii), we have that M does not accept w^* in time T^*, hence $\overline{M}$ does not accepts h^*w^* in time $\tilde{T}^*$ where $\tilde{T}^*$ is the upper bound of the running time of $\overline{M}$ constructed from M. In this case, $\mathcal{B}$ issues a set of signing queries that corresponds to the transition function of $\overline{M}$, which $\mathcal{B}$ then provides as the signing key to $\mathcal{A}$. Suppose the second case has occurred. Let (M, T, w, m) be the signing query where $\mathcal{B}$ uses τ^* as the random integer to create the signature. By the change we made in Game 3, there exists at most one signing query that satisfies this. In this case, owing to the change we made in Game 1, to respond to this signing query, $\mathcal{B}$ uses the Turing machine $M[h]$ where $h = \mathsf{Hash}(\mathsf{hk}, \langle T, w, m \rangle)$. Due to the winning conditions (iii) and (iv), the Turing machine $M[h]$ does not accept h^*w^*, since $M[h]$ accepts h^*w^* only when $h^* = h$, but $h^* \neq h$. Note that similarly to the first case, $\mathcal{B}$ issues a set of signing queries that corresponds to the transition function of $M[h]$ to its own challenger.

In any case, $\mathcal{B}$ only issues a set of signing queries which correspond to some Turing machine M^* (which is either $\overline{M}$ or $M[h]$ mentioned above) that does not accept h^*w^*. From now on we will argue that in these cases there is a signature θ^* in the extracted $\theta^*_{i,j}$'s whose message is not issued by $\mathcal{B}$ as a signing query to its own challenger.

Let $t^*_i = t^*_{i,0} \cdots t^*_{i,\tilde{T}^*+1}$ for all $i \in \{0, \ldots, \tilde{T}\}$. Notice that t^*_0 is the valid initial configuration of M^* with input h^*w^*, and $t^*_{\tilde{T}^*}$ is the configuration whose state is q_{acc}. Then since M^* does not accept h^*w^*, there exists i that satisfies $t^*_i \underset{M^*}{\not\longrightarrow} t^*_{i+1}$. Let i^* be the smallest index satisfying $t^*_{i^*} \underset{M^*}{\not\longrightarrow} t^*_{i^*+1}$. Observe that $t^*_0 \in \Gamma^* \times Q \times \Gamma^*$ and that $t^*_0 \underset{M^*}{\longrightarrow} t^*_1 \underset{M^*}{\longrightarrow} \cdots \underset{M^*}{\longrightarrow} t^*_{i^*}$. It is trivial to check that, if $s \underset{M^*}{\longrightarrow} t$, and $s \in \Gamma^* \times Q \times \Gamma^*$, then $t \in \Gamma^* \times Q \times \Gamma^*$, since a state cannot split into two states as long as $s \underset{M^*}{\longrightarrow} t$. Therefore, we have that $t^*_{i^*} \in \Gamma^* \times Q \times \Gamma^*$ and that $t^*_{i^*} \underset{M^*}{\not\longrightarrow} t^*_{i^*+1}$, and hence we can apply Lemma 1. Lemma 1 ensures that the pair $(t^*_{i^*}, t^*_{i^*+1})$ is not authorized at some position j^* with respect to M^*. Since $\mathcal{B}$ only issues signing queries of the forms that appear in Definition 5, the tuple $(\tau^*, t^*_{i^*,j^*-1}, t^*_{i^*,j^*}, t^*_{i^*,j^*+1}, t^*_{i^*,j^*+2}, t^*_{i^*+1,j^*})$ is never issued as a signing query by $\mathcal{B}$. Thus $\theta^*_{i^*,j^*}$ is a valid forgery for the structure-preserving signature scheme.

To sum up, in any case, that $\mathcal{A}$ satisfies the winning conditions, $\mathcal{B}$ successfully finds a forgery. Therefore, the probability $\Pr[W_4]$ is negligible due to the unforgeability of the structure-preserving signature scheme. □

Finally, we have that all the terms in Eq. (8) are negligible, which implies that $\Pr[W_0]$ is negligible. □

6 Attribute-Based Signature Scheme for Nondeterministic Finite Automata

In this section, we present an attribute-based signature scheme for nondeterministic finite automata. As mentioned in the introduction, this is the first scheme supporting nondeterministic computation as the policy. The syntax and security definitions are similar to those of Turing machines, thus we defer those definitions to the full version.

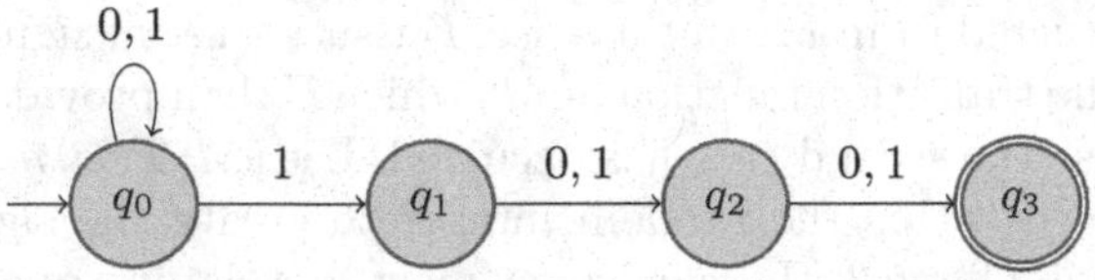

Fig. 2. An example of NFA: it accepts all strings over $\{0, 1\}$ containing a 1 in the third position from the last.

6.1 Nondeterministic Finite Automata

We give a syntactic definition of finite automata. Let Σ be a finite set of alphabet.

Definition 6. *A nondeterministic finite automaton (NFA) over Σ is defined by the tuple $M = (Q, \delta, q_0, F)$ where: (1) Q is a finite set of states, (2) $\delta\colon Q \times \Sigma \to \mathcal{P}(Q)$ is a transition function, (3) $q_0 \in Q$ is the initial state, and (4) $F \subseteq Q$ is a set of accepting states. We say that a nondeterministic finite automaton $M = (Q, \delta, q_0, F)$ accepts a string $w = w_1 \cdots w_n$ if there exists a sequence $(r_0, r_1, \ldots, r_n)$ of states satisfying (1) $r_0 = q_0$, (2) $\delta(r_{i-1}, w_i) \ni r_i$ for all $i \in \{1, \ldots, n\}$, and (3) $r_n \in F$.*

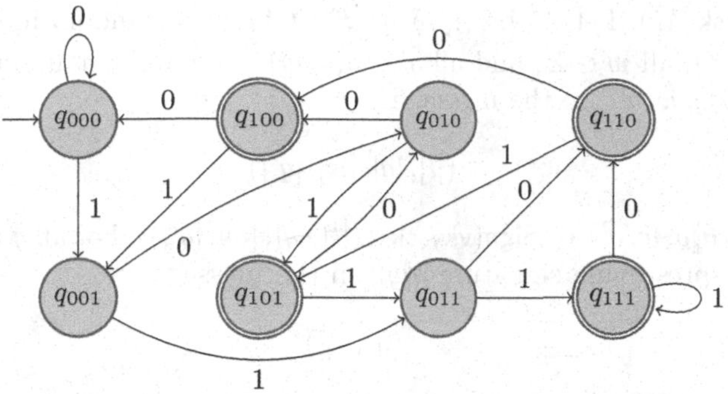

Fig. 3. The smallest DFA that is equivalent to the NFA of Fig. 2.

We remark that the above definition does not allow an automaton to have ε-transitions, i.e., a transition which moves to a new state without reading a symbol. However, it is well known that we can convert any nondeterministic finite automata having ε-transitions into a nondeterministic finite automaton which falls into the above definition, without increasing the number of the states.

For self-containment and ease of understanding, we provide an example of NFA in Fig. 2. This NFA accepts all strings over $\{0, 1\}$ containing a 1 in the third position from the last. It is well known that any NFA can be converted into an equivalent DFA but with an exponential blowup in the number of states (see, for example, [Sip96]). We provide in Fig. 3 such an equivalent DFA to the NFA of Fig. 2. These examples are copied almost verbatim from Sipser's book [Sip96].

6.2 Notations

We define some notations. For an alphabet Σ, let $\hat{\Sigma}$ be $\Sigma \cup \{-1, -2\}$. We assume that the hash function Hash has as its range $\{-1, -2\}^\ell$ instead of $\{0, 1\}^\ell$ to separate the alphabet for hash values from the alphabet for attribute strings. For an NFA $M = (Q, \delta, q_0, F)$, we define an NFA $\hat{M} = (Q, \hat{\delta}, q_0, F)$ over $\hat{\Sigma}$ as follows:

$$\hat{\delta}(q, w) = \begin{cases} \delta(q, w) & (w \in \Sigma), \\ \{q\} & (w \in \{-1, -2\}). \end{cases}$$

6.3 The Scheme

The construction of our scheme is as follows.

$\mathsf{AttrSetup}(1^k, 1^N)$. Given a security parameter 1^k and the size 1^N of an alphabet, generate a bilinear group parameter $\mathsf{gk} = (p, \mathbb{G}_1, \mathbb{G}_2, \mathbb{G}_T, e, g, \tilde{g}) \leftarrow \mathcal{G}(1^k)$, a common reference string $\mathsf{crs} \leftarrow \mathsf{WISetup}(\mathsf{gk})$, two key pairs $(\mathsf{vk}_\delta, \mathsf{sk}_\delta) \leftarrow \mathsf{Kg}(\mathsf{gk}, 1^4)$ and $(\mathsf{vk}_F, \mathsf{sk}_F) \leftarrow \mathsf{Kg}(\mathsf{gk}, 1^2)$ of the structure-preserving signature, and a hashing key $\mathsf{hk} \leftarrow \mathcal{H}(1^k)$. Let $\mathsf{pp} \leftarrow (N, \mathsf{gk}, \mathsf{crs}, \mathsf{vk}_\delta, \mathsf{vk}_F, \mathsf{hk})$ and $\mathsf{msk} \leftarrow (\mathsf{sk}_\delta, \mathsf{sk}_F)$ and output $(\mathsf{pp}, \mathsf{msk})$.

$\mathsf{AttrGen}(\mathsf{pp}, \mathsf{msk}, M)$. Let $\hat{M}$ be $(Q, \hat{\delta}, q_0, F)$. Choose a random integer $t \leftarrow \mathbb{Z}_p$. For all $q \in Q$, all $w \in \hat{\Sigma}$, and all $q' \in \hat{\delta}(q, w)$ generate a structure-preserving signature $\theta[\![q, w, q']\!]$ on the message

$$([t], [q], [w], [q'])$$

by running $\theta[\![q, w, q']\!] \leftarrow \mathsf{Sign}(\mathsf{vk}_\delta, \mathsf{sk}_\delta, ([t], [q], [w], [q']))$. For all $q \in F$ generate a structure-preserving signature $\rho[\![q]\!]$ on the message

$$([t], [q])$$

by running $\rho[\![q]\!] \leftarrow \mathsf{Sign}(\mathsf{vk}_\rho, \mathsf{sk}_\rho, ([t], [q]))$. Let sk be

$$(M, t, (\theta[\![q, w, q']\!])_{q \in Q, w \in \hat{\Sigma}, q' \in \hat{\delta}(q,w)}, (\rho[\![q]\!])_{q \in F})$$

and output sk.

$\mathsf{AttrSign}(\mathsf{pp}, \mathsf{sk}, w, m)$. Let $w_1 \cdots w_n$ be w.

1. Compute $h \leftarrow \mathsf{Hash}(\mathsf{hk}, \langle w, m \rangle)$. Let $\hat{w} = \hat{w}_1 \cdots \hat{w}_{n+\ell}$ be wh.
2. Let $(\hat{q}_0, \hat{q}_1, \ldots, \hat{q}_{n+\ell})$ be one of the sequence of the states that $\hat{M}$ takes when $\hat{M}$ accepts $\hat{w}$.
3. Let $\hat{\theta}_i$ be $\theta[\![\hat{q}_{i-1}, \hat{w}_i, \hat{q}_i]\!]$ for each $i \in \{1, \ldots, n+\ell\}$.
4. Let $\hat{\rho}$ be $\hat{\rho}[\![\hat{q}_{n+\ell}]\!]$.
5. Compute
   - a Groth-Sahai commitment $\psi^{(t)}$ to $[t]$,
   - a Groth-Sahai commitment $\psi_i^{(q)}$ to $[\hat{q}_i]$ for each $i \in \{1, \ldots, n+\ell\}$,
   - a Groth-Sahai commitment $\psi_i^{(\theta)}$ to $\hat{\theta}_i$ for each $i \in \{1, \ldots, n+\ell\}$, and
   - a Groth-Sahai commitment $\psi^{(\rho)}$ to $\hat{\rho}$.
6. Compute a proof $\pi_i^{(\theta)}$ of the equation
$$\mathsf{Verify}(\mathsf{vk}_\delta, ([t], [\hat{q}_{i-1}], [\hat{w}_i], [\hat{q}_i]), \hat{\theta}_i) = 1$$
   for each $i \in \{1, \ldots, n+\ell\}$.
7. Compute a proof $\pi^{(\rho)}$ of the equation
$$\mathsf{Verify}(\mathsf{vk}_F, ([t], [\hat{q}_{n+\ell}]), \hat{\rho}) = 1.$$
8. Let σ be
$$(\psi^{(t)}, \psi_1^{(q)}, \ldots, \psi_{n+\ell}^{(q)}, \psi_1^{(\theta)}, \ldots, \psi_{n+\ell}^{(\theta)}, \psi^{(\rho)}, \pi_1^{(\theta)}, \ldots, \pi_{n+\ell}^{(\theta)}, \pi^{(\rho)})$$
   and output σ.

$\mathsf{AttrVerify}(\mathsf{pp}, w, m, \sigma)$. Compute $h \leftarrow \mathsf{Hash}(\mathsf{hk}, \langle w, m \rangle)$ and let $\hat{w}$ be wh. Under this $\hat{w}$ verify all the proofs included in σ where the initial state q_0 is treated as a public constant in the non-interactive proofs. If all the proofs are verified as valid, output 1. Otherwise output 0.

The security of the scheme is postponed to the full version.

7 Conclusion

In this paper, we formalize a new cryptographic primitive, attribute-based signatures for Turing machines. We also present an efficient instantiation of this primitive using the Groth-Sahai proof system, a structure-preserving signature scheme, and a collision-resistant hash function family. In addition, we present an attribute-based signature scheme for NFA, which is more efficient than our first scheme, while less expressive. These two schemes provide a trade-off between efficiency and expressiveness.

Acknowledgment. The first author is supported by JSPS KAKENHI Grant Number 18K18055. The second author was partially supported by JST CREST Grant Number JPMJCR1302 and JSPS KAKENHI Grant Number 17J05603. The first, third, and fourth authors are partially supported by JST CREST Grant Number JPMJCR1688.

References

[AS16] Ananth, P., Sahai, A.: Functional encryption for turing machines. In: Kushilevitz, E., Malkin, T. (eds.) TCC 2016. LNCS, vol. 9562, pp. 125–153. Springer, Heidelberg (2016). https://doi.org/10.1007/978-3-662-49096-9_6

[BF14] Bellare, M., Fuchsbauer, G.: Policy-based signatures. In: Krawczyk, H. (ed.) PKC 2014. LNCS, vol. 8383, pp. 520–537. Springer, Heidelberg (2014). https://doi.org/10.1007/978-3-642-54631-0_30

[BGI14] Boyle, E., Goldwasser, S., Ivan, I.: Functional signatures and pseudorandom functions. In: Krawczyk, H. (ed.) PKC 2014. LNCS, vol. 8383, pp. 501–519. Springer, Heidelberg (2014). https://doi.org/10.1007/978-3-642-54631-0_29

[DDM17] Datta, P., Dutta, R., Mukhopadhyay, S.: Attribute-based signatures for Turing machines. Cryptology ePrint Archive, Report 2017/801 (2017). http://eprint.iacr.org/2017/801

[GKP+13] Goldwasser, S., Kalai, Y.T., Popa, R.A., Vaikuntanathan, V., Zeldovich, N.: How to run turing machines on encrypted data. In: Canetti, R., Garay, J.A. (eds.) CRYPTO 2013. LNCS, vol. 8043, pp. 536–553. Springer, Heidelberg (2013). https://doi.org/10.1007/978-3-642-40084-1_30

[GS12] Groth, J., Sahai, A.: Efficient noninteractive proof systems for bilinear groups. SIAM J. Comput. **41**(5), 1193–1232 (2012)

[KPW15] Kiltz, E., Pan, J., Wee, H.: Structure-preserving signatures from standard assumptions, revisited. In: Gennaro, R., Robshaw, M. (eds.) CRYPTO 2015. LNCS, vol. 9216, pp. 275–295. Springer, Heidelberg (2015). https://doi.org/10.1007/978-3-662-48000-7_14

[MPR11] Maji, H.K., Prabhakaran, M., Rosulek, M.: Attribute-based signatures. In: Kiayias, A. (ed.) CT-RSA 2011. LNCS, vol. 6558, pp. 376–392. Springer, Heidelberg (2011). https://doi.org/10.1007/978-3-642-19074-2_24

[NP15] Nandi, M., Pandit, T.: On the power of pair encodings: Frameworks for predicate cryptographic primitives. Cryptology ePrint Archive, Report 2015/955 (2015). http://eprint.iacr.org/

[OT11] Okamoto, T., Takashima, K.: Efficient attribute-based signatures for non-monotone predicates in the standard model. In: Catalano, D., Fazio, N., Gennaro, R., Nicolosi, A. (eds.) PKC 2011. LNCS, vol. 6571, pp. 35–52. Springer, Heidelberg (2011). https://doi.org/10.1007/978-3-642-19379-8_3

[SAH16] Sakai, Y., Attrapadung, N., Hanaoka, G.: Attribute-based signatures for circuits from bilinear map. In: Cheng, C.-M., Chung, K.-M., Persiano, G., Yang, B.-Y. (eds.) PKC 2016. LNCS, vol. 9614, pp. 283–300. Springer, Heidelberg (2016). https://doi.org/10.1007/978-3-662-49384-7_11

[Sip96] Sipser, M.: Introduction to the Theory of Computation, 1st edn. International Thomson Publishing, Stamford (1996)

[SSN09] Shahandashti, S.F., Safavi-Naini, R.: Threshold attribute-based signatures and their application to anonymous credential systems. In: Preneel, B. (ed.) AFRICACRYPT 2009. LNCS, vol. 5580, pp. 198–216. Springer, Heidelberg (2009). https://doi.org/10.1007/978-3-642-02384-2_13

[TLL14] Tang, F., Li, H., Liang, B.: Attribute-Based Signatures for Circuits from Multilinear Maps. In: Chow, S.S.M., Camenisch, J., Hui, L.C.K., Yiu, S.M. (eds.) ISC 2014. LNCS, vol. 8783, pp. 54–71. Springer, Cham (2014). https://doi.org/10.1007/978-3-319-13257-0_4

Asiacrypt 2018 Award Paper II

Learning Strikes Again: The Case of the DRS Signature Scheme

Yang Yu[1(✉)] and Léo Ducas[2]

[1] Department of Computer Science and Technology, Tsinghua University, Beijing, China
yang.yu0986@gmail.com

[2] Cryptology Group, CWI, Amsterdam, The Netherlands
ducas@cwi.nl

Abstract. Lattice signature schemes generally require particular care when it comes to preventing secret information from leaking through signature transcript. For example, the Goldreich-Goldwasser-Halevi (GGH) signature scheme and the NTRUSign scheme were completely broken by the parallelepiped-learning attack of Nguyen and Regev (Eurocrypt 2006). Several heuristic countermeasures were also shown vulnerable to similar statistical attacks.

At PKC 2008, Plantard, Susilo and Win proposed a new variant of GGH, informally arguing resistance to such attacks. Based on this variant, Plantard, Sipasseuth, Dumondelle and Susilo proposed a concrete signature scheme, called DRS, that has been accepted in the round 1 of the NIST post-quantum cryptography project.

In this work, we propose yet another statistical attack and demonstrate a weakness of the DRS scheme: one can recover some partial information of the secret key from sufficiently many signatures. One difficulty is that, due to the DRS reduction algorithm, the relation between the statistical leak and the secret seems more intricate. We work around this difficulty by training a statistical model, using a few features that we designed according to a simple heuristic analysis.

While we only recover partial information on the secret key, this information is easily exploited by lattice attacks, significantly decreasing their complexity. Concretely, we claim that, provided that 100 000 signatures are available, the secret key may be recovered using BKZ-138 for the first set of DRS parameters submitted to the NIST. This puts the security level of this parameter set below 80-bits (maybe even 70-bits), to be compared to an original claim of 128-bits.

Keywords: Cryptanalysis · Lattice based signature
Statistical attack · Learning · BDD

1 Introduction

At Crypto'97, Goldreich, Goldwasser and Halevi proposed the encryption and signature schemes [16] whose security relies on the hardness of lattice problems. Concurrently, a practical scheme, NTRUEncrypt was proposed, and adapted

T. Peyrin and S. Galbraith (Eds.): ASIACRYPT 2018, LNCS 11273, pp. 525–543, 2018.
https://doi.org/10.1007/978-3-030-03329-3_18

for signatures a few years later (NTRUSign [18]). In 2006, Nguyen and Regev presented a celebrated statistical attack [23] and completely broke GGH and NTRUSign in practice. The starting point of NR attack is a basic observation that any difference between signature and message always lies in the parallelepiped spanned by secret key. Thus each signature leaks partial information about the secret key, which allows to fully recover the secret key from sufficiently many signatures. In 2012, Ducas and Nguyen revisited NR attack [13] and showed that it could be generalized to defeat several heuristic countermeasures [18,19].

Designing secure and efficient lattice based signatures remains a challenging problem. To get rid of information leaks, the now standard method is to use a delicate sampling algorithm for trapdoor inversion [15,25].[1] Following such setting, it can be proved that signatures are independent of the secret key. Yet this provable guarantee doesn't come cheap in terms of efficiency and simplicity: it remains very tempting to make more aggressive design choices.

Such a design was proposed by Plantard, Susilo and Win [27]. It is very close to the original GGH scheme, with a modified reduction algorithm that produces signatures falling in a known hypercube, independent of the secret key. According to the authors, such property should prevent the NR attack. The main idea of [27] is to reduce vectors under ℓ_∞-norm instead of Euclidean norm. Recently, Plantard, Sipasseuth, Dumondelle and Susilo updated this scheme, and submitted it to the NIST post-quantum cryptography project, under the name of DRS [26], standing for Diagonal-dominant Reduction Signature. Currently DRS is in the list of round 1 submissions to the NIST post-quantum cryptography project.

Our results. In this work, we present a statistical attack against the DRS scheme [26,27]. We first notice that while the support of the transcript distribution is indeed fixed and known, the distribution itself is not, and is related to the secret key. More concretely, in the DRS signature, the reduction algorithm will introduce some correlations among coordinates w_i's of the signature, and these correlations are strongly related to certain coefficients of the secret key $\mathbf{S}$.

In more details, we assume that the coefficient $\mathbf{S}_{i,j}$ can be well approximated by some function of the distribution of (w_i, w_j) and proceed to profile such a function according to known instances (the training phase). Once we have the function, we can measure over sufficient signatures and obtain the guess for an unknown secret $\mathbf{S}$.

With a few extra amplification tricks, we show this attack to be rather effective: for the first set of parameters, 100 000 signatures suffice to locate all the large coefficients of the secret matrix $\mathbf{S}$ and to determine most of their signs as well. Finally, we can feed this leaked information back into lattice attacks (BDD-uSVP attack), significantly decreasing their cost. Concretely, we claim that the first set of parameters offers at most 80-bits of security, significantly less than the original claim of 128-bits.

---

[1] Alternatively, one may resort to the (trapdoorless) Fiat-Shamir with aborts approach such as done in [12,21], yet for simplicity, we focus our discussion on the Hash-then-Sign approach.

As a by-product, we formalize how to accelerate BDD attack when given some known coefficients of the solution. More specifically, we are able to construct a lattice of the same volume but smaller dimension for this kind of BDD instances.

Our scripts are open source for checking, reproduction or extension purposes, available at https://github.com/yuyang-Tsinghua/DRS_Cryptanalysis.

Related work. Very recently, Li, Liu, Nitaj and Pan proposed a chosen message attack [17] against the randomized version of Plantard-Susilo-Win GGH signature variant [27]. Their starting observation is that the difference between two signatures of a same message is a relatively short lattice vector in the randomized Plantard-Susilo-Win scheme, then from enough such short lattice vectors one may recover some short vectors of the secret matrix by lattice reduction. The randomized modification is a crucial weakness of Plantard-Susilo-Win scheme exploited by the attack in [17]. To fix such weakness, the authors mentioned two strategies: storing previous messages and padding a random nonce in the hash function. In comparison, our targeted scheme and technical idea are different from those in [17]. More importantly, the weakness of the DRS scheme that we demonstrate does not seem to be easily fixed.

Roadmap. In Sect. 2, we introduce notations and background on lattices. In Sect. 3, we provide a brief description of DRS signature scheme. Then we explain how to learn large coefficients of the secret matrix in Sect. 4, and how to combine partial information and lattice techniques to recover the full key in Sect. 5. Finally, we conclude and discuss potential countermeasure in Sect. 6.

2 Preliminaries

We use bold lowercase letters for vectors and denote by v_i the i-th entry of the vector $\mathbf{v}$. We denote by $\|\mathbf{v}\|$ (resp. $\|\mathbf{v}\|_\infty$) the Euclidean norm (resp. ℓ_∞-norm) of $\mathbf{v}$. For simplicity and matching programming, we assume the script of each entry of $\mathbf{v} \in \mathbb{R}^n$ is an element of $\mathbb{Z}_n = \{0, \cdots, n-1\}$.

Let $\mathbf{rot}_i(\mathbf{v}) = (v_{-i}, \cdots, v_{-i+n-1})$ be a rotation of $\mathbf{v} \in \mathbb{R}^n$. We denote by $\mathbf{srot}_i(\mathbf{v})$ the vector generated by $\mathbf{rot}_i(\mathbf{v})$ with each entry changing the sign independently with probability 1/2. We define the set

$$\mathcal{T}(n, b, N_b, N_1) = \left\{ \mathbf{v} \in \mathbb{Z}^n \,\middle|\, \begin{array}{r l} & N_b \text{ entries equal } b; \\ \mathbf{v} \text{ is a vector with exactly} & N_1 \text{ entries equal } 1; \\ & \text{and the rest of entries equal } 0. \end{array} \right\}.$$

We use bold capital letters for matrices and denote by $\mathbf{v}_i$ the i-th row of the matrix $\mathbf{V}$, i.e. $\mathbf{V} = (\mathbf{v}_0, \cdots, \mathbf{v}_{n-1})$. We use $\mathbf{V}_{i,j}$ to represent the entry in the i-th row and j-th column of $\mathbf{V}$. Let $\mathbf{I}_n$ be the n-dimensional identity matrix. We denote by $\mathbf{ROT}(\mathbf{v})$ (resp. $\mathbf{SROT}(\mathbf{v})$) the matrix $(\mathbf{rot}_0(\mathbf{v}), \cdots, \mathbf{rot}_{n-1}(\mathbf{v}))$ (resp. $(\mathbf{srot}_0(\mathbf{v}), \cdots, \mathbf{srot}_{n-1}(\mathbf{v}))$). Note that all $\mathbf{srot}_i(\mathbf{v})$'s in $\mathbf{SROT}(\mathbf{v})$ are generated independently. A matrix $\mathbf{V}$ is diagonal dominant if $\mathbf{V}_{i,i} > \sum_{j \neq i} |\mathbf{V}_{i,j}|$ for all i.

For a distribution D, we write $X \leftarrow D$ when the random variable X is sampled from D. Given a finite set S, let $U(S)$ be the uniform distribution over S. We denote by $\mathbb{E}(X)$ the expectation of random variable X.

A (full-rank) n-dimensional lattice $\mathcal{L}$ is the set of all integer combinations of linearly independent vectors $\mathbf{b}_0, \cdots, \mathbf{b}_{n-1} \in \mathbb{R}^n$, i.e. $\mathcal{L} = \{\sum_{i=0}^{n-1} x_i \mathbf{b}_i \mid x_i \in \mathbb{Z}\}$. We call $\mathbf{B} = (\mathbf{b}_0, \cdots, \mathbf{b}_{n-1})$ a basis of $\mathcal{L}$ and write $\mathcal{L} = \mathcal{L}(\mathbf{B})$. For a unimodular matrix $\mathbf{U} \in \mathbb{Z}^{n \times n}$, we have $\mathbf{UB}$ is also a basis of $\mathcal{L}(\mathbf{B})$, i.e. $\mathcal{L}(\mathbf{B}) = \mathcal{L}(\mathbf{UB})$. Let $(\mathbf{b}_0^*, \cdots, \mathbf{b}_{n-1}^*)$ be the Gram-Schmidt vectors of $\mathbf{B}$. The volume of the lattice $\mathcal{L}(\mathbf{B})$ is $\mathrm{vol}(\mathcal{L}(\mathbf{B})) = \prod_i \|\mathbf{b}_i^*\|$ that is an invariant of the lattice. Given $\mathcal{L} \subseteq \mathbb{R}^n$ and $\mathbf{t} \in \mathbb{R}^n$, the distance between $\mathbf{t}$ and $\mathcal{L}$ is $\mathrm{dist}(\mathbf{t}, \mathcal{L}) = \min_{\mathbf{v} \in \mathcal{L}} \|\mathbf{t} - \mathbf{v}\|$.

Lattice reduction is an important tool for solving lattice problems and estimating the security of lattice-based cryptosystems. The goal of lattice reduction is to find a basis of high quality. The quality of a basis $\mathbf{B}$ is related to its root Hermite factor $\mathbf{rhf}(\mathbf{B}) = \left(\frac{\|\mathbf{b}_0\|}{\mathrm{vol}(\mathcal{L}(\mathbf{B}))^{1/n}}\right)^{1/n}$. Currently, the most practical lattice reduction algorithms are BKZ [28] and BKZ 2.0 [10]. We denote by BKZ-β the BKZ/BKZ 2.0 with blocksize β. In general, we assume the root Hermite factor of a BKZ-β basis is bounded by

$$\delta_\beta \approx \left(\frac{(\pi\beta)^{\frac{1}{\beta}}\beta}{2\pi e}\right)^{\frac{1}{2(\beta-1)}}$$

when $n \gg \beta > 50$.

3 The DRS Signature Scheme

In this section, we are to make a brief description of the DRS scheme. We may omit some details that are unnecessary for understanding our attack. For more details on the algorithms and implementations we refer to [26].

To start with, we introduce several public parameters of DRS:

- n : the dimension
- D : the diagonal coefficient of the secret key
- b : the magnitude of the large coefficients (i.e. $\{\pm b\}$) in the secret key
- N_b : the number of large coefficients per vector in the secret key
- N_1 : the number of small coefficients (i.e. $\{\pm 1\}$) per vector in the secret key

Following the setting provided in [26], the parameter D is chosen to be n and satisfies that $D > b \cdot N_b + N_1$.

The secret key of DRS is a matrix

$$\mathbf{S} = D \cdot \mathbf{I}_n - \mathbf{M}$$

where $\mathbf{M} = \mathbf{SROT}(\mathbf{v})$ with $\mathbf{v} \leftarrow U\left(\mathcal{T}(n, b, N_b, N_1) \bigcap \{\mathbf{v} \in \mathbb{Z}^n \mid v_0 = 0\}\right)$ is the noise matrix. It is easily verified that $\mathbf{S}$ is diagonal dominant. The public key is a matrix $\mathbf{P}$ such that $\mathcal{L}(\mathbf{P}) = \mathcal{L}(\mathbf{S})$ and the vectors in $\mathbf{P}$ are much longer than those in $\mathbf{S}$.

Hash space. The specification submitted to the NIST [26] is rather unclear about the message space. Namely, only a bound of 2^{28} is mentioned, which suggests a hash space $\mathcal{M} = (-2^{28}, 2^{28})^n$, following the original scheme [27]. Yet, we noted that the implementation seems to instead use the message space $\mathcal{M} = (0, 2^{28})^n$: the sign randomization is present, but commented out. Discussion with the designers[2] led us to consider this as an implementation bug, and we therefore focus on the analysis with $\mathcal{M} = (-2^{28}, 2^{28})^n$, following both the original scheme [27] and the intention of [26].

We strongly suspect that taking $\mathcal{M} = (0, 2^{28})^n$ would not be an effective countermeasure against the kind attack analyzed in this paper. Preliminaries experiments on this variant suggested that leak was stronger, but its relation to the secret key seemed more intricate.

For our experiments, we generated directly uniform points in that space rather than hashing messages to this space; according to the Random Oracle Model, this should make no difference.

Signature. The signature algorithm of DRS follows the one in [27] and its main component is a message reduction procedure in ℓ_∞-norm. It is summarized below as Algorithm 1.

Algorithm 1. Message reduction in DRS signature algorithm

Input: a message $\mathbf{m} \in \mathbb{Z}^n$, the secret matrix $\mathbf{S}$
Output: a reduced message $\mathbf{w} \in \mathbb{Z}^n$ such that $\mathbf{w} - \mathbf{m} \in \mathcal{L}(\mathbf{S})$

$\mathbf{w} \leftarrow \mathbf{m}, i \leftarrow 0, k \leftarrow 0$
repeat
  $q \leftarrow \lfloor w_i/D \rceil_{\rightarrow 0}$, (Rounding toward 0)
  if $q \neq 0$ **then**
    $\mathbf{w} \leftarrow \mathbf{w} - q\mathbf{s}_i$
    $k = 0$
  end if
  $k \leftarrow k+1$, $i \leftarrow (i+1) \bmod n$
until $k = n$
return $\mathbf{w}$

In brief, the message reduction is reducing successively each large coefficient m_i of the message $\mathbf{m}$ by qD such that $|m_i - qD| < D$ but adding $\pm q, \pm qb$ to m_j with $j \neq i$ according to the entries of $\mathbf{M}$, until all coefficients of the reduced message are within $(-D, D)$. Since $\mathbf{S}$ is diagonal dominant, the message can be reduced within bounded steps as proved in [26,27].

Besides the reduced message $\mathbf{w}$, an auxiliary vector $\mathbf{k}$ is also included in the signature and used to accelerate the verification. To verify the signature, one would first check whether $\|\mathbf{w}\|_\infty < D$ and then check whether $\mathbf{m} - \mathbf{w} = \mathbf{kP}$. In later discussions, we shall ignore the auxiliary vector, because it can be calculated in polynomial time from $\mathbf{w}, \mathbf{m}$ and the public key $\mathbf{P}$.

[2] https://csrc.nist.gov/CSRC/media/Projects/Post-Quantum-Cryptography/documents/round-1/official-comments/DRS-official-comment.pdf.

4 Learning Coefficients of the Secret Matrix

All DRS signatures $\mathbf{w}$ lie in and fill the region $(-D, D)^n$. Unlike the GGH scheme, the signature region is a known hypercube and independent of the secret matrix, thus the DRS scheme was deemed to resist statistical attacks. However, the distribution of random signature in $(-D, D)^n$ may be still related to the secret key, which would leak some key information.

In later discussion, we aim at a concrete parameter set

$$(n, D, b, N_b, N_1) = (912, 912, 28, 16, 432)$$

that is submitted to the NIST and claimed to provide at least 128-bits of security in [26].

4.1 Intuition on a Potential Leak

Our approach is to try to recover $\mathbf{S}_{i,j}$ by studying the distribution $W_{i,j}$ of (w_i, w_j). Indeed, when a reduction happens at index i: $\mathbf{w} \leftarrow \mathbf{w} - q\mathbf{s}_i$, and when $\mathbf{S}_{i,j} \neq 0$ some correlation is introduced between w_i and w_j. Symmetrically, correlation is also introduced when $\mathbf{S}_{j,i} \neq 0$. Another source of correlations is created by other reductions at index $k \notin \{i, j\}$ when both $\mathbf{S}_{k,i}$ and $\mathbf{S}_{k,j}$ are non-zero; these events create much less correlations since the diagonal coefficients are much larger, but those correlations accumulate over many k's. One is tempted to model the accumulated correlations as those of some bi-variate Gaussians with a certain covariance.

Of course, there are complicated "cascading" phenomena: by modifying a coefficient, a reduction may trigger another reduction at an other index. But let us ignore such phenomena, and just assume that several reductions at indices $k \neq i, j$ occur, followed by one reduction at index i with $q = \pm 1$, before the algorithm terminates. We depict our intuition as Fig. 1.

In this simple model, we note that there are 4 degrees of liberty, 3 for the shape of the ellipsoid, and 1 for $\mathbf{S}_{i,j} = -b, 0, b$.[3] Therefore, one may expect to be able to recover all the parameters using 4 statistical measures. One natural choice is the following. First, measure the covariance matrix of the whole distribution, which gives 3 parameters. Assuming the clipped caps have small weights, this would roughly give the shape of the ellipsoid. For the last measure, one would select only sample for which $|w_i|$ is small, so as to focus on the superimposed displaced caps. With a bit of effort one would find an appropriate measurement.

Unfortunately, it seems rather hard to determine mathematically what will precisely happen in the full reduction algorithm, and to construct by hand a measurement on the distribution of (w_i, w_j) directly giving $\mathbf{S}_{i,j}$, i.e. a function f such that $f(W_{i,j}) = \mathbf{S}_{i,j}$.

[3] In fact, two of those degrees are fixed by the shape of the secret matrix: each rows of $\mathbf{S}$ has fixed Euclidean length, fixing the variance of w_i and w_j.

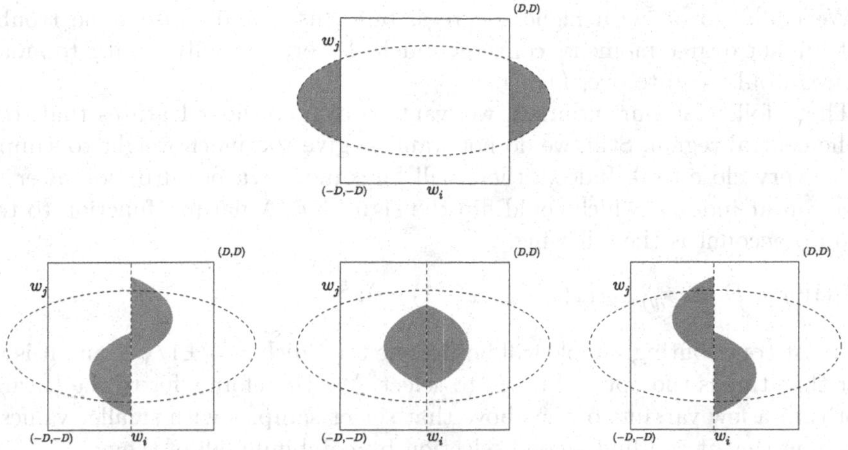

Fig. 1. Figures in the second row show the regions to which (w_i, w_j) in two cap regions will be moved by reduction at index i when $\mathbf{S}_{i,j} = -b, 0, b$ respectively from left to right.

4.2 Training

While constructing such a function f by a mathematical analysis may be hard, our hope is that such function may be easy to learn using standard techniques, ranging from least-square method to convolutional neural networks. Indeed, going back to Fig. 1, recovering $\mathbf{S}_{i,j}$ from $W_{i,j}$ can essentially be viewed as a grey-scale image classification problem (the lightness of the pixel (x, y) corresponding to the density of $W_{i,j}$ at (x, y)).

Features. We therefore proceed to design a few *features*, according to the intuition built above. The average of each w_i is supposed to be 0, thus we do not treat it as a feature. Certainly, the covariance information is helpful, but we also introduce extra similar statistics to allow the learning algorithm to handle extra perturbations not captured by our simple intuition. We restrict our features to being symmetric: a sample (x, y) should have the same impact as $(-x, -y)$. Indeed, while quite involved, the whole reduction process preserves this symmetry.

More specifically, by scaling a factor of D, consider the distribution W to have support $(-1, 1)^2$. For a function f over $(-1, 1)^2$, we write $f(W) = \mathbb{E}_{(x,y)\leftarrow W}(f(x))$. The features mentioned before are listed below[4]:

- $f_1(W) = D \cdot \mathbb{E}_{(x,y)\leftarrow W}(x \cdot y)$;
- $f_2(W) = D \cdot \mathbb{E}_{(x,y)\leftarrow W}(x \cdot |x|^{1/2} \cdot y)$;
- $f_3(W) = D \cdot \mathbb{E}_{(x,y)\leftarrow W}(x \cdot |x| \cdot y)$;

[4] We introduced a re-normalization factor D in our experiments. We keep it in this paper for consistency.

We could go on with higher degrees, but this would cause some trouble. First, higher degree moments converge much slower. Secondly, taking too many features would lead to over-fitting.

Then, following our intuition, we want to also consider features that focus on the central region. Still, we do not want to give too much weight to samples with x very close to 0. Indeed, there will be some extra perturbation after the reduction at index i, which could flip the sign of x. A natural function to take this into account is the following.

- $f_4(W) = D \cdot \mathbb{E}_{(x,y)\leftarrow W}(x(x-1)(x+1) \cdot y)$. [5]

The most contributing sample will be the one for which $x = \pm 1/\sqrt{3}$, and it is not clear that this is the optimal range to select. We therefore offer to the learning algorithm a few variants of the above that select samples with smaller values of x, hoping that it can find a good selection by combining all of them:

- $f_5(W) = D \cdot \mathbb{E}_{(x,y)\leftarrow W}(2x(2x-1)(2x+1) \cdot y \mid |2x| \leq 1)$;
- $f_6(W) = D \cdot \mathbb{E}_{(x,y)\leftarrow W}(4x(4x-1)(4x+1) \cdot y \mid |4x| \leq 1)$;
- $f_7(W) = D \cdot \mathbb{E}_{(x,y)\leftarrow W}(8x(8x-1)(8x+1) \cdot y \mid |8x| \leq 1)$;

For any function f over $\mathbb{R}^2$, we call $f^t : (x,y) \mapsto f(y,x)$ the transpose of f. So far, we have introduced 13 different features, i.e. $f_1, \cdots, f_7$ and their transposes $f_8 = f_2^t, \cdots, f_{13} = f_7^t$.[6] We plot these functions in Fig. 2.

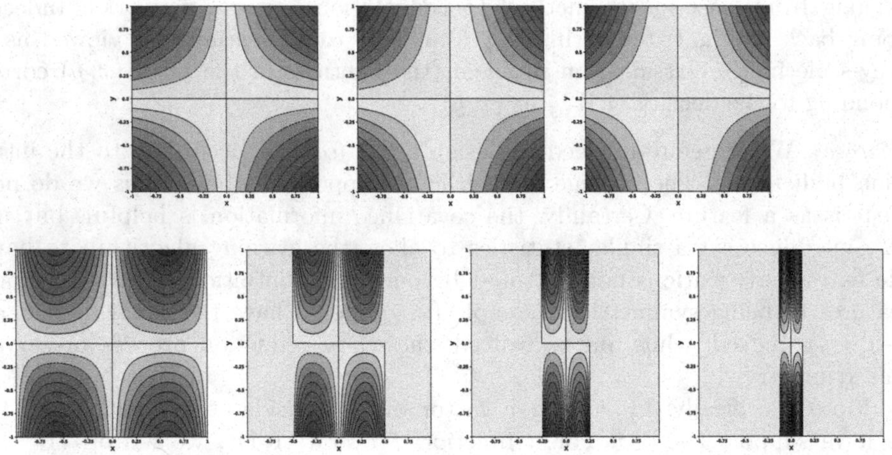

Fig. 2. The color matrices for $f_1, \cdots, f_7$. For any pixel at (x,y), its color is red (full-line contour), blue (dashed-line contour) when $f_i(x,y) > 0, \leq 0$ respectively. The deeper the color is, the larger $|f_i(x,y)|$ is. (Color figure online)

[5] As we are only going to consider linear models in our features, we could equivalently replace this feature by $\mathbb{E}_{(x,y)\leftarrow W}(x^3 \cdot y)$ because of the presence of f_1.

[6] Since f_1 is a symmetric function of (w_i, w_j), we did not count its transpose.

Generating data. Then, we proceed to measure each $W_{i,j}$ for known values of $\mathbf{S}_{i,j}$, say, using 400 000 samples for each key $\mathbf{S}$, and using 30 different keys $\mathbf{S}$. This is implemented by our script `gen_training.py`. This took about 38 core-hours.

Training. We naturally considered using advanced machine learning techniques (support vector regression [7], random forest regression [20] and artificial neural networks) to construct a model, with the precious support of Han Zhao. Despite some effort, he was unable to find a method that outperforms what we achieved with a linear model $f = \sum_{\ell=1}^{13} x_\ell f_\ell$ trained using the *least-square fit* method. Yet his exploration was certainly far from exhaustive, and we do not conclude that least-square fit is the best method.

Evaluating and refining our model. After preliminary experiments, we noted that, depending on their position $i-j$, some coefficients $\mathbf{S}_{i,j}$ seem easier to learn than others. In this light, it is not clear that one should use the same function f for all indices i, j. Instead, we constructed two functions $f^+ = \sum x_\ell^+ f_\ell$, $f^- = \sum x_\ell^- f_\ell$ respectively for indices such that $i - j \bmod n \geq n/2$ and $i - j \bmod n < n/2$. The model obtained by the least-square fit method is provided in Table 1 and plotted in Fig. 3. Moreover, the distributions of $f^+(W_{i,j})$, $f^-(W_{i,j})$ for $\mathbf{S}_{i,j} = \pm b, \pm 1, 0$ are illustrated in Figs. 4 and 5.

Table 1. The model trained from 30 keys and 400 000 signatures per key. This is implemented by our script `gen_model.py`.

i	1	2	3	4	5	6	7
x_i^-	−48.3640	354.9788	−289.1598	58.7149	−3.7709	−2.9138	2.3777
i		8	9	10	11	12	13
x_i^-		−21.2574	6.6581	3.5598	1.0255	0.4835	−0.3637
i	1	2	3	4	5	6	7
x_i^+	−67.9781	324.8442	−248.7882	44.6268	−4.1116	−2.6163	2.8288
i		8	9	10	11	12	13
x_i^+		−9.0923	3.1639	−0.8145	0.5204	0.3486	0.4920

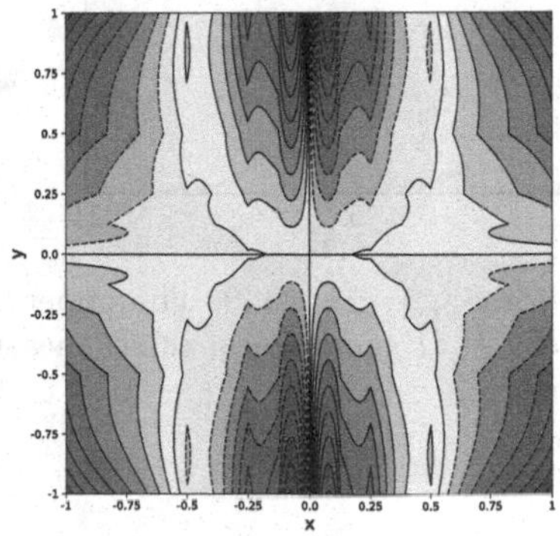

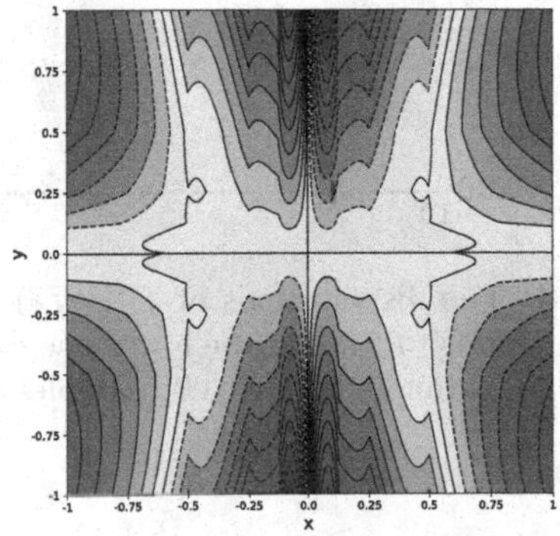

Fig. 3. The left graph is the color matrix for f^-, and the right one is for f^+. (Color figure online)

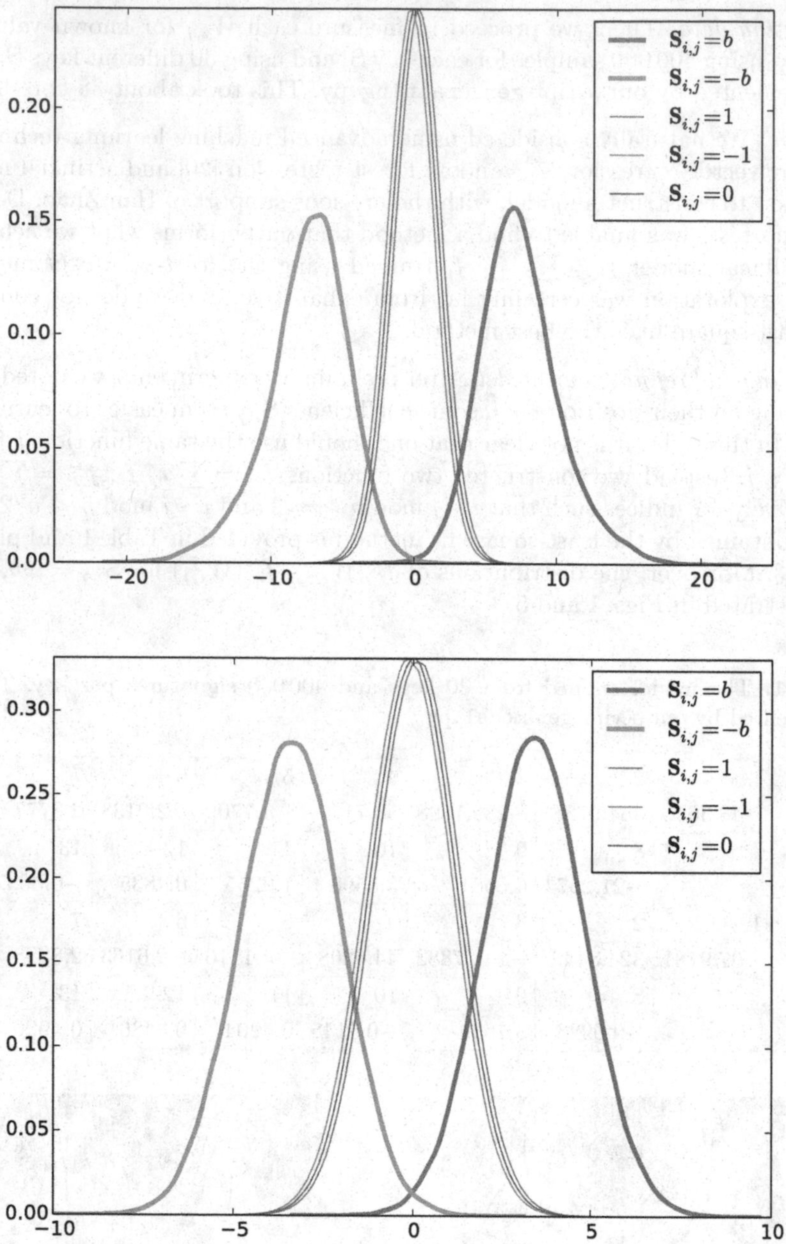

Fig. 4. The distributions of $f^-(W_{i,j})$, $f^+(W_{i,j})$ for $\mathbf{S}_{i,j} = \pm b, \pm 1, 0$. The upper one corresponds to f^- and the lower one corresponds to f^+. Experimental values measure over 20 instances and 400 000 samples per instance.

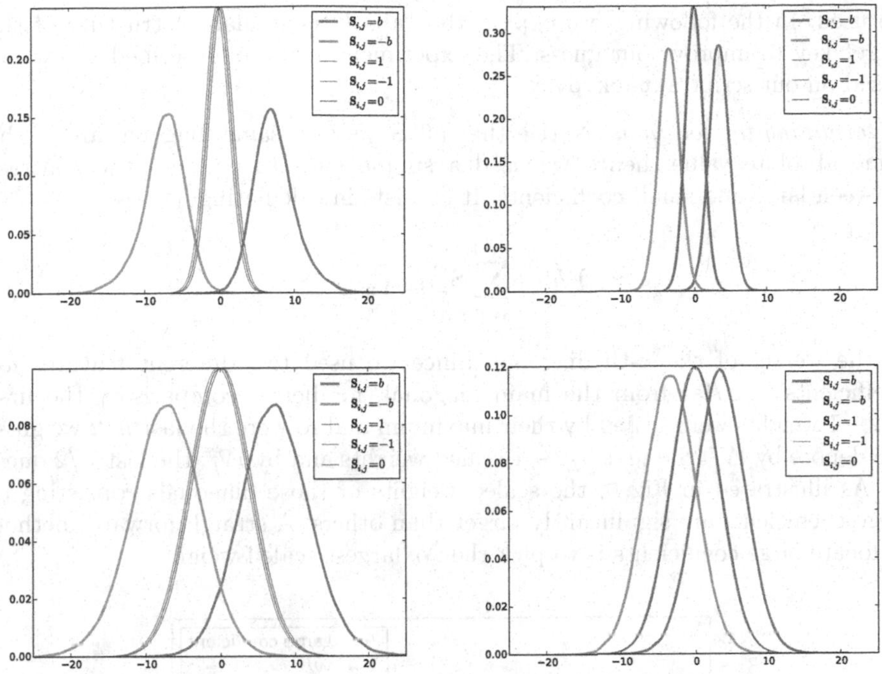

Fig. 5. The impact from sample sizes on the measured distributions of $f^-(W_{i,j})$, $f^+(W_{i,j})$. The left graphs correspond to f^- and the right graphs correspond to f^+. The upper graphs measure over 20 instances and 400 000 samples per instance, and the lower graphs measure over 20 instances and 50 000 samples per instance.

Remark 1. For other set of parameters, or even to refine our attack and recover more secret information, it is of course possible to cut our modeling in more than 2 pieces, but this requires more training data, and therefore more computational resources.

Remark 2. As shown in Figs. 4 and 5, predicted values $f(W_{i,j})$ for large coefficients are usually of larger size than those for $-1, 0, 1$. Compared with large coefficients far from the main diagonal, those near the main diagonal tend to be predicted as a number of larger size. Furthermore, the variances of $f(W_{i,j})$ decrease with sample size growing, which provides a sanity check for our models.

4.3 Learning

Following the previous method, we obtain a matrix $\mathbf{S}'$ consisting of all guesses of $\mathbf{S}_{i,j}$'s.[7] While clear correlations between the guess $\mathbf{S}'$ and $\mathbf{S}$ were observed, the guess was not good enough by itself for the limited number of samples that

[7] We ignore diagonal elements because they are public.

we used. In the following, we exploit the "absolute-circulant" structure of the secret key to improve our guess. The experimental results described below are based on our script `attack.py`.

Determining the locations. Notice that all $\mathbf{S}_{i,j}$'s in a same diagonal are of the same absolute value, hence we used a simple trick to enhance the contrast between large and small coefficients. It consists in calculating

$$\mathcal{W}_k = \sum_{i=0}^{n-1} \mathbf{S}'^2_{i,(i+k) \bmod n}$$

as the weight of the k-th diagonal. Since we used two different features for coefficients near/far from the main diagonal, for better comparison, the first $n/2-1$ weights were scaled by their maximum and so were the last $n/2$ weights. We denote by $\mathcal{W}_k^-$ the first $n/2-1$ scaled weights and by $\mathcal{W}_k^+$ the last $n/2$ ones.

As illustrated in Fig. 6, the scaled weights of those diagonals consisting of large coefficients are significantly larger than others. A straightforward method to locate large coefficients is to pick the N_b largest scaled weights.

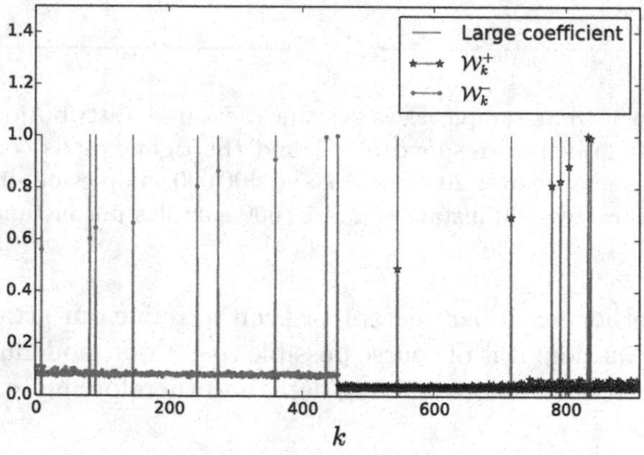

Fig. 6. Large coefficients and scaled weights. Experimental values measure over 400 000 samples.

Verified by experimental results, we were able to perfectly locate all large coefficients, provided we collected sufficient signatures. For different sample size, i.e. the number of signatures, we respectively tested 20 instances and checked the accuracy of locations for large coefficients. All experimental data is illustrated in Table 2.

Determining the signs. We straightforward assumed the sign of measured feature $f(W_{i,j})$ is the same as that of $\mathbf{S}_{i,j}$, when $\mathbf{S}_{i,j} = \pm b$. Unlike guessing locations, we could not recover all signs of large coefficients exactly, but as the sample size grows, we were still able to get a high accuracy, denoted by p. Then, we

Table 2. Experimental measure of location accuracy. The column, labeled by $K/16$, shows the number of tested instances in which the largest N_b scaled weights corresponded to exactly K large coefficient diagonals.

#signs	13/16	14/16	15/16	16/16
50 000	5	3	6	6
100 000	-	-	-	20
200 000	-	-	-	20
400 000	-	-	-	20

Table 3. Experimental measures for p_l, p_u, p and p_{row}. All values measure over 20 instances.

#signs	p_l	p_u	p	p_{row}
400 000	0.9975	0.9939	0.9956	0.9323
200 000	0.9920	0.9731	0.9826	0.7546
100 000	0.9722	0.9330	0.9536	0.4675
50 000	0.9273	0.8589	0.8921	0.1608

may expect to recover all signs of large coefficients in each row exactly with a probability $p_{row} = p^{N_b}$ (in our case $N_b = 16$).

Moreover, we noticed that the accuracy of guessing signs for large coefficients in the lower triangle, i.e. $\mathbf{S}_{i,j}$ with $i > j$, is higher than that for large coefficients in the upper triangle, thus we denote by p_l and p_u the accuracy corresponding to the lower and upper triangle. That may suggest us to guess the signs of large coefficients from the last row to the first row. Table 3 exhibits the experimental data for p_l, p_u, p and p_{row}.

Comparing guessing locations, guessing signs is much more sensitive to the number of signatures. That is because the sign information of $\mathbf{S}_{i,j}$ only comes from $f(W_{i,j})$ rather than all features in the same diagonal so that it requires a more precise measurement. Furthermore, we tried a modified model for guessing signs: in training phase, we mapped $\mathbf{S}_{i,j}$ to $\lfloor \mathbf{S}_{i,j}/b \rceil$ and then find x_ℓ's determining the global feature. Intuitively, the modified model further emphasizes large coefficients, but it performed almost the same as the current model in practice.

5 Exploiting Partial Secret Key Knowledge in Lattice Attacks

Using the technique described in last section, we are able to recover exactly all off-diagonal large coefficients in a row, with high probability (in addition to the diagonal coefficient D). First, we show how to adapt the BDD-uSVP attack, by exploiting the known coefficients of a row $\mathbf{s}_k$ to decrease the distance of the BDD target to the lattice, making the problem easier. Then, we show a more involved version, where we also decrease the dimension of the lattice while maintaining its volume. While not much is gained to recover a first secret row $\mathbf{s}_k$, this technique makes guessing the rest of the key much faster.

In later discussion, assume that we have already successfully determined all $-b, b$ and D coefficients in $\mathbf{s}_k$. Let $M = \{m_0, \cdots, m_{N_b}\}$ be the set of all m's such that $\mathbf{S}_{k,m} \in \{-b, b, D\}$ where $m_0 < \cdots < m_{N_b}$. We still focus on the concrete parameter set $(n, D, b, N_b, N_1) = (912, 912, 28, 16, 432)$.

5.1 Direct BDD-uSVP Attack

Let $\mathbf{t} \in \mathbb{Z}^n$ such that, if $|\mathbf{S}_{k,i}| > 1$, $t_i = \mathbf{S}_{k,i}$, otherwise $t_i = 0$, then $\text{dist}(\mathbf{t}, \mathcal{L}) = \sqrt{N_1}$. We construct a new lattice $\mathcal{L}'$ with a basis

$$\mathbf{P}' = \begin{pmatrix} \mathbf{t} & 1 \\ \mathbf{P} & 0 \end{pmatrix} \in \mathbb{Z}^{(n+1)\times(n+1)},$$

we have $\text{vol}(\mathcal{L}') = \text{vol}(\mathcal{L}) \approx D^n$ and $\mathcal{L}'$ contains a vector of Euclidean norm $\sqrt{N_1 + 1} \ll D$. Thus, to recover $\mathbf{s}_k$, it suffices to solve uSVP on $\mathcal{L}'$.

New estimations of the blocksize required by BKZ to solve uSVP were given in [4] and have been confirmed by theoretical analysis and experiments in [2]. Following these results, we claim that $\mathbf{s}_k$ could be recovered by BKZ-β when β satisfies:

$$\sqrt{\frac{\beta}{n+1}} \cdot \sqrt{N_1 + 1} \leq \delta_\beta^{2\beta-n-1} \cdot D^{\frac{n}{n+1}}.$$

We conclude that running BKZ-β with $\beta = 146$ should be sufficient to break the scheme. Typically [1,8], it is estimated that BKZ-β converges after about 16 tours, therefore making $16(n+1)$ calls to SVP-β:

$$C_{\text{BKZ-}\beta} = 16(n+1) \cdot C_{\text{SVP-}\beta}.$$

Though the factor 16 may shrink by increasing the blocksize β' progressively from 2 to β. Estimation of the cost of $C_{\text{SVP-}\beta}$ varies a bit in the literature, also depending on the algorithm used. The standard reference for estimating the cost enumeration is [10], which gives a cost of $2^{0.270\beta\ln\beta - 1.019\beta + 16.10}$ [3,9] clock-cycles. Alternatively, the Gauss-Sieve algorithm [22] with dimension for free and other tricks showed a running time of $2^{0.396\beta+8.4}$ clock cycles [11].

Those two methods lead respectively to estimates of 2^{78} and 2^{80} clock-cycles to recover one secret row. One could of course repeat the attack over each row, but below, we present a strategy that slightly reduces the cost of guessing a first row, and greatly reduces the cost of guessing all the other rows.

Remark 3. These numbers are likely to be over-estimates. Indeed, while cost predictions have not been provided, the enumeration algorithms have been sped up in practice recently with the discrete-pruning technique [5,14,29]. Unfortunately, the record timing on SVP challenges up to SVP-150 are difficult to use, as they only solve SVP up to an approximation factor of 1.05, which is significantly easier than the exact SVP typically used in BKZ. Similarly, avenues for improvements are discussed in [11], such as using a faster sieve, or amortizing certain costs inside the BKZ loop. Moreover, a long-standing question remains open: could it be more efficient to use an approx-SVP oracle with a larger blocksize in BKZ to achieve similar reduction faster.

5.2 BDD-uSVP Attack with Dimension Reduction

Next we detail how to also reduce the dimension of $\mathcal{L}'$ but maintain its volume, when exploiting known coefficients of a BDD solution.

Let $\mathbf{H} = (h_{i,j})_{i,j}$ be the HNF (Hermite Normal Form) of $\mathbf{P}$ satisfying:

- $h_{i,i} > 0$;
- $h_{j,i} \in \mathbb{Z}_{h_{i,i}}$ for any $j > i$.
- $h_{j,i} = 0$ for any $j < i$.

Let $I = \{i \mid h_{i,i} > 1\}$. In general, $|I|$ is very small (say ≤ 5), for example $|I| = 1$ if $\det(\mathbf{H})$ is square-free. Thus we have, with a high probability, that $I \cap M = \emptyset$, i.e. $h_{m,m} = 1$ for any $m \in M$. If not so, we choose another row $\mathbf{s}_{k'}$ of $\mathbf{S}$. Let $\{l_0, \cdots, l_{n-2-N_b}\} = \mathbb{Z}_n \setminus M$ where $l_0 < \cdots < l_{n-2-N_b}$.

Let $\mathbf{H}' = (h'_{i,j})_{i,j}$ be a matrix of size $(n - N_b - 1) \times (n - N_b - 1)$, in which $h'_{i,j} = h_{l_i,l_j}$. Let $\mathbf{a} = (a_0, \cdots, a_{n-N_b-2})$ where $a_i = \sum_{m \in M} \mathbf{S}_{k,m} h_{m,l_i}$. Let $\mathcal{L}'$ be the lattice generated by

$$\mathbf{B} = \begin{pmatrix} \mathbf{H}' & \\ \mathbf{a} & 1 \end{pmatrix} \in \mathbb{Z}^{(n-N_b)\times(n-N_b)}.$$

We first have that

$$\mathrm{vol}(\mathcal{L}') = \det(\mathbf{H}') = \frac{\det(\mathbf{H})}{\prod_{m \in M} h_{m,m}} = \det(\mathbf{H}) = \mathrm{vol}(\mathcal{L}).$$

Secondly, we can prove that $\mathcal{L}'$ has an unusually short vector corresponding to all small coefficients of $\mathbf{s}_k$. Indeed, let $\mathbf{c} \in \mathbb{Z}^n$ such that $\mathbf{cH} = \mathbf{s}_k$, then $c_m = \mathbf{S}_{k,m}$ for any $m \in M$ thanks to $h_{m,m} = 1$. Let $\mathbf{c}' = (c_{l_0}, \cdots, c_{l_{n-2-N_b}})$, then

$$(\mathbf{c}', 1)\mathbf{B} = (\mathbf{c}'\mathbf{H}' + \mathbf{a}, 1) = (s_{l_0}, \cdots, s_{l_{n-2-N_b}}, 1) := \mathbf{v}'.$$

Notice that $\|\mathbf{v}'\| = \sqrt{N_1 + 1} \ll \mathrm{vol}(\mathcal{L}')^{\frac{1}{n-N_b}} \approx D^{\frac{n}{n-N_b}}$, we may use uSVP oracle to find $\mathbf{v}'$.

Using the same argument as in the previous subsection, we could recover $\mathbf{v}'$, namely $\mathbf{s}_k$, by BKZ-β when β satisfies:

$$\sqrt{\frac{\beta}{n - N_b}} \cdot \sqrt{N_1 + 1} \leq \delta_\beta^{2\beta - n + N_b} \cdot D^{\frac{n}{n-N_b}}.$$

This condition is satisfied for $\beta = 138$. Based respectively on [10] and [11], this gives attack in 2^{73} and 2^{77} clock-cycles. Again, these numbers should be taken with a grain of salt (see Remark 3).

5.3 Cheaply Recovering All the Other Rows

Once a vector $\mathbf{s}_k$ has been fully recovered, we have much more information on all the other secret rows. In particular, we know all the positions of the 0, and this allows to decrease the dimension from n to $N_b + N_1 + 1$.

As in previous section we are able to construct a $(N_b + N_1 + 1)$-dimensional lattice $\mathcal{L}'$ of the same volume as $\mathcal{L}$ and containing a vector of length $\sqrt{N_b \cdot b^2 + N_1 + 1}$. Then, using BKZ-50 is enough[8] to recover the target vector and the cost is negligible compared to the cost of the first step.

6 Conclusion

We have shown that the DRS scheme is in principle susceptible to a statistical attack: signatures do leak information about the secret key. More concretely, for the first set of parameters submitted to the NIST [26], we have shown its security should be considered below 80-bits after $100\,000 \approx 2^{17}$ signatures have been released, contradicting the original claim of 128-bits of security. While such a large number of signatures may not be released in many applications, it remains much lower than the bound of 2^{64} signatures given by the NIST call for proposal [24, Sect. 4.A.4].

We also warn the reader that for demonstrating the principle of our attack, we have only focused on the easiest secret coefficients. But from Fig. 4, it seems also possible to deduce more information on the key. We strongly suspect that, focusing on the very near-diagonal coefficients, it could be possible to get the locations of a few 0's and ±1's as well, using more signatures, a more focused statistical model, and the diagonal amplification trick. This may lead to a full break in practice of this parameter set. Moreover, our estimates do not take account of the recent discrete pruning technique for enumeration [5,14,29], that has unfortunately not yet been the object of easily usable predictions.

While we view it likely that the attack can be pushed further, it is not clear how much effort this question deserves. In our view, our current attack suffices to demonstrate the need to fix the leak of the DRS scheme [26], and maybe to re-parametrize it.

In addition, we would like to clarify our views on lattice-based crypto security estimates. While we did stick to the best known attack methodology in this paper so as to not overclaim our cryptanalytic result, we do not recommend this approach for design and security claims, considering that the state of the art in lattice reduction is still making significant progress [5,11,14,29].

6.1 Viability of the DRS Design, and Potential Countermeasure

We note nevertheless that this statistical attack seems much less powerful than the statistical attacks presented in [13,23] against the original schemes GGH [16]

[8] The required blocksize can be much smaller, but we should use a different estimation for δ_β for small β [10,30].

and NTRUSign [18]. Indeed, our attack requires much more signatures, and still only recovers partial secret key information. In this light, we *do not* conclude that the approach of [26] is to be discarded at once, at least if it shows competitive performances. We therefore suggest several directions to improve the security of the scheme.
Disclaimer. These suggestions should however not be understood as a pledge for the DRS scheme [26]. We believe a much more thorough analysis of the statistical properties of the scheme should be provided to sustain its security. We think that a statistical argument would be much more reassuring than the experimental failure of the type of attack described in this paper.

Randomization. In [26,27], it is suggested that the orders of the indices j for the reductions $\mathbf{w} \leftarrow \mathbf{w} - q\mathbf{s}_j$ could be randomized. As claimed in [17], this modification should not be applied directly. For our attack, such randomization does not affect the intuition developed in Sect. 4.1. We suspect it might make the attack somewhat simpler. Indeed, in the current deterministic version, the coefficients far from the diagonal seemed harder to learn, forcing us to use two different models f^- and f^+. We believe that this complication could be removed against the randomized variant.

Set of secret coefficients. Rather than a sparse yet wide set $\{0, \pm 1, \pm b\}$ for the coefficients of $\mathbf{S}$, we recommend an interval of integers $\{-u, \ldots, u\}$, where u is chosen such that the Euclidean length of the rows is maintained (say, on average). As we saw (Fig. 4), larger coefficients are easier to detect, and the gap between 1 and b allows one to make a guess with much more confidence. Note that this could only mitigate the attack, but would not fully seal the leak.

Structure of the secret matrix. Secondly, the "absolute-circulant" structure could be removed without affecting the size of the secret key; indeed, the whole matrix, could be streamed by a PRG, only keeping the seed as the new secret key.[9] Again, this may only mitigate the attack, but would not fully seal the leak.

Perturbation/drowning. Depending on the situation, adding well-designed perturbation may [25] or may not [13,18] be an effective countermeasure against statistical attacks. Given the track record of heuristic countermeasures, we find the formal approach preferable. Drowning is a similar idea in spirit, but the added noise has a fixed distribution, typically much larger than what is to be hidden.

We note that the problem of directly trying to forge a signature seems harder than recovering the secret key with the current parameters of DRS [26]. This means that allowing larger vectors for signatures (up to a certain cross-over point) should not affect security. This gives a lot of room for perturbation or drowning, for which ad-hoc concrete statistical statements could plausibly be made, maybe exploiting Rényi divergence as in [4,6].

Acknowledgements. We thank Thomas Plantard, Arnaud Sipasseuth, and Han Zhao for helpful discussions and comments. We are also grateful to Yanbin Pan for sharing

[9] Variants can be designed so that each row can be generated on demand.

their work. Yang Yu is supported by the National Key Research and Development Program of China (No. 2017YFA0303903) and Zhejiang Province Key R & D Project (No. 2017C01062). Léo Ducas is supported by a Veni Innovational Research Grant from NWO under project number 639.021.645.

References

1. Albrecht, M.R.: On dual lattice attacks against small-secret LWE and parameter choices in HElib and SEAL. In: Coron, J.-S., Nielsen, J.B. (eds.) EUROCRYPT 2017. LNCS, vol. 10211, pp. 103–129. Springer, Cham (2017). https://doi.org/10.1007/978-3-319-56614-6_4
2. Albrecht, M.R., Göpfert, F., Virdia, F., Wunderer, T.: Revisiting the expected cost of solving uSVP and applications to LWE. In: Takagi, T., Peyrin, T. (eds.) ASIACRYPT 2017. LNCS, vol. 10624, pp. 297–322. Springer, Cham (2017). https://doi.org/10.1007/978-3-319-70694-8_11
3. Albrecht, M.R., Player, R., Scott, S.: On the concrete hardness of learning with errors. J. Math. Cryptol. **9**(3), 169–203 (2015)
4. Alkim, E., Ducas, L., Pöppelmann, T., Schwabe, P.: Post-quantum key exchange—a new hope. In: USENIX Security 2016, pp. 327–343 (2016)
5. Aono, Y., Nguyen, P.Q.: Random sampling revisited: lattice enumeration with discrete pruning. In: Coron, J.-S., Nielsen, J.B. (eds.) EUROCRYPT 2017. LNCS, vol. 10211, pp. 65–102. Springer, Cham (2017). https://doi.org/10.1007/978-3-319-56614-6_3
6. Bai, S., Langlois, A., Lepoint, T., Stehlé, D., Steinfeld, R.: Improved security proofs in lattice-based cryptography: Using the rényi divergence rather than the statistical distance. In: Iwata, T., Cheon, J.H. (eds.) ASIACRYPT 2015. LNCS, vol. 9452, pp. 3–24. Springer, Heidelberg (2015). https://doi.org/10.1007/978-3-662-48797-6_1
7. Basak, D., Pal, S., Patranabis, D.C.: Support vector regression. Neural Inf. Process. Lett. Rev. **11**(10), 203–224 (2007)
8. Chen, Y.: Réduction de réseau et sécurité concrète du chiffrement complètement homomorphe. PhD thesis (2013)
9. Chen, Y., Nguyen, P.Q.: BKZ 2.0: Better lattice security estimates (full version). http://www.di.ens.fr/~ychen/research/Full_BKZ.pdf
10. Chen, Y., Nguyen, P.Q.: BKZ 2.0: better lattice security estimates. In: Lee, D.H., Wang, X. (eds.) ASIACRYPT 2011. LNCS, vol. 7073, pp. 1–20. Springer, Heidelberg (2011). https://doi.org/10.1007/978-3-642-25385-0_1
11. Ducas, L.: Shortest vector from lattice sieving: a few dimensions for free. In: Nielsen, J.B., Rijmen, V. (eds.) EUROCRYPT 2018. LNCS, vol. 10820, pp. 125–145. Springer, Cham (2018). https://doi.org/10.1007/978-3-319-78381-9_5
12. Ducas, L., Durmus, A., Lepoint, T., Lyubashevsky, V.: Lattice signatures and bimodal Gaussians. In: Canetti, R., Garay, J.A. (eds.) CRYPTO 2013. LNCS, vol. 8042, pp. 40–56. Springer, Heidelberg (2013). https://doi.org/10.1007/978-3-642-40041-4_3
13. Ducas, L., Nguyen, P.Q.: Learning a zonotope and more: cryptanalysis of NTRUSign countermeasures. In: Wang, X., Sako, K. (eds.) ASIACRYPT 2012. LNCS, vol. 7658, pp. 433–450. Springer, Heidelberg (2012). https://doi.org/10.1007/978-3-642-34961-4_27
14. Fukase, M., Kashiwabara, K.: An accelerated algorithm for solving SVP based on statistical analysis. J. Inf. Process. **23**(1), 67–80 (2015)

15. Gentry, C., Peikert, C., Vaikuntanathan, V.: Trapdoors for hard lattices and new cryptographic constructions. In: STOC 2008, pp. 197–206 (2008)
16. Goldreich, O., Goldwasser, S., Halevi, S.: Public-key cryptosystems from lattice reduction problems. In: Kaliski, B.S. (ed.) CRYPTO 1997. LNCS, vol. 1294, pp. 112–131. Springer, Heidelberg (1997). https://doi.org/10.1007/BFb0052231
17. Li, H., Liu, R., Nitaj, A., Pan, Y.: Cryptanalysis of the randomized version of a lattice-based signature scheme from PKC'08. In: Susilo, W., Yang, G. (eds.) ACISP 2018. LNCS, vol. 10946, pp. 455–466. Springer, Cham (2018). https://doi.org/10.1007/978-3-319-93638-3_26
18. Hoffstein, J., Howgrave-Graham, N., Pipher, J., Silverman, J.H., Whyte, W.: NTRUSign: digital signatures using the NTRU lattice. In: Joye, M. (ed.) CT-RSA 2003. LNCS, vol. 2612, pp. 122–140. Springer, Heidelberg (2003). https://doi.org/10.1007/3-540-36563-X_9
19. Hu, Y., Wang, B., He, W.: NTRUSign with a new perturbation. IEEE Trans. Inf. Theor. **54**(7), 3216–3221 (2008)
20. Liaw, A., Wiener, M., et al.: Classification and regression by randomforest. R News **2**(3), 18–22 (2002)
21. Lyubashevsky, V.: Fiat-Shamir with aborts: applications to lattice and factoring-based signatures. In: Matsui, M. (ed.) ASIACRYPT 2009. LNCS, vol. 5912, pp. 598–616. Springer, Heidelberg (2009). https://doi.org/10.1007/978-3-642-10366-7_35
22. Micciancio, D., Voulgaris, P.: Faster exponential time algorithms for the shortest vector problem. In: SODA 2010, pp. 1468–1480 (2010)
23. Nguyen, P.Q., Regev, O.: Learning a parallelepiped: cryptanalysis of GGH and NTRU signatures. In: Vaudenay, S. (ed.) EUROCRYPT 2006. LNCS, vol. 4004, pp. 271–288. Springer, Heidelberg (2006). https://doi.org/10.1007/11761679_17
24. NIST: Submission requirements and evaluation criteria for the post-quantum cryptography standardization process, December 2016. https://csrc.nist.gov/CSRC/media/Projects/Post-Quantum-Cryptography/documents/call-for-proposals-final-dec-2016.pdf
25. Peikert, C.: An efficient and parallel gaussian sampler for lattices. In: Rabin, T. (ed.) CRYPTO 2010. LNCS, vol. 6223, pp. 80–97. Springer, Heidelberg (2010). https://doi.org/10.1007/978-3-642-14623-7_5
26. Plantard, T., Sipasseuth, A., Dumondelle, C., Susilo, W.: DRS : diagonal dominant reduction for lattice-based signature. Submitted to the NIST Post-Quantum Cryptography Project. https://csrc.nist.gov/projects/post-quantum-cryptography/round-1-submissions
27. Plantard, T., Susilo, W., Win, K.T.: A digital signature scheme based on CVP_∞. In: Cramer, R. (ed.) PKC 2008. LNCS, vol. 4939, pp. 288–307. Springer, Heidelberg (2008). https://doi.org/10.1007/978-3-540-78440-1_17
28. Schnorr, C.P., Euchner, M.: Lattice basis reduction: improved practical algorithms and solving subset sum problems. Math. Program. **66**(1–3), 181–199 (1994)
29. Teruya, T., Kashiwabara, K., Hanaoka, G.: Fast lattice basis reduction suitable for massive parallelization and its application to the shortest vector problem. In: Abdalla, M., Dahab, R. (eds.) PKC 2018. LNCS, vol. 10769, pp. 437–460. Springer, Cham (2018). https://doi.org/10.1007/978-3-319-76578-5_15
30. Yu, Y., Ducas, L.: Second order statistical behavior of LLL and BKZ. In: Adams, C., Camenisch, J. (eds.) SAC 2017. LNCS, vol. 10719, pp. 3–22. Springer, Cham (2018). https://doi.org/10.1007/978-3-319-72565-9_1

Leakage-Resilient Cryptography

How to Securely Compute with Noisy Leakage in Quasilinear Complexity

Dahmun Goudarzi[1,2(✉)], Antoine Joux[3], and Matthieu Rivain[1]

[1] CryptoExperts, Paris, France
{dahmun.goudarzi,matthieu.rivain}@cryptoexperts.com
[2] ENS, CNRS, Inria and PSL Research University, Paris, France
[3] Sorbonne Université, Institut de Mathématiques de Jussieu–Paris Rive Gauche, CNRS, Inria, Univ Paris Diderot, Paris, France
antoine.joux@m4x.org

Abstract. Since their introduction in the late 90's, side-channel attacks have been considered as a major threat against cryptographic implementations. This threat has raised the need for formal leakage models in which the security of implementations can be proved. At Eurocrypt 2013, Prouff and Rivain introduced the *noisy leakage model* which has been argued to soundly capture the physical reality of power and electromagnetic leakages. In their work, they also provide the first formal security proof for a masking scheme in the noisy leakage model. However their work has two important limitations: (i) the security proof relies on the existence of a leak-free component, (ii) the tolerated amount of information in the leakage (aka *leakage rate*) is of $O(1/n)$ where n is the security parameter (*i.e.* the number of shares in the underlying masking scheme). The first limitation was nicely tackled by Duc, Dziembowski and Faust one year later (Eurocrypt 2014). Their main contribution was to show a security reduction from the noisy leakage model to the conceptually simpler *random-probing model*. They were then able to prove the security of the well-known Ishai-Sahai-Wagner scheme (Crypto 2003) in the noisy leakage model. The second limitation was addressed in a paper by Andrychowicz, Dziembowski and Faust (Eurocrypt 2016) which makes use of a construction due to Ajtai (STOC 2011) to achieve security in the strong adaptive probing model with a leakage rate of $O(1/\log n)$. The authors argue that their result can be translated into the noisy leakage model with a leakage rate of $O(1)$ by using secret sharing based on algebraic geometric codes. In terms of complexity, the protected program scales from $|P|$ arithmetic instructions to $\tilde{O}(|P|\,n^2)$. According to the authors, this $\tilde{O}(n^2)$ blow-up could be reduced to $\tilde{O}(n)$ using *packed secret sharing* but no details are provided. Moreover, such an improvement would only be possible for a program of *width* at least linear in n. The issue of designing an explicit scheme achieving $\tilde{O}(n)$ complexity blow-up for *any* arithmetic program is hence left open.

In this paper, we tackle the above issue: we show how to securely compute in the presence of noisy leakage with a leakage rate $\tilde{O}(1)$ and complexity blow-up $\tilde{O}(n)$. Namely, we introduce a transform that turns any program P composed of arithmetic instructions on some filed $\mathbb{F}$ into

T. Peyrin and S. Galbraith (Eds.): ASIACRYPT 2018, LNCS 11273, pp. 547–574, 2018.
https://doi.org/10.1007/978-3-030-03329-3_19

a (functionally equivalent) program Π composed of $|\Pi| = O(|P| n \log n)$ arithmetic instructions which can tolerate some (quasi-constant) amount of noisy leakage on its internal variables (while revealing negligible information). We use a polynomial encoding allowing quasilinear multiplication based on the fast Number Theoretic Transform (NTT). We first show that our scheme is secure in the random-probing model with leakage rate $O(1/\log n)$. Using the reduction by Duc *et al.* this result can be translated in the noisy leakage model with a $O(1/|\mathbb{F}|^2 \log n)$ leakage rate. However, a straight application of this reduction is not satisfactory since our construction requires $|\mathbb{F}| = O(n)$. In order to bypass this issue (which is shared with the construction of Andrychowicz *et al.*), we provide a generic security reduction from the noisy leakage model at the logical-instruction level to the random-probing model at the arithmetic level. This reduction allows us to prove the security of our construction in the noisy leakage model with leakage rate $\tilde{O}(1)$.

1 Introduction

Side-channel attacks have been considered as a major threat against cryptographic implementations since their apparition in the late 90's. It was indeed shown that even a tiny dependence between the data processed by a device and its *side-channel leakage* (*e.g.* running time, power consumption, electromagnetic emanation) could allow devastating key-recovery attacks against the implementation of any cryptosystem secure in the *black-box* model (*i.e.* the model in which the adversary only sees the input-output behaviour of the cryptosystem) [15,18,19]. The so-called physical security of cryptographic implementations has then become a very active research area and many efficient countermeasures have been proposed to mitigate these side-channel attacks. However, most of these countermeasures are only empirically validated or they are proven secure in a weak adversarial model where, for instance, an attacker only exploits a small part of the available leakage.

An important step towards a more formal treatment of side-channel security was made by Micali and Reyzin in 2004 in their *physically observable cryptography* framework [20]. In particular, they formalized the assumptions that a cryptographic device can at least keep some secrets and that *only computation leaks information.* This framework was then specialized into the *leakage resilient cryptography* model introduced by Dziembowski and Pietrzak in [14] which gave rise to a huge amount of subsequent works. In this model, a leaking computation is divided into elementary operations that are assumed to leak some information about their inputs through a leakage function whose range is bounded (*i.e.* taking values in $\{0,1\}^\lambda$ for some parameter λ). Many new leakage-resilient cryptographic primitives were proposed as well as so-called *compilers* that can make any computation secure in this model [16].

While the leakage resilient literature has achieved considerable theoretical advances, the considered model does not fully capture the physical reality of power or electromagnetic leakages (see for instance [24]). In particular for a leakage function $f : \{0,1\}^m \to \{0,1\}^\lambda$, the parameter λ must be (significantly) smaller than m. This means, for instance, that the leakage of an AES computation should be smaller than 128 bits, whereas in practice a power trace resulting from an AES computation can take several kilobytes (or even megabytes). On the other hand, it is fair to assume that the side-channel leakage is *noisy* in such a way that the information $f(x)$ leaked by an elementary operation on a variable x is not enough to fully recover x. This intuition was formalized in the *noisy leakage model* introduced by Prouff and Rivain in 2013 [21]. In a nutshell, this model considers that an elementary operation with some input x leaks a *noisy leakage function* $f(x)$ (with a random tape parameter which is omitted from the presentation). The noisy feature is then captured by assuming that an observation of $f(x)$ only implies a bounded bias in the probability distribution of x. Namely the statistical distance between the distribution of x and the distribution of x given the observation $f(x)$ is bounded by some parameter δ which shall be called the *leakage rate* in the following. The function f is then said to be a δ-noisy leakage function. Notably, this model does not imply any restriction on the leakage size (*i.e.* on the range of f) but only on the amount of useful information it contains.

1.1 Related Works

Probing-Secure Circuits. In a seminal paper of 2003, Ishai, Sahai and Wagner considered the problem of building Boolean circuits secure against *probing attacks* [17]. In the so-called *probing model*, an adversary is allowed to adaptively probe up to t wires of the circuit. They show how to transform any circuit C with q logic gates into a circuit C' with $O(qt^2)$ logic gates that is secure against a t-probing adversary. Their scheme consists in encoding each Boolean variable x as a random sharing $(x_1, x_2, \ldots, x_n)$ satisfying $x_1 + x_2 + \ldots + x_n = x$ over $\mathbb{F}_2$, where $n = 2t + 1$. They show how to transform each logic gate into a *gadget* that work on encoded variables. Their construction is actually secure against an adversary that can adaptively place up to t probes per such gadget. The so-called ISW construction has since then served as a building block in many practical side-channel countermeasures known as *higher-order masking schemes* (see for instance [10,11,22]). Its efficiency has also been improved in recent works [5,6] which respectively show how to optimize the randomness consumption and the number of multiplications (while conserving similar asymptotic complexity).

Towards Noisy-Leakage Security. In [21], Prouff and Rivain proposed the first formal security proof for an ISW-like masking scheme in the noisy leakage model. In particular they generalize the previous work of Chari *et al.* [7] and show that in the presence of noisy leakage on the shares x_1, x_2, $\ldots$, x_n the information on x becomes negligible as n grows. Specifically, they show that for any δ-noisy leakage function f, the mutual information between x and the leakage $(f(x_1), f(x_2), \ldots, f(x_n))$ is of order $O(\delta^n)$. They also provide a security proof for full masked computation in the noisy leakage model, however their result has two important limitations. First they assume the existence of a *leak-free component* that can refresh a sharing without leaking any information. Second, their proof can only tolerate an δ-noisy leakage with $\delta = O(1/n)$. Namely, the leakage rate must decrease linearly with the number of shares. Note that this second limitation is inherent to masking schemes based on the ISW construction since it implies that each share leaks $O(n)$ times. Some practical attacks have been exhibited that exploit this issue [4].

Avoiding Leak-Free Components. In [13], Duc, Dziembowski and Faust tackled the first of these two limitations. Namely they show how to avoid the requirement for a leak-free component with a nice and conceptually simpler security proof. Applying the Chernoff bound, they show that the ISW scheme is secure in the *δ-random probing model* in which each operation leaks its full input with a given probability $\delta = O(1/n)$ (and leaks nothing with probability $1 - \delta$). Their main contribution is then to show that any δ'-noisy leakage $f(x)$ can be simulated from a δ-random probing leakage $\phi(x)$ with $\delta' \leq \delta \cdot |\mathcal{X}|$, where $\mathcal{X}$ denotes the definition space of x. In other words, if the δ-random probing leakage of a computation contains no significant information, then neither does any δ'-noisy leakage of this computation as long as $\delta \leq \delta' \cdot |\mathcal{X}|$. The ISW scheme is therefore secure against δ'-noisy leakage for $\delta' = O(1/n|\mathcal{X}|)$. Note that for an arithmetic program working over some field $\mathbb{F}$, each elementary operation takes up to two inputs on $\mathbb{F}$, meaning $\mathcal{X} = \mathbb{F}^2$ and $\delta' = O(1/n|\mathbb{F}|^2)$. This way, the work of Duc *et al.* avoid the strong requirement of leak-free components. However, it still requires a leakage rate of $O(1/n)$.

Towards a Constant Leakage Rate. This second limitation was addressed by Andrychowicz, Dziembowski, and Faust [3]. They propose a scheme –that we call *ADF scheme* hereafter– which is based on Shamir's secret sharing [23] and a refreshing algorithm from expander graphs due to Ajtai [1]. The number of instructions in the protected program is multiplied by a factor $O(n^3)$ which can be reduced to $O(n^2 \log n)$ using an FFT-based multiplication. They show that this construction achieves security in the strong probing model where an adversary can adaptively place up to $O(1/\log n)$ probes per elementary operation. In the random probing model, the result is improved to a constant ratio. Applying the reduction from [13] they obtain the security in the noisy model for a leakage rate $\delta = O(1/|\mathbb{F}|^2)$.[1] For the standard version of their scheme based on Shamir's secret sharing, the base field $\mathbb{F}$ must be of size $O(n)$ which implies a leakage rate $\delta = O(1/n^2)$ in the noisy leakage model. Fortunately, their scheme can be improved by using secret sharing based on algebraic geometric codes [8] (at the cost of weaker parameters). As argued in [3], these codes operate over fields of

[1] Note that they obtain a leakage rate $O(1/|\mathbb{F}|)$ in the restrictive model where input variables leak independently. In the present paper, we make the more realistic assumption that the leakage function applies to the full input of each elementary operation.

constant size and hence there basic operations can be implemented by constant size Boolean circuits, which gives a $\delta = O(1)$ noisy leakage rate with the reduction from [13]. We show in this paper that a simple reduction actually exists to achieve $\delta = \tilde{O}(1)$ noisy leakage security from a random-probing secure scheme on a field $\mathbb{F} = O(n)$. This reduction could also be used to get tight noisy-leakage security for the ADF scheme without algebraic geometric codes (*i.e.* with simple Shamir's secret sharing).

Towards a Quasilinear Complexity. The leakage-secure schemes in the current state-of-the-art imply a (quasi)quadratic blow-up of the complexity: the protected program (or circuit) scales from $|P|$ arithmetic instructions to $\tilde{O}(|P|\, n^2)$. Another challenging issue is hence to bridge the gap between this $\tilde{O}(n^2)$ blow-up and the theoretically achievable $\tilde{O}(n)$ blow-up. In [3], the authors claim that the complexity of their scheme can be improved by using *packed secret sharing* [2,12]. As explained in [2], the use of packed secret sharing allows to securely compute (in the presence of leakage) an addition or a multiplication on several encoded values in parallel at the same asymptotic cost as a single operation with a standard secret sharing. Using the transform of [12], one can improve the complexity of the ADF scheme on an arithmetic program P from $O(|P|\, n^2 \log n)$ to $O(|P| \log |P|\, n^2 \log n/w)$ where w denotes the *width* of P. Roughly speaking, the width of P is the number of operations that can be computed in parallel throughout an execution of P which satisfies $w = O(|P|/d)$ where d is the depth of P (considered as a circuit). For a circuit of width $w = \Theta(n)$, this approach hence results in a complexity blow-up quasilinear in n. For a constant-size circuit (as the AES cipher) on the other hand, only a constant factor can be saved and the complexity blow-up remains (quasi)quadratic.

1.2 Our Contribution

In this paper we show how to securely compute *any* arithmetic program (or circuit) in the noisy leakage model with a leakage rate $\tilde{O}(1)$ and with complexity blow-up $\tilde{O}(n)$. Our scheme is conceptually very simple and also practically efficient provided that the computation relies on a base field $\mathbb{F}$ with appropriate structure.

We consider an *arithmetic program* P that executes basic arithmetic instructions over some prime field $\mathbb{F}$ (additions, subtractions, and multiplications) satisfying $|\mathbb{F}| = \alpha \cdot n + 1$ for n being a power of 2 (in particular $|\mathbb{F}| = O(n)$ as in [3]). Note that we prefer the terminology of (arithmetic) program composed of instructions to the terminology of (arithmetic) circuit composed of gates but the two notions are strictly equivalent.

Each internal variable $a \in \mathbb{F}$ of the computation is encoded into a random tuple $(a_0, a_1, \ldots, a_{n-1})$ that satisfies the relation $a = \sum_{i=0}^{n-1} a_i \omega^i$ for some random element $\omega \in \mathbb{F}$. In other words, a is encoded as the coefficient of a random n-degree polynomial Q satisfying $Q(\omega) = a$. It is worth noting that the security of our scheme does not rely on the secrecy of ω but on its random distribution. We then show how to transform each arithmetic instruction of P into a corresponding secure gadget that works on encoded variables. Using a fast Number Theoretic Transform (NTT), we then achieve a multiplication gadget with $O(n \log n)$ instructions.

We first show that our scheme is secure in the δ-random-probing model for a parameter $\delta = O(1/\log n)$. Specifically, we show that for any program P with a constant number of instructions $|P|$, the advantage of a δ-random-probing adversary can be upper bounded by $\mathsf{negl}(\lambda) + \mathsf{negl}'(n)$ where negl and negl' are some negligible functions and where λ denotes some security parameter that impact the size of $\mathbb{F}$ (specifically we have $\lambda = \log \alpha$ where $|\mathbb{F}| = \alpha \cdot n + 1$). This is shown at the level of a single NTT-based secure multiplication in a first place. Then we show how to achieve compositional security, by interleaving each gadget by a refreshing procedure that has some *input-output separability* property. Using the Chernoff bound as in [13] we can then statistically bound the number of leaking intermediate variables in each gadget. Specifically, we show that the leakage in each gadget can be expressed as linear or quadratic combinations of the input shares that do not reveal any information with overwhelming probability (over the random choice of ω).

From our result in the random probing model, the security reduction of Duc *et al.* [13] directly implies that our construction is secure in the δ'-noisy leakage model for $\delta' = O(1/|\mathbb{F}|^2 \log n)$. However, since we require $|\mathbb{F}| = O(n)$ (as in the standard ADF scheme) this reduction is not satisfactory. We then refine the granularity of our computation by considering the noisy leakage model on *logical instructions* working on constant-size machine words. In this model, we provide a generic reduction from the random-probing model over $\mathbb{F}$ to the noisy leakage model on logical instructions. Namely we show that any arithmetic program Π secure under a δ-random-probing leakage gives rise to a functionally equivalent program Π' that is secure under a δ'-noisy leakage at the logical instruction level where $\delta' = \delta/O(\log|\mathbb{F}| \log\log|\mathbb{F}|)$. Applying this reduction, our construction achieves security in the δ'-noisy leakage model with $\delta' = O\big(1/((\log n)^2 \log\log n)\big)$ for a complexity blow-up of $O(n \log n)$.

Table 1 hereafter gives a asymptotic comparison of our scheme and the previous schemes in the literature (with noisy leakage security): the ISW scheme [17] with the reduction from [13], the ADF scheme with algebraic geometric codes [3], the ADF scheme improved with packed secret sharing [2,3] (ADF-PSS). We emphasize that for the latter case no detailed description and analysis have been provided.

Table 1. Asymptotic comparison of secure schemes in the noisy leakage model.

	ISW	ADF	ADF-PSS*	Our result
Leakage rate	$O(1/n)$	$O(1)$	$O(1)$	$\tilde{O}(1)$
Complexity blow-up	$O(n^2)$	$\tilde{O}(n^2)$	$\tilde{O}(n^2/w)$	$\tilde{O}(n)$

*w stands for the width of the protected program.

The paper is organized as follows. Section 2 provides background notions on the noisy leakage model and the considered adversary. In Sect. 3 we describe our secure quasilinear multiplication scheme and we prove its security in the random probing model. Section 4 then presents the refreshing procedure used to get compositional security and provides a security proof for a full arithmetic program. In Sect. 5 we give our generic reduction from the random-probing model over $\mathbb{F}$ to the noisy leakage model on logical instructions and we apply this reduction to our scheme to get our final result. We finally discuss practical aspects of our scheme and related open problems in Sect. 6.

2 Leakage and Adversary

In the rest of the paper, we shall denote by $x \leftarrow \mathcal{X}$ the action of picking x uniformly at random over some set $\mathcal{X}$. Similarly, for a probabilistic algorithm $\mathcal{A}$, we denote by $y \leftarrow \mathcal{A}(x)$ the action of running $\mathcal{A}$ on input x with a fresh random tape and setting y to the obtained result.

2.1 Noisy Leakage Model

The noisy leakage model introduced by Prouff and Rivain in [21] follows the *only computation leaks* paradigm [20]. In this paradigm, the computation is divided into subcomputations; each works on a subpart x of the current computation state and leaks some information $f(x)$, where f is called the *leakage function*. In practice, f is a so-called *randomized function* that takes two arguments, the input variable x and a random tape ρ that is large enough to model the leakage noise. A subcomputation with input variable x hence leaks $f(x, \rho)$ for a fresh random tape ρ. For the sake of simplicity, in the sequel we shall omit the parameter ρ and see $f(x)$ as a random realization of $f(x, \rho)$. Moreover, the definition space of the input x shall be called the *domain* of f, and we shall write $f : \mathcal{X} \to \mathcal{Y}$ for a randomized function with domain $\mathcal{X}$ and image space $\mathcal{Y}$.

In the noisy leakage model [21], a *noisy leakage function* f is defined as a randomized function such that an observation $f(x)$ only implies a bounded bias in the probability distribution of x. Namely, the statistical distance between the distributions of x and $(x \mid f(x))$ is assumed to be bounded by some bias δ. Let X and X' be two random variables defined over some set $\mathcal{X}$. We recall that the *statistical distance* between X and X' is defined as:

$$\Delta(X; X') = \frac{1}{2} \sum_{x \in \mathcal{X}} |\Pr(X = x) - \Pr(X' = x)|. \tag{1}$$

The notion of noisy leakage function is then formalized as follows:

Definition 1 ([21]). *A* δ-noisy leakage function *is a randomized function* f : $\mathcal{X} \to \mathcal{Y}$ *satisfying*

$$\sum_{y \in \mathcal{Y}} \Pr(f(X) = y) \cdot \Delta(X; (X \mid f(X) = y)) \leq \delta, \tag{2}$$

where X *is a uniform random variable over* $\mathcal{X}$.

In practice, the leaking input x might not be uniformly distributed but one must specify a distribution to have a consistent definition, and as argued in [21], the uniform distribution is a natural choice. Also note that in the original paper [21], the L_2 norm was used for the definition of the statistical distance while, as argued in [13], the L_1 norm is a more standard choice (that we also adopt in this paper).

A conceptually simpler model, known as the *random probing model*, was first used in [17] and formalized in the work of Duc, Dziembowski, and Faust [13]. Informally speaking, this model restricts the noisy leakage model to leakage functions that leak their entire input with a given probability. These *random-probing leakage functions* are formalized in the following definition.[2]

Definition 2. *A* δ-random-probing leakage function *is a randomized function* $\phi : \mathcal{X} \to \mathcal{X} \cup \{\perp\}$ *satisfying*

$$\phi(x) = \begin{cases} \perp & \text{with probability } 1 - \delta \\ x & \text{with probability } \delta \end{cases} \tag{3}$$

It can be checked that such a function is a special case of δ-noisy leakage function.[3] Moreover, it has been shown by Duc, Dziembowski, and Faust [13] that every noisy leakage function f can be expressed as a composition $f = f' \circ \phi$ where ϕ is a random-probing leakage function. This important result enables to reduce noisy-leakage security to random-probing security. It is recalled hereafter:

Lemma 1 ([13]). *Let* $f : \mathcal{X} \to \mathcal{Y}$ *be a* δ*-noisy leakage function with* $\delta < \frac{1}{|\mathcal{X}|}$. *There exists a* δ'*-random-probing leakage function* $\phi : \mathcal{X} \to \mathcal{X} \cup \{\perp\}$ *and a randomized function* $f' : \mathcal{X} \cup \{\perp\} \to \mathcal{Y}$ *such that for every* $x \in \mathcal{X}$ *we have*

$$f(x) = f'(\phi(x)) \quad \text{and} \quad \delta' \leq \delta \cdot |\mathcal{X}|. \tag{4}$$

In the random-probing model, the total number of leaking operations can be statistically bounded using the Chernoff bound as suggested in [13,17]. We shall follow this approach in the present paper by using the following corollary.

Corollary 1 (Chernoff bound [9]**).** *The* δ*-random probing leakage of a computation composed of* N *elementary operations reveals the input of* $\ell > \delta N$ *of these elementary operations with probability lower than*

$$\psi(\ell, N) = \exp\Big(-\frac{(\ell - \delta N)^2}{\ell + \delta N}\Big). \tag{5}$$

If $\ell \leq \alpha n$ *and* $N = \beta n$, *for some* α, β *and* n *with* $\alpha/\beta > \delta$, *the above gives*

$$\psi(\alpha n, \beta n) = \exp\Big(-\frac{(\alpha - \delta\beta)^2}{\alpha + \delta\beta}\, n\Big). \tag{6}$$

[2] Note that we use a different terminology from [13] where these are called δ*-identity functions*.

[3] To be tighter, a δ-random-probing leakage function is a $\delta\,(1 - \frac{1}{|\mathcal{X}|})$-noisy function. This can be simply checked by evaluating (2).

2.2 Leakage Adversary

We consider computation schemes that *encode* the data of a program in order to make the leakage on the encoded data useless. An *encoding* Enc is a randomized function that maps an element $x \in \mathbb{F}$ to a n-tuple $\mathsf{Enc}(x) \in \mathbb{F}^n$, where n is called the encoding length, and for which a deterministic function $\mathsf{Dec} : \mathbb{F}^n \to \mathbb{F}$ exists that satisfies $\Pr(\mathsf{Dec}(\mathsf{Enc}(x)) = x) = 1$ for every $x \in \mathbb{F}$ (where the latter probability is taken over the encoding randomness).

Consider an *arithmetic program* P taking a string $\boldsymbol{x} \in \mathbb{F}^s$ as input and executing a sequence of instructions of the form $\mu_i \leftarrow \mu_j * \mu_k$, where $*$ denotes some operations over $\mathbb{F}$ (addition, subtraction, or multiplication) and where $[\mu_0, \mu_1, \ldots, \mu_T]$ denotes the memory of the program which is initialized with $\boldsymbol{x}$ (and some constants). To achieve leakage security, the program P is transformed into a functionally equivalent arithmetic program Π taking as input an encoded string $\mathsf{Enc}(\boldsymbol{x})$ (where the encoding simply applies to each coordinate of $\boldsymbol{x}$). According to the defined leakage model, each executed instruction of Π is then assumed to leak some noisy function $f(\mu_j, \mu_k)$ of its pair of inputs. It is further assumed that Π includes random sampling instructions $\mu_i \leftarrow \mathbb{F}$ that each leaks a noisy function of the generated random element $f(\mu_i)$. We denote the overall leakage by $\mathcal{L}(\Pi, \boldsymbol{x})$. The compiler is then said to be *leakage secure* if an observation of $\mathcal{L}(\Pi, \boldsymbol{x})$ does not reveal significant information about $\boldsymbol{x}$. More specifically, the leakage $\mathcal{L}(\Pi, \boldsymbol{x})$ must be indistinguishable from the leakage $\mathcal{L}(\Pi, \boldsymbol{x}')$ for every $\boldsymbol{x}' \in \mathbb{F}^s$. This security notion is formalized as follows:

Definition 3 (Leakage Security). *The program Π is* ε-leakage secure *(w.r.t. leakage functions $\mathcal{L}$) if every adversary $\mathcal{A}$ has advantage at most ε of distinguishing $\mathcal{L}(\Pi, \boldsymbol{x}_0)$ from $\mathcal{L}(\Pi, \boldsymbol{x}_1)$ for chosen $\boldsymbol{x}_0$ and $\boldsymbol{x}_1$, i.e. we have:*

$$\mathrm{Adv}_{\mathcal{A}}^{\Pi, \mathcal{L}} := \left| \mathrm{Succ}_{\mathcal{A}}^{\Pi, \mathcal{L}} - \frac{1}{2} \right| \leq \varepsilon \tag{7}$$

where

$$\mathrm{Succ}_{\mathcal{A}}^{\Pi, \mathcal{L}} = \Pr \left(\begin{array}{c} (\boldsymbol{x}_0, \boldsymbol{x}_1, \mu) \leftarrow \mathcal{A}(\perp) \\ b \leftarrow \{0,1\} \\ \boldsymbol{\ell} \leftarrow \mathcal{L}(\Pi, \boldsymbol{x}_b) \end{array} : \mathcal{A}(\boldsymbol{x}_0, \boldsymbol{x}_1, \mu, \boldsymbol{\ell}) = b \right). \tag{8}$$

In the above definition, $\mu \in \{0,1\}^*$ denotes any auxiliary information computed by the adversary during the first round when she chooses the inputs $\boldsymbol{x}_0$ and $\boldsymbol{x}_1$. Note that for the definition to be sound, we only consider adversaries $\mathcal{A}$ such that $\mathcal{A}(\perp)$ takes values over $\mathbb{F}^s \times \mathbb{F}^s \times \{0,1\}^*$ and $\mathcal{A}(\boldsymbol{x}_0, \boldsymbol{x}_1, \mu, \boldsymbol{\ell})$ takes values over $\{0,1\}$ for every input $(\boldsymbol{x}_0, \boldsymbol{x}_1, \mu, \boldsymbol{\ell}) \in \mathbb{F}^s \times \mathbb{F}^s \times \{0,1\}^* \times \mathrm{span}(\mathcal{L})$.

Lemma 1 provides a security reduction from the noisy leakage model to the random probing model. This is formalized in the following corollary:

Corollary 2. *Let Π be an arithmetic program that is ε-leakage secure w.r.t δ-random-probing leakage functions. Then Π is ε-leakage secure w.r.t δ'-noisy leakage functions, where $\delta' = \delta\,|\mathbb{F}|^2$.*

Note that in the original version of Lemma 1 (see [13]), the authors need the additional requirement that f' is efficiently *decidable* so that $f'(\phi(x))$ is computable in polynomial time in $|\mathcal{X}|$. We ignore this property in the present paper since our security statements consider adversaries with unlimited computational power.

3 Secure Multiplication in Quasilinear Complexity

In this section, we describe our encoding scheme and the associated secure multiplication. An important requirement of our construction is that the size n of the underlying encoding must divide $\frac{p-1}{2}$ where p is the characteristic of $\mathbb{F}$, that is $\mathbb{F}$ must contain the $2n$-th roots of unity. This implies that the size of the elements of $\mathbb{F}$ is in $\Omega(\log n)$. Without loss of generality, we further assume that n is a power of 2.

3.1 Our Encoding

Let ξ denote a primitive $2n$th root of unity in $\mathbb{F}$. Our encoding is based on a random element $\omega \in \mathbb{F}^*$ and is defined as follows:

Definition 4. *Let $\omega \in \mathbb{F}^*$ and $a \in \mathbb{F}$. An ω-encoding of a is a tuple $(a_i)_{i=0}^{n-1} \in \mathbb{F}^n$ satisfying $\sum_{i=0}^{n-1} a_i \omega^i = a$.*

Our encoding function Enc maps an element $a \in \mathbb{F}$ to a random element $\omega \in \mathbb{F}^*$ and a random uniform ω-encoding of a:

$$\mathsf{Enc}(a) = \langle \omega, (a_0, a_1, \ldots, a_{n-1}) \rangle. \tag{9}$$

The corresponding decoding function Dec is defined as:

$$\mathsf{Dec}\big(\langle \omega, (a_0, a_1, \ldots, a_{n-1}) \rangle\big) := \mathsf{Dec}_\omega(a_0, a_1, \ldots, a_{n-1}) := \sum_{i=0}^{n-1} a_i \omega^i \tag{10}$$

It is easy to check that we have $\Pr(\mathsf{Dec}(\mathsf{Enc}(a)) = a) = 1$ for every $a \in \mathbb{F}$. It is worth noting that the security of our scheme does not rely on the secrecy of ω but on its uniformity. Besides, we will consider that ω is systematically leaked to the adversary.

3.2 Multiplication of Encoded Variables

Let $(a_i)_{i=0}^{n-1}$ be an ω-encoding of a and $(b_i)_{i=0}^{n-1}$ be an ω-encoding of b. To compute an ω-encoding $(c_i)_{i=0}^{n-1}$ of $c = a \cdot b$ we use the NTT-based polynomial multiplication.

Specifically, we first apply the NTT on $(a_i)_i$ and $(b_i)_i$ to obtain the polynomial evaluations $u_j = \sum_{i=0}^{n-1} a_i (\xi^j)^i$ and $v_j = \sum_{i=0}^{n-1} b_i (\xi^j)^i$ for $j \in [\![0, 2n-1]\!]$. These evaluations are then pairwisely multiplied to get evaluations of the product $s_j = (2n)^{-1} u_j \cdot v_j$ for $j \in [\![0, 2n-1]\!]$ (with a multiplicative factor $(2n)^{-1}$). Afterwards, we apply the inverse NTT to get coefficients t_i that satisfy $\sum_{i=0}^{2n-1} t_i \omega^i = (\sum_{i=0}^{n-1} a_i \omega^i) \cdot (\sum_{i=0}^{n-1} b_i \omega^i)$. Eventually, we apply a compression procedure to recover an n-size ω-encoding from the $2n$-size ω-encoding $(t_i)_i$. Due to the particular form of roots of unity, an NTT can be evaluated with a divide and conquer strategy in $3\, n \log n$ arithmetic instructions (a detailed description is given in Appendix A).

The overall process is summarized as follows:

$$\begin{aligned}
(u_0, u_1, \ldots, u_{2n-1}) &\leftarrow \mathsf{NTT}_\xi(a_0, a_1, \ldots, a_{n-1}, 0, \ldots, 0) \\
(r_0, r_1, \ldots, r_{2n-1}) &\leftarrow \mathsf{NTT}_\xi(b_0, b_1, \ldots, b_{n-1}, 0, \ldots, 0) \\
(s_0, s_1, \ldots, s_{2n-1}) &\leftarrow (2n)^{-1}(u_0 \cdot r_0, u_1 \cdot r_1, \ldots, u_{2n-1} \cdot r_{2n-1})) \\
(t_0, t_1, \ldots, t_{2n-1}) &\leftarrow \mathsf{NTT}_{\xi^{-1}}(s_0, s_1, \ldots, s_{2n-1}) \\
(c_0, c_1, \ldots, c_{n-1}) &\leftarrow \mathsf{compress}(t_0, t_1, \ldots, t_{2n-1})
\end{aligned}$$

Compression Procedure. After computing the inverse NTT, we get a double-size encoding $(t_i)_{i=0}^{2n-1}$ satisfying $\sum_{i=0}^{2n-1} t_i\, \omega^i = a \cdot b$. In order to obtain a standard encoding with n shares, we simply set $c_i = t_i + t_{n+i} \omega^n$ for $i \in [\![0, n-1]\!]$. It is not hard to see that the result is consistent.

3.3 Security in the Random Probing Model

We first focus on the NTT leakage security as it is the most complex part of our scheme, and then provide a security proof for the whole multiplication.

Security of the NTT. We have the following result:

Theorem 1. *Let ω be a uniform random element of $\mathbb{F}^*$, let $(a_i)_{i=0}^{n-1}$ be a uniform ω-encoding of some variable a and let $\delta < 1/(6 \log n)$. The NTT_ξ procedure on input $(a_i)_{i=0}^{n-1}$ is ε-leakage secure in the δ-random-probing leakage model, where*

$$\varepsilon = \frac{n}{|\mathbb{F}|} + \exp\Big(- \frac{(1 - 6\delta \log n)^2}{4}\, n \Big). \tag{11}$$

The rest of the section gives a proof of Theorem 1. During the computation of the NTT on an ω-encoding $(a_i)_{i=0}^{n-1}$ of a, all the leaking intermediate variables (*i.e.* the inputs of arithmetic instructions) are linear combinations of the a_i's. Specifically, every intermediate variable v occurring in the NTT computation can be expressed as

$$v = \sum_{i=0}^{n-1} \alpha_i a_i \tag{12}$$

where the α_i's are constant coefficients over $\mathbb{F}$. In the following, we shall use the notation

$$[v] = (\alpha_0, \alpha_1, \ldots, \alpha_{n-1})^{\mathrm{t}} \tag{13}$$

for the column vector of coefficients of such an intermediate variable. Similarly, we shall denote $[a] = (1, \omega, \omega^2, \ldots, \omega^{n-1})^{\mathrm{t}}$ since we have $a = \sum_{i=0}^{n-1} \omega^i a_i$ by definition. Moreover, we will denote by $[v_0, v_1, \ldots, v_\ell]$ the matrix with column vectors $[v_0]$, $[v_1]$, ..., $[v_\ell]$. In particular, we have $[a_0, a_1, \ldots, a_{n-1}] = I_n$ (where I_n stands for the identity matrix of dimension n over $\mathbb{F}$) and for $u_i = \sum_{j=0}^{n-1} a_j (\xi^i)^j$ (the output elements of the NTT), the matrix $[u_0, u_1, \ldots, u_{n-1}]$ is a Vandermonde matrix.

First consider an adversary that recovers $\ell < n$ intermediate variables in the computation of the NTT, denoted $v_1, v_2, \ldots, v_\ell$. Without loss of generality, we assume that these intermediate variables are linearly independent (otherwise the adversary equivalently gets less than ℓ intermediate variables), which means that the matrix $[v_1, v_2, \ldots, v_\ell]$ has full rank. The following lemma gives a necessary and sufficient condition for such a leakage to be statistically independent of a.

Lemma 2. *Let $v_1, v_2, \ldots, v_\ell$ be a set of $\ell < n$ intermediate variables of the NTT on input a uniform ω-encoding of a variable a. The distribution of the tuple $(v_1, v_2, \ldots, v_\ell)$ is statistically independent of a iff*

$$[a] \notin \mathrm{span}([v_1, \ldots, v_\ell]) \,, \tag{14}$$

where span(·) *refers to the linear span of the input matrix.*

Proof. If $[a] \in \mathrm{span}([v_1, \ldots, v_\ell])$ then there exists constants γ_1, γ_2, ..., γ_ℓ such that $[a] = \sum_i \gamma_i [v_i]$ implying $a = \sum_i \gamma_i v_i$, and the distribution $(v_1, v_2, \ldots, v_\ell)$ is hence statistically dependent on a. On the other hand, if $[a] \notin \mathrm{span}([v_1, \ldots, v_\ell])$, then the system

$$\begin{cases} a = \sum_{j=0}^{n-1} \omega^j a_j & = \gamma_0 \\ v_1 = \sum_{j=0}^{n-1} \alpha_{1,j} a_j & = \gamma_1 \\ v_2 = \sum_{j=0}^{n-1} \alpha_{2,j} a_j & = \gamma_2 \\ \vdots & \\ v_\ell = \sum_{j=0}^{n-1} \alpha_{t,j} a_j & = \gamma_\ell \end{cases}$$

has $|\mathbb{F}|^{n-(\ell+1)}$ solutions $(a_0, a_1, \ldots, a_{n-1})$ for every $(\gamma_0, \gamma_1, \ldots, \gamma_\ell) \in \mathbb{F}^{\ell+1}$. This implies the statistical independence between a and $(v_1, v_2, \ldots, v_\ell)$. □

The following lemma gives an upper bound on the probability that the above condition is not fulfilled.

Lemma 3. *Let ω be a uniform random element in $\mathbb{F}^*$ and let $v_1, v_2, \ldots, v_\ell$ be a set of $\ell < n$ linearly independent intermediate variables of the NTT on input an ω-encoding of a variable a. We have:*

$$\Pr\left([a] \in \mathrm{span}([v_1, \ldots, v_\ell])\right) \leq \frac{\ell}{|\mathbb{F}| - 1} < \frac{n}{|\mathbb{F}|} \,, \tag{15}$$

where the above probability is taken over a uniform random choice of ω.

Proof. Let us denote $A(x) = \sum_{i=0}^{n-1} a_i x^i$ so that $[A(\alpha)] = (1, \alpha, \alpha^2, \dots, \alpha^{n-1})^{\mathrm{t}}$ for every $\alpha \in \mathbb{F}$, and in particular $[a] = [A(\omega)]$. For any distinct $\ell + 1$ elements $\alpha_1, \alpha_2, \cdots \alpha_{\ell+1} \in \mathbb{F}^*$, the matrix $[A(\alpha_1), A(\alpha_2), \dots, A(\alpha_{\ell+1})]$ has full rank since it is a Vandermonde matrix with distinct input entries. This directly implies:

$$\underbrace{\mathrm{span}([A(\alpha_1), A(\alpha_2), \dots, A(\alpha_{\ell+1})])}_{\dim\ \ell+1} \not\subseteq \underbrace{\mathrm{span}([v_1, \dots, v_\ell])}_{\dim\ \ell}, \tag{16}$$

hence the set $\Omega = \{\alpha \mid [A(\alpha)] \in \mathrm{span}([v_0, v_1, \dots, v_\ell])\}$ has cardinality at most ℓ. By the uniform distribution of ω, we then have a probability at most $\ell/(|\mathbb{F}|-1) \leq n/|\mathbb{F}|$ to have $\omega \in \Omega$ that is to have $[a] \in \mathrm{span}([v_1, \dots, v_\ell])$. $\square$

We now have all the ingredients to prove Theorem 1.

Proof. (Theorem 1) We will show that for any adversary $\mathcal{A}$, the advantage $\mathrm{Adv}_{\mathcal{A}}^{\mathsf{NTT},\mathcal{L}}$ in distinguishing $\mathcal{L}(\mathsf{NTT}, \mathsf{Enc}(a^{(0)}))$ from $\mathcal{L}(\mathsf{NTT}, \mathsf{Enc}(a^{(1)}))$ for any chosen elements $a^{(0)}, a^{(1)} \in \mathbb{F}$ is lower than ε, where $\mathcal{L}(\mathsf{NTT}, \mathsf{Enc}(a))$ denotes the δ-random-probing leakage of the procedure NTT_ξ on input $\mathsf{Enc}(a) = \langle \omega, (a_i)_{i=0}^{n-1} \rangle$. Note that this leakage is a tuple in which each coordinate corresponds to an arithmetic instruction in the computation of NTT_ξ that either equals $\perp$ (with probability $1 - \delta$) or the input of the instruction. We recall that the advantage is defined as $\mathrm{Adv}_{\mathcal{A}}^{\mathsf{NTT},\mathcal{L}} = \left|\mathrm{Succ}_{\mathcal{A}}^{\mathsf{NTT},\mathcal{L}} - \frac{1}{2}\right|$ where

$$\mathrm{Succ}_{\mathcal{A}}^{\mathsf{NTT},\mathcal{L}} = \Pr\left(\begin{array}{c} (a^{(0)}, a^{(1)}, \mu) \leftarrow \mathcal{A}(\perp) \\ b \leftarrow \{0,1\} \\ \boldsymbol{\ell} \leftarrow \mathcal{L}(\mathsf{NTT}, a^{(b)}) \end{array} : \mathcal{A}(a^{(0)}, a^{(1)}, \mu, \boldsymbol{\ell}) = b\right) \tag{17}$$

Without loss of generality, we assume $\mathrm{Succ}_{\mathcal{A}}^{\mathsf{NTT},\mathcal{L}} \geq \frac{1}{2}$. Indeed, for any adversary with success probability $\frac{1}{2} - \mathrm{Adv}_{\mathcal{A}}^{\mathsf{NTT},\mathcal{L}}$, there exists an adversary $\mathcal{A}'$ with success probability $\frac{1}{2} + \mathrm{Adv}_{\mathcal{A}}^{\mathsf{NTT},\mathcal{L}}$ (defined as $\mathcal{A}'(a^{(0)}, a^{(1)}, \boldsymbol{\ell}) = 1 - \mathcal{A}(a^{(0)}, a^{(1)}, \mu, \boldsymbol{\ell})$).

The procedure NTT_ξ is composed of $N = 3n \log n$ arithmetic instructions. In the δ-random-probing model, each of these instructions leaks its input(s) with probability δ. The number of instructions that leak hence follows a binomial distribution with parameters N and δ. Let us denote by max_ℓ the event that ℓ or less instructions leak in the random-probing leakage $\mathcal{L}(\mathsf{NTT}, \mathsf{Enc}(a))$. Since each instruction takes at most two inputs over $\mathbb{F}$, the adversary gets the values of at most 2ℓ intermediate variables whenever max_ℓ occurs. By the Chernoff bound (see Corollary 1), the probability that more than $\ell > N\delta$ arithmetic instructions leak, namely the probability that $\neg\mathsf{max}_\ell$ occurs, satisfies:

$$\Pr(\neg\mathsf{max}_\ell) \leq \psi(\ell, N). \tag{18}$$

From $N = 3n \log n$ and $\ell < \frac{n}{2}$, we get that:

$$\Pr(\neg\mathsf{max}_\ell) \leq \exp\Big(-\frac{(1 - 6\delta \log n)^2}{2 + 12\delta \log n}\, n\Big) \leq \exp\Big(-\frac{(1 - 6\delta \log n)^2}{4}\, n\Big). \tag{19}$$

Now let assume that max_ℓ occurs for some $\ell < \frac{n}{2}$ and let denote $v_1, v_2, \ldots, v_{2\ell}$ the recovered intermediate variables. Without loss of generality, we assume that the recovered intermediate variables are linearly independent. Let us then denote by free the event that $[a] \notin \mathrm{span}([v_1, \ldots, v_\ell])$. By Lemma 3, we have

$$\Pr(\neg\mathsf{free}) < \frac{n}{|\mathbb{F}|}. \tag{20}$$

And let finally denote by succ the event that $\mathcal{A}$ outputs the right bit b on input $(a^{(0)}, a^{(1)}, \mu, \boldsymbol{\ell})$ so that $\mathrm{Succ}_{\mathcal{A}}^{\mathsf{NTT},\mathcal{L}} = \Pr(\mathsf{succ})$. We can then write:

$$\begin{aligned}\mathrm{Succ}_{\mathcal{A}}^{\mathsf{NTT},\mathcal{L}} = \Pr(\mathsf{max}_\ell)\Pr(\mathsf{succ} \mid \mathsf{max}_\ell) &+ \Pr(\neg\mathsf{max}_\ell)\Pr(\mathsf{succ} \mid \neg\mathsf{max}_\ell)\\ &\leq \Pr(\mathsf{succ} \mid \mathsf{max}_\ell) + \Pr(\neg\mathsf{max}_\ell). \end{aligned} \tag{21}$$

In the same way, we have

$$\Pr(\mathsf{succ} \mid \mathsf{max}_\ell) \leq \Pr(\mathsf{succ} \mid \mathsf{max}_\ell \cap \mathsf{free}) + \Pr(\neg\mathsf{free}). \tag{22}$$

By Lemma 2, we have that the leakage $\boldsymbol{\ell}$ is statistically independent of $a^{(b)}$ in (17) whenever $\mathsf{max}_\ell \cap \mathsf{free}$ occurs. This directly implies $\Pr(\mathsf{succ} \mid \mathsf{max}_\ell \cap \mathsf{free}) = \frac{1}{2}$, which gives

$$\mathrm{Succ}_{\mathcal{A}}^{\mathsf{NTT},\mathcal{L}} < \frac{1}{2} + \Pr(\neg\mathsf{max}_\ell) + \Pr(\neg\mathsf{free}). \tag{23}$$

Hence, we finally get

$$\mathrm{Adv}_{\mathcal{A}}^{\mathsf{NTT},\mathcal{L}} < \Pr(\neg\mathsf{max}_\ell) + \Pr(\neg\mathsf{free}) = \frac{n}{|\mathbb{F}|} + \exp\Big(-\frac{(1-6\delta\log n)^2}{4}\, n\Big), \tag{24}$$

which concludes the proof. □

Security of the Full Multiplication. We now prove the security of the full multiplication. We have the following result:

Theorem 2. *Let ω be a uniform random element of $\mathbb{F}^*$, let $(a_i)_{i=0}^{n-1}$ and $(b_i)_{i=0}^{n-1}$ be uniform ω-encodings of some variables a and b, and let $\delta < 1/(21\log n)$. The above NTT-based multiplication procedure on input $(a_i)_{i=0}^{n-1}$ and $(b_i)_{i=0}^{n-1}$ is ε-leakage secure in the δ-random-probing leakage model, where*

$$\varepsilon = \frac{2n}{|\mathbb{F}|} + 5\exp\Big(-\frac{(1-21\delta\log n)^2}{14}\, n\Big). \tag{25}$$

Proof. The full multiplication is composed of five successive steps:

1. the NTT on input $(a_i)_i$,
2. the NTT on input $(b_i)_i$,
3. the pairwise multiplications $(2n)^{-1} \cdot u_i \cdot r_i$,
4. the NTT on input $(s_i)_i$,
5. the final compression on input $(t_i)_i$.

Let us denote by ℓ_1, ℓ_2, ..., ℓ_5 the number of operations that leak at each of these steps. Since each operation takes up to 2 input variables, the adversary then gets:

- up to $2\ell_1$ variables from the first NTT, each variable providing a linear equation in the a_i's;
- up to $2\ell_2$ variables from the second NTT, each variable providing a linear equation in the b_i's;
- up to ℓ_3 pairs (u_i, r_i);[4] each pair providing a linear equation in the a_i's and a linear equation in the b_i's;
- up to $2\ell_4$ variables in the third NTT (the inverse NTT), each variable providing a linear equation in the s_j's;
- up to ℓ_5 pairs (t_i, t_{i+n}),[5] each pair providing two linear equations in the s_j's.

To sum up, the adversary gets a system composed of

- up to $\ell_1^* = 2\ell_1 + \ell_3$ linear equations of the form

$$\sum_{i=1}^{n} \alpha_{k,i} \cdot a_i = \eta_k \quad \text{for } k = 1, \ldots, \ell_1^* \tag{26}$$

- up to $\ell_2^* = 2\ell_2 + \ell_3$ linear equations of the form

$$\sum_{i=1}^{n} \beta_{k,i} \cdot b_i = \nu_k \quad \text{for } k = 1, \ldots, \ell_2^* \tag{27}$$

- up to $\ell_3^* = 2\ell_4 + 2\ell_5$ linear equations of the form

$$\sum_{j=1}^{2n} \gamma_{k,j} \cdot s_j = \chi_k \quad \text{for } k = 1, \ldots, \ell_3^* \tag{28}$$

we have $s_j = (2n)^{-1} u_j r_j$ for every j, and since u_j and r_j can be expressed as linear combinations of $(a_i)_i$ and of $(b_i)_i$ respectively, for every j, the last ℓ_3^* equations can be rewritten as:

$$\sum_{i=1}^{n} \gamma'_{k,i} \cdot b_i = \chi_k \quad \text{for } k = 1, \ldots, \ell_3^* \tag{29}$$

where the $\gamma'_{k,i}$'s are coefficients that depend on the a_i's.

From these equations, the attacker gains the knowledge that:

[4] Either a multiplication of the form $(2n)^{-1} \cdot u_i$ or a multiplication of the form $(2n)^{-1} u_i \cdot r_i$ leaks. In both cases we consider that the pair (u_i, r_i) is revealed to the adversary.

[5] Either a multiplication $\omega^n \cdot t_{i+n}$ or an addition $t_i + \omega^n t_{i+n}$ leaks. In both cases we consider that the pair (t_i, t_{i+n}) is revealed to the adversary.

1. the encoding $(a_i)_{i=0}^{n-1}$ belongs to some vectorial space
$$\mathcal{S}_1 = \{\boldsymbol{x} \in \mathbb{F}^n \ ; \ M_1 \cdot \boldsymbol{x} = \boldsymbol{\eta}\} \tag{30}$$
of dimension at least $n - \ell_1^*$ where M_1 is the matrix with coefficients $\alpha_{k,i}$'s, and $\boldsymbol{\eta}$ is the vector with coordinates η_k,
2. the encoding $(b_i)_{i=0}^{n-1}$ then belongs to some vectorial space
$$\mathcal{S}_2 = \{\boldsymbol{x} \in \mathbb{F}^n \ ; \ M_2 \cdot \boldsymbol{x} = (\boldsymbol{\nu}, \boldsymbol{\chi})\} \tag{31}$$
of dimension at least $n - \ell_2^* - \ell_3^*$ where M_2 is the matrix with coefficients $\beta_{k,i}$'s and $\gamma'_{k,i}$'s and $(\boldsymbol{\nu}, \boldsymbol{\chi})$ is the vector with coordinates ν_k and χ_k.

Following the demonstration of Lemma 2, it can be checked that if
$$(1, \omega, \ldots, \omega^{n-1}) \notin \text{span}(M_1) \quad \text{and} \quad (1, \omega, \ldots, \omega^{n-1}) \notin \text{span}(M_2),$$
then the full leakage of the multiplication is statistically independent of a and b, namely the leakage security holds. These two events are denoted free_1 and free_2 hereafter.

Then, following the demonstration of Lemma 3, free_1 occurs with probability at least $1 - \frac{n}{|\mathbb{F}|}$ over a random choice of ω, provided that we have $\text{rank}(M_1) < n$. Then, since the vectorial space $\mathcal{S}_1$ is independent of ω, any possible choice of $(a_i)_{i=0}^{n-1} \in \mathcal{S}_1$ gives rise to some coefficients $\gamma'_{k,i}$'s independent of ω and we have that free_2 occurs with probability at least $1 - \frac{n}{|\mathbb{F}|}$ over a random choice of ω as long as we have $\text{rank}(M_2) < n$. The two conditions on the ranks of M_1 and M_2 are then fulfilled whenever we have
$$\ell_1^* = 2\ell_1 + \ell_3 < n, \tag{32}$$
and
$$\ell_2^* + \ell_3^* = 2\ell_2 + \ell_3 + 2\ell_4 + 2\ell_5 < n. \tag{33}$$
Let us denote max_i the event that the number of leaking operations ℓ_i at step i is lower than $n/7$, for every i. If max_i occurs for every $i \in \{1, 2, 3, 4, 5\}$, then two above inequalities are well satisfied.

By applying the Chernoff bound, we hence get:
$$\Pr(\neg \mathsf{max}_i) \leq \psi\left(\frac{n}{7}, N_i\right), \tag{34}$$
where N_i is the number of operations at step i, which satisfies $N_i \leq 3n \log n$, which gives
$$\Pr(\neg \mathsf{max}_i) \leq \psi\left(\frac{n}{7}, 3n \log n\right) \leq \exp\left(- \frac{(1 - 21\delta \log n)^2}{14} \, n \right). \tag{35}$$
We finally get that the multiplication is ε-leakage secure with
$$\begin{aligned} \varepsilon < \; & \Pr(\neg \mathsf{max}_1) + \Pr(\neg \mathsf{max}_2) + \cdots + \Pr(\neg \mathsf{max}_5) \\ & + \underbrace{\Pr(\neg \mathsf{free}_1 \mid \mathsf{max}_1 \wedge \ldots \wedge \mathsf{max}_5)}_{< n/|\mathbb{F}|} + \underbrace{\Pr(\neg \mathsf{free}_2 \mid \mathsf{max}_1 \wedge \ldots \wedge \mathsf{max}_5)}_{< n/|\mathbb{F}|}. \end{aligned} \tag{36}$$

□

4 Compositional Security for Arithmetic Programs

In this section we show how to obtain leakage security for a full arithmetic program, composed of several multiplications, additions and subtractions. Since computing addition and subtraction on encoded variables is quite simple, our main contribution is to describe a refreshing procedure which allows us to achieve compositional security.

We first describe our refreshing procedure before explaining how to transform an arithmetic program into a leakage-secure equivalent arithmetic program. Then we provide our compositional security proof.

4.1 Refreshing Procedure

Our refreshing procedure is based on the common approach of adding an encoding of 0. Let $(a_i)_{i=0}^{n-1}$ be an ω-encoding of a variable a. We refresh it into an ω-encoding $(a'_i)_{i=0}^{n-1}$ of a as follows:

1. sample a random ω-encoding $(r_0, r_1, \ldots, r_{n-1}) \leftarrow \mathsf{Enc}_\omega(0)$
2. set $a'_i = a_i + r_i$ for $i = 0$ to $n-1$

The main issue with such an approach is the design of a scheme to sample an encoding of 0 which has the right features for the compositional security. As detailed later, we can prove the compositional security as long as our construction satisfies the two following properties:

- **Uniformity:** it outputs a uniform ω-encoding of 0;
- **Output linearity:** its intermediate variables (*i.e.* the input of elementary operations in the sampler) can each be expressed as a linear combination of the output shares $(r_i)_i$.

We now describe an $\mathsf{Enc}_\omega(0)$ sampler which satisfies these two properties.

Sampling Encodings of 0. At the beginning of the computation of Π, a random ω-encoding of 0 is generated. This is simply done by randomly picking $n-1$ of the n shares and computing the last one accordingly. We will denote by $(e_i)_{i=0}^{n-1}$ this encoding. Note that just as for ω, this encoding can be fully leaked to the adversary. Our sampler then works as follows:

1. pick $n-1$ random values $u_0, u_1, \ldots, u_{n-2}$ over $\mathbb{F}$,
2. output $(r_i)_{i=0}^{n-1} = \mathsf{NTTMult}((u_0, u_1, \ldots, u_{n-2}, 0), (e_0, e_1, \ldots, e_{n-1}))$

where NTTMult is the NTT-based multiplication described in Sect. 3.

It is not hard to see that the result is indeed an encoding of 0: since the $(e_i)_i$ encode a 0, then the encoded product is also a 0. The uniformity is slightly more tricky to see. We claim that with overwhelming probability (over the random choice of $(e_i)_i$), the function:

$$(u_0, u_1, \ldots, u_{n-2}) \mapsto \mathsf{NTTMult}((u_0, u_1, \ldots, u_{n-2}, 0), (e_0, e_1, \ldots, e_{n-1})), \quad (37)$$

is invertible. This function is indeed linear and it can be seen as a multiplication by an $(n-1)\times n$ matrix. We empirically validated that this matrix is of rank $n-1$ with overwhelming probability.[6] By discarding one column we can get a full-rank square matrix of dimension $n-1$, allowing the recovery of the $(u_0, u_1, \ldots, u_{n-2})$ from output encoding. Therefore, we have a one-to-one mapping between the vectors $(u_0, u_1, \ldots, u_{n-2}) \in \mathbb{F}^{n-1}$ and the ω-encodings of 0, $(r_i)_{i=0}^{n-1} \in \mathbb{F}^n$ with $\mathsf{Dec}_\omega((r_i)_{i=0}^{n-1}) = 0$.

The output linearity is a direct consequence of the above. Since the u_i's can be expressed as linear combinations of the r_i's, then all the intermediate variables of the sampling procedure can be expressed as such linear combinations as well.

4.2 Arithmetic Program Compiler

We consider an arithmetic program P processing variables defined over a prime field $\mathbb{F}$. We show how to transform such a program into a leakage-secure arithmetic program Π. Each arithmetic instruction of P gives rise to a corresponding *gadget* in Π that works on encodings. We describe these different gadgets hereafter.

Copy Gadget. The copy gadget simply consists in applying a refreshing procedure to copy an encoded variable into the same freshly encoded variable. Let $(a_i)_{i=0}^{n-1}$ be an ω-encoding of a. The copy gadget compute an ω-encoding $(a'_i)_{i=0}^{n-1}$ of a as:

$$(a'_0, a'_1, \ldots, a'_{n-1}) \leftarrow \mathsf{refresh}(a_0, a_1, \ldots, a_{n-1})$$

The copy gadget is used whenever an output ω-encoding $(a_i)_{i=0}^{n-1}$ from some previous gadget is used as an input of several following gadgets. If $(a_i)_{i=0}^{n-1}$ is to be used in input of N following gadgets, one makes $N-1$ extra copies (in such a way that each new copy enters the next copy gadget):

$$(a_i)_{i=0}^{n-1} \rightarrow (a_i^{(2)})_{i=0}^{n-1} \rightarrow \cdots \rightarrow (a_i^{(N)})_{i=0}^{n-1}$$

This way, each fresh encoding $(a_i^{(j)})_{i=0}^{n-1}$ enters at most two different gadgets: the copy gadget and one of the N computation gadgets.

Addition Gadget. Let $(a_i)_{i=0}^{n-1}$ be an ω-encoding of a and $(b_i)_{i=0}^{n-1}$ be an ω-encoding of b. To compute an ω-encoding $(c_i)_{i=0}^{n-1}$ of $c = a + b$, we simply compute:

$$(c_0, c_1, \ldots, c_{n-1}) \leftarrow \mathsf{refresh}(a_0 + b_0, a_1 + b_1, \ldots, a_{n-1} + b_{n-1})$$

[6] To avoid to rely on an empirical assumption, one could easily check whether the generated encoding $(e_i)_i$ gives rise to a full-rank linear transformation.

Subtraction Gadget. Let $(a_i)_{i=0}^{n-1}$ be an ω-encoding of a and $(b_i)_{i=0}^{n-1}$ be an ω-encoding of b. To compute an ω-encoding $(c_i)_{i=0}^{n-1}$ of $c = a + b$, we simply compute:

$$(c_0, c_1, \ldots, c_{n-1}) \leftarrow \mathsf{refresh}(a_0 - b_0, a_1 - b_1, \ldots, a_{n-1} - b_{n-1})$$

Multiplication Gadget. Let $(a_i)_{i=0}^{n-1}$ be an ω-encoding of a and $(b_i)_{i=0}^{n-1}$ be an ω-encoding of b. To compute an ω-encoding $(c_i)_{i=0}^{n-1}$ of $c = a \cdot b$, we simply compute:

$$(c_0, c_1, \ldots, c_{n-1}) \leftarrow \mathsf{refresh}\big(\mathsf{NTTMult}((a_0, a_1, \ldots, a_{n-1}), (b_0, b_1, \ldots, b_{n-1}))\big)$$

where NTTMult denotes the NTT-based multiplication described in Sect. 3.

4.3 Compositional Security

The compositional security of our construction is based on the two following properties of the refreshing procedure:

- **Uniformity:** for a given $\omega \in \mathbb{F}^*$ and a given value $a \in \mathbb{F}$, the ω-encoding $(a'_i)_{i=0}^{n-1}$ in output of the refreshing procedure is uniformly distributed and independent of the input ω-encoding $(a_i)_{i=0}^{n-1}$;
- **I/O linear separability:** the intermediate variables of the refreshing procedure can each be expressed as a deterministic function of a linear combination of the $(a_i)_i$ and a linear combination of the $(a'_i)_i$.

The uniformity property is a direct consequence of the uniformity of the $\mathsf{Enc}_\omega(0)$ sampler. The I/O linear separability holds from the output linearity of the $\mathsf{Enc}_\omega(0)$ sampler since the shares $(r_i)_i$ output by the sampler satisfy $r_i = a'_i - a_i$ for every i, implying that any linear combination $\sum_i \gamma_i r_i$ equals $\sum_i \gamma_i a'_i - \sum_i \gamma_i a_i$ and is hence a deterministic function of a linear combination $\sum_i \gamma_i a'_i$ and a linear combination $\sum_i \gamma_i a_i$.

The I/O linear separability of the refreshing procedure implies that its leakage can be split into some leakage depending only on its input encoding, which is the output (before refreshing) from a previous gadget, and some leakage depending only on its output encoding, which is the input of a next gadget. This way, the full leakage can be split into subleakages each depending on the input/output of one gadget. Moreover, the uniformity property implies that all these subleakages are mutually independent. They can hence be analyzed separately: if none of them reveal information, then the full leakage does not reveal information either.

The compositional security of our construction is formalized in the following theorem.

Theorem 3. *Let P be an arithmetic program taking some input $\boldsymbol{x} \in \mathbb{F}^s$ and let Π denotes the corresponding program protected with n-size encodings as described* *above. For every $\delta < 1/(33\log n)$, Π is ε-leakage secure in the δ-random-probing model where*

$$\varepsilon = 3|P| \cdot \left(2\exp\left(-\frac{(1-33\delta\log n)^2}{22}\,n\right) + \frac{2n}{|\mathbb{F}|}\right), \tag{38}$$

where $|P|$ denotes the size of P i.e. its number of arithmetic instructions.

Proof. Let $|\Pi|$ denotes the number of gadgets in Π. Since the output of each gadget is refreshed (and nothing more), the number of call to the refreshing procedure is also $|\Pi|$. Each arithmetic instruction in P gives rise to one associated gadget, plus up to 2 copy gadgets if necessary. We hence deduce $|\Pi| \leq 3|P|$.

Let us denote by rmax the event that at most $\frac{n}{11}$ operations leak in each refreshing. By applying the Chernoff bound (see Corollary 1), we have

$$\Pr(\neg\mathsf{rmax}) \leq |\Pi| \cdot \psi(\frac{n}{11}, N_{\text{ref}}), \tag{39}$$

where N_{ref} denotes the number of elementary operations in the refreshing procedure. Let us further denote by gmax the event that at most $\frac{n}{11}$ operations leak in each gadget (without refreshing). In the same way as above, we have

$$\Pr(\neg\mathsf{gmax}) \leq \sum_{i=1}^{|\Pi|} \psi(\frac{n}{11}, N^{(i)}) \leq |\Pi| \cdot \psi(\frac{n}{11}, N_{\text{gad}}), \tag{40}$$

where $N^{(i)}$ denotes the number of elementary operations in the ith gadget and where N_{gad} denotes the max (which is reached by the multiplication gadget).

In the following, we shall denote by $(a_j^{(i)})_j$ and $(b_j^{(i)})_j$ the input encodings of the ith gadget of Π and by $(c_j^{(i)})_j$ the output encoding (before refreshing) of the ith gadget of Π. Let us further denote by $\mathcal{L}$ the full δ-random-probing leakage of Π, so that we have:

$$\mathcal{L} = \bigcup_{i=1}^{|\Pi|} \mathcal{G}^{(i)} \cup \bigcup_{i=1}^{|\Pi|} \mathcal{R}^{(i)} \tag{41}$$

where $\mathcal{G}^{(i)}$ denotes the leakage from the ith gadget (without refreshing) and where $\mathcal{R}^{(i)}$ denotes the leakage of the ith refresh. Specifically, $\mathcal{G}^{(i)}$ and $\mathcal{R}^{(i)}$ are families of intermediate variables (inputs of elementary operations) that are revealed by the δ-random-probing leakage. If rmax and gmax occurs, we have $|\mathcal{G}^{(i)}| \leq \frac{2n}{11}$ and $|\mathcal{R}^{(i)}| \leq \frac{2n}{11}$.

According the the I/O linear separability property of the refreshing procedure, we can define a *separated leakage* $\mathcal{L}'$ as

$$\mathcal{L}' = \bigcup_{i=1}^{|\Pi|} (\mathcal{G}^{(i)} \cup \mathcal{A}^{(i)} \cup \mathcal{B}^{(i)} \cup \mathcal{C}^{(i)}) \tag{42}$$

where $\mathcal{A}^{(i)}$ is a set of linear combinations of $(a_j^{(i)})_j$, $\mathcal{B}^{(i)}$ is a set of linear combinations of $(b_j^{(i)})_j$, $\mathcal{C}^{(i)}$ is a set of linear combinations of $(c_j^{(i)})_j$, such that $\mathcal{L}$ is a deterministic function of $\mathcal{L}'$. This implies that if $\mathcal{L}'$ is statistically independent of the program input $\boldsymbol{x}$, then so is $\mathcal{L}$. The remaining of the proof consists in showing that the former occurs with overwhelming probability (for a sound choice of the parameters).

We shall bound the probability (over the distribution of ω) that the family $\mathcal{L}'$ is statistically dependent on $\boldsymbol{x}$, hereafter denoted $\boldsymbol{x} \triangledown \mathcal{L}'$. We have

$$\boldsymbol{x} \triangledown \mathcal{L}' = \bigvee_{i=1}^{|\Pi|} \left(\boldsymbol{x} \triangledown \mathcal{G}^{(i)} \cup \mathcal{A}^{(i)} \cup \mathcal{B}^{(i)} \cup \mathcal{C}^{(i)}\right). \tag{43}$$

By the uniformity property of the refreshing, we have that, given the program input $\boldsymbol{x}$, the different families of input/output shares $\{(a_j^{(i)})_{j=0}^{n-1}, (b_j^{(i)})_{j=0}^{n-1}, (c_j^{(i)})_{j=0}^{n-1}\}$ are mutually independent. We hence get

$$\Pr(\boldsymbol{x} \triangledown \mathcal{L}') \le \sum_{i=1}^{|\Pi|} \Pr\left(\boldsymbol{x} \triangledown \mathcal{G}^{(i)} \cup \mathcal{A}^{(i)} \cup \mathcal{B}^{(i)} \cup \mathcal{C}^{(i)}\right). \tag{44}$$

We can then upper bound the probability $\Pr\left(\boldsymbol{x} \triangledown \mathcal{G}^{(i)} \cup \mathcal{A}^{(i)} \cup \mathcal{B}^{(i)} \cup \mathcal{C}^{(i)}\right)$ when the ith gadget is a secure multiplication by following the proof of Theorem 2. The only difference is that the attacker gets additional linear combinations of the input/output shares from the refreshing procedures. Specifically, we would have

- up to $\ell_1^* = 2\ell_1 + \ell_3 + 2\ell_1'$ linear combinations of the form $\sum_i \alpha_{k,i} a_i$, for $1 \le k \le \ell_1^*$;
- up to $\ell_2^* = 2\ell_2 + \ell_3 + 2\ell_2'$ linear combinations of the form $\sum_i \beta_{k,i} b_i$, for $1 \le k \le \ell_2^*$;
- up to $\ell_3^* = 2\ell_4 + 2\ell_5 + 2\ell_3'$ linear combinations of the form $\sum_{i,j} \gamma_{k,j} s_j$, for $1 \le k \le \ell_3^*$;

where ℓ_1', ℓ_2' and ℓ_3', are the number of leaking operations in the input/output refreshing procedures. Taking the constraint $\ell_i < \frac{n}{11}$ and $\ell_i' < \frac{n}{11}$ for every i, we still get $\ell_1^* + \ell_3^* < n$ and $\ell_2^* + \ell_3^* < n$. That is, if rmax and gmax occurs, we get

$$\Pr\left(\boldsymbol{x} \triangledown \mathcal{G}^{(i)} \cup \mathcal{A}^{(i)} \cup \mathcal{B}^{(i)} \cup \mathcal{C}^{(i)} \mid \mathsf{rmax} \wedge \mathsf{gmax}\right) \le \frac{2n}{|\mathbb{F}|}. \tag{45}$$

For copy, addition and subtraction gadgets, the proof is quite simple. When an operation leaks in such a gadget, it reveals one shares from each input encoding. We hence get less that $\frac{n}{11}$ linear combinations on each input encoding (from the gadget leakage), plus $\frac{2n}{11}$ linear combinations on each input encoding (from their respective refreshing), plus $\frac{2n}{11}$ linear combinations on the output encoding, which can be split into independent linear combinations on the two input encodings. We clearly get less than n linear combinations on each encoding, which allows us to apply Lemma 3 and to obtain (45) for every kind of gadget.

We finally get

$$\Pr(\boldsymbol{x} \triangledown \mathcal{L}') \le \Pr(\neg\mathsf{rmax}) + \Pr(\neg\mathsf{gmax}) + \sum_{i=1}^{|\Pi|} \Pr\left(\boldsymbol{x} \triangledown \mathcal{G}^{(i)} \cup \mathcal{A}^{(i)} \cup \mathcal{B}^{(i)} \cup \mathcal{C}^{(i)} \mid \mathsf{rmax} \wedge \mathsf{gmax}\right) \le |\Pi| \cdot \left(\psi(\frac{n}{11}, N_{\text{ref}}) + \psi(\frac{n}{11}, N_{\text{gad}}) + \frac{2n}{|\mathbb{F}|}\right),$$

which together with $N_{\text{ref}}, N_{\text{gad}} < 3n \log n$ concludes the proof. □

5 From Arithmetic Random Probing to Noisy Leakage

5.1 Logical Programs

The definition of a *logical program* is analogous to the definition of an arithmetic program but it is composed of logical instructions over $\{0,1\}^w$ such as the bitwise AND, OR, XOR, logical shifts and rotations, as well as the addition, subtraction, and multiplication modulo 2^w (namely typical instructions of a w-bit processor). In the ε-noisy leakage model, a logical program leaks an ε-noisy leakage function $f(\mu_j, \mu_k)$ of the pair of inputs of each logical instruction $\mu_i \leftarrow \mu_j * \mu_k$.

The security reduction of Duc *et al.* (Lemma 1) then implies that a logical program Π that is secure against δ-random-probing leakage is also secure against δ'-noisy leakage with $\delta' = \delta/2^{2w}$.

5.2 A Generic Reduction

We then have the following reduction of random-probing model for a logical programs, to the random-probing model for an arithmetic programs:

Lemma 4. *Let Π be a ε-leakage secure arithmetic program in the δ-random-probing model, then there exists a functionally equivalent logical program Π' that is ε-leakage secure in the δ'-random-probing model for some δ' satisfying*

$$\delta' = 1 - (1-\delta)^{1/N} \ge \frac{\delta}{N} \quad \text{with} \quad N = O\Big(\frac{1}{w} \log|\mathbb{F}| \log\big(\frac{1}{w}\log|\mathbb{F}|\big)\Big). \tag{46}$$

Proof. The logical program Π' is simply the program Π where arithmetic instructions are built from several w-bit logical instructions. It is well known that the addition and subtraction on $\mathbb{F}$ can be computed in $N = O(\frac{1}{w}\log|\mathbb{F}|)$ elementary (w-bit) operations, and that the multiplication on $\mathbb{F}$ can be computed from $N = O(\frac{1}{w}\log|\mathbb{F}|\log(\frac{1}{w}\log|\mathbb{F}|))$ elementary (w-bit) operations.

Assume that there exists an adversary $\mathcal{A}'$ with advantage ε that makes use of a δ'-random-probing leakage on Π', then we show that there exists an adversary $\mathcal{A}$ with advantage ε that makes use of a δ-random-probing leakage on Π. Since by assumption no such adversary $\mathcal{A}$ exists, then by contraposition neither does such adversary $\mathcal{A}'$, meaning that Π' is indeed ε-leakage secure in the δ'-random-probing model.

We construct an adversary $\mathcal{A}$ that is given the full input to an arithmetic instruction of Π whenever at least one of the corresponding logical instruction leaks in Π'. Informally, it is clear that this can only increase the success probability. To make this reasoning formal, we need to construct an adversary $\mathcal{A}$ that receives the strengthened leakage, resamples it to make its distribution identical to that of the δ'-random-probing leakage on Π' and then call $\mathcal{A}'$. When $\mathcal{A}$ receives $\perp$ as leakage for an arithmetic instruction, it simply sends $\perp$ to $\mathcal{A}'$ for all the corresponding logical instructions. When it receives the full input of the arithmetic instruction (meaning that at least one corresponding logical instruction of Π' must leak), it can compute all the inputs of the corresponding logical instructions in Π', and reveal each of them to $\mathcal{A}'$ with some (biased) given probability. Since we do not consider the computational complexity of the adversaries, the easiest way to achieve a perfect simulation is to use rejection sampling. Namely, for every logical instruction in the group, the input is revealed with probability δ'. If at the end of the group, no input was revealed, simply restart the revealing process for the same group. This way, we have constructed an adversary $\mathcal{A}$ using a δ-random-probing leakage on Π where

$$\delta = 1 - (1 - \delta')^N,$$

for $N = O\big(\log |\mathbb{F}| \log\log |\mathbb{F}|\big)$. Since by assumption no such adversary exists, this means that no adversary $\mathcal{A}'$ exists with advantage ε that makes use of a δ'-random-probing leakage on Π'. □

Combining the above lemma with Lemma 1, and considering a constant word-size w, we get a tight reduction of the security in the noisy leakage model for logical program to the security in the random-probing model for arithmetic program:

Lemma 5. *Let Π be a ε-leakage secure arithmetic program in the δ-random-probing model, then there exists a functionally equivalent logical program Π' that is ε-leakage secure in the δ'-noisy leakage model for some δ' satisfying*

$$\delta' = \frac{\delta}{O(\log |\mathbb{F}| \log\log |\mathbb{F}|)}. \tag{47}$$

5.3 Application to Our Scheme

In the previous section we have shown that for $\delta = O(1/\log n)$ our construction is ε-leakage secure in the δ-random-probing model with

$$\varepsilon = \mathsf{negl}(\lambda) + \mathsf{negl}'(n) \tag{48}$$

where negl and negl' are some negligible functions and where λ is some security parameter such that $\log |\mathbb{F}| = \lambda + \log n$.

By applying the above reduction to our construction (and recalling that we have $|\mathbb{F}| = O(n)$), we obtain the following corollary of Theorem 3:

Corollary 3. *Let Π' denotes the secure logical program corresponding to our construction (see Sect. 4). Π' is ε-leakage secure in the δ-noisy leakage model where $\varepsilon = \mathsf{negl}(\lambda) + \mathsf{negl}'(n)$ and $\delta' = O\big(1/((\log n)^2 \log\log n)\big)$.*

6 Practical Aspects and Open Problems

Securing Arbitrary Computation. Although our scheme is described to work on a finite field $\mathbb{F}$ with specific structure, it can be used to secure any arbitrary computation represented as a Boolean circuit. Indeed, it is possible to embed a Boolean circuit into an arithmetic program over $\mathbb{F}$. Each bit is simply represented by an element $a \in \{0,1\} \subseteq \mathbb{F}$. The binary multiplication then matches with the $\mathbb{F}$-multiplication over this subset. Regarding the binary addition $\oplus$, it can be implemented with operations over $\mathbb{F}$ as:

$$a \oplus b = a + b - 2ab, \tag{49}$$

for every $a, b \in \{0,1\} \subseteq \mathbb{F}$. Of course such an embedding comes at a high cost in practice and our scheme would not be efficient to protect *e.g.* an AES computation. However, our scheme is asymptotically more efficient than previous ISW-based schemes meaning that there exists some masking order n for which an implementation of our scheme would be more efficient than an implementation of a previous scheme. Moreover and as discussed hereafter, we think that our scheme could be practically improved in many ways.

Practical Efficiency. For any cryptographic computation on a base field $\mathbb{F}$ with appropriate structure, our scheme should be very efficient in practice. We recall that the field should be such that $|\mathbb{F}| = \alpha \cdot n + 1$, for n being a power of 2 and α being large enough so that n/α is negligible. A 256-bit prime field such as those used in Elliptic Curve Cryptography could for instance satisfy these criteria. An interesting open issue would be to extend our scheme to work on other algebraic structures and in particular on binary fields (*e.g.* to efficiently secure the AES) or on rings used in lattice-based cryptography.

On the Size of the Field. We note that we need a 'big' field (typically of size $128 + 2\log n$) in order to have enough randomness when picking ω. However this might be a proof artefact and the scheme could be secure for some constant ω and/or using smaller fields. Another direction of improvement would be to mitigate or remove this constraint with an improved construction and/or proof technique.

Packing Encodings. Finally our scheme could also probably be improved by using the principle of packed secret sharing as suggested in [2,3] since our encoding is a kind of randomized Shamir's secret sharing.

A Number Theoretic Transform

The Number Theoretic Transform (NTT) is essentially a (Fast) Fourier Transform defined in a finite field (or ring) where inaccurate floating point or complex arithmetic can be avoided. The NTT can be used to multiply two polynomials over a finite field in quasilinear complexity. Let $\mathbb{F}_p$ be a prime finite field such that $d \mid p-1$ for some integer d ($\mathbb{F}_p$ contains d-th roots of unity) and let A be a $(d-1)$-degree polynomial over $\mathbb{F}_p[x]$ such that $A(x) = a_0 + a_1 x + a_2 x^2 + \cdots + a_{d-1} x^{d-1}$. For a given primitive d-th root of unity ξ, the NTT maps the coefficients of A to the evaluations $A(\xi^i)$ with $1 \leq i \leq d$:

$$\mathsf{NTT}_\xi : (a_0, a_1, \ldots, a_{d-1}) \mapsto (A(\xi^1), A(\xi^2), \ldots, A(\xi^d)). \tag{50}$$

For d being a power of two, the NTT can be computed in time complexity $O(d \log d)$. To show this, let us define A_0 and A_1, the two $(\frac{d}{2} - 1)$-degree polynomials

$$\begin{aligned} A_0(x) &= a_0 + a_2 x + a_4 x^2 + \cdots + a_{d-2} x^{\frac{d}{2}-1} \\ A_1(x) &= a_1 + a_3 x + a_5 x^2 + \cdots + a_{d-1} x^{\frac{d}{2}-1} \end{aligned}$$

which satisfy

$$A(x) = A_0(x^2) + x A_1(x^2).$$

The problem of evaluating $A(x)$ at each d-th root of unity ξ^i, for $1 \leq i \leq d$, is reduced to the problem of evaluating $A_0(x)$ and $A_1(x)$ at the points ξ^{2i}, for $1 \leq i \leq \frac{d}{2}$, and we can combine the results with $A(\xi) = A_0(\xi^2) + \xi A_1(\xi^2)$. The polynomials $A_0(x)$ and $A_1(x)$ can also be evaluated at the points ξ^{2i} with the same divide and conquer strategy, using the polynomials A_{00}, A_{01}, A_{10}, A_{11} satisfying

$$A_0(x) = A_{00}(x^2) + x A_{01}(x^2) \quad \text{and} \quad A_1(x) = A_{01}(x^2) + x A_{11}(x^2).$$

This divide and conquer strategy can be iterated $\log_2(d)$ times. At the t-th step we have 2^t polynomials $A_{\boldsymbol{u}}$ of degree $\frac{d}{2^t}$ for $\boldsymbol{u} \in \{0,1\}^t$ that must be evaluated in ξ^j for $j = 2^t, 2 \cdot 2^t, \ldots, \frac{d}{2^t} \cdot 2^t$, which makes a total of $2^t \cdot \frac{d}{2^t} = d$ evaluations. Moreover, from $\xi^{j+\frac{d}{2}} = -\xi^j$ we have

$$A_{\boldsymbol{u}}(\xi^j) = A_{\boldsymbol{u}|0}(\xi^{2j}) + \xi^j A_{\boldsymbol{u}|1}(\xi^{2j}) \text{ and } A_{\boldsymbol{u}}(\xi^{j+\frac{d}{2}}) = A_{\boldsymbol{u}|0}(\xi^{2j}) - \xi^j A_{\boldsymbol{u}|1}(\xi^{2j}) \tag{51}$$

implying that the number of evaluations can be merely divided by two.

In practice, we start with $t = \log_2(d)$, where we have $2^t = d$ constant polynomials $A_{\boldsymbol{u}} = a_{\varphi(\boldsymbol{u})}$ with $\varphi(\boldsymbol{u})$ denoting the integer corresponding to the binary expansion $\boldsymbol{u} \in \{0,1\}^{\log_2(d)}$. Then we iterate (51) for t from $\log_2(d)$ down to 1 where we have our d evaluations of A. The overall process is summarized hereafter:

1. $(c_0, c_1, \ldots, c_{d-1}) \leftarrow (a_0, a_1, \ldots, a_{d-1})$
2. for $t = \log_2(d) - 1$ down to 1:
3. $\quad j = 2^t$; $k = 2^{d-t-1}$
4. $\quad$ for $i \in \bigcup_{\ell=0}^{k-1} U_{j,\ell}$
5. $\quad\quad (c_i, c_{i+j}) \leftarrow (c_i + \xi^j c_{i+j}, c_i - \xi^j c_{i+j})$

where $U_{j,\ell} = \{(2\ell j, \ldots, (2\ell+1)j - 1)\}$ and where the index shiftings of c are done modulo d, *i.e.* $c_{i+j} = c_{i+j \bmod d}$. It can be checked that the above evaluation of NTT_ξ takes a total of $\frac{d \log d}{2}$ multiplications, $\frac{d \log d}{2}$ additions and $\frac{d \log d}{2}$ subtractions.

Using the NTT with a dth root of unity, we can efficiently compute the product $C(x) = A(x) \cdot B(x)$ for any two polynomials $A, B \in \mathbb{F}_p[x]$ of degree up to $n-1$ with $d = 2n$. We first apply the NTT to get d evaluations of both polynomials:

$$(A(\xi^1), A(\xi^2), \ldots, A(\xi^d)) = \mathsf{NTT}_\xi(a_0, a_1, \ldots, a_{n-1}, 0, \ldots, 0)$$
$$(B(\xi^1), B(\xi^2), \ldots, B(\xi^d)) = \mathsf{NTT}_\xi(b_0, b_1, \ldots, b_{n-1}, 0, \ldots, 0)$$

from which we get d evaluations of C by $C(\xi^i) = A(\xi^i) \cdot B(\xi^i)$ for $1 \leq i \leq d$. Finally, we can recover the coefficients of the output polynomial C by computing the inverse NTT on $(C(\xi), C(\xi^1), \ldots, C(\xi^d))$, which satisfies

$$\begin{aligned}(c_0, c_1, \ldots, c_d) &= \mathsf{NTT}_\xi^{-1}(C(\xi^1), C(\xi^2), \ldots, C(\xi^d)) \\ &= \mathsf{NTT}_{\xi^{-1}}(\frac{1}{d}C(\xi^1), \frac{1}{d}C(\xi^2), \ldots, \frac{1}{d}C(\xi^d)).\end{aligned}$$

References

1. Ajtai, M.: Secure computation with information leaking to an adversary. In: Fortnow, L., Vadhan, S.P. (eds.) 43rd ACM STOC, pp. 715–724. ACM Press, June 2011
2. Andrychowicz, M., Damgård, I., Dziembowski, S., Faust, S., Polychroniadou, A.: Efficient leakage resilient circuit compilers. In: Nyberg, K. (ed.) CT-RSA 2015. LNCS, vol. 9048, pp. 311–329. Springer, Cham (2015). https://doi.org/10.1007/978-3-319-16715-2_17
3. Andrychowicz, M., Dziembowski, S., Faust, S.: Circuit compilers with $O(1/\log(n))$ leakage rate. In: Fischlin, M., Coron, J.-S. (eds.) EUROCRYPT 2016, Part II. LNCS, vol. 9666, pp. 586–615. Springer, Heidelberg (2016). https://doi.org/10.1007/978-3-662-49896-5_21
4. Battistello, A., Coron, J.-S., Prouff, E., Zeitoun, R.: Horizontal side-channel attacks and countermeasures on the ISW masking scheme. In: Gierlichs, B., Poschmann, A.Y. (eds.) CHES 2016. LNCS, vol. 9813, pp. 23–39. Springer, Heidelberg (2016). https://doi.org/10.1007/978-3-662-53140-2_2
5. Belaïd, S., Benhamouda, F., Passelègue, A., Prouff, E., Thillard, A., Vergnaud, D.: Randomness complexity of private circuits for multiplication. In: Fischlin, M., Coron, J.-S. (eds.) EUROCRYPT 2016, Part II. LNCS, vol. 9666, pp. 616–648. Springer, Heidelberg (2016). https://doi.org/10.1007/978-3-662-49896-5_22

6. Belaïd, S., Benhamouda, F., Passelègue, A., Prouff, E., Thillard, A., Vergnaud, D.: Private multiplication over finite fields. In: Katz, J., Shacham, H. (eds.) CRYPTO 2017, Part III. LNCS, vol. 10403, pp. 397–426. Springer, Cham (2017). https://doi.org/10.1007/978-3-319-63697-9_14
7. Chari, S., Jutla, C.S., Rao, J.R., Rohatgi, P.: Towards sound approaches to counteract power-analysis attacks. In: Wiener, M. (ed.) CRYPTO 1999. LNCS, vol. 1666, pp. 398–412. Springer, Heidelberg (1999). https://doi.org/10.1007/3-540-48405-1_26
8. Chen, H., Cramer, R.: Algebraic geometric secret sharing schemes and secure multi-party computations over small fields. In: Dwork, C. (ed.) CRYPTO 2006. LNCS, vol. 4117, pp. 521–536. Springer, Heidelberg (2006). https://doi.org/10.1007/11818175_31
9. Chernoff, H.: A measure of asymptotic efficiency for tests of a hypothesis based on the sum of observations. Ann. Math. Stat. **23**(4), 493–507 (1952)
10. Coron, J.-S., Prouff, E., Rivain, M., Roche, T.: Higher-order side channel security and mask refreshing. In: Moriai, S. (ed.) FSE 2013. LNCS, vol. 8424, pp. 410–424. Springer, Heidelberg (2014). https://doi.org/10.1007/978-3-662-43933-3_21
11. Coron, J.-S., Roy, A., Vivek, S.: Fast evaluation of polynomials over binary finite fields and application to side-channel countermeasures. In: Batina, L., Robshaw, M. (eds.) CHES 2014. LNCS, vol. 8731, pp. 170–187. Springer, Heidelberg (2014). https://doi.org/10.1007/978-3-662-44709-3_10
12. Damgård, I., Ishai, Y., Krøigaard, M.: Perfectly secure multiparty computation and the computational overhead of cryptography. In: Gilbert, H. (ed.) EUROCRYPT 2010. LNCS, vol. 6110, pp. 445–465. Springer, Heidelberg (2010). https://doi.org/10.1007/978-3-642-13190-5_23
13. Duc, A., Dziembowski, S., Faust, S.: Unifying leakage models: from probing attacks to noisy leakage. In: Nguyen, P.Q., Oswald, E. (eds.) EUROCRYPT 2014. LNCS, vol. 8441, pp. 423–440. Springer, Heidelberg (2014). https://doi.org/10.1007/978-3-642-55220-5_24
14. Dziembowski, S., Pietrzak, K.: Leakage-resilient cryptography. In: 49th FOCS, pp. 293–302. IEEE Computer Society Press, October 2008
15. Gandolfi, K., Mourtel, C., Olivier, F.: Electromagnetic analysis: concrete results. In: Koç, Ç.K., Naccache, D., Paar, C. (eds.) CHES 2001. LNCS, vol. 2162, pp. 251–261. Springer, Heidelberg (2001). https://doi.org/10.1007/3-540-44709-1_21
16. Goldwasser, S., Rothblum, G.N.: How to compute in the presence of leakage. In: 53rd FOCS, pp. 31–40. IEEE Computer Society Press, October 2012
17. Ishai, Y., Sahai, A., Wagner, D.: Private circuits: securing hardware against probing attacks. In: Boneh, D. (ed.) CRYPTO 2003. LNCS, vol. 2729, pp. 463–481. Springer, Heidelberg (2003). https://doi.org/10.1007/978-3-540-45146-4_27
18. Kocher, P.C.: Timing attacks on implementations of Diffie-Hellman, RSA, DSS, and other systems. In: Koblitz, N. (ed.) CRYPTO 1996. LNCS, vol. 1109, pp. 104–113. Springer, Heidelberg (1996). https://doi.org/10.1007/3-540-68697-5_9
19. Kocher, P., Jaffe, J., Jun, B.: Differential power analysis. In: Wiener, M. (ed.) CRYPTO 1999. LNCS, vol. 1666, pp. 388–397. Springer, Heidelberg (1999). https://doi.org/10.1007/3-540-48405-1_25
20. Micali, S., Reyzin, L.: Physically observable cryptography (extended abstract). In: Naor, M. (ed.) TCC 2004. LNCS, vol. 2951, pp. 278–296. Springer, Heidelberg (2004). https://doi.org/10.1007/978-3-540-24638-1_16

21. Prouff, E., Rivain, M.: Masking against side-channel attacks: a formal security proof. In: Johansson, T., Nguyen, P.Q. (eds.) EUROCRYPT 2013. LNCS, vol. 7881, pp. 142–159. Springer, Heidelberg (2013). https://doi.org/10.1007/978-3-642-38348-9_9
22. Rivain, M., Prouff, E.: Provably secure higher-order masking of AES. In: Mangard, S., Standaert, F.-X. (eds.) CHES 2010. LNCS, vol. 6225, pp. 413–427. Springer, Heidelberg (2010). https://doi.org/10.1007/978-3-642-15031-9_28
23. Shamir, A.: How to share a secret. Commun. Assoc. Comput. Mach. **22**(11), 612–613 (1979)
24. Standaert, F.-X., Pereira, O., Yu, Y., Quisquater, J.-J., Yung, M., Oswald, E.: Leakage resilient cryptography in practice. Cryptology ePrint Archive, Report 2009/341 (2009). http://eprint.iacr.org/2009/341

Leakage-Resilient Cryptography from Puncturable Primitives and Obfuscation

Yu Chen[1,2,3], Yuyu Wang[4,5,6](✉), and Hong-Sheng Zhou[7]

[1] State Key Laboratory of Information Security, Institute of Information Engineering, Chinese Academy of Sciences, Beijing 100093, China
chenyu@iie.ac.cn

[2] State Key Laboratory of Cryptology, P.O. Box 5159, Beijing 100878, China

[3] School of Cyber Security, University of Chinese Academy of Sciences, Beijing, China

[4] Tokyo Institute of Technology, Tokyo, Japan
wang.y.ar@m.titech.ac.jp

[5] IOHK, Hong Kong, China

[6] National Institute of Advanced Industrial Science and Technology, Tokyo, Japan

[7] Virginia Commonwealth University, Richmond, USA
hszhou@vcu.edu

Abstract. In this work, we develop a framework for building leakage-resilient cryptosystems in the bounded leakage model from puncturable primitives and indistinguishability obfuscation ($i\mathcal{O}$). The major insight of our work is that various types of puncturable pseudorandom functions (PRFs) can achieve leakage resilience on an obfuscated street.

First, we build leakage-resilient weak PRFs from weak puncturable PRFs and $i\mathcal{O}$, which readily imply leakage-resilient secret-key encryption. Then, we build leakage-resilient publicly evaluable PRFs (PEPRFs) from puncturable PEPRFs and $i\mathcal{O}$, which readily imply leakage-resilient key encapsulation mechanism and thus public-key encryption. As a building block of independent interest, we realize puncturable PEPRFs from either newly introduced puncturable objects such as puncturable trapdoor functions and puncturable extractable hash proof systems or existing puncturable PRFs with $i\mathcal{O}$. Finally, we construct the first leakage-resilient public-coin signature from selective puncturable PRFs, leakage-resilient one-way functions and $i\mathcal{O}$. This settles the open problem posed by Boyle, Segev, and Wichs (Eurocrypt 2011).

By further assuming the existence of lossy functions, all the above constructions achieve optimal leakage rate of $1 - o(1)$. Such a leakage rate is not known to be achievable for weak PRFs, PEPRFs and public-coin signatures before. This also resolves the open problem posed by Dachman-Soled, Gordon, Liu, O'Neill, and Zhou (PKC 2016, JOC 2018).

T. Peyrin and S. Galbraith (Eds.): ASIACRYPT 2018, LNCS 11273, pp. 575–606, 2018.
https://doi.org/10.1007/978-3-030-03329-3_20

1 Introduction

A main line in cryptography is to design cryptosystems in security models that capture a wide range of possible attacks. Based on the idealized assumption that software/hardware implementations of cryptosystems perfectly hide the internal secrets, traditional security models (following the seminal work of Goldwasser and Micali [GM84]) only give an adversary "black-box" access to cryptosystems. However, advancements of cryptanalysis indicate that such an idealized assumption is false in real world: an adversary can launch a variety of *key leakage attacks* (such as [Koc96,BDL97,BS97,KJJ99,HSH+08]) to get some partial information about secret keys.

To thwart key leakage attacks in a systematic manner, the research community has paid extensive efforts on the design of provably secure leakage-resilient cryptosystems in the last decade, spreading from basic primitives (including one-way functions, pseudorandom functions, message authentication codes, encryptions, and signatures) to advanced protocols (including identifications, authenticated key agreements, and zero-knowledge proof systems).

Leakage Models. Briefly speaking, leakage models are defined by strengthening standard models with a leakage oracle $\mathcal{O}_{\mathsf{leak}}(\cdot)$, from which an adversary can (adaptively) specify a series of *leakage functions* $f_i : \{0,1\}^* \to \{0,1\}^{\ell_i}$ and learn the result of f_i applied to the internal secret state. Over the years, several leakage models have been proposed in the literature, differing in the specifications of f_i. In this work we focus on a simple yet general model called *bounded leakage* model, introduced by Akavia et al. [AGV09]. In the bounded leakage model, all secrets in memory are subject to leakage, i.e., the input of f_i could be entire secret key sk, while f_i could be arbitrary subjected to the natural restriction that $\sum_i \ell_i$ is bounded by some parameter ℓ, called the leakage bound. The leakage rate is defined as the ratio of ℓ to the secret key size $|sk|$, i.e., $\ell/|sk|$. Obviously, the optimal leakage rate is $1 - o(1)$ since otherwise the adversary can trivially learn the entire secret via querying $\mathcal{O}_{\mathsf{leak}}(\cdot)$.

To date, the bounded leakage model has been widely adopted in many works [NS09,KV09,CDRW10,BG10,GKPV10,HL11,BK12,BCH12]. The results from the bounded leakage model are usually used as building blocks for leakage-resilient schemes in more complex leakage models.

Approach Towards Leakage Resilience. From the perspective of provable security, the main technical hurdle to achieve leakage-resilience is that the reduction must be able to handle leakage queries w.r.t. arbitrary functions chosen from $\mathcal{L}$, where $\mathcal{L}$ is the ensemble of admissible leakage functions. This seemingly stipulates that the reduction should know the secret key while typically this is not the case because the underlying intractable problems is usually embedded in the secret key. This intuition has been formalized as "useless attacker paradox" in [Wic13]. Prior works overcome this paradox by taking the following two approaches.

One approach is directly resorting to *leakage-resilient* assumptions (which might be well packed as advanced assumptions). Following this approach, the reduction can easily handle leakage queries by simply forwarding them to its own challenger. Goldwasser et al. [GKPV10] proved that the LWE assumption itself is leakage-resilient and then built a leakage-resilient secret-key encryption from it. Akavia et al. [AGV09] proved that meaningful and meaningless public keys are computationally indistinguishable even in the presence of secret key leakage based on the LWE assumption, and then utilized this leakage-resilient "assumption" to show that Regev's PKE [Reg05] is actually leakage-resilient. Katz and Vaikuntanathan [KV09] built a leakage-resilient signature from universal one-way hash functions (UOWHFs)[1] together with PKE and simulation-sound non-interactive zero knowledge (NIZK) proof system, where the UOWHFs are actually used as leakage-resilient one-way functions. Similar strategy is also adopted for constructing other leakage-resilient signature schemes [DHLW10, BSW11, MTVY11].

Another approach is combining *key detached* strategy and *leakage-resilient* facts/assumptions, which is mainly used in the constructions of leakage-resilient PKE. Informally, the key detached strategy means the underlying intractable problems are not embedded to the secret keys, but to the ciphertexts. Following this approach, the reduction can easily handle key leakage queries by either owning the secret key or relying on leakage-resilient assumptions. Naor and Segev [NS09] utilized hash proof system (HPS) as a powerful tool to construct leakage-resilient PKE. In the security proof, valid ciphertexts are first switched to invalid ones (such switching is computationally indistinguishable even given the whole secret key because the underlying subset membership problem and secret keys are detached) to ensure that the hash proof π has high min-entropy, then the leftover hash lemma is used to prove the session key of the form $\mathsf{ext}(\pi, s)$ is random even in the presence of bounded key leakage.[2] Subsequently, Alwen et al. [ADN+10] and Hazay et al. [HLWW13] extended HPS to the identity-based and symmetric-key setting respectively, and used them to construct leakage-resilient identity-based encryption and secret-key encryption. Dodis et al. [DGK+10] constructed leakage-resilient PKE in the auxiliary input model via a similar method. In the security proof, valid ciphertexts are also first switched to invalid ones, then the generalized Goldreich-Levin theorem is used to argue that the session key of the form $\mathsf{hc}(sk)$ is pseudorandom even given auxiliary-input of the secret key sk.[3]

---

[1] This is sometimes called second pre-image resistant functions.

[2] Leftover hash lemma could be interpreted as a leakage-resilient fact, which stipulates $\mathsf{ext}(x, s)$ is close to uniform even given a correlated value z, as long as s is a random seed chosen independently and x still has high min-entropy given leakage z.

[3] Goldreich-Levin theorem can be interpreted as a leakage-resilient assumption, which states that if h is one-way then $\mathsf{hc}(x)$ is pseudorandom even in the presence of $h(x)$. Here hc serves as a computational randomness extractor and $h(x)$ could be viewed as leakage on x.

1.1 Motivation

So far, a broad range of leakage-resilient cryptographic schemes under various leakage models have been proposed in the literature. Nevertheless, several interesting problems are still left open around lower-level, "workhorse" primitives like SKE, PKE, and signature under the basic bounded leakage model.

For leakage-resilient SKE, the task can be reduced to constructing leakage-resilient weak PRFs (wPRFs) in the bounded leakage model. However, the literature on this topic is sparse. [Pie09, DY13] showed that any wPRF is already leakage-resilient for a logarithmic leakage bound $\ell = O(\log \lambda)$. Hazay et al. [HLWW13] built leakage-resilient wPRF from any one-way functions. Their construction only requires minimal assumption, but its leakage rate is $O(\log(\lambda)/|sk|)$, which is rather poor. To date, essentially nothing better was known for generic construction of leakage-resilient SKE with optimal leakage rate, beyond simply using leakage-resilient PKE in the symmetric-key setting.

For leakage-resilient PKE, existing constructions [AGV09, BG10, DGK+10, NS09, ADN+10] are based on either specific assumptions such as LWE, DDH, DCR, QR, or somewhat more generally the hash proof systems[4]. It is intriguing to know if there is a generic construction. In particular, whether the generic constructions of PKE based on trapdoor functions/relations [PW08, RS09, KMO10, Wee10] can be made leakage-resilient is still unclear. On the other hand, semantic security against chosen-ciphertext attacks (CCA) is the strongest notion for PKE in the traditional security model [GM84]. Several previous works [NS09, LWZ13, QL13, QL14, CQX18] studied how to achieve leakage-resilience and CCA security simultaneously via dedicated composition of separate techniques. Nevertheless, no prior work considered the orthogonal problem: whether we can acquire leakage-resilience from CCA security. We observe that in the CCA security experiment, responses to decryption queries can be viewed as a certain form of key leakage (the leakage function f is tied to decryption algorithm but with unbounded output length). It is interesting to know whether there is a general connection between the two important security notions for PKE.

For leakage-resilient signature, achieving *fully leakage-resilience* is of particular interest since it better captures real attacks [KV09]. This notion requires a signature to remain existentially unforgeable under chosen-message attacks even when an adversary obtains bounded leakage information on all intermediate states, including the secret keys and internal random coins. Clearly, if the signing procedure is deterministic or public-coin[5], standard leakage resilience automatically implies fully leakage resilience. To date, all the known fully leakage-resilient

[4] Following current conventions, we do not regard hash proof systems [CS02] as a general assumption.

[5] A signature is *secret-coin* if its security breaks down when the randomness used in the signing procedure is revealed. On the contrary, a signature is *public-coin* if it stays secure even when the random coins used in the signing procedure are revealed (i.e., provided in-the-clear by the signature). In other words, public-coin signature is secure even when the *entire* random coins used for signing are leaked.

signature schemes [BSW11, MTVY11, LLW11, GJS11] in the standard model are randomized and secret-coin. The existence of leakage-resilient deterministic or public-coin signature is unclear and was left as an open problem by Boyle et al. [BSW11]. Earlier, the leakage-resilient signature scheme by Katz and Vaikuntanathan [KV09] is deterministic but only "one-time" secure. Recently, Wang et al. [WMHT16] proposed a leakage-resilient public-coin signature scheme. However, their construction is only secure against selective leakage attacks, i.e., an adversary has to declare the leakage function before seeing the verification key. Besides, their construction requires differing-input obfuscation [BGI+12], whose existence is seriously cast in doubt [GGHW14, BSW16]. From this perspective, the problem posed by Boyle et al. [BSW11] is still largely open.

1.2 Our Contributions

With the preceding discussion in mind, in this work we focus on generic constructions of leakage-resilient encryption and signature in the bounded leakage model. The major insight of our work is that various kinds of puncturable PRFs can achieve leakage-resilience on an obfuscated street. We summarize our main results (depicted in Fig. 1) as below.

Leakage-Resilient SKE. As shown in [HLWW13], the classic construction of CPA-secure SKE from wPRF is leakage-resilience-preserving. So, we restrict our attention to constructing leakage-resilient wPRFs. Towards this goal, in Sect. 3.2 we first put forward a new notion called weak puncturable PRFs (wPPRFs), which could be thought of as the puncturable version of wPRFs. We then show wPPRFs and selective puncturable PRFs (sPPRFs) [SW14] imply each other, while the latter is implied by the GGM-tree based PRFs [GGM86]. Finally, in Sect. 3.3 we build leakage-resilient wPRFs from wPPRFs and $i\mathcal{O}$.

Leakage-Resilient KEM. The KEM-DEM paradigm (here KEM stands for key encapsulation mechanism, DEM stands for data encapsulation mechanism) is a modular and efficient approach for building PKE. In the leakage setting, one can build a leakage-resilient PKE by combining a leakage-resilient KEM with a standard DEM. In the rest of this work, we only focus on the construction of leakage-resilient KEM. Chen and Zhang [CZ14] put forward the notion of publicly evaluable PRFs (PEPRFs), which encompasses almost all the known constructions of KEM. We observe that leakage-resilient PEPRFs naturally imply leakage-resilient KEM. So, the task is reduced to acquiring leakage resilience for PEPRFs.

To this end, in Sect. 4.2 we first put forward the notion of puncturable PEPRFs, then build leakage-resilient PEPRFs from puncturable PEPRFs and $i\mathcal{O}$ in Sect. 4.3. Moreover, we instantiate puncturable PEPRFs from either newly introduced primitives such as puncturable trapdoor functions and puncturable extractable hash proof systems, or existing puncturable PRFs with $i\mathcal{O}$.

This result provides a unified framework for constructing leakage-resilient KEM, which not only clarifies and encompasses the construction by Dachman-Soled et al. [DGL+16, Sect. 5.1], but also indicates that the PKE constructions based on "puncturable" trapdoor functions/relations (which in turn implied by correlated-product trapdoor functions [RS09] or extractable hash proof systems [Wee10] with puncturable property) can be made leakage resilient! Recently, Matsuda and Hanaoka [MH15] introduced a new primitive called puncturable KEM (PKEM), which captures a common pattern towards CCA security underlying many constructions of CCA-secure PKE. We remark that PPEPRFs imply PKEM with perfect strong punctured decapsulation soundness. This result establishes a somewhat surprising connection between CCA security and leakage resilience, that is, CCA security obtained along the puncturable road can be converted to leakage-resilience in a non-black-box manner via obfuscation.

Leakage-Resilient Signature. In Sect. 5, we show how to build leakage-resilient signature from selective puncturable PRFs, $i\mathcal{O}$, and leakage-resilient one-way functions. Our basic scheme is deterministic but only achieves selective security[6]. To attain adaptive security, several bootstrapping techniques can be used without compromising leakage resilience. More precisely, one can either use the magic method enabled by extremely lossy function [Zha16], obtaining the first deterministic leakage-resilient signature scheme, or apply the "prefix-guessing technique" [HW09, RW14], yielding the first public-coin leakage-resilient signature scheme. We postpone the details to the full version [CWZ18].

We highlight that in our construction the signature size is exactly the output size of a puncturable PRF[7], which is very close to the leakage bound. Clearly, signature size cannot be shorter than leakage bound, since otherwise an adversary can directly obtain a forged signature from leakage. In this sense, our constructions also enjoy the almost optimal signature size.

All the basic constructions described above can tolerate L bits of leakage for any polynomial L of security parameter λ. However, the leakage rate is low due to the fact that secret keys are obfuscated programs, which could be very huge. By further assuming the existence of lossy functions [PW08], we can remarkably shrink the size of secret keys and achieve optimal leakage rate $1 - o(1)$. Such a leakage rate is not known to be achievable for weak PRFs, PEPRFs and deterministic/public-coin signatures before.

1.3 Overview of Our Techniques

As we summarized before, a common theme of the two main approaches towards leakage resilience in the literature is that the reduction always try to simulate leakage oracle *perfectly*, i.e., answering leakage queries with *real* leakage. To do so, we have to either rely on leakage-resilient assumptions or resort to sophisticated design with specific structure. It is interesting to investigate the possibility of simulating leakage oracle *computationally*, namely answering leakage queries

[6] In selective security model, the adversary must declare the message m^* on which it will make a forgery before seeing the verification key, but then can adaptively make signing queries on messages distinct from m^*.

[7] In the case of our adaptively secure construction, a signature additionally contains a public coin of size λ^c for any constant $c < 1$.

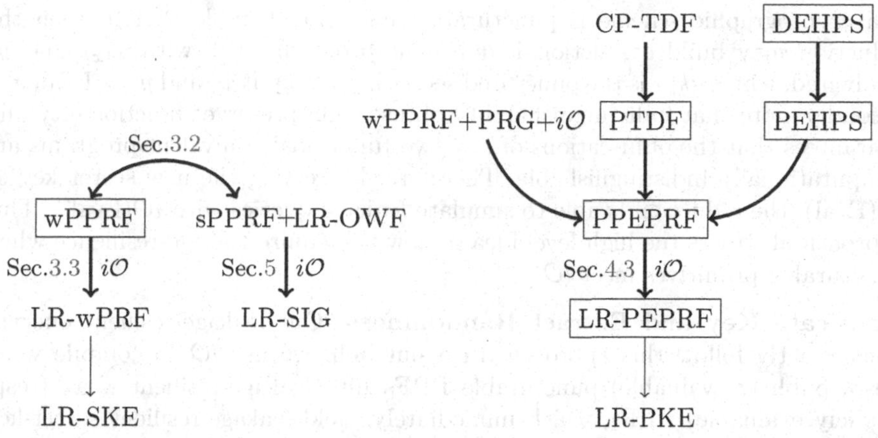

Fig. 1. The bold lines and rectangles denote our contributions (the thin lines denote those that are straightforward or follow readily from previous work).

with *simulated* leakage, as long as it is computationally indistinguishable from *real* leakage. This would possibly lend new techniques to address the unsolved problems in leakage-resilient cryptography.

Very recently, Dachman-Soled et al. [DGL+16] discovered powerful applications of $i\mathcal{O}$ to leakage-resilient cryptography. In the continual leakage model, they presented an $i\mathcal{O}$-based compiler that transforms any public-key encryption or signature scheme with *consecutive* continual leakage-resilience to continual leakage resilience allowing leakage on key updates. In the bounded leakage model, they showed how to modify the Sahai-Waters PKE to be leakage-resilient. We observe that their work essentially embodies the idea of simulating leakage oracle computationally.

Simulate Leakage via Obfuscation. At the heart of our leakage-resilient encryptions and signatures is a general approach of simulating leakages enabled by puncturable primitives and obfuscation, which is largely inspired by the leakage-resilient variant of Sahai-Waters PKE due to Dachman-Soled et al. [DGL+16]. Next, we first distill and extend the idea underlying the work of [DGL+16], then carry out a systematic study of its applicability to leakage-resilient cryptography.

Recall that the common technical hurdle towards leakage resilience is to handle leakage queries. As opposed to the naive strategy of answering leakage queries with real secret keys, another promising strategy is simulating leakage with "faked" secret keys. By the composition lemma, as long as the faked secret keys are indistinguishable from the real ones, the simulated leakages are also indistinguishable from the real leakages because all leakage functions are efficiently computable.

Our approach adopts the second strategy. First, a secret key *sk* of any cryptographic scheme can always be expressed as a program Eval with *sk* hardwired.

If a cryptographic scheme is puncturable (e.g., puncturable PRFs), then the reduction may build a functional-equivalent program Eval′ with sk_{x^*} and y^* hardwired, where sk_{x^*} is the punctured secret key at input x^* and $y^* = \text{Eval}(x^*)$. Secondly, note that indistinguishability obfuscation preserves functionality and guarantees that the obfuscations of any two functional-equivalent programs are computationally indistinguishable. Therefore, by setting the new secret key as $i\mathcal{O}(\text{Eval})$, the reduction is able to simulate leakage queries with $i\mathcal{O}(\text{Eval}')$. This approach abstracts the high-level idea of how to acquire leakage-resilience when puncturable primitives meet $i\mathcal{O}$.

Obfuscate Key and Extract Randomness. Our leakage-resilient encryptions exactly follow this approach. In a nutshell, we use $i\mathcal{O}$ to compile weak (resp. publicly evaluable) puncturable PRFs into leakage-resilient weak (resp. publicly evaluable) PRFs, which immediately yield leakage-resilient secret-key (resp. public-key) encryption.

To best illustrate our approach, we focus here on the secret-key setting, as it already emphasizes the main ideas underlying our approach. Starting from a weak puncturable PRF $F : K \times X \rightarrow \{0,1\}^n$, we use $i\mathcal{O}$ to compile it into a leakage-resilient weak PRF with a randomness extractor $\mathsf{ext} : \{0,1\}^n \times S \rightarrow Z$. The construction is instructive: (1) generate a secret key k for F, then create a program Eval with k hardwired, which on input x and s outputs $\mathsf{ext}(F_k(x), s)$; (2) set the secret key as $i\mathcal{O}(\text{Eval})$. This defines a weak PRF $\hat{F} : \{0,1\}^n \times S \rightarrow Z$. To establish security, the hybrid argument starts with the real game for leakage-resilient wPRF, where leakage and evaluation queries are handled with real secret key $i\mathcal{O}(\text{Eval})$. In the next game, the challenger picks the challenge input x^* and s^* at the very beginning, create a program Eval′ with the same input-output behavior as Eval, where k_{x^*} is the punctured key for k w.r.t. x^* and $y^* = F_k(x^*)$. The leakage and evaluation queries are thus handled with $i\mathcal{O}(\text{Eval}')$. Such modifications are undetectable by the security of $i\mathcal{O}$. In the final game, the challenger switches y^* from $F_k(x^*)$ to a random value. This transition is undetectable by the weak pseudorandomness of the starting puncturable PRF. An important fact is that the responses to evaluation queries are determined by k_{x^*}, and thus do not leak any information about y^*. Now, we can argue the desired security in purely information-theoretic way. By appropriate parameter choice, y^* still retains high min-entropy in the presence of leakage, and thus the value $\mathsf{ext}(y^*, s^*)$ is statistically close to uniform distribution.

In the public-key setting, our construction essentially follows the same approach. We use $i\mathcal{O}$ to compile puncturable PEPRF into leakage-resilient PEPRF, which readily yield leakage-resilient CPA-secure KEM. The main technical novelty lies in realizing puncturable PEPRFs from a variety of puncturable primitives. More precisely, we build puncturable PEPRFs from: (1) newly introduced notion of puncturable TDFs, which is in turn implied by correlated-product TDFs [RS09]; (2) newly introduced notion of puncturable EHPS, which is implied by EHPS [Wee10] satisfying derivable property; (3) selective puncturable PRFs, pseudorandom generator, and $i\mathcal{O}$ (adapted from the Sahai-Waters PKE [SW14]). This provides us a unified method to build leakage-resilient KEM from various puncturable primitives and $i\mathcal{O}$.

Obfuscate Key and Translate Leakage. Along our approach towards leakage resilience, we investigate the possibility of building leakage-resilient signature from puncturable primitives and $i\mathcal{O}$. We choose the short "hash-and-sign" selectively secure signature by Sahai and Waters [SW14] as our starting point, since it inherits the puncturable property from its underlying selective puncturable PRFs. To best illustrate the idea of our adaption, we first briefly review the Sahai-Waters signature scheme.

The Sahai-Waters signature is essentially a PRF-based MAC with public verifiability. The signing key sk is simply a secret key of selective puncturable PRF (sPPRF), and the signature on m is $\sigma \leftarrow F_k(m)$. The verification key vk is set as $i\mathcal{O}(\text{Vefy})$ where Vefy is a program that can check the MAC publicly. To excise out the information about $F_k(m^*)$ (here m^* denotes the target message), Vefy computes $g(F_k(m))$ and compares the result for equality to $g(\sigma)$, where g is a one-way function and σ is the claimed signature on m. To establish security, the hybrid argument starts with the real game for selective signature. The intermediate hybrid game builds an equivalent verification program using a punctured key k_{m^*} and $y^* \leftarrow g(\sigma^*)$ where $\sigma^* = F_k(m^*)$. The final hybrid game replaces σ^* with a random value. The first transition is undetectable by the security of $i\mathcal{O}$, while the second transition is undetectable by the pseudorandomness of sPPRF. In the final game, no PPT adversary is able to output a valid forgery (find the preimage σ^*) with non-negligible advantage by the one-wayness of g.

Following the new approach of simulating leakage, a tempting idea to make the Sahai-Waters signature leakage-resilient is setting the signing key as $i\mathcal{O}(\text{Sign})$, where Sign is a program that on input m outputs $F_k(m)$. Among the transitions of hybrid games, Sign is replaced by Sign$'$ (with k_{m^*} and σ^* hardwired). In this way, leakage and signing queries can be handled with "faked" signing key. However, we are unable to reduce the leakage-resilient unforgeability to the one-wayness of g. This is because in addition to $y^* = g(\sigma^*)$ revealed in vk, the information of σ^* may also be leaked via leakage queries on signing key $i\mathcal{O}(\text{Sign}')$. Therefore, the security proof breaks down in the final game, i.e., the reduction has to build Sign$'$ while σ^* is unknown.[8] We overcome this obstacle by using *leakage-resilient* OWF to replace standard OWF. Briefly, OWF is *leakage-resilient* if one-wayness remains in the presence of certain leakage on the preimage. Also observe that a leakage function f about the signing key $i\mathcal{O}(\text{Sign}')$ can be efficiently translated to leakage about σ^*, since both f and $i\mathcal{O}$ are efficiently computable. With such enhancement, in the final game the reduction can handle signing queries using k_{m^*} and handle leakage queries on signing key $i\mathcal{O}(\text{Sign}')$ by translating them to leakage queries on preimage σ^* to the underlying leakage-resilient OWF. See Sect. 5 for technical details.

Improving Leakage Rate via Lossy Functions. Applying the above approach in a straightforward manner will incur poor leakage rate, because the secret keys are obfuscated programs, which could be very large.

---

[8] Note that this dilemma does not occur in the case of encryption, since the argument in the final game is information-theoretic.

In [DGL+16], the authors showed how to modify their basic leakage-resilient PKE construction to achieve optimal leakage rate. Next, we briefly revisit their technique in the context of our construction of leakage-resilient wPRF. Now, the key generation algorithm works as follows: (1) pick a random key k_e for a SKE scheme and generate a dummy ciphertext $ct \leftarrow \mathsf{Enc}(k_e, 0^n)$ as the secret key sk; (2) pick a collision-resistant hash h and compute $\eta^* \leftarrow h(ct)$; (3) pick a random key k for the underlying weak PRF, obfuscate a program Eval and store the obfuscated result C_{eval} into public parameters. Here, the program Eval is hardwired with k and t^*, which on input sk and (x, s) outputs $\mathsf{ext}(F_k(x), s)$ if and only if $h(sk) = \eta^*$. Intuitively, ct acts as a trigger of C_{eval}, which only works when $h(ct)$ matches η^*. In this way, the size of secret key is greatly reduced.

In the security proof, the first game is the real game. In the next game, ct is switched to an encryption of the PRF value $y^* \leftarrow F_k(x^*)$. This modification is undetectable by the semantic security of SKE. Then, C_{eval} is switched to C'_{eval}, which is an obfuscation of program Eval$'$. With k_e and a punctured PRF key k_{x^*} hardwired, Eval' works if and only if the hash value of its input ct matches η^*. When $h(ct) = t^*$, it evaluates with k_{x^*} if $x \neq x^*$, otherwise it evaluates after decrypting ct to y^*. In the final game, y^* is switched to a uniformly random value. The rest security analysis is routine. A subtle problem arised is that now Eval and Eval$'$ have differing inputs, because h is compressing and thus a collision ct' (i.e., $h(ct') = \eta^* = h(ct)$) that encrypts a value $y' \neq y^*$ is likely to exist. Therefore, they have to rely on public-coin differing-input obfuscation [IPS15], which is stronger than indistinguishability obfuscation.

As analyzed above, the usage of CRHF leads to the reliance on differing-input obfuscation, while the choice of CRHF seems necessary to ensure that η^* only leaks partial information about y^* (encrypted in ct), which is crucial to achieve high leakage rate. Can we achieve higher leakage rate without resorting to differing-input obfuscation? The answer is affirmative. Our idea is to replace CRHFs with lossy functions [PW08]. In the real construction, h is generated as an injective function. By this choice, η^* uniquely fixes its preimage ct and thus the value y^*. With this setting, Eval and Eval$'$ agree on all inputs, and $i\mathcal{O}$ suffices to guarantee the switching from Eval to Eval$'$ is undetectable. To argue the high leakage rate we can attain, in the last game we switches h to a lossy function that significantly lose the information about y^*. By the security of lossy functions, this change is undetectable. Clearly, in the last game y^* still maintains sufficiently large min-entropy even in the presence of η^* and leakage. By appropriate choice of parameter, optimal leakage rate is achievable. The above technique carries over to the constructions of leakage-resilient PEPRF and signature as well.

We believe that the our technique of improving leakage rate by interplaying $i\mathcal{O}$ with lossy functions will also be instructive for avoiding using differing-input obfuscation in other places.

1.4 Related Work

Leakage Models. Several leakage models have been proposed in the literature. In the seminal work, Micali and Reyzin [MR04] initiated the formal study of side-channel attacks by introducing the "only computation leaks information" model. Unfortunately, it fails to capture many practical leakage attacks, such as the cold-boot attack of [HSH+08].

To capture more general side-channel attacks known as memory attacks, Akavia et al. [AGV09] introduced the bounded leakage model, in which the adversary can obtain arbitrary length-bounded leakage. The follow-up works considered various strengthenings to accommodate more complex and general leakage scenarios. Naor and Segev [NS09] generalized the bounded leakage model to noisy leakage model (also known as entropy leakage model), where length-bounded leakage is relaxed to entropy-bounded leakage. Alwen et al. [ADW09, ADN+10] suggested the bounded-retrieval model, which imposes an additional requirement that the tolerated leakage amount can grow by proportionally expanding the secret key without increasing the size of public key, or computation/bandwidth efficiency. Dodis et al. [DHLAW10] and Brakerski et al. [BKKV10] introduced the continual leakage model for public-key schemes, where the secret key can be periodically self-refreshed while the public key remains the same. This model allows bounded leakage between any two successive refreshes without a-priori bound on the overall amount of leakage throughout the lifetime of the system.

The bottomline of the bounded leakage model and its variants interpret the following restriction on the leakage: it is information-theoretically impossible to recover the secret key from the leakage. Dodis et al. [DKL09, DGK+10] introduced the auxiliary input model (AIM), in which the total amount of leakage could be unbounded, as long as the secret key remains hard-to-invert given the leakage (but even if the secret key is fully determined in an information-theoretic sense). As noted in [KV09], a drawback of this model is that given some collection of leakage functions $\{f_i\}$ there is no way to tell, in general, whether they satisfy the stated requirement or not. Furthermore, existing constructions in this model require super-polynomial hardness assumptions.

Leakage-Resilient Cryptosystems. There is a large body of constructions of leakage-resilient cryptosystems in various models. In the bounded leakage model, there are OWF [KV09, Kom16], MAC and SKE [HLWW13], PKE [AGV09, NS09, LWZ13, QL13, QL14, CQX18], IBE [AGV09, ADN+10, CDRW10], signature [KV09, ADW09], AKE [ADW09], and zero-knowledge proofs [GJS11]. In the continual leakage model, there are PKE [DHLAW10, BKKV10], IBE [LRW11, YCZY12, YXZ+15], and signature [BSW11, MTVY11, LLW11]. In the auxiliary input model, there are SKE [DKL09], PKE [DGK+10], and signature [WMHT16].

2 Preliminaries

Notation. For a distribution or random variable X, we write $x \xleftarrow{\text{R}} X$ to denote the operation of sampling a random x according to X. For a set X, we use $x \xleftarrow{\text{R}} X$ to denote the operation of sampling x uniformly at random from X, and use $|X|$ to denote its size. We use U_X to denote the uniform distribution over X. For a positive integer n, we use $[n]$ to denote the set $\{1, \ldots, n\}$. Unless described otherwise, all quantities are implicitly functions of a security parameter denoted λ. We say that a quantity is negligible, written $\mathsf{negl}(\lambda)$, if it vanishes faster than the inverse of any polynomial in λ. A probabilistic polynomial time (PPT) algorithm is a randomized algorithm that runs in time $\mathsf{poly}(\lambda)$. If $\mathcal{A}$ is a randomized algorithm, we write $z \leftarrow \mathcal{A}(x_1, \ldots, x_n; r)$ to indicate that $\mathcal{A}$ outputs z on inputs $(x_1, \ldots, x_n)$ and random coins r. For notational clarity we usually omit r and write $z \leftarrow \mathcal{A}(x_1, \ldots, x_n)$.

Due to space limitations, we postpone the background of randomness extraction, definitions of lossy functions, leakage-resilient one-way functions/symmetric encryption/key encapsulation mechanism/signature to the full version [CWZ18].

2.1 Puncturable Pseudorandom Functions

Puncturable PRFs (PPRFs) is the simplest type of constrained PRFs [KPTZ13, BW13, BGI14]. In a PPRF, the constrained key is associated with an element $x^* \in X$, which allows evaluation on all elements $x \neq x^*$. Next, we recall the definition and security notion of PPRFs from [SW14] as below.

Definition 1 (PPRFs). *A PPRF $F : K \times X \rightarrow Y$ consists of four polynomial time algorithms:*

- $\mathsf{Gen}(\lambda)$: *on input λ, output public parameter pp and a secret key $k \xleftarrow{\text{R}} K$. pp will be used as an implicit input of* $\mathsf{PrivEval}$, $\mathsf{Puncture}$ *and* $\mathsf{PuncEval}$.
- $\mathsf{PrivEval}(k, x)$: *on input a secret key k and $x \in X$, output $F(k, x)$.*
- $\mathsf{Puncture}(k, x^*)$: *on input a secret key k and $x^* \in X$, output a punctured key $k(\{x^*\})$.*[9]
- $\mathsf{PuncEval}(k_{x^*}, x)$: *on input a punctured key k_{x^*} and an element $x \in X$, output $F(k, x)$ if $x \neq x^*$ and a special reject symbol $\perp$ otherwise.*

For ease of notation, we write k_{x^*} to represent $k(\{x^*\})$, write $F_k(x)$ and $F(k, x)$ interchangeably and write $F_{k_{x^*}}(x)$ or $F(k_{x^*}, x)$ to represent $\mathsf{PuncEval}(k_{x^*}, x)$.

Sahai and Waters [SW14] defined selective pseudorandomness for PPRFs, which is weaker than full pseudorandomness in that the adversary must commit to the target input x^* even before seeing the public parameter.

Selective Pseudorandomness. Let $\mathcal{A} = (\mathcal{A}_1, \mathcal{A}_2)$ be an adversary against PPRFs and define its advantage in the following experiment:

$$\mathsf{Adv}_{\mathcal{A}}(\lambda) = \Pr\left[\beta = \beta' : \begin{array}{l} (state, x^*) \leftarrow \mathcal{A}_1(\lambda); \\ (pp, k) \leftarrow \mathsf{Gen}(\lambda); \\ k_{x^*} \leftarrow \mathsf{Puncture}(k, x^*); \\ y_0^* \leftarrow F_k(x^*), y_1^* \xleftarrow{\text{R}} Y; \\ \beta \xleftarrow{\text{R}} \{0,1\}; \\ \beta' \leftarrow \mathcal{A}_2(state, pp, k_{x^*}, y_\beta^*); \end{array}\right] - \frac{1}{2}.$$

[9] Without loss of generality, we assume that $k(\{x^*\})$ includes the information of x^* in plain.

A PPRF is said to be selectively pseudorandom if for any PPT adversary $\mathcal{A}$ its advantage defined as above is negligible in λ. For simplicity, we refer to selectively pseudorandom PPRFs as sPPRFs. sPPRFs with fixed-length domain are easily obtained from the GGM tree-based PRFs [GGM86], as observed in [BW13, BGI14, KPTZ13]. Ramchen and Waters [RW14] also showed the existence of sPPRFs with variable-length domain.

2.2 Indistinguishability Obfuscation for Circuits

We recall the definition and security notion of indistinguishability obfuscator from [GGH+13] as below.

Definition 2 (Indistinguishability Obfuscator ($i\mathcal{O}$)). *A uniform PPT machine $i\mathcal{O}$ is called an indistinguishability obfuscator for a circuit class $\{\mathcal{C}_\lambda\}$ if the following conditions are satisfied:*

- *(Preserving Functionality) For all security parameter $\lambda \in \mathbb{N}$, for all $C \in \mathcal{C}_\lambda$, and for all inputs $x \in \{0,1\}^*$, we have:*

$$\Pr[C'(x) = C(x) : C' \leftarrow i\mathcal{O}(\lambda, C)] = 1$$

- *(Indistinguishability of Obfuscation) For any PPT adversaries $(\mathcal{S}, \mathcal{D})$, there exists a negligible function α such that the following holds: if $\Pr[\forall x, C_0(x) = C_1(x) : (C_0, C_1, aux) \leftarrow \mathcal{S}(\lambda)] \geq 1 - \alpha(\lambda)$, then we have:*

$$|\Pr[\mathcal{D}(aux, i\mathcal{O}(\lambda, C_0)) = 1] - \Pr[\mathcal{D}(aux, i\mathcal{O}(\lambda, C_1)) = 1]| \leq \alpha(\lambda)$$

3 Leakage-Resilient SKE

We begin this section by recalling the notion of leakage-resilient wPRFs and their application in building leakage-resilient CPA-secure SKE from [HLWW13]. We then introduce a new notion called weak puncturable PRFs (weak PPRFs), and show how to compile weak PPRFs to leakage-resilient wPRFs via $i\mathcal{O}$.

3.1 Leakage-Resilient Weak PRFs

Standard PRFs require full pseudorandomness: given polynomially many *arbitrarily* inputs $x_1, \ldots, x_q$, the outputs $F_k(x_1), \ldots, F_k(x_q)$ look pseudorandom. Sometimes, the full power of PRFs is not needed and it is sufficient to have weak PRFs which only claim weak pseudorandomness, where pseudorandomness holds for *uniformly random* choice of inputs $\{x_i\}$. The corresponding leakage-resilient notion requires that weak pseudorandomness holds even if the adversary can learn some leakage about the secret key k. Now, we recall the formal definition of leakage-resilient weak pseudorandomness from [HLWW13].

Leakage-Resilient Weak Pseudorandomness. Let $\mathcal{A} = (\mathcal{A}_1, \mathcal{A}_2)$ be a PPT adversary against PRFs and define its advantage in the following experiment.

$$\mathsf{Adv}_{\mathcal{A}}(\lambda) = \Pr\left[\beta = \beta' : \begin{array}{l} (pp, k) \leftarrow \mathsf{Gen}(\lambda); \\ state \leftarrow \mathcal{A}_1^{\mathcal{O}_{\mathsf{leak}}(\cdot), \mathcal{O}_{\mathsf{eval}}(\$)}(pp); \\ x^* \xleftarrow{\mathrm{R}} X; \\ y_0^* \leftarrow F_k(x^*), y_1^* \xleftarrow{\mathrm{R}} Y; \\ \beta \xleftarrow{\mathrm{R}} \{0,1\}; \\ \beta' \leftarrow \mathcal{A}_2^{\mathcal{O}_{\mathsf{eval}}(\$)}(state, x^*, y_\beta^*); \end{array}\right] - \frac{1}{2}.$$

Here $\mathcal{O}_{\mathsf{leak}}(\cdot)$ is a leakage oracle that on input leakage function $f : K \to \{0,1\}^*$ returns $f(k)$, subjected to the restriction that the sum of its output lengths is at most ℓ. $\mathcal{O}_{\mathsf{eval}}(\$)$ is an evaluation oracle that does not take any input and on each invocation, chooses a freshly random $x \in X$ and outputs $(x, F_k(x))$. A PRF is ℓ-leakage-resilient weakly pseudorandom if no PPT adversary has non-negligible advantage in the above experiment.

Remark 1. As pointed out in [HLWW13], since the adversary can always learn a few bits of $F_k(x)$ for some x of its choice (via leakage query), we cannot hope to achieve full pseudorandomness in the presence of leakage, and hence setting for weak pseudorandomness is a natural choice.

Leakage-Resilient SKE. The construction of LR CPA-secure SKE from LR wPRF is obvious. We sketch the construction from [HLWW13] for completeness. Assume $F : K \times X \to Y$ is a leakage-resilient wPRF, whose range Y is an additive group (e.g., bit-strings under XOR). The secret key is exactly the key of the underlying wPRF. To encrypt a message $m \in Y$, one samples $x \xleftarrow{\mathrm{R}} X$ and outputs the ciphertext $(x, F_k(x) + m)$. The decryption process is obvious. The desired LR CPA security of SKE follows readily from the LR weak pseudorandomness of the wPRF.

3.2 Weak Puncturable PRFs

Towards the construction of leakage-resilient wPRFs, we put forward a new notion called weak PPRFs by introducing weak pseudorandomness for PPRFs. We show that weak PPRFs and selective PPRFs imply each other, while the latter is directly implied by the GGM-tree based PRFs [GGM86].

Next, we formally introduce weak pseudorandomness for PPRFs, which differs from selective pseudorandomness (cf. definition in Sect. 2.1) in that the target input x^* is uniformly chosen by the challenger, rather than being arbitrarily chosen by the adversary before seeing the public parameter.

Weak Pseudorandomness. Let $\mathcal{A} = (\mathcal{A}_1, \mathcal{A}_2)$ be an adversary against PPRFs and define its advantage in the following experiment:

$$\mathsf{Adv}_{\mathcal{A}}(\lambda) = \Pr\left[\beta = \beta' : \begin{array}{l} (pp, k) \leftarrow \mathsf{Gen}(\lambda); \\ x^* \xleftarrow{\text{R}} X; \\ k_{x^*} \leftarrow \mathsf{Puncture}(k, x^*); \\ y_0^* \leftarrow F_k(x^*), y_1^* \xleftarrow{\text{R}} Y; \\ \beta \xleftarrow{\text{R}} \{0,1\}; \\ \beta' \leftarrow \mathcal{A}(pp, x^*, k_{x^*}, y_\beta^*); \end{array}\right] - \frac{1}{2}.$$

A PPRF is weakly pseudorandom if no PPT adversary has non-negligible advantage in the above experiment. For simplicity, we refer to weakly pseudorandom PPRFs as wPPRFs.

Interestingly, we show that wPPRFs and sPPRFs imply each other.

Theorem 1. *wPPRFs and sPPRFs imply each other.*

Proof. We first show that "wPPRFs imply sPPRFs" by building sPPRFs from wPPRFs. Let $F : K \times X \to Y$ be a wPPRF, we build a sPPRF $\hat{F} : K \times X \to Y$ from F as below.

- $\mathsf{Gen}(\lambda)$: run $(pp, k) \leftarrow F.\mathsf{Gen}(\lambda)$, pick $r^* \xleftarrow{\text{R}} X$, set $\hat{pp} = (pp, r^*)$ and k as the secret key.
- $\mathsf{PrivEval}(k, x)$: on input k and x, output $\hat{y} \leftarrow F_k(x + r^*)$ via computing $F.\mathsf{PrivEval}(k, x + r^*)$. This algorithm defines $\hat{F}_k(x) := F_k(x + r^*)$.
- $\mathsf{Puncture}(k, x^*)$: compute $k_{x^*+r^*} \leftarrow F.\mathsf{Puncture}(k, x^* + r^*)$, output $\hat{k}_{x^*} = k_{x^*+r^*}$.
- $\mathsf{PuncEval}(\hat{k}_{x^*}, x)$: parse $\hat{k}_{x^*}$ as $k_{x^*+r^*}$, if $x \neq x^*$ output $y \leftarrow F_{k_{x^*+r^*}}(x + r^*)$ via computing $F.\mathsf{PuncEval}(k_{x^*+r^*}, x + r^*)$, else output $\perp$.

We now reduce the selective pseudorandomness of the above construction to the weak pseudorandomness of the underlying wPPRF. Let $\mathcal{A}$ be an adversary against sPPRF with advantage $\mathsf{Adv}_{\mathcal{A}}(\lambda)$, we build an adversary $\mathcal{B}$ that breaks wPPRF with the same advantage. $\mathcal{B}$ interacts with $\mathcal{A}$ in the selective pseudorandomness experiment of sPPRF as below:

1. Commit: $\mathcal{A}$ submits its target input $\hat{x^*}$.
2. Setup and Challenge: $\mathcal{B}$ invokes its wPPRF challenger and receives back the wPPRF challenge instance $(pp, k_{x^*}, x^*, y_\beta^*)$ where x^* is randomly chosen from X, y_β^* is either $F_k(x^*)$ if $\beta = 0$ or randomly chosen from Y if $\beta = 1$. $\mathcal{B}$ then sets $r^* = x^* - \hat{x^*}$, $\hat{pp} = (pp, r^*)$, $\hat{k}_{\hat{x^*}} = k_{x^*}$, sends $(\hat{pp}, \hat{k}_{\hat{x^*}}, y_\beta^*)$ to $\mathcal{A}$ as the sPPRF challenge.
3. Guess: $\mathcal{A}$ outputs its guess β' for β and $\mathcal{B}$ forwards β' to its own challenger.

Note that x^* is distributed uniformly at random over X, thereby so is r^*. According to the construction, the punctured key $\hat{k}_{\hat{x^*}}$ at point $\hat{x^*}$ in sPPRF $\hat{F}$ equals the punctured key $k_{\hat{x^*}+r^*} = k_{x^*}$ at point x^* in wPPRF F. Therefore, $\mathcal{B}$'s simulation is perfect and has the same advantage as $\mathcal{A}$. This proves the forward implication.

The reverse direction that "sPPRFs imply wPPRFs" follows by a simple reduction of weak pseudorandomness to selective pseudorandomness. Let $\mathcal{A}$ be an adversary against wPPRF with advantage $\mathsf{Adv}_{\mathcal{A}}(\lambda)$, we build an adversary $\mathcal{B}$ that breaks sPPRF with the same advantage. $\mathcal{B}$ interacts with $\mathcal{A}$ in the weak pseudorandomness experiment of wPPRF as below:

1. Setup and Challenge: $\mathcal{B}$ picks $x^* \xleftarrow{R} X$ and submits x^* to its own sPPRF challenger. Upon receiving back (pp, k_{x^*}, y^*_β) where y_β is either $F_k(x^*)$ if $\beta = 0$ or randomly chosen from Y if $\beta = 1$, $\mathcal{B}$ sends $(pp, x^*, k_{x^*}, y^*_\beta)$ to $\mathcal{A}$ as the wPPRF challenge.
2. Guess: $\mathcal{A}$ outputs its guess β' for β and $\mathcal{B}$ forwards β' to its own challenger.

Note that x^* is distributed uniformly over X. Therefore, $\mathcal{B}$'s simulation is perfect and has the same advantage as $\mathcal{A}$. This proves the inverse implication.

The theorem immediately follows.

3.3 Leakage-Resilient wPRFs from wPPRFs and $i\mathcal{O}$

Now, we show how to construct leakage-resilient wPRFs from wPPRFs and $i\mathcal{O}$. Let $F : K \times X \to Y$ be a wPPRF, $i\mathcal{O}$ be an indistinguishability obfuscator, and $\mathsf{ext} : Y \times S \to Z$ be an average-case (n, ϵ)-strong extractor. In what follows, we build a LR wPRF $\hat{F} : \hat{K} \times \hat{X} \to Z$, where $\hat{X} = X \times S$.

- $\mathsf{Gen}(\lambda)$: run $(pp, k) \leftarrow F.\mathsf{Gen}(\lambda)$, output pp and $\hat{k} \leftarrow i\mathcal{O}(\text{PrivEval})$, where PrivEval is the program defined in Fig. 2.

PrivEval

Constants: wPPRF key k
Input: $\hat{x} = (x, s)$
1. Output $z \leftarrow \mathsf{ext}(F_k(x), s)$.

Fig. 2. Program PrivEval. This program is appropriately padded to the maximum of the size of itself and program PrivEval* defined in Fig. 3.

PrivEval*

Constants: wPPRF punctured key k_{x^*}, x^*, y^*
Input: $\hat{x} = (x, s)$
1. If $x = x^*$, output $z \leftarrow \mathsf{ext}(y^*, s)$.
2. Else, output $z \leftarrow \mathsf{ext}(F_{k_{x^*}}(x), s)$.

Fig. 3. Program PrivEval*

– $\mathsf{PrivEval}(\hat{k}, \hat{x})$: on input $\hat{k}$ and $\hat{x} = (x, s) \in X \times S$, output $y \leftarrow \hat{k}(x, s)$. This algorithm implicitly defines $\hat{F}_{\hat{k}}(\hat{x}) := \mathsf{ext}(F_k(x), s)$.

Theorem 2. *If F is a secure wPPRF, $i\mathcal{O}$ is indistinguishably secure,* ext *is an average-case (n, ϵ)-strong extractor, the above construction is an ℓ-LR wPRF as long as $\ell \leq \log |Y| - n$.*

Proof. We proceed via a sequence of games. Let S_i be the event that $\mathcal{A}$ wins in Game i.

Game 0. This game is the standard leakage-resilient weak pseudorandomness game for wPRFs. $\mathcal{CH}$ interacts with $\mathcal{A}$ as below:

Setup: $\mathcal{CH}$ runs $(pp, k) \leftarrow F.\mathsf{Gen}(\lambda)$, creates $\hat{k} \leftarrow i\mathcal{O}(\text{PrivEval})$, where the program PrivEval is defined in Fig. 2. $\mathcal{CH}$ then sends pp to $\mathcal{A}$.
Phase 1: $\mathcal{A}$ can make evaluation queries and leakage queries. For each evaluation query, $\mathcal{CH}$ chooses $x \xleftarrow{R} X$ and $s \xleftarrow{R} S$ and returns $(x, s, \hat{k}(x, s))$. For each leakage query $\langle f \rangle$, $\mathcal{CH}$ responds with $f(\hat{k})$.
Challenge: $\mathcal{CH}$ chooses $x^* \xleftarrow{R} X$, $s^* \xleftarrow{R} S$ and computes $y^* \leftarrow F_k(x^*)$, then computes $z_0^* \leftarrow \mathsf{ext}(y^*, s^*)$, picks $z_1^* \xleftarrow{R} Z$ and $\beta \xleftarrow{R} \{0, 1\}$, sends z_β^* to $\mathcal{A}$.
Phase 2: $\mathcal{A}$ continues to make evaluation queries. $\mathcal{CH}$ responds the same way as in Phase 1.
Guess: $\mathcal{A}$ outputs its guess β' for β and wins if $\beta' = \beta$.

According to the definition, we have:

$$\mathsf{Adv}_{\mathcal{A}}(\lambda) = |\Pr[S_0] - 1/2|$$

Game 1. Same as Game 0 except that $\mathcal{CH}$ chooses $x^* \xleftarrow{R} X$, $s^* \xleftarrow{R} S$ and computes $y^* \leftarrow F_k(x^*)$ in the Setup stage. This change is only conceptual and thus we have:

$$\Pr[S_1] = \Pr[S_0]$$

Game 2. Same as Game 1 except that $\mathcal{CH}$ directly aborts when handling evaluation queries for $x = x^*$.

Let E be the event that there exists one random sample x that equals x^* when $\mathcal{CH}$ emulates evaluation oracle. Clearly, if E never happens, then Game 1 and Game 2 are identical. Suppose $\mathcal{A}$ makes at most q_e evaluation queries. Since $\mathcal{A}$ is a PPT adversary, q_e is bounded by a polynomial in λ. Therefore, $\Pr[E] \leq q_e/|X| \leq \mathsf{negl}(\lambda)$, we have:

$$|\Pr[S_2] - \Pr[S_1]| \leq \Pr[E] \leq \mathsf{negl}(\lambda)$$

Game 3. Same as Game 2 except that $\mathcal{CH}$ computes $k_{x^*} \leftarrow F.\mathsf{Puncture}(k, x^*)$, $y^* \leftarrow F_k(x^*)$, and creates $\hat{k} \leftarrow i\mathcal{O}(\text{PrivEval}^*)$ in the Setup stage. Here, the program PrivEval* (defined in Fig. 3) is built from constants k_{x^*}, x^*, y^*.

By the correctness of wPPRFs, the two programs PrivEval and PrivEval* agree on all inputs. By the security of $i\mathcal{O}$, we have:

$$|\Pr[S_3] - \Pr[S_2]| \leq \mathsf{Adv}_{\mathcal{A}}^{i\mathcal{O}}$$

Game 4. Same as Game 3 except that $\mathcal{CH}$ picks $y^* \xleftarrow{\text{R}} Y$ rather than setting $y^* \leftarrow F_k(x^*)$ in the Setup stage.

By a simple reduction to the weak pseudorandomness of wPPRFs, this modification is undetectable for all PPT adversaries. Thus, we have:

$$|\Pr[S_4] - \Pr[S_3]| \leq \mathsf{Adv}_{\mathcal{A}}^{\text{wPPRF}}$$

Game 5. Same as Game 4 except that $\mathcal{CH}$ picks $z_0^* \xleftarrow{\text{R}} Z$ rather than setting $z_0^* \leftarrow \mathsf{ext}(y^*, s^*)$ in the Challenge stage.

We denote by V the set of public parameter pp, (x^*, s^*), the responses to all evaluation queries (determined by k_{x^*}), z_1^* and β. In both Game 4 and Game 5, y^* is uniformly chosen from Y (independent of V), thus $\mathsf{H}_\infty(y^*|V) = \log|Y|$. Observe that $\mathcal{A}$ also obtains at most ℓ bits leakage on $\hat{k}$ (denoted by $leak$) which is correlated to y^*, it follows by the chain rule that $\tilde{\mathsf{H}}_\infty(y^*|(V, leak)) \geq \mathsf{H}_\infty(y^*|V) - \ell = \log|Y| - \ell$. Since ext is an average-case (n, ϵ)-strong extractor, we conclude that $\mathsf{ext}(y^*, s^*)$ is ϵ-close to a uniformly random $z_0^* \xleftarrow{\text{R}} Z$, even given V and leakage. Note that $\mathcal{A}$'s view in Game 4 and Game 5 is fully determined by z_0^*, V and $leak$, while V and $leak$ are distributed identically in Game 4 and Game 5. Thereby, $\mathcal{A}$'s view in Game 4 and Game 5 are $\epsilon/2$-close. Thus, we have:

$$|\Pr[S_5] - \Pr[S_4]| \leq \epsilon/2 \leq \mathsf{negl}(\lambda)$$

In Game 5, both z_0^* and z_1^* are randomly chosen from Z. Therefore, we have:

$$\Pr[S_5] = 1/2$$

Putting all the above together, the theorem immediately follows. □

We have sketched how to achieve optimal leakage rate in Sect. 1.3. To avoid repetition, we omit the details here.

Comparison with Prior Constructions. [Pie09, DY13] showed that any wPRF is already leakage-resilient for a logarithmic leakage bound $\ell = O(\log \lambda)$. Hazay et al. [HLWW13] showed a black-box construction of LR wPRF from any wPRF $F : K \times X \rightarrow Y$. Their construction takes two steps: (1) construct symmetric-key weak HPS from wPRF; (2) build LR wPRF by parallel repetition of symmetric-key weak HPS. The consequence is that it is not flexible and efficient. To make the output size larger than $n \log|Y|$, they have to invoke n independent copies of the basic wPRF, and the domain size must be larger than $n(|X| + \log|Y|)$. Besides, its leakage rate is rather poor, say, $O(\log(\lambda)/|k|)$. In contrast, our construction enjoys flexible parameter choice and optimal leakage rate, which is benefited from the non-black-box use of underlying wPPRF via $i\mathcal{O}$.

4 Leakage-Resilient KEM

We begin this section by formally defining leakage-resilient PEPRFs. We then show that leakage-resilient PEPRFs naturally yield leakage-resilient KEM. Towards achieving leakage-resilience for PEPRFs, we first introduce a new notion called puncturable PEPRFs, and construct them from various puncturable primitives, which we believe is of independent interest. Finally, we show how to compile puncturable PEPRFs to leakage-resilient PEPRFs via $i\mathcal{O}$.

4.1 Leakage-Resilient PEPRFs

Chen and Zhang [CZ14] put forwarded the notion of PEPRFs, which is best viewed as a counterpart of weak PRFs in the public-key setting. In PEPRFs, each secret key is associated with a public key, and there is a collection of $\mathcal{NP}$ languages (indexed by public key) defined over domain. For any element in the language, in addition to evaluating its PRF value using secret key, one can also evaluate it publicly with public key and the associated witness.

PEPRFs neatly capture the essence of KEM, and they can be instantiated from either specific assumptions or more general assumptions such as (extractable) hash proof systems and trapdoor functions. In what follows, we recall the standard definition of PEPRFs from [CZ14] and proceed to introduce leakage resilience for them.

Definition 3 (PEPRFs). *Let $L = \{L_{pk}\}_{pk \in PK}$ be a collection of $\mathcal{NP}$ languages defined over X. A PEPRF $F : SK \times X \to Y \cup \perp$*[10] *for L consists of three polynomial time algorithms as below:*

- $\mathsf{Gen}(\lambda)$: *on input λ, output a public key pk and a secret key sk.*
- $\mathsf{PrivEval}(sk, x)$: *on input sk and $x \in X$, output $y \leftarrow F_{sk}(x) \in Y \cup \perp$.*
- $\mathsf{PubEval}(pk, x, w)$: *on input pk and $x \in L_{pk}$ together with a witness w, output $y \leftarrow F_{sk}(x) \in Y$.*

To be applicable, L is required to be efficiently samplable, i.e., for each $pk \in PK$, there exists an efficient sampling algorithm SampRel *that on input pk outputs a random element $x \in L_{pk}$ together with a witness w.*

Leakage-Resilient Weak Pseudorandomness. Let $\mathcal{A}$ be an adversary against PEPRFs and define its advantage as below:

$$\mathsf{Adv}_{\mathcal{A}}(\lambda) = \Pr\left[\beta' = \beta : \begin{array}{l} (pk, sk) \leftarrow \mathsf{Gen}(\lambda); \\ state \leftarrow \mathcal{A}^{\mathcal{O}_{\mathsf{leak}}(\cdot)}(pk); \\ (x^*, w^*) \leftarrow \mathsf{SampRel}(pk); \\ y_0^* \leftarrow F_{sk}(x^*), y_1^* \xleftarrow{\text{R}} Y; \\ \beta \xleftarrow{\text{R}} \{0,1\}; \\ \beta' \leftarrow \mathcal{A}(pk, x^*, y_\beta^*); \end{array}\right] - \frac{1}{2}.$$

[10] In a PEPRF, when the input x is not in L_{pk}, its PRF value $F_{sk}(x)$ may not be well defined and will be denoted by a distinguished symbol $\perp$.

Here $\mathcal{O}_{\mathsf{leak}}(\cdot)$ is a leakage oracle that on input $f : SK \rightarrow \{0,1\}^*$ returns $f(sk)$, subjected to the restriction that the sum of its output lengths is at most ℓ. A PEPRF is ℓ-leakage-resilient weakly pseudorandom if no PPT adversary has non-negligible advantage in the above experiment. As pointed out in [CZ14], full pseudorandomness is impossible due to the publicly evaluable property.

Leakage-Resilient KEM. [CZ14] showed that weakly pseudorandom PEPRF naturally implies CPA-secure KEM. We observe that this implication applies in the leakage setting as well. We sketch the construction here for completeness. Assume $F : SK \times X \rightarrow Y$ is a leakage-resilient PEPRF for $L = \{L_{pk}\}_{pk \in PK}$, where the range Y is an additive group. The key pair is exactly the key pair of the underlying PEPRF. To encrypt a message $m \in Y$, one picks $x \xleftarrow{\text{R}} L_{pk}$ with a witness w, computes $k \leftarrow \mathsf{PubEval}(pk, x, w)$ and outputs ciphertext $(x, k+m)$. The decryption process re-computes k via $\mathsf{PrivEval}(k, x)$. The LR CPA security of KEM readily follows from the LR weak pseudorandomness of the underlying PEPRF. The resulting LR CPA-secure KEM can be boosted to LR CPA-secure PKE by combining data encapsulation mechanism (DEM) with appropriate security properties [CS02].

4.2 Puncturable PEPRFs

To construct leakage-resilient PEPRFs, we first introduce the puncturable version of PEPRFs, called puncturable PEPRFs (PPEPRFs), which could also be viewed as an extension of PPRFs in the public-key setting. We formally define PPEPRFs as below and postpone their realizations to the full version [CWZ18].

Definition 4 (PPEPRFs). *Let $L = \{L_{pk}\}$ be a collection of $\mathcal{NP}$ languages defined over X. A PPEPRF $F : SK \times X \rightarrow Y \cup \perp$ for L consists of the following polynomial time algorithms:*

- $\mathsf{Gen}(\lambda)$*: on input λ, output a public key pk and a secret key sk.*
- $\mathsf{PrivEval}(sk, x)$*: on input sk and $x \in X$, output $y \leftarrow F_{sk}(x) \in Y \cup \perp$.*
- $\mathsf{Puncture}(sk, x^*)$*: on input sk and $x^* \in L_{pk}$, output a punctured key sk_{x^*}.*
- $\mathsf{PuncEval}(sk_{x^*}, x)$*: on input a punctured key sk_{x^*} and $x \neq x^*$, output $y \leftarrow F_{sk}(x) \in Y \cup \perp$.*
- $\mathsf{PubEval}(pk, x, w)$*: on input pk and $x \in L_{pk}$ together with a witness w, output $y \leftarrow F_{sk}(x) \in Y$.*

For security, we require that weak pseudorandomness remains even when the adversary is given a punctured secret key.

Weak Pseudorandomness. Let $\mathcal{A}$ be an adversary against PPEPRFs and define its advantage as below:

$$\mathsf{Adv}_{\mathcal{A}}(\lambda) = \Pr\left[\beta' = \beta : \begin{array}{l} (pk, sk) \leftarrow \mathsf{Gen}(\lambda); \\ (x^*, w^*) \leftarrow \mathsf{SampRel}(pk); \\ sk_{x^*} \leftarrow \mathsf{Puncture}(sk, x^*); \\ y_0^* \leftarrow F_{sk}(x^*), y_1^* \xleftarrow{\text{R}} Y; \\ \beta \xleftarrow{\text{R}} \{0,1\}; \\ \beta' \leftarrow \mathcal{A}(pk, sk_{x^*}, x^*, y_\beta^*); \end{array}\right] - \frac{1}{2}.$$

A PPEPRF is weakly pseudorandom if for any PPT adversary $\mathcal{A}$ its advantage in the above experiment is negligible in λ.

4.3 Leakage-Resilient PEPRFs from PPEPRFs and $i\mathcal{O}$

Let $F : SK \times X \to Y \cup \perp$ be a PPEPRF for $L = \{L_{pk}\}_{pk \in PK}$, $i\mathcal{O}$ be an indistinguishability obfuscation, and $\mathsf{ext} : Y \times S \to Z$ be an average-case (n, ϵ)-strong extractor. Without loss of generality, we assume that $Y = \{0,1\}^\rho$. In what follows, we build a leakage-resilient PEPRF $\hat{F} : \hat{SK} \times \hat{X} \to Z \cup \perp$ for $\hat{L} = \{\hat{L}_{pk}\}_{pk \in PK}$, where $\hat{X} = X \times S$ and $\hat{L}_{pk} = \{\hat{x} = (x, s) : x \in L_{pk} \wedge s \in S\}$. According to the definition of $\hat{L}$, a witness w for $x \in L_{pk}$ is also a witness for $\hat{x} = (x, s) \in \hat{L}_{pk}$, where s could be any seed from S.

- $\mathsf{Gen}(\lambda)$: run $F.\mathsf{Gen}(\lambda)$ to obtain (pk, sk), create $\hat{sk} \leftarrow i\mathcal{O}(\text{PrivEval})$, where the program PrivEval is defined in Fig. 4; output $(pk, \hat{sk})$.
- $\mathsf{PrivEval}(\hat{sk}, \hat{x})$: on input $\hat{sk}$ and $\hat{x} = (x, s) \in \hat{X}$, output $\hat{y} \leftarrow \hat{sk}(\hat{x})$. This actually defines $\hat{F}_{\hat{sk}}(\hat{x}) := \mathsf{ext}(F_{sk}(x), s)$, where $\hat{x} = (x, s)$.
- $\mathsf{PubEval}(pk, \hat{x}, w)$: on input pk, $\hat{x} = (x, s) \in \hat{L}_{pk}$ and a witness w for $\hat{x}$, compute $y \leftarrow F_{sk}(x)$ via $F.\mathsf{PubEval}(pk, x, w)$, output $\hat{y} \leftarrow \mathsf{ext}(y, s)$.

PrivEval

Constants: PPEPRF secret key sk
Input: $\hat{x} = (x, s)$

1. Output $\mathsf{ext}(F_{sk}(x), s)$.

Fig. 4. Program PrivEval. The program is appropriately padded to the maximum of the size of itself and program PrivEval* described in Fig. 5.

PrivEval*

Constants: PPEPRF punctured secret key sk_{x^*}, x^* and y^*
Input: $\hat{x} = (x, s)$

1. If $x = x^*$, output $\mathsf{ext}(y^*, s)$.
2. Else, output $\mathsf{ext}(F_{sk_{x^*}}(x), s)$.

Fig. 5. Program PrivEval*

Theorem 3. *If F is a secure PPEPRF, $i\mathcal{O}$ is indistinguishably secure, and* ext *is an average-case (n, ϵ)-strong extractor, the above PEPRF construction is ℓ-leakage-resilient weakly pseudorandom as long as $\ell \leq \rho - n$.*

The security proof is somewhat similar to that in Sect. 3. We postpone the details to the full version [CWZ18].

4.4 Construction with Improved Leakage Rate

The leakage rate of the above basic construction is low. Next, we show how to modify it to achieve optimal leakage rate. We need two extra primitives: (1) an IND-CPA secure SKE with message space $\{0,1\}^\rho$ and ciphertext space $\{0,1\}^v$; (2) a family of (v, τ)-lossy functions. The construction is as below.

- $\mathsf{Gen}(\lambda)$: run $(pk, sk) \leftarrow F.\mathsf{Gen}(\lambda)$, $h \leftarrow \mathsf{LF.GenInj}(\lambda)$, $k_e \leftarrow \mathrm{SKE.Gen}(\lambda)$, generate a dummy ciphertext $ct \leftarrow \mathrm{SKE.}\mathsf{Enc}(k_e, 0^\rho)$ as $\hat{sk}$, compute $\eta^* \leftarrow h(ct)$, create $C_{\text{eval}} \leftarrow i\mathcal{O}(\text{PrivEval})$ (here the program PrivEval is defined in Fig. 6 and η^* acts as its trigger), set $\hat{pk} = (pk, C_{\text{eval}})$, output $(\hat{pk}, \hat{sk})$.
- $\mathsf{PrivEval}(\hat{sk}, \hat{x})$: on input $\hat{sk}$ and $\hat{x} = (x, s) \in \hat{X}$, output $\hat{y} \leftarrow C_{\text{eval}}(\hat{sk}, \hat{x})$. This actually defines $\hat{F}_{\hat{sk}}(\hat{x}) := \mathsf{ext}(F_{sk}(x), s)$, where $\hat{x} = (x, s)$.
- $\mathsf{PubEval}(\hat{pk}, \hat{x}, w)$: on input $\hat{pk} = (pk, C_{\text{eval}}, t)$, $\hat{x} = (x, s) \in \hat{L}_{pk}$ and a witness w for $\hat{x}$, compute $y \leftarrow F_{sk}(x)$ via $F.\mathsf{PubEval}(pk, x, w)$, output $\hat{y} \leftarrow \mathsf{ext}(y, s)$.

PrivEval

Constants: PPEPRF secret key sk, η^*
Input: $\hat{sk}$, $\hat{x} = (x, s)$

1. If $h(\hat{sk}) \neq \eta^*$, output $\perp$.
2. Else, output $\mathsf{ext}(F_{sk}(x), s)$.

Fig. 6. Program PrivEval. This program is appropriately padded to the maximum of the size of itself and the program PrivEval* described in Fig. 7.

PrivEval*

Constants: PPEPRF punctured secret key sk_{x^*}, k_e, x^* and η^*
Input: $\hat{sk}$, $\hat{x} = (x, s)$

1. If $h(\hat{sk}) \neq \eta^*$, output $\perp$.
2. If $x = x^*$, set $y^* \leftarrow \mathrm{SKE.}\mathsf{Dec}(k_e, \hat{sk})$, output $\mathsf{ext}(y^*, s)$.
3. Else, output $\mathsf{ext}(F_{sk_{x^*}}(x), s)$.

Fig. 7. Program PuncEval

Theorem 4. *If F is a secure PPEPRF, $i\mathcal{O}$ is indistinguishably secure, SKE is an IND-CPA secure secret-key encryption, LF is a family of (v, τ)-lossy functions,* ext *is an average-case (n, ϵ)-strong extractor. the above PEPRF construction is ℓ-leakage-resilient weakly pseudorandom as long as $\ell \leq \rho - n - \tau$.*

Proof. By appropriate parameter choice (e.g. setting $v = \rho + o(\rho)$, $n = o(\rho)$, $\tau = o(v)$), we have $|\hat{sk}| = v = \rho + o(\rho)$ and $\ell = \rho - o(\rho)$ and thus the leakage rate is optimal.

We proceed via a sequence of games. Let S_i be the event that $\mathcal{A}$ succeeds in Game i.

Game 0. This is the standard leakage-resilient weak pseudorandomness game for PEPRFs. $\mathcal{CH}$ interacts with $\mathcal{A}$ as below.

1. Setup: $\mathcal{CH}$ runs $(pk, sk) \leftarrow F.\mathsf{Gen}(\lambda)$, $h \leftarrow \mathsf{LF.GenInj}(\lambda)$, samples $k_e \leftarrow \mathsf{SKE.Gen}(\lambda)$, generates a dummy ciphertext $ct \leftarrow \mathsf{SKE.Enc}(k_e, 0^\rho)$ as $\hat{sk}$, computes $\eta^* \leftarrow h(ct)$, creates $C_{\text{eval}} \leftarrow i\mathcal{O}(\text{PrivEval})$. $\mathcal{CH}$ sets $\hat{pk} = (pk, C_{\text{eval}})$ and sends it to $\mathcal{A}$.
2. Leakage Query: Upon receiving leakage query $\langle f \rangle$, $\mathcal{CH}$ responds with $f(\hat{sk})$ as long as the total leakage is less than ℓ.
3. Challenge: $\mathcal{CH}$ samples $(x^*, w^*) \leftarrow \mathsf{SampRel}(pk)$, picks $s^* \xleftarrow{\text{R}} S$, computes $y^* \leftarrow F_{sk}(x^*)$ via $F.\mathsf{PubEval}(pk, x^*, w^*)$, $z_0^* \leftarrow \mathsf{ext}(y^*, s^*)$, samples $z_1^* \xleftarrow{\text{R}} Z$, $\beta \xleftarrow{\text{R}} \{0,1\}$. Finally, $\mathcal{CH}$ sends $\hat{x}^* = (x^*, s^*)$ and z_β^* to $\mathcal{A}$.
4. Guess: $\mathcal{A}$ outputs a guess β' for β and wins if $\beta' = \beta$.

According to the definition, we have:

$$\mathsf{Adv}_{\mathcal{A}}(\lambda) = |\Pr[S_0] - 1/2|$$

Game 1. Same as Game 0 except that $\mathcal{CH}$ samples x^*, w^* and computes $y^* \leftarrow F_{sk}(x^*)$ in the Setup stage. This change is purely conceptual and thus we have:

$$\Pr[S_1] = \Pr[S_0]$$

Game 2. Same as Game 1 except that $\mathcal{CH}$ computes $ct \leftarrow \mathsf{SKE.Enc}(k_e, y^*)$ rather than $ct \leftarrow \mathsf{SKE.Enc}(k_e, 0^\rho)$ in the Setup stage. By a direct reduction to the IND-CPA security of SKE, we have:

$$|\Pr[S_2] - \Pr[S_1]| \leq \mathsf{Adv}_{\mathcal{A}}^{\text{SKE}}$$

Game 3. Same as Game 2 except that $\mathcal{CH}$ computes $sk_{x^*} \leftarrow F.\mathsf{Puncture}(sk, x^*)$ and creates $C_{\text{eval}} \leftarrow i\mathcal{O}(\text{PrivEval})$ in the Setup stage. Here, the program PrivEval* (defined in Fig. 7) is built from constants (sk_{x^*}, x^*, y^*).

By the injectivity of h and the correctness of SKE and PPEPRF, the two programs PrivEval and PuncPriv agree on all inputs. By a direct reduction to the security of $i\mathcal{O}$, we conclude that:

$$|\Pr[S_3] - \Pr[S_2]| \leq \mathsf{Adv}_{\mathcal{A}}^{i\mathcal{O}}$$

Game 4. Same as Game 3 except that in the Setup stage $\mathcal{CH}$ picks $y^* \xleftarrow{\text{R}} Y$ rather than setting $y^* \leftarrow F_{sk}(x^*)$.

Assuming the weak pseudorandomness of the underlying PPEPRF, this modification is undetectable by all PPT adversaries. Thus, we have:

$$|\Pr[S_4] - \Pr[S_3]| \leq \mathsf{Adv}_{\mathcal{A}}^{\mathrm{PPEPRF}}$$

Game 5. Same as Game 4 except that $\mathcal{CH}$ samples a lossy function h via LF.GenLossy(λ) rather than sampling an injective function in the Setup stage. By a direct reduction to the security of lossy functions, we conclude that:

$$|\Pr[S_5] - \Pr[S_4]| \leq \mathsf{Adv}_{\mathcal{A}}^{\mathrm{LF}}$$

Game 6. Same as Game 5 except that $\mathcal{CH}$ picks $z_0^* \xleftarrow{\mathrm{R}} Z$ rather than setting $z_0^* \leftarrow \mathsf{ext}(y^*, s^*)$ in the Challenge stage.

We denote by V the set of public key $\hat{pk} = (pk, C_{\mathrm{eval}})$, x^* and s^*. In both Game 5 and Game 6, y^* is uniformly chosen from Y (independent of sk_{x^*}, x^* and s^*) but is correlated to η^* which has at most 2^τ values, we have $\mathsf{H}_\infty(y^*|V) \geq \rho - \tau$ by the chain rule. Observe that $\mathcal{A}$ also obtains at most ℓ bits leakage on $\hat{sk}$ (denote by $leak$) which is correlated to y^*, it follows by the chain rule that $\tilde{\mathsf{H}}_\infty(y^*|(V, leak)) \geq \mathsf{H}_\infty(y^*|V) - \ell = \rho - \tau - \ell$, which is greater than n by the parameter choice. Since ext is an average-case (n, ϵ)-strong extractor, we conclude that $\mathsf{ext}(y^*, s^*)$ is ϵ-close to a uniformly random $z_0^* \in Z$, even given V and leakage. Observe that $\mathcal{A}$'s view in Game 5 and Game 6 are fully determined by z_0^*, z_1^*, β^*, V and $leak$, while z_1^*, β^*, V and $leak$ are distributed identically in Game 5 and Game 6. Thereby, $\mathcal{A}$'s view in Game 5 and Game 6 are $\epsilon/2$-close. Thus, we have:

$$|\Pr[S_6] - \Pr[S_5]| \leq \epsilon/2 \leq \mathsf{negl}(\lambda)$$

In Game 6, both z_0^* and z_1^* are randomly chosen from Z. Therefore, we have:

$$\Pr[S_6] = 1/2$$

Putting all the above together, the theorem immediately follows. □

5 Leakage-Resilient Signature

To best illustrate our idea, in the section we only present the construction with selective security. We postpone the constructions with adaptive security and optimal leakage rate to the full version [CWZ18].

5.1 Selective Construction from sPPRFs, Leakage-Resilient OWFs and $i\mathcal{O}$

Let $F : K \times M \to \{0,1\}^n$ be a sPPRF, $i\mathcal{O}$ be an indistinguishability obfuscator, $g : \{0,1\}^n \to \{0,1\}^\mu$ be a leakage-resilient OWF. We build a leakage-resilient signature as below.

- $\mathsf{Gen}(\lambda)$: run $(pp, k) \leftarrow F.\mathsf{Gen}(\lambda)$, create $sk \leftarrow i\mathcal{O}(\mathrm{Sign})$ and $vk \leftarrow i\mathcal{O}(\mathrm{Verify})$. The programs Sign and Verify are defined in Figs. 8 and 10 respectively.

- $\mathsf{Sign}(sk, m)$: output $\sigma \leftarrow sk(m)$.
- $\mathsf{Verify}(vk, m, \sigma)$: output $vk(m, \sigma)$.

Theorem 5. *If F is a secure sPPRF, $i\mathcal{O}$ is indistinguishably secure, g is ℓ-leakage-resilient one-way, the above construction is ℓ-leakage-resilient EUF-CMA in the selective sense.*

Proof. We proceed via a sequence of games. Let S_i be the probability that $\mathcal{A}$ wins in Game i.

> Sign
>
> **Constants:** sPPRF key k
> **Input:** message m
>
> 1. Compute $\sigma \leftarrow F(k, m)$.

Fig. 8. Program Sign. This program is appropriately padded to the maximum of the size of itself and program Sign* defined in Fig. 9.

> Sign*
>
> **Constants:** sPPRF punctured key k_{m^*}, m^*, σ^*
> **Input:** message m
>
> 1. If $m = m^*$, output σ^*.
> 2. Else, output $\sigma \leftarrow F(k_{m^*}, m)$.

Fig. 9. Program Sign*

> Verify
>
> **Constants:** sPPRF key k
> **Input:** message m and signature σ
>
> 1. Test if $g(\sigma) = g(F(k, m))$, output 1 if true and 0 if false.

Fig. 10. Program Verify. This program is appropriately padded to the maximum of the size of itself and the program Verify* defined in Fig. 11.

> Verify*
>
> **Constants:** sPPRF punctured key k_{m^*}, m^* and y^*
> **Input:** message m and signature σ
>
> 1. If $m = m^*$, test whether $g(\sigma) = y^*$. Output 1 if true and 0 if false.
> 2. Else, test if $g(\sigma) = g(F(k_{m^*}, m))$. Output 1 if true and 0 if false.

Fig. 11. Program Verify*

Game 0. This is the standard leakage-resilient selective EUF-CMA game for signature. $\mathcal{CH}$ interacts with $\mathcal{A}$ as follows:

1. Commit: $\mathcal{A}$ submits the target message m^* to $\mathcal{CH}$.
2. Setup: $\mathcal{CH}$ runs $(pp, k) \leftarrow F.\mathsf{Gen}(\lambda)$, creates $sk \leftarrow i\mathcal{O}(\text{Sign})$, $vk \leftarrow i\mathcal{O}(\text{Verify})$. $\mathcal{CH}$ sends vk to $\mathcal{A}$.
3. Signing Query: Upon receiving signing query $\langle m \rangle \neq \langle m^* \rangle$, $\mathcal{CH}$ responds with $\sigma \leftarrow sk(m)$.
4. Leakage Query: Upon receiving leakage query $\langle f \rangle$, $\mathcal{CH}$ responds with $f(sk)$.
5. Forge: $\mathcal{A}$ outputs a forgery σ' and wins if $\mathsf{Verify}(vk, m^*, \sigma') = 1$.

According to the definition of $\mathcal{A}$, we have:

$$\mathsf{Adv}_{\mathcal{A}}(\lambda) = \Pr[S_0]$$

Game 1. Same as Game 0 except that in the Setup stage $\mathcal{CH}$ computes $\sigma^* \leftarrow F(k, m^*)$, $y^* \leftarrow g(\sigma^*)$, and $k_{m^*} \leftarrow F.\mathsf{Puncture}(k, m^*)$, creates $vk \leftarrow i\mathcal{O}(\text{Verify}^*)$, where the program Verify* is defined in Fig. 11.

It is easy to check that the programs Verify and Verify* agree on all inputs. By the security of $i\mathcal{O}$, we have:

$$|\Pr[S_1] - \Pr[S_0]| \leq \mathsf{Adv}_{\mathcal{A}}^{i\mathcal{O}}$$

Game 2. Same as Game 1 except that $\mathcal{CH}$ uses k_{m^*} to handle signing queries, i.e., returning $\sigma \leftarrow F(k_{m^*}, m)$ for $m \neq m^*$.

By the correctness of sPPRF, Game 1 and Game 2 are identical in $\mathcal{A}$'s view. Thus, we have:

$$\Pr[S_2] = \Pr[S_1]$$

Game 3. Same as Game 2 except that $\mathcal{CH}$ creates $sk \leftarrow i\mathcal{O}(\text{Sign}^*)$ in the Setup stage. Here the program Sign* (defined in Fig. 9) is built from constants k_{m^*}, m^* and σ^*.

It is easy to check that the two programs Sign and Sign* agree on all inputs. By the security of $i\mathcal{O}$, we have:

$$|\Pr[S_3] - \Pr[S_2]| \leq \mathsf{Adv}_{\mathcal{A}}^{i\mathcal{O}}$$

Game 4. Same as Game 3 except that in Setup stage $\mathcal{CH}$ picks $\sigma^* \xleftarrow{R} \{0,1\}^n$ rather than setting $\sigma^* \leftarrow F(k, m^*)$.

By the selective pseudorandomness of sPPRF, we have:

$$|\Pr[S_4] - \Pr[S_3]| \leq \mathsf{Adv}_{\mathcal{A}}^{\text{sPPRF}} \tag{1}$$

It remains to analyze $\Pr[S_4]$. We have the following claim.

Claim. If g is an ℓ-leakage-resilient OWF, then the advantage of any PPT adversary in Game 4 is negligible in λ.

Proof. Let $\mathcal{A}$ be a PPT adversary wins Game 4 with advantage $\mathsf{Adv}_{\mathcal{A}}(\lambda)$. We construct an adversary $\mathcal{B}$ that breaks the assumed leakage-resilient one-wayness of g with the same advantage, implying that $\Pr[S_4]$ must be negligible.

Given (g, y^*) where $y^* \leftarrow g(\sigma^*)$ for some $\sigma^* \xleftarrow{R} \{0,1\}^n$, $\mathcal{B}$ interacts with $\mathcal{A}$ in Game 4 with the aim to output σ' such that $g(\sigma') = y^*$.

1. Commit: $\mathcal{A}$ submits the target message m^* to $\mathcal{CH}$.
2. Setup: $\mathcal{B}$ runs $(pp, k) \leftarrow F.\mathsf{Gen}(\lambda)$, computes $k_{m^*} \leftarrow F.\mathsf{Puncture}(k, m^*)$, creates $vk \leftarrow i\mathcal{O}(\mathsf{Verify}^*)$, and sends vk to $\mathcal{A}$. $\mathcal{B}$ also picks random coins r used for obfuscating the program Sign* (with constants k_{m^*}, m^*, σ^* hardwired) for later simulation. Note that the constant σ^* is unknown to $\mathcal{B}$.
3. Signing Query: Upon receiving signing query $\langle m \rangle \neq \langle m^* \rangle$, $\mathcal{B}$ responds with $\sigma \leftarrow F(k_{m^*}, m)$ using k_{m^*}.
4. Leakage Query: Note that the signing key $sk \leftarrow i\mathcal{O}(\mathsf{Sign}^*_{k_{m^*}, m^*, \sigma^*}; r)$ could be viewed as the value of some function $\psi(\cdot)$ at point σ^*, where $\psi(\cdot)$ on input σ outputs $i\mathcal{O}(\mathsf{Sign}^*_{k_{m^*}, m^*, \sigma}; r)$. Since $i\mathcal{O}$ is efficiently computable, so is $\psi(\cdot)$. Based on this observation, $\mathcal{B}$ can transform any leakage queries on sk to leakage queries on σ^*. Upon receiving leakage query $\langle f \rangle$, $\mathcal{B}$ makes leakage query $\langle f \circ \psi \rangle$ to its own challenger and forwards the reply to $\mathcal{A}$.
5. Forge: $\mathcal{A}$ outputs a forgery σ' and wins if $\mathsf{Verify}(vk, m^*, \sigma') = 1$.

Finally, $\mathcal{B}$ forwards σ' to its challenger. It is straightforward to verify that $\mathcal{B}$'s simulation for Game 4 is perfect. If $\mathcal{A}$ succeeds, according to the definition of algorithm Verify in Game 4, σ' is indeed a preimage of y^* under g, thus $\mathcal{B}$ also succeeds. This proves the claim.

Putting all the above together, the theorem immediately follows. ☐

Acknowledgments. We thank the anonymous reviewers of Asiacrypt 2018 for their helpful comments. The first author is supported by National Natural Science Foundation of China (Grant No. 61772522), Youth Innovation Promotion Association CAS, Key Research Program of Frontier Sciences, CAS (Grant No. QYZDB-SSW-SYS035). The second author is partially supported by Nomura Research Institute, JST CREST JPMJCR14D6, JST OPERA. The third author is partially supported by NSF grant 1801470.

References

[ADN+10] Alwen, J., Dodis, Y., Naor, M., Segev, G., Walfish, S., Wichs, D.: Public-key encryption in the bounded-retrieval model. In: Gilbert, H. (ed.) EUROCRYPT 2010. LNCS, vol. 6110, pp. 113–134. Springer, Heidelberg (2010). https://doi.org/10.1007/978-3-642-13190-5_6

[ADW09] Alwen, J., Dodis, Y., Wichs, D.: Leakage-resilient public-key cryptography in the bounded-retrieval model. In: Halevi, S. (ed.) CRYPTO 2009. LNCS, vol. 5677, pp. 36–54. Springer, Heidelberg (2009). https://doi.org/10.1007/978-3-642-03356-8_3

[AGV09] Akavia, A., Goldwasser, S., Vaikuntanathan, V.: Simultaneous hardcore bits and cryptography against memory attacks. In: Reingold, O. (ed.) TCC 2009. LNCS, vol. 5444, pp. 474–495. Springer, Heidelberg (2009). https://doi.org/10.1007/978-3-642-00457-5_28

[BCH12] Bitansky, N., Canetti, R., Halevi, S.: Leakage-tolerant interactive protocols. In: Cramer, R. (ed.) TCC 2012. LNCS, vol. 7194, pp. 266–284. Springer, Heidelberg (2012). https://doi.org/10.1007/978-3-642-28914-9_15

[BDL97] Boneh, D., DeMillo, R.A., Lipton, R.J.: On the importance of checking cryptographic protocols for faults. In: Fumy, W. (ed.) EUROCRYPT 1997. LNCS, vol. 1233, pp. 37–51. Springer, Heidelberg (1997). https://doi.org/10.1007/3-540-69053-0_4

[BG10] Brakerski, Z., Goldwasser, S.: Circular and leakage resilient public-key encryption under subgroup indistinguishability - (or: quadratic residuosity strikes back). In: Rabin, T. (ed.) CRYPTO 2010. LNCS, vol. 6223, pp. 1–20. Springer, Heidelberg (2010). https://doi.org/10.1007/978-3-642-14623-7_1

[BGI+12] Barak, B., Goldreich, O., Impagliazzo, R., Rudich, S., Sahai, A., Vadhan, S.P., Yang, K.: On the (im)possibility of obfuscating programs. J. ACM **59**(2), 6 (2012)

[BGI14] Boyle, E., Goldwasser, S., Ivan, I.: Functional signatures and pseudorandom functions. In: Krawczyk, H. (ed.) PKC 2014. LNCS, vol. 8383, pp. 501–519. Springer, Heidelberg (2014). https://doi.org/10.1007/978-3-642-54631-0_29

[BK12] Brakerski, Z., Kalai, Y.T.: A parallel repetition theorem for leakage resilience. In: Cramer, R. (ed.) TCC 2012. LNCS, vol. 7194, pp. 248–265. Springer, Heidelberg (2012). https://doi.org/10.1007/978-3-642-28914-9_14

[BKKV10] Brakerski, Z., Kalai, Y.T., Katz, J., Vaikuntanathan, V.: Overcoming the hole in the bucket: public-key cryptography resilient to continual memory leakage. In: FOCS, pp. 501–510 (2010)

[BS97] Biham, E., Shamir, A.: Differential fault analysis of secret key cryptosystems. In: Kaliski, B.S. (ed.) CRYPTO 1997. LNCS, vol. 1294, pp. 513–525. Springer, Heidelberg (1997). https://doi.org/10.1007/BFb0052259

[BSW11] Boyle, E., Segev, G., Wichs, D.: Fully leakage-resilient signatures. In: Paterson, K.G. (ed.) EUROCRYPT 2011. LNCS, vol. 6632, pp. 89–108. Springer, Heidelberg (2011). https://doi.org/10.1007/978-3-642-20465-4_7

[BSW16] Bellare, M., Stepanovs, I., Waters, B.: New negative results on differing-inputs obfuscation. In: Fischlin, M., Coron, J.-S. (eds.) EUROCRYPT 2016, Part II. LNCS, vol. 9666, pp. 792–821. Springer, Heidelberg (2016). https://doi.org/10.1007/978-3-662-49896-5_28

[BW13] Boneh, D., Waters, B.: Constrained pseudorandom functions and their applications. In: Sako, K., Sarkar, P. (eds.) ASIACRYPT 2013, Part II. LNCS, vol. 8270, pp. 280–300. Springer, Heidelberg (2013). https://doi.org/10.1007/978-3-642-42045-0_15

[CDRW10] Chow, S.S.M., Dodis, Y., Rouselakis, Y., Waters, B.: Practical leakage-resilient identity-based encryption from simple assumptions. In: ACM CCS, pp. 152–161 (2010)

[CQX18] Chen, Y., Qin, B., Xue, H.: Regularly lossy functions and applications. In: Smart, N.P. (ed.) CT-RSA 2018. LNCS, vol. 10808, pp. 491–511. Springer, Cham (2018). https://doi.org/10.1007/978-3-319-76953-0_26

[CS02] Cramer, R., Shoup, V.: Universal hash proofs and a paradigm for adaptive chosen ciphertext secure public-key encryption. In: Knudsen, L.R. (ed.) EUROCRYPT 2002. LNCS, vol. 2332, pp. 45–64. Springer, Heidelberg (2002). https://doi.org/10.1007/3-540-46035-7_4

[CWZ18] Chen, Y., Wang, Y., Zhou, H.-S.: Leakage-resilient cryptography from puncturable primitives and obfuscation (2018). http://eprint.iacr.org/2018/781

[CZ14] Chen, Y., Zhang, Z.: Publicly evaluable pseudorandom functions and their applications. In: Abdalla, M., De Prisco, R. (eds.) SCN 2014. LNCS, vol. 8642, pp. 115–134. Springer, Cham (2014). https://doi.org/10.1007/978-3-319-10879-7_8

[DGK+10] Dodis, Y., Goldwasser, S., Kalai, Y.T., Peikert, C., Vaikuntanathan, V.: Public-key encryption schemes with auxiliary inputs. In: Micciancio, D. (ed.) TCC 2010. LNCS, vol. 5978, pp. 361–381. Springer, Heidelberg (2010). https://doi.org/10.1007/978-3-642-11799-2_22

[DGL+16] Dachman-Soled, D., Dov Gordon, S., Liu, F.-H., O'Neill, A., Zhou, H.-S.: Leakage-resilient public-key encryption from obfuscation. In: Cheng, C.-M., Chung, K.-M., Persiano, G., Yang, B.-Y. (eds.) PKC 2016, Part II. LNCS, vol. 9615, pp. 101–128. Springer, Heidelberg (2016). https://doi.org/10.1007/978-3-662-49387-8_5

[DHLAW10] Dodis, Y., Haralambiev, K., López-Alt, A., Wichs, D.: Cryptography against continuous memory attacks. In: FOCS, pp. 511–520 (2010)

[DHLW10] Dodis, Y., Haralambiev, K., López-Alt, A., Wichs, D.: Efficient public-key cryptography in the presence of key leakage. In: Abe, M. (ed.) ASIACRYPT 2010. LNCS, vol. 6477, pp. 613–631. Springer, Heidelberg (2010). https://doi.org/10.1007/978-3-642-17373-8_35

[DKL09] Dodis, Y., Kalai, Y.T., Lovett, S.: On cryptography with auxiliary input. In: STOC, pp. 621–630 (2009)

[DY13] Dodis, Y., Yu, Y.: Overcoming weak expectations. In: Sahai, A. (ed.) TCC 2013. LNCS, vol. 7785, pp. 1–22. Springer, Heidelberg (2013). https://doi.org/10.1007/978-3-642-36594-2_1

[GGH+13] Garg, S., Gentry, C., Halevi, S., Raykova, M., Sahai, A., Waters, B.: Candidate indistinguishability obfuscation and functional encryption for all circuits. In: FOCS, pp. 40–49 (2013)

[GGHW14] Garg, S., Gentry, C., Halevi, S., Wichs, D.: On the implausibility of differing-inputs obfuscation and extractable witness encryption with auxiliary input. In: Garay, J.A., Gennaro, R. (eds.) CRYPTO 2014, Part I. LNCS, vol. 8616, pp. 518–535. Springer, Heidelberg (2014). https://doi.org/10.1007/978-3-662-44371-2_29

[GGM86] Goldreich, O., Goldwasser, S., Micali, S.: How to construct random functions. J. ACM **33**(4), 792–807 (1986)

[GJS11] Garg, S., Jain, A., Sahai, A.: Leakage-resilient zero knowledge. In: Rogaway, P. (ed.) CRYPTO 2011. LNCS, vol. 6841, pp. 297–315. Springer, Heidelberg (2011). https://doi.org/10.1007/978-3-642-22792-9_17

[GKPV10] Goldwasser, S., Kalai, Y.T., Peikert, C., Vaikuntanathan, V.: Robustness of the learning with errors assumption. In: ICS, pp. 230–240 (2010)

[GM84] Goldwasser, S., Micali, S.: Probabilistic encryption. J. Comput. Syst. Sci. **28**(2), 270–299 (1984)

[HL11] Halevi, S., Lin, H.: After-the-fact leakage in public-key encryption. In: Ishai, Y. (ed.) TCC 2011. LNCS, vol. 6597, pp. 107–124. Springer, Heidelberg (2011). https://doi.org/10.1007/978-3-642-19571-6_8

[HLWW13] Hazay, C., López-Alt, A., Wee, H., Wichs, D.: Leakage-resilient cryptography from minimal assumptions. In: Johansson, T., Nguyen, P.Q. (eds.) EUROCRYPT 2013. LNCS, vol. 7881, pp. 160–176. Springer, Heidelberg (2013). https://doi.org/10.1007/978-3-642-38348-9_10

[HSH+08] Alex Halderman, J., et al.: Lest we remember: cold boot attacks on encryption keys. In: USENIX Security Symposium, pp. 45–60 (2008)

[HW09] Hohenberger, S., Waters, B.: Short and stateless signatures from the RSA assumption. In: Halevi, S. (ed.) CRYPTO 2009. LNCS, vol. 5677, pp. 654–670. Springer, Heidelberg (2009). https://doi.org/10.1007/978-3-642-03356-8_38

[IPS15] Ishai, Y., Pandey, O., Sahai, A.: Public-coin differing-inputs obfuscation and its applications. In: Dodis, Y., Nielsen, J.B. (eds.) TCC 2015, Part II. LNCS, vol. 9015, pp. 668–697. Springer, Heidelberg (2015). https://doi.org/10.1007/978-3-662-46497-7_26

[KJJ99] Kocher, P., Jaffe, J., Jun, B.: Differential power analysis. In: Wiener, M. (ed.) CRYPTO 1999. LNCS, vol. 1666, pp. 388–397. Springer, Heidelberg (1999). https://doi.org/10.1007/3-540-48405-1_25

[KMO10] Kiltz, E., Mohassel, P., O'Neill, A.: Adaptive trapdoor functions and chosen-ciphertext security. In: Gilbert, H. (ed.) EUROCRYPT 2010. LNCS, vol. 6110, pp. 673–692. Springer, Heidelberg (2010). https://doi.org/10.1007/978-3-642-13190-5_34

[Koc96] Kocher, P.C.: Timing attacks on implementations of Diffie-Hellman, RSA, DSS, and other systems. In: Koblitz, N. (ed.) CRYPTO 1996. LNCS, vol. 1109, pp. 104–113. Springer, Heidelberg (1996). https://doi.org/10.1007/3-540-68697-5_9

[Kom16] Komargodski, I.: Leakage resilient one-way functions: the auxiliary-input setting. In: Hirt, M., Smith, A. (eds.) TCC 2016, Part I. LNCS, vol. 9985, pp. 139–158. Springer, Heidelberg (2016). https://doi.org/10.1007/978-3-662-53641-4_6

[KPTZ13] Kiayias, A., Papadopoulos, S., Triandopoulos, N., Zacharias, T.: Delegatable pseudorandom functions and applications. In: ACM CCS, pp. 669–684 (2013)

[KV09] Katz, J., Vaikuntanathan, V.: Signature schemes with bounded leakage resilience. In: Matsui, M. (ed.) ASIACRYPT 2009. LNCS, vol. 5912, pp. 703–720. Springer, Heidelberg (2009). https://doi.org/10.1007/978-3-642-10366-7_41

[LLW11] Lewko, A.B., Lewko, M., Waters, B.: How to leak on key updates. In: STOC, pp. 725–734 (2011)

[LRW11] Lewko, A., Rouselakis, Y., Waters, B.: Achieving leakage resilience through dual system encryption. In: Ishai, Y. (ed.) TCC 2011. LNCS, vol. 6597, pp. 70–88. Springer, Heidelberg (2011). https://doi.org/10.1007/978-3-642-19571-6_6

[LWZ13] Liu, S., Weng, J., Zhao, Y.: Efficient public key cryptosystem resilient to key leakage chosen ciphertext attacks. In: Dawson, E. (ed.) CT-RSA 2013. LNCS, vol. 7779, pp. 84–100. Springer, Heidelberg (2013). https://doi.org/10.1007/978-3-642-36095-4_6

[MH15] Matsuda, T., Hanaoka, G.: Constructing and understanding chosen ciphertext security via puncturable key encapsulation mechanisms. In: Dodis, Y., Nielsen, J.B. (eds.) TCC 2015, Part I. LNCS, vol. 9014, pp. 561–590. Springer, Heidelberg (2015). https://doi.org/10.1007/978-3-662-46494-6_23

[MR04] Micali, S., Reyzin, L.: Physically observable cryptography (extended abstract). In: Naor, M. (ed.) TCC 2004. LNCS, vol. 2951, pp. 278–296. Springer, Heidelberg (2004). https://doi.org/10.1007/978-3-540-24638-1_16

[MTVY11] Malkin, T., Teranishi, I., Vahlis, Y., Yung, M.: Signatures resilient to continual leakage on memory and computation. In: Ishai, Y. (ed.) TCC 2011. LNCS, vol. 6597, pp. 89–106. Springer, Heidelberg (2011). https://doi.org/10.1007/978-3-642-19571-6_7

[NS09] Naor, M., Segev, G.: Public-key cryptosystems resilient to key leakage. In: Halevi, S. (ed.) CRYPTO 2009. LNCS, vol. 5677, pp. 18–35. Springer, Heidelberg (2009). https://doi.org/10.1007/978-3-642-03356-8_2

[Pie09] Pietrzak, K.: A leakage-resilient mode of operation. In: Joux, A. (ed.) EUROCRYPT 2009. LNCS, vol. 5479, pp. 462–482. Springer, Heidelberg (2009). https://doi.org/10.1007/978-3-642-01001-9_27

[PW08] Peikert, C., Waters, B.: Lossy trapdoor functions and their applications. In: STOC, pp. 187–196 (2008)

[QL13] Qin, B., Liu, S.: Leakage-resilient chosen ciphertext secure public-key encryption from hash proof system and one-time lossy filter. In: Sako, K., Sarkar, P. (eds.) ASIACRYPT 2013, Part II. LNCS, vol. 8270, pp. 381–400. Springer, Heidelberg (2013). https://doi.org/10.1007/978-3-642-42045-0_20

[QL14] Qin, B., Liu, S.: Leakage-flexible cca-secure public-key encryption: simple construction and free of pairing. In: Krawczyk, H. (ed.) PKC 2014. LNCS, vol. 8383, pp. 19–36. Springer, Heidelberg (2014). https://doi.org/10.1007/978-3-642-54631-0_2

[Reg05] Regev, O.: On lattices, learning with errors, random linear codes, and cryptography. In: STOC, pp. 84–93 (2005)

[RS09] Rosen, A., Segev, G.: Chosen-ciphertext security via correlated products. In: Reingold, O. (ed.) TCC 2009. LNCS, vol. 5444, pp. 419–436. Springer, Heidelberg (2009). https://doi.org/10.1007/978-3-642-00457-5_25

[RW14] Ramchen, K., Waters, B.: Fully secure and fast signing from obfuscation. In: ACM CCS, pp. 659–673 (2014)

[SW14] Sahai, A., Waters, B.: How to use indistinguishability obfuscation: deniable encryption, and more. In: STOC, pp. 475–484 (2014)

[Wee10] Wee, H.: Efficient chosen-ciphertext security via extractable hash proofs. In: Rabin, T. (ed.) CRYPTO 2010. LNCS, vol. 6223, pp. 314–332. Springer, Heidelberg (2010). https://doi.org/10.1007/978-3-642-14623-7_17

[Wic13] Wichs, D.: Barriers in cryptography with weak, correlated and leaky sources. In: Innovations in Theoretical Computer Science, ITCS, pp. 111–126 (2013)

[WMHT16] Wang, Y., Matsuda, T., Hanaoka, G., Tanaka, K.: Signatures resilient to uninvertible leakage. In: Zikas, V., De Prisco, R. (eds.) SCN 2016. LNCS, vol. 9841, pp. 372–390. Springer, Cham (2016). https://doi.org/10.1007/978-3-319-44618-9_20

[YCZY12] Yuen, T.H., Chow, S.S.M., Zhang, Y., Yiu, S.M.: Identity-based encryption resilient to continual auxiliary leakage. In: Pointcheval, D., Johansson, T. (eds.) EUROCRYPT 2012. LNCS, vol. 7237, pp. 117–134. Springer, Heidelberg (2012). https://doi.org/10.1007/978-3-642-29011-4_9

[YXZ+15] Yang, R., Xu, Q., Zhou, Y., Zhang, R., Hu, C., Yu, Z.: Updatable hash proof system and its applications. In: Pernul, G., Ryan, P.Y.A., Weippl, E. (eds.) ESORICS 2015, Part I. LNCS, vol. 9326, pp. 266–285. Springer, Cham (2015). https://doi.org/10.1007/978-3-319-24174-6_14

[Zha16] Zhandry, M.: The magic of ELFs. In: Robshaw, M., Katz, J. (eds.) CRYPTO 2016, Part I. LNCS, vol. 9814, pp. 479–508. Springer, Heidelberg (2016). https://doi.org/10.1007/978-3-662-53018-4_18

Functional/Inner Product/Predicate Encryption

Unbounded Inner Product Functional Encryption from Bilinear Maps

Junichi Tomida[1(✉)] and Katsuyuki Takashima[2(✉)]

[1] NTT, Tokyo, Japan
tomida.junichi@lab.ntt.co.jp
[2] Mitubishi Electric, Kanagawa, Japan
Takashima.Katsuyuki@aj.MitsubishiElectric.co.jp

Abstract. Inner product functional encryption (IPFE), introduced by Abdalla et al. (PKC2015), is a kind of functional encryption supporting only inner product functionality. All previous IPFE schemes are bounded schemes, meaning that the vector length that can be handled in the scheme is fixed in the setup phase. In this paper, we propose the first unbounded IPFE schemes, in which we do not have to fix the lengths of vectors in the setup phase and can handle (a priori) unbounded polynomial lengths of vectors. Our first scheme is private-key based and fully function hiding. That is, secret keys hide the information of the associated function. Our second scheme is public-key based and provides adaptive security in the indistinguishability based security definition. Both our schemes are based on SXDH, which is a well-studied standard assumption, and secure in the standard model. Furthermore, our schemes are quite efficient, incurring an efficiency loss by only a small constant factor from previous bounded function hiding schemes.

Keywords: Functional encryption · Inner product · Function hiding
Unbounded · Bilinear maps

1 Introduction

Functional encryption (FE) [9,27] is an advanced cryptographic paradigm that is expected to drastically enhance the availability of encrypted data. Traditional encryption schemes can provide only "all-or-nothing" decryption capability over encrypted data, i.e., an owner of a legitimate decryption key can learn the entire data from a ciphertext and the others can learn nothing. In contrast, FE allows a legitimate user to learn some computed results from encrypted data without revealing any other information. More precisely, FE supporting a function class $\mathcal{F}$ allows an owner of a master secret key msk to issue a secret key sk_f for any function $f \in \mathcal{F}$, and decrypting a ciphertext ct_m of a message m with sk_f reveals only $f(m)$ and nothing else.

Although there are several constructions of FE for all circuits [17,18,30], all are based on currently impractical cryptographic primitives such as indistinguishability obfuscation [17] or multi-linear maps [16]. As a result, such general

T. Peyrin and S. Galbraith (Eds.): ASIACRYPT 2018, LNCS 11273, pp. 609–639, 2018.
https://doi.org/10.1007/978-3-030-03329-3_21

purpose FEs are far from practical, and this is why Abdalla et al. [1] initiated the study of a more specific and practical FE, i.e., inner product functional encryption (IPFE). In IPFE, an owner of a master secret key msk can issue a secret key $\mathsf{sk}_{\mathbf{y}}$ for a vector $\mathbf{y}$ and decrypting a ciphertext $\mathsf{ct}_{\mathbf{x}}$ of a vector $\mathbf{x}$ with $\mathsf{sk}_{\mathbf{y}}$ reveals only the inner product $\langle \mathbf{x}, \mathbf{y} \rangle$. The inner product is a simple but interesting function, because it is sufficient to directly compute weighted means over numerical data and useful for statistical computations. Furthermore, we can evaluate any polynomial over the data by encrypting all monomials appearing in the desired family of polynomials beforehand.

Following the work of Abdalla et al., there arose two main streams of works on IPFE. The first stream is for public-key based IPFE [2,5], aiming to obtain the adaptive security, and the second stream is for private-key based IPFE [8,13, 21,22,24,28], aiming to obtain function privacy and better efficiency. Function privacy is an important property of FE when it is used to delegate computation to another party. Recently, a multi-input version of IPFE has also been considered in [3,4,14].

Although most above (single-input) IPFE schemes are efficient and based on standard assumptions, all have one inconvenient property: they are *bounded*. That is, we need to fix the maximum length of vectors to be handled in the scheme at the beginning. After fixing the maximum length, we cannot handle vectors whose lengths exceed it. This is very inconvenient because it is almost impossible in the setup phase to predict which data will be encrypted. One may think that we can solve the problem by setting the maximum length to a quite large value. However, the size of a public parameter of bounded schemes expands at least linearly with the fixed maximum length, and such a solution incurs an unnecessary efficiency loss. Hence, it is desirable that we do not need to declare the maximum length of vectors to be handled in the scheme at the beginning and can make encryption or key generation for vectors with unbounded lengths. In the context of inner product predicate encryption (IPPE) [20] and attribute-based encryption [19], there exist unbounded schemes [10,11,23,26], whose public parameters do not impose a limit on the maximum length of vectors or number of attributes used in the scheme. Thus, we naturally have the following question:

Can we construct IPFE schemes that can handle vectors with unbounded lengths?

Our Contributions. We answer the question affirmatively. More precisely, we construct two concrete unbounded IPFE (UIPFE) schemes on the basis of the standard SXDH assumption that are both secure in the standard model.

1. The first scheme is private-key IPFE with fully function hiding, which is the strongest indistinguishability based security notion when considering function privacy [13].
2. The second scheme is public-key IPFE with adaptive security, which is a standard and desirable indistinguishability based security notion [5].

Table 1. Comparison among private-key schemes that are fully function hiding and public-key schemes with adaptive security in the standard model. Although Lin also presented a construction of function hiding scheme [24], her scheme is the selective secure one and we do not adopt it here. A natural number $m \in \mathbb{N}$ denotes a length of a vector associated with the ciphertext or secret key. In our schemes, α denotes a bit length that is necessary to specify an index set associated with a vector. In the ALS16 scheme, β denotes a bit length that is necessary to specify a vector to be embed into a secret key. In this table, we omit a group description in a public key.

Private-key scheme						
Scheme	$\lvert\mathsf{msk}\rvert$		$\lvert\mathsf{ct}\rvert$	$\lvert\mathsf{sk}\rvert$	Pairing	Assumption
DDM16 [13]	$(8m^2+12m+28)\lvert\mathbb{Z}_p\rvert$		$(4m+8)\lvert G_1\rvert$	$(4m+8)\lvert G_2\rvert$	Yes	SXDH
TAO16 [28]	$(4m^2+18m+20)\lvert\mathbb{Z}_p\rvert$		$(2m+5)\lvert G_1\rvert$	$(2m+5)\lvert G_2\rvert$	Yes	XDLIN
KKS17 [22]	$(6m+8)\lvert\mathbb{Z}_p\rvert$		$(2m+8)\lvert G_1\rvert$	$(2m+8)\lvert G_2\rvert$	Yes	SXDH
Ours 1	|PRF key|		$4m\lvert G_1\rvert$	$4m\lvert G_2\rvert+\alpha$	Yes	SXDH
Public-key scheme						
Scheme	$\lvert\mathsf{pk}\rvert$	$\lvert\mathsf{msk}\rvert$	$\lvert\mathsf{ct}\rvert$	$\lvert\mathsf{sk}\rvert$	Pairing	Assumption
ALS16 [5]	$(m+1)\lvert G\rvert$	$2m\lvert\mathbb{Z}_p\rvert$	$(m+2)\lvert G\rvert$	$2\lvert\mathbb{Z}_p\rvert+\beta$	No	DDH
Ours 2	$28\lvert G_1\rvert$	$28\lvert\mathbb{Z}_p\rvert$	$7m\lvert G_1\rvert$	$7m\lvert G_2\rvert+\alpha$	Yes	SXDH

Table 1 compares efficiency among private-key schemes that are fully function hiding and public-key schemes with adaptive security in the standard model. Both our schemes achieve almost the same efficiency as the previous bounded fully function hiding IPFE schemes except the small constant factor. Note that previous public-key based schemes do not need pairing when instantiated from a cyclic group [1,5]. However, we do not know how to construct unbounded public-key based IPFE schemes *without pairing*.

In UIPFE schemes, we can consider various conditions about encryption, key generation, and decryption. It is another important merit of UIPFE. For encryption and key generation, we can consider two cases, *consecutive* and *separate*. In the consecutive setting, each element of a vector is automatically indexed to its position when the vector is input to an encryption or key generation algorithm, i.e., for a vector (a, b, c), a's index is set to 1, b's index to 2, and c's index to 3. On the other hand, in the separate setting, an index set is attached to a vector and encryption and key generation are executed correspondingly to its index set. In other words, a vector (a, b, c) is indexed by some set, e.g., $\{1, 5, 6\}$, and the indices of a, b and c are set to 1, 5, and 6, respectively. A separate scheme obviously suggests a consecutive scheme with respect to encryption or key generation. Next, we focus on the conditions of decryption. Similar to [26], we can classify the decryptable condition of IPFE schemes into three types: *ct-dominant*, *sk-dominant*, and *equal*. Let S_{ct} be an index set of a ciphertext ct and S_{sk} be an index set of a secret key sk. Then ct is decryptable with sk iff $S_{\mathsf{ct}} \supseteq S_{\mathsf{sk}}$ in ct-dominant schemes, $S_{\mathsf{ct}} \subseteq S_{\mathsf{sk}}$ in sk-dominant schemes, and $S_{\mathsf{ct}} = S_{\mathsf{sk}}$ in equal schemes. We denote the type of the schemes described above as (E:xx, K:yy, D:zz) where xx, yy $\in$ {con, sep}, and zz $\in$ {ct-dom, sk-dom, eq}, which means that encryption is xx setting, key generation is yy setting, and decryption is zz setting. It is not difficult to observe that the setting (E:sep, K:con, D:ct-dom) is meaningless because only the *consecutive* part of *separate* ciphertexts can be decrypted with any *consecutive* secret key. For example, for a ciphertext with an index set $\{1, 2, 4\}$, the element indexed as 4 is never used for decryption in the K:con setting. Hence, it is the same as the (E:con, K:con, D:ct-dom) setting. Similarly, (E:con, K:sep, D:sk-dom), (E:con, K:sep, D:eq), and (E:sep, K:con, D:eq) are also meaningless. Thus, we can consider eight types of UIPFE schemes.

In this paper, we focus on the D:ct-dom setting because we believe it is the most convenient for real applications. Consider the situation where Alice holds a huge encrypted database in an untrusted server. When she wants the server to make some computation over the database, she can obtain the result by sending a corresponding secret key to the server. If the necessary part of the database for the computation is very small, the D:ct-dom setting allows Alice to issue a compact secret key. This is because the size of a secret key of IPFE schemes typically grows linearly to the length of the corresponding vector. In the other settings, Alice needs to issue a secret key that is at least larger than some constant multiple of the size of the database, and this incurs a big efficiency loss.

Both our schemes are the (E:con, K:sep, D:ct-dom) setting, which suggests (E:con, K:con, D:ct-dom). Some readers may wonder why we do not consider the most general setting of D:ct-dom, (E:sep, K:sep, D:ct-dom), which suggests all D:ct-dom schemes. The reason is we can prove the security of our schemes against adaptive adversaries only in the (E:con, K:sep, D:ct-dom) setting. The intuitive reason for this limitation is that, in security proofs, reduction algorithms need to guess the contents of an index set with which an adversary queries an encryption oracle. This is possible in the E:con setting because the length of vectors queried by an adversary is a polynomial and a reduction algorithm can correctly guess the length with a non-negligible probability. In the E:sep setting, however, the possibility of index sets is exponential and is unpredictable for reduction algorithms. For this reason, our schemes are secure against selective adversaries in the (E:sep, K:sep, D:ct-dom) setting. In particular, our public-key scheme is semi-adaptively secure in the (E:sep, K:sep, D:ct-dom) setting, which means that the adversary declares a challenge message right after obtaining a public key in a security game [12]. Note that the fully function hiding private-key IPFE scheme in the (E:sep, K:con, D:sk-dom) setting is trivial with our scheme because the roles of ciphertexts and secret keys are the same in fully function hiding private-key IPFE. In addition, the fully function hiding private-key IPFE in the (E:con, K:con, D:eq) setting is easily constructible and we describe it in full version. We summarize our result in Table 2.

1.1 Our Techniques

We use bracket notation to denote elements on the exponent of a group element, i.e., for $\iota \in \{1, 2, T\}$, $[x]_\iota$ denotes g_ι^x where g_ι is a generator of a cyclic group G_ι.

Table 2. Summary of our result. A symbol $\perp$ indicates that the scheme is meaningless.

Private-key scheme				
	E:con, K:con	E:sep, K:con	E:con, K:sep	E:sep, K:sep
D:ct-dom	full	$\perp$	full	selective
D:sk-dom	full	full	$\perp$	selective
D:eq	full	$\perp$	$\perp$	open
Public-key scheme				
	E:con, K:con	E:sep, K:con	E:con, K:sep	E:sep, K:sep
D:ct-dom	adaptive	$\perp$	adaptive	semi-adaptive
D:sk-dom	open	open	$\perp$	open
D:eq	open	$\perp$	$\perp$	open

Private-Key UIPFE. Our starting point is the fully function hiding unbounded multi-input IPFE (MIPFE) scheme proposed by Datta et al. [14]. In an unbounded MIPFE scheme, an index space for slots are not determined in the setup phase. Then, roughly speaking, an encryption algorithm can generate a ciphertext that corresponds to a vector $\mathbf{x}$ and an arbitrary index $i \in \mathbb{N}$. Also, a key generation algorithm can issue a secret key that is associated with indexed vectors $(S, \{\mathbf{y}_i\}_{i \in S})$ for an arbitrary set $S \subset \mathbb{N}$. Only if a decryptor has all ciphertexts corresponding to elements of the set S, i.e., $\{\mathsf{ct}_i := \mathsf{MIPFE.Enc}(\mathsf{pp}, \mathsf{msk}, i, \mathbf{x}_i)\}_{i \in S}$, the secret key for S can be used for legitimate decryption and reveals $\sum_{i \in S} \langle \mathbf{x}_i, \mathbf{y}_i \rangle$. Their scheme is based on the dual pairing vector spaces (DPVS) framework introduced by Okamoto and Takashima [25] and utilizes a pseudorandom function (PRF) to handle an unbounded index space. Consider the unbounded MIPFE scheme in which the vector length is set to 1 and observe that such a scheme already serves the function of UIPFE in the D:ct-dom setting. More precisely, to encrypt $\mathbf{x} := (x_1, \ldots, x_m) \in \mathbb{Z}^m$, the encryption algorithm computes $\mathsf{ct}_i := \mathsf{MIPFE.Enc}(\mathsf{pp}, \mathsf{msk}, i, x_i)$ for all $i \in [m]$ and set $\mathsf{ct} := (\mathsf{ct}_1, \ldots, \mathsf{ct}_m)$. In key generation for an indexed vector $(S, \mathbf{y} := (y_i)_{i \in S} \in \mathbb{Z}^S)$, the key generation algorithm computes $\mathsf{sk} := \mathsf{MIPFE.KeyGen}(\mathsf{pp}, \mathsf{msk}, S, \mathbf{y})$. Then $\mathsf{MIPFE.Dec}(\mathsf{pp}, \mathsf{ct}, \mathsf{sk})$ outputs $\sum_{i \in S} x_i y_i$. However, this construction allows recomposition of ciphertexts due to the property of MIPFE. That is, for $\mathsf{ct}_1 := (\mathsf{ct}_{1,1}, \ldots, \mathsf{ct}_{1,m})$ and $\mathsf{ct}_2 := (\mathsf{ct}_{2,1}, \ldots, \mathsf{ct}_{2,m})$, we can decrypt a ciphertext like $(\mathsf{ct}_{1,1}, \mathsf{ct}_{2,2}, \ldots, \mathsf{ct}_{2,m})$ correctly whereas UIPFE should not allow such recomposition of ciphertexts.

To prevent such recomposition, each ciphertext of our scheme has a unique randomness that all elements in a ciphertext share. Decryption is possible only if an input ciphertext has a consistent randomness, so this unique randomness prevents recomposed ciphertexts from being decrypted correctly. Essentially, a ciphertext for index i of the MIPFE scheme by Datta et al. has a form like $[\mathbf{c}_i]_1 := [(x_i, 1)\mathbf{B}_i]_1$ and each element of a secret key has a form like $[\mathbf{k}_i]_2 := [(y_i, r_i)\mathbf{B}_i^*]_2$, where $\mathbf{B}_i$ is a 2×2 regular matrix, $\mathbf{B}_i^* := (\mathbf{B}_i^{-1})^\top$, and r_i are random elements in $\mathbb{Z}_p$ s.t. $\sum_{i \in S} r_i = 0$. Bases $\mathbf{B}_i$ are generated unboundedly with a PRF. A decryption algorithm computes $[\sum_{i \in S}\langle \mathbf{c}_i, \mathbf{k}_i \rangle]_T$ and it reveals the inner product $\sum_{i \in S}(x_i y_i + r_i) = \sum_{i \in S} x_i y_i$. In this construction, switching elements of one ciphertext that have the same indices as others does not affect the correct decryption. On the other hand, an element of one ciphertext corresponding to index i of our scheme has a form like $[\mathbf{c}_i]_1 := [(x_i, z)\mathbf{B}_i]_1$ where z is a unique randomness for each ciphertext, whereas each element of a secret key is the same as in the MIPFE scheme. Then it is easy to confirm that unless all $\mathbf{c}_i$ for $i \in S$ have the same randomness, $[\sum_{i \in S}\langle \mathbf{c}_i, \mathbf{k}_i \rangle]_T$ does not reveal the inner product $\sum_{i \in S} x_i y_i$ and this construction prevents recomposition of ciphertexts.

Although the concept of the construction is simple, the security proof of the scheme is rather complicated. The basic proof strategy of our scheme is the same as that by Tomida et al. [28], who proposed a fully function hiding *bounded* IPFE scheme, and this strategy is also employed in [14]. In the case of unbounded MIPFE and UIPFE, however, we encounter a new challenging problem that does not appear in *bounded* IPFE: how to prove collusion resistance against illegitimate secret keys queried by an adversary. More precisely, in the D:ct-dom setting, secret keys whose index sets are not included in the index set of a ciphertext must be useless to decrypt the ciphertext even if their owners collude. For example, an owner of a ciphertext ct_1 for a index set $\{1, 2, 3\}$ and two secret keys sk_1 and sk_2 for index sets $\{1, 2, 4\}$ and $\{3, 4\}$ respectively must not learn any information about underlying vectors in the ciphertext and secret keys.

In the context of unbounded MIPFE, the problem was solved by cleverly utilizing symmetric key encryption (SKE). Briefly, ciphertexts for index i contain a secret key of SKE that is unique to the index i. On the other hand, a secret key of unbounded MIPFE for an index set S is iteratively encrypted by SKE with all secret keys of SKE in the set S. Then, unless an owner of the secret key for a set S has all ciphertexts in the set S, he or she cannot decrypt the secret key of unbounded MIPFE encrypted by SKE and the secret key is useless to derive information from ciphertexts corresponding to any proper subset of S. Due to UIPFE not allowing the recomposition of ciphertexts, however, we cannot apply a similar technique to UIPFE schemes.

To solve this problem, we introduce a new proof strategy. In fully function hiding scheme, we consider an adversary that can query many ciphertexts and secret keys. First, we generate a situation where it is sufficient to consider only one ciphertext and all secret keys by using hidden spaces of DPVS framework. We can consider that this is a kind of dual system methodology by Waters [29], which allows us to reduce the problem of a security for many keys to that for one key [31]. Then what we need to do next is to ensure that illegitimate keys are useless to decrypt the ciphertext. For the purpose, we randomize all elements in illegitimate secret keys whose indices are out of the index set of the ciphertext by computational argument. That is, the randomization is indistinguishable for all probabilistic polynomial time (PPT) adversaries under the SXDH assumption. In the above simple example, it means that the elements for index 4 in both secret keys are randomized. The intuitive reason to take this step is to ensure that partial decryption does not leak any information on underlying vectors. That is, in the above example, one can correctly compute the term $x_i y_i$ for indices 1 and 2 with sk_1 and 3 with sk_2, which is masked by the term zr_i. What we want to prove here is that the all zr_i terms are indistinguishable from independently random elements in $\mathbb{Z}_p$ and they completely hide the terms $x_i y_i$. Recall that elements in each secret key contain the random numbers r_i such that $\sum_{i \in S} r_i = 0$. Then, if at least one of r_is in each secret key is randomized, entire r_is become completely random elements in $\mathbb{Z}_p$. At this point, partial decryption with illegitimate secret keys reveals no meaningful information and we can complete the proof.

Public-Key UIPFE. Our public-key UIPFE scheme is technically more intricate than our private-key one. Because we do not need to publish any information for encryption in the private-key UIPFE scheme, we can utilize PRFs to generate dual orthonormal bases unboundedly, which is necessary for encryption. More precisely, an encryption algorithm generates a basis for index i as $F_K(i)$ where F_K is a PRF, and encode the i-th element of the vector using the basis. In the public-key setting, however, a setup algorithm needs to publish information that is needed to encrypt vectors. Thus an encryptor cannot utilize PRFs to generate bases because if a key of a PRF is public, the output is no longer pseudorandom.

Our approach to overcome this problem is an indexing technique [26], which is introduced to construct unbounded inner product *predicate* encryption (IPPE) and attribute based encryption (ABE) schemes. Briefly, we add a two-dimensional prefix that specifies an index to a vector to be encoded, and only if the indices of a ciphertext and a secret key are equal, the correct inner product value is computable. In a ciphertext side, an encoding of the i-th element of a vector $\mathbf{x} := (x_1, \ldots, x_m)$ is the form like $[\mathbf{c}_i]_1 := [(\pi_i(1, i), x_i, z)\mathbf{B}]_1$ and in a secret key side, the index j of an indexed vector $(S, \mathbf{y} := (y_j)_{j \in S})$ is encoded as $[\mathbf{k}_j]_2 := [(\rho_j(-j, 1), y_j, r_j)\mathbf{B}^*]_2$. Then, although all indices share the same dual orthonormal bases, $[\langle \mathbf{c}_i, \mathbf{k}_j \rangle]_T$ reveals the meaningful value only if $i = j$. By this construction, each element in ciphertexts and secret keys is encoded as if dual orthonormal bases that are unique to each index were used.

The basic concept of the security proof of our public-key scheme is also similar to that in [26]. That is, we prove lemmas that say that normal ciphertexts and secret keys are indistinguishable from ones encoded on "somewhat" random dual orthonormal bases for each index by amplifying the entropy of the two-dimensional prefix. More concretely, we use a kind of the following relation in the security proof. Note that it is just a toy example for an intuitive explanation and an informal one. That is, for any polynomial $m := m(\lambda)$, we have the computational indistinguishability:

$$\left\{ \begin{matrix} [(\pi_i(1, i), x_i, z, \ldots)\mathbf{B}]_1 \\ [(\rho_i(-i, 1), y_i, r_i, \ldots)\mathbf{B}^*]_2 \end{matrix} \right\}_{i \in [m]} \approx_c \left\{ \begin{matrix} [(\pi_i(1, i), x_i, z, \ldots)\mathbf{D}_i]_1 \\ [(\rho_i(-i, 1), y_i, r_i, \ldots)\mathbf{D}_i^*]_2 \end{matrix} \right\}_{i \in [m]},$$

where $\{\pi_i\}_{i \in [m]}, \{\rho_i\}_{i \in [m]} \xleftarrow{\mathsf{U}} \mathbb{Z}_p$ and $\mathbf{D}_i := \mathbf{W}_i \mathbf{B}$. LHS represents normal elements of a ciphertext and secret key, and RHS represents elements of ones encoded on "somewhat" random dual orthonormal bases for each index. Here, each $\mathbf{W}_i$ need not be a completely random matrix, and it is sufficient if $\mathbf{W}_i$ is chosen from some specific distribution for our security proof. This is why we call $\mathbf{D}_i$ "somewhat" random. At this point, we can use the proof strategy similar to that of the private-key IPFE scheme because dual orthonormal bases are generated somewhat randomly for each index and we have a similar situation to the private-key IPFE scheme. Although the top-level concept of the techniques are similar to [26], i.e., indexing and entropy amplification, we cannot directly use their techniques because the security proof of our scheme is completely different from that of their scheme. Therefore, we managed to tailor lemmas of entropy amplification suitable for our scheme.

1.2 Discussion

In this work, we cannot achieve the schemes that have the following two features. We quickly discuss the difficulty about them.

Public-Key UIPFE Scheme Without Pairing. We briefly explain the reason why constructing unbounded public-key IPFE without pairing is difficult. First, we recall the bounded scheme without pairing by Abdalla et al. in [1] (and the scheme in [5] essentially follows the construction of Abdalla et al.). In their scheme, a master secret key is a randomly chosen vector $\mathbf{s} \in \mathbb{Z}_p^n$ and a public key is a vector of group elements $g^{\mathbf{s}} \in G^n$. To encrypt a vector $\mathbf{x} \in \mathbb{Z}^n$, an encryption algorithm choose a random number $r \in \mathbb{Z}_p$ and compute the ciphertext as $\mathsf{ct} := (g^r, g^{r\mathbf{s}+\mathbf{x}}) \in G^{n+1}$. On the other hand, a secret key for a vector $\mathbf{y} \in \mathbb{Z}^n$ is set as $\mathsf{sk} := (\langle \mathbf{y}, \mathbf{s} \rangle, \mathbf{y}) \in \mathbb{Z}_p^{n+1}$, and a decryption algorithm computes $g^{\langle r\mathbf{s}+\mathbf{x}, \mathbf{y} \rangle} / g^{r\langle \mathbf{y}, \mathbf{s} \rangle} = g^{\langle \mathbf{x}, \mathbf{y} \rangle}$. To handle vectors with unbounded lengths, an encryption algorithm or a key generation algorithm needs to generate an element s.t. $g^{r\mathbf{s}+\mathbf{x}}$ or $\langle \mathbf{y}, \mathbf{s} \rangle$ respectively for a vector $\mathbf{s}$ with an arbitrary length from a fixed public key or master secret key.

As we explained in the technical section, we obtain such a situation by entropy amplification and it requires computational arguments. However, if secret keys consist of elements in $\mathbb{Z}_p$ likely to the scheme by Abdalla et al., we cannot apply computational arguments to secret keys. Therefore, it seems inevitable to encode elements in secret keys on the exponent of group elements to leverage computational arguments, and it incurs the necessity of pairing in decryption.

Adaptively Secure (E:sep, K:sep) UIPFE Schemes. As we mentioned, our proof strategy needs to guess an index set of a ciphertext and inherently we cannot apply it to (E:sep, K:sep) schemes with adaptive security. We consider that this difficulty is similar to that to prove adaptive security of multi-use KP-ABE from static assumptions (this problem is solved in the semi-adaptive setting [12]). That is, the reduction algorithm needs to embed the instance of an underlying problem into secret keys depending on the instance that the adversary outputs in the challenge phase. Hence, the difficulty disappears in the semi-adaptive setting because the reduction knows the challenge instance before it simulates secret keys. We know that we can obtain adaptively secure multi-use KP-ABE from so-called q-type assumptions [6,7], then we might be able to obtain adaptively secure (E:sep, K:sep) schemes from q-type assumptions similarly.

1.3 Concurrent Work

Concurrently and independently, Dufour Sans and Pointcheval also presented UIPFE schemes [15]. In our term, they proposed public-key (E:sep, K:sep, D:eq) and (E:sep, K:sep, D:ct-dom) schemes in their paper. Their schemes have short secret keys, meaning that they contain one group element and a corresponding vector. However, their schemes rely on the random oracle model and achieve only the selective security, and their (E:sep, K:sep, D:ct-dom) scheme also relies on a new interactive assumption. More precisely, they assume that a kind of problem is hard for all PPT adversaries even if they are allowed to access some oracles. In addition, their (E:sep, K:sep, D:ct-dom) scheme does not have collusion resistance of illegitimate secret keys, which means that a combination of illegitimate keys can become a legitimate key.

2 Preliminary

2.1 Notations

For a prime p, $\mathbb{Z}_p$ denotes a field $\mathbb{Z}/p\mathbb{Z}$. For natural numbers $n, m \in \mathbb{N}$, $[n]$ denotes a set $\{1, \ldots, n\}$, and $[m, n]$ denotes a set $\{m, \ldots, n\}$ (if $m > n$, $[m, n] := \phi$). For a set S, $s \xleftarrow{\mathsf{U}} S$ denotes that s is uniformly chosen from S. We treat vectors as row vectors. For a vector $\mathbf{x}$, $||\mathbf{x}||_\infty$ denotes its infinity norm. For a field K, $\mathsf{M}_n(K)$ and $\mathsf{GL}_n(K)$ denote a set of all $n \times n$ matrices and all $n \times n$ regular matrices whose elements are in K, respectively. We use a bold upper-case letter to denote a matrix, e.g., $\mathbf{A}$, and a bold lower-case version of the same letter with subscript i to denote the i-th row of the matrix, e.g., $\mathbf{a}_i$. For example, $\mathbf{a}_i$ denotes the i-th row of $\mathbf{A}$. For a regular matrix $\mathbf{A}$, $\mathbf{A}^*$ denotes $(\mathbf{A}^{-1})^\top$. For a generator g_ι of a cyclic group G_ι, a matrix $\mathbf{A}$, and vector $\mathbf{a}$, $[\mathbf{A}]_\iota$ and $[\mathbf{a}]_\iota$ denote the corresponding matrix and vector on the exponent of g_ι, respectively. For vectors $\mathbf{x} := (x_1, \ldots, x_n)$ and $\mathbf{y} := (y_1, \ldots, y_n) \in \mathbb{Z}_p^n$, let $e([\mathbf{x}]_1, [\mathbf{y}]_2) := e(g_1, g_2)^{\langle \mathbf{x}, \mathbf{y} \rangle}$ be a function that computes the inner product on the exponent by $\prod_{i \in [n]} e([x_i]_1, [y_i]_2)$. A function $f : \mathbb{N} \to \mathbb{R}$ is called negligible if $f(\lambda) = \lambda^{-\omega(1)}$ and denotes $f(\lambda) \leq \mathsf{negl}(\lambda)$.

2.2 Basic Notions

Definition 2.1 (Pseudorandom Functions). A pseudorandom function (PRF) family $\mathcal{F} := \{F_K\}_{K \in \mathcal{K}_\lambda}$ with a key space $\mathcal{K}_\lambda$, a domain $\mathcal{X}_\lambda$, and a range $\mathcal{Y}_\lambda$ is a function family that consists of functions $F_K : \mathcal{X}_\lambda \to \mathcal{Y}_\lambda$. Let $\mathcal{R}_\lambda$ be a set of functions consisting of all functions whose domain and range are $\mathcal{X}_\lambda$ and $\mathcal{Y}_\lambda$ respectively. For any PPT adversary $\mathcal{A}$, the following condition holds,

$$\mathsf{Adv}_{\mathcal{A}}^{\mathsf{PRF}}(\lambda) := \left|\Pr[1 \leftarrow \mathcal{A}^{F_K(\cdot)}] - \Pr[1 \leftarrow \mathcal{A}^{R(\cdot)}]\right| \le \mathsf{negl}(\lambda),$$

where $K \xleftarrow{\mathsf{U}} \mathcal{K}_\lambda$ and $R \xleftarrow{\mathsf{U}} \mathcal{R}_\lambda$.

Definition 2.2 (Bilinear Groups). Bilinear groups $\mathbb{G}:=(p, G_1, G_2, G_T, g_1, g_2, e)$ consist of a prime p, cyclic groups G_1, G_2, G_T of order p, generators g_1 and g_2 of G_1 and G_2 respectively, and a bilinear map $e : G_1 \times G_2 \rightarrow G_T$, which has two properties.

- (Bilinearity): $\forall h_1 \in G_1, h_2 \in G_2, a, b \in \mathbb{Z}_p, e(h_1^a, h_2^b) = e(h_1, h_2)^{ab}$.
- (Non-degeneracy): For generators g_1 and g_2, $e(g_1, g_2)$ is a generator of G_T.

A bilinear group generator $\mathcal{G}_{\mathsf{BG}}(1^\lambda)$ takes security parameter 1^λ and outputs bilinear groups $\mathbb{G}$ with a λ-bit prime p.

Definition 2.3 (SXDH Assumption). For $\iota \in \{1, 2\}$, we define the following distribution,

$$\mathbb{G} \leftarrow \mathcal{G}_{\mathsf{BG}}(1^\lambda), \;\; a, e, f \xleftarrow{\mathsf{U}} \mathbb{Z}_p, \;\; D := (\mathbb{G}, [a]_\iota, [e]_\iota)$$
$$[t_\beta]_\iota := [ae + \beta f]_\iota \;\text{ for } \beta \in \{0, 1\}.$$

We say the SXDH assumption holds if for any PPT adversary $\mathcal{A}$ and both $\iota \in \{1, 2\}$,

$$\mathsf{Adv}_{\mathcal{A}}^{\mathsf{SXDH}}(\lambda) := |\Pr[1 \leftarrow \mathcal{A}(D, [t_0]_\iota)] - \Pr[1 \leftarrow \mathcal{A}(D, [t_1]_\iota)]| \le \mathsf{negl}(\lambda).$$

2.3 Unbounded Inner Product Functional Encryption for (E:con, K:sep, D:ct-dom)

In this paper, we propose two unbounded inner product functional encryption schemes. The first scheme is private-key unbounded IPFE that is fully function hiding and the second one is public-key unbounded IPFE with adaptive security. Both our schemes can handle (a-priori) unbounded polynomial lengths of vectors for encryption and key generation, and support a function that we call limited-norm inner product. As explained in the introduction, our schemes support inner product in the (E:con, K:sep, D:ct-dom) setting. Informally, for a ciphertext of a vector whose length is m and a secret key with a set S, only if $S \subseteq [m]$, we can decrypt the ciphertext with the secret key and learn the inner product value over the set S. Note that in previous works [3,4], the term *bounded-norm* is used, but in this paper, *bounded* generally refers to vector length. Therefore, we use *limited-norm* for the functionality in this paper.

Definition 2.4 (Limited-Norm Inner Product). This function family $\mathcal{F}$ consists of functions $f_{S,\mathbf{y}}^{X,Y} : \mathbb{Z}^m \rightarrow \mathbb{Z}$ where $X, Y \in \mathbb{N}$, $S \subset \mathbb{N}$, $\mathbf{y} := (y_i)_{i \in S} \in \mathbb{Z}^S$

s.t. $||\mathbf{y}||_\infty \le Y$, and $m \in \mathbb{N}$ s.t. $S \subseteq [m]$. We define the function for every $\mathbf{x} := (x_1, \ldots, x_m) \in \mathbb{Z}^m$ s.t. $||\mathbf{x}||_\infty \le X$ as

$$f_{S,\mathbf{y}}^{X,Y}(\mathbf{x}) := \sum_{i \in S} x_i y_i.$$

Definition 2.5 (Private-Key Unbounded Inner Product Functional Encryption). Let $\mathcal{X} := \{X_\lambda\}_{\lambda \in \mathbb{N}}, \mathcal{Y} := \{Y_\lambda\}_{\lambda \in \mathbb{N}}$ be ensembles of norm-limit. Private-key unbounded inner product functional encryption (Priv-UIPFE) consists of four algorithms.

$\mathsf{Setup}(1^\lambda)$**:** This algorithm takes a security parameter 1^λ, and outputs a public parameter pp and a master secret key msk.

$\mathsf{Enc}(\mathsf{pp}, \mathsf{msk}, \mathbf{x})$**:** This algorithm takes $\mathsf{pp}, \mathsf{msk}$, and a vector $\mathbf{x} := (x_1, \ldots, x_m) \in \mathbb{Z}^m$ where $m := m(\lambda)$ is any polynomial. It outputs a ciphertext ct_m.

$\mathsf{KeyGen}(\mathsf{pp}, \mathsf{msk}, S, \mathbf{y})$**:** This algorithm takes $\mathsf{pp}, \mathsf{msk}$, a non-empty index set $S \subseteq [s]$ where $s := s(\lambda)$ is any polynomial, and an indexed vector $\mathbf{y} := (y_i)_{i \in S} \in \mathbb{Z}^S$. It outputs a secret key sk_S.

$\mathsf{Dec}(\mathsf{pp}, \mathsf{ct}_m, \mathsf{sk}_S)$**:** This algorithm takes $\mathsf{pp}, \mathsf{ct}_m$ and sk_S and outputs a decrypted value $d \in \mathbb{Z}$ or a symbol $\perp$.

Correctness. Priv-UIPFE is *correct* if it satisfies the following condition. For any $\lambda \in \mathbb{N}$, $\mathbf{x} \in \mathbb{Z}^m$ s.t. $m := m(\lambda)$ is any polynomial and $||\mathbf{x}||_\infty \le X_\lambda$, index set $S \subseteq [s]$ s.t. $s := s(\lambda)$ is any polynomial and $S \subseteq [m]$, and $\mathbf{y} \in \mathbb{Z}^S$ s.t. $||\mathbf{y}||_\infty \le Y_\lambda$, we have

$$\Pr\left[d = \sum_{i \in S} x_i y_i \;\middle|\; \begin{array}{l} (\mathsf{pp}, \mathsf{msk}) \leftarrow \mathsf{Setup}(1^\lambda) \\ \mathsf{ct}_m \leftarrow \mathsf{Enc}(\mathsf{pp}, \mathsf{msk}, \mathbf{x}) \\ \mathsf{sk}_S \leftarrow \mathsf{KeyGen}(\mathsf{pp}, \mathsf{msk}, S, \mathbf{y}) \\ d := \mathsf{Dec}(\mathsf{pp}, \mathsf{ct}_m, \mathsf{sk}_S) \end{array} \right] \ge 1 - \mathsf{negl}(\lambda).$$

Security. Priv-UIPFE is *fully function hiding* if it satisfies the following condition. That is, the advantage of $\mathcal{A}$ against Priv-UIPFE defined as follows is negligible in λ for any PPT adversary $\mathcal{A}$,

$$\mathsf{Adv}_{\mathcal{A}}^{\mathsf{Priv\text{-}UIPFE}}(\lambda) := \left| \begin{array}{l} \Pr\left[\begin{array}{l} 1 \leftarrow \mathcal{A}^{\mathcal{O}_{\mathsf{Enc},0}(\mathsf{pp},\mathsf{msk},\cdot), \mathcal{O}_{\mathsf{KG},0}(\mathsf{pp},\mathsf{msk},\cdot,\cdot)}(\mathsf{pp}) : \\ (\mathsf{pp}, \mathsf{msk}) \leftarrow \mathsf{Setup}(1^\lambda) \end{array} \right] \\ -\Pr\left[\begin{array}{l} 1 \leftarrow \mathcal{A}^{\mathcal{O}_{\mathsf{Enc},1}(\mathsf{pp},\mathsf{msk},\cdot), \mathcal{O}_{\mathsf{KG},1}(\mathsf{pp},\mathsf{msk},\cdot,\cdot)}(\mathsf{pp}) : \\ (\mathsf{pp}, \mathsf{msk}) \leftarrow \mathsf{Setup}(1^\lambda) \end{array} \right] \end{array} \right|.$$

Here, $\mathcal{O}_{\mathsf{Enc},\beta}(\mathsf{pp}, \mathsf{msk}, \cdot)$ with $\beta \in \{0,1\}$ is an encryption oracle that takes a pair of vectors $(\mathbf{x}^0, \mathbf{x}^1) \in (\mathbb{Z}^m)^2$ with the same polynomial length m, and outputs $\mathsf{Enc}(\mathsf{pp}, \mathsf{msk}, \mathbf{x}^\beta)$. $\mathcal{O}_{\mathsf{KG},\beta}(\mathsf{pp}, \mathsf{msk}, \cdot, \cdot)$ with $\beta \in \{0,1\}$ is a key generation oracle that takes a set S including polynomial indices and a pair of indexed vectors $(\mathbf{y}^0, \mathbf{y}^1) \in (\mathbb{Z}^S)^2$ associated with the index set S, and outputs

$\mathsf{KeyGen}(\mathsf{pp}, \mathsf{msk}, S, \mathbf{y}^{\beta})$. To avoid a trivial attack of $\mathcal{A}$, we have the following condition on $\mathcal{A}$'s queries. Let q_{ct} (resp. q_{sk}) be a total number of ciphertext query (resp. secret key query) of $\mathcal{A}$. For all $j \in [q_{\mathsf{ct}}]$ and $\ell \in [q_{\mathsf{sk}}]$, if $S_\ell \subseteq [m_j]$, then

$$\sum_{i \in S_\ell} x^0_{j,i} y^0_{\ell,i} = \sum_{i \in S_\ell} x^1_{j,i} y^1_{\ell,i}. \tag{1}$$

Consider the modified game where the adversary queries all vectors in one-shot, i.e., $\{(\mathbf{x}^0_j, \mathbf{x}^1_j)\}_{j \in [q_{\mathsf{ct}}]}$ and $\{(\mathbf{y}^0_\ell, \mathbf{y}^1_\ell)\}_{\ell \in [q_{\mathsf{sk}}]}$, right after obtaining a public parameter, and then the adversary receive all ciphertexts and secret keys for queried vectors for β-side. If the advantage of all PPT adversary against the modified game is negligible, we say that Priv-UIPFE is *selectively function hiding*.

Definition 2.6 (Public-key Unbounded Inner Product Functional Encryption). Let $\mathcal{X} := \{X_\lambda\}_{\lambda \in \mathbb{N}}, \mathcal{Y} := \{Y_\lambda\}_{\lambda \in \mathbb{N}}$ be ensembles of norm-limit. Public-key unbounded inner product functional encryption (Pub-UIPFE) consists of four algorithms.

$\mathsf{Setup}(1^\lambda)$**:** This algorithm takes a security parameter 1^λ, and outputs a public key pk and a master secret key msk.

$\mathsf{Enc}(\mathsf{pk}, \mathbf{x})$**:** This algorithm takes pk and a vector $\mathbf{x} := (x_1, \ldots, x_m) \in \mathbb{Z}^m$ where $m := m(\lambda)$ is any polynomial. It outputs a ciphertext ct_m.

$\mathsf{KeyGen}(\mathsf{pk}, \mathsf{msk}, S, \mathbf{y})$**:** This algorithm takes $\mathsf{pk}, \mathsf{msk}$, a non-empty index set $S \subseteq [s]$ where $s := s(\lambda)$ is any polynomial, and an indexed vector $\mathbf{y} := (y_i)_{i \in S} \in \mathbb{Z}^S$. It outputs a secret key sk_S.

$\mathsf{Dec}(\mathsf{pk}, \mathsf{ct}_m, \mathsf{sk}_S)$**:** This algorithm takes $\mathsf{pk}, \mathsf{ct}_m$ and sk_S and outputs a decrypted value $d \in \mathbb{Z}$ or a symbol $\perp$.

Correctness. Pub-UIPFE is *correct* if it satisfies the following condition. For any $\lambda \in \mathbb{N}$, $\mathbf{x} \in \mathbb{Z}^m$ s.t. $m := m(\lambda)$ is any polynomial and $||\mathbf{x}||_\infty \leq X_\lambda$, index set $S \subseteq [s]$ s.t. $s := s(\lambda)$ is any polynomial and $S \subseteq [m]$, and $\mathbf{y} \in \mathbb{Z}^S$ s.t. $||\mathbf{y}||_\infty \leq Y_\lambda$, we have

$$\Pr\left[d = \sum_{i \in S} x_i y_i \;\middle|\; \begin{array}{l} (\mathsf{pk}, \mathsf{msk}) \leftarrow \mathsf{Setup}(1^\lambda) \\ \mathsf{ct}_m \leftarrow \mathsf{Enc}(\mathsf{pk}, \mathbf{x}) \\ \mathsf{sk}_S \leftarrow \mathsf{KeyGen}(\mathsf{pk}, \mathsf{msk}, S, \mathbf{y}) \\ d := \mathsf{Dec}(\mathsf{pk}, \mathsf{ct}_m, \mathsf{sk}_S) \end{array} \right] \geq 1 - \mathsf{negl}(\lambda).$$

Security. Pub-UIPFE is *adaptively secure* if it satisfies the following condition. That is, the advantage of $\mathcal{A}$ against Pub-UIPFE defined as follows is negligible in λ for any stateful PPT adversary $\mathcal{A}$,

$$\mathsf{Adv}_{\mathcal{A}}^{\mathsf{Pub\text{-}UIPFE}}(\lambda) := \left| \begin{array}{l} \Pr\left[\beta = 1 \left| \begin{array}{l} (\mathsf{pk}, \mathsf{msk}) \leftarrow \mathsf{Setup}(1^\lambda) \\ (\mathbf{x}^0, \mathbf{x}^1) \leftarrow \mathcal{A}^{\mathsf{KeyGen}(\mathsf{pk},\mathsf{msk},\cdot,\cdot)}(\mathsf{pk}) \\ \mathsf{ct}_{m^*} \leftarrow \mathsf{Enc}(\mathsf{pk}, \mathbf{x}^0) \\ \beta \leftarrow \mathcal{A}^{\mathsf{KeyGen}(\mathsf{pk},\mathsf{msk},\cdot,\cdot)}(\mathsf{pk}, \mathsf{ct}_{m^*}) \end{array} \right. \right] \\ -\Pr\left[\beta = 1 \left| \begin{array}{l} (\mathsf{pk}, \mathsf{msk}) \leftarrow \mathsf{Setup}(1^\lambda) \\ (\mathbf{x}^0, \mathbf{x}^1) \leftarrow \mathcal{A}^{\mathsf{KeyGen}(\mathsf{pk},\mathsf{msk},\cdot,\cdot)}(\mathsf{pk}) \\ \mathsf{ct}_{m^*} \leftarrow \mathsf{Enc}(\mathsf{pk}, \mathbf{x}^1) \\ \beta \leftarrow \mathcal{A}^{\mathsf{KeyGen}(\mathsf{pk},\mathsf{msk},\cdot,\cdot)}(\mathsf{pk}, \mathsf{ct}_{m^*}) \end{array} \right. \right] \end{array} \right|.$$

Here, the challenge vectors $\mathbf{x}^0$ and $\mathbf{x}^1$ that $\mathcal{A}$ outputs must have the same length m^*. To avoid a trivial attack of $\mathcal{A}$, we have the following condition on $\mathcal{A}$'s queries. Let q_{sk} be a total number of secret key query of $\mathcal{A}$. For all $\ell \in [q_{\mathsf{sk}}]$, if $S_\ell \subseteq [m^*]$, then

$$\sum_{i \in S_\ell} x_i^0 y_{\ell,i} = \sum_{i \in S_\ell} x_i^1 y_{\ell,i}. \tag{2}$$

Consider the modified game where the adversary is prohibited to make a secret-key query before outputting challenge vectors $(\mathbf{x}^0, \mathbf{x}^1)$. If the advantage of all PPT adversary against the modified game is negligible, we say that Pub-UIPFE is *semi-adaptively secure*.

3 Private-Key Unbounded Inner Product Functional Encryption

Our schemes are based on the DPVS framework introduced by Okamoto and Takashima [25]. We use the following lemma in our Priv-IPFE scheme, which is implicitly shown in [14].

Lemma 3.1. *Let p be a λ-bit prime. For any polynomial $m := m(\lambda)$ and $n := n(\lambda)$, we have*

$$\Pr[\exists i, \det \mathbf{B}_i = 0 | \mathbf{B}_1, \ldots, \mathbf{B}_m \xleftarrow{\mathsf{U}} \mathsf{M}_n(\mathbb{Z}_p)] = 2^{-\Omega(\lambda)}.$$

3.1 Construction

In the following scheme, norm limits X_λ, Y_λ are some polynomials in λ. Let $\mathcal{F} := \{F_K\}_{K \in \mathcal{K}_\lambda}$ be a PRF family with a key space $\mathcal{K}_\lambda$ consisting of functions $F_K : \{0,1\}^\lambda \to \mathsf{M}_4(\mathbb{Z}_p)$.

$\mathsf{Setup}(1^\lambda)$: Takes a security parameter 1^λ and chooses bilinear groups $\mathbb{G} \leftarrow \mathcal{G}_{\mathsf{BG}}(1^\lambda)$ and a PRF key $K \xleftarrow{\mathsf{U}} \mathcal{K}_\lambda$. Outputs

$$\mathsf{pp} := \mathbb{G}, \quad \mathsf{msk} := K.$$

$\mathsf{Enc}(\mathsf{pp}, \mathsf{msk}, \mathbf{x})$: Takes $\mathsf{pp}, \mathsf{msk}$ and $\mathbf{x} := (x_1, \ldots, x_m) \in \mathbb{Z}^m$ where $m := m(\lambda)$ is any polynomial. Sets $\mathbf{B}_i := F_K(i)$ and $\mathbf{c}_i := (x_i, 0, z, 0)\mathbf{B}_i \in \mathbb{Z}_p^4$ for all $i \in [m]$, where $z \xleftarrow{\mathsf{U}} \mathbb{Z}_p$. Outputs

$$\mathsf{ct}_m := ([\mathbf{c}_1]_1, \ldots, [\mathbf{c}_m]_1).$$

If there exists $i \in [m]$ such that $\mathbf{B}_i$ is a singular matrix, outputs $\perp$.

$\mathsf{KeyGen}(\mathsf{pp}, \mathsf{msk}, S, \mathbf{y})$: Takes pp, msk, a non-empty index set $S \subseteq [s]$ where $s := s(\lambda)$ is any polynomial, and an indexed vector $\mathbf{y} := (y_i)_{i \in S} \in \mathbb{Z}^S$. Chooses $\{r_i\}_{i \in S} \xleftarrow{\mathsf{U}} \mathbb{Z}_p$ s.t. $\sum_{i \in S} r_i = 0$. Sets $\mathbf{B}_i := F_K(i)$ and $\mathbf{k}_i := (y_i, 0, r_i, 0)\mathbf{B}_i^* \in \mathbb{Z}_p^4$ for all $i \in S$. Outputs

$$\mathsf{sk}_S := (S, \{[\mathbf{k}_i]_2\}_{i \in S}).$$

If there exists $i \in S$ such that $\mathbf{B}_i$ is a singular matrix, outputs $\perp$.

$\mathsf{Dec}(\mathsf{pp}, \mathsf{ct}_m, \mathsf{sk}_S)$: Takes pp, a ciphertext ct_m for m dimensional vector, and a secret key sk_S for a index set S. If $S \subseteq [m]$, then computes

$$h := \prod_{i \in S} e([\mathbf{c}_i]_1, [\mathbf{k}_i]_2),$$

and searches for d s.t. $e(g_1, g_2)^d = h$ exhaustively in the range of $-|S|X_\lambda Y_\lambda$ to $|S|X_\lambda Y_\lambda$. If such d is found, outputs d. Otherwise, outputs $\perp$.

Correctness. Our Priv-UIPFE scheme is correct if $\mathcal{F}$ is a PRF family. We consider the case where for a natural number $m \in \mathbb{N}$, $\mathbf{B}_i := F_K(i)$ for all $i \in [m]$ is invertible. Then, we observe that if $S \subseteq [m]$,

$$h = \prod_{i \in S} e([\mathbf{c}_i]_1, [\mathbf{k}_i]_2) = e(g_1, g_2)^{\sum_{i \in S} \langle \mathbf{c}_i, \mathbf{k}_i \rangle} = e(g_1, g_2)^{\sum_{i \in S} (x_i y_i + z r_i)}.$$

Here we have $\sum_{i \in S} r_i = 0$, then $h = e(g_1, g_2)^{\sum_{i \in S} x_i y_i}$. If $||\mathbf{x}||_\infty \leq X_\lambda$ and $||\mathbf{y}||_\infty \leq Y_\lambda$, $|\sum_{i \in S} x_i y_i| \leq |S|X_\lambda Y_\lambda$ and Dec outputs $\sum_{i \in S} x_i y_i$. Hence, if $\mathbf{B}_i$ for all $i \in [m]$ is invertible without a negligible probability, our scheme is correct. Let $m := m(\lambda)$ be any polynomial. For $i \in [m]$, we have $\Pr[\exists i, \det \mathbf{B}_i = 0 | \mathbf{B}_i \xleftarrow{\mathsf{U}} \mathsf{M}_4(\mathbb{Z}_p)] = 2^{-\Omega(\lambda)}$ from Lemma 3.1 and $|\Pr[\exists i, \det \mathbf{B}_i = 0 | \mathbf{B}_i \xleftarrow{\mathsf{U}} \mathsf{M}_4(\mathbb{Z}_p)] - \Pr[\exists i, \det \mathbf{B}_i = 0 | K \xleftarrow{\mathsf{U}} \mathcal{K}_\lambda, \mathbf{B}_i := F_K(i)]| \leq \mathsf{negl}(\lambda)$ from the definition of PRF. Consequently, $\Pr[\exists i, \det \mathbf{B}_i = 0 | K \xleftarrow{\mathsf{U}} \mathcal{K}_\lambda, \mathbf{B}_i := F_K(i)] \leq \mathsf{negl}(\lambda)$.

Remark 3.1. Similarly to all previous IPFE schemes based on a cyclic group or bilinear groups, the decryption algorithm of our schemes need to solve the small discrete logarithm problem. As pointed out in [21], however, this step does not affect efficiency so much in many practical applications.

3.2 Security

Theorem 3.1. *Assume that the SXDH assumption holds and $\mathcal{F}$ is a PRF family, then our Priv-UIPFE is fully function hiding. More formally, let m_{max} be the maximum length of vectors with which $\mathcal{A}$ makes a query to the encryption oracle, then for any PPT adversary $\mathcal{A}$ and security parameter λ, there exists a PPT adversary $\mathcal{B}_1$ for the SXDH and $\mathcal{B}_2$ for the PRF family, we have*

$$\mathsf{Adv}_{\mathcal{A}}^{\mathsf{Priv\text{-}UIPFE}}(\lambda) \leq \{4q_{\mathsf{sk}} + 2(m_{\mathsf{max}} + 1)q_{\mathsf{ct}} + 2\}\mathsf{Adv}_{\mathcal{B}_1}^{\mathsf{SXDH}}(\lambda) + 2\mathsf{Adv}_{\mathcal{B}_2}^{\mathsf{PRF}}(\lambda) + 2^{-\Omega(\lambda)}.$$

Proof Outline. The top-level strategy of the proof is similar to that of the proof by Tomida et al. [28], although the order of changing the forms of ciphertexts and secret keys is the opposite. In the security proof, we employ a usual hybrid argument and gradually change the forms of ciphertexts and secret keys queried by an adversary from the case of $\beta = 0$ to $\beta = 1$ defined in Definition 2.5. We use the spaces not used in the actual function, i.e., the second and fourth spaces, for the security proof. Intuitively, the second space is a kind of a working space to handle intermediate states between $\beta = 0$ and $\beta = 1$, and the fourth space is utilized to make a situation where we can focus on only one query even if an adversary makes multiple queries. In other words, we can see the fourth space as a semi-functional space of dual system methodology proposed by Waters [29]. First, the form of secret keys is changed from $[(y^0_{\ell,i}, 0, r_{\ell,i}, 0)\mathbf{B}^*_i]_2$ to $[(y^0_{\ell,i}, y^1_{\ell,i}, r_{\ell,i}, 0)\mathbf{B}^*_i]_2$ in the Game 1 sequence. Next, we change the form of ciphertexts from $[(x^0_{j,i}, 0, z_j, 0)\mathbf{B}_i]_1$ to $[(0, x^1_{j,i}, z_j, 0)\mathbf{B}_i]_1$ in the Game 3 sequence, and here we leverage the game condition Eq. (1). Then we switch the first space with the second space as $[(x^1_{j,i}, 0, z_j, 0)\mathbf{B}_i]_1$ and $[(y^1_{\ell,i}, y^0_{\ell,i}, r_{\ell,i}, 0)\mathbf{B}^*_i]_2$. Finally, the form of secret keys is changed from $[(y^1_{\ell,i}, y^0_{\ell,i}, r_{\ell,i}, 0)\mathbf{B}^*_i]_2$ to $[(y^1_{\ell,i}, 0, r_{\ell,i}, 0)\mathbf{B}^*_i]_2$ as the reverse of the Game 1 sequence. The most complicated and important part is the Game 3 sequence, in which we need to deal with the ciphertexts and secret keys that do not satisfy the condition Eq. (1). In Game 3 sequence, we change the ciphertexts from 0-side to 1-side one by one, and in the ν-th iteration of Game 3 sequence, we change the ν-th ciphertexts from 0-side to 1-side. For the ν-th ciphertext, we can classify secret keys queried by an adversary into three types. Let m_ν be the length of the ciphertext.

1. The index set S of the secret key is included in $[m_\nu]$, i.e., $\max S \leq m_\nu$.
2. A part of the index set S is included in $[m_\nu]$, i.e., $(\max S > m_\nu) \wedge (\min S \leq m_\nu)$.
3. The index set S and $[m_\nu]$ are disjoint, i.e., $\min S > m_\nu$.

The cumbersome secret keys are type 2 keys because they can correctly decrypt a part of the ciphertext even though they may not satisfy the condition Eq. (1). We want to change the form of the ν-th ciphertext from 0-side to 1-side by information-theoretical change in Game 3-ν-1-4, but it does not work without any treatment due to the above property of type 2 keys. Therefore, we manage to randomize or "sanitize" type 2 keys from Game 3-ν-1-1 to Game 3-ν-1-3.

Proof. We prove Theorem 3.1 by a series of games. For each game transition, we prove that the difference between probabilities that the adversary $\mathcal{A}$ outputs 1 in both games is negligible.

Game 0: This game is the same as the real security game when $\beta = 0$ in Definition 2.5. That is, the j-th ciphertext query with a pair of vectors $(\mathbf{x}_j^0, \mathbf{x}_j^1) \in (\mathbb{Z}^{m_j})^2$ is replied as

$$\mathbf{c}_{j,i} := (x_{j,i}^0, 0, z_j, 0)\mathbf{B}_i \text{ for all } i \in [m_j]$$
$$\mathsf{ct}_{j,m_j} := ([\mathbf{c}_{j,1}]_1, \ldots, [\mathbf{c}_{j,m_j}]_1).$$

The ℓ-th secret key query with an index set S_ℓ and a pair of vectors $(\mathbf{y}_\ell^0, \mathbf{y}_\ell^1) \in (\mathbb{Z}^{S_\ell})^2$ is replied as

$$\mathbf{k}_{\ell,i} := (y_{\ell,i}^0, 0, r_{\ell,i}, 0)\mathbf{B}_i^* \text{ for all } i \in S_\ell$$
$$\mathsf{sk}_{\ell,S_\ell} := (S_\ell, \{[\mathbf{k}_{\ell,i}]_2\}_{i \in S_\ell}).$$

Game 0': This game is the same as Game 0 except for the way of making dual orthonormal bases. In Game 0, the dual orthonormal bases for the i-th element are made as $(\mathbf{B}_i, \mathbf{B}_i^*)$ where $\mathbf{B}_i := F_K(i)$, but in Game 0', they are made as $\mathbf{B}_i \xleftarrow{\mathsf{U}} \mathsf{GL}_4(\mathbb{Z}_p)$. More precisely, the cipertext oracle and secret key oracle have the same list $\mathcal{L}$ for bases. When the oracle needs a basis for the i-th element, it searches for $(i, \mathbf{B}_i)$ from $\mathcal{L}$. If the oracle find it, the oracle uses the bases, and if not, it generates $\mathbf{B}_i \xleftarrow{\mathsf{U}} \mathsf{GL}_4(\mathbb{Z}_p)$ and records them as $(i, \mathbf{B}_i)$ into $\mathcal{L}$.

Game 1-μ-1 ($\mu \in [q_{\mathsf{sk}}]$) **:** We define Game 1-0-3 as equivalent to Game 0'. This game is the same as Game 1-($\mu-1$)-3 except that in the μ-th secret key query, $\mathbf{k}_{\mu,i}$ is set as

$$w \xleftarrow{\mathsf{U}} \mathbb{Z}_p, \ \mathbf{k}_{\mu,i} := (y_{\mu,i}^0, 0, r_{\mu,i}, \boxed{wr_{\mu,i}})\mathbf{B}_i^* \text{ for all } i \in S_\mu.$$

Game 1-μ-2 ($\mu \in [q_{\mathsf{sk}}]$)**:** This game is the same as Game 1-μ-1 except that in the μ-th secret key query, $\mathbf{k}_{\mu,i}$ is set as

$$w \xleftarrow{\mathsf{U}} \mathbb{Z}_p, \ \mathbf{k}_{\mu,i} := (y_{\mu,i}^0, \boxed{y_{\mu,i}^1}, r_{\mu,i}, wr_{\mu,i})\mathbf{B}_i^* \text{ for all } i \in S_\mu.$$

Game 1-μ-3 ($\mu \in [q_{\mathsf{sk}}]$)**:** This game is the same as Game 1-μ-2 except that in the μ-th secret key query, $\mathbf{k}_{\mu,i}$ is set as

$$\mathbf{k}_{\mu,i} := (y_{\mu,i}^0, y_{\mu,i}^1, r_{\mu,i}, \boxed{0})\mathbf{B}_i^* \text{ for all } i \in S_\mu.$$

Game 2: This game is the same as Game 1-q_{sk}-3 except that in all secret key queries, $\mathbf{k}_{\ell,i}$ for all $\ell \in [q_{sk}]$ is set as

$$\mathbf{k}_{\ell,i} := (y_{\ell,i}^0, y_{\ell,i}^1, r_{\ell,i}, \boxed{\tilde{r}_{\ell,i}})\mathbf{B}_i^* \text{ for all } i \in S_\ell,$$

where $\tilde{r}_{\ell,i} \xleftarrow{\mathsf{U}} \mathbb{Z}_p$ s.t. $\sum_{i \in S_\ell} \tilde{r}_{\ell,i} = 0$.

Game 3-ν-1 ($\nu \in [q_{\mathsf{ct}}]$): Game 2 is equivalent to Game 3-0-3. This game is the same as Game 3-$(\nu-1)$-3 except that in the ν-th ciphertext query, $\mathbf{c}_{\nu,i}$ is set as

$$\tilde{z}_\nu \xleftarrow{\mathsf{U}} \mathbb{Z}_p, \quad \mathbf{c}_{\nu,i} := (x^0_{\nu,i}, 0, z_\nu, \boxed{\tilde{z}_\nu})\mathbf{B}_i \text{ for all } i \in [m_\nu].$$

Game 3-ν-2 ($\nu \in [q_{\mathsf{ct}}]$) **:** This game is the same as Game 3-ν-1 except that in the ν-th ciphertext query, $\mathbf{c}_{\nu,i}$ is set as

$$\tilde{z}_\nu \xleftarrow{\mathsf{U}} \mathbb{Z}_p, \quad \mathbf{c}_{\nu,i} := (\boxed{0, x^1_{\nu,i}}, z_\nu, \tilde{z}_\nu)\mathbf{B}_i \text{ for all } i \in [m_\nu].$$

Game 3-ν-3 ($\nu \in [q_{\mathsf{ct}}]$) **:** This game is the same as Game 3-ν-2 except that in the ν-th ciphertext query, $\mathbf{c}_{\nu,i}$ is set as

$$\mathbf{c}_{\nu,i} := (0, x^1_{\nu,i}, z_\nu, \boxed{0})\mathbf{B}_i \text{ for all } i \in [m_\nu].$$

Game 4: This game is the same as Game 3-q_{ct}-5 except that in all ciphertext and secret key queries, $\mathbf{c}_{j,i}$ and $\mathbf{k}_{\ell,i}$ are set as

$$\mathbf{c}_{j,i} := (\boxed{x^1_{j,i}, 0}, z_j, 0)\mathbf{B}_i \text{ for all } i \in [m_j],$$
$$\mathbf{k}_{\ell,i} := (\boxed{y^1_{\ell,i}, y^0_{\ell,i}}, r_{\ell,i}, \tilde{r}_{\ell,i})\mathbf{B}^*_i, \text{ for all } i \in S_\ell.$$

Game 5: This game is the same as the real security game when $\beta = 1$ in Definition 2.5. That is, the j-th ciphertext query with a pair of vectors $(\mathbf{x}^0_j, \mathbf{x}^1_j) \in (\mathbb{Z}^{m_j})^2$ is replied as

$$\mathbf{c}_{j,i} := (x^1_{j,i}, 0, z_j, 0)\boxed{\mathbf{B}_i} \text{ for all } i \in [m_j]$$
$$\mathsf{ct}_{j,m_j} := ([\mathbf{c}_{j,1}]_1, \ldots, [\mathbf{c}_{j,m_j}]_1).$$

The ℓ-th secret key query with an index set S_ℓ and a pair of vectors $(\mathbf{y}^0_\ell, \mathbf{y}^1_\ell) \in (\mathbb{Z}^{S_\ell})^2$ is replied as

$$\mathbf{k}_{\ell,i} := (y^1_{\ell,i}, \boxed{0}, r_{\ell,i}, \boxed{0})\boxed{\mathbf{B}^*_i} \text{ for all } i \in S_\ell$$
$$\mathsf{sk}_{\ell,S_\ell} := (S_\ell, \{[\mathbf{k}_{\ell,i}]_2\}_{i \in S_\ell}).$$

Note that $\mathbf{B}_i$ is generated as $\mathbf{B}_i := F_K(i)$ in Game 5.

Thanks to Lemma 3.2 to Lemma 3.11, we can conclude the proof of Theorem 3.1. □

In the following, we denote the event that $\mathcal{A}$ outputs 1 in Game ι by E_ι.

Lemma 3.2. *For any PPT adversary $\mathcal{A}$, there exists a PPT adversary $\mathcal{B}$ for PRFs s.t.*

$$|\Pr[\mathsf{E}_0] - \Pr[\mathsf{E}_{0'}]| \leq \mathsf{Adv}^{\mathsf{PRF}}_{\mathcal{B}}(\lambda) + 2^{-\Omega(\lambda)}.$$

Proof. First, we consider Game 0_{M}, which is the same as Game 0 except that $\mathbf{B}_i$ is generated as $\mathbf{B}_i \xleftarrow{\mathsf{U}} \mathsf{M}_4(\mathbb{Z}_p)$ for each i. The following inequality directly follows from the property of PRF s.t. $|\Pr[\mathsf{E}_0] - \Pr[\mathsf{E}_{0_{\mathsf{M}}}]| \le \mathsf{Adv}_{\mathcal{B}}^{\mathsf{PRF}}(\lambda)$. Next, we have $|\Pr[\mathsf{E}_{0_{\mathsf{M}}}] - \Pr[\mathsf{E}_{0'}]| \le 2^{-\Omega(\lambda)}$ from Lemma 3.1. Then Lemma 3.2 holds. □

Lemma 3.3. *For any PPT adversary $\mathcal{A}$, there exists a PPT adversary $\mathcal{B}$ for the SXDH s.t.*

$$|\Pr[\mathsf{E}_{\mathit{1}\text{-}(\mu-1)\text{-}\mathit{3}}] - \Pr[\mathsf{E}_{\mathit{1}\text{-}\mu\text{-}\mathit{1}}]| \le \mathsf{Adv}_{\mathcal{B}}^{\mathsf{SXDH}}(\lambda) + 2^{-\Omega(\lambda)}.$$

Proof. We show that we can make a reduction algorithm $\mathcal{B}$ for the SXDH using $\mathcal{A}$. $\mathcal{B}$ obtains an instance of SXDH with $\iota := 2$, i.e., $(\mathbb{G}, [a]_2, [e]_2, [t_\beta]_2)$, and sets $\mathsf{pp} := \mathbb{G}$. $\mathcal{B}$ defines random dual orthonormal bases $\mathbf{B}_i, \mathbf{B}_i^*$ as follows,

$$\mathbf{W}_i \xleftarrow{\mathsf{U}} \mathsf{GL}_4(\mathbb{Z}_p),\ \ \mathbf{B}_i := \begin{pmatrix} 1 & & & \\ & 1 & & \\ & & 0 & 1 \\ & & 1 & -a \end{pmatrix} \mathbf{W}_i,\ \ \mathbf{B}_i^* := \begin{pmatrix} 1 & & & \\ & 1 & & \\ & & a & 1 \\ & & 1 & 0 \end{pmatrix} \mathbf{W}_i^* \in \mathsf{GL}_4(\mathbb{Z}_p).$$

Then $\mathcal{B}$ simulates all ciphertext queries and all secret key queries except the μ-th one as follows.

$$[\mathbf{c}_{j,i}]_1 := [(x_{j,i}^0, 0, z_{j,i}, 0)\mathbf{B}_i]_1 \ \text{ for all } i \in [m_j],$$

$$[\mathbf{k}_{\ell,i}]_2 := \begin{cases} [(y_{\ell,i}^0, y_{\ell,i}^1, r_{\ell,i}, 0)\mathbf{B}_i^*]_2 \ \text{ for all } i \in S_\ell & (\ell < \mu) \\ [(y_{\ell,i}^0, 0, r_{\ell,i}, 0)\mathbf{B}_i^*]_2 \ \text{ for all } i \in S_\ell & (\ell > \mu). \end{cases}$$

Note that $\mathcal{B}$ cannot compute $[\mathbf{b}_{i,4}]_1$ because it does not know $[a]_1$, but the above instances are computable without $[\mathbf{b}_{i,4}]_1$. For the μ-th secret key query, $\mathcal{B}$ replies to $\mathcal{A}$ for all $i \in S_\mu$ as

$$r_i' \xleftarrow{\mathsf{U}} \mathbb{Z}_p \ \text{ s.t. } \sum_{i \in S_\mu} r_i' = 0,$$

$$[\mathbf{k}_{\mu,i}]_2 := [(y_{\mu,i}^0, 0, 0, 0)\mathbf{B}_i^* + r_i'(0, 0, t_\beta, e)\mathbf{W}_i^*]_2 = [(y_{\mu,i}^0, 0, er_i', \beta f r_i')\mathbf{B}_i^*]_2.$$

Observe that we can implicitly set $r_{\mu,i} := er_i'$ and $w := f/e$ unless $e = 0$, then $\mathcal{A}$'s view is the same as in Game 1-$(\mu-1)$-3 (resp. Game 1-μ-1) if $\beta = 0$ (resp. $\beta = 1$). □

Lemma 3.4. *For any PPT adversary $\mathcal{A}$, we have*

$$|\Pr[\mathsf{E}_{\mathit{1}\text{-}\mu\text{-}\mathit{1}}] - \Pr[\mathsf{E}_{\mathit{1}\text{-}\mu\text{-}\mathit{2}}]| \le 2^{-\Omega(\lambda)}.$$

Proof. We define $(\mathbf{D}_i, \mathbf{D}_i^*)$ as

$$\mathbf{D}_i := \begin{pmatrix} 1 & & & 0 \\ & 1 & & \frac{y_{\mu,i}^1}{wr_{\mu,i}} \\ & & 1 & 0 \\ & & & 1 \end{pmatrix} \mathbf{B}_i,\ \ \mathbf{D}_i^* := \begin{pmatrix} 1 & & & \\ & 1 & & \\ & & 1 & \\ 0 & -\frac{y_{\mu,i}^1}{wr_{\mu,i}} & 0 & 1 \end{pmatrix} \mathbf{B}_i^* \in \mathsf{GL}_4(\mathbb{Z}_p).$$

Observe that $(\mathbf{D}_i, \mathbf{D}_i^*)$ are random dual orthonormal bases. Then, for all $j \in [q_{\mathsf{ct}}]$ and $\ell \in [q_{\mathsf{sk}}]$, we have

$$\mathbf{c}_{j,i} = (x_{j,i}^0, 0, z_{j,i}, 0)\mathbf{B}_i = (x_{j,i}^0, 0, z_{j,i}, 0) \begin{pmatrix} 1 & & & 0 \\ & & 1 & -\frac{y_{\mu,i}^1}{wr_{\mu,i}} \\ & 1 & & 0 \\ & & & 1 \end{pmatrix} \mathbf{D}_i = (x_{j,i}^0, 0, z_{j,i}, 0)\mathbf{D}_i,$$

$$\mathbf{k}_{\ell,i} = (y_{\ell,i}^0, \beta_\ell y_{\ell,i}^1, r_{\ell,i}, \hat{\beta}_\ell w r_{\mu,i})\mathbf{B}_i^* = (y_{\ell,i}^0, \beta_\ell y_{\ell,i}^1, r_{\ell,i}, \hat{\beta}_\ell w r_{\mu,i}) \begin{pmatrix} 1 & & & \\ & 1 & & \\ & & 1 & \\ 0 & \frac{y_{\mu,i}^1}{wr_{\mu,i}} & 0 & 1 \end{pmatrix} \mathbf{D}_i^*$$

$$= (y_{\ell,i}^0, (\beta_\ell + \hat{\beta}_\ell) y_{\ell,i}^1, r_{\ell,i}, \hat{\beta}_\ell w r_{\mu,i})\mathbf{D}_i^*,$$

where $\beta_\ell = 0$ if $\ell \geq \mu$ and $\beta_\ell = 1$ if $\ell < \mu$, and $\hat{\beta}_\ell = 0$ if $\ell \neq \mu$ and $\hat{\beta}_\ell = 1$ if $\ell = \mu$. Then if $w \neq 0$ and $r_{\mu,i} \neq 0$, $\mathcal{A}$'s view is identically distributed in Game 1-μ-2 and Game 1-μ-3. □

Lemma 3.5. *For any PPT adversary $\mathcal{A}$, there exists a PPT adversary $\mathcal{B}$ for the SXDH s.t.*

$$|\Pr[\mathsf{E}_{1\text{-}\mu\text{-}2}] - \Pr[\mathsf{E}_{1\text{-}\mu\text{-}3}]| \leq \mathsf{Adv}_{\mathcal{B}}^{\mathsf{SXDH}}(\lambda) + 2^{-\Omega(\lambda)}.$$

This lemma can be proven almost the same as Lemma 3.3, so we omit the proof.

Lemma 3.6. *For any PPT adversary $\mathcal{A}$, there exists a PPT adversary $\mathcal{B}$ for the SXDH s.t.*

$$|\Pr[\mathsf{E}_{1\text{-}q_{\mathsf{sk}}\text{-}3}] - \Pr[\mathsf{E}_2]| \leq \mathsf{Adv}_{\mathcal{B}}^{\mathsf{SXDH}}(\lambda) + 2^{-\Omega(\lambda)}$$

Proof. We show that we can make a reduction algorithm $\mathcal{B}$ for the SXDH using $\mathcal{A}$. $\mathcal{B}$ obtains an instance of SXDH with $\iota := 2$, i.e., $(\mathbb{G}, [a]_2, [e]_2, [t_\beta]_2)$, and sets $\mathsf{pp} := \mathbb{G}$. $\mathcal{B}$ defines random dual orthonormal bases $\mathbf{B}_i, \mathbf{B}_i^*$ as follows,

$$\mathbf{W}_i \xleftarrow{\mathsf{U}} \mathsf{GL}_4(\mathbb{Z}_p), \quad \mathbf{B}_i := \begin{pmatrix} 1 & & & \\ & 1 & & \\ & & 0 & 1 \\ & & 1 & -a \end{pmatrix} \mathbf{W}_i, \quad \mathbf{B}_i^* := \begin{pmatrix} 1 & & & \\ & 1 & & \\ & & a & 1 \\ & & 1 & 0 \end{pmatrix} \mathbf{W}_i^* \in \mathsf{GL}_4(\mathbb{Z}_p).$$

Then $\mathcal{B}$ simulates all ciphertext queries and all secret key queries as follows.

$$[\mathbf{c}_{j,i}]_1 := [(x_{j,i}^0, 0, z_{j,i}, 0)\mathbf{B}_i]_1 \text{ for all } i \in [m_j],$$

$$r'_{\ell,i}, r''_{\ell,i} \xleftarrow{\mathsf{U}} \mathbb{Z}_p \text{ s.t. } \sum_{i \in S_\ell} r'_{\ell,i} = \sum_{i \in S_\ell} r''_{\ell,i} = 0,$$

$$[\mathbf{k}_{\ell,i}]_2 := [(y_{\ell,i}^0, y_{\ell,i}^1, r'_{\ell,i}, 0)\mathbf{B}_i^* + r''_{\ell,i}(0, 0, t_\beta, e)\mathbf{W}_i^*]_2$$
$$= [(y_{\ell,i}^0, y_{\ell,i}^1, r'_{\ell,i} + e r''_{\ell,i}, \beta f r''_{\ell,i})\mathbf{B}_i^*]_2 \text{ for all } i \in S_\ell.$$

Note that $\mathcal{B}$ cannot compute $[\mathbf{b}_{i,4}]_1$ because it does not know $[a]_1$, but the above instances are computable without $[\mathbf{b}_{i,4}]_1$. Observe that we can implicitly set $r_{\ell,i} := r'_{\ell,i} + er''_{\ell,i}$ and $\tilde{r}_{\ell,i} := fr''_{\ell,i}$ unless $f = 0$, then $\mathcal{A}$'s view is the same as in Game 1-q_{sk}-3 (resp. Game 2) if $\beta = 0$ (resp. $\beta = 1$). □

Lemma 3.7. *For any PPT adversary $\mathcal{A}$, there exists a PPT adversary $\mathcal{B}$ for the SXDH s.t.*

$$|\Pr[\mathsf{E}_{3\text{-}(\nu-1)\text{-}3}] - \Pr[\mathsf{E}_{3\text{-}\nu\text{-}1}]| \leq \mathsf{Adv}_{\mathcal{B}}^{\mathsf{SXDH}}(\lambda).$$

Proof. We show that we can make a reduction algorithm $\mathcal{B}$ for the SXDH using $\mathcal{A}$. $\mathcal{B}$ obtains an instance of SXDH with $\iota := 1$, i.e., $(\mathbb{G}, [a]_1, [e]_1, [t_\beta]_1)$, and sets $\mathsf{pp} := \mathbb{G}$. $\mathcal{B}$ defines random dual orthonormal bases $\mathbf{B}_i, \mathbf{B}_i^*$ as follows,

$$\mathbf{W}_i \xleftarrow{\mathsf{U}} \mathsf{GL}_4(\mathbb{Z}_p),\ \ \mathbf{B}_i := \begin{pmatrix} 1 & & & \\ & 1 & & \\ & & a & 1 \\ & & 1 & 0 \end{pmatrix} \mathbf{W}_i,\ \ \mathbf{B}_i^* := \begin{pmatrix} 1 & & & \\ & 1 & & \\ & & 0 & 1 \\ & & 1 & -a \end{pmatrix} \mathbf{W}_i^* \in \mathsf{GL}_4(\mathbb{Z}_p).$$

Then $\mathcal{B}$ simulates all ciphertext queries except the ν-th one and all secret key queries as follows,

$$[\mathbf{c}_{j,i}]_1 := \begin{cases} [(0, x_{j,i}^1, z_{j,i}, 0)\mathbf{B}_i]_1 & \text{for all } i \in [m_j] \quad (j < \nu) \\ [(x_{j,i}^0, 0, z_{j,i}, 0)\mathbf{B}_i]_1 & \text{for all } i \in [m_j] \quad (j > \nu), \end{cases}$$

$$r'_{\ell,i}, r''_{\ell,i} \xleftarrow{\mathsf{U}} \mathbb{Z}_p \text{ s.t. } \sum_{i \in S_\ell} r'_{\ell,i} = \sum_{i \in S_\ell} r''_{\ell,i} = 0,$$

$$\begin{aligned} [\mathbf{k}_{\ell,i}]_2 &:= [(y_{\ell,i}^0, y_{\ell,i}^1, r'_{\ell,i}, 0)\mathbf{B}_i^* + (0, 0, r''_{\ell,i}, 0)\mathbf{W}_i^*]_2 \\ &= [(y_{\ell,i}^0, y_{\ell,i}^1, r'_{\ell,i} + ar''_{\ell,i}, r''_{\ell,i})\mathbf{B}_i^*]_2 \ \text{ for all } i \in S_\ell. \end{aligned}$$

Note that $\mathcal{B}$ cannot compute $[\mathbf{b}_{i,4}^*]_2$ because it does not know $[a]_2$, but the above instances are computable without $[\mathbf{b}_{i,4}^*]_2$. Observe that we can implicitly set $r_{\ell,i} := r'_{\ell,i} + ar''_{\ell,i}$ and $\tilde{r}_{\ell,i} := r''_{\ell,i}$, so $\mathcal{B}$ correctly simulates the answer for queries. For the ν-th ciphertext query, $\mathcal{B}$ replies to $\mathcal{A}$ for all $i \in [m_\nu]$ as

$$[\mathbf{c}_{\nu,i}]_1 := [(x_{\nu,i}^0, 0, 0, 0)\mathbf{B}_i + (0, 0, t_\beta, e)\mathbf{W}_i]_1 = [(x_{\nu,i}^0, 0, e, \beta f)\mathbf{B}_i]_1.$$

Observe that we can implicitly set $z_\nu := e$ and $\tilde{z}_\nu := f$, then $\mathcal{A}$'s view is the same as in Game 3-$(\nu - 1)$-3 (resp. Game 3-ν-1) if $\beta = 0$ (resp. $\beta = 1$). □

Lemma 3.8. *Let m_{max} be the maximum length of vectors with which $\mathcal{A}$ makes a query to the encryption oracle. For any PPT adversary $\mathcal{A}$, there exists a PPT adversary $\mathcal{B}$ for the SXDH s.t.*

$$|\Pr[\mathsf{E}_{3\text{-}\nu\text{-}1}] - \Pr[\mathsf{E}_{3\text{-}\nu\text{-}2}]| \leq 2m_{\mathsf{max}}\mathsf{Adv}_{\mathcal{B}}^{\mathsf{SXDH}}(\lambda) + 2^{-\Omega(\lambda)}.$$

Proof. To prove Lemma 3.8, we consider the following intermediate games between Game 3-ν-1 and 3-ν-2. In each intermediate game, the challenger chooses a random element $m'_\nu \xleftarrow{\mathsf{U}} [m_{\mathsf{max}}]$ as a guess of m_ν at the beginning of the games.

Game 3-ν-1-1 ($\nu \in [q_{\mathsf{ct}}]$)**:** This game is the same as Game 3-ν-1 except that the challenger aborts the game immediately if the vector length of the ν-th ciphertext query is not m'_ν i.e., $m'_\nu \neq m_\nu$. We define that $\mathcal{A}$'s output is $\perp$ when the game is aborted.

Game 3-ν-1-2 ($\nu \in [q_{\mathsf{ct}}]$)**:** This game is the same as Game 3-ν-1-1 except the following. In the ℓ-th secret key query for all ℓ s.t. whose index set S_ℓ contains both elements that are greater than m'_ν and not greater than m'_ν, i.e., $(\max S_\ell > m'_\nu) \wedge (\min S_\ell \leq m'_\nu)$, $\mathbf{k}_{\ell,i}$ is set as

$$\mathbf{k}_{\ell,i} := \begin{cases} (y^0_{\ell,i}, y^1_{\ell,i}, r_{\ell,i}, \tilde{r}_{\ell,i})\mathbf{B}^*_i & (i \in S_\ell, i \leq m'_\nu) \\ (y^0_{\ell,i}, y^1_{\ell,i}, r_{\ell,i}, \boxed{a\tilde{r}_{\ell,i}})\mathbf{B}^*_i & (i \in S_\ell, i > m'_\nu) \end{cases}$$

where $a \xleftarrow{\mathsf{U}} \mathbb{Z}_p, \tilde{r}_{\ell,i} \xleftarrow{\mathsf{U}} \mathbb{Z}_p$ s.t. $\sum_{i \in S_\ell} \tilde{r}_{\ell,i} = 0$.

Game 3-ν-1-3 ($\nu \in [q_{\mathsf{ct}}]$)**:** This game is the same as Gamc 3-ν-1-2 except that in the ℓ-th secret key query for all ℓ s.t. $(\max S_\ell > m'_\nu) \wedge (\min S_\ell \leq m'_\nu)$, $\mathbf{k}_{\ell,i}$ is set as

$$\bar{r}_{\ell,i} \xleftarrow{\mathsf{U}} \mathbb{Z}_p, \quad \mathbf{k}_{\ell,i} := (y^0_{\ell,i}, y^1_{\ell,i}, r_{\ell,i}, \boxed{\bar{r}_{\ell,i}})\mathbf{B}^*_i \text{ for all } i \in S_\ell.$$

Game 3-ν-1-4 ($\nu \in [q_{\mathsf{ct}}]$)**:** This game is the same as Game 3-ν-1-3 except that in the ν-th ciphertext query, $\mathbf{c}_{\nu,i}$ is set as

$$\tilde{z}_\nu \xleftarrow{\mathsf{U}} \mathbb{Z}_p, \quad \mathbf{c}_{\nu,i} := (\boxed{0, x^1_{\nu,i}}, z_\nu, \tilde{z}_\nu)\mathbf{B}_i \text{ for all } i \in [m'_\nu].$$

Game 3-ν-1-5 ($\nu \in [q_{\mathsf{ct}}]$)**:** This game is the same as Game 3-ν-1-4 except that in all secret key queries, $\mathbf{k}_{\ell,i}$ are set as

$$\mathbf{k}_{\ell,i} := (y^0_{\ell,i}, y^1_{\ell,i}, r_{\ell,i}, \boxed{\tilde{r}_{\ell,i}})\mathbf{B}^*_i \text{ for all } i \in S_\ell,$$

where $\tilde{r}_{\ell,i} \xleftarrow{\mathsf{U}} \mathbb{Z}_p$ s.t. $\sum_{i \in S_\ell} \tilde{r}_{\ell,i} = 0$.

Next we consider the probability that $\mathcal{A}$ outputs 1 in each game. Thanks to Claim 1 to Claim 6, we have

$$\begin{aligned} |\Pr[\mathsf{E}_{3\text{-}\nu\text{-}1}] - \Pr[\mathsf{E}_{3\text{-}\nu\text{-}2}]| &= m_{\mathsf{max}} |\Pr[\mathsf{E}_{3\text{-}\nu\text{-}1\text{-}1}] - \Pr[\mathsf{E}_{3\text{-}\nu\text{-}1\text{-}5}]| \\ &\leq 2m_{\mathsf{max}} \mathsf{Adv}^{\mathsf{SXDH}}_{\mathcal{B}}(\lambda) + 2^{-\Omega(\lambda)} \end{aligned}$$

This concludes the proof of Lemma 3.8. □

Claim 1. For any PPT adversary $\mathcal{A}$, we have

$$\Pr[\mathsf{E}_{3\text{-}\nu\text{-}1\text{-}1}] = \frac{1}{m_{\mathsf{max}}} \Pr[\mathsf{E}_{3\text{-}\nu\text{-}1}]$$

Proof. First, we consider the game (denoted by Game X) that is the same as Game 3-ν-1 except that $\mathcal{A}$'s output is defined as $\perp$ when $m'_\nu \neq m_\nu$. Note that the challenger does not abort the game in Game X in contrast to Game 3-ν-1-1. It is obvious that the probabilities that $\mathcal{A}$ outputs 1 are equal in Game X and Game 3-ν-1-1 respectively. Then, we have

$$\begin{aligned}\Pr[\mathsf{E}_{3\text{-}\nu\text{-}1\text{-}1}] = \Pr[\mathsf{E}_X] &= \sum_{i\in[m_{\max}]} \Pr[m'_\nu = i]\Pr[m_\nu = i \wedge \mathsf{E}_{3\text{-}\nu\text{-}1}|m'_\nu = i] \\ &= \frac{1}{m_{\max}} \sum_{i\in[m_{\max}]} \Pr[m_\nu = i \wedge \mathsf{E}_{3\text{-}\nu\text{-}1}] \\ &= \frac{1}{m_{\max}} \Pr[\mathsf{E}_{3\text{-}\nu\text{-}1}].\end{aligned}$$

The second line follows from the fact that m'_ν is chosen independently from $\mathcal{A}$'s view in Game X and its value does not affect $\mathcal{A}$'s behavior. □

Claim 2. For any PPT adversary $\mathcal{A}$, we have

$$|\Pr[\mathsf{E}_{3\text{-}\nu\text{-}1\text{-}1}] - \Pr[\mathsf{E}_{3\text{-}\nu\text{-}1\text{-}2}]| \leq 2^{-\Omega(\lambda)}.$$

Proof. For $i > m'_\nu$, we define $(\mathbf{D}_i, \mathbf{D}^*_i)$ as

$$\mathbf{D}_i := \begin{pmatrix} 1 & & & \\ & 1 & & \\ & & 1 & \\ & & & a \end{pmatrix} \mathbf{B}_i, \ \mathbf{D}^*_i := \begin{pmatrix} 1 & & & \\ & 1 & & \\ & & 1 & \\ & & & 1/a \end{pmatrix} \mathbf{B}^*_i \in \mathsf{GL}_4(\mathbb{Z}_p).$$

Ciphertexts except the ν-th one and secret keys that have indices greater than m'_ν are changed as

$$\begin{aligned}\mathbf{c}_{j,i} &= (\beta_j x^0_{j,i}, (1-\beta_j)x^1_{j,i}, z_j, 0)\mathbf{B}_i = (\beta_j x^0_{j,i}, (1-\beta_j)x^1_{j,i}, z_j, 0) \begin{pmatrix} 1 & & & \\ & 1 & & \\ & & 1 & \\ & & & 1/a \end{pmatrix} \mathbf{D}_i \\ &= (\beta_j x^0_{j,i}, (1-\beta_j)x^1_{j,i}, z_j, 0)\mathbf{D}_i \ \text{ for all } i > m'_\nu,\end{aligned}$$

$$\begin{aligned}\mathbf{k}_{\ell,i} &= (y^0_{\ell,i}, y^1_{\ell,i}, r_{\ell,i}, \tilde{r}_{\ell,i})\mathbf{B}^*_i = (y^0_{\ell,i}, y^1_{\ell,i}, r_{\ell,i}, \tilde{r}_{\ell,i}) \begin{pmatrix} 1 & & & \\ & 1 & & \\ & & 1 & \\ & & & a \end{pmatrix} \mathbf{D}^*_i \\ &= (y^0_{\ell,i}, y^1_{\ell,i}, r_{\ell,i}, a\tilde{r}_{\ell,i})\mathbf{D}^*_i \ \text{ for all } i > m'_\nu,\end{aligned}$$

where $\beta_j = 0$ if $j < \nu$ and $\beta_j = 1$ if $j \geq \nu$. Note that secret keys whose all indices are greater than m'_ν are not affected by the basis change because $\{\tilde{r}_{\ell,i}\}_{i\in S_\ell}$ s.t. $\sum_{i\in S_\ell} \tilde{r}_{\ell,i} = 0$ and $\{a\tilde{r}_{\ell,i}\}_{i\in S_\ell}$ s.t. $\sum_{i\in S_\ell} \tilde{r}_{\ell,i} = 0$ are identically distributed. Finally, when $m'_\nu = m_\nu$, this basis change does not affect ct_{ν,m_ν} because it is applied only for the bases with indices $i > m_\nu$. Hence, in Game 3-ν-1-1 and Game 3-ν-1-2, $\mathcal{A}$'s view is identically distributed unless $a = 0$. □

Claim 3. For any PPT adversary $\mathcal{A}$, there exists a PPT adversary $\mathcal{B}$ for the SXDH s.t.

$$|\Pr[\mathsf{E}_{3\text{-}\nu\text{-}1\text{-}2}] - \Pr[\mathsf{E}_{3\text{-}\nu\text{-}1\text{-}3}]| \leq \mathsf{Adv}_{\mathcal{B}}^{\mathsf{SXDH}}(\lambda) + 2^{-\Omega(\lambda)}.$$

Proof. We show that we can make a reduction algorithm $\mathcal{B}$ for the SXDH using $\mathcal{A}$. In the beginning of the simulation, $\mathcal{B}$ chooses a $m'_\nu \xleftarrow{\mathsf{U}} [m_{\mathsf{max}}]$ as a guess of m_ν. If the guess is incorrect, $\mathcal{B}$ aborts and outputs 0. Otherwise, $\mathcal{B}$ outputs $\mathcal{A}$'s output as it is. $\mathcal{B}$ obtains an SXDH instance with $\iota := 2$, i.e., $(\mathbb{G}, [a]_2, [e]_2, [t_\beta]_2)$ and gives $\mathsf{pp} := \mathbb{G}$ to $\mathcal{A}$. $\mathcal{B}$ defines dual orthonormal bases as $\mathbf{B}_i \xleftarrow{\mathsf{U}} \mathsf{GL}_4(\mathbb{Z}_p)$ for each index i. Then, all ciphertexts and the ℓ-th secret key s.t. $(\max S_\ell \leq m'_\nu) \vee (\min S_\ell > m'_\nu)$ can be generated by using $\mathbf{B}_i$ and $\mathbf{B}^*_i$. For the ℓ-th secret key s.t. $(\max S_\ell > m'_\nu) \wedge (\min S_\ell \leq m'_\nu)$, $\mathcal{B}$ computes secret keys as follows.

$$u_{\ell,i}, u'_{\ell,i} \xleftarrow{\mathsf{U}} \mathbb{Z}_p \text{ s.t. } \sum_{i \in S_\ell} u_{\ell,i} = \sum_{i \in S_\ell} u'_{\ell,i} = 0,$$

$$[\mathbf{k}_{\ell,i}]_2 := \begin{cases} [(y^0_{\ell,i}, y^1_{\ell,i}, r_{\ell,i}, eu_{\ell,i} + u'_{\ell,i})\mathbf{B}^*]_2 & (i \in S_\ell, i \leq m'_\nu) \\ [(y^0_{\ell,i}, y^1_{\ell,i}, r_{\ell,i}, t_\beta u_{\ell,i} + au'_{\ell,i})\mathbf{B}^*]_2 & \\ = [(y^0_{\ell,i}, y^1_{\ell,i}, r_{\ell,i}, a(eu_{\ell,i} + u'_{\ell,i}) + \beta f u_{\ell,i})\mathbf{B}^*]_2 & (i \in S_\ell, i > m'_\nu) \end{cases}$$

Then, we can define $\tilde{r}_{\ell,i} := eu_{\ell,i} + u'_{\ell,i}$. In the case of $\beta = 0$, $[\mathbf{k}_{\ell,i}]_2$ is distributed identically to Game 3-ν-1-2. Next, we consider the case $\beta = 1$. First, $\{\tilde{r}_{\ell,i}\}_{i \in S_\ell}$ and $\{u_{\ell,i}\}_{i \in S_\ell}$ are independently distributed because the information of $\{u_{\ell,i}\}_{i \in S_\ell}$ in $\{\tilde{r}_{\ell,i}\}_{i \in S_\ell}$ is completely hidden by $\{u'_{\ell,i}\}_{i \in S_\ell}$. Therefore, we can set $\bar{r}_{\ell,i} := \begin{cases} \tilde{r}_{\ell,i} & (i \in S_\ell, i \leq m'_\nu) \\ a\tilde{r}_{\ell,i} + fu_{\ell,i} & (i \in S_\ell, i > m'_\nu) \end{cases}$, unless $f = 0$. Hence, $[\mathbf{k}_{\ell,i}]_2$ is distributed identically to Game 3-ν-1-3 if $\beta = 1$. □

Claim 4. For any PPT adversary $\mathcal{A}$, we have

$$|\Pr[\mathsf{E}_{3\text{-}\nu\text{-}1\text{-}3}] - \Pr[\mathsf{E}_{3\text{-}\nu\text{-}1\text{-}4}]| \leq 2^{-\Omega(\lambda)}.$$

Proof. Here, we denote the event such that $m'_\nu = m_\nu$ in Game ι by X_ι. By the game definition, we have

$$\begin{aligned} &|\Pr[\mathsf{E}_{3\text{-}\nu\text{-}1\text{-}3}] - \Pr[\mathsf{E}_{3\text{-}\nu\text{-}1\text{-}4}]| \\ =&|\Pr[\mathsf{X}_{3\text{-}\nu\text{-}1\text{-}3}]\Pr[\mathsf{E}_{3\text{-}\nu\text{-}1\text{-}3}|\mathsf{X}_{3\text{-}\nu\text{-}1\text{-}3}] - \Pr[\mathsf{X}_{3\text{-}\nu\text{-}1\text{-}4}]\Pr[\mathsf{E}_{3\text{-}\nu\text{-}1\text{-}4}|\mathsf{X}_{3\text{-}\nu\text{-}1\text{-}4}]| \\ =&|\Pr[\mathsf{X}_{3\text{-}\nu\text{-}1\text{-}3}](\Pr[\mathsf{E}_{3\text{-}\nu\text{-}1\text{-}3}|\mathsf{X}_{3\text{-}\nu\text{-}1\text{-}3}] - \Pr[\mathsf{E}_{3\text{-}\nu\text{-}1\text{-}4}|\mathsf{X}_{3\text{-}\nu\text{-}1\text{-}4}])|. \end{aligned}$$

In the third line, we use the fact that $\mathcal{A}$'s view is identical before the ν-th ciphertext query and then we have $\Pr[\mathsf{X}_{3\text{-}\nu\text{-}1\text{-}3}] = \Pr[\mathsf{X}_{3\text{-}\nu\text{-}1\text{-}4}]$. Therefore, it is sufficient to prove that $|\Pr[\mathsf{E}_{3\text{-}\nu\text{-}1\text{-}3}|\mathsf{X}_{3\text{-}\nu\text{-}1\text{-}3}] - \Pr[\mathsf{E}_{3\text{-}\nu\text{-}1\text{-}4}|\mathsf{X}_{3\text{-}\nu\text{-}1\text{-}4}])| \leq 2^{-\Omega(\lambda)}$. For the purpose, we analyze $\mathcal{A}$'s view under the condition such that $m'_\nu = m_\nu$.

We define $(\mathbf{D}_i, \mathbf{D}_i^*)$ for all $i \in [m_\nu]$ as

$$\mathbf{D}_i := \begin{pmatrix} 1 & & & \\ & 1 & & \\ & & 1 & \\ \frac{x^0_{\nu,i}}{\tilde{z}_\nu} & -\frac{x^1_{\nu,i}}{\tilde{z}_\nu} & 0 & 1 \end{pmatrix} \mathbf{B}_i, \; \mathbf{D}_i^* := \begin{pmatrix} 1 & & & -\frac{x^0_{\nu,i}}{\tilde{z}_\nu} \\ & 1 & & \frac{x^1_{\nu,i}}{\tilde{z}_\nu} \\ & & 1 & 0 \\ & & & 1 \end{pmatrix} \mathbf{B}_i^* \in \mathsf{GL}_4(\mathbb{Z}_p).$$

Observe that $(\mathbf{D}_i, \mathbf{D}_i^*)$ are random dual orthonormal bases. Then, for all $j \in [q_{\mathrm{ct}}]$, we have

$$\begin{aligned} \mathbf{c}_{j,i} &= (\beta_j x^0_{j,i}, (1-\beta_j)x^1_{j,i}, z_j, \hat{\beta}_j \tilde{z}_\nu)\mathbf{B}_i \\ &= (\beta_j x^0_{j,i}, (1-\beta_j)x^1_{j,i}, z_j, \hat{\beta}_j \tilde{z}_\nu) \begin{pmatrix} 1 & & & \\ & 1 & & \\ & & 1 & \\ -\frac{x^0_{\nu,i}}{\tilde{z}_\nu} & \frac{x^1_{\nu,i}}{\tilde{z}_\nu} & 0 & 1 \end{pmatrix} \mathbf{D}_i \\ &= ((\beta_j - \hat{\beta}_j)x^0_{j,i}, (1-\beta_j+\hat{\beta}_j)x^1_{j,i}, z_j, \hat{\beta}_j \tilde{z}_\nu)\mathbf{D}_i, \end{aligned}$$

where $\beta_j = 0$ if $j < \nu$ and $\beta_j = 1$ if $j \geq \nu$, and $\hat{\beta}_j = 0$ if $j \neq \nu$ and $\hat{\beta}_j = 1$ if $j = \nu$. On the other hand, for all ℓ s.t. $\max S_\ell \leq m_\nu$, we have

$$\begin{aligned} \mathbf{k}_{\ell,i} &= (y^0_{\ell,i}, y^1_{\ell,i}, r_{\ell,i}, \tilde{r}_{\ell,i})\mathbf{B}_i^* = (y^0_{\ell,i}, y^1_{\ell,i}, r_{\ell,i}, \tilde{r}_{\ell,i}) \begin{pmatrix} 1 & & & \frac{x^0_{\nu,i}}{\tilde{z}_\nu} \\ & 1 & & -\frac{x^1_{\nu,i}}{\tilde{z}_\nu} \\ & & 1 & 0 \\ & & & 1 \end{pmatrix} \mathbf{D}_i^* \\ &= (y^0_{\ell,i}, y^1_{\ell,i}, r_{\ell,i}, \tilde{r}_{\ell,i} + \frac{1}{\tilde{z}_\nu}(x^0_{\nu,i}y^0_{\ell,i} - x^1_{\nu,i}y^1_{\ell,i}))\mathbf{D}_i^*. \end{aligned}$$

Here, we have the condition Eq. (1) s.t. $\sum_{i \in S_\ell}(x^0_{\nu,i}y^0_{\ell,i} - x^1_{\nu,i}y^1_{\ell,i}) = 0$, because $S_\ell \subseteq [m_\nu]$. Hence, we can set $\tilde{r}'_{\ell,i} := \tilde{r}_{\ell,i} + \frac{1}{\tilde{z}_\nu}(x^0_{\nu,i}y^0_{\ell,i} - x^1_{\nu,i}y^1_{\ell,i})$. Observe that $\tilde{r}'_{\ell,i}$ is randomly distributed s.t. $\sum_{i \in S_\ell} \tilde{r}'_{\ell,i} = 0$. In the same way, for all ℓ s.t. $(\max S_\ell > m_\nu) \wedge (\min S_\ell \leq m_\nu)$, we have

$$\mathbf{k}_{\ell,i} = \begin{cases} (y^0_{\ell,i}, y^1_{\ell,i}, r_{\ell,i}, \bar{r}_{\ell,i} + \frac{1}{\tilde{z}_\nu}(x^0_{\nu,i}y^0_{\ell,i} - x^1_{\nu,i}y^1_{\ell,i}))\mathbf{D}_i^* & (i \leq m_\nu) \\ (y^0_{\ell,i}, y^1_{\ell,i}, r_{\ell,i}, \bar{r}_{\ell,i})\mathbf{B}_i^* & (i > m_\nu) \end{cases}$$

In this case, there is no condition on $(x^0_{\nu,i}y^0_{\ell,i} - x^1_{\nu,i}y^1_{\ell,i})$. However, because $\bar{r}_{\ell,i}$ are chosen randomly from $\mathbb{Z}_p$, then $\bar{r}'_{\ell,i} := \bar{r}_{\ell,i} + \frac{1}{\tilde{z}_\nu}(x^0_{\nu,i}y^0_{\ell,i} - x^1_{\nu,i}y^1_{\ell,i})$ are also random elements in $\mathbb{Z}_p$. Note that for all ℓ s.t. $\min S_\ell > m_\nu$, this basis change does not affect $\mathsf{sk}_{\ell,S_\ell}$ because we only change the bases for $i \leq m_\nu$. Then, in Game 3-ν-1-3 and Game 3-ν-1-4, $\mathcal{A}$'s view is identically distributed unless $\tilde{z}_\nu = 0$ under the condition such that $m'_\nu = m_\nu$. □

Claim 5. For any PPT adversary $\mathcal{A}$, there exists a PPT adversary $\mathcal{B}$ for the SXDH s.t.

$$|\Pr[\mathsf{E}_{3\text{-}\nu\text{-}1\text{-}4}] - \Pr[\mathsf{E}_{3\text{-}\nu\text{-}1\text{-}5}]| \leq \mathsf{Adv}^{\mathsf{SXDH}}_{\mathcal{B}}(\lambda) + 2^{-\Omega(\lambda)}.$$

Claim 5 can be proven by just the reverse of Game 3-($\nu-1$)-1-1 to Game 3-ν-1-3, so we omit the proof.

Claim 6. For any PPT adversary $\mathcal{A}$, we have

$$\Pr[\mathsf{E}_{3\text{-}\nu\text{-}1\text{-}5}] = \frac{1}{m_{\max}}\Pr[\mathsf{E}_{3\text{-}\nu\text{-}2}]$$

The difference between Game 3-ν-1-5 and 3-ν-2 is just the existence of the abort condition introduced in Game 3-ν-1-1. Then, we can prove Claim 6 similarly to Claim 1.

Lemma 3.9. *For any PPT adversary $\mathcal{A}$, there exists a PPT adversary $\mathcal{B}$ for the SXDH s.t.*

$$|\Pr[\mathsf{E}_{3\text{-}\nu\text{-}2}] - \Pr[\mathsf{E}_{3\text{-}\nu\text{-}3}]| \leq \mathsf{Adv}_{\mathcal{B}}^{\mathsf{SXDH}}(\lambda).$$

This lemma can be proven by just the reverse of Game 3-($\nu-1$)-3 to Game 3-ν-1, so we omit the proof.

Lemma 3.10. *For any PPT adversary $\mathcal{A}$, we have*

$$\Pr[\mathsf{E}_{3\text{-}q_{\mathsf{ct}}\text{-}3}] = \Pr[\mathsf{E}_4].$$

Proof. We define $(\mathbf{D}_i, \mathbf{D}_i^*)$ as

$$\mathbf{D}_i := \begin{pmatrix} & 1 & & \\ 1 & & & \\ & & 1 & \\ & & & 1 \end{pmatrix}\mathbf{B}_i,\ \mathbf{D}_i^* := \begin{pmatrix} & 1 & & \\ 1 & & & \\ & & 1 & \\ & & & 1 \end{pmatrix}\mathbf{B}_i^* \in \mathsf{GL}_4(\mathbb{Z}_p).$$

Observe that $(\mathbf{D}_i, \mathbf{D}_i^*)$ are random dual orthonormal bases. Then, for all $j \in [q_{\mathsf{ct}}]$ and $\ell \in [q_{\mathsf{sk}}]$, we have

$$\begin{aligned} \mathbf{c}_{j,i} &= (0, x_{j,i}^1, z_j, 0)\mathbf{B}_i = (x_{j,i}^1, 0, z_j, 0)\mathbf{D}_i \ \text{ for all } i \in [m_j], \\ \mathbf{k}_{\ell,i} &= (y_{\ell,i}^0, y_{\ell,i}^1, r_{\ell,i}, \tilde{r}_{\ell,i})\mathbf{B}_i^* = (y_{\ell,i}^1, y_{\ell,i}^0, r_{\ell,i}, \tilde{r}_{\ell,i})\mathbf{D}_i^* \ \text{ for all } i \in S_\ell. \end{aligned}$$

Then, in Game 3-q_{ct}-3 and Game 4, $\mathcal{A}$'s view is identically distributed. □

Lemma 3.11. *For any PPT adversary $\mathcal{A}$, there exists a PPT adversary $\mathcal{B}_1$ for the SXDH and $\mathcal{B}_2$ for PRF s.t.*

$$|\Pr[\mathsf{E}_4] - \Pr[\mathsf{E}_5]| \leq (2q_{\mathsf{sk}} + 1)\mathsf{Adv}_{\mathcal{B}_1}^{\mathsf{SXDH}}(\lambda) + \mathsf{Adv}_{\mathcal{B}_2}^{\mathsf{PRF}}(\lambda) + 2^{-\Omega(\lambda)}.$$

This lemma can be proven by just the reverse of Games 0 to 2, so we omit the proof.

4 Public-Key Unbounded Inner Product Functional Encryption

In the following scheme, norm limits X_λ, Y_λ are some polynomials in λ.

4.1 Construction

$\mathsf{Setup}(1^\lambda)$**:** Takes a security parameter 1^λ and generates $\mathbb{G} \leftarrow \mathcal{G}_{\mathsf{BG}}(1^\lambda)$ and $\mathbf{B} \xleftarrow{\mathsf{U}} \mathsf{GL}_7(\mathbb{Z}_p)$. Outputs

$$\mathsf{pk} := (\mathbb{G}, [\mathbf{b}_1]_1, \ldots, [\mathbf{b}_4]_1), \;\; \mathsf{msk} := (\mathbf{b}_1^*, \ldots, \mathbf{b}_4^*),$$

where $\mathbf{b}_i$ (resp. $\mathbf{b}_j^*$) denotes the i-th row of $\mathbf{B}$ (resp. j-th row of $\mathbf{B}^*$).

$\mathsf{Enc}(\mathsf{pk}, \mathbf{x})$**:** Takes pk and $\mathbf{x} := (x_1, \ldots, x_m) \in \mathbb{Z}^m$ where $m = m(\lambda)$ is any polynomial. Defines $\mathbf{c}_i := (\pi_i(1, i), x_i, z, 0, 0, 0)\mathbf{B} \in \mathbb{Z}_p^7$ for all $i \in [m]$, where $\pi_i, z \xleftarrow{\mathsf{U}} \mathbb{Z}_p$. Outputs

$$\mathsf{ct}_m := ([\mathbf{c}_1]_1, \ldots, [\mathbf{c}_m]_1).$$

$\mathsf{KeyGen}(\mathsf{pk}, \mathsf{msk}, S, \mathbf{y})$**:** Takes pk, msk, a non-empty index set $S \subseteq [s]$ where $s = s(\lambda)$ is any polynomial, and an indexed vector $\mathbf{y} := (y_i)_{i \in S} \in \mathbb{Z}^S$. Chooses $\{r_i\}_{i \in S} \xleftarrow{\mathsf{U}} \mathbb{Z}_p$ s.t. $\sum_{i \in S} r_i = 0$ and $\rho_i \xleftarrow{\mathsf{U}} \mathbb{Z}_p$, and defines $\mathbf{k}_i := (\rho_i(-i, 1), y_i, r_i, 0, 0, 0)\mathbf{B}^* \in \mathbb{Z}_p^7$ for all $i \in S$. Outputs

$$\mathsf{sk}_S := (S, \{[\mathbf{k}_i]_2\}_{i \in S}).$$

$\mathsf{Dec}(\mathsf{pk}, \mathsf{ct}_m, \mathsf{sk}_S)$**:** Takes pk, a ciphertext ct_m for m dimensional vector, and a secret key sk_S for a index set S. If $S \subseteq [m]$, then computes

$$h := \prod_{i \in S} e([\mathbf{c}_i]_1, [\mathbf{k}_i]_2),$$

and searches for d s.t. $e(g_1, g_2)^d = h$ exhaustively in the range of $-|S|X_\lambda Y_\lambda$ to $|S|X_\lambda Y_\lambda$. If such d is found, outputs d. Otherwise, outputs $\perp$.

Correctness. Observe that if $S \subseteq [m]$,

$$h = \prod_{i \in S} e([\mathbf{c}_i]_1, [\mathbf{k}_i]_2) = e(g_1, g_2)^{\sum_{i \in S} \langle \mathbf{c}_i, \mathbf{k}_i \rangle} = e(g_1, g_2)^{\sum_{i \in S}(x_i y_i + z r_i)}.$$

Here we have $\sum_{i \in S} r_i = 0$, then $h = e(g_1, g_2)^{\sum_{i \in S} x_i y_i}$. If $||\mathbf{x}||_\infty \leq X_\lambda$ and $||\mathbf{y}||_\infty \leq Y_\lambda$, then $|\sum_{i \in S} x_i y_i| \leq |S| X_\lambda Y_\lambda$ and Dec outputs $\sum_{i \in S} x_i y_i$.

4.2 Security

Theorem 4.1. *Assume that the SXDH assumption holds, then our Pub-UIPFE is adaptively secure. More formally, let m_{max} be the maximum length of the challenge vector that $\mathcal{A}$ outputs and s_{max} be the maximum index with which $\mathcal{A}$ queries the key generation oracle, then for any PPT adversary $\mathcal{A}$ and security parameter λ, there exists a PPT adversary $\mathcal{B}$ for the SXDH s.t.*

$$\mathsf{Adv}_{\mathcal{A}}^{\mathsf{Pub\text{-}UIPFE}}(\lambda) \leq \{16 m_{\mathsf{max}}^2 + 8 m_{\mathsf{max}}(s_{\mathsf{max}} - 1) + 4\} \mathsf{Adv}_{\mathcal{B}}^{\mathsf{SXDH}}(\lambda) + 2^{-\Omega(\lambda)}.$$

Proof Outline. The top-level strategy of the security proof is simple. Consider a world where an encryption algorithm could magically generate unbounded random dual orthonormal bases for each index. Then we observe that only one loop of the Game 3 sequence in the Priv-UIPFE scheme suffices for the Pub-UIPFE scheme because there is one challenge ciphertext query and no challenge secret key query. To generate such a situation, we utilize an entropy-amplification technique like [26] and show that PPT adversaries cannot distinguish the real world from the "magical" world under the SXDH assumption. In the following, we provide a more concrete overview of the proof. Similarly to the Game 3 sequence in the Priv-UIPFE scheme, we first change the challenge ciphertext and all secret keys into the following form,

$$\tilde{z}, \{\tilde{r}_{\ell,i}\}_{i \in S_\ell} \xleftarrow{\mathsf{U}} \mathbb{Z}_p \text{ s.t. } \sum_{i \in S_\ell} \tilde{r}_{\ell,i} = 0,$$

$$\mathbf{c}_i := (\pi_i(1,i), x_i^0, z, \boxed{\tilde{z}}, 0, 0)\mathbf{B}, \;\; \mathbf{k}_{\ell,i} := (\rho_{\ell,i}(-i,1), y_{\ell,i}, r_{\ell,i}, \boxed{\tilde{r}_{\ell,i}}, 0, 0)\mathbf{B}^*.$$

Next, we change $\mathbf{k}_{\ell,i}$ for all ℓ s.t. $(\max S_\ell > m') \wedge (\min S_\ell \leq m')$, where m' is the guess of the vector length for the challenge ciphertext, as

$$\{\tilde{r}_{\ell,i}\}_{i \in S_\ell} \xleftarrow{\mathsf{U}} \mathbb{Z}_p, \;\; \mathbf{k}_{\ell,i} := (\rho_{\ell,i}(-i,1), y_{\ell,i}, r_{\ell,i}, \boxed{\tilde{r}_{\ell,i}}, 0, 0)\mathbf{B}^*. \tag{3}$$

Then, we change $\mathbf{c}_i$ as

$$\mathbf{c}_i := (\pi_i(1,i), \boxed{x_i^1}, z, \tilde{z}, 0, 0)\mathbf{B}, \tag{4}$$

similar to Priv-UIPFE. The remaining sequence is just the reverse. In the case of the Priv-UIPFE scheme, recall that we perform distinct basis changes for each index in the steps of Eqs. (3) and (4). However, we cannot perform such basis changes in Pub-UIPFE, because all indices share the same dual orthonormal bases. To overcome this difficulty, we conduct this step by computational change on the basis of the SXDH assumption. Specifically, we introduce the following two lemmas and use them in the proof as a kind of basis change in Priv-UIPFE. Especially, it is relatively easy to see that Lemma 4.2 can be used for showing that PPT adversaries cannot distinguish the real world, i.e., $\beta = 0$, from the "magical" world, i.e., $\beta = 1$, where dual orthonormal bases for each index are "somewhat" random. In other words, in the case of $\beta = 1$, dual orthonormal bases for index i is generated as

$$\mathbf{D}_i := \begin{pmatrix} \mathbf{I}_2 & & & & \\ & 1 & & & \\ & & 1 & & \\ & w_i & 1 & & \\ & & & & \mathbf{I}_2 \end{pmatrix} \mathbf{B}, \;\; \mathbf{D}_i^* := \begin{pmatrix} \mathbf{I}_2 & & & & \\ & 1 & & -w_i & \\ & & 1 & & \\ & & & 1 & \\ & & & & \mathbf{I}_2 \end{pmatrix} \mathbf{B}^*. \tag{5}$$

Lemma 4.1 is used for the step of Eq. (3), which corresponds to Games 3-ν-2 and 3-ν-3 in the proof of Priv-UIPFE, and Lemma 4.2 is used for the step of

Eq. (4), which corresponds to Game 3-ν-4 in the proof of Priv-UIPFE. In our Pub-UIPFE scheme, there are three-dimensional subspaces that are not used in the actual function: the 5-7th spaces. The fifth space is a kind of a semi-functional space that is similar to the fourth space of our Priv-UIPFE scheme. The sixth and seventh spaces are necessary to amplify the entropy of the two dimensional prefix for the proof of the lemmas. Similar to here, adding extra spaces other than the semi-functional space and amplifying the entropy in the space are also done in [11,23,26].

Lemma 4.1. *For any polynomial $m := m(\lambda)$ and $n := n(\lambda)$, we define the following distribution,*

$$\begin{aligned}
&\mathbb{G} \leftarrow \mathcal{G}_{\mathsf{BG}}(1^\lambda),\ \ \mathbf{B} \xleftarrow{\mathsf{U}} \mathsf{GL}_7(\mathbb{Z}_p),\ \ \{\pi_i\}_{i\in[m]}, \tilde{z} \xleftarrow{\mathsf{U}} \mathbb{Z}_p,\\
&\mathbf{u}_i := (\pi_i(1,i), 0, 0, \tilde{z}, 0, 0)\mathbf{B} \quad \text{for all } i \in [m],\\
&D := (\mathbb{G}, [\mathbf{b}_1]_1, \ldots, [\mathbf{b}_4]_1, [\mathbf{b}_1^*]_2, \ldots, [\mathbf{b}_5^*]_2, [\mathbf{u}_1]_1, \ldots, [\mathbf{u}_m]_1),\\
&\{\rho_i'\}_{i\in[m+1,n]}, \{r_i'\}_{i\in[m+1,n]} \xleftarrow{\mathsf{U}} \mathbb{Z}_p,\\
&\mathbf{u}_{i,\beta}^* := (\rho_i'(-i,1), 0, 0, \beta r_i', 0, 0)\mathbf{B}^* \quad \text{for all } i \in [m+1,n],\\
&U_\beta := \{[\mathbf{u}_{i,\beta}^*]_2\}_{i\in[m+1,n]}.
\end{aligned}$$

For any PPT adversary $\mathcal{A}$, there exists a PPT adversary $\mathcal{B}$ for the SXDH s.t.

$$\begin{aligned}
\mathsf{Adv}_{\mathcal{A}}^{\mathsf{P1}}(\lambda) :=& |\Pr[1 \leftarrow \mathcal{A}(D, U_0)] - \Pr[1 \leftarrow \mathcal{A}(D, U_1)]|\\
\leq& 4(n-m)\mathsf{Adv}_{\mathcal{B}}^{\mathsf{SXDH}}(\lambda) + 2^{-\Omega(\lambda)}.
\end{aligned}$$

Lemma 4.2. *For any polynomial $m := m(\lambda)$ and $n := n(\lambda)$, we define the following distribution,*

$$\begin{aligned}
&\mathbb{G} \leftarrow \mathcal{G}_{\mathsf{BG}}(1^\lambda),\ \ \mathbf{B} \xleftarrow{\mathsf{U}} \mathsf{GL}_7(\mathbb{Z}_p),\ \ \{\rho_i'\}_{i\in[m+1,n]} \xleftarrow{\mathsf{U}} \mathbb{Z}_p,\\
&\mathbf{u}_i^* := (\rho_i'(-i,1), 1, 0, 0, 0, 0)\mathbf{B}^* \quad \text{for all } i \in [m+1,n],\\
&D := (\mathbb{G}, [\mathbf{b}_1]_1, \ldots, [\mathbf{b}_4]_1, [\mathbf{b}_1^*]_2, [\mathbf{b}_2^*]_2, [\mathbf{b}_4^*]_2, [\mathbf{b}_5^*]_2, \{[\mathbf{u}_i^*]_2\}_{i\in[m+1,n]}),\\
&\{\pi_i'\}_{i\in[m]}, \{\rho_i'\}_{i\in[m]}, \{w_i\}_{i\in[m]} \xleftarrow{\mathsf{U}} \mathbb{Z}_p,\\
&\mathbf{u}_{i,\beta} := (\pi_i'(1,i), \beta w_i, 0, 1, 0, 0)\mathbf{B} \quad \text{for all } i \in [m],\\
&\mathbf{u}_{i,\beta}^* := (\rho_i'(-i,1), 1, 0, -\beta w_i, 0, 0)\mathbf{B}^* \quad \text{for all } i \in [m],\\
&U_\beta := \{[\mathbf{u}_{i,\beta}]_1, [\mathbf{u}_{i,\beta}^*]_2\}_{i\in[m]}.
\end{aligned}$$

For any PPT adversary $\mathcal{A}$, there exists a PPT adversary $\mathcal{B}$ for the SXDH s.t.

$$\mathsf{Adv}_{\mathcal{A}}^{\mathsf{P2}}(\lambda) := |\Pr[1 \leftarrow \mathcal{A}(D, U_0)] - \Pr[1 \leftarrow \mathcal{A}(D, U_1)]| \leq 8m\mathsf{Adv}_{\mathcal{B}}^{\mathsf{SXDH}}(\lambda) + 2^{-\Omega(\lambda)}.$$

The formal proofs of Theorem 4.1, Lemmas 4.1, and 4.2 are presented in the full version of this paper.

Acknowledgments. We are very grateful to Pratish Datta and Tatsuaki Okamoto for giving us a chance to start this work. We also would like to thank anonymous reviewers for their helpful comments.

References

1. Abdalla, M., Bourse, F., De Caro, A., Pointcheval, D.: Simple functional encryption schemes for inner products. In: Katz, J. (ed.) PKC 2015. LNCS, vol. 9020, pp. 733–751. Springer, Heidelberg (2015). https://doi.org/10.1007/978-3-662-46447-2_33
2. Abdalla, M., Bourse, F., De Caro, A., Pointcheval, D.: Better security for functional encryption for inner product evaluations. Cryptology ePrint Archive, Report 2016/011 (2016). http://eprint.iacr.org/2016/011
3. Abdalla, M., Catalano, D., Fiore, D., Gay, R., Ursu, B.: Multi-input functional encryption for inner products: function-hiding realizations and constructions without pairings. Cryptology ePrint Archive, Report 2017/972 (2017). http://eprint.iacr.org/2017/972
4. Abdalla, M., Gay, R., Raykova, M., Wee, H.: Multi-input inner-product functional encryption from pairings. In: Coron, J.-S., Nielsen, J.B. (eds.) EUROCRYPT 2017, Part I. LNCS, vol. 10210, pp. 601–626. Springer, Cham (2017). https://doi.org/10.1007/978-3-319-56620-7_21
5. Agrawal, S., Libert, B., Stehlé, D.: Fully secure functional encryption for inner products, from standard assumptions. In: Robshaw, M., Katz, J. (eds.) CRYPTO 2016, Part III. LNCS, vol. 9816, pp. 333–362. Springer, Heidelberg (2016). https://doi.org/10.1007/978-3-662-53015-3_12
6. Attrapadung, N.: Dual system encryption via doubly selective security: framework, fully secure functional encryption for regular languages, and more. In: Nguyen, P.Q., Oswald, E. (eds.) EUROCRYPT 2014. LNCS, vol. 8441, pp. 557–577. Springer, Heidelberg (2014). https://doi.org/10.1007/978-3-642-55220-5_31
7. Attrapadung, N.: Dual system encryption framework in prime-order groups via computational pair encodings. In: Cheon, J.H., Takagi, T. (eds.) ASIACRYPT 2016, Part II. LNCS, vol. 10032, pp. 591–623. Springer, Heidelberg (2016). https://doi.org/10.1007/978-3-662-53890-6_20
8. Bishop, A., Jain, A., Kowalczyk, L.: Function-hiding inner product encryption. In: Iwata, T., Cheon, J.H. (eds.) ASIACRYPT 2015, Part I. LNCS, vol. 9452, pp. 470–491. Springer, Heidelberg (2015). https://doi.org/10.1007/978-3-662-48797-6_20
9. Boneh, D., Sahai, A., Waters, B.: Functional encryption: definitions and challenges. In: Ishai, Y. (ed.) TCC 2011. LNCS, vol. 6597, pp. 253–273. Springer, Heidelberg (2011). https://doi.org/10.1007/978-3-642-19571-6_16
10. Brakerski, Z., Vaikuntanathan, V.: Circuit-ABE from LWE: unbounded attributes and semi-adaptive security. In: Robshaw, M., Katz, J. (eds.) CRYPTO 2016, Part III. LNCS, vol. 9816, pp. 363–384. Springer, Heidelberg (2016). https://doi.org/10.1007/978-3-662-53015-3_13
11. Chen, J., Gong, J., Kowalczyk, L., Wee, H.: Unbounded ABE via bilinear entropy expansion, revisited. In: Nielsen, J.B., Rijmen, V. (eds.) EUROCRYPT 2018, Part I. LNCS, vol. 10820, pp. 503–534. Springer, Cham (2018). https://doi.org/10.1007/978-3-319-78381-9_19
12. Chen, J., Wee, H.: Semi-adaptive attribute-based encryption and improved delegation for Boolean formula. In: Abdalla, M., De Prisco, R. (eds.) SCN 2014. LNCS, vol. 8642, pp. 277–297. Springer, Cham (2014). https://doi.org/10.1007/978-3-319-10879-7_16
13. Datta, P., Dutta, R., Mukhopadhyay, S.: Functional encryption for inner product with full function privacy. In: Cheng, C.-M., Chung, K.-M., Persiano, G., Yang, B.-Y. (eds.) PKC 2016, Part I. LNCS, vol. 9614, pp. 164–195. Springer, Heidelberg (2016). https://doi.org/10.1007/978-3-662-49384-7_7

14. Datta, P., Okamoto, T., Tomida, J.: Full-Hiding (Unbounded) Multi-input Inner Product Functional Encryption from the k-Linear Assumption. In: Abdalla, M., Dahab, R. (eds.) PKC 2018, Part II. LNCS, vol. 10770, pp. 245–277. Springer, Cham (2018). https://doi.org/10.1007/978-3-319-76581-5_9
15. Dufour Sans, E., Pointcheval, D.: Unbounded inner product functional encryption, with succinct keys. Cryptology ePrint Archive, Report 2018/487 (2018). https://eprint.iacr.org/2018/487
16. Garg, S., Gentry, C., Halevi, S.: Candidate multilinear maps from ideal lattices. In: Johansson, T., Nguyen, P.Q. (eds.) EUROCRYPT 2013. LNCS, vol. 7881, pp. 1–17. Springer, Heidelberg (2013). https://doi.org/10.1007/978-3-642-38348-9_1
17. Garg, S., Gentry, C., Halevi, S., Raykova, M., Sahai, A., Waters, B.: Candidate indistinguishability obfuscation and functional encryption for all circuits. In: 54th FOCS, pp. 40–49. IEEE Computer Society Press, October 2013
18. Garg, S., Gentry, C., Halevi, S., Zhandry, M.: Functional encryption without obfuscation. In: Kushilevitz, E., Malkin, T. (eds.) TCC 2016, Part II. LNCS, vol. 9563, pp. 480–511. Springer, Heidelberg (2016). https://doi.org/10.1007/978-3-662-49099-0_18
19. Goyal, V., Pandey, O., Sahai, A., Waters, B.: Attribute-based encryption for fine-grained access control of encrypted data. In: Juels, A., Wright, R.N., Vimercati, S. (eds.) ACM CCS 2006, pp. 89–98. ACM Press, October–November 2006. Available as Cryptology ePrint Archive Report 2006/309
20. Katz, J., Sahai, A., Waters, B.: Predicate encryption supporting disjunctions, polynomial equations, and inner products. In: Smart, N. (ed.) EUROCRYPT 2008. LNCS, vol. 4965, pp. 146–162. Springer, Heidelberg (2008). https://doi.org/10.1007/978-3-540-78967-3_9
21. Kim, S., Lewi, K., Mandal, A., Montgomery, H., Roy, A., Wu, D.J.: Function-hiding inner product encryption is practical. Cryptology ePrint Archive, Report 2016/440 (2016). http://eprint.iacr.org/2016/440
22. Kim, S., Kim, J., Seo, J.H.: A new approach for practical function-private inner product encryption. Cryptology ePrint Archive, Report 2017/004 (2017). http://eprint.iacr.org/2017/004
23. Lewko, A., Waters, B.: Unbounded HIBE and attribute-based encryption. In: Paterson, K.G. (ed.) EUROCRYPT 2011. LNCS, vol. 6632, pp. 547–567. Springer, Heidelberg (2011). https://doi.org/10.1007/978-3-642-20465-4_30
24. Lin, H.: Indistinguishability obfuscation from SXDH on 5-linear maps and locality-5 PRGs. In: Katz, J., Shacham, H. (eds.) CRYPTO 2017, Part I. LNCS, vol. 10401, pp. 599–629. Springer, Cham (2017). https://doi.org/10.1007/978-3-319-63688-7_20
25. Okamoto, T., Takashima, K.: Fully secure functional encryption with general relations from the decisional linear assumption. In: Rabin, T. (ed.) CRYPTO 2010. LNCS, vol. 6223, pp. 191–208. Springer, Heidelberg (2010). https://doi.org/10.1007/978-3-642-14623-7_11
26. Okamoto, T., Takashima, K.: Fully secure unbounded inner-product and attribute-based encryption. In: Wang, X., Sako, K. (eds.) ASIACRYPT 2012. LNCS, vol. 7658, pp. 349–366. Springer, Heidelberg (2012). https://doi.org/10.1007/978-3-642-34961-4_22
27. O'Neill, A.: Definitional issues in functional encryption. Cryptology ePrint Archive, Report 2010/556 (2010). http://eprint.iacr.org/2010/556

28. Tomida, J., Abe, M., Okamoto, T.: Efficient functional encryption for inner-product values with full-hiding security. In: Bishop, M., Nascimento, A.C.A. (eds.) ISC 2016. LNCS, vol. 9866, pp. 408–425. Springer, Cham (2016). https://doi.org/10.1007/978-3-319-45871-7_24
29. Waters, B.: Dual system encryption: realizing fully secure IBE and HIBE under simple assumptions. In: Halevi, S. (ed.) CRYPTO 2009. LNCS, vol. 5677, pp. 619–636. Springer, Heidelberg (2009). https://doi.org/10.1007/978-3-642-03356-8_36
30. Waters, B.: A punctured programming approach to adaptively secure functional encryption. In: Gennaro, R., Robshaw, M. (eds.) CRYPTO 2015, Part II. LNCS, vol. 9216, pp. 678–697. Springer, Heidelberg (2015). https://doi.org/10.1007/978-3-662-48000-7_33
31. Wee, H.: Dual system encryption via predicate encodings. In: Lindell, Y. (ed.) TCC 2014. LNCS, vol. 8349, pp. 616–637. Springer, Heidelberg (2014). https://doi.org/10.1007/978-3-642-54242-8_26

Adaptively Simulation-Secure Attribute-Hiding Predicate Encryption

Pratish Datta[1(✉)], Tatsuaki Okamoto[1], and Katsuyuki Takashima[2]

[1] NTT Secure Platform Laboratories,
3-9-11 Midori-cho, Musashino-shi, Tokyo 180-8585, Japan
pratish.datta.yg@hco.ntt.co.jp, tatsuaki.okamoto@gmail.com
[2] Mitsubishi Electric, 5-1-1 Ofuna, Kamakura, Kanagawa 247-8501, Japan
Takashima.Katsuyuki@aj.MitsubishiElectric.co.jp

Abstract. This paper demonstrates how to achieve *simulation-based strong attribute hiding* against *adaptive* adversaries for *predicate encryption* (PE) schemes supporting *expressive* predicate families under *standard* computational assumptions in bilinear groups. Our main result is a *simulation-based adaptively strongly partially-hiding* PE (PHPE) scheme for predicates computing *arithmetic branching programs* (ABP) on *public* attributes, followed by an *inner-product predicate* on *private* attributes. This simultaneously generalizes attribute-based encryption (ABE) for boolean formulas and ABP's as well as strongly attribute-hiding PE schemes for inner products. The proposed scheme is proven secure for *any a priori bounded* number of ciphertexts and an *unbounded* (polynomial) number of decryption keys, which is the *best possible* in the simulation-based adaptive security framework. This directly implies that our construction also achieves *indistinguishability-based strongly partially-hiding* security against adversaries requesting an *unbounded* (polynomial) number of ciphertexts and decryption keys. The security of the proposed scheme is derived under (asymmetric version of) the *well-studied decisional linear* (DLIN) assumption. Our work resolves an open problem posed by Wee in TCC 2017, where his result was limited to the *semi-adaptive* setting. Moreover, our result advances the current state of the art in both the fields of simulation-based and indistinguishability-based strongly attribute-hiding PE schemes. Our main technical contribution lies in extending the strong attribute hiding methodology of Okamoto and Takashima [EUROCRYPT 2012, ASIACRYPT 2012] to the framework of simulation-based security and beyond inner products.

Keywords: Predicate encryption · Partially-hiding
Simulation-based adaptive security · Arithmetic branching programs
Inner products

1 Introduction

Functional encryption (FE) is a new vision of modern cryptography that aims to overcome the potential limitation of the traditional encryption schemes, namely, the all or nothing control over decryption capabilities. FE supports restricted

T. Peyrin and S. Galbraith (Eds.): ASIACRYPT 2018, LNCS 11273, pp. 640–672, 2018.
https://doi.org/10.1007/978-3-030-03329-3_22

decryption keys which enable decrypters to learn specific functions of encrypted messages, and nothing else. More precisely, a (public-key) FE scheme for a function family $\mathcal{F}$ involves a setup authority which holds a master secret key and publishes public system parameters. An encrypter uses the public parameters to encrypt its message M belonging to some supported message space $\mathbb{M}$, creating a ciphertext CT. A decrypter may obtain a private decryption key $\text{SK}(F)$ for some function $F \in \mathcal{F}$ from the setup authority, provided the authority deems that the decrypter is entitled for that key. Such a decryption key $\text{SK}(F)$ can be used to decrypt CT to recover $F(M)$, but nothing more about M.

The most intuitive security requirement for an FE scheme is *collusion resistance*, i.e., a group of decrypters cannot jointly retrieve any more information about an encrypted message beyond the union of what each of them is allowed to learn individually. This intuitive notion has been formalized by Boneh et al. [12] and O'Neill [37] in two distinct frameworks, namely, (a) *indistinguishability-based security* and (b) *simulation-based security*. The former stipulates that distinguishing encryptions of any two messages is infeasible for a group of colluders which do not have a decryption key that decrypts the ciphertext to distinct values. The latter, on the other hand, stipulates the existence of a polynomial-time simulator that given $F_1(M), \ldots, F_{q_{\text{KEY}}}(M)$ for any message $M \in \mathbb{M}$ and functions $F_1, \ldots, F_{q_{\text{KEY}}} \in \mathcal{F}$, outputs the view of the colluders which are given an encryption of M together with decryption keys for $F_1, \ldots, F_{q_{\text{KEY}}}$. Both of the above notions can be further refined, depending on how the queries of the adversary to the decryption key generation and encryption oracles depend on one another as well as on the public parameters of the system, as *adaptive* vs *semi-adaptive* vs *selective*. Boneh et al. [12] and O'Neill [37] showed that in general, simulation-based security provides a stronger guarantee than indistinguishability-based security, i.e., simulation-based security of some kind, e.g., adaptive, semi-adaptive, or selective, implies indistinguishability-based security of the same kind; but the converse does not hold in general. In fact, Boneh et al. pointed out that indistinguishability-based security is vacuous for certain circuit families, which indicates that we should opt for simulation-based security whenever possible. On the other hand, it is known that while security for single and multiple ciphertexts are equivalent in the indistinguishability-based setting [12], this is not the case in the simulation-based setting [3,9,12,16]. In particular, it has been demonstrated by Boneh et al. [12] that in the adaptive or semi-adaptive simulation-based setting, where the adversary is allowed to make decryption key queries even after receiving the queried ciphertexts, achieving security for an unbounded number of ciphertexts is impossible.

An important subclass of FE is *predicate encryption* (PE). In recent years, with the rapid advancement of Internet communication and cloud technology, there has been an emerging trend among individuals and organizations to outsource potentially sensitive private data to external untrusted servers, and to perform selective computations on the outsourced data by remotely querying the server at some later point in time, or to share specific portions of the outsourced data to other parties of choice. PE is an indispensable tool for performing such operations on outsourced sensitive data without compromising the confidentiality of the data.

Consider a predicate family $R = \{R(Y, \cdot) : \mathcal{X} \rightarrow \{0,1\} \mid Y \in \mathcal{Y}\}$, where $\mathcal{X}$ and $\mathcal{Y}$ are two collections of indices or attributes. In a PE scheme for some predicate family R, the associated message space $\mathbb{M}$ is of the form $\mathcal{X} \times \mathcal{M}$, where $\mathcal{M}$ contains the actual payloads. The functionality F_{R_Y} associated with a predicate $R(Y, \cdot) \in R$ is defined as $F_{R_Y}(X, \mathsf{msg}) = \mathsf{msg}$ if $R(Y, X) = 1$, or in other words, Y is authorized for X, and $F_{R_Y}(X, \mathsf{msg}) = \perp$ (a special empty string) if $R(Y, X) = 0$, or in other words, Y is not authorized for X for all $(X, \mathsf{msg}) \in \mathbb{M} = \mathcal{X} \times \mathcal{M}$.

The standard security notion for FE described above, when adopted in the context of PE, stipulates that recovering the payload from a ciphertext generated with respect to some attribute $X \in \mathcal{X}$ should be infeasible for a group of colluders none of which possesses a decryption key corresponding to an attribute authorized for X, also referred to as an authorized decryption key; and moreover, the ciphertext should conceal X from any group of colluders, even those in possession of authorized decryption keys. In the context of PE, this security notion is referred to as *strongly attribute-hiding* security. A weakening of the above notion, called *weakly attribute-hiding* security requires that X should only remain hidden to colluders in possession of unauthorized keys. An even weaker notion, which only demands the payload to remain hidden to colluders with unauthorized keys, is known as *payload-hiding* security, and a payload-hiding PE scheme is often referred to as an *attribute-based encryption* (ABE) scheme in the literature.

Over the last decade, a long sequence of works have developed extremely powerful techniques for realizing indistinguishability-based ABE and weakly attribute-hiding PE schemes supporting more and more expressive predicate families under well-studied computational assumptions in bilinear groups and lattices, culminating into schemes that can now support general polynomial-size circuits [7,11,14,19,20,22,26,30,31,33,34,41]. However, very little is known for strongly attribute-hiding PE schemes, even in the indistinguishability-based setting. The situation is even worse when security against an unbounded (polynomial) number of authorized-key-possessing colluders under standard computational assumption is considered. In fact, until very recently, the known candidates were restricted to only inner products or even simpler predicates [13,16,29,32,34,36], out of which the schemes designed in the more efficient and secure prime order bilinear groups being only the works of Okamoto and Takashima [32,34,36]. One big reason for this state of the art is that unlike payload-hiding or weakly attribute-hiding, for proving strongly attribute-hiding security, one must argue about an adversary that gets hold of authorized decryption keys, something cryptographers do not have a good understanding of so far. Moreover, there are indeed reasons to believe that constructing strongly attribute-hiding PE schemes for sufficiently expressive predicate classes such as NC^1 under standard computational assumptions could be very difficult. In fact, it is known that a strongly attribute-hiding PE scheme for NC^1 predicates, even in the weakest selective setting, can lead all the way to indistinguishability

obfuscation (IO) for general circuits, the new holy grail of modern cryptography [5,6,10]. In view of this state of affairs, it is natural to ask the following important question:
Can we realize "the best of both worlds", i.e., can we design PE *scheme for some sufficiently expressive predicate family (e.g.,* NC^1*) that is secure against an unbounded (polynomial) number of colluders under standard computational assumptions (without* IO*), such that the strongly attribute-hiding guarantee holds for a limited segment (e.g., one belonging to some subclass of* NC^1*) of each predicate in the predicate family?*

Towards answering this question, in TCC 2017, Wee [40] put forward a new PE scheme for an NC^1 predicate family in bilinear groups of prime order that is secure against an unbounded (polynomial) number of colluders under the well-studied *k-linear* (k-LIN) assumption, where the strongly attribute-hiding property is achieved only for an inner product evaluating segment of each predicate of the predicate class. More precisely, in his proposed PE system, the ciphertext attribute set $\mathcal{X}$ is given by $\mathbb{F}_q^{n'} \times \mathbb{F}_q^n$ for some finite field $\mathbb{F}_q$ and $n', n \in \mathbb{N}$, while the decryption key attribute set $\mathcal{Y}$ is given by the function family $\mathcal{F}_{\text{ABP}\circ\text{IP}}^{(q,n',n)}$. Any function $f \in \mathcal{F}_{\text{ABP}\circ\text{IP}}^{(q,n',n)}$ operates on a pair $(\vec{x}, \vec{z}) \in \mathbb{F}_q^{n'} \times \mathbb{F}_q^n$ by first computing n arithmetic branching programs (ABP) $f_1, \ldots, f_n : \mathbb{F}_q^{n'} \to \mathbb{F}_q$ on $\vec{x}$ to obtain a vector $(f_1(\vec{x}), \ldots, f_n(\vec{x})) \in \mathbb{F}_q^n$, and then evaluating the inner product of the computed vector and $\vec{z}$. The predicate family $R^{\text{ABP}\circ\text{IP}}$ associated with the PE scheme is defined as $R^{\text{ABP}\circ\text{IP}} = \{R^{\text{ABP}\circ\text{IP}}(f, (\cdot, \cdot)) : \mathbb{F}_q^{n'} \times \mathbb{F}_q^n \to \{0,1\} \mid f \in \mathcal{F}_{\text{ABP}\circ\text{IP}}^{(q,n',n)}\}$, where $R^{\text{ABP}\circ\text{IP}}(f, (\vec{x}, \vec{z})) = 1$ if $f(\vec{x}, \vec{z}) = 0$, and 0 if $f(\vec{x}, \vec{z}) \neq 0$ for any $f \in \mathcal{F}_{\text{ABP}\circ\text{IP}}^{(q,n',n)}$ and $(\vec{x}, \vec{z}) \in \mathbb{F}_q^{n'} \times \mathbb{F}_q^n$. The security property of Wee's PE scheme guarantees that other than hiding the payload, a ciphertext generated for some attribute pair $(\vec{x}, \vec{z}) \in \mathbb{F}_q^{n'} \times \mathbb{F}_q^n$ also conceals the attribute $\vec{z}$ (but not the attribute $\vec{x}$). Moreover, the concealment of the attribute $\vec{z}$ is strong, i.e., even against colluders possessing authorized keys. Wee termed this security notion as *strongly partially-hiding* security, while the attributes $\vec{x} \in \mathbb{F}_q^{n'}$ and $\vec{z} \in \mathbb{F}_q^n$ as the *public* and *private* attributes respectively.

This PE scheme simultaneously generalizes ABE for boolean formulas and ABP's, as well as strongly attribute-hiding inner-product PE (IPE). For instance, unlike standard IPE schemes, where an inner-product predicate is evaluated between the (private) attribute vector $\vec{z}$ associated with a ciphertext and the attribute vector $\vec{y}$ hardwired within a decryption key, this PE scheme evaluates inner-product predicate between $\vec{z}$ and $\vec{y}$ obtained as the result of complicated ABP computations on a public attribute string $\vec{x}$, which is now associated in addition to the private attribute vector $\vec{z}$ with the ciphertext. This in turn means that this PE scheme can be deployed in richer variants of the applications captured by IPE schemes. For example, it is well-known that inner-product predicates can be used to evaluate conjunctive comparison predicates of the form $R^{\text{COMP}}((c_1, \ldots, c_n), (z_1, \ldots, z_n)) = \bigwedge_{j \in [n]} [z_j \geq c_j]$, where c_j's and z_j's lie in polynomial-size domains [13]. In case of standard IPE schemes, $c_1, \ldots, c_n$ are fixed constants which are specified within the decryption key. On the contrary, in case of a PE scheme for $R^{\mathrm{ABP}\circ\mathrm{IP}}$, we can carry out more complex computation, where instead of being fixed constants, $c_1, \ldots, c_n$ can be derived as the outputs of ABP evaluations on public ciphertext attributes. Of course, fixed $c_1, \ldots, c_n$ is a special case of this more expressive computation, since one can have ABP's that ignore the public ciphertext attributes, and simply output hardwired constants. Similarly, standard IPE schemes can be employed for evaluating polynomials with constant coefficients, where the coefficients are specified within the decryption keys [29]. In contrast, in case of a PE scheme for $R^{\mathrm{ABP}\circ\mathrm{IP}}$, the polynomial coefficients can be generated as outputs of ABP computations on public ciphertext attributes.

Partially-hiding PE (PHPE) schemes for similar type of predicate families were considered in [2,19] in the lattice setting, and those PHPE schemes are in fact capable of evaluating general polynomial-size circuits, as opposed to ABP's in Wee's construction, over public ciphertext attributes prior to evaluating inner-product predicates over private ciphertext attributes. However, those constructions are either only weakly partially-hiding, i.e., the security of the private attributes of the ciphertexts are only guaranteed against unauthorized colluders [19], or strongly partially-hiding against a priori bounded number of authorized colluders [2]. In contrast, Wee's PHPE scheme is strongly partially-hiding against an unbounded (polynomial) number of authorized colluders. Another strong aspect of the PHPE construction of Wee is that its security is proven in the (unbounded) simulation-based framework [3], while except [16], all prior PE constructions with strongly attribute-hiding security against an unbounded (polynomial) number of authorized colluders were proven in the weaker indistinguishability-based framework.

However, the PHPE scheme proposed by Wee [40] only achieves semi-adaptive security [15], i.e., against an adversary that is restricted to submit its ciphertext queries immediately after viewing the public parameters, and can make decryption key queries only after that. While semi-adaptive security seems somewhat stronger, it has recently been shown by Goyal et al. [21] that it is essentially equivalent to the selective security, the weakest notion of security in which the adversary is bound to declare its ciphertext queries even before the system is setup. Their result also indicates that the gap between semi-adaptive and adaptive security, the strongest and most reasonable notion in which the adversary is allowed to make ciphertext and decryption key queries at any point during the security experiment, is in fact much wider than was previously thought. While Ananth et al. [4] have demonstrated how to generically transform an FE scheme that supports arbitrary polynomial-size circuits from selective security to one that achieves adaptive security, their conversion does not work for ABE or PE schemes which fall below this threshold in functionality. In view of this state of affairs, it is interesting to explore *whether it is possible to construct an efficient adaptively simulation-secure strongly partially-hiding* PE *scheme for the predicate family* $R^{\mathrm{ABP}\circ\mathrm{IP}}$ *that is secure against an unbounded (polynomial) number of colluders under well-studied computational assumption.* Note that while several impossibility results exist against the achievability of simulation-based security in certain settings [3,9,12,16], those results do not overrule the existence of such a construction, provided of course we bound the number of allowed ciphertext queries by the adversary. In fact, Wee has posed the realization of such a PHPE construction as an open problem in his paper [40].

Our Contributions. In this paper, we resolve the above open problem. Specifically, our main result is a PE scheme for the predicate family $R^{\mathsf{ABP}\circ\mathsf{IP}}$ that achieves *simulation-based adaptively strongly partially hiding* security against adversaries making *any a priori bounded* number of ciphertext queries while requesting an *unbounded* (polynomial) number of decryption keys both before and after the ciphertext queries, which is the *best* one could hope for in the simulation-based framework when the adversary is allowed to make decryption key queries even after making the ciphertext queries [12]. From the relation between simulation-based and indistinguishability-based security as well as that between single and multiple ciphertext security in the indistinguishability-based setting as mentioned above, it is immediate that the proposed scheme is also *adaptively strongly partially-hiding* in the *indistinguishability-based* framework against adversaries making an *unbounded* number of queries to both the encryption and the decryption key generation oracles. Thus, our work advances the state of the art in both the fields of simulation-based and indistinguishability-based strongly attribute-hiding PE schemes. Our construction is built in *asymmetric* bilinear groups of *prime* order. The security of our PHPE scheme is derived under the *simultaneous external decisional linear* (SXDLIN) assumption [1,38], which is a natural extension of the *well-studied decisional linear* (DLIN) assumption in asymmetric bilinear group setting, and as noted in [1], the two assumptions are in fact *equivalent* in the generic bilinear group model. Nevertheless, our scheme can be readily generalized to one that is secure under the k-LIN assumption.

Similar to [40], we only consider security against a single ciphertext query for the construction presented in this paper to keep the exposition simple. However, we explain in Remark 3.1 how our techniques can be readily extended to design a PHPE scheme that is secure for any a priori bounded number of ciphertexts. Following [16], here we present our construction in the attribute-only mode (i.e., without any actual payload). However, in the full version of this paper we also provide a key-encapsulation mechanism (KEM) version (i.e., one that uses a symmetric session key as the payload) of our scheme similar to [40]. For the attribute-only version, we design a simulator that runs in polynomial time, and thus this version of our scheme is secure in the standard simulation-based security framework. On the other hand, for the KEM version, similar to Wee [40], our simulator needs to perform a brute force discrete log computation, and thus requires super-polynomial (e.g., sub-exponential) computational power. Nonetheless, this is still stronger than the indistinguishability-based framework [3,40].

In terms of efficiency, our PHPE scheme is fairly practical. The length of ciphertexts and decryption keys of our scheme grow linearly with the total length of the associated attribute strings and the ABP-size of the associated functions respectively. This is the same as that of [40] except for a constant blow-up, which is common in the literature for semi-adaptive vs adaptive security. Moreover, asymmetric bilinear groups of prime order, which are used for implementing our scheme, are now considered to be both faster and more secure in the cryptographic community following the recent progress in analysing bilinear groups of composite order [17,23] and symmetric bilinear groups instantiated with elliptic curves of small characteristics [8,18,27,28].

As a byproduct of our main result, we also obtain the *first simulation-based* adaptively strongly attribute-hiding IPE scheme in asymmetric bilinear groups of prime order under the SXDLIN assumption. The only prior simulation-based strongly attribute-hiding IPE scheme, also due to Wee [40], only achieves semi-adaptive security.

On the technical side, our approach is completely different from that of Wee [40]. More precisely, Wee's technique consists of two steps, namely, first building a private-key scheme, and then bootstrapping it to a public-key one by applying a private-key to public-key compiler similar to [14,41], built on Water's dual system encryption methodology [39]. In contrast, we *directly* construct our scheme in the public-key setting by extending the technique of Okamoto and Takashima [32,34,36], a more sophisticated methodology than the dual system encryption originally developed for designing adaptively strongly attribute-hiding IPE schemes in the indistinguishability-based setting, to the scenario of simulation-based adaptively strongly attribute-hiding security for a much expressive predicate class. Also, in order to incorporate the information of the session keys within the ciphertexts in the KEM version of our scheme, which is presented in the full version of this paper, we adopt an idea along the lines of the works of Okamoto and Takashima [32,34,36], that deviates from that of Wee [40]. Thus, our work further demonstrates the power of the technique introduced by Okamoto and Takashima [32,34,36] in achieving very strong security for highly expressive predicate families. We also believe that our work will shed further light on one of the longstanding questions of modern cryptography:
What is the most expressive function or predicate family for which it is possible to construct FE *or strongly attribute-hiding* PE *schemes with adaptive security against adversaries making an unbounded (polynomial) number of decryption key queries under standard computational assumptions?*

Overview of Our Techniques. We now proceed to explain the key technical ideas underlying our construction. For simplicity, here we will only deal with the IPE scheme, which is a special case of our PHPE construction for $R^{\mathrm{ABP}\circ\mathrm{IP}}$. The proposed PHPE scheme for $R^{\mathrm{ABP}\circ\mathrm{IP}}$ is obtained via a more sophisticated application of the techniques described in this section, and is formally presented in full details in the sequel.

In this overview, we will consider IPE in the attribute-only mode. For IPE, the ciphertext attribute set $\mathcal{X} = \mathbb{F}_q^n$, the decryption key attribute set $\mathcal{Y} = \mathbb{F}_q^n$ for some finite field $\mathbb{F}_q$ and $n \in \mathbb{N}$, and the predicate family is given by $R^{\mathrm{IP}} = \{R^{\mathrm{IP}}(\vec{y}, \cdot) : \mathbb{F}_q^n \to \{0,1\} \mid \vec{y} \in \mathbb{F}_q^n\}$, where $R^{\mathrm{IP}}(\vec{y}, \vec{z}) = 1$ if $\vec{z} \cdot \vec{y} = 0$, and 0, if

$\vec{z} \cdot \vec{y} \neq 0$ for any $\vec{z}, \vec{y} \in \mathbb{F}_q^n$. Observe that the predicate family R^{IP} is subclass of the predicate family $R^{\text{ABP}\circ\text{IP}}$, where we set $n' = 0$, and the component ABP's $f_1, \ldots, f_n$ of a function $f \in \mathcal{F}_{\text{ABP}\circ\text{IP}}^{(q,n',n)}$ to simply output hardwired constants. In the attribute-only mode, a ciphertext is associated with only a vector $\vec{z} \in \mathbb{F}_q^n$ but no payload, and decryption with a key for some vector $\vec{y} \in \mathbb{F}_q^n$ only reveals the predicate, i.e., whether $\vec{z} \cdot \vec{y} = 0$ or not, but not the exact value of $\vec{z} \cdot \vec{y}$.

Just like [32,34,36], we make use of the machinery of the *dual pairing vector spaces* (DPVS) [33,35]. A highly powerful feature of DPVS is that one can completely or partially hide a linear subspace of the whole vector space by concealing the basis of that subspace or the basis of its dual from the public parameters respectively. In DPVS-based constructions, a pair of mutually dual vector spaces $\mathbb{V}_1$ and $\mathbb{V}_2$, along with a bilinear pairing $e : \mathbb{V}_1 \times \mathbb{V}_2 \rightarrow \mathbb{G}_T$ constructed from a standard bilinear group $(q, \mathbb{G}_1, \mathbb{G}_2, \mathbb{G}_T, g_1, g_2, e)$ of prime order q is used. Typically a pair of dual orthonormal bases $(\mathbb{B}, \mathbb{B}^*)$ of the vector spaces $(\mathbb{V}_1, \mathbb{V}_2)$ are generated during setup, using random linear transformations, and a portion of $\mathbb{B}$, say $\widehat{\mathbb{B}}$, is used as the public parameters. Thus, the corresponding segment of $\mathbb{B}^*$, say $\widehat{\mathbb{B}}^*$ remains partially hidden (its dual subspace is disclosed), while the part $\mathbb{B} \backslash \widehat{\mathbb{B}}$ of the basis $\mathbb{B}$ and the corresponding portion $\mathbb{B}^* \backslash \widehat{\mathbb{B}}^*$ of the basis $\mathbb{B}^*$ remain completely hidden to an adversary that is given the public parameters, ciphertexts, and decryption keys. This provides a strong framework for various kinds of information-theoretic tricks in the public-key setting by exploiting various nice properties of linear transformations.

In the proposed IPE scheme, we consider a $(4n+1)$-dimensional DPVS. During setup, we generate a random pair of dual orthonormal bases $(\mathbb{B}, \mathbb{B}^*)$, and use as the public parameters the subset $\widehat{\mathbb{B}}$ consisting of the first n and the last $n+1$ vectors of the basis $\mathbb{B}$, while as the master secret key the corresponding portion of the dual basis $\mathbb{B}^*$. Thus, the linear subspaces spanned by the remaining $2n$ vectors of the bases $\mathbb{B}$ and $\mathbb{B}^*$ are kept completely hidden. Intuitively, we will use the first n-dimensional subspaces of these $2n$-dimensional subspaces for simulating the post-ciphertext decryption key queries, while the latter n-dimensional subspaces for simulating the pre-ciphertext decryption key queries in the ideal experiment. A ciphertext for some vector $\vec{z} \in \mathbb{F}_q^n$ in the proposed scheme has the form $\text{CT} = \boldsymbol{c}$ such that

$$\boldsymbol{c} = (\omega \vec{z}, \vec{0}^n, \vec{0}^n, \vec{0}^n, \varphi)_{\mathbb{B}},$$

where $\omega, \varphi \xleftarrow{\mathsf{U}} \mathbb{F}_q$, and $(\vec{v})_{\mathbb{W}}$ represents the linear combination of the elements of $\mathbb{W}$ with the entries of $\vec{v}$ as coefficients for any $\vec{v} \in \mathbb{F}_q^n$ and any basis $\mathbb{W}$ of DPVS. Similarly, a decryption key corresponding to some vector $\vec{y} \in \mathbb{F}_q^n$ is given by $\text{SK}(\vec{y}) = (\vec{y}, \boldsymbol{k})$ such that

$$\boldsymbol{k} = (\zeta \vec{y}, \vec{0}^n, \vec{0}^n, \vec{\kappa}, 0)_{\mathbb{B}^*},$$

where $\zeta \xleftarrow{\mathsf{U}} \mathbb{F}_q$ and $\vec{\kappa} \xleftarrow{\mathsf{U}} \mathbb{F}_q^n$. Decryption computes $e(\boldsymbol{c}, \boldsymbol{k})$ to obtain $g_T^{\omega\zeta(\vec{z}\cdot\vec{y})} \in \mathbb{G}_T$, which equals to the identity element of the group $\mathbb{G}_T$ if $\vec{z} \cdot \vec{y} = 0$, and a uniformly random element of $\mathbb{G}_T$ if $\vec{z} \cdot \vec{y} \neq 0$. Observe that this IPE construction is essentially the same as that presented by Okamoto and Takashima in [32]. However, they only proved the strongly attribute-hiding security of this construction in the indistinguishability-based framework, while we prove this construction to be strongly attribute-hiding in the simulation-based framework, by extending their techniques. Let us start with describing our simulation strategy.

In the semi-adaptive case, as considered in [40], the simulation strategy is relatively simple. In fact, for designing an IPE in the semi-adaptive setting, only a $(3n+1)$-dimensional DPVS with n-dimensional hidden subspace would suffice. Note that in the semi-adaptive setting, the adversary is restricted to make the ciphertext query immediately after seeing the public parameters, and there is no pre-ciphertext decryption key query. So, in the semi-adaptive setting, when the adversary makes a ciphertext query, the simulator has no constraint arising from the pre-ciphertext queries of the adversary, and can simply simulate the ciphertext as $\text{CT} = \boldsymbol{c}$ such that

$$\boldsymbol{c} = (\vec{0}^n, (\vec{0}^{n-1}, \tau), \vec{0}^n, \varphi)_{\mathbb{B}},$$

where $\tau, \varphi \xleftarrow{\mathsf{U}} \mathbb{F}_q$, i.e., the simulator puts nothing in the subspace spanned by the public segment of the basis $\mathbb{B}$, and merely puts a random value in a one-dimensional subspace spanned by the hidden segment of the basis. Later, when the adversary queries a decryption key for some vector $\vec{y} \in \mathbb{F}_q^n$, the simulator gets $\vec{y}$ along with the inner product relation of $\vec{y}$ with $\vec{z}$, and the simulator can simply hardwire this information in the corresponding hidden subspace of the decryption key. More precisely, it can simply generate the decryption key as $\text{SK}(\vec{y}) = (\vec{y}, \boldsymbol{k})$ such that

$$\boldsymbol{k} = (\zeta\vec{y}, (\vec{\eta}, \nu), \vec{\kappa}, 0)_{\mathbb{B}^*},$$

where $\zeta \xleftarrow{\mathsf{U}} \mathbb{F}_q$, $\vec{\eta} \xleftarrow{\mathsf{U}} \mathbb{F}_q^{n-1}$, $\vec{\kappa} \xleftarrow{\mathsf{U}} \mathbb{F}_q^n$, and $\nu = 0$ if $\vec{z} \cdot \vec{y} = 0$, and $\nu \xleftarrow{\mathsf{U}} \mathbb{F}_q$ if $\vec{z} \cdot \vec{y} \neq 0$. Observe that when the simulated ciphertext is decrypted using this simulated decryption key, one obtains the identity element of $\mathbb{G}_T$, or a random element of $\mathbb{G}_T$ according as the inner product relation is satisfied or not, i.e., decryption correctness clearly holds. At this point, please note that the simulator cannot put anything in the subspace of the ciphertext corresponding to the public segment of $\mathbb{B}$, since it must put the actual attribute vectors in the corresponding dual subspace of the decryption keys to ensure correct decryption with other honestly generated ciphertexts.

In the adaptive setting, the situation is much more complex, and we need a $(4n+1)$-dimensional DPVS with $2n$-dimensional hidden subspace. Now, the simulator should also correctly simulate the pre-ciphertext decryption key queries of the adversary. The difference between the pre-ciphertext and post-ciphertext decryption key queries is that unlike the post-ciphertext ones, the information about whether the inner product relation between the associated attribute vector and the attribute vector $\vec{z}$ corresponding to the ciphertext query of the adversary is not supplied when the decryption key is queried. In fact, $\vec{z}$ is not even declared at that time. On the contrary, the information about predicate satisfaction for all the pre-ciphertext decryption key vectors become available to the simulator when the ciphertext query is made by the adversary. The main hurdle for the simulator is to compactly embed this huge amount of information (note that we are considering an unbounded number of pre-ciphertext decryption key queries) in the simulated ciphertext, so that when the simulated ciphertext is decrypted using any pre-ciphertext decryption key, one should get the proper information about predicate satisfaction.

Towards overcoming this difficulty, we observe that it has already been demonstrated by O'Neill [37] that the inner-product predicate family is *pre-image samplable*, i.e., given a set of vectors and their inner-product relation with another fixed vector (but not the vector itself), one can efficiently sample a vector that satisfies all those inner-product relations with high probability. To simulate the ciphertext queried by the adversary, our simulator does exactly this, i.e., it samples a vector $\vec{s} \in \mathbb{F}_q^n$ that has the same inner-product relations as the original queried ciphertext attribute vector $\vec{z}$ with all the attribute vectors corresponding to the pre-ciphertext decryption key queries of the adversary. However, $\vec{s}$ may not have the same inner-product relation as $\vec{z}$ with the attribute vectors corresponding to the post-ciphertext decryption key queries. Therefore, it cannot be embedded in the hidden subspace of the ciphertext devoted for handling the post-ciphertext decryption key queries. Therefore, the simulator needs another n-dimensional subspace to embed $\vec{s}$. Thus, the simulator simulates the queried ciphertext as $\mathrm{CT} = \boldsymbol{c}$ such that

$$\boldsymbol{c} = (\vec{0}^n, (\vec{0}^{n-1}, \tau), \theta\vec{s}, \vec{0}^n, \varphi)_{\mathbb{B}},$$

where $\theta \xleftarrow{\mathsf{U}} \mathbb{F}_q$. On the other hand, it simulates a decryption key corresponding to some vector $\vec{y} \in \mathbb{F}_q^n$ as $\mathrm{SK}(\vec{y}) = (\vec{y}, \boldsymbol{k})$ such that

$$\boldsymbol{k} = \begin{cases} (\zeta\vec{y}, \vec{0}^n, \widehat{\zeta}\vec{y}, \vec{\kappa}, 0)_{\mathbb{B}^*} & \text{(pre-ciphertext)}, \\ (\zeta\vec{y}, (\vec{\eta}, \nu), \vec{0}^n, \vec{\kappa}, 0)_{\mathbb{B}^*} & \text{(post-ciphertext)}, \end{cases}$$

where $\zeta, \widehat{\zeta} \xleftarrow{\mathsf{U}} \mathbb{F}_q$.

Here, we would like to emphasize that while we make use of the pre-image samplability property introduced by O'Neill [37] to design our simulator, our result is not a mere special case of the result that O'Neill obtained using that property. Specifically, O'Neill showed that indistinguishability-based and simulation-based security notions are equivalent in case of FE schemes for function families which are pre-image samplable, provided the adversary is constrained from making any decryption key query after making a ciphertext query. His result does not apply if the adversary is allowed to make decryption key queries even after making ciphertext queries, as is the case in this paper. Moreover, note that there is no known PE scheme for the predicate family $R^{\mathrm{ABP}\circ\mathrm{IP}}$, the actual focus of this paper, even with indistinguishability-based strongly partially-hiding security against adversaries that are allowed to make decryption key queries prior to making ciphertext queries.

Let us continue with the technical overview. It remains to argue that the above simulated forms of ciphertexts and decryption keys are indistinguishable from their real forms. In order to accomplish these changes, we design elaborate hybrid transitions over different forms of ciphertext and decryption keys. In fact, the $2n$-dimensional hidden subspace not only allows us to simulate the pre-ciphertext and post-ciphertext queries differently, but are also crucially leveraged to realize the various forms of ciphertext and decryption keys throughout our hybrid transitions. The hybrid transitions are alternatively computational and information-theoretic. Also, note that not only our simulation strategy for pre-ciphertext and post-ciphertext decryption key queries are different, rather in our hybrid transitions, we handle the pre-ciphertext and post-ciphertext decryption key queries differently, and thereby achieve a security loss that is only proportional to the number of pre-ciphertext decryption key queries.

We start by changing the pre-ciphertext decryption keys to their simulated form. For making these changes, we use the first n-dimensional subspace of the $2n$-dimensional hidden subspace as the *working space*, where we generate the simulated components, and the next n-dimensional subspace as the *storing space*, where we transfer and store the simulated components once they are generated. Note that in the simulated pre-ciphertext decryption keys, the additional simulated components are placed in the second n-dimensions subspace of the $2n$-dimensional hidden subspace. For the hybrid transitions of this part, we make use of the first two of the three types of information-theoretic tricks, namely, Type I, Type II, and Type III introduced in [32,34,36], in conjunction with the three types of computational tricks based on the SXDLIN assumption also used in those works. The Type I trick is to apply a linear transformation inside a hidden subspace on the ciphertext side, while the more complex Type II trick is to apply a linear transformation inside a hidden subspace on the ciphertext side preserving the predicate relation with the entries in the corresponding dual subspace of a specific decryption key.

After the transformation of the pre-ciphertext queries is completed, we turn our attention to vanish the component of the ciphertext in the subspace spanned by the public portion of the basis $\mathbb{B}$. For doing this, we apply one of the three computational tricks followed by a Type III information-theoretic trick, which amounts to applying a linear transformation across a hidden and a partially public subspace on both the ciphertext and decryption key sides. While, this enables us to achieve our target for the ciphertext, the forms of the pre-ciphertext decryption keys get distorted. To bring the pre-ciphertext decryption keys to their correct simulated form, we then apply an extension of one of the computational tricks mentioned above.

Once the component in the public subspace of the ciphertext is vanished and pre-ciphertext decryption keys are brought back to their correct simulated form, we turn our attention to the post-cipertext decryption keys. Note that the Type III trick applied for the ciphertext, has already altered the forms of the post-ciphertext queries to something else. Starting with these modified forms, we apply a more carefully crafted variant of the Type II information-theoretic trick, followed by another computational trick based on the SXDLIN assumption to alter the post-ciphertext decryption keys to their simulated forms. This step is reminiscent of the *one-dimensional localization of the inner-product values* used in [36]. This step also alters the ciphertext to its simulated form. At this point we arrive at the simulated experiment, and our security analysis gets complete.

2 Preliminaries

In this section we present the backgrounds required for the rest of this paper.

2.1 Notations

Let $\lambda \in \mathbb{N}$ denotes the security parameter and 1^λ be its unary encoding. Let $\mathbb{F}_q$ for any prime $q \in \mathbb{N}$, denotes the finite field of integers modulo q. For $d \in \mathbb{N}$ and $c \in \mathbb{N} \cup \{0\}$ (with $c < d$), we let $[d] = \{1, \ldots, d\}$ and $[c, d] = \{c, \ldots, d\}$. For any set Z, $z \xleftarrow{\mathsf{U}} Z$ represents the process of uniformly sampling an element z from the set Z, and $\sharp Z$ signifies the size or cardinality of Z. For a probabilistic algorithm $\mathcal{U}$, we denote by $\Pi = \mathcal{U}(\Theta; \Phi)$ the output of $\mathcal{U}$ on input Θ with the content of the random tape being Φ, while by $\Pi \xleftarrow{\mathsf{R}} \mathcal{U}(\Theta)$ the process of sampling Π from the output distribution of $\mathcal{U}$ with a uniform random tape on input Θ. Similarly, for any deterministic algorithm $\mathcal{V}$, we write $\Pi = \mathcal{V}(\Theta)$ to denote the output of $\mathcal{V}$ on input Θ. We use the abbreviation PPT to mean probabilistic polynomial-time. We assume that all the algorithms are given the unary representation 1^λ of the security parameter λ as input and will not write 1^λ explicitly as input of the algorithms when it is clear from the context. For any finite field $\mathbb{F}_q$ and $d \in \mathbb{N}$, let $\vec{v}$ denotes the (row) vector $(v_1, \ldots, v_d) \in \mathbb{F}_q^d$, where $v_i \in \mathbb{F}_q$ for all $i \in [d]$. The all zero vectors in $\mathbb{F}_q^d$ will be denoted by $\vec{0}^d$. For any two vectors $\vec{v}, \vec{w} \in \mathbb{F}_q^d$, $\vec{v} \cdot \vec{w}$ stands for the inner product of the vectors $\vec{v}$ and $\vec{w}$, i.e., $\vec{v} \cdot \vec{w} = \sum_{i \in [d]} v_i w_i \in \mathbb{F}_q$. For any multiplicative cyclic group $\mathbb{G}$ of order q and any generator $g \in \mathbb{G}$, let $\boldsymbol{v}$ represents a d-dimensional (row) vector of group elements, i.e., $\boldsymbol{v} = (g^{v_1}, \ldots, g^{v_d}) \in \mathbb{G}^d$ for some $d \in \mathbb{N}$, where $\vec{v} = (v_1, \ldots, v_d) \in \mathbb{F}_q^d$. We use $\boldsymbol{M} = (m_{i,k})$ to represent a matrix with entries $m_{i,k} \in \mathbb{F}_q$. By $\boldsymbol{M}^\intercal$ we will signify the transpose of the matrix $\boldsymbol{M}$. The determinant of a matrix $\boldsymbol{M}$ is denoted by $\det(\boldsymbol{M})$. Let $\mathsf{GL}(d, \mathbb{F}_q)$ denotes the set of all $d \times d$ invertible matrices over $\mathbb{F}_q$. A function $\mathsf{negl} : \mathbb{N} \to \mathbb{R}^+$ is said to be *negligible* if for every $c \in \mathbb{N}$, there exists $T \in \mathbb{N}$ such that for all $\lambda \in \mathbb{N}$ with $\lambda > T$, $|\mathsf{negl}(\lambda)| < 1/\lambda^c$.

2.2 Arithmetic Branching Programs

A *branching program* (BP) Γ is defined by a 5-tuple $\Gamma = (V, E, v_0, v_1, \phi)$, where (V, E) is a directed acyclic graph, $v_0, v_1 \in V$ are two special vertices called the source and the sink respectively, and ϕ is a labeling function for the edges in E. An *arithmetic branching program* (ABP) Γ over a finite field $\mathbb{F}_q$ computes a function $f : \mathbb{F}_q^d \to \mathbb{F}_q$ for some $d \in \mathbb{N}$. In this case, the labeling function ϕ assigns to each edge in E either a degree one polynomial function in one of the input variables with coefficients in $\mathbb{F}_q$ or a constant in $\mathbb{F}_q$. Let $\wp$ be the set of all v_0-v_1 paths in Γ. The output of the function f computed by the ABP Γ on some input $\vec{w} = (w_1, \ldots, w_d) \in \mathbb{F}_q^d$ is defined as $f(\vec{w}) = \sum_{P \in \wp} \left[\prod_{e \in P} \phi(e)|_{\vec{w}} \right]$, where for any $e \in E$, $\phi(e)|_{\vec{w}}$ represents the evaluation of the function $\phi(e)$ at $\vec{w}$. We refer to $\sharp V + \sharp E$ as the size of the ABP Γ. Ishai and Kushilevitz [24,25] showed how to relate the computation performed by an ABP to the computation of the determinant of a matrix.

Lemma 2.1 ([24]): *Given an ABP $\Gamma = (V, E, v_0, v_1, \phi)$ computing a function $f : \mathbb{F}_q^d \to \mathbb{F}_q$, we can efficiently and deterministically compute a function $\mathbf{L}$ mapping an input $\vec{w} \in \mathbb{F}_q^d$ to a $(\sharp V - 1) \times (\sharp V - 1)$ matrix $\mathbf{L}(\vec{w})$ over $\mathbb{F}_q$ such that the following holds:*

- $\det(\mathbf{L}(\vec{w})) = f(\vec{w})$.
- *Each entry of $\mathbf{L}(\vec{w})$ is either a degree one polynomial in a single input variable w_i $(i \in [d])$ with coefficients in $\mathbb{F}_q$ or a constant in $\mathbb{F}_q$.*
- *$\mathbf{L}(\vec{w})$ contains only -1's in the second diagonal, i.e., the diagonal just below the main diagonal, and 0's below the second diagonal.*

Specifically, $\mathbf{L}$ is obtained by removing the column corresponding to v_0 and the row corresponding to v_1 in the matrix $\mathbf{A}_\Gamma - \mathbf{I}$, where $\mathbf{A}_\Gamma$ is the adjacency matrix for Γ and $\mathbf{I}$ is the identity matrix.

Note that there is a linear-time algorithm that converts any Boolean formula, Boolean branching program, or arithmetic formula to an ABP with a constant blow-up in the representation size. Thus, ABP's can be viewed as a stronger computational model than all the others mentioned above.

2.3 The Function Family $\mathcal{F}_{\mathsf{ABP}\circ\mathsf{IP}}^{(q,n',n)}$ and the Algorithm PGB

Here, we formally describe the function family $\mathcal{F}_{\mathsf{ABP}\circ\mathsf{IP}}^{(q,n',n)}$ which our PHPE scheme supports, and an algorithm PGB for this function class that will be used as a sub-routine in our PHPE construction. Parts of this section is taken verbatim from [26,40].

■ The Function Family $\mathcal{F}_{\mathsf{ABP}\circ\mathsf{IP}}^{(q,n',n)}$

The function class $\mathcal{F}_{\mathsf{ABP}\circ\mathsf{IP}}^{(q,n',n)}$, parameterized by a prime q and $n', n \in \mathbb{N}$, contains functions of the form $f : \mathbb{F}_q^{n'} \times \mathbb{F}_q^n \to \mathbb{F}_q$ defined by $f(\vec{x}, \vec{z}) = \sum_{j \in [n]} f_j(\vec{x}) z_j$ for all $\vec{x} = (x_1, \ldots, x_{n'}) \in \mathbb{F}_q^{n'}$ and $\vec{z} = (z_1, \ldots, z_n) \in \mathbb{F}_q^n$, where $f_1, \ldots, f_n : \mathbb{F}_q^{n'} \to \mathbb{F}_q$ are functions computed by some ABP's $\Gamma_1, \ldots, \Gamma_n$ respectively. We will view the input $\vec{x} = (x_1, \ldots, x_{n'})$ as the *public attribute string*, while $\vec{z} = (z_1, \ldots, z_n)$ as the *private attribute string*. Please refer to [40] for some illustrative examples. A simple but crucial property of the function f is that for any $\zeta \in \mathbb{F}_q$ and any $(\vec{x}, \vec{z}) \in \mathbb{F}_q^{n'} \times \mathbb{F}_q^n$, we have $f(\vec{x}, \zeta\vec{z}) = \zeta f(\vec{x}, \vec{z})$.

Observe that the function f can itself be realized by an ABP Γ constructed as follows: First, marge the source vertices of all the component ABP's $\{\Gamma_j\}_{j\in[n]}$ together to form a single vertex, and designate it as the source vertex of the ABP Γ. Next, generate a new sink vertex for Γ, and for each $j \in [n]$, connect the sink vertex of the component ABP Γ_j to that newly formed sink vertex with a directed edge labeled with z_j. For ease of notations, we will denote the size of the ABP Γ computing the function f as $m+n+1$, where 1 corresponds to the sink vertex of Γ, n accounts for the number of edges directed to that sink vertex, and m accounts for the number of other vertices and edges in Γ. Also, note that the ABP Γ can be further modified to another ABP Γ' in which each vertex has at most one outgoing edge having a label of degree one, by replacing each edge e in Γ with a pair of edges labeled 1 and $\phi(e)$ respectively, where ϕ is the labeling function of the ABP Γ. It is clear that the number of vertices in this modified ABP Γ' is $m+n+1$, since Γ' is obtained by adding a fresh vertex for each edge in Γ as a result of replacing each edge in Γ with a pair of edges. Throughout this paper, whenever we will talk about the ABP computing the function f, we will refer to the ABP Γ' just described, unless otherwise specified.

■ **The Algorithm PGB**

► **Syntax and Properties:**

PGB$(f;\vec{r})$: PGB is a PPT algorithm takes as input a function $f \in \mathcal{F}^{(q,n',n)}_{\text{ABP}\circ\text{IP}}$, uses randomness $\vec{r} \in \mathbb{F}_q^{m+n-1}$, and outputs a collection of constants $(\{\sigma_j\}_{j\in[n]}, \{\alpha_{j'}, \gamma_{j'}\}_{j'\in[m]}) \in \mathbb{F}_q^n \times (\mathbb{F}_q^2)^m$ along with a function $\rho : [m] \rightarrow [n']$. Together with some $\vec{x} \in \mathbb{F}_q^{n'}$ and $\vec{z} \in \mathbb{F}_q^n$, this specifies a collection of $n+m$ *shares*

$$(\{z_j + \sigma_j\}_{j\in[n]}, \{\alpha_{j'} x_{\rho(j')} + \gamma_{j'}\}_{j'\in[m]}). \tag{2.1}$$

Here, $m+n+1$ is the number of vertices in the ABP computing f and ρ is deterministically derived from f.

The algorithm PGB satisfies the following properties:

- **Linearity**: For a fixed $f \in \mathcal{F}^{(q,n',n)}_{\text{ABP}\circ\text{IP}}$, PGB$(f;\cdot)$ computes a linear function of its randomness over $\mathbb{F}_q$.
- **Reconstruction**: There exists a deterministic polynomial-time algorithm REC that on input any $f \in \mathcal{F}^{(q,n',n)}_{\text{ABP}\circ\text{IP}}$ and any $\vec{x} \in \mathbb{F}_q^{n'}$, outputs a collection of coefficients $(\{\Omega_j\}_{j\in[n]}, \{\Omega'_{j'}\}_{j'\in[m]}) \in \mathbb{F}_q^n \times \mathbb{F}_q^{n'}$. These coefficients can be used in combination with any set of shares of the form as in Eq. (2.1), computed by combining the output of PGB(f) with $\vec{x}$ and any $\vec{z} \in \mathbb{F}_q^n$, to recover $f(\vec{x},\vec{z})$. Moreover, the recovery procedure is linear in the shares used.
- **Privacy**: There exists a PPT simulator SIM such that for all $f \in \mathcal{F}^{(q,n',n)}_{\text{ABP}\circ\text{IP}}, \vec{x} \in \mathbb{F}_q^{n'}, \vec{z} \in \mathbb{F}_q^n$, the output of SIM on input f, $\vec{x}$, and $f(\vec{x},\vec{z})$ is identically distributed to the shares obtained by combining the output of PGB$(f;\vec{r})$ for uniformly random $\vec{r}$, with $\vec{x}$ and $\vec{z}$ as in Eq. (2.1).

► **Instantiation of the Algorithm:** We now sketch an instantiation of the algorithm PGB following [26,40]. This instantiation will be utilized in our PHPE construction.

PGB(f): The algorithm takes as input a function $f \in \mathcal{F}_{\text{ABP}\circ\text{IP}}^{(q,n',n)}$, and proceeds as follows:

1. Let Γ' denotes the ABP computing f as described above. Recall that in the ABP Γ', there are $m+n+1$ vertices, the variables z_j's only appear on edges leading into the sink vertex, and any vertex has at most one outgoing edge with a label of degree one. It first computes the matrix representation $\boldsymbol{L} \in \mathbb{F}_q^{(m+n)\times(m+n)}$ of the ABP Γ' using the efficient algorithm of Lemma 2.1. Then as per Lemma 2.1, the matrix $\boldsymbol{L}$ satisfies the following properties:
   - $\det(\boldsymbol{L}(\vec{x}, \vec{z})) = f(\vec{x}, \vec{z})$ for all $(\vec{x}, \vec{z}) \in \mathbb{F}_q^{n'} \times \mathbb{F}_q^{n}$.
   - For $j' \in [m]$, each entry in the j'^{th} row of $\boldsymbol{L}$ is either a degree one polynomial function in one (and the same) input variable $x_{\iota'}$ ($\iota' \in [n']$), with coefficients in $\mathbb{F}_q$ or a constant in $\mathbb{F}_q$.
   - $\boldsymbol{L}$ contains only -1's in the second diagonal, and 0's below the second diagonal.
   - The last column of $\boldsymbol{L}$ is $(0, \ldots, 0, z_1, \ldots, z_n)^{\mathsf{T}}$.
   - $\boldsymbol{L}$ has 0's everywhere else in the last n rows.

   It defines the function $\rho : [m] \to [n']$ as $\rho(j') = \iota'$ if the entries of the j'^{th} row of $\boldsymbol{L}$ involves the variable $x_{\iota'}$ for $j' \in [m]$.
2. Next, it chooses $\vec{r} \xleftarrow{\mathsf{U}} \mathbb{F}_q^{m+n-1}$, and computes
$$\boldsymbol{L}\begin{pmatrix}\vec{r}^{\mathsf{T}}\\ 1\end{pmatrix} = (\alpha_1 x_{\rho(1)} + \gamma_1, \ldots, \alpha_m x_{\rho(m)} + \gamma_m, z_1 + \sigma_1, \ldots, z_n + \sigma_n)^{\mathsf{T}}.$$
3. It outputs $((\{\sigma_j\}_{j\in[n]}, \{\alpha_{j'}, \gamma_{j'}\}_{j'\in[m]}), \rho : [m] \to [n'])$.

It is straightforward to verify that each of $\{\sigma_j\}_{j\in[n]}, \{\alpha_{j'}, \gamma_{j'}\}_{j'\in[m]}$ are indeed linear functions of the randomness $\vec{r}$.

REC($f, \vec{x}$): This algorithm takes as input a function $f \in \mathcal{F}_{\text{ABP}\circ\text{IP}}^{(q,n',n)}$ and a vector $\vec{x} \in \mathbb{F}_q^{n'}$. It proceeds as follows:

1. It first executes Step 1 of the algorithm PGB described above to generate the matrix representation $\boldsymbol{L}$ of f.
2. Next, it computes the cofactors of each entry in the last column of $\boldsymbol{L}$. Let $(\{\Omega'_{j'}\}_{j'\in[m]}, \{\Omega_j\}_{j\in[n]}) \in \mathbb{F}_q^{m+n}$ be the collection of all the cofactors in the order of the entries. Note that the first $m+n-1$ columns of $\boldsymbol{L}$ involve only the variables $\{x_{\iota'}\}_{\iota'\in[n']}$. Hence, it can compute all the cofactors using the input $\vec{x}$.
3. It outputs $(\{\Omega_j\}_{j\in[n]}, \{\Omega'_{j'}\}_{j'\in[m]})$.

The output of REC($f, \vec{x}$) can be used in conjunction with a collection of shares $(\{z_j + \sigma_j\}_{j\in[n]}, \{\alpha_{j'} x_{\rho(j')} + \gamma_{j'}\}_{j'\in[m]})$ for any $\vec{z} \in \mathbb{F}_q^n$, to compute $f(\vec{x}, \vec{z})$ as

$$f(\vec{x}, \vec{z}) = \sum_{j'\in[m]} \Omega'_{j'}(\alpha_{j'} x_{\rho(j')} + \gamma_{j'}) + \sum_{j\in[n]} \Omega_j(z_j + \sigma_j). \tag{2.2}$$

Observe that the RHS of Eq. (2.2) corresponds to computing $\det(\boldsymbol{L}'(\vec{x},\vec{z}))$, where the matrix $\boldsymbol{L}'$ is obtained by replacing the last column of the matrix $\boldsymbol{L}$ with the column $(\alpha_1 x_{\rho(1)} + \gamma_1, \ldots, \alpha_m x_{\rho(m)} + \gamma_m, z_1 + \sigma_1, \ldots, z_n + \sigma_n)^{\mathsf{T}}$, where $\boldsymbol{L}$ is the matrix representation of the ABP Γ' computing the function $f \in \mathcal{F}^{(q,n',n)}_{\mathrm{ABP}\circ\mathrm{IP}}$, obtained by applying the algorithm of Lemma 2.1. Hence, the correctness of Eq. (2.2) follows from the fact that

$$\det(\boldsymbol{L}'(\vec{x},\vec{z})) = \det(\boldsymbol{L}(\vec{x},\vec{z}))\begin{vmatrix} 1 & & r_1 \\ & \ddots & \vdots \\ & 1 & r_{m+n-1} \\ & & 1 \end{vmatrix} = \det(\boldsymbol{L}(\vec{x},\vec{z}))\cdot 1 = f(\vec{x},\vec{z}).$$

Here, $\vec{r} = (r_1, \ldots, r_{m+n-1}) \in \mathbb{F}_q^{m+n-1}$ is the randomness used by PGB while generating the constants $(\{\sigma_j\}_{j\in[n]}, \{\alpha_{j'}, \gamma_{j'}\}_{j'\in[m]})$. In fact, an augmented version of Eq. (2.2) also holds. More precisely, for any $\Upsilon, \widetilde{\Upsilon} \in \mathbb{F}_q$, we have

$$\Upsilon f(\vec{x},\vec{z}) = \sum_{j'\in[m]} \Omega'_{j'}\widetilde{\Upsilon}(\alpha_{j'}x_{\rho(j')} + \gamma_{j'}) + \sum_{j\in[n]} \Omega_j(\Upsilon z_j + \widetilde{\Upsilon}\sigma_j). \tag{2.3}$$

This follows by observing that

$$\det(\boldsymbol{L}(\vec{x},\vec{z})) = \sum_{j\in[n]} \Omega_j z_j, \text{(since the first } m \text{ entries in the last column is 0)}$$

and hence, the RHS of Eq. (2.3) can be written as

$$\begin{aligned} &\widetilde{\Upsilon}\Big[\sum_{j'\in[m]} \Omega'_{j'}(\alpha_{j'}x_{\rho(j')} + \gamma_{j'}) + \sum_{j\in[n]} \Omega_j(z_j + \sigma_j)\Big] + (\Upsilon - \widetilde{\Upsilon})\sum_{j\in[n]} \Omega_j z_j \\ &= \widetilde{\Upsilon}\det(\boldsymbol{L}'(\vec{x},\vec{z})) + (\Upsilon - \widetilde{\Upsilon})\det(\boldsymbol{L}(\vec{x},\vec{z})) = \Upsilon\det(\boldsymbol{L}(\vec{x},\vec{z})), \end{aligned}$$

as $\det(\boldsymbol{L}'(\vec{x},\vec{z})) = \det(\boldsymbol{L}(\vec{x},\vec{z}))$. This fact will be used to justify the correctness of our PHPE construction.

$\mathsf{SIM}(f, \vec{x}, \epsilon)$: The simulator takes as input a function $f \in \mathcal{F}^{(q,n',n)}_{\mathrm{ABP}\circ\mathrm{IP}}$, a vector $\vec{x} \in \mathbb{F}_q^{n'}$, and a value $\epsilon \in \mathbb{F}_q$. It proceeds as follows:

1. At first, it executes Step 1 of the algorithm PGB described above to obtain the matrix representation $\boldsymbol{L}$ of f together with the function $\rho : [m] \to [n']$.
2. Next, it constructs a matrix $\widehat{\boldsymbol{L}}$ from the matrix $\boldsymbol{L}$ by replacing its last column with $(\epsilon, 0, \ldots, 0)^{\mathsf{T}}$.
3. Next, it samples $\vec{r} \xleftarrow{\mathsf{U}} \mathbb{F}_q^{m+n-1}$, and computes

$$\widehat{\boldsymbol{L}}\begin{pmatrix} \vec{r}^{\mathsf{T}} \\ 1 \end{pmatrix} = (\mu_1, \ldots, \mu_m, \nu_1, \ldots, \nu_n)^{\mathsf{T}}.$$

4. It outputs $((\{\nu_j\}_{j\in[n]}, \{\mu_{j'}\}_{j'\in[m]}), \rho : [m] \to [n'])$.

It readily follows from Theorem 3, Corollary 1 of [26] that for all $f \in \mathcal{F}_{\text{ABP}\circ\text{IP}}^{(q,n',n)}$, $\vec{x} \in \mathbb{F}_q^{n'}$, and $\vec{z} \in \mathbb{F}_q^n$, the output of $\mathsf{SIM}(f, \vec{x}, f(\vec{x}, \vec{z}))$ is identically distributed to the shares obtained by combining with $(\vec{x}, \vec{z})$ the output of $\mathsf{PGB}(f)$ with uniform randomness, thereby establishing the privacy property of the algorithm PGB described above. We omit the details here. Clearly the determinant value of the matrix $\widehat{\boldsymbol{L}}(\vec{x}, \vec{z})$ generated by SIM on input any $f \in \mathcal{F}_{\text{ABP}\circ\text{IP}}^{(q,n',n)}$, $\vec{x} \in \mathbb{F}_q^{n'}$, and $f(\vec{x}, \vec{z})$ for any $\vec{z} \in \mathbb{F}_q^n$ is $f(\vec{x}, \vec{z})$.

2.4 Bilinear Groups and Dual Pairing Vector Spaces

In this section, we will provide the necessary backgrounds on bilinear groups and dual pairing vector spaces, which are the primary building blocks of our PHPE construction.

Definition 2.1 (Bilinear Group): A bilinear group $\mathsf{params}_{\mathbb{G}} = (q, \mathbb{G}_1, \mathbb{G}_2, \mathbb{G}_T, g_1, g_2, e)$ is a tuple of a prime integer $q \in \mathbb{N}$; cyclic multiplicative groups $\mathbb{G}_1, \mathbb{G}_2, \mathbb{G}_T$ of order q each with polynomial-time computable group operations; generators $g_1 \in \mathbb{G}_1$, $g_2 \in \mathbb{G}_2$; and a polynomial-time computable non-degenerate bilinear map $e : \mathbb{G}_1 \times \mathbb{G}_2 \to \mathbb{G}_T$, i.e., e satisfies the following two properties:

- *Bilinearity*: $e(g_1^{\delta}, g_2^{\hat{\delta}}) = e(g_1, g_2)^{\delta\hat{\delta}}$ for all $\delta, \hat{\delta} \in \mathbb{F}_q$.
- *Non-degeneracy*: $e(g_1, g_2) \neq 1_{\mathbb{G}_T}$, where $1_{\mathbb{G}_T}$ denotes the identity element of the group $\mathbb{G}_T$.

A bilinear group is said to be asymmetric if no efficiently computable isomorphism exists between $\mathbb{G}_1$ and $\mathbb{G}_2$. Let $\mathcal{G}_{\text{BPG}}$ be an algorithm that on input the unary encoding 1^λ of the security parameter λ, outputs a description $\mathsf{params}_{\mathbb{G}} = (q, \mathbb{G}_1, \mathbb{G}_2, \mathbb{G}_T, g_1, g_2, e)$ of a bilinear group.

Definition 2.2 (Dual Pairing Vector Spaces: DPVS [33,35]): A dual pairing vector space (DPVS) $\mathsf{params}_{\mathbb{V}} = (q, \mathbb{V}_1, \mathbb{V}_2, \mathbb{G}_T, \mathbb{A}_1, \mathbb{A}_2, e)$ formed by the direct product of a bilinear group $\mathsf{params}_{\mathbb{G}} = (q, \mathbb{G}_1, \mathbb{G}_2, \mathbb{G}_T, g_1, g_2, e)$ is a tuple of a prime integer q; d-dimensional vector spaces $\mathbb{V}_t = \mathbb{G}_t^d$ over $\mathbb{F}_q$ for $t \in [2]$ under vector addition and scalar multiplication defined componentwise in the usual manner; canonical bases $\mathbb{A}_t = \{\boldsymbol{a}^{(t,\ell)} = (\overbrace{1_{\mathbb{G}_t}, \ldots, 1_{\mathbb{G}_t}}^{\ell-1}, g_t, \overbrace{1_{\mathbb{G}_t}, \ldots, 1_{\mathbb{G}_t}}^{d-\ell})\}_{\ell \in [d]}$ of $\mathbb{V}_t$ for $t \in [2]$, where $1_{\mathbb{G}_t}$ is the identity element of the group $\mathbb{G}_t$ for $t \in [2]$; and a pairing $e : \mathbb{V}_1 \times \mathbb{V}_2 \to \mathbb{G}_T$ defined by $e(\boldsymbol{v}, \boldsymbol{w}) = \prod_{\ell \in [d]} e(g_1^{v_\ell}, g_2^{w_\ell}) \in \mathbb{G}_T$ for all $\boldsymbol{v} = (g_1^{v_1}, \ldots, g_1^{v_d}) \in \mathbb{V}_1$, $\boldsymbol{w} = (g_2^{w_1}, \ldots, g_2^{w_d}) \in \mathbb{V}_2$. Observe that the newly defined map e is also non-degenerate bilinear, i.e., e also satisfies the following two properties:

- *Bilinearity*: $e(\delta\boldsymbol{v}, \hat{\delta}\boldsymbol{w}) = e(\boldsymbol{v}, \boldsymbol{w})^{\delta\hat{\delta}}$ for all $\delta, \hat{\delta} \in \mathbb{F}_q$, $\boldsymbol{v} \in \mathbb{V}_1$, and $\boldsymbol{w} \in \mathbb{V}_2$.
- *Non-degeneracy*: If $e(\boldsymbol{v}, \boldsymbol{w}) = 1_{\mathbb{G}_T}$ for all $\boldsymbol{w} \in \mathbb{V}_2$, then $\boldsymbol{v} = (\overbrace{1_{\mathbb{G}_1}, \ldots, 1_{\mathbb{G}_1}}^{d})$. Similar statement also holds with the vectors $\boldsymbol{v}$ and $\boldsymbol{w}$ interchanged.

For any ordered basis $\mathbb{W} = \{\boldsymbol{w}^{(1)}, \ldots, \boldsymbol{w}^{(d)}\}$ of $\mathbb{V}_t$ for $t \in [2]$, and any vector $\vec{v} \in \mathbb{F}_q^d$, let $(\vec{v})_{\mathbb{W}}$ represents the vector in $\mathbb{V}_t$ formed by the linear combination of the members of $\mathbb{W}$ with the components of $\vec{v}$ as the coefficients, i.e., $(\vec{v})_{\mathbb{W}} = \sum_{\ell \in [d]} v_\ell \boldsymbol{w}^{(\ell)} \in \mathbb{V}_t$. The DPVS generation algorithm $\mathcal{G}_{\mathsf{DPVS}}$ takes as input the unary encoded security parameter 1^λ, a dimension value $d \in \mathbb{N}$, along with a bilinear group $\mathsf{params}_{\mathbb{G}} = (q, \mathbb{G}_1, \mathbb{G}_2, \mathbb{G}_T, g_1, g_2, e) \xleftarrow{\mathsf{R}} \mathcal{G}_{\mathsf{BPG}}()$, and outputs a description $\mathsf{params}_{\mathbb{V}} = (q, \mathbb{V}_1, \mathbb{V}_2, \mathbb{G}_T, \mathbb{A}_1, \mathbb{A}_2, e)$ of DPVS with d-dimensional $\mathbb{V}_1$ and $\mathbb{V}_2$.

We now describe random *dual orthonormal basis* generator $\mathcal{G}_{\mathsf{OB}}$ [33,35] in Fig. 1. This algorithm will be utilized as a sub-routine in our PHPE construction.

$\mathcal{G}_{\mathsf{OB}}(N, (d_0, \ldots, d_N))$: This algorithm takes as input the unary encoded security parameter 1^λ, a number $N \in \mathbb{N}$, and the respective dimensions $d_0, \ldots, d_N \in \mathbb{N}$ of the $N+1$ pairs of bases to be generated. It executes the following operations:

1. It first generates $\mathsf{params}_{\mathbb{G}} = (q, \mathbb{G}_1, \mathbb{G}_2, \mathbb{G}_T, g_1, g_2, e) \xleftarrow{\mathsf{R}} \mathcal{G}_{\mathsf{BPG}}()$.
2. Next, it samples $\psi \xleftarrow{\mathsf{U}} \mathbb{F}_q \backslash \{0\}$ and computes $g_T = e(g_1, g_2)^\psi$.
3. Then, for $\imath \in [0, N]$, it performs the following:
   (a) It constructs $\mathsf{params}_{\mathbb{V}_\imath} = (q, \mathbb{V}_{\imath,1}, \mathbb{V}_{\imath,2}, \mathbb{G}_T, \mathbb{A}_{\imath,1}, \mathbb{A}_{\imath,2}, e) \xleftarrow{\mathsf{R}} \mathcal{G}_{\mathsf{DPVS}}(d_\imath, \mathsf{params}_{\mathbb{G}})$.
   (b) It samples $\boldsymbol{B}^{(\imath)} = (b_{\ell,k}^{(\imath)}) \xleftarrow{\mathsf{U}} \mathsf{GL}(d_\imath, \mathbb{F}_q)$.
   (c) It computes $\boldsymbol{B}^{*(\imath)} = (b_{\ell,k}^{*(\imath)}) = \psi((\boldsymbol{B}^{(\imath)})^{-1})^\intercal$.
   (d) For all $\ell \in [d_\imath]$, let $\vec{b}^{(\imath,\ell)}$ and $\vec{b}^{*(\imath,\ell)}$ represent the ℓth rows of $\boldsymbol{B}^{(\imath)}$ and $\boldsymbol{B}^{*(\imath)}$ respectively. It computes $\boldsymbol{b}^{(\imath,\ell)} = (\vec{b}^{(\imath,\ell)})_{\mathbb{A}_{\imath,1}}, \boldsymbol{b}^{*(\imath,\ell)} = (\vec{b}^{*(\imath,\ell)})_{\mathbb{A}_{\imath,2}}$ for $\ell \in [d_\imath]$, and sets
   $$\mathbb{B}_\imath = \{\boldsymbol{b}^{(\imath,1)}, \ldots, \boldsymbol{b}^{(\imath,d_\imath)}\}, \mathbb{B}_\imath^* = \{\boldsymbol{b}^{*(\imath,1)}, \ldots, \boldsymbol{b}^{*(\imath,d_\imath)}\}.$$
   Clearly $\mathbb{B}_\imath$ and $\mathbb{B}_\imath^*$ form bases of the vector spaces $\mathbb{V}_{\imath,1}$ and $\mathbb{V}_{\imath,2}$ respectively. Also, note that $\mathbb{B}_\imath$ and $\mathbb{B}_\imath^*$ are dual orthonormal in the sense that for all $\ell, \ell' \in [d_\imath]$,
   $$e(\boldsymbol{b}^{(\imath,\ell)}, \boldsymbol{b}^{*(\imath,\ell')}) = \begin{cases} g_T & \text{if } \ell = \ell', \\ 1_{\mathbb{G}_T} & \text{otherwise.} \end{cases}$$
4. Next, it sets $\mathsf{params} = (\{\mathsf{params}_{\mathbb{V}_\imath}\}_{\imath \in [0,N]}, g_T)$.
5. It returns $(\mathsf{params}, \{\mathbb{B}_\imath, \mathbb{B}_\imath^*\}_{\imath \in [0,N]})$.

Fig. 1. Dual orthonormal basis generator $\mathcal{G}_{\mathsf{OB}}$

2.5 Complexity Assumption

For realizing our PHPE construction in asymmetric bilinear groups, we rely on the natural extension of the well-studied decisional linear (DLIN) assumption to the asymmetric bilinear group setting, called the external decisional linear (XDLIN) assumption.

Assumption (External Decisional Linear: XDLIN [1,38]**):** For $t \in [2]$, the XDLIN_t problem is to guess the bit $\widehat{\beta} \xleftarrow{\mathsf{U}} \{0,1\}$ given $\varrho_{\widehat{\beta}}^{\mathrm{XDLIN}_t} = (\mathsf{params}_{\mathbb{G}}, g_1^{\varpi}, g_1^{\xi}, g_1^{\varkappa\varpi}, g_1^{\varsigma\xi}, g_2^{\varpi}, g_2^{\xi}, g_2^{\varkappa\varpi}, g_2^{\varsigma\xi}, \Re_{t,\widehat{\beta}})$, where

$$\begin{aligned}&\mathsf{params}_{\mathbb{G}} = (q, \mathbb{G}_1, \mathbb{G}_2, \mathbb{G}_T, g_1, g_2, e) \xleftarrow{\mathsf{R}} \mathcal{G}_{\mathrm{BPG}}();\\ &\varpi, \xi, \varkappa, \varsigma, \varepsilon \xleftarrow{\mathsf{U}} \mathbb{F}_q;\\ &\Re_{t,0} = g_t^{(\varkappa+\varsigma)}, \Re_{t,1} = g_t^{(\varkappa+\varsigma)+\varepsilon}.\end{aligned}$$

The XDLIN_t assumption states that for any PPT algorithm $\mathcal{E}$, for any security parameter λ, the advantage of $\mathcal{E}$ in deciding the XDLIN_t problem, defined as

$$\mathsf{Adv}_{\mathcal{E}}^{\mathrm{XDLIN}_t}(\lambda) = |\mathsf{Pr}[1 \xleftarrow{\mathsf{R}} \mathcal{E}(\varrho_0^{\mathrm{XDLIN}_t}) - \mathsf{Pr}[1 \xleftarrow{\mathsf{R}} \mathcal{E}(\varrho_1^{\mathrm{XDLIN}_t})]|,$$

is negligible in λ, i.e., $\mathsf{Adv}_{\mathcal{E}}^{\mathrm{XDLIN}_t}(\lambda) \leq \mathsf{negl}(\lambda)$, where negl is some negligible function. The simultaneous XDLIN (SXDLIN) assumption states that both XDLIN_1 and XDLIN_2 assumptions hold at the same time. For any security parameter λ, we denote the advantage of any probabilistic algorithm $\mathcal{E}$ against SXDLIN as $\mathsf{Adv}_{\mathcal{E}}^{\mathrm{SXDLIN}}(\lambda)$.

2.6 The Notion of Partially-Hiding Predicate Encryption

Here, we formally present the syntax and simulation-based security notion of a partially-hiding predicate encryption (PHPE) scheme for the function family $\mathcal{F}_{\mathrm{ABP}\circ\mathrm{IP}}^{(q,n',n)}$ for some prime q and $n', n \in \mathbb{N}$. Following [40], we define the ABP∘IP predicate family $R^{\mathrm{ABP}\circ\mathrm{IP}}$ as $R^{\mathrm{ABP}\circ\mathrm{IP}} = \{R^{\mathrm{ABP}\circ\mathrm{IP}}(f, (\cdot,\cdot)) : \mathbb{F}_q^{n'} \times \mathbb{F}_q^n \to \{0,1\} \mid f \in \mathcal{F}_{\mathrm{ABP}\circ\mathrm{IP}}^{(q,n',n)}\}$, where $R^{\mathrm{ABP}\circ\mathrm{IP}}(f, (\vec{x}, \vec{z})) = 1$ if $f(\vec{x}, \vec{z}) = 0$, and $R^{\mathrm{ABP}\circ\mathrm{IP}}(f, (\vec{x}, \vec{z})) = 0$ if $f(\vec{x}, \vec{z}) \neq 0$ for all $f \in \mathcal{F}_{\mathrm{ABP}\circ\mathrm{IP}}^{(q,n',n)}$ and $(\vec{x}, \vec{z}) \in \mathbb{F}_q^{n'} \times \mathbb{F}_q^n$.

► **Syntax:** An *attribute-only/key-encapsulation mechanism* (KEM) *partially-hiding predicate encryption* (PHPE) scheme for the function family $\mathcal{F}_{\mathrm{ABP}\circ\mathrm{IP}}^{(q,n',n)}$ consists of the following polynomial-time algorithms:

PHPE.Setup($1^{n'}, 1^n$): The setup algorithm takes as input the security parameter λ along with the public and private attribute lengths n' and n respectively (all encoded in unary). It outputs the public parameters MPK and the master secret key MSK.

PHPE.Encrypt(MPK, $(\vec{x}, \vec{z})$): The encryption algorithm takes as input the public parameters MPK, a pair of public-private attribute strings $(\vec{x}, \vec{z}) \in \mathbb{F}_q^{n'} \times \mathbb{F}_q^n$. It outputs a ciphertext CT. In the KEM mode, it additionally outputs a session key KEM.

PHPE.KeyGen(MPK, MSK, f): On input the public parameters MPK, the master secret key MSK, along with a function $f \in \mathcal{F}_{\mathrm{ABP}\circ\mathrm{IP}}^{(q,n',n)}$, the key generation algorithm outputs a decryption key SK(f).

$\mathsf{PHPE.Decrypt}(\text{MPK}, (f, \text{SK}(f)), (\vec{x}, \text{CT}))$: The decryption algorithm takes as input the public parameters MPK, a pair of a function $f \in \mathcal{F}_{\text{ABP}\circ\text{IP}}^{(q,n',n)}$ and a decryption key $\text{SK}(f)$ for f, along with a pair of a public attribute $\vec{x} \in \mathbb{F}_q^{n'}$ and a ciphertext CT associated with $\vec{x}$ and some private attribute string. In the attribute-only mode, it outputs either 1 or 0, while in the KEM mode, it outputs a session key $\widetilde{\text{KEM}}$. For notational convenience, we will think of f and $\vec{x}$ as parts of $\text{SK}(f)$ and CT respectively, and will not write them explicitly in the argument of PHPE.Decrypt.

The algorithm PHPE.Decrypt is deterministic, while all the others are probabilistic.

► **Correctness:** A PHPE scheme for the function family $\mathcal{F}_{\text{ABP}\circ\text{IP}}^{(q,n',n)}$ is said to be correct if for any security parameter λ, any $(\vec{x}, \vec{z}) \in \mathbb{F}_q^{n'} \times \mathbb{F}_q^n$, any $f \in \mathcal{F}_{\text{ABP}\circ\text{IP}}^{(q,n',n)}$, any $(\text{MPK}, \text{MSK}) \xleftarrow{R} \mathsf{PHPE.Setup}(1^{n'}, 1^n)$, and any $\text{SK}(f) \xleftarrow{R} \mathsf{PHPE.KeyGen}(\text{MPK}, \text{MSK}, f)$, the following holds:

- (*Authorized*) If $R^{\text{ABP}\circ\text{IP}}(f, (\vec{x}, \vec{z})) = 1$, then

$$\Pr[\mathsf{PHPE.Decrypt}(\text{MPK}, \text{SK}(f), \text{CT}) = 1 : \text{CT} \xleftarrow{R} \mathsf{PHPE.Encrypt}(\text{MPK}, (\vec{x}, \vec{z}))] \geq 1 - \mathsf{negl}(\lambda) \text{ (attribute-only mode)},$$
$$\Pr[\mathsf{PHPE.Decrypt}(\text{MPK}, \text{SK}(f), \text{CT}) = \text{KEM} : (\text{CT}, \text{KEM}) \xleftarrow{R} \mathsf{PHPE.Encrypt}(\text{MPK}, (\vec{x}, \vec{z}))] \geq 1 - \mathsf{negl}(\lambda) \text{ (KEM mode)}.$$

- (*Unauthorized*) If $R^{\text{ABP}\circ\text{IP}}(f, (\vec{x}, \vec{z})) = 0$, then

$$\Pr[\mathsf{PHPE.Decrypt}(\text{MPK}, \text{SK}(f), \text{CT}) = 0 : \text{CT} \xleftarrow{R} \mathsf{PHPE.Encrypt}(\text{MPK}, (\vec{x}, \vec{z}))] \geq 1 - \mathsf{negl}(\lambda) \text{ (attribute-only mode)},$$
$$\Pr[\mathsf{PHPE.Decrypt}(\text{MPK}, \text{SK}(f), \text{CT}) \neq \text{KEM} : (\text{CT}, \text{KEM}) \xleftarrow{R} \mathsf{PHPE.Encrypt}(\text{MPK}, (\vec{x}, \vec{z}))] \geq 1 - \mathsf{negl}(\lambda) \text{ (KEM mode)}.$$

Here, negl is some negligible function, and the probabilities are taken over the random coins of PHPE.Encrypt.

► **Simulation-Based Security:** The simulation-based adaptively strongly partially-hiding security notion for a PHPE scheme is formulated by considering the following two experiments involving a stateful probabilistic adversary $\mathcal{A}$ and a stateful probabilistic simulator $\mathcal{S}$:

$\mathsf{Exp}_{\mathcal{A}}^{\text{PHPE,REAL}}(\lambda)$:

1. $(\text{MPK}, \text{MSK}) \xleftarrow{R} \mathsf{PHPE.Setup}(1^{n'}, 1^n)$.
2. $\{(\vec{x}^{(i)}, \vec{z}^{(i)})\}_{i \in [q_{\text{CT}}]} \xleftarrow{R} \mathcal{A}^{\mathsf{PHPE.KeyGen}(\text{MSK}, \cdot)}(\text{MPK})$.
3. (a) (attribute-only case) $\text{CT}^{(i)} \xleftarrow{R} \mathsf{PHPE.Encrypt}(\text{MPK}, (\vec{x}^{(i)}, \vec{z}^{(i)}))$ for $i \in [q_{\text{CT}}]$.

(b) (KEM case) $(\text{CT}^{(i)}, \text{KEM}^{(i)}) \xleftarrow{R} \mathsf{PHPE.Encrypt}(\text{MPK}, (\vec{x}^{(i)}, \vec{z}^{(i)}))$ for $i \in [q_{\text{CT}}]$.

4. (a) (attribute-only case) $\mathfrak{I} \xleftarrow{R} \mathcal{A}^{\mathsf{PHPE.KeyGen}(\text{MSK},\cdot)}(\text{MPK}, \{\text{CT}^{(i)}\}_{i\in[q_{\text{CT}}]})$.
   (b) (KEM case) $\mathfrak{I} \xleftarrow{R} \mathcal{A}^{\mathsf{PHPE.KeyGen}(\text{MSK},\cdot)}(\text{MPK}, \{(\text{CT}^{(i)}, \text{KEM}^{(i)})\}_{i\in[q_{\text{CT}}]})$.
5. Output $\varrho_{\mathcal{A}}^{\text{PHPE,REAL}} = (\text{MPK}, \{(\vec{x}^{(i)}, \vec{z}^{(i)})\}_{i\in[q_{\text{CT}}]}, \mathfrak{I})$.

$\mathsf{Exp}_{\mathcal{A},\mathcal{S}}^{\text{PHPE,IDEAL}}(\lambda)$:

1. $\text{MPK} \xleftarrow{R} \mathcal{S}(1^{n'}, 1^n)$.
2. $\{(\vec{x}^{(i)}, \vec{z}^{(i)})\}_{i\in[q_{\text{CT}}]} \xleftarrow{R} \mathcal{A}^{\mathcal{S}(\cdot)}(\text{MPK})$.
3. (a) (attribute-only case) $\{\text{CT}^{(i)}\}_{i\in[q_{\text{CT}}]} \xleftarrow{R} \mathcal{S}(q_{\text{CT}}, \{(\vec{x}^{(i)}, R^{\text{ABP}\circ\text{IP}}(f_h, (\vec{x}^{(i)}, \vec{z}^{(i)})))\}_{i\in[q_{\text{CT}}], h\in[q_{\text{KEY-PRE}}]})$.
   (b) (KEM case) $\{\text{KEM}^{(i)}\}_{i\in[q_{\text{CT}}]} \xleftarrow{U} \mathbb{K}$, where $\mathbb{K}$ = session key space $\{\text{CT}^{(i)}\}_{i\in[q_{\text{CT}}]} \xleftarrow{R} \mathcal{S}(q_{\text{CT}}, \{(\vec{x}^{(i)}, \overline{\text{KEM}}^{(i,h)})\}_{i\in[q_{\text{CT}}], h\in[q_{\text{KEY-PRE}}]})$, where for all $i \in [q_{\text{CT}}], h \in [q_{\text{KEY-PRE}}]$, $\overline{\text{KEM}}^{(i,h)} = \text{KEM}^{(i)}$ if $R^{\text{ABP}\circ\text{IP}}(f_h, (\vec{x}^{(i)}, \vec{z}^{(i)})) = 1$, and $\perp$ if $R^{\text{ABP}\circ\text{IP}}(f_h, (\vec{x}^{(i)}, \vec{z}^{(i)})) = 0$.
4. (a) (attribute-only case) $\mathfrak{I} \xleftarrow{R} \mathcal{A}^{\mathcal{S}^{\mathcal{O}_{R^{\text{ABP}\circ\text{IP}}}(\{(\vec{x}^{(i)}, \vec{z}^{(i)})\}_{i\in[q_{\text{CT}}]},\cdot)}(\cdot)}(\text{MPK}, \{\text{CT}^{(i)}\}_{i\in[q_{\text{CT}}]})$.
   (b) (KEM case) $\mathfrak{I} \xleftarrow{R} \mathcal{A}^{\mathcal{S}^{\mathcal{O}_{R^{\text{ABP}\circ\text{IP}}}(\{((\vec{x}^{(i)}, \vec{z}^{(i)}), \text{KEM}^{(i)})\}_{i\in[q_{\text{CT}}]},\cdot)}(\cdot)}(\text{MPK}, \{(\text{CT}^{(i)}, \text{KEM}^{(i)})\}_{i\in[q_{\text{CT}}]})$.
5. Output $\varrho_{\mathcal{A},\mathcal{S}}^{\text{PHPE,IDEAL}} = (\text{MPK}, \{(\vec{x}^{(i)}, \vec{z}^{(i)})\}_{i\in[q_{\text{CT}}]}, \mathfrak{I})$.

Here, the simulator $\mathcal{S}$ accepts as input a function $f \in \mathcal{F}_{\text{ABP}\circ\text{IP}}^{(q,n',n)}$ when it acts as an oracle to $\mathcal{A}$. Also, q_{CT} and $q_{\text{KEY-PRE}}$ respectively denotes the number of ciphertext queries made by $\mathcal{A}$ and number of decryption key queries made by $\mathcal{A}$ prior to submitting the ciphertext queries. Further, in the attribute-only case, the oracle $\mathcal{O}_{R^{\text{ABP}\circ\text{IP}}}$ receives as its second argument a function $f \in \mathcal{F}_{\text{ABP}\circ\text{IP}}^{(q,n',n)}$, and outputs $\{R^{\text{ABP}\circ\text{IP}}(f, (\vec{x}^{(i)}, \vec{z}^{(i)}))\}_{i\in[q_{\text{CT}}]}$. On the other hand, in the KEM case, the oracle $\mathcal{O}_{R^{\text{ABP}\circ\text{IP}}}$ takes as its second argument a function $f \in \mathcal{F}_{\text{ABP}\circ\text{IP}}^{(q,n',n)}$, and outputs $\text{KEM}^{(i)}$ if $R^{\text{ABP}\circ\text{IP}}(f, (\vec{x}^{(i)}, \vec{z}^{(i)})) = 1$, and $\perp$ if $R^{\text{ABP}\circ\text{IP}}(f, (\vec{x}^{(i)}, \vec{z}^{(i)})) = 0$ for $i \in [q_{\text{CT}}]$. A simulator $\mathcal{S}$ is said to be admissible if on each decryption key query $f \in \mathcal{F}_{\text{ABP}\circ\text{IP}}^{(q,n',n)}$ of $\mathcal{A}$ in the post-ciphertext query phase, $\mathcal{S}$ makes just a single query to the oracle $\mathcal{O}_{R^{\text{ABP}\circ\text{IP}}}$ on f itself. Let the number of decryption key queries made by $\mathcal{A}$ after receiving the queried ciphertexts be $q_{\text{KEY-POST}}$.

For any security parameter λ, for any probabilistic distinguisher $\mathcal{D}$, the advantage of $\mathcal{D}$ in distinguishing the above two experiments is defined as

$$\mathsf{Adv}_{\mathcal{D}}^{\text{PHPE,SIM-AH}}(\lambda) = |\mathsf{Pr}[1 \xleftarrow{R} \mathcal{D}(\varrho_{\mathcal{A}}^{\text{PHPE,REAL}})] - \mathsf{Pr}[1 \xleftarrow{R} \mathcal{D}(\varrho_{\mathcal{A},\mathcal{S}}^{\text{PHPE,IDEAL}})]|.$$

Definition 2.3: A PHPE scheme is called $(q_{\text{KEY-PRE}}, q_{\text{CT}}, q_{\text{KEY-POST}})$-simulation-based adaptively strongly partially hiding if there exists an admissible stateful PPT simulator $\mathcal{S}$ such that for any stateful PPT adversary $\mathcal{A}$ making at most

q_{CT} ciphertext queries, $q_{\text{KEY-PRE}}$ decryption key queries in the pre-ciphertext query phase, while $q_{\text{KEY-POST}}$ decryption key queries in the post-ciphertext query phase, any PPT distinguisher $\mathcal{D}$, and any security parameter λ, $\mathsf{Adv}_{\mathcal{D}}^{\text{PHPE,SIM-AH}}(\lambda) \leq \mathsf{negl}(\lambda)$, where negl is some negligible function. Further, a PHPE scheme is said to be $(\mathsf{poly}, q_{\text{CT}}, \mathsf{poly})$-simulation-based adaptively strongly partially hiding if it is $(q_{\text{KEY-PRE}}, q_{\text{CT}}, q_{\text{KEY-POST}})$-simulation-based adaptively strongly partially hiding as well as $q_{\text{KEY-PRE}}$ and $q_{\text{KEY-POST}}$ are unbounded polynomials in the security parameter λ.

Remark 2.1: Consider an adversary $\mathcal{H}$ that first invokes $\mathcal{A}$ and then invokes $\mathcal{D}$ once the transcript ($\varrho_{\mathcal{A}}^{\text{PHPE,REAL}}$ or $\varrho_{\mathcal{A},\mathcal{S}}^{\text{PHPE,IDEAL}}$) of the experiment is obtained. Consider the experiments $\mathsf{Exp}_{\mathcal{H}}^{\text{PHPE,REAL}}(\lambda)$ and $\mathsf{Exp}_{\mathcal{H},\mathcal{S}}^{\text{PHPE,IDEAL}}(\lambda)$ which are obtained from the experiments $\mathsf{Exp}_{\mathcal{A}}^{\text{PHPE,REAL}}(\lambda)$ and $\mathsf{Exp}_{\mathcal{A},\mathcal{S}}^{\text{PHPE,IDEAL}}(\lambda)$ respectively by applying the corresponding augmentations. Let us define the outputs of the augmented experiments as the output of $\mathcal{H}$ in those experiments, and the advantage of $\mathcal{H}$ as

$$\mathsf{Adv}_{\mathcal{H}}^{\text{PHPE,SIM-AH}}(\lambda) = |\mathsf{Pr}[1 \xleftarrow{\mathsf{R}} \mathsf{Exp}_{\mathcal{H}}^{\text{PHPE,REAL}}(\lambda)] - \mathsf{Pr}[1 \xleftarrow{\mathsf{R}} \mathsf{Exp}_{\mathcal{H},\mathcal{S}}^{\text{PHPE,IDEAL}}(\lambda)]|.$$

Then, clearly $\mathsf{Adv}_{\mathcal{H}}^{\text{PHPE,SIM-AH}}(\lambda) = \mathsf{Adv}_{\mathcal{D}}^{\text{PHPE,SIM-AH}}(\lambda)$. We make use of this combined adversary $\mathcal{H}$ as well as the associated augmented experiments $\mathsf{Exp}_{\mathcal{H}}^{\text{PHPE,REAL}}(\lambda)$ and $\mathsf{Exp}_{\mathcal{H},\mathcal{S}}^{\text{PHPE,IDEAL}}(\lambda)$ in the security proof of our PHPE construction, both the attribute-only and KEM versions.

3 The Proposed PHPE Scheme

3.1 Construction

In this section, we will present our PHPE scheme for the function family $\mathcal{F}_{\text{ABP}\circ\text{IP}}^{(q,n',n)}$. This construction is presented in the attribute-only mode, i.e., without any actual payload. A key-encapsulation mechanism (KEM) version of this construction is presented in the full version of this paper. In the proposed scheme, we assume that the function ρ outputted by $\mathsf{PGB}(f)$ for any $f \in \mathcal{F}_{\text{ABP}\circ\text{IP}}^{(q,n',n)}$ is injective. This restriction can be readily overcome using standard techniques along the lines of [30,34].

$\mathsf{PHPE.Setup}(1^{n'}, 1^{n})$: The setup algorithm takes as input the security parameter λ together with the lengths n' and n of the public and private attribute strings respectively. It proceeds as follows:

1. It first generates $(\mathsf{params}, \{\mathbb{B}_\imath, \mathbb{B}_\imath^*\}_{\imath\in[n'+n]}) \xleftarrow{\mathsf{R}} \mathcal{G}_{\text{OB}}(n'+n, (0, \overbrace{9, \ldots, 9}^{n'+n}))$.
2. For $\imath \in [n'+n]$, it sets $\widehat{\mathbb{B}}_\imath = \{\boldsymbol{b}^{(\imath,1)}, \boldsymbol{b}^{(\imath,2)}, \boldsymbol{b}^{(\imath,9)}\}, \widehat{\mathbb{B}}_\imath^* = \{\boldsymbol{b}^{*(\imath,1)}, \boldsymbol{b}^{*(\imath,2)}, \boldsymbol{b}^{*(\imath,7)}, \boldsymbol{b}^{*(\imath,8)}\}$.
3. It outputs the public parameters $\text{MPK} = (\mathsf{params}, \{\widehat{\mathbb{B}}_\imath\}_{\imath\in[n'+n]})$ and the master secret key $\text{MSK} = \{\widehat{\mathbb{B}}_\imath^*\}_{\imath\in[n'+n]}$.

$\mathsf{PHPE.Encrypt}(\text{MPK}, (\vec{x}, \vec{z}))$: The encryption algorithm takes as input the public parameters MPK and a pair of public-private attribute strings $(\vec{x}, \vec{z}) \in \mathbb{F}_q^{n'} \times \mathbb{F}_q^n$. It executes the following:

1. First, it samples $\omega \xleftarrow{\mathsf{U}} \mathbb{F}_q$.
2. Next, for $\iota' \in [n']$, it samples $\varphi'_{\iota'} \xleftarrow{\mathsf{U}} \mathbb{F}_q$, and computes
$$\boldsymbol{c}'^{(\iota')} = (\omega(1, x_{\iota'}), \vec{0}^4, \vec{0}^2, \varphi'_{\iota'})_{\mathbb{B}_{\iota'}}.$$
3. Then, for $\iota \in [n]$, it samples $\varphi_\iota \xleftarrow{\mathsf{U}} \mathbb{F}_q$, and computes
$$\boldsymbol{c}^{(\iota)} = (\omega(1, z_\iota), \vec{0}^4, \vec{0}^2, \varphi_\iota)_{\mathbb{B}_{n'+\iota}}.$$
4. It outputs the ciphertext $\text{CT} = (\vec{x}, \{\boldsymbol{c}'^{(\iota')}\}_{\iota' \in [n']}, \{\boldsymbol{c}^{(\iota)}\}_{\iota \in [n]})$.

$\mathsf{PHPE.KeyGen}(\text{MPK}, \text{MSK}, f)$: The key generation algorithm takes as input the public parameters MPK, the master secret key MSK, along with a function $f \in \mathcal{F}_{\text{ABP}\circ\text{IP}}^{(q,n',n)}$. It operates as follows:

1. It first generates $((\{\sigma_j\}_{j \in [n]}, \{\alpha_{j'}, \gamma_{j'}\}_{j' \in [m]}), \rho : [m] \to [n']) \xleftarrow{\mathsf{R}} \mathsf{PGB}(f)$.
2. Next, it samples $\zeta \xleftarrow{\mathsf{U}} \mathbb{F}_q$.
3. Then, for $j' \in [m]$, it samples $\vec{\kappa}'^{(j')} \xleftarrow{\mathsf{U}} \mathbb{F}_q^2$, and computes
$$\boldsymbol{k}'^{(j')} = ((\gamma_{j'}, \alpha_{j'}), \vec{0}^4, \vec{\kappa}'^{(j')}, 0)_{\mathbb{B}^*_{\rho(j')}}.$$
4. Then, for $j \in [n]$, it samples $\vec{\kappa}^{(j)} \xleftarrow{\mathsf{U}} \mathbb{F}_q^2$, and computes
$$\boldsymbol{k}^{(j)} = ((\sigma_j, \zeta), \vec{0}^4, \vec{\kappa}^{(j)}, 0)_{\mathbb{B}^*_{n'+j}}.$$
5. It outputs the decryption key $\text{SK}(f) = (f, \{\boldsymbol{k}'^{(j')}\}_{j' \in [m]}, \{\boldsymbol{k}^{(j)}\}_{j \in [n]})$.

$\mathsf{PHPE.Decrypt}(\text{MPK}, \text{SK}(f), \text{CT})$: The decryption algorithm takes in the public parameters MPK, a decryption key $\text{SK}(f) = (f, \{\boldsymbol{k}'^{(j')}\}_{j' \in [m]}, \{\boldsymbol{k}^{(j)}\}_{j \in [n]})$, and a ciphertext $\text{CT} = (\vec{x}, \{\boldsymbol{c}'^{(\iota')}\}_{\iota' \in [n']}, \{\boldsymbol{c}^{(\iota)}\}_{\iota \in [n]})$. It proceeds as follows:

1. It first computes $\Lambda'_{j'} = e(\boldsymbol{c}'^{(\rho(j'))}, \boldsymbol{k}'^{(j')})$ for $j' \in [m]$, and $\Lambda_j = e(\boldsymbol{c}^{(j)}, \boldsymbol{k}^{(j)})$ for $j \in [n]$.
2. Next, it determines the coefficients $(\{\Omega_j\}_{j \in [n]}, \{\Omega'_{j'}\}_{j' \in [m]}) = \mathsf{REC}(f, \vec{x})$.
3. Then, it computes $\Lambda = \left(\prod_{j' \in [m]} \Lambda_{j'}'^{\Omega'_{j'}}\right)\left(\prod_{j \in [n]} \Lambda_j^{\Omega_j}\right)$.
4. It outputs 1 if $\Lambda = 1_{\mathbb{G}_T}$, and 0 otherwise, where $1_{\mathbb{G}_T}$ is the identity element in $\mathbb{G}_T$.

► **Correctness:** For any decryption key $\text{SK}(f) = (f, \{\boldsymbol{k}'^{(j')}\}_{j' \in [m]}, \{\boldsymbol{k}^{(j)}\}_{j \in [n]})$ for a function $f \in \mathcal{F}_{\text{ABP}\circ\text{IP}}^{(q,n',n)}$, and any ciphertext $\text{CT} = (\vec{x}, \{\boldsymbol{c}'^{(\iota')}\}_{\iota' \in [n']}, \{\boldsymbol{c}^{(\iota)}\}_{\iota \in [n]})$ encrypting a pair of public-private attribute strings $(\vec{x}, \vec{z}) \in \mathbb{F}_q^{n'} \times \mathbb{F}_q^n$, we have

$$\Lambda'_{j'} = g_T^{\omega(\alpha_{j'} x_{\rho(j')} + \gamma_{j'})} \text{ for } j' \in [m],$$
$$\Lambda_j = g_T^{\omega(\zeta z_j + \sigma_j)} \text{ for } j \in [n].$$

The above follows from the expressions of $\{\boldsymbol{k}'^{(j')}\}_{j'\in[m]}$, $\{\boldsymbol{k}^{(j)}\}_{j\in[n]}$, $\{\boldsymbol{c}'^{(\iota')}\}_{\iota'\in[n']}$, $\{\boldsymbol{c}^{(\iota)}\}_{\iota\in[n]}$, and the dual orthonormality property of $\{\mathbb{B}_\imath, \mathbb{B}_\imath^*\}_{\imath\in[n'+n]}$. Hence, from Eq. (2.3) it follows that

$$\Lambda = g_T^{\omega\zeta f(\vec{x},\vec{z})}.$$

Therefore, if $R^{\mathrm{ABP\circ IP}}(f,(\vec{x},\vec{z})) = 1$, i.e., $f(\vec{x},\vec{z}) = 0$, then $\Lambda = 1_{\mathbb{G}_T}$, while if $R^{\mathrm{ABP\circ IP}}(f,(\vec{x},\vec{z})) = 0$, i.e., $f(\vec{x},\vec{z}) \neq 0$, then $\Lambda \neq 1_{\mathbb{G}_T}$ with all but negligible probability $2/q$, i.e., except when $\omega = 0$ or $\zeta = 0$.

Remark 3.1 (On Multi-Ciphertext Scheme): The PHPE scheme described above is only secure against adversaries that are allowed to make a single ciphertext query. However, we can readily extend the above scheme to one that is secure for any a priori bounded number of ciphertext queries of the adversary. The extension is as follows: Suppose we want to design a scheme that is secure for q_{CT} number of ciphertext queries. Then, we would introduce a $4q_{\mathrm{CT}}$-dimensional hidden subspace on each of the ciphertext and the decryption key sides, where each 4-dimensional hidden subspace on the ciphertext side and its corresponding 4-dimensional dual subspace on the decryption key side will be used to handle each ciphertext query in the security reduction. Clearly the size of ciphertexts, decryption keys, and public parameters would scale linearly with q_{CT}.

3.2 Security

We now present our main theorem:

Theorem 3.1: *The proposed* PHPE *scheme is* (poly, 1, poly)*-simulation-based adaptively strongly partially hiding (as per the security model described in Sect. 2.6) under the* SXDLIN *assumption.*

Following corollary is immediate from the relation between indistinguishability-based and simulation-based security for FE, as mentioned in the Introduction as well as the equivalence of the single- and multi-ciphertext security in the indistinguishability-based setting for FE:

Corollary 3.1: *The proposed* PHPE *scheme is* (poly, poly, poly)*-indistinguishability-based adaptively strongly partially hiding (as per the security model described in [12] and the full version of this paper) under the* SXDLIN *assumption.*

In order to prove Theorem 3.1, we consider a sequence of hybrid experiments which differ from one another in the construction of the ciphertext and/or the decryption keys queried by the augmented adversary $\mathcal{H}$ (described in Remark 2.1). The first hybrid corresponds to the experiment $\mathsf{Exp}_{\mathcal{H}}^{\mathrm{PHPE,REAL}}(\lambda)$ (described in Sect. 2.6), while the last one corresponds to the experiment $\mathsf{Exp}_{\mathcal{H},\mathcal{S}}^{\mathrm{PHPE,IDEAL}}(\lambda)$ (also described in Sect. 2.6) with the simulator $\mathcal{S}$ described below. We argue that $\mathcal{H}$'s probability of outputting 1 changes only by a negligible amount in each successive hybrid experiment, thereby establishing Theorem 3.1. Note that we are considering only one ciphertext query made by the adversary $\mathcal{H}$. Let,

$q_{\text{KEY-PRE}}, q_{\text{KEY-POST}}$ be respectively the number of decryption key queries made by $\mathcal{H}$ before and after making the ciphertext query, and $q_{\text{KEY}} = q_{\text{KEY-PRE}} + q_{\text{KEY-POST}}$. Note that we consider $q_{\text{KEY-PRE}}$ and $q_{\text{KEY-POST}}$ to be arbitrary polynomials in the security parameter λ.

▪ Description of the Simulator

The simulator $\mathcal{S}$ is described below.

- In order to generate the public parameters, $\mathcal{S}$ proceeds as follows:
  1. It first generates $(\mathsf{params}, \{\mathbb{B}_\imath, \mathbb{B}^*_\imath\}_{\imath \in [n'+n]}) \xleftarrow{\mathsf{R}} \mathcal{G}_{\text{OB}}(n'+n, (0, \overbrace{9, \ldots, 9}^{n'+n}))$.
  2. For $\imath \in [n'+n]$, it sets $\widehat{\mathbb{B}}_\imath = \{\boldsymbol{b}^{(\imath,1)}, \boldsymbol{b}^{(\imath,2)}, \boldsymbol{b}^{(\imath,9)}\}$.
  3. It outputs the public parameters $\text{MPK} = (\mathsf{params}, \{\widehat{\mathbb{B}}_\imath\}_{\imath \in [n'+n]})$.
- For $h \in [q_{\text{KEY-PRE}}]$, $\mathcal{S}$ simulates the hth decryption key queried by $\mathcal{H}$ corresponding to some function $f_h \in \mathcal{F}^{(q,n',n)}_{\text{ABP}\circ\text{IP}}$ as follows:
  1. At first, it generates $((\{\sigma_{h,j}\}_{j\in[n]}, \{\alpha_{h,j'}, \gamma_{h,j'}\}_{j'\in[m_h]}), \rho_h : [m_h] \to [n'])$, $((\{\widehat{\sigma}_{h,j}\}_{j\in[n]}, \{\widehat{\alpha}_{h,j'}, \widehat{\gamma}_{h,j'}\}_{j'\in[m_h]}), \rho_h : [m_h] \to [n']) \xleftarrow{\mathsf{R}} \mathsf{PGB}(f_h)$.
  2. Next, it samples $\zeta_h, \widehat{\zeta}_h \xleftarrow{\mathsf{U}} \mathbb{F}_q$.
  3. Then, for $j' \in [m_h]$, it samples $\vec{\kappa}'^{(h,j')} \xleftarrow{\mathsf{U}} \mathbb{F}_q^2$, and computes
  $$\boldsymbol{k}'^{(h,j')} = ((\gamma_{h,j'}, \alpha_{h,j'}), \vec{0}^2, (\widehat{\gamma}_{h,j'}, \widehat{\alpha}_{h,j'}), \vec{\kappa}'^{(h,j')}, 0)_{\mathbb{B}^*_{\rho_h(j')}}.$$
  4. Then, for $j \in [n]$, it samples $\vec{\kappa}^{(h,j)} \xleftarrow{\mathsf{U}} \mathbb{F}_q^2$, and computes
  $$\boldsymbol{k}^{(h,j)} = ((\sigma_{h,j}, \zeta_h), \vec{0}^2, (\widehat{\sigma}_{h,j}, \widehat{\zeta}_h), \vec{\kappa}^{(h,j)}, 0)_{\mathbb{B}^*_{n'+j}}.$$
  5. It outputs $\text{SK}(f_h) = (f_h, \{\boldsymbol{k}'^{(h,j')}\}_{j'\in[m_h]}, \{\boldsymbol{k}^{(h,j)}\}_{j\in[n]})$.
- When $\mathcal{H}$ queries a ciphertext for some pair of public-private attribute strings $(\vec{x}, \vec{z}) \in \mathbb{F}_q^{n'} \times \mathbb{F}_q^n$, $\mathcal{S}$ receives $\vec{x}$ and $\{R^{\text{ABP}\circ\text{IP}}(f_h, (\vec{x}, \vec{z}))\}_{h\in[q_{\text{KEY-PRE}}]}$. It simulates the ciphertext as follows:
  1. At first, it samples $\vec{s} \xleftarrow{\mathsf{U}} S = \{\vec{s} \in \mathbb{F}_q^n \mid R^{\text{ABP}\circ\text{IP}}(f_h, (\vec{x}, \vec{s})) = R^{\text{ABP}\circ\text{IP}}(f_h, (\vec{x}, \vec{z})) \forall h \in [q_{\text{KEY-PRE}}]\}$. Observe that the set S is exactly identical to the set $\widetilde{S} = \{\vec{s} \in \mathbb{F}_q^n \mid R^{\text{IP}}((f_{h,1}(\vec{x}), \ldots, f_{h,n}(\vec{x})), \vec{s}) = R^{\text{IP}}((f_{h,1}(\vec{x}), \ldots, f_{h,n}(\vec{x})), \vec{z}) \forall h \in [q_{\text{KEY-PRE}}]\}$, where R^{IP} represents the inner-product predicate family defined as $R^{\text{IP}} = \{R^{\text{IP}}(\vec{w}, \cdot) : \mathbb{F}_q^n \to \{0,1\} \mid \vec{w} \in \mathbb{F}_q^n\}$ such that $R^{\text{IP}}(\vec{w}, \vec{v}) = 1$ if $\vec{v} \cdot \vec{w} = 0$, and 0 if $\vec{v} \cdot \vec{w} \neq 0$ for $\vec{v}, \vec{w} \in \mathbb{F}_q^n$, and $f_{h,j}$ is the jth component ABP of f_h for $h \in [q_{\text{KEY-PRE}}], j \in [n]$. It has already been demonstrated by O'Neill [37] that the inner-product predicate family R^{IP} is *pre-image-samplable*, which essentially means that we can efficiently sample from the set $\widetilde{S}$. In fact, he provided an explicit algorithm for doing this. Thus, given $\{f_h\}_{h\in[q_{\text{KEY-PRE}}]}$ and $\vec{x}$, $\mathcal{S}$ can efficiently sample from S by first determining the vectors $\{(f_{h,1}(\vec{x}), \ldots, f_{h,n}(\vec{x}))\}_{h\in[q_{\text{KEY-PRE}}]}$ and then sampling from the set $\widetilde{S}$ using the algorithm described in [37].

2. Then, it samples $\tau, \theta, \xleftarrow{\mathsf{U}} \mathbb{F}_q$.
3. Next, for $\iota' \in [n']$, it samples $\varphi'_{\iota'} \xleftarrow{\mathsf{U}} \mathbb{F}_q$, and computes

$$\boldsymbol{c}'^{(\iota')} = (\vec{0}^3, \tau, \theta(1, x_{\iota'}), \vec{0}^2, \varphi'_{\iota'})_{\mathbb{B}_{\iota'}}.$$

4. Then, for $\iota \in [n]$, it samples $\varphi_\iota \xleftarrow{\mathsf{U}} \mathbb{F}_q$, and computes

$$\boldsymbol{c}^{(\iota)} = (\vec{0}^3, \tau, \theta(1, s_\iota), \vec{0}^2, \varphi_\iota)_{\mathbb{B}_{n'+\iota}}.$$

5. It outputs the ciphertext $\text{CT} = (\vec{x}, \{\boldsymbol{c}'^{(\iota')}\}_{\iota' \in [n']}, \{\boldsymbol{c}^{(\iota)}\}_{\iota \in [n]})$.

- For $h \in [q_{\text{KEY-PRE}} + 1, q_{\text{KEY}}]$, in response to the hth decryption key query of $\mathcal{H}$ corresponding to some function $f_h \in \mathcal{F}^{(q,n',n)}_{\text{ABP}\circ\text{IP}}$, $\mathcal{S}$ executes the following steps:
  1. It first generates $((\{\sigma_{h,j}\}_{j\in[n]}, \{\alpha_{h,j'}, \gamma_{h,j'}\}_{j'\in[m_h]}), \rho_h : [m_h] \to [n']) \xleftarrow{\mathsf{R}} \mathsf{PGB}(f_h)$.
  2. Next, it samples $\zeta_h \xleftarrow{\mathsf{U}} \mathbb{F}_q$.
  3. After that, it queries its oracle $\mathcal{O}_{R^{\text{ABP}\circ\text{IP}}}((\vec{x}, \vec{z}), \cdot)$ with the function f_h, and receives back $R^{\text{ABP}\circ\text{IP}}(f_h, (\vec{x}, \vec{z}))$. If $R^{\text{ABP}\circ\text{IP}}(f_h(\vec{x}, \vec{z})) = 1$, i.e., $f_h(\vec{x}, \vec{z}) = 0$, it forms $((\{\nu_{h,j}\}_{j\in[n]}, \{\mu_{h,j'}\}_{j'\in[m_h]}), \rho_h : [m_h] \to [n']) \xleftarrow{\mathsf{R}} \mathsf{SIM}(f_h, \vec{x}, 0)$. Otherwise, if $R^{\text{ABP}\circ\text{IP}}(f_h, (\vec{x}, \vec{z})) = 0$, i.e., $f_h(\vec{x}, \vec{z}) \neq 0$, then it samples $\check{\zeta}_h \xleftarrow{\mathsf{U}} \mathbb{F}_q$, and generates $((\{\nu_{h,j}\}_{j\in[n]}, \{\mu_{h,j'}\}_{j'\in[m_h]}), \rho_h : [m_h] \to [n']) \xleftarrow{\mathsf{R}} \mathsf{SIM}(f_h, \vec{x}, \check{\zeta}_h)$.
  4. Then, for $j' \in [m_h]$, it samples $\eta'_{h,j'} \xleftarrow{\mathsf{U}} \mathbb{F}_q, \vec{\kappa}'^{(h,j')} \xleftarrow{\mathsf{U}} \mathbb{F}_q^2$, and computes

$$\boldsymbol{k}'^{(h,j')} = ((\gamma_{h,j'}, \alpha_{h,j'}), (\eta'_{h,j'}, \mu_{h,j'}), \vec{0}^2, \vec{\kappa}'^{(h,j')}, 0)_{\mathbb{B}^*_{\rho_h(j')}}.$$

  5. Then, for $j \in [n]$, it samples $\eta_{h,j} \xleftarrow{\mathsf{U}} \mathbb{F}_q, \vec{\kappa}^{(h,j)} \xleftarrow{\mathsf{U}} \mathbb{F}_q^2$, and computes

$$\boldsymbol{k}^{(h,j)} = ((\sigma_{h,j}, \zeta_h), (\eta_{h,j}, \nu_{h,j}), \vec{0}^2, \vec{\kappa}^{(h,j)}, 0)_{\mathbb{B}^*_{n'+j}}.$$

  6. It outputs $\text{SK}(f_h) = (f_h, \{\boldsymbol{k}'^{(h,j')}\}_{j'\in[m_h]}, \{\boldsymbol{k}^{(h,j)}\}_{j\in[n]})$.

▪ Sequence of Hybrid Experiments

The hybrid experiments are described below. In the description of these hybrids, a part framed by a box indicates coefficients that are altered in a transition from its previous hybrid.

Hyb$_0$: This experiment corresponds to the experiment $\mathsf{Exp}^{\text{PHPE,REAL}}_{\mathcal{H}}(\lambda)$ defined in Sect. 2.6. Thus, in this experiment, the ciphertext queried by $\mathcal{H}$ corresponding to a pair of public-private attribute strings $(\vec{x}, \vec{z}) \in \mathbb{F}_q^{n'} \times \mathbb{F}_q^n$ is generated as $\text{CT} = (\vec{x}, \{\boldsymbol{c}'^{(\iota')}\}_{\iota'\in[n']}, \{\boldsymbol{c}^{(\iota)}\}_{\iota\in[n]})$ such that

$$\begin{aligned} \boldsymbol{c}'^{(\iota')} &= (\omega(1, x_{\iota'}), \vec{0}^2, \vec{0}^2, \vec{0}^2, \varphi'_{\iota'})_{\mathbb{B}_{\iota'}} \text{ for } \iota' \in [n'], \\ \boldsymbol{c}^{(\iota)} &= (\omega(1, z_\iota), \vec{0}^2, \vec{0}^2, \vec{0}^2, \varphi_\iota)_{\mathbb{B}_{n'+\iota}} \text{ for } \iota \in [n], \end{aligned} \tag{3.1}$$

where $\omega, \{\varphi'_{\iota'}\}_{\iota' \in [n']}, \{\varphi_\iota\}_{\iota \in [n]} \xleftarrow{\mathsf{U}} \mathbb{F}_q$, while for $h \in [q_{\text{KEY}}]$, the hth decryption key queried by $\mathcal{H}$ corresponding to the function $f_h \in \mathcal{F}^{(q,n',n)}_{\text{ABP}\circ\text{IP}}$ is generated as $\text{SK}(f_h) = (f_h, \{\boldsymbol{k}'^{(h,j')}\}_{j' \in [m_h]}, \{\boldsymbol{k}^{(h,j)}\}_{j \in [n]})$ such that

$$\begin{aligned} \boldsymbol{k}'^{(h,j')} &= ((\gamma_{h,j'}, \alpha_{h,j'}), \vec{0}^2, \vec{0}^2, \vec{\kappa}'^{(h,j')}, 0)_{\mathbb{B}^*_{\rho_h(j')}} \text{ for } j' \in [m_h], \\ \boldsymbol{k}^{(h,j)} &= ((\sigma_{h,j}, \zeta_h), \vec{0}^2, \vec{0}^2, \vec{\kappa}^{(h,j)}, 0)_{\mathbb{B}^*_{n'+j}} \text{ for } j \in [n], \end{aligned} \quad (3.2)$$

where $\zeta_h \xleftarrow{\mathsf{U}} \mathbb{F}_q$, $\{\vec{\kappa}'^{(h,j')}\}_{j' \in [m_h]}, \{\vec{\kappa}^{(h,j)}\}_{j \in [n]} \xleftarrow{\mathsf{U}} \mathbb{F}_q^2$, $m_h + n + 1$ is the number of vertices in the ABP Γ'_h computing the function f_h as described in Sect. 2.3, and $((\{\sigma_{h,j}\}_{j \in [n]}, \{\alpha_{h,j'}, \gamma_{h,j'}\}_{j' \in [m_h]}), \rho_h : [m_h] \to [n']) \xleftarrow{\mathsf{R}} \mathsf{PGB}(f_h)$. Here, $\{\mathbb{B}_\iota, \mathbb{B}^*_\iota\}_{\iota \in [n'+n]}$ is the collection of dual orthonormal bases generated by executing $\mathcal{G}_{\text{OB}}(n'+n, (0, \overbrace{9, \ldots, 9}^{n'+n}))$ during setup.

Hyb_1 : This experiment is analogous to Hyb_0 except that in this experiment, the ciphertext queried by $\mathcal{H}$ corresponding to the pair of public-private attribute strings $(\vec{x}, \vec{z}) \in \mathbb{F}_q^{n'} \times \mathbb{F}_q^n$ is generated as $\text{CT} = (\vec{x}, \{\boldsymbol{c}'^{(\iota')}\}_{\iota' \in [n']}, \{\boldsymbol{c}^{(\iota)}\}_{\iota \in [n]})$ such that

$$\begin{aligned} \boldsymbol{c}'^{(\iota')} &= (\omega(1, x_{\iota'}), (\boxed{\vartheta}, 0), \vec{0}^2, \vec{0}^2, \varphi'_{\iota'})_{\mathbb{B}_{\iota'}} \text{ for } \iota' \in [n'], \\ \boldsymbol{c}^{(\iota)} &= (\omega(1, z_\iota), (\boxed{\vartheta}, 0), \vec{0}^2, \vec{0}^2, \varphi_\iota)_{\mathbb{B}_{n'+\iota}} \text{ for } \iota \in [n], \end{aligned} \quad (3.3)$$

where $\vartheta \xleftarrow{\mathsf{U}} \mathbb{F}_q$, and all the other variables are generated as in Hyb_0.

$\mathsf{Hyb}_{2\text{-}\chi\text{-}1}$ ($\chi \in [q_{\text{KEY-PRE}}]$): The experiment $\mathsf{Hyb}_{2\text{-}0\text{-}4}$ coincides with Hyb_1. This experiment is analogous to $\mathsf{Hyb}_{2\text{-}(\chi-1)\text{-}4}$ except that in this experiment, the ciphertext queried by $\mathcal{H}$ corresponding to the pair of public-private attribute strings $(\vec{x}, \vec{z}) \in \mathbb{F}_q^{n'} \times \mathbb{F}_q^n$ is generated as $\text{CT} = (\vec{x}, \{\boldsymbol{c}'^{(\iota')}\}_{\iota' \in [n']}, \{\boldsymbol{c}^{(\iota)}\}_{\iota \in [n]})$ such that

$$\begin{aligned} \boldsymbol{c}'^{(\iota')} &= (\omega(1, x_{\iota'}), \boxed{\tau(1, x_{\iota'}), \theta(1, x_{\iota'})}, \vec{0}^2, \varphi'_{\iota'})_{\mathbb{B}_{\iota'}} \text{ for } \iota' \in [n'], \\ \boldsymbol{c}^{(\iota)} &= (\omega(1, z_\iota), \boxed{\tau(1, z_\iota), \theta(1, s_\iota)}, \vec{0}^2, \varphi_\iota)_{\mathbb{B}_{n'+\iota}} \text{ for } \iota \in [n], \end{aligned} \quad (3.4)$$

where $\tau, \theta \xleftarrow{\mathsf{U}} \mathbb{F}_q$, $\vec{s} \xleftarrow{\mathsf{U}} S = \{\vec{s} \in \mathbb{F}_q^n \mid R^{\text{ABP}\circ\text{IP}}(f_h, (\vec{x}, \vec{s})) = R^{\text{ABP}\circ\text{IP}}(f_h, (\vec{x}, \vec{z})) \forall h \in [q_{\text{KEY-PRE}}]\}$, and all the other variables are generated as in $\mathsf{Hyb}_{2\text{-}(\chi-1)\text{-}4}$.

$\mathsf{Hyb}_{2\text{-}\chi\text{-}2}$ ($\chi \in [q_{\text{KEY-PRE}}]$): This experiment is the same as $\mathsf{Hyb}_{2\text{-}\chi\text{-}1}$ with the only exception that the χth decryption key queried by $\mathcal{H}$ corresponding to the function $f_\chi \in \mathcal{F}^{(q,n',n)}_{\text{ABP}\circ\text{IP}}$ is formed as $\text{SK}(f_\chi) = (f_\chi, \{\boldsymbol{k}'^{(\chi,j')}\}_{j' \in [m_\chi]}, \{\boldsymbol{k}^{(\chi,j)}\}_{j \in [n]})$ such that

$$\begin{aligned} \boldsymbol{k}'^{(\chi,j')} &= ((\gamma_{\chi,j'}, \alpha_{\chi,j'}), \boxed{(\widetilde{\gamma}_{\chi,j'}, \widetilde{\alpha}_{\chi,j'})}, \vec{0}^2, \vec{\kappa}'^{(\chi,j')}, 0)_{\mathbb{B}^*_{\rho_\chi(j')}} \text{ for } j' \in [m_\chi], \\ \boldsymbol{k}^{(\chi,j)} &= ((\sigma_{\chi,j}, \zeta_\chi), \boxed{(\widetilde{\sigma}_{\chi,j}, \widetilde{\zeta}_\chi)}, \vec{0}^2, \vec{\kappa}^{(\chi,j)}, 0)_{\mathbb{B}^*_{n'+j}} \text{ for } j \in [n], \end{aligned} \quad (3.5)$$

where $\widetilde{\zeta}_\chi \xleftarrow{\mathsf{U}} \mathbb{F}_q$, $((\{\widetilde{\sigma}_{\chi,j}\}_{j \in [n]}, \{\widetilde{\alpha}_{\chi,j'}, \widetilde{\gamma}_{\chi,j'}\}_{j' \in [m_\chi]}), \rho_\chi : [m_\chi] \to [n']) \xleftarrow{\mathsf{R}} \mathsf{PGB}(f_\chi)$, and all the other variables are generated as in $\mathsf{Hyb}_{2\text{-}\chi\text{-}1}$.

$\mathsf{Hyb}_{2\text{-}\chi\text{-}3}$ ($\chi \in [q_{\text{KEY-PRE}}]$): This experiment is analogous to $\mathsf{Hyb}_{2\text{-}\chi\text{-}2}$ except that in this experiment, the ciphertext queried by $\mathcal{H}$ for the pair of public-private attribute strings $(\vec{x}, \vec{z}) \in \mathbb{F}_q^{n'} \times \mathbb{F}_q^n$ is formed as $\text{CT} = (\vec{x}, \{\boldsymbol{c}'^{(\iota')}\}_{\iota' \in [n']}, \{\boldsymbol{c}^{(\iota)}\}_{\iota \in [n]})$ such that $\{\boldsymbol{c}'^{(\iota')}\}_{\iota' \in [n']}$ are given by Eq. (3.4) and

$$\boldsymbol{c}^{(\iota)} = (\omega(1, z_\iota), \tau(1, \boxed{s_\iota}), \theta(1, s_\iota), \vec{0}^2, \varphi_\iota)_{\mathbb{B}_{n'+\iota}} \text{ for } \iota \in [n], \tag{3.6}$$

where all the variables are generated as in $\mathsf{Hyb}_{2\text{-}\chi\text{-}2}$.

$\mathsf{Hyb}_{2\text{-}\chi\text{-}4}$ ($\chi \in [q_{\text{KEY-PRE}}]$): This experiment is identical to $\mathsf{Hyb}_{2\text{-}\chi\text{-}3}$ except that the χth decryption key queried by $\mathcal{H}$ corresponding to the function $f_\chi \in \mathcal{F}_{\text{ABP}\circ\text{IP}}^{(q,n',n)}$ is generated as $\text{SK}(f_\chi) = (f_\chi, \{\boldsymbol{k}'^{(\chi,j')}\}_{j' \in [m_\chi]}, \{\boldsymbol{k}^{(\chi,j)}\}_{j \in [n]})$ such that

$$\begin{aligned} \boldsymbol{k}'^{(\chi,j')} &= ((\gamma_{\chi,j'}, \alpha_{\chi,j'}), \boxed{\vec{0}^2, (\widehat{\gamma}_{\chi,j'}, \widehat{\alpha}_{\chi,j'})}, \vec{\kappa}'^{(\chi,j')}, 0)_{\mathbb{B}^*_{\rho_\chi(j')}} \text{ for } j' \in [m_\chi], \\ \boldsymbol{k}^{(\chi,j)} &= ((\sigma_{\chi,j}, \zeta_\chi), \boxed{\vec{0}^2, (\widehat{\sigma}_{\chi,j}, \widehat{\zeta}_\chi)}, \vec{\kappa}^{(\chi,j)}, 0)_{\mathbb{B}^*_{n'+j}} \text{ for } j \in [n], \end{aligned} \tag{3.7}$$

where $\widehat{\zeta}_\chi \xleftarrow{\mathsf{U}} \mathbb{F}_q$, $((\{\widehat{\sigma}_{\chi,j}\}_{j \in [n]}, \{\widehat{\alpha}_{\chi,j'}, \widehat{\gamma}_{\chi,j'}\}_{j' \in [m_\chi]}), \rho_\chi : [m_\chi] \to [n']) \xleftarrow{\mathsf{R}} \mathsf{PGB}(f_\chi)$, and all the other variables are generated in the same manner as that in $\mathsf{Hyb}_{2\text{-}\chi\text{-}3}$.

Hyb_3: This experiment is analogous to $\mathsf{Hyb}_{2\text{-}q_{\text{KEY-PRE}}\text{-}4}$ except that in this experiment, the ciphertext queried by $\mathcal{H}$ for the pair of public-private attribute strings $(\vec{x}, \vec{z}) \in \mathbb{F}_q^{n'} \times \mathbb{F}_q^n$ is formed as $\text{CT} = (\vec{x}, \{\boldsymbol{c}'^{(\iota')}\}_{\iota' \in [n']}, \{\boldsymbol{c}^{(\iota)}\}_{\iota \in [n]})$, where $\{\boldsymbol{c}'^{(\iota')}\}_{\iota' \in [n']}, \{\boldsymbol{c}^{(\iota)}\}_{\iota \in [n]}$ are given by Eq. (3.4), while for $h \in [q_{\text{KEY}}]$, the hth decryption key queried by $\mathcal{H}$ for $f_h \in \mathcal{F}_{\text{ABP}\circ\text{IP}}^{(q,n',n)}$ is generated as $\text{SK}(f_h) = (f_h, \{\boldsymbol{k}'^{(h,j')}\}_{j' \in [m_h]}, \{\boldsymbol{k}^{(h,j)}\}_{j \in [n]})$ such that

$$\begin{aligned} \boldsymbol{k}'^{(h,j')} &= \begin{cases} ((\gamma_{h,j'}, \alpha_{h,j'}), \boxed{(\widetilde{\gamma}_{h,j'}, \widetilde{\alpha}_{h,j'})}, (\widehat{\gamma}_{h,j'}, \widehat{\alpha}_{h,j'}), \vec{\kappa}'^{(h,j')}, 0)_{\mathbb{B}^*_{\rho_h(j')}} \\ \qquad \text{for } j' \in [m_h] \text{ if } h \in [q_{\text{KEY-PRE}}], \\ ((\gamma_{h,j'}, \alpha_{h,j'}), \boxed{(\widetilde{\gamma}_{h,j'}, \widetilde{\alpha}_{h,j'})}, \vec{0}^2, \vec{\kappa}'^{(h,j')}, 0)_{\mathbb{B}^*_{\rho_h(j')}} \\ \qquad \text{for } j' \in [m_h] \text{ if } h \in [q_{\text{KEY-PRE}} + 1, q_{\text{KEY}}], \end{cases} \\ \boldsymbol{k}^{(h,j)} &= \begin{cases} ((\sigma_{h,j}, \zeta_h), \boxed{(\widetilde{\sigma}_{h,j}, \widetilde{\zeta}_h)}, (\widehat{\sigma}_{h,j}, \widehat{\zeta}_h), \vec{\kappa}^{(h,j)}, 0)_{\mathbb{B}^*_{n'+j}} \\ \qquad \text{for } j \in [n] \text{ if } h \in [q_{\text{KEY-PRE}}], \\ ((\sigma_{h,j}, \zeta_h), \boxed{(\widetilde{\sigma}_{h,j}, \widetilde{\zeta}_h)}, \vec{0}^2, \vec{\kappa}^{(h,j)}, 0)_{\mathbb{B}^*_{n'+j}} \\ \qquad \text{for } j \in [n] \text{ if } h \in [q_{\text{KEY-PRE}} + 1, q_{\text{KEY}}], \end{cases} \end{aligned} \tag{3.8}$$

where $\{\widetilde{\zeta}_h\}_{h \in [q_{\text{KEY}}]} \xleftarrow{\mathsf{U}} \mathbb{F}_q$, $((\{\widetilde{\sigma}_{h,j}\}_{j \in [n]}, \{\widetilde{\alpha}_{h,j'}, \widetilde{\gamma}_{h,j'}\}_{j' \in [m_h]}), \rho_h : [m_h] \to [n']) \xleftarrow{\mathsf{R}} \mathsf{PGB}(f_h)$ for $h \in [q_{\text{KEY}}]$, and all the other variables are formed as in $\mathsf{Hyb}_{2\text{-}q_{\text{KEY-PRE}}\text{-}4}$.

Hyb$_4$: This experiment is analogous to Hyb$_3$ except that in this experiment, the ciphertext queried by $\mathcal{H}$ for the pair of public-private attribute strings $(\vec{x}, \vec{z}) \in \mathbb{F}_q^{n'} \times \mathbb{F}_q^n$ is generated as $\text{CT} = (\vec{x}, \{c'^{(\iota')}\}_{\iota' \in [n']}, \{c^{(\iota)}\}_{\iota \in [n]})$ such that

$$\begin{aligned} c'^{(\iota')} &= (\boxed{\vec{0}^2}, \tau(1, x_{\iota'}), \theta(1, x_{\iota'}), \vec{0}^2, \varphi'_{\iota'})_{\mathbb{B}_{\iota'}} \text{ for } \iota' \in [n'], \\ c^{(\iota)} &= (\boxed{\vec{0}^2}, \tau(1, z_\iota), \theta(1, s_\iota), \vec{0}^2, \varphi_\iota)_{\mathbb{B}_{n'+\iota}} \text{ for } \iota \in [n], \end{aligned} \tag{3.9}$$

where all the variables are generated as in Hyb$_3$.

Hyb$_5$: This experiment is identical to Hyb$_4$ except that in this experiment, for $h \in [q_{\text{KEY-PRE}}]$, the hth decryption key queried by $\mathcal{H}$ corresponding to the function $f_h \in \mathcal{F}_{\text{ABP}\circ\text{IP}}^{(q,n',n)}$ is generated as $\text{SK}(f_h) = (f_h, \{k'^{(h,j')}\}_{j' \in [m_h]}, \{k^{(h,j)}\}_{j \in [n]})$ such that $\{k'^{(h,j')}\}_{j' \in [m_h]}$ and $\{k^{(h,j)}\}_{j \in [n]}$ are given by Eq. (3.7).

Hyb$_6$: This experiment is the same as Hyb$_5$ except that in this experiment, the ciphertext queried by $\mathcal{H}$ for the pair of public-private attribute strings $(\vec{x}, \vec{z}) \in \mathbb{F}_q^{n'} \times \mathbb{F}_q^n$ is generated as $\text{CT} = (\vec{x}, \{c'^{(\iota')}\}_{\iota' \in [n']}, \{c^{(\iota)}\}_{\iota \in [n]})$ such that

$$\begin{aligned} c'^{(\iota')} &= (\vec{0}^2, \boxed{(0, \tau)}, \theta(1, x_{\iota'}), \vec{0}^2, \varphi'_{\iota'})_{\mathbb{B}_{\iota'}} \text{ for } \iota' \in [n'], \\ c^{(\iota)} &= (\vec{0}^2, \boxed{(0, \tau)}, \theta(1, s_\iota), \vec{0}^2, \varphi_\iota)_{\mathbb{B}_{n'+\iota}} \text{ for } \iota \in [n], \end{aligned} \tag{3.10}$$

while for $h \in [q_{\text{KEY-PRE}} + 1, q_{\text{KEY}}]$, the hth decryption key queried by $\mathcal{H}$ for $f_h \in \mathcal{F}_{\text{ABP}\circ\text{IP}}^{(q,n',n)}$ is generated as $\text{SK}(f_h) = (f_h, \{k'^{(h,j')}\}_{j' \in [m_h]}, \{k^{(h,j)}\}_{j \in [n]})$ such that

$$\begin{aligned} k'^{(h,j')} &= ((\gamma_{h,j'}, \alpha_{h,j'}), \boxed{(\widetilde{\gamma}_{h,j'}, \widetilde{\alpha}_{h,j'}) U'^{(\rho_h(j'))}}, \vec{0}^2, \vec{\kappa}'^{(h,j')}, 0)_{\mathbb{B}^*_{\rho_h(j')}} \text{ for } j' \in [m_h], \\ k^{(h,j)} &= ((\sigma_{h,j}, \zeta_h), \boxed{(\widetilde{\sigma}_{h,j}, \widetilde{\zeta}_h) U^{(j)}}, \vec{0}^2, \vec{\kappa}^{(h,j)}, 0)_{\mathbb{B}^*_{n'+j}} \text{ for } j \in [n], \end{aligned} \tag{3.11}$$

where $Z'^{(\iota')} \xleftarrow{\mathsf{U}} \{Z \in \mathsf{GL}(2, \mathbb{F}_q) \mid (1, x_{\iota'}) Z = \vec{e}^{(2)} = (0,1)\}$, $U'^{(\iota')} = ((Z'^{(\iota')})^{-1})^{\intercal}$ for $\iota' \in [n']$, $Z^{(\iota)} \xleftarrow{\mathsf{U}} \{Z \in \mathsf{GL}(2, \mathbb{F}_q \mid (1, z_\iota) Z = \vec{e}^{(2)} = (0,1)\}$, $U^{(\iota)} = ((Z^{(\iota)})^{-1})^{\intercal}$ for $\iota \in [n]$, and all the other variables are generated as in Hyb$_5$.

Hyb$_7$: This experiment is identical to Hyb$_6$ with the only exception that for $h \in [q_{\text{KEY-PRE}}+1, q_{\text{KEY}}]$, the hth decryption key queried by $\mathcal{H}$ corresponding to the function $f_h \in \mathcal{F}_{\text{ABP}\circ\text{IP}}^{(q,n',n)}$ is generated as $\text{SK}(f_h) = (f_h, \{k'^{(h,j')}\}_{j' \in [m_h]}, \{k^{(h,j)}\}_{j \in [n]})$ such that

$$\begin{aligned} k'^{(h,j')} &= ((\gamma_{h,j'}, \alpha_{h,j'}), \boxed{(\eta'_{h,j'}, \widetilde{\alpha}_{h,j'} x_{\rho_h(j')} + \widetilde{\gamma}_{h,j'})}, \vec{0}^2, \vec{\kappa}'^{(h,j')}, 0)_{\mathbb{B}^*_{\rho_h(j')}} \\ &\qquad \text{for } j' \in [m_h], \\ k^{(h,j)} &= ((\sigma_{h,j}, \zeta_h), \boxed{(\eta_{h,j}, \widetilde{\zeta}_h z_j + \widetilde{\sigma}_{h,j})}, \vec{0}^2, \vec{\kappa}^{(h,j)}, 0)_{\mathbb{B}^*_{n'+j}} \text{ for } j \in [n], \end{aligned} \tag{3.12}$$

where $\{\eta'_{h,j'}\}_{h \in [q_{\text{KEY-PRE}}+1, q_{\text{KEY}}], j' \in [m_h]}, \{\eta_{h,j}\}_{h \in [q_{\text{KEY-PRE}}+1, q_{\text{KEY}}], j \in [n]} \xleftarrow{\mathsf{U}} \mathbb{F}_q$, and all the other variables are generated as in Hyb$_6$.

Hyb_8: This experiment is analogous to Hyb_7 with the only exception that for $h \in [q_{\text{KEY-PRE}}+1, q_{\text{KEY}}]$, the hth decryption key queried by $\mathcal{H}$ corresponding to the function $f_h \in \mathcal{F}^{(q,n',n)}_{\text{ABP}\circ\text{IP}}$ is formed as $\text{SK}(f_h) = (f_h, \{\boldsymbol{k}'^{(h,j')}\}_{j' \in [m_h]}, \{\boldsymbol{k}^{(h,j)}\}_{j\in[n]})$ such that

$$\begin{aligned} \boldsymbol{k}'^{(h,j')} &= ((\gamma_{h,j'}, \alpha_{h,j'}), (\eta'_{h,j'}, \boxed{\mu_{h,j'}}), \vec{0}^2, \vec{\kappa}'^{(h,j')}, 0)_{\mathbb{B}^*_{\rho_h(j')}} \quad \text{for } j' \in [m_h], \\ \boldsymbol{k}^{(h,j)} &= ((\sigma_{h,j}, \zeta_h), (\eta_{h,j}, \boxed{\nu_{h,j}}), \vec{0}^2, \vec{\kappa}^{(h,j)}, 0)_{\mathbb{B}^*_{n'+j}} \quad \text{for } j \in [n], \end{aligned} \tag{3.13}$$

where $\{\widetilde{\zeta}_h\}_{h\in[q_{\text{KEY-PRE}}+1, q_{\text{KEY}}]} \xleftarrow{\mathsf{U}} \mathbb{F}_q$, $((\{\nu_{h,j}\}_{j\in[n]}, \{\mu_{h,j'}\}_{j'\in[m_h]}), \rho_h : [m_h] \to [n'])$ $\xleftarrow{\mathsf{R}} \mathsf{SIM}(f_h, \vec{x}, f_h(\vec{x}, \widetilde{\zeta}_h \vec{z}))$ for $h \in [q_{\text{KEY-PRE}}+1, q_{\text{KEY}}]$, and all the other variables are generated as in Hyb_7. Observe that for any $h \in [q_{\text{KEY-PRE}}] + 1, q_{\text{KEY}}]$ if $R^{\text{ABP}\circ\text{IP}}(f_h, (\vec{x}, \vec{z})) = 1$, i.e., $f_h(\vec{x}, \vec{z}) = 0$, then $f_h(\vec{x}, \widetilde{\zeta}_h\vec{z}) = \widetilde{\zeta}_h f_h(\vec{x}, \vec{z}) = 0$, while if $R^{\text{ABP}\circ\text{IP}}(f_h(\vec{x}, \vec{z})) = 0$, i.e., $f_h(\vec{x}, \vec{z}) \neq 0$, then due to the uniform and independent (of the other variables) choice of $\widetilde{\zeta}_h$, it follows that $f_h(\vec{x}, \widetilde{\zeta}_h\vec{z}) = \widetilde{\zeta}_h f_h(\vec{x}, \vec{z})$ is uniformly and independently (of the other variables) distributed in $\mathbb{F}_q$. Thus, this experiment coincides with the experiment $\mathsf{Exp}^{\text{PHPE,IDEAL}}_{\mathcal{H},\mathcal{S}}(\lambda)$ with the simulator $\mathcal{S}$ as described above.

▪ **Analysis**

Let us now denote by $\mathsf{Adv}^{(\jmath)}_{\mathcal{H}}(\lambda)$ the probability that $\mathcal{H}$ outputs 1 in $\mathsf{Hyb}_\jmath$ for $\jmath \in \{0, 1, \{2\text{-}\chi\text{-}k\}_{\chi\in[q_{\text{KEY-PRE}}], k\in[4]}, 3, \ldots, 8\}$. By definition of the hybrids, we clearly have $\mathsf{Adv}^{\text{PHPE-SIM-AH}}_{\mathcal{H}}(\lambda) = |\mathsf{Adv}^{(0)}_{\mathcal{H}}(\lambda) - \mathsf{Adv}^{(8)}_{\mathcal{H}}(\lambda)|$. Hence, we have

$$\begin{aligned} \mathsf{Adv}^{\text{PHPE,SIM-AH}}_{\mathcal{H}}(\lambda) \leq {} & |\mathsf{Adv}^{(0)}_{\mathcal{H}}(\lambda) - \mathsf{Adv}^{(1)}_{\mathcal{H}}(\lambda)| + \\ & \sum_{\chi\in[q_{\text{KEY-PRE}}]} \Big[|\mathsf{Adv}^{(2\text{-}(\chi-1)\text{-}4)}_{\mathcal{H}}(\lambda) - \mathsf{Adv}^{(2\text{-}\chi\text{-}1)}_{\mathcal{H}}(\lambda)| + \\ & \sum_{k\in[3]} |\mathsf{Adv}^{(2\text{-}\chi\text{-}k)}_{\mathcal{H}}(\lambda) - \mathsf{Adv}^{(2\text{-}\chi\text{-}(k+1))}_{\mathcal{H}}(\lambda)| \Big] + \\ & |\mathsf{Adv}^{(2\text{-}q_{\text{KEY-PRE}}\text{-}4)}_{\mathcal{H}}(\lambda) - \mathsf{Adv}^{(3)}_{\mathcal{H}}(\lambda)| + \sum_{\jmath\in[3,7]} |\mathsf{Adv}^{(\jmath)}_{\mathcal{H}}(\lambda) - \mathsf{Adv}^{(\jmath+1)}_{\mathcal{H}}(\lambda)|. \end{aligned}$$

It can be shown that each term on the RHS of the above equation is negligible in λ, and hence Theorem 3.1 follows. The details are provided in the full version.

References

1. Abe, M., Chase, M., David, B., Kohlweiss, M., Nishimaki, R., Ohkubo, M.: Constant-size structure-preserving signatures: generic constructions and simple assumptions. In: Wang, X., Sako, K. (eds.) ASIACRYPT 2012. LNCS, vol. 7658, pp. 4–24. Springer, Heidelberg (2012). https://doi.org/10.1007/978-3-642-34961-4_3
2. Agrawal, S.: Stronger security for reusable garbled circuits, general definitions and attacks. In: Katz, J., Shacham, H. (eds.) CRYPTO 2017. LNCS, vol. 10401, pp. 3–35. Springer, Cham (2017). https://doi.org/10.1007/978-3-319-63688-7_1

3. Agrawal, S., Gorbunov, S., Vaikuntanathan, V., Wee, H.: Functional encryption: new perspectives and lower bounds. In: Canetti, R., Garay, J.A. (eds.) CRYPTO 2013. LNCS, vol. 8043, pp. 500–518. Springer, Heidelberg (2013). https://doi.org/10.1007/978-3-642-40084-1_28
4. Ananth, P., Brakerski, Z., Segev, G., Vaikuntanathan, V.: From selective to adaptive security in functional encryption. In: Gennaro, R., Robshaw, M. (eds.) CRYPTO 2015. LNCS, vol. 9216, pp. 657–677. Springer, Heidelberg (2015). https://doi.org/10.1007/978-3-662-48000-7_32
5. Ananth, P., Jain, A.: Indistinguishability obfuscation from compact functional encryption. In: Gennaro, R., Robshaw, M. (eds.) CRYPTO 2015. LNCS, vol. 9215, pp. 308–326. Springer, Heidelberg (2015). https://doi.org/10.1007/978-3-662-47989-6_15
6. Ananth, P., Jain, A., Sahai, A.: Indistinguishability obfuscation from functional encryption for simple functions. Cryptology ePrint Archive, Report 2015/730
7. Attrapadung, N.: Dual system encryption via doubly selective security: framework, fully secure functional encryption for regular languages, and more. In: Nguyen, P.Q., Oswald, E. (eds.) EUROCRYPT 2014. LNCS, vol. 8441, pp. 557–577. Springer, Heidelberg (2014). https://doi.org/10.1007/978-3-642-55220-5_31
8. Barbulescu, R., Gaudry, P., Joux, A., Thomé, E.: A heuristic quasi-polynomial algorithm for discrete logarithm in finite fields of small characteristic. In: Nguyen, P.Q., Oswald, E. (eds.) EUROCRYPT 2014. LNCS, vol. 8441, pp. 1–16. Springer, Heidelberg (2014). https://doi.org/10.1007/978-3-642-55220-5_1
9. Bellare, M., O'Neill, A.: Semantically-secure functional encryption: possibility results, impossibility results and the quest for a general definition. In: Abdalla, M., Nita-Rotaru, C., Dahab, R. (eds.) CANS 2013. LNCS, vol. 8257, pp. 218–234. Springer, Cham (2013). https://doi.org/10.1007/978-3-319-02937-5_12
10. Bitansky, N., Vaikuntanathan, V.: Indistinguishability obfuscation from functional encryption. In: FOCS 2015, pp. 171–190. IEEE (2015)
11. Boneh, D., et al.: Fully key-homomorphic encryption, arithmetic circuit ABE and compact garbled circuits. In: Nguyen, P.Q., Oswald, E. (eds.) EUROCRYPT 2014. LNCS, vol. 8441, pp. 533–556. Springer, Heidelberg (2014). https://doi.org/10.1007/978-3-642-55220-5_30
12. Boneh, D., Sahai, A., Waters, B.: Functional encryption: definitions and challenges. In: Ishai, Y. (ed.) TCC 2011. LNCS, vol. 6597, pp. 253–273. Springer, Heidelberg (2011). https://doi.org/10.1007/978-3-642-19571-6_16
13. Boneh, D., Waters, B.: Conjunctive, subset, and range queries on encrypted data. In: Vadhan, S.P. (ed.) TCC 2007. LNCS, vol. 4392, pp. 535–554. Springer, Heidelberg (2007). https://doi.org/10.1007/978-3-540-70936-7_29
14. Chen, J., Gay, R., Wee, H.: Improved dual system ABE in prime-order groups via predicate encodings. In: Oswald, E., Fischlin, M. (eds.) EUROCRYPT 2015. LNCS, vol. 9057, pp. 595–624. Springer, Heidelberg (2015). https://doi.org/10.1007/978-3-662-46803-6_20
15. Chen, J., Wee, H.: Semi-adaptive attribute-based encryption and improved delegation for boolean formula. In: Abdalla, M., De Prisco, R. (eds.) SCN 2014. LNCS, vol. 8642, pp. 277–297. Springer, Cham (2014). https://doi.org/10.1007/978-3-319-10879-7_16
16. De Caro, A., Iovino, V., Jain, A., O'Neill, A., Paneth, O., Persiano, G.: On the achievability of simulation-based security for functional encryption. In: Canetti, R., Garay, J.A. (eds.) CRYPTO 2013. LNCS, vol. 8043, pp. 519–535. Springer, Heidelberg (2013). https://doi.org/10.1007/978-3-642-40084-1_29

17. Freeman, D.M.: Converting pairing-based cryptosystems from composite-order groups to prime-order groups. In: Gilbert, H. (ed.) EUROCRYPT 2010. LNCS, vol. 6110, pp. 44–61. Springer, Heidelberg (2010). https://doi.org/10.1007/978-3-642-13190-5_3
18. Göloğlu, F., Granger, R., McGuire, G., Zumbrägel, J.: On the function field sieve and the impact of higher splitting probabilities. In: Canetti, R., Garay, J.A. (eds.) CRYPTO 2013. LNCS, vol. 8043, pp. 109–128. Springer, Heidelberg (2013). https://doi.org/10.1007/978-3-642-40084-1_7
19. Gorbunov, S., Vaikuntanathan, V., Wee, H.: Predicate encryption for circuits from LWE. In: Gennaro, R., Robshaw, M. (eds.) CRYPTO 2015. LNCS, vol. 9216, pp. 503–523. Springer, Heidelberg (2015). https://doi.org/10.1007/978-3-662-48000-7_25
20. Gorbunov, S., Vaikuntanathan, V., Wee, H.: Attribute-based encryption for circuits. J. ACM (JACM) **62**(6), 45 (2015)
21. Goyal, R., Koppula, V., Waters, B.: Semi-adaptive security and bundling functionalities made generic and easy. In: Hirt, M., Smith, A. (eds.) TCC 2016. LNCS, vol. 9986, pp. 361–388. Springer, Heidelberg (2016). https://doi.org/10.1007/978-3-662-53644-5_14
22. Goyal, V., Pandey, O., Sahai, A., Waters, B.: Attribute-based encryption for fine-grained access control of encrypted data. In: CCS 2006, pp. 89–98. ACM (2006)
23. Guillevic, A.: Comparing the pairing efficiency over composite-order and prime-order elliptic curves. In: Jacobson, M., Locasto, M., Mohassel, P., Safavi-Naini, R. (eds.) ACNS 2013. LNCS, vol. 7954, pp. 357–372. Springer, Heidelberg (2013). https://doi.org/10.1007/978-3-642-38980-1_22
24. Ishai, Y., Kushilevitz, E.: Perfect constant-round secure computation via perfect randomizing polynomials. In: Widmayer, P., Eidenbenz, S., Triguero, F., Morales, R., Conejo, R., Hennessy, M. (eds.) ICALP 2002. LNCS, vol. 2380, pp. 244–256. Springer, Heidelberg (2002). https://doi.org/10.1007/3-540-45465-9_22
25. Ishai, Y., Kushilevitz, E.: Private simultaneous messages protocols with applications. In: Proceedings of the Fifth Israeli Symposium on Theory of Computing and Systems, pp. 174–184. IEEE (1997)
26. Ishai, Y., Wee, H.: Partial garbling schemes and their applications. In: Esparza, J., Fraigniaud, P., Husfeldt, T., Koutsoupias, E. (eds.) ICALP 2014. LNCS, vol. 8572, pp. 650–662. Springer, Heidelberg (2014). https://doi.org/10.1007/978-3-662-43948-7_54
27. Joux, A.: Faster index calculus for the medium prime case application to 1175-bit and 1425-bit finite fields. In: Johansson, T., Nguyen, P.Q. (eds.) EUROCRYPT 2013. LNCS, vol. 7881, pp. 177–193. Springer, Heidelberg (2013). https://doi.org/10.1007/978-3-642-38348-9_11
28. Joux, A.: A new index calculus algorithm with complexity $L(1/4 + o(1))$ in small characteristic. In: Lange, T., Lauter, K., Lisoněk, P. (eds.) SAC 2013. LNCS, vol. 8282, pp. 355–379. Springer, Heidelberg (2014). https://doi.org/10.1007/978-3-662-43414-7_18
29. Katz, J., Sahai, A., Waters, B.: Predicate encryption supporting disjunctions, polynomial equations, and inner products. In: Smart, N. (ed.) EUROCRYPT 2008. LNCS, vol. 4965, pp. 146–162. Springer, Heidelberg (2008). https://doi.org/10.1007/978-3-540-78967-3_9
30. Lewko, A., Okamoto, T., Sahai, A., Takashima, K., Waters, B.: Fully secure functional encryption: attribute-based encryption and (hierarchical) inner product encryption. In: Gilbert, H. (ed.) EUROCRYPT 2010. LNCS, vol. 6110, pp. 62–91. Springer, Heidelberg (2010). https://doi.org/10.1007/978-3-642-13190-5_4

31. Lewko, A., Waters, B.: New proof methods for attribute-based encryption: achieving full security through selective techniques. In: Safavi-Naini, R., Canetti, R. (eds.) CRYPTO 2012. LNCS, vol. 7417, pp. 180–198. Springer, Heidelberg (2012). https://doi.org/10.1007/978-3-642-32009-5_12
32. Okamoto, T., Takashima, K.: Adaptively attribute-hiding (hierarchical) inner product encryption. In: Pointcheval, D., Johansson, T. (eds.) EUROCRYPT 2012. LNCS, vol. 7237, pp. 591–608. Springer, Heidelberg (2012). https://doi.org/10.1007/978-3-642-29011-4_35
33. Okamoto, T., Takashima, K.: Fully secure functional encryption with general relations from the decisional linear assumption. In: Rabin, T. (ed.) CRYPTO 2010. LNCS, vol. 6223, pp. 191–208. Springer, Heidelberg (2010). https://doi.org/10.1007/978-3-642-14623-7_11
34. Okamoto, T., Takashima, K.: Fully secure unbounded inner-product and attribute-based encryption. In: Wang, X., Sako, K. (eds.) ASIACRYPT 2012. LNCS, vol. 7658, pp. 349–366. Springer, Heidelberg (2012). https://doi.org/10.1007/978-3-642-34961-4_22
35. Okamoto, T., Takashima, K.: Hierarchical predicate encryption for inner-products. In: Matsui, M. (ed.) ASIACRYPT 2009. LNCS, vol. 5912, pp. 214–231. Springer, Heidelberg (2009). https://doi.org/10.1007/978-3-642-10366-7_13
36. Okamoto, T., Takashima, K.: Efficient (hierarchical) inner-product encryption tightly reduced from the decisional linear assumption. IEICE Trans. Fundam. Electron. Commun. Comput. Sci. **96**(1), 42–52 (2013)
37. O'Neill, A.: Definitional issues in functional encryption. Cryptology ePrint Archive, Report 2010/556
38. Tomida, J., Abe, M., Okamoto, T.: Efficient functional encryption for inner-product values with full-hiding security. In: Bishop, M., Nascimento, A.C.A. (eds.) ISC 2016. LNCS, vol. 9866, pp. 408–425. Springer, Cham (2016). https://doi.org/10.1007/978-3-319-45871-7_24
39. Waters, B.: Dual system encryption: realizing fully secure IBE and HIBE under simple assumptions. In: Halevi, S. (ed.) CRYPTO 2009. LNCS, vol. 5677, pp. 619–636. Springer, Heidelberg (2009). https://doi.org/10.1007/978-3-642-03356-8_36
40. Wee, H.: Attribute-hiding predicate encryption in bilinear groups, revisited. In: Kalai, Y., Reyzin, L. (eds.) TCC 2017. LNCS, vol. 10677, pp. 206–233. Springer, Cham (2017). https://doi.org/10.1007/978-3-319-70500-2_8
41. Wee, H.: Dual system encryption via predicate encodings. In: Lindell, Y. (ed.) TCC 2014. LNCS, vol. 8349, pp. 616–637. Springer, Heidelberg (2014). https://doi.org/10.1007/978-3-642-54242-8_26

Improved Inner-Product Encryption with Adaptive Security and Full Attribute-Hiding

Jie Chen[1], Junqing Gong[2(✉)], and Hoeteck Wee[3]

[1] East China Normal University, Shanghai, China
s080001@e.ntu.edu.sg
[2] ENS de Lyon, Laboratoire LIP (U. Lyon, CNRS, ENSL, INRIA, UCBL), Lyon, France
junqing.gong@ens-lyon.fr
[3] CNRS and ENS, PSL, Paris, France
wee@di.ens.fr

Abstract. In this work, we propose two IPE schemes achieving both adaptive security and full attribute-hiding in the prime-order bilinear group, which improve upon the unique existing result satisfying both features from Okamoto and Takashima [Eurocrypt '12] in terms of efficiency.

- Our first IPE scheme is based on the standard k-LIN assumption and has shorter master public key and shorter secret keys than Okamoto and Takashima's IPE under weaker DLIN = 2-LIN assumption.
- Our second IPE scheme is adapted from the first one; the security is based on the XDLIN assumption (as Okamoto and Takashima's IPE) but now it also enjoys shorter ciphertexts.

Technically, instead of starting from composite-order IPE and applying existing transformation, we start from an IPE scheme in a very restricted setting but already in the *prime-order* group, and then gradually upgrade it to our full-fledged IPE scheme. This method allows us to integrate Chen *et al.*'s framework [Eurocrypt '15] with recent new techniques [TCC '17, Eurocrypt '18] in an optimized way.

1 Introduction

Attribute-based encryption (ABE) is an advanced public-key encryption system supporting fine-grained access control [20,31]. In an ABE system, an authority

J. Chen—School of Computer Science and Software Engineering. Supported by the National Natural Science Foundation of China (Nos. 61472142, 61632012, U1705264) and the Young Elite Scientists Sponsorship Program by CAST (2017QNRC001). Homepage: http://www.jchen.top.

J. Gong—Supported in part by the French ANR ALAMBIC Project (ANR-16-CE39-0006).

H. Wee—Supported in part by the European Union's Horizon 2020 Research and Innovation Programme under grant agreement 780108 (FENTEC).

T. Peyrin and S. Galbraith (Eds.): ASIACRYPT 2018, LNCS 11273, pp. 673–702, 2018.
https://doi.org/10.1007/978-3-030-03329-3_23

publishes a master public key mpk for encryption and issues secret keys to users for decryption; a ciphertext for message m is associated with an attribute x while a secret key is associated with a policy f, a boolean function over the set of all attributes; when $f(x) = 1$, the secret key can be used to recover message m. The basic security requirement for ABE is *message-hiding*: an adversary holding a secret key with $f(x) = 0$ cannot infer any information about m from the ciphertext; furthermore, this should be ensured when the adversary has more than one such secret key, which is called *collusion resistance*.

In some applications, an additional security notion *attribute-hiding* [10,22] is desirable, which concerns the privacy of attribute x instead of message m. In the literature, there are two levels of attribute-hiding: (1) *weak* attribute-hiding is against an adversary who holds multiple secret keys with $f(x) = 0$; (2) *full* attribute-hiding is against an adversary holding any kind of secret keys including those with $f(x) = 1$. Nowadays we have seen many concrete ABE schemes [7,9,18–21,24–26,30,33]. Based on the seminal *dual system method* [32], we even reached generic frameworks for constructing and analyzing ABE [2–6,11,12,35] in bilinear groups. Many of them, including both concrete ABE schemes and generic frameworks, have already achieved weak attribute-hiding [9,11,12,18,19,21].

However it is much harder to obtain ABE with the *full* attribute-hiding feature. In fact, all known schemes only support so-called inner-product encryption (IPE), in which both ciphertexts and secret keys are associated with vectors and the decryption procedure succeeds when the two vectors has zero inner-product. Furthermore, almost all of them are selectively or semi-adaptively secure which means the adversary has to choose the vectors associated with the challenge ciphertext (called challenge vector/attribute) before seeing mpk or before seeing any secret keys [10,22,29,36]. Both of them are much weaker than the standard *adaptive security* (i.e., the one we have mentioned in the prior paragraph) where the choice can be made at any time. (Note that Wee achieved *simulation-based* security in [36].) What's worse, some schemes [10,22] are built on the composite-order group, on which group operations are slower and more memory space is required to store group elements. The best result so far comes from Okamoto and Takashima [27]: the IPE scheme is adaptively secure and fully attribute-hiding based on external decisional linear assumption[1] (XDLIN) in efficient prime-order bilinear groups.

1.1 Our Results

In this work, we propose two IPE schemes in prime-order bilinear groups achieving both adaptive security and full attribute-hiding, which improve upon Okamoto and Takashima's IPE scheme [27] in terms of space efficiency:

[1] The construction is originally based on the decisional linear assumption in *symmetric* prime-order bilinear group. In this paper, we will work with asymmetric bilinear group where their proof will be translated into a proof based on the external decisional linear assumption. Note that XDLIN assumption is stronger than DLIN assumption.

- Our first construction is proven secure under standard k-Linear (k-LIN) assumption. When instantiating with $k = 2$ (i.e., DLIN assumption), it enjoys shorter master public key and secret keys under weaker assumption than Okamoto and Takashima's IPE, but we have slightly larger ciphertexts. With parameter $k = 1$ (i.e., SXDH assumption), we can also achieve shorter ciphertexts but at the cost of basing the security on a stronger assumption.
- Our second construction is proven secure under the XDLIN assumption, which is stronger than DLIN assumption. This gives another balance point between (space) efficiency and assumption. Now we can get better efficiency than Okamoto and Takashima's IPE in terms of master public key, ciphertext and secret keys without sacrificing anything — Okamoto and Takashima also worked with XDLIN.

A detailed comparison is provided in Table 1.

Table 1. Comparison among our two IPE schemes and Okamoto and Takashima's IPE [27]. All schemes are built on an asymmetric prime-order bilinear group $(p, G_1, G_2, G_T, e : G_1 \times G_2 \to G_T)$. In the table, $|G_1|, |G_2|, |G_T|$ denote the sizes of group elements in G_1, G_2, G_T.

Scheme	|mpk|	|ct|	|sk|	Assumption
OT12 [27]	$(12n+16)\|G_1\| + \|G_T\|$	$(5n+1)\|G_1\| + \|G_T\|$	$11\|G_2\|$	XDLIN
Section 3.4	$(10n+16)\|G_1\| + 2\|G_T\|$	$(5n+3)\|G_1\| + \|G_T\|$	$8\|G_2\|$	DLIN
	$(3n+5)\|G_1\| + \|G_T\|$	$(3n+2)\|G_1\| + \|G_T\|$	$5\|G_2\|$	SXDH
Section 4.4	$(8n+14)\|G_1\| + 2\|G_T\|$	$(4n+3)\|G_1\| + \|G_T\|$	$7\|G_2\|$	XDLIN

1.2 Our Technique in Composite-Order Groups

As a warm-up, we present a scheme in asymmetric composite-order bilinear groups. Here, we will rely on composite-order groups whose order is the product of *four* primes; this is different from the settings of adaptively secure ABE schemes and selectively secure full attribute-hiding inner product encryption where it suffices to use *two* primes.

The Scheme. Assume an asymmetric composite-order bilinear group $\mathbb{G} = (N, G_N, H_N, G_T, e : G_N \times H_N \to G_T)$ where $N = p_1p_2p_3p_4$. Let g_1, h_{14} be respective random generators of subgroups $G_{p_1}, H_{p_1p_4}$. Pick $\alpha, u, w_1, \ldots, w_n \leftarrow \mathbb{Z}_N$. We describe an IPE scheme for n dimensional space over $\mathbb{Z}_N$ as follows.

$$\begin{aligned}
\mathsf{mpk} &: g_1,\, g_1^u,\, g_1^{w_1}, \ldots, g_1^{w_n},\, e(g_1, h_{14})^\alpha \\
\mathsf{sk}_{\mathbf{y}} &: h_{14}^{\alpha + (y_1w_1 + \cdots + y_nw_n)r},\, h_{14}^r \\
\mathsf{ct}_{\mathbf{x}} &: g_1^s,\, g_1^{s(u \cdot x_1 + w_1)}, \ldots, g_1^{s(u \cdot x_n + w_n)},\, \mathsf{H}(e(g_1, h_{14})^{\alpha s}) \cdot m
\end{aligned} \tag{1}$$

where $\mathbf{x} = (x_1, \ldots, x_n) \in \mathbb{Z}_N^n$ and $\mathbf{y} = (y_1, \ldots, y_n) \in \mathbb{Z}_N^n$. The construction is adapted from Chen *et al.* IPE [11] (without attribute-hiding feature) by embedding it into groups with four subgroups. This allows us to carry out the proof strategy introduced by Okamoto and Takashima [27], which involves a non-trivial extension of the standard dual system method [32]. We only give a high-level sketch for the proof below but show the complete game sequence in Fig. 1 for reference.

As is the case for adaptively secure ABE [32,35], we will rely on the following private-key one-ciphertext one-key fully attribute-hiding inner product encryption scheme in the proof of security. Here, g_3, h_3 denote the respective generators for the subgroups of order p_3.

$$\begin{aligned} \mathsf{sk}_{\mathbf{y}} &: h_3^{\alpha + y_1 w_1 + \cdots + y_n w_n} \\ \mathsf{ct}_{\mathbf{x}} &: g_3^{u \cdot x_1 + w_1}, \ldots, g_3^{u \cdot x_n + w_n}, g_3^{\alpha} \cdot m \end{aligned} \tag{2}$$

Note that the scheme satisfies (simulation-based) information-theoretic security in the selective setting, which immediately yields (indistinguishability-based) adaptive security via complexity leveraging.

In the proof of security (outlined in Fig. 1), we will first switch the ciphertext to having just a $p_2p_3p_4$-component via the subgroup decision assumption. At the beginning of the proof, all the secret keys will have a p_4-component, and at the end, all the secret keys will have a p_2-component; throughout, the secret keys will also always have a p_1-component but no p_3-components at the beginning or the end. To carry out the change in the secret keys from p_4-components to p_2-components, we will switch the keys one by one. For the switch, we will introduce a p_3-component into one secret key and then invoke security of the above private-key one-ciphertext one-key scheme in the p_3-subgroup. It is important here that throughout the hybrids, at most one secret key has a p_3-component.

1.3 Our Technique in Prime-Order Groups

Assume a prime-order bilinear group $\mathbb{G} = (p, G_1, G_2, G_T, e : G_1 \times G_2 \to G_T)$ and let $[\cdot]_1, [\cdot]_2, [\cdot]_T$ denote the entry-wise exponentiation on G_1, G_2, G_T, respectively. Naively, we simulate a composite-order group whose order is the product of four primes using vectors of dimension $4k$ "in the exponent" under k-LIN assumption. That is, we replace

$$g_1, h_{14} \mapsto [\mathbf{A}_1]_1, [\mathbf{B}_{14}]_2$$

where $\mathbf{A}_1 \leftarrow \mathbb{Z}_p^{4k \times k}, \mathbf{B}_{14} \leftarrow \mathbb{Z}_p^{4k \times 2k}$. However, the resulting IPE scheme is less efficient than Okamoto and Takashima's scheme [27]. Instead, we will show that it suffices to use

$$\mathbf{A}_1 \leftarrow \mathbb{Z}_p^{(k+1) \times k}, \ \mathbf{B}_{14} \leftarrow \mathbb{Z}_p^{(2k+1) \times k} \tag{3}$$

Then, with the correspondence by Chen *et al.* [11,13,16]:

$$\begin{array}{llll} \alpha \mapsto \mathbf{k} \in \mathbb{Z}_p^{k+1} & u, w_i \mapsto \mathbf{U}, \mathbf{W}_i \in \mathbb{Z}_p^{(k+1) \times (2k+1)} & \forall i \in [n] \\ s \mapsto \mathbf{s} \in \mathbb{Z}_p^k, & r \mapsto \mathbf{r} \in \mathbb{Z}_p^k & \\ g_1^s \mapsto [\mathbf{s}^\top \mathbf{A}_1^\top]_1, & h_{14}^r \mapsto [\mathbf{B}_{14}\mathbf{r}]_2 & \\ g_1^{sw} \mapsto [\mathbf{s}^\top \mathbf{A}_1^\top \mathbf{W}]_1, & h_{14}^{wr} \mapsto [\mathbf{W}\mathbf{B}_{14}\mathbf{r}]_2 & \end{array} \tag{4}$$

Game	ct				κth sk: $H_{p_1} \times ?$			Remark
	$g_1^{s(u\cdot ?+w_i)}$	$g_2^{s(u\cdot ?+w_i)}$	$g_3^{s(u\cdot ?+w_i)}$	$g_4^{s(u\cdot ?+w_i)}$	$\kappa < j$	$\kappa = j$	$\kappa > j$	
0	$x_{i,b}$	—			H_{p_4}			Real game
1	—	$x_{i,b}$			H_{p_4}			$p_1 \mapsto p_2p_3p_4$ in G
$2.j-1$	—	$x_{i,0}$	$x_{i,b}$	$x_{i,b}$	H_{p_2}	H_{p_4}	H_{p_4}	
$2.j-1.1$	—	$x_{i,0}$	$x_{i,b}$	$x_{i,b}$	H_{p_2}	H_{p_3}	H_{p_4}	$p_4 \mapsto p_3$ in H
$2.j-1.2$	—	$x_{i,0}$	$x_{i,0}$	$x_{i,b}$	H_{p_2}	H_{p_3}	H_{p_4}	private-key scheme in p_3
$2.j-1.3$	—	$x_{i,0}$	$x_{i,0}$	$x_{i,b}$	H_{p_2}	H_{p_2}	H_{p_4}	$p_3 \mapsto p_2$ in H
3	—	$x_{i,0}$	$x_{i,0}$	$x_{i,0}$	H_{p_2}			statistical in p_3, p_4

Fig. 1. Game sequence for composite-order IPE. In the table, $\mathbf{x}_0 = (x_{1,0}, \ldots, x_{n,0})$ and $\mathbf{x}_1 = (x_{1,1}, \ldots, x_{n,1})$ are the challenge vectors; $b \in \{0,1\}$ is the secret bit we hope to hide against the adversary. The gray background highlights the difference between adjacent games. The column "ct" shows the structure of the challenge ciphertext on four subgroups whose generators are g_1, g_2, g_3, g_4, while the next column gives the subgroup where every secret keys lie in. In the last column, the notation "$p_1 \mapsto p_2p_3p_4$ in G" is indicating the subgroup decision assumption stating that $G_{p_1} \approx_c G_{p_2p_3p_4}$.

we have the following prime-order IPE scheme:

$$\begin{aligned}
\mathsf{mpk} &: [\mathbf{A}^\top]_1, [\mathbf{A}^\top\mathbf{U}]_1, [\mathbf{A}^\top\mathbf{W}_1]_1, \ldots, [\mathbf{A}^\top\mathbf{W}_n]_1, [\mathbf{A}^\top\mathbf{k}]_T \\
\mathsf{sk}_\mathbf{y} &: [\mathbf{k} + (y_1 \cdot \mathbf{W}_1 + \cdots + y_n \cdot \mathbf{W}_n)\mathbf{B}_{14}\mathbf{r}]_2, \; [\mathbf{B}_{14}\mathbf{r}]_2 \\
\mathsf{ct}_\mathbf{x} &: [\mathbf{s}^\top\mathbf{A}_1^\top]_1, [\mathbf{s}^\top\mathbf{A}_1^\top(x_1 \cdot \mathbf{U} + \mathbf{W}_1)]_1, \ldots, [\mathbf{s}^\top\mathbf{A}_1^\top(x_n \cdot \mathbf{U} + \mathbf{W}_n)]_1, [\mathbf{c}^\top\mathbf{k}]_T \cdot m
\end{aligned} \tag{5}$$

Note that, with matrices $\mathbf{A}_1 \in \mathbb{Z}_p^{(k+1)\times k}$ and $\mathbf{B} \in \mathbb{Z}_p^{(2k+1)\times k}$, we only simulate two and three subgroups, respectively, rather than four subgroups; meanwhile some of them are simulated as low-dimension subspaces. Although it has become a common optimization technique to adjust dimensions of subspaces, it is not direct to justify that we can work with less subspaces. In fact, these optimizations are based on elaborate investigations of the proof strategy sketched in Sect. 1.2. In the rest of this section, we explain our method leading to the optimized parameter shown in (3).

Our Translation. We start from an IPE scheme in a very restricted setting and then gradually upgrade it to our full-fledged IPE scheme in the *prime-order* group. In particular, we follow the roadmap

$$\text{private-key one-key IPE} \xrightarrow[\text{[11,13]}]{\text{Step 1}} \text{private-key IPE} \xrightarrow[\text{[11,36]}]{\text{Step 2}} \text{public-key IPE}$$

The private key one-key IPE corresponds to scheme (2) over p_3-subgroup (cf. $\mathsf{Game}_{2.j-1.2}$ in Fig. 1). In Step 1, we move from one-key to multi-key model using the technique from [13], which is related to the argument just after we change ciphertext in proof of scheme (1) (cf. $\mathsf{Game}_{2.0}$ to $\mathsf{Game}_{2.q}$ and Game_3 in Fig. 1). In Step 2, we move from private-key to public-key setting with the compiler in [36], which is related to the change of ciphertext at the beginning of the proof (cf. Game_1 in Fig. 1). By handling these proof techniques underlying the proof sketched in Sect. 1.2 (cf. Fig. 1) one by one as above, we are able to integrate Chen *et al.*'s framework [11] with recent new techniques [13,36] in an optimized way.

Private-key IPE in One-key Setting. We start from a *private-key* IPE where the ciphertext is created from msk rather than mpk. We also consider a weaker *one-key* model where the adversary can get only one secret key. Pick $\alpha, u, w_1, \ldots, w_n \leftarrow_{\mathrm{R}} \mathbb{Z}_p$ and let message $m \in \mathbb{Z}_p$. We give the following private-key IPE over $\mathbb{Z}_p$:

$$\begin{aligned} &\mathsf{msk} : \alpha, u, w_1, \ldots, w_n \\ &\mathsf{sk}_{\mathbf{y}} : \alpha + (y_1 \cdot w_1 + \cdots + y_n \cdot w_n) \\ &\mathsf{ct}_{\mathbf{x}} : x_1 \cdot u + w_1, \ldots, x_n \cdot u + w_n, \alpha \cdot m \end{aligned} \tag{6}$$

Analogous to scheme (2), the scheme satisfies (simulation-based) information-theoretic security in the selective setting (cf. [36]). By the implication from simulation-based security to indistinguishability-based security and standard complexity leveraging technique, we have the following statement: For adaptively chosen $\mathbf{x}_0 = (x_{1,0}, \ldots, x_{n,0}) \in \mathbb{Z}_p^n$, $\mathbf{x}_1 = (x_{1,1}, \ldots, x_{n,1}) \in \mathbb{Z}_p^n$ and $\mathbf{y} = (y_1, \ldots, y_n) \in \mathbb{Z}_p^n$ satisfying either $\langle \mathbf{x}_0, \mathbf{y} \rangle \neq 0 \wedge \langle \mathbf{x}_1, \mathbf{y} \rangle \neq 0$ or $\langle \mathbf{x}_0, \mathbf{y} \rangle = \langle \mathbf{x}_1, \mathbf{y} \rangle = 0$ and all $b \in \{0,1\}$, we have

$$\begin{aligned} &\{ \boxed{x_{1,b}} \cdot u + w_1, \ldots, \boxed{x_{n,b}} \cdot u + w_n,\ y_1 \cdot w_1 + \cdots + y_n \cdot w_n \} \\ \equiv &\{ \boxed{x_{1,1-b}} \cdot u + w_1, \ldots, \boxed{x_{n,1-b}} \cdot u + w_n,\ y_1 \cdot w_1 + \cdots + y_n \cdot w_n \} \end{aligned} \tag{7}$$

Note that the statement here is different from that used in Fig. 1 (where $x_{i,0}$ is in the place of $x_{i,1-b}$). Looking ahead, this choice is made to employ the "change of basis" technique when moving from one-key to multi-key model (see the next paragraph).

Private-key IPE in Multi-key Setting. To handle multiple keys revealed to the adversary, we employ Chen *et al.*'s prime-order generic framework[2] [11] based on the dual system method [32] to scheme (6). The framework works with prime-order finite cyclic group G on which the k-LIN assumption holds. Let $[\cdot]$ denote the entry-wise exponentiation on G. In order to avoid collusion of multiple secret keys, we will re-randomize each secret key [8,31,34] using fresh vector $\mathbf{d} \leftarrow \mathsf{span}(\mathbf{B}_1)$ where $\mathbf{B}_1 \leftarrow \mathbb{Z}_p^{(k+1)\times k}$, which supports standard dual system method [32] with a hidden subspace $\mathbf{B}_2 \leftarrow \mathbb{Z}_p^{k+1}$. For this purpose, we need to do the following "scalar to vector" substitutions:

$$u \in \mathbb{Z}_p \mapsto \mathbf{u} \in \mathbb{Z}_p^{1\times(k+1)} \quad \text{and} \quad w_i \in \mathbb{Z}_p \mapsto \mathbf{w}_i \in \mathbb{Z}_p^{1\times(k+1)} \quad \forall i \in [n].$$

[2] Note that, with their framework, we can work out a *public key* IPE directly, but we focus on the technique handling multiple secret keys at the moment.

Then the re-randomization is done by multiplying $\mathbf{u}$ and each $\mathbf{w}_i$ in secret keys by $\mathbf{d}$ and moving them from $\mathbb{Z}_p$ to G. This yields the following private-key IPE:

$$\begin{aligned} &\mathsf{msk} : \alpha, \mathbf{u}, \mathbf{w}_1, \ldots, \mathbf{w}_n \\ &\mathsf{sk}_{\mathbf{y}} : [\alpha + (y_1 \cdot \mathbf{w}_1 + \cdots + y_n \cdot \mathbf{w}_n)\mathbf{d}],\ [\mathbf{d}] \quad \text{where} \quad \mathbf{d} \leftarrow \mathsf{span}(\mathbf{B}_1) \\ &\mathsf{ct}_{\mathbf{x}} : x_1 \cdot \mathbf{u} + \mathbf{w}_1, \ldots, x_n \cdot \mathbf{u} + \mathbf{w}_n, [\alpha] \cdot m \end{aligned} \tag{8}$$

To carry out the non-trivial extension by Okamoto and Takashima [27] which involves three subgroups of H_N (cf. game sequence from $\mathsf{Game}_{2.0}$ to $\mathsf{Game}_{2.q}$), we increase the dimension of vectors $\mathbf{u}, \mathbf{w}_1, \ldots, \mathbf{w}_n$, $\mathbf{d}$ in secret keys by k (i.e., from $k+1$ to $2k+1$) as in [13] such that the support of $\mathbf{d}$ can accommodate three subspaces defined by

$$(\mathbf{B}_1, \mathbf{B}_2, \mathbf{B}_3) \leftarrow \mathbb{Z}_p^{(2k+1)\times k} \times \mathbb{Z}_p^{2k+1} \times \mathbb{Z}_p^{(2k+1)\times k}$$

where $\mathbf{B}_1, \mathbf{B}_2, \mathbf{B}_3$ play the roles similar to p_4, p_2, p_3-subgroup respectively. Following the proof strategy in [13] and statement (7) for the one-key scheme (6), we can change secret keys and the challenge ciphertext revealed to the adversary into the form:

$$\begin{aligned} &\mathsf{sk}_{\mathbf{y}} : [\alpha + (y_1 \cdot \mathbf{w}_1 + \cdots + y_n \cdot \mathbf{w}_n)\mathbf{d}],\ [\mathbf{d}] \quad \text{where} \quad \mathbf{d} \leftarrow \mathsf{span}(\mathbf{B}_1, \boxed{\mathbf{B}_2}) \\ &\mathsf{ct}^* : \{x_{i,b} \cdot \mathbf{u}^{(1)} + \boxed{x_{i,1-b} \cdot \mathbf{u}^{(2)}} + x_{i,b} \cdot \mathbf{u}^{(3)} + \mathbf{w}_i\}_{i \in [n]},\ [\alpha] \cdot m \end{aligned}$$

where $\mathbf{u}^{(1)}$ (resp. $\mathbf{u}^{(2)}$, $\mathbf{u}^{(3)}$) is a random vector orthogonal to $\mathsf{span}(\mathbf{B}_2, \mathbf{B}_3)$ (resp. $\mathsf{span}(\mathbf{B}_1, \mathbf{B}_3)$, $\mathsf{span}(\mathbf{B}_1, \mathbf{B}_2)$). Finally, by the "change of basis" commonly appeared in the proof with dual pairing vector space [23,27] (and a simple statistical argument), we claim that ct^* has the same distribution as

$$\boxed{x_{1,0} \cdot \mathbf{u}_0 + x_{1,1} \cdot \mathbf{u}_1} + \mathbf{w}_1, \ldots, \boxed{x_{n,0} \cdot \mathbf{u}_0 + x_{n,1} \cdot \mathbf{u}_1} + \mathbf{w}_n,\ [\alpha] \cdot m$$

where $\mathbf{u}_0, \mathbf{u}_1 \leftarrow \mathbb{Z}_p^{1\times(2k+1)}$. This means that ct^* hides b and scheme (8) is fully attribute-hiding.

Note that the support of randomness $\mathbf{d}$ (after the change) is $\mathsf{span}(\mathbf{B}_1, \mathbf{B}_2)$ rather than $\mathsf{span}(\mathbf{B}_2)$, which simulates p_2-subgroup in the composite-order scheme (1). This is crucial to derive more efficient IPE scheme but slightly complicates the final argument above where "change of basis" technique has to be used to deal with $x_{i,b} \cdot \mathbf{u}^{(1)}$ interplaying with $\mathbf{B}_1$-component in $\mathsf{sk}_{\mathbf{y}}$.

(Public-key) IPE scheme. To upgrade our private-key IPE to public-key IPE, we will employ the "private-key to public-key" compiler in [36]. The compiler relies on bilinear groups $(p, G_1, G_2, G_T, e : G_1 \times G_2 \to G_T)$ in which the k-LIN assumption holds. In detail, we do the following "vector to matrix"/"scalar to vector" substitution for entries in msk and secret keys:

$$\begin{aligned} \mathbf{u}, \mathbf{w}_1, \ldots, \mathbf{w}_n \in \mathbb{Z}_p^{1\times(2k+1)} &\mapsto \mathbf{U}, \mathbf{W}_1, \ldots, \mathbf{W}_n \in \mathbb{Z}_p^{(k+1)\times(2k+1)} \\ \alpha \in \mathbb{Z}_p &\mapsto \mathbf{k} \in \mathbb{Z}_p^{k+1} \end{aligned}$$

and publish them as parts of mpk in the form of

$$[\mathbf{A}^\top \mathbf{U}]_1, [\mathbf{A}^\top \mathbf{W}_1]_1, \ldots, [\mathbf{A}^\top \mathbf{W}_n]_1, [\mathbf{A}^\top \mathbf{k}]_T \quad \text{where} \quad \mathbf{A} \leftarrow \mathbb{Z}_p^{(k+1)\times k}.$$

In the ciphertext, we translate $\mathbf{u}, \mathbf{w}_1, \ldots, \mathbf{w}_n$ into $[\mathbf{c}^\top \mathbf{U}]_1, [\mathbf{c}^\top \mathbf{W}_1]_1, \ldots, [\mathbf{c}^\top \mathbf{W}_n]_1$ where $\mathbf{c} \leftarrow \mathsf{span}(\mathbf{A})$ and translate $[\alpha]_2$ into $[\mathbf{c}^\top \mathbf{k}]_T$. Finally, secret keys are now moved to group G_2. This results in the following IPE scheme:

$$\begin{aligned} \mathsf{mpk} &: [\mathbf{A}]_1, [\mathbf{A}^\top \mathbf{U}]_1, [\mathbf{A}^\top \mathbf{W}_1]_1, \ldots, [\mathbf{A}^\top \mathbf{W}_n]_1, [\mathbf{A}^\top \mathbf{k}]_T \\ \mathsf{sk}_\mathbf{y} &: [\mathbf{k} + (y_1 \cdot \mathbf{W}_1 + \cdots + y_n \cdot \mathbf{W}_n)\mathbf{d}]_2,\ [\mathbf{d}]_2 \quad \text{where} \quad \mathbf{d} \leftarrow \mathsf{span}(\mathbf{B}_1) \\ \mathsf{ct}_\mathbf{x} &: [\mathbf{c}^\top]_1, [x_1 \cdot \mathbf{c}^\top \mathbf{U} + \mathbf{c}^\top \mathbf{W}_1]_1, \ldots, [x_n \cdot \mathbf{c}^\top \mathbf{U} + \mathbf{c}^\top \mathbf{W}_n]_1, [\mathbf{c}^\top \mathbf{k}]_T \cdot m \\ &\qquad \text{where} \quad \mathbf{c} \leftarrow \mathsf{span}(\mathbf{A}) \end{aligned} \tag{9}$$

Note that the translation does not involve $(\mathbf{B}_1, \mathbf{B}_2, \mathbf{B}_3)$ we just introduced.

To prove the security of the resulting public-key IPE scheme, we first show that we can change the support of $\mathbf{c}$ from $\mathsf{span}(\mathbf{A})$ to $\mathbb{Z}_p^{k+1}$ by the following statement implied by the k-LIN assumption:

$$(\,[\mathbf{A}]_1, [\mathbf{c} \leftarrow \mathsf{span}(\mathbf{A})]_1\,) \approx_c (\,[\mathbf{A}]_1, [\mathbf{c} \leftarrow \mathbb{Z}_p^{k+1}]_1\,).$$

Since $(\mathbf{A} \mid \mathbf{c})$ is full-rank with overwhelming probability, we can see that

$$\begin{aligned} \widetilde{\mathsf{msk}} &= (\,\mathbf{A}^\top \mathbf{U}, \mathbf{A}^\top \mathbf{W}_1, \ldots, \mathbf{A}^\top \mathbf{W}_n, \mathbf{A}^\top \mathbf{k}\,) \\ \text{and} \quad \mathsf{msk}^* &= (\,\mathbf{c}^\top \mathbf{U}, \mathbf{c}^\top \mathbf{W}_1, \ldots, \mathbf{c}^\top \mathbf{W}_n, \mathbf{c}^\top \mathbf{k}\,) \end{aligned}$$

are distributed independently. Then the security of scheme (9) can be reduced to that of private-key scheme (8) by observations: (i) $\widetilde{\mathsf{msk}}$ is necessary for generating mpk in scheme (9); (ii) we can view a ciphertext in scheme (9) as a ciphertext of our private-key IPE scheme under master secret key msk^*; (iii) a secret key in scheme (9) can be produced from a secret key of private-key IPE scheme (8) under master secret key msk^* with the help of $\widetilde{\mathsf{msk}}$.

How to Shorten the Ciphertext. The ciphertext size of our IPE scheme (9) mainly depends on the width of matrix $\mathbf{U}$ and $\mathbf{W}_i$, which is further determined by the dimensions of subspaces defined by $\mathbf{B}_1, \mathbf{B}_2, \mathbf{B}_3$. Therefore, in order to reduce the ciphertext size, we employ the "dimension compress" technique used in [16]. The basic idea is to let $\mathbf{B}_1$ and $\mathbf{B}_3$ "share some dimensions" and finally decrease the width of $\mathbf{U}$ and $\mathbf{W}_i$, the cost is that we have to use the XDLIN assumption. Compared with our first scheme, a qualitative difference is that the private-key variant now works with bilinear maps. This is not needed when we work with the k-LIN assumption in the first scheme.

Organization. The paper is organized as follows. In Sect. 2, we review some basic notions. The next two sections, Sects. 3 and 4, will be devoted to our two IPE schemes, respectively. In both sections, we will first develop a private-key scheme and then transform it to the public-key version as [36].

2 Preliminaries

Notation. Let $\mathbf{A}$ be a matrix over $\mathbb{Z}_p$. We use $\mathsf{span}(\mathbf{A})$ to denote the column span of $\mathbf{A}$, use $\mathsf{basis}(\mathbf{A})$ to denote a basis of $\mathsf{span}(\mathbf{A})$, and use $(\mathbf{A}_1|\mathbf{A}_2)$ to denote the concatenation of matrices $\mathbf{A}_1, \mathbf{A}_2$. By $\mathsf{span}(\mathbf{A}^\top)$, we are indicating the row span of $\mathbf{A}^\top$. We let $\mathbf{I}_n$ be the n-by-n identity matrix and $\mathbf{0}$ be a zero matrix of proper size. Given an invertible matrix $\mathbf{B}$, we use $\mathbf{B}^*$ to denote its dual satisfying $\mathbf{B}^\top \mathbf{B}^* = \mathbf{I}$.

2.1 Inner-Product Encryption

Algorithms. An inner-product encryption (IPE) scheme consists of four algorithms $(\mathsf{Setup}, \mathsf{KeyGen}, \mathsf{Enc}, \mathsf{Dec})$:

$\mathsf{Setup}(1^\lambda, n) \to (\mathsf{mpk}, \mathsf{msk})$. The setup algorithm gets as input the security parameter λ and the dimension n of the vector space. It outputs the master public key mpk and the master key msk.

$\mathsf{KeyGen}(\mathsf{msk}, \mathbf{y}) \to \mathsf{sk}_\mathbf{y}$. The key generation algorithm gets as input msk and a vector $\mathbf{y}$. It outputs a secret key $\mathsf{sk}_\mathbf{y}$ for vector $\mathbf{y}$.

$\mathsf{Enc}(\mathsf{mpk}, \mathbf{x}, m) \to \mathsf{ct}_\mathbf{x}$. The encryption algorithm gets as input mpk, a vector $\mathbf{x}$ and a message m. It outputs a ciphertext $\mathsf{ct}_\mathbf{x}$ for vector $\mathbf{x}$.

$\mathsf{Dec}(\mathsf{ct}_\mathbf{x}, \mathsf{sk}_\mathbf{y}) \to m$. The decryption algorithm gets as a ciphertext $\mathsf{ct}_\mathbf{x}$ for $\mathbf{x}$ and a secret key $\mathsf{sk}_\mathbf{y}$ for vector $\mathbf{y}$ satisfying $\langle \mathbf{x}, \mathbf{y} \rangle = 0$. It outputs message m.

Correctness. For all vectors $\mathbf{x}, \mathbf{y}$ satisfying $\langle \mathbf{x}, \mathbf{y} \rangle = 0$ and all m, it holds that

$$\Pr[\mathsf{Dec}(\mathsf{ct}_\mathbf{x}, \mathsf{sk}_\mathbf{y}) = m] = 1,$$

where $(\mathsf{mpk}, \mathsf{msk}) \leftarrow \mathsf{Setup}(1^\lambda, n)$, $\mathsf{ct}_\mathbf{x} \leftarrow \mathsf{Enc}(\mathsf{mpk}, \mathbf{x}, m)$, $\mathsf{sk}_\mathbf{y} \leftarrow \mathsf{KeyGen}(\mathsf{msk}, \mathbf{y})$.

Security. For a stateful adversary $\mathcal{A}$, we define the advantage function

$$\mathsf{Adv}^{\mathrm{IPE}}_{\mathcal{A}}(\lambda) := \left| \Pr\left[b = b' : \begin{array}{l} (\mathsf{mpk}, \mathsf{msk}) \leftarrow \mathsf{Setup}(1^\lambda, n); \\ (\mathbf{x}_0, \mathbf{x}_1, m_0, m_1) \leftarrow \mathcal{A}^{\mathsf{KeyGen}(\mathsf{msk},\cdot)}(\mathsf{mpk}); \\ b \leftarrow_{\mathrm{R}} \{0,1\};\ \mathsf{ct}^* \leftarrow \mathsf{Enc}(\mathsf{mpk}, \mathbf{x}_b, m_b); \\ b' \leftarrow \mathcal{A}^{\mathsf{KeyGen}(\mathsf{msk},\cdot)}(\mathsf{ct}^*) \end{array} \right] - \frac{1}{2} \right|$$

with the following restrictions on all queries $\mathbf{y}$ that $\mathcal{A}$ submitted to $\mathsf{KeyGen}(\mathsf{msk}, \cdot)$:

- if $m_0 \neq m_1$, we require that $\langle \mathbf{x}_0, \mathbf{y} \rangle \neq 0 \wedge \langle \mathbf{x}_1, \mathbf{y} \rangle \neq 0$;
- if $m_0 = m_1$, we require that either $\langle \mathbf{x}_0, \mathbf{y} \rangle \neq 0 \wedge \langle \mathbf{x}_1, \mathbf{y} \rangle \neq 0$ or $\langle \mathbf{x}_0, \mathbf{y} \rangle = \langle \mathbf{x}_1, \mathbf{y} \rangle = 0$.

An IPE scheme is *adaptively secure* and *fully attribute-hiding* if for all PPT adversaries $\mathcal{A}$, the advantage $\mathsf{Adv}^{\mathrm{IPE}}_{\mathcal{A}}(\lambda)$ is a negligible function in λ.

Private-key IPE. In a private-key IPE, the Setup algorithm does not output mpk; and the Enc algorithm takes msk instead of mpk as input. The adaptive security and full attribute-hiding can be defined analogously except that $\mathcal{A}$ only gets ct^* and has access to $\mathsf{KeyGen}(\mathsf{msk}, \cdot)$. The advantage function is denoted by $\mathsf{Adv}^{\mathrm{IPE}^*}_{\mathcal{A}}(\lambda)$. Accordingly, we may call the standard IPE *public-key IPE*.

2.2 Prime-Order Groups and Matrix Diffie-Hellman Assumptions

A group generator $\mathcal{G}$ takes as input security parameter λ and outputs group description $\mathbb{G} = (p, G_1, G_2, G_T, e)$, where p is a prime of $\Theta(\lambda)$ bits, G_1, G_2 and G_T are cyclic groups of order p, and $e : G_1 \times G_2 \to G_T$ is a non-degenerate bilinear map. We require that group operations in G_1, G_2 and G_T as well the bilinear map e are computable in deterministic polynomial time with respect to λ. Let $g_1 \in G_1$, $g_2 \in G_2$ and $g_T = e(g_1, g_2) \in G_T$ be the respective generators. We employ the *implicit representation* of group elements: for a matrix $\mathbf{M}$ over $\mathbb{Z}_p$, we define $[\mathbf{M}]_1 = g_1^{\mathbf{M}}, [\mathbf{M}]_2 = g_2^{\mathbf{M}}, [\mathbf{M}]_T = g_T^{\mathbf{M}}$, where exponentiations are carried out component-wise. Given $\mathbf{A}$ and $[\mathbf{B}]_2$, we let $\mathbf{A} \odot [\mathbf{B}]_2 = [\mathbf{AB}]_2$; for $[\mathbf{A}]_1$ and $[\mathbf{B}]_2$, we let $e([\mathbf{A}]_1, [\mathbf{B}]_2) = [\mathbf{AB}]_T$.

We review the matrix Diffie-Hellman (MDDH) assumption on G_1 [14]. The $\text{MDDH}_{k,\ell}$ assumption on G_2 can be defined analogously and it is known that $k\text{-LIN} \Rightarrow \text{MDDH}_{k,\ell}$ [14].

Assumption 1 ($\text{MDDH}_{k,\ell}$ Assumption). *Let $\ell > k \geq 1$. We say that the $\text{MDDH}_{k,\ell}$ assumption holds with respect to $\mathcal{G}$ if for all PPT adversaries $\mathcal{A}$, the following advantage function is negligible in λ.*

$$\mathsf{Adv}_{\mathcal{A}}^{\text{MDDH}_{k,\ell}}(\lambda) := \left| \Pr[\mathcal{A}(\mathbb{G}, [\mathbf{M}]_1, [\mathbf{Ms}]_1) = 1] - \Pr[\mathcal{A}(\mathbb{G}, [\mathbf{M}]_1, [\mathbf{u}]_1) = 1] \right|$$

where $\mathbb{G} \leftarrow \mathcal{G}(1^\lambda)$, $\mathbf{M} \leftarrow \mathbb{Z}_p^{\ell \times k}$, $\mathbf{s} \leftarrow \mathbb{Z}_p^k$ and $\mathbf{u} \leftarrow \mathbb{Z}_p^\ell$.

We also use the external decisional linear (XDLIN) assumption on G_2 [1]:

Assumption 2 (XDLIN Assumption). *We say that the XDLIN assumption holds with respect to $\mathcal{G}$ if for all PPT adversaries $\mathcal{A}$, the following advantage function is negligible in λ.*

$$\mathsf{Adv}_{\mathcal{A}}^{\text{XDLIN}}(\lambda) := \left| \Pr[\mathcal{A}(\mathbb{G}, D, T_0 = [a_3(s_1 + s_2)]_2) = 1] - \Pr[\mathcal{A}(\mathbb{G}, D, T_1 \leftarrow G_2) = 1] \right|$$

where $\mathbb{G} \leftarrow \mathcal{G}(1^\lambda)$ and $D = ([a_1, a_2, a_3, a_1 s_1, a_2 s_2]_1, [a_1, a_2, a_3, a_1 s_1, a_2 s_2]_2)$ with $a_1, a_2, a_3, s_1, s_2 \leftarrow \mathbb{Z}_p$.

3 Construction from k-LIN Assumption

3.1 Preparation

Fix parameters $\ell_1, \ell_2, \ell_3 \geq 1$ and let $\ell := \ell_1 + \ell_2 + \ell_3$. We use basis

$$\mathbf{B}_1 \leftarrow \mathbb{Z}_p^{\ell \times \ell_1},\ \mathbf{B}_2 \leftarrow \mathbb{Z}_p^{\ell \times \ell_2},\ \mathbf{B}_3 \leftarrow \mathbb{Z}_p^{\ell \times \ell_3},$$

and its dual basis $(\mathbf{B}_1^{\|}, \mathbf{B}_2^{\|}, \mathbf{B}_3^{\|})$ such that $\mathbf{B}_i^\top \mathbf{B}_i^{\|} = \mathbf{I}$ (known as *non-degeneracy*) and $\mathbf{B}_i^\top \mathbf{B}_j = \mathbf{0}$ if $i \neq j$ (known as *orthogonality*), as depicted in Fig. 2.

Assumption. We review the $\text{SD}^{G_2}_{\mathbf{B}_1 \mapsto \mathbf{B}_1, \mathbf{B}_2}$ assumption [13,15,17] as follows. By symmetry, one may permute the indices for subspaces.

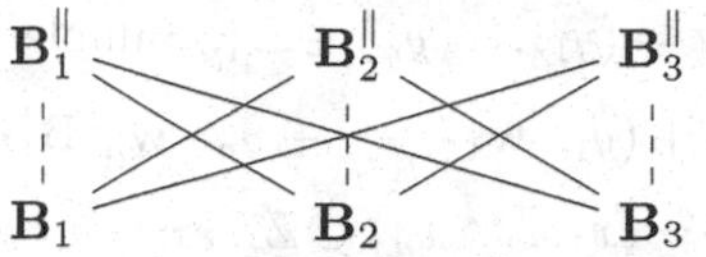

Fig. 2. Basis relations. Solid lines mean orthogonal, dashed lines mean non-degeneracy.

Lemma 1 ($\text{MDDH}_{\ell_1,\ell_1+\ell_2} \Rightarrow \text{SD}^{G_2}_{\mathbf{B}_1 \mapsto \mathbf{B}_1,\mathbf{B}_2}$). *Under the* $\text{MDDH}_{\ell_1,\ell_1+\ell_2}$ *assumption in* G_2*, there exists an efficient sampler outputting random* $([\mathbf{B}_1]_2, [\mathbf{B}_2]_2, [\mathbf{B}_3]_2)$ *(as described above) along with base* $\mathsf{basis}(\mathbf{B}_3^{\|})$ *and* $\mathsf{basis}(\mathbf{B}_1^{\|}, \mathbf{B}_2^{\|})$ *(of arbitrary choice) such that the following advantage function is negligible in* λ.

$$\mathsf{Adv}_{\mathcal{A}}^{\text{SD}^{G_2}_{\mathbf{B}_1 \mapsto \mathbf{B}_1,\mathbf{B}_2}}(\lambda) := \big|\Pr[\mathcal{A}(\mathbb{G}, D, [\mathbf{t}_0]_1) = 1] - \Pr[\mathcal{A}(\mathbb{G}, D, [\mathbf{t}_1]_1) = 1]\big|$$

where

$$D := (\ [\mathbf{B}_1]_2, [\mathbf{B}_2]_2, [\mathbf{B}_3]_2, \mathsf{basis}(\mathbf{B}_1^{\|}, \mathbf{B}_2^{\|}), \mathsf{basis}(\mathbf{B}_3^{\|})\ )$$
$$\mathbf{t}_0 \leftarrow \mathsf{span}(\mathbf{B}_1),\ \mathbf{t}_1 \leftarrow \mathsf{span}(\mathbf{B}_1, \mathbf{B}_2).$$

Facts. With basis $(\mathbf{B}_1, \mathbf{B}_2, \mathbf{B}_3)$, we can uniquely decompose $\mathbf{w} \in \mathbb{Z}_p^{1\times\ell}$ as

$$\mathbf{w} = \textstyle\sum_{\beta\in[3]} \mathbf{w}^{(\beta)} \quad \text{where} \quad \mathbf{w}^{(\beta)} \in \mathsf{span}(\mathbf{B}_\beta^{\|\top}).$$

In the paper, we use notation $\mathbf{w}^{(\beta)}$ to denote the projection of $\mathbf{w}$ onto $\mathsf{span}(\mathbf{B}_\beta^{\|\top})$ and define $\mathbf{w}^{(\beta_1\beta_2)} = \mathbf{w}^{(\beta_1)} + \mathbf{w}^{(\beta_2)}$ for $\beta_1, \beta_2 \in [3]$. Furthermore, we highlight two facts: (1) For $\beta \in [3]$, it holds that $\mathbf{w}\mathbf{B}_\beta = \mathbf{w}^{(\beta)}\mathbf{B}_\beta$; (2) For all $\beta^* \in [3]$, it holds that

$$\{\boxed{\mathbf{w}^{(\beta^*)}}, \{\mathbf{w}^{(\beta)}\}_{\beta\neq\beta^*}\} \equiv \{\boxed{\mathbf{w}^*}, \{\mathbf{w}^{(\beta)}\}_{\beta\neq\beta^*}\}$$

when $\mathbf{w} \leftarrow \mathbb{Z}_p^{1\times\ell}$ and $\mathbf{w}^* \leftarrow \mathsf{span}(\mathbf{B}_{\beta^*}^{\|\top})$.

3.2 Step One: A Private-Key IPE in Prime-Order Groups

Our first prime-order private-key IPE is described as follows. We use the basis described in Sect. 3.1 with $(\ell_1, \ell_2, \ell_3) = (k, 1, k)$. As mentioned in Sect. 1.2, we do not need bilinear map for this private-key IPE. However, for our future use in Sect. 3.4, we describe the IPE in bilinear groups and note that only one of source groups is used.

– $\mathsf{Setup}(1^\lambda, n)$: Run $\mathbb{G} = (p, G_1, G_2, G_T, e) \leftarrow \mathcal{G}(1^\lambda)$. Sample $\mathbf{B}_1 \leftarrow \mathbb{Z}_p^{(2k+1)\times k}$ and pick $\mathbf{u}, \mathbf{w}_1, \ldots, \mathbf{w}_n \leftarrow \mathbb{Z}_p^{1\times(2k+1)}$, $\alpha \leftarrow \mathbb{Z}_p$. Output

$$\mathsf{msk} = (\ \mathbb{G}, \alpha, \mathbf{u}, \mathbf{w}_1, \ldots, \mathbf{w}_n, \mathbf{B}_1\ ).$$

- $\mathsf{KeyGen}(\mathsf{msk}, \mathbf{y})$: Let $\mathbf{y} = (y_1, \ldots, y_n) \in \mathbb{Z}_p^n$. Sample $\mathbf{r} \leftarrow \mathbb{Z}_p^k$ and output

$$\mathsf{sk}_{\mathbf{y}} = (\, K_0 = [\alpha + (y_1 \cdot \mathbf{w}_1 + \cdots + y_n \cdot \mathbf{w}_n)\mathbf{B}_1\mathbf{r}]_2,\ K_1 = [\mathbf{B}_1\mathbf{r}]_2 \,)$$

- $\mathsf{Enc}(\mathsf{msk}, \mathbf{x}, m)$: Let $\mathbf{x} = (x_1, \ldots, x_n) \in \mathbb{Z}_p^n$ and $m \in G_2$. Output

$$\mathsf{ct}_{\mathbf{x}} = (\, C_1 = x_1 \cdot \mathbf{u} + \mathbf{w}_1,\ \ldots,\ C_n = x_n \cdot \mathbf{u} + \mathbf{w}_n,\ C = [\alpha]_2 \cdot m \,)$$

- $\mathsf{Dec}(\mathsf{ct}_{\mathbf{x}}, \mathsf{sk}_{\mathbf{y}})$: Parse $\mathsf{ct}_{\mathbf{x}} = (C_1, \ldots, C_n, C)$ and $\mathsf{sk}_{\mathbf{y}} = (K_0, K_1)$ for $\mathbf{y} = (y_1, \ldots, y_n) \in \mathbb{Z}_p^n$. Output

$$m' = C \cdot ((y_1 \cdot C_1 + \cdots + y_n \cdot C_n) \odot K_1) \cdot K_0^{-1}.$$

The correctness is straightforward.

3.3 Security of Private-Key IPE

We will prove the following theorem.

Theorem 1. *Under the k-LIN assumption, the private-key IPE scheme described in Sect. 3.2 is adaptively secure and fully attribute-hiding (cf. Sect. 2.1).*

Following [11,35], we can reduce the case $m_0 \neq m_1$ to the case $m_0 = m_1$ by arguing that an encryption for m_b is indistinguishable with an encryption for m_0. Therefore it is sufficient to prove the following lemma for $m_0 = m_1$.

Lemma 2. *For any adversary $\mathcal{A}$ that makes at most Q key queries and outputs $m_0 = m_1$, there exists adversaries $\mathcal{B}_1, \mathcal{B}_2, \mathcal{B}_3$ such that*

$$\mathsf{Adv}_{\mathcal{A}}^{\text{IPE}^*}(\lambda) \leq Q \cdot \mathsf{Adv}_{\mathcal{B}_1}^{\text{SD}^{G_2}_{\mathbf{B}_1 \mapsto \mathbf{B}_1,\mathbf{B}_3}}(\lambda) + Q \cdot \mathsf{Adv}_{\mathcal{B}_2}^{\text{SD}^{G_2}_{\mathbf{B}_3 \mapsto \mathbf{B}_3,\mathbf{B}_2}}(\lambda) + \ Q \cdot \mathsf{Adv}_{\mathcal{B}_3}^{\text{SD}^{G_2}_{\mathbf{B}_1 \mapsto \mathbf{B}_1,\mathbf{B}_3}}(\lambda)$$

and $\mathsf{Time}(\mathcal{B}_1), \mathsf{Time}(\mathcal{B}_2), \mathsf{Time}(\mathcal{B}_3) \approx \mathsf{Time}(\mathcal{A})$.

Game sequence. We prove Lemma 2 via the following game sequence, which is summarized in Fig. 3.

- Game_0 is the real game in which the challenge ciphertext for $\mathbf{x}_b = (x_{1,b}, \ldots, x_{n,b})$ is of the form

$$x_{1,b} \cdot \mathbf{u} + \mathbf{w}_1,\ \ldots,\ x_{n,b} \cdot \mathbf{u} + \mathbf{w}_n,\ [\alpha]_2 \cdot m_0.$$

  Here $b \leftarrow \{0, 1\}$ is a secret bit.
- Game_1 is identical to Game_0 except that the challenge ciphertext is

$$x_{1,b} \cdot \mathbf{u}^{(13)} + \boxed{x_{1,1-b} \cdot \mathbf{u}^{(2)}} + \mathbf{w}_1,\ \ldots,\ x_{n,b} \cdot \mathbf{u}^{(13)} + \boxed{x_{n,1-b} \cdot \mathbf{u}^{(2)}} + \mathbf{w}_n,\ [\alpha]_2 \cdot m_0.$$

  We claim that $\mathsf{Game}_1 \equiv \mathsf{Game}_0$. This follows from facts that (1) secret keys will not reveal $\mathbf{w}_1^{(2)}, \ldots, \mathbf{w}_n^{(2)}$; (2) for all $\mathbf{x}_0, \mathbf{x}_1 \in \mathbb{Z}_p^n$ and $\mathbf{u}^{(2)} \in \mathsf{span}(\mathbf{B}_2^{\|^\top})$, it holds

$$\{ \boxed{x_{i,b} \cdot \mathbf{u}^{(2)}} + \mathbf{w}_i^{(2)} \}_{i \in [n]} \equiv \{ \boxed{x_{i,1-b} \cdot \mathbf{u}^{(2)}} + \mathbf{w}_i^{(2)} \}_{i \in [n]}$$

  when $\mathbf{w}_1^{(2)}, \ldots, \mathbf{w}_n^{(2)} \leftarrow \mathsf{span}(\mathbf{B}_2^{\|^\top})$. See Lemma 4 for more details.

Game	ct			κ-th sk ($\mathbf{d} \leftarrow$ span(?))			Remark
	$?^{(1)} + \mathbf{w}_i^{(1)}$	$?^{(2)} + \mathbf{w}_i^{(2)}$	$?^{(3)} + \mathbf{w}_i^{(3)}$	$\kappa < j$	$\kappa = j$	$\kappa > j$	
0	$x_{i,b} \cdot \mathbf{u}$			$\mathbf{B}_1$			Real game
1	$x_{i,b} \cdot \mathbf{u}$	$x_{i,1-b} \cdot \mathbf{u}$	$x_{i,b} \cdot \mathbf{u}$	$\mathbf{B}_1$			statistical argument: $\{x_{i,b} \cdot \mathbf{u}^{(2)} + \mathbf{w}_i^{(2)}\}_{i\in[n]} \equiv \{x_{i,1-b} \cdot \mathbf{u}^{(2)} + \mathbf{w}_i^{(2)}\}_{i\in[n]}$
$2.j-1$	$x_{i,b} \cdot \mathbf{u}$	$x_{i,1-b} \cdot \mathbf{u}$	$x_{i,b} \cdot \mathbf{u}$	$\mathbf{B}_1, \mathbf{B}_2$	$\mathbf{B}_1$	$\mathbf{B}_1$	$\mathsf{Game}_{2.0} = \mathsf{Game}_1$, $\mathsf{Game}_{2.j} = \mathsf{Game}_{2.j-1.5}$
$2.j-1.1$	$x_{i,b} \cdot \mathbf{u}$	$x_{i,1-b} \cdot \mathbf{u}$	$x_{i,b} \cdot \mathbf{u}$	$\mathbf{B}_1, \mathbf{B}_2$	$\mathbf{B}_1, \mathbf{B}_3$	$\mathbf{B}_1$	$\mathsf{SD}^{G_2}_{\mathbf{B}_1 \mapsto \mathbf{B}_1, \mathbf{B}_3}$: $[\mathsf{span}(\mathbf{B}_1)]_2 \approx_c [\mathsf{span}(\mathbf{B}_1, \mathbf{B}_3)]_2$ given $\mathsf{basis}(\mathbf{B}_2^{\parallel})$, $\mathsf{basis}(\mathbf{B}_1^{\parallel}, \mathbf{B}_3^{\parallel})$
$2.j-1.2$	$x_{i,b} \cdot \mathbf{u}$	$x_{i,1-b} \cdot \mathbf{u}$	$x_{i,1-b} \cdot \mathbf{u}$	$\mathbf{B}_1, \mathbf{B}_2$	$\mathbf{B}_1, \mathbf{B}_3$	$\mathbf{B}_1$	statistical argument: $\{x_{i,b} \cdot \mathbf{u}^{(3)} + \mathbf{w}_i^{(3)}\}_{i\in[n]} \equiv \{x_{i,1-b} \cdot \mathbf{u}^{(3)} + \mathbf{w}_i^{(3)}\}_{i\in[n]}$ given $y_1 \cdot \mathbf{w}_1^{(3)} + \cdots + y_n \cdot \mathbf{w}_n^{(3)}$
$2.j-1.3$	$x_{i,b} \cdot \mathbf{u}$	$x_{i,1-b} \cdot \mathbf{u}$	$x_{i,1-b} \cdot \mathbf{u}$	$\mathbf{B}_1, \mathbf{B}_2$	$\mathbf{B}_1, \mathbf{B}_2, \mathbf{B}_3$	$\mathbf{B}_1$	$\mathsf{SD}^{G_2}_{\mathbf{B}_3 \mapsto \mathbf{B}_3, \mathbf{B}_2}$: $[\mathsf{span}(\mathbf{B}_3)]_2 \approx_c [\mathsf{span}(\mathbf{B}_2, \mathbf{B}_3)]_2$ given $\mathsf{basis}(\mathbf{B}_1^{\parallel})$, $\mathsf{basis}(\mathbf{B}_2^{\parallel}, \mathbf{B}_3^{\parallel})$
$2.j-1.4$	$x_{i,b} \cdot \mathbf{u}$	$x_{i,1-b} \cdot \mathbf{u}$	$x_{i,b} \cdot \mathbf{u}$	$\mathbf{B}_1, \mathbf{B}_2$	$\mathbf{B}_1, \mathbf{B}_2, \mathbf{B}_3$	$\mathbf{B}_1$	statistical argument: analogous to $\mathsf{Game}_{2.j-1.2}$
$2.j-1.5$	$x_{i,b} \cdot \mathbf{u}$	$x_{i,1-b} \cdot \mathbf{u}$	$x_{i,b} \cdot \mathbf{u}$	$\mathbf{B}_1, \mathbf{B}_2$	$\mathbf{B}_1, \mathbf{B}_2$	$\mathbf{B}_1$	$\mathsf{SD}^{G_2}_{\mathbf{B}_1 \mapsto \mathbf{B}_1, \mathbf{B}_3}$: analogous to $\mathsf{Game}_{2.j-1.1}$
3	$x_{i,0} \cdot \mathbf{u}_0 + x_{i,1} \cdot \mathbf{u}_1$		$x_{i,b} \cdot \mathbf{u}$	$\mathbf{B}_1, \mathbf{B}_2$			$\mathbf{u}_0, \mathbf{u}_1 \leftarrow \mathbb{Z}_p^{1\times(2k+1)}$; statistical argument: change of basis w.r.t. $\mathsf{span}(\mathbf{B}_1, \mathbf{B}_2)$
4	$x_{i,0} \cdot \mathbf{u}_0 + x_{i,1} \cdot \mathbf{u}_1$			$\mathbf{B}_1, \mathbf{B}_2$			statistical argument: analogous to $\mathsf{Game}_{2.j-1}$

Fig. 3. Game sequence for private-key IPE based on k-LIN assumption. The gray background highlights the difference between adjacent games. Here, $\mathbf{B}_1, \mathbf{B}_2, \mathbf{B}_3$ play a role similar to the p_4, p_2, p_3-subgroups in Fig. 1.

- $\mathsf{Game}_{2.j}$ for $j \in [0, q]$ is identical to Game_1 except that the first j secret keys are

$$[\alpha + (y_1 \cdot \mathbf{w}_1 + \cdots + y_n \cdot \mathbf{w}_n)\mathbf{d}]_2,\ [\mathbf{d}]_2 \quad \text{where} \quad \boxed{\mathbf{d} \leftarrow \mathsf{span}(\mathbf{B}_1, \mathbf{B}_2)}.$$

We claim that $\mathsf{Game}_{2.j-1} \approx_c \mathsf{Game}_{2.j}$ for $j \in [q]$ and give a proof sketch later.
- Game_3 is identical to $\mathsf{Game}_{2.q}$ except that the challenge ciphertext is

$$\{\boxed{x_{i,0} \cdot \mathbf{u}_0^{(12)} + x_{i,1} \cdot \mathbf{u}_1^{(12)}} + x_{i,b} \cdot \mathbf{u}^{(3)} + \mathbf{w}_i\}_{i\in[n]}, [\alpha]_2 \cdot m_0.$$

where $\mathbf{u}_0, \mathbf{u}_1 \leftarrow \mathbb{Z}_p^{1\times(2k+1)}$. We claim that $\mathsf{Game}_{2.q} \equiv \mathsf{Game}_3$. This follows from the "change of basis" technique used in dual pairing vector spaces [23,28]. In particular, we argue that

$$(\overbrace{\mathbf{u}^{(1)}}^{x_{i,b}}, \overbrace{\mathbf{u}^{(2)}}^{x_{i,1-b}}) \equiv (\mathbf{u}_0^{(12)}, \mathbf{u}_1^{(12)})$$

when $\mathbf{u}, \mathbf{u}_0, \mathbf{u}_1$ and basis $\mathbf{B}_1, \mathbf{B}_2$ are chosen at random. Here we use the fact that randomness $\mathbf{d}$ in secret keys reveals no information about the basis of $\mathsf{span}(\mathbf{B}_1, \mathbf{B}_2)$. See Lemma 5 for more details.
- Game_4 is identical to Game_3 except that the challenge ciphertext is

$$\boxed{x_{1,0} \cdot \mathbf{u}_0 + x_{1,1} \cdot \mathbf{u}_1} + \mathbf{w}_1,\ \ldots,\ \boxed{x_{n,0} \cdot \mathbf{u}_0 + x_{n,1} \cdot \mathbf{u}_1} + \mathbf{w}_n,\ [\alpha]_2 \cdot m_0$$

in which the adversary has no advantage in guessing b. We claim that $\mathsf{Game}_3 \equiv \mathsf{Game}_4$. The proof is similar to that for $\mathsf{Game}_1 \equiv \mathsf{Game}_0$. See Lemma 6 for details.

Proving $\mathsf{Game}_{2.j-1} \approx_c \mathsf{Game}_{2.j}$. We now prove $\mathsf{Game}_{2.j-1} \approx_c \mathsf{Game}_{2.j}$ and thus complete the proof for Lemma 2. For all $j \in [q]$, we employ the following game sequence, which has been included in Fig. 3.

- $\mathsf{Game}_{2.j-1.1}$ is identical to $\mathsf{Game}_{2.j-1}$ except that the jth secret key is

$$[\alpha + (y_1 \cdot \mathbf{w}_1 + \cdots + y_n \cdot \mathbf{w}_n)\mathbf{d}]_2,\ [\mathbf{d}]_2 \quad \text{where} \quad \boxed{\mathbf{d} \leftarrow \mathsf{span}(\mathbf{B}_1, \mathbf{B}_3)}.$$

We claim that $\mathsf{Game}_{2.j-1.1} \approx_c \mathsf{Game}_{2.j-1}$. This follows from the $\mathrm{SD}^{G_2}_{\mathbf{B}_1 \mapsto \mathbf{B}_1, \mathbf{B}_3}$ assumption: given $[\mathbf{B}_1]_2, [\mathbf{B}_2]_2, [\mathbf{B}_3]_2, \mathsf{basis}(\mathbf{B}_2^{\|}), \mathsf{basis}(\mathbf{B}_1^{\|}, \mathbf{B}_3^{\|})$, it holds that

$$[\mathbf{t} \leftarrow \mathsf{span}(\mathbf{B}_1)]_2 \approx_c [\mathbf{t} \leftarrow \mathsf{span}(\mathbf{B}_1, \mathbf{B}_3)]_2.$$

In the reduction, we sample $\alpha \leftarrow \mathbb{Z}_p$, $\mathbf{w}_1, \ldots, \mathbf{w}_n \leftarrow \mathbb{Z}_p^{1 \times (2k+1)}$ and pick

$$\mathbf{u}^{(13)} \leftarrow \mathsf{span}((\mathbf{B}_1^{\|} | \mathbf{B}_3^{\|})^\top) \quad \text{and} \quad \mathbf{u}^{(2)} \leftarrow \mathsf{span}(\mathbf{B}_2^{\|\top})$$

using $\mathsf{basis}(\mathbf{B}_1^{\|}, \mathbf{B}_3^{\|})$ and $\mathsf{basis}(\mathbf{B}_2^{\|})$, respectively. The challenge ciphertext is generated using

$$\{ x_{i,b} \cdot \mathbf{u}^{(13)} + x_{i,1-b} \cdot \mathbf{u}^{(2)} + \mathbf{w}_i \}_{i \in [n]};$$

the jth secret key is created from $\mathbf{w}_1, \ldots, \mathbf{w}_n$ and $[\mathbf{t}]_2$ while the remaining keys can be generated using $[\mathbf{B}_1]_2$ and $[\mathbf{B}_2]_2$ along with $\alpha, \mathbf{w}_1, \ldots, \mathbf{w}_n$. See Lemma 7 for more details.
- $\mathsf{Game}_{2.j-1.2}$ is identical to $\mathsf{Game}_{2.j-1.1}$ except that the challenge ciphertext is

$$\{ x_{i,b} \cdot \mathbf{u}^{(1)} + x_{i,1-b} \cdot \mathbf{u}^{(2)} + \boxed{x_{i,1-b} \cdot \mathbf{u}^{(3)}} + \mathbf{w}_i \}_{i \in [n]}, [\alpha]_2 \cdot m_0.$$

We claim that $\mathsf{Game}_{2.j-1.2} \equiv \mathsf{Game}_{2.j-1.1}$. This follows from facts that: (1) $\mathbf{u}^{(3)}$ and $\mathbf{w}_i^{(3)}$ are only revealed from the challenge ciphertext and the jth secret key; (2) for all $\mathbf{x}_0$, $\mathbf{x}_1$ and $\mathbf{y}$ with the restriction that (a) $\langle \mathbf{x}_0, \mathbf{y} \rangle = \langle \mathbf{x}_1, \mathbf{y} \rangle = 0$; or (b) $\langle \mathbf{x}_0, \mathbf{y} \rangle \neq 0 \wedge \langle \mathbf{x}_1, \mathbf{y} \rangle \neq 0$, it holds that

$$\begin{aligned} &(\overbrace{x_{1,b} \cdot \mathbf{u}^{(3)} + \mathbf{w}_1^{(3)}, \ldots, x_{n,b} \cdot \mathbf{u}^{(3)} + \mathbf{w}_n^{(3)}}^{\mathsf{ct}}, \overbrace{y_1 \cdot \mathbf{w}_1^{(3)} + \cdots + y_n \cdot \mathbf{w}_n^{(3)}}^{\mathsf{sk}}) \\ \equiv &(\boxed{x_{1,1-b} \cdot \mathbf{u}^{(3)}} + \mathbf{w}_1^{(3)}, \ldots, \boxed{x_{n,1-b} \cdot \mathbf{u}^{(3)}} + \mathbf{w}_n^{(3)}, y_1 \cdot \mathbf{w}_1^{(3)} + \cdots + y_n \cdot \mathbf{w}_n^{(3)}). \end{aligned}$$

See Lemma 8 for more details.

- $\mathsf{Game}_{2.j-1.3}$ is identical to $\mathsf{Game}_{2.j-1.2}$ except that the jth secret key is

$$[\alpha + (y_1 \cdot \mathbf{w}_1 + \cdots + y_n \cdot \mathbf{w}_n)\mathbf{d}]_2,\ [\mathbf{d}]_2 \quad \text{where} \quad \boxed{\mathbf{d} \leftarrow \mathsf{span}(\mathbf{B}_1, \mathbf{B}_2, \mathbf{B}_3)}.$$

We claim that $\mathsf{Game}_{2.j-1.3} \approx_c \mathsf{Game}_{2.j-1.2}$. This follows from the $\mathrm{SD}^{G_2}_{\mathbf{B}_3 \mapsto \mathbf{B}_3, \mathbf{B}_2}$ assumption: given $[\mathbf{B}_1]_2, [\mathbf{B}_2]_2, [\mathbf{B}_3]_2, \mathsf{basis}(\mathbf{B}_1^\parallel), \mathsf{basis}(\mathbf{B}_2^\parallel, \mathbf{B}_3^\parallel)$, it holds that

$$[\mathbf{t} \leftarrow \mathsf{span}(\mathbf{B}_3)]_2 \approx_c [\mathbf{t} \leftarrow \mathsf{span}(\mathbf{B}_2, \mathbf{B}_3)]_2.$$

In the reduction, we sample $\alpha \leftarrow \mathbb{Z}_p$, $\mathbf{w}_1, \ldots, \mathbf{w}_n \leftarrow \mathbb{Z}_p^{1\times(2k+1)}$ and pick

$$\mathbf{u}^{(1)} \leftarrow \mathsf{span}(\mathbf{B}_1^{\parallel\top}) \quad \text{and} \quad \mathbf{u}^{(23)} \leftarrow \mathsf{span}((\mathbf{B}_2^\parallel | \mathbf{B}_3^\parallel)^\top)$$

using $\mathsf{basis}(\mathbf{B}_1^\parallel)$ and $\mathsf{basis}(\mathbf{B}_2^\parallel, \mathbf{B}_3^\parallel)$, respectively. The challenge ciphertext is generated using

$$\{\, x_{i,b} \cdot \mathbf{u}^{(1)} + x_{i,1-b} \cdot \mathbf{u}^{(23)} + \mathbf{w}_i \,\}_{i\in[n]}$$

the jth secret key is created from $\alpha, \mathbf{w}_1, \ldots, \mathbf{w}_n$ and $[\mathbf{B}_1]$, $[\mathbf{t}]_2$ while the remaining keys can be generated using $[\mathbf{B}_1, \mathbf{B}_2]_2$ along with $\alpha, \mathbf{w}_1, \ldots, \mathbf{w}_n$. See Lemma 9 for more details.
- $\mathsf{Game}_{2.j-1.4}$ is identical to $\mathsf{Game}_{2.j-1.3}$ except that the challenge ciphertext is

$$\{\, x_{i,b} \cdot \mathbf{u}^{(1)} + x_{i,1-b} \cdot \mathbf{u}^{(2)} + \boxed{x_{i,b} \cdot \mathbf{u}^{(3)}} + \mathbf{w}_i \,\}_{i\in[n]}, [\alpha]_2 \cdot m_0.$$

We claim that $\mathsf{Game}_{2.j-1.4} \equiv \mathsf{Game}_{2.j-1.3}$. The proof is identical to that for $\mathsf{Game}_{2.j-1.2} \equiv \mathsf{Game}_{2.j-1.1}$. See Lemma 10 for more details.
- $\mathsf{Game}_{2.j-1.5}$ is identical to $\mathsf{Game}_{2.j-1.4}$ except that the jth secret key is

$$[\alpha + (y_1 \cdot \mathbf{w}_1 + \cdots + y_n \cdot \mathbf{w}_n)\mathbf{d}]_2,\ [\mathbf{d}]_2 \quad \text{where} \quad \boxed{\mathbf{d} \leftarrow \mathsf{span}(\mathbf{B}_1, \mathbf{B}_2)}.$$

We claim that $\mathsf{Game}_{2.j-1.5} \approx_c \mathsf{Game}_{2.j-1.4}$. The proof is identical to that for $\mathsf{Game}_{2.j-1} \approx_c \mathsf{Game}_{2.j-1.1}$. See Lemma 11 for more details. Note that $\mathsf{Game}_{2.j-1.5} = \mathsf{Game}_{2.j}$.

3.4 Step Two: From Private-Key to Public-Key

We describe our prime-order full-fledged IPE, which is derived from our private-key IPE in Sect. 3.2 via the "private-key to public-key" compiler [36].

- $\mathsf{Setup}(1^\lambda, n)$: Run $\mathbb{G} = (p, G_1, G_2, G_T, e) \leftarrow \mathcal{G}(1^\lambda)$. Sample $\mathbf{A} \leftarrow \mathbb{Z}_p^{(k+1)\times k}$, $\mathbf{B}_1 \leftarrow \mathbb{Z}_p^{(2k+1)\times k}$ and pick

$$\mathbf{U}, \mathbf{W}_1, \ldots, \mathbf{W}_n \leftarrow \mathbb{Z}_p^{(k+1)\times(2k+1)} \quad \text{and} \quad \mathbf{k} \leftarrow \mathbb{Z}_p^{k+1}.$$

Output

$$\mathsf{mpk} = (\,\mathbb{G}, [\mathbf{A}^\top]_1, [\mathbf{A}^\top\mathbf{U}]_1, [\mathbf{A}^\top\mathbf{W}_1]_1, \ldots, [\mathbf{A}^\top\mathbf{W}_n]_1, [\mathbf{A}^\top\mathbf{k}]_T\,)$$
$$\mathsf{msk} = (\,\mathbf{k}, \mathbf{W}_1, \ldots, \mathbf{W}_n, \mathbf{B}_1\,).$$

- $\mathsf{KeyGen}(\mathsf{msk}, \mathbf{y})$: Let $\mathbf{y} = (y_1, \ldots, y_n) \in \mathbb{Z}_p^n$. Sample $\mathbf{r} \leftarrow \mathbb{Z}_p^k$ and output

$$\mathsf{sk}_{\mathbf{y}} = (\, K_0 = [\mathbf{k} + (y_1 \cdot \mathbf{W}_1 + \cdots + y_n \cdot \mathbf{W}_n)\mathbf{B}_1\mathbf{r}]_2, K_1 = [\mathbf{B}_1\mathbf{r}]_2\,)$$

- $\mathsf{Enc}(\mathsf{mpk}, \mathbf{x}, m)$: Let $\mathbf{x} = (x_1, \ldots, x_n) \in \mathbb{Z}_p^n$ and $m \in G_T$. Sample $\mathbf{s} \leftarrow \mathbb{Z}_p^k$ and output

$$\mathsf{ct}_{\mathbf{x}} = (\, C_0 = [\mathbf{s}^\top \mathbf{A}^\top]_1, \{\, C_i = [\mathbf{s}^\top \mathbf{A}^\top (x_i \cdot \mathbf{U} + \mathbf{W}_i)]_1 \,\}_{i \in [n]}, C = [\mathbf{s}^\top \mathbf{A}^\top \mathbf{k}]_T \cdot m\,)$$

- $\mathsf{Dec}(\mathsf{ct}_{\mathbf{x}}, \mathsf{sk}_{\mathbf{y}})$: Parse $\mathsf{ct}_{\mathbf{x}} = (C_0, C_1, \ldots, C_n, C)$ and $\mathsf{sk}_{\mathbf{y}} = (K_0, K_1)$ for $\mathbf{y} = (y_1, \ldots, y_n)$. Output

$$m' = C \cdot e(y_1 \odot C_1 \cdots y_n \odot C_n, K_1) \cdot e(C_0, K_0)^{-1}.$$

The correctness is straightforward.

Security. We will prove the following theorem.

Theorem 2. *Under the k-LIN assumption, the IPE scheme described above is adaptively secure and fully attribute-hiding (cf. Sect. 2.1).*

For the same reason as in Sect. 3.3, we prove the lemma for the $m_0 = m_1$, which shows that the security of the IPE described above is implied by that of our private-key IPE in Sect. 3.2 and the MDDH_k assumption.

Lemma 3. *For any adversary $\mathcal{A}$ that makes at most Q key queries and outputs $m_0 = m_1$, there exists adversaries $\mathcal{B}_0, \mathcal{B}$ such that*

$$\mathsf{Adv}_{\mathcal{A}}^{\text{IPE}}(\lambda) \le \mathsf{Adv}_{\mathcal{B}_0}^{\text{MDDH}_k}(\lambda) + \mathsf{Adv}_{\mathcal{B}}^{\text{IPE}^*}(\lambda)$$

and $\mathsf{Time}(\mathcal{B}_0), \mathsf{Time}(\mathcal{B}) \approx \mathsf{Time}(\mathcal{A})$.

We prove Lemma 3 via the following game sequence.

- Game_0 is the real game in which the challenge ciphertext for $\mathbf{x}_b = (x_{1,b}, \ldots, x_{n,b})$ is of the form

$$[\mathbf{c}^\top]_1, [\mathbf{c}^\top(x_{1,b} \cdot \mathbf{U} + \mathbf{W}_1)]_1, \;\ldots,\; [\mathbf{c}^\top(x_{n,b} \cdot \mathbf{U} + \mathbf{W}_n)]_1, e([\mathbf{c}^\top]_1, [\mathbf{k}]_2) \cdot m_0$$

  where $\mathbf{c} \leftarrow \mathsf{span}(\mathbf{A})$. Here $b \leftarrow \{0,1\}$ is a secret bit.
- Game_1 is identical to Game_0 except that we pick $\mathbf{c} \leftarrow \mathbb{Z}_p^{k+1}$ when generating the challenge ciphertext. We claim that $\mathsf{Game}_1 \approx_c \mathsf{Game}_0$. This follows from the MDDH_k assumption:

$$[\mathbf{c} \leftarrow \mathsf{span}(\mathbf{A})]_1 \approx_c [\mathbf{c} \leftarrow \mathbb{Z}_p^{k+1}] \quad \text{given} \quad [\mathbf{A}]_1.$$

  In the reduction, we sample $\mathbf{k}, \mathbf{U}, \mathbf{W}_1, \ldots, \mathbf{W}_n$ and $\mathbf{B}_1$. The master public key mpk and the challenge ciphertext are simulated using $\mathbf{k}, \mathbf{U}, \mathbf{W}_1, \ldots, \mathbf{W}_n$ along with $[\mathbf{A}]_1$, $[\mathbf{c}]_1$; all secret keys can be created honestly. See Lemma 12 for details.

It remains to show that the advantage in guessing $b \in \{0,1\}$ in Game_1 is negligible. This follows from the security of our private-key IPE in Sect. 3.2. For $\mathbf{A}$ and $\mathbf{c}$, define

$$\begin{array}{lll} \mathbf{A}^\top \mathbf{U} = \widetilde{\mathbf{U}} \in \mathbb{Z}_p^{k\times(2k+1)} & \mathbf{A}^\top \mathbf{W}_i = \widetilde{\mathbf{W}}_i \in \mathbb{Z}_p^{k\times(2k+1)} & \mathbf{A}^\top \mathbf{k} = \widetilde{\mathbf{k}} \in \mathbb{Z}_p^k \\ \mathbf{c}^\top \mathbf{U} = \mathbf{u} \in \mathbb{Z}_p^{1\times(2k+1)} & \mathbf{c}^\top \mathbf{W}_i = \mathbf{w}_i \in \mathbb{Z}_p^{1\times(2k+1)} & \mathbf{c}^\top \mathbf{k} = \alpha \in \mathbb{Z}_p \end{array}$$

We can then rewrite mpk as

$$[\mathbf{A}^\top]_1, [\widetilde{\mathbf{U}}]_1, [\widetilde{\mathbf{W}}_1]_1, \ldots, [\widetilde{\mathbf{W}}_n]_1, [\widetilde{\mathbf{k}}]_T;$$

the challenge ciphertext (in Game_1) becomes

$$[\mathbf{c}^\top]_1, \underline{[\,x_{1,b} \cdot \mathbf{u} + \mathbf{w}_1\,]_1}, \ldots, \underline{[\,x_{n,b} \cdot \mathbf{u} + \mathbf{w}_n\,]_1}, e([1]_1, \underline{[\alpha]_2}) \cdot m_0.$$

Assume that $(\mathbf{A}|\mathbf{c})$ is full-rank which occurs with high probability and define $\mathbf{T} = \begin{pmatrix} \mathbf{A}^\top \\ \mathbf{c}^\top \end{pmatrix}^{-1}$, we have $\mathbf{W}_i = \mathbf{T}\begin{pmatrix} \widetilde{\mathbf{W}}_i \\ \mathbf{w}_i \end{pmatrix}$ and $\mathbf{k} = \mathbf{T}\begin{pmatrix} \widetilde{\mathbf{k}} \\ \alpha \end{pmatrix}$, a secret key can be rewritten as

$$\mathbf{T} \odot \begin{pmatrix} [\widetilde{\mathbf{k}} + (y_1 \cdot \widetilde{\mathbf{W}}_1 + \cdots + y_n \cdot \widetilde{\mathbf{W}}_n)\mathbf{d}]_2 \\ \underline{[\alpha + (y_1 \cdot \mathbf{w}_1 + \cdots + y_n \cdot \mathbf{w}_n)\mathbf{d}]_2} \end{pmatrix}, \underline{[\mathbf{d}]_2}.$$

Observe that the underlined parts are *exactly* the ciphertext and secret keys of our private-key IPE in Sect. 3.2; and $(\widetilde{\mathbf{U}}, \widetilde{\mathbf{W}}_i, \widetilde{\mathbf{k}})$, $(\mathbf{u}, \mathbf{w}_i, \alpha)$ are distributed uniformly and *independently*. This means we can simulate mpk honestly and transform a ciphertext/secret key from our private-key IPE to its public-key counterpart using $\mathbf{A}$, $\mathbf{c}$, $\widetilde{\mathbf{U}}$, $\widetilde{\mathbf{W}}_i$, $\widetilde{\mathbf{k}}$. This is sufficient for the reduction from the public-key IPE to private-key IPE. See Lemma 13 for more details.

3.5 Lemmas for Private-Key IPE

Let Adv_x be the advantage function with respect to $\mathcal{A}$ in Game_x. We prove the following lemma for the game sequence in Sect. 3.3.

Lemma 4 ($\mathsf{Game}_0 \equiv \mathsf{Game}_1$). $\mathsf{Adv}_0(\lambda) = \mathsf{Adv}_1(\lambda)$.

Proof. It is sufficient to prove that, for all $\mathbf{u} \leftarrow \mathbb{Z}_p^{1\times(2k+1)}$, it holds that

$$\begin{aligned} &(\overbrace{\mathbf{w}_1\mathbf{B}_1, \ldots, \mathbf{w}_n\mathbf{B}_1}^{\mathsf{sk}}, \overbrace{\{\, x_{i,b} \cdot \mathbf{u}^{(13)} + \boxed{x_{i,b}} \cdot \mathbf{u}^{(2)} + \mathbf{w}_i \,\}_{i\in[n]}}^{\mathsf{ct}}) \\ \equiv\ &(\mathbf{w}_1\mathbf{B}_1, \ldots, \mathbf{w}_n\mathbf{B}_1, \{\, x_{i,b} \cdot \mathbf{u}^{(13)} + \boxed{x_{i,1-b}} \cdot \mathbf{u}^{(2)} + \mathbf{w}_i \,\}_{i\in[n]}) \end{aligned}$$

when $\mathbf{w}_1, \ldots, \mathbf{w}_n \leftarrow \mathbb{Z}_p^{1\times(2k+1)}$. By the facts shown in Sect. 3.1, it is implied by the statement that, for all $\mathbf{u}^{(2)} \in \mathsf{span}(\mathbf{B}_2^{\|\top})$, it holds that

$$\{\, x_{i,b} \cdot \mathbf{u}^{(2)} + \mathbf{w}_i^{(2)} \,\}_{i\in[n]} \equiv \{\, \mathbf{w}_i^{(2)} \,\}_{i\in[n]} \equiv \{\, x_{i,1-b} \cdot \mathbf{u}^{(2)} + \mathbf{w}_i^{(2)} \,\}_{i\in[n]}$$

when $\mathbf{w}_1^{(2)}, \ldots, \mathbf{w}_n^{(2)} \leftarrow \mathsf{span}(\mathbf{B}_2^{\|\top})$. This completes the proof. □

Lemma 5 ($\mathsf{Game}_{2.q} \equiv \mathsf{Game}_3$). $\mathsf{Adv}_{2.q}(\lambda) = \mathsf{Adv}_3(\lambda)$.

Proof. We simulate $\mathsf{Game}_{2.q}$ as follows:

Setup. We alternatively prepare basis $(\mathbf{B}_1, \mathbf{B}_2, \mathbf{B}_3)$ as follows: Sample $\widetilde{\mathbf{B}}_1, \mathbf{B}_3 \leftarrow \mathbb{Z}_p^{(2k+1)\times k}$, $\widetilde{\mathbf{B}}_2 \leftarrow \mathbb{Z}_p^{2k+1}$ and compute dual basis $\widetilde{\mathbf{B}}_1^{\|}, \widetilde{\mathbf{B}}_2^{\|}, \mathbf{B}_3^{\|}$ as usual. Pick $\mathbf{R} \leftarrow \mathrm{GL}_{k+1}(\mathbb{Z}_p)$ and define

$$(\mathbf{B}_1|\mathbf{B}_2) = (\widetilde{\mathbf{B}}_1|\widetilde{\mathbf{B}}_2)\mathbf{R} \quad \text{and} \quad (\mathbf{B}_1^{\|}|\mathbf{B}_2^{\|}) = (\widetilde{\mathbf{B}}_1^{\|}|\widetilde{\mathbf{B}}_2^{\|})\mathbf{R}^*.$$

This does not change the distribution of basis. We then sample $\alpha, \mathbf{u}, \mathbf{w}_1, \ldots, \mathbf{w}_n$ honestly.

Key queries. On input $\mathbf{y} = (y_1, \ldots, y_n)$, output

$$[\alpha + (y_1 \cdot \mathbf{w}_1 + \cdots + y_n \cdot \mathbf{w}_n)\mathbf{d}]_2,\ [\mathbf{d}]_2 \quad \text{where} \quad \mathbf{d} \leftarrow \mathsf{span}(\widetilde{\mathbf{B}}_1, \widetilde{\mathbf{B}}_2).$$

Although we sample $\mathbf{d}$ using $\widetilde{\mathbf{B}}_1, \widetilde{\mathbf{B}}_2$, the vector is uniformly distributed over $\mathsf{span}(\mathbf{B}_1, \mathbf{B}_2)$ as required and our simulation is perfect.

Ciphertext. On input $(\mathbf{x}_0, \mathbf{x}_1, m_0, m_1)$ with $m_0 = m_1$, we create the challenge ciphertext honestly using $(\mathbf{B}_1^{\|}, \mathbf{B}_2^{\|}, \mathbf{B}_3^{\|})$. That is, we pick $b \leftarrow \{0,1\}$ and output

$$\{\, x_{i,b} \cdot \mathbf{v}_0 + x_{i,1-b} \cdot \mathbf{v}_1 + x_{i,b} \cdot \mathbf{u}^{(3)} + \mathbf{w}_i \,\}_{i\in[n]},\ [\alpha]_2 \cdot m_0$$

where $\mathbf{u}^{(3)} \leftarrow \mathsf{span}(\mathbf{B}_3^{\|\top})$ and

$$\mathbf{v}_0 = \mathbf{u}^{(1)} \leftarrow \mathsf{span}(\mathbf{B}_1^{\|\top}) \quad \text{and} \quad \mathbf{v}_1 = \mathbf{u}^{(2)} \leftarrow \mathsf{span}(\mathbf{B}_2^{\|\top}).$$

Observe that, we have a 2-by-$(k+1)$ matrix $\mathbf{V}$ of rank 2 such that

$$\begin{pmatrix} -\mathbf{v}_0- \\ -\mathbf{v}_1- \end{pmatrix} = \mathbf{V}(\mathbf{B}_1^{\|}|\mathbf{B}_2^{\|})^\top = \underbrace{\mathbf{V}\mathbf{R}^{-1}}_{\text{uniformly over } \mathbb{Z}_p^{2\times(k+1)}} (\widetilde{\mathbf{B}}_1^{\|}|\widetilde{\mathbf{B}}_2^{\|})^\top.$$

Since $\mathbf{R}$ is independent of other part of simulation, $\mathbf{V}\mathbf{R}^{-1}$ are uniformly distributed over $\mathbb{Z}_p^{2\times(k+1)}$ and thus it is equivalent to sample $\mathbf{v}_0, \mathbf{v}_1 \leftarrow \mathsf{span}((\widetilde{\mathbf{B}}_1^{\|}|\widetilde{\mathbf{B}}_2^{\|})^\top)$ when creating the challenge ciphertext. This leads to the simulation of Game_3 (with respect to $\widetilde{\mathbf{B}}_1, \widetilde{\mathbf{B}}_2, \mathbf{B}_3$). □

Lemma 6 ($\mathsf{Game}_3 \equiv \mathsf{Game}_4$). $\mathsf{Adv}_3(\lambda) = \mathsf{Adv}_4(\lambda)$.

Proof The proof is similar to that for Lemma 4, except that we work with $\mathbf{u}^{(3)}$, $\mathbf{u}_0^{(3)}$, $\mathbf{u}_1^{(3)}$, $\mathbf{w}_i^{(3)}$ instead. □

Lemma 7 ($\mathsf{Game}_{2.j-1} \approx_c \mathsf{Game}_{2.j-1.1}$). *There exists adversary* $\mathcal{B}_1$ *with* $\mathsf{Time}(\mathcal{B}_1) \approx \mathsf{Time}(\mathcal{A})$ *such that*

$$|\,\mathsf{Adv}_{2.j-1.1}(\lambda) - \mathsf{Adv}_{2.j-1}(\lambda)\,| \le \mathsf{Adv}_{\mathcal{B}_1}^{\mathrm{SD}^{G_2}_{\mathbf{B}_1 \mapsto \mathbf{B}_1,\mathbf{B}_3}}(\lambda).$$

Proof. This follows from the $\mathrm{SD}^{G_2}_{\mathbf{B}_1 \mapsto \mathbf{B}_1, \mathbf{B}_3}$ assumption stating that, given $[\mathbf{B}_1]_2, [\mathbf{B}_2]_2, [\mathbf{B}_3]_2, \mathsf{basis}(\mathbf{B}_2^{\parallel}), \mathsf{basis}(\mathbf{B}_1^{\parallel}, \mathbf{B}_3^{\parallel})$, it holds that

$$[\mathbf{t} \leftarrow \mathsf{span}(\mathbf{B}_1)]_2 \approx_c [\mathbf{t} \leftarrow \mathsf{span}(\mathbf{B}_1, \mathbf{B}_3)]_2.$$

On input $[\mathbf{B}_1]_2, [\mathbf{B}_2]_2, [\mathbf{B}_3]_2, \mathsf{basis}(\mathbf{B}_2^{\parallel}), \mathsf{basis}(\mathbf{B}_1^{\parallel}, \mathbf{B}_3^{\parallel})$ and $[\mathbf{t}]_2$, the adversary $\mathcal{B}_1$ works as follows:

Setup. Sample $\alpha \leftarrow \mathbb{Z}_p$, $\mathbf{w}_1, \ldots, \mathbf{w}_n \leftarrow \mathbb{Z}_p^{1 \times (2k+1)}$. Implicitly sample $\mathbf{u}$ by picking

$$\mathbf{u}^{(13)} \leftarrow \mathsf{span}((\mathbf{B}_1^{\parallel} | \mathbf{B}_3^{\parallel})^{\top}) \quad \text{and} \quad \mathbf{u}^{(2)} \leftarrow \mathsf{span}(\mathbf{B}_2^{\parallel\top})$$

using $\mathsf{basis}(\mathbf{B}_1^{\parallel}, \mathbf{B}_3^{\parallel})$ and $\mathsf{basis}(\mathbf{B}_2^{\parallel})$, respectively.

Key Queries. On the κth query $\mathbf{y} = (y_1, \ldots, y_n)$, output

$$[\alpha + (y_1 \cdot \mathbf{w}_1 + \cdots + y_n \cdot \mathbf{w}_n)\mathbf{d}]_2, [\mathbf{d}]_2 \quad \text{where} \quad \mathbf{d} \leftarrow \begin{cases} \mathsf{span}(\mathbf{B}_1, \mathbf{B}_2) & \kappa < j; \\ \mathbf{t} & \kappa = j; \\ \mathsf{span}(\mathbf{B}_1) & \kappa > j; \end{cases}$$

using $[\mathbf{B}_1]_2$, $[\mathbf{B}_2]_2$ and $[\mathbf{t}]_2$

Ciphertext. On input $(\mathbf{x}_0, \mathbf{x}_1, m_0, m_1)$ with $m_0 = m_1$, pick $b \leftarrow \{0,1\}$ and output

$$x_{1,b} \cdot \mathbf{u}^{(13)} + x_{1,1-b} \cdot \mathbf{u}^{(2)} + \mathbf{w}_1, \ldots, x_{n,b} \cdot \mathbf{u}^{(13)} + x_{n,1-b} \cdot \mathbf{u}^{(2)} + \mathbf{w}_n, [\alpha]_2 \cdot m_0$$

Observe that, when $\mathbf{t}$ is uniformly distributed over $\mathsf{span}(\mathbf{B}_1)$, the simulation is identical to $\mathsf{Game}_{2.j-1}$; otherwise, when $\mathbf{t}$ is uniformly distributed over $\mathsf{span}(\mathbf{B}_1, \mathbf{B}_3)$, the simulation is identical to $\mathsf{Game}_{2.j-1.1}$. This proves the lemma. □

Lemma 8 ($\mathsf{Game}_{2.j-1.1} \equiv \mathsf{Game}_{2.j-1.2}$). $\mathsf{Adv}_{2.j-1.1} = \mathsf{Adv}_{2.j-1.2}$.

Proof. By complexity leveraging and the facts shown in Sect. 3.1, it is sufficient to prove the following statement: for all $\mathbf{x}_0$, $\mathbf{x}_1$ and $\mathbf{y}$ (corresponding to the jth key query) satisfying that (a) $\langle \mathbf{x}_0, \mathbf{y} \rangle = \langle \mathbf{x}_1, \mathbf{y} \rangle = 0$; or (b) $\langle \mathbf{x}_0, \mathbf{y} \rangle \neq 0 \wedge \langle \mathbf{x}_1, \mathbf{y} \rangle \neq 0$, it holds that

$$\begin{aligned} &(\overbrace{x_{1,b} \cdot \mathbf{u}^{(3)} + \mathbf{w}_1^{(3)}, \ldots, x_{n,b} \cdot \mathbf{u}^{(3)} + \mathbf{w}_n^{(3)}}^{\mathsf{ct}}, \overbrace{y_1 \cdot \mathbf{w}_1^{(3)} + \cdots + y_n \cdot \mathbf{w}_n^{(3)}}^{\mathsf{sk}}) \\ \equiv &(\boxed{x_{1,1-b}} \cdot \mathbf{u}^{(3)} + \mathbf{w}_1^{(3)}, \ldots, \boxed{x_{n,1-b}} \cdot \mathbf{u}^{(3)} + \mathbf{w}_n^{(3)}, y_1 \cdot \mathbf{w}_1^{(3)} + \cdots + y_n \cdot \mathbf{w}_n^{(3)}) \end{aligned}$$

when $\mathbf{u}^{(3)}, \mathbf{w}_1^{(3)}, \ldots, \mathbf{w}_n^{(3)} \leftarrow \mathsf{span}(\mathbf{B}_3^{\parallel\top})$. By the linearity, it in turn follows from the following statement

$$\begin{aligned} &\{x_{1,b} \cdot u + w_1, \ldots, x_{n,b} \cdot u + w_n, \ y_1 \cdot w_1 + \cdots + y_n \cdot w_n\} \\ \equiv &\{\boxed{x_{1,1-b}} \cdot u + w_1, \ldots, \boxed{x_{n,1-b}} \cdot u + w_n, \ y_1 \cdot w_1 + \cdots + y_n \cdot w_n\} \end{aligned}$$

where $u, w_1, \ldots, w_n \leftarrow \mathbb{Z}_p$. This follows from the statistical argument for all $\mathbf{x} = (x_1, \ldots, x_n)$ which is implicitly used in the proof of Wee's simulation-based selectively secure IPE [36]: by programming $\tilde{w}_i = x_i \cdot u + w_i$ for all $i \in [n]$, we have

$$\begin{aligned} &\{\, x_1 \cdot u + w_1, \ldots, x_n \cdot u + w_n,\ y_1 \cdot w_1 + \cdots + y_n \cdot w_n \,\} \\ \equiv &\{\, \tilde{w}_1, \ldots, \tilde{w}_n,\ (y_1 \cdot \tilde{w}_1 + \cdots + y_n \cdot \tilde{w}_n) - u \cdot (x_1 y_1 + \cdots + x_n y_n) \,\} \end{aligned}$$

which means that the left-hand side distributions for all vector $\mathbf{x}$ not orthogonal to $\mathbf{y}$ are identical (since u hides the information about the inner-product) and so do all vector $\mathbf{x}$ orthogonal to $\mathbf{y}$. This proves the above statement and thus proves the lemma. □

Lemma 9 ($\mathsf{Game}_{2.j-1.2} \approx_c \mathsf{Game}_{2.j-1.3}$). *There exists adversary* $\mathcal{B}_2$ *with* $\mathsf{Time}(\mathcal{B}_2) \approx \mathsf{Time}(\mathcal{A})$ *such that*

$$|\, \mathsf{Adv}_{2.j-1.3}(\lambda) - \mathsf{Adv}_{2.j-1.2}(\lambda) \,| \leq \mathsf{Adv}_{\mathcal{B}_2}^{\mathrm{SD}^{G_2}_{\mathbf{B}_3 \mapsto \mathbf{B}_3, \mathbf{B}_2}}(\lambda).$$

Proof. The proof is analogous to that for Lemma 7 ($\mathsf{Game}_{2.j-1} \approx_c \mathsf{Game}_{2.j-1.1}$). □

Lemma 10 ($\mathsf{Game}_{2.j-1.3} \equiv \mathsf{Game}_{2.j-1.4}$). $\mathsf{Adv}_{2.j-1.3} = \mathsf{Adv}_{2.j-1.4}$.

Proof. The proof is identical to that for Lemma 8 ($\mathsf{Game}_{2.j-1.1} \approx_c \mathsf{Game}_{2.j-1.2}$). □

Lemma 11 ($\mathsf{Game}_{2.j-1.4} \approx_c \mathsf{Game}_{2.j-1.5}$). *There exists adversary* $\mathcal{B}_3$ *with* $\mathsf{Time}(\mathcal{B}_3) \approx \mathsf{Time}(\mathcal{A})$ *such that*

$$|\, \mathsf{Adv}_{2.j-1.5}(\lambda) - \mathsf{Adv}_{2.j-1.4}(\lambda) \,| \leq \mathsf{Adv}_{\mathcal{B}_3}^{\mathrm{SD}^{G_2}_{\mathbf{B}_1 \mapsto \mathbf{B}_1, \mathbf{B}_3}}(\lambda).$$

Proof. The proof is analogous to that for Lemma 7 ($\mathsf{Game}_{2.j-1} \approx_c \mathsf{Game}_{2.j-1.1}$). □

3.6 Lemmas for Public-Key IPE

Let Adv_x be the advantage function with respect to $\mathcal{A}$ in Game_x. We prove the following lemma for the game sequence in Sect. 3.4.

Lemma 12 ($\mathsf{Game}_0 \equiv \mathsf{Game}_1$). *There exists adversary* $\mathcal{B}_0$ *with* $\mathsf{Time}(\mathcal{B}_0) \approx \mathsf{Time}(\mathcal{A})$ *such that*

$$|\, \mathsf{Adv}_1(\lambda) - \mathsf{Adv}_0(\lambda) \,| \leq \mathsf{Adv}_{\mathcal{B}_0}^{\mathrm{MDDH}_k}(\lambda).$$

Proof. The proof is direct, we omit it here and refer the reader to the full paper. □

Lemma 13 (Advantage in Game_1**).** *There exists adversary* $\mathcal{B}$ *with* $\mathsf{Time}(\mathcal{B}) \approx \mathsf{Time}(\mathcal{A})$ *such that*

$$\mathsf{Adv}_1(\lambda) \leq \mathsf{Adv}_{\mathcal{B}}^{\mathrm{IPE}^*}(\lambda).$$

Proof. We construct the adversary $\mathcal{B}$ as below:

Setup. Sample $(\mathbf{A}, \mathbf{c}) \leftarrow \mathbb{Z}_p^{(k+1)\times k} \times \mathbb{Z}_p^{k+1}$ and compute $\mathbf{T} = \begin{pmatrix} \mathbf{A}^\top \\ \mathbf{c}^\top \end{pmatrix}^{-1}$. Since $(\mathbf{A}|\mathbf{c})$ is full-rank which occurs with high probability, $\mathbf{T}$ is well-defined. Pick

$$\widetilde{\mathbf{U}}, \widetilde{\mathbf{W}}_1, \ldots, \widetilde{\mathbf{W}}_n \leftarrow \mathbb{Z}_p^{k\times(2k+1)} \quad \text{and} \quad \widetilde{\mathbf{k}} \leftarrow \mathbb{Z}_p^k$$

and output

$$\mathsf{mpk} = ([\mathbf{A}^\top]_1, [\widetilde{\mathbf{U}}]_1, [\widetilde{\mathbf{W}}_1]_1, \ldots, [\widetilde{\mathbf{W}}_n]_1, [\widetilde{\mathbf{k}}]_T).$$

Key Queries. On input $\mathbf{y}$, adversary $\mathcal{B}$ forwards the query to its environment and receives (K_0, K_1). Compute

$$\widetilde{K}_0 = [\widetilde{\mathbf{k}}]_2 \cdot ((y_1 \cdot \widetilde{\mathbf{W}}_1 + \cdots + y_n \cdot \widetilde{\mathbf{W}}_n) \odot K_0)$$

and output

$$\mathsf{sk}_{\mathbf{y}} = (\mathbf{T} \odot \begin{pmatrix} \widetilde{K}_0 \\ K_0 \end{pmatrix}, \; K_1).$$

Ciphertext. On input $(\mathbf{x}_0, \mathbf{x}_1, m_0, m_1)$, adversary $\mathcal{B}$ sends query $(\mathbf{x}_0, \mathbf{x}_1, 1, 1)$ to its environment and receives $(C_1, \ldots, C_n, C)$. Create the challenge ciphertext as

$$[\mathbf{c}^\top]_1, [C_1]_1, \; \ldots, \; [C_n]_1, e([1]_1, C) \cdot m_0.$$

The adversary $\mathcal{B}$ outputs $\mathcal{A}$'s guess bit. By the observation in Sect. 3.4, mpk is simulated perfectly; if (K_0, K_1) is a private-key IPE secret key, secret keys we computed is for our public-key IPE; if $(C_1, \ldots, C_n, C)$ is a private-key IPE ciphertext for $b = 0$, the ciphertext we created is a public-key IPE ciphertext for $b = 0$; this also holds for $b = 1$. This readily proves the lemma. □

4 Construction from XDLIN Assumption

In this section, we improve the IPE scheme presented in Sect. 3 by the optimization technique in [16]. As in Sect. 3, we will first develop a private-key IPE from that in Sect. 3.2 and then compile it into the public-key setting.

4.1 Correspondence

Applying the technique in [16] to our private-key IPE in Sect. 3.2, we basically overlap $\mathsf{span}(\mathbf{B}_1)$ and $\mathsf{span}(\mathbf{B}_3)$ so that the total dimension decreases. Technically, we work with basis

$$\mathbf{B}_1 \leftarrow \mathbb{Z}_p^{\ell\times\ell_1}, \; \mathbf{B}_2 \leftarrow \mathbb{Z}_p^{\ell\times\ell_2}, \; \mathbf{B}_3 \leftarrow \mathbb{Z}_p^{\ell\times\ell_3}, \; \mathbf{B}_4 \leftarrow \mathbb{Z}_p^{\ell\times\ell_4}$$

where $\ell_1, \ell_2, \ell_3, \ell_4 \geq 1$ and $\ell := \ell_1 + \ell_2 + \ell_3 + \ell_4$, and follow the correspondence:

$$\begin{array}{ccc} \text{Sec 3.1} & & \text{this section} \\ \mathbf{B}_1 & \mapsto & (\mathbf{B}_1 \mid \mathbf{B}_4) \\ \mathbf{B}_2 & \mapsto & \mathbf{B}_2 \\ \mathbf{B}_3 & \mapsto & (\mathbf{B}_3 \mid \mathbf{B}_4) \end{array} \tag{10}$$

saying that $\mathbf{B}_1$ and $\mathbf{B}_3$ used in Sect. 3 are replaced by $(\mathbf{B}_1|\mathbf{B}_4)$ and $(\mathbf{B}_3|\mathbf{B}_4)$, respectively, whose spans interact at $\mathsf{span}(\mathbf{B}_4)$. Analogous to Sect. 3.1, we can define its dual basis $(\mathbf{B}_1^{\|}, \mathbf{B}_2^{\|}, \mathbf{B}_3^{\|}, \mathbf{B}_4^{\|})$ and decompose $\mathbf{w} \in \mathbb{Z}_p^{1\times\ell}$ as $\mathbf{w}^{(1)} + \mathbf{w}^{(2)} + \mathbf{w}^{(3)} + \mathbf{w}^{(4)}$.

Assumptions. With the correspondence (10), the assumption $\text{SD}^{G_2}_{\mathbf{B}_1 \mapsto \mathbf{B}_1, \mathbf{B}_3}$ used in Sect. 3.3 will be replaced by $\text{SD}^{G_2}_{\mathbf{B}_1, \mathbf{B}_4 \mapsto \mathbf{B}_1, \mathbf{B}_3, \mathbf{B}_4}$ defined as follows.

Lemma 14 ($\text{MDDH}_{\ell_1+\ell_4, \ell_1+\ell_3+\ell_4} \Rightarrow \text{SD}^{G_2}_{\mathbf{B}_1, \mathbf{B}_4 \mapsto \mathbf{B}_1, \mathbf{B}_3, \mathbf{B}_4}$). *Under* $\text{MDDH}_{\ell_1+\ell_4, \ell_1+\ell_3+\ell_4}$ *assumption in* G_2*, there exists an efficient sampler outputting random* $([\mathbf{B}_1]_2, [\mathbf{B}_2]_2, [\mathbf{B}_3]_2, [\mathbf{B}_4]_2)$ *along with base* $\mathsf{basis}(\mathbf{B}_2^{\|})$ *and* $\mathsf{basis}(\mathbf{B}_1^{\|}, \mathbf{B}_3^{\|}, \mathbf{B}_4^{\|})$ *(of arbitrary choice) such that the following advantage function is negligible in* λ.

$$\mathsf{Adv}_{\mathcal{A}}^{\text{SD}^{G_2}_{\mathbf{B}_1, \mathbf{B}_4 \mapsto \mathbf{B}_1, \mathbf{B}_3, \mathbf{B}_4}}(\lambda) := \big| \Pr[\mathcal{A}(\mathbb{G}, D, [\mathbf{t}_0]_1) = 1] - \Pr[\mathcal{A}(\mathbb{G}, D, [\mathbf{t}_1]_1) = 1] \big|$$

where

$$D := (\, [\mathbf{B}_1]_2, [\mathbf{B}_2]_2, [\mathbf{B}_3]_2, [\mathbf{B}_4]_2, \mathsf{basis}(\mathbf{B}_2^{\|}), \mathsf{basis}(\mathbf{B}_1^{\|}, \mathbf{B}_3^{\|}, \mathbf{B}_4^{\|}) \,),$$
$$\mathbf{t}_0 \leftarrow \mathsf{span}(\mathbf{B}_1, \mathbf{B}_4), \;\; \mathbf{t}_1 \leftarrow \mathsf{span}(\mathbf{B}_1, \mathbf{B}_3, \mathbf{B}_4).$$

The proof is analogous to that for Lemma 1 (cf. [13]).

Also, we replace $\text{SD}^{G_2}_{\mathbf{B}_3 \mapsto \mathbf{B}_2, \mathbf{B}_3}$ assumption in Sect. 3.3 with *external subspace decision assumption* $\text{XSD}^{G_2}_{\mathbf{B}_3, \mathbf{B}_4 \mapsto \mathbf{B}_2, \mathbf{B}_3, \mathbf{B}_4}$ defined as below.

Assumption 3 ($\text{XSD}^{G_2}_{\mathbf{B}_3, \mathbf{B}_4 \mapsto \mathbf{B}_2, \mathbf{B}_3, \mathbf{B}_4}$). *We say that* $\text{XSD}^{G_2}_{\mathbf{B}_3, \mathbf{B}_4 \mapsto \mathbf{B}_2, \mathbf{B}_3, \mathbf{B}_4}$ *assumption holds if there exists an efficient sampler outputting random* $([\mathbf{B}_1]_2, [\mathbf{B}_2]_2, [\mathbf{B}_3]_2, [\mathbf{B}_4]_2)$ *along with base* $\mathsf{basis}(\mathbf{B}_1^{\|}), \mathsf{basis}(\mathbf{B}_4^{\|})$ *and* $[\mathsf{basis}(\mathbf{B}_2^{\|}, \mathbf{B}_3^{\|})]_1$ *(of arbitrary choice) such that the following advantage function is negligible in* λ.

$$\mathsf{Adv}_{\mathcal{A}}^{\text{XSD}^{G_2}_{\mathbf{B}_3, \mathbf{B}_4 \mapsto \mathbf{B}_2, \mathbf{B}_3, \mathbf{B}_4}}(\lambda) := \big| \Pr[\mathcal{A}(\mathbb{G}, D, [\mathbf{t}_0]_1) = 1] - \Pr[\mathcal{A}(\mathbb{G}, D, [\mathbf{t}_1]_1) = 1] \big|$$

where

$$D := (\, [\mathbf{B}_1]_2, [\mathbf{B}_2]_2, [\mathbf{B}_3]_2, [\mathbf{B}_4]_2, \mathsf{basis}(\mathbf{B}_1^{\|}), [\mathsf{basis}(\mathbf{B}_2^{\|}, \mathbf{B}_3^{\|})]_1, \mathsf{basis}(\mathbf{B}_4^{\|}) \,),$$
$$\mathbf{t}_0 \leftarrow \mathsf{span}(\mathbf{B}_3, \mathbf{B}_4), \;\; \mathbf{t}_1 \leftarrow \mathsf{span}(\mathbf{B}_2, \mathbf{B}_3, \mathbf{B}_4).$$

We note that we do not give out $\mathsf{basis}(\mathbf{B}_2^{\|}, \mathbf{B}_3^{\|}, \mathbf{B}_4^{\|})$ as usual; instead, $\mathsf{basis}(\mathbf{B}_4^{\|})$ on $\mathbb{Z}_p$ and $[\mathsf{basis}(\mathbf{B}_2^{\|}, \mathbf{B}_3^{\|})]_1$ on G_1 are provided. We then prove the following lemma saying that, for a specific set of parameters, the assumption is implied by XDLIN assumption.

Lemma 15 (XDLIN $\Rightarrow$ XSD$^{G_2}_{\mathbf{B}_3,\mathbf{B}_4 \mapsto \mathbf{B}_2,\mathbf{B}_3,\mathbf{B}_4}$). *Under the external decisional linear assumption (XDLIN) [1] (cf. Sect. 2.2), the* XSD$^{G_2}_{\mathbf{B}_3,\mathbf{B}_4 \mapsto \mathbf{B}_2,\mathbf{B}_3,\mathbf{B}_4}$ *assumption holds for parameter $\ell_2 = \ell_3 = \ell_4 = 1$.*

Proof. For any PPT adversary $\mathcal{A}$, we construct an algorithm $\mathcal{B}$ with $\mathsf{Time}(\mathcal{B}) \approx \mathsf{Time}(\mathcal{A})$ such that

$$\mathsf{Adv}_{\mathcal{A}}^{\mathrm{XSD}^{G_2}_{\mathbf{B}_3,\mathbf{B}_4 \mapsto \mathbf{B}_2,\mathbf{B}_3,\mathbf{B}_4}}(\lambda) \leq \mathsf{Adv}_{\mathcal{B}}^{\mathrm{XDLIN}}(\lambda).$$

On input $([a_1, a_2, a_3, a_1 s_1, a_2 s_2]_1, [a_1, a_2, a_3, a_1 s_1, a_2 s_2]_2, T)$ where $a_1, a_2, a_3, s_1, s_2 \leftarrow \mathbb{Z}_p$ and T is either $[a_3(s_1 + s_2)]_2$ or uniformly distributed over G_2, algorithm $\mathcal{B}$ works as follows:

Programming $\mathbf{B}_1, \mathbf{B}_2, \mathbf{B}_3, \mathbf{B}_4$ and $\mathbf{B}_1^{\|}, \mathbf{B}_2^{\|}, \mathbf{B}_3^{\|}, \mathbf{B}_4^{\|}$. Sample $\widetilde{\mathbf{B}} \leftarrow \mathrm{GL}_{3+\ell_1}(\mathbb{Z}_p)$ and define

$$(\mathbf{B}_1, \mathbf{B}_2, \mathbf{B}_3, \mathbf{B}_4) = \widetilde{\mathbf{B}} \begin{pmatrix} \mathbf{I}_{\ell_1} & & & \\ & 1 & a_3 & a_3 \\ & & a_2 & \\ & & & a_1 \end{pmatrix}$$

$$\text{and} \quad (\mathbf{B}_1^{\|}, \mathbf{B}_2^{\|}, \mathbf{B}_3^{\|}, \mathbf{B}_4^{\|}) = \widetilde{\mathbf{B}}^* \begin{pmatrix} \mathbf{I}_{\ell_1} & & & \\ & 1 & & \\ & -a_3 a_2^{-1} & a_2^{-1} & \\ & -a_3 a_1^{-1} & & a_1^{-1} \end{pmatrix}$$

Algorithm $\mathcal{B}$ can simulate $[\mathbf{B}_1, \mathbf{B}_2, \mathbf{B}_3, \mathbf{B}_4]_2$ using $[a_1, a_2, a_3]_2$.

Simulating $\mathsf{basis}(\mathbf{B}_1^{\|}), \mathsf{basis}(\mathbf{B}_4^{\|})$. We define

$$\mathsf{basis}(\mathbf{B}_1^{\|}) = \widetilde{\mathbf{B}}^* \begin{pmatrix} \mathbf{I}_{\ell_1} \\ \mathbf{0} \end{pmatrix} \quad \text{and} \quad \mathsf{basis}(\mathbf{B}_4^{\|}) = \widetilde{\mathbf{B}}^*(a_1^{-1}\mathbf{e}_{3+\ell_1})a_1 = \widetilde{\mathbf{B}}^*\mathbf{e}_{3+\ell_1},$$

both of which can be simulated using $\widetilde{\mathbf{B}}^*$.

Simulating $[\mathsf{basis}(\mathbf{B}_2^{\|}, \mathbf{B}_3^{\|})]_1$. We define

$$\mathsf{basis}(\mathbf{B}_2^{\|}, \mathbf{B}_3^{\|}) = \widetilde{\mathbf{B}}^* \begin{pmatrix} \mathbf{0} & \\ 1 & \\ -a_3 a_2^{-1} & a_2^{-1} \\ -a_3 a_1^{-1} & \end{pmatrix} \begin{pmatrix} a_1 & \\ a_1 a_3 & a_2 \end{pmatrix} = \widetilde{\mathbf{B}}^* \begin{pmatrix} \mathbf{0} & \\ a_1 & \\ & 1 \\ -a_3 & \end{pmatrix}$$

such that $[\mathsf{basis}(\mathbf{B}_2^{\|}, \mathbf{B}_3^{\|})]_1$ (over G_1) can be simulated using $\widetilde{\mathbf{B}}^*$ and $[a_1, a_3]_1$.

Simulating the challenge. Output the challenge

$$\begin{pmatrix} [\mathbf{0}]_2 \\ T \\ [a_2 s_2]_2 \\ [a_1 s_1]_2 \end{pmatrix}.$$

Observe that if $T = [a_3(s_1 + s_2)]_2$, the output challenge is uniformly distributed over $[\mathsf{span}(\mathbf{B}_3, \mathbf{B}_4)]_2$; if T is uniformly distributed over G_2, the output challenge is then uniformly distributed over $[\mathsf{span}(\mathbf{B}_2, \mathbf{B}_3, \mathbf{B}_4)]_2$. This readily proves the lemma. □

4.2 Step One: A Private-Key IPE from XDLIN Assumption

Our second private-key IPE is described as follows, which is translated from the private-key IPE in Sect. 3.2 with the correspondence (10). Here we employ the basis defined in Sect. 4.1 with parameter $(\ell_1, \ell_2, \ell_3, \ell_4) = (1, 1, 1, 1)$.

- $\mathsf{Setup}(1^\lambda, n)$: Run $\mathbb{G} = (p, G_1, G_2, G_T, e) \leftarrow \mathcal{G}(1^\lambda)$. Sample $\mathbf{B}_{14} = (\mathbf{B}_1|\mathbf{B}_4) \leftarrow \mathbb{Z}_p^{4\times 2}$ and pick $\mathbf{u}, \mathbf{w}_1, \ldots, \mathbf{w}_n \leftarrow \mathbb{Z}_p^{1\times 4}$, $\alpha \leftarrow \mathbb{Z}_p$. Output
$$\mathsf{msk} = (\,\mathbb{G}, \alpha, \mathbf{u}, \mathbf{w}_1, \ldots, \mathbf{w}_n, \mathbf{B}_{14}\,).$$
- $\mathsf{KeyGen}(\mathsf{msk}, \mathbf{y})$: Let $\mathbf{y} = (y_1, \ldots, y_n) \in \mathbb{Z}_p^n$. Sample $\mathbf{r} \leftarrow \mathbb{Z}_p^2$ and output
$$\mathsf{sk}_{\mathbf{y}} = (\,K_0 = [\alpha + (y_1 \cdot \mathbf{w}_1 + \cdots + y_n \cdot \mathbf{w}_n)\mathbf{B}_{14}\mathbf{r}]_2,\, K_1 = [\mathbf{B}_{14}\mathbf{r}]_2\,)$$
- $\mathsf{Enc}(\mathsf{msk}, \mathbf{x}, m)$: Let $\mathbf{x} = (x_1, \ldots, x_n) \in \mathbb{Z}_p^n$ and $m \in G_T$. Output
$$\mathsf{ct}_{\mathbf{x}} = (\,C_1 = [x_1 \cdot \mathbf{u} + \mathbf{w}_1]_1,\, \ldots,\, C_n = [x_n \cdot \mathbf{u} + \mathbf{w}_n]_1,\, C = [\alpha]_T \cdot m\,)$$
- $\mathsf{Dec}(\mathsf{ct}_{\mathbf{x}}, \mathsf{sk}_{\mathbf{y}})$: Parse $\mathsf{ct}_{\mathbf{x}} = (C_1, \ldots, C_n, C)$ and $\mathsf{sk}_{\mathbf{y}} = (K_0, K_1)$ for $\mathbf{y} = (y_1, \ldots, y_n) \in \mathbb{Z}_p^n$. Output
$$m' = C \cdot e(y_1 \odot C_1 \cdots y_n \odot C_n, K_1) \cdot e([1]_1, K_0)^{-1}.$$

The correctness is straightforward. Compared with the construction in Sect. 3.2, we now have ciphertexts over G_1 instead of $\mathbb{Z}_p$ and the bilinear map is required for decryption procedure. However the total dimension $\ell = 4$ is smaller than that in Sect. 3.1 when $k = 2$ (corresponding to DLIN assumption), which is $\ell = 5$.

4.3 Security

We will prove the following theorem.

Theorem 3. *Under the* XDLIN *assumption, the private-key IPE scheme described in Sect. 4.2 is adaptively secure and fully attribute-hiding (cf. Sect. 2.1).*

As before, we only need to prove the following lemma for $m_0 = m_1$.

Lemma 16. *For any adversary $\mathcal{A}$ that makes at most Q key queries and outputs $m_0 = m_1$, there exists adversaries $\mathcal{B}_1, \mathcal{B}_2, \mathcal{B}_3$ such that*

$$\mathsf{Adv}_{\mathcal{A}}^{\mathrm{IPE}^*}(\lambda) \le Q \cdot \mathsf{Adv}_{\mathcal{B}_1}^{\mathrm{SD}^{G_2}_{\mathbf{B}_1,\mathbf{B}_4 \mapsto \mathbf{B}_1,\mathbf{B}_3,\mathbf{B}_4}}(\lambda) + Q \cdot \mathsf{Adv}_{\mathcal{B}_2}^{\mathrm{XSD}^{G_2}_{\mathbf{B}_3,\mathbf{B}_4 \mapsto \mathbf{B}_2,\mathbf{B}_3,\mathbf{B}_4}}(\lambda) + Q \cdot \mathsf{Adv}_{\mathcal{B}_3}^{\mathrm{SD}^{G_2}_{\mathbf{B}_1,\mathbf{B}_4 \mapsto \mathbf{B}_1,\mathbf{B}_3,\mathbf{B}_4}}(\lambda)$$

and $\mathsf{Time}(\mathcal{B}_1), \mathsf{Time}(\mathcal{B}_2), \mathsf{Time}(\mathcal{B}_3) \approx \mathsf{Time}(\mathcal{A})$.

Game sequence. With the correspondence in Sect. 4.1, the proof for Lemma 16 is almost the same as that for Lemma 2 presented in Sect. 3. Here we only give the game sequence, summarized in Fig. 4.

Game	ct			κ-th sk ($\mathbf{d} \leftarrow \mathsf{span}(?)$)			Remark
	$?^{(14)} + \mathbf{w}_i^{(14)}$	$?^{(2)} + \mathbf{w}_i^{(2)}$	$?^{(3)} + \mathbf{w}_i^{(3)}$	$\kappa < j$	$\kappa = j$	$\kappa > j$	
0	$x_{i,b} \cdot \mathbf{u}$			$\mathbf{B}_1, \mathbf{B}_4$			real game
1	$x_{i,b} \cdot \mathbf{u}$	$x_{i,1-b} \cdot \mathbf{u}$	$x_{i,b} \cdot \mathbf{u}$	$\mathbf{B}_1, \mathbf{B}_4$			statistical argument: analogous to Fig 3
$2.j-1$	$x_{i,b} \cdot \mathbf{u}$	$x_{i,1-b} \cdot \mathbf{u}$	$x_{i,b} \cdot \mathbf{u}$	$\mathbf{B}_1, \mathbf{B}_2, \mathbf{B}_4$	$\mathbf{B}_1, \mathbf{B}_4$	$\mathbf{B}_1, \mathbf{B}_4$	$\mathsf{Game}_{2.0} = \mathsf{Game}_1$, $\mathsf{Game}_{2.j} = \mathsf{Game}_{2.j-1.5}$
$2.j-1.1$	$x_{i,b} \cdot \mathbf{u}$	$x_{i,1-b} \cdot \mathbf{u}$	$x_{i,b} \cdot \mathbf{u}$	$\mathbf{B}_1, \mathbf{B}_2, \mathbf{B}_4$	$\mathbf{B}_1, \mathbf{B}_3, \mathbf{B}_4$	$\mathbf{B}_1, \mathbf{B}_4$	$\mathrm{SD}^{G_2}_{\mathbf{B}_1,\mathbf{B}_4 \mapsto \mathbf{B}_1,\mathbf{B}_3,\mathbf{B}_4}$: given $\mathsf{basis}(\mathbf{B}_2^{\parallel})$, $\mathsf{basis}(\mathbf{B}_1^{\parallel}, \mathbf{B}_3^{\parallel}, \mathbf{B}_4^{\parallel})$, $[\mathsf{span}(\mathbf{B}_1, \mathbf{B}_4)]_2 \approx_c [\mathsf{span}(\mathbf{B}_1, \mathbf{B}_3, \mathbf{B}_4)]_2$
$2.j-1.2$	$x_{i,b} \cdot \mathbf{u}$	$x_{i,1-b} \cdot \mathbf{u}$	$x_{i,1-b} \cdot \mathbf{u}$	$\mathbf{B}_1, \mathbf{B}_2, \mathbf{B}_4$	$\mathbf{B}_1, \mathbf{B}_3, \mathbf{B}_4$	$\mathbf{B}_1, \mathbf{B}_4$	statistical argument: analogous to Fig 3
$2.j-1.3$	$x_{i,b} \cdot \mathbf{u}$	$x_{i,1-b} \cdot \mathbf{u}$	$x_{i,1-b} \cdot \mathbf{u}$	$\mathbf{B}_1, \mathbf{B}_2, \mathbf{B}_4$	$\mathbf{B}_1, \mathbf{B}_2, \mathbf{B}_3, \mathbf{B}_4$	$\mathbf{B}_1, \mathbf{B}_4$	$\mathrm{XSD}^{G_2}_{\mathbf{B}_3,\mathbf{B}_4 \mapsto \mathbf{B}_2,\mathbf{B}_3,\mathbf{B}_4}$: given $[\mathsf{basis}(\mathbf{B}_2^{\parallel}, \mathbf{B}_3^{\parallel})]_1$, $\mathsf{basis}(\mathbf{B}_1^{\parallel})$, $\mathsf{basis}(\mathbf{B}_4^{\parallel})$, $[\mathsf{span}(\mathbf{B}_3, \mathbf{B}_4)]_2 \approx_c [\mathsf{span}(\mathbf{B}_2, \mathbf{B}_3, \mathbf{B}_4)]_2$
$2.j-1.4$	$x_{i,b} \cdot \mathbf{u}$	$x_{i,1-b} \cdot \mathbf{u}$	$x_{i,b} \cdot \mathbf{u}$	$\mathbf{B}_1, \mathbf{B}_2, \mathbf{B}_4$	$\mathbf{B}_1, \mathbf{B}_2, \mathbf{B}_3, \mathbf{B}_4$	$\mathbf{B}_1, \mathbf{B}_4$	statistical argument: analogous to $\mathsf{Game}_{2.j-1.2}$
$2.j-1.5$	$x_{i,b} \cdot \mathbf{u}$	$x_{i,1-b} \cdot \mathbf{u}$	$x_{i,b} \cdot \mathbf{u}$	$\mathbf{B}_1, \mathbf{B}_2, \mathbf{B}_4$	$\mathbf{B}_1, \mathbf{B}_2, \mathbf{B}_4$	$\mathbf{B}_1, \mathbf{B}_4$	$\mathrm{SD}^{G_2}_{\mathbf{B}_1,\mathbf{B}_4 \mapsto \mathbf{B}_1,\mathbf{B}_3,\mathbf{B}_4}$: analogous to $\mathsf{Game}_{2.j-1.1}$
3	$x_{i,0} \cdot \mathbf{u}_0 + x_{i,1} \cdot \mathbf{u}_1$		$x_{i,b} \cdot \mathbf{u}$	$\mathbf{B}_1, \mathbf{B}_2, \mathbf{B}_4$			$\mathbf{u}_0, \mathbf{u}_1 \leftarrow \mathbb{Z}_p^{1\times(2k+1)}$; change of basis
4	$x_{i,0} \cdot \mathbf{u}_0 + x_{i,1} \cdot \mathbf{u}_1$			$\mathbf{B}_1, \mathbf{B}_2, \mathbf{B}_4$			statistical argument: analogous to Game_1

Fig. 4. Game sequence for Private-key IPE based on XDLIN. The gray background highlights the difference between adjacent games.

- Game_0 is the real game in which the challenge ciphertext for $\mathbf{x}_b = (x_{1,b}, \ldots, x_{n,b})$ is of the form

$$[x_{1,b} \cdot \mathbf{u} + \mathbf{w}_1]_1, \ldots, [x_{n,b} \cdot \mathbf{u} + \mathbf{w}_n]_1, [\alpha]_T \cdot m_0.$$

  Here $b \leftarrow \{0,1\}$ is a secret bit.
- Game_1 is identical to Game_0 except that the challenge ciphertext is

$$\{\, [x_{i,b} \cdot \mathbf{u}^{(134)} + \boxed{x_{i,1-b} \cdot \mathbf{u}^{(2)}} + \mathbf{w}_i]_1 \,\}_{i \in [n]},\ [\alpha]_T \cdot m_0.$$

  We claim that $\mathsf{Game}_1 \equiv \mathsf{Game}_0$. The proof is analogous to that for $\mathsf{Game}_1 \equiv \mathsf{Game}_0$ in Sect. 3.3.
- $\mathsf{Game}_{2.j}$ for $j \in [0, q]$ is identical to Game_1 except that the first j secret keys are

$$[\alpha + (y_1 \cdot \mathbf{w}_1 + \cdots + y_n \cdot \mathbf{w}_n)\mathbf{d}]_2,\ [\mathbf{d}]_2 \quad \text{where} \quad \boxed{\mathbf{d} \leftarrow \mathsf{span}(\mathbf{B}_1, \mathbf{B}_2, \mathbf{B}_4)}.$$

  We claim that $\mathsf{Game}_{2.j-1} \approx_c \mathsf{Game}_{2.j}$ for $j \in [q]$ and give a proof sketch later.
- Game_3 is identical to $\mathsf{Game}_{2.q}$ except that the challenge ciphertext is

$$\{\, [\boxed{x_{i,0} \cdot \mathbf{u}_0^{(124)} + x_{i,1} \cdot \mathbf{u}_1^{(124)}} + x_{i,b} \cdot \mathbf{u}^{(3)} + \mathbf{w}_i]_1 \,\}_{i \in [n]},\ [\alpha]_T \cdot m_0.$$

  where $\mathbf{u}_0, \mathbf{u}_1 \leftarrow \mathbb{Z}_p^{1\times(k+1)}$. We claim that $\mathsf{Game}_{2.q} \equiv \mathsf{Game}_3$. The proof is analogous to that for $\mathsf{Game}_{2.q} \equiv \mathsf{Game}_3$ in Sect. 3.3 using "change of basis" technique [23,28], except that we now work with subspace $\mathsf{span}(\mathbf{B}_1, \mathbf{B}_2, \mathbf{B}_4)$ corresponding to $\mathsf{span}(\mathbf{B}_1, \mathbf{B}_2)$ there (cf. Section 4.1).
- Game_4 is identical to Game_3 except that the challenge ciphertext is

$$[\boxed{x_{1,0} \cdot \mathbf{u}_0 + x_{1,1} \cdot \mathbf{u}_1} + \mathbf{w}_1]_1, \ldots, [\boxed{x_{n,0} \cdot \mathbf{u}_0 + x_{n,1} \cdot \mathbf{u}_1} + \mathbf{w}_n]_1, [\alpha]_T \cdot m_0$$

We claim that $\mathsf{Game}_3 \equiv \mathsf{Game}_4$ and the adversary has no advantage in guessing b in Game_4. The proof for the former claim is similar to that for $\mathsf{Game}_1 \equiv \mathsf{Game}_0$.

Proving $\mathsf{Game}_{2.j-1} \approx_c \mathsf{Game}_{2.j}$. We now proves $\mathsf{Game}_{2.j-1} \approx_c \mathsf{Game}_{2.j}$ which completes the proof for Lemma 16. For all $j \in [q]$, we employ the following game sequence, which has been included in Fig. 4.

- $\mathsf{Game}_{2.j-1.1}$ is identical to $\mathsf{Game}_{2.j-1}$ except that the jth secret key is

$$[\alpha + (y_1 \cdot \mathbf{w}_1 + \cdots + y_n \cdot \mathbf{w}_n)\mathbf{d}]_2,\ [\mathbf{d}]_2 \quad \text{where} \quad \boxed{\mathbf{d} \leftarrow \mathsf{span}(\mathbf{B}_1, \mathbf{B}_3, \mathbf{B}_4)}.$$

We claim that $\mathsf{Game}_{2.j-1.1} \approx_c \mathsf{Game}_{2.j-1}$. This follows from the $\mathrm{SD}^{G_2}_{\mathbf{B}_1,\mathbf{B}_4 \mapsto \mathbf{B}_1,\mathbf{B}_3,\mathbf{B}_4}$ assumption with a reduction analogous to that for $\mathsf{Game}_{2.j-1.1} \approx_c \mathsf{Game}_{2.j-1}$ in Sect. 3.3.
- $\mathsf{Game}_{2.j-1.2}$ is identical to $\mathsf{Game}_{2.j-1.1}$ except that the challenge ciphertext is

$$\{\, [x_{i,b} \cdot \mathbf{u}^{(14)} + x_{i,1-b} \cdot \mathbf{u}^{(2)} + \boxed{x_{i,1-b} \cdot \mathbf{u}^{(3)}} + \mathbf{w}_i]_1 \,\}_{i \in [n]},\ [\alpha]_T \cdot m_0.$$

We claim that $\mathsf{Game}_{2.j-1.2} \equiv \mathsf{Game}_{2.j-1.1}$. The proof is analogous to that for $\mathsf{Game}_{2.j-1.2} \equiv \mathsf{Game}_{2.j-1.1}$ in Sect. 3.3.
- $\mathsf{Game}_{2.j-1.3}$ is identical to $\mathsf{Game}_{2.j-1.2}$ except that the j-th secret key is

$$[\alpha + (y_1 \cdot \mathbf{w}_1 + \cdots + y_n \cdot \mathbf{w}_n)\mathbf{d}]_2,\ [\mathbf{d}]_2 \quad \text{where} \quad \boxed{\mathbf{d} \leftarrow \mathsf{span}(\mathbf{B}_1, \mathbf{B}_2, \mathbf{B}_3, \mathbf{B}_4)}.$$

We claim that $\mathsf{Game}_{2.j-1.3} \approx_c \mathsf{Game}_{2.j-1.2}$. This follows from $\mathrm{XSD}^{G_2}_{\mathbf{B}_3,\mathbf{B}_4 \mapsto \mathbf{B}_2,\mathbf{B}_3,\mathbf{B}_4}$ assumption. The proof is analogous to that for $\mathsf{Game}_{2.j-1.3} \equiv \mathsf{Game}_{2.j-1.2}$ in Sect. 3.3. Note that, in the reduction, we simulate the challenge ciphertext over G_1 using $[\mathsf{basis}(\mathbf{B}_2^{\|}, \mathbf{B}_3^{\|})]_1$.
- $\mathsf{Game}_{2.j-1.4}$ is identical to $\mathsf{Game}_{2.j-1.3}$ except that the challenge ciphertext is

$$\{\, [x_{i,b} \cdot \mathbf{u}^{(14)} + x_{i,1-b} \cdot \mathbf{u}^{(2)} + \boxed{x_{i,b} \cdot \mathbf{u}^{(3)}} + \mathbf{w}_i]_1 \}_{i \in [n]},\ [\alpha]_T \cdot m_0.$$

We claim that $\mathsf{Game}_{2.j-1.4} \equiv \mathsf{Game}_{2.j-1.3}$. The proof is identical to that for $\mathsf{Game}_{2.j-1.2} \equiv \mathsf{Game}_{2.j-1.1}$.
- $\mathsf{Game}_{2.j-1.5}$ is identical to $\mathsf{Game}_{2.j-1.4}$ except that the jth secret key is

$$[\alpha + (y_1 \cdot \mathbf{w}_1 + \cdots + y_n \cdot \mathbf{w}_n)\mathbf{d}]_2,\ [\mathbf{d}]_2 \quad \text{where} \quad \boxed{\mathbf{d} \leftarrow \mathsf{span}(\mathbf{B}_1, \mathbf{B}_2, \mathbf{B}_4)}.$$

We claim that $\mathsf{Game}_{2.j-1.5} \approx_c \mathsf{Game}_{2.j-1.4}$. The proof is identical to that for $\mathsf{Game}_{2.j-1} \approx_c \mathsf{Game}_{2.j-1.1}$. Note that $\mathsf{Game}_{2.j-1.5} = \mathsf{Game}_{2.j}$.

4.4 Step Two: From Private-Key to Public-Key

Following the "private-key to public-key" compiler [36], we transform the private-key IPE in Sect. 4.2 to the following public-key IPE:

- $\mathsf{Setup}(1^\lambda, n)$: Run $\mathbb{G} = (p, G_1, G_2, G_T, e) \leftarrow \mathcal{G}(1^\lambda)$. Sample $\mathbf{A} \leftarrow \mathbb{Z}_p^{3\times 2}, \mathbf{B}_{14} \leftarrow \mathbb{Z}_p^{4\times 2}$ and pick

$$\mathbf{U}, \mathbf{W}_1, \ldots, \mathbf{W}_n \leftarrow \mathbb{Z}_p^{3\times 4} \quad \text{and} \quad \mathbf{k} \leftarrow \mathbb{Z}_p^3.$$

  Output

$$\begin{aligned} \mathsf{mpk} &= (\,\mathbb{G}, [\mathbf{A}^\top]_1, [\mathbf{A}^\top\mathbf{U}]_1, [\mathbf{A}^\top\mathbf{W}_1]_1, \ldots, [\mathbf{A}^\top\mathbf{W}_n]_1, [\mathbf{A}^\top\mathbf{k}]_T\,) \\ \mathsf{msk} &= (\,\mathbf{k}, \mathbf{W}_1, \ldots, \mathbf{W}_n, \mathbf{B}_{14}\,). \end{aligned}$$

- $\mathsf{KeyGen}(\mathsf{msk}, \mathbf{y})$: Let $\mathbf{y} = (y_1, \ldots, y_n) \in \mathbb{Z}_p^n$. Sample $\mathbf{r} \leftarrow \mathbb{Z}_p^2$ and output

$$\mathsf{sk}_\mathbf{y} = (\,K_0 = [\mathbf{k} + (y_1 \cdot \mathbf{W}_1 + \cdots + y_n \cdot \mathbf{W}_n)\mathbf{B}_{14}\mathbf{r}]_2, K_1 = [\mathbf{B}_{14}\mathbf{r}]_2\,)$$

- $\mathsf{Enc}(\mathsf{mpk}, \mathbf{x}, m)$: Let $\mathbf{x} = (x_1, \ldots, x_n) \in \mathbb{Z}_p^n$ and $m \in G_T$. Sample $\mathbf{s} \leftarrow \mathbb{Z}_p^2$ and output

$$\mathsf{ct}_\mathbf{x} = (\,C_0 = [\mathbf{s}^\top\mathbf{A}^\top]_1, \{C_i = [\mathbf{s}^\top\mathbf{A}^\top(x_i \cdot \mathbf{U} + \mathbf{W}_i)]_1\}_{i\in[n]}, C = [\mathbf{s}^\top\mathbf{A}^\top\mathbf{k}]_T \cdot m\,)$$

- $\mathsf{Dec}(\mathsf{ct}_\mathbf{x}, \mathsf{sk}_\mathbf{y})$: Parse $\mathsf{ct}_\mathbf{x} = (C_0, C_1, \ldots, C_n, C)$ and $\mathsf{sk}_\mathbf{y} = (K_0, K_1)$ for $\mathbf{y} = (y_1, \ldots, y_n)$. Output

$$m' = C \cdot e(y_1 \odot C_1 \cdots y_n \odot C_n, K_1) \cdot e(C_0, K_0)^{-1}.$$

The correctness is straightforward.
Security. We will prove the following theorem.

Theorem 4. *Under the* XDLIN *assumption, the IPE scheme described above is adaptively secure and fully attribute-hiding (cf. Sect. 2.1).*

Concretely, we prove the following lemma, showing that the security of the above IPE is implied by that of our private-key IPE in Sect. 4.2 and the MDDH_2 assumption.

Lemma 17. *For any adversary $\mathcal{A}$ that makes at most Q key queries, there exists adversaries $\mathcal{B}_0, \mathcal{B}$ such that*

$$\mathsf{Adv}_\mathcal{A}^{\text{IPE}}(\lambda) \le \mathsf{Adv}_{\mathcal{B}_0}^{\text{MDDH}_2}(\lambda) + \mathsf{Adv}_\mathcal{B}^{\text{IPE}^*}(\lambda)$$

and $\mathsf{Time}(\mathcal{B}_0), \mathsf{Time}(\mathcal{B}) \approx \mathsf{Time}(\mathcal{A})$.

We prove Lemma 17 via the following game sequence, as in Sect. 3.4.

- Game_0 is the real game in which the challenge ciphertext for $\mathbf{x}_b = (x_{1,b}, \ldots, x_{n,b})$ is of the form

$$[\mathbf{c}^\top]_1, [\mathbf{c}^\top(x_{1,b} \cdot \mathbf{U} + \mathbf{W}_1)]_1,\ \ldots,\ [\mathbf{c}^\top(x_{n,b} \cdot \mathbf{U} + \mathbf{W}_n)]_1, e([\mathbf{c}^\top]_1, [\mathbf{k}]_2) \cdot m_b$$

  where $\mathbf{c} \leftarrow \mathsf{span}(\mathbf{A})$. Here $b \leftarrow \{0,1\}$ is a secret bit.

– Game_1 is identical to Game_0 except that we sample $\mathbf{c} \leftarrow \mathbb{Z}_p^{k+1}$ when generating the challenge ciphertext. We claim that $\mathsf{Game}_1 \approx_c \mathsf{Game}_0$. This follows from MDDH_2 assumption and the proof is analogous to that for $\mathsf{Game}_1 \approx_c \mathsf{Game}_0$ in Sect. 3.4.

Analogous to Sect. 3.4 and Sect. 3.6, we can prove that adversary's advantage in Game_1 is bounded by that against our private-key IPE in Sect. 4.2.

Acknowledgement. We thank the reviewers for their detailed and constructive feedback.

References

1. Abe, M., Chase, M., David, B., Kohlweiss, M., Nishimaki, R., Ohkubo, M.: Constant-size structure-preserving signatures: generic constructions and simple assumptions. In: Wang, X., Sako, K. (eds.) ASIACRYPT 2012. LNCS, vol. 7658, pp. 4–24. Springer, Heidelberg (2012). https://doi.org/10.1007/978-3-642-34961-4_3
2. Agrawal, S., Chase, M.: A study of pair encodings: predicate encryption in prime order groups. In: Kushilevitz, E., Malkin, T. (eds.) TCC 2016. LNCS, vol. 9563, pp. 259–288. Springer, Heidelberg (2016). https://doi.org/10.1007/978-3-662-49099-0_10
3. Agrawal, S., Chase, M.: Simplifying design and analysis of complex predicate encryption schemes. In: Coron, J.-S., Nielsen, J.B. (eds.) EUROCRYPT 2017. LNCS, vol. 10210, pp. 627–656. Springer, Cham (2017). https://doi.org/10.1007/978-3-319-56620-7_22
4. Attrapadung, N.: Dual system encryption via doubly selective security: framework, fully secure functional encryption for regular languages, and more. In: Nguyen, P.Q., Oswald, E. (eds.) EUROCRYPT 2014. LNCS, vol. 8441, pp. 557–577. Springer, Heidelberg (2014). https://doi.org/10.1007/978-3-642-55220-5_31
5. Attrapadung, N.: Dual system encryption framework in prime-order groups via computational pair encodings. In: Cheon, J.H., Takagi, T. (eds.) ASIACRYPT 2016. LNCS, vol. 10032, pp. 591–623. Springer, Heidelberg (2016). https://doi.org/10.1007/978-3-662-53890-6_20
6. Attrapadung, N., Yamada, S.: Duality in ABE: converting attribute based encryption for dual predicate and dual policy via computational encodings. In: Nyberg, K. (ed.) CT-RSA 2015. LNCS, vol. 9048, pp. 87–105. Springer, Cham (2015). https://doi.org/10.1007/978-3-319-16715-2_5
7. Bethencourt, J., Sahai, A., Waters, B.: Ciphertext-policy attribute-based encryption. In: 2007 IEEE Symposium on Security and Privacy, pp. 321–334. IEEE Computer Society Press, May 2007
8. Boneh, D., Boyen, X.: Efficient selective-ID secure identity-based encryption without random oracles. In: Cachin, C., Camenisch, J.L. (eds.) EUROCRYPT 2004. LNCS, vol. 3027, pp. 223–238. Springer, Heidelberg (2004). https://doi.org/10.1007/978-3-540-24676-3_14
9. Boneh, D., et al.: Fully key-homomorphic encryption, arithmetic circuit ABE and compact garbled circuits. In: Nguyen, P.Q., Oswald, E. (eds.) EUROCRYPT 2014. LNCS, vol. 8441, pp. 533–556. Springer, Heidelberg (2014). https://doi.org/10.1007/978-3-642-55220-5_30

10. Boneh, D., Waters, B.: Conjunctive, subset, and range queries on encrypted data. In: Vadhan, S.P. (ed.) TCC 2007. LNCS, vol. 4392, pp. 535–554. Springer, Heidelberg (2007). https://doi.org/10.1007/978-3-540-70936-7_29
11. Chen, J., Gay, R., Wee, H.: Improved dual system ABE in prime-order groups via predicate encodings. In: Oswald, E., Fischlin, M. (eds.) EUROCRYPT 2015. LNCS, vol. 9057, pp. 595–624. Springer, Heidelberg (2015). https://doi.org/10.1007/978-3-662-46803-6_20
12. Chen, J., Gong, J.: ABE with tag made easy. In: Takagi, T., Peyrin, T. (eds.) ASIACRYPT 2017. LNCS, vol. 10625, pp. 35–65. Springer, Cham (2017). https://doi.org/10.1007/978-3-319-70697-9_2
13. Chen, J., Gong, J., Kowalczyk, L., Wee, H.: Unbounded ABE via bilinear entropy expansion, revisited. In: Nielsen, J.B., Rijmen, V. (eds.) EUROCRYPT 2018. LNCS, vol. 10820, pp. 503–534. Springer, Cham (2018). https://doi.org/10.1007/978-3-319-78381-9_19
14. Escala, A., Herold, G., Kiltz, E., Ràfols, C., Villar, J.: An algebraic framework for Diffie-Hellman assumptions. In: Canetti, R., Garay, J.A. (eds.) CRYPTO 2013. LNCS, vol. 8043, pp. 129–147. Springer, Heidelberg (2013). https://doi.org/10.1007/978-3-642-40084-1_8
15. Gay, R., Hofheinz, D., Kiltz, E., Wee, H.: Tightly CCA-secure encryption without pairings. In: Fischlin, M., Coron, J.-S. (eds.) EUROCRYPT 2016. LNCS, vol. 9665, pp. 1–27. Springer, Heidelberg (2016). https://doi.org/10.1007/978-3-662-49890-3_1
16. Gong, J., Chen, J., Dong, X., Cao, Z., Tang, S.: Extended nested dual system groups, revisited. In: Cheng, C.-M., Chung, K.-M., Persiano, G., Yang, B.-Y. (eds.) PKC 2016. LNCS, vol. 9614, pp. 133–163. Springer, Heidelberg (2016). https://doi.org/10.1007/978-3-662-49384-7_6
17. Gong, J., Dong, X., Chen, J., Cao, Z.: Efficient IBE with tight reduction to standard assumption in the multi-challenge setting. In: Cheon, J.H., Takagi, T. (eds.) ASIACRYPT 2016. LNCS, vol. 10032, pp. 624–654. Springer, Heidelberg (2016). https://doi.org/10.1007/978-3-662-53890-6_21
18. Gorbunov, S., Vaikuntanathan, V., Wee, H.: Attribute-based encryption for circuits. In: Boneh, D., Roughgarden, T., Feigenbaum, J. (eds.) 45th ACM STOC, pp. 545–554. ACM Press, June 2013
19. Gorbunov, S., Vaikuntanathan, V., Wee, H.: Predicate encryption for circuits from LWE. In: Gennaro, R., Robshaw, M. (eds.) CRYPTO 2015. LNCS, vol. 9216, pp. 503–523. Springer, Heidelberg (2015). https://doi.org/10.1007/978-3-662-48000-7_25
20. Goyal, V., Pandey, O., Sahai, A., Waters, B.: Attribute-based encryption for fine-grained access control of encrypted data. In: Juels, A., Wright, R.N., Vimercati, S. (eds.) ACM CCS 2006, pp. 89–98. ACM Press, October/November 2006. Cryptology ePrint Archive Report 2006/309
21. Ishai, Y., Wee, H.: Partial garbling schemes and their applications. In: Esparza, J., Fraigniaud, P., Husfeldt, T., Koutsoupias, E. (eds.) ICALP 2014. LNCS, vol. 8572, pp. 650–662. Springer, Heidelberg (2014). https://doi.org/10.1007/978-3-662-43948-7_54
22. Katz, J., Sahai, A., Waters, B.: Predicate encryption supporting disjunctions, polynomial equations, and inner products. In: Smart, N. (ed.) EUROCRYPT 2008. LNCS, vol. 4965, pp. 146–162. Springer, Heidelberg (2008). https://doi.org/10.1007/978-3-540-78967-3_9

23. Lewko, A.: Tools for simulating features of composite order bilinear groups in the prime order setting. In: Pointcheval, D., Johansson, T. (eds.) EUROCRYPT 2012. LNCS, vol. 7237, pp. 318–335. Springer, Heidelberg (2012). https://doi.org/10.1007/978-3-642-29011-4_20
24. Lewko, A., Okamoto, T., Sahai, A., Takashima, K., Waters, B.: Fully secure functional encryption: attribute-based encryption and (hierarchical) inner product encryption. In: Gilbert, H. (ed.) EUROCRYPT 2010. LNCS, vol. 6110, pp. 62–91. Springer, Heidelberg (2010). https://doi.org/10.1007/978-3-642-13190-5_4
25. Lewko, A., Waters, B.: New proof methods for attribute-based encryption: achieving full security through selective techniques. In: Safavi-Naini, R., Canetti, R. (eds.) CRYPTO 2012. LNCS, vol. 7417, pp. 180–198. Springer, Heidelberg (2012). https://doi.org/10.1007/978-3-642-32009-5_12
26. Okamoto, T., Takashima, K.: Fully secure functional encryption with general relations from the decisional linear assumption. In: Rabin, T. (ed.) CRYPTO 2010. LNCS, vol. 6223, pp. 191–208. Springer, Heidelberg (2010). https://doi.org/10.1007/978-3-642-14623-7_11
27. Okamoto, T., Takashima, K.: Adaptively attribute-hiding (hierarchical) inner product encryption. In: Pointcheval, D., Johansson, T. (eds.) EUROCRYPT 2012. LNCS, vol. 7237, pp. 591–608. Springer, Heidelberg (2012). https://doi.org/10.1007/978-3-642-29011-4_35
28. Okamoto, T., Takashima, K.: Fully secure unbounded inner-product and attribute-based encryption. In: Wang, X., Sako, K. (eds.) ASIACRYPT 2012. LNCS, vol. 7658, pp. 349–366. Springer, Heidelberg (2012). https://doi.org/10.1007/978-3-642-34961-4_22
29. Okamoto, T., Takashima, K.: Efficient (hierarchical) inner-product encryption tightly reduced from the decisional linear assumption. IEICE Trans. **96–A**(1), 42–52 (2013)
30. Ostrovsky, R., Sahai, A., Waters, B.: Attribute-based encryption with non-monotonic access structures. In: Ning, P., di Vimercati, S.D.C., Syverson, P.F. (eds.) ACM CCS 07, pp. 195–203. ACM Press, October 2007
31. Sahai, A., Waters, B.: Fuzzy identity-based encryption. In: Cramer, R. (ed.) EUROCRYPT 2005. LNCS, vol. 3494, pp. 457–473. Springer, Heidelberg (2005). https://doi.org/10.1007/11426639_27
32. Waters, B.: Dual system encryption: realizing fully secure IBE and HIBE under simple assumptions. In: Halevi, S. (ed.) CRYPTO 2009. LNCS, vol. 5677, pp. 619–636. Springer, Heidelberg (2009). https://doi.org/10.1007/978-3-642-03356-8_36
33. Waters, B.: Ciphertext-policy attribute-based encryption: an expressive, efficient, and provably secure realization. In: Catalano, D., Fazio, N., Gennaro, R., Nicolosi, A. (eds.) PKC 2011. LNCS, vol. 6571, pp. 53–70. Springer, Heidelberg (2011). https://doi.org/10.1007/978-3-642-19379-8_4
34. Waters, B.: Efficient identity-based encryption without random oracles. In: Cramer, R. (ed.) EUROCRYPT 2005. LNCS, vol. 3494, pp. 114–127. Springer, Heidelberg (2005). https://doi.org/10.1007/11426639_7
35. Wee, H.: Dual system encryption via predicate encodings. In: Lindell, Y. (ed.) TCC 2014. LNCS, vol. 8349, pp. 616–637. Springer, Heidelberg (2014). https://doi.org/10.1007/978-3-642-54242-8_26
36. Wee, H.: Attribute-hiding predicate encryption in bilinear groups, revisited. In: Kalai, Y., Reyzin, L. (eds.) TCC 2017. LNCS, vol. 10677, pp. 206–233. Springer, Cham (2017). https://doi.org/10.1007/978-3-319-70500-2_8

Decentralized Multi-Client Functional Encryption for Inner Product

Jérémy Chotard[1,2,3], Edouard Dufour Sans[2,3], Romain Gay[2,3], Duong Hieu Phan[1], and David Pointcheval[2,3(✉)]

[1] XLIM, University of Limoges, CNRS, Limoges, France
[2] DIENS, École normale supérieure, CNRS, PSL University, Paris, France
{jeremy.chotard,edufoursans,romain.gay,phan,david.pointcheval}@ens.fr
[3] Inria, Paris, France

Abstract. We consider a situation where multiple parties, owning data that have to be frequently updated, agree to share weighted sums of these data with some aggregator, but where they do not wish to reveal their individual data, and do not trust each other. We combine techniques from Private Stream Aggregation (PSA) and Functional Encryption (FE), to introduce a primitive we call Decentralized Multi-Client Functional Encryption (DMCFE), for which we give a practical instantiation for Inner Product functionalities. This primitive allows various senders to *non-interactively* generate ciphertexts which support inner-product evaluation, with functional decryption keys that can also be generated *non-interactively*, in a distributed way, among the senders. Interactions are required during the setup phase only. We prove adaptive security of our constructions, while allowing corruptions of the clients, in the random oracle model.

Keywords: Decentralized · Multi-Client · Functional encryption Inner product

1 Introduction

Functional Encryption (FE) [9,15,18,28] is a new paradigm for encryption which extends the traditional "all-or-nothing" requirement of Public-Key Encryption in a much more flexible way. FE allows users to learn specific functions of the encrypted data: for any function f from a class $\mathcal{F}$, a functional decryption key dk_f can be computed such that, given any ciphertext c with underlying plaintext x, using dk_f, a user can efficiently compute $f(x)$, but does not get any additional information about x. This is the most general form of encryption as it encompasses identity-based encryption, attribute-based encryption, broadcast encryption.

However, whereas the input can be large, like a high-dimensional vector, the basic definition of FE implies that the input data comes from only one party: all the coordinates of the vector are provided by one party, and all are encrypted

T. Peyrin and S. Galbraith (Eds.): ASIACRYPT 2018, LNCS 11273, pp. 703–732, 2018.
https://doi.org/10.1007/978-3-030-03329-3_24

at the same time. In many practical applications, the data are an aggregation of information that comes from different parties that may not trust each other.

A naive way to distribute the ciphertext generation would be to take an FE scheme and to have a trusted party handling the setup and the key generation phases, while the encryption procedure would be left to many clients to execute by Multi-Party Computation (MPC). This straw man construction has two obvious weaknesses:

1. Generating any ciphertext requires potentially heavy interactions, with everybody simultaneously on line, and the full ciphertext has to be generated at once, with all the components being known at the same time;
2. Some authority (the trusted third party) reserves the power to recover every client's private data.

Multi-Client Functional Encryption [16,20] addresses the former issue of independent generation of the ciphertext, and we introduce Decentralized Multi-Client Functional Encryption to address the latter, without any central authority nor master secret key.

Multi-Client Functional Encryption. In Multi-Client Functional Encryption (MCFE), as defined in [16,20], the single input x to the encryption procedure is broken down into an input vector $(x_1, \ldots, x_n)$ where the components are independent. An index i for each client and a (typically time-based) label ℓ are used for every encryption: $(c_1 = \mathsf{Encrypt}(1, x_1, \ell), \ldots, c_n = \mathsf{Encrypt}(n, x_n, \ell))$. Anyone owning a functional decryption key dk_f, for an n-ary function f and multiple ciphertexts *for the same label* ℓ, $c_1 = \mathsf{Encrypt}(1, x_1, \ell), \ldots, c_n = \mathsf{Encrypt}(n, x_n, \ell)$, can compute $f(x_1, \ldots, x_n)$ but nothing else about the individual x_i's. The combination of ciphertexts generated for different labels does not give a valid global ciphertext and the adversary learns nothing from it. MCFE is similar to the naive construction described above with MPC, except that ciphertext generation now simply takes one round, and each ciphertext c_i can also be generated independently for the others.

Decentralized Multi-Client Functional Encryption. Still, MCFE requires a trusted party to generate a master key msk and to distribute the encryption keys ek_i to the clients and the functional decryption keys dk_f to the decryptors. In our scenario, however, the clients do not want to rely on any authority. We would thus be interested in a decentralized version of MCFE, where no authority is involved, but the generation of functional decryption keys remains an efficient process under the control of the clients themselves. We introduce the notion of Decentralized Multi-Client Functional Encryption (DMCFE), in which the authority is removed and the clients work together to generate appropriate functional decryption keys. We stress that the authority is not simply *distributed* to a larger number of parties, but that the resulting protocol is indeed *decentralized*: each client has complete control over their individual data and the functional keys they authorize the generation of.

1.1 A Use Case

Consider a financial firm that wants to compute aggregates of several companies' private data (profits, number of sales) so that it can better understand the dynamics of a sector. The companies may be willing to help the financial firm understand the sector as whole, or may be offered compensation for their help, but they don't trust the financial firm or each other with their individual data. After setting up a DMCFE, each company encrypts its private data with a time-stamp label under its private key. Together, they can give the financial firm a decryption aggregation key that only reveals a sum on the companies' private data weighted by public information (employee count, market value) for a given time-stamp. New keys can retroactively decrypt aggregates on old data.

1.2 Related Work

In their more general form, FE and MCFE schemes have been introduced in [5,6, 10,16–19,27,30] but unfortunately, they all rely on non standard cryptographic assumptions (indistinguishability obfuscation, single-input FE for circuits, or multilinear maps). It is more important in practice, and it is an interesting challenge, to build FE for restricted (but concrete) classes of functions, satisfying standard security definitions, under well-understood assumptions.

Inner-Product Functional Encryption. In 2015, Abdalla, Bourse, De Caro, and Pointcheval [1] considered the question of building FE for inner-product functions. In their paper, they show that inner-product functional encryption (IP-FE) can be efficiently realized under standard assumptions like the Decisional Diffie-Hellman (DDH) and Learning-with-Errors (LWE) assumptions [26], but in a weak security model, named *selective security*. Later on, Agrawal, Libert and Stehlé [4] considered *adaptive security* for IP-FE and proposed constructions whose security is based on DDH, LWE or Paillier's Decisional Composite Residuosity (DCR) [25] assumptions.

Private Stream Aggregation (PSA). This notion, also referred to as Privacy-Preserving Aggregation of Time-Series Data, is an older primitive introduced by Shi *et al.* [29]. It is quite similar to our target DMCFE scheme, however PSA does not consider the possibility of adaptively generating different keys for different inner-product evaluations, but only enables the aggregator to compute the *sum* of the clients' data for each time period. PSA also typically involves a Differential Privacy component, which has yet to be studied in the larger setting of DMCFE. Further research on PSA has focused on achieving new properties or better efficiency [8,11,13,21,23,24] but not on enabling new functionalities.

Multi-Input Functional Encryption. Goldwasser *et al.* [16] introduced the notion of Multi-Input Functional Encryption (MIFE) which breaks down a single input x into an input vector $(x_1, \dots, x_n)$ where the components are independent (as does MCFE), but for which there is no notion of ciphertext index or label: user i can enter x_i and encrypt it as $c_i = \mathsf{Encrypt}(x_i)$. Anyone owning a functional decryption key dk_f, for an n-ary function f and multiple ciphertexts

$c_1 = \mathsf{Encrypt}(x_1), \ldots, c_n = \mathsf{Encrypt}(x_n)$, can compute $f(x_1, \ldots, x_n)$ but nothing else about the individual x_i's. Numerous applications of MIFE have been given in detail in [16].

As with MCFE, general purpose MIFE schemes rely on indistinguishability obfuscation or multilinear maps, which we currently do not know how to instantiate under standard cryptographic assumptions. Extending IP-FE to the multi-input setting has proved technically challenging. [3] builds the first Multi-Input IP-FE, that is, each input slot encrypts a vector $\boldsymbol{x}_i \in \mathbb{Z}_p^m$ for some dimension m, each functional decryption key is associated with a vector $\boldsymbol{y}$, and decryption recovers $\langle \boldsymbol{x}, \boldsymbol{y} \rangle$ where $\boldsymbol{x} := (\boldsymbol{x}_i \| \cdots \| \boldsymbol{x}_n)$, $\boldsymbol{y} \in \mathbb{Z}_p^{n \cdot m}$, and n denotes the number of slots, which can be set up arbitrarily. They prove their construction secure under standard assumptions (SXDH, and in fact, k-Lin for any $k \geq 1$) in bilinear groups. Concurrently, [22] build a two-input (i.e. $n = 2$) FE using similar assumptions in bilinear groups. Very recently, [2,12] gave a *function-hiding* multi-input FE for inner products, where the functional decryption keys do not reveal their underlying functions. [2] also gives a generic transformation from single to multi-input for IP-FE, which gives the first multi-input constructions whose security rely on DDH, LWE, or DCR.

In multi-input FE, every ciphertext for every slot can be combined with any other ciphertext for any other slot, and used with functional decryption keys to decrypt an exponential number of values, as soon as there are more than one ciphertext per slot. This "mix-and-match" feature is crucial for some of the applications of MIFE, such as building Indistinguishability Obfuscation [16]. However, it also means the information leaked about the underlying plaintext is enormous, and in many applications, the security guarantees simply become void, especially when many functional decryption keys are queried. In the case of inner product, as soon as m well-chosen functional decryption keys are queried (i.e. for linearly independent vectors), the plaintexts are completely revealed. In the multi-client setting however, since only ciphertexts with the same label (think of it as a time-stamp, for instance) can be combined for decryption, information leakage of the plaintext is much reduced.

The fact that clients have more control over how much information is leaked about their data, and that we remove the need for a central authority in the case of DMCFE, makes our schemes better suited for real-world use.

1.3 Multi-Client Functional Encryption

We remark that, as for MIFE, private-key MCFE is more relevant than its public-key counterpart (this is explained in [16], or [3] in the context of IP-FE).

Essentially, in a public-key MCFE, an encryption of unknown plaintext x_i (for some label ℓ) can be used together with encryptions of arbitrarily chosen values x'_j for each slot $j \in [n]$ (for the same label ℓ) and a functional decryption key for some function f, to obtain the value $f(x'_1, \cdots, x'_{i_1}, x_i, x'_{i+1}, \cdots, x'_n)$. Since the values x'_j for $j \neq i$ are arbitrarily chosen, this reveals typically too much information on x_i for practical uses. In the case of inner product, that means that, from $\mathsf{Enc}(i, x_i, \ell)$, $\mathsf{dk}_{\boldsymbol{y}}$, and the public key, one can efficiently extract the values $x_i y_i + \sum_{j \neq i} x'_j y_j$ for chosen x'_j, which exactly reveals the partial inner product $x_i y_i$ (see [3] for more details on the limitations of public-key IP-FE in the multi-input setting).

Security is defined with an indistinguishability game, where the adversary has to distinguish between encryptions of chosen plaintexts $(x_i^0)_{i \in [n]}$ and $(x_i^1)_{i \in [n]}$. The inherent leakage of information about the plaintext given by functional decryption keys dk_f is captured by a Finalize procedure in the security game, where the advantage is set to zero if the adversary performed a trivial attack, in the sense that correctness allows the adversary to distinguish encryptions of $(x_i^0)_{i \in [n]}$ from $(x_i^1)_{i \in [n]}$, simply because the underlying functions f of the decryption keys tell apart these plaintexts, i.e. $f(x_1^0, \cdots, x_n^0) \neq f(x_1^1, \cdots, x_n^1)$.

In the public-key setting, in order to prevent the adversary from a trivial win, one should make the restriction that the adversary is only allowed to ask functional decryption keys dk_f for functions f that satisfy $f(x_1^0, \cdot, \ldots, \cdot) = f(x_1^1, \cdot, \ldots, \cdot)$, $f(\cdot, x_2^0, \ldots, \cdot) = f(\cdot, x_2^1, \ldots, \cdot)$, $\ldots$, $f(\cdot, \cdot, \ldots, x_n^0) = f(\cdot, \cdot, \ldots, x_n^1)$. Again, this would essentially exclude any function. A private-key encryption solves this issue, and is still well-suited for practical applications.

In this paper, we will thus consider this private-key setting which naturally fits the MCFE (and DMCFE) model as each component in the plaintext is separately provided by a different client. In such a case, the corruption of some clients is an important issue, since several of them could collude to learn information about other clients' inputs. More precisely, we propose such an MCFE for Inner-Product functions in Sect. 4, that is secure even against adaptive corruptions of the senders.

1.4 Decentralized Multi-Client Functional Encryption

While it allows independent generation of the ciphertexts, MCFE (like MIFE) still assumes the existence of a trusted third-party who runs the SetUp algorithm and distributes the functional decryption keys. This third-party, if malicious or corrupted, can easily undermine any client's privacy. We are thus interested in building a scheme in which such a third-party is entirely taken out of the equation.

We thus introduce the notion of Decentralized Multi-Client Functional Encryption (DMCFE), in which the setup phase and the generation of functional decryption keys are decentralized among the same clients as the ones that generate the ciphertexts. We are interested in minimizing interactions during those operations. While one can do it, in a generic way, using MPC, our target is *at least* a non-interactive generation of the functional decryption keys, that we achieve in Sect. 5, again for Inner-Product functions. The one-time setup phase might remain interactive, but this has to be done once only.

1.5 Technical Overview

We briefly showcase the techniques that allow us to build efficient MCFE and DMCFE schemes. The schemes we introduce later enjoy adaptive security (aka full security), where encryption queries are made adaptively by the adversary against the security game, but for the sake of clarity, we will here give an informal description of a selectively-secure scheme from the DDH assumption, where queries are made beforehand. Namely, the standard security notion for FE is indistinguishability-based, where the adversary has access to a Left-or-Right oracle, that on input (m_0, m_1) either always encrypts m_0 or always encrypts m_1. While for the adaptive security, the adversary can query this oracle adaptively, in the *selective* setting, all queries are made at the beginning, before seeing the public parameters.

We first design a secret-key MCFE scheme building up from the public-key FE scheme introduced by Abdalla *et al.* [1] (itself a selectively-secure scheme) where we replace the global randomness with a hash function (modeled as a random oracle for the security analysis), in order to make the generation of the ciphertexts independent for each client. The comparison is illustrated in Fig. 1. Note that for the final decryption to be possible, one needs the function evaluation γ to be small enough, within this discrete logarithm setting. This is one limitation, which is still reasonable for real-world applications that use concrete numbers, that are not of cryptographic size.

Scheme	MCFE	ABDP15 [1]
SetUp	Pick $(s_i)_{i\in[n]}$ at random	Pick $(s_i)_{i\in[n]}$ at random and set $v_i = g^{s_i}$
Encrypt	Each client i, on input (x_i, s_i, ℓ), return $c_i = g^{x_i} \cdot \mathcal{H}(\ell)^{s_i}$	On input $((x_i)_i, (v_i)_i)$, pick $r \xleftarrow{\$} \mathbb{Z}_p$, return $(c_0 = g^r, (c_i = g^{x_i} \cdot v_i^r)_i)$
DKeyGen	On input $((y_i)_i, (s_i)_i)$, return $\mathsf{dk}_{\boldsymbol{y}} = \sum_i y_i s_i$	On input $((y_i)_i, (s_i)_i)$, return $\mathsf{dk}_{\boldsymbol{y}} = \sum_i y_i s_i$
Decrypt	Discrete logarithm on $g^\gamma = \frac{\prod_i c_i^{y_i}}{\mathcal{H}(\ell)^{\mathsf{dk}_{\boldsymbol{y}}}}$	Discrete logarithm on $g^\gamma = \frac{\prod_i c_i^{y_i}}{c_0^{\mathsf{dk}_{\boldsymbol{y}}}}$

Fig. 1. Comparison of the Inner-Product FE scheme from Abdalla *et al.* [1] and a similar MCFE obtained by introducing a hash function $\mathcal{H}$.

If we write $c_0 = g^r$ in the single input case and $c_0 = \mathcal{H}(\ell)$ in the Multi-Client case, we have $c_i = g^{x_i} {c_0}^{s_i}$ for $i \in [n]$ in both cases. In the public-key scheme from [1], s_i was private, and only $v_i = g^{s_i}$ was known to the encryptor. Since we are now dealing with private encryption, the encryptor can use s_i. Correctness then follows from

$$g^\gamma = \frac{\prod_i c_i^{y_i}}{{c_0}^{\mathsf{dk}_{\boldsymbol{y}}}} = \frac{\prod_i (g^{x_i} {c_0}^{s_i})^{y_i}}{{c_0}^{\mathsf{dk}_{\boldsymbol{y}}}} = \frac{g^{\sum_i x_i y_i} {c_0}^{\sum_i y_i s_i}}{{c_0}^{\mathsf{dk}_{\boldsymbol{y}}}} = \frac{g^{\sum_i x_i y_i} {c_0}^{\mathsf{dk}_{\boldsymbol{y}}}}{{c_0}^{\mathsf{dk}_{\boldsymbol{y}}}} = g^{\langle \boldsymbol{x}, \boldsymbol{y} \rangle}.$$

We further define this MCFE scheme and prove it selectively secure under the DDH assumption in Appendix B.

We can easily decentralize the above protocol using standard MPC techniques, but as we mentioned, our main goal is to minimize interactions during the DKeyGen protocol. This simple protocol can illustrate our main insight: we need to provide the aggregator with the decryption key $\langle \boldsymbol{s}, \boldsymbol{y} \rangle$. Since the s_i's are owned individually by the clients, we are interested in a protocol that would let them send shares from which the decryptor would recover an agreed upon Inner Product on their individual inputs. This sounds like a job for MCFE.

More precisely, sending $\mathsf{Encrypt}(s_i)$ under some other key t_i would not solve our problem, because we would still need to provide $\langle \boldsymbol{t}, \boldsymbol{y} \rangle$ to enable decryption, so we send $\mathsf{Encrypt}(y_i s_i)$ under t_i. Now we only need to compute one decryption key: the key for the inner product with vector $\mathbf{1} = (1, \ldots, 1)$, namely $\sum_i t_i$.

There is one final caveat. The result of the inner product evaluation requires a final discrete logarithm computation, and we are no longer operating on real-world data, but on random elements from $\mathbb{Z}_p$. Any attempt to recover the discrete logarithm is hopeless, and we are stuck with $g^{\langle \boldsymbol{s}, \boldsymbol{y} \rangle}$. We work around this issue by using pairings, which effectively enable us to decrypt using only $g^{\langle \boldsymbol{s}, \boldsymbol{y} \rangle}$. The standard SXDH assumption on pairing groups states that the DDH assumption holds in both groups, so introducing pairings doesn't compromise the security of our scheme. Our fully-secure DMCFE from pairings, that inherits from this approach, is described in Sect. 5.

1.6 Contributions

Practical constructions of functional encryption for specific classes of functions is of high interest. In this paper, we focus on MCFE and DMCFE for Inner Product.

We present the first solutions for Inner-Product Functional Encryption in the Multi-Client and Decentralized Multi-Client settings:

1. **Efficiency:** the proposed schemes are highly practical as their efficiency is comparable to that of the DDH-based IP-FE scheme from [4]. A value x_i is encrypted as a unique group element C_i. The setup phase, key generation and decryption all take time linear in the number of participants, and encryption takes time linear in its input.
2. **Security under a standard assumption:** our schemes are all adaptively secure under either the classical DDH assumption or the standard SXDH assumption.
3. **Security against adaptive corruptions:** In addition, we successfully address corruptions of clients, even adaptive ones in the MCFE setting, exploring what Goldwasser *et al.* [16] highlighted as an "interesting direction".
4. **Non interactivity:** The DMCFE scheme we present in Sect. 5 has a key generation protocol that does not require interactions.

Refer to Fig. 2 for a comparison of the different schemes mentioned here. We leave open the problems of considering LWE-based or Paillier-based constructions and of extending this work beyond inner-product functions.

Scheme	Multiple Inner Products	Non Interactive Setup	Non Interactive Encrypt	Non Interactive KeyGen	Decentralized
PSA [29]	✗	✓	✓	N/A	✗
Section 1: Straw man Distributed FE	✓	✓	✗	✓	✗
Section 4: MCFE	✓	✓	✓	✓	✗
Section 5: DMCFE	✓	✗	✓	✓	✓

Fig. 2. Comparison of different cryptographic solutions to the problem of linearly aggregating Private Multi-Client data.

2 Definitions and Security Models

This section is devoted to defining MCFE and DMCFE and the security models that are appropriate for those primitives, in the indistinguishability setting.

2.1 Multi-Client Functional Encryption

An MCFE scheme encrypts vectors of data from several senders and allows the controlled computation of functions on these heterogeneous data. We now define a private-key MCFE as in [16,20]:

Definition 1 (Multi-Client Functional Encryption). *A multi-client functional encryption on $\mathcal{M}$ over a set of n senders is defined by four algorithms:*

- $\mathsf{SetUp}(\lambda)$: *Takes as input the security parameter λ, and outputs the public parameters* mpk, *the master secret key* msk *and the n encryption keys* ek_i*;*
- $\mathsf{Encrypt}(\mathsf{ek}_i, x_i, \ell)$: *Takes as input a user encryption key* ek_i*, a value x_i to encrypt, and a label ℓ, and outputs the ciphertext $C_{\ell,i}$;*
- $\mathsf{DKeyGen}(\mathsf{msk}, f)$: *Takes as input the master secret key* msk *and a function $f : \mathcal{M}^n \to \mathcal{R}$, and outputs a functional decryption key* dk_f*;*
- $\mathsf{Decrypt}(\mathsf{dk}_f, \ell, \boldsymbol{C})$: *Takes as input a functional decryption key* dk_f*, a label ℓ, and an n-vector ciphertext $\boldsymbol{C}$, and outputs $f(\boldsymbol{x})$, if $\boldsymbol{C}$ is a valid encryption of $\boldsymbol{x} = (x_i)_i \in \mathcal{M}^n$ for the label ℓ, or $\perp$ otherwise.*

We make the assumption that mpk is included in msk and in all the encryption keys ek_i as well as the functional decryption keys dk_f. The correctness property states that, given $(\mathsf{mpk}, \mathsf{msk}, (\mathsf{ek}_i)_i) \leftarrow \mathsf{SetUp}(\lambda)$, for any label ℓ, any function $f : \mathcal{M}^n \to \mathcal{R}$, and any vector $\boldsymbol{x} = (x_i)_i \in \mathcal{M}^n$, if $C_{\ell,i} \leftarrow \mathsf{Encrypt}(\mathsf{ek}_i, x_i, \ell)$, for $i \in \{1, \ldots, n\}$, and $\mathsf{dk}_f \leftarrow \mathsf{DKeyGen}(\mathsf{msk}, f)$, then $\mathsf{Decrypt}(\mathsf{dk}_f, \ell, \boldsymbol{C}_\ell = (C_{\ell,i})_i) = f(\boldsymbol{x} = (x_i)_i)$.

The security model is quite similar to the one defined for FE, but as noted in [16,20], one has to consider corruptions, since the senders do not trust each other, and they can collude and give their secret keys to the adversary who will play on their behalf.

Definition 2 (IND-Security Game for MCFE). *Let us consider an MCFE scheme over a set of n senders. No adversary $\mathcal{A}$ should be able to win the following security game against a challenger $\mathcal{C}$:*

- *Initialization: the challenger $\mathcal{C}$ runs the setup algorithm $(\mathsf{mpk}, \mathsf{msk}, (\mathsf{ek}_i)_i) \leftarrow \mathsf{SetUp}(\lambda)$ and chooses a random bit $b \xleftarrow{\$} \{0,1\}$. It provides mpk to the adversary $\mathcal{A}$;*
- *Encryption queries $\mathsf{QEncrypt}(i, x^0, x^1, \ell)$: $\mathcal{A}$ has unlimited and adaptive access to a Left-or-Right encryption oracle, and receives the ciphertext $C_{\ell,i}$ generated by $\mathsf{Encrypt}(\mathsf{ek}_i, x^b, \ell)$. We note that any further query for the same pair (ℓ, i) will later be ignored;*
- *Functional decryption key queries $\mathsf{QDKeyGen}(f)$: $\mathcal{A}$ has unlimited and adaptive access to the $\mathsf{DKeyGen}(\mathsf{msk}, f)$ algorithm for any input function f of its choice. It is given back the functional decryption key dk_f;*
- *Corruption queries $\mathsf{QCorrupt}(i)$: $\mathcal{A}$ can make an unlimited number of adaptive corruption queries on input index i, to get the encryption key ek_i of any sender i of its choice;*
- *Finalize: $\mathcal{A}$ provides its guess b' on the bit b, and this procedure outputs the result β of the security game, according to the analysis given below.*

The output β of the game depends on some conditions, where $\mathcal{CS}$ is the set of corrupted senders (the set of indexes i input to $\mathsf{QCorrupt}$ during the whole game), and $\mathcal{HS}$ the set of honest (non-corrupted) senders. We set the output to $\beta \leftarrow b'$, unless one of the three cases below is true, in which case we set $\beta \xleftarrow{\$} \{0,1\}$:

1. *some $\mathsf{QEncrypt}(i, x_i^0, x_i^1, \ell)$-query has been asked for an index $i \in \mathcal{CS}$ with $x_i^0 \neq x_i^1$;*
2. *for some label ℓ, an encryption-query $\mathsf{QEncrypt}(i, x_i^0, x_i^1, \ell)$ has been asked for some $i \in \mathcal{HS}$, but encryption-queries $\mathsf{QEncrypt}(j, x_j^0, x_j^1, \ell)$ have not all been asked for all $j \in \mathcal{HS}$;*
3. *for some label ℓ and for some function f asked to $\mathsf{QDKeyGen}$, there exists a pair of vectors $(\boldsymbol{x}^0 = (x_i^0)_i, \boldsymbol{x}^1 = (x_i^1)_i)$ such that $f(\boldsymbol{x}^0) \neq f(\boldsymbol{x}^1)$, when*
   - *$x_i^0 = x_i^1$, for all $i \in \mathcal{CS}$;*
   - *$\mathsf{QEncrypt}(i, x_i^0, x_i^1, \ell)$-queries have been asked for all $i \in \mathcal{HS}$.*

We say this MCFE is IND-secure if for any adversary $\mathcal{A}$, $\mathsf{Adv}^{\mathit{IND}}(\mathcal{A}) = |P[\beta = 1|b = 1] - P[\beta = 1|b = 0]|$ is negligible.

Informally, this is the usual Left-or-Right indistinguishability [7], but where the adversary should not be able to get ciphertexts or functional decryption keys that trivially help distinguish the encrypted vectors:

1. since the encryption might be deterministic, if we allow Left-or-Right encryption queries even for corrupted encryption keys, these queries should be on identical messages: with the encryption key, the adversary could simply re-encrypt and compare in case of deterministic encryption;
2. intuitively, if some input is missing, no function evaluation can be done by the adversary, so we enforce the adversary to ask QEncrypt-queries for all the non-corrupted keys (since the adversary can generate any ciphertext itself for the corrupted components) as soon as one label is used;

3. for any functional decryption key, all the possible evaluations should not trivially allow the adversary to distinguish the ciphertexts generated through QEncrypt-queries (on honest components).

In all these cases, the guess of the adversary is not considered (a random bit β is output). Otherwise, this is a legitimate attack, and the guess b' of the adversary is output. We stress that we bar the adversary from querying several ciphertexts under the same pair (ℓ, i). In real life, it is of course the responsibility of the senders not to encrypt under the same label twice (as explained in the introduction, the labels are typically time-stamps, only used once).

Remark 3. While the third constraint aims at preventing the adversary from trivially winning by guessing the bit b from the evaluation of a functional decryption, the two first might look artificial, but they are required for our proof to go through with our constructions:

- with a probabilistic encryption scheme, one could hope to remove the first one, but up to now, we only have deterministic constructions, which is quite classical in the private-key setting (such as symmetric encryption);
- depending on the scheme, an encryption on an "inactive" component (a component that has no impact on the value of a function f, for instance the ith ciphertext in the case of $f_{\boldsymbol{y}} : \boldsymbol{x} \rightarrow \langle \boldsymbol{x}, \boldsymbol{y} \rangle$ when $y_i = 0$) might not be needed for a complete evaluation, as is the case in our schemes (see Sect. 4). Moreover, our keys are homomorphic: from $\mathsf{dk}_{f_{\boldsymbol{y}}}$ and $\mathsf{dk}_{f_{\boldsymbol{y}'}}$, one can easily obtain $\mathsf{dk}_{f_{\boldsymbol{y}+\boldsymbol{y}'}}$. Rather than defining the inactivity of components of functions in the span of those queried, we simply require that ciphertexts be obtained for every component for a given label (either through an explicit query to QEncrypt or thanks to the encryption key obtained from QCorrupt), which is consistent with the use-case we outlined in Sect. 1.1. One could also enforce, by construction, all the queries to be asked and otherwise guarantee that no information is leaked about the plaintexts, which is not the case of our schemes.

Weaker Notions. One may define weaker variants of indistinguishability, where some queries can only be sent *before* the initialization phase:

- Selective Security (`sel-IND`): the encryption queries (QEncrypt) are sent before the initialization;
- Static Security (`sta-IND`): the corruption queries (QCorrupt) are sent before the initialization.

2.2 Decentralized Multi-Client Functional Encryption

In MCFE, an authority owns a master secret key msk to generate the functional decryption keys. We would like to avoid such a powerful authority, and make the scheme totally decentralized among the owners of the data (the senders). We thus define DMCFE, for Decentralized Multi-Client Functional Encryption.

In this context, there are n senders $(\mathcal{S}_i)_i$, for $i = 1, \dots, n$, who will play the role of both the encrypting players and the functional decryption key generators, for a functional decryptor $\mathcal{FD}$. Of course, the senders do not trust each other and they want to control the functional decryption keys that will be generated. There may be several functional decryptors, but since they could collude and combine all the functional decryption keys, in the description below, and in the security model, we will consider only one functional decryptor $\mathcal{FD}$. As already noticed, we could simply use the definition of MCFE [16,20], where the setup and the functional decryption key algorithms are replaced by MPC protocols among the clients. But this could lead to a quite interactive process. We thus focus on efficient one-round key generation protocols DKeyGen that can be split in a first step DKeyGenShare that generates partial keys and the combining algorithm DKeyComb that combines partial keys into the functional decryption key.

Definition 4 (Decentralized Multi-Client Functional Encryption). *A decentralized multi-client functional encryption on $\mathcal{M}$ between a set of n senders $(\mathcal{S}_i)_i$, for $i = 1, \dots, n$, and a functional decrypter $\mathcal{FD}$ is defined by the setup protocol and four algorithms:*

- $\mathsf{SetUp}(\lambda)$: *This is a protocol between the senders $(\mathcal{S}_i)_i$ that eventually generate their own secret keys sk_i and encryption keys ek_i, as well as the public parameters mpk;*
- $\mathsf{Encrypt}(\mathsf{ek}_i, x_i, \ell)$: *Takes as input a user encryption key ek_i, a value x_i to encrypt, and a label ℓ, and outputs the ciphertext $C_{\ell,i}$;*
- $\mathsf{DKeyGenShare}(\mathsf{sk}_i, \ell_f)$: *Takes as input a user secret key sk_i and a label ℓ_f, and outputs the partial functional decryption key $\mathsf{dk}_{f,i}$ for a function $f : \mathcal{M}^n \to \mathcal{R}$ that is described in ℓ_f;*
- $\mathsf{DKeyComb}((\mathsf{dk}_{f,i})_i, \ell_f)$: *Takes as input the partial functional decryption keys and eventually outputs the functional decryption key dk_f;*
- $\mathsf{Decrypt}(\mathsf{dk}_f, \ell, \boldsymbol{C})$: *Takes as input a functional decryption key dk_f, a label ℓ, and an n-vector ciphertext $\boldsymbol{C}$, and outputs $f(\boldsymbol{x})$, if $\boldsymbol{C}$ is a valid encryption of $\boldsymbol{x} = (x_i)_i \in \mathcal{M}^n$ for the label ℓ, or $\perp$ otherwise;*

We make the assumption that mpk is included in all the secret and encryption keys, as well as the (partial) functional decryption keys. Similarly, the function f might be included in the (partial) functional decryption keys. The correctness property states that, given $(\mathsf{mpk}, (\mathsf{sk}_i)_i, (\mathsf{ek}_i)_i) \leftarrow \mathsf{SetUp}(\lambda)$, for any label ℓ, any function $f : \mathcal{M}^n \to \mathcal{R}$, and any vector $\boldsymbol{x} = (x_i)_i \in \mathcal{M}^n$, if $C_{\ell,i} \leftarrow \mathsf{Encrypt}(\mathsf{ek}_i, x_i, \ell)$, for $i \in \{1, \dots, n\}$, and $\mathsf{dk}_f \leftarrow \mathsf{DKeyComb}((\mathsf{DKeyGenShare}(\mathsf{sk}_i, \ell_f))_i, \ell_f)$, then we have $\mathsf{Decrypt}(\mathsf{dk}_f, \ell, \boldsymbol{C}_\ell = (C_{\ell,i})_i) = f(\boldsymbol{x} = (x_i)_i)$.

The security model is quite similar to the one defined above for MCFE, except that for the DKeyGen protocol, the adversary has access to transcripts of the communications and can make some senders play maliciously. Corrupt-queries additionally reveal the secret keys sk_i.

Definition 5 (IND-Security Game for DMCFE). *Let us consider a DMCFE scheme between a set of n senders. No adversary $\mathcal{A}$ should be able to win the following security game against a challenger $\mathcal{C}$:*

- *Initialization: the challenger* $\mathcal{C}$ *runs the setup protocol* $(\mathsf{mpk}, (\mathsf{sk}_i)_i, (\mathsf{ek}_i)_i) \leftarrow \mathsf{SetUp}(\lambda)$ *and chooses a random bit* $b \xleftarrow{\$} \{0,1\}$. *It provides* mpk *to the adversary* $\mathcal{A}$;
- *Encryption queries* $\mathsf{QEncrypt}(i, x^0, x^1, \ell)$: $\mathcal{A}$ *has unlimited and adaptive access to a Left-or-Right encryption oracle, and receives the ciphertext* $C_{\ell,i}$ *generated by* $\mathsf{Encrypt}(\mathsf{ek}_i, x^b, \ell)$. *We note that any further query for the same pair* (ℓ, i) *will later be ignored;*
- *Functional decryption key queries* $\mathsf{QDKeyGen}(i, f)$: $\mathcal{A}$ *has unlimited and adaptive access to the (non-corrupted) senders running the* $\mathsf{DKeyGenShare}(\mathsf{sk}_i, f)$ *algorithm for any input function* f *of its choice. It is given back the partial functional decryption key* $\mathsf{dk}_{f,i}$;
- *Corruptions queries* $\mathsf{QCorrupt}(i)$: $\mathcal{A}$ *can make an unlimited number of adaptive corruption queries on input index* i, *to get the secret and encryption keys* $(\mathsf{sk}_i, \mathsf{ek}_i)$ *of any sender* i *of its choice.*
- *Finalize:* $\mathcal{A}$ *provides its guess* b' *on the bit* b, *and this procedure outputs the result* β *of the security game, according to the analysis given below.*

The output β *of the game depends on some conditions, where* $\mathcal{CS}$ *is the set of corrupted senders (the set of indexes* i *input to* $\mathsf{QCorrupt}$ *during the whole game), and* $\mathcal{HS}$ *the set of honest (non-corrupted) senders. We set the output to* $\beta \leftarrow b'$, *unless one of the three cases below is true, in which case we set* $\beta \xleftarrow{\$} \{0,1\}$:

1. *some* $\mathsf{QEncrypt}(i, x_i^0, x_i^1, \ell)$*-query has been asked for an index* $i \in \mathcal{CS}$ *with* $x_i^0 \neq x_i^1$;
2. *for some label* ℓ, *an encryption-query* $\mathsf{QEncrypt}(i, x_i^0, x_i^1, \ell)$ *has been asked for some* $i \in \mathcal{HS}$, *but encryption-queries* $\mathsf{QEncrypt}(j, x_j^0, x_j^1, \ell)$ *have not all been asked for all* $j \in \mathcal{HS}$;
3. *for some label* ℓ *and for some function* f *asked to* $\mathsf{QDKeyGen}$ *for all* $i \in \mathcal{HS}$, *there exists a pair of vectors* $(\boldsymbol{x}^0 = (x_i^0)_i, \boldsymbol{x}^1 = (x_i^1)_i)$ *such that* $f(\boldsymbol{x}^0) \neq f(\boldsymbol{x}^1)$, *when*
   - $x_i^0 = x_i^1$, *for all* $i \in \mathcal{CS}$;
   - $\mathsf{QEncrypt}(i, x_i^0, x_i^1, \ell)$*-queries have been asked for all* $i \in \mathcal{HS}$.

We say this DMCFE is IND*-secure if for any adversary* $\mathcal{A}$, $\mathsf{Adv}^{\mathit{IND}}(\mathcal{A}) = |P[\beta = 1|b = 1] - P[\beta = 1|b = 0]|$ *is negligible.*

We define `sel-IND` (selective) and `sta-IND` (static) security for DMCFE as we did for MCFE.

3 Notations and Assumptions

3.1 Groups

Prime Order Group. We use a prime-order group generator GGen, a probabilistic polynomial time (PPT) algorithm that on input the security parameter 1^λ returns a description $\mathcal{G} = (\mathbb{G}, p, P)$ of an additive cyclic group $\mathbb{G}$ of order p for a 2λ-bit prime p, whose generator is P.

We use implicit representation of group elements as introduced in [14]. For $a \in \mathbb{Z}_p$, define $[a] = aP \in \mathbb{G}$ as the *implicit representation* of a in $\mathbb{G}$. More generally, for a matrix $\mathbf{A} = (a_{ij}) \in \mathbb{Z}_p^{n\times m}$ we define $[\mathbf{A}]$ as the implicit representation of $\mathbf{A}$ in $\mathbb{G}$:

$$[\mathbf{A}] := \begin{pmatrix} a_{11}P \dots a_{1m}P \\ \\ a_{n1}P \dots a_{nm}P \end{pmatrix} \in \mathbb{G}^{n\times m}$$

We will always use this implicit notation of elements in $\mathbb{G}$, i.e., we let $[a] \in \mathbb{G}$ be an element in $\mathbb{G}$. Note that from a random $[a] \in \mathbb{G}$ it is generally hard to compute the value a (discrete logarithm problem in $\mathbb{G}$). Obviously, given $[a], [b] \in \mathbb{G}$ and a scalar $x \in \mathbb{Z}_p$, one can efficiently compute $[ax] \in \mathbb{G}$ and $[a+b] = [a] + [b] \in \mathbb{G}$.

Pairing Group. We also use a pairing group generator PGGen, a PPT algorithm that on input 1^λ returns a description $\mathcal{PG} = (\mathbb{G}_1, \mathbb{G}_2, p, P_1, P_2, e)$ of asymmetric pairing groups where $\mathbb{G}_1$, $\mathbb{G}_2$, $\mathbb{G}_T$ are additive cyclic groups of order p for a 2λ-bit prime p, P_1 and P_2 are generators of $\mathbb{G}_1$ and $\mathbb{G}_2$, respectively, and $e : \mathbb{G}_1 \times \mathbb{G}_2 \to \mathbb{G}_T$ is an efficiently computable (non-degenerate) bilinear map. Define $P_T := e(P_1, P_2)$, which is a generator of $\mathbb{G}_T$. We again use implicit representation of group elements. For $s \in \{1, 2, T\}$ and $a \in \mathbb{Z}_p$, define $[a]_s = aP_s \in \mathbb{G}_s$ as the implicit representation of a in G_s. Given $[a]_1$, $[a]_2$, one can efficiently compute $[ab]_T$ using the pairing e. For two matrices $\mathbf{A}$, $\mathbf{B}$ with matching dimensions define $e([\mathbf{A}]_1, [\mathbf{B}]_2) := [\mathbf{AB}]_T \in \mathbb{G}_T$.

Compatibility. Our construction from Sect. 4 uses a prime-order group, while the one from Sect. 5 uses pairing groups. Since the latter use the former as a building block, we must use groups that are compatible with each other. Notice that one can generate a prime-order group either with $\mathcal{G} := (\mathbb{G}, p, P) \xleftarrow{\$} \mathsf{GGen}(1^\lambda)$, but also using $\mathcal{PG} := (\mathbb{G}_1, \mathbb{G}_2, p, P_1, P_2, e) \xleftarrow{\$} \mathsf{PGGen}(1^\lambda)$, and setting $\mathbb{G} := \mathbb{G}_1$. This is possible here because we use asymmetric pairings and rely on the SXDH assumption in the pairing group, which is DDH in $\mathbb{G}_1$ and $\mathbb{G}_2$. More details on computational assumptions follow.

3.2 Computational Assumptions

Definition 6 (Decisional Diffie-Hellman Assumption). *The Decisional Diffie-Hellman Assumption states that, in a prime-order group $\mathcal{G} \xleftarrow{\$} \mathsf{GGen}(1^\lambda)$, no PPT adversary can distinguish between the two following distributions with non-negligible advantage:*

$$\{([a], [r], [ar]) \mid a, r \xleftarrow{\$} \mathbb{Z}_p\} \text{ and } \{([a], [r], [s]) \mid a, r, s \xleftarrow{\$} \mathbb{Z}_p\}.$$

Equivalently, this assumption states it is hard to distinguish, knowing $[a]$, a random element from the span of $[\boldsymbol{a}]$ for $\boldsymbol{a} = \binom{1}{a}$, from a random element in $\mathbb{G}^2$: $[\boldsymbol{a}] \cdot r = [\boldsymbol{a}r] = \binom{[r]}{[ar]} \approx \binom{[r]}{[s]}$.

Definition 7 (Symmetric eXternal Diffie-Hellman Assumption). *The Symmetric eXternal Diffie-Hellman (SXDH) Assumption states that, in a pairing group* $\mathcal{PG} \xleftarrow{\$} \mathsf{PGGen}(1^\lambda)$, *the DDH assumption holds in both* $\mathbb{G}_1$ *and* $\mathbb{G}_2$.

4 A Fully-Secure MCFE for Inner Product

After the first construction drafted in the introduction, from the Abdalla *et al.* [1] selectively-secure FE, we propose another construction of MCFE for inner product adapted from the Agrawal *et al.* [4] scheme. We also provide the full security analysis under the DDH assumption, since the security proof of our DMCFE construction will rely on it.

Overview of the Construction. This construction is an extension of the previous one proposed in the introduction: we first extended the scheme from Abdalla *et al.* [1] in the multi-client setting with a hash function. Because of the selective security of the underlying scheme, our first proposal was just selectively secure too. We now adapt the Agrawal *et al.* [4] scheme, in the same manner. This construction and its proof of adaptive security are for the sake of clarity, since the proof of our next DMCFE will be made clearer when reducing to this one.

4.1 Description

We use a prime-order group, and the bracket notation, as defined in Sect. 3.1.

- $\mathsf{SetUp}(\lambda)$: Takes as input the security parameter, and generates prime-order group $\mathcal{G} := (\mathbb{G}, p, P) \xleftarrow{\$} \mathsf{GGen}(1^\lambda)$, and $\mathcal{H}$ a full-domain hash function onto $\mathbb{G}^2$. It also generates the encryption keys $\boldsymbol{s}_i \xleftarrow{\$} \mathbb{Z}_p^2$, for $i = 1, \ldots, n$. The public parameters mpk consist of $(\mathbb{G}, p, g, \mathcal{H})$, while the encryption keys are $\mathsf{ek}_i = \boldsymbol{s}_i$ for $i = 1, \ldots, n$, and the master secret key is $\mathsf{msk} = ((\mathsf{ek}_i)_i)$, (in addition to mpk, which is omitted);
- $\mathsf{Encrypt}(\mathsf{ek}_i, x_i, \ell)$: Takes as input the value x_i to encrypt, under the key $\mathsf{ek}_i = \boldsymbol{s}_i$ and the label ℓ. It computes $[\boldsymbol{u}_\ell] := \mathcal{H}(\ell) \in \mathbb{G}^2$, and outputs the ciphertext $[c_i] = [\boldsymbol{u}_\ell^\top \boldsymbol{s}_i + x_i] \in \mathbb{G}$;
- $\mathsf{DKeyGen}(\mathsf{msk}, \boldsymbol{y})$: Takes as input $\mathsf{msk} = (\boldsymbol{s}_i)_i$ and an inner-product function defined by $\boldsymbol{y}$ as $f_{\boldsymbol{y}}(\boldsymbol{x}) = \langle \boldsymbol{x}, \boldsymbol{y} \rangle$, and outputs the functional decryption key $\mathsf{dk}_{\boldsymbol{y}} = (\boldsymbol{y}, \sum_i \boldsymbol{s}_i \cdot y_i) \in \mathbb{Z}_p^n \times \mathbb{Z}_p^2$;
- $\mathsf{Decrypt}(\mathsf{dk}_{\boldsymbol{y}}, \ell, ([c_i])_{i\in[n]})$: Takes as input a functional decryption key $\mathsf{dk}_{\boldsymbol{y}} = (\boldsymbol{y}, \boldsymbol{d})$, a label ℓ, and ciphertexts. It computes $[\boldsymbol{u}_\ell] := \mathcal{H}(\ell)$, $[\alpha] = \sum_i [c_i] \cdot y_i - [\boldsymbol{u}_\ell^\top] \cdot \boldsymbol{d}$, and eventually solves the discrete logarithm to extract and return α.

Note that, as for [4], the result α must be polynomially bounded to efficiently compute the discrete logarithm in the last decryption step: let $\boldsymbol{x}, \boldsymbol{y} \in \mathbb{Z}_p^n$, we have:

$$\begin{aligned}[\alpha] &= \sum_i [c_i] \cdot y_i - [\boldsymbol{u}_\ell^\top] \cdot \boldsymbol{d} = \sum_i [\boldsymbol{u}_\ell^\top \boldsymbol{s}_i + x_i] \cdot y_i - [\boldsymbol{u}_\ell^\top] \cdot \sum_i y_i \boldsymbol{s}_i \\ &= \sum_i [\boldsymbol{u}_\ell^\top] \cdot \boldsymbol{s}_i y_i + \sum_i [x_i] \cdot y_i - [\boldsymbol{u}_\ell^\top] \cdot \sum_i y_i \boldsymbol{s}_i = [\sum_i x_i y_i].\end{aligned}$$

4.2 Security Analysis

Theorem 8 (IND-Security). *The above MCFE protocol (see Sect. 4.1) is IND-secure under the DDH assumption, in the random oracle model. More precisely, we have*

$$\mathsf{Adv}^{\mathit{IND}}(\mathcal{A}) \leq 2Q \cdot \mathsf{Adv}^{\mathit{ddh}}_{\mathbb{G}}(t) + \mathsf{Adv}^{\mathit{ddh}}_{\mathbb{G}}(t + 4Q \times t_{\mathbb{G}}) + \frac{2Q}{p},$$

for any adversary $\mathcal{A}$, running within time t, where Q is the number of (direct and indirect—asked by QEncrypt*-queries—) queries to $\mathcal{H}$ (modeled as a random oracle), and $t_{\mathbb{G}}$ is the time for an exponentiation in $\mathbb{G}$.*

We stress that this Theorem supports both adaptive encryption queries and adaptive corruptions.

Proof Technique. To obtain adaptive security, we use a technique that consists of first proving perfect security in the selective variant of the involved games, then, using a guessing (a.k.a. complexity leveraging) argument, which incurs an exponential security loss, we obtain the same security guarantees in the adaptive games. Since the security in the selective game is perfect (the advantage of any adversary is exactly zero), the exponential security loss is multiplied by a zero term, and the overall adaptive security is preserved. This technique has been used before in [31] in the context of Attribute-Based Encryption, or more recently, in [2,3] in the context of multi-input IP-FE. We defer to [31, Remark 1] and [3, Remark 5] for more details on this proof technique.

Proof. We proceed using hybrid games, described in Fig. 3. Let $\mathcal{A}$ be a PPT adversary. For any game G_{index}, we denote by $\mathsf{Adv}_{\mathsf{index}} := |\Pr[G_{\mathsf{index}}(\mathcal{A})|b = 1] - \Pr[G_{\mathsf{index}}(\mathcal{A})|b = 0]|$, where the probability is taken over the random coins of G_{index} and $\mathcal{A}$. Also, by event $G_{\mathsf{index}}(\mathcal{A})$, or just G_{index} when there is no ambiguity, we mean that the Finalize procedure in game G_{index} (defined as in Definition 2) returns $\beta = 1$ from the adversary's answer b' when interacting with $\mathcal{A}$.

Game G_0: This is the IND-security game as given in Definition 2. Note that the hash function $\mathcal{H}$ is modeled as a random oracle RO onto $\mathbb{G}^2$. This is essentially used to generate $[\boldsymbol{u}_\ell] = \mathcal{H}(\ell)$.

Game G_1: We simulate the answers to any new RO-query by a truly random pair in $\mathbb{G}^2$, on the fly. The simulation remains perfect, and so $\mathsf{Adv}_0 = \mathsf{Adv}_1$.

Game G_2: We simulate the answers to any new RO-query by a truly random pair in the span of $[\boldsymbol{a}]$ for $\boldsymbol{a} := \binom{1}{a}$, with $a \xleftarrow{\$} \mathbb{Z}_p$. This uses the Multi-DDH assumption, which tightly reduces to the DDH assumption using the random-self reducibility (see Lemma 10, in Appendix A): $\mathsf{Adv}_1 - \mathsf{Adv}_2 \leq \mathsf{Adv}^{\mathsf{ddh}}_{\mathbb{G}}(t + 4Q \times t_{\mathbb{G}})$, where Q is the number of RO-queries and $t_{\mathbb{G}}$ the time for an exponentiation.

Game G_3: We simulate any QEncrypt query as the encryption of x_i^0 instead of x_i^b and go back for the answers to any new RO query by a truly random pair in $\mathbb{G}^2$.

Games G_0, G_1, $\boxed{G_2, (G_{3.q.1})_{q\in[Q+1]}, (G_{3.q.2}, G_{3.q.3})_{q\in[Q]}}$

$\mathcal{G} \leftarrow \mathsf{GGen}(1^\lambda)$, for all $i \in [n]$, $\boldsymbol{s}_i \xleftarrow{\$} \mathbb{Z}_p^2$, $\mathsf{ek}_i := \boldsymbol{s}_i$, $\mathsf{msk} := (\boldsymbol{s}_i)_i$, $\mathsf{mpk} := (\mathbb{G}, p, g)$.

$\boxed{a \xleftarrow{\$} \mathbb{Z}_p,\ \boldsymbol{a} := \binom{1}{a},\ \boldsymbol{a}^\perp := \binom{-a}{1}}$

Sample a full-domain hash function $\mathcal{H}$ onto $\mathbb{G}^2$, and a bit $b \xleftarrow{\$} \{0,1\}$.

$b' \leftarrow \mathcal{A}^{\mathsf{QEncrypt}(\cdot,\cdot,\cdot,\cdot),\mathsf{QDKeyGen}(\cdot),\mathsf{QCorrupt}(\cdot),\mathsf{RO}(\cdot)}(\mathsf{mpk})$.

Run Finalize on b'.

$\underline{\mathsf{RO}(\ell)}$: // G_0, G_1, $\boxed{G_2, G_{3.q.1}, G_{3.q.2}, G_{3.q.3}}$

$[\boldsymbol{u}_\ell] := \mathcal{H}(\ell)$, $[\boldsymbol{u}_\ell] := \mathsf{RF}(\ell)$, $\boxed{[\boldsymbol{u}_\ell] := [\boldsymbol{a} \cdot r_\ell], \text{ with } r_\ell := \mathsf{RF}'(\ell)}$

On the q'th (fresh) query: $[\boldsymbol{u}_\ell] := \mathsf{RF}'(\ell) \cdot \boldsymbol{a} + \mathsf{RF}''(\ell) \cdot \boldsymbol{a}^\perp$

Return $[\boldsymbol{u}_\ell]$.

$\underline{\mathsf{QEncrypt}(i, x_i^0, x_i^1, \ell)}$: // G_0, G_1, G_2, $\boxed{G_{3.q.1}, G_{3.q.2}, G_{3.q.3}}$

$[\boldsymbol{u}_\ell] := \mathsf{RO}(\ell)$,

$[c_i] := [\boldsymbol{u}_\ell^\top] \cdot \boldsymbol{s}_i + [x_i^b]$

$\boxed{\text{If } [\boldsymbol{u}_\ell] \text{ is computed on the } j \text{ RO-query, for } j < q\text{: } [c_i] := [\boldsymbol{u}_\ell^\top] \cdot \boldsymbol{s}_i + [x_i^0]}$

If $[\boldsymbol{u}_\ell]$ is computed on the q-th RO-query: $[c_i] := [\boldsymbol{u}_\ell^\top] \cdot \boldsymbol{s}_i + [x_i^0]$

Return $[c_i]$

$\underline{\mathsf{QDKeyGen}(\boldsymbol{y})}$: Return $\sum_i y_i \boldsymbol{s}_i$. //$G_0$, G_1, G_2, $G_{3.q.1}$, $G_{3.q.2}$, $G_{3.q.3}$

$\underline{\mathsf{QCorrupt}(i)}$: Return $\boldsymbol{s}_i$. // G_0, G_1, G_2, $G_{3.q.1}$, $G_{3.q.2}$, $G_{3.q.3}$

Fig. 3. Games for the proof of Theorem 8. Here, RF, RF', RF'' are random functions onto $\mathbb{G}^2$, $\mathbb{Z}_p$, and $\mathbb{Z}_p^*$, respectively, that are computed on the fly. In each procedure, the components inside a solid (dotted, gray) frame are only present in the games marked by a solid (dotted, gray) frame. The Finalize procedure is defined as in Definition 2.

While it is clear that in this last game the advantage of any adversary is exactly 0 since b does not appear anywhere, the gap between G_2 and G_3 will be proven using a hybrid technique on the RO-queries. We thus index the following games by q, where $q = 1, \ldots, Q$. Note that only distinct RO-queries are counted, since a second similar query is answered as the first one. We detail this proof because the technique is important.

$G_{3.1.1}$: This is exactly game G_2. Thus, $\mathsf{Adv}_2 = \mathsf{Adv}_{3.1.1}$.

$G_{3.q.1} \rightsquigarrow G_{3.q.2}$: We first change the distribution of the output of the q-th RO-query, from uniformly random in the span of $[\boldsymbol{a}]$ to uniformly random over $\mathbb{G}^2$, using the DDH assumption. Then, we use the basis $(\binom{1}{a}, \binom{-a}{1})$ of $\mathbb{Z}_p^2$, to write a uniformly random vector over $\mathbb{Z}_p^2$ as $u_1 \cdot \boldsymbol{a} + u_2 \cdot \boldsymbol{a}^\perp$, where $u_1, u_2 \xleftarrow{\$} \mathbb{Z}_p$. Finally, we switch to $u_1 \cdot \boldsymbol{a} + u_2 \cdot \boldsymbol{a}^\perp$ where $u_1 \xleftarrow{\$} \mathbb{Z}_p$, and $u_2 \xleftarrow{\$} \mathbb{Z}_p^*$, which only changes the adversary view by a statistical distance of $1/p$: $\mathsf{Adv}_{3.q.1} - \mathsf{Adv}_{3.q.2} \leq \mathsf{Adv}_{\mathbb{G}}^{\mathsf{ddh}}(t) + 1/p$. The last step with $u_2 \in \mathbb{Z}_p^*$ will be important to guarantee that $\boldsymbol{u}_\ell^\top \boldsymbol{a}^\perp \neq 0$.

Games $(G^\star_{3.q.2}, G^\star_{3.q.3})_{q\in[Q]}$:

$(\mathsf{state}, (z_i \in \mathbb{Z}_p^2 \cup \{\perp\})_{i\in[n]}) \leftarrow \mathcal{A}(1^\lambda, 1^n)$

$\mathcal{G} \leftarrow \mathsf{GGen}(1^\lambda)$, for all $i \in [n]$, $\boldsymbol{s}_i \xleftarrow{\$} \mathbb{Z}_p^2$, $\mathsf{ek}_i := \boldsymbol{s}_i$, $\mathsf{msk} := (\boldsymbol{s}_i)_i$, $\mathsf{mpk} := (\mathbb{G}, p, g)$.

$a \xleftarrow{\$} \mathbb{Z}_p$, $\boldsymbol{a} := \binom{1}{a}$, $\boldsymbol{a}^\perp := \binom{-a}{1}$, $b \xleftarrow{\$} \{0,1\}$.

$b' \leftarrow \mathcal{A}^{\mathsf{QEncrypt}(\cdot,\cdot,\cdot,\cdot),\mathsf{QDKeyGen}(\cdot),\mathsf{QCorrupt}(\cdot),\mathsf{RO}(\cdot)}(\mathsf{mpk}, \mathsf{state})$.

Run Finalize on b'.

$\mathsf{RO}(\ell)$: // $G^\star_{3.q.2}$, $G^\star_{3.q.3}$

$[\boldsymbol{u}_\ell] := [\boldsymbol{a} \cdot r_\ell]$, with $r_\ell := \mathsf{RF}'(\ell)$

On the q'th (fresh) query: $[\boldsymbol{u}_\ell] := [\mathsf{RF}'(\ell) \cdot \boldsymbol{a} + \mathsf{RF}''(\ell) \cdot \boldsymbol{a}^\perp]$

Return $[\boldsymbol{u}_\ell]$.

$\mathsf{QEncrypt}(i, x_i^0, x_i^1, \ell)$: // $\boxed{G^\star_{3.q.2}}$, $G^\star_{3.q.3}$ (gray)

$[\boldsymbol{u}_\ell] := \mathsf{RO}(\ell)$,

$[c_i] := [\boldsymbol{u}_\ell^\top] \cdot \boldsymbol{s}_i + [x_i^b]$

If $[\boldsymbol{u}_\ell]$ is computed on the j-th RO-query with $j < q$: $[c_i] := [\boldsymbol{u}_\ell^\top] \cdot \boldsymbol{s}_i + [x_i^0]$.

If $[\boldsymbol{u}_\ell]$ is computed on the q-th RO-query, then:

- if $(x_i^0, x_i^1) \neq z_i$, the game ends and returns $\beta \xleftarrow{\$} \{0,1\}$.
- otherwise, $[c_i] := [\boldsymbol{u}_\ell^\top] \cdot \boldsymbol{s}_i \boxed{+[x_i^b]}$ $+[x_i^0]$ (gray), $\mathcal{S} := \mathcal{S} \cup \{i\}$.

Return $[c_i]$.

$\mathsf{QDKeyGen}(\boldsymbol{y})$: Return $\sum_i y_i \boldsymbol{s}_i$. // $G^\star_{3.q.2}$, $G^\star_{3.q.3}$

$\mathsf{QCorrupt}(i)$: // $G^\star_{3.q.2}$, $G^\star_{3.q.3}$

If $z_i = (x_i^0, x_i^1)$ with $x_i^0 \neq x_i^1$, the game ends, and returns $\beta \xleftarrow{\$} \{0,1\}$.

Return $\boldsymbol{s}_i$.

Fig. 4. Games $G^\star_{3.q.2}$ and $G^\star_{3.q.3}$, with $q \in [Q]$, for the proof of Theorem 8. Here, RF, RF' are random functions onto $\mathbb{G}^2$, and $\mathbb{Z}_p$, respectively, that are computed on the fly. In each procedure, the components inside a solid (gray) frame are only present in the games marked by a solid (gray) frame.

$G_{3.q.2} \rightsquigarrow G_{3.q.3}$: We now change the generation of the ciphertext $[c_i] := [\boldsymbol{u}_\ell^\top] \cdot \boldsymbol{s}_i + [x_i^b]$ by $[c_i] := [\boldsymbol{u}_\ell^\top] \cdot \boldsymbol{s}_i + [x_i^0]$, where $[\boldsymbol{u}_\ell]$ corresponds to the q-th RO-query. We then prove this does not change the adversary's view.

Note that if the output of the q-th RO-query is not used by QEncrypt-queries, then the games $G_{3.q.2}$ and $G_{3.q.3}$ are identical. But we can show this is true too when there are RO-queries that are really involved in QEncrypt-queries, and show that $\mathsf{Adv}_{3.q.2} = \mathsf{Adv}_{3.q.3}$ in that case too, in two steps. In Step 1, we show that there exists a PPT adversary $\mathcal{B}^\star$ such that $\mathsf{Adv}_{3.q.t} = (p^2 + 1)^n \cdot \mathsf{Adv}^\star_{3.q.t}(\mathcal{B}^\star)$, for $t = 2, 3$, where the games $G^\star_{3.q.2}$ and $G^\star_{3.q.3}$ are selective variants of games $G_{3.q.2}$ and $G_{3.q.3}$ respectively (see Fig. 4), where QCorrupt queries are asked before the initialization phase. In Step 2, we show that for all PPT adversaries $\mathcal{B}^\star$, we have $\mathsf{Adv}^\star_{3.q.2}(\mathcal{B}^\star) = \mathsf{Adv}^\star_{3.q.3}(\mathcal{B}^\star)$. This will conclude the two steps.

Step 1. We build a PPT adversary $\mathcal{B}^\star$ playing against $G^\star_{3.q.t}$ for $t = 2, 3$, such that $\mathsf{Adv}_{3.q.t} = (p^2 + 1)^n \cdot \mathsf{Adv}^\star_{3.q.t}(\mathcal{B}^\star)$.

Adversary $\mathcal{B}^\star$ first guesses for all $i \in [n]$, $z_i \xleftarrow{\$} \mathbb{Z}_p^2 \cup \{\bot\}$, which it sends to its selective game $G^\star_{3.q.t}$. That is, each guess z_i is either a pair of values (x_i^0, x_i^1) queried to QEncrypt, or $\bot$, which means no query to QEncrypt. Then, it simulates $\mathcal{A}$'s view using its own oracles. When $\mathcal{B}^\star$ guesses successfully (call E that event), it simulates $\mathcal{A}$'s view exactly as in $G_{3.q.t}$. If the guess was not successful, then $\mathcal{B}^\star$ stops the simulation and outputs a random bit β. Since event E happens with probability $(p^2+1)^{-n}$ and is independent of the view of adversary $\mathcal{A}$: $\mathsf{Adv}^\star_{3.q.t}(\mathcal{B}^\star)$ is equal to

$$\left|\Pr[G^\star_{3.q.t}|b=0,E]\cdot\Pr[E]+\frac{\Pr[\neg E]}{2}-\Pr[G^\star_{3.q.t}|b=1,E]\cdot\Pr[E]-\frac{\Pr[\neg E]}{2}\right|$$
$$=\Pr[E]\cdot|\Pr[G^\star_{3.q.t}|b=0,E]-\Pr[G^\star_{3.q.t}|b=1,E]|=(p^2+1)^{-n}\cdot\mathsf{Adv}_{3.q.t}.$$

Step 2. We assume the values $(z_i)_{i\in[n]}$ sent by $\mathcal{B}^\star$ are consistent, that is, they don't make the game end and return a random bit, and Finalize on b' does not return a random bit independent of b' (call E' this event).
We show that games $G^\star_{3.q.2}$ and $G^\star_{3.q.3}$ are identically distributed, conditioned on E'. To prove it, we use the fact that the two following distributions are identical, for any choice of γ:

$$(\boldsymbol{s}_i)_{i\in[n],z_i=(x_i^0,x_i^1)} \text{ and } \left(\boldsymbol{s}_i+\boldsymbol{a}^\perp\cdot\gamma(x_i^b-x_i^0)\right)_{i\in[n],z_i=(x_i^0,x_i^1)},$$

where $\boldsymbol{a}^\perp := \binom{-a}{1} \in \mathbb{Z}_p^2$ and $\boldsymbol{s}_i \xleftarrow{\$} \mathbb{Z}_p^2$, for all $i=1,\ldots,n$. This is true since the $\boldsymbol{s}_i$ are independent of the z_i (note that this is true because we are in a selective setting, while this would not necessarily be true with adaptive QEncrypt-queries). Thus, we can re-write $\boldsymbol{s}_i$ into $\boldsymbol{s}_i+\boldsymbol{a}^\perp\cdot\gamma(x_i^b-x_i^0)$ without changing the distribution of the game.
We now take a look at where the extra terms $\boldsymbol{a}^\perp\cdot\gamma(x_i^b-x_i^0)$ actually appear in the adversary's view:

- They do not appear in the output of QCorrupt, because we assume event E' holds, which implies that if $z_i \neq \bot$, then i is not queried to QCorrupt or $x_i^1 = x_i^0$.
- They might appear in QDKeyGen($\boldsymbol{y}$) as

$$\mathsf{dk}_{\boldsymbol{y}} = \sum_{i\in[n]} \boldsymbol{s}_i\cdot y_i + \boldsymbol{a}^\perp\cdot\gamma\textstyle\sum_{i:z_i=(x_i^0,x_i^1)} y_i(x_i^b-x_i^0).$$

But the gray term equals $\mathbf{0}$ by the constraints for E' in Definition 2: for all $i\in\mathcal{HS}$, $z_i\neq\bot$; if $i\in\mathcal{CS}$ and $z_i\neq\bot$, $x_i^1=x_i^0$; and $f(\boldsymbol{x}^0)=f(\boldsymbol{x}^1)$, hence $\sum_{i:z_i=(x_i^0,x_i^1)} y_i(x_i^b-x_i^0)=0$.
- Eventually, they appear in the output of the QEncrypt-queries which use $[\boldsymbol{u}_\ell]$ computed on the q-th RO-query, since for all others, the vector $[\boldsymbol{u}_\ell]$ lies in the span of $[\boldsymbol{a}]$, and $\boldsymbol{a}^\top\boldsymbol{a}^\perp=0$. We thus have $[c_i]:=[\boldsymbol{u}_\ell^\top]\cdot\boldsymbol{s}_i+(x_i^b-x_i^0)\gamma[\boldsymbol{u}_\ell^\top]\boldsymbol{a}^\perp+[x_i^b]$. Since $\boldsymbol{u}_\ell^\top\boldsymbol{a}^\perp\neq0$, we can choose $\gamma=-1/\boldsymbol{u}_\ell^\top\boldsymbol{a}^\perp \bmod p$, and then $[c_i]=[\boldsymbol{u}_\ell^\top]\cdot\boldsymbol{s}_i+[x_i^0]$, which is the encryption of x_i^0. We stress that

γ is independent of the index i, and so this simultaneously converts all the encryptions of x_i^b into encryptions of x_i^0. Finally, reverting these statistically perfect changes, we obtain that $[c_i]$ is identically distributed to $[\boldsymbol{u}_\ell^\top] \cdot \boldsymbol{s}_i + [x_i^0]$, as in game $G^\star_{3.q.3}$.

Thus, when event E' happens, the games are identically distributed. When $\neg E$ happens, the games both return $\beta \stackrel{\$}{\leftarrow} \{0,1\}$: $\mathsf{Adv}^\star_{3.q.2}(\mathcal{B}^\star) = \mathsf{Adv}^\star_{3.q.3}(\mathcal{B}^\star)$. As a conclusion, we get $\mathsf{Adv}_{3.q.2} = \mathsf{Adv}_{3.q.3}$.

$G_{3.q.3} \rightsquigarrow G_{3.q+1.1}$: This transition is the reverse of $G_{3.q.1} \rightsquigarrow G_{3.q.2}$, namely, we use the DDH assumption to switch back the distribution of $[\boldsymbol{u}_\ell]$ computed on the q-th RO-query from uniformly random over $\mathbb{G}^2$ (conditioned on the fact that $\boldsymbol{u}_\ell^\top \boldsymbol{a}^\perp \neq 0$) to uniformly random in the span of $[\boldsymbol{a}]$: $\mathsf{Adv}_{3.q.3} - \mathsf{Adv}_{3.q+1.1} \leq \mathsf{Adv}^{\mathsf{ddh}}_{\mathbb{G}}(t) + 1/p$.

As a conclusion, since $G_{3.Q+1.1} = G_3$, we have $\mathsf{Adv}_2 - \mathsf{Adv}_3 \leq 2Q(\mathsf{Adv}^{\mathsf{ddh}}_{\mathbb{G}}(t) + 1/p)$. In addition, $\mathsf{Adv}_3 = 0$, which concludes the proof.

5 A Statically-Secure DMCFE for Inner Product

Overview of the Scheme. Our construction of MCFE for inner product uses functional decryption keys $\mathsf{dk}_{\boldsymbol{y}} = (\boldsymbol{y}, \langle \boldsymbol{s}, \boldsymbol{y}\rangle) = (\boldsymbol{y}, \boldsymbol{d})$, where $\boldsymbol{d} = \langle \boldsymbol{s}, \boldsymbol{y}\rangle = \sum_i s_i y_i = \langle \boldsymbol{t}, \boldsymbol{1}\rangle$, with $t_i = s_i y_i$, for $i = 1, \ldots, n$, and $\boldsymbol{1} = (1, \ldots, 1)$. Hence, one can split $\mathsf{msk} = \boldsymbol{s}$ into $\mathsf{msk}_i = s_i$, define $T(\mathsf{msk}_i, \boldsymbol{y}) = t_i = s_i y_i$ and $F(\boldsymbol{t}) = \langle \boldsymbol{t}, \boldsymbol{1}\rangle$. We could thus wish to use the above generic construction from the introduction with our MCFE for inner product, that is self-enabling, to describe a DMCFE for inner product. However, this is not straightforward as our MCFE only allows small results for the function evaluations, since a discrete logarithm has to be computed. While, for real-life applications, it might be reasonable to assume the plaintexts and any evaluations on them are small enough, it is impossible to recover such a large scalar as $\boldsymbol{d} = \langle \boldsymbol{s}, \boldsymbol{y}\rangle$, which comes up when we use our scheme to encrypt encryption keys.

Nevertheless, following this idea we can overcome the concern above with pairings: One can only recover $[\boldsymbol{d}]$, but using a pairing $e : \mathbb{G}_1 \times \mathbb{G}_2 \to \mathbb{G}_T$, one can use our MCFE in both $\mathbb{G}_1$ and $\mathbb{G}_2$. This allows us to compute the functional decryption in $\mathbb{G}_T$, to get $[\langle \boldsymbol{x}, \boldsymbol{y}\rangle]_T$, which is decryptable as $\langle \boldsymbol{x}, \boldsymbol{y}\rangle$ is small enough.

5.1 Construction

Let us describe the new construction, using an asymmetric pairing group, as in Sect. 3.1.

- $\mathsf{SetUp}(\lambda)$: Generates $\mathcal{PG} := (\mathbb{G}_1, \mathbb{G}_2, p, P_1, P_2, e) \stackrel{\$}{\leftarrow} \mathsf{PGGen}(1^\lambda)$. Samples two full-domain hash functions $\mathcal{H}_1$ and $\mathcal{H}_2$ onto $\mathbb{G}_1^2$ and $\mathbb{G}_2^2$ respectively. Each sender $\mathcal{S}_i$ generates $\boldsymbol{s}_i \stackrel{\$}{\leftarrow} \mathbb{Z}_p^2$ for all $i \in [n]$, and interactively generates $\mathbf{T}_i \stackrel{\$}{\leftarrow} \mathbb{Z}_p^{2\times 2}$ such that $\sum_{i\in[n]} \mathbf{T}_i = \mathbf{0}$. One then sets $\mathsf{mpk} \leftarrow (\mathcal{PG}, \mathcal{H}_1, \mathcal{H}_2)$, and for $i = 1, \ldots, n$, $\mathsf{ek}_i = \boldsymbol{s}_i$, $\mathsf{sk}_i = (\boldsymbol{s}_i, \mathbf{T}_i)$;

- $\mathsf{Encrypt}(\mathsf{ek}_i, x_i, \ell)$: Takes as input the value x_i to encrypt, under the key $\mathsf{ek}_i = \boldsymbol{s}_i$ and the label ℓ. It computes $[\boldsymbol{u}_\ell]_1 := \mathcal{H}_1(\ell) \in \mathbb{G}_1^2$, and outputs the ciphertext $[c_i]_1 = [\boldsymbol{u}_\ell^\top \boldsymbol{s}_i + x_i]_1 \in \mathbb{G}_1$;
- $\mathsf{DKeyGenShare}(\mathsf{sk}_i, \boldsymbol{y})$: on input $\boldsymbol{y} \in \mathbb{Z}_p^n$ that defines the function $f_{\boldsymbol{y}}(\boldsymbol{x}) = \langle \boldsymbol{x}, \boldsymbol{y} \rangle$, and the secret key $\mathsf{sk}_i = (\boldsymbol{s}_i, \mathbf{T}_i)$, it computes $[\boldsymbol{v}_{\boldsymbol{y}}]_2 := \mathcal{H}_2(\boldsymbol{y}) \in \mathbb{G}_2^2$, $[\boldsymbol{d}_i]_2 := [y_i \cdot \boldsymbol{s}_i + \mathbf{T}_i \boldsymbol{v}_{\boldsymbol{y}}]_2$, and returns the partial decryption key as $\mathsf{dk}_{\boldsymbol{y},i} := ([\boldsymbol{d}_i]_2)$.
- $\mathsf{DKeyComb}((\mathsf{dk}_{\boldsymbol{y},i})_{i \in [n]}, \boldsymbol{y})$: the partial decryption keys $(\mathsf{dk}_{\boldsymbol{y},i} = ([\boldsymbol{d}_i]_2))_{i \in [n]}$, lead to $\mathsf{dk}_{\boldsymbol{y}} := (\boldsymbol{y}, [\boldsymbol{d}]_2)$, where $[\boldsymbol{d}]_2 = \sum_{i \in [n]} [\boldsymbol{d}_i]_2$;
- $\mathsf{Decrypt}(\mathsf{dk}_{\boldsymbol{y}}, \ell, ([c_i]_1)_{i \in [n]})$: on input the decryption key $\mathsf{dk}_{\boldsymbol{y}} = [\boldsymbol{d}]_2$, the label ℓ, and ciphertexts $([c_i]_1)_{i \in [n]}$, it computes $[\alpha]_T := \sum_{i \in [n]} e([c_i]_1, [y_i]_2) - e([\boldsymbol{u}_\ell]_1^\top, [\boldsymbol{d}]_2)$, and eventually solve the discrete logarithm in basis $[1]_T$ to extract and return α.

Correctness: Let $\boldsymbol{x}, \boldsymbol{y} \in \mathbb{Z}_p^n$, we have:

$$\begin{aligned}[\boldsymbol{d}]_2 &= \sum_{i \in [n]} [\boldsymbol{d}_i]_2 = \sum_{i \in [n]} [y_i \cdot \boldsymbol{s}_i + \mathbf{T}_i \boldsymbol{v}_{\boldsymbol{y}}]_2 \\ &= [\sum_{i \in [n]} y_i \cdot \boldsymbol{s}_i]_2 + [\boldsymbol{v}_{\boldsymbol{y}}]_2 \cdot \sum_{i \in [n]} \mathbf{T}_i = [\sum_{i \in [n]} y_i \cdot \boldsymbol{s}_i]_2.\end{aligned}$$

Thus:

$$\begin{aligned}[\alpha]_T &:= \sum_{i \in [n]} e([c_i]_1, [y_i]_2) - e([\boldsymbol{u}_\ell]_1^\top, [\boldsymbol{d}]_2) \\ &= \sum_i [(\boldsymbol{u}_\ell^\top \boldsymbol{s}_i + x_i) y_i]_T - [\sum_{i \in [n]} y_i \boldsymbol{u}_\ell^\top \boldsymbol{s}_i]_T = [\sum_i x_i y_i]_T.\end{aligned}$$

5.2 Security Analysis

Theorem 9 (sta-IND-Security). *The above DMCFE protocol (see Sect. 5.1) is* sta-IND *secure under the SXDH assumption, in the random oracle model. Namely, for any PTT adversary $\mathcal{A}$, there exist PPT adversaries $\mathcal{B}_1$ and $\mathcal{B}_2$ such that:*

$$\begin{aligned}\mathsf{Adv}^{\mathit{IND}}(\mathcal{A}) \leq\ & 2Q_1 \cdot \mathsf{Adv}^{\mathit{ddh}}_{\mathbb{G}_1}(t) + 2Q_2 \cdot \mathsf{Adv}^{\mathit{ddh}}_{\mathbb{G}_2}(t) + \frac{2Q_1 + 2Q_2}{p} \\ & + \mathsf{Adv}^{\mathit{ddh}}_{\mathbb{G}_1}(t + 4Q_1 \times t_{\mathbb{G}_1}) + 2 \cdot \mathsf{Adv}^{\mathit{ddh}}_{\mathbb{G}_2}(t + 4Q_2 \times t_{\mathbb{G}_2}),\end{aligned}$$

where Q_1 and Q_2 are the number of (direct and indirect) queries to $\mathcal{H}_1$ and $\mathcal{H}_2$ respectively (modeled as random oracles). The former being asked by QEncrypt-*queries and the latter being asked by* QDKeyGen-*queries.*

We stress that this Theorem supports adaptive encryption queries, but static corruptions only.

Proof. We proceed using hybrid games, described in Fig. 5, with similar notations as in the previous proof.

Game G_0: This is the sta-IND-security game as given in Definition 5, but with the set $\mathcal{CS}$ of corrupted senders known from the beginning. Note that the hash functions $\mathcal{H}_1$ and $\mathcal{H}_2$ are modeled as random oracles. The former is used to generate $[\boldsymbol{u}_\ell]_1 := \mathcal{H}_1(\ell) \in \mathbb{G}_1^2$ and the latter $[\boldsymbol{v_y}]_2 := \mathcal{H}_2(\boldsymbol{y}) \in \mathbb{G}_2^2$.

Game G_1: We replace the hash function $\mathcal{H}_2$ by a random oracle RO_2 that generates random pairs from $\mathbb{G}_2^2$ on the fly. In addition, for any QDKeyGen-query on a corrupted index $i \in \mathcal{CS}$, one generates the partial functional decryption key by itself, without explicitly querying QDKeyGen. Hence, we can assume that $\mathcal{A}$ does not query QCorrupt and QDKeyGen on the same indices $i \in [n]$. The simulation remains perfect, and so $\mathsf{Adv}_0 = \mathsf{Adv}_1$.

Game G_2: Now, the outputs of RO_2 are uniformly random in the span of $[\boldsymbol{b}]_2$ for $\boldsymbol{b} := \binom{1}{a'}$, with $a' \xleftarrow{\$} \mathbb{Z}_p$. As in the previous proof, we have $\mathsf{Adv}_1 - \mathsf{Adv}_2 \leq \mathsf{Adv}_{\mathbb{G}_2}^{\mathsf{ddh}}(t + 4Q_2 \times t_{\mathbb{G}_2})$, where Q_2 is the number of RO_2-queries and $t_{\mathbb{G}_2}$ the time for an exponentiation.

Game G_3: We replace all the partial key decryption answers by $\mathsf{dk}_{\boldsymbol{y},i} := [y_i \cdot \boldsymbol{s}_i + \boldsymbol{w}_i \cdot (\boldsymbol{b}^\perp)^\top \boldsymbol{v_y} + \mathbf{T}_i \boldsymbol{v_y}]_2$, for new $\boldsymbol{w}_i \xleftarrow{\$} \mathbb{Z}_p^2$, such that $\sum_i \boldsymbol{w}_i = \mathbf{0}$, for each $\boldsymbol{y}$. We show below that $\mathsf{Adv}_2 = \mathsf{Adv}_3$.

Game G_4: We switch back the distribution of all the vectors $[\boldsymbol{v_y}]_2$ output by RO_2, from uniformly random in the span of $[\boldsymbol{b}]_2$, to uniformly random over $\mathbb{G}_2^2$, thus back to $\mathcal{H}_2(\boldsymbol{y})$. This transition is reverse to the two first transitions of this proof: $\mathsf{Adv}_3 - \mathsf{Adv}_4 \leq \mathsf{Adv}_{\mathbb{G}_2}^{\mathsf{ddh}}(t + 4Q_2 \times t_{\mathbb{G}_2})$.

In order to prove the gap between G_2 and G_3, we do a new hybrid proof:

Game $G_{3.1.1}$: This is exactly game G_2. Thus, $\mathsf{Adv}_2 = \mathsf{Adv}_{3.1.1}$.

$G_{3.q.1} \rightsquigarrow G_{3.q.2}$: As in the previous proof, we first change the distribution of the output of the q-th RO_2-query, from uniformly random in the span of $[\boldsymbol{b}]$ to uniformly random over $\mathbb{G}^2$, using the DDH assumption. Then, we use the basis $(\binom{1}{a'}, \binom{-a'}{1})$ of $\mathbb{Z}_p^2$, to write a uniformly random vector over $\mathbb{Z}_p^2$ as $v_1 \cdot \boldsymbol{b} + v_2 \cdot \boldsymbol{b}^\perp$, where $v_1, v_2 \xleftarrow{\$} \mathbb{Z}_p$. Finally, we switch to $v_1 \cdot \boldsymbol{b} + v_2 \cdot \boldsymbol{b}^\perp$ where $v_1 \xleftarrow{\$} \mathbb{Z}_p$, and $v_2 \xleftarrow{\$} \mathbb{Z}_p^*$, which only changes the adversary view by a statistical distance of $1/p$: $\mathsf{Adv}_{3.q.1} - \mathsf{Adv}_{3.q.2} \leq \mathsf{Adv}_{\mathbb{G}}^{\mathsf{ddh}}(t) + 1/p$. The last step with $v_2 \in \mathbb{Z}_p^*$ will be important to guarantee that $\boldsymbol{v_y}^\top \boldsymbol{b}^\perp \neq 0$.

$G_{3.q.2} \rightsquigarrow G_{3.q.3}$: We now change the simulation of $\mathsf{dk}_{\boldsymbol{y},i}$ from $\mathsf{dk}_{\boldsymbol{y},i} = [y_i \cdot \boldsymbol{s}_i + \mathbf{T}_i \boldsymbol{v_y}]_2$ to $\mathsf{dk}_{\boldsymbol{y},i} = [y_i \cdot \boldsymbol{s}_i + \mathsf{RF}_i(\boldsymbol{y}) + \mathbf{T}_i \boldsymbol{v_y}]_2$, with some RF_i functions onto $\mathbb{Z}_p^2$ such that $\sum_i \mathsf{RF}_i(\boldsymbol{y}) = 0$ for any input $\boldsymbol{y}$. We prove $\mathsf{Adv}_{3.q.2} = \mathsf{Adv}_{3.q.3}$. To this aim, we use the fact that the two following distributions are identical, for any choice of $\boldsymbol{w}_i \xleftarrow{\$} \mathbb{Z}_p^2$, such that $\sum_i \boldsymbol{w}_i = \mathbf{0}$:

$$(\mathbf{T}_i)_{i \in \mathcal{HS}} \text{ and } (\mathbf{T}_i + \boldsymbol{w}_i (\boldsymbol{b}^\perp)^\top)_{i \in \mathcal{HS}},$$

where for all $i \in [n]$, $\mathbf{T}_i \xleftarrow{\$} \mathbb{Z}_p^{2\times 2}$ such that $\sum_i \mathbf{T}_i = \mathbf{0}$, and $\boldsymbol{b}^\perp := \binom{-a'}{1}$. The extra terms $(\boldsymbol{w}_i (\boldsymbol{b}^\perp)^\top)_{i \in \mathcal{HS}}$ only appear in the output of the queries to QDKeyGen which use the vector $[\boldsymbol{v_y}]_2$ computed on the q-th RO_2-query (if

Games G_0, G_1, $\boxed{G_2, (G_{3.q.1})_{q\in[Q_{dk}+1]}, \boxed{(G_{3.q.2}, G_{3.q.3})_{q\in[Q_{dk}]}}}$, G_4

$\mathcal{PG} \leftarrow \mathsf{PGGen}(1^\lambda)$, $\forall i \in [n]$: $\boldsymbol{s}_i \xleftarrow{\$} \mathbb{Z}_p^2$, $\mathbf{T}_i \xleftarrow{\$} \mathbb{Z}_p^{2\times 2}$, such that $\sum_{i\in[n]} \mathbf{T}_i = \mathbf{0}$
$\mathsf{ek}_i := \boldsymbol{s}_i$, $\mathsf{sk}_i := (\boldsymbol{s}_i, \mathbf{T}_i)$, $\mathsf{mpk} := (\mathbb{G}, p, g)$.
$\boxed{a' \xleftarrow{\$} \mathbb{Z}_p, \boldsymbol{b} := \binom{1}{a'}}$
Sample full-domain hash functions $\mathcal{H}_1$ onto $\mathbb{G}_1^2$ and $\mathcal{H}_2$ onto $\mathbb{G}_2^2$.
Sample a bit $b \xleftarrow{\$} \{0,1\}$.
$b' \leftarrow \mathcal{A}^{\mathsf{QEncrypt}(\cdot,\cdot,\cdot,\cdot),\mathsf{QDKeyGen}(\cdot,\cdot),\mathsf{QCorrupt}(\cdot),\mathsf{RO}_1(\cdot),\mathsf{RO}_2(\cdot)}(\mathsf{mpk})$.
Run Finalize on b'.

$\mathsf{RO}_1(\ell)$: // G_0, G_1, G_2, $G_{3.q.1}$, $G_{3.q.2}$, $G_{3.q.3}$
Return $\mathcal{H}_1(\ell)$.

$\mathsf{RO}_2(\boldsymbol{y})$: // G_0, $\boxed{G_1}$ (dotted), $\boxed{G_2, G_{3.q.1}, \boxed{G_{3.q.2}, G_{3.q.3}}}$, G_4
$[\boldsymbol{v_y}]_2 := \mathcal{H}_2(\boldsymbol{y})$, $\boxed{[\boldsymbol{v_y}]_2 := \mathsf{RF}(\boldsymbol{y})}$ (dotted), $\boxed{[\boldsymbol{v_y}]_2 := [\boldsymbol{b} \cdot t_{\boldsymbol{y}}]_2, \text{ with } t_{\boldsymbol{y}} := \mathsf{RF}'(\boldsymbol{y})}$
$\boxed{\text{On the } q\text{-th } \mathsf{RO}_2\text{-query: } [\boldsymbol{v_y}]_2 := \mathsf{RF}(\boldsymbol{y})}$ (gray)
Return $[\boldsymbol{v_y}]_2$.

$\mathsf{QEncrypt}(i, x_i^0, x_i^1, \ell)$: // G_0, G_1, G_2, $G_{3.q.1}$, $G_{3.q.2}$, $G_{3.q.3}$, G_4
$[\boldsymbol{u}_\ell]_1 := \mathsf{RO}_1(\ell)$,
$[c_i]_1 := [\boldsymbol{u}_\ell^\top]_1 \cdot \boldsymbol{s}_i + [x_i^b]_1$
Return $[c_i]$

$\mathsf{QDKeyGen}(\boldsymbol{y}, i)$: // G_0, G_1, G_2, $\boxed{G_{3.q.1}, G_{3.q.2}, \boxed{G_{3.q.3}}}$, $\boxed{G_4}$ (dotted)
Compute $[\boldsymbol{v_y}]_2 := \mathsf{RO}_2(\boldsymbol{y})$, $\mathsf{dk}_{\boldsymbol{y},i} := [y_i \cdot \boldsymbol{s}_i + \mathbf{T}_i \boldsymbol{v_y}]_2$, set $\mathcal{S} := \mathcal{S} \cup \{i\}$.
$\boxed{\text{If } [\boldsymbol{v_y}]_2 \text{ is computed on the } j\text{-th } \mathsf{RO}_2\text{-query, for } j < q\text{: } \mathsf{dk}_{\boldsymbol{y},i} := [y_i \cdot \boldsymbol{s}_i + \mathsf{RF}_i(\boldsymbol{y}) + \mathbf{T}_i \boldsymbol{v_y}]_2.}$
$\boxed{\text{If } [\boldsymbol{v_y}]_2 \text{ is computed on the } q\text{-th } \mathsf{RO}_2\text{-query: } \mathsf{dk}_{\boldsymbol{y},i} := [y_i \cdot \boldsymbol{s}_i + \mathsf{RF}_i(\boldsymbol{y}) + \mathbf{T}_i \boldsymbol{v_y}]_2.}$ (gray)
$\boxed{\mathsf{dk}_{\boldsymbol{y},i} := [y_i \cdot \boldsymbol{s}_i + \mathsf{RF}_i(\boldsymbol{y}) + \mathbf{T}_i \boldsymbol{v_y}]_2.}$ (dotted)
Return $\mathsf{dk}_{\boldsymbol{y},i}$.

$\mathsf{QCorrupt}(i)$: Return $(\boldsymbol{s}_i, \mathbf{T}_i)$. // G_0, G_1, G_2, $G_{3.q.1}$, $G_{3.q.2}$, $G_{3.q.3}$, G_4

Fig. 5. Games for the proof of Theorem 9. Here, RF, RF' are random functions onto $\mathbb{G}_2^2$ and $\mathbb{Z}_p$, respectively, that are computed on the fly. The RF_i are random functions conditioned on the fact that $\sum_{i\in[n]} \mathsf{RF}_i$ is the zero function. In each procedure, the components inside a solid (dotted, gray) frame are only present in the games marked by a solid (dotted, gray) frame. The Finalize procedure is defined as in Definition 5

there are such queries), because for all other queries, $[\boldsymbol{v_y}]_2$ lies in the span of $[\boldsymbol{b}]_2$, and $\boldsymbol{b}^\top \boldsymbol{b}^\perp = 0$. We thus have $\mathsf{dk}_{\boldsymbol{y},i} := [y_i \cdot \boldsymbol{s}_i + \boldsymbol{w}_i \cdot (\boldsymbol{b}^\perp)^\top \boldsymbol{v_y} + \mathbf{T}_i \boldsymbol{v_y}]_2$. Since $\boldsymbol{v_y}$ is such that $\boldsymbol{v_y}^\top \boldsymbol{b}^\perp \neq 0$, $(\boldsymbol{b}^\perp)^\top \boldsymbol{v_y} \neq 0$. In that case, the vectors

$\boldsymbol{w}_i \cdot (\boldsymbol{b}^\perp)^\top \boldsymbol{v}_{\boldsymbol{y}}$ are uniformly random over $\mathbb{Z}_p^2$ such that $\sum_i \boldsymbol{w}_i \cdot (\boldsymbol{b}^\perp)^\top \boldsymbol{v}_{\boldsymbol{y}} = \mathbf{0}$, which is as in $G_{3.q.3}$, by setting $\mathsf{RF}_i(\boldsymbol{y}) := \boldsymbol{w}_i \cdot (\boldsymbol{b}^\perp)^\top \boldsymbol{v}_{\boldsymbol{y}}$.

$G_{3.q.3} \rightsquigarrow G_{3.q+1.1}$: This transition is the reverse of $G_{3.q.1} \rightsquigarrow G_{3.q.2}$, namely, we use the DDH assumption to switch back the distribution of $[\boldsymbol{v}_{\boldsymbol{y}}]_2$ to uniformly random in the span of $[\boldsymbol{b}]_2$: $\mathsf{Adv}_{3.q.3} - \mathsf{Adv}_{3.q+1.1} \leq \mathsf{Adv}_{\mathbb{G}_2}^{\mathsf{ddh}}(t) + 1/p$.

Then one can note that $G_{3.Q_2+1.1} = G_3$, but also that in Game G_4, all the $\mathsf{dk}_{\boldsymbol{y},i}$ output by QDKeyGen can be computed only knowing $\sum_{i\in[n]} \boldsymbol{s}_i \cdot y_i$, which is exactly the functional decryption key $\mathsf{dk}_{\boldsymbol{y}}$ from our MCFE in Sect. 4.1. This follows from the fact that the values $\mathsf{RF}_i(\boldsymbol{y})$ perfectly mask the vectors $\boldsymbol{s}_i \cdot y_i$, up to revealing $\sum_{i\in[n]} \boldsymbol{s}_i \cdot y_i$ (as the RF_i must sum up to the zero function). Thus, we can reduce to the IND-security of the MCFE from Sect. 4.1 (or even sta-IND-security) by designing an adversary $\mathcal{B}$ against the MCFE from Sect. 4.1: Adversary $\mathcal{B}$ first samples $\mathbf{T}_i \xleftarrow{\$} \mathbb{Z}_p^{2\times 2}$ for all $i \in [n]$, such that $\sum_{i\in[n]} \mathbf{T}_i = \mathbf{0}$. It sends $\mathcal{CS}$ given by $\mathcal{A}$ (set of static corruptions), then it receives mpk from the MCFE security game, as well as the secret keys $\boldsymbol{s}_i$ for $i \in \mathcal{CS}$. It forwards mpk as well as $(\boldsymbol{s}_i, \mathbf{T}_i)$ for $i \in \mathcal{CS}$ to $\mathcal{A}$. Then

- $\mathcal{B}$ answers oracle calls to RO_1, RO_2 and QEncrypt from $\mathcal{A}$ using its own oracles.
- To answer QDKeyGen$(i, \boldsymbol{y})$: if i is the last non-corrupted index for $\boldsymbol{y}$, $\mathcal{B}$ queries its own QDKeyGen oracle on $\boldsymbol{y}$, to get $\mathsf{dk}_{\boldsymbol{y}} := \sum_i \boldsymbol{s}_i \cdot y_i \in \mathbb{Z}_p^2$, computes $[\boldsymbol{v}_{\boldsymbol{y}}]_2 := \mathcal{H}_2(\boldsymbol{y})$, and returns $\mathsf{dk}_{\boldsymbol{y},i} := [\mathsf{dk}_{\boldsymbol{y}} + \mathsf{RF}_i(\boldsymbol{y}) + \mathbf{T}_i \boldsymbol{v}_{\boldsymbol{y}}]_2$ to $\mathcal{A}$. Otherwise, it computes $[\boldsymbol{v}_{\boldsymbol{y}}]_2 := \mathcal{H}_2(\boldsymbol{y})$, and returns $\mathsf{dk}_{\boldsymbol{y},i} := [\mathsf{RF}_i(\boldsymbol{y}) + \mathbf{T}_i \boldsymbol{v}_{\boldsymbol{y}}]_2$ to $\mathcal{A}$. The random functions RF_i are computed on the fly, such that their sum is the zero function.

We stress that this last simulation requires to know $\mathcal{CS}$ and $\mathcal{HS}$, hence static corruptions only. From this reduction, one gets

$$\mathsf{Adv}_4 \leq 2Q_1 \cdot \mathsf{Adv}_{\mathbb{G}_1}^{\mathsf{ddh}}(t) + \mathsf{Adv}_{\mathbb{G}_1}^{\mathsf{ddh}}(t + 4Q_1 \times t_{\mathbb{G}_1}) + \frac{2Q_1}{p},$$

where Q_1 denotes the number of calls to RO_1, $t_{\mathbb{G}_1}$ denotes the time to compute an exponentiation in $\mathbb{G}_1$. This concludes the proof.

6 Conclusion

Multi-Client Functional Encryption and Decentralized Cryptosystems are invaluable tools for many emerging applications such as cloud services or big data. These applications often involve many parties who contribute their data to enable the extraction of knowledge, while protecting their individual privacy with minimal trust in the other parties, including any central authority. We make an important step towards combining the desired functionalities and properties by introducing the notion of Decentralized Multi-Client Functional Encryption. It opens some interesting directions:

- For inner-product, in the DDH-based setting with ElGamal-like encryption, we have a strong restriction on the plaintexts, since the inner-product has to be small, in order to allow complete decryption of the scalar evaluation. It is an interesting problem to consider whether the LWE-based and DCR-based schemes can address this issue.
- Getting all the desired properties, namely efficiency, new functionalities and the strongest security level, is a challenging problem. One of the main challenges is to construct an efficient, non-interactive DMCFE which is fully secure (adaptive encryptions and adaptive corruptions), for a larger class of functions than that of inner-product functions. The security analyses of our concrete constructions heavily rely on the linear properties of inner-product functions, however, the global methodology of the constructions themselves is not restricted to the inner-product setting. Therefore, new constructions could follow it.

Acknowledgments. This work was supported in part by the European Community's Seventh Framework Programme (FP7/2007-2013 Grant Agreement no. 339563 – CryptoCloud), the European Community's Horizon 2020 Project FENTEC (Grant Agreement no. 780108), the Google PhD fellowship, the ANR ALAMBIC (ANR16-CE39-0006) and the French FUI ANBLIC Project.

A Multi DDH Assumption

Theorem 10. *For any distinguisher $\mathcal{A}$ running within time t, the best advantage $\mathcal{A}$ can get in distinguishing*

$$\mathcal{D}_m = \{(X, (Y_j, Z_j = \mathsf{CDH}(X, Y_j))_j) \mid X, Y_j \xleftarrow{\$} \mathbb{G}, j = 1, \ldots, m\}$$
$$\mathcal{D}'_m = \{(X, (Y_j, Z_j)_j) \mid X, Y_j, Z_j \xleftarrow{\$} \mathbb{G}, j = 1, \ldots, m\}.$$

is bounded by $\mathsf{Adv}^{\mathsf{ddh}}(t + 4m \times t_{\mathbb{G}})$*, where* $t_{\mathbb{G}}$ *is the time for an exponentiation in* $\mathbb{G}$.

Proof. One can first note that the best advantage one can get, within time t, between

$$\mathcal{D} = \{(X, Y, Z = \mathsf{CDH}(X, Y)) \mid X, Y \xleftarrow{\$} \mathbb{G}\}$$
$$\mathcal{D}' = \{(X, Y, Z) \mid X, Y, Z \xleftarrow{\$} \mathbb{G}\}.$$

is bounded by $\mathsf{Adv}^{\mathsf{ddh}}(t)$. This is actually the DDH assumption. One can note that $\mathcal{D}_m$ and $\mathcal{D}'_m$ can be rewritten as

$$\mathcal{D}_m = \{(X, (Y_j = g^{u_j} Y^{v_j}, Z_j = X^{u_j} \cdot \mathsf{CDH}(X, Y)^{v_j})_j) \mid X, Y \xleftarrow{\$} \mathbb{G}, u_j, v_j \xleftarrow{\$} \mathbb{Z}_p\}$$
$$\mathcal{D}'_m = \{(X, (Y_j = g^{u_j} Y^{v_j}, Z_j = X^{u_j} \cdot Z^{v_j})_j) \mid X, Y, Z \xleftarrow{\$} \mathbb{G}, u_j, v_j \xleftarrow{\$} \mathbb{Z}_p\},$$

Since, from (X, Y, Z), the m tuples require 4 additional exponentiations per index j, one get the expected bound.

B A Selectively-Secure MCFE

B.1 Description

In this section, we formally present the selectively secure MCFE scheme for inner product we described in Sect. 1. It is inspired by Abdalla *et al.*'s scheme [1]:

- SetUp(λ): Takes as input the security parameter, and generates a group $\mathbb{G}$ of prime order $p \approx 2^\lambda$, $g \in \mathbb{G}$ a generator, and $\mathcal{H}$ a full-domain hash function onto $\mathbb{G}$. It also generates the encryption keys $s_i \xleftarrow{\$} \mathbb{Z}_p$, for $i = 1, \ldots, n$, and sets $\boldsymbol{s} = (s_i)_i$. The public parameters mpk consist of $(\mathbb{G}, p, g, \mathcal{H})$, while the master secret key is $\mathsf{msk} = \boldsymbol{s}$ and the encryption keys are $\mathsf{ek}_i = s_i$ for $i = 1, \ldots, n$ (in addition to mpk, which is omitted);
- Encrypt(ek_i, x_i, ℓ): Takes as input the value x_i to encrypt, under the key $\mathsf{ek}_i = s_i$ and the label ℓ. It computes $[u_\ell] := \mathcal{H}(\ell) \in \mathbb{G}$, and outputs the ciphertext $[c_i] = [u_\ell s_i + x_i] \in \mathbb{G}$;
- DKeyGen(msk, $\boldsymbol{y}$): Takes as input $\mathsf{msk} = (s_i)_i$ and an inner-product function defined by $\boldsymbol{y}$ as $f_{\boldsymbol{y}}(\boldsymbol{x}) = \langle \boldsymbol{x}, \boldsymbol{y} \rangle$, and outputs the functional decryption key $\mathsf{dk}_{\boldsymbol{y}} = (\boldsymbol{y}, \sum_i s_i y_i) \in \mathbb{Z}_p^n \times \mathbb{Z}_p$;
- Decrypt($\mathsf{dk}_{\boldsymbol{y}}, \ell, ([c_i])_{i \in [n]}$): Takes as input a decryption key $\mathsf{dk}_{\boldsymbol{y}} = (\boldsymbol{y}, d)$, a label ℓ. It computes $[u_\ell] := \mathcal{H}(\ell)$, $[\alpha] = \sum_i y_i \cdot [c_i] - d \cdot [u_\ell]$, and eventually solves the discrete logarithm to extract and return α.

As for Abdalla *et al.*'s scheme [1], the result α should not be too large to allow the final discrete logarithm computation.

Correctness: if the scalar dk in the decryption functional key $\mathsf{dk}_{\boldsymbol{y}} = (\boldsymbol{y}, dk)$ is indeed $dk = \langle \boldsymbol{s}, \boldsymbol{y} \rangle$, then

$$\begin{aligned} [\alpha] &= \sum_i y_i \cdot [c_i] - d \cdot [u_\ell] = \sum_i y_i \cdot [u_\ell s_i + x_i] - [u_\ell] \cdot \sum_i s_i y_i \\ &= [u_\ell] \cdot \sum_i s_i y_i + [\sum_i x_i y_i] - [u_\ell] \cdot \sum_i s_i y_i = [\sum_i x_i y_i]. \end{aligned}$$

B.2 Selective Security

Like Abdalla *et al.*'s original scheme [1], our protocol can only be proven secure in the weaker security model, where the adversary has to commit in advance to all of the pairs of messages for the Left-or-Right encryption oracle (QEncrypt-queries). However, it can adaptively ask for functional decryption keys (QDKeyGen-queries) and encryption keys (QCorrupt-queries). Concretely, the challenger is provided (plaintext,label) pairs: $(x_{j,i}^b, \ell_j)_{b \in \{0,1\}, i \in [n], j \in [Q]}$, where Q is the number of query to QEncrypt$(i, \cdot, \cdot)$, each one for a different label ℓ_j (note that in the security model, we assume each slots are queried the same number of time, on different labels). The challenge ciphertexts $C_{i,j} = \mathsf{Encrypt}(\mathsf{ek}_i, x_{j,i}^b, \ell_j)$, for the random bit b, are returned to the adversary.

Note that the adversary committing to challenge ciphertexts also limits its ability to corrupt users during the game: it must corrupt clients for which it didn't ask a ciphertext and cannot corrupt any client from which it asked a ciphertext for $x_{j,i}^0 \neq x_{j,i}^1$.

B.3 Security Analysis

Theorem 11 (sel-IND Security). *The MCFE protocol described above (see Appendix B.1) is* sel-IND *secure under the DDH assumption, in the random oracle model. More precisely, we have*

$$\mathsf{Adv}^{IND}(\mathcal{A}) \leq 2Q \cdot \mathsf{Adv}^{ddh}_{\mathbb{G}}(t),$$

for any adversary $\mathcal{A}$, running within time t, where Q is the number of encryption queries per slot.

Games G_0, G_1, $(G_{2.q})_{q\in[Q+1]}$

$(\mathsf{state}, (\ell_j, z_{j,i})_{i\in[n],j\in[Q]}) \leftarrow \mathcal{A}(1^\lambda, 1^n)$
where each $z_{j,i} = (x^0_{j,i}, x^1_{j,i}) \in \mathbb{Z}_p^2$, or $z_{j,i} = \perp$, which stands for no query.
$\mathcal{G} \leftarrow \mathsf{GGen}(1^\lambda)$, for all $i \in [n]$, $s_i \stackrel{\$}{\leftarrow} \mathbb{Z}_p$,$\mathsf{ek}_i := s_i$, $\mathsf{msk} := (s_i)_i$, $\mathsf{mpk} := (\mathbb{G}, p, g)$.
$C_{j,i} = \mathsf{QEncrypt}(i, x^0_{j,i}, x^1_{j,i}, \ell_j)$ for $i \in [n], j \in [Q]$ such that $z_{j,i} = (x^0_{j,i}, x^1_{j,i})$.
$b' \leftarrow \mathcal{A}^{\mathsf{QDKeyGen}(\cdot),\mathsf{QCorrupt}(\cdot),\mathsf{RO}(\cdot)}(\mathsf{mpk}, \mathsf{state})$.
Run Finalize on b'.

$\mathsf{RO}(\ell)$: // G_0, $\boxed{G_1, G_{2.q}}$

$[u_\ell] := \mathcal{H}(\ell)$, $\boxed{[u_\ell] := \mathsf{RF}(\ell)}$.
Return $[u_\ell]$.

$\mathsf{QEncrypt}(i, x^0_i, x^1_i, \ell)$: // G_0, G_1, $\boxed{G_{2.q}}$

$[u_\ell] := \mathsf{RO}(\ell)$,
$[c_i] := [u_\ell] \cdot s_i + [x^b_i]$
$\boxed{\text{If } \ell = \ell_j \text{ with } j < q\text{: } [c_i] := [u_\ell s_i + x^0_i]}$
Return $[c_i]$.

$\mathsf{QDKeyGen}(\boldsymbol{y})$: // G_0, G_1, $G_{2.q}$

Return $\sum_i y_i s_i$.

$\mathsf{QCorrupt}(i)$: // G_0, G_1, $G_{2.q}$

Return s_i.

Fig. 6. Games G_0, G_1, $(G_{2.})_{q\in[Q+1]}$, for the proof of Theorem 11. Here, RF is a random function onto $\mathbb{G}$, that is computed on the fly. Note that QEncrypt is only used as a subroutine of the initialization of the game and is not accessible to the adversary. In each procedure, the components inside a solid frame are only present in the games marked by a solid frame.

Proof. We proceed using hybrid games, described in Fig. 6, with the same notations as in the previous proofs.

Game G_0: This is the sel-IND security game as given in Definition 2 (see the paragraph about weaker models), with all the encryption queries being sent first: they are stored in $z_{j,i} = (x^0_{j,i}, x^1_{j,i})$, for $j \in [Q]$ and $i \in [n]$, where j is for the j-th $\mathcal{H}$-query that specifies the label ℓ_j and i is for the index of the sender. If the query is not asked, we have $z_{j,i} = \perp$. Note that the hash function $\mathcal{H}$ is modeled as a random oracle RO onto $\mathbb{G}$. This is used to generate $[u_\ell] = \mathcal{H}(\ell)$.

Game G_1: We simulate the answers to any new RO query by computing a truly random element of $\mathbb{G}$, on the fly. The simulation remains perfect, so $\mathsf{Adv}_0 = \mathsf{Adv}_1$.

Game G_2: We simulate every encryption as the encryption of x^0_i instead of x^b_i.

While it is clear that in this last game the advantage of any adversary is exactly 0 since b does not appear anywhere, the gap between G_1 and G_2 will be proven using an hybrid argument on the RO-queries. We thus index the following games by q, where $q = 1, \ldots, Q$. Note that only distinct RO-queries are counted, since a second similar query is answered as the first one.

$G_{2.1}$: This is exactly game G_1. Thus, $\mathsf{Adv}_1 = \mathsf{Adv}_{2.1}$.

$G_{2.q} \rightsquigarrow G_{2.q+1}$: We change the generation of the ciphertexts from $[c_{q,i}] := [u_{\ell_q} s_i + x^b_{q,i}]$ to $[c_{q,i}] := [u_{\ell_q} s_i + x^0_{q,i}]$. We proceed in three steps:

Step 1. We use the fact that the two following distributions are identical, for any choice of γ:

$$(s_i)_{i \in [n], z_{q,i} = (x^0_{q,i}, x^b_{q,i})} \text{ and } \left(s_i + \gamma(x^0_{q,i} - x^b_{q,i})\right)_{i \in [n], z_{q,i} = (x^0_{q,i}, x^1_{q,i})},$$

where $s_i \xleftarrow{\$} \mathbb{Z}_p$, for all $i \in [n]$. This is true since the s_i are independent of the $z_{q,i}$ (we are in a selective setting, so the s_i's are generated after the $z_{q,i}$'s have been chosen). Thus, we can re-write s_i into $s_i + \gamma(x^0_{q,i} - x^b_{q,i})$ without changing the distribution of the game.

Note that when Finalize does not output a random bit $\beta \xleftarrow{\$} \{0,1\}$ independent of the guess b', γ does not appear in the outputs of $\mathsf{QCorrupt}(i)$, since it must be that $x^0_i = x^1_i$ or $z_{q,i} = \perp$, and it does not appear in the output of $\mathsf{QDKeyGen}(\boldsymbol{y})$ either, since $\sum_i s_i \cdot y_i + \sum_i \gamma(x^0_{q,i} - x^b_{q,i}) y_i$, where the gray term equals zero by Definition 1. The fact that γ does not appear in the outputs of these oracles will be crucial for step 2, which applies DDH on $[\gamma]$.

Step 2. We use the DDH assumption to replace the $[u_{\ell_q} \gamma]$ that appear in the output of the q-th query to $\mathsf{QEncrypt}$ queries with $[r_{\ell_q} + 1]$ with $r_{\ell_q} \xleftarrow{\$} \mathbb{Z}_p$. This is possible since the rest of the adversary view can be generated only from $[\gamma]$ and $[r_{\ell_q} + 1]$. This increases the adversary's advantage by no more than $\mathsf{Adv}^{\mathsf{ddh}}_{\mathbb{G}}(t)$. We now have:

$$\begin{aligned}[c_{q,i}] :=& [u_{\ell_q} s_i + (x^0_{q,i} - x^b_{q,i})(r_{\ell_q} + 1) + x^b_{q,i}] \\ =& [u_{\ell_q} s_i + r_{\ell_q}(x^0_{q,i} - x^b_{q,i}) + x^0_{q,i} - x^b_{q,i} + x^b_{q,i}] \\ =& [u_{\ell_q} s_i + r_{\ell_q}(x^0_{q,i} - x^b_{q,i}) + x^0_{q,i}].\end{aligned}$$

Step 3. We switch $[r_{\ell_q}]$ in the output of the q-query to $\mathsf{QEncrypt}$ back to $[u_{\ell_q} \gamma]$, using the DDH assumption again. This is possible since the adversary's view is simulatable solely from $[\gamma]$, $[u_{\ell_q}]$, and $[r_{\ell_q}]$. We finally undo the distribution change on the s_i, which brings us to $G_{2.q+1}$.

As a conclusion, since $G_{2.Q+1} = G_2$, we have $\mathsf{Adv}_1 - \mathsf{Adv}_2 \leq 2Q \cdot \mathsf{Adv}_{\mathbb{G}}^{\mathsf{ddh}}(t)$. In addition, $\mathsf{Adv}_2 = 0$, which concludes the proof.

References

1. Abdalla, M., Bourse, F., De Caro, A., Pointcheval, D.: Simple functional encryption schemes for inner products. In: Katz, J. (ed.) PKC 2015. LNCS, vol. 9020, pp. 733–751. Springer, Heidelberg (2015). https://doi.org/10.1007/978-3-662-46447-2_33
2. Abdalla, M., Catalano, D., Fiore, D., Gay, R., Ursu, B.: Multi-input functional encryption for inner products: function-hiding realizations and constructions without pairings. In: Shacham, H., Boldyreva, A. (eds.) CRYPTO 2018, part I. LNCS, vol. 10991, pp. 597–627. Springer, Cham (2018). https://doi.org/10.1007/978-3-319-96884-1_20
3. Abdalla, M., Gay, R., Raykova, M., Wee, H.: Multi-input inner-product functional encryption from pairings. In: Coron, J.-S., Nielsen, J.B. (eds.) EUROCRYPT 2017, part I. LNCS, vol. 10210, pp. 601–626. Springer, Cham (2017). https://doi.org/10.1007/978-3-319-56620-7_21
4. Agrawal, S., Libert, B., Stehlé, D.: Fully secure functional encryption for inner products, from standard assumptions. In: Robshaw, M., Katz, J. (eds.) CRYPTO 2016, part III. LNCS, vol. 9816, pp. 333–362. Springer, Heidelberg (2016). https://doi.org/10.1007/978-3-662-53015-3_12
5. Ananth, P., Brakerski, Z., Segev, G., Vaikuntanathan, V.: From selective to adaptive security in functional encryption. In: Gennaro, R., Robshaw, M.J.B. (eds.) CRYPTO 2015, part II. LNCS, vol. 9216, pp. 657–677. Springer, Heidelberg (2015). https://doi.org/10.1007/978-3-662-48000-7_32
6. Badrinarayanan, S., Goyal, V., Jain, A., Sahai, A.: Verifiable functional encryption. In: Cheon, J.H., Takagi, T. (eds.) ASIACRYPT 2016, part II. LNCS, vol. 10032, pp. 557–587. Springer, Heidelberg (2016). https://doi.org/10.1007/978-3-662-53890-6_19
7. Bellare, M., Desai, A., Jokipii, E., Rogaway, P.: A concrete security treatment of symmetric encryption. In: 38th FOCS, pp. 394–403. IEEE Computer Society Press, October 1997
8. Benhamouda, F., Joye, M., Libert, B.: A new framework for privacy-preserving aggregation of time-series data. ACM Trans. Inf. Syst. Secur. **18**(3), 10:1–10:21 (2016)
9. Boneh, D., Sahai, A., Waters, B.: Functional encryption: definitions and challenges. In: Ishai, Y. (ed.) TCC 2011. LNCS, vol. 6597, pp. 253–273. Springer, Heidelberg (2011). https://doi.org/10.1007/978-3-642-19571-6_16
10. Brakerski, Z., Komargodski, I., Segev, G.: Multi-input functional encryption in the private-key setting: stronger security from weaker assumptions. In: Fischlin, M., Coron, J.-S. (eds.) EUROCRYPT 2016, part II. LNCS, vol. 9666, pp. 852–880. Springer, Heidelberg (2016). https://doi.org/10.1007/978-3-662-49896-5_30
11. Chan, T.-H.H., Shi, E., Song, D.: Privacy-preserving stream aggregation with fault tolerance. In: Keromytis, A.D. (ed.) FC 2012. LNCS, vol. 7397, pp. 200–214. Springer, Heidelberg (2012). https://doi.org/10.1007/978-3-642-32946-3_15
12. Datta, P., Okamoto, T., Tomida, J.: Full-hiding (unbounded) multi-input inner product functional encryption from the k-linear assumption. In: Abdalla, M., Dahab, R. (eds.) PKC 2018, part II. LNCS, vol. 10770, pp. 245–277. Springer, Cham (2018). https://doi.org/10.1007/978-3-319-76581-5_9

13. Emura, K.: Privacy-preserving aggregation of time-series data with public verifiability from simple assumptions. In: Pieprzyk, J., Suriadi, S. (eds.) ACISP 2017. LNCS, vol. 10343, pp. 193–213. Springer, Cham (2017). https://doi.org/10.1007/978-3-319-59870-3_11
14. Escala, A., Herold, G., Kiltz, E., Ràfols, C., Villar, J.: An algebraic framework for diffie-hellman assumptions. In: Canetti, R., Garay, J.A. (eds.) CRYPTO 2013, part II. LNCS, vol. 8043, pp. 129–147. Springer, Heidelberg (2013). https://doi.org/10.1007/978-3-642-40084-1_8
15. Garg, S., Gentry, C., Halevi, S., Raykova, M., Sahai, A., Waters, B.: Candidate indistinguishability obfuscation and functional encryption for all circuits. In: 54th FOCS, pp. 40–49. IEEE Computer Society Press, October 2013
16. Goldwasser, S., et al.: Multi-input functional encryption. In: Nguyen, P.Q., Oswald, E. (eds.) EUROCRYPT 2014. LNCS, vol. 8441, pp. 578–602. Springer, Heidelberg (2014). https://doi.org/10.1007/978-3-642-55220-5_32
17. Goldwasser, S., Kalai, Y.T., Popa, R.A., Vaikuntanathan, V., Zeldovich, N.: How to run turing machines on encrypted data. In: Canetti, R., Garay, J.A. (eds.) CRYPTO 2013, part II. LNCS, vol. 8043, pp. 536–553. Springer, Heidelberg (2013). https://doi.org/10.1007/978-3-642-40084-1_30
18. Goldwasser, S., Kalai, Y.T., Popa, R.A., Vaikuntanathan, V., Zeldovich, N.: Reusable garbled circuits and succinct functional encryption. In: Boneh, D., Roughgarden, T., Feigenbaum, J. (eds.) 45th ACM STOC, pp. 555–564. ACM Press, June 2013
19. Gorbunov, S., Vaikuntanathan, V., Wee, H.: Functional encryption with bounded collusions via multi-party computation. In: Safavi-Naini, R., Canetti, R. (eds.) CRYPTO 2012. LNCS, vol. 7417, pp. 162–179. Springer, Heidelberg (2012). https://doi.org/10.1007/978-3-642-32009-5_11
20. Gordon, S.D., Katz, J., Liu, F.H., Shi, E., Zhou, H.S.: Multi-input functional encryption. Cryptology ePrint Archive, Report 2013/774 (2013). http://eprint.iacr.org/2013/774
21. Joye, M., Libert, B.: A scalable scheme for privacy-preserving aggregation of time-series data. In: Sadeghi, A.-R. (ed.) FC 2013. LNCS, vol. 7859, pp. 111–125. Springer, Heidelberg (2013). https://doi.org/10.1007/978-3-642-39884-1_10
22. Lee, K., Lee, D.H.: Two-input functional encryption for inner products from bilinear maps. IACR Cryptology ePrint Archive 2016, 432 (2016). http://eprint.iacr.org/2016/432
23. Li, Q., Cao, G.: Efficient and privacy-preserving data aggregation in mobile sensing. In: ICNP 2012, pp. 1–10. IEEE Computer Society (2012)
24. Li, Q., Cao, G.: Efficient privacy-preserving stream aggregation in mobile sensing with low aggregation error. In: De Cristofaro, E., Wright, M. (eds.) PETS 2013. LNCS, vol. 7981, pp. 60–81. Springer, Heidelberg (2013). https://doi.org/10.1007/978-3-642-39077-7_4
25. Paillier, P.: Public-key cryptosystems based on composite degree residuosity classes. In: Stern, J. (ed.) EUROCRYPT 1999. LNCS, vol. 1592, pp. 223–238. Springer, Heidelberg (1999). https://doi.org/10.1007/3-540-48910-X_16
26. Regev, O.: On lattices, learning with errors, random linear codes, and cryptography. In: Gabow, H.N., Fagin, R. (eds.) 37th ACM STOC, pp. 84–93. ACM Press, May 2005
27. Sahai, A., Seyalioglu, H.: Worry-free encryption: functional encryption with public keys. In: Al-Shaer, E., Keromytis, A.D., Shmatikov, V. (eds.) ACM CCS 2010, pp. 463–472. ACM Press, October 2010

28. Sahai, A., Waters, B.R.: Fuzzy identity-based encryption. In: Cramer, R. (ed.) EUROCRYPT 2005. LNCS, vol. 3494, pp. 457–473. Springer, Heidelberg (2005). https://doi.org/10.1007/11426639_27
29. Shi, E., Chan, T.H.H., Rieffel, E.G., Chow, R., Song, D.: Privacy-preserving aggregation of time-series data. In: NDSS 2011. The Internet Society, February 2011
30. Waters, B.: A punctured programming approach to adaptively secure functional encryption. In: Gennaro, R., Robshaw, M. (eds.) CRYPTO 2015, part II. LNCS, vol. 9216, pp. 678–697. Springer, Heidelberg (2015). https://doi.org/10.1007/978-3-662-48000-7_33
31. Wee, H.: Dual system encryption via predicate encodings. In: Lindell, Y. (ed.) TCC 2014. LNCS, vol. 8349, pp. 616–637. Springer, Heidelberg (2014). https://doi.org/10.1007/978-3-642-54242-8_26

Practical Fully Secure Unrestricted Inner Product Functional Encryption Modulo p

Guilhem Castagnos[1](✉), Fabien Laguillaumie[2], and Ida Tucker[2]

[1] Université de Bordeaux, Inria, CNRS, IMB UMR 5251, 33405 Talence, France
guilhem.castagnos@math.u-bordeaux.fr

[2] Univ Lyon, CNRS, Université Claude Bernard Lyon 1, ENS de Lyon, Inria, LIP UMR 5668, 69007 Lyon Cedex 07, France
{fabien.laguillaumie,ida.tucker}@ens-lyon.fr

Abstract. Functional encryption (FE) is a modern public-key cryptographic primitive allowing an encryptor to finely control the information revealed to recipients from a given ciphertext. Abdalla, Bourse, De Caro, and Pointcheval (PKC 2015) were the first to consider FE restricted to the class of linear functions, i.e. inner products. Though their schemes are only secure in the *selective* model, Agrawal, Libert, and Stehlé (CRYPTO 16) soon provided *adaptively* secure schemes for the same functionality. These constructions, which rely on standard assumptions such as the Decision Diffie-Hellman (DDH), the Learning-with-Errors (LWE), and Paillier's Decision Composite Residuosity (DCR) problems, do however suffer of various practical drawbacks. Namely, the DCR based scheme only computes inner products modulo an RSA integer which is oversized for many practical applications, while the computation of inner products modulo a prime p either requires, for their DDH based scheme, that the inner product be contained in a sufficiently small interval for decryption to be efficient, or, as in the LWE based scheme, suffers of poor efficiency due to impractical parameters.

In this paper, we provide adaptively secure FE schemes for the inner product functionality which are both efficient and allow for the evaluation of unbounded inner products modulo a prime p. Our constructions rely on new natural cryptographic assumptions in a cyclic group containing a subgroup where the discrete logarithm (DL) problem is easy which extend Castagnos and Laguillaumie's assumption (RSA 2015) of a DDH group with an easy DL subgroup. Instantiating our generic constructions using class groups of imaginary quadratic fields gives rise to the most efficient FE for inner products modulo an arbitrary large prime p. One of our schemes outperforms the DCR variant of Agrawal *et al.*'s protocols in terms of size of keys and ciphertexts by factors varying between 2 and 20 for a 112-bit security.

Keywords: Inner product functional encryption · Adaptive security Diffie-Hellman assumptions

T. Peyrin and S. Galbraith (Eds.): ASIACRYPT 2018, LNCS 11273, pp. 733–764, 2018.
https://doi.org/10.1007/978-3-030-03329-3_25

1 Introduction

Traditional public key encryption (PKE) provides an all-or-nothing approach to data access. This somewhat restricting property implies that a receiver can either recover the entire message with the appropriate secret key, or learns nothing about the encrypted message. In many real life applications however, the encryptor may wish for a more subtle encryption primitive, allowing him to disclose distinct and restricted information on the encrypted data according to the receivers privileges. For instance, in a cloud-based email service, users may want the cloud to perform spam filtering on their encrypted emails but learn nothing more about the contents of these emails. Here the cloud should only learn one bit indicating whether or not the message is spam, but nothing more.

Functional encryption (FE) [BSW11, O'N10] emerged from a series of refinements of PKE, starting with identity based encryption [Sha84], which was later extended to fuzzy identity-based encryption by Sahai and Waters [SW05]. This work also introduced attribute-based encryption, where a message is encrypted for all users that have a certain set of attributes. FE encompasses all three of these primitives, and goes further still, as it allows not only to devise policies regulating which users can decrypt, but also provides control over which piece or function of the data each user can recover. Specifically, FE allows for a receiver to recover a function $f(y)$ of the encrypted message y, without learning anything else about y. The primitive requires a trusted authority, which possesses a master secret key msk, to deliver secret keys sk_{f_i} – associated to specific functionalities f_i – to the appropriate recipients. The encryptor computes a single ciphertext associated to the plaintext $c = \mathsf{Encrypt}(y)$, from which any user, given a decryption key sk_{f_i}, can recover $f_i(y) = \mathsf{Decrypt}(sk_i, c)$.

There exist two main security definitions for FE, indistinguishability-based and a stronger simulation-based security. The former – which is the model we adopt throughout this paper – requires that no efficient adversary, having chosen plaintext messages y_0 and y_1, can guess, given the encryption of one of these, which is the underlying message with probability significantly greater than 1/2. The adversary can query a key derivation oracle for functionalities f, with the restriction that $f(y_0) = f(y_1)$, otherwise one could trivially tell apart both ciphertexts. Though constructions for general FE have been put forth, these schemes are far from practical, and only allow the adversary to request an a priori bounded number of secret keys [GKP+13b, SS10], or rely on non-standard and ill-understood cryptographic assumptions such as indistinguishability obfuscation or multilinear maps [ABSV15, BGJS16, GKP+13a, GVW12, Wat15, GGHZ16].

The problem thus arose of building efficient FE schemes for restricted classes of functions; such constructions could be of great use for many practical applications, while developing our understanding of FE.

Inner Product Functional Encryption (IPFE). The restriction of FE to linear functions, i.e. the inner product functionality yields many interesting applications. Among other uses, linear functions allow for the computation of weighted averages and sums, useful for statistical analysis on encrypted data, where the statistical analysis itself has sensitive information. As mentioned by Katz, Sahai and Waters [KSW08], another application is the evaluation of polynomials over encrypted data. Agrawal, Libert and Stehlé [ALS16, Sect. 6] motivate FE for computing linear functions modulo a prime p by demonstrating that such a scheme can be turned into a bounded collusion FE scheme for all circuits[1]. And as a final example, Agrawal, Bhattacherjee, Phan, Stehlé and Yamada provide a generic transformation from FE for linear functions to trace-and-revoke systems in [ABP+17]. As they are performing linear algebra, their transformation requires the modulus to be prime and preferably quite large (~128 or 256 bits).

The primitive can succinctly be defined as follows: plaintexts are vectors $\boldsymbol{y} \in \mathcal{R}^\ell$, where $\mathcal{R}$ is a ring. Function specific secret keys $sk_{\boldsymbol{x}}$ are derived from vectors $\boldsymbol{x} \in \mathcal{R}^\ell$ and allow to recover $\langle \boldsymbol{y}, \boldsymbol{x} \rangle \in \mathcal{R}$ but reveal no further information about $\boldsymbol{y}$. It is worth noting that due to the linearity of inner products, if the adversary requests decryption keys derived from independent vectors $\boldsymbol{x}_i$ for $i \in \{1, \ldots, \ell\}$, it can recover $\boldsymbol{y}$ by resolving a simple system of linear equations resulting from $\langle \boldsymbol{y}, \boldsymbol{x}_i \rangle$ for $i \in \{1, \ldots, \ell\}$.

This specific line of research was initiated by Abdalla, Bourse, De Caro and Pointcheval in 2015 [ABDP15]. They provided the first IPFE schemes which rely on standard assumptions such as learning with errors (LWE) and decision Diffie Hellman (DDH). However their schemes are only *selectively* secure, i.e. the adversary must commit to challenge messages before having access to the schemes' public parameters. Though of great theoretical interest, such schemes are not sufficiently secure for practical applications, indeed selective security is often considered a first step towards proving full *adaptive security*. The first fully secure schemes were put forth by Agrawal et al. [ALS16] under the LWE, DDH and Paillier's Decision Composite Residuosity (DCR, *cf.* [Pai99]) assumptions. Abdalla *et al.* in [ABCP16] also put forth an adaptively secure generic construction and provide instantiations from the DDH, DCR and LWE assumptions. However, their instantiation from Elgamal gives the same construction as the DDH based scheme of [ALS16], and their obtained schemes from LWE are restricted to the computation of inner products over the integers $\mathbf{Z}$, and are less efficient than those of [ALS16]. Finally Benhamouda *et al.* [BBL17,Bou17] provided generic constructions from hash proof systems to both chosen plaintext and chosen ciphertext secure IPFE schemes. The resulting schemes are again restricted to the computation of inner products over the integers $\mathbf{Z}$ and the sizes of secret keys are larger than those of [ALS16] (see details at the end of this introduction).

These brilliant developments do however still suffer of practical drawbacks. Namely the computation of inner products modulo a prime p are restricted, in that they require that the inner product $\langle \boldsymbol{y}, \boldsymbol{x} \rangle$ be small for decryption to be efficient (as is the case for the schemes of [ABDP15], [ABCP16], and the DDH

[1] We note however that this application of linear FE modulo a prime p can not be instantiated with our schemes, as we require p to be at least a 112-bit prime, whereas this application typically calls for small values of p (e.g. $p = 2$).

based scheme of [ALS16]). To our knowledge, the only scheme that allows for decryption of inner products of any size modulo a prime p is the LWE based scheme of [ALS16], which suffers of poor efficiency since the modulus should be exponentially large in the dimension of encrypted vectors while the size of ciphertexts is cubic in this dimension.

Our Contributions. In this paper we put forth IPFE schemes which resolve the aforementioned issue. Our constructions compute inner products over the integers and modulo a prime p, and rely on novel cryptographic assumptions defined in Sect. 3.1. These are variants of the [CL15] assumption, which supposes the existence of a DDH *group with an easy* DL *subgroup*: a cyclic group $G = \langle g \rangle$ where the DDH assumption holds together with a subgroup $F = \langle f \rangle$ of G where the discrete logarithm (DL) problem is easy.

The first assumption we introduce relies on a *hard subgroup membership* (HSM) problem (according to Gjøsteen's terminology [Gjø05]), and somewhat generalises Paillier's DCR assumption, which follows a long line of assumptions of distinguishing powers in $\mathbf{Z}/N\mathbf{Z}$. Known attacks for these require computing the groups' order which reduces to factoring N. In the [CL15] framework, the group G is cyclic of order ps where s is unknown and $\gcd(p, s) = 1$. We denote $G^p = \langle g_p \rangle$ the subgroup of p−th powers in G. In this setting one has $G = F \times G^p$. The assumption is that it is hard to distinguish the elements of G^p in G.

We then define the DDH-f assumption, which is *weaker* than both the DDH assumption of [CL15], and the aforementioned HSM assumption. Denoting $\mathcal{D}$ a distribution statistically close to the uniform distribution modulo ps, this assumption states that it is hard to distinguish distributions $\{(g^x, g^y, g^{xy}), x, y \hookleftarrow \mathcal{D}\}$ (i.e. Diffie-Hellman triplets in G) and $\{(g^x, g^y, g^{xy} f^u), x, y \hookleftarrow \mathcal{D}, u \hookleftarrow \mathbf{Z}/p\mathbf{Z}\}$. We prove this assumption is *equivalent* to the semantic security of the generic CL homomorphic encryption scheme of [CL15], an Elgamal variant in G where messages are encoded in the exponent in the subgroup F. In fact, the DDH-f assumption is better suited to mask elements of F, thus providing clearer proofs.

These new assumptions allow us to construct generic, linearly homomorphic encryption schemes over $\mathbf{Z}/p\mathbf{Z}$ which are semantically secure under chosen plaintext attacks (ind-cpa), which we call HSM-CL and Modified CL (*cf.* Sect. 3.2). The reductions between their semantic security and the underlying assumptions are given in Fig. 1, where $A \to B$ indicates that assumption B holds if assumption A holds, i.e. A is a stronger assumption than B.

We then use the homomorphic properties of the above schemes to construct generic IPFE schemes over the integers and over $\mathbf{Z}/p\mathbf{Z}$, both from the weaker DDH-f assumption in Sect. 4, and from the HSM assumption in Sect. 5, somewhat generalising the scheme based on DCR of [ALS16]. Since the inner product is encoded in the exponent in the subgroup F, it can efficiently be recovered, whatever its size. We thereby present the first IPFE schemes which are both efficient and recover $\langle \boldsymbol{y}, \boldsymbol{x} \rangle \mod p$ whatever its size.

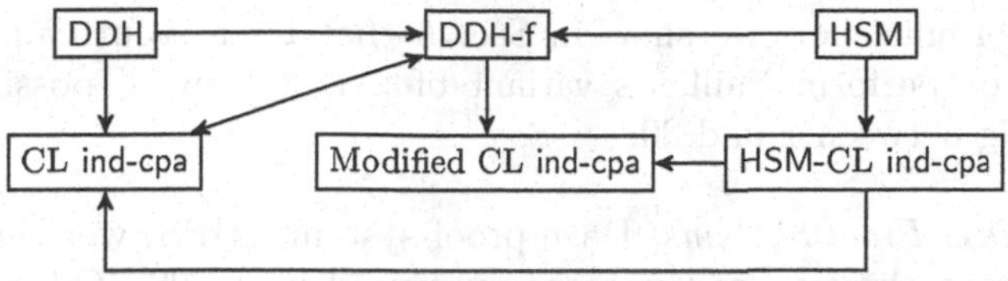

Fig. 1. Reductions between assumptions and ind-cpa security of CL variants

Our security proofs for the HSM based schemes follow a similar logic to those of [ALS16], analysing the entropy loss that occurs via queried keys, and demonstrating that there is enough residual entropy left for the challenge ciphertext to appear uniform to the adversary. However, significant difficulties occur for the schemes arising from the weaker DDH-f assumption. As in the DDH based scheme of [ALS16], we use a variant of Elgamal *à la* Cramer-Shoup. But unlike previous uses of this approach, the order of our group is unknown *and* may have small factors, so with constant probability an element may not be a generator. This calls for various subtleties: any element of the group can not be masked, however, if p is large enough, elements of the subgroup F of order p can be.

Moreover, in order to handle the information given by private key queries, instead of computing the global distribution of the master secret keys, we carefully simplify the description of the adversary's view, since merely restricting the adversary's view modulo p could potentially result in a loss of information.

We note that for our schemes over $\mathbf{Z}/p\mathbf{Z}$, vectors $\boldsymbol{x}_i$ from which keys are derived are in $\mathbf{Z}/p\mathbf{Z}$, whereas decryption keys are computed in $\mathbf{Z}$, so a lift of the $\boldsymbol{x}_i$ in $\mathbf{Z}$ must be done. Since lifting does not preserve linear dependencies, it is essential (as in [ALS16]) the key generation algorithm be stateful to lift vectors while maintaining linear dependencies. Without this restriction an adversary could learn a combination of the master key components which is singular modulo p but invertible over $\mathbf{Z}$, thus revealing the whole master key.

To instantiate our generic constructions we use class groups of imaginary quadratic fields. Although the devastating attack from [CL09] eliminates a whole family of protocols built from such groups, this attack applies to schemes whose security is based on factoring a discriminant while here this factorisation is public. Moreover [CL15] showed that designing with care DL based cryptosystems within such groups is still possible and allows for efficient and versatile protocols (*Encryption switching protocols* for instance, *cf.* [CIL17]). The problem of computing a DL in class groups of imaginary quadratic fields has been extensively studied since the 80's, and the complexity of best known subexponential algorithms is[2] $\mathcal{O}(L_{1/2})$ (*cf.* [BJS10]) as opposed to $\mathcal{O}(L_{1/3})$ (*cf.* [Adl94]) for the DL problem in finite field or factoring. In particular this implies that our keys can be chosen shorter and corroborates the above claim that the assumptions on which we rely are indeed weak.

[2] L_α is a shortcut to denote $L_{\alpha,c}(x) = \exp(c \log(x)^\alpha \log(\log(x))^{1-\alpha})$.

In terms of efficiency, we show in Sect. 6 that for a security parameter of $\lambda = 112$ we outperform Paillier's variant of [ALS16] on all possible sizes by factors varying between 2 and 20.

Relation to Hash Proof Systems. Hash proof systems (HPS) were introduced in [CS02] as a generalisation of the techniques used in [CS98]. Consider a set of words $\mathcal{X}$, an NP language $\mathcal{L} \subset \mathcal{X}$ such that $\mathcal{L} = \{x \in \mathcal{X} \mid w : (x, w) \in \mathsf{R}\}$ where R is the relation defining the language, $\mathcal{L}$ is the language of true statements in $\mathcal{X}$, and for $(x, w) \in \mathsf{R}$, w is a witness for $x \in \mathcal{L}$. A HPS defines a key generation algorithm which outputs a secret hashing key hk and a public projection key hp such that hk defines a hash function $\mathcal{H}_{\mathsf{hk}} : \mathcal{X} \mapsto \Pi$, and hp allows for the (public) evaluation of the hash function on words $x \in \mathcal{L}$, i.e. $\mathcal{H}_{\mathsf{hp}}(x, w) = \mathcal{H}_{\mathsf{hk}}(x)$ for $(x, w) \in \mathsf{R}$. The *smoothness* property requires that for any $x \notin \mathcal{L}$, the value $\mathcal{H}_{\mathsf{hk}}(x)$ be uniformly distributed knowing hp.

The DDH and DCR assumptions yield smooth HPSs where the languages $\mathcal{L} \subset \mathcal{X}$ define hard subset membership problems. Such HPSs, endowed with homomorphic properties over the key space, underly the IPFE schemes of [ALS16]. In fact Benhamouda, Bourse, and Lipmaa in [BBL17, Bou17], present a generic construction from a key homomorphic HPS (satisfying various properties) to an IPFE scheme in $\mathbf{Z}$ which is secure under chosen plaintext attacks. They instantiate it from DDH and from DCR but leave out LWE due to the complexity of the resulting scheme, as simpler constructions can be attained without using HPSs.

We note that though our constructions resemble the above – one can deduce new subset membership problems from the assumptions in Sect. 3.1 and associated HPSs – our proof techniques are very different to those of [Bou17], to achieve adaptive security, their game challenger must *guess* the difference between challenge ciphertexts prior to generating the public/private key pair. If the hash key is *not* sampled uniformly at random from the key space (as in our constructions), then in order to maintain a level of security equivalent to that of the HPS the size of the secret keys increases substantially. Indeed, to encrypt ℓ-dimensional vectors whose coordinates are bounded by Y, their proof techniques cause an additional $\ell \log(Y)$-bit term to appear in each coordinate of the secret key, whereas in our constructions over $\mathbf{Z}$, the bit length of the coordinates is independent of ℓ. Consequently, this approach leads to less efficient schemes.

Our goal has been to build *practical* IPFE schemes, therefore we avoid this genericity and the key blow up it entails, carefully evaluating the information leaked to the adversary by the public key, the secret key queries and the challenge ciphertext, thus ensuring that the challenge bit remains statistically hidden. This style of proof is closer to those of [ALS16], it allows us to obtain constructions for IPFE over $\mathbf{Z}$ that are substantially more efficient than those of [BBL17, Bou17], and constructions for IPFE modulo a prime p that do not restrict the size of the resulting inner product, which are the most efficient such schemes to date.

2 Background

Notations. We denote sets by uppercase letters, vectors by bold lowercase letters, and $\langle \boldsymbol{x}, \boldsymbol{y} \rangle$ denotes the inner product of vectors $\boldsymbol{x}$ and $\boldsymbol{y}$. For a distribution $\mathcal{D}$, we write $d \hookleftarrow \mathcal{D}$ to refer to d being sampled from $\mathcal{D}$. We overload the notation as $b \hookleftarrow B$ to say that b is sampled uniformaly at random in the set B. For an integer x, we denote its size by $|x|$, and by $[x]$ the set of integers $\{1, \ldots, x\}$. For any $\mathbf{c} \in \mathbf{R}^\ell$, real $\sigma > 0$, and ℓ-dimensional lattice Λ, $\mathcal{D}_{\Lambda,\sigma,\mathbf{c}}$ will denote the usual discrete Gaussian distribution over Λ.

Definition of Inner Product Functional Encryption. This is a special case of functional encryption, as first formalised by Boneh, Sahai and Waters in [BSW11]. To start with, we provide the definition of a *functionality.*

Definition 1 (Functionality). *A functionality F defined over $(\mathcal{K}, \mathcal{Y})$ is a function $F : \mathcal{K} \times \mathcal{Y} \to \Sigma \cup \{\perp\}$, where $\mathcal{K}$ is a key space, $\mathcal{Y}$ is a message space and Σ is an output space, which does not contain the special symbol $\perp$.*

In this article, we consider the inner product functionality, s.t. decrypting the encryption of a vector $\mathbf{y}$ with a key associated to a vector $\mathbf{x}$ only reveals $\langle \mathbf{x}, \mathbf{y} \rangle$. So we consider the function $F : (\mathbf{Z}/p\mathbf{Z})^\ell \times (\mathbf{Z}/p\mathbf{Z})^\ell \to \mathbf{Z}/p\mathbf{Z} \cup \{\perp\}$ s.t. $F(\mathbf{x}, \mathbf{y}) = \langle \mathbf{x}, \mathbf{y} \rangle$. The syntax of a functional encryption scheme is described below.

Definition 2 (Functional encryption scheme). *Let λ be a positive integer. A functional encryption (FE) scheme for a functionality F over $(\mathcal{K}, \mathcal{Y})$ is a tuple* (Setup, KeyDer, Encrypt, Decrypt) *of algorithms with the following specifications:*

- Setup *on input a security parameter 1^λ, outputs a master key pair (mpk, msk);*
- KeyDer *on input the master key msk and a key $K \in \mathcal{K}$, outputs a key sk_K;*
- Encrypt *on input the master public key mpk and a message $Y \in \mathcal{Y}$, outputs a ciphertext C;*
- Decrypt *takes as input the master public key mpk, a key sk_K and a ciphertext C and outputs $v \in \Sigma \cup \{\perp\}$.*

Correctness requires that for all $(mpk, msk) \leftarrow$ Setup(1^λ), all keys $K \in \mathcal{K}$ and all messages $Y \in \mathcal{Y}$, if $sk_K \leftarrow$ KeyDer(msk, K) and $C \leftarrow$ Encrypt(mpk, Y), with overwhelming probability it holds that, if $v \leftarrow$ Decrypt(mpk, sk_K, C) then $v = F(K, Y)$ whenever $F(K, Y) \neq \perp$.

Security. We define below the security notion for FE, which states that given the ciphertext of a message Y, the only information obtained from the secret key sk_K is the evaluation of the function $f(K, Y)$. More precisely, no adversary can distinguish an encryption of Y_0 from an encryption of Y_1 even with the knowledge of secret keys sk_K chosen adaptatively but satisfying $F(K, Y_0) = F(K, Y_1)$. The following definition is that of *adaptive* security, meaning that the adversary has access to the systems' public parameters, and can perform a series of secret key requests *before* choosing Y_0 and Y_1. We consider an indistinguishability-based definition instead of the simulation-based security definition of [BSW11]. This adaptive indistinguishability notion is easier to handle, and it is also the strongest adaptive notion of security that can be achieved for numerous interesting functionalities. In particular, it has been demonstrated in [BSW11, AGVW13, BO13] that the strong simulation-based definition cannot be met in the standard model, while O'Neill showed in [O'N10] that indistinguishability-based security is equivalent to non-adaptive simulation-based security for a class of functions that includes the inner product. Moreover, De Caro *et al.* [DIJ+13] describe a method to transform an FE achieving an indistinguishability-based security notion into an FE attaining a certain simulation-based security.

Definition 3 (Indistinguishability-based security). *A functional encryption scheme* $\mathsf{FE} = (\mathsf{Setup}, \mathsf{KeyDer}, \mathsf{Encrypt}, \mathsf{Decrypt})$ *provides semantic security under chosen-plaintext attacks (*ind-fe-cpa*) if no PPT adversary* $\mathcal{A}$ *has non-negligible advantage* $\mathsf{Adv}_{\mathcal{A}}(\lambda)$*, under the constraints that* $\mathcal{A}$*'s secret-key queries before and after its choice of challenge messages* Y_0 *and* Y_1 *satisfy* $F(K, Y_0) = F(K, Y_1)$ *for all* K *in the set of key queries.* $\mathcal{A}$*'s advantage is defined as:*

$$\mathsf{Adv}_{\mathcal{A}}(\lambda) = \Big| \Pr\big[\beta = \beta' : mpk, msk \leftarrow \mathsf{Setup}(1^\lambda), Y_0, Y_1 \leftarrow \mathcal{A}^{\mathsf{KeyDer}(msk,\cdot)}(mpk),$$
$$\beta \xleftarrow{\$} \{0,1\}, C^\star \leftarrow \mathsf{Encrypt}(mpk, Y_\beta), \beta' \leftarrow \mathcal{A}^{\mathsf{KeyDer}(msk,\cdot)}(C^\star)\big] - \frac{1}{2}\Big|.$$

Backgound on Lattices. We recall some definitions and basic results on Gaussian distributions. These are useful for our security proofs, in which we evaluate the distribution of an inner product when one of the two vectors follows a Gaussian distribution. We also recall a result from [GPV08] giving the conditions for a Gaussian distribution over a lattice, which is reduced modulo a sublattice, to be close to a uniform distribution, another crucial point of our proofs.

Definition 4 (Gaussian Function). *For any* $\sigma > 0$ *define the Gaussian function on* $\mathbf{R}^\ell$ *centred at* $\mathbf{c}$ *with parameter* σ*:* $\forall \boldsymbol{x} \in \mathbf{R}^\ell, \rho_{\sigma,\mathbf{c}}(\boldsymbol{x}) = \exp(-\pi||\boldsymbol{x} - \mathbf{c}||^2/\sigma^2)$*. If* $\sigma = 1$ *(resp.* $\mathbf{c} = \boldsymbol{0}$*), then the subscript* σ *(resp.* $\mathbf{c}$*) is omitted.*

Definition 5 (Discrete Gaussian). *For any* $\mathbf{c} \in \mathbf{R}^\ell$*, real* $\sigma > 0$*, and* ℓ*-dimensional lattice* Λ*, define the discrete Gaussian distribution over* Λ *as:* $\forall \boldsymbol{x} \in \Lambda, \quad \mathcal{D}_{\Lambda,\sigma,\mathbf{c}}(\boldsymbol{x}) = \rho_{\sigma,\mathbf{c}}(\boldsymbol{x})/\rho_{\sigma,\mathbf{c}}(\Lambda)$*, where* $\rho_{\sigma,\mathbf{c}}(\Lambda) = \sum_{\boldsymbol{x}\in\Lambda} \rho_{\sigma,\mathbf{c}}(\boldsymbol{x})$*.*

Lemma 1. *Let* $\boldsymbol{x} \in \mathbf{R}^\ell \setminus \{\boldsymbol{0}\}$*,* $\mathbf{c} \in \mathbf{R}^\ell$*,* $\sigma \in \mathbf{R}$ *with* $\sigma > 0$ *and* $\sigma' = \sigma/||\boldsymbol{x}||_2$*,* $c' = \frac{\langle \mathbf{c}, \boldsymbol{x}\rangle}{\langle \boldsymbol{x}, \boldsymbol{x}\rangle}$*. A random variable* K *is distributed according to* $\mathcal{D}_{\mathbf{Z},\sigma',c'}$ *if and only if* $V := K\boldsymbol{x}$ *is distributed according to* $\mathcal{D}_{\boldsymbol{x}\mathbf{Z},\sigma,\mathbf{c}}$*.*

In dimension 1, Lemma 1 implies that if $x \in \mathbf{R}$, then Kx is distributed according to $\mathcal{D}_{x\mathbf{Z},\sigma,c}$ iff. K is distributed according to $\mathcal{D}_{\mathbf{Z},\sigma/|x|,c/x}$. Lemma 2 gives the distribution of the inner product resulting from a constant vector $\boldsymbol{x}$, and a vector with coordinates sampled from a Gaussian distribution over the lattice $\boldsymbol{x} \cdot \mathbf{Z}$. Please refer to the full version [CLT18, Aux. Material I] for proofs of Lemmas 1 and 2.

Lemma 2. *Let $\boldsymbol{x} \in \mathbf{R}^\ell$ with $\boldsymbol{x} \neq \boldsymbol{0}$, $\mathbf{c} \in \mathbf{R}^\ell$, $\sigma \in \mathbf{R}$ with $\sigma > 0$. Let V be a random variable distributed according to $\mathcal{D}_{\boldsymbol{x}\cdot\mathbf{Z},\sigma,\mathbf{c}}$. Then the random variable S defined as $S = \langle \boldsymbol{x}, V \rangle$ is distributed according to $\mathcal{D}_{||\boldsymbol{x}||_2^2\cdot\mathbf{Z},\sigma\cdot||\boldsymbol{x}||_2,\langle c,\boldsymbol{x}\rangle}$.*

Lemma 3 ([GPV08]). *Let $\Lambda_0' \subset \Lambda_0 \subset \mathbf{R}^\ell$ be two lattices with the same dimension. Let $\epsilon \in (0, 1/2)$ and $\eta_\epsilon(\Lambda_0')$ be the* smoothing parameter *of Λ_0' (cf. [MR04]). Then for any $c \in \mathbf{R}^\ell$ and any $\sigma \geq \eta_\epsilon(\Lambda_0')$, the distribution $D_{\Lambda_0,\sigma,c}$ mod Λ_0' is within statistical distance 2ϵ from the uniform distribution over Λ_0/Λ_0'.*

3 Variants of CL: Assumptions and ind-cpa Schemes

In [CL15], Castagnos and Laguillaumie introduced the framework of a DDH *group with an easy* DL *subgroup*: a cyclic group G where the DDH assumption holds along with a subgroup F of G where the DL problem is easy. Within this framework, they designed a linearly homomorphic variant of Elgamal [CL15], denoted CL. Moreover, they gave an instantiation using class groups of quadratic fields allowing for the computation of linear operations modulo a prime p.

Their protocol is similar to the one of Bresson *et. al.* [BCP03] whose ind-cpa security relies on the DDH assumption in $(\mathbf{Z}/N^2\mathbf{Z})^\times$, where $N = pq$, using the arithmetic ideas of Paillier's encryption [Pai99]. Another encryption scheme based on Elgamal over $(\mathbf{Z}/N^2\mathbf{Z})^\times$ was proposed by Camenisch and Shoup in [CS03]. Its ind-cpa security relies on the Decision Composite Residuosity assumption (DCR), which consists in distinguishing the $N-$th powers in $(\mathbf{Z}/N^2\mathbf{Z})^\times$.

In the following subsection, we recall the framework of [CL15] and then generalise the DCR assumption to fit this framework of a DDH *group with an easy* DL *subgroup* with a hard subgroup membership problem (following [Gjø05]'s terminology). We also introduce a new DDH-like assumption which is weaker than the original DDH in G. Then, in Subsect. 3.2, we give generic encryption schemes whose ind-cpa security are based on these assumptions. In particular we give a generalisation of the scheme of [CS03] in a DDH *group with an easy* DL *subgroup*, and a modification of CL *à la* Cramer-Shoup. Finally, in Subsect. 3.3, we discuss the relations between these assumptions.

3.1 Algorithmic Assumptions

We first define the generator GenGroup used in the framework of a DDH group with an easy DL subgroup [CL15], with a few modifications as discussed below.

Definition 6 (Generator for a DDH group with an easy DL subgroup). *Let* GenGroup *be a pair of algorithms* (Gen, Solve). *The* Gen *algorithm is a group generator which takes as inputs two parameters λ and μ and outputs a tuple $(p, \tilde{s}, g, f, g_p, G, F, G^p)$. The set $(G, \cdot)$ is a cyclic group of order ps where s is an integer, p is a μ-bit prime, and $\gcd(p, s) = 1$. The algorithm* Gen *only outputs an upper bound $\tilde{s}$ of s. The set $G^p = \{x^p, x \in G\}$ is the subgroup of order s of G, and F is the subgroup of order p of G, so that $G = F \times G^p$. The algorithm*

Gen *outputs* f, g_p *and* $g = f \cdot g_p$ *which are respective generators of* F, G^p *and* G. *Moreover, the* DL *problem is easy in* F, *which means that the* Solve *algorithm is a deterministic polynomial time algorithm that solves the* DL *problem in* F:

$$\Pr\big[x = x^\star : (p, \tilde{s}, g, f, g_p, G, F, G^p) \leftarrow \mathsf{Gen}(1^\lambda, 1^\mu), x \hookleftarrow \mathbf{Z}_p, X = f^x,$$
$$x^\star \leftarrow \mathsf{Solve}(p, \tilde{s}, g, f, g_p, G, F, G^p, X)\big] = 1.$$

Remark 1. In practice the size of s is chosen so that computing discrete logarithms in G^p takes time $\mathcal{O}(2^\lambda)$.

We note that this definition differs slightly from the original definition of [CL15]. Here F is of prime order p as our agenda is to use the instantiation with class groups of quadratic fields so as to have $\mathbf{Z}/p\mathbf{Z}$ as the message space. This means that our generic constructions do not encompass the schemes built from Paillier where the message space is $\mathbf{Z}/N\mathbf{Z}$, with $N = pq$. If using $N = pq$ as the order of F, the proofs must rely on factoring assumptions to deal with the non-zero non-invertible elements of $\mathbf{Z}/N\mathbf{Z}$. Consequently, this restriction simplifies the proofs, since an element of $\mathbf{Z}/p\mathbf{Z}$ is invertible if and only if it is non-zero.

Another modification is outputting the element g_p that generates G^p to define the HSM assumption below, and setting $g = f \cdot g_p$. In practice, the instantiation of [CL15] with class groups of quadratic fields already computes an element g_p and thus defines the generator g of G. Note that this explicit definition of g is only needed in proof of Theorem 4, for the relation between the HSM, DDH-f (defined below) and DDH [CL15, Definition 1] assumptions. A last modification is that Gen only outputs an upper bound $\tilde{s}$ of s and not n. This is more accurate than the original definition as n is not used in the applications and actually, the instantiation does not compute n as it is a class number that requires sub-exponential time (with an $\mathcal{O}(L_{1/2})$ complexity) to be computed. This implies that in the following assumptions, exponents are sampled from distributions statistically close to uniform distributions. We discuss this in Remark 2.

We now define a *hard subgroup membership* (HSM) problem, which somewhat generalises Paillier's DCR assumption. In Definition 6, one has $G = F \times G^p$, the assumption is that it is hard to distinguish the elements of G^p in G.

Definition 7 (HSM **assumption**). *Let* GenGroup = (Gen, Solve) *be a generator for* DDH *groups with an easy* DL *subgroup. Using the notations introduced in Definition 6, the* HSM *assumption requires that the* HSM *problem is hard in* G *even with access to the* Solve *algorithm. Let* $\mathcal{D}$ *(resp.* $\mathcal{D}_p$*) be a distribution over the integers such that the distribution* $\{g^x, x \hookleftarrow \mathcal{D}\}$ *(resp.* $\{g_p^x, x \hookleftarrow \mathcal{D}_p\}$*) is at distance less than* $2^{-\lambda}$ *from the uniform distribution in* G *(resp. in* G^p*). Let* $\mathcal{A}$ *be an adversary for the* HSM *problem, its advantage is defined as:*

$$\mathsf{Adv}_{\mathcal{A}}^{\mathsf{HSM}}(\lambda, \mu) = \Big| 2 \cdot \Pr\big[b = b^\star : (p, \tilde{s}, g, f, g_p, G, F, G^p) \leftarrow \mathsf{Gen}(1^\lambda, 1^\mu),$$
$$x \hookleftarrow \mathcal{D}, x' \hookleftarrow \mathcal{D}_p, b \hookleftarrow \{0,1\}, Z_0 = g^x, Z_1 = g_p^{x'},$$
$$b^\star \leftarrow \mathcal{A}(p, \tilde{s}, g, f, g_p, G, F, G^p, Z_b, \mathsf{Solve}(.))\big] - 1 \Big|$$

The HSM *problem is said to be hard in* G *if for all probabilistic polynomial time attacker* $\mathcal{A}$, $\mathsf{Adv}_{\mathcal{A}}^{\mathsf{HSM}}(\lambda, \mu)$ *is negligible.*

Remark 2. In contrast to the traditional formulation of DDH or DCR, we can not sample uniformly elements in G^p or G as the order s (resp. ps) of G^p (resp. of G) is unknown. As a result we use the upper bound $\tilde{s}$ of s to instantiate the distributions $\mathcal{D}_p$ and $\mathcal{D}$ of Definition 7. Choosing $\mathcal{D}$ and $\mathcal{D}_p$ statistically close to the uniform distributions in G and G^p allows for more flexibility in our upcoming proofs, which is of interest, since it is easy to see that the DDH and HSM assumptions do not depend on the choice of the distribution.

In practice, we will instantiate $\mathcal{D}_p$ and $\mathcal{D}$ thanks to Lemma 4 (proved in the full version [CLT18, Aux. Material III.]). We use folded gaussians as they provide better efficiency than folded uniforms, and allow us to apply Lemma 3 in our security proofs.

Lemma 4. *Distributions* $\mathcal{D}_p$ *and* $\mathcal{D}$ *can be implemented from the output of* Gen*:*

1. *One can choose* $\mathcal{D}$ *to be the uniform distribution over* $\{0, \ldots, 2^{\lambda-2} \cdot \tilde{s} \cdot p\}$.
2. *Alternatively, choosing* $\mathcal{D} = \mathcal{D}_{\mathbf{Z},\sigma}$ *with* $\sigma = \tilde{s} \cdot p \cdot \sqrt{\lambda}$ *allows for more efficient constructions as the sampled elements will tend to be smaller.*
3. *Likewise, one can choose* $\mathcal{D}_p = \mathcal{D}_{\mathbf{Z},\sigma'}$ *with* $\sigma' = \tilde{s} \cdot \sqrt{\lambda}$
4. *One can also, less efficiently, define* $\mathcal{D}_p = \mathcal{D}$.
5. *Conversely, one can also define* $\mathcal{D}$ *from* $\mathcal{D}_p$ *and the uniform distribution modulo p: the distribution* $\{g_p^x \cdot f^a, x \hookleftarrow \mathcal{D}_p, a \hookleftarrow \mathbf{Z}_p\}$ *is statistically close to the uniform distribution in* G.

Finally, we introduce a new assumption called DDH-f. Roughly speaking, it means that it is hard to distinguish the distributions:

$$\{(g^x, g^y, g^{xy}), x, y \hookleftarrow \mathcal{D}\} \text{ and } \{(g^x, g^y, g^{xy}f^u), x, y \hookleftarrow \mathcal{D}, u \hookleftarrow \mathbf{Z}/p\mathbf{Z}\}.$$

In other words, we have on the left, a Diffie-Hellman (DH) triplet in G, and on the right, a triplet whose components in G^p form a DH triplet, and whose components in F form a random triplet: (f^x, f^y, f^{xy+u}) since $g = g_p \cdot f$ (as noted in Remark 2, $\mathcal{D}$ induces distributions statistically close to the uniform in G^p and F).

We will see in the next subsection that the security of the CL encryption scheme is actually *equivalent* to this assumption and that this assumption is *weaker* than the DDH assumption and the HSM assumption (see Theorem 4). As a side effect, using this assumption will simplify the forthcoming proofs as it is tightly related to the ind-cpa security of the underlying encryption scheme.

We note that DDH-f can be seen as an instance of the Extended-DDH (EDDH) problem defined by Hemenway and Ostrovsky [HO12]. They show that QR and DCR imply two different instantiations of EDDH, our implication from HSM to DDH-f somewhat generalises their proof as DDH-f is more generic than either of the hardness assumptions obtained from their reductions.

Definition 8 (DDH-f assumption). *Let* GenGroup = (Gen, Solve) *be a generator for* DDH *groups with an easy* DL *subgroup. Using the notations of Definition 6, the* DDH-f *assumption requires that the* DDH-f *problem is hard in G even with access to the* Solve *algorithm. Let $\mathcal{D}$ be a distribution over the integers such that $\{g^x, x \hookleftarrow \mathcal{D}\}$ is at distance less than $2^{-\lambda}$ of the uniform distribution in G. Let $\mathcal{A}$ be an adversary for the* DDH-f *problem, its advantage is defined as:*

$$\mathsf{Adv}_{\mathcal{A}}^{\mathsf{DDH\text{-}f}}(\lambda, \mu) = \Big| 2 \cdot \Pr\big[b = b^\star : (p, \tilde{s}, g, f, g_p, G, F, G^p) \leftarrow \mathsf{Gen}(1^\lambda, 1^\mu),$$
$$x, y \hookleftarrow \mathcal{D}, u \hookleftarrow \mathbf{Z}/p\mathbf{Z}, X = g^x, Y = g^y, b \hookleftarrow \{0,1\}, Z_0 = g^{xy}, Z_1 = g^{xy} f^u,$$
$$b^\star \leftarrow \mathcal{A}(p, \tilde{s}, g, f, g_p, G, F, G^p, X, Y, Z_b, \mathsf{Solve}(.))\big] - 1 \Big|.$$

The DDH-f *problem is said to be hard in G if for all probabilistic polynomial time attacker $\mathcal{A}$, $\mathsf{Adv}_{\mathcal{A}}^{\mathsf{DDH\text{-}f}}(\lambda, \mu)$ is negligible.*

3.2 Some Variants of the CL Generic Encryption Scheme

The Original Castagnos-Laguillaumie Encryption Scheme. Castagnos and Laguillaumie put forth in [CL15, Sect. 2.3] a generic construction for a linearly homomorphic encryption scheme over $\mathbf{Z}/p\mathbf{Z}$ based on a cyclic group with a subgroup of order p where the DL problem is easy, as given by the GenGroup generator of Definition 6. They prove this scheme is ind-cpa under the DDH assumption [CL15, Definition 1]. We demonstrate below that we can be more precise and prove that the security of this scheme is equivalent to the DDH-f assumption of Definition 8: the key idea is to perform a one-time pad in F, instead of in the whole group G.

Theorem 1. *The* CL *encryption scheme is semantically secure under chosen plaintext attacks (*ind-cpa*) if and only if the* DDH-f *assumption holds.*

Proof (sketch). Suppose that the DDH-f assumption holds. Let us consider the ind-cpa game, with a public key, $h = g^x$, $x \hookleftarrow \mathcal{D}$, and a challenge ciphertext $(c_1, c_2) = (g^r, f^{m_\beta} h^r)$ with $r \hookleftarrow \mathcal{D}$ and $\beta \hookleftarrow \{0,1\}$, $m_0, m_1 \in \mathbf{Z}/p\mathbf{Z}$. We can replace $(h, c_1, h^r) = (g^x, g^r, g^{xr})$ by $(g^x, g^r, g^{xr} f^u) = (g^x, g^r, h^r f^u)$ with $u \hookleftarrow \mathbf{Z}/p\mathbf{Z}$. As a result $c_2 = h^r f^{u+m_\beta}$. For the adversary, the value of r modulo n is fixed by $c_1 = g^r$ as g is a generator, so the value of h^r is fixed. As a result from c_2 an unbounded adversary can infer $u + m_\beta \in \mathbf{Z}/p\mathbf{Z}$ but as u is uniformly distributed in $\mathbf{Z}/p\mathbf{Z}$, he will have no information on β.

Conversely, we construct an ind-cpa adversary from a distinguisher for the DDH-f problem. Choose $m_0 \in \mathbf{Z}_p$ and $m_1 := m_0 + u$ with $u \hookleftarrow \mathbf{Z}/p\mathbf{Z}$. From the public key and the challenge ciphertext, construct the triplet

$$(h, c_1, c_2/f^{m_0}) = (g^x, g^r, g^{xr} f^{m_\beta - m_0}).$$

This gives a DH triplet if and only $\beta = 0$ and the exponent of f is uniformly distributed in $\mathbf{Z}/p\mathbf{Z}$ if and only $\beta = 1$. As a result, one can use the output of a distinguisher for the DDH-f problem to win the ind-cpa game. □

A linearly homomorphic encryption scheme from HSM. As noted in this section's introduction, the CL scheme was inspired by the scheme of [BCP03]. We here slightly modify the CL scheme so that it relies on the HSM assumption of Definition 7 and somewhat generalises the approach of Camenisch and Shoup's scheme in [CS03]. This ind-cpa scheme will be the basis of the IPFE scheme of Sect. 5.

Setting the parameters. We use the output $(p, \tilde{s}, g, f, g_p, G, F, G^p)$ of the GenGroup generator of Definition 6, ignoring the generator g which is useless here. Following Lemma 4, Item 3, we require $\sigma' > \tilde{s}\sqrt{\lambda}$ so that $\{g_p^r, r \hookleftarrow \mathcal{D}_{\mathbf{Z},\sigma'}\}$ is at distance less than $2^{-\lambda}$ from the uniform distribution in G^p. The plaintext space is $\mathbf{Z}/p\mathbf{Z}$, where p is a μ bit prime, with $\mu \geq \lambda$. The scheme is depicted in Fig. 2a.

Theorem 2 *The scheme described in Fig. 2a is semantically secure under chosen plaintext attacks (*ind-cpa*) under the* HSM *assumption.*

Please see the full version [CLT18, Aux. Material IV] for the proof.

Algorithm $\mathsf{KeyGen}(1^\lambda, 1^\mu)$

1. $(p, \tilde{s}, f, g_p, G, F, G^p) \leftarrow \mathsf{Gen}(1^\lambda, 1^\mu)$
2. Pick $x \hookleftarrow \mathcal{D}_{\mathbf{Z},\sigma'}$ and $h = g_p^x$
3. Set $pk = (\tilde{s}, g_p, f, p, h)$
4. Set $sk = x$
5. Return (pk, sk)

Algorithm $\mathsf{Encrypt}(pk, m)$

1. Pick $r \hookleftarrow \mathcal{D}_{\mathbf{Z},\sigma'}$
2. Return $(g_p^r, f^m h^r)$

Algorithm $\mathsf{Decrypt}(sk, (c_1, c_2))$

1. Compute $M = c_2/c_1^x$
2. Return $\mathsf{Solve}(M)$

(a) HSM-CL

Algorithm $\mathsf{KeyGen}(1^\lambda, 1^\mu)$

1. $(p, \tilde{s}, g, f, G, F) \leftarrow \mathsf{Gen}(1^\lambda, 1^\mu)$
2. Pick $x, y, \alpha \hookleftarrow \mathcal{D}_{\mathbf{Z},\sigma}$
3. Compute $h = g^\alpha$
4. Compute $\eta = g^x h^y$
5. Set $pk = (g, h, \eta)$
6. Set $sk = (x, y)$
7. Return (pk, sk)

Algorithm $\mathsf{Encrypt}(pk, m)$

1. Pick $r \hookleftarrow \mathcal{D}_{\mathbf{Z},\sigma}$
2. Return $(g^r, h^r, \eta^r f^m)$

Algorithm $\mathsf{Decrypt}(sk, (c_1, c_2, c_3))$

1. Compute $M = c_3/(c_1^x c_2^y)$
2. Return $\mathsf{Solve}(M)$

(b) Modified CL

Fig. 2. Description of our variants of the CL encryption

Enhanced variant of the CL encryption scheme. We here modify the original CL scheme by adding a key *à la* Cramer-Shoup (*cf.* [CS98]). The security of this scheme also relies on the DDH-f assumption. This ind-cpa scheme will be the basis of the IPFE scheme of Sect. 4.

This modification incurs some challenges: consider the vanilla Elgamal encryption scheme defined over a cyclic group of prime order q, generated by g. The modification leading to the [CS03] encryption scheme uses a second generator h to create a key $\eta = g^x h^y$ where $x, y \hookleftarrow \mathbf{Z}/q\mathbf{Z}$. Then η^r, with $r \hookleftarrow \mathbf{Z}/q\mathbf{Z}$ is used to mask the message. In the proof under the DDH assumption, one replaces the DH triplet (h, g^r, h^r) built from the public key and the ciphertext by a random triplet and proves that the mask η^r is then uniformly distributed and acts as a one-time pad for the plaintext, even knowing η. The triplet (h, g^r, h^r) is indeed a DH triplet, because if h is a generator, $h = g^\alpha$ with $\alpha \in (\mathbf{Z}/q\mathbf{Z})^*$. As a result, α is almost uniformly distributed in $\mathbf{Z}/q\mathbf{Z}$ ($\alpha \hookleftarrow \mathbf{Z}/q\mathbf{Z}$ is s.t. $\alpha \neq 0$ with overwhelming probability if q is large). The same happens in a composite group of order N' where N' is an RSA integer as in [Luc02], under the factoring assumption.

In our case, we use the GenGroup generator of Definition 6, i.e. a cyclic group G of order $n = p \cdot s$ generated by g, where s is unknown and may have small factors. As a result, a random element $h = g^\alpha$, with $\alpha \hookleftarrow \mathcal{D}_{\mathbf{Z},\sigma}$ may not be a generator with constant probability. Consequently, the padding η^r where $r \hookleftarrow \mathcal{D}_{\mathbf{Z},\sigma}$ and $\eta = g^x h^y$, with $x, y \hookleftarrow \mathcal{D}_{\mathbf{Z},\sigma}$ may not be uniformly distributed in G knowing η. However, we only need η^r to act as a one-time pad in the subgroup $F = \langle f \rangle$ of G of order p, since the message $m \in \mathbf{Z}/p\mathbf{Z}$ is encoded as $f^m \in F$. Supposing that p is a μ-bit prime, with $\mu \geq \lambda$ is sufficient to prove this. As the exponents are taken close to uniform modulo n and $n = p \cdot s$ with $\gcd(p, s) = 1$, they behave independently and close to uniform mod p and mod s. As we are interested only in what happens mod p, we can ignore the behaviour mod s and get ind-cpa security under the DDH-f assumption. Note that the use of this assumption instead of the stronger DDH assumption greatly simplifies the proof.

Setting the parameters. We use the output $(p, \tilde{s}, g, f, g_p, G, F, G^p)$ of the generator GenGroup of Definition 6, ignoring the group G^p and its generator. Following Lemma 4, Item 2 we require $\sigma > p\tilde{s}\sqrt{\lambda}$ to ensure that $\{g^r, r \hookleftarrow \mathcal{D}_{\mathbf{Z},\sigma}\}$ is at distance less than $2^{-\lambda}$ from the uniform distribution in G. The plaintext space is $\mathbf{Z}/p\mathbf{Z}$, where p is a μ bit prime, with $\mu \geq \lambda$. The scheme is depicted in Fig. 2b.

Theorem 3. *The scheme described in Fig. 2b is semantically secure under chosen plaintext attacks (*ind-cpa*) under the* DDH-f *assumption.*

Please see the full version [CLT18, Aux. Material V] for the proof.

3.3 Relations Between the Assumptions

Although one can establish direct reductions from the problems underlying the DDH, DDH-f and HSM assumptions, it is easier to use intermediate results on the ind-cpa security of the schemes defined in Subsect. 3.2 to see these reductions.

Theorem 1 states that the original CL cryptosystem is ind-cpa iff. the DDH-f assumption holds. In [CL15], it was proven that this scheme is ind-cpa under the DDH assumption. As a result, DDH-f is a weaker assumption than DDH. Furthermore, if the HSM scheme of Fig. 2a is ind-cpa then the original CL cryptosystem is ind-cpa: from a public key $h = g_p^x$, $x \hookleftarrow \mathcal{D}_{\mathbf{Z},\sigma'}$ and a ciphertext $c = (c_1, c_2) = (g_p^r, f^m \cdot h^r)$, $r \hookleftarrow \mathcal{D}_{\mathbf{Z},\sigma'}$ for the HSM scheme, one can chose $a, b \hookleftarrow \mathbf{Z}/p\mathbf{Z}$ and construct $h' = h \cdot f^a$, and the ciphertext $c' = (c_1', c_2') = (c_1 \cdot f^b, c_2 \cdot f^{ab})$. According to Lemma 4, Item 5 h' and c_1' are statistically indistinguishable from the uniform distribution in G. Furthermore, $h' = g_p^x f^a = g^\alpha$ where α is defined mod n from the Chinese remainder theorem, such that $\alpha \equiv x \pmod{s}$ and $\alpha \equiv a \pmod{p}$. Likewise, $c_1' = g_p^r f^b = g^\beta$ for some β defined equivalently. Finally, one has $c_2'/f^m = g_p^{xr} f^{ab} = g_p^{\alpha\beta \bmod s} f^{\alpha\beta \bmod p} = g^{\alpha\beta}$. As a result, $(h', c_1', c_2'/f^m)$ is a DH triplet in G, so h', c' are a public key and a ciphertext for m for the CL cryptosystem. Consequently, an ind-cpa attacker against the cryptosystem based on HSM can be built from an ind-cpa attacker against CL. Now, if the HSM assumption holds, from Theorem 2, the HSM scheme is ind-cpa, so the CL scheme is also ind-cpa and the DDH-f assumption holds. We sum up these results in Theorem 4 (see also Fig. 1).

Theorem 4. *The* DDH *assumption implies the* DDH-f *assumption. Furthermore, the* HSM *assumption implies the* DDH-f *assumption.*

4 Inner Product FE Relying on the DDH-f Assumption

In this section, we build an IPFE scheme from the DDH-f assumption (Definition 8). As proven in Theorem 4, this assumption is weaker than both the DDH and the HSM assumptions and yields simple proofs as it is suited to deal with the encoding of the message into a subgroup of prime order p. We use the formalism of a cyclic group with an easy DL subgroup. Our approach is based on the enhanced variant of the CL scheme, described in Fig. 2b. The resulting scheme over $\mathbf{Z}/p\mathbf{Z}$ can be viewed as an adaptation of the DDH scheme of [ALS16] to this setting, thereby removing the restriction on the size of the inner product.

The proof technique somewhat differs from the general approach of [ALS16]. We start from the ind-cpa proof of the enhanced variant of CL and then deal with the information leaked by key queries. Instead of computing the global distribution of the keys given this information, so as to make the proof go through, we carefully simplify the description of the adversary's view. A technical point is that even if we are only interested in what happens mod p, as the plaintexts are defined in $(\mathbf{Z}/p\mathbf{Z})^\ell$, we cannot restrict the adversary's view mod p: this could potentially result in a loss of information, as the key queries are defined in $\mathbf{Z}$.

We first present an FE scheme for inner products over $\mathbf{Z}$ (Sect. 4.1) and then consider a scheme for inner products over $\mathbf{Z}/p\mathbf{Z}$ (Sect. 4.2).

4.1 DDH-f-Based FE for Inner Product over Z

Setting the parameters. As in the ind-cpa scheme of Fig. 2b, we use the output $(p, \tilde{s}, g, f, g_p, G, F, G^p)$ of the GenGroup generator of Definition 6, ignoring the group G^p and its generator g_p. We require that p is a μ-bit prime, with $\mu \geq \lambda$.

From Lemma 4, Item 2 choosing $\sigma > \tilde{s} \cdot p \cdot \sqrt{\lambda}$ suffices to ensure that the distribution $\{g^x, x \hookleftarrow \mathcal{D}_{\mathbf{Z},\sigma}\}$ is at distance less than $2^{-\lambda}$ from the uniform distribution in G, however for security we must take a larger $\sigma > \tilde{s} \cdot p^{3/2} \cdot \sqrt{2\lambda}$ (*cf.* proof of Theorem 5). The Encrypt algorithm operates on plaintext messages $\boldsymbol{y} \in \mathbf{Z}^\ell$ and the key derivation algorithm derives keys from vectors $\mathbf{x} \in \mathbf{Z}^\ell$. Norm bounds X and Y are chosen s.t. $X, Y < (p/2\ell)^{1/2}$ to ensure decryption correctness. Indeed key vectors $\mathbf{x}$ and message vectors $\mathbf{y}$ are assumed to be of bounded norm $||\mathbf{x}||_\infty \leq X$ and $||\mathbf{y}||_\infty \leq Y$. The decryption algorithm recovers $\langle \mathbf{x}, \mathbf{y} \rangle \mod p$ (using a centered modulus), which is exactly $\langle \mathbf{x}, \mathbf{y} \rangle$ over the integers, thanks to the Cauchy–Schwarz inequality and the norm bounds, since $X \cdot Y < p/2\ell$.

Construction. Figure 3 depicts the FE scheme for inner products in $\mathbf{Z}$ secure under the DDH-f assumption (*cf.* Definition 8).

Algorithm $\mathsf{Setup}(1^\lambda, 1^\mu, 1^\ell)$

1. $(p, \tilde{s}, g, f, G, F) \leftarrow \mathsf{Gen}(1^\lambda, 1^\mu)$
2. Pick $\alpha \hookleftarrow \mathcal{D}_{\mathbf{Z},\sigma}$
3. Compute $h = g^\alpha$
4. Pick $\boldsymbol{s}, \boldsymbol{t} \hookleftarrow \mathcal{D}_{\mathbf{Z}^\ell,\sigma}$
5. For $1 \leq i \leq \ell$:
6. Compute $h_i = g^{s_i} h^{t_i}$
7. Return $msk = (\boldsymbol{s}, \boldsymbol{t})$ and $mpk = (\tilde{s}, g, h, f, p, \{h_i\}_{i \in [\ell]})$

Algorithm $\mathsf{KeyDer}(msk, \boldsymbol{x})$

1. Compute in $\mathbf{Z}$: $sk_{\mathbf{x}} = (s_{\mathbf{x}}, t_{\mathbf{x}}) = (\langle \mathbf{x}, \mathbf{s} \rangle, \langle \mathbf{x}, \mathbf{t} \rangle)$
2. Return $sk_{\boldsymbol{x}} = (s_{\mathbf{x}}, t_{\mathbf{x}})$

Algorithm $\mathsf{Encrypt}(mpk, \boldsymbol{y})$

1. Pick $r \hookleftarrow \mathcal{D}_{\mathbf{Z},\sigma}$
2. Set $C = g^r$ and $D = h^r$
3. For $1 \leq i \leq \ell$:
4. Compute $E_i = f^{y_i} h_i^r$
5. Return $C_{\mathbf{y}} = (C, D, \{E_i\}_{i \in [\ell]})$

Algorithm $\mathsf{Decrypt}(mpk, C_{\mathbf{y}}, sk_{\boldsymbol{x}})$

1. Compute $C_{\mathbf{x}} = (\prod_{i \in [\ell]} E_i^{x_i}) / (C^{s_{\mathbf{x}}} \cdot D^{t_{\mathbf{x}}})$
2. $\mathsf{sol} = \mathsf{Solve}(C_{\mathbf{x}})$
3. If $\mathsf{sol} \geq p/2$:
4. Return $(\mathsf{sol} - p)$
5. Else:
6. Return sol

Fig. 3. FE scheme for inner product over $\mathbf{Z}$ under the DDH-f assumption.

Correctness. We have

$$\begin{aligned}\prod_{i \in [\ell]} E_i^{x_i} / (C^{s_{\mathbf{x}}} \cdot D^{t_{\mathbf{x}}}) &= \prod_{i \in [\ell]} (f^{y_i} (g^{s_i} \cdot h^{t_i})^r)^{x_i} / ((g^r)^{\langle \mathbf{x}, \mathbf{s} \rangle} \cdot (h^r)^{\langle \mathbf{x}, \mathbf{t} \rangle}) \\ &= (f^{\sum_{i=1}^{\ell} y_i x_i})(g^{r \sum_{i=1}^{\ell} s_i x_i})(h^{r \sum_{i=1}^{\ell} t_i x_i}) / (g^{r \langle \mathbf{x}, \mathbf{s} \rangle} \cdot h^{r \langle \mathbf{x}, \mathbf{t} \rangle}) \\ &= f^{\langle x, y \rangle}.\end{aligned}$$

Applying the Solve algorithm to $C_{\mathbf{x}}$ yields $\langle \boldsymbol{x}, \boldsymbol{y} \rangle \mod p$, which, thanks to the norm bounds, is either $\langle \mathbf{x}, \mathbf{y} \rangle$ or $\langle \mathbf{x}, \mathbf{y} \rangle + p$. Since the absolute value of $\langle \mathbf{x}, \mathbf{y} \rangle$ is lower than $p/2$, if $\mathsf{sol} < p/2$ then $\langle \mathbf{x}, \mathbf{y} \rangle = \mathsf{sol}$ in $\mathbf{Z}$, otherwise $\langle \mathbf{x}, \mathbf{y} \rangle = (\mathsf{sol} - p)$.

Theorem 5. *Under the* DDH-f *assumption, the functional encryption scheme for inner products over* $\mathbf{Z}$ *of Fig. 3 provides full security (*ind-fe-cpa*).*

Proof. The proof proceeds as a sequence of games, starting in Game 0 with the real ind-fe-cpa game and ending in a game where the ciphertext statistically hides the random bit β chosen by the challenger from the adversary $\mathcal{A}$'s point of view. The beginning of the proof is similar to the proof of Theorem 3 on ind-cpa security. Then we take into account the fact that $\mathcal{A}$ has access to a key derivation oracle. For each Game i, we denote S_i the event $\beta = \beta'$.

Game 1	Game 2
1. $mpk, msk \leftarrow \mathsf{Setup}(1^\lambda, 1^\mu, 1^\ell)$	1. $mpk, msk \leftarrow \mathsf{Setup}(1^\lambda, 1^\mu, 1^\ell)$
2. $\mathbf{y}_0, \mathbf{y}_1 \leftarrow \mathcal{A}^{\mathsf{KeyDer}(msk,\cdot)}(mpk)$	2. $\mathbf{y}_0, \mathbf{y}_1 \leftarrow \mathcal{A}^{\mathsf{KeyDer}(msk,\cdot)}(mpk)$
3. Pick $\beta \hookleftarrow \{0,1\}$	3. Pick $\beta \hookleftarrow \{0,1\}$
4. Pick $r \hookleftarrow \mathcal{D}_{\mathbf{Z},\sigma}$	4. Pick $r \hookleftarrow \mathcal{D}_{\mathbf{Z},\sigma}$ and $u \hookleftarrow \mathbf{Z}/p\mathbf{Z}$
5. Compute $C = g^r, D = h^r$	5. Compute $C = g^r, D = h^r f^u$
6. For $1 \leq i \leq \ell$:	6. For $1 \leq i \leq \ell$:
7. Compute $E_i = f^{y_{\beta,i}} C^{s_i} D^{t_i}$	7. Compute $E_i = f^{y_{\beta,i}} C^{s_i} D^{t_i}$
8. $C_{\mathbf{y}} = (C, D, \{E_i\}_{i \in [\ell]})$	8. $C_{\mathbf{y}} = (C, D, \{E_i\}_{i \in [\ell]})$
9. $\beta' \leftarrow \mathcal{A}^{\mathsf{KeyDer}(msk,\cdot)}(C_{\mathbf{y}})$	9. $\beta' \leftarrow \mathcal{A}^{\mathsf{KeyDer}(msk,\cdot)}(C_{\mathbf{y}})$
10. Return $(\beta = \beta')$	10. Return $(\beta = \beta')$

Game 0 ⇒ Game 1: In Game 1 the challenger, who has access to the master secret key msk, computes the ciphertext using msk instead of mpk. The resulting ciphertext has exactly the same distribution therefore $\Pr[S_0] = \Pr[S_1]$.
Game 1 ⇒ Game 2: In Game 1, the tuple $(h = g^\alpha, C = g^r, D = h^r = g^{\alpha r})$, with $\alpha, r \hookleftarrow \mathcal{D}_{\mathbf{Z},\sigma}$, is a DH triplet as $\sigma > p^{3/2} \cdot \tilde{s} \cdot \sqrt{2\lambda}$ ensures that the induced distribution is at distance less than $2^{-\lambda}$ of the uniform distribution in G. In Game 2, the challenger samples a random $u \hookleftarrow \mathbf{Z}/p\mathbf{Z}$ and computes $D = h^r f^u$. Both games are indistinguishable under the DDH-f assumption: $|\Pr[S_2] - \Pr[S_1]| = \mathsf{Adv}_{\mathcal{B}}^{\mathsf{DDH\text{-}f}}(\lambda, \mu)$. Now in Game 2 the challenge ciphertext is:

$$(C = g^r,\ D = h^r f^u,\ \{E_i = f^{y_{\beta,i}} \cdot C^{s_i} \cdot D^{t_i} = f^{y_{\beta,i} + ut_i} h_i^r\}_{i \in [\ell]}).$$

Lemma 5. *In Game 2 the ciphertext* $(C, D, E_1, \ldots, E_\ell) \in G^{\ell+2}$ *statistically hides* β *such that* $|Pr[S_2] - 1/2| \leq 2^{-\lambda}$.

INTUITION. Following the proof methodology of [ALS16], we first delimit the information that is leaked in the challenge ciphertext by only considering the dimension in which both potential challenge ciphertexts differ. Indeed, denoting $\mathbf{z}_\beta = \mathbf{y}_\beta + u \cdot \boldsymbol{t} \mod p$, then projecting $\mathbf{z}_\beta$ onto the subspace generated by $\mathbf{y}_0 - \mathbf{y}_1$ encapsulates all the information revealed by the challenge ciphertext.
Next, we consider the distribution of the projection of the secret key component $\mathbf{t}$ on the subspace generated by $\mathbf{y}_0 - \mathbf{y}_1$, conditionally on $\mathcal{A}$'s view (i.e. on the information leaked by private key queries and the public key). This amounts to a

distribution over a one dimensional lattice Λ_0. We then reduce this distribution modulo a sub-lattice Λ_0' such that $\Lambda_0/\Lambda_0' \simeq \mathbf{Z}/n\mathbf{Z}$, and using Lemma 3 we demonstrate that for an appropriate choice of the standard deviation σ (which defines $\mathcal{D}_{\mathbf{Z}^\ell,\sigma}$, from which $\boldsymbol{t}$ is sampled), the projection of $\boldsymbol{t}$ on the subspace generated by $\mathbf{y}_0 - \mathbf{y}_1$ is statistically close to the uniform distribution over $\mathbf{Z}/n\mathbf{Z}$. As a result, $\langle \mathbf{y}, \boldsymbol{t}\rangle$ modulo p is also close to the uniform distribution over $\mathbf{Z}/p\mathbf{Z}$, and thus $\mathbf{y}_\beta$ (and therefore β) is statistically hidden in $\mathbf{z}_\beta$.

Proof (Lemma 5). The ciphertext component $C = g^r$ information theoretically reveals $r \mod n$. Furthermore, $\forall i \in [\ell]$, E_i information theoretically reveals $y_{\beta,i} + ut_i \mod p$ as the value of h_i^r is fixed from C and the public key. Therefore the challenge ciphertext information theoretically reveals $\boldsymbol{z}_\beta = \boldsymbol{y}_\beta + u \cdot \boldsymbol{t} \mod p$.

Throughout the rest of this proof we demonstrate that $\boldsymbol{y}_\beta$ is statistically hidden mod p, thanks to the distribution of $\boldsymbol{t}$ conditioned on $\mathcal{A}$'s view.

We denote $\boldsymbol{x}_i$ $\mathcal{A}$'s ith query to the key derivation oracle. It must hold that, for all i, $\langle \boldsymbol{x}_i, \boldsymbol{y}_0\rangle = \langle \boldsymbol{x}_i, \boldsymbol{y}_1\rangle$. Let $d \neq 0$ be the gcd of the coefficients of $\boldsymbol{y}_1 - \boldsymbol{y}_0$ and define $\boldsymbol{y} = (y_1, \ldots, y_\ell) = 1/d \cdot (\boldsymbol{y}_1 - \boldsymbol{y}_0) \in \mathbf{Z}^\ell$. It holds that $\langle \boldsymbol{x}_i, \boldsymbol{y}\rangle = 0$ over $\mathbf{Z}$ for all i. Therefore if we consider the lattice $\boldsymbol{y}^\perp = \{\boldsymbol{x} \in \mathbf{Z}^\ell : \langle \boldsymbol{x}, \boldsymbol{y}\rangle = 0\}$, all the queries $\boldsymbol{x}_i$ must belong to that lattice. W.l.o.g., we assume the n_0 first coordinates of $\boldsymbol{y}$ are zero (for some n_0), and all remaining entries are non-zero. Further, the rows of the following matrix form a basis of $\boldsymbol{y}^\perp$:

$$\mathbf{X}_{\mathsf{top}} = \left[\begin{array}{c|ccccc} \mathbf{I}_{n_0} & & & & & \\ \hline & -y_{n_0+2} & y_{n_0+1} & & & \\ & & -y_{n_0+3} & y_{n_0+2} & & \\ & & & \ddots & \ddots & \\ & & & & -y_\ell & y_{\ell-1} \end{array}\right] \in \mathbf{Z}^{(\ell-1)\times\ell}.$$

We define the matrix:

$$\mathbf{X} = \begin{bmatrix} \mathbf{X}_{\mathsf{top}} \\ \boldsymbol{y}^T \end{bmatrix} \in \mathbf{Z}^{\ell\times\ell}, \tag{1}$$

and claim that $\mathbf{X}$ is invertible mod p (proof provided in the full version [CLT18, Aux. Material VI]). Now since $\mathbf{X}$ does not depend on $\beta \in \{0,1\}$, it suffices to show that $\mathbf{X} \cdot \mathbf{z}_\beta \in (\mathbf{Z}/p\mathbf{Z})^\ell$ is statistically independent of β. Moreover by construction $\mathbf{X}_{\mathsf{top}} \cdot \boldsymbol{y}_0 = \mathbf{X}_{\mathsf{top}} \cdot \boldsymbol{y}_1$ (over the integers), so $\mathbf{X}_{\mathsf{top}} \cdot \mathbf{z}_\beta$ is clearly independent of β and we only need to worry about the last row of $\mathbf{X} \cdot \mathbf{z}_\beta$ mod p, i.e. the information about β leaked by the challenge ciphertext is contained in:

$$\langle \boldsymbol{y}, \boldsymbol{z}_\beta\rangle = \langle \boldsymbol{y}, \boldsymbol{y}_\beta\rangle + u \cdot \langle \boldsymbol{y}, \boldsymbol{t}\rangle \mod p. \tag{2}$$

We hereafter prove that, from $\mathcal{A}$'s perspective, $\langle \boldsymbol{y}, \boldsymbol{t}\rangle$ follows a distribution statistically close to the uniform distribution mod p, thus proving that β is statistically hidden: since u is sampled uniformly at random from $\mathbf{Z}/p\mathbf{Z}$, $u \neq 0 \mod p$ with all but negligible probability as p is a μ-bit prime, with $\mu \geq \lambda$. To this end, we analyse the information that $\mathcal{A}$ gains on $\boldsymbol{t}$ mod n. From this, we will prove that the distribution of $\langle \boldsymbol{y}, \boldsymbol{t} \rangle$ is close to uniform mod n, and thus, mod p.

As in the proof of Theorem 3, $\mathcal{A}$ learns $\boldsymbol{z} = \boldsymbol{s} + \alpha \boldsymbol{t}$ mod n from the public key as $\forall i \in [\ell], h_i = g^{s_i} h^{t_i}$. Knowing $\boldsymbol{z}$, the joint distribution of $(\boldsymbol{s}, \boldsymbol{t})$ mod n is $(\boldsymbol{z} - \alpha \boldsymbol{t} \mod n, \boldsymbol{t} \mod n)$ where $\boldsymbol{t} \hookleftarrow \mathcal{D}_{\mathbf{Z}^\ell, \sigma}$. As a result, knowing $\boldsymbol{z}$ does not give more information on $\boldsymbol{t}$ modulo n to $\mathcal{A}$.

One may assume that through its secret key queries, the information learned by $\mathcal{A}$ is completely determined by $\mathbf{X}_{\mathsf{top}} \cdot \boldsymbol{s}$ and $\mathbf{X}_{\mathsf{top}} \cdot \boldsymbol{t} \in \mathbf{Z}^{(\ell-1)}$, as all the queried vectors $\boldsymbol{x}_i$ can be obtained as linear combinations of the rows of $\mathbf{X}_{\mathsf{top}}$.

The value of $\mathbf{X}_{\mathsf{top}} \cdot \boldsymbol{s}$ does not give $\mathcal{A}$ more information on $\boldsymbol{t}$ mod n than what he obtains from $\mathbf{X}_{\mathsf{top}} \cdot \boldsymbol{t}$. Indeed the remainder of the Euclidean division of $\mathbf{X}_{\mathsf{top}} \cdot \boldsymbol{s}$ by n can be deduced from $\boldsymbol{z}$ and $\mathbf{X}_{\mathsf{top}} \cdot \boldsymbol{t}$; while the quotient is independent of $\boldsymbol{t}$ mod n and $\mathbf{X}_{\mathsf{top}} \cdot \boldsymbol{t}$, as $\boldsymbol{s}$ and $\boldsymbol{t}$ are sampled independently and $\boldsymbol{z}$ only brings a relation mod n. It is thus sufficient to analyse the distribution of $\boldsymbol{t}$ mod n knowing $\mathbf{X}_{\mathsf{top}} \cdot \boldsymbol{t}$.

Let $\boldsymbol{t}_0 \in \mathbf{Z}^\ell$ be an arbitrary vector s.t. $\mathbf{X}_{\mathsf{top}} \cdot \boldsymbol{t}_0 = \mathbf{X}_{\mathsf{top}} \cdot \boldsymbol{t}$. Knowing $\mathbf{X}_{\mathsf{top}} \cdot \boldsymbol{t}$, the distribution of $\boldsymbol{t}$ is $\boldsymbol{t}_0 + \mathcal{D}_{\Lambda, \sigma, -\boldsymbol{t}_0}$ where $\Lambda = \{\mathrm{t} \in \mathbf{Z}^\ell : \mathbf{X}_{\mathsf{top}} \cdot \mathrm{t} = \mathbf{0}\}$. This lattice has dimension 1 and contains $\boldsymbol{y} \cdot \mathbf{Z}$. In fact, as $\gcd(y_1, \ldots, y_\ell) = 1$, one has $\boldsymbol{y} \cdot \mathbf{Z} = \Lambda$ (there exits $\boldsymbol{y}' \in \mathbf{Z}^\ell$ s.t. $\Lambda = \boldsymbol{y}' \cdot \mathbf{Z}$ and $\boldsymbol{y} = \alpha \boldsymbol{y}'$ so α must divide $\gcd(y_1, \ldots, y_\ell) = 1$). Therefore, applying Lemma 2, we see that conditioned on $\mathbf{X}_{\mathsf{top}} \cdot \boldsymbol{t}$, $\langle \boldsymbol{y}, \boldsymbol{t} \rangle$ is distributed according to $\langle \boldsymbol{y}, \boldsymbol{t}_0 \rangle + \mathcal{D}_{||\boldsymbol{y}||_2^2 \mathbf{Z}, ||\boldsymbol{y}||_2 \sigma, -\langle \boldsymbol{t}_0, \boldsymbol{y} \rangle}$.

Now consider the distribution obtained by reducing $\mathcal{D}_{||\boldsymbol{y}||_2^2 \mathbf{Z}, ||\boldsymbol{y}||_2 \sigma, -\langle \boldsymbol{t}_0, \boldsymbol{y} \rangle}$ over $\Lambda_0 = ||\boldsymbol{y}||_2^2 \cdot \mathbf{Z}$ modulo the sublattice $\Lambda_0' = n \cdot ||\boldsymbol{y}||_2^2 \cdot \mathbf{Z}$. In order to apply Lemma 3 we need $||\boldsymbol{y}||_2 \cdot \sigma > \eta_\epsilon(\Lambda_0')$, which – applying a bound on the smoothing parameter from [MR07] for $\epsilon = 2^{-\lambda-1}$ – is guaranteed by choosing $||\boldsymbol{y}||_2 \cdot \sigma > \lambda_1(\Lambda_0') \cdot \sqrt{\lambda}$. Moreover since $\lambda_1(\Lambda_0') = n \cdot ||\boldsymbol{y}||_2^2$, we require $||\boldsymbol{y}||_2 \cdot \sigma > p \cdot \tilde{s} \cdot ||\boldsymbol{y}||_2^2 \cdot \sqrt{\lambda}$, thus $\sigma > p \cdot \tilde{s} \cdot ||\boldsymbol{y}||_2 \cdot \sqrt{\lambda}$. Now from the norm bounds on $\boldsymbol{y}_0$ and $\boldsymbol{y}_1$ it holds that $||\boldsymbol{y}||_2 < \sqrt{2p}$, so choosing $\sigma > p^{3/2} \cdot \tilde{s} \cdot \sqrt{2\lambda}$ suffices to ensure that from $\mathcal{A}$'s view, $\langle \boldsymbol{y}, \boldsymbol{t} \rangle$ modulo n is within distance $2^{-\lambda}$ from the uniform distribution over $\Lambda_0 / \Lambda_0' \simeq \mathbf{Z}/n\mathbf{Z}$. As a result, $\langle \boldsymbol{y}, \boldsymbol{t} \rangle$ modulo p is also close to the uniform distribution over $\mathbf{Z}/p\mathbf{Z}$.

We have therefore demonstrated that with overwhelming probability the term $\langle \boldsymbol{y}, \boldsymbol{y}_\beta \rangle$ in Eq. (2) is statistically hidden modulo p and $|Pr[S_2] - 1/2| \leq 2^{-\lambda}$. □

Combining the different transition probabilities provides a bound for $\mathcal{A}$'s advantage, thus concluding the proof: $\mathsf{Adv}_{\mathcal{A}}^{\mathsf{ind\text{-}fe\text{-}cpa}}(\lambda, \mu) \leq \mathsf{Adv}_{\mathcal{B}}^{\mathsf{DDH\text{-}f}}(\lambda, \mu) + 2^{-\lambda}$. □

4.2 DDH-f-Based FE for Inner Product over $\mathbf{Z}/p\mathbf{Z}$

As in the LWE and Paillier-based IPFE modulo p of [ALS16], the main problem here is that private key queries are performed over $\mathbf{Z}$. An adversary may therefore query keys for vectors that are linearly dependent over $(\mathbf{Z}/p\mathbf{Z})^\ell$ but independent over $\mathbf{Z}^\ell$. To solve this issue we require, as in [ALS16], that the authority distributing private keys keeps track of previously revealed private keys.

Setting the parameters. We use the output $(p, \tilde{s}, f, g_p, G, F, G^p)$ of the GenGroup generator of Definition 6, with p a μ bit prime, and with $\mu \geq \lambda$. We sample the coordinates of the secret key from $\mathcal{D}_{\mathbf{Z}^\ell,\sigma}$. Choosing $\sigma > \tilde{s} \cdot p^\ell \cdot \sqrt{\lambda} \cdot (\sqrt{\ell})^{\ell-1}$ suffices for security to hold (*cf.* proof of Theorem 6), and ensures the distribution $\{g^x, x \leftarrow \mathcal{D}_{\mathbf{Z},\sigma}\}$ is at distance less than $2^{-\lambda}$ from the uniform distribution in G (*cf.* Lemma 4, Item 2. The Encrypt algorithm encrypts plaintexts $\boldsymbol{y} \in (\mathbf{Z}/p\mathbf{Z})^\ell$ and the key derivation algorithm derives keys from vectors $\mathbf{x} \in (\mathbf{Z}/p\mathbf{Z})^\ell$.

Construction. Algorithms Setup and Encrypt proceed exactly as in the construction for inner products over $\mathbf{Z}$ under DDH-f (*cf.* Fig. 3). Algorithms KeyDer and Decrypt, which differ from those of the previous construction, are defined in Fig. 4. Again, correctness follows from the linearity of the inner product.

Theorem 6. *Under the* DDH-f *assumption, the functional encryption scheme for inner products over* $\mathbf{Z}/p\mathbf{Z}$ *of Fig. 4 provides full security (*ind-fe-cpa*).*

Proof. The proof proceeds similarly to that of Theorem 5, only we must define the matrix $\mathbf{X}_{\mathsf{top}}$ differently, as we can no longer guarantee that it is invertible modulo p. So we here follow the same steps as in the previous proof up until the definition of Game 2. The only difference being that the adversary $\mathcal{A}$ queries the *stateful* key derivation algorithm. We denote Game i' the variant of Game i in which the key derivation algorithm is stateful. From the proof of Theorem 5, it holds that $|\Pr[S_2'] - \Pr[S_0']| = \mathsf{Adv}_{\mathcal{B}}^{\mathsf{DDH\text{-}f}}(\lambda, \mu)$.

As in the original Game 2, here in Game 2′ the challenge ciphertext information theoretically reveals $\boldsymbol{z}_\beta = \boldsymbol{y}_\beta + u \cdot \boldsymbol{t} \mod p$.

Algorithm KeyDer$(msk, \boldsymbol{x}, st)$

Answering the jth key request $sk_{\boldsymbol{x}}$ where $\boldsymbol{x} \in (\mathbf{Z}/p\mathbf{Z})^\ell$. At any time the internal state st contains at most ℓ tuples $(\boldsymbol{x}_i, \overline{\mathbf{x}}_i, z_{\mathbf{x}_i})$ where $(\overline{\mathbf{x}}_i, z_{\mathbf{x}_i})$ are previously queried secret keys and the $\boldsymbol{x}_i$'s are corresponding vectors.

1. If $\boldsymbol{x}$ is linearly independent of the $\boldsymbol{x}_i$'s modulo p :
2. Set $\overline{\mathbf{x}} \in \{0, \ldots, p-1\}^\ell$ with $\overline{\mathbf{x}} = \boldsymbol{x} \mod p$
3. $z_{\mathbf{x}} = (s_{\mathbf{x}}, t_{\mathbf{x}}) = (\langle \overline{\mathbf{x}}, \boldsymbol{s}\rangle, \langle \overline{\mathbf{x}}, \mathbf{t}\rangle) \in \mathbf{Z} \times \mathbf{Z}$
4. $st = (st, (\boldsymbol{x}, \overline{\mathbf{x}}, z_{\mathbf{x}}))$
5. If $\exists \{k_i\}_{1 \leq i \leq j-1} \in \mathbf{Z}^{j-1}$ s.t. $\boldsymbol{x} = \sum_{i=1}^{j-1} k_i \boldsymbol{x}_i \in (\mathbf{Z}/p\mathbf{Z})^\ell$ then:
6. $\overline{\mathbf{x}} = \sum_{i=1}^{j-1} k_i \overline{\mathbf{x}}_i \in \mathbf{Z}^\ell$
7. $z_{\mathbf{x}} = (\sum_{i=1}^{j-1} k_i s_{\boldsymbol{x}_i}, \sum_{i=1}^{j-1} k_i t_{\boldsymbol{x}_i}) \in \mathbf{Z} \times \mathbf{Z}$
8. Return $sk_{\boldsymbol{x}} = (\overline{\mathbf{x}}, z_{\mathbf{x}})$

Algorithm Decrypt$(mpk, C_{\mathbf{y}}, sk_{\boldsymbol{x}})$

1. Parse $(\overline{\mathbf{x}} = (\overline{x}_1, \ldots, \overline{x}_\ell);\ z_{\mathbf{x}} = (s_{\mathbf{x}}, t_{\mathbf{x}})) = sk_{\boldsymbol{x}}$
2. Compute $C_{\mathbf{x}} = (\prod_{i \in [\ell]} E_i^{\overline{x}_i})/(C^{s_{\mathbf{x}}} \cdot D^{t_{\mathbf{x}}})$
3. Return Solve$(C_{\boldsymbol{x}})$

Fig. 4. Stateful FE scheme for inner products over $\mathbf{Z}/p\mathbf{Z}$ from DDH-f.

We define $\boldsymbol{y} = (y_1, \ldots, y_\ell) = \boldsymbol{y}_1 - \boldsymbol{y}_0 \in (\mathbf{Z}/p\mathbf{Z})^\ell$; and, assuming $\mathcal{A}$ has performed j private key queries, for $1 \leq i \leq j$, we denote $\boldsymbol{x}_i \in (\mathbf{Z}/p\mathbf{Z})^\ell$ the vectors for which keys have been derived.

We want to demonstrate that from $\mathcal{A}$'s view, the bit β is statistically hidden in Game 2′. However we cannot use the same matrix $\mathbf{X}_{\mathsf{top}}$ as in the proof of Theorem 5; indeed, if we define $\boldsymbol{X}$ as in Eq. (1) we cannot guarantee that $\boldsymbol{X}$ is invertible modulo p, since $\det(\boldsymbol{X}\boldsymbol{X}^T)$ could be a multiple of p. Therefore, so as to ensure that the queried vectors $\boldsymbol{x}_i$ do not in some way depend on β, we prove via induction that after the j first private key queries (where $j \in \{0, \ldots, \ell-1\}$), $\mathcal{A}$'s view remains statistically independent of β, thus proving that the challenge ciphertext in Game 2′ statistically hides β such that $|Pr[S_2'] - 1/2| \leq 2^{-\lambda}$. The induction proceeds on the value of j.

Recall that Game 2 and Game 2′ are identical but for the key derivation algorithm. Therefore if $\mathcal{A}$ can make no calls to its key derivation oracle, the indistinguishability of ciphertexts in Game 2′ follows immediately from that in Game 2, demonstrated in proof of Theorem 5, thus the induction hypothesis holds for $j = 0$. Now consider $j \in \{0, \ldots, \ell-1\}$. From the induction hypothesis one may assume that at this point the state $st = \{(\boldsymbol{x}_i, \overline{\mathbf{x}}_i, z_{\mathbf{x}_i})\}_{i \in [j]}$ is independent of β. Indeed if $\mathcal{A}$'s view after $j-1$ requests is independent of β then the jth request performed by $\mathcal{A}$ must be so.

W.l.o.g. we assume that the key requests $\boldsymbol{x}_i$ performed by $\mathcal{A}$ are linearly independent. This implies that the $\overline{\mathbf{x}}_i$'s are linearly independent mod p and generate a subspace of $\boldsymbol{y}^{\perp_p} = \{\boldsymbol{x} \in (\mathbf{Z}/p\mathbf{Z})^\ell : \langle \boldsymbol{x}, \boldsymbol{y} \rangle = 0 \mod p\}$. The set $\{\overline{\mathbf{x}}_i\}_{i \in [j]}$ can be extended to a basis $\{\overline{\mathbf{x}}_i\}_{i \in [\ell-1]}$ of $\boldsymbol{y}^{\perp_p}$. We define $\mathbf{X}_{\mathsf{top}} \in \mathbf{Z}^{(\ell-1)\times\ell}$ to be the matrix whose rows are the vectors $\overline{\mathbf{x}}_i$ for $i \in [\ell-1]$. Let $\boldsymbol{x}' \in (\mathbf{Z}/p\mathbf{Z})^\ell$ be a vector chosen deterministically, $\boldsymbol{x}' \notin \boldsymbol{y}^{\perp_p}$, such that $\mathcal{A}$ can also easily compute $\boldsymbol{x}'$. We define $\mathbf{x}_{\mathsf{bot}}$ to be the canonical lift of $\boldsymbol{x}'$ over $\mathbf{Z}$, and $\mathbf{X}$ as:

$$\mathbf{X} = \begin{bmatrix} \mathbf{X}_{\mathsf{top}} \\ \mathbf{x}_{\mathsf{bot}}^T \end{bmatrix} \in \mathbf{Z}^{\ell \times \ell}.$$

The matrix $\mathbf{X}$ is invertible mod p, statistically independent of β by induction and by construction, and computable by $\mathcal{A}$, thus we need only prove that $\mathbf{X} \cdot \boldsymbol{z}_\beta$ is statistically independent of β. And since $\mathbf{X}_{\mathsf{top}} \cdot (\boldsymbol{y}_1 - \boldsymbol{y}_0) = 0 \mod p$, we need only consider $\langle \mathbf{x}_{\mathsf{bot}}, \boldsymbol{z}_\beta \rangle = \langle \mathbf{x}_{\mathsf{bot}}, \boldsymbol{y}_\beta \rangle + u \cdot \langle \mathbf{x}_{\mathsf{bot}}, \boldsymbol{t} \rangle \mod p$.

We hereafter prove that, from $\mathcal{A}$'s view, $\langle \mathbf{x}_{\mathsf{bot}}, \boldsymbol{t} \rangle$ follows a distribution statistically close to the uniform distribution mod p, thus proving that β is statistically hidden (since u is sampled uniformly at random from $\mathbf{Z}/p\mathbf{Z}$, $u \neq 0 \mod p$ with all but negligible probability as p is a μ bit prime, with $\mu \geq \lambda$). To this end, we analyse the information $\mathcal{A}$ gets on $\boldsymbol{t} \bmod n$, so as to prove that $\boldsymbol{t} \bmod p$ follows a distribution statistically close to the uniform distribution over $\boldsymbol{y} \cdot \mathbf{Z}/p\mathbf{Z}$, thus proving that $\langle \mathbf{x}_{\mathsf{bot}}, \boldsymbol{t} \rangle$ follows a distribution statistically close to uniform mod p.

As in the proof of Theorem 3, $\mathcal{A}$ learns $\boldsymbol{z} := \boldsymbol{s} + \alpha \boldsymbol{t} \bmod n$ from the public key as $\forall i \in [\ell], h_i = g^{s_i} h^{t_i}$. Knowing $\boldsymbol{z}$, the joint distribution of $(\boldsymbol{s}, \boldsymbol{t}) \bmod n$ is $(\boldsymbol{z} - \alpha \boldsymbol{t} \mod n, \boldsymbol{t} \mod n)$ where $\boldsymbol{t} \hookleftarrow \mathcal{D}_{\mathbf{Z}^\ell, \sigma}$. As a result, knowing $\boldsymbol{z}$ does not give $\mathcal{A}$ more information on $\boldsymbol{t} \bmod n$. Then, as in the proof of Theorem 5, private key queries give $\mathcal{A}$ the knowledge of $\mathbf{X}_{\mathsf{top}} \cdot \boldsymbol{s}$ and $\mathbf{X}_{\mathsf{top}} \cdot \boldsymbol{t}$ in $\mathbf{Z}^{\ell-1}$. The value of $\mathbf{X}_{\mathsf{top}} \cdot \boldsymbol{s}$ does not give $\mathcal{A}$ more information on $\boldsymbol{t}$ mod n than what he obtains from $\mathbf{X}_{\mathsf{top}} \cdot \boldsymbol{t}$. It thus suffices to analyse the distribution of $\boldsymbol{t}$ mod n knowing $\mathbf{X}_{\mathsf{top}} \cdot \boldsymbol{t}$.

We define $\Lambda = \{\boldsymbol{x} \in \mathbf{Z}^{\ell} | \mathbf{X}_{\mathsf{top}} \cdot \boldsymbol{x} = \boldsymbol{0} \in \mathbf{Z}^{\ell}\}$. This one dimensional lattice can equivalently be defined as $\Lambda = \boldsymbol{y}' \cdot \mathbf{Z}$ where $\boldsymbol{y}' = \gamma \cdot \boldsymbol{y} \mod p$ for some $\gamma \in (\mathbf{Z}/p\mathbf{Z})^*$. One should note that all the coefficients of $\boldsymbol{y}'$ are co-prime since $\boldsymbol{y}' / \gcd(y'_1, \ldots, y'_\ell) \in \Lambda$.

Let $\boldsymbol{t}_0 \in \mathbf{Z}^{\ell}$ be an arbitrary vector such that $\mathbf{X}_{\mathsf{top}} \cdot \boldsymbol{t}_0 = \mathbf{X}_{\mathsf{top}} \cdot \boldsymbol{t}$. Knowing $\mathbf{X}_{\mathsf{top}} \cdot \boldsymbol{t}$, the distribution of $\boldsymbol{t}$ is $\boldsymbol{t}_0 + \mathcal{D}_{\Lambda,\sigma,-\boldsymbol{t}_0}$. Now consider the distribution obtained by reducing the distribution $\mathcal{D}_{\Lambda,\sigma,-\boldsymbol{t}_0}$ over Λ modulo the sublattice $\Lambda' := n \cdot \Lambda$. We first bound $||\boldsymbol{y}'||_2$ so as to bound $\lambda_1(\Lambda')$. We can then apply Lemma 3 by imposing a lower bound for σ.

Since $\Lambda = \boldsymbol{y}' \cdot \mathbf{Z}$, it holds that $||\boldsymbol{y}'||_2 = \det(\Lambda)$. We define Λ_{top} as the lattice generated by the rows of $\mathbf{X}_{\mathsf{top}}$, then applying results from [Mar03] and [Ngu91], one gets $||\boldsymbol{y}'||_2 = \det(\Lambda) \leq \det(\Lambda_{\mathsf{top}})$. We now apply Hadamard's bound, which tells us that, since the coordinates of each $\overline{\mathbf{x}}_i$ are smaller than p and since we assumed all requested $\overline{\mathbf{x}}_i$'s are linearly independent, $\det(\Lambda_{\mathsf{top}}) \leq \prod_{i=1}^{\ell-1} ||\overline{\mathbf{x}}_i||_2 \leq (\sqrt{\ell}p)^{\ell-1}$. Therefore $||\boldsymbol{y}'||_2 \leq (\sqrt{\ell}p)^{\ell-1}$, this implies $\lambda_1(\Lambda') \leq n \cdot (\sqrt{\ell}p)^{\ell-1} < \tilde{s} \cdot p^{\ell} \cdot (\sqrt{\ell})^{\ell-1}$. From [MR07] we know that the smoothing parameter verifies $\eta_\epsilon(\Lambda') \leq \sqrt{\frac{\ln(2(1+1/\epsilon))}{\pi}} \cdot \lambda_1(\Lambda')$. Thus for $\epsilon = 2^{-\lambda-1}$, we have $\eta_\epsilon(\Lambda') \leq \tilde{s} \cdot p^{\ell} \cdot \sqrt{\lambda} \cdot (\sqrt{\ell})^{\ell-1}$. Therefore setting $\sigma > \tilde{s} \cdot p^{\ell} \cdot \sqrt{\lambda} \cdot (\sqrt{\ell})^{\ell-1}$ and applying Lemma 3 ensures that the distribution $\mathcal{D}_{\Lambda,\sigma,-\boldsymbol{t}_0} \mod \Lambda'$, and therefore that of $\boldsymbol{t}$ mod n is within distance $2^{-\lambda}$ from the uniform distribution over $\Lambda/\Lambda' \simeq \boldsymbol{y}' \cdot \mathbf{Z}/n\mathbf{Z}$. This entails that $\boldsymbol{t}$ mod p is within distance $2^{-\lambda}$ from the uniform distribution over $\boldsymbol{y}' \cdot \mathbf{Z}/p\mathbf{Z} \simeq \boldsymbol{y} \cdot \mathbf{Z}/p\mathbf{Z}$ since $\boldsymbol{y}' = \gamma \cdot \boldsymbol{y} \mod p$ for some $\gamma \in (\mathbf{Z}/p\mathbf{Z})^*$.

Since by construction $\langle \mathbf{x}_{\mathsf{bot}}, \boldsymbol{y} \rangle \neq 0 \mod p$, we get that $\langle \mathbf{x}_{\mathsf{bot}}, \boldsymbol{t} \rangle$ mod p is statistically close to the uniform distribution over $\mathbf{Z}/p\mathbf{Z}$. Moreover, with overwhelming probability $u \neq 0 \mod p$, so $u \cdot \langle \mathbf{x}_{\mathsf{bot}}, \boldsymbol{t} \rangle$ statistically hides $\langle \mathbf{x}_{\mathsf{bot}}, \boldsymbol{y}_\beta \rangle$ which implies that $\langle \mathbf{x}_{\mathsf{bot}}, \boldsymbol{z}_\beta \rangle$ does not carry significant information about β, thus concluding the proof. □

5 Inner Product FE Relying on the HSM Assumption

We here build IPFE schemes from the HSM assumption and the ind-cpa scheme described in Fig. 2a, using the formalism of a cyclic group with an easy DL subgroup. Our approach is inspired by, and somewhat generalises, the approach of [ALS16] with Paillier's DCR assumption (an RSA integer N plays the role of p in this scheme so one should invoke the factoring assumption in our proof in order to encompass this construction). We first present an FE scheme for inner products over $\mathbf{Z}$ and then consider a scheme for inner products over $\mathbf{Z}/p\mathbf{Z}$.

5.1 HSM-Based FE for Inner Product over Z

Setting the parameters. As in the ind-cpa scheme of Fig. 2a, we use the output $(p, \tilde{s}, g, f, g_p, G, F, G^p)$ of the GenGroup generator of Definition 6, ignoring the generator g. We require that p is a μ bit prime, with $\mu \geq \lambda$. The message space and decryption key space is $\mathbf{Z}^\ell$. As in Subsect. 4.1 norm bounds $X, Y < (p/2\ell)^{1/2}$ are chosen to ensure decryption correctness. Key vectors $\mathbf{x}$ and message vectors $\mathbf{y}$ are of bounded norm $||\mathbf{x}||_\infty \leq X$ and $||\mathbf{y}||_\infty \leq Y$. The decryption algorithm uses a centered modulus to recover $\langle \mathbf{x}, \mathbf{y} \rangle$ over $\mathbf{Z}$. To guarantee the scheme's security we sample the coordinates of the secret key $\boldsymbol{s} = (s_1, \ldots, s_\ell)^T \hookleftarrow \mathcal{D}_{\mathbf{Z}^\ell,\sigma}$ with discrete Gaussian entries of standard deviation $\sigma > \sqrt{2\lambda} \cdot p^{3/2} \cdot \tilde{s}$. Setting $\sigma' > \tilde{s}\sqrt{\lambda}$ ensures that $\{g_p^r, r \hookleftarrow \mathcal{D}_{\mathbf{Z}^\ell,\sigma'}\}$ is at distance less than $2^{-\lambda}$ from the uniform distribution in G^p.

Construction. Figure 5 depicts our IPFE construction over $\mathbf{Z}$ relying on the HSM assumption. The proof of correctness is similar to that of the DDH-f construction.

Theorem 7. *Under the* HSM *assumption, the functional encryption scheme for inner products over* $\mathbf{Z}$ *depicted in Fig. 5 provides full security (*ind-fe-cpa*).*

Proof. The proof proceeds as a sequence of games, starting with the real ind-fe-cpa game (Game 0) and ending in a game where the ciphertext statistically hides the random bit β chosen by the challenger from the adversary $\mathcal{A}$'s point of view. The beginning of the proof is similar to the proof of Theorem 2 on ind-cpa security. Then we take into account the fact that $\mathcal{A}$ has access to a key derivation oracle. For each Game i, we denote S_i the event $\beta = \beta'$.

Game 0 ⇒ Game 1: In Game 1 the challenger uses the secret key $\boldsymbol{s} = (s_1, \ldots, s_\ell)$ to compute ciphertext elements $C_i = f^{y_{\beta,i}} \cdot (g_p^r)^{s_i} = f^{y_{\beta,i}} \cdot C_0^{s_i}$. This does not impact the distribution of the obtained ciphertext, therefore $\mathcal{A}$'s success probability in both games is identical: $Pr[S_0] = Pr[S_1]$.

Algorithm $\mathsf{Setup}(1^\lambda, 1^\mu, 1^\ell, X, Y)$

1. $(p, \tilde{s}, f, g_p, G, F, G^p) \leftarrow \mathsf{Gen}(1^\lambda, 1^\mu)$
2. $\boldsymbol{s} = (s_1, \ldots, s_\ell)^T \hookleftarrow \mathcal{D}_{\mathbf{Z}^\ell,\sigma}$
3. For $1 \leq i \leq \ell$:
4. Compute $h_i = g_p^{s_i}$
5. Return $mpk = (\tilde{s}, g_p, f, p, \{h_i\}_{i\in[\ell]})$, $msk = \boldsymbol{s}$.

Algorithm $\mathsf{KeyDer}(msk, \mathbf{x})$

$\mathbf{x} = (x_1, \ldots, x_\ell)^T \in \mathbf{Z}^\ell$,

1. Compute $sk_{\boldsymbol{x}} = \langle \boldsymbol{s}, \boldsymbol{x} \rangle$ over $\mathbf{Z}$.
2. Return $sk_{\boldsymbol{x}}$

Algorithm $\mathsf{Encrypt}(mpk, \mathbf{y})$

$\mathbf{y} = (y_1, \ldots, y_\ell)^T \in \mathbf{Z}^\ell$,

1. Pick $r \hookleftarrow \mathcal{D}_{\mathbf{Z},\sigma'}$
2. Compute $C_0 = g_p^r$
3. For $1 \leq i \leq \ell$:
4. Compute $C_i = f^{y_i} \cdot h_i^r$
5. Return $C_\mathbf{y} = (C_0, C_1, \ldots, C_\ell)$

Algorithm $\mathsf{Decrypt}(mpk, C_\mathbf{y}, sk_{\boldsymbol{x}})$

1. Compute $C_\mathbf{x} = \left(\prod_{i\in[\ell]} C_i^{x_i}\right) \cdot C_0^{-sk_{\boldsymbol{x}}}$
2. $\mathsf{sol} \leftarrow \mathsf{Solve}(C_\mathbf{x})$
3. If $\mathsf{sol} \geq p/2$:
4. Return $(\mathsf{sol} - p)$
5. Else return sol

Fig. 5. FE scheme for inner product over $\mathbf{Z}$ from the HSM assumption.

Game 1 ⇒ Game 2: In Game 1, the distribution of C_0 is at distance less than $2^{-\lambda}$ of the uniform distribution in the subgroup G^p. Thus under the HSM assumption, we can, in Game 2, substitute C_0 by $g_p^r \cdot f^a \in G$, with $r \hookleftarrow \mathcal{D}_p, a \hookleftarrow \mathbf{Z}/p\mathbf{Z}$, which, as stated in Lemma 4, Item 5 is also at distance less than $2^{-\lambda}$ of the uniform distribution in G. Therefore, $|Pr[S_2] - Pr[S_1]| \leq \mathsf{Adv}_{\mathcal{B}}^{\mathsf{HSM}}(\lambda, \mu)$. Now in Game 2 we have, for $a \hookleftarrow \mathbf{Z}/p\mathbf{Z}$ and $r \hookleftarrow \mathcal{D}_{\mathbf{Z},\sigma'}$:

$$\begin{cases} C_0 = f^a \cdot g_p^r \\ C_i = f^{y_{\beta,i} + a \cdot s_i} \cdot h_i^r \end{cases} . \tag{3}$$

Game 1

1. $mpk, msk \leftarrow \mathsf{Setup}(1^\lambda, 1^\mu, 1^\ell, X, Y)$
2. $\mathbf{y}_0, \mathbf{y}_1 \leftarrow \mathcal{A}^{\mathsf{KeyDer}(msk,\cdot)}(mpk)$
3. Pick $\beta \hookleftarrow \{0, 1\}$
4. Pick $r \hookleftarrow \mathcal{D}_{\mathbf{Z},\sigma'}$
5. Compute $C_0 = g_p^r \in G^p$
6. For $1 \leq i \leq \ell$:
7. Compute $C_i = f^{y_{\beta,i}} \cdot C_0^{s_i}$
8. $C_{\mathbf{y}} = (C_0, C_1, \ldots, C_\ell)$
9. $\beta' \leftarrow \mathcal{A}^{\mathsf{KeyDer}(msk,\cdot)}(C_{\mathbf{y}})$
10. Return $(\beta = \beta')$

Game 2

1. $mpk, msk \leftarrow \mathsf{Setup}(1^\lambda, 1^\mu, 1^\ell, X, Y)$
2. $\mathbf{y}_0, \mathbf{y}_1 \leftarrow \mathcal{A}^{\mathsf{KeyDer}(msk,\cdot)}(mpk)$
3. Pick $\beta \hookleftarrow \{0, 1\}$
4. Pick $r \hookleftarrow \mathcal{D}_{\mathbf{Z},\sigma'}$ and $a \hookleftarrow \mathbf{Z}/p\mathbf{Z}$
5. Compute $C_0 = f^a \cdot g_p^r \in G$
6. For $1 \leq i \leq \ell$:
7. Compute $C_i = f^{y_{\beta,i}} \cdot C_0^{s_i}$
8. $C_{\mathbf{y}} = (C_0, C_1, \ldots, C_\ell)$
9. $\beta' \leftarrow \mathcal{A}^{\mathsf{KeyDer}(msk,\cdot)}(C_{\mathbf{y}})$
10. Return $(\beta = \beta')$

Lemma 6. *In Game 2 the ciphertext $C_{\mathbf{y}} = (C_0, C_1, \ldots, C_\ell) \in G^{\ell+1}$ statistically hides β such that $|Pr[S_2] - 1/2| \leq 2^{-\lambda}$.*

Proof (sketch). We here give an overview of the proof, details are deferred to the full version [CLT18]. As in proof of Lemma 5, we first delimit the information leaked via the challenge ciphertext by considering the dimension in which both potential challenge ciphertexts differ. Indeed, denoting $\mathbf{z}_\beta = \mathbf{y}_\beta + a\mathbf{s} \mod p$, then projecting $\mathbf{z}_\beta$ onto the subspace generated by $\mathbf{y}_0 - \mathbf{y}_1$ encapsulates all the information revealed by the challenge ciphertext.

Next, we consider the distribution of the projection of the secret key $\mathbf{s}$ on the subspace generated by $\mathbf{y}_0 - \mathbf{y}_1$, conditionally on $\mathcal{A}$'s view (given the information leaked by private key queries and the public key). This amounts to a distribution over a one dimensional lattice Λ_0. We then reduce this distribution modulo a sub-lattice Λ_0' s.t. $\Lambda_0/\Lambda_0' \simeq \mathbf{Z}/p\mathbf{Z}$, and Lemma 3 tells us that choosing $\sigma > \sqrt{2\lambda} \cdot \tilde{s} \cdot p^{3/2}$ suffices to ensure the distribution of the projection of $\boldsymbol{s}$ on the subspace generated by $\mathbf{y}_0 - \mathbf{y}_1$ is within distance $2^{-\lambda}$ of the uniform distribution over $\mathbf{Z}/p\mathbf{Z}$, and thus $\mathbf{y}_\beta$ (and therefore β) is statistically hidden in $\mathbf{z}_\beta$. □

Over all game transitions, after adding up the different probabilities, we find that $\mathcal{A}$'s advantage in the real game can be bounded as $|Pr[S_0] - 1/2| \leq \mathsf{Adv}_{\mathcal{B}}^{\mathsf{HSM}}(\lambda, \mu) + 2^{-\lambda}$ which is negligible if the HSM assumption holds in G. □

5.2 HSM-Based FE for Inner Product over $\mathbf{Z}/p\mathbf{Z}$

As in the DDH-f based scheme for inner products over $\mathbf{Z}/p\mathbf{Z}$ of Sect. 4.2, the key generation algorithm is stateful to ensure the adversary cannot query keys for vectors that are linearly dependant over $(\mathbf{Z}/p\mathbf{Z})^\ell$ but independent over $\mathbf{Z}^\ell$.

Setting the parameters. As in the previous construction, we use the output $(p, \tilde{s}, f, g_p, G, F, G^p)$ of the GenGroup generator of Definition 6, with p a μ-bit prime, and $\mu \geq \lambda$. The message space and vector space from which decryption keys are derived are now $(\mathbf{Z}/p\mathbf{Z})^\ell$. Given an encryption of $\boldsymbol{y} \in (\mathbf{Z}/p\mathbf{Z})^\ell$ and a decryption key for $\boldsymbol{x} \in (\mathbf{Z}/p\mathbf{Z})^\ell$, the decryption algorithm recovers $\langle \mathbf{x}, \mathbf{y} \rangle \in \mathbf{Z}/p\mathbf{Z}$. To guarantee the scheme's security we sample the coordinates of the secret key $\boldsymbol{s}$ from $\mathcal{D}_{\mathbf{Z}^\ell,\sigma}$ with discrete Gaussian entries of standard deviation $\sigma > \sqrt{\lambda} \cdot p \cdot \tilde{s} \cdot (\sqrt{\ell p})^{\ell-1}$. We require $\sigma' > \tilde{s}\sqrt{\lambda}$ to ensure that $\{g_p^r, r \hookleftarrow \mathcal{D}_{\mathbf{Z}^\ell,\sigma'}\}$ is at distance less than $2^{-\lambda}$ from the uniform distribution in G^p.

Construction. The Setup and Encrypt algorithms proceed exactly as in Fig. 5, only Encrypt operates on message vectors $\boldsymbol{y} \in (\mathbf{Z}/p\mathbf{Z})^\ell$ instead of $\boldsymbol{y} \in \mathbf{Z}^\ell$. In Fig. 6 we only define algorithms KeyDer and Decrypt, since they differ from those of the previous construction.

Algorithm KeyDer($msk, \boldsymbol{x}, st$)

Answering the jth key request $sk_{\boldsymbol{x}}$ where $\boldsymbol{x} \in (\mathbf{Z}/p\mathbf{Z})^\ell$. At any time the internal state st contains at most ℓ tuples $(\boldsymbol{x}_i, \overline{\mathbf{x}}_i, z_{\mathbf{x}_i})$ where $(\overline{\mathbf{x}}_i, z_{\mathbf{x}_i})$ are previously queried secret keys and the $\boldsymbol{x}_i$'s are corresponding vectors.

1. If $\boldsymbol{x}$ is linearly independent of the $\boldsymbol{x}_i$'s modulo p :
2. $\quad$ Set $\overline{\mathbf{x}} \in \{0, \ldots, p-1\}^\ell$ with $\overline{\mathbf{x}} = \boldsymbol{x} \mod p$
3. $\quad$ $z_{\mathbf{x}} = \langle \boldsymbol{s}, \overline{\mathbf{x}} \rangle \in \mathbf{Z}$; $st = (st, (\boldsymbol{x}, \overline{\mathbf{x}}, z_{\mathbf{x}}))$
4. If $\exists \{k_i\}_{1 \leq i \leq j-1} \in \mathbf{Z}^{j-1}$ such that $\boldsymbol{x} = \sum_{i=1}^{j-1} k_i \boldsymbol{x}_i \in (\mathbf{Z}/p\mathbf{Z})^\ell$ then:
5. $\quad$ $\overline{\mathbf{x}} = \sum_{i=1}^{j-1} k_i \overline{\mathbf{x}}_i \in \mathbf{Z}^\ell$; $z_{\mathbf{x}} = \sum_{i=1}^{j-1} k_i z_{\mathbf{x}_i} \in \mathbf{Z}$
6. Return $sk_{\boldsymbol{x}} = (\overline{\mathbf{x}}, z_{\mathbf{x}})$

Algorithm Decrypt($mpk, C_{\boldsymbol{y}}, sk_{\boldsymbol{x}}$)

1. Parse $(\overline{\mathbf{x}} = (\overline{x}_1, \ldots, \overline{x}_\ell), z_{\mathbf{x}}) = sk_{\boldsymbol{x}}$
2. Compute $C_{\boldsymbol{x}} = \left(\prod_{i \in [\ell]} C_i^{\overline{x}_i}\right) \cdot (C_0^{-z_{\mathbf{x}}})$
3. Return Solve($C_{\boldsymbol{x}}$)

Fig. 6. Functional encryption scheme for inner products over $\mathbf{Z}/p\mathbf{Z}$ from HSM.

Theorem 8. *Under the* HSM *assumption the above stateful functional encryption scheme for inner products over* $\mathbf{Z}/p\mathbf{Z}$ *provides full security (*ind-fe-cpa*).*

The proof resembles that of Theorem 7 and is adapted from the proofs of [ALS16], so we defer it to the full version [CLT18]. The main issue is that we can no longer guarantee $\boldsymbol{X}$ is invertible modulo p. We need to compute on-the-fly a basis for $\{\boldsymbol{x} \in (\mathbf{Z}/p\mathbf{Z})^\ell : \langle \boldsymbol{x}, \boldsymbol{y} \rangle = 0 \mod p\}$ to apply the same techniques as in Theorem 7. The analysis gives significantly larger standard deviations as mentioned above due a bad approximation of the determinant of a related matrix.

6 Instantiation and Efficiency Considerations

Both generic constructions we put forth of IPFE are based on variants of Elgamal in the same group and both sample their master secret keys from Gaussian distributions with the same standard deviation. As a result their asymptotic complexities are the same. The second scheme's security relies on a hard subgroup membership assumption (HSM) and this scheme appears to be the most efficient FE evaluating inner products modulo a prime p. At the (small) expense of a single additional element in the keys and in the ciphertext, the first scheme's security relies on a weaker DDH-like assumption, which is also weaker than the DDH assumption in the group. We compare, in Table 1, an implementation of our HSM-based IPFE mod p of Subsect. 5.2 within the class group of an imaginary quadratic field and Paillier's variant of [ALS16]. This is the most relevant comparison since their DDH variant does not allow a full recovery of large inner products over $\mathbf{Z}/p\mathbf{Z}$, and, as detailed in the following paragraph, the LWE variant is far from being efficient, as ciphertexts are computed using arithmetic modulo $q = 2^\ell$ where ℓ is the dimension of the plaintext vectors.

Comparison with the LWE *based scheme of* [ALS16]. Parameter choices for lattice-based cryptography are complex, indeed [ALS16] do not provide a concrete set of parameters. This being said, using [ALS16, Theorem 3], and setting $\log p = \lambda$ as in Table 1, we give rough bit sizes for their LWE based scheme over $\mathbf{Z}/p\mathbf{Z}$. Basic elements are integers mod q of size ℓ since $q \approx 2^\ell$ for security to hold. The largest component in the public key mpk consists of $\lambda^2\ell^3$ elements, so mpk is of size greater than $\lambda^2\ell^4$. The component $z_{\boldsymbol{x}}$ in secret keys is the product of a vector of $(\mathbf{Z}/p\mathbf{Z})^\ell$ with a matrix, resulting in a vector made up of $\lambda\ell^2$ inner products, where each inner product is of size $\ell\lambda$. Thus these keys are of size $\lambda^2\ell^3$. Finally ciphertexts consist of $\lambda\ell^2$ elements, and are thus of size $\lambda\ell^3$. As a result, although it is hard to compare the complexities in λ, for a fixed security level, the complexity in ℓ for all the parameters of the LWE based scheme is in ℓ^3 or ℓ^4 whereas we are linear in ℓ (see Table 1). For example, for $\lambda = 128, \ell = 100$, their $sk_{\boldsymbol{x}}$ is of approximately 2^{34} bits vs. 13852 bits in our instantiation.

Instantiation. To instantiate the protocol of Sect. 5.2, we must first define the algorithm GenGroup of Definition 6. We follow the lines of [CL15], starting from a fundamental discriminant $\Delta_K = -p \cdot q$ with its class group $Cl(\Delta_K)$, where q is a prime such that $p \cdot q \equiv -1 \pmod 4$ and $(p/q) = -1$. Then, we consider a non-maximal order of discriminant $\Delta_p = p^2 \cdot \Delta_K$ and its class group $Cl(\Delta_p)$. The order of $Cl(\Delta_p)$ is $h(\Delta_p) = p \cdot h(\Delta_K)$. It is known [Coh00, p. 295], that $h(\Delta_K) < \frac{1}{\pi} \log |\Delta_K| \sqrt{|\Delta_K|}$ which is the bound we take for $\tilde{s}$ (a slightly better bound can be computed from the analytic class number formula, *cf.* [McC89]).

In [CL15, Fig. 2] the authors show how to build a generator of a cyclic group of order ps of the class group of discriminant Δ_p and a generator for the subgroup of order p (in which the DL problem is easy). We need to modify their generator s.t. it outputs a generator g_p of the subgroup of p–th powers. The computation of such an element is actually implicit in their generator: this is done by computing an ideal $\mathfrak{r}$ in the maximal order with norm a small prime r such that $\left(\frac{\Delta_K}{r}\right) = 1$. Then the ideal $\mathfrak{r}^2$ is lifted into a class of $Cl(\Delta_p)$ which is then raised to the power p to define g_p. A second modification is to output $\tilde{s}$ instead of their larger bound B (since they sampled elements using a folded uniform distribution). We refer to [CL15] for a full description of the implementation. The manipulated objects are reduced ideals represented by two integers smaller than $\sqrt{p^3 q}$, and the arithmetic operations in class groups are very efficient, since the reduction and composition of quadratic forms have a quasi linear time complexity using fast arithmetic (see for instance [Coh00]).

The sole restriction on the size of the prime p is that it must have at least λ bits, where λ is the security parameter. The size of Δ_K, and thus of q, is chosen to thwart the best practical attack, which consists in computing discrete logarithms in $Cl(\Delta_K)$ (or equivalently the class number $h(\Delta_K)$). An index-calculus method to solve the DL problem in a class group of imaginary quadratic field of discriminant Δ_K was proposed in [Jac00]. It is conjectured in [BJS10] that a state of the art implementation of this algorithm has complexity $\mathcal{O}(L_{|\Delta_K|}[1/2, o(1)])$. They estimate that the DL problem with a discriminant Δ_K of 1348 (resp. 1828 bits) is as hard as factoring a 2048 (resp. 3072 bits) RSA integer. This is our reference to estimate the bit size of the different elements in Table 1.

Table 1. Comparing our IPFE from HSM and the [ALS16] IPFE from DCR

size	$\lambda = 112$		$\lambda = 128$	
	this work	[ALS16]	this work	[ALS16]
$(p, \tilde{s})$	$(112, 684)$	$(1024, 2046)$	$(128, 924)$	$(1536, 3070)$
group element	1572	4096	2084	6144
secret key* ($z_{\boldsymbol{x}}$)	$112(\ell+1)+684$	$2048(\ell+2)$	$128(\ell+1)+924$	$3072(\ell+2)$
ciphertext	$1572(\ell+1)$	$4096(\ell+1)$	$2084(\ell+1)$	$6144(\ell+1)$
enc. expo.	687	2046	928	3070
dec. expo.	$112(\ell+1)+684$	$2048(\ell+2)$	$128(\ell+1)+924$	$3072(\ell+2)$

*ignoring an additive term $(\ell \pm 1)\log(\sqrt{\ell})$

Note that in this case, the size of our group elements (reduced ideals in the class group of discriminant $p^3 q$), are significantly smaller than those of the Paillier variant of [ALS16] (elements of $\mathbf{Z}/N^2\mathbf{Z}$). This is also the case for ciphertexts (which consist in both protocols of $\ell + 1$ group elements). We have the same situation with secret keys: to simplify the comparison we consider linearly independent queries (thus ignoring the vectors in $\mathbf{Z}^\ell$). As a result, we have, for our scheme, the inner product of a vector from $(\mathbf{Z}/p\mathbf{Z})^\ell$ with a vector sampled from a discrete Gaussian with standard deviation greater than $\sqrt{\lambda} p \tilde{s} (\sqrt{\ell} p)^{\ell-1}$ over $\mathbf{Z}^\ell$ vs. the inner product of a vector of $(\mathbf{Z}/N\mathbf{Z})^\ell$ with a vector sampled from a discrete Gaussian with standard deviation greater than $\sqrt{\lambda}(\sqrt{\ell}N)^{\ell+1}$ over $\mathbf{Z}^\ell$.

We note however that our underlying message space $\mathbf{Z}/p\mathbf{Z}$ is much smaller than their message space $\mathbf{Z}/N\mathbf{Z}$. Using larger message spaces would be more favorable to their Paillier based scheme. But in practice, a 128 bits message space is large enough, if for instance, one needs to perform computations with double or quadruple precision. Our protocols are the most suited for such intermediate computations, since Paillier's construction from [ALS16] would add a large overhead cost, while their DDH construction could not decrypt the result.

In terms of timings, a fair comparison is difficult since to our knowledge, no library for the arithmetic of quadratic forms is as optimized as a standard library for the arithmetic of modular integers. Nevertheless, we note that the exponents involved in the (multi-)exponentiations for encryption and decryption are significantly smaller than those in [ALS16], as is the group size. Indeed, the encryption of Paillier's variant involves $(\ell+1)$ exponentiations to the power a $(|N|-2)$-bit integer modulo N^2, whereas our protocol involves one exponentiation to the power a $|\sigma'|$-bit integer in $Cl(p^3q)$, where $\sigma' > \tilde{s}\sqrt{\lambda}$ and ℓ (multi-)exponentiations whose maximum exponent size is also $|\sigma'|$. Decryptions involve respectively a multi-exponentiation whose maximum exponent size is lower than $\ell\sigma N = \ell\sqrt{\lambda}(\sqrt{\ell}N)^{\ell+1}N$ for [ALS16] and $\ell p \sigma = \ell p \sqrt{\lambda} p \tilde{s} (\sqrt{\ell} p)^{\ell-1}$ for our protocol. We performed timings with Sage 8.1 on a standard laptop with a straight-forward implementation. Using the settings of [CL15], the exponentiation in class groups uses a PARI/GP function (qfbnupow), which is far less optimised than the exponentiation in $\mathbf{Z}/N\mathbf{Z}$, implying a huge bias in favour of Paillier. Despite this bias, the efficiency improvement we expected from our protocols is reflected in practice, as showed in Table 2. We gain firstly from the fact that we can use smaller parameters for the same security level and secondly, because our security reductions allow to replace N^ℓ with p^ℓ in the derived keys. Thus the gain is not only in the constants and our scheme becomes more and more interesting as the security level and the dimension ℓ increase.

Table 2. Timings: our IPFE from HSM *vs.* [ALS16]'s IPFE from DCR

	$\lambda = 112, \ell = 10^*$		$\lambda = 128, \ell = 10^*$	
	this work	[ALS16]	this work	[ALS16]
secret key bitsize	1920	24592	2340	36876
encryption time	40 ms	**27 ms**	**78 ms**	85 ms
decryption time	**110 ms**	301 ms	**193 ms**	964 ms

* For all parameters our dependency in ℓ is linear which allows to extrapolate timings for $\ell > 10$.

Acknowledgements. The authors would like to thank both Benoît Libert and Damien Stehlé for fruitful discussions. This work was supported by the French ANR ALAMBIC project (ANR-16-CE39-0006), and by ERC Starting Grant ERC-2013-StG-335086-LATTAC.

References

[ABCP16] Abdalla, M., Bourse, F., Caro, A.D., Pointcheval, D.: Better security for functional encryption for inner product evaluations. Cryptology ePrint Archive, Report 2016/011 (2016). http://eprint.iacr.org/2016/011

[ABDP15] Abdalla, M., Bourse, F., De Caro, A., Pointcheval, D.: Simple functional encryption schemes for inner products. In: Katz, J. (ed.) PKC 2015. LNCS, vol. 9020, pp. 733–751. Springer, Heidelberg (2015). https://doi.org/10.1007/978-3-662-46447-2_33

[ABP+17] Agrawal, S., Bhattacherjee, S., Phan, D.H., Stehlé, D., Yamada, S.: Efficient public trace and revoke from standard assumptions: extended abstract. In: ACM CCS 17, pp. 2277–2293. ACM Press (2017)

[ABSV15] Ananth, P., Brakerski, Z., Segev, G., Vaikuntanathan, V.: From selective to adaptive security in functional encryption. In: Gennaro, R., Robshaw, M. (eds.) CRYPTO 2015, Part II. LNCS, vol. 9216, pp. 657–677. Springer, Heidelberg (2015). https://doi.org/10.1007/978-3-662-48000-7_32

[Adl94] Adleman, L.M.: The function field sieve. In: Adleman, L.M., Huang, M.-D. (eds.) ANTS 1994. LNCS, vol. 877, pp. 108–121. Springer, Heidelberg (1994). https://doi.org/10.1007/3-540-58691-1_48

[AGVW13] Agrawal, S., Gorbunov, S., Vaikuntanathan, V., Wee, H.: Functional encryption: new perspectives and lower bounds. In: Canetti, R., Garay, J.A. (eds.) CRYPTO 2013, Part II. LNCS, vol. 8043, pp. 500–518. Springer, Heidelberg (2013). https://doi.org/10.1007/978-3-642-40084-1_28

[ALS16] Agrawal, S., Libert, B., Stehlé, D.: Fully secure functional encryption for inner products, from standard assumptions. In: Robshaw, M., Katz, J. (eds.) CRYPTO 2016, Part III. LNCS, vol. 9816, pp. 333–362. Springer, Heidelberg (2016). https://doi.org/10.1007/978-3-662-53015-3_12

[BBL17] Benhamouda, F., Bourse, F., Lipmaa, H.: CCA-secure inner-product functional encryption from projective hash functions. In: Fehr, S. (ed.) PKC 2017, Part II. LNCS, vol. 10175, pp. 36–66. Springer, Heidelberg (2017). https://doi.org/10.1007/978-3-662-54388-7_2

[BCP03] Bresson, E., Catalano, D., Pointcheval, D.: A simple public-key cryptosystem with a double trapdoor decryption mechanism and its applications. In: Laih, C.-S. (ed.) ASIACRYPT 2003. LNCS, vol. 2894, pp. 37–54. Springer, Heidelberg (2003). https://doi.org/10.1007/978-3-540-40061-5_3

[BGJS16] Badrinarayanan, S., Goyal, V., Jain, A., Sahai, A.: Verifiable functional encryption. In: Cheon, J.H., Takagi, T. (eds.) ASIACRYPT 2016, Part II. LNCS, vol. 10032, pp. 557–587. Springer, Heidelberg (2016). https://doi.org/10.1007/978-3-662-53890-6_19

[BJS10] Biasse, J.-F., Jacobson, M.J., Silvester, A.K.: Security estimates for quadratic field based cryptosystems. In: Steinfeld, R., Hawkes, P. (eds.) ACISP 2010. LNCS, vol. 6168, pp. 233–247. Springer, Heidelberg (2010). https://doi.org/10.1007/978-3-642-14081-5_15

[BO13] Bellare, M., O'Neill, A.: Semantically-secure functional encryption: possibility results, impossibility results and the quest for a general definition. In: Abdalla, M., Nita-Rotaru, C., Dahab, R. (eds.) CANS 2013. LNCS, vol. 8257, pp. 218–234. Springer, Cham (2013). https://doi.org/10.1007/978-3-319-02937-5_12

[Bou17] Bourse, F.: Functional encryption for inner-product evaluations. Ph.D. thesis, PSL Research University, France (2017)

[BSW11] Boneh, D., Sahai, A., Waters, B.: Functional encryption: definitions and challenges. In: Ishai, Y. (ed.) TCC 2011. LNCS, vol. 6597, pp. 253–273. Springer, Heidelberg (2011). https://doi.org/10.1007/978-3-642-19571-6_16

[CIL17] Castagnos, G., Imbert, L., Laguillaumie, F.: Encryption switching protocols revisited: switching modulo p. In: Katz, J., Shacham, H. (eds.) CRYPTO 2017, Part I. LNCS, vol. 10401, pp. 255–287. Springer, Cham (2017). https://doi.org/10.1007/978-3-319-63688-7_9

[CL09] Castagnos, G., Laguillaumie, F.: On the security of cryptosystems with quadratic decryption: the nicest cryptanalysis. In: Joux, A. (ed.) EUROCRYPT 2009. LNCS, vol. 5479, pp. 260–277. Springer, Heidelberg (2009). https://doi.org/10.1007/978-3-642-01001-9_15

[CL15] Castagnos, G., Laguillaumie, F.: Linearly homomorphic encryption from DDH. In: Nyberg, K. (ed.) CT-RSA 2015. LNCS, vol. 9048, pp. 487–505. Springer, Cham (2015). https://doi.org/10.1007/978-3-319-16715-2_26

[CLT18] Castagnos, G., Laguillaumie, F., Tucker, I.: Practical fully secure unrestricted inner product functional encryption modulo p. Cryptology ePrint Archive, Report 2018/791 (2018). https://eprint.iacr.org/2018/791

[Coh00] Cohen, H.: A Course in Computational Algebraic Number Theory. Springer, Heidelberg (2000)

[CS98] Cramer, R., Shoup, V.: A practical public key cryptosystem provably secure against adaptive chosen ciphertext attack. In: Krawczyk, H. (ed.) CRYPTO 1998. LNCS, vol. 1462, pp. 13–25. Springer, Heidelberg (1998). https://doi.org/10.1007/BFb0055717

[CS02] Cramer, R., Shoup, V.: Universal hash proofs and a paradigm for adaptive chosen ciphertext secure public-key encryption. In: Knudsen, L.R. (ed.) EUROCRYPT 2002. LNCS, vol. 2332, pp. 45–64. Springer, Heidelberg (2002). https://doi.org/10.1007/3-540-46035-7_4

[CS03] Camenisch, J., Shoup, V.: Practical verifiable encryption and decryption of discrete logarithms. In: Boneh, D. (ed.) CRYPTO 2003. LNCS, vol. 2729, pp. 126–144. Springer, Heidelberg (2003). https://doi.org/10.1007/978-3-540-45146-4_8

[DIJ+13] De Caro, A., Iovino, V., Jain, A., O'Neill, A., Paneth, O., Persiano, G.: On the achievability of simulation-based security for functional encryption. In: Canetti, R., Garay, J.A. (eds.) CRYPTO 2013, Part II. LNCS, vol. 8043, pp. 519–535. Springer, Heidelberg (2013). https://doi.org/10.1007/978-3-642-40084-1_29

[GGHZ16] Garg, S., Gentry, C., Halevi, S., Zhandry, M.: Functional encryption without obfuscation. In: Kushilevitz, E., Malkin, T. (eds.) TCC 2016, Part II. LNCS, vol. 9563, pp. 480–511. Springer, Heidelberg (2016). https://doi.org/10.1007/978-3-662-49099-0_18

[Gjø05] Gjøsteen, K.: Symmetric subgroup membership problems. In: Vaudenay, S. (ed.) PKC 2005. LNCS, vol. 3386, pp. 104–119. Springer, Heidelberg (2005). https://doi.org/10.1007/978-3-540-30580-4_8

[GKP+13a] Goldwasser, S., Kalai, Y.T., Popa, R.A., Vaikuntanathan, V., Zeldovich, N.: How to run turing machines on encrypted data. In: Canetti, R., Garay, J.A. (eds.) CRYPTO 2013, Part II. LNCS, vol. 8043, pp. 536–553. Springer, Heidelberg (2013). https://doi.org/10.1007/978-3-642-40084-1_30

[GKP+13b] Goldwasser, S., Kalai, Y.T., Popa, R.A., Vaikuntanathan, V., Zeldovich, N.: Reusable garbled circuits and succinct functional encryption. In: 45th ACM STOC, pp. 555–564. ACM Press (2013)

[GPV08] Gentry, C., Peikert, C., Vaikuntanathan, V.: Trapdoors for hard lattices and new cryptographic constructions. In: 40th ACM STOC, pp. 197–206. ACM Press (2008)

[GVW12] Gorbunov, S., Vaikuntanathan, V., Wee, H.: Functional encryption with bounded collusions via multi-party computation. In: Safavi-Naini, R., Canetti, R. (eds.) CRYPTO 2012. LNCS, vol. 7417, pp. 162–179. Springer, Heidelberg (2012). https://doi.org/10.1007/978-3-642-32009-5_11

[HO12] Hemenway, B., Ostrovsky, R.: Extended-DDH and lossy trapdoor functions. In: Fischlin, M., Buchmann, J., Manulis, M. (eds.) PKC 2012. LNCS, vol. 7293, pp. 627–643. Springer, Heidelberg (2012). https://doi.org/10.1007/978-3-642-30057-8_37

[Jac00] Jacobson Jr., M.J.: Computing discrete logarithms in quadratic orders. J. Cryptol. **13**(4), 473–492 (2000)

[KSW08] Katz, J., Sahai, A., Waters, B.: Predicate encryption supporting disjunctions, polynomial equations, and inner products. In: Smart, N. (ed.) EUROCRYPT 2008. LNCS, vol. 4965, pp. 146–162. Springer, Heidelberg (2008). https://doi.org/10.1007/978-3-540-78967-3_9

[Luc02] Lucks, S.: A variant of the Cramer-Shoup cryptosystem for groups of unknown order. In: Zheng, Y. (ed.) ASIACRYPT 2002. LNCS, vol. 2501, pp. 27–45. Springer, Heidelberg (2002). https://doi.org/10.1007/3-540-36178-2_2

[Mar03] Martinet, J.: Perfect Lattices in Euclidean Spaces. Grundlehren der mathematischen Wissenschaften, vol. 327, 1st edn. Springer, Heidelberg (2003). https://doi.org/10.1007/978-3-662-05167-2

[McC89] McCurley, K.S.: Cryptographic key distribution and computation in class groups. In: Number Theory and Applications (Proc. NATO Advanced Study Inst. on Number Theory and Applications, Banff, 1988). Kluwer (1989)

[MR04] Micciancio, D., Regev, O.: Worst-case to average-case reductions based on Gaussian measures. In: 45th FOCS, pp. 372–381. IEEE Computer Society Press (2004)

[MR07] Micciancio, D., Regev, O.: Worst-case to average-case reductions based on Gaussian measures. SIAM J. Comput. **37**(1), 267–302 (2007)

[Ngu91] Nguyen, P.Q.: La Géométrie des Nombres en Cryptologie. Ph.D. thesis, École Normale Supérieure (1991)

[O'N10] O'Neill, A.: Definitional issues in functional encryption. Cryptology ePrint Archive, Report 2010/556 (2010). http://eprint.iacr.org/2010/556

[Pai99] Paillier, P.: Public-key cryptosystems based on composite degree residuosity classes. In: Stern, J. (ed.) EUROCRYPT 1999. LNCS, vol. 1592, pp. 223–238. Springer, Heidelberg (1999). https://doi.org/10.1007/3-540-48910-X_16

[Sha84] Shamir, A.: Identity-based cryptosystems and signature schemes. In: Blakley, G.R., Chaum, D. (eds.) CRYPTO 1984. LNCS, vol. 196, pp. 47–53. Springer, Heidelberg (1985). https://doi.org/10.1007/3-540-39568-7_5
[SS10] Sahai, A., Seyalioglu, H.: Worry-free encryption: functional encryption with public keys. In: ACM CCS 10, pp. 463–472. ACM Press (2010)
[SW05] Sahai, A., Waters, B.: Fuzzy identity-based encryption. In: Cramer, R. (ed.) EUROCRYPT 2005. LNCS, vol. 3494, pp. 457–473. Springer, Heidelberg (2005). https://doi.org/10.1007/11426639_27
[Wat15] Waters, B.: A punctured programming approach to adaptively secure functional encryption. In: Gennaro, R., Robshaw, M. (eds.) CRYPTO 2015, Part II. LNCS, vol. 9216, pp. 678–697. Springer, Heidelberg (2015). https://doi.org/10.1007/978-3-662-48000-7_33

Author Index

Printed in the United States
By Bookmasters